D1615680

DIVES AND PAUPER

VOLUME II

EARLY ENGLISH TEXT SOCIETY

No. 323

2004

DIVES AND PAUPER

VOLUME II

BY

PRISCILLA HEATH BARNUM

Published for
THE EARLY ENGLISH TEXT SOCIETY
by the
OXFORD UNIVERSITY PRESS
2004

OXFORD
UNIVERSITY PRESS

Great Clarendon Street, Oxford OX2 6DP

Oxford University Press is a department of the University of Oxford.
It furthers the University's objective of excellence in research, scholarship,
and education by publishing worldwide in

Oxford New York

Auckland Bangkok Buenos Aires Cape Town Chennai
Dar es Salaam Delhi Hong Kong Istanbul Karachi Kolkata
Kuala Lumpur Madrid Melbourne Mexico City Mumbai Nairobi
São Paulo Shanghai Singapore Taipei Tokyo Toronto

Oxford is a registered trade mark of Oxford University Press
in the UK and in certain other countries

Published in the United States
by Oxford University Press Inc., New York

British Library Cataloguing in Publication Data

Data available

Library of Congress Cataloging in Publication Data

Data applied for

ISBN 0-19-722326-5

1 3 5 7 9 10 8 6 4 2

Typeset by Anne Joshua, Oxford
Printed in Great Britain
on acid-free paper by
Print Wright Ltd., Ipswich

ACKNOWLEDGEMENTS

I owe a very great debt of gratitude to the late Pamela Gradon for many rereadings over the years and for a large fund of patience; to Anne Hudson for always asking the hard questions and always rejecting the easy answers; to the late John Fines, who never stopped believing that one day the edition would be finished; to Theodore Draper for his patient insistence on clear writing. I owe much gratitude also to A. Ian Doyle for advice and encouragement from the beginning of the work as well as for unearthing manuscript fragment W of *D&P*. Without the trenchant criticism of EETS's 'second reader' and Helen Spencer's tactful, erudite and patient editorial advice, the final volume would have remained too long and too diffuse to publish.

I owe thanks to many institutions: the librarians of the Hunterian Collection in the Glasgow University Library; to the staffs of the Bodleian's Duke Humfrey's Library; to the staffs of the British Museum (now British Library) manuscript collection; to Dr Barbara Shailor of the Beinecke Collection, Yale University Library; to Father Cousins of Oscott College for allowing me (in 1973) to copy the pastedown containing text of *D&P*; to Richard Beadle for alerting me to the *D&P* fragment in MS Bodley Ashmole 750; to the late Reverend Prebendary Baylis of Lichfield Cathedral for welcoming me to the manuscript collection of the cathedral library; to Daniel Huws of the National Library of Wales, Aberystwyth, for sending a photocopy of MS fragment W and offprints of material related to the manuscript, and to Dr Paul Saenger, Curator of Special Collections in the Newberry Library, for bringing to light a manuscript fragment of *D&P*. And, finally, I owe a debt to the unknown author of *Dives and Pauper* for keeping my interest focused for so many years on all that is known and all that remains to be discovered about late fourteenth and early fifteenth century England.

CONTENTS

ABBREVIATIONS AND SHORT TITLES   ix

INTRODUCTION   xv
- 1. Genre   xv
- 2. Historical setting, date and authorship   xvii
- 3. *D&P* as a literary work   xxxi
- 4. Theology   xxxix
- 5. Paths of Less and More Perfection   li
- 6. Manuscripts, MS Fragments and Printed Texts of *D&P*   liv
- 7. Relationships Among the MSS of *D&P*   lxxvi

EXPLANATORY NOTES
- Tables (A & B), 'Holy Poverty' Prologues (A & B)   1
- Commandment I   22
- Commandment II   99
- Commandment III   117
- Commandment IV   138
- Commandment V   164
- Commandment VI   193
- Commandment VII   225
- Commandment VIII   271
- Commandment IX   298
- Commandment X   312

GLOSSARY   325

INDEX OF BIBLICAL REFERENCES   394

INDEX OF NON-BIBLICAL REFERENCES   404

INDEX OF CANON LAW CITATIONS   407

BIBLIOGRAPHY
- Manuscripts   410
- Primary Sources   411
- Secondary Sources   426

ERRATA AND CORRIGENDA FOR VOLS. 1: 1 AND 1: 2   447

ABBREVIATIONS AND SHORT TITLES

ABD	*Anchor Bible Dictionary*. 6 vols., ed. D. N. Freedman *et al.* (1992)
Add.	Additional manuscript (BL)
BIHR	*Bulletin of the Institute of Historical Research* (London, 1923–)
BL	British Library
BRUO	A. B. Emden, *Biographical Register of the University of Oxford*, 3 vols. (Oxford, repr. 1989)
CA	Thomas Aquinas, *Catena Aurea in Quatuor Evangelia*, 2 vols. (Turin, Rome, 1953)
CCCM	*Corpus Christianorum continuatio medievalis* (Turnhout, 1952–)
CCL	*Corpus Christianorum, series Latina* (Turnhout, 1953–)
Chevalier *Repertorium*	Ulysse Chevalier, *Repertorium hymnologicum*, 6 vols. (Louvain, 1892–1920)
CMA	*Catalogi librorum manuscriptorum Angliae et Hiberniae*, ed. E. Bernard (Oxford, 1697)
Councils and Synods	*Councils and Synods, with other Documents relating to the English Church*, II, AD 1205–1313, ed. F. M. Powicke and C. R. Cheney (Oxford, 1964)
CSEL	*Corpus scriptorum ecclesiasticorum Latinorum* (Vienna, 1866–)
CT	Chaucer, *Canterbury Tales*, 3rd Riverside ed., ed. L. D. Benson (Boston, 1987)
DACL	*Dictionnaire d'archéologie et de liturgie*
DML	*Dictionary of Medieval Latin from British Sources*, 5 vols., A–L, ed. R. E. Latham (Oxford, 1975-)
DNB	*The Compact Edition of the Dictionary of National Biography*, 2 vols. (Oxford, 1975)
Dom. Stud.	*Dominican Studies*
Doyle *Survey*	A. I. Doyle, 'A Survey of the Origins and Circulation of Theological Writings in English in the 14th, 15th and early 16th centuries' 2 vols. (PhD thesis, Cambridge, 1953–4)
D&P	*Dives and Pauper* (text), 2 vols., ed. P. H. Barnum (EETS 275, 280)
Drèves	G. M. Drèves and C. Blume, *Analecta hymnica medii aevi*, 55 vols. (Leipzig, 1886–1922)

DTC	*Dictionnaire de Théologie Catholique*, 15 vols, ed. A. Vacant *et al.* (Paris 1899–1950
Du Cange	*Glossarium mediae et infimae Latinitatis*, 7 vols. (Paris, 1840–50)
Durandus *Rationale*	William Durandus, *Rationale divinorum officiorum*, 3 vols. ed. A. Davril and M. Thibodeau (CCCM cxl, cxlA, cxlB; Turnhout, 1995–2000)
ECBH	M. B. Parkes, *English Cursive Book Hands* (Oxford, 1969)
EETS	*Early English Text Society* (London, 1868–) (OS Original Series, ES Extra Series, SS Supplementary Series)
EHR	*English Historical Review* (London, 1886)
EV	Early Version of the Wycliffite Bible (FM)
EWS	*English Wycliffite Sermons*, 5 vols., ed. A. Hudson and P. Gradon (Oxford, 1983–96)
EWW	*Selections from English Wycliffite Writings*, ed. A. Hudson (Cambridge, 1978)
FM	*The Wycliffite Bible*, 4 vols.. ed. Forshall & Madden (N.Y., 1850)
Fran. Stud.	*Franciscan Studies*
Friedberg	*Corpus iuris canonici*, 2 vols., ed. Æ. Friedberg (repr. Graz, 1959)
	Canon law citations:
	Decretum:
	Distinctiones: D.1 c.1
	Causae: C.1 q. 1 c. 1
	Tractatus de Poenitentia: De poen. D. 1 c. 1
	Tractatus de Consecratione: De cons. D. 1 c. 1
	Liber Extra: X 1.1.1
FZ	*Fasciculi Zizaniorum*, ed. W. W. Shirley (RS, 1858)
GL	Jacobus de Voragine, *The Golden Legend*, 2 vols., tr. W. G. Ryan (Princeton, 1993)
GO	*Biblia Latina cum glossa ordinaria*, 4 vols. (Strassburg, 1480–1 facs.)
Graesse	J. A. de Voragine, *Legenda aurea*, 3rd edn. (Bratislava, 1890) (followed by Legend numbers in this edn.)
Hartung *Manual*	*A Manual of the Writings in Middle English 1050–1500*, 9 vols., gen. ed. A. E. Hartung (New Haven, Ct., 1967-)
Historia	Peter Comestor, *Historia scholastica*, *PL* 198, pp. 1054–1844
Horstman	*Yorkshire Writers*, 2 vols., ed. C. Horstman (London, 1895–6)
HP-A,B	The first (A) and second (B) prologues to *D&P*

HUO	*History of the University of Oxford*: Vol. II, *Late Medieval Oxford*, ed. J. I. Catto and T. A. R. Evans (Oxford, 1992)
IMEP	*Index of Middle English Prose*, Handlist Series, gen. ed. A. S. G. Edwards *et al.* (D. S. Brewer, Cambridge, 1984–)
IMEV	Brown & Robbins, *Index of Middle English Verse* (N.Y., 1943; Supp. 1965)
IPMEP	*Index of Printed Middle English Prose*. ed. R. E. Lewis *et al.* (N.Y. and London, 1985)
Isidore, *Etym.*	Isidore of Seville, *Isidori Etymologiarum*, 2 vols., ed. W. M. Lindsay (Oxford, 1911; repr. 1971) (cited by section numbers)
JEGP	*Journal of English and Germanic Theology*
JEH	*Journal of Ecclesiastical History* (London, 1950–)
JHI	*Journal of the History of Ideas*
Jolliffe, Checklist	P. S. Jolliffe, *A Checklist of Middle English Prose Writings of Spiritual Guidance* (PIMS, Toronto, 1974)
KJV	King James version of the English Bible
LALME	*A Linguistic Atlas of Late Mediaeval English*, 4 vols., ed. A. McIntosh *et al.* (Aberdeen, 1986)
LCC	Library of Christian Classics (Philadelphia)
LCL	Loeb Classical Library (Cambridge, Mass., 1912–)
LL4	MS Longleat 4 (unedited sermons by the author of *D&P*)
LNPF	Library of the Nicene and Post-Nicene Fathers of the Christian Church
LXX	Septuagint (edition used: *Septuaginta*, A. Rahlfs, 2 vols. in 1 (Stuttgart, 1935–79)
LV	Later Version of the Wycliffite Bible (FM)
Mansi	*Sacrorum conciliorum nova et amplissima collectio*, 31 vols., ed. J. D. Mansi (Florence, 1759–98)
MÆ	*Medium Ævum* (Oxford, 1931-)
Med. Stud.	*Medieval Studies*
ME Sermons	*Middle English Sermons*, ed. W. O. Ross, EETS 209 (1960)
MED	*Middle English Dictionary*, ed. H. Kurath et al. (Ann Arbor, Mich, 1982–2001)
MET	*Middle English Texts*, Heidelberg
Monumenta	*Monumenta Franciscana* ed. S. Brewer (RS, 1958)
MRS	*Medieval and Renaissance Studies*
MRTS	*Medieval and Renaissance Texts and Studies*
NAPF	A Select Library of the Nicene and Post-Nicene Fathers
NQ	*Notes and Queries*
Novum Testamentum	3 vols., ed. J. Wordsworth and H. J. White (Oxford, 1898– 1954)

OCD	*Oxford Classical Dictionary*, ed. S. Hornblower and A. Spawforth (3rd edn., Oxford, 1996)
OCL	*Oxford Companion to Law*, ed. D. M. Walker (Oxford, 1980)
ODCC	*Oxford Dictionary of the Christian Church*, ed. F. L. Cross (3rd edn. Oxford, 1997)
ODEP	*Oxford Dicltionary of English Proverbs*, ed. F. P. Wilson (3rd edn., Oxford, 1970
ODS	*Oxford Dictionary of Saints*, ed. D. H. Farmer (Oxford, 1978)
ODP	*Oxford Dictionary of Popes*, ed. J. N. D. Kelly (Oxford, 1986)
OED	*Oxford English Dictionary*, 13 vols. & Supp. (Oxford, 1933–86)
OLD	*Oxford Latin Dictionary* ed. P. G. W. Glare (Oxford, 1982)
OMT	Oxford Medieval Texts
Oxford Aristotle	*The Complete Works of Aristotle*, 2 vols., tr. J. Barnes (Oxford, 1984; 1991)
Peñaforte, *Summa*	Raymond of Peñaforte, *Summa de Poenetentia . . . cum glossis Joanis Friburgo* (Rome, 1603; facs. 1967)
PG	J.-P. Migne, *Patrologia Graeca*, 161 vols. (Paris, 1857–)
PIMS	Pontifical Institute of Medieval Studies (Toronto)
PL	J.-P. Migne, *Patrologia Latina*, 221 vols. (Paris, 1857–)
PMLA	*Publications of the Modern Language Association of America* (N.Y., 1884)
Pollock & Maitland	*History of English Law*, 2 vols. (Cambridge, 1895; rev. edn. S. F. C. Milsom, 1968)
Postilla	Nicolaus de Lyra, *Postilla super totam bibliam*, 4 vols. (Strassburg, 1492; repr. Frankfurt/Main, 1972)
PP	William Langland, *Piers Plowman* (edition specified in Notes)
PR	A. Hudson, *The Premature Reformation* (Oxford, 1988)
Properties	John Trevisa, tr., *On the Properties of Things*, 4 vols., ed. M. C. Seymour (Oxford, 1975–88)
Rationale	Durandus of Mende, *Rationale divinorum officiorum*, 3 vols., *CCL* cxl, cxlA, cxlB.
The Riverside Chaucer	ed. L. D. Benson (3rd edn., Boston, Mass., 1987)
Register	*The Register of Henry Chichele*, 4 vols., ed. E. F. Jacob (Oxford, 1943–7)
RHDFE	*Nouvelle revue historique de droit français et étranger*
Rock	Daniel Rock, *The Church of our Fathers*, 4 vols. (London, 1849; repr. 1905)

RS	Rolls Series (London, 1858–1911)
RSV	The Revised Standard Version of the Bible
RTAM	Recherches de théologie ancienne et médiévale (Louvain, 1929–)
Royal Catalogue	Sir George Warner & J. P. Gilson, Catalogue of Western Manuscripts in the Old Royal and King's Collection, 3 vols. (London, 1921)
SAC	Studies in the Age of Chaucer, series ed. T. Hefernan (Knoxville, Tenn., 1978-)
Sarum Missal	ed. J. Wickham Legg (Oxford, 1916; repr. 1969)
SC	F. Madan, Summary Catalogue of Western Manuscripts . . . Bodleian Library
SCH	Studies in Church History, Ecclesiastical History Society, Cambridge
Sermons, ed. Devlin	The Sermons of Thomas Brinton, 2 vols., ed. M. A. Devlin (London, 1954)
Sources and Analogues	Sources and Analogues of Chaucer's Canterbury Tales, ed. W. F. Bryan and G. Dempster (N.Y., 1951; repr. 1958)
Speculum	Journal of the Medieval Academy of America (Cambridge, Mass., 1825-)
SSEL	Salzburg Studies in English Literature
ST	Aquinas, Summa theologica (edition specified in Notes; cited by Part (Roman numerals), Question (Arabic number), Article (Arabic number)
STC	Short Title Catalogue, 2 vols., ed. Pollard & Redgrave (2nd edn. London, 1986)
Tanner, Heresy	Norman P. Tanner, ed., Heresy Trials in the Diocese of Norwich, 1423–31 Camden Society 19 ser., 20 (London, 1977)
Text	Transactions of the Society for Textual Scholarship, ed. D. C. Gretham et al. (N.Y.)
Traité . . . S. Luc	St Ambrose, Traité sur L'Evangile de S. Luc, 2 vols., ed. and tr. G. Tissot (Paris, 1971–6)
TWT	Two Wycliffite Texts, ed. A. Hudson (EETS, 301)
VL	Vulgar Latin
Vulgate	Biblia sacra iuxta Vulgatem versionem, 2 vols., ed. R. Weber (3rd edn., Stuttgart, 1983)
Walther	Proverbia, sententiaeque latinitatis medii aevi, 9 vols., ed. P. G. Schmidt (Göttingen, 1963–9)
Whiting	Proverbs, Sentences, and Proverbial Phrases from English Writings Mainly Before 1500, ed. B. J. and H. W. Whiting (Cambridge, 1968)

Wilkins	*Concilia Magnae Britanniae et Hiberniae*, 4 vols., ed. D. Wilkins (London, 1737)
WLP	*Works of a Lollard Preacher*, ed. A. Hudson (EETS 317)
WS	Wyclif Society (fl. London 1882–1924)
Wyclif	John Wyclif: refs. to individual works: *De servitute civili et dominio seculari*, WS 1913 (*De civ. dom.*); *De eucharistia*, WS 1892 (*De euch.*); *De mandatis divinis*, WS 1922 (*De mand.*); *Polemical Works*, 2 vols., WS 1883 (*Pol. Works*); *De veritate sacrae scripturae*, WS 1905–7 (*De veritate*); *Trialogus*, ed. G. Lechler, Oxford, 1869 (*Trialogus*); *Sermones*, 4 vols., WS 1887–90 (*Serm.*). Dates cited from W. R. Thomson, *The Latin Writings of John Wyclyf* (PIMS, Toronto, 1983).

INTRODUCTION

1. GENRE

In the early fifteenth century, *Dives and Pauper*[1] was a work that had no close analogues, and after nearly six hundred years, it remains hard to classify. It sits uncomfortably among the short expositions of the Decalogue with which it has been classed,[2] because it is too long and too full of stories, poems, and miscellaneous lore. Among Middle English religious tracts of comparable length and inclusiveness,[3] it is out of place as too learned, too controversially theological and too topical.

An early printer of *D&P*, Thomas Berthelet, in his colophon of 1536, called the work 'a compendiouse treatyse'. It is indeed a compendium of knowledge. But 'treatise' in the ordinary modern sense of the word does not quite describe it. *D&P* is both a treatise and a dialogue. If the modern word 'treatise' retained its Middle English connotations—cognate with 'treaty'—'colloquy' or 'negotiating session' or, especially, a 'meeting for discussion', it would be a better fit.[4] When the author of *D&P* himself, in the prologue to his later sermon cycle, called his earlier work a 'tretys' he may well have had in mind the wider Middle English sense of the word. Perhaps it is best not to argue with the author: *D&P* is a treatise that treats of many things and leads, in the end, to a treaty of peace between two contentious interlocutors.

No Middle English treatise—understanding the word in the dual sense of 'compendiousness' and 'dialogue'—on the Commandments is available for comparison with *D&P*. Large-scale treatments of this

---

[1] Ed. P. H. Barnum (2 vols., EETS 275, 280, 1976–80); referred to hereafter as *D&P*. Page references in the text to Vol. I:1 will be written page/line; page references to Vol. I:2 will be written 2–page/line.

[2] As in the Hartung *Manual*, 7:2287–8. P. S. Jolliffe explains why he cannot find a place for it among 'prose writings of spiritual guidance' (*Check-list*, p. 29, note 81). H. G. Pfander also rejects *D&P* from the class of 'manuals of religious instruction' (*JEGP* 35 (1936), 244, note 1). On the other hand, A. I. Doyle says: 'The author of *Dives & Pauper* seems to have had a better sense of the general conditions of his time' (*Survey*, 1:93).

[3] e.g., Mirk's *Festial*; *Jacob's Well*; *Handlyng Synne*.

[4] Definitions from *MED*, sv. 'tretis(e', 1 and 2; *MED* cites Trevisa's use of the word in both senses in the *Polychronicon* 1:7, and in his *On the Properties of Things* 2:1204/36–8.

topic survive only in Latin. John Wyclif's *De mandatis divinis* (1375/6) may be the only contemporary work on the Commandments of comparable length and inclusiveness. His *De mandatis* has a central feature in common with *D&P*: it discusses the Commandments in the contexts both of Church law and the laws of civil society. The large general topic it proposes for itself is the exploration of justice, *ius*, in light of the seemingly double standard offered by the Old and New Testaments of the Bible: Old Testament *ius* and New Testament *caritas*. Can God's laws and man's laws be harmonized? In his summing-up, Wyclif asks the question with which *D&P* opens: What do the scriptures teach the Christian about wealth or *temporalia*? The rich man (Wyclif says) is more strongly tempted by mammon than the poor man; it is harder for him to obey the law of Christ; his cupidity leads him to the ultimate sin of pride.[5] Read in light of Wyclif's concluding peroration, *D&P* can seem very much like a long reply to the question, If what John Wyclif says about the possession of wealth is true, is there any hope that I—a rich man— can avoid damnation?

From this point of view, *D&P*'s 'Holy Poverty' prologue is a cleric's debate with a layman over how to reconcile property and powerful social position with salvation. When the poor man's (Pauper's) case for 'poverty' is totally rejected by the rich man (Dives), the rich man suggests:

The same tale tolde me þin brothir twenty wynter hens, but we spokyn þanne most of the hye perfeccioun of excelencye. I preye þe, lete vs now a qhyle spekyn of the *lesse perfeccioun* þat is nedeful to alle, for sythin I may nought atteynyn to the *more perfeccioun* I wolde as me must kepyn and heldyn wel the lesse perfeccioun. (italics added)[6]

The 'poor man' then undertakes to prescribe a way of life for a man who is leading the 'lyf actyf . . . in doyngge and trauayl and besynes of

---

[5] *De mandatis*.: 'Deus enim semper torquet ad contrarium quod avarus intenderit, et est pena non modica servire mammone, ymmo peccato, quod est infinitum abieccius quam aliqua creatura. . . . hiat namque ad superbiam dives seculo' (p. 473/6–11). An indication of the form in which Wyclif's *De mandatis* circulated *c.*1400 and of the continuing interest in his writings is the abridgement described by Rachel Pyper, *MÆ* 52 (1983), 306–9: MS Bodley Laud misc. 524. Wyclif's earlier writings (less polemical and theologically orthodox) are referred to here and in the Explanatory Notes as a source of contemporary views of many topics discussed in *D&P*.

[6] *D&P*, I:1, 66/22–7. Wyclif, unlike the author of *D&P*, addresses himself to a clerical audience and does not hesitate to recommend voluntary poverty as a sovereign remedy against such temptations.

body and soule' (69/54–5). Thus *D&P* is describable only in part as a treatise (in either sense) on the Commandments. It spills over into another genre when it presents itself as a layman's guide to the practical uses of the Commandments.

The Latin and vernacular guides to the development of the life of the spirit were written primarily for those who were in or who were intending to pursue a religious life, in a convent or monastery or as recluses. Ordinarily such guides contain a passage in which the styles of life are laid out as 'active', 'mixed' or 'contemplative', after which the writer goes on to develop the requirements of the last. Walter Hilton's tract of 1370–80, 'On the Mixed Life', is exceptional in taking account of the spiritual needs and aspirations of the lay Christian, especially those who

han souereynte wiþ moche auere [possession] of wordli goodis, and hauen also as it were lordschipe ouere oþere men for to gouerne and sustene hem, as a fader haþ ouer his children, a maister ouer his seruauntes, and a lord ouere his tenantes, þe which men han also receyued of oure lordis ȝift grace of deuocioun, and in partie sauoure of goostli occupacioun. Vnto þise men also longeþ þis medeled [mixed] lif, þat is both actif and contemplatif.[7]

Such a passage in such a tract could have suggested to the author of *D&P* the possibility of combining a treatise on the Commandments with a more extended answer to the neglected question of how the active life was actually to be led, if kept within the limits of the *lex Christi*.

But is *D&P* a dialogue with a single theme—the 'active' life of the lay Christian? The 'Holy Poverty' prologue brings about a meeting between *two* persons who need one another. The life of the poor mendicant preacher is just as much an 'active' life as that of the rich layman. The friar-preacher's pursuit of 'hye perfeccioun' in the uncloistered settings of parish churchyards, village streets, great manor houses and London thoroughfares is likewise an uncharted possibility. The quest is therefore a dual one. Each participant needs

[7] Walter Hilton's 'Mixed Life', SSEL 92:15 (1986), p. 12/122–131. The tract, which may have been addressed to a nobleman, assumes a desire for an active life combined with a degree of religious devotion. See Explanatory Notes 68/43–5. For a less admiring view of the active life, Aelred of Rievaulx, *De Institutione Inclusarum*, EETS, 287 (1984): 'Let hem þat beþ more contemptible and rude to spirituale . . . bysie hem wit þe wordle, let hem cleppe to hem carayne and dung . . .', p. 37/474–6. On devotional works aimed at lay as well as clerical readers, G. R. Keiser, 'Nought how long man lifs; bot how wele', in *De Cella in Seculum*, ed. M. G. Sargent (Cambridge, 1989), pp, 145–59.

something the other is able to give. The rich man begs the poor man for moral instruction; the poor man begs the rich man for sustenance—perhaps also for protection—so that he can preach and teach the truth without fear. In the *vita activa* chosen by both, each will follow his own path to the goal of salvation.

D&P also has some claim to the status of a literary work. Much of it is written in a clear, vigorous style, and it undertakes with no little success to dramatize its complex subject by means of personification and dialogue.[8] The Vulgate Bible,[9] cited copiously and translated with care and artistry, provides a running backdrop to the argument; this is supplemented by secular tales and poems from a wide variety of sources.[10] According to each of the genres or contexts in which it is placed—or according to the particular interests of the reader—*D&P* presents different faces; thus its several aspects are best described separately. *D&P* will first be discussed in its historical setting, then (briefly) as literature, then as a theological work and finally evaluated by its author's own criterion—as a delineation of the paths of 'less and more perfection'.

2. HISTORICAL SETTING, DATE AND AUTHORSHIP

D&P was written in England during the long-continued papal schism (1378–1417), half a century after the Great Plague (1348–50), a quarter century after the Peasants' Revolt (1381–2), and only a few years after the deposition of Richard II (1399). The author, by giving two easily dateable references to external events, indicates that he began to write at some time after 1402, and that in 1405 he was at work on *D&P*. The first of these references is to the spectacular, Europe-wide appearance of a comet in 1402: '. . . þat wondyrful comete and sterre queche apperydde vpon þis lond þe ʒer of oure lord M CCCC II, from þe Ephiphanye tyl too wokys aftryn tyl myd Aperyl'[11] This provides a *terminus post quem* for the date of composition. The second piece of internal evidence is a reference to the fact that in 1400 'þe kalendis of Ieneuer [January] fellyn on þe Thursday.

---

[8] Noticed long ago by G. R. Owst, *Literature and Pulpit* (1933; repr. 1966), esp. pp. 543–5.
[9] See Scriptural Index for *D&P*.   [10] See Non-scriptural Index for *D&P*.
[11] *D&P* 147/20–148/23; see Explanatory Notes 147/5–20.

. . . and þis ʒer [i.e., 1405] ben comyn aʒen on þe Thursday' (183/14–20). Both these references appear in Commandment I, which also contains allusions to troubles that fell to the lot of the English 'nacioun' at or near the same time:

And so I drede me that God wile maken an ende of this lond, for we louen no pees, we seken no mercy, but oure lykyngge is al in warre and wo, in mordre and shedyng of blood, in robrie and falshed. . . . And ouermore, so welawey, they haue ordeyned a *comoun lawe* that what man speke with the trewthe aʒens here falshed he shal be *hangen, drawen and heueded* (148–9/39–46).

The 'comoun lawe' referred to is probably (because of 'common' and the imposition of the death penalty) the *De heretico comburendo*, a law passed by Parliament in 1401 making heresy, for the first time in England, a capital crime.[12] This reference provides an additional *terminus post quem* for *D&P*.

Protests expressed by the author of *D&P* against recent laws restricting preaching and the distribution of Bible translations also have a bearing on the date of *D&P*. Before 1407, the Englishing of the Bible text was urged openly and not only by Wyclif, Lollards and their sympathisers. The debate was so lively and open, especially in Oxford, from the last decade or so of the fourteenth century that Oxford became a byword for such controversy: 'Syche dowtis we schulden sende to þe scole of Oxenforde'[13]—and conservative churchmen became alarmed. In 1407, Archbishop Arundel chose Oxford—the source of the trouble—as the venue for the first announcement of his famous Constitutions, which sought to enforce licensing of translations of the scriptures into English and also of preachers.[14] The text of *D&P* refers to this recent effort to

[12] See Explanatory Notes 148/44. The mistake about what the penalty for heresy would be is puzzling; perhaps the novelty of the penalty in England was slow to sink in compared to the shock of finding heresy a capital crime. The possibility that another capital offense is being referred to here, one especially concerning Franciscans, is discussed in the Notes, 148/44 and 149/57.

[13] EWS, 1:370/47–8. On the entire period of the Oxford debate on Wyclif's views (1381–1413), see A. Hudson, *PR* (1988), pp. 60–119; see also, idem, 'Wycliffism in Oxford 1381–1411', in *Wyclif and his Times* (1986), pp. 67–84; see Explanatory Notes 327/10.

[14] Wilkins, 3:314–9; for the text of the 1408 Constitutions, William Lyndwood *Provinciale seu constitutiones Angliae* [completed in 1433] (Oxford, 1679), s.v. 'Constitutiones Provinciales in concilio Oxon. celebratae', pp. 64–8. On Thomas Arundel (d. 1414), including a summary of his conflict with the Oxford community, *BRUO*, 1:15–3. A recent article surveys the background of the controversy: N. Watson, 'Censorship and Cultural Change in Late Medieval Englsnd: Vernacular Theology, the Oxford Translation Debate, and Arundel's Constitutions of 1409', *Speculum* 70:4 (1995), 822–64.

restrict access to the vernacular Bible, though without naming Arundel:

But now men seyyn þat þer schulde no lewyd folc ent[yr]mettyn hem of Godis lawe ne of þe gospel ne of holy writ, neyþer to connyn it ne to techyn it (327/3–5).

. . .

Godis lawe [the Bible] is forȝetyn and defendyd [forbidden] þat men schul nout connyn it ne han it in her moder tunge (2–64/68–9).

D&P protests even more bitterly against restrictions on preaching:

. . . alle þo þat lettyn Godis word and lettyn hem þat han autorite to prechyn & techyn . . . þei ben mansleeris gostlyche . . . & namely þese proude couetous prelatis & curatis þat neyþer connyn techyn ne wiln techin ne suffryn oþir þat connyn techyn & woldyn techin & han auctorite to techyn but lettyn hem for dred þat þei schuldyn han þe lesse of her sogetis ȝif ony of hem ȝeue þe prechour ony elmesse (2–22/39–47).

Whether *D&P*'s protests against restrictions on preaching predated or followed—or both—the Arundel Constitutions is uncertain.[15] The rivalry between Franciscans and the secular clergy certainly predated 1407.

Neither author nor patron of *D&P* has so far been identified. The author's intentions in writing, the years when he wrote, his religious affiliation, his milieu, and who, apart from his patron, his readership was expected to be, must be surmised mainly from internal evidence and the historical setting. In 1933, H. G. Pfander agreed with H. G. Richardson that John Bale[16] had been mistaken in attributing *D&P* to the Carmelite friar, Henry Parker. It seemed most probable to Pfander that the author was a Franciscan friar who flourished much earlier in the fifteenth century.[17] He noted the praise of poverty, the emphasis on preaching, the attacks on prelates and recluses, the complaisance about expenditure on burial rites and on churches—all of which could fit members of any of the orders of mendicants. He opts for a Franciscan on the basis of mention of a life of St Francis (319/71).[18]

---

[15] See Explanatory Notes, 327/10.

[16] John Bale (1495–1568), Reformation playwright and polemicist, author of *Illustrium majoris Britannias scriptorum . . .* (1548), notable for its early compilation of information about British writers, as well as for its many inaccuracies.

[17] 'Dives et Pauper', *The Library* 14 (1933), pp. 299–312.

[18] He did not see another mention, in the 'Coventry' story found only in MS G (2–193/25–194/61); nor the description of the Apostles' footware: 'gallochis, a soole benethyn wyt a festyng aboutyn þe foot' (93/5–6), which takes the Conventual Franciscan side of a controversy about the poverty of Christ.

In 1934, H. G. Richardson[19] responded to Pfander and introduced
some speculations that tended to cloud the issue of authorship.
Richardson argued first that the Holy Poverty prologue was a separate
work, basing this on his inspection of the acephalous Harleian manuscript; this manuscript is, however (as I have shown in my edition of
the text), a later, rather careless copy and one of the worst witnesses to
the original. The discovery of the Longleat sermons in 1984 (see
below) finally disposed of this speculation when it was found that the
author of *D&P* himself referred to his earlier work as 'diues et
pauper'—the *incipit* of the 'Holy Poverty' Prologue—indicating that
he considered this the beginning of the First Commandment portion
of the treatise.

Richardson had also been reluctant to agree with Pfander that the
work was written by a Franciscan. This was impossible, he said,
because of the opposition of the Order to translations of the Bible into
the vernacular.[20] But it is now not as clear as Richardson then
assumed that the author of *D&P* was in fact writing 'with a view
to publication and distribution', nor that in *c.*1405 (two years before
the first of Arundel's Constitutions) all minds had been changed and
all open interest in a vernacular text of the Bible had been snuffed out.
The Regent Master of the Oxford convent cited by Richardson,
William Butler,[21] wrote his *determinacio* against translation of the
Bible into English in 1401 in the context of a long-running Oxford
debate on the issue, from which his happens to be one of the few
surviving manuscripts. In Margaret Deanesly's account of the debate
(relied on by Richardson), John Purvey[22] features as a leading Lollard
proponent of translation (as well as author of the prologue to the
Wycliffite Bible and secretary to Wyclif); but serious doubts about all

[19] In an article which, read many years later, led to my starting work on an edition of the
text, Richardson wrote: 'I had undertaken to edit *Dives and Pauper* . . . not long before the
War [World War I] . . . But when I was prepared to resume in 1919, times were not
propitious . . . and an accumulation of commitments forbids all thought of my ever taking
Dives and Pauper in hand again. The field is therefore clear': *The Library* 15 (1934), 31.
[20] He cites A. C. Paves, *A Fourteenth-Century English Biblical Version* (1904), pp. xxxi ff.;
and M. Deanesly, *The Lollard Bible and Other Medieval Biblical Versions* (1920; repr. 1969),
pp. 268; 289 ff.
[21] William Butler (d. 1410?) was the thirteenth Provincial of the Franciscans in England;
see *DNB* s.v.; *BRUO*, 1:329; *Monumenta* (RS, 1858), pp. 538; 561; M. Deanesly, op. cit.,
pp. 317; 320; 399–418; C. L. Kingsford, *The Grey Friars of London* (Aberdeen, 1915), p. 194;
A. Hudson, *Lollards and their Books* (London, 1985), pp. 67–8; 150; 155–7. The early
information about Butler comes from John Bale, *Scriptorium*, 2 vols. (Basel, 1557–90), pt. i,
pp. 536–7. The *determinacio* is found in Oxford, Merton Coll. MS 68, fos. 202–4ᵛ.
[22] On John Purvey, see BRUO, 3:1526–7.

these propositions have subsequently arisen.[23] With the discovery of a manuscript of the Latin original, the 'Purvey' tract defending vernacular translation and distribution of the Bible to the laity has now been reascribed to Richard Ullerston (d. 1425), a prominent and quite orthodox cleric, who at about the same date (1401) also wrote a tract against the Lollards on the question of Church dominion over property.[24] Anne Hudson sums up: 'It . . . seems clear that interest in questions which had been raised by Wyclif and which later became identified with Lollardy continued in Oxford up to 1407'.[25]

Thus around the turn of the century there were many views of the matter, all quite freely expressed, and to ascribe the view of one Franciscan to the whole Order is untenable. During the two centuries since the founding of the Order, in fact, internal controversy had been the rule rather than the exception.[26]

The discovery, announced in 1984 by Anne Hudson and H. L. Spencer, of a manuscript (Longleat 4) containing a sermon cycle by the author of *D&P* removed several more misconceptions. The discoverers noted that on the first leaf of the manuscript was written: 'But of þis mater I spak more largely in þe tretys which

---

[23] Deanesly was interested in Butler primarily because of her interest in the career of Purvey, whom she considered to be a leader in the movement for vernacular scriptures and a leading Lollard (*The Lollard Bible*, pp. 268–97); Butler is mentioned pp. 289–90. Subsequent investigation by Anne Hudson has cast serious doubt on this view ('The Debate on Bible Translation, Oxford 1401', *EHR* 90 (1975), 1–18; 'John Purvey: a Reconsideration of his Life and Writings', *Viator* xii, 1981, pp. 355–80; both repr. in her *Lollards* (London, 1985), pp. 67–110). She writes: 'I see no reason whatever to assign to Purvey any particular association with the Lollard Bible, or with any of the texts advocating vernacular scriptures', idem, p. 108.

[24] Anne Hudson discusses the Latin text and identifies its author from a MS fragment (the final page) with a colophon attributing the authorship to Richard Ullerston ('The Debate on Bible Translation': *Lollards*, pp. 74–6). An English version of the tract, with revisions and additions, is printed in Arber's *English Reprints* (London, 1871), pp. 170–84). Curt Bühler edited a Middle English version of the tract in 'A Lollard Tract on Translating the Bible into English', *MÆ*, 7:3 (1938), 167–83. On Purvey, see A. Hudson, 'John Purvey: a Reconsideeration of the Evidence', *Lollards*, pp. 85–110. Deanesly's treatment of the views of Innocent III on Bible translation has been corrected by L. E. Boyle, 'Innocent III and Vernacular Versions of Scripture', *SCH*, Subsidia 4, ed. K. Walsh and D. Wood (1985), pp. 97–107.

[25] A. Hudson, *Lollards* (1985), p. 83.

[26] See, e.g., J. Moorman (Oxford, 1968), *passim*. On the Continent, friars, as agents of papal power, were leading lights in the Inquisition; on the other hand, in England, Franciscan dissidents ranged from the group involved in maintaining that Richard II still lived (see E. F. Jacob, *The Fifteenth Century*, Oxford, 1961, pp. 27–9) to those such as William Russell (warden of the friars minor in London) tried for heresy (see *BRUOi*, 3:1611–12; *Chichele Register*, ed. E. F. Jacob (Oxford, 1943–7), 1:cxlii–cxliii; 3:104–5; 118–38; 151–7; 175–7). See also F. S. Haydon, ed. *Eulogium* (RS, 1858–63), pp. 390–4.

begynnyth diues et pauper in þe fyrste comaundement'. The manuscript contains five further specific references to *D&P* and is
otherwise consistent with common authorship.[27] The prologue to
the sermons contains a vivid suggestion that their author had *not*
intended his work for wide distribution and that he was, at the very
time of writing, in some sort of hiding (possibly under the wing of a
powerful protector) because of his expressed views. He wrote
defiantly:

. . . euery man & womman . . . schulde connyn þe gospel . . . in euery
language þat þe peple myȝte connyn þe gospel & vnderstonden it . . . And
þerfore þoȝu it be þese dayis defendit [forbidden] & inhybyȝt be somme
prelatis þat men schulde techin þe gospel in englych . I answere & sey to
hem. . . . it behouith in þis cas more to obeyȝin to god þanne to men (LL4,
fo. 1rb).

As in *D&P*, he addresses himself to his 'leue frend' and—to judge
from the Prologue alone—he is at this date even more dependent on
his patron and more explicit about his opposition to 'some prelatis' on
the questions of preaching and teaching, translation of the Bible, and
the proper use of images in churches:

And þerfore leue frend . alþoȝu somme prelatis han defendyt me to techin þe
gospel & to writin it in englych . ȝet non of hem hath defendit ȝou ne may
defendin ȝou to connyn þe gospel in englych þat is ȝoure kendely language.
. . . And sitthe I haue wretin þe gospel to ȝou in wol gret drede &
persecucioun ȝe þat ben in swych sekyrnesse þat non prelat may lettin
[hinder] ȝou ne dishesin ȝou for connynge ne for kepinge of þe gospel .
connyth it & kepith it with good deuocioun. . . . & þoȝu þe persecucioun of
deoclician & maximian be now newly begonnyn to lettin techinge &
prechinge of goddys word & goddis lawe & to *compellin men to worschepin
grauyn ymagis* of ston & of tre . stonde ȝe stif in þe feyth & worschepith ȝe
ȝoure god abouyn alle þinge . . . (LL4, fos. 1[rb–va]; ital. add.).

Early in Commandment I of *D&P*, it becomes clear that the author
has marked out for his Pauper a path of 'more perfection' that leads
him to make some stringent criticism of the clergy. It is also clear that
the author is not asking for the reform, still less the restructuring of
the Church. Rather he points members of the clergy to the Bible, to
canon law and their glossators, and to the weight of patristic and

---

[27] 'Old Author, New Work', *MÆ* 53, No. 2 (1984), 220–38. A partial edition of the text
has been made by Adrian Willmott: 'An Edition of Selected Sermons from MS. Longleat'
(Ph.D. thesis, Bristol, 1994).

scholastic theological exegesis: Try, he keeps repeating, to live up to these exemplars!

The author makes his complaints about the Church and clergy directly and indirectly. There is direct mention of the mystagogy (as he sees it)[28] surrounding images and the clerics who profit from it (101/45–56; 2–133/1–134/18); of corrupt judges in the ecclesiastical courts (2–210/109–111); of priests who bargain for the highest price for singing masses for souls in purgatory (2–186/1 ff.); and of recipients of benefices who 'absentyn hem from her chirchis only for ese or for couetyse or for lust of þe flech' (2–163/124–5). And there is also far more telling indirect criticism of clerical behaviour in the form of extended translations of passages from commentators on Church law (largely Raymond of Peñafort and John of Freiburg) on simony (2–180/1–183/100), usury (2–198/1–206/80),[29] clerical 'bigamy' (2–115/124–116/131),[30] tithes (2–165/13 ff.), and the qualifications of legal witnesses (2–235/21 ff.). These are the statutes, intended for internal use, which spell out the infractions of Church law for Church authorities to correct and punish.

In addition to the author's negative view of the secular clergy, the guess that he was a Franciscan[31] is based also on what Pauper says about himself at the outset:

Sum tyme I was free as othere been but for Cristys sake, to wynnyn the soulys þat he boughte so dere, I haue mad me seruaunt to alle meen ryche and pore to seruyn hem of soule bote. And for my trauayl I begge myn mete and myn clothyng; oþir hyre aske I noon but þat þey welyn frely ʒeuyn for þe loue of God. (53/15–19)

Friars are the only clerical group mentioned favorably in *D&P* and omitted from the list of clerical groups criticized (317/17–23). Of founders of mendicant Orders, only St Francis is named (319/71, 2–194/61). The writer's stance is that of a freelance cleric who offers preaching and Christian instruction (and perhaps burial rites) to the laity, while keeping up a litany of criticism of the beneficed secular clergy.

Taking the evidence of *D&P* and the Longleat sermons together,

---

[28] Cf. K. Thomas, *Religion and the Decline of Magic* (N.Y., 1971), pp. 33–6; *D&P* is cited on p. 34.

[29] See Explanatory Notes to Com. VII, caps. 24–28..

[30] In the figurative sense of compromising the unity between Christ and the Church; see Explanatory Notes 2–111/1–4.

[31] See Explanatory Notes 51/HOLY POVERT and 54/46–52.

one could also guess that the writer, as a friar, was employed as a member of the household staff of an English magnate. In this period, friars were commonly members of large noble households in both a religious capacity, as confessors, and in a legal capacity, in dealings with the ecclesiastical courts (e.g., 245/1–9), as a normal part of manorial administration. There is in Commandment IV a clear suggestion that the author has in mind for his fictional patron (Dives) the assumption of certain responsibilities for the Christian education of his own household:

[Iche] man & woman is boundyn aftir his degre to don his besynesse to knowyn Godis lawe [i.e., the Bible] þat he is bondyn to kepyn. And *fadris &* *moodris, godfadris & godmoodris are boundyn to techyn her childryn Godis lawe* or ellys don hem be tauȝt. (327/6–10, ital. add.)

He cites St Augustine:

And Sent Austyn seith þat iche man in his owyn houshold schulde don þe offys of þe buschop in techinge & correctynge of comoun þingis. (328/23–5)

and canon law:

And þerfor seith þe lawe þat þe offys of teching & chastysyng longyth nout only to þe buschop but to euery gouernour aftir his name & his degre, to þe pore man gouernynge his pore houshold, to þe riche man gouernynge his mene . . . (328/25–8)[32]

Since the text shows a writer well-read in both theology and canon law, one might also guess that he had been trained in the Oxford convent, with its notable library.[33] A specific indication of this is that among the books cited by him is Thomas Docking's commentary on Deuteronomy. Docking (d. *c.*1270), seventh Lector to the Friars Minor at Oxford, spent his entire career there, and his works probably did not circulate beyond Oxford until, in the second half of the fifteenth century, William Gray, Bishop of Ely, had them copied.[34]

The text of *D&P* reflects the author's awareness that civil life was

---

[32] He cites Deut. 6:6–9; the canon law reference is C.23 q.4 c.35 (Friedberg 1:915–6); and C.23 q.5 c.41 (Friedberg 1:940). Cf. Augustine, *Enarrationes in Psalmos*, 32.12 (*CCL* xxxviii, pp. 256–7/1–43; PL 36:285–6).

[33] See M. B. Parkes, 'The Provision of Books' in *HUO* (1992), 2:431–83.

[34] The friars were criticized in the period for reluctance to lend books, cf. *Jack Upland,* ed. P. L. Heyworth (Oxford, 1968), p. 70/373–6; see also R. H. & M. A. Rouse, 'The Franciscans and Books: Lollard Accusations' in *From Ockham to Wyclif* SCH 24 (1987), pp. 369–84. On Docking, see Explanatory Notes 266/32.

governed by both civil and canon law. Commandment I, cap. xxxv
(159/1), for example, opens with Dives' question whether it was
lawful for anyone who catches a thief red-handed to kill him. Pauper
replies:

It is nou3t leful to ony man for to slen a þef a3ens þe kyngis lawe and
withoutyn proces of londis lawe and withoutyn *autoritie of hese lyche lord* ne
withoutyn a lawful iuge ordeynyd of hys lyche lord (159–60/3–6; ital. add.).

When Dives has assented to this, he continues:

Syth men don so mychil reuerence to þe kyngys lawe and londis lawe to flen
myscheuys þat schuldyn fallyn but þe lawis were kept, mychil mor reuerence
schuldyn þey don to Goddis lawe and holy chyrche lawe . . . for *Goddis lawys
and holy chyrche lawis ben as resonable and as goode as þe kyngis lawis of
Engelond* . . . þe kyngys lawys, 3if it [they] ben iust, it [they] arn Goddis lawis
(160/10–18; ital. add.).

This exchange illustrates both the fragmented character of civil law
and the potential for unification offered (as Pauper sees it) by the
centralized administrative machinery of the Church's canon law.

But Pauper is fully aware of the strains between the two codes.[35] In
the fifth Commandment forbidding killing, it emerges that human
law and God's law sometimes conflict. Dives asks Pauper whether
there is any case in which it is legal ('leful') to kill an innocent person.
Pauper answers that it is legal 'in no cas' and cites canon law as his
authority (C.23 q.5 c.9; 2–49/1–2): 'legal' here apparently means
'moral'. But when Dives asks, 'What if a jury condemns a man the
judge knows is innocent? Shall the judge sentence him to execution?',
'legal' here is taken to mean 'procedurally correct according to civil
law' (2–49/3–5). Pauper repeats his citation of canon law, but Dives
persists: 'What schal he don þan?' forcing Pauper to tackle the issue
as one of civil law. The judge (he now says) has the following choices:
if there is no court of appeal, the judge may overturn the jury's
verdict and save the man; if there is a court of appeal, he may appeal
the case, informing the higher court judge of the facts (2–49–51/8–
50). In the course of the discussion of 'non occides', the precept is
repeatedly shown to apply on a gradient from the absolute immorality
of deliberate killing of humans (God's law) to the permissability of

---

[35] In the late fourteenth century, John Trevisa translated Ockham's 'Dialogus inter
militem et clericum', in which the gap between the two codes is a theme of the early part of
the dialogue (*Dialogus inter Militem et Clericum*, ed. A. J. Perry (EETS 167), pp. 1–38).

killing humans for a variety of reasons (civil law). According to Pauper, a woman (for example) may legally be killed for adultery if civil law permits it (2–53/26–54/39); men who rebel or break the peace may be killed in just wars (2–55/15–41); and though 'clerkis schul nout fyȝtyn for non wordly goodis', even they may kill in self defense (2–56/42–5). In the end, Pauper shows that he is conscious of a divide between his own and Dives' standards: 'Y [Pauper] am sekyr þat God dampnyth mychil manslaute þat ȝe [Dives] and oþere iustyfyyn' (2–57/78–9). A diversion between the two 'paths' is here clearly marked, and the impasse is allowed to stand.

Specific references to political events are all too few in *D&P*, but it is clear that the writer felt he was living in a time of wars and threats of war. God (he felt) was offended with the people of England (148/23–4), whose 'lykyngge is al in warre and wo, in mordre and shedyng of blood' (148/41–2). They pray for peace, but in their hearts they 'preyyn al aȝens þe pes' (198/11–12). Fears of invasion by foreign nations are expressed: '[M]any cuntrees in þis reme ben destroied and chaunged into oþer lordchipe of oþer nacioun' (149/54–6). Continued war has weakened the nation, to the point where a second conquest by the French is to be feared: '[I]t is wol mychil to dredyn þat þis rewme in schort tyme . . . schal ben translatyd aȝen to þe Bretonys' (258/59–61). In 1403, the Bretons in fact briefly took Plymouth, and in 1404 made raids on the Devon coast. In August 1405 French naval forces made a landing at Milford Haven, and the danger from the French did not subside until 1406. During the same period, anti-Lancastrian conspiracies intensified the mood of uncertainty. The activities of certain friars against Henry IV, as well as the trials and executions of a number of them in 1402, may also have a bearing on the dark outlook of the writer of *D&P*.[36]

Danger also threatened the polity from 'comoun clamour of the people' (150/21). The Peasants' Revolt of 1381–2 is the probable referent of the lament:

For pride & rebellion of þe pore peple is cause of destruccion of þis lond, for syth þey aresyn aȝenys her lordis & her souereynys was þer neuyr stabilite in þis lond but alwey sythyn þe tre of þe peple of þis lond & þe rewme hat stondyn in fallynge. (358/37–40)

---

[36] See Explanatory Notes 148/44, 149/53–4, 149/57. A long passage, found only in MS G of *D&P*, deploring the abuse of confessors may possibly be linked to this incident, see Explanatory Notes 250/18–251/58.

The author's social philosophy is expressed in his speech near the close of Commandment IV:

. . . as longe as ony peple is buxum & meke to her souereyns & wiln folwyn her good gouernance & worchepyn men aftir her degre . . . so longe þat peple is able to kepyn þat lond þat God hat ȝouyn hem & to lyuyn good lyf. But whan þei wiln rebellyn her souereyns & nout wiln stondyn to her ordinance but euery man wil ben his owyn man & folwyn his owyn fantasyys & despysyn her souereynys . . . þat peple is able to þe swerd & able sone to lesyn his lond. (357/5–17)

Other nations, the author says sadly, surveying the English civil wars, 'slen us in euery syde & robbyn us and we han lytil sped or non but only to slen our owyn nacion' (2–57/84–6).

The author comes close to alluding to a specific event when, in speaking of martyrdom in general, he says that the English have made many martyrs, sparing 'neyþer here owyn kyng ne her buschopys, no dignyte, non ordre, no staat, no degre but indifferently slen as hem lykyth' (209/21–7). The allusion is almost certainly to the execution of Richard Scrope in York in 1405, the Archbishop having sided with the opposition to Henry IV by the Percies and others. The reference is slightly muffled by the subsequent mention of the murder of Thomas Becket at the behest of Henry II in 1170. The cult of St Thomas Becket set a precedent for the popularization of a political cause under cover of religious veneration, and Scrope's execution 'provoked an immediate and widespread veneration of the cleric as a martyr'.[37] D&P's 'þey woldyn be comoun clamor & comoun assent han slayn here owyn kyng' (209/26–7) depends on its context. There is some evidence (mentioned above) that among Franciscans especially there was a persisting loyalty to Richard II, deposed in 1399. But the 'comoun clamor' could also and more plausibly be read as aimed against Henry IV, especially if Scrope's execution is the intended reference, as 'now' (209/21) indicates.

The plague is mentioned as an expected calamity among other calamities: 'auenture of hungyr, of moreyn, of tempest, of droughte, of whet [too much rain]' (143/45–6), but the special terror it caused is suggested by the description:

Sumtyme is moreyn general, sumtyme parcyal, in on contree nought in anothir; sumtyme in on toun and nought in þe nexte; sumtyme in þe to syde

---

[37] J. W. McKenna, 'Popular Canonization as Political Propaganda', *Speculum* 45:4 (1970), p. 611. See Explanatory Notes 209/21–7. See also Note 192/54–193/75.

of þe strete and nought in þe tothir. Sum houshold it taky3t vp al hool; at þe
nexte it taky3t noon. Summe dey3yn in 3ougthe, summe in elde, summe in
medyl age, summe wel, summe wol euele, summe wyt lytil peyne, summe
wyt mechil peyne. (146/73–147/79)[38]

In England, the Black Death had first appeared in 1348 in Bristol.
There were four major recurrences, in 1361, 1369, 1374–9 and
1390–3. Thus for the author of *D&P* it was not a tale told by
elders but an ever-present reality.

Plague is one of the dire social ills that, with 'hungyr . . . tempest . . .
sekenesse . . . and werre [war]' (117/14–15) people endeavour by one
means or another to predict. The author of *D&P* seems to have been
particularly exercised about astrology, which he saw as a kind of *lèse
majesté*, or effort to be 'of Godys preuy counseyl, wyl God nyl God'
(117/7). He spends over half of Commandment I (itself the longest
part of the treatise) attacking astrology and related methods of
prognostication. When *D&P* was written 'astronomy' comprised
the objective study of the heavens as well as the casting of horoscopes,
and the terms 'astronomy' and 'astrology' were more or less interchangeable. 'Judicial' astronomy referred more narrowly to predictions of individual fates. Though opposed by the Church since
Augustine,[39] the belief and the practice persisted.[40] In *D&P*, the
author allows Dives to express what was for the period the enlightened view that horoscopes were foolish but that the stars have a
general influence on human affairs, a view shared by the respected
astronomer Nicholas Oresme (*c.*1320–82).[41] Pauper, however, is made
to express more sweeping condemnation:

þis maner of speche is nought ellys but a meyntenyngge of lesynggys and of
fayterye and an hydyng of folye and a synful excusacioun of synne and a
neeth [net] to lacchyn wyt mannys soule . . . and to drawyn mannys herte, his
loue and his trost from God. (125/17–21)

Pauper not only argues that astrology competes with God but also
that it deflects man's attention from God's own handiwork, nature.
Human diversity in people results, he says, from many natural causes:
'excees of mete and drynk' (129/49), 'mysdyetyngge of þe moder
qhyl she is wyt childe' (129/52–3), carelessness in watching over

---

[38] See Explanatory Notes 146/73–147/81.
[39] Cf. *De civ. dei*, Bk. V, e.g.
[40] See Explanatory Notes 117/3–43.
[41] See Explanatory Notes 125/6–7.

children, who are inclined to put anything into their mouths and so 'venymyn hemself and hurtyn hemself in many wyse' (129/58), and from parents who love their children too much 'and welyn goon to helle to makyn hem riche and grete in þis word [world]' (129/61–2). He takes the common sense view that children born near the sea are likely to become fishermen; those born inland, farmers, shepherds, miners or vintners (131/14–27), despite their horoscopes. Nor is astrology helpful in weather forecasting. Rather, observation should indicate that sweating of stones, melting of salt, smoke in the house, a halo around the candle flame, and a blue glow to the fire predict rain. The best meteorologists are sailors, shepherds and farmers who experience its effects most directly (141/48–50). It is God, not the stars, who ordains the seasons and the endless diversity in 'tree, in gres, in best, fysh and foul' (146/62–3).

Pauper also gives common sense explanations for soothsayers' apparent knowledge of private matters: they are persons who 'slyleche kunnen appose the shepherd and the ploughman in the feld or som eld symple folk or childreyn at þe tounys ende and asken how it stant amonges neygheboures and abouten in the contre, and after that they tellen hem they maken hem wyse as thowe they knewen it be astronomye or be prophesye or be nigromaunsye' (151/47–51). But, he complains, 'þese dayys' the English people 'nouȝt with-stondynge þat þey fyndyn þe fendys talys and his craftis wol false be gret and oftyn experience' continue to believe in such soothsayers (161/52–9). He scoffs at calendar magic, pointing out that the kalends of January, which fell on a supposedly lucky Thursday in 1400 and again in 1405, brought nothing but hunger, pestilence and war in the first of these years and even worse in the second (183/14–22). And he disposes of alchemy by observing that alchemists are ordinarily 'wol pore and wol nedy' (185/8–9).

In the change of subject (in cap. li of the first Commandment) from superstitions to architecture, Dives is made to comment on the 'fayre chirchys' of England, surpassing those in other lands (188/12–15). Though Pauper replies that it is all a hollow show, this passage may nevertheless be read as a reflection of the historical fact that there had been an architectural flowering in the reign of Edward III (1328–1377). Under the King's generous patronage and that of his friends, Yeveley and other important architects devised the Perpendicular style and undertook the refashioning of Norman churches. By 1400, the nave of Canterbury Cathedral was nearly complete; the remodel-

ling of Westminster Hall was nearly finished; and work on the nave at
Winchester was underway.[42]

Recent changes in musical taste are also noted in the dialogue.
When Dives complains about polyphonic singing of the service (206/
28–30), Pauper defends it: 'Godis offys schulde ben seyd & songyn
lyflyche, distynctlych, deuoutlych, with gladnesse of herte' (207/59–
61); he contrasts this lively musical style with the older chant, which
is sung so 'heuylyche' and 'dedlyche' that it 'loþith [disgusts] boþe þe
synger and þe hereris and bryngith folc into heuynesse & distraccion'
(207/62).[43]

The author of *D&P* is also on the side of the use of drama for
moral and religious instruction. In Commandment III, cap. xvii,
Pauper extols 'steraclis'—mystery plays—and more specifically the
'pleyynge at Christenmesse Heroudis & þe thre kyngis & oþir proces
of the gospel boþin þan & at Estryn' (293/12–24; 22–4). While Dives'
doubts about such 'merthe-makynge' expressed here (294/35–7, 49–
56; 296/1–2; 296/1–2; 21 ff.) might possibly be thought to reflect
Lollard opposition to plays and dances on religious themes, Pauper
defends this form of religious instruction for the people.[44] But the
author felt obliged to cite canon law to bolster his argument,
indicating that he was aware that the matter was controversial.[45]

3. *D&P* AS A LITERARY WORK

In the broadest sense, *D&P* exists on a borderline between the Latin
language, classical and medieval, and Middle English. The Middle
English dialogue rests lightly on an ancient foundation: the Latin of
the Christian writers of the classical period, the Latin of the scholastic
writers, the Latin of Church law and its glossators, the Latin of the
penitential handbooks, the Latin of popular tales and natural history,
the Latin of saints' legends, the Latin of the liturgy, and—above all—

---

[42] See Explanatory Notes 188/14–45 and 202/42–3.

[43] See Explanatory Notes 206/28–33 and 206/30.

[44] Wyclif opposed the more boisterous forms of rest and recreation on Sundays but did
not allude to religious drama: 'Sed, heu hodie in ecclesia diebus festivis populus plus gule,
luxurie, contencionibus et maleficiis intentus quam per totum residuum septimane. . . .
Tempus enim quod est Dei servicio specialiter deputatum est econtra per ipsos appropriate
servicio dyaboli dedicatum', *De mandatis* (WS, London, 1907), p. 223/23–9. Anne Hudson
(1988) points out, however, that much of what is tagged as Lollard 'could be matched from
orthodox preaching' *PR*, p. 387.

[45] See Explanatory Notes 293/21–2.

the Latin of the Vulgate and its glossators. *D&P* is very far from being a free-standing work in Middle English. In judging its literary qualities, or lack of them, two questions are central: How good a translator is the author? And does he add anything of his own—anything native—to his work?

The answer to the first question is that the author of *D&P* was a fluent and adroit translator. He knew how to borrow an old tale and adapt it to new uses, For him, the Vulgate text was a plastic medium to be shaped to fit an argument—a preacher's approach to the text.[46] On occasion, he makes metrical versions of the text (2–245/5–8), and he does not hesitate to rearrange or omit verses in order to achieve better poetry or a more pointed argument. His translation of Ecclesiasticus 26:1–24 (for example) omits verses 4–15, 18, 20, and 22 in order to avoid intrusive comments on the 'bad' wife and to transform the passage into a poetical paean to the ideal wife:

Blyssyd is þat man þat hat a good woman to hys wyf;
hys ȝerys schul ben dublyd & he schal endyn hys ȝerys in pes.
A good woman is a good part in a good part of hem þat dredyn God
& she schal ben ȝouyn to a man for his goode dedis.
The grace of þe besy woman shal lykyn hyr housebonde
& make his bonys fette.
Hyr disciplyne & hyr norture is þe ȝifte of God,
& þe holy woman & chast is grace upon grace.
As þe sonne schynyng illumynyth þe world in þe heiþe of þe day
so þe bewte of a good woman is in confort & aray of hyr houshold.
And as goldene pylerys set on sylueren baas,
so ben sekyr feet on þe solys of þe stable woman,
& endeles groundys on a sykyr ston
ben Godis comandementis in þe herte of an holy woman. (2–89/24–33)[47]

The author of *D&P* clearly read the Latin Bible not only as a theological but also as a literary work. His sensitivity to its language is shown in his rewordings of his biblical citations. His cuts and amplifications tailor his texts to the contexts in which they appear.[48] A translation of Ezek. 34:2–8 in *D&P* (for example) can be compared with the same author's translation of the text in his sermon cycle and with the Wycliffite Bible translation. The Wycliffite Bible:

[46] Comparison can be made with the 'earlier and later' translations in the Wycliffite Bible dating from the last two decades of the fourteenth century (FM 3:173–4).

[47] In the manuscripts of *D&P*, the lines are set as prose. See text 2–102/74–91 for another fine verse translation.

[48] This is true also of the biblical texts cited in his sermon cycle in MS Longleat 4.

Wo to the schepherdis of Israel, that fedden hym silf; whether flockis ben not fed of schepherdis? ȝe eeten mylk, and weren hilid with wollis, and ȝe killiden that that was fat; but ȝe fedden nout my floc. ȝe maden not sad that that was vnstidfast, and ȝe maden not hool that that was sijk; ȝe bounden not that that was brokun, and ȝe brouȝten not aȝen that that was cast awei, and ȝe souȝten nout that that perischide; but ȝe comaundiden to hem with sturnenesse, and with power. And my scheep weren scaterid, for no sheepherde was. (FM 3:580–1)

In this faithful translation, the 'shepherds' remain safely distanced in 'Israel', and their sin is chiefly weakness or indifference rather than positive cruelty and tyranny on the part of prelates of the Church. The *D&P* version is expanded in the context of Commandment V ('non occides') to support an attack on prelates who fail to preach and teach as offenders against the Commandment:

Wo be to þe schepherdys of Israel, *þat is to seye, to þe prelatis & curatis of holy chirche, whyche schuldyn ben schepperdis of Goddis schep & of þo soulys þat he bouȝte so dere. Wo be to þese cheperdis, for þei fedyn hemself & of þe pore peple ȝeuyn þei no tale.* Ȝe etyn, *seyth he,* þe mylc & claddyn ȝou with þe wulle, & þat was fet ȝe slowyn *to fedyn wel ȝoure wombe,* but ȝe feddyn nout my floc *of myn peple.* Þat was feble ȝe holpyn it nout ne confortyn it nout, and þat was sor & sek ȝe heledyn it nout, & þat was brokyn ȝe boundyn it nout aȝen, and þat was cast awey & fordryfyn ȝe fettyn it nout aȝen ne leddyn it nout aȝen; and þat was perchyd ȝe soutyn it nout, but with fyrshed & hardnesse & be power *withoutyn pyte* ȝe comandedyn to hem *many grete þingis & greuous & regnedyn amongis hem as emperouris, & so* myn schep ben discateryd, for þer is no schepperde *þat ȝeuyt ony tale of hem* (2–17/43–18/57; *D&P* author's additions italicized)

When Ezek. 34:2–8 is cited in the Longleat sermons, the wording is different, and the application to the prelates of the Church is made more explicit within the translation itself:

Wo be to þo schepperdys þat fedin hemself. Be not þe flokkys fedde of here schepperdys . ȝe eetin þe mylk & weren wryyd in þe wolle *of ȝoure type* . . . but ȝe feddin not myn flok. That was feble *in temptacioun* ȝe strencthedin it not & þat was seek *in synne* ȝe heledin it not & þat was brokin *in dyspeyr* ȝe boundin it not aȝen & þat was caste awey *be wyllyng in tempest* ȝe leddin it not aȝen & þat was perschyd *be euyl custom* ȝe souȝtyn it not but wiþ fershed *ȝe regnedyn as emperouris vpon myn peple* & so myn schep ben dysparplyid & *deuourid of bestis þo be þe fendis be rekleshed & slepinge of prelatis.* (LL 4, fo. 24ra–24rb; author's additions italicized)

The author's own consciousness of the problems of translation is expressed in the Longleat 4 sermons, where he makes an early (*c*.1415?) use of 'English' as a verb meaning 'translate': he says the word 'amen' may be '*englyschyd* in þre maneris, ffyrst þus . . . or ellys þus . . . or ellys þus' (fo. 43va, italics added).[49]

Among biblical narratives, the author of *D&P* draws most often on the story of King David, clearly relying on the fact that the story was a popular one, as well-known to a Dives as to a Pauper. (He even has Dives cite it back to Pauper on one occasion.) Episodes from David's life are selected and shaped to show how the precepts of the Commandments can or should be fitted to the exigencies of everyday life. In Commandment I, the author of *D&P* supports his argument in favour of fine Church architecture by referring to God's decision that Solomon (a man of peace) not David (a man of war) should build him 'a wol costful temple' (192/59–193/75). In Commandment III, the story of David dancing before the ark (to the scorn of his wife, Michal) supports Pauper's argument for Sunday merry-making (297/33–46). In Commandment IV, the story of David and Absalom warns against the disobedience of children (307/15–35). In Commandment VI, the story of David and Bathsheba is used to show the ill effects of adultery on the body politic (2–64/75–65/92); to suggest that lechery is more powerful in men than in women (2–85/19–86/43); and again to warn that adulterous behaviour will have dire social effects (2–105/27–30). In Commandment VII, the story of David, Abigail and Nabal contrasts the alms-giving Abigail with the stingy Nabal: in helping David, Abigail is not breaking the Commndment by stealing (from her husband) but rather doing God's will (2–142/53–89). In Commandment VIII, David was not bearing false witness when he

---

[49] The *MED* gives as first use of 'English' as a verb the prologue of the Wycliffite Bible, 'a1397'. Another hesitation over translation is recorded in the Longleat 4 sermons: how should Luke 1:51 'Dispersit superbos mente cordis sui' be rendered? as 'He has destroyed and dispersed those who were proud of heart' or as 'He has destroyed the proud by means of his thoughts'? Following Bede's gloss, the writer says that the destroying arm, *brachio suo*, is both God and 'also . . . his sone be whom he werkith', and he (the Longleat translator) draws from this perception of an ambiguity in the Vulgate text a lesson about the double nature of the mind of God: God is all-wise as well as all-powerful; in his might, he dooms the 'proude fendis', but in his wisdom he holds open to proud men the chance of redemption (LL4, fo. 134vb).In recently edited tracts, the first of which (C1) may have been written (in part) by the Longleat friar, the author uses both noun and verb and makes a distinction between 'worde for worde' and 'sentence for sentence' translation (Simon Hunt, 'An Edition of 'Tracts in Favour of Translation and of Some Texts connected with Lollard Vernacular Biblical Scholarship' (D.Phil. thesis, Oxford 1954), 2:264/233–4. See Explanatory Notes 327/10.

pretended to be mad in order to escape his enemies—thus supporting
Pauper's argument for common sense in fulfilling this Commandment: '. . . whan fenyyng in dede is profytable to þe doere & to his
euene cristene & to þe worchepe of God it is leful' (2–218/26–30). In
Commandment IX, David's behaviour during the illness and death of
his first child by Bathsheba is used to make the point that the
'covetousness' warned against by the Commandment extends to
excessive love of anything, even of one's own child (2–261/68–73).
In Commandment X, Dives cites the story of Bethsheba in his
attempt to sort out the difference between covetousness of eye and
covetousness of deed (2–297/55–72).

Beyond fine translation, did the author of *D&P* add something
more to his treatise on the Commandments? I think it can be said that
he managed to invest his solemn and unwieldy topic with real
dramatic tension. His choice of the dialogue form was the first
important decision. Here the relative inertness of Chaucer's mono-
logic 'Parson's Tale' makes an instructive comparison. Comparison
may also be made with the popular *Elucidarium* of Honorius
Augustodunensis.[50] This teacher-pupil dialogue, aims at imparting
the fundamentals of Christian dogma to young *literati*, perhaps boys
in a cathedral school. The brief questions put by the *discipulus* serve to
break up the exposition nicely and facilitate reference to particular
topics. But *D&P*'s author takes a further step: he presents not just
two speakers but two speakers with distinct and often clashing points
of view. (This open disagreement on matters of dogma may be one
reason why the work later acquired a heretical reputation.) While the
author's 'Pauper' is the teacher throughout the dialogue, his 'Dives' is
not a docile young pupil. Dives is presented from the outset as at least
the equal in age and the social superior of the *magister* in the dialogue.
Even though Dives has far less to say, his views carry weight. More
than that, his views add up to a point of view that is sharply
distinguishable from that of his 'teacher'. It is this difference that
brings the dialogue to life.

All these matters are settled very early. The 'Holy Poverty' prologue begins with a confrontation. Pauper (the 'pore man') says that
Dives (the 'ryche man') is one of those who answer the 'meke preyere'
of poor mendicants with harsh words and call them destroyers of the

---

[50] Early twelfth century; PL 172:1109–1176. A closer analogue might be St Anselm's
(d. 1109) *Cur deus homo*, in which 'Boso' has a point of view of his own; the disputants are,
however, not otherwise distinguishable in any personal way.

land (51/19–52/20).[51] The rich man, Dives, angered, snaps back: 'For þin gredynesse þu schalt han the lesse. And þu myghtist, þu woldyst be weye of elmesse han al þat I haue' (52/36–8). In this way, from the very start, sides are taken; divergent interests are stated; and the book promises to be about a contest. As the work unfolds and the two speakers become acquainted, they now agree, now disagree, and sometimes agree to disagree. In the end, they differ as friends and look forward to a continuation of the dialogue in the Heavenly Kingdom.

Though it would be too much to expect that by this means alone the long (and often formless) mass of D&P could be turned into a dramatic work, the establishment of two points of view at the outset draws the reader into the subject matter. Dives emerges as a self-assured member of the English ruling class who has lived long enough to form his own opinions on many subjects. He is literate and can (and does) cite the Bible in Latin (57/24–5), as well as canon law (319/1–320/12; 2–16/17; 2–110/21–2; 2–185/52–3). Aristotle (171/59; 337/14), and Augustine (135/15; 294/35–7); he knows of Jerome (166/13) and also of Ptolemy (125/6). Probably he has gathered many of his ideas by word of mouth from the better-educated, since he refers to what 'clerkys seyn' or to what 'clerkys arguyn aȝenys þe' (124/1; 2–121/1–7). For himself, he is indifferent to the 'hye perfeccioun' of Matt. 19:21; the 'lesse perfeccioun' is quite enough (66/24; 27). The Franciscan author does not show his Dives as persuaded of the rightness of mendicancy; Dives replies to Pauper's fervent peroration on the subject merely: 'þin speche is skylful but nought plesaunt to ryche folk' (65/1) and changes the subject.[52] He thinks the images in churches encourage idolatry.[53] He is in deep perplexity about astrology.[54] He thinks the Devil ('the fend') has extensive and malign powers.[55] He is curious about dice, witchcraft, spells, ghosts, dreams, divination, alchemy, the efficacy of prayer, and miracles.[56] He has a Lollard-leaning (or perhaps merely fashionable)

[51] Prov. 18:23: 'Cum obsecrationibus loquetur pauper et dives effabitur rigide' is extended by the addition in direct address of what the obsecrations of the rich man might be.

[52] Cf. 2–160/22–34, where Dives claims: it is harder for rich men to give alms, because it is so costly to maintain their 'stat of dispensacion'.

[53] Pauper answers Dives' objections to many forms of worship that appear to him to be idolatrous in the following fifteen chapters of Commandment I.

[54] Commandment I, caps. 17–27.

[55] Commandment I, caps. 31–6.

[56] Commandment I, caps. 37–42.

INTRODUCTION xxxvii

suspicion of expensive burial rites, arguing that many 'letyn it a gret perfeccion þese dayys' to give the money to the poor instead (214/12–13). He is dubious about enjoying 'steraclis, pleyys and dauncis' on Sundays (293/12–11, 294/35–7;49–56, 296–7/21–2;21–2). He begins, but is soon bored by, arguments about religious possessioners (321/1–2). He is appalled by the new restrictions on preaching and the distribution of vernacular Bibles (327/1–5). He is doubtful about obedience to wicked prelates (340–1/1–2; 12–15). He digs in his heels against Pauper's assertion that fornication between single persons is a deadly sin (2–76/1–5; 2–80/1–8). He knows the flesh is frail and blames women's tempting attire, which 'steryt mychil folc to lecherye' (2–90/1). He cannot believe that Adam was guiltier than Eve (2–121/1–7; 2–126/1–3).[57] He wonders whether tithes should be paid to a church whose curate is an open fornicator, thief or murderer (2–168/20–4; 2–169/29–32; 2–170/55–66). He thinks Pauper is too stringent about an heir's obligation to return property acquired less than honestly by his forebears (2–257/1–5; 2–268/1–2).

To all this the author opposes his friar, a man deeply learned in the Bible, the Fathers, and the scholastic theologians, a student of canon and civil law and of the *artes praedicandi*, who has chosen for himself the path of 'more perfection' in a life of mendicancy. Pauper soon buries Dives' protests under a mountain of sermons on subjects more interesting to clerics, such as (in Commandments VII and VIII) simony, tithes, trentals, usury, and laws governing witnesses in church courts.

The balance shifts towards the end of Commandment VIII xiv, when Christ and the Doom are invoked. Pauper warns that while Christ is now a meek lamb, at the Doom he will be a 'lyon, dredful & sterne' (2–241/15–16). From this point forward, the text is less dialogic, more preacherly and shaped to create an apocalyptic mood. The sermonizing tone becomes increasingly fervent. In a striking image,[58] Christ has drawn the great bow of the Judgement; and when he looses the string, the 'ryȝtful lyuerys' will be on his right hand and the 'wrong lyuerys' on his left (2–246/22–31). The Last Judgement projected as a great courtroom trial scene dominates the remainder of *D&P*. Chapter xvi recounts the Fifteen Signs of Doom.[59] ('It is a dredful þing to þinkyn on þis dom' says Dives [2–251/1]) Pauper

<hr/>

[57] See Explanatory Notes 2–121/2–3, 2–126/1–128/92, 2–129/90.
[58] See Explanatory Notes 2–245/13–246/39.
[59] See Explanatory Notes 2–247/13–44.

tells in quick succession the biblical story of Nabal's vineyard, the 'three gallows' tale, the archer and nightingale tale, ('What is þis to purpoos?' says Dives at this point [2–260/40]), and the story of Balaam and his ass, relating them all to the coming Doom. The theme, appropriate to Commandment IX, is covetousness, briefly personified as if recalled from a performance of a morality play (2–264/46–9).[60] Dives is thus warned that his riches will be useless to him after he dies; worldly wealth is as unsteady as a juggler's horse (2–267/53–63) or Dame Fortune's wheel (2–270/10–29). Pauper points out that man's life is, like a ship, narrow at both ends (2–271/41–272/85), like a rose that fades (2–273/1–9), like a fox who listens to water running beneath the ice and avoids the treacherous crossing (2–276/1–5), like the knight whose nephew fails to say masses for his soul (2–280/45–281/71), and like Everyman and his faithless friends (2–281/2–282/26). A chastened Dives now pleads: 'To whom schal Y don myn elmesse?' (2–284/1).

Pauper replies with a great final sermon, which invokes the Deuteronomic curses and blessings, shouted from the hilltops.[61] He draws on the Book of Revelation for descriptions of the Heavenly City (2–318/1 ff.). And finally (in reply to Dives' rather barbed comment that if people were truly certain that their good deeds would bring such rewards, they would never sin) Pauper answers him with St Gregory's story of the mother who bears her child in a deep dungeon; when she tells the child of the light and beauty of the world outside the prison walls, he refuses to believe her.[62] It is an effective and moving coda.

The partial withdrawal of the dramatic element and thickening of the texture with stories and allegorizations perhaps seemed unavoidable to the writer of *D&P*, who may have blenched at the prospect of continuing to set his speakers at odds about such solemn matters as preparations for the Last Assize and appearance before the supreme Judge. By the end of the treatise, the solemn poetry of religious belief has taken precedence over both dialogue and explication of the Church's code of laws.

---

[60] See Explanatory Notes 2–264/46–9.
[61] Deut. 27:11–26, Deut. 28:2–68; see Explanatory Notes 2–313/20–314/53.
[62] See Explanatory Note 2–323/4–324/37.

4. QUESTIONS OF THEOLOGY

Dives and Pauper is fundamentally a religious tract. All of its questions about behavior return to a single source: the nature of God. Here the problems of translation are redoubled. The university-trained Franciscan author takes for granted ideas about God shaped by his Latin learning. He knows—not only Augustine—but also the great scholastic theologians who, under presssure of the twelfth-century European rediscovery of Aristotle, once again pursued the philosophy of religion. The author of *D&P* saw clearly that the vernacular concepts of God of his time and place were helpless against the world of popular superstition. Only a far wider and grander concept of God as Prime Mover and Absolute Power—and a concept of God requiring worship in spirit and truth—would be capable of driving back the shadows of superstition and fear.

After the two speakers have introduced themselves to each other in the Holy Poverty prologue, Commandment I goes straight to the heart of the matter—first, the nature of God, second, the nature of superstition. The Commandment falls into three parts: (1) *chapters i–xvi* (81–117), on worship; (2) *chapters xvii–l* (117–187), on superstitions, and (3) *chapters li–lxiv* (188–220), on parish life. A fairly close reading of just the first two parts will be enough to show the author's point of view on the topic closest to his heart.

In the first part, Dives is shown trying to enter Pauper's world of Christian devotion and dogma but holding back because of what he sees as the connivance of some clerics in the idolatrous behaviour of the common people. Pauper argues against Dives' literalism and for a more inward notion of God. In the second part, Pauper enters Dives' world, where he, in turn, recoils from the superstititious practices he finds there. This world, Pauper concludes, must be under the sway of the Devil, and he argues against Dives' (partial) credulity.

Dives opens the discussion by reciting Exod. 20:3–4 in good idiomatic English:

þu shalt . . . haue noon othere straunge godys aforn me. þu shalt makyn the noo grauyn þing, no maument, noo lyknesse þat is abouyn in heuene ne þat is benethyn in erthe ne of noo thyng þat is in þe water vnder þe erthe (81/2–5).

But in his version of Exod. 20:5 he adds a few highly significant words not found in the Latin text:

þu shalt nought wurshepyn hem wyt þin *body outward* ne wyt þin *herte inward* (81/5–6, italics added).

The Vulgate 'non adorabis ea neque coles' is translated in the Wycliffite Bible, 'thou schalt not herie tho, nether thou schalt worschipe' and rendered in the Tyndale and King James translations, Do not 'bow down nor worship'.[63] Dives' version tends to put into high relief the distinction between 'adorare' and 'colere' and to suggest that there is a conflict between them. The author may have been relying on the *Glossa ordinaria*, which does in fact interpret the difference between the two Latin verbs as the difference between outward action and inner affect: a person may be compelled by force or fear to 'adorare' but can never be forced to 'colere'.[64] In *D&P*, this distinction structures the dialogue on images: in the first sixteen chapters of Commandment I, Dives persistently questions Pauper about the acts of worship of the 'body outward', while Pauper elaborates on worship as the act of the 'herte inward'. Levels or grades of 'inward' worship do not enter into the discussion until cap. xi (pp. 101 ff.).

Dives' questions are blunt: the churches are full of material images, even though God's law plainly says, Do not make them. He feels great social pressure to 'doo in þat as alle meen don' and worship them. But that is idolatry and plainly against God's law. All these images, he exclaims, should be burned! (81/11; 82/36–7) Pauper responds by telling him about the images in the biblical tabernacle[65] and about some of the symbolic meanings of images of saints, angels and Evangelists. He makes the time-honoured argument that images are the layman's 'book'.[66] As an exercise, he recommends *meditatio* before the image of Christ on the cross: Dives should stand before the image of the crucified Christ and imagine himself actually present at the scene of the crucifixion.[67] When Dives has heard enough of this, he says it is still nothing more than image-worship, 'and so weny3t mechil of þe peple' (85–6/1–7). Pauper's counter-argument is that

[63] FM, 1:238b (LV).

[64] 'Aliud est colere, aliud adorare . . . Colere vero est toto his affectu & studio manicipari' GO (1:152).

[65] Exod. 24:12–30:21. Bede's (672/3–735) commentary on the decor of the OT tabernacle is the conventional riposte to the prohibition against graven images ('De tabernaculo', *PL* 91 (2):735 ff.).

[66] St John of Damascus (c675–c749) was one of the first to call images the books of the unlettered; see Explanatory Notes 82 /42–4.

[67] See Explanatory Notes 82/44–5 and 83/1–84/38.

the worshipper must distinguish between worshipping God in front of the image ('aforn') and offering worship 'to' the image (85/3). This does not meet Dives' objection that the Commandment forbids such worship *either* with the outward body *or* with the inward heart.

Whether or not Pauper's effort to bridge the gap by means of an emotional or aesthetic appeal ultimately fails,[68] it quiets Dives while he listens to examples of Church rituals that are (he is repeatedly told) neither inner nor outer *worship* but rather 'mende makyng'— reminders—of an unseen reality. The priest at the altar, above which hangs the crucifix, kneels and kisses his bible; he may even weep (86/14–15); in the outward form of bread and wine, he offers the highest sacrifice, that of Christ (87/35–7); the Passion hymn 'O crux aue, spes vnica' is sung (88/8); and at the Palm Sunday procession, when the cross is unveiled, the people fall to their knees and chant, 'Ave rex!' (89/43–4). In a comparison likely to appeal to a 'Dives', Pauper says the cross is like the device on a knight's shield, a token of his identity and rank (88/24–30). The beauty of the setting and ritual of the public worship of the 'Church of our Fathers'[69] is powerfully evoked. Only after all this is said does Dives assent that the image is 'noothyng ellys but a book and a tokene to þe lewyd peple, as þu sayde ferst' (90/22–3).

Now that the author has enunciated the two extremes and pointed to a moderate, and orthodox, middle way, he turns to the specific nature of the act of worship. For this purpose, he introduces scholastic terminology. With the one English word, 'worship', it is difficult, he says, to make the fine distinctions that are needed:

And forasmechil as alle þese manerys of wurshepe so dyuers been clepid wyt on name of wurshepe on Englysh tonge, and often þe Latyn of wurshepe is takyn and vsyd vnpropyrly & to comounly, þerfore meen fallyn in mechil doughte and errour in redyngge and nought wel vnderstondyn qhat þey redyn (109/60–5).

He needs the Latin terms *latria*, *dulia*, and *hyperdulia* to make distinctions among *levels* of worship—between the level of worship owed to God alone and worship owed to angels and to some reasonable creatures (102–4/15–76). There is no difficulty in agreeing that *latria*, the highest form of worship, is owed to God. Controversy

---

[68] Fails, that is, in Commandment I. In Commandment X, there are no more scholastic arguments, and imagery and emotion prevail.

[69] Cf. Daniel Rock, whose *Church of Our Fathers*, 4 vols. (London, 1849; new edn. 1905) throughout cites relevant passages from *D&P*.

arises over the images of Christ, because Christ is truly God and truly man ('verey God & verey man' 2–221/64–6). Here the scholastic philosophers differed among themselves, and what promised to be a useful division of the senses of 'worship' falls short. A third term is needed, Pauper explains, and *hyperdulia* may cover the intermediate cases lying somewhere between God and man (108/41–50). These cases certainly include Mary, the mother of Jesus, as well as the human nature of Christ. Now the question arises whether the cross on which Christ died should also be given *hyperdulia*. Pauper says that some academics ('clerkys') say yes, but he thinks this would be improper—though if any material object were worthy of *hyperdulia*, the true cross would be that object (108/45–9). Though the subject has been left in something of a muddle,[70] Pauper has said enough to convince Dives ('I am out of doughte', 109/4).[71]

While Dives himself is now 'out of doubt', he puts himself in the place of his fellow parishoners who see 'þe ymage þat þe carpenteer hatȝ mad and þe peyntour peyntyd' (89/45–6). It is not easy for them, he says, to understand that the priest holding up his Bible before the cross and weeping is not worshipping the cross and the book. Even though he finally answers Pauper's question with a docile acknowledgement that the priest prays 'to God and nought to þe book' (86/17), he continues to worry about the beliefs and practises he observes in his own church:

Me merueylyȝt mechil qhy meen been so besy *to doon þe peple wurshepyn ymagys* . . . I haue herd seyd þat manye grete clerkys . . . seyn þat meen shuldyn wurshepyn ymagys. . . . [but] men shuldyn nought wurshepyn seer drye trees þat han noo vertue at al. (107/1–2, 4–6, 21–3; ital. add.)

In the fifteenth century, the few Paupers able and willing to steer their parishoners towards a finely discriminating 'inward' worship of religious images were greatly outnumbered by a tide of naysayers, plain folks who, like Dives, saw what they saw and clergy who were quite content with how matters stood.

The author of *D&P* seems, however, to have been even more disturbed by the deplorable persistence of paganism—as he saw it— in fifteenth-century England than by the threat of heresy. In the second part of Commandment I, astronomy, astrology and other kinds of forecasting and witchery are dealt with. These topics were normally included in expositions of Commandment I, following an

[70] Cf. Aston (1988), 1:413.   [71] See Explanatory Notes 108/47.

ancient pattern.[72] During the early centuries, in its long struggle with paganism, the Church accumulated a large library of diatribes against late classical worship of the sun, moon and planets, use of horoscopes, lewd theatre performances, jugglers and acrobats, and the like. These writings were handed down by the Fathers and incorporated into canon law, to be drawn upon by commentators and glossators whether they fitted current local conditions or not. In *D&P*, the author is unconventional only in treating the topic at such length and including in his diatribe a few descriptions of practices he has actually seen or heard of in his own society.[73]

Dives leads the discussion towards astrology with a question about God's power (117/1–118/43). He can plainly see that the King of England is powerful enough to make a page of a yeoman or to have any of his enemies executed. The king does not have to consult the stars; he does not have to ask the astrologers to make calculations; he decides and acts. What about God? Does He rule the stars, or is He ruled by them? Pauper patiently explains that the heavenly bodies are God's instruments; they are like lanterns (119/23; 120/38–40), clocks (120/34–45)[74] or the grindstone of the blacksmith (120/48–121/60). This opens the way to the question that Dives really wants an answer to: can we learn the future by watching the operations of God's instruments and 'dyuynyn of thynggys þat been to come'? (121/7)[75]

Now Pauper must take on the double-sided question of God's power and man's freedom—and in the simplest possible vernacular terms. If God is unchangeable, is man's fate predestined? He does not explicitly invoke Boethius's distinction between God's Providence and human Destiny—still less the theory of future contingents—but he does so implicitly when he says: '[A]fter þat meen chaungyn here lyuyngge so chaungyȝt he [God] hese domys to punishyn or to spare, to wele or to woo, to heuene or to helle' (122/24–6). The way Pauper constructs his argument is typical of many others in *D&P*. He begins with 'holy wryȝt' (122/32: Jonah 3:5–10; 2 Kings 20:2–7). Both texts

[72] Cf. Grosseteste, *De decem mand.*, ed. R. C. Dales and E. B. King (British Academy, Oxford, 1987), pp. 9–11; he, in turn, cites Augustine, Isidore of Seville, Rabanus Maurus, and Jerome. See also Peter Brown, 'Sorcery', in his *Religion and Society* (London, 1972), pp. 119–146.

[73] See Explanatory Notes 156/11, 157/6–7, 162/19–20, for example.

[74] See Explanatory Notes 120/34–41.

[75] This too is topical: Chaucer's 'Nun's Priest's Tale' alludes to Bishop Bradwardine (*c.*1290–1349), who had published a controversial work on God's foreknowledge, *De Causa Dei contra Pelagium . . .* (1344). See Explanatory Notes 121/1–7.

tell stories of God's condemnation, a sinner's repentance, and God's revocation of the threatened punishment. The king of Nineveh repents in sackcloth and ashes, and God changes his mind about the calamities he had promised to inflict on his city. Isaiah prophesies that king Hezekiah will soon die of his illness. But when Hezekiah turns his face to the wall and prays, reminding the Lord of his faithfulness and good behaviour, God stops Isaiah before he has left the palace and tells him to return to the King and prophesy his recovery. The latter story—showing God's use of the sun as a token of good faith—also fits neatly into Pauper's arguments against astrology: 'ryght as þe sonne chaungede his cours after þe repentaunce of the kyng, ryght so God chaungyȝt his sentence onon as man or womman repentyȝt hym of his synne and is in wyl to amendyn hym' (123/53).

Pauper next invokes patristic authority—but by the indirect route of canon law. His legal citation (*De poen.* D.1 c.64) comprises a sentence from Ambrose's *In Lucam*: '*nouit Deus mutare sentenciam si tu noueris emendare delictum,*' God can chaungyn his sentence and his doom onon as þu canst amendyn þin trespas' (123/54–6).[76] And he caps the argument with a verse from St Paul—'For who hath known the mind of the Lord? (Rom. 11:34)—stressing God's transcendence. It is a careful balancing act between, on the one side, the pitfalls of predestination and, on the other side, the simplistic notion that God is ruled either by the planets or by human prayers. When a man obeys God's commands he conforms his own destiny to God's unchanging will to reward him; when he disobeys, he conforms his own destiny to God's unchanging will to punish him.

God's supreme power and authority having been established, Pauper next confronts man's disobedience. He begins with the disobedience of some members of the elite: those learned men who practise the 'craft of astronomye', or that speciality of it, astrology (117/3). They 'presume' to know God's decisions; thus they commit the sin of pride; they are 'folys of alle folys' (124/86). But (Dives wants to know) is it not true that the heavenly bodies indicate in a *general* way what will happen in the future? Did Ptolemy not say as much? (124–5/1–10). Nonsense, says Pauper; astronomy/astrology is 'a stryng to drawyn meen to helle' (125/20). After some commonsensical lessons in basic astronomy, hygiene, social psychology, and

---

[76] Friedberg 1:1177; *PL* 15:1645.

other practical causes of human outcomes (128–9/33–46),[77] Pauper
(in nine chapters) winds up his denunciation of astrology/astronomy
by equating the 'iudicial' (or future-forecasting) astronomers with
Lucifer:

Lucyfor seyde in his herte þat he shulde styyn up into heuene and settyn his
seete abouyn þe sterrys and syttyn in þe mount of þe testament, and þat he
shulde wendyn vp abouyn þe heyghte of þe skyis, þat is to seye, abouyn alle
aungelys and been lyke hym þat is hey3est. But onon he fel doun to helle, and
so shullyn sueche astronomyenys and wycchis, but þey amendyn hem. (cf.
Isa. 14:12; *D&P* I:1, 136/21–7)

This serves to introduce the long-deferred question of evil, which
(after a detour of five chapters)[78] occupies the subsequent six chapters
of part two of Commandment I.

Pauper draws on 'De divinatione daemonium' (159/54),[79] in which
Augustine attributes the existence of the Devil to man's sinfulness
and God's justice ('. . . et ratione judicii ejus ab omnipotente
permitti'). Unlike God, the Devil (the 'fend') is a changeable, earthly
creature, who is able to torment and deceive because his senses are
finer and his ability to move about is superior to that of humans. But
the Devil, says Pauper, is merely God's agent: he does everything 'be
the sufferaunce of God'; he may do nothing without the 'graunt and
permission of God' (153/18–20).[80] Dives then poses the key question:
'Whi suffreþ God hym [the devil] so muche to temptyn mankynde?'
(154/24–5). Pauper's answer evades the question of God's justice and
places the burden on mankind: humans, he says, have been given a
chance to fight for their salvation. He follows this up with a catchy
rhymed translation of James 1:12: 'þere is no man worthy to haue þe
coroune of lyf but he wythstonde þe fend in gostly stryf'. Thus in

[77] He uses St John Chrysostom (PG 56:61) to quash the notion that the Star of
Bethlehem validates astrology by making Christ the first astrologer, a question he puts in
Dives' mouth in cap. xxiv (134–1–2); see Explanatory Notes 133/29–34.

[78] These chapters return to questions of forecasting events on earth and discuss weather
forecasting, the tides (related to the moon), ominous signs in the heavens, and use of the
astrolabe to find lost articles (chapters 26–30, pp. 139–151).

[79] Augustine is found in C.26 q.3 c.2 (Friedberg, 1:1025); ed. in PL 40:581–92. All of
Causa 26 is on divination, citing the decrees of the Councils and drawing on Augustine,
Isidore of Seville, Chrysostom, and papal letters.

[80] Cf. Wyclif, *Trialogus*, Bk. 2, c. xiii: 'Regulam autem in omnibus istis oportet de
beneplacito Dei accipere, cum diaboli ex fide non plus possunt tentare homines quam de
Dei beneplacito permittuntur, cum Dei iusticia non permittit nos tentari supra id quod
possumus, vel sic resistere non sufficimus, peccatum nostrum primum est causa' (ed.
G. Lechler, Oxford, 1869).

D&P's school of theological studies, not all questions are pushed to
the limits of a university *disputatio*.[81] Throughout his work, in fact,
the friar persistently searches for a middle way, justified by reason
and natural law. He says:

[W]hatsoeuere man or woman do be weye of kende and of reason, ʒif he use
ony craft of iaperye and of fayterie to blendyn [blind] þe peple for to don
hem leuyn þat he were a wyche and þat he dede it nouʒt be weye of kende
but be charmys and sorcerye, he þat is a wyche in Godis syʒthe. (168/17–21;
cf. 169/10–15)

He draws a line between *Christian* incantations (over herbs, candles,
ill persons), which are allowable, and rituals that directly or indirectly
invoke the Devil or lead the recipient to believe in the supernatural
powers of the speaker. In Commandment VII, he says bluntly:

[A]s men don þese dayys [they] fenyedyn miracles of ymagis . . . to
meynteþin [promote] ydolatrye for lucre of offerynge & false miraclys of
wyckyd lyuerys & seyn þat God doth miracles for hem & so blendyn [blind]
þe peple in falsnesse. (2–133–4/7–10)

While combating lay literalism about images and clerical oppor-
tunism in profiting from such literalism, Pauper—unlike the
Lollards—defends fine church buildings and the furniture of worship, church music, and the ritual of worship (188/16–20; 190/10–
36). Yes, the poor must be helped, but it is also 'wol medful to
arayyn wel Godys hous and maynteþyn and moryn [enhance] Godys
seruyce' (191/42–3). It is hypocritical—even Judas-like—to
begrudge the cost of maintaining the Church (193/17–19). Pauper
adds some special pleading for the mendicant cause, 'hem þat [like
himself] trauaylyyn in Godis seruyse and studyin in Godys lawe
nyʒt and day and prechyn it fortʒ to þe peple in dede and worde,
and han nede of bodyly almesse . . . [these are] Godys knyʒthis'
(194–5/25–48).[82] He underlines this self-praise with a little tale of
two friars gleefully walking towards London, leaving behind them in
the deep ditch where they had shoved him the arrogant mounted

[81] Wyclif's answer to the question of evil is the same, even if more soberly put: 'Et sic
eternaliter ordinavit Deus peccatores omnes vinci et puniri pro sua vecordia, cum sit
iustum' *De mandatis* (WS, 1922), p. 36, lines 15–17. Wyclif goes on to say that God 'ponit in
libertate arbitrii utramque partem contradiccionis, licet necessitet ad passionem converti-
bilem . . . sed non vult quod homo peccet sive deficiat'.

[82] There are textual suggestions that some of this may have seemed overemphatic or
over-Franciscan to some readers: 'and prechyn . . . almesse' (194/30–1) and 'Neþeles . . .
reprouyd' (194–5/45–8) were excised from MS G.

'getter', who had superstitiously insisted that he must pass them on the right hand. Pauper indicates that it is a prefiguration of how 'rich' and 'poor' will be treated at the final Judgement (186–7/17–43). The story may suggest that the author of *D&P* was sometimes exasperated by his struggle to harmonize nature, reason and Christian worship.

Questions of theology raise questions of orthodoxy. Questions about the orthodoxy of *D&P* (in its own time) were always questions about whether it was Wycliffite or Lollard.[83] The *D&P* author's position can be outlined under the headings of doctrine and the sacraments, and beliefs about the Church as an institution.

The writer's attitude towards the sacraments of the Church, to the extent that he discusses them at all, is unexceptionably orthodox: baptism is defined at the beginning of Commandment II as a rite in which Christians forsake the Devil and unite themselves with Christ assuming the name of Christian (221/7–15). Confirmation is not mentioned. The eucharist is described as the 'heyest sacrifyse . . . Crist, Godys sone of heuene vnder forme of bred and of wyn' (87/35–7; 235/44–5; 2–38–9/37–52). Confession is assumed to be the normal recourse for the Christian sinner, who is advised to put himself 'in þe dom of Goddys iuge þat is þin confessour and makyn amendys aftir his doom and be his assent' (154/31; 2–240–1/87–90). The only further discussion of this sacrament concerns practise not doctrine: Dives raises the question of secrecy, and while Pauper confirms that a confessor is bound by his oath to keep what he is told in the confessional secret, he also vents the complaint that 'men in schrifte lyyn al day' (251/29–30), and the more serious complaint that confessors 'in þis lond' have been persecuted and even 'banchid, drenchid' and 'brent' to make them betray the secrets of the confessional (251/36–58). Holy orders are mentioned by implication only: clerics who are flagrant, open sinners are not to receive tithes (2–168–71/20–100); they are, however, to be obeyed in other matters

[83] M. Teresa Brady (1989), 'Lollard Interpolations' (in *De Cella in Seculum*, ed. M. G. Sargent (Cambridge, 1980), pp. 183–203), usefully distinguishes the orthodox 'Pore Caitif' manuscripts from the copies with Lollard interpolations on grounds of doctrine, worship, confession, oaths, the Creed, preaching and persecution. Also helpful in ascertaining what was then legally considered heretical (esp. in Norwich in 1438–41) is N. Tanner, *Heresy*, esp. pp. 10–22. For grounds on which heretics were prosecuted in Lincoln diocese in the 1380s, see A. K. McHardy, 'Bishop Buckingham and the Lollards of the Lincoln Diocese', *SCH* 9 (1972), pp. 131–45. On Oldcastle's trial, *FZ*, pp. 433–50; See also A. Hudson, 'The Examination of Lollards', *BIRR* 46 (1973), 145–59; repr. in *Lollards* (London, 1985), pp. 125–39.

(340/1–12). Extreme Unction is not alluded to.[84] Matrimony is described as a sacrament representing the unity between the Godhead and manhood in Christ, the love between Christ and the soul, and the love between Christ and the Church (2–60/1–18).

Attitudes to the Church and the clergy in *D&P* take the form of complete acceptance of the historical and contemporary institution and nearly total rejection of the behaviour of most categories of its personnel. The acceptance of the institution includes acceptance of the efficacy of the office of the priest, whether the priest himself lives up to his vows or not (338/39–44),[85]acceptance of the lordship, or dominion, of both civil and Church rulers (317/18, 320/28, 2–138/ 1–5, 2–140/76–8), and acceptance of the doctrine of purgatory and the efficacy of prayers for the dead (170/42–4, 214/19, 328/36, 2– 187/50–4, 2–188–9/80–97). As to the papacy itself, nothing is said directly. A passage on the doctrine of the 'keys' (found in all manuscripts except G, the base manuscript of *D&P*) might seem to suggest Wycliffian sympathies: 'But ȝyt afterwardys Cryst ȝaf þe keyes to alle þe apostlys, as þe gospellys wytnessyn, Matthei xvii [18] et Iohanni xx [23]' (92/13–15).[86] That the passage is not an interpolation but represents the author's view is indicated by one of the author's later sermons:

And in þis ȝyfte of þe holy gost crist ȝaf hese apostolys þe keyȝes of holy chyrche to byndin & vnbyndin . . . Aforn hys passcioun he hyȝt [promised] hem þe keyȝys of holy chyrche but aftyr hys pascioun whanne he was rysin as at þis tyme he ȝaf hem þe keyȝis of holy chyrche. (LL4, fo. 50ra–b)

But it is doubtful whether the view was Lollard-influenced: the question of papal authority was part of an ongoing controversy in which Franciscans figured prominently. Most Christians at the date of writing were hoping that a way out of the papal schism would be found, and theories of papal power that seemed to allow for a conciliar solution were given wide credence.

[84] Unless the *exemplum* about the procrastinating tyrant of 'Oxsynford' who is killed by a fall from his horse before he could ask for God's mercy implies the necessity of the sacrament (2–25–6/46–56).

[85] The only passage in the text where two views on this point are given is the discussion of tithes, in which canonists and glossators are cited as supporting the view that 'open lechourys & malefactouris' should be deposed 'tyl þei amendyn hem' (2–169/48–51).

[86] See Explanatory Notes 92/13–15. For Franciscan involvement in the controversy over papal sovereignty, see B. Tierney, *Origins of Papal Infallibility* (Leiden, 1972), pp. 64– 92 and *passim*; this study makes clear that the doctrine of papal infallibility was in a state of flux at the time when *D&P* was written.

Other signs of Lollard sympathies can include opposition to oaths.[87] *D&P*, however, approves oaths sworn on the Bible (235/31–43); asserts that only the Pope may dispense from a vow to go on pilgrimage to the Holy Land (249/68–9);[88] and describes a vow as an act of *latria* towards God (248/33). Pilgrimages, opposition to which was another Lollard shibboleth, are assumed as a fact of medieval life (249/72–80). Mendicancy, opposed by Wyclif (in his later years) and the Lollards, is described in *D&P* as the path of 'hye perfeccioun' (66/23).

Dives' question about burials (213/1–4)[89] has Lollard resonances: why should there be such costly burials? Why not instead give the money to the poor? Pauper's defence of largesse-dispensing public funeral rites is consistent with the well-known practice of many Franciscan convents of opening their grounds for burial—for a fee—to lay persons.[90]

The question might, however, be raised, Did the author of *D&P*, in choosing to express his views in dialogue form, intend to promote the views of 'Dives' rather than the views of 'Pauper'? At some periods of intense heresy-hunting in the fifteenth century some persons may have thought it plausible that a writer should try to circulate Lollard views by this means. It is more likely though that suspicions about *D&P*, even in that period, were based not on its content but on the fact that it was a book.[91] But the best answer to the question is another question, Which set of views, those of Dives or those of Pauper, does the author strive to make attractive? Would a reader find Dives' (initial) snobbery, his wide array of superstitions, and his biblical

[87] In Lollard William Thorpe's early fifteenth century interrogation before Archbishop Arundel, a point is made of the difference between swearing on a book, where the physical book is the guarantor of the oath, and swearing by God; Thorpe's view was that 'to swere vpon a book or bi a book is to swere bi creaturis': *TWT*, ed. A. Hudson (EETS 301), p. 76/1685–6.

[88] The Lollard view: '. . . hym nediþ not go to Rome to parforme þis medful dede'—i.e., get papal permission to change his oath, *EWS*, 1:352/48–9.

[89] See Explanatory Notes 213/1–3..

[90] 'The struggle between the friars and the secular clergy over . . . the burial of the dead . . . was wholly financial. . . . Friary churches and cemeteries became popular burial grounds . . .': J. R. H. Moorman, *Church Life* (Cambridge, 1955), pp. 391–2; see Explanatory Notes 213/1–3..

[91] Or perhaps a book with a bad reputation, see N. Tanner, *Heresy*, pp. 22, 95, 102. Anne Hudson discusses this issue very thoroughly, pointing out that within the same time period a hapless Robert Bert was accused of heresy for possessing a copy of *D&P*, and the abbot of St Albans was comissioning a copy for his library; she sums up the *D&P* author's position as 'radical orthodoxy': *PR* (1988), pp. 417–21.

literalism—as the author presents them—more attractive than the alternatives presented to him by Pauper? I think not.

In *D&P*, in sum, we are in a parochial world that, with all its complaints about lazy or corrupt clerics, seems less embattled and less broadly ideological than that of the later Lollard movement. The ignorance and credulity of nominal Christians was equally damaging to the health of the Church. The author believed that if God's laws were rationally understood and inwardly felt they would be obeyed by a people 'buxum & meke' to their 'souereyns' and to all the precepts of 'holy chirche' (305/28). Orthodox though his views were—and he himself seems confident of this throughout his treatise[92]—he also showed that he knew that the way he expressed them put him in mortal danger. He had reason to fear the 'pharisees' and 'satraps' of the Church inquisition, and he addressed himself prudently to his 'leue frend', his upper-class patron and protector.[93] If the author could be identified with any certainty, the particulars of his life might answer the question why one Franciscan might hold views for which many of his fellow friars were helping to pursue other men as heretics,

symple men þat ben clepude heretykys for þei [the heretics] tellon Godis lawe; for þei ben somownede and reprouede monye weyes, and aftur put in prisoun, and brende or kyllude, as worse þan þeues. And maistres of þis purseewyng ben preestis, more and lasse, and moste pryue frerys . . . (*EWS*, 2:65/106–10).

The Lollards were the most vehement castigators of the friars, especially the mendicants, and especially for their perceived hostility to the circulation of the vernacular scriptures.[94] Yet the Franciscan writer of *D&P* made common cause with the Lollards in committing himself to this 'English heresy'.[95]

---

[92] Or he is willing, when unsure, to submit to 'þe doom of oþir clerkis ȝif þey connyn seyn bettere' (2–129/88–92).

[93] Wyclif (*c*.1383/4): 'Cum satrape et pharisei nostri dicunt, quod homo non debet predicare nec colligere ewangelium in wlgari, ne forte ex eius diwlgacione in anglico sit suspectum, sed septem peccata mortalia et mandatorum decalogus sunt in anglico populo explananda, videndum est, quid probabiliter sit ex observancia decalogi viris istis specialiter inferendum: 'De nova praevaricantia mandatorum', *Polemical Works*, 2 vols., ed. Biuddensieg (London 1883), 1:126/4–9.

[94] *EWS*, 1:425/36–9. Among members of the council of 1382 which condemned the twenty-four Conclusions of the Lollards were four Franciscans (*FZ*, p. 499).

[95] The apt, punning phrase for a foundational premiss of Lollardy: that the legitimacy of the Church depended on the dissemination of the scriptures in English; see A. Hudson, 'Lollardy: the English Heresy?', SCH 9 (1972), 147–57; repr. in *Lollards* (1985), pp. 141–63. See also M. Aston, 'Lollardy and Sedition' (1960, in R. H. Hilton, ed., *Peasants, Knights and Heretics* (London, 1976), pp. 290–1.

5. THE DECALOGUE AND PATHS OF 'LESS AND MORE PERFECTION'

The author of *D&P* began his treatise with the evident intention of spelling out the requirements of an active life both for a religious mendicant and an educated upper-class layman. In the course of the dialogue—as might be expected—the boundary separating the two paths is crossed and recrossed numerous times. Perjury (oath-breaking), for example, is a sin that falls under the ban of the second Commandment.[96] But perjury is not a matter of bad language, white lies, or scatalogical jokes. In the period in which *D&P* was written, it was a political crime. In the fifteenth century, the rule of law depended on oath-taking.[97] For lack of one man's trust in another man's oath, social order could be threatened and kingdoms destroyed (253/47–54; 257/43–5). Enforcement of a basic standard of trust was the prerogative and obligation of a Dives. The tale Pauper tells of the aborted duel between a Scot and an Englishman (255/86–96), in a setting entirely outside the province of the Church—is intended not only to show that 'periurie is gretist of alle synnys nest [next to] idolatrie' (252/10) but also that it is a sin for which the lay world ought to take primary responsibility. Dives is exhorted to fight against abuses in the courts of law, where, for numbers of people, the bearing of false witness was a regular, paid occupation (253/53; 2–221/61–3) and where 'men of lawe' were buyable (2–224/1–4).

Pauper, for his part, expands the meaning of the fourth Commandment to include honoring spiritual 'fathers' and launches a diatribe against monks who live in luxury and ride out with their entourages on horses with saddles 'al gold-begon' (321/43–4) but will not relieve the poor. He grows so vehement in his denunciations of those clerics who 'vndir þe colour of pouert . . . menteþin [maintain] her pryde & her auarice & occupyyn greter lordchepys þan don many dukys, arlys & baronys' (320/15–16) that Dives implores him to change the subject. Dives'question about lay rulers ('me marvaylyth mychil why God ӡeuyth wyckyd men swyche power in þis world' (336/2–3) gets far less attention from Pauper. Dives is told he should simply accept God's decision to use lay rulers, even wicked ones, as pillars of social order (337/21–338/23). Dives' obligations would seem not to extend very far beyond governing his own household and local parish affairs. With the sanction of the Church, he may, of course, fight in a 'just war' (2–55/15–17). But about this, Pauper is discouraging: 'Y am sekyr þat God dampnyth mychil manslaute þat ʒe [Dives] & oþere men iustyfyyn' (2–57/78–9).

The wide gap between lay and clerical standards of sexual behaviour is the occasion for some of the lighter reading in the treatise as a whole. Dives, whose marital status is unclear, is quite sure that fornication between unmarried persons is not a sin, and he admits that 'it is wol hard to me for to kepyn me' from the snares of women (2–80/1–5). Pauper replies with an attack on male philandering in the vein of St Augustine's sermon 'De decem cordis'.[98] This leads quite naturally to the question, Who was guiltier of the Fall, Adam or Eve? The long argument that follows has the flavour of a well-worn academic debate (2–66/27 ff.; 2–81/29 ff.; 2–121/1 ff.). But it leads to the less conventional conclusion (by Pauper) that, of the two, Eve was the more innocent party.[99] Dives' worries about the sexual temptations of everyday life are left unappeased.

Finally we come to the question, why was *D&P* written? Why this immense, anonymous, impassioned work of vernacular theology, in which explanations and complaints tumble over one another and point fingers in many directions? The author appears to have thought that the multifarious troubles of his time and place had many immediate and intermediate causes but that all could be traced to a single underlying cause: the diminished—or distorted or mistaken or merely untutored—conception of God in the minds of too many of his lettered and unlettered contemporaries. He chose the Decalogue as the appropriate framework within which to expound his thinking about God, and Commandment I as the place to set out his thesis. Prayer to God should be an acknowledgement of the suppliant's need (203/13) and an exercise in inward change, above all change of heart. For the worshipper to look no higher than the stars—or worse, no farther than the nearest wonderworker—was to become a creature of the Devil. Churches were too full of credulous adorers of images—or too often emptied by the greater drawing power of the tavern (189/ 38–41). Unchecked, such ignorance could soon destroy the roots supporting the tree of social order (cf. 357/21–2).

[98] Passages from which are translated in *D&P* Com. VI, cap. v–vi, as part of Pauper's lecture on the superior goodness of women; see Explanatory Notes 2–67/10–71/113.

[99] In Table B of *D&P* a scribal dissent is appended: 'for that was þe opynyen of hym þat drewe þis boke' (1:1, 42/xxv cap.). See Explanatory Note 25/TABLE(B).

The true Commandment breakers, to whom Pauper gives his final curse in Commandment X,[100] are the clerics who receive offerings for images (2–133–4/7–13), give perjured evidence in court cases (2–232/15–17), and make their churches inhospitable to the laity (196/28 ff.); curates who fail to preach or teach in a language the people understand and who oppose others who do (2–22/39–40, 2–134/13–22, 2–163/124–6);[101] prelates who foment war and become men of arms themselves (2–38/19–20, 2–39/62–4, 2–40/1–8); monks who are immensely rich administrators of tithes but forget the poor (320/14–16). These are the true blasphemers, Sabbath breakers, thieves, murderers, adulterers, and bearers of false witness.

Thus for Pauper to follow the path of 'more perfection' was to hold up the mirror of the Decalogue before Church and clergy, while at the same time serving as a moral preceptor to the lay Christian. Pauper guides Dives along an active path of 'less perfection' that entails a degree of self-discipline and a shouldering of personal and civic responsibility for those of his 'even Christians' who are needy, lazy, venal, ignorant or weak. He tries to steer Dives between the errors of laxity and the errors of excess rigour. Pauper finds that Dives' moral perplexities stem more often than not from the narrow literalism of his reading of the Bible and his despair of finding a way to follow even the necessary minimum required for the salvation of his soul. Pauper, as his 'trainer',[102] repeatedly encourages Dives to look beyond the words of the Bible to their wider contexts, as well as to his 'herte inward'. His pupil is willing but often perplexed. How can I pray, complains Dives (for example), when you tell me that 'preyere withoutyn deuocion is but ded, as seyn þese clerkys', and when it is impossible for me to keep my mind fixed on each and every word of my prayer? 'Take it nout so streyte', replies Pauper; with good intentions, it is quite enough to do your best (2–20–1/53–68).[103]

---

[100] It is suggestive that the Lollard tract, the *Opus arduum*, of *c*.1390 'devotes a long section to the friars' abuse of each of the Ten Commandments': Penn Szittya, *The Antifraternal Tradition* (Princeton, 1986), p. 182.

[101] Wyclif concurs: 'Et de isto homicidio timerent se clerici et prelati qui . . . omnino subtrahunt predicacionem evangelii et spirituale suffragium', *De mandatis*, p. 335/3–7.

[102] '. . . you who are haughty and powerful and rich should appoint . . . some man of God as trainer and pilot': 'The Rich Man's Salvation', *Clement of Alexandria*, tr. G. W. Butterworth, LCL 92, p. 355. ¶ 41.

[103] Pauper's 'man & woman owyth to don hys deuer [do his best] . . .' here echoes Robert Holcot's (d. 1349] 'Nam si homo facit quod in se est satis informabitur de illis qui sunt necessaria ad salutem suam' (*Super libros Sapientiae*, Lect. 28B (Habenau, 1494), which, as the principle of 'facere quod in se est', was seen as a guide to a middle way between the

History was not on the side of the author of *D&P*. Clerical laxity and lay literalism chafed one another increasingly during the remainder of the fifteenth century. Social order was not restored for long by the Lancastrian ascendancy. Instead of running smoothly side by side, the paths of less and more perfection collided. Neither churchmen nor laymen were then prepared to listen to the lessons of social quietism and ecclesiastical activism embodied in this 'compendiouse treatyse'.

6. THE MANUSCRIPTS, MANUSCRIPT FRAGMENTS AND EARLY PRINTED TEXTS OF *DIVES AND PAUPER*

The manuscripts (except MS fragments W and N) are listed in vol. 1:1, xi-xii, of the edition of the text, with references to the catalogues in which they are described. An expanded description will be given here. The manuscripts are listed in the order GRDTBYLH and the manuscript fragments in the order EAOMWN.

(1) G: Glasgow University Library, MS Hunterian 270, the base manuscript for the edition.[104]

270 vellum leaves, size 235 mm by 150 mm, written frame 160 to 168 mm by 98 to 103 mm, in single columns, 32 lines to a column. Collation: four paper flyleaves (i^4), two marbled paper flyleaves (ii^2), two vellum flyleaves (iii^2). The quires are 1^{10}, 2^8–33^8, 34^4. Regular catchwords appear, beginning on fo. 26^v. At the end of the written text are four paper flyleaves (iv^4) and two marbled paper flyleaves (v^2). The regular, single foliation begins on fo. 1^r, with the Table, and continues in ink in a large bold eighteenth-century hand through fo. 99^v; This foliation may have been the work of Thomas Martin of

extremes of predestination and Pelagianism by such later theologians as Jean Gerson (d. 1429) and Gabriel Biel (d. 1495). That the author of *D&P* read Holcot seems attested by the fact that he drew the *exemplum* of the fox on ice (2–276/1–5) from its source in Holcot's *De sapientia*, Lect. 17: Beryl Smalley, 'Robert Holcot, O.P.', *Archivum Fratrum Praedicatorym* 26 (1956), 5–97. On 'facere quod in se est' see H. A. Oberman, 'Facientibus quod in se est deus non denegat gratiam: Robert Holcot, O.P. and the Beginnings of Luther's Theology', *Harvard Theological Review* 55 (Boston, 1962), 317–42; H. A. Oberman, *The Harvest of Medieval Theology* (North Carolina, 1983), pp. 235–48.

[104] John Young and P. Henderson Aitken, *A Catalogue of the Manuscripts in the Library of the Hunterian Museum in the University of Glasgow* (Glasgow, 1908), pp. 217–8.

Palgrave (1691–1771), whose ex libris appears on iii^r. The foliation continues, in a smaller hand, without error from fo. 100^r to fo. 270^v.

Contents:

1. Flyleaves: iii^1 contains the ex libris of Thomas Martin (see above) and on iii^2 his remarks on the authorship of D&P, derived from Bale and Leland (see Introduction on authorship). He refers to his possession of a printed edition by Wynkyn de Worde, the existence of an edition by Pynson, and the possibility that the book was once in the collection of the antiquary, John Theyer (1597–1678); cf. the remarks below on BL MS Royal 17C.xxi. Other brief jottings, all eighteenth-century, on succeeding flyleaves are fully transcribed in the catalogue. The end flyleaves are blank.

2. fos. 1^r–10^r contain the Table, beginning þis table leue frend . . . (edn. I:1,1/1) and ending . . . þer is swiche blysse (edn. I:1,24/26); fo. 10^v is blank.

3. fos. 11^r–20^v contain the Holy Poverty prologue (A), headed in the upper margin holy povert. and beginning Diues et pauper obviauerunt . . . (edn. I:1,51/1), ending . . . Qhat doute hast þu þerinne (edn. I:1,69/80).

4. fos. 20^v–270^v contain the dialogue on the Commandments headed in the upper margins 1^m/p[re]cep[tum] and beginning (marked by a floral design in the left margin) In þe ferste commandment . . . (edn. I:1,81/1) and ending . . . for me deyyd on tre amen (edn. I:2, 326/80).

The manuscript is written by three scribes in a hand formerly called textualis with cursive influences but now termed Anglicana formata.[105] Though the manuscript is the work of three scribes, the handwriting is fairly uniform in appearance throughout. Scribe 1 writes the Table (fos. 1^r–10^r), the marginal emendations, and the main body of the text from fo. 51^r through fo. 270^v (edn. I:1, pp. 1–24, pp. 154–359; 1:2, pp. 1–326.). Scribe 2 writes the Holy Poverty Prologue, fos. 11^r–20^v, and part of the first Commandment, fos. 20^v–48^r (edn. I:1. pp. 51–69, pp. 81–148). Scribe 3 writes part of fo. 48$_r$ and through fo. 50^v (edn. I:1, pp. 148–54). The textual notes record changes of hand by all scribes. In Vol. 1:1, the Frontispiece shows Hunterian MS. 270, fo. 11^r, scribe 2.

Successive sections of the manuscript, beginning with the Table, open with large capital letters decorated in blue and red. The first page of the Prologue is floriated. On each page of the text, the letters

---

[105] ECBH, pp. xxii–xxv and Plate 5 (1), opp. p. 5, written in Oxford, dated 1380.

'*b*', '*h*','*k*', and '*l*' in the upper margins are decoratively elongated and coloured, with hooks to the right at the top.[106] On twenty-one pages of the text, usually on the verso (five are on the recto), a scribal hand has drawn male, usually bearded, profiles. Each is unique, occuring at irregular intervals (i.e. not connected with the catch words), from fo. 21^v to fo. 266^v. Latin quotations are underlined. Chapter numbers appear in the side margins. Textual corrections are usually marginal and are in the hands of the scribes. The binding is eighteenth-century. The manuscript is not known to have been in a medieval library.

The three scribes who write MS G are distinguishable mainly on the basis of spellings. Scribe 1 spells: *chyrche, kende, menteþyn, muchil, nouȝt, seyth, schal, schulde, swyche, whanne, world*; scribe 2 spells: *cherche, kende, mayntene, mechil, nought, seyȝt, shal/shul, shulde, sueche, qhanne, word*. Scribe 2 is fond of doubled vowels: *goo, moodir, woord, meen, woot, waar* and the like. Scribe 3 spells: *chirche, kynde, meyntenen, muche, nought, seith, shal, shulde, sweche/swyche/sueche, whenne*. The line of demarcation is a vague one, even though in reading the manuscript it is always clear which scribe is writing which part of the text. The most recent survey of late Middle English dialects (*LALME*) lists Hunterian 270 as a manuscript written in an East Anglian dialect but does not provide a separate linguistic profile.[107] See Explanatory Notes, 2–278/9, on the rare word 'whor' (whether), which occurs in both MS G and the Longleat sermons (LL4). *LALME*, Map 570, indicates for it a south and southwest location (1:447). A note on the word 'wyndounne' (window), which occurs twice in MS G (scribe 1; all other manuscripts 'windowe'), identifies the form as specifically Norfolk.[108]

(2) R: British Library MS Royal 17 C.xxi[109]

249 leaves, the first two quires and flyleaf are velum, the remainder paper. The size of the leaves is 221 mm. by 140 mm.; the written frame, 153 mm. by 102 mm., in single columns, 36 to 39 lines to a column. Collation: 3 paper flyleaves i^3, quires 1^{12}, 2^{10}, 3^{12}, 4^{16}–13^{16}, 14^{14}, 15^{12}–17^{12}, 3 paper flyleaves, ii^3. Catchwords are now visible only

---

[106] Cf. *ECBH*, Plate 5 (ii), dated ca.1394–7.

[107] *LALME*, 1:89.

[108] A. McIntosh and M. Laing, 'Middle English *wyndown*, 'Window'' *Neuphilologische Mitteilungen* 97 (1998), 295–300, ref. to *D&P* p. 296.

[109] *Royal Catalogue*, 2:247.

on fos. 12ᵛ, 180ᵛ, 225ᵛ, and 236ᵛ. Between fos. 118ᵛ and 119ᵛ are 6 stubs; again between fos. 154ᵛ–155ᵛ. There are two foliations: the first, in black ink, numbers each side of the leaf; a pencilled foliation beneath numbers by folios; I have followed the latter. After the last page of text, fo. 245ʳ, there is on fos. 245ᵛ–248ʳ a Latin scriptural index; these pages are defective and repaired. The final page is a sheet from a musical manuscript, which is counted as fo. 249ʳ⁻ᵛ.

Contents:

1. fos. 1ʳ–11ʳ, headed in a contemporary hand 'Diues et paup[er]', begin (the Holy Poverty prologue) *Diues et paup[er] obuiaueru[n]t . . .* (edn. I:1,51/1) and end . . .*What douȝte hast þu þ[er]in[n]e* (edn. I:1,69/80). Fo. 1ʳ contains in the lower margin a seventeenth-century inscription: 'Henricus Parker Monachus qui Claruit Anno Dm. 1470 Author fuit istius libri'. On fo. 11ʳ, the heading in the upper margin changes, still in a hand contemporary with the manuscript, to *Pri[mu]m Mandatu[m]* (subsequently further abbreviated).

2. fos.11ʳ–245ʳ contain the dialogue on the Commandments, beginning *In þe fyrst commaundement as I haue lernyd . . .*, ending . . .*per for dyid on þe rode tre . Amen.* Below the end of the text, in the hand of the writer of the ascription of authorship on fo. 11ʳ, is a repetition: *Explicit dialogus . . . . . per Henricus Parker . . . 1470.* In a Gothic script below this is an inscription ending . . . *tristi saluer pia passio Xristi..* On fo. 183ʳ. the name Richard Messinge (as read by the Warner and Gibson catalogue, which adds '17th cent.?') is scribbled in the lower margin. A second name is illegible.

3. fos. 245ᵛ–248ᵛ contain an index of scriptural passages, the Latin arranged alphabetically, followed by the biblical source; this index is not keyed to the text of *D&P*.

The hand is an Anglicana formata, cf. *ECBH*, Pl. 5 (i), written in Oxford in *c.*1380; in *D&P* I:1, see Plate opposite p. 81. The manuscript is written by a single scribe. *LALME* dates it as 'earlier 15th century' and states that 'the scribal language looks to be of S. Norfolk or N. Suffolk' (1:115).

MS Royal 17 C. xxi has capital letters in blue with red flourishing. Latin citations are underlined in red. The smaller 'D's' and 'P's' are black with red decoration. Chapter numbers are in the side margins. Non-scribal marginal annotations, two to ten per page, date from the post-medieval period, except for two (one in Latin), on fos. 235ʳ and

237^r in a fifteenth-century hand. On the last page, fo. 245^r, the attribution to Henry Parker is repeated in the same hand as on fo. 1^r. Both inscriptions may be the work of John Theyer, the antiquary (1597–1678), whose much-reduced library reached the British Museum in the eighteenth century.[110] Hence this manuscript, like Hunterian 270 (MS G, see above) may once have been in Theyer's collection. A. I. Doyle[111] observes that this manuscript shares 'textual features' with the *D&P* extract found in BL, Add. 10053, a South-West Midland copy' (MS A in edn., see below). The binding is dated 1757.

(3) D: Bodleian Library MS Douce 295[112]

222 parchment leaves, 250 mm by 170 mm, written frame 170 mm by 113 mm, in single columns, 39 to 41 lines each. Collation: 1 paper flyleaf i^r, quires 1^2, 2^8–27^8, 2^3, and a final paper flyleaf, numbered '222 ult.'. Catchwords begin on fo. 11^v and continue throughout. No visible foliation until fo. 126^r; text foliated by editor consistent with this numbering, beginning on the first page of written text and concluding with the last page of written text, fo. 221^v.

Contents:

1. fos. 1^r–6^r contain the Table, beginning imperfectly from T, Com. I, cap. 29, to the end. The written text begins . . . -*moun corse of kende & whan* . . . (edn. I:1,3/58), ending . . . *þer is suche blisse* (edn. I:1,24/27). The 'Explicit' and the recipe below it are in other, later hands. Fo. 6^v is blank except for some alphabet practice in a later hand.

2. fos. 7^r–10^r contain the Holy Poverty Prologue (A), beginning *Diues et pauper obuiauerunt* . . . (edn. I:1.51/1) and ending . . . *what doute hast thou ther inne* (edn. I:1,69/80). No transition is indicated in the text; the next word, *Diues*, marks the beginning of the dialogue on the Commandments.

3. fos. 10^r–222^r contain the dialogue, beginning *Diues In the ferst comaundement* . . . (edn. I:1,81/1) and ending (imperfectly) . . . *And þer for he longith not peraftir*, in Com. X, cap. 13 (edn. I:2,324/20). The final text page is damaged; fo. 222^r is blank.

The manuscript appears to have been written by one scribe. The hand is a variant of Anglicana formata, cf. *ECBH*, Pl. 5 (i), written in

---

[110] Samples of the handwriting of John Theyer can be found in *Royal Catalogue*, Vol. 4, Plate 125.

[111] Doyle *Survey*, 1:96.

[112] *SC*, 4:583.

Oxford c1380; see Plate of fo. 80^v in Frontispiece of *D&P* 1:2. Capital letters are decorated in red; Latin quotations are underlined in red, and capital D's and P's at the beginnings of chapters are decorated in blue and red. No corrections appear. Two (later) hands contribute marginalia throughout. A number of margins are cut away (fos. 88, 90, 107, 147, 185, 192 and 198). Fos. 219, 220 and 221 are severely damaged. On fo. 60^r a name in the margin may be 'John gabriall' or 'gabrielle'; below it (dubiously) 'paliter marial'. The date 1640 appears in the lower margin of fo. 78^r. On fos. 85^v and 99^r is scrawled the name 'Jonas Kingardson' (?). From fos. 123^r to 137^v, the pages are puckered and browned, as are the final pages of the manuscript. Inside the front cover is the bookplate of Francis Douce. A. I. Doyle found evidence that the manuscript was owned by a parish priest in 1502.[113] Douce 295 is listed in the linguistic atlas (*LALME*), which places the scribal dialect in 'SW Norfolk, or Ely border, Norfolk' (I:148).

(4) T: British Library MS Royal 17 C. xx.[114]

273 leaves (but see below on foliation), paper except for vellum flyleaves. The size is 215 mm by 135 mm, written frame 163 mm by 102 to 106 mm. The text is in single columns, from 26 to 43 lines each. Collation: 3 paper flyleaves, i^3, 3 vellum flyleaves, ii^3; quires 1^{12}–11^{12}, 12^{10}–22^{10}, 23^{12}–24^{12}; 3 vellum flyleaves, iii^3. Catchwords begin sporadically (visible on fos. 16^v and 18^v) but are regular from fo. 51^v to the end of the manuscript. The foliation is dual: the flyleaves are numbered 1 to 3; the text (part of the Table) begins on a leaf numbered 5 (hence on fo. 4^v); a second numbering begins on fo. 14^r with '2' and continues by page. The first numbering (which I have followed in the edition) continues through fo. 269^r. In order to be consistent with the first numbering in the manuscript I have numbered the first page of text fo. 4^v; the vellum flyleaves are numbered 1^r–4^r. Thus the last page of text is 269^v, and the vellum flyleaves are in my foliation 270^r–273^v.

Contents:

1. fos. i^3–13^r contain the opening flyleaves and two fragments of the Table. Flyleaf i^2 (2^r) contains the signature and date (1640) indicating that the manuscript was once (like MS R) in the library of John Theyer, the antiquary, whose hand appears to be responsible

---

[113] Doyle *Survey*, 1:96.   [114] *Royal Catalogue*, 2:246–7.

for the reiterated attribution of *D&P* to Henry Parker. The name Thomas Patten and date 1587 appear below; he had connections to Magdalen College, Oxford and was Theyer's apparent source for the manuscript. A portion of the Table begins on fo. 4^v, *Whi crist enformyd more* . . . (edn. I:1,26/x cap.), ending on fo. 12^r . . . *suche blisse / Explicit* (edn. I:1,24/27). Fo. 12^v is blank but seems to be pasted over a page of the second Table fragment. This fragment begins on 13^r: *Of fals borowerys* . . . (edn. I:1,22/15) and ends . . . *blysse–xii^{co}/ Explicit* (edn. I:1,24/27).

2. fos. 13^v–21^v contain the (later-titled) Holy Poverty (A) Prologue, beginning *d: leue frend þese wordys* . . . (edn. I:1,49/2), ending . . .*What douȝte hast þou þerynne* (edn. I:1,69/80).

3. fos. 21^v–269^v contain the dialogue on the Commandments. This begins without a break on fo. 21^v, *d. In þe ferste commaundement* . . . (edn. I:1,81/1) and ends . . . *þat for vs dyed on þe rode tre.A.M.E.N* (edn. I:2,326/79–80).

4. fos. 270^r–274^{r-v}: 270^{r-v} are blank. Fo. 271^r contains four short notes giving page references. Fo. 272^r contains the note '270 folios'. Fos. 272^v–273^r are blank.

Three hands can be clearly distinguished. A fourth is possible; it is most similar to, but distinguishable from, hand 3. These divide the manuscript in the following way: hand 1, fos. 4^v–12^r; fos. 33^r–34^v, fo. 39^r (half), fos. 67^v–245^v; and all corrections. Hand 2, fos. 13^r–18^v, fos. 29^r–32^v, fos. 35^r–38^v, fos. 246^r–269^v. Hand 3, fos. 19^r–28^r. Hand 4 (possible), fos. 40^r–67^r. Hand 1 is a secretary book hand, cf. *ECBH*, Pl. 13 (i), dated 1470; hand 2 is also a secretary book hand but closer to Parkes's Pl. 17 (i), Oxford, 1429; hand 3 is a somewhat carelesss (or late) version of Parkes's 'bastard secretary' hand, Pl.14 (i), written c1415; hand 4 is a blend of Anglicana and secretary hands, Pl. 17 (i), written in Oxford, dated 1429. A plate of manuscript T was not included in the edition.

A misplacement of text occurs between fos. 24^v and 25^r, resulting in the omission of part of cap. 4, all of cap. 5, and the first part of cap. 6 of the first Commandment and its transfer to fos. 27^{r-v}. Again, at the top of fo. 29^r, with a change of hand, a lacuna of about 20 lines occurs.

The manuscript appears to have been intended for private use. The scribal hands are not self-consistent as to letter sizes or as to how much text is crowded onto a given page. The manuscript is undecorated; A. I. Doyle lists MS T as 'another East Anglian copy' and finds the marginal name 'John Wellys of Norwich'.[115] The manuscript has recently been elegantly rebound. MS Royal 17 C xx is not listed in *LALME*.

(5) B: Bodleian Library MS Eng.th.d.36.[116]

204 parchment leaves, size 260 mm by 185 mm, written frame 185 mm by 135 mm in double columns of 37 lines, ruled. Collation: i², 1¹, 2⁸–26⁸, 27³, ii²; catchwords are mostly visible. The existing foliation begins with fo. 10ʳ and continues through 213ʳ (blank). The foliator has noted the duplication of fo. 95 and has numbered these 'ff. 95a and 95b'. In the edition, I have retained the manuscript numbering.

Contents:.

1.   Foliation begins on fo. 10ʳ; what would be fo. 9ᵛ contains notes on the text in a later hand. Fo. 10ʳ⁻ᵛ, the last leaf of Table, begins on fo. 10ʳ: *iiii c. what ve[n]iau[n]ce hap fallen* . . . (edn. I:1,47/iv cap.) and ends . . . *petir & poul & moyses/ amen.*(edn. I:1,50/85); in the lower margin in a later hand: *Regnum Potestas Gloria Trinitati.*

2.   fos. 11ʳ–17ʳ (as numbered) contain the Holy Poverty Prologue (B), beginning, after heading, *Of holy pou[er]te, Of hooli pouertee/ þe firste c. Diues* . . . (edn. I:1,70/1) and ending . . . *what doute hast þ[o]u þerynne* . . . (edn. I:1,69/80).

3.   fos. 17ʳ–212ᵛ (as numbered) contain the dialogue on the Commandments, beginning *Diues In þe firste commaundement* . . . (edn. I:1,81/1), ending (imperfectly) . . . *þi speche skilful good* . . . (edn. I:2,295/1).

The manuscript is imperfect at both ends.[117] It is carefully written, by a single scribe, in a book hand classifiable as 'fere-textura', cf. *ECBH*, Plate 8 (ii), dated c1500; see Plate of fo. 17ʳ in *D&P* 1:1 opposite p. 81. Corrections are made by the scribe, usually in the lower margins. The

---

[115] Doyle *Survey*, 1:96.

[116] *Bodleian Catalogue of Medieval Manuscripts, Typescript Supplement*, s.v. 'Holkhammisc'; *IMEP*, Handlist XII, ed. Hanna, pp. 10–11. MS B is the basis of all of the printed editions of *D&P*, as shown by Margery M. Morgan in her article 'Pynson's Manuscripts of *Dives and Pauper*', *The Library*, 5th Ser., Vol. VIII, No. 4 (1953), 217–28 (see below 'Early Printed Texts'). In her work on MS B, Dr Morgan was misled by its existing foliation; she noted the duplication of fo. 95 but misread the final numbering as fo. 219 and miscounted the manuscript leaves; see corrected foliation.

[117] The *IMEP* finds that the first nine folios of MS B have been lost, and that 'stubs of five leaves are visible at the the rear' and 'one additional quire followed these', Handlist XII, ed. Hanna, p. 11.

capital letters are decorated in black and red ink; chapter numbers are
in red ink in the margins. The opening page (11^r) of the Holy Poverty
Prologue is floreated. In the lower margin of fo. 148^r is scrawled
'Miles Berne', identified by Margery M. Morgan as a rector of
Lyminge in the early seventeenth century.[118] In the same article,
Dr Morgan notes that the manuscript was formerly in the Ashburn-
ham collection, then bought by Leicester Harmsworth, then by
Maggs Bros., from whom it was acquired by the Bodleian in 1950
(idem, pp. 217–8). In an article of 1909, H. R. Plomer provided
evidence of ownership of the manuscript by John Russhe (d. 1498) of
London and Essex.[119] The *IMEP* dates the hand s. $xv^{3/4}$ *LALME*
does not list MS B. The binding is a rough calf of the eighteenth
century.

(6) Y: Yale University Library MS Beinecke 228.[120]

199 leaves on unlined paper, size 298 mm by 209 mm, written frame
214 mm by 146 mm. Written in single columns of 36 to 40 lines each.
Collation: i^1 (parchment stub) + ii^3 (paper), 1^{16}–12^{16}, 13^7 + iii^1
(paper), iv^1 (parchment stub); catchwords generally visible. No
consistent foliation appears in the manuscript; I have numbered
from the first to the last folio on which there is written text, fos.
1^r–199^r. A '70' appears on my fo. 54^r and continues numbering by
tens. By this numbering, the last leaf containing text would be
fo. 215^r. Adding to the confusion, most upper margins in the
manuscript (those not cut off) contain '210F' (see Plate of fo. 199^r
in edition, I:2, opposite p. 325; note that the misprinted caption
beneath the Plate has been corrected (see Explanatory Notes 2–326/
note 78–80). The colophon is ambiguous: 'ii^d x levis' (not as I
transcribed it in the edition '5 4 lebir'), and can be translated as
either '204 leaves' or '210 leaves' depending on whether the 'x' is read
as an arabic '4' or a Roman 'x': the number is made with a loop and
might be either; on (my) fo. 124^r a similar looped number is, however,
unquestionably '4' (see Explanatory Notes 2–326/note 78–80).

---

[118] Morgan, 'Pynson's Manuscript', p. 227.

[119] 'Two Lawsuits of Richard Pynson', *The Library*, New Ser. No. 38, Vol. 10 (1909),
115–33.

[120] Barbara Shailor, *Catalogue of Medieval and Renaissance Manuscripts in the Beinecke
Rare Book and Manuscript Library, Yale University, Vol. I, MSS 1–250*, MRTS 34
(Binghamton, N.Y.,1984–92) 321. MS 228 is listed in Seymour de Ricci, *The Supplement
to the Census of Medieval & Renaissance Manuscripts in the United States & Canada* (N.Y.,
1962), p. 43, No. 228, as 'Henry Parker . . . Dives and Pauper'.

Contents:

1. ii³, fos. 1ʳ–7ʳ: The flyleaves contain the semilegible signature of 'Philip Emily' or 'Smily', with the date July 4, 1614. The last flyleaf (ii³) contains in a non-scribal hand *Animae vita virtus: sensus charitas: Bern[ard]*. The text of the Holy Poverty Prologue (B) begins on fo. 1ʳ, with the heading *p[rimum] p[re]ceptu[m] Ooff holy pouert/ca[pitulum] p[rimu]m/ Diues & paup[er]* . . . (edn. I:1,70/1) and ends . . . *What dout has þu þer inne* (edn. I:1,69/80).

2. fos. 7ʳ–199ʳ contain the dialogue on the Commandments, beginning *Diues In þe first com[m]andement as I haue lerned* . . . (edn. I:1,81/1), ending . . . *and þer bith writyn w[ith] þe calander ii^d x lebis* (edn. I:2,326 note). Fo. 199ᵛ contains a business account not in a scribal hand.

The manuscript was written by a single scribe, with the exception of a few short passages. The second scribal hand appears on fos. 2ᵛ, 4ᵛ, 7ᵛ, 14ʳ⁻ᵛ, 36ᵛ, and the colophon, 199ʳ (edn. 1:1, 73/26–33, 78/17–38, 83/45–84, 108/45–111, 186/4–8, and 2–326/note 80). The first scribe adds two short passages, reflecting conditions in Lisbon, to the text of MS Y; these are found on 26ʳ and 56ᵛ (edn. 1:1, 146/60 and 256/26). Both scribal hands are an English secretary, cf. *ECBH*, Pl. 12 (ii), dated *c*.1470; see Plate in *D&P* 1:2, fo. 199ʳ, opposite p. 325. The manuscript has very few corrections, usually above the line, marked with a caret. It is informal in appearance. Some red and brown ink is used to touch up capital letters; biblical and other quotations and page headings are underlined in red. Occasional simple scroll-work extends a short line to the edge of the written frame. The watermark in the paper on which the manuscript is written is a tulip-like flower nearest to Briquet, Vol. III, No. 6654 (of 1452), a Roman paper.[121] The colophon (in the hand of the second scribe) indicates that the time and place of writing was St Katherine's monastery in Lisbon, Portugal, in 1465. An indication that the secondary scribe may have been Spanish or Portuguese-speaking is his use of '*b*' for '*v*' in spelling such words as 'Dibes'. He also writes 'Lisboa' for the first scribe's 'Luxbon'. The manuscript is not listed in *LALME*. The Beinecke Library acquired the manuscript in 1954 from Maggs Bros., via C. A. Stonehill. The manuscript is in a seventeenth-century calf binding.

[121] C. M. Briquet, *Les Filigranes*, 4 vols., ed. A. Stevenson (Amsterdam, 1968), 3:No. 6654. Other marks that are close to: 3:No. 6655 (1462, Palermo), and 3:No. 6656 (1468, Perpignon-Lugano-Venice).

(7) L: Lichfield Cathedral Library MS 35 (formerly 5)[122]

216 vellum leaves, size 290 mm by 196 mm, written frame size 200 mm by 112 mm, single column, 34–41 lines to the page. Collation: i², 1⁸–27⁸, ii²; regular catchwords. A single foliation, but with several repeated folio numbers, results in a page count of 214 leaves; the actual number is 216. For editorial purposes I have renumbered the leaves from 95–216.

Contents:

1. fos. 1ʳ–10ᵛ contain a Table (B), beginning *The table* [missing capital R]*iche and pore* . . . (edn. I:1,25/1, ending . . . *peter and powle & moyses / Explicit* (edn. I:1,50/85). There are no early names or dates on the flyleaves.

2. fos. 11ʳ–17ᵛ contain the Holy Poverty Prologue (B) beginning *Of holy pouerte / Diues* . . . (edn. I:1,70/1), ending . . . *what don₃t[is] hast þow therynne* (edn. I:1,69/80).

3. fos. 17ᵛ–216ᵛ contain the dialogue on the Commandments, beginning [*space for missing capital D*]*ives In þe fyrst comawndment as I have* . . ., ending (imperfectly) in Com. VIII, cap. 5 . . . *Ffor þe wyse man seyth Qui cito* . . . (edn. I:2,220/15–16); the following word, *credit*, appears as a catchword at the foot of the page.

The manuscript appears to have been written by a single scribe, though his hand varies considerably throughout. The hand may be classified as 'bastard secretary', cf. *ECBH*, Pl. 14 (ii), mid fifteenth century; see Plate of fo. 182ʳ in *D&P* 1:2 opposite p. 129. The manuscript is undecorated. Spaces for capital letters are often left unfilled. The margins contain chapter numbers in the scribal hand. The few longer marginalia by other hands are noted in the edition.

A distinctive feature of the spellings is the doubling of vowels, as, e.g., in *leest, oon, seeknesse, feends, moost, feelde, eende*. *LALME* finds that the 'language seems to be mixed, but may have a Northants element' (I:98).

How the manuscript arrived in Lichfield Cathedral is far from clear. A note on a flyleaf of BL MS Harley 149 (MS H, see below) dated 1802 states that Lichfield Cathedral library owns a 'finely

---

[122] N. R. Ker, *Medieval Manuscripts in British Libraries*, 4 Vols., (Oxford, 1969–92), 3:124–5; see also S. S. Benedikz, *Lichfield Cathedral Library: A Catalogue of the Cathedral Library Manuscripts*, rev. version (Birmingham University Library, 1978), p. 20; An earlier listing appears in J. C. Cox, *Catalogue of the Muniments & Manuscript Books Pertaining to the Dean and Chapter of Lichfield*, William Salt Archaeological Society, vi (ii), 1886, p. 204.

written copy' of *D&P*. The bulk of the small manuscript collection in the library was donated to the Cathedral in the seventeenth century by the Duchess of Somerset. Her handwritten catalogue does not list *D&P*, but it does list one 'untitled MS'. Subsequent early catalogues fail to list it, however. The present binding is an eighteenth-century gold-tooled brown calf.

(8) H: British Library MS Harley 149 (olim Savile 46)[123]

281 leaves overall; *D&P* is contained in the first 182 leaves; size 275 mm by 225 mm, written frame 240 mm by 155 mm, on paper, written in single columns 30 to 45 lines each. Collation (first 182 leaves): flyleaves i⁴, quires 1⁶, 2¹⁶–12¹⁶, ii², iii². Catchwords (in the *D&P* portion) are visible from fo. 22ᵛ on. Regular single foliation, in pencil, begins with fo. 1ʳ, at the beginning of written text.

Contents:

1. i⁴: i³ contains a handwritten note dated 1802 by R. E. Nares citing the existence of a *D&P* manuscript in the Lichfield Cathedral Library (see above). i⁴ contains in large Gothic letters: *Hic Exposition /in English auntient and large upo[n] the ten Commandements.*

2. fos. 1ʳ–6ᵛ: the Table, incomplete at the beginning, headed in a non-scribal hand (perhaps to obscure the incompleteness) *A Table of the Exposition of the 10 com[m]andements.* The scribal hand begins . . . *that þe fende knowith* . . . (edn. I:1,4/62: Com. I, cap. 31). The Table ends midway down fo. 6ᵛ: . . . *forth in derknesse* (edn. I:1,24/textual note 26–7). The rest of the page contains a prescription for sciatica in Latin, in a hand similar to the scribal hand (another such prescription appears on fo. 41ʳ).

3. fos. 7ʳ–182ᵛ contain the dialogue on the Commandments, beginning at the top of the page with an interpolated (see below on owners) heading: *An Exposition on the 10 com[m]andements / Dives/ Pauper/ Interlocutors.* The scribal hand begins *DIVES -in þe fyrst com[m]aundement as I haue lernyd* . . . (edn. I:1/81/1) and ends, imperfectly, near the end of Com. X, cap. 3: . . . *on thin hert* . . . (edn. I:2,303/93, note); '*And*' has been inked out and '*finis*' has been written at the bottom of the page.

4. fos. 183ʳ–252ʳ: an unnumbered parchment leaf separates *D&P* from

[123] H. Wanley and R. Nares, *A Catalogue of the Harleian Manuscripts in the British Museum*, 3 vols. (London, 1808–12), 1:44.

Caxton's *Book of Good Manners*,[124] This work opens with a Table beginning [*H*]*ere begynneth the table* . . . and ends (fo. 184^r) . . . *gretly dysplesaunt to godd*. Caxton's text begins on the same page *And now we wyl speke of the fyrst chapytre* . . . and ends . . . *the worlde shal endure longe*. At the bottom of the same page, in the same hand, . . . *here endyth the book of goode manners or of goode conditiouns*.

5. fos. 252^r–262^v begin with the title of the ensuing work: *hereaftyr folweth þe cene þat oure lorde made wyth hys dyssyplys*. In the same scribal hand the text begins on fo. 252^v [*O*]*ure lorde Ihesu cryst was sory* . . . ending . . . *and so he ended hys unthryfty lyfe*.

6. fos. 263^r–275^v begin *here endyth the passyoun* . . . [*T*]*he constable of the Iewes* . . ., ending . . . *et sic est finis dei gratias*.

7. fos. 275^v–279^r begin *hereaftyr folweth a story of þe veronycle* . . ., ending . . . *trewe louers of Ihu cryst/ Amen*.

8. fos. 279^r–280^v begin *here begynneth a tretys betwene saynt Petre and Symon Magus to the deth of Tybery Cesar* . . ., ending . . . *eternal glory /AMEN/EXPLICIT*.

9. fo. 281^r contains, in a different hand, a short macaronic verse (six pairs of lines), one line Latin, the next a Middle English translation. It begins *Iudici* . . . *Respice Digna* . . . and ends . . . *pourge alle this world*. On the third end flyleaf, in a later hand, is the name W. Marsh and the date 1875.

The handwritings in the *D&P* portion may be classified as secretary bookhands (cf. *ECBH*, Plates 12–13, mid to late fifteenth century); see Plate of MS H in *D&P* 1:1, fo. 7^r, facing p. 81. Two, possibly three, hands can be distinguished. These divide the text in the following way: hand 1, fos.1^r–6^v; hand 2, fos.7^r–22^v; hand 1, fos.23^r–41^r; hand 2, fos.41^r–43^v (half); hand 1, fos.43^v–59^v; hand 3, fos.60^r (only); hand 1, fos. 60^v–182^v. Hand 3 is a phantom, appearing only on the lower three fourths of fo. 60^r. Its general appearance is larger and more open than the other hands, but its letter forms are closely similar, in their details, to hand 1.

MS H contains a hierarchy of marginal notations. The earliest are in Latin and are in a hand closely similar to the scribal hands. A hint that some may be scribal (hand 1) is that a frequent scribal flourish consisting of a descending curled-ribbon design is also found on a marginal note on fo. 88^v. The early marginalia consist of biblical or

---

[124] William Caxton's (?1415–?1491) *Book of Good Manners* is a translation of Jacques Legrand's *Livre de bonnes moeurs* (of *c*.1410). Caxton's translation received several early printings, see *STC*, 2:55, nos. 15394–15399.

legal references and brief *nota bene* remarks. Marginalia in later hands
are in English, are usually longer, and usually consist of restatements
of what is in the text, for ready reference. The more recent marginalia
have been attributed to the previous owners of fos. 1–182 of the
manuscript, the Savile's, father and son, who acquired the two parts
of the present manuscript separately in 1624 and 1625. The *D&P*
portion was acquired from Sir Simonds D'Ewes, who may have been
responsible for the heading on fo. 1ʳ.[125]

Harley 149 is not listed in *LALME*. A. I Doyle's *Survey* (op. cit.,
I:62) observes that the language shows 'marked E. Anglian features
(x-, qw-, -yn, etc.)'. The manuscript, lopped off at beginning and end
and minus a Prologue, is otherwise notable for its omissions and for
its free variation on the text of *D&P*.

(9) E: Bodleian Library MS Eng.th.e.1, 'Scraps'.[126]

14 leaves, the *D&P* portion comprising two vellum leaves, which
have been cut away on top, bottom and outer margins. The width of
each of the inner margins is *c.*27 mm; the size of the written frame is
now about 182 mm by 118 mm; some text on the lower margins has
been cut away. The text is written in single columns, 43–45 lines
each. No foliation is visible. I refer to the leaves on which *D&P*
appears as fos. 1ʳ–2ᵛ, describing first the outer sides of the bifolium
then the inner sides.

Contents:

1. fos. 1ʳ–2ᵛ contain two discontinuous portions of the text of *D&P*:
   fo. 1ʳ⁻ᵛ: *. . . ʒif þei ben not harmyd . . .* (Com. VII, cap. 25, edn.
   I:2,198/26), ending *. . . in tyme of nede to . . .* (edn. I:2,201/32).
   Fo. 2ʳ⁻ᵛ: *. . . and for consuetude of lesyng . . .* (Com. VIII, cap. 2, edn.
   I:2,213/24), ending *. . . done in dede / þer for it . . .* (edn. I:2,216/36).
2. fo. 3ʳ⁻ᵛ: lower portion of a larger leaf, 197 mm by 140 mm, written
   in an early fifteenth-century hand: *. . . bisshop . and nowe to Cayphas
   . . .*, ending *. . . rynen oute of þe citee at alle ʒates to þe citeseyns and
   strangers . . .* (a description of the trial of Jesus). On the verso, *. . .
   come and make þe . . .*, ending *. . . Firste his moder see* [several final

[125] See Andrew G. Watson, *The Library of Sir Simonds D'Ewes*, The Trustees of the British Museum (London, 1966), p. 115; Andrew G. Watson, *The Manuscripts of Henry Savile of Banke*, London Bibliographical Society (London, 1969), p. 27. The Saviles' catalogues are in the BL, MS Add.35213, fo. 31; MS Harley 1879, fo. 2.
[126] *SC*, 5:824, no.30521; *IMEP*, Handlist XII, ed. Hanna, p. 11, no. 1.

words illeg.] . . . : fragments of Nicholas Love, *Mirror of the Blessed Life of Jesus Christ*.[127]

3. fo. 4^{r-v}: size 163 mm by 122 mm; a fragment of 'Hors eiþer armour of hevene' from 'Pore Caitif'.[128] Fo. 4^r begins *Hors eiþer armour . . .* and ends *. . . but if his hors be to him buxum*; fo. 4^v begins *. . . þe charter of heuene . . .* and ends *. . . þt y gete* [*illeg. word*] *þt y speke*.

4. fos. 5^r–6^v: paper, size approx. 152 mm by 100 mm. Text begins *. . . gods great love . . .* [remainder illeg.].

5. fo. 7^{r-v}: paper leaf, 130 mm by 85 mm, containing calligraphy practice in Latin and English, in post-medieval hands.

6. fos. 8^r–11^v: 200 mm by 150 mm; four paper sheets containing eighteenth-century writing in English and Latin.

7. fos. 12^r–13^v:, folded paper containing a letter dated July 2, 1892.

8. fo. 14^{r-v}: two paper sheets pasted together, 197 mm by 125 mm containing, on the recto, in a hand of the later fifteenth century, a poem, rhyming on alternate lines marked in red, on the martyrdom of St Margaret. On the verso, a poem on a romance of Mary Magdalene.

The hand of the *D&P* fragment is similar to 'bastard secretary', cf. *ECBH*, Plate 14 (i); *IMEP*, Handlist XII (ed. Hanna), p. 11, dates it s.xv^1. The hand is indistinguishable from that of MS D (Douce 295, cf. Plate of fo. 180^v in *D&P* 1:2 Frontispiece), as is the language (see textual notes in the edition). No corrections are visible. Quotations are underlined in red; double virgules in red ink separate sentences. Small capital letters are slashed through in red.

(10) O: Oscott College Library, pastedown in Robert Persons (or Parsons), *A Christian Directorie* (1585)[129]

Three scraps of vellum once pasted into the binding of Persons's book containing small portions of the text of *D&P* from Commandments

---

[127] *The Mirror* by Nicholas Love (d. 1423/4) is ed. by M. G. Sargent (N.Y., 1993).

[128] On 'Pore Caitif' manuscripts see Jolliffe *Checklist*, pp. 65–7; *IMEP*, Handlist XII, ed. Hanna, pp. 9, 11, 18. See also Explanatory Notes, 227/1.

[129] In a letter of April 10, 1951, Margery M. Morgan thanked the Reverend F. Davis, then Librarian of Oscott College, for lending her Robert Persons' book containing the three velum fragments. Owing to her work on the Pynson edition (see below, Early Printed Texts), she was able to identify the manuscript fragments as parts of *Dives and Pauper*, Commandments II and V. The Oscott fragments were catalogued by N. R. Ker, *Fragments of Medieval Manuscripts used as Pastedowns in Oxford Bindings with a Survey of Oxford Bindings c. 1515–1620*, Oxford Bibliographical Society Publications, n.s., v (1951–2), (Oxford, 1954), 174. See also G. F. Pullen, *Recusant Books at St. Mary's, Oscott* (St. Mary's Seminary, New Oscott, Warwickshire, 1974), p. 60 (see Note after No. 651). I owe thanks to Father Cousins, former Librarian of Oscott College, for allowing me, in May, 1973, to transcribe the text of the manuscript fragments in the Oscott College library.

II and V. The writing is in double columns. The portions of the handwriting that can be read are collated with the edited text as follows:

Contents:

1. The fragment from the front cover of the book contains, on the recto, column 1, portions of *D&P*, Commandment II, cap. 11, beginning . . . *Seyst þu of hem þat sweryn* . . . (edn. I:1,238/8), ending . . . *hede ne by no party of* . . . (edn. I:1,239/15). Column 2, recto, begins . . . *wepte salte watir w*^{t hs} y^{en} . . . (edn. I:1,240/38), and ends . . . *bones ne his blode And* . . . (edn. I:1,240/45). On the verso, column 1 begins: . . . *some by* [ ] *bodye some* . . . (edn. I:1,241/3), and ends: . . . *suche othis not for deciete* . . . (edn. I:1,241/10). Column 2, verso, begins: . . . *drawe othir to þ*^t *same synne* . . . (edn. I:1,242/34), and ends: . . . *mor charge And therfor I* . . . (edn. I:1,242–3/44).

2. The larger fragment from the back cover contains portions of Commandment V. Column 1, recto, begins . . . *legge and barefote and* . . . (edn. I:2,43/81) and ends . . . what þ^t þ^uwulne . . . (edn. I:2,43/1). Column 2, recto, begins . . . *to afere the*[ ] . . . (edn. I:2,44/23) and ends . . . [ ]*gular If a clerk* . . . (edn. I:2,45/38). Column 1, verso, begins . . . [ ]*an he is not* . . . (edn. I:2,45/61) and ends . . . [ ]*lle her clothys* . . . (edn. I:2,46/4). Column 2, verso, begins . . . *why ne to wha*[ ] . . . (edn. I:2,47/28) and ends . . . *londe of byheste* . . . (edn. I:2,47/39).

3. The recto of the smaller scrap in the back cover begins . . . *colde or tak* . . . (edn. I:2,43/82) and ends . . . / *Sey [forth] DIUES* . . . (edn. I:2,43/1). The verso of a smaller scrap in the back cover (part of col. 2, verso, of larger scrap in the back cover) begins . . . [ ]*de bodin*[*g*] *h*[*ese*] . . . (edn. I:2,47/30) and ends . . . -*ficit tibi / It is* . . . (edn. I:2,47/39).

All three fragments are written in a small, somewhat irregular, secretary hand. References to canon law are underlined in red. 'Dives' and 'Pauper' are in larger capitals, in a book hand, and also coloured red. The text on the verso, column 2, of the first fragment is nearly continuous with the text on the recto, column 1, of a manuscript fragment now found in the Newberry Library, Chicago (now MS Newberry 167)—if allowance is made for the fact that the top three eighths of the written frame of the Newberry fragment is missing. The gap between the end of the larger O fragment (fragment 1) and the beginning of the Newberry fragment is approximately 18 printed lines of text. The handwriting in all four fragments is closely similar. Their dialect assigns them, or their scribal source, to the South Midlands area. Distinctive spellings shared by the O/N fragments include: *hit*, (it), *moche, suche, ellis, wul-* (will), *sey-, hem, myght, schulde,* double-'t' spellings in *nott, thatt, butt,* and *yett,* and consistent *ir-, -id,* and *-is* endings. The variants against the text of *Dives and Pauper* (MS G) found in the O and N fragments are consistent with the BYL (or later) group of manuscripts of *D&P*.

(11) A: British Library MS Add. 10053.[130]

110 vellum leaves, size 200 mm by 130 mm, written frame 145 mm by 90 mm (in *D&P* portion), in single columns 27 lines each. Collation: i³ (paper), 1⁹, 2¹⁶–7¹⁶, 8⁵, ii³ (paper). This collation is a best guess; the manuscript has been tightly rebound in a modern binding, and no visible catchwords remain. Of the three pencilled foliations, I have used the middle one. A note on an opening flyleaf states that the correct order of fos. 47–51 should be fos. 47, 49, 48, 51, 50.

Contents:

1. fos. 1ʳ–27ᵛ: St Edmund's *Mirror*, ending . . . *more þan of þyself.*[131]

2. fos. 28ʳ–40ʳ, beginning *here beginnyþ a tretes necessarie for men þat ȝeuen hem vnto perfeccioun whiche was foundyn in maister lowys de fontibus bok at cambrigge & torned into englisshe be maister walter hilton chanon of thorgorton. . . .*[132]

3. fos. 40ʳ–68ᵛ begin *here follwyn a pystyl of seynt jerome The first besynesse and the first studie of a mayden ought for to be to know the work of our lord*[133] . . ., followed by a description of hell.

---

[130] *List of Additions to the MSS in the British Museum in the years 1836–1840* (London, 1843): 'the fragment of the text of *D&P* is contained in the 'Speculum S. Edmundi': subsection of 'a treatise on the seven deadly sins [impf.]', p. 7. See also Doyle *Survey*, 1:45–6. 95–6, who says the manuscript was made for an Austin Canon of Holy Trinity, London and shares 'textual features with a South-West Midland copy, Royal 17 c.xxi' (*D&P* MS R); *IMEP*, Handlist V, ed. Brown and Higgs, pp. 6–9 (*D&P* is item 7).

[131] A translation of St Edmund of Abingdon's thirteenth-century *Speculum ecclesie*, ed. George G. Perry, in *Religious Pieces in Prose and Verse*, EETS, os 26 (1905; repr. 1969), 16–50; Hartung *Manual* 9:3116–7; on editions; *IPMEP*, pp. 269–70, Nos. 799, 800.

[132] From Walter Hilton's late fourteenth-century *Eight Chapters on Perfection*; on editions, see *IPMEP*, p. 229, no. 677; on manuscripts, Hartung *Manual*, 9: 3435–6.

[133] Probably from St Jerome's letter to Theodosia, Ep. CXXX (*PL* 22, cols. 1107–24).

4. fos. 69ʳ–83ʳ contain a poem in 8-line alternating rhyme stanzas
    beginning *Consciens clere this lesen I rede þe lere Al-mighty god in
    trinite . . .*[134] ending with a 3-line Latin prayer and . . . *amen.*

5. fos. 83ᵛ–84ᵛ contain a Latin passage, in a different hand, beginning
    duodecim abuciones claustralium.

6. fos. 85ʳ–94ʳ begin *Euery cristen man and woman that ȝeuyth to be saved
    hath grete nede to be ware . . .* : a short treatise on the seven deadly
    sins.

7. fos. 94ᵛ–98ᵛ contain the extract from *D&P* (Com. VI, cap. 16–18),
    beginning *Ferst take hede what veniaunce god hath taken for symple
    fornycacioun . . .* (edn. I:2,104/2), ending *. . . for whi þe grete [sic] his
    benefice is & þe more . . .* (edn. I:2,110/38).

8. fos. 99ʳ–110ʳ, after an unnumbered blank leaf, contain short tracts
    on the Pater noster, creed, Commandments, the seven works of
    mercy, etc., begining *sacerdotes parochialis tenetur per casti[gat]iones
    docere et predicare in lingua materna in anno septem petitiones in ordine
    dominica . . .,* ending *. . . and not for drede of payne.*

The *D&P* fragment is written in bastard anglicana, compare *ECBH*.
Plates 8 (i and ii), dated the second half of the fifteenth century and
c.1500. Some capital letters are decorated with red ink; others are left
unfinished. The language of the fragment places it in the B group of
manuscripts of *D&P*. The manuscript is not listed in *LALME*.
Add. 10053 is listed in the *CMA* s.v. 'Caroli Theyere', 6591.221. It
was acquired by the British Museum in 1876.

(12) M: Bodleian Library MS Ashmole 750 (5)[135]

203 paper leaves, size 210 mm by 140 mm, written frame size 175 mm
by 135 mm (in *D&P* portion); written in single columns 27 to 31 lines
each. Collation: i⁴, ii¹ (vellum), 1¹¹, 2¹⁶–13¹⁶, iii¹ (vellum), iv⁴; a
vellum leaf (unnumbered) and four paper leaves are inserted at
fo. 100. Foliation begins on the recto of the first parchment leaf.

---

[134] Listed in *IMEV*, p. 40, No. 244. It is printed from MS Reg.17 B xvii in Horstman,
Yorkshire Writers (1895), 2:36–45.

[135] *SC*, 2, Part 1:1115–62; W. H. Black, *Catalogue of the MSS Bequeathed unto the
University of Oxford by Elias Ashmole* (Oxford, 1845), cols. 357–62 (*D&P* is listed as item 5,
of 53 items). I am indebted to Dr Richard Beadle for bringing to my attention (in 1975) the
fact that Ashmole 750 (5) contains a series of extracts from *D&P*..

Contents:

1. Ashmole 750 has been described as a 'clerical miscellany'.[136] The more important contents are in Latin[137] The hymn, 'Angele qui meus es . . .' (fos. 102^v-103^r) is cited in *D&P* 1:1, 351/14. A hymn beginning *Mary moder welle the be. . . .* (fo. 100^{rv}) is found in the *Speculum Christiani*.[138] In Middle English, in addition to the *D&P* extracts (fos. 42^v-48^v), the Handlist notes the sermon of Richard Lavynham (fos. 89^v-96^r).[139] Ashmole 750 also contains the *Romance of Ypotis* (fos. 148^r-159^v);[140] a religious lyric beginning *ihesus thy swetnes wo . . .'* (fo. 100^v,[141] a satirical verse beginning *Wytte is trechery . . .* (fos. 100^{rv},[142] and a mystery play fragment (fo. 168^r).[143]

2. The *D&P* portion of Ashmole 750 comprises a series of extracts from Commandments IV, VI, IX, I, and II (in that order). The locations and incipits and explicits of the extracts are as follows: fos. 42^v-48^v contain a passage beginning *It farit be age of man & woman . . .* (Com. IV, cap. 27, edn. I:1,358/52), ending *. . . to þe syȝth* (edn. I:2,359/62); a passage beginning *We fyndyn . . .* (Com. VI, cap. 15, edn. I:2,994), ending *. . . mannys loue* (edn. I:2,102/91); a passage beginning *Two þingis . . .* (Com. IX, cap. 8–9, edn. I:2,270/1), ending *. . . endeles mysch*[ef] cut off at edge of page *. . .* (edn. I:2,277/35); a passage beginning *Qhy be þe ymagys . . .* (Com. I, cap. 10, edn. I:1,99/1), ending *. . . amendyn hem* (edn. I:1,99/9); a passage beginning *Wherfor . . .* (Com. II, caps. 9–11, edn. I:1,237/1), ending *. . . þe fer of helle w^{t}oute*[n] *ende* (edn. I:1,241/66).

The hand of the *D&P* contributor is a secretary book hand of the second quarter of the fifteenth century; compare *ECBH*, Plate 11 (ii).

[136] A. J. Fletcher, 'The Preaching of the Pardoner', SAC, 11 (1988), 27–35; see pp. 27–9 for discussion of the *D&P* extracts.
[137] *IMEP*, Handlist IX, ed. L. M. Eldredge, p. 191, no. 11; description is limited mainly to jottings, recipes and marginalia; *D&P* is listed but only the *incipit* and *explicit* are given.
[138] EETS 182, ed. Holmstedt, pp. 336–40.
[139] Richard Lavynham (d. *c*.1383), 'A Little Tretys on the Seven Deadly Sins'; ed. J. P. W. M. van Zutphen (Rome, 1956); Hartung *Manual* 7:2306; 2527; *IPMEP*, pp. 266–7, no. 789.
[140] L'Enfant sage' (Ypotis), listed in Hartung *Manual* 3:740–1; B898–9, which says MS Ashmole 750 may be the best manuscript source for this text. Chaucer's 'Prologue of Sir Thopas' (*CT*, p. 216, l. 898) alludes to the tale; *IMEV*, p.36, no. 220, lists 14 manuscripts, not including Ashmole 750.
[141] *IMEV*, no. 1781.
[142] *IMEV*, p. 280, no. 906. The poem is listed under such titles as 'The Abuses of the Age' or 'Perversions of the Age'; it is translated from the Latin given here.
[143] Ed. Norman Davis, *Non-cycle Plays*, EETS s.s. 1 (1970), pp. cxviii–cxx; 120.

There are no corrections; Latin is underlined; the margins are heavily scribbled over. On the basis of distinctive spellings, manuscript fragment M may be classified with the A group of manuscripts of *D&P*. *LALME* assigns the fragment (MS M) to 'Hand B', a Suffolk scribe (1:145). On ownership, *LALME* points to indications that in *c*.1445 the manuscript was 'in the neighborhood of Preston, Kettlebaston, Gedding and Monks Eleigh, all in Suffolk' (III:49).

(13) W: The National Library of Wales MS Peniarth 541C[144]

One parchment leaf 225 mm by 160 mm, written frame 205 mm by 130 mm; single columns, 37 lines each. The lower righthand side (recto) of the leaf is damaged and partly repaired, with the loss of some of the text. The text is faded but readable under ultra-violet light.

Contents:

> Fo. 1[r-v] contains a portion of *D&P* beginning . . . *to hym þat þe ymage* . . . (Com. I, cap. 3, edn. I:1,86/22) and ending . . . *for þe ymage* . . . (edn. I:1,90/21).

The handwriting is a 'calligraphic' Anglicana formata, compare Parkes *ECBH*, Plate 5 (ii), dated 1394–7 The language is similar to that of the second scribe of MS G, except for the occasional use of *wh-* spellings rather than the *qh-* spellings in this portion of G. In his note on the fragment, J. Simons cites the following variants: G (I:1/87/41–2) *Goddys sone, Crist hymself*, W *crist hymself goddis sone*; G (89/35) *spekyn, om.* W; G (89/42) *þe, om.* W, and omission of *þat cros* (G 88/18–19), which omission occurs only in G and W. I would add the variants G (88/17) *heldʒt, hast* W; G (89/42) *at þe, atte* W; and G (89/50) *shappere of, al add.* W. The conclusion may be that the leaf is part of a manuscript in direct line of descent, or ascent, from or to MS G.

---

[144] The manuscript fragment was identified by Dr A. I. Doyle in a letter to me of January 12, 1980 as an uncatalogued leaf from a manuscript of *D&P*. His student, J. Simons, concurred in this identification; see J. Simons, 'A Fragment of *Dives and Pauper* in MS Peniarth 541c', *The National Library of Wales Journal*, Biographica et Bibliographica 22 (Aberystwyth, 1982), p. 347. I should also like to thank Daniel Huws for sending a photocopy of the manuscript as well as an offprint of Mr Simons's article.

(14) N: The Newberry Library (Chicago), MS 167:[145]

A parchment fragment of a single manuscript leaf. Three other
fragments of the same manuscript are described above under the
heading Oscott, MS O. The Newberry fragment measures *c.*182 x
150 mm. The written columns are 70 mm. in breadth. Column a,
recto (and correspondingly b, verso), has been cut off on the inner
margin and now measures about 50 mm. in breadth. The fragment
comprises approximately the lower five eighths of the origninal
manuscript page. No line rulings are visible; the pages appear to
have been frame ruled. The fragment of parchment was formerly a
pastedown for a small book.

Contents:
   Fo. 1ra begins (imperfectly) . . . *swere* þ[u] *false . Butt yett* (Com. II,
   cap. 13, edn. 1:1, 243/7) and ends . . . *householde or out of house-*
   (Com. II, cap. 13, edn. 1:1, 244/24). Fo. 1rb begins . . . *If þe lorde be*
   pacient and skyl- (Com. II, cap. 13, edn. 1:1, 244/39) and ends . . .
   desese . DIUES . whenne a / commonte or a collage sweret hem &
   (Com. II, cap.14, edn. 1:1, 245/1). Fo. 1va begins (imperfectly) . . .
   of þe man þ[t] *he sweryth* . . . (Com. II, cap. 14, edn. 1:1, 245/15) and
   ends . . . *of thatt synne for to auoyde slaundir* (Com. II, cap. 14, edn.
   246/29). Fo. 1vb begins, after two blacked-out lines) . . . *to be holpene*
   be [blacked out]/ *to fullfylle* þ[t] *vowe* (Com. II, cap. 15, edn. 1:1, 247/
   4) and ends . . . *If sche* . . . / *the vowe . Nathe-* . . . / *husbonde may*
   un- (Com. II, cap. 15, edn. 1:1, 247/13–14).

The text contained in the N fragment begins after about the equivalent of seventeen lines of printed text comprising the end of *D&P*
Com. I, cap. 12 and the beginning of cap. 13. This amount of text
would be enough to fill the missing top portion of the original folio,
hence it seems likely that the first fragment of MS O and MS
fragment N were once contiguous.

   The handwriting is a small, irregular secretary hand, which is
identical to the handwriting of MS O. It is informal in appearance,
not the hand of a professional scribe. The red, rather than black,
underlining of canon law references and some passages of text is

---

[145] Dr Paul Saenger, George A. Poole III Curator of Rare Books and Collection
Development Librarian of the Newberry Library, is responsible for the discovery and
recataloguing of the manuscript fragment of *D&P* and has very kindly supplied a
photocopy and the measurements of the text given above. I have quoted from his letter
to me of December 19, 2003 the descriptions of Newberry's copy of the Pynson edition and
of the bookplate and letter found in the book.

somewhat unusual. The transition between *D&P* chapters 13 and 14 (between 'desese' and '*DIVES*', fo. 1rb line 22) is not indicated in the text nor in what remains of the margin. The dialect appears to place the scribal origin of manuscript O/N in the South Midlands (see MS O above).

The parchment fragment was found by Dr Paul Saenger, Curator of Rare Books at the Newberry Library, in the Newberry's copy of the Pynson (1493) edition of *D&P*, (now Inc. 9782). This copy is now in a nineteenth-century binding, but, in Dr Saenger's view, the original binding of the Pynson volume was not the source of the parchment fragment. The Newberry Library acquired Inc. 9782 in 1964 'from the estate of Louis H. Silver, the great mid-century Chicago collector'. The 'red leather bookplate on the front pastedown bearing the stamp of a lion holding a banner, placed above and beneath two differently shaped crowns' now found in the Pynson volume is, according to a letter also found in the book, that of Lord Mornington. The writer of the letter, who signs himself H. F. but is otherwise unidentified, says that he acquired the book at auction in Dublin on April 23, 1832. It is more likely, however, that the O/N fragments were once part of the binding of Robert Persons' *A Christian Directorie*.

(15) Early printed texts:

Three early printings of *Dives and Pauper* were made.[146] A sizeable number of copies of each printing are available in major libraries.[147] The first printing was made by Richard Pynson at Temple Bar, London, in 1493 (STC, no. 19212).[148] In 1953, Margery M. Morgan demonstrated that Pynson had set up the type for his edition from a manuscript now in the Bodleian Library, Eng.th.d.36 (MS B).Her article shows that the printers' marks in the manuscript correspond to the pagination of Pynson's printed text and shows further that the variants from MS B are consistent with printers' habits and practises of the period. She concluded (p. 227) that no other manuscript was

---

[146] *STC*, 2:213, nos. 19212–19214. I have used a copy of the Pynson edition in the New York Public Library (and a microfilm of it supplied by the Library); a copy of the Wynken de Worde edition from the Pierpont Morgan Library (and microfilm supplied by the Library); and a copy of the Berthelet edition supplied in microfilm by University Microfilms, Inc., Ann Arbor, Michigan.

[147] See E. Gordon Duff, *Fifteenth Century English Books*, Bibliographical Society (Oxford, 1917), pp. 94–5.

[148] An account of this printing is given in H. R. Plomer, *Wynkyn de Worde & his Contemporaries* (London, 1925), pp. 115–16.

used as a source for the printed text.[149] A second printing was made by Wynkyn de Worde at Westminster in 1496 (*STC*, no. 19213). This was set up from a copy of the Pynson edition, as is made clear by the fact that it repeats printer's emendations found in the Pynson text. A third (and last) early printing was produced by Thomas Berthelet in 'Fletestreet' at the 'sign of the Lucrece' in 1536 (*STC*, no.19214). The basis of his text seemed to have been the Wynkyn de Worde printing, but Berthelet abbreviated the Table and freely modernized spellings and wordings. That the second two printings were based on the Pynson edition is, however, now made certain by the discovery that Pynson's compositor at Com. VI, cap. 17 (edn. I:2, 108/38) after ... *prestis* by mistake inserted a page from Com. VI, cap. 18 (edn. I:2, 110/9–38) *And perfor þe lawe . . . . . . & þe mor*. In this slip, Pynson's edition was followed to the letter by Wynkyn de Worde and Berthelet.

7. RELATIONSHIPS AMONG THE MANUSCRIPTS OF *DIVES AND PAUPER*

The manuscripts of *Dives and Pauper* divide into two main groups, which will be referred to as Group A and Group B. To Group A (RDT) is appended a subgroup (GH), which will be called A_1. Group B comprises manuscripts BYL. The manuscripts are classified on the basis of three kinds of evidence: (1) the versions of the Prologues and Tables they contain, (2) consistent differences in dialect in respect to certain commonly used words, and (3) agreements in scribal errors, omissions, or additions, based on comparison with the text of the base manuscript, MS G.

Two differently worded Tables are now attached, in whole or part, to six of the eight manuscripts (manuscripts RY lack Tables). The two Tables are entirely independent. The first is attached to the Group A and A_1 manuscripts GDTH and the second to the Group B manuscripts BL.[150] Neither Table is by the author of *D&P*. The author of Table A begins with what amounts to an apology for the work that follows. Evidently unsettled by *D&P*'s opening salvo

[149] 'Pynson's Manuscript . . .', *The Library*, 5th Series, Vol. 8,No. 4 (1953), 217–28.
[150] Table B, in MS B, was complete when Pynson set his printed text from it. It is now a fragment, see 'Early Printed Texts' above.

against a social hierarchy based on rank and riches (Pauper to Dives: 'Or ȝow muste been pore or beyȝyn [buy] heuene [heaven] of the pore ȝyf ȝe welyn comyn in heuene' [I:1/54/13–14]), the author of the Table begins by imploring readers not to be offended because in the dialogue that follows the 'pore man is principal techere' (1/7). It is unlikely that the author of D&P would make such an apology (see Explanatory Notes 1/TABLE A).

The writer of Table B still more openly shows himself to be independent by distancing himself from his author's defense of Eve in Commandment VI, commenting: '. . . for that was þe opynyen of hym þat drewe þis boke' (I:1,42/cap.xxv). He again refers to the author in the third person: 'He rehersith the.x.commaundmentys' (25/cap. ix). Clearly neither Table is authorial.

Two Tables were written because there are also two versions of the Holy Poverty prologue. Holy Poverty prologue B (HP-B) is a shortened and revised version of HP prologue A, with only a few minor additions to the text, extant in manuscripts BYL. HP-A is about 7500 words long, HP-B about 5500 words long, or about one fourth shorter. HP-A, in manuscripts GRDT, is also clearly the earlier of the two versions in respect to content. What has been cut from HP-A is mainly its idealization of poverty as practised by poor preachers who wander from place to place and depend for their sustenance upon begging, or, in other words, clerics who follow the Franciscan ideal. Allusions to such mendicants occur only in the portions of HP-A omitted from HP-B (e.g., I:1,54/47, 64/27–32, 65/54/3–6). HP-A, cap. 2 and 6, missing in HP-B, are the sections containing the most explicit references to the mendicant ideal. In contrast to the Franciscan sense of 'poverty' found in HP-A, HP-B effectively redefines poverty as an involuntary condition of neediness or misfortune. In the B recension of the Prologue, poverty is 'holy' merely because it offers the rich man an opportunity to buy heaven for himself (I:1,75/12–13), not because it is a freely-chosen ideal of religious life. 'Pauper', in HP-B, is no longer a preaching friar but is redefined as a 'pore caitif' (I:1,70/19). Admittedly, passages favourable to preaching and to poor preachers also occur in the main body of the text of D&P, but they appear there in the context of an exposition of the Commandments; perhaps in that context, they were assumed by the reviser to be less exposed to controversy.[151]

---

[151] Cf. A. I Doyle's view (in 1953–4) that manuscripts B and L represented a 'second recension' of the original state of the text (*Survey*, 1:96).

A further detail provides evidence that HP-B is a revision of HP-A. In all the B versions of the Prologue, the rather long tenth chapter of HP-A is divided into two chapters numbered 10 and 11. After cutting, many of the other chapters of HP-B were shorter than those of HP-A. Since all of HP-A's long cap. 10 is retained in HP-B, it is likely that it was divided because after the revision it seemed disproportionately long.

The discovery of the sermons of the Longleat friar (see Introduction)[152] has provided evidence that in the original state of *D&P* the Holy Poverty prologue was an integral part of the treatise. Some earlier critics had speculated that Holy Poverty was a tract by a different author, which had been added to the dialogue on the Commandments. But the friar of the Longleat sermons, expressing pride in his authorship of *D&P*, cited Proverbs 22:22, beginning 'Dives et pauper . . .', as the incipit of his treatise. A guess can be made that in the holograph no separation was marked out between 'Holy Poverty' and the dialogue on the Commandments. The manuscripts of Group A and A₁ appear on several other grounds to predate the manuscripts of Group B, and in two of these (possibly) earlier manuscripts, D and T, there is no 'Holy Poverty' heading and little or no break in the text to mark the transition to the dialogue on the Commandments. In the Group B manuscripts B and L (Y precedes the *incipit* 'Dives et pauper' with 'Holy Poverty', but lacks top of page headings), the heading is 'Holy Poverty', and the transition to the dialogue on the Commanments is set off by large decorated capitals. In the extant manuscripts, however, chapters in HP and in the dialogue on the Commandments are numbered separately, and no evidence exists to show the chapter numbering was not authorial.

Vocabulary provides another mark of separation between Group A and B manuscripts. Certain common words and suffixes, taken as a group, differentiate manuscripts RDT (and fragments EAMW) from manuscripts BYL (and fragments O and N). The manuscripts in Group A use, predominantly, *wol, þou3, defend, -hed* (suffix), while the manuscripts in Group B, for the same forms, use *-ful, 3it, biforn, forbed* and *-nesse*. (Readings in manuscripts GH (A₁) deviate from Groups A and B and from each other.) To this may be added the evidence of additions of explanatory words to difficult or rare words in the manuscripts of Group B. For example, the rare word *borow*

---

[152] Anne Hudson and H. L. Spencer, 'Old Author, New Work' *MÆ* 53, No. 2 (1984), 220–38. See Introduction, p. xxii.

(halo around a candle flame) is explained in manuscripts BYL by the addition to the text of *eiþer sercle* [*aboute*] (I:1,142/14); the word *steraclis* (I:1, 293/12, 13 ,18) in Group A manuscripts is changed to *miraclis* in manuscripts BY and omitted in H (see Explanatory Notes 293/12–20). Such differences point to different provenances and probably later dates for the copying of the B group.

The evidence of variant readings also points to a division of the manuscripts into groups A and B. By 'variant reading' I mean semantic differences, differences in morphology, errors, omissions, and additions to the text. For the present purpose, I do not include spelling differences that do not affect morphology. The number of times groups of manuscripts agree in variant readings of the base text in MS G can be taken as an indicator of filiation. The evidence, based on a large sample of the edition of the text (I:1,81–220), consists of the total number of times manuscript groups vary together as a group. When variant groups of manuscripts are tabulated, two clusters of manuscripts stand out: manuscripts BYL and manuscripts RDT. In a variant-group total of 1204, manuscripts BYL vary together 711 times, mnuscripts RDT vary together 188 times, and all other combinations of two or more manuscripts (of which there are fifty) total 305.

In summary, manuscript Group A contains a core cluster of manuscripts, RDT, that vary together with high frequency and include the 'A' version of the Holy Poverty prologue. Manuscripts D and T also contain the 'A' version of the Table. Manuscripts G and H are added to this group (as a subgroup) because, though they deviate on the basis of variant readings, they are similar to RDT in dialect type, and both contain all or part of the 'A' version of the Table. MS H has a fragmentary A Table but lacks a 'Holy Poverty' prologue. The manuscript fragments EAMW are included with this group solely on the basis of similarities in dialect. Manuscript group B comprises manuscripts BYL, which are similar in dialect and vary together with high frequency. Manuscripts B and L include the 'B' versions of the Table and HP-B prologue. MS Y includes the HP-B prologue but lacks a Table. The manuscript fragments O and N (from the same manuscript) are classed with this group on the basis of dialect type.

The sorting of six of the manuscripts of *D&P* into two groups that seem fairly clearly separated on grounds of vocabulary and content raises the question whether it might or might not be possible to construct a stemma. The most that can be done, in my view, is to give evidence that all eight complete or nearly complete manuscripts derive from a single exemplar. The best evidence for this is an eyeskip error that occurs in Commandment X, cap. ii (1:2, 298/19–23). The phrase *of þe eye & of wordly good þan to couetyse* in line 22 is repeated in line 20 above, where it does not belong. The eyeskip appears in all mnuscripts in which Commandment X is extant or attested, GRDTHBY (L is defective at this point). In manuscripts GRD, the error is left uncorrected. In MS T, the scribe makes a rather awkward attempt to correct it by cancelling *eye* in line 20, scribbling over *of wordly good* and, in the next line, omitting *flesch* and inserting *ey* above the line. The scribe of H omits the third *to couetyse* (line 22). The scribe of Y, seeing the eyeskip, or something askew in the sense of the text, attempts a correction by adding *raþþer* after *good* in line 22. Though MS B is defective at this point, the Pynson edition made from this text reproduces the eyeskip without change.[153] The passage in MS G with the unrevised eyeskip reads as follows:

. . . man and woman in hys ȝougþe and in his begynnyng is soner temptyd to couetyse *of þe eye & of wordly good þan to couetyse* of þe flesch and in his endyng & in his age lattere temptyd to couetyse of þe eye & of wordly good þan to coueytyse of þe flesch (I:2, 298/19–23; eyeskip italicised)

All this indicates that seven of the eight mauscripts of *D&P*, for which the portion of the text containing the eyeskip is extant (or attested) descend from a single exemplar. If there is added to this the evidence of revised Tables and the revised Holy Poverty prologues, it would appear likely that manuscripts RDT derive fairly directly from an eyeskip manuscript. Manuscripts BYL follow the eyeskip exemplar but include the revised Table and shorter prologue HP-B. MS L, though defective from Com. VIII, cap. v, on, includes the revised Table and the shortened HP-B prologue. Manuscripts BYL exhibit the same dialect revision.

To this should be added a further complication. Two longer passages appear only in MS G—the Coventry story (I:2, 193/25–194/61, see Explanatory Notes) and the complaint about betrayals of the confessional (I:1, 250/18–58, see Explanatory Notes). Both of these passages may seem more likely to have been excised than to have been added. The first is explicitly Franciscan and the second is politically controversial on a topic then of special interest to

[153] See 'Manuscripts . . . and Early Printed Texts' above, pp. liv ff.

Franciscans. This suggests two possibilities, either that MS G like the other manuscripts was copied from the single eyeskip source manuscript, and the copier (or his editor) added the two 'Franciscan' passages, or that MS G was copied from a different exemplar but one so closely related to the exemplar of all the other manuscripts that it contained both the eyeskip error and the two 'Franciscan' passages. In any case, if there were in fact two exemplars for the manuscripts of *D&P*, they were very closely related.

More evidence of manuscript filiation may appear in future, but present data leads to the conclusion that all extant manuscripts of *D&P* derive from a single non-authorial source. It cannot be shown that any extant manuscript of *D&P* was copied from any other extant manuscript. Thus the relationships among the manuscripts may be shown most clearly in tabular form in the following layout.

CRITERIA FOR SORTING MANUSCRIPTS OF *D&P*

1. eyeskip in Commandment X
2. manuscript defective in Commandment X
3. first version of Table
4. second version of Table
5. lacking Table
6. HP-A prologue, longer version
7. HP-B prologue, shorter version
8. lacking HP prologue
9. two long excisions of text (vis-à-vis MS G)
10. dialect shift

MANUSCRIPTS SORTED BY CRITERIA:

X (1 non-extant source of eyeskip)
G 1, 3, 6
R 1, 5, 6, 9
D 1, 3, 6, 9
T 1, 3, 6, 9
H 1, 3, 8, 9
B 1, 4 (attested), 7, 9, 10
Y 1, 5, 7, 9, 10
L 2, 4, 7, 9, 10

The history of *Dives and Pauper* during the period between its composition in 1405–10 and its printing by Pynson in 1493 largely remains to be written. Dr A. Ian Doyle, in his wide-ranging study of the manuscripts of religious instruction (1954), was less interested in their 'origins' than in their 'circulation'. He paired *D&P* with *Jacob's Well* and posed the question, Why had tbe latter remained uncopied and obscure while the former was very soon circulating widely enough to inspire, on the one hand, Abbot Whethamstede of St Albans (in *c.*1420–1430) to pay to have a copy made for his Chapter and, on the other hand, for a copy of *D&P* in the hands of a simple layman to inspire accusations of heresy by an ecclesiastical court?[154] In his answer to his own question, Dr Doyle pointed out the usefulness of *D&P* to preachers. It was a work, he said, 'full of sermon-phraseology and materials, as well as academic theology and science'. He also documented owners ranging in rank from the Duke of Norfolk to an obscure parish priest. He pointed to the 'flourishing network of the several mendicant orders' in East Anglia as a possible conduit to a wider world.[155]

Since the mid 1950s, evidence has come to light that the author of *D&P* was an active controversialist and a prolific sermon writer.[156] It is becoming clearer that at the time of writing the author was by no means an obscure figure, and that, even if we take literally his presentation of his work as a private conversation with a highly-placed patron, he also had a circle of well-placed friends—and enemies—who wanted to know what his views were on a wide range of topics. The present study of the manuscripts of *D&P* adds a few corroborating details. References in the text to Thomas Docking's commentary on Deuteronomy go far toward confirming that the author of *D&P* was, or had been, a member of the Oxford *studium*, hence at the center of academic discussion of issues surrounding Church teachings and practises.[157]Manuscript fragments E, A and M (described in the previous section, pp. lxvii–lxxiii) show how early the work acquired readers who wanted to include extracts from it in their commonplace books. During the latter half of the period Anne Hudson has called the 'Premature Reformation',[158] when tracts of religious instruction were reaching a wider reading public, *D&P* was sufficiently in the public domain to be used as a quarry. The (still unedited) tracts known as 'Pore Caitif' borrowed

---

[154] In 1429; Tanner, *Heresy*, p. 99.
[155] Doyle, *Survey*, 1: 93–7.
[156] See Explanatory Notes 327/10 and Introduction, pp. xxii ff.
[157] See Introduction, p. xiii and Explanatory Notes 266/32.
[158] Her foundational work on the development and spread of the 'Wycliffite heresy', *The Premature Reformation* (1988), deals with *D&P* and its author's sermon cycle on pp. 417–21

freely from *D&P*,[159] as did the writer of the tract, 'A Tretyse of Gostly Batayle'.[160]

All such scraps of evidence, however, provide little more than a starting point for future scholars. What we do know is that by 1490, *D&P* was popular enough to inspire a London merchant, John Russhe, to put up half the cost of a first printing of six hundred copies. Thus a manuscript of *D&P* (now MS Bodley Eng.th.d.36) joined such other notable manuscripts as those of *The Canterbury Tales*, Mirk's *Festial*, and Lydgate's *Fall of Princes* in Richard Pynson's London printing shop. The success of this first printing inspired a second printing by a better-established printer of many popular works, Wynkyn de Worde, in 1496—while Richard Pynson, his former apprentice, went on to become King's Printer in 1508.[161]

The popularity of *Dives and Pauper* did not, of course, survive the Reformation. But that it was influential during much of the fiercely-embattled century that led up to the English breakaway from the Church of Rome seems clear. The full story remains to be discovered.

---

[159] See Explanatory Notes 227/1. Surviving manuscripts of this work, in 1974, numbered 56, see Jolliffe, *Check-list*, pp. 65–7.

[160] See Explanatory Notes 2–304–12/cap. v–vi. Nine manuscripts of this work are listed in Jolliffe, *Checklist*, p. 92.

[161] H. R. Plomer, *Wynkyn de Worde* (1917): on John Russhe and Pynson, pp. 115–17; on Wynkyn de Worde, pp. 43–105. Records of a lawsuit between Russhe and Pynson make clear that the printed copies were for sale, and profit, not for Russhe's private collection.

EXPLANATORY NOTES FOR
DIVES AND PAUPER

(1) VOL. I: 1, TABLES, HOLY POVERTY A-B,
pp. 1–80

Notes to Vol. I: 1 are listed by page and line; notes to Vol. I: 2 have '2-' before page numbers. The aim of the Explanatory Notes is to supply references, as needed, to works, authors or subjects mentioned in the text of *D&P*. To avoid duplication, most of the notes to the Tables are cross-referenced to notes on the Prologues and Commandments. Frequently-cited works are referred to by author, abbreviated title (if needed) and year of publication, with full reference given in the Bibliography. Unless otherwise noted, translations are by the editor.

1/*TABLE* (A)–11: The preamble to this Table (extant only in manuscript G) is written in the style of the body of the text, including an instance of a rare form occurring elsewhere in the text ('it' as a third person plural pronoun, see Gloss. s.v. 'he'). The apology for the fact that the 'poor man' is the 'teacher' in the dialogue may, however, indicate that the preamble is not authorial. Cf. 25/TABLE (B) below.

1/1a *Leue frend*: For a general discussion of addresses in sermons see H. L. Spencer, *English Preaching in the Late Middle Ages* (1993), pp. 112–113. On forms of address in the MS Longleat 4 sermons, written later by the author of *D&P*, see A. Willmott, 'An Edition of Selected Sermons from MS Longleat 4' (D.Phil. thesis, 1994), pp. 7–8. The Longleat sermons are cited below as LL4. On other forms of address see 52/21 and 324/17 below.

1/8a *as Sent Powyl seyth*: 2 Cor. 8: 9: 'Iesu Christi . . . propter vos egenus factus est cum esset dives ut illius cum esset dives ut illius inopia vos divites essetis'. LL4: 'Breþerin, ȝe knowyn þe charite & þe grace of oure lord Iesu crist, for whanne he was riche & lord of al he becam nedy & pore for vs þat we schulde ben riche with his pouert & his nede' (fo. 99va). On the Longleat sermons, see Introduction, pp. xxii ff. In the text, line 8a, a comma after 'lore' might have made it clearer that 'whyche' here refers to Christ. Cited below 2–226/66–9.

1/11a *Ecclesiastes ix* [: *15*]: 'Inventusque est in ea [civitas parva] vir pauper et sapiens, et liberavit urbem per sapientiam suam; et nullus deinceps recordatus est hominis illius pauperis.' Cited in LL4: '[A] pore man with his wisdam deliueryd a cytee þat was besechid with his enmyys, & fro þat tyme forth no man hadde meende of þat pore man' (fo.118rb).

1/1b *euene in kende*: See 51/6 below.

1/2b *a pilgrymage*: Ps. 38: 13; see 53/12 below.

1/6b–7b *nedelys eye*: Matt. 19: 24; see 55/30–49, 75/18 below.

1/11b–12b *Crist . . . þu schalt nout temptyn*: Matt. 4: 7; see 61/29 below.

1/14b *Panem nostrum cotidianum*: Luke 11: 3; see 62/3 below.

2/16a *Cristys word*: Acts 20: 35; see 63/2, 72/2 (emended reference), and 73/27 (emended reference) below.

2/1b *booc . . . lewyd folc*: See 82/42–4 below.

2/5b *crepyn to þe cros*: See 87/2 below.

3/49 *iudicial*: See 117/3–43 below.

4/86 *our ladyys fast newe comyn*: See note 172/1–70 below.

7/147 (64) *keche hem out of þe temple*: The reference is to Matt. 21: 12 (see 218/15–18 below), Mark 11: 15 and Luke 19: 45 (218/15–18 below), John 2: 13–17 (219/36–8 below).

14/31 *red*: See Glossary s.v. 'red'; *MED* s.v. 'ridden' 2: 'clear, free (of)'; the sense here is: 'are thereby deprived of the mercy of God'.

25/*TABLE* (B): That Table B is not authorial is indicated by its two third-person references to the author of *D&P*: 'He rehersith the x commaundmentys' (24/ix cap.), and 'þe opynyen of hym þat drewe þis boke' (42/xxv cap). Table B's ordering of the chapters was revised to correspond to the reordering and compression of HP Prologue B.

28/xxx cap. *wyles*: Not 'wyses': MS L clearly has 'l', not 's'; in this manuscript, medial 's' extends below the line.

31/1 cap. *Crist veyn*: Sic: the Pynson ed. (see *D&P* 1: 1, p. xiii) adds 'in' after 'Crist'.

38/xxvi cap. *ȝouyn*: manuscript L omits 'with', required by the sense here.

51/*HOLY POUERT*: The title of the Prologue points to the Franciscan provenance of *D&P*. In founding his Order, St Francis had laid down the central principle of absolute rejection of ownership: 'And my bretherne must be welle ware and welle advysed in ony wyse that they resceyve no churches nor dwellynge playcys, or ony thingis but yf they be as semythe [befits] holy pouerte, the whiche in our rewle we haue vowed and promised alweys longyng [staying] and biding ther in those places but as pilgryms and straungers' (from a fifteenth-century translation of his Testament

Monumenta, ed. Brewer, p. 564). In the course of the first century of the Order, this ideal was gradually institutiionalized. St Bonaventure, the 'second founder' of the Franciscan Order, argued for a moderate *usus pauper* in his 'Apologia pauperum' of 1269–70 (*Opera* VIII, Chs. 3–10/ 244–304; 12.28.33/325–8). Pope Nicholas III in 1279 redefined Franciscan poverty as *usus moderatus*, a compromise between extreme poverty and use of material things—legitimating, for example, the use of books for study ('Exiit qui seminat', X 5.12.3: Friedberg 2: 1109–21). See J. Moorman, *Franciscan Order* (1968), pp. 184–5, 367–8, 477–8.

By the time *Piers Plowman* was written in the second half of the fourteenth century, the Order had spread and established itself to the point where its high ideals were generally appreciated but where friars were often seen to be falling short of them:

> And in a freres frokke he [Piers] was yfounden ones,
> Ac it is fern and fele yeer in Franceis tyme;
> In þat secte siþþe to selde haþ he ben knowe.
>
> (*PP*, B-Text, XV/229–31)

51/1–2 *Diues et pauper . . . Prouer. xxii* [2]: Nicolaus de Lyra's postil on Proverbs 22: 2 stresses the reciprocity between the two speakers, citing the story of St Martin and the beggar. When St Martin divided his cloak with the beggar he earned the merit of mercifulness, but the beggar in turn earned the merit of patience. The author of *D&P* at the outset establishes that the ensuing dialogue will not follow the usual teacher-pupil conventions but will be an exchange in which each participant has something to offer the other.

Nicolaus de Lyra (1270–1349), whose postils on the Bible will be followed throughout the Explanatory Notes, was a Franciscan, a regent master at the University of Paris, and a champion of the literal sense of the biblical text, based on his knowledge of Hebrew and his familiarity with such Jewish expositors as Rashi (1040–1105). His *Postilla literalis* (*c.*1340), first printed in 1471, was added to the GO in some manuscript bibles. See H. de Lubac (1964), II: 2/344–67; S. Ozment, *Age of Reform* (1980), pp. 69–72; *Nicholas of Lyra*, ed. P. D. Krey and L. Smith (2000), pp. 1–118 and *passim*. On St Martin (c316–397), Graesse, No.166; *GL* 2: 292–300.

51/2 *Leue frend*: The opening of the dialogue is somewhat puzzling. One interpretation may be that two mendicants have encountered a rich man. The first friar launches into a begging sermon which ends in rather tactless denunciation of rich men ('ȝe dyshesyn alle meen' 52/20). The second friar PAUPER, 52/20) remonstrates ('beth waar qhat ȝe seyn') but continues the sermon himself, in less harsh terms. The first mendicant then drops out of the story. As it was customary for the Franciscans to travel in pairs preaching and begging, the opening may have been intended as a nod towards the reader's expectations here. On the HP-B revision of the prologue, see 70/1 below.

51/4 *ryche . . . pore*: Clement of Alexandria's (*c.*150 - *c.*215) 'The Rich Man's Salvation' ('Quis dives salvetur?'), like *D&P*, softens the extreme moral demand of Mark 10: 17–31: the rich man may be permitted to keep his wealth, but on condition that he become 'poor in spirit' and use his wealth for the benefit of the needy (*PG* 9: 603–652; LCL *92, Clement*, ed. Butterworth, pp. 265–367). Cf. J. A. McGuckin, 'The Vine . . .', SCH 24 (1987), 1–14.

51/6 *lyke in kende*: Human beings differ in 'estate' or rank but are equal in respect to natural law, a theme that recurs in *D&P*; cf. John of Wales: 'Omnes homines natura sunt equales', *Communiloquium* 3.3.1; on John of Wales (d. 1285), see J. Swanson, *John of Wales* (1989). Cf. 1/1b above

51/8 *nakyd and pore*: Job 1: 21: 'Nudus egressus sum de utero matris meae, et nudus revertar illus.' The GO interprets 'matris meae' in a mystical sense as the 'synagogue': 'Sed nudus revertetur, cum in fine mundi reliquiis Israel Deus innotescet' (2: 379). Job 1: 21 is cited below 56/62–8, HP-B 71/45, HP-B 77/12, 2–272/65–273/95, 2–306/65, and twice in LL4: 'Nakyd I cam out of myn modrys wombe & nakyd I schal wendin aȝen þedyr' (fos. 21vb and 8rb). It is a standard biblical text in sermons about the Doom. Cf. Gregory's *Moralia* 2.36.59, in which the 'uterus matris' is also interpreted as the synagogue from which the Church sprang (*CCL* cxliii, pp. 96–7; *PL* 75: 585).

51/12 *Sapien. vii* [*:5*]: Sap. [Wisd.] 7: 5: 'Nemo enim ex regibus aliud habuit nativitatis initium.' Cited below 70/9 (HP-B).

51/16 *as seyȝt Salomon*: An expansion of Prov. 18: 23: 'Cum obsecrationibus loquetur pauper et dives effabitur rigide', providing a scriptural parallel to the friction between rich man and poor man at their first encounter.

52/21 *ȝe*: Here Pauper addresses his social superior with the formal 'you'; in turn, Dives addresses his inferior with the informal 'thou'. This usage is not adhered to throughout, however. A few lines below, Pauper uses 'þu' six times in one sentence in addressing his superior (ll. 52/39–41), See 1/1a above.

52/23 *Prouer.* [*17: 5*]: 'Qui despicit pauperem exproboret factori eius, et qui in ruina laetatur alterius non erit inpunitus'

52/23–32 *Dyspyse nout . . . Ecclesiastici iv* [*: 1–6*]: Ecclus. 4: 2–6: 'Animam esurientem ne despexeris, et non exasperes pauperem in inopia sua,/ cor inopis ne adflixeris et non protrahas datum angustianti,/ rogationem contribulati ne abicias et non avertas faciem tuam ab egeno,/ ab inope ne avertas oculos propter iram et non relinquas quaerentibus tibi retro maledicere,/ maledicentis enim te in amaritudine exaudietur precati-

illius exaudiet autem eum qui fecit illum.' A somewhat different translation of this text is given in Com. VII iv (2–136/31–45). The GO: 'Elemosina autem facienda est non ex tristicia aut ex necessitatem. Hilarem enim daturem diligit deus. . . . Non per iram exasperandus est pauper sed blanda locutione placandus', etc. (2: 748a).

52/32 *Seynt Pouyl*: 2 Cor. 9: 7: '. . . hilarem enim datorem diligit Deus'. Cited below 2–136/45–6; GO: 'Qui dat vt careat tedio interpellantis non vt reficiat viscera indigentis & meritum & rem perdit' (4: 348–9).

52/35–6 *And for his loue . . . per charite*: Rhyming tag, a conventional way to conclude a sermon, cf. LL4, fo. 14vb; *ME Sermons*, ed. Ross (EETS, 209), p. 110/10; *CT*, 215/890; *PP*, B-Text, VI/253.

52/41–7 *For he þat fedyȝt*: Pauper gives a free-ranging expansion of the sense of Matt. 6: 28–34: 'Considerate lilia agri, quomodo crescunt', etc. The praise of the natural world here may be compared with similar passages in *D&P* below, 119/19, 145/37–42, and with *PP* (B-Text, XI/327–330). John of Wales's *Communiloquium* refers to the joy that should accompany a religious vocation: 'Tertius est hilariter obedire, que hilarem datorem diligit deus, ut hilaritas sit in vultu et dulcedo in affata et promptitudo in effectu' (6.4.2), and its Franciscan author goes on to refer to David dancing before the ark (2 Sam. 6: 14–23, cf. 297/32 below).

53/6–8 *Seynt Pouyl . . . II ad Corinth v [8]*: 'Audemus autem et bonam voluntatem habemus magis peregrinari a corpore et praesentes esse ad Deum'. Here *D&P* summarizes the sense of 2 Cor. 5: 1–8.

53/9–10 *Seynt Pouyl . . . a cyte*: Heb. 13: 14: 'Non enim habemus hic manentem civitatem, sed futuram inquirimus'.

53/12 *[Ps. 38: 13]*: On 'peregrinus' and 'inquilinus' ('boarder', 'lodger') see the GO: 'Iam apud te, sed adhuc inquilinus, que hinc transiturus ad eterna vbi non ero inquilinus' (2: 502). St Augustine: 'Hic autem ubi dicturus est Dominus domus: Migra, et quando dicturus est nescis, paratus esto. Desiderando autem domum aeternam paratus eris. Nec succenseas ei, quia cum uult dicit: Migra . . . quando uult dominus eius, migraturus es' (*Enarr.* 38.21; *CCL* xxxviii, p. 421/14–20; *PL* 36: 429).

53/14–19 *PAUPER . . . I begge myn mete and myn clothyng . . .*: His profession of voluntary poverty ('I haue mad me seruaunt') and mendicancy is one of the indications that the writer of HP-A and the rest of *D&P* was a Franciscan friar. John of Wales, in his *Communiloquium*, says: 'Sed paupertas voluntaria propter christum assumpta primum est religiounis fundamentum' (6.2.4). *D&P* resembles the *Communiloquum* in combining discussion of civil society with discussion of the requirements of a religious vocation.

53/22–3 *a lettryd man and a clerk*: Cf. *Jack Upland* (*c*.1390), which begins: 'For God þat is almyȝti . . . he sette mannes state: in lordis to represente þe power of þe Fadir; preestis to represente þe wisdom of þe Sone; and þe comouns to presente þe good lastinge wille of þe Holi Goost' (p. 54/4–10). Some of the other 'estates' are cited by *Mum and the Sothsegger* (1403–6):

> To bonde-men and bourgois and many oþer barnes,
> To knightz and to comunes and craftz -men eeke,
> To citezeyns and souurayns and to many grete sires,
> To bachilliers, to benerettz, to barons and erles,
> To princes and peris and alle maniere estatz.
>
>   (ed. Day and Steele, EETS, 199, p. 50/789–93)

On the 'estate ideal' of Chaucer's Clerk of Oxenford, see Mann, *Chaucer and Medieval Estates Satire* (1973), pp. 74–85. See also Constable, 'The Orders of Society', in *Three Studies* (1995), pp. 251–360; and Fletcher, *Preaching* (1998), p. 221, (comparing 'estates thinking' in *PP* with its use in *D&P*).

53/31–2 *Seynt Pouyl . . . I ad Thimo. iii* [:*13*]: 'Qui enim bene ministraverint gradum sibi bonum adquirent'.

53/33–5 *I am a beggere . . . in mechil trauayl from myn ʒuugthe*: Possibly an echo of Ps. 21: 7–8: 'Ego autem sum vermis et non homo, obprobrium hominum et dispectio plebis./ Omnes videntes me subsannant me'. Pauper suggests that his religious mendicant vocation places him outside conventional social rankings.

53/35–6 *a lettryd man*: On the rebirth of 'literacy' in eleventh and twelfth-century Europe, see Stock (1983); see also R. N. Swanson, (1994), pp. 279–293.

53/38 *a iape and a scorn to al the peple*: Not all beggars were religious mendicants, and not everyone approved of even religious mendicants. The opinion of Richard Wyche, heretic, *c*.1420, was: '. . . mallem terram comedere quam mendicare vere, quia scriptum est . . . "Divitias et mendicitatem ne dederis mihi"' (*FZ*, p. 372; on Prov. 30: 8, see 59/3–9 below); cf. *PP*, B-Text, XV/202–8. For William of St Amour's mid thirteenth-century attack on mendicancy, see Szittya, *Antifraternal Tradition* (*1986*), pp. 11–122. For Archbishop Richard FitzRalph's (c.1290–1360) anti-mendicant campaign, see Walsh, *A Fourteenth Century Scholar* (1981), pp. 374–406. On late medieval fear of the poor, Rubin, *Charity and Community* (1987), pp. 71 ff. See below, 57/20–1.

53/39 *As seyʒt Seynt Pouyl*: 1 Cor. 1: 27–9: 'Sed quae stulta sunt mundi elegit Deus ut confundat sapientes, et infirma mundi elegit Deus ut confundat fortia / et ignobilia mundi et contemptibilia elegit Deus, et quae non sunt ut ea quae sunt destrueret, / ut non glorietur omnis caro in conspectu eius.' The GO: 'Qui etsi primum elegerit pauperes, indoctos, infirmos; non tamen relinquit sapientes, diuites, nobiles, sed si eos primos eligeret merito talium rerum sibi viderent eligi & ita superbia qua homo cecidit, nisi procederet piscator, non humilis sequeretur orator. Vnde Nathanahel doctus in apostolum non est electus' (4: 309). On Nathanahel, *ABD* 4: 1030–1.

54/45–6 *I Corinth*. [*3: 19*]: 'Sapientia enim huius mundi, stultitia est apud Deum.' The GO (Ambrose): 'Abusine ponitur sapientia per astutia' (4: 312).

54/46–52 *be sueche prechyngge*: The core of the Franciscan claim to legitimacy within the Church: 'S. Francis, from the moment of his conversion, regarded himself as essentially a preacher', J. Moorman, (1968), p. 272. See Bonaventure: 'Apologia pauperum' (*Opera* VIII, 12.9/319–22) on the preaching of the friars. Compare the preamble to John of Wales's *Communiloquium*: 'Saluatore demandante praedicare euangelium omni creature, sedula diligentia prouidere debet vt sciat omnes instruere doctrinaliter, et admonere efficaciter, non solum in praedicatione declamatoria sed in collatione familiari et mutua' ('Prologus'). On the friars and the revival of preaching, d'Avray, *Preaching of the Friars* (1985), pp. 29–63. See 290/7, 2–23/56–7 below.

54/2–3 *Beati* . . . [*Mt. 5: 3*]: The whole text of Matt. 5: 3 reads: 'Beati pauperes spiritu quoniam ipsorum est regnum caelorum.' Pauper's omission of 'spiritu' simplifies the argument he is making in favour of mendicancy; when the text is next cited (HP-A iii 56/79, and HP-B vi 77/22 (where the citation should be emended to read Matt. 5: 3), the word 'spiritu' has been restored. Cf. Luke 6: 20, 'Beati pauperes quia vestrum est regnum Dei' cited below, 75/3. The GO stresses the difference between voluntary and involuntary poverty; below the word 'pauperes' the word 'voluntate' is supplied, and in the margin the gloss, 'Pauperes spiritu his sunt qui omnia habent et nichil possident' (4: 17). Wordsworth does not record substantive variants in the Vulgate texts (*Novum testamentum*, 1: 1/54–9). See also Edmund of Abingdon's *Speculum* (*ante* 1220) on this same text: 'Pauperes sunt qui habent paupertatem et illam diligunt; aut qui possident divicias et diligunt paupertatem, et divicias contempnunt', ed. H. P. Forshaw (1973), pp. 72–73. Cited below, 56/79, 77/22 (HP-B, where Luke 6: 20 should be Matt. 5: 3), 2–289/85; also referred to in LL4, fo. 133ra.

54/8 [*Mt. 18: 28*]: This should be emended to *19: 28*: '. . . vos qui secuti estis me, in regeneratione cum sederit Filius hominis in sede maiestatis suae, sedebitus et vos super sedes duodecim, iudicantes duodecim tribus Israhel'. The GO: 'per duodecim sedes vniversitas iudicandorum intelligitur. Qui reliquerunt omnia et secuti sunt dominum, hi iudices erunt qui licita habentes recte vsi sunt; iudicabuntur quibus dicetur, "Venite. . . "' etc. (4: 63). Cf. *CA* 1: 289–90. On poor men judging rich men, see also *Speculum christiani* (1360's–1370's), EETS os 182, ed. Holmstedt, pp. 184–5; and 'Hou a man schal lyue parfytly', a translation, *c.*1400, of Edmund's *Speculum*

in *The Minor Poems of the Vernon MS* (ed. Horstmann, EETS os 98), 1: 249/
1077–8. Matt. 29: 28 is cited in HP-B 75/7–8, and 2–250/74 below.

54/11 *the deuelshene of wyckydnesse*: Luke 16: 9: '. . . facite vos amicos de
mammona iniquitatis: ut, cum defeceritis, recipiant vos in aeterna tabernacula'; LL4: 'Makyth ꝫow frendys of rychessys of wyckydnesse þat whanne
ꝫe schul faylyn þey moun receyuyn ꝫow into endeles tabernaculis' (fo. 81ᵛᵃ).
The GO: '"Mammona" lingua syrorum: diuitie iniquitatas, quia de
iniquitate collecte sunt. Si ergo iniquitas bene dispensata vertitur in
iusticiam . . .' (4: 198). Pauper's explanation of the meaning of 'mammon
of iniquity' slides over the question whether the eleemosynary use of ill-
gotten gains is or is not morally efficacious, or even licit. In the earlier
Middle Ages, Bede in 'De tabernaculo' cites Luke 16: 9 as a simple
injunction to give alms (*CCL*, 199A, p. 37; tr. Holder (1994), p. 40). In
the later Middle Ages, the rise of usury and the Church's campaign against
it brought to the fore questions about the limits of almsgiving. Thomas
Aquinas explicates Luke 16: 9 to mean that all riches present moral
temptations, but that alms may be given from all gains which are strictly
lawful. A borderline case would be the prostitute who engages in activity
that may or may not be lawful but who lawfully receives payment and so
lawfully may give alms (*ST*, II–II, 32.7). Nicolaus de Lyra comments
evenhandedly: 'Mammon est nomen demonis tentantis de diuitiis male
acquirendis et ideo nomen eius ad diuitias significandas deriuatur . . . facere
igitur amicos de mammona iniquiatis est dare diuitias pauperibus (*Postilla*
4). Bonaventure's 'Apologia pauperum' warns churchmen against temptation by the 'mammon' of contributions from the rich (*Opera* VIII, 8.16) and
reminds them that the 'poor in spirit' are more worthy recipients of such
alms than the merely 'poor' (idem, 12.38/329). John of Wales's *Communiloquium* defines 'mammon' as riches acquired 'per rapinas, vsuras, dolosas,
mercaturas, vel per alios modos illicitos' (3.4.1) and cites Luke 16: 9 against
giving usurious profits to the poor (2.6.4). Raymond of Peñafort likewise
holds that illicit gains from usury, 'rapina', theft, simony, acting, prostitution, gaming, or the like must not be given as alms, *Summa*, Bk. 2, ¶ 7. Lk.
16: 9 is cited below 75/10, 272/42–4, 2–156/14, 2–158/54–5, 2–a85/41–8.

54/18–55/28 *Matthei 19* [: *16–22*] . . . *rychesse*: Alluded to at 65/6 below,
cited 66/20, 75/18 (HP-B), 2–313/5, 2–322/10 below, and summed up in
LL4: 'ꝫif þu wilt entrin into þe liif wiþouten ende, kepe þe comaundementis
& loue þin god abouyn alle þinge & þin neyꝫhebore as þinself' (fo. 113ʳᵇ).
GO: '. . . ille non est bonus qui querit de bono, sed qui facit quod bonum
est' (4: 62). Nicolaus de Lyra: 'Hoc docet paupertatem voluntariam &
diuiditur in duas partes, que primo docet id quod est necessitatis, secundo
id quod est supererogationis' (*Postilla* 4).

55/30–49 '*a chamel to pasyn be the nedelys eye . . .* ': Matt. 19: 24: 'Facilius est camelum per foramen acus transire, quam divitem intrare in regnum caelorum.' Pauper's literal explanation of the meaning of 'needle's eye' is found in Peter Comestor's *Historia*: 'Fuerunt qui dicerent, in Jerusalem parvam fuisse portam, quae Acus dicebatur, ad quam cum veniebant cameli, pro compendio viae cum oneribus suis, non poterant transire, vel subire eam. . . . Oportet enim avarum amorem opum dimittere, si vult ingredi ad vitam' (*PL* 198: 1588). On Comestor, see Morey, *Speculum* 68: 1 (1993), 6–35. The *CA* gives the story but attributes it to the GO, where it is not found (1: 288a). The GO provides a 'mystical' interpretation of the camel as Christ who, humiliating himself, bears our infirmities; and an interpretation of the needle as the Passion, which stitches up the clothing of mankind torn by the Fall, etc. (4: 62–3). See 77/25–6 below.

55/36 *soundyn wol harde*: The sense is: 'penetrate my mind with difficulty', see Glossary s.v. 'soundyn' 2. Cf. 76/34, 2–141/2–3 below. The forms of the two Middle English verbs, 'sounen' (*MED*, s.v. 'sounen': bespeak, signify), and 'sounden' (*MED*, s.v. 'sounden' 1: penetrate, sink in), are often indistinguishable.

55/50–1 *Nisi . . .* [*Lc. 14: 23*]: Read [*Lc. 14: 33*]. Perhaps cited from memory; the Vulgate text is: 'Sic ergo omnis ex vobis qui non renuntiat omnibus quae possidet non potest meus esse discipulus'. Cited in HP-B, 76/49 below. The GO makes a distinction between 'renunciare omnibus' and 'relinquere omnia': 'relinquere', to give up a claim to, is weaker than 'renunciare', to abandon and leave behind (4: 194). The LV translates 'forsakith' (FM 4: 198b).

56/58 [*Ps. 61: 11*]: Augustine: 'Non uides quia si ibi cor posueris, et tu flues? Diues es, et ecce iam non concupiscis adhuc habere, quia multa habes . . .' (*Enarr.* 61.16; *CCL* xxxix, p. 785/36–8; *PL* 36: 741). Cited in HP-B, 76/2–3 below.

56/62,68 [*Job 1: 21*]: See 51/8 above.

56/79 [*Mt. 5: 3*]: For the 'and in wyl' here added to the translation of the biblical text, the interlinear GO giving 'voluntate' above the word 'spiritu' may be responsible. See 54/2–3 above.

56/80 *nedele . . . Seynt Pouyl*: The reference is possibly to 2 Thess. 1: 4–5: 'Ita ut et nos ipsi in vobis gloriemur in Ecclesiis Dei, pro patientia vestra; et fide, et in omnibus persecutionibus vestris, et tribulationibus, quas sustinetis / in exemplum iusti iudicii Dei, ut digni habeamini in regno Dei, pro quo et patimini.' Cf. Eph. 3: 13.

56/87 *Matthei vii* [: *13–14*]: '. . . quia lata porta, et spatiosa via est, quae ducit ad perditionem, et multi sunt qui intrant per eam. / Quam angusta porta, et arcta via est, quae ducit ad vitam: et pauci sunt qui inveniunt eam.'

Cited in LL4: '. . þe way whiche ledith to liif is wol streyt & few pasin þerby' (fo. 112rb). The GO links the 'narrow way' with the wound in Christ's side: 'Quid angustius illo foramine quod vnus ex militibus in latere christi aperuit, per quas tamen angustas portas iam pene totus mundus intrauit' (4: 32). The *CA* cites Jerome's comment: '[L]atum enim non quaerimus, nec inventione opus est, quia sponte se offert, et errantium via est; angustam vero nec omnes inveniunt, nec qui invenerint, statim ingrediuntur per eam. Siquidem multi, inventa vertitatis via, capti volupta-tibus saeculi, de medio itinere revertuntur' (1: 127a).

57/91 *seyde Crist*: See above 55/30–49.

57/10 *Ambrose*: 'In Lucam', VIII, 13: 'neque enim sancta omnis paupertas, aut diuitiae criminosae; sed ut luxuria infamat diuitias, ita paupertatem commendat sanctitas' (*PL* 15: 1859; *Traité . . . S. Luc*, 2: 105). Cited below, 2–209/82–6.

57/20–1 *For more shrewys . . . but þey nought the word*: The sense is: 'I find no persons so wicked as those poor destitute beggars whom the world has forsaken but who have not forsaken the world'. See above 53/38, below 151/41, and Com. IX, xiii–xvi (on almsgiving): 2–284/1–294/64 below. See also 'Hou a man schal lyue parfytly' (a tr. *c.*1400 of Edmund's *Speculum*, where the invidious sense of 'rich men' is expanded to include those who are poor but covet wealth, as well as certain prelates:

> þe caytyf beggers þat nouȝwher wol dwelle,
> But euer þei reyken aboute to craue,
> Al þat þei seon þei wolde hit haue;
> Also wiþ hem sette we moun
> þis fals folk of Religioun.
> þeos ben as riche in vnquerte [wickedness]
> As þeos oþure and as proude of herte.
>   (ed. Horstmann, EETS os 98, 1: 250/1116–22)

57/25–6 *Ecclesiastici [27: 1]*: GO: 'Hac compartione exprimit angustiam auari, cui equam videtur deesse quod habet & quod non habet, dominum timet amittere quod possidet & aliena rapere incessanter ardet; spiritus enim sollicitudo torquet & in futuro paena aeterna manet' (2: 772). Cited HP-B 78/24 below.

58/34 [*I Tim. 6: 10*]: 'Radix enim omnium malorum est cupiditas.' LL4: 'for coueytse is roote of al euyl' (fo. 95va; cited also idem, fo. 34vb). Cited 78/32 (HP-B), 2–120/40, 2–253/14, and 2–296/38 below. Verses 9 and 10 are cited 71/31–6 (HP-B) and 2–265/82 below. Verse 9 is cited 2–158/59–60, 2–274/21 below. The GO points out that elsewhere pride is said to be the root of all evil, but there is no contradiction, because cupidity stems from pride and leads to pride (4: 412). Bonaventure's 'Apologia pauperum' stresses covetousness, root of all evil, as the antitype to poverty, the source of all spiritual goods (*Opera*, VIII, 10.1/304, 12.40/317).

58/39 [*Eccles. 5: 9*]: 'Avarus non implebitur pecunia.' The Preacher says love of riches is vanity, not that the avaricious man will lose his soul, as in the *D&P* translation. Cited below 78/37 (HP-B), 80/36 (HP-B), 2–158/73–4.

58/41 *the ryche man hat3 more nede*: Cf. 2–160/31–2 below.

59/63–4 *hous . . . heye on hille*: Matt. 5: 14: 'Vos estis lux mundi; non potest civitas abscondi supra montem posita.' Cited 2–318/1 and in LL4: 'And crist seyde to his disciplis . . . 3e ben ly3t of þe world' (fo. 138rb).

59/70 *Apoc. iii* [:*17*]: Rev. 3: 17: 'Quia dicis quod dives sum et locupletatus et nullius egeo, et nescis quia tu es miser et miserabilis et pauper et caecus et nudus.' Cited HP-B 75/39 below. LL4: 'þu seyst þat þu art ryche & plenteuous & hast nede of non/ good, & þu knowyst not þat þu art wrechyd & most henous, pore blynd & nakyd' (fo. 21$^{ra–rb}$); also cited fos. 32$^{rb–va}$, 72vb, and 134$^{va–vb}$). On 'diues sum' the GO comments: 'Purgatus in baptismo, vel diues scientie diuine vel secularis' (4: 554). The tenor of the argument is to convert Dives, the rich man, to the view that it is he who, in a spiritual sense, is the pauper.

59/1 *3et contra*: Dives uses the standard opening of the opposing argument in a university *disputatio*, cf. *PP*, A-Text, IX/16, B-Text, X/349–50; the early fifteenth-century *Mum and the Sothsegger* (ed. Day and Steele (EETS os 199), p. 36/300. See text 63/4, 73/43 (HP-B) below. Cf. J. I. Catto, *HUO*, 1: 188–9; 477–8.

59/3–9 *Prov. 30: 8–9*: Dives quotes a part of the passage only: 'Vanitatem et verba mendacia longe fac a me, *mendicitatem et divitias* ne dederis mihi, tribue tantum victui meo necessaria,/ ne forte saturatus inliciar ad negandum et dicam, Quis est Dominus? et egestate conpulsus, furer, et peierem nomen Dei mei' (italics added). Prov. 30: 8 could, in this period, be read as an anti-mendicant argument and is thus appropriately put into the mouth of Dives, who uses it to argue that 'povert, beggerye and myschef' are calamities to be avoided at all costs (see Scase (1989), pp. 57–8). Pauper gives the mendicant counter-argument that 'poverty' is a matter of an inner, moral attitude towards possessions: covetousness makes for beggery no matter how rich one is. Bonaventure's 'Apologia pauperum', citing Prov. 30: 8 three times, uses 'paupertates' once and 'mendicitatem' twice and supports the interpretation that Solomon is not rejecting mendicity but rather advocating a mean between the extremes of rich and poor (*Opera*, VIII, 9.16/298, 12.19/322, 12.26/325). The Carmelite friar, Richard Maidstone argues (*c*.1380) in defence of mendicancy that the two Latin words are equivalent in meaning and that the meaning is 'poverty *and* beggery' (as Pauper puts it in his reply); Solomon was therefore not condemning mendicancy as practised by the begging friars. On the other side of the argument, Wyclif, *De civ. dom.* (*c.*1377), in quoting Prov. 30: 8 cites both 'mendicitatem' (3: 152) and 'paupertatem' (3: 159), following the second citation with: 'Paupertas ergo sicut mendicitas fuit in testamento veteri reprobata, non sic divicie, ergo racio est earum, qua ad par virtutis prestancior'. In citing Prov. 30: 8, the reviser of HP-A adds further exegesis, see 79/24 below.

59/6 *diuicias et paupertates ne dederis mihi*: A liturgical text, based on Prov. 30: 8, for use on the feast day of St Augustine of Hippo (August 28). The text of the Responsory given by Carl Marbach is: 'Verbum iniquum et dolosum longe fac a me, Domine: Divitias et paupertatem ne dederis mihi, sed tantum victui meo tribue necessaria' etc. (*Carmina scriptuarum* (1963), p. 263). Richard Maidstone's *Protectorium Paupertatis* contains a marginal note opposite this text in a hand other than the scribe's: 'Sic canit ecclesia in historia mensis Augusti' (ed. A. Williams, *Carmelus* 5 (1958), 148, note 13).

59/18–19 *Ecclesiastes [9;16]*: For [9;16] read [5: 9;16]. Eccles. 5: 9 is cited above, 58/39. Eccles. 5: 16: 'Cunctus diebus vitae suae comedit in tenebris et in curis multis et in aerumna atque tristia.' The GO: 'Melius est autem spiritualem escam et potum et laeticiam a deo datam intelligere & videre bonitatem domini et habere iocunditatem cordis in labore bonorum operum spe futurae retributionis & haec pars nostra quam uis non plena, donec videamus facie ad faciem . . .' (2: 701).

59/23 *Ecclesiastes vi [: 2]*: 'Vir cui dedit Deus divitias, et substantium, et honorem, et nihil deest animae eius, ex omnibus quae desiderat, nec tribuit ei potestatem Deus ut comedat ex eo, sed homo extraneus vorabit illud: hoc vanitas et magna miseria est.' GO: 'Potest hoc de populis israel accipi, cui dedit dominus legem et prophetas et promissiones. Vnde . . .' (2: 701). Cited HP-B, 80/40–1 below.

60/38 [*Ps. 39: 18*]: LL4: 'Therfore dauid seyde, I am a beggere, I am wol pore, & as a lost man, & oure lord is wol besy of me to sauyn me' (fo. 70vb). On Ps. 39 (40): 18, the interlinear GO: 'De hoc constat Aug[ustinus] quod orat hic corpus christi, unus mendicus, unus pauper cum eo'; the marginal GO: 'Cassi[odorus]: Hic christus ex forma serui, ne quis gloriam predicte leticie sibi arrogaret, mendicus qui petit, pauper qui sibi non sufficit' (2: 503b). Augustine adds: 'Et quid facturus es, o egene et pauper? Mendica ante ianuam Dei; pulsa, et aperietur tibi' (*Enarr.* 39.27; *CCL* xxxviii, p. 444/ 14–15; *PL* 36: 450). Nicolaus de Lyra's postil: 'Si hoc refertur ad personam cristi, certum est que vitam valde pauperem duxit in hoc mundo, sicut patet ex euangelio, si autem referatur ad corpus christi mysticum, sic certus est que fuerunt et sunt multi fideles, propter christum paupertatem eligentes' (*Postilla* 3). Cf. John Audelay's comment on Ps. 39: 18 and the friars in the second quarter of the fifteenth century: 'Hit is aȝayns Godys ordenans/ To couet more þen ȝoure sustynans' (*Poems*, ed. E. K. Whiting, EETS, 184, p. 27/478–9).

60/39 *the glose*: The pioneering work on the nature and history of the *Glossa Ordinaria* was done by Beryl Smalley, beginning with her articles in *RTAM* (1935, 7: 235–62; 1936, 8: 24–64; 1937: 365–400). See also idem, *Study of the Bible* (1952; repr. 1964), pp. 46–52 and *passim*. A thorough revision of Migne, *PL* 113–114, has not been achieved. See M. T. Gibson, 'The Place of the *Glossa ordinaria* in Medieval Exegesis' in *Ad Litteram* ed. Jordan and Emery (1992), pp. 5–77. Mary Dove's edition and translation of the GO on the Song of Songs, based on the twelfth-century manuscripts of the Glossa (edition based on eight manuscripts selected from an extant ca.seventy) is also a pioneering effort. Her Introduction surveys both the manuscript tradition and the interpretive history of the text, pp. 3–53 (*Glossa ordinaria, In canticum canticorum*, *CCL* clxx, pars 22, Turnhout, 1997).

60/50 *nede . . . lawe of kende . . . Godys lawe . . .* : On 'lawe' see 63/10–16 below. On 'nede' (Necessitas legem non habet), see 287/24, 2–141/13–14 and 2–141/23 below.

60/60 *Austyn*: This is the message of St Augustine's sermon 14, his 'poverty' sermon, which takes as its texts Ps. 9: 14: 'Tibi derelictus est pauper;/ Orphano [pupillo] tu eris adiutor'; Ecclus. 29: 15: 'Conclude eleemosynam in corde pauperis'; and Matt. 5: 3: 'Beati pauperes spiritu'. Augustine says: 'Lauda diuitem humilem, lauda diuitem pauperem. . . .Audi ergo me. Esto uerus pauper, esto pius, esto humilis' (*CCL* xli, pp. 185–6; *PL* 38: 111–112).

61/1–7 *Non temptabis . . . [Mt. 4: 7]*: LL4: 'Cryst aleggyd þese wordys trewly aȝens þe fend . . . and seyde, It is wrytyn & bodyn to euery man, þou schal nouȝt temptyn þyn lord god' (fo. 34rb). The GO: 'Dauid golyam tribus lapidibus de torrente prostrauit & Christus dyabolum tribus testimoniis de lege' (4: 14). Nicolaus de Lyra's postil cites the OT text, Deut. 6: 16, 'Non temptabis Dominum Deum tuum' and says that it is sinful to tempt God to do what a man can do for himself; hence Jesus's reply to the Devil that if he was able to descend from the pinnacle by human means he was morally obliged to do so (*Postilla* 4). Bonaventure, in his 'Apologia' (1269/70), vigorously rebuts Dives' charge that Franciscan mendicity tempts God, pointing out that 'for over sixty years' the mendicants 'have been living in great numbers, while God's promise was being so well fulfilled in them . . . that we have never heard any one of them ever to have been in danger of death from lack of food or clothing' (*Opera* VIII, 12.22/323).

61/3–4 *he þat . . . he þat*: This construction in this passage has been noted by Bengt Lindström: 'Duplication of *he* or *she* by *this* is not uncommon in Middle English writings (157) . . . [d]uplication by *that* . . . is exceedingly rare (155)', *Stud. Neophil.* 46 (1974 [2]), 151–8. He also notes the use in

D&P of the plural form '*þey þoo . . . þat*', see 61/7 and /27 above and 158/
39, 181/6, and 2–14/21 below for examples, and Glossary s.v. '*he*'. Cf. *EWS*
3, p. lxxxi, where the editor discusses the use of '*he þis*' as a translation of
Latin *hic*.

61/19 *golys . . . Malachie iii [10]*: The use of 'golys' to translate Vulgate
'cataractas' is unusual. EV has 'gutters' and LV has 'goteris' (3: 771b). For
'golys' see Glossary. In using a Middle English word with the meanings
'gullet' and 'narrow inlet of the sea' the author of *D&P* has chosen to make
a richer metaphorical interpretation of the passage. See *ABD* 4: 478–85,
where this passage is interpreted in context.

61/29 [*Mt. 4: 7*]: See 61/1–7 above.

62/52 *Alþey*: I would now repunctuate, reading: '. . . it is wol medeful, alþey
in caas it be nought nedeful . . .'.

62/58 [*Ps. 33: 11*]: Ps. 33 (34): 11; the Vulgate does not give 'deficient' as a
variant of 'minuentur'. LL4: 'Worldli riche men han had myschef & gret
hungger, for þey moun nout ben fild ne han inoȝw, but þey þat sekin god
schul nout faylin of euery good' (fo. 134vb). Augustine's exposition of this
passage, like Pauper's, stresses the poverty of the rich man who dies in his
burnished bed surrounded by his weeping family but who lacks the true
bread of life, 'Egunt ergo illi diuites, egent; et, quod est grauius, pane [sc.
panis uiuus] egent' (*Enarr. in Ps.*, 33.2.15; *CCL* xxxviii, p. 292/24–5; *PL*
36: 316).

62/3 [*Lc. 11: 3*]: LL4: 'Graunte þu vs þis day oure eche dayys bred'
(fo. 32rb). The *CA* cites Augustine: 'Non iste est panis qui vadit in corpus,
sed ille panis vitae aeternae, qui animae nostrae substantiam fulcit' (2: 159b).

63/9 *Dominiamini*: Read *Dominamini*.

63/10 [*Gen. 1: 28*]: In his literal exegesis, Dives fails to note that man's
dominion over birds and fishes preceded the Fall; in the GO, Bede is cited
on this point (1: 16). In his reply, Pauper does not refer to the relationship
between humans, birds and fishes before the Fall. Cited 72/10 (HP-B) and
2–78/48, 2–79/2 below.

63/13–18 *Lordshepe*: Gratian's Decretals (*c.*1150) begin with the distinction
between natural and civil law: 'Humanum genus duobus regitur, naturali
uidelicet iure et moribus . . . Omnes leges aut diuinae sunt, aut humanae'
(D. 1 c. 1: Friedberg 1: 1). See also Gratian, D. 8, Pars. 1: 'Nam iure
naturae sunt omnia communia omnibus' (idem, 1: 12). The Franciscans
made expedient use of the distinction. Cf. Bonaventure's 'Apologia' (1269/
70) on the Franciscan view of use and dominion (*Opera* VIII, 10.13–16/309;
11.5/312). John of Wales, in *c.*1265–75: 'Prima causa seruitutis est
peccatum, proinde numque in scripturis legimus seruum antequam hoc
vocabulo Noe iustus pecccatum filii iudicaret, Gen. ix. Nomen itaque illud

culpa meruit non natura' (*Communiloquium*, 2.1.1). Wyclif's *De civ. dom.*
(1376–7) has been thought to reflect the turn from theological to political
discussion of the issues, beginning as it does with discussion of the *lex
Christi* and concluding with the right of the Church to own property (4:v–
viii). Cf. Coleman, 'The Two Jurisdictions', SCH 25 (1987), pp. 75–110;
Doe, *Fundamental Authority* (1990), pp. 60–83. See further below: 63/17,
160/11–15, 2–336/47, 2–138/1,

63/17 *euene in lordshepe*: Gratian (*c.*1150): 'Differt etiam ius naturae a
consuetutine et constitutione. Nam iure naturae sunt omnia communia
omnibus. . . . Unde apud Platonem illa ciuitas iustissime ordinata traditur,
in qua quisque proprios nescit affectus. Iure uero consuetudinis uel
constitutionis hoc meum est, illud uero alterius' (D.8 c.1; Friedberg 1: 12–
13). Distinction 8 is followed by a citation from Augustine's 'In Ioannis
Evangelium', 6.25: 'Pauperes et diuites Deus de uno limo facit, et pauperes
et diuites una terra supportat. Iure ergo humano dicitur: hec uilla mea est,
hec domus mea est, hic seruus meus est' etc. (*CCL* xxxvi, p. 66/18–21; *PL*
35: 1437). Distinction 8 was the focus of much controversy in the Middle
Ages and after, see Kuttner, 'Gratian and Plato' in *Church and Government*
ed. Brooke, Martin and Owen (1976; repr. 1980), pp. 93–118. Cf. 63/13–18
above and Com. VII iv–v below for further reference to 'lordship', or
dominion.

63/30 *Seynt Austyn . . . diues et pauper*: Augustine's Sermon 39.6 has the
sense but not the exact wording ('necessaria') (*CCL* xli, pp. 491–2/90–2; *PL*
38: 243), The word appears in Ps.-Augustine: 'Dives et pauper duo sibi sunt
contraria: sed iterum duo sibi sunt *necessaria*. Nullus indigeret, si se invicem
supportarent; et nemo laboret, si se ambo juvarent. Dives propter pauperem
factus, et pauper propter divitem factus est; pauperis est orare, et divitis
erogare', etc. (*Sermo* 367, *PL* 39: 1651). This may also be the intended
reference in Pecham's 'Tractatus tres de Pauperis' (*c.*1270), ed. C. L.
Kingsford *et al.* (1910), p. 71. Bishop Brinton's Sermon 44 (?1377) deals
with the same topic and also uses 'necessaria'; the editor's note refers to Ps.-
Augustine's sermon (*Sermons*, ed. Devlin, 1: 194). Cited in HP-B, 74/12–14
below.

63/2 *Actus Apostolorum xx* [*35*]: Dives cites scripture against scripture. The
GO points out that the text is not found in the gospels, but that Paul could
have heard words spoken by the Apostles or derived them from the Holy
Spirit (4: 498). Nicolaus de Lyra comments that while it is always
praiseworthy to give to the poor, the last word in the argument was
spoken by Christ: 'Vade et vende omnia quod habes . . .', and that the
gospels have greater authority than Acts (*Postilla* 4). Cited in HP-B 72/2
(emended ref.), and HP-B 73/27 (emended ref.) below.

64/10–12 Seynt Gregorie . . . Quanto dona: Homily IX ('Homiliarum in Evangelia', Lib. I; *PL* 76 (2): 1106). Also cited by Wyclif in *De mand.* (1376), p. 63/22. See 188/16 and 2–251/5 below.

64/15 [I Cor. 4: 7]: 'Ryght nought but synne' does not translate the next sentence in the biblical text ('Si autem accepisti, quid gloriaris quasi non acceperis?') but is added as interpretation by the writer of HP-A. The GO: 'Aliud genus arrogantie amonere conat, scilicet, ne homo superbiat propter aliquam gratiam a deo sibi datam; putans se eam habere a se, vel a ministro' etc. (4: 313). Cited in HP-B, 73/14–15 below.

64/20 Luce xxi [: 1–4]: Luke 21: 2–4 'Vidit autem et quandam viduam pauperculam mittentem aera minuta duo, et dixit: Vere dico vobis, quia vidua haec pauper plus quam omnes misit, nam omnes hi ex abundanti sibi miserunt in munera Dei, haec autem ex eo quod deest illi omnem victum suum quem habuit misit.' The GO allegorizes: the widow is the Church: 'pro qua vir ipsius mortem pertulit & in celi penetralibus ab oculis eius occultus quasi in parte alterius regionis venit.' (4: 210). Cited in HP-B, 73/20 below.

64/39 Beati pauperes: Matt. 5: 3: 'Beati pauperes spiritu'; see 54/2–3 above.

64/40 God sey3t in the gospel: Luke 16: 9, see 54/11 above.

65/54 pore meen, prechourys of Godys woord: See 53/14–19 and 54/46–52 above; cf. d'Avray, (1985), p. 11 and *passim*; M. E. O'Carroll, *A Fourteenth Century Preacher's Handbook* (1997), pp. 15–34 and *passim*.

65/56 [I Cor. 9: 11]: 'Si nos vobis spirituali seminavimus, magnum est si nos carnalia vestra metamus?' LL4: '3if we sowyn to 3ow gostly þyngis why schulde we nout repyn 3oure fleschly þyngis, þat is to seye, þyngis nedful to sustenaunce of þe flesch? For as cryst ordeynyd þe prest to leuyn be þe auter, so ordeynyd he þe prechour to leuyn be his prechynge' (fo. 41vb). Cited 194/33 and 2–291/37–8 below.

65/3 Twenty 3eer hens: The words evoke Luke 18: 18, in which the 'rich young ruler' is given a counsel of perfection by Jesus but cannot follow it. In this biblical passage, the paths of 'more and less perfection' are laid out. In *c*.1383, Wyclif remarked that he was undertaking a compendious exposition of the Commandments 'ut mandatus sum a quodam devoto layco' (*Serm.*, I: 89/22–4). See Introduction, pp. xvi ff.

65/6 tale of þat 3onge man: Matt. 19: 16–22: see 54/18–55/28 above.

66/12 taughte: Read [taughte]: manuscript G has 'thaughte'.

66/15 Deutero. xviii [: 13]: 'Perfectus eris, et absque macula cum Domino Deo tuo.' The passage is taken somewhat out of context, since it refers to warnings against witchcraft and the command that in the land of behest none shall engage in such practises. 'Criminali' is not found in Deut. 18: 13 nor among canon law titles.

66/20 [*Mt. 19: 21*]: 'Ait illi Iesus: Si vis perfectus esse, vade, uende quae habes et da pauperibus, et habebis thesaurum in caelo, et veni sequere me.' The GO interlinear: 'Ecce contemplatiua que ad euangelium pertinet. Non sufficit relinquere mala nisi sequatur dominum, id est, imitetur' (4: 62). The *CA* cites Rabanus Maurus (d. 856), who more clearly connects this text with the choice between active and contemplative lives: 'Ecce duas vitas hominibus propositas audivimus: activam, ad quam pertinet "Non occides", et cetera legis mandata; et contemplativam, ad quam pertinet "Si vis perfectus esse". Activa ad legem pertinet, contemplativa ad Evangelium: quia sicut vetus novum praecessit testamentum, ita bona actio praecedit contemplationem' (1: 286a). Cf. Bonaventure's 'Apologia pauperum' in *Opera*, VIII, 7.13/276; 3.17/248–9. See below 68/43–5.

66/22–7 *The same tale . . . perfeccioun*: Dives' request for instruction in how to follow the path of 'the lesse perfeccioun' sets the course of the dialogue as a whole; see Introduction, pp. xvi ff. See 65/3 above.

66/28 *Serua mandata*: Matt. 19: 17–19: 'Iesus autem dixit: Non homicidium facies: Non adulterabis: Non facies furtum: Non falsum testimonium dices: / Honora patrem tuum, et matrem tuam, et diliges proximum tuum sicut teipsum.' LL4: 'Ȝyf þu wilt entrin into þe liif wiþouten ende, kepe þe comaundementis & loue þin god abouyn alle þinge & þin neyȝhebore as þinself' (fo. 113ʳᵇ).

67/56 [*Mt. 22: 40*]: Matt. 22: 37–40: 'Diliges Dominum Deum tuum ex toto corde tuo et in tota anima tua et in tota mente tua. / Hoc est maximum, et primum mandatum./ Secundum autem simile est huic: diliges proximum tuum sicut teipsum;/in his duobus mandatis universa lex pendet et prophetae.' LL4: '& þerfore crist seyth, þu schalt louyn þi lord god wiþ alle þin herte, with al þi soule, with al þin mende, wiþ al þin myȝt, & þin neȝhebore as þiself; in þese two preceptis hangith al þe lawe & prophecye' (fo. 27ᵛᵇ). Cited below 2–27/30–1 and twice more in LL4: fo. 90ᵛᵇ; fo. 127ʳᵃ. Augustine comments that love of self is not omitted in this prescription: '[D]e dilectione tua nihil dictum uidetur, sed cum dictum est, "Diliges proximum tuum . . .", simul et tui abs te dilectio non praetermissa est' (*De Doctr. Christ.* 1.27; *CCL* xxxii, pp. 21–2/17–19; *PL* 34: 29). Cited in *CA* 1: 326–7.

67/57 [*Gal. 5: 14*]: 'Omnis enim lex in uno sermone impletur: Diliges proximum tuum sicut teipsum.' LL4: 'And þerfore seynt poul seyth þat al þe lawe is fulfild in þis word, þu schalt louyn þin neyȝebore as þinself' fo. 102ᵛᵇ.

68/26 [*Lc. 18: 18*]: 'Et interrogavit eum quidam princeps . . .'; cf. Luke 18: 23: 'His ille auditis constristatus est quia dives erat valde.'

68/43–5 *lyf contemplatyf . . . actyf*: A distinction made by Augustine, *De civ. dei* (XIX.19: *CCL* xlviii, p. 686; *PL* 41: 647). Peter Lombard cites Augustine's *De trinitate* in making a parallel distinction between 'sapientia' and 'scientia': ' "In hoc ergo differentia est, quia ad contemplationem sapientia, ad actionem vero scientia pertinet" ' (*De trin.* 14.22; *CCL* l, p. 375; *PL* 42: 1009; in *Sententiae* III, D. 35, c. 1 (2: 199). See Gregory, *PL* 76: 953; Ambrose, *PL*, 46: 2–11 ff. The distinction is usually referred back to the contrasted roles of Martha and Mary, Luke 10: 41–2, as in the *Ayenbite of Inwyt* (*c.*1340):

> þanne þe uerste [active life] is be-tokned be marþen / þet wes bisy uor to uede oure lhord / ase zayþ þet godspel. þe oþer [contemplative life] is betokned be Marie / þet hire zette ate uet [feet] of Iesu crist / and lheste his wordes. (ed. Gradon, EETS, 23, p. 199/30–4).

Giles Constable surveys the Martha and Mary tradition from the earliest biblical exegetes to the painters of the renaissance, *Three Studies* (1995), pp. 3–141. See also Aelred of Rivaulx (*c.*1160), *De Institutione*, ed. Ayto and Barratt (EETS, 287), p. 16/634–6; the *Ancrene Riwle*, ed. Mack (EETS, 252), p. 155/11–23; Bonaventure, 'Apologia pauperum' (*Opera* VIII, 2.15/243–4. See 280/17–19 below.

70/1 *POUERTEE*: The HP-B revision of the HP-A prologue removes the explicit references to begging, presenting 'Pauper' simply as a poor man not a mendicant. This second 'Pauper' says: 'Neþeles, whiles we lyuen heere we mai not vtterly caste alle temporal goodis awei' (71/49). The purpose of such a revision may have been to make *D&P*, originally written for a single patron, acceptable to a wider audience.

70/2 *Proverb. xxii* [2]: See 51/1–2 (HP-A).

70/5 *Bede*: Bede on Prov. 22: 2: 'Neque diuitem propter diuitias honores neque pro inopia pauperem despicias sed in utroque merito uenerare quia opus sunt diuinum, quia ad imagem Dei et similitudinem facti' ('In proverbia Salomonis', *CCL* cxixB, p. 111; *PL* 91: 1001).

70/9 *Sapience vii* [5]: Cited 51/12 (HP-A) above; here the reviser of the HP-A prologue continues to the next verse: 'Unus ergo introitus est omnibus ad vitam et similis exitus.'

70/19 *pore caitif*: Pauper's self-description here is echoed by the title of a popular work of elementary religious instruction. The work, originally orthodox, was given a Lollard revision. The date of the original version is uncertain but may fall within the first quarter of the fifteenth century. The tracts borrow freely from earlier works, including *D&P*; see Hartung *Manual*, 9: 3135; B3470–1. See further 227/1 below.

70/25 *Iob v* [6]: 'Nihil in terra sine causa fit, et de humo non oritur dolor.' Gregory: 'Nihil ergo est in terra sine causa quando et studioso tarditas ad

praemium proficit et desidioso uelocitas ad supplicium crescit. Ad intelle-
genda autem quae recta sunt, aliquando laboris studio, aliquando uero
dolore percussionis erudimur' (*Moralia* 6.11; *CCL* cxliii, p. 293/6–10; *PL*
75: 736). Nicolaus de Lyra cautions: 'Que licet aliqui effectus sint fortuiti et
casuales respectu secundarum causarum, tamen respectu prime cause, que
Deus est, nihil est fortuitum & nihil casuale' (*Postilla* 3).

71/28 *ad Roman. viii* [*28*]: 'Scimus autem quoniam diligentibus Deum
omnia cooperantur in bonum, iis qui secundum propositum vocati sunt
sancti.' The HP-B reviser of the prologue, in translating Rom. 8: 28,
telescopes the senses of verses 28–30, evidently reading 'diligentibus' as
'deligentibus' and importing the predestinarian content of the succeeding
verses. It is notable that the 'Pauper' of HP-A follows his mendicant life for
love of Christ, 'to wynnyn the soulys þat he boughte so dere' while the
'Pauper' of the HP-B revision justifies his poverty (not mendicancy) on the
ground that he is one of God's 'chosen'. The GO interlinear note to the first
phrase of Rom. 8: 28 ('diligentibus Deum') stresses perseverance: 'Que non
recedentibus sed vsque in finem perseuerantibus'; the interlinear note to
'secundum propositum' stresses predestination: 'secundum prescientiam &
predestinationem' (4: 292). In the LV, the translation of the second phrase
is: 'to hem that *aftir purpos* ben clepid seyntis', and a marginal gloss explains
'after purpos' as 'predestynacioun ether bifore ordeynyng by grace', citing
glosses by Nicolaus de Lyra, Augustine and the GO (FM 4: 320b). In citing
Rom. 8: 28, LL4 translates more acccurately: 'To hem þat louyn god alle
þinge turnyth to gode' but attributes the saying to 'salomon' (fo. 102vb).

71/31–6 *Seynt Poul . . . I ad Thymoth. vi* [*: 9–10*]: 1 Tim. 6: 9–10: 'Nam qui
volunt divites fieri incidunt in temptationem et laqueum et desideria multa
inutilia et nociva quae mergunt homines in interitum et perditionem./
Radix enim omnium malorum est cupiditas, quam quidam appetentes
erraverunt a fide et inseruerunt se doloribus multis.' Verse 9 is cited
below, 2–158/59–60, 2–274/21. Verse 10 is cited 58/34 (HP-A) above,
and 78/32 (HP-B), 2–120/40–1, 2–253/14 and 2–296/38 below. Verses 9
and 10 are cited below, 2–265/82, and twice in LL4, fos. 34vb and 95va.

71/38 *comyn as þe carteweye*: Whiting, C64, in which *PP* (a1376) A-Text,
III/127 is cited, as well as this instance in *D&P* (with old dating a1470).
MED, s.v. 'cart' 7, cites *Topias* (1402), ed. T. Wright (RS, 1859–61), 2: 39–
114; now see *Jack Upland*, ed. P. L. Heyworth (1968), p. 100/882.

71/42 *can seie hoo*: See *MED* s.v. 'ho'. See also Whiting, E28, which gives
this instance under the old dating of *D&P* (a1470).

71/45 *Job i* [*21*]: See 51/8 (HP-A) above.

71/50 [*I Tim.6: 8*]: 'Habentes autem alimenta, et quibus tegamur, his
contenti simus.' LL4 cites 1 Tim. 7–10 (fo. 95va). A Latin paraphrase is
given in the citation below, 2–137/71–2. Cited twice by Bonaventure in his

'Apologia pauperum' (1269/70) in support of Franciscan poverty as a *usus moderatus* (*Opera* VIII, 7.3/272, 12.20–1/322–3).

71/1 *folis bolt*: See Whiting, F408, where this instance is given (dated a1470). See also *ODEP*, p. 276.

72/10 *Dominiamini*: Text should read *Dominamini*. [Gen. 1: 28] is cited 63/10 above, 2–78/48 and 2–79/2 below.,

72/17–30 *Lordschip*: In HP-A, Pauper alludes to the traditional distinction between lay and clerical dominion; in HP-B, the reviser adds a tendentious interpretation, 'lordschip pretense', defined as usurpation of power by tyrants and 'false oppressouris'. See 63/10–16 (HP-A), 63/17 (HP-A) above and 336/1 below.

72/2 *Act. xx* [*25*]: Text should read [35]. See 63/2 (HP-A) above and 73/27 below.

72/7 *Ergo*: Dives maintains the academic form of argument: 'Ergo' and 'nunc tibi concluditur'; see 59/1 (HP-A), 63/2 (HP-A) above and 73/27 below.

73/11 *Gregori*: See 64/10–12 (HP-A) above.

73/14–15 [*I Cor. 4: 7*]: See 64/15 (HP-A) above.

73/20 *Luce xxi* [*1–4*]: See 64/20 (HP-A) above.

73/27 *Bede seiþ . . . Act. xx* [*38*]: Read [35]; cited 63/2 (HP-A) and 72/2 above. Bede on Acts 20: 35 says: 'Non illis qui relictis omnibus secuti sunt dominum, diuites etiam elemosynarios praeponit, sed illos quam maxime glorificat qui cunctis quae possident in semel renuntiatis, nihilominus laborant operando manibus, quod bonum est, ut habeant unde tribuant necessitatem patienti' ('Expositio Actuum Apostolorum', *CCL* cxxi, p. 84/101–6; *PL* 92: 986). The addition of Bede's commentary to the citation of Acts 20: 35 enjoining manual labour (73/31)—the text now cited by Pauper, not Dives—is a further indication of the anti-mendicant slant of the reviser of the HP prologue.

73/36 *pore widewe*: See 64/20 (HP-A) above.

74/12–14 *Seint Austyn . . . diues et pauper*: See 63/30 (HP-A) above.

75/39 *Apoc. 3* [*: 17*]: See 59/70 (HP-A) above.

75/3 *Luce vi* [*: 20*]: For 'celorum' the Vulgate has 'dei'; Wordsworth finds two manuscripts with the variant 'caelorum' and one with 'caeli'; a number of manuscripts, influenced by Matt. 5: 3, add 'spiritu' to 'pauperes' (*Novum Testamentum*, Pt. I, fasc. 3/342). Note that [Lc. 6: 20] 77/22 below is emended to Matt. 5: 3, for which see 54/2–3 (HP-A) above.

75/7–8 [*Mt. 19: 28*]: See 54/8 (HP-A) above.

75/10 *deuelshene . . .* [*Lc. 16: 9*]: See 54/11 (HP-A) above.

75/18 *Matheu xix* [: *16–26*]: See 54/8–55/28 (HP-A) above.

76/34 *sownen*: See 55/36 above.

76/37 *expositouris*: See 55/30–49 (HP-A) above.

76/49 [*Lc. 14: 33*]: See 55/50–1 (HP-A) above.

76/2–3 [*Ps. 61: 11*]: See 56/58 (HP-A) above.

77/12 *Iob i* [*21*]: See 51/8 (HP-A) above.

77/21–2 *Beati . . . * [*Lc.6: 20*]: Read [Mt. 5: 3]. See 54/2–3, 56/79 (HP-A) above.

77/25–6 *Doctor de Lira . . . such a ȝate*: In his commentary on Mt. 19: 24. Nicolaus de Lyra states that there is no evidence that a gate called the 'Needle's Eye' ever existed in Jerusalem. Hence the gate must be understood figuratively as a warning against the Pelagian view that a man can achieve salvation by his own efforts. In his further (cross-referenced) commentary on Mark 10: 24, Nicolaus de Lyra suggests that the gate stands for the severe difficulty of achieving salvation by way of voluntary poverty (*Postilla* 4). See 55/30–49 above.

78/9 *Ambrosè*: See 57/10 (HP-A) above.

78/24 *Ecclesiastici* [*27: 1*]: See 57/25–6 (HP-A) above.

78/32 [*1 Tim.6: 10*]: See 58/34 (HP-A) above.

78/37 [*Eccl. 5: 9*]: See 58/39 (HP-A) above.

79/2–16 *Proverb. xxx* [*8–9*] . . . *fantasie*: Cited 59/3–9 (HP-A). HP-B here sharpens the complaint about mistranslation of scripture and the picking and choosing of texts to prove any argument (cf. 60/39 HP-A above). To Dives' assertion that Solomon advises men to flee from poverty, Pauper answers that the whole passage (with added exegesis by Bede and Nicolaus de Lyra, see 79/24 below) is Solomon's prayer that anyone—rich or poor—should avoid the niggardliness of heart that might tempt him to forswear his God. Though elsewhere Pauper seems to advocate distribution of the Bible in the vernacular (cf. 2–64/69 below), here he expresses the more conservative, and Franciscan, view that preaching was safer than unlimited distribution of the scriptures in English. For this the friars were criticized in Wycliffite writings: '[F]reris wolden lede þe puple in techinge hem goddis lawe & þus þei wolden teche sum, & sum hide, & docke sum' etc. ('De officio pastorali', ed. Matthew (EETS os 74), p. 430). This would seem to be further evidence that the revision of HP-B was not authorial.

79/24 *Bede and Lire*: The HP-B revision of the Prologue adds Bede and Nicolaus de Lyra to the discussion of the meaning of 'mendicitatem' in Prov. 30: 8 (see 59/3–9 and 53/14–19 above). Bede comments: 'Haec adhuc uir cum quo est Deus sermonis eius igne radiatus ad ipsum dominum conuersa uoce profatur obsecrans ne uanitatem saeculi umquam uel uerba

mendacia ueritati caelestium praeponat scripturarum, nec rursum uel copia
uel inopia transeuntium rerum in obliuionem decidat aeternorum' ('In
proverbia salomonis', *CCL*, cxixB, p. 142; *PL* 91: 1024). The EV and LV
translate 'mendicitatem' as 'beggery' and the LV provides a marginal extract
from Nicolaus de Lyra's gloss: 'He [Salomon] spekith this in the persoone of
a siyk man, that kan not wel vse prosperites with out pride, nether aduersite
with out grucching' (FM 3: 49). Nicolaus de Lyra's postil: 'Salomon . . .
loquitur hic in persona infirmi qui nescit bene vti fortunis prosperis vel
aduersis, que prosperis nimis eleuatur & aduersis per impatientiam frangi-
tur, & ideo tali magis eligibilis status mediocris . . .' (*Postilla* 3).

80/36 *Ecclesiastes þe v.c.* [9]: See 58/39 (HP-A) above.

80/40–1 *Ecclesiastes vi* [2]: See 59/23 (HP-A) above.

80/46–7 *Salomon . . . richessis and beggerie*: See 59/3–9 (HP-A) above.

80/53 [*Ps. 39: 17*]: Text should read: [Ps. 39: 18]; see 60/38 (HP-A) above.

80/65 *Seint Austyn*: See 60/60 (HP-A) above.

VOL. I: 1, COMMANDMENT I, CAP. 1–29
(pp. 81–149)

81/7 *Exodi xx* [*3–5*]: Exod. 20: 3–5: 'Non habebis deos alienos coram me./
Non facies tibi sculptile, neque omnem similitudinem quae est in caelo
desuper et quae in terra deorsum, nec eorum quae sunt in aquis sub terra./
Non adorabis ea neque coles.' Augustine (in the GO) asks: 'Queritur
quomodo decem precepta legis diuidenda sint'; he recognized that to
divide the first Commandment into two would mean combining the ninth
and tenth into one (equating 'domum' and 'uxorem') and would also
produce a structure less adapted to figurative interpretation ('mihi autem
congruentius videtur accipi illa tria & ista septem'. The three-to-seven
division would equate the first subgroup to the Trinity and align the second
subgroup with other 'sevens': the cardinal virtues, deadly sins, sacraments,
etc. The gloss also cites Origen, who assumes that the 'first' Commandment
of Exod. 20: 3–5 comprises the first two Commandments of the decalogue
(GO 1: 151–2). Though Origen's view remained that of the Greek Orthodox
Church and was also accepted by St Jerome, Augustine prevailed. The
argument is summarized by Reginald Pecock in *The Donet* (1443–9), ed.
Hitchcock (EETS os 156), p. 157/21–31. See Aston (1988), pp. 371–92. On
Augustine's less consistent view of how the proscriptions of the ninth and
tenth Commandments should be allocated, see 2–253/4–5 below.

    In the *D&P* translation, the addition 'noo maument' is traditional,
derived from the name Mohammed and the belief that Mohammed was

an idol worshipped by the Saracens. Cf. *Speculum christiani* (1360's-70's), in which 'maumtrye' translates VL 'ydola' (ed. Holmstedt, EETS, 182, pp. 18–19). Compare Chaucer's 'Parson's Tale': 'al þat worschipen þe crosse or ymages . . . done mawmentri' (*CT*, p. 313/745–50); and *EWW*, p. 19/33.

81/8–12 *meen doon makyn þese dayis ymagys*: Dives asks whether making a likeness ('similitudinem') is the same as worshipping an idol (cf. Introduction, pp. xxxix–xlii); the GO: 'Aliud est ergo facere ydolum, aliud similitudinem' 1: 152a; Origen, 'De fide', Bk. 4.16). An ancient predesssor of the debate in *D&P* is St Theodore of Studios's (759–826) dialogue between an 'Orthodoxus' and a 'Haereticus'. Theodore's 'Haereticus' is a Dives who wants to know where in the Old or New Testament it says images must be adored. His Pauper is an 'Orthodoxus', who explains that Christ's Incarnation—as an image of God the Father—has altered the meaning of the Commandment. Not the material image but the 'prototype' of the images of Christ (including the prototype of images of the cross) may legitimately be adored (*Antirrheticus II*, PG 99: 351–87). Nicolaus de Lyra adds a postil to his commentary on Exod. 20 in which he makes the same argument: it is false to believe that the first Commandment forbade the making of images of sentient, rational beings. Such images in ancient Hebrew places of worship did not lead to priestly idolatry. In the 'time of grace', the prohibition has become merely 'ceremonial'; images are not to be worshipped per se but for what they represent ('ratione rei significate, que est ipse cristus vere deus' (*Postilla* 1). Pauper's orthodox view was shared by Wyclif (*De mand.* (1375–6), pp. 152 ff.) but not by the Lollards (*EWW*, pp. 27, 179–81; *PR* (1988), pp. 301–7 and *passim*. On the history of 'the longest sustained doctrinal controversy in Christian history', see Pelikan (1974), 2: 91–145. See further 82/42–4 and 102/17–21 below.

81/13–15 *he bad Moyses . . . Exodi xxxvii [7–9]*: Exod. 37: 7–9: 'Duos etiam cherubim ex auro ductili, quos posuit ex utraque parte propitiatorii', etc. The GO (interlinear) gives a symbolic interpretation: ' "Cherub" interpretatur plenitudo scientie dilectio, scilicet dei et proximi' (1: 204). Nicolaus de Lyra's commentary points to controversy about the placement of these images in the ancient sanctuary (*Postilla* 1).

81/16–18 *And Salomon . . . þe thredde book of Kynggys vii [29;36]*: 1 Kgs. 7: 29; 36: '. . . et inter coronulas et plectas, leones et boves et cherubin. . . ./ Sculpsit quoque in tabulatis illis quae erant ex aere et in angulis cherubin et leones et palmas, quasi in similitudinem stantis hominis, ut non celata sed adposita per circuitum viderentur'. In defense of images, it was standard practise to point to these descriptions of temple decorations in the OT; see, e.g., Reginald Pecock, cited above (81/8–12), p. 125.

82/19–21 *tabernacle . . . Exodi xv [1–40]*: Read Exod. 25: 8 ff.: 'Facientque mihi sanctuarium, et habitabo in medio eorum; /iuxta omnem similitudinem tabernaculi quod ostendam tibi, et omnium vasorum in cultum eius sicque facietis illud', etc. Bede, in his 'De tabernaculo' 1.3, discusses this passage as a prefiguration of the heavenly city, in which the blessed will enjoy fellowship with angels (*CCL* 119A, p. 12/275–96; *PL* 91: 400).

82/32–4 *Ysaie xlii* [*8*] . . . *And in the same chapetle*: Note that 'ne to peyntyd ymagys' is added to the translation in *D&P*. Isa. 42: 8 is cited in LL4: 'I schal nout ȝeuyn myn worschepe to ony oþere ne ȝeuyn myn preysinge to grauyn ymagys' (fo. 104ᵛᵃ). Isa. 42: 17: 'Conversi sunt retrorsum, confundantur confusione qui confidunt in sculptili', tr. in LV: 'Thei ben turned abac; be thei schent with schenschipe, that trusten in a grauun ymage' (FM 3: 300b).

82/37 *I wold . . . brent euerychon*: In 1382, two Lollards, Richard Waytestathe and William Smith, boasted that they had used a wooden statue of St Catherine for firewood over which to cook their cabbage stew (Knighton's *Chronicle: 1337–1396*, ed. and tr. G. H. Martin, pp. 296–7).

82/42–4 *tokene . . . boke*: St John of Damascus (d. *c.*749) was one of the first to call images the books of the unlettered; he said

Imago siquidem monimentum quoddam est: ac quidquid liber est iis qui litteras didicerunt: hoc imago est illitteratis et rudibus: et quod auditui praestat oratio, hoc visui confert imago: per mentem vero ipsi conjungimur (*De Imaginibus*, Oratio 10: *PG* 94: 1247–8).

In the thirteenth century, Grosseteste (citing Bede) makes Pauper's argument in his *De decem mand.*, p. 13/17–21); cf. Durandus, *Rationale* 1.3.1 (*CCCM* cxl, p. 34/1). *Jacob's Well* in the early fifteenth century:

. . . ymagys in cherchys arn ordeynyd to ȝour syȝt for to be bokys to laymen to se and knowyn þerby in ȝour herte þe seyntys þat ar figuryd by þo imagys . as clerkys knowyn & se be here bokys how þei schul serue and worschepe god . . . (Salisbury MS 174: fo. 185ʳ)

Cf. See also Lyndwood, *Provinciale* (*c.*1470–80), p. 252b (1679 edn.); and *The Pilgrimage of the Life of Man*, tr. John Lydgate, ed. Furnivall (EETS es 77, 83, 92), p. 560/21006–21015). Early Lollards were sometimes temperate on the issue, as for example the early fifteenth-century *Lanterne of Light*, ed. Swinburn, EETS os 151, p. 85/19–21; and the fourteenth-century *Rosarium*, ed. von Nolcken, MET 10 (1979), p. 99. See also Joy M. Russell-Smith, 'Walter Hilton and a Tract in Defence of the Veneration of Images', *Dominican Studies* 7 (1954), 180–214; and W. R. Jones on the Oxford 'iconodules', *JHI* 37 (1973), 27–50. See 81/8–12 above and 90/23, 91/1 and 102/17–21 below.

82/44–5 *De con. di iii Perlatum*: Pope Gregory I (590–604) wrote to Bishop Serenus of Marseilles that he had heard of the destruction of certain images by persons having an excess of zeal. This act he deplores, because it is one thing to adore an image, and quite another to learn from a picture what ought to be adored; the illiterate especially need images: 'in ipsa legunt qui litteras nesciunt' (Gregory, 'Epistola', Ep. 105; *PL* 77: 1027–8; De cons. D 3 c. 27; Friedberg 1: 1360). See also Aston, (1988), p. 185.

83/1–84/38 *How shulde I rede*: Cf. Augustine: 'Vulnere etiam percussus a capite usque ad pedes, integer tamen intus, respondit tentatrici, de limine uiuentium, de limine cordis sui . . .' (*Enarr.*, 55.20; *CCL* xxxix, p. 693/36–8; *PL* 36: 660). Lines 4–37 of cap. ii provided material for a short tract by an anonymous author, 'A Tretyse of Gostly Batayle'. A survey of the genre may be found in R. R. Raymo's section of the Hartung *Manual*, 7: 2254–2378; 2467–2582. The tract, dating from the mid to late fifteenth century, is printed in *Yorkshire Writers*, ed. Horstman, where it is loosely attributed to Richard Rolle. For three more borrowings from *D&P* found in 'A Tretyse of Gostly Batayle' see below 2–304–12/cap. v–vi, 2–323/4–324/37, and 2–324/43–325/66 (text). For brief comment on the nature of the tract, Bloomfield (1952), p. 220.

84/39 *as Seynt Bernard bydd3t*: Ps.-Bernard's 'Instructio sacerdotis':

> Imaginare hic, o homo, quo, quali et quanto pretio redemptus es. . . .In cruce distentitur, membra distrahuntur, dorsum adhuc plagosum de recentibus plagis flagellorum recenti adhuc sanguine stillans, rigido patibulo crucis atteritur; manus et pedes perforiuntur, clavi maleis incutiuntur, et quanto altius clavi penetrant . . . (*PL* 184: 778–9).

A closer parallel is found in Bishop Brinton's sermon 54 (of 1375): *Sermons*, ed. Devlin, 2: 243, but there attributed to Augustine; the editor refers to Ps.-Augustine *Manuale*, in which the wording is again different:

> Extendit brachia sua in cruce, et expandit manus suas paratus in amplexus peccatorum. Inter brachia Salvatoris mei et vivere volo, et mori cupio. Ibi securus decantabo . . . Salvator noster caput inclinavit in morte, ut oscula daret suis dilectis. Toties Deum osculamur, quoties in ejus amore compungimur. (*PL* 40: 961)

Meditation on the sufferings of Christ was widely recommended as a cure for many kinds of sin and as an adjunct to penance. See, e.g., Aelred of Rievaulx, *De Institutione Inclusarum* (1160–2), ed. Ayto and Barratt (EETS, 287), p. 35/380–1; the *Ancrene Wisse* (first half of the thirteenth century), ed. Tolkien (EETS, 249), p. 205/19–20; *English Lyrics of the Thirteenth Century*, ed. C. Brown, No.69, p. 128; the fourteenth-century Ps.-Bonventure's Franciscan *Meditationes vitae Christi*, pp. 317–358; Chaucer's 'Parson's Tale', *CT*, pp. 234–5/268 ff.; the late fourteenth-century *Chastising of God's Children*, ed. Bazire and Colledge, p. 202; Mirk's *Festial*, ed. Erbe (EETS es 96), I: 112/32–6; *Jacob's Well* (Salisbury MS, fos. 160ᵇ, 173ᵃ); the fifteenth-century *Orchard of Syon*, ed. Hodgson and Liegey (EETS, 258), 1: 294/28–31; St Bridget's *Liber*, ed. Ellis (EETS os 291),

1: 49/17–50/8–31 and *passim*. See also Thomas H. Bestul, 'Chaucer's Parson's Tale and the Late-medieval Tradition of Religious Meditation' *Speculum* 64: 3 (1989), 600–619. See 2–99/2–4 below.

85/54–5 *Doo þin wurshepe . . . ymage*: Cf. 'The Vision of William of Stranton' (1400): '. . . bifore an ymage, not for þe ymage, but in worship of þat seint þat þe ymage bitokened', in *St Patrick's Purgatory*, ed. Easting, EETS, 298, pp. lxxxi–lxxxviii, 110/611–13.

85/3 *and so wenyȝt mechil of þe peple*: Dives candidly expresses a view, shared by the Lollards, that became steadily more popular in the century before the Reformation, see Aston (1984), pp. 135–92.

87/37 *vnder forme of bred and of wyn*: There is no extended discussion of the eucharist in *D&P*, cf. 235/44–5 and 2–38/37–39/47 below. Two good reasons for the author of *D&P* to have avoided questions about the eucharist are, first, that Wyclif and the Lollards had become identified with opposition to transsubstantiation (*PR*, pp. 281–90); and, second, from the late thirteenth century, Franciscan scholastics (e.g. John Pecham, Richard of Middleton, Duns Scotus) had been arguing the finer points of the eucharistic presence and raising numerous philosophic questions about the standard Thomist-Bonaventuran rationale; see Burr, *Eucharistic Presence and Controversy* (1986), pp. 32–75. In *c*.1405, it was not a topic for casual discussion, especially in the vernacular.

87/2 *crepyn to þe croos*: As a sign of devotion, to 'creep to the cross' was to approach the cross on one's knees during the Good Friday service; see Rock (4: 99 ff.; 287–8), where the rite is described and where further references are given. *Jacob's Well* alludes to the rite in a miracle tale (ed. Brandeis, EETS os 115, 1: 153), as does *PP*'s Long Will (B-Text, XVIII/427–9). See also *Mum and the Sothsegger*, ed. M. Day and R. Steele (EETS, 199), p. 41/ 483 and note pp. 114–5. See Duffy (1992), p. 29, for a description, citing *Missale ad usum Insignis Sarum*, ed. Dickinson, cols. 316–333. For the later history of the rite, see Aston (1988), pp. 230, 237, 244–5, 262; see also Hutton (1996), pp. 189–90.

87/5 *Beda*: The reference is not to Bede but to Honorius Augustodunensis' *Gemma animae* (early twelfth century), Lib. iii: 'Post passionem Christi crucifixus oculis nostris repraesentatur, quem Ecclesia imitari adhortatur . . . Et nullus sapiens crucem sed Christum crucifixum adorat, crucem tamen venerando salutat' (*PL* 172: 667). On Honorius, see Y. Lefèvre, *L'Elucidarium et les Lucidaires* (Paris, 1954); V. I. J Flint, 'The Place and the Purpose of the Works of Honorius Augustodunensis', *Révue Bénédictine* 87 (1977), 97–127.

88/8 *O crux aue, spes vnica*: The first line of an eighth stanza added later to the Passion hymn 'Vexilla regis, prodeunt' written by Fortunatus (ca.530–600):

O crux ave, spes unica,
Hoc passionis tempore,
Auge piis iustitiam,
Reisque dona veniam.

Listed in Drèves, *Analecta* 43, No. 87, stanza 8, p. 56. See Ruth
E. Messenger, *The Medieval Latin Hymn* (1953), pp. 85–6; Raby, *Christian
Latin Poetry* (1953), pp. 88–90; Chevalier *Repertorium*, 4: 186, No. 12842–
12843. 'O crux aue' is alluded to in 'The Rewle of Sustris Menouresses' in
Courtesy Book, ed. Chambers and Seton, EETS, 198, p. 106/24. Julian,
Hymnology, says this stanza of the hymn is not by Fortunatus but added
later (2: 1219–22).

88/12 *O crux splendidior*: Listed in Drèves, *Analecta* 7, No. 91, p. 105; this
line appears in Stanza 8 of the hymn, beginning: 'Prodeunt et fulget/ Crucis
mysterium':

O crux veneranda
quae sola fuisti
digna portare regem
coelorum et dominum.
O crux
splendidior cunctis astris
mundi hominibus
multumque amabilis,
quod meruisti
portare talentum mundi.

88/24–30 *And as euery lord and knyȝt . . . his special tokene*: The passage may
be translated: 'And just as every lord and knight has a special token on his
armour, or else accompanying his armour, by which he is known and famed,
and just as he is often called by the name of his token—as when his deeds
are recounted under this name by heralds and goliards who do not know his
real name or person—so in the scriptures Christ is often referred to as the
cross, for the cross is his special token.' That Christ is 'often' referred to in
the scriptures as the cross is something of an overstatement; while passages
such as 'nos autem praedicamus Christum crucifixum' (1 Cor. 1: 23) not
infrequently juxtapose the words 'Christ', 'cross', and 'crucified' there is no
example of the use of 'cross' to mean Christ.

In an analogous scene in *PP*, Will dreams he sees Piers 'peynted al blody'
in procession carrying a cross (C text, XXII; Skeat edn., 1: 551/10–14).
Skeat's note (2: 266) to this passage suggests that Langland was depending
on a false etymology of the word 'Christ' as 'conquerour'; Skeat also refers
to conventional representations of Christ after the resurrection as bearing a
long staff/cross with a banner, citing Rock (3: 226). See also *PP* Prologue to
the B-Text (Skeat 1: 14/139), and editor's note pointing out a connection

between goliard and king (2: 15–16). *PP*'s 'Christ' is greeted by 'an heraud of armes when Auentrous comeþ to Iustes' (B-Text, XVIII/16). See 98/51 below.

Christine of Pisan's contemporary *Othéa* (*c.*1400) combines an exposition of the ten Commandments with chivalric allegory, ed. Bühler (EETS, 264), pp. 46–56. See also her *Book of Fayttes*, Caxton translation, ed. Byles (EETS, 189), pp. 289–90.

89/40 *antiphene*: See 88/12 above.

89/43 *þe veyl aforn þe rode*: Rock, drawing on Leland, *Collectanea* iv. 235, says that

> [t]he Lenten curtain hung down between the people and holy of holies. In cathedrals, it parted the presbytery from the choir; in parish churches, the chancel from the nave (4: 257–68).

Rock cites *D&P* 89/42–4. Durandus says that 'depending on local custom', on the first Sunday of Quadragesime or on Passion Sunday two curtains should be suspended, one around the choir the other between the altar and the choir, to signify that before Christ's Passion the meaning of the Old Law was hidden; both to be removed on Easter Sunday (*Rationale* 1.3.36; *CCCM* cxl, pp. 46–7/424–36). Aelred of Rievaulx's *De Institutione* (1160–2): 'To reduce to oure mynde that we ben letted from heuenly desire, ther is [during Lent] hanged bitwene us and Crist, his flesshe and his blood, the sacrament of the autere, a veyl', ed. Ayto and Barratt (EETS, 287), p. 7/277–9. See also King, *Liturgies* (1955), p. 152; Duffy (1992), p. 111; and R. Hutton (1996), p. 171.

90/20 *De conse. di.iii.c.28*: The canon 'Venerabiles' warns that images must not be worshipped as gods, and hopes of salvation must not be placed in them; they may, however, be venerated as memorials. The source is a ninth-century Synod (De cons. D.3 c.28: Friedberg 1: 1360). Cited below, 108/36.

90/23 *book and a tokene*: See 82/42–4 above.

91/26 *crossys made be þe weye*: W. W. Seymour: 'Wayside crosses are almost a peculiar feature of the Western Church. . . . Some idea may be formed of the immense number of crosses, wayside, market, etc., formerly in Great Britain from noticing the number of places which retain the name of the cross although the structure itself has disappeared' *The Cross, in Tradition, History and Art* (N.Y. and London, 1898), pp. 324; 326. See Rock, 1: 254–5. Also see Owst (1926, repr. 1965) on 'preaching crosses', pp. 148; 195–9.

91/37 *Eccl. 2: 14*: LL4: '. . . liftyn vp here understondinge & here loue to god for þese two ben oure gostli eyȝin of whiche eyȝyn salomon seyth þat þe eyȝin of þe wise man ben in his hefd þat is to seye in crist hefd of holi cherche (fo. 117ᵛᵃ). The interpretation of 'hefd' as Christ appears in the interlinear GO (2: 697a). Cited again below 327/88.

91/1 *tokene and a book*: See 82/42–4 above.

91/3–4 *in special . . . in comoun*: Pauper begins his course of instruction with an academic *divisio* of the subject matter. See 59/1 above.

91/5 *peyntyd*: The Franciscan Archbishop Pecham, may 'have inspired the pictures on the walls of medieval churches', see Decima L. Douie, *Archbishop Pecham* (London, 1952), p.135. *Jacob's Well* refers to the walls of churches 'wyth peynture of bry3tnesse, schynyng wyth gaynesse', ed. Brandeis (EETS, os 115), 1: 306.

91–3/11–43 *Saints Peter . . . and Margaret*: See G. Ferguson, *Signs and Symbols* (repr. 1956) for a summary of the iconography with illustrations. See Duffy (1992), pp. 155–205.

92/13–15 *keyes . . . Mt.18: 18, Io.20: 23*: '. . . quaecumque alligaveritis super terram, erunt ligata et in caelo: et quaecumque solveritis super terram erunt soluta in caelo' (Matt. 18: 18) . . . quorum remiseritis peccata, remittuntur eis: et quorum retinueritis, retenta sunt' (John 20: 23). These passages bear on the moot question whether Christ gave the 'keys' (the power to absolve from sin) to Peter alone or to all the disciples. Wyclif (and later the Lollards) believed the 'keys' had been given to all the apostles: 'þe same eiþer euene power of byndynge and assoilinge was 3ouene of Crist generally to þe apostles' (see *EWW*, p. 123/50–1; *EWS* 2, Serm. 74/81–3). Wyclif's argument is that just as Peter merited the 'keys' which Christ gave him, so should all clerics who exercise priestly powers; see *De pot. pap.* (1379), pp. 97–8; 140–1. MS G (and only G) omits the qualifying 'But 3it afterwardys' clause that contains the two biblical references. That the omission was not authorial is clearly shown by the Longleat friar's sermon: 'And in þis 3yfte of þe holy gost crist 3af / hese apostolys þe key3es of holy chyrche to byndin & vnbyndin . . . Aforn hys pascioun he hy3t hem þe key3ys of holy chyrche but aftyr hys pascioun whanne he was rysin as at þis tyme he 3af hem þe key3is of holy chyrche' (LL4, fo. 50ra–b). Cf. 94/25–6 and 342/49 below.

92/30 [*Io. 1: 29*]: LL4: 'Seeth goodis lomb . seth hym þat doth awey synnys of þe world' (fo. 6ra; also fo. 131vb). On 'lamb', the GO: 'Tria ministrat agnum possidentibus se, lac simplicis doctrinae quo paruli nutriuntur, lanam, i.e., incrementa virtutum, esum carnis suae' (4: 226).

92/31–4 *Seynt Katerine . . . Maxence*: The story of St Catherine's martyrdom is found in the *Legenda aurea*: Graesse, No.172; *GL*, 2: 334–41. See *ODS*, pp. 69–70.

93/37–40 *Seynt Margarete . . . hool*: The story of St Margaret and the dragon is found in the *Legenda aurea*: Graesse, No. 151; *GL*, 2: 232–3. See *ODS*, pp. 260–1.

93/4–5 *barefoot . . . gallochis*: Pauper refers indirectly to the controversy about the poverty of Christ that divided the Franciscan order. After a long struggle, the view that Christ and the apostles had no possessions was declared heretical, and before the first half of the fourteenth century the Franciscans who held that view had become schismatic. When the question came down to footwear, the attempt to follow the barefoot practise of St Francis himself seemed less practical as the Order spread into northern Europe. A controversy between Archbishop Pecham (d. 1292) and Robert Kilwardby (d. 1279) over Franciscan poverty in *c.*1272 touched on the wearing of shoes, with Pecham asserting against Kilwardby that Franciscans were free either to wear or not wear shoes according to their circumstances and needs (*Fratris Johannis Pecham*, ed. C. L. Kingsford *et al.*. (1910; repr. 1966), pp. 112, 121–47, esp. p. 124–5). In *Mum and the Sothsegger*, the friars are accused of 'smale semyd sockes . . . of softe wolle', ed. Day and Steele (EETS, 199), p. 39/424–8). The word 'gallochis' is connected with the word 'clog' and seems to have meant a wooden sole fastened onto the foot with a strap; the meaning 'waterproof overshoe' is a later development; see *DML* s.v. 'galocha'. See 93/6, and 2–228/56 below.

93/6 *Beda*: The point of Bede's commentary on Acts 12: 8 ('calcea te caligas tuas') is that strict rules of attire may and should be modified according to circumstances: Peter, in prison, loosened his belt and wrapped his tunic around his feet to keep them warm ('Super Acta Apostolorum', c. xii: *PL* 92: 972). Cited by John Pecham (*c.*1270s) in his 'Contra Kilwardby', ed. Kingsford *et al.* (1910; repr. 1966), p. 124. See also Bonaventure, 'Apologia' on Bede and 'caligulae' (*Opera* VIII x: 7–8). The VL 'caligas' originally meant Roman army boots, but Pauper's description of this footwear makes clear that he understands the word as 'sandals', the meaning having been assimilated by exegesis to the 'sandaliis' of Mark 6: 9 (DuCange 2: 31–2). The word also means 'hose' and is so translated in the EV and LV: 'ho(o)sis' (FM 4: 543a/7, 543b/9.

93/10 *Gregory*: The reference is possibly to Gregory's Homily VI: 'Nemo ergo existimet in fluxu atque studio vestium peccatum deesse, quia si hoc culpa non esset, nullo modo Joanem Dominus de vestimenti sui asperitate laudasset. Si hoc culpa non esset, nequaquam Petrus apostolas per epistolam, feminas a pretiosarum vestium appetitu compesceret, dicens: *Non in veste pretiosa*', *PL* 76 (1): 1097. St Bridget's *Liber* contrasts real mantles with the spiritual mantle of meekness (ed. Ellis, EETS, 291, pp. 178/34–179/4). See 2–228/38(2) below.

94/22–34 *Ysaye*: Isa. 51: 11: The remainder of the verse is: '. . . Gaudium et laetitiam tenebunt;/ fugiet dolor et gemitus'.

94/25–6 *þey weryn nought so gay*: In manuscript G, the discussion appears to have been cut short, with something of a non sequitur (lines 32–4) substituted for the views expressed in the other manuscripts. Apart from G, each of the two manuscript groups (RDTH and BYL) ends the chapter with a plea for an honest mean to be kept between over-ornate and over-crude styles of representation. Cf. 92/13–15 above, where there is another possible softening of the meaning by the scribe of G.

94/29–32 *Seynt Powyl . . . ba*u*seynys . . .* [*Heb. 11: 37*]: The *MED* defines *D&P* 'bauseyn' as 'badger' and 'beaver (?by confusion)' and the *D&P* variant 'brocke' as both 'badger' and 'beaver'. The *Catholicon* makes 'bawson' and 'broke' equivalent and defines them as 'beaver', Latin: '*taxus, castor*', pp. 24, 44 (ed. Herrtage, EETS os 75). The *Prompt. Parv.* has 'bawston' and 'broke' and follows suit (ed. Mayhew, EETS os 102), pp. 26, 50. The fullest account is in du Cange s.v. 'melote'. See 2–98/75 (text) below.

95/1–17 *aungelys*: The details about angels are drawn from Trrevisa's translation of Bartholomaeus 2.3–19, which, like *D&P*, begins with how angels are to be painted: 'Payntoures peyntith aungels with winges in swiftnes of fliȝt; wiþ winges is betokened þe swift werchinge of aungels, and so simple men knowiþ þe swift werchinge of angelis bi þat maner of peyntinge'; they are painted 'wiþ longe lockes and crisp here' and with chariots and wheels, and with armour; a good angel 'is iȝeue to men for help and kepinge, so euery man hath an euel angel to assailinge and temptinge' (*Properties*, 1: 59/13–16, 64/2, 84/18–19).

95/16 *towalyis*: In an article published a year before the Oxford edition of Trevisa's translation of Bartholomaeus, Bengt Lindström, noting this passage in *D&P*, speculated about whether or not 'towles' was a corruption of 'tools' ('Two Notes', *Stud. Neophil.* 46, 335–7). He failed to find a basis for the meaning 'towels' in the Latin text of Bartholomaeus.

95/18 *ad Hebreos i* [*14*]: Heb. 1: 14: 'Nonne omnes sunt administratorii spiritus, in ministerium misse propter eos, qui haereditatem capient salutis?' The GO (marginal): 'Intellige igitur quantos honor nobis existit vt ad nos sicut ad amicos ministros angelos suos destinet deus. Quamuis enim multum intersit inter angelos & homines, propinquos tamen eos nobiscum fecit: quia nostre saluti student, propter nos discurrunt, nobis suo funguntur officio; hoc est opus angelicum' (4: 415a).

95/26 *þe Phylosofre*: Aristotle is certainly the source of the notion that the heavenly bodies move in circular orbits (*De Caelo*, 2.6–12; *Oxford Aristotle*, tr. J. Barnes, 1: 476–82; *On the Heavens* (tr. W. K. C. Guthrie, LCL 338, II.iv, 152–67) but that angels were the motive power is a medieval conception: 'During the Middle Ages a celestial mover was conceived in a variety of ways: as an intelligence, an angel, a form, or a soul', Grant (1996), p. 525; cf. Robertus Anglicus' commentary on 'The Sphere of Sacrobosco',

Thorndike (1949), pp. 153; 207; cf. Aquinas, 'In de caelo et mundo Aristotelis', Bk. 2, lec. 3, par. 3, *Opera* (Parma edn.), XIX, p. 156.

96/1 ff. *Euaungelystys*: Dives refers to the symbols of the Evangelists: a man, an eagle, an ox, and a lion. The ultimate source is biblical, Ezek. 1: 5–10, Dan. 7: 3–27, and Rev. 4: 7–8. St Ambrose connects Rev. 4 with the Evangelists in his introduction to *In Lucam* (*PL* 15: 1611). St Jerome lists the standard symbols ('Ad Jovin.', *PL* 23: 259). Honorius Augustodunensis (early twelfth century) relates the four to Christ: 'Christus erat homo nascendo, vitulus moriendo, leo resurgendo, aquile ascendo' (*PL* 172: 956). See also Peter of Riga (d. 1209), *Aurora: Petri Rigae Biblia Versificata*, ed. P. E. Beichner, 2: 421/15–22. Mirk's *Festial* discusses the meanings of the symbols of the evangelists in relation to painting: '. . . þes foure euangelystys ben lyknet to foure dyuerse bestys, and soo byn paynted yn fowre partyes of Cryst, þat ys: for Marke a lyon, for Mathew a man, for Luke a calfe, and for Ion an eron [eagle]. Wherfor mony lewde men wenen þat þay wern suche bestys and not men' (ed. Erbe, EETS es 96), 1: 261/8–11. Mirk's comment on 'lewde men' could serve to distinguish Dives as a more literate person who instead wonders why men were painted as animals. Durandus connects the Evangelists with other 'fours': the four rivers of Paradise; prophets Isaiah, Jeremiah, Ezechial and Daniel; wise men Job, David, Solomon and 'iesus Syrach'; doctors Jerome, Augustine, Ambrose and Gregory (cf. Durandus' *Rationale*, CCCM, cxlB, 7.44.3–4; pp. 117–19).

97/23 ff. *leon*: Isidore of Seville (c.560–637): 'Cum genuerint catulum, tribus diebus et tribus noctibus catulus dormire fertur; tunc deinde patris fremitu vel rugitu veluti tremefactus cubilis locus suscitare dicitur catulum dormientem' (*Etym.* XII, ii, 5). The thirteenth-century English translation of the Latin *Physiologus* contains this story of the birth of the lion and its Christological interpretation (ed. Wirtjes, EETS, 299, pp. 3/8–11), Alexander Neckam (d.1217) makes the identification of the lion with Christ: 'Christus etiam dormiens secundum humanitatem, vigilavit in natura divinitatis', followed by the fable of the lion's whelps, born in an inert state and brought to life on the third day by the lion's roar ('nunc rugitu patris moveantur'), *De naturis rerum*, ed. T. Wright (RS, 1863), p. 228. The legend appears in *An Old English Miscellany* (c.1250), ed. Richard Morris, EETS os 49, p. 1/17–22; in the *Fasciculus morum*, ed. Wenzel, pp. 274–6; Mirk's *Festial*, ed. Erbe, EETS es 96, I: 261; and in Trevisa's Bartholomaeus 18.65: 'And it is ytrowe þat þe leoun whelp whanne he is ywhelped slepeþ þre dayes and þre nightes and it is yseyde þat þe place of þe couche trembleþ and schakeþ by grontynge and rorynge of þe fader and wakeþ þe whelpe þat slepeþ (*Properties*, 2: 1214/18–21). For another reference to the legend, 2–241/17 below.

97/31 *Estryn day*: Mark 16: 1–7; see *Sarum Missal*, ed. Legg, p. 136. The same lection precedes the Easter sermon of the Longleat friar (LL4, fo. 48rb).

98/43–4 *foure endys of þe cros*: A fine example is the Bury St Edmund's cross (now in the Cloisters, in New York), shown in Beckwith (1972), plates 187–88; a frontispiece shows an ivory and gold crucifix of the late tenth century (now in the Victoria and Albert Museum) with stylized symbols of the four evangelists in enamel work. See also Delaruelle (1980), pp. 27–42, esp. bibliog. pp. 40–2. On the symbolism of 'fours' see de Lubac (1964), II 2: 26–40. See 98/54–67 below.

98/51 *kynggys in kende*: In his interpretation, Pauper reverts to the idea of Christ in Triumph broached earlier (88/24–30 above), so that the evangelical symbols now stand for kingship. This idea can be traced to the description of the four 'animals' in Rev. 5: 6–10, which closes on the vision of an earthly kingdom ('. . . et fecisti nos Deo nostro regnum, et sacerdotes: et regnabimus super terram'). The idea is carried further in the apocryphal 'Gospel of Nicodemus', in which Christ confronts Satan and 'Inferus' as a king, 'Rex Gloriae', and rescues the kings and heroes of ancient times from hell; see Middle English edition by W. H. Hulme (EETS es 100), pp. 111–12; and Latin edition by H. C. Kim (1973), pp. 40 ff. Some historians have seen in the Franciscan ideal a renewal of chivalry; St Francis spoke of himself as a 'chevalier du Christ', and, according to E. Delaruelle, St Francis 'a intériorisé l'héroisme du XIIIème siècle, a révélé aux lecteurs du *Roland* qui'il admirait lui-même, le caractère épique de la vie chrétienne': *La piété populaire* (1980), p. 458). R. B. Brooke in the introduction to her edition of the writings of the companions of St Francis says that St Francis 'used the literature of the day, the Chansons de Geste and the Arthurian cycle and projected his vision of poverty in the language of romance and chivalry': *The Writings of Leo*, p. 22. In *PP*, Jesus enters Jerusalem like a 'kynght þat comeþ to be dubbed,/ To geten hym gilte spores [and] galoches ycouped' (B-Text, XVIII/13–14). With the suggestion provided by Eph. 6: 11–18 ('Induite vos armaturam Dei'), the imagery of knighthood often appears in the sermon literature, as in the late fourteenth-century Wycliffite sermon on this text: 'What good kny3t shulde drede hym to fy3te in þe armes of þis Lord?' (*EWS* 1, Serm. 51/6–7). See further R. Woolf, 'The Theme of Christ the Lover-knight' (1962), pp. 2–16; R. A. Waldron, Langland's . . . the Christ-Knight' (1986), pp. 66–81, and A. Finlay, 'The Warrior Christ' (1986), pp. 19–29. Further references to the theme: 88/24–30 above and 2–99/5 ff, 2–227/4, 2–304/-12/cap. v–vi, and 2–307/57–308/38 (text) below.

98/54–67 *be þese foure been vnderstondyn*: The OT foundation for this interpretation of the symbols of the four Evangelists is Ezek. 1: 5–28 and Dan. 7: 3–27, see note 96/1 ff. above. Both prophets had visions of four superterrestial creatures with the faces of a lion, an ox, a man, and an eagle, which, according to Dan. 7: 17, are 'four kingdoms, which shall arise out of the earth (Douai)'. Hugh of St Victor (ca.1096–1141), *De Arca Noe Morali*: 'Item post diluvium principium regnororum et caput mundi in Assyriis, et Chaldaeis, et Medis in partibus Orientis fuit. Deinde ad Graecos venit, postremo circa finem saeculi ad Romanos in Occidente, quasi in fine mundi habitantes, potestas summa descendit' (*PL* 176: 677–8). The connection between the evangelists and the four kingdoms is a commonplace for Peter Comestor: 'similitudinem . . . hominis, leonis et vituli et aquilae [Ezech. 1] non solum ad praefigurandum evangelistas, sed ut ostenderet Deum Israel Dominum esse totius creaturae' (*Historia, PL* 198: 1442). Peter of Riga lists the four realms as Assyria, Persia, Greece and Rome (*Aurora*, ed. Beichner, 1: 346–8). Henri de Lubac discusses the medieval exegesis of the number four (de Lubac, II 2: 26–40), and the idea of *mutatio regnorum* (idem, II 1: 520 ff.). Cf. 99/12–100/15 below.

98/58 *may*: In Middle English, the verb 'may' can mean 'may be', 'may do' or 'may go', see *MED*, s.v. 'mouen' 6. In Chaucer, for example, 'gon' is implied: 'For it was nyght, and forther myghte they noght' (*CT*, 'The Reeve's Tale', p. 81/A4117); in Gower, 'don' is implied: 'Ther is no sleihte at thilke nede,/ Which eny loves faitour mai' (*Confessio*, 1: 688–9). The *MED* does not record an instance of 'may' with the implied sense 'may reach', as would seem required here. Either this is a rare instance of an omitted word in manuscript G or an example of an unrecorded use of 'may' in the requisite extended sense. See Glossary s.v. 'moun'.

99/66 *Seynt Pouyl*: Phil. 2: 10: 'ut in nomine Iesu omne genu flectatur caelestium, terrestrium et infernorum'. The GO: 'Hic aperit cui datum sit nomen dei, cui omnis creatura flectit genu, id est, deo. Sed forte diceretur quod homo adoptione debemus esset. Et sic Christis ex parte verus deus, ex parte adoptiuus erit. Adoptiuo autem deo non flectit genu creatura, sed vero. Constat autem Christum verus deus esse cui flectitur genu, non adoptiuum' (4: 383b).

99/68 *foure partyis of þe hous*: The use of the evangelical symbols as charms to ward off bad weather and evil spirits probably originates in the popular use of gospel extracts as good luck spells. The late-medieval 'primers' containing short texts from each of the gospels are discussed by Duffy (1992), pp. 214–7. See *The Oxford Dictionary of Nursery Rhymes*, No. 346, pp. 303–5, for the 'nursery prayer' known as the 'White Paternoster'; the Opies' bibliography attests to its popularity. Cf. F. J. Mone, 'Quadriforme crucis signum', *Lateinische Hymnen*, 1: 144. See also Rock, who gives an example of the prayer (3: 108–9, and note 49). It is notable that Pauper, for all his theological sophistication, here gives a sympathetic word to the use of the apostolic symbols as good luck charms against the Devil.

99/1 *ymages so hydde*: See 89/42 above.

99/12–100/15 *Lentoun . . . Adamis synne*: The liturgy connects the four seasons of the year with the four ages of human history. Durandus specifies the four ages as Adam to Moses (winter), Moses to Christ (spring), life of Christ and the early Church (summer), and Ascension to Judgement (autumn): *Rationale, CCCM* cxlA, 6.1.1–5 (pp. 120 ff.).

100/15–16 *Septuagesyme*: So-called because it is (or is approximately) the seventieth day before Easter; it is the third Sunday before Lent and the ninth before Easter. It marks the beginning of the 'winter' season of the Church year.

100/33 *ad Colocens. iii [5]*: The GO argues that covetousness is a form of idolatry because the greedy man attempts to take for himself what is freely given to all who ask (4: 392b). Cf. 166/12–13, 2–78/60, 2–264/57 below.

100/37 *shoon of syluer*: Dugdale's *Monasticon* provides an inventory of some of the possessions of pre-Reformation Lincoln Cathedral, s.v. 'Imagines':

A gret Image of our Lady sitting in a Chair, Silver and Gilt, with four Polls, two of them having Arms in the top before, having upon her Head a Crown, Silver and Gilt, set with Stones and Pearls about her Neck, and an Owche depending thereby, having in her hand a Scepter with one Flower, set with Stones & Pearls, and one Bird in the top thereof; and her Child sitting upon his Knee, with one Crown on his Head with a Diadem set with Pearls and Stones; having a Ball with a Cross, Silver and Gilt, in his Left-hand, and at either of his Feet a Scutcheon of Arms, with Arms . . . Relicks of the Eleven thousands Virgins closed in a head of Silver and Gilt, and standing upon a Foot of Copper and Gilt, having a Garland with Stones of divers colours, weithing Seventy one Ounces . . . (3: 273).

Among thefts from London churches in 1393, *The Westminster Chronicle* records '500 marks' worth of jewels' and 'a very valuable cross and jewels and fabrics, some of silk and others of velvet, worth altogether 1,000 marks' (ed. Hector and Harvey, pp. 512–13).

101/46 *þe feet*: Dives' claim that Pauper had once told him that 'feet' symbolized 'mannys loue and his affeccioun' is perhaps an in-joke: there may be a hidden reference to Ps. 35 [36]: 12: 'Non veniat mihi pes superbiae' and perhaps further to St Augustine's exegesis of it, in which he explains that the Fall of Man began with the 'foot of pride' (*Enarr.*, 35.17; *CCL* xxxviii, pp. 334–6; *PL* 36: 353). Interpretation of the feet as man's love and affection is found in Wyclif's Latin sermons and also in the Wycliffite sermons (Wyclif, *Serm.* 3: 466/7 ff.; *EWS* 1, E51/68–70; *EWS* 3, xv; *WLP*, p. 140/2980–1).

101/2 *Matthei iv* [*10*]: The GO (marginal) here introduces the terms *latria* and *dulia*: 'Grece latreosis latria seruitus dicitur. Seruitus communis deo et homini & cuicumque grece dulia dicitur. Illa vero soli deo debetur: latria distincte, vnde ydolatria, que quod soli deo debet ydolis dat' (4: 15a). See 102/17–21 below.

101/4 *Deutero. vi* [*13–14*]: Deut. 6: 13–14: '. . . cave diligenter ne obliviscaris Domini, qui eduxit te de terra Aegypti, de domo servitutis. Dominum Deum tuum timebis, et illi soli servies, ac per nomen illius iurabis./ Non ibitis post deos alienos cunctarum gentium quae in circuitu vestro sunt.' It is the phrase 'illi soli servies' that puzzles Dives. LL4: 'þu schalt dredin þin lord god & seruyn hym aloone, & þu schalt swerin be his name whanne þee nedith to swerin' (fo. 102ᵛᵃ). Deut. 6: 13–14 cited below 232/84.

102/9 *ad Gala. v* [*13*]: Ad Gal. 5: 13: GO, citing Augustine: 'Non per affectus carnis charitas habenda est sed per spiritum' (4: 366a).

102/11 [*I Pet. 2: 18*]: 'Servi subditi in omni timore dominis, non tantum bonis et modestis sed etiam discolis'; the GO: Huc usque exhortatus est liberos ad subjectionem nunc servis loquitur, vt et ipsi subiecti sint dominus (4: 523). '[I]n þe same place' (102/13 below) refers to the previous verse, I Pet. 2: 17: 'Omnes honorate, fraternitatem diligite, Deum timete, regem honorificate'; see 106/55 below.

102/17–21 *latria . . . dulia*: Augustine advocated (for lack of satisfactory Latin terms) the use of Greek λατρεια and δυλια to distinguish the worship of God from the honour owed to men (*De civ. dei*, 10.3; *CCL* xlvii, p. 275; *PL* 41: 280; *Quest. in Hepta.* 2: 94 [*PL* 34: 631). Thomas Aquinas distinguished *latria* from *dulia*: '. . . alia veneratione veneramur Deum, quod pertinet ad latriam; et alia veneratione quasdam excellentes creaturas, quod pertinet ad duliam' (*ST*, II–II.84.1), taking account of the Incarnation: '. . . quia in novo Testamento Deus factus est homo, potest in sui imagine corporali adorari'. He distinguished between the *latria* owed to Christ or images of Christ and the absence of any honour owed to the stone or wood of which the image is made (*ST*, III. 25. 3). Aquinas' argument depends on a time-honoured threefold distinction: there is (1) the ultimate object of worship (God), (2) the immaterial *image* of the object of worship (God suggested or depicted by the material image, and (3) the material out of which the image is fashioned (wood, stone, silver). The first two are owed *latria*; the third (at best) *dulia*. For a historical survey, Pelikan (1974) 2: 91–145.

102/35 *Autisioderensis*: William of Auxerre (d. 1231) distinguishes between the divine and human aspects of Christ, reserving *latria* for the divine and *superdulia* for the human aspect of Christ (and for angels). He is aware of differing opinons, but says:

Iste due opiniones possunt reduci ad concordiam vt illa que dicit que
caro christi adoranda est latria loquatur per accidens. Aliis que dicit que
dulia loquatur per se. Concedimus enim que caro christi est adoranda
tantum dulia per se, sed per accidens latria (*Summa aurea*, facs. edn.,
fo. 170rb).

He thus makes use of the formula of transubstantiation, but he notes that
dulia is 'duplex'

> vna que dicitur conperdulia quasi superior dulia, qua honoratur caro
> cristi et crux cristi, conperdulia, qua adoratur caro cristi, nichil aliud est
> quam professio, que caro cristi est causa redemptionis nostre (idem).

Pauper draws on this same text for the word 'protestacyoun' (William's
'protestatio'), and for 'herte, speche and dede' (103/42–3 below): 'corde/
ore/opera, corde profitemur diuinam maiestatem, per fidem et sapientam . . .
Ore profitemur diuinam maiestatem orando deum vt fontem omnium
honorum, opere profitemur sacrificando / genuflectendo et similibus'
(idem, fo. 169ra).

103/54 *Mt. 5: 33*: Referred to at greater length in the context of
Commandment II (see, e.g., 232/81, 233/17–18 below).

103/60–1 [*Ps. 75: 12*] . . . *stockys ne stonys*: Note that 'nought to ymagys,
stockys ne stonys' is added to the translation. The line is drawn between 'to'
the image and 'before' the image. Augustine: 'Non sitis pigri ad uouendum;
non enim uiribus uestris implebitis' (*Enarr.*, 75.16; *CCL* xxxix, p. 1048/3–4;
PL 36: 967). Cf. the trial of Johannes Burell in Tanner (1977), p. 73.

104/9–10 *Ricardus de Media Villa*: The passage referred to here appears in
Richard of Middleton's (d. c1300–9) *Commentum super IV Sententianum* in
the context of a discussion of *latria* and *dulia*: 'Cum enim homo per latriam
genuaflectit, recognoscit se non posse stare in virtute, nisi per Deum; tum se
prosternit, recogniscit se, que caderet in nihil, nisi manu teneretur a Deo:
cum autem per duliam praedicta exhibentur, recognoscit homo aliquam
superioritatem in illo, cui ista exhibet, per quam eum potest vivere, non
tamen sicut principalis actor' (Bk. III, c. 9, qu. 5; facs. *Manuscripta*, St
Louis, Mo., p. 95). See below 2–221/43–4.

106/38 *Doctor Halys*: Alexander of Hales (c1185-c1245), in his discussion of
the first Commandment in his *Summa theologica*, says: 'Dicendum quod
latria vel servitus uno modo dicitur vel accipitur pro illis quae exhibentur in
cultu, sicut sunt thurificationes, oblationes, genuiflexiones et huismodi' (De
primo precaepto, q. 2, ti. 1; edn. p. 444b), and 'Honor qui debetur Deo est
honor latriae, qua homo protestatur Deum sicut suum conditorem; honor
vero qui debetur homini est honor duliae' (De quarto praecepto, art. 3; edn.
p. 509a). Modern scholars doubt Alexander of Hale's authorship of this
work; see Glorieux, 2: 15–24; *ODCC*, s.v.. I have been unable to find

specific mention of the symbolism of kneeling on one or two knees. Cf. 104/ 9–10 above.

106/50 *Seynt Austyn vp þe Sauteer*: The reference is to Augustine's *Enarr. in Ps.* (in *CCL* xxxviii, cccix, xl; *PL* 36, 37), but I have not found a passage closely paralleling the sense of: No person is so wicked that he does not serve God in something.

106/55 [*I Pet. 2: 17*]: Referred to above 102/11 and below, 334/37–60, 347/18–26, 354/16–18, and LL4, fo. 34vb.

106/56–7 [*Rom. 12: 10*] . . . *qhoso may ferst*: 'Caritatem fraternitatis invicem diligentes honore invicem praevenientes'. The sense of the Middle English is perhaps 'Be the first, if you can, to honour others', an awkward English rendering of Latin 'prevenientes': coming first or anticipating. The translation in LL4, fo. 132ra is: 'be ʒe besi eche of ʒow fyrst to worschepin oþer be weye of charite'. Cf. the EV: '. . . comynge bifore to gidere in honour' (FM 4: 329a), and the Douai-Rheims tr.: '. . . with honour preventing one another' (1899 edn.; repr. 1989). All other manuscripts of *D&P* omit 'ferst'.

107/7–8 *latria . . . dulia*: See 102/17–21 above.

107/9 *Philosofre*: Pauper refers (however indirectly) to Aristotle's *Nicomachean Ethics*, section 3 on pride: 'Nor, again, would he be worthy of honour if he were bad; for, honour is the prize of excellence, and it is to the good that it is rendered' (*Oxford Aristotle*, 2: 1774/21–2. Cited below 337/14–18.

108/29 *þe lewyd mannys book*: See 82/42–4 above.

108/29note *as kalendyrs*: The scribe of H adds 'as kalendyrs' to amplify the meaning of 'bokys'; the meaning of 'kalendyrs' here is 'guides, patterns, or models'. In William Thorpe's 'Testimony' (early fifteenth century), the word 'kalender' is used in an argument on one side of the debate about the legitimacy of church images:

> But þe keruynge, þe ʒetynge, neiþer þe peyntynge of ymagerie wiþ mannus hond, al be it þat þis doinge be accept of men of hiʒeste astaat and dignite, and ordeyned of hem to be a kalender to lewde men . . . owiþ not to be worschipid in þis foorme. . . . (*TWT*, p. 36/1071–76).

108/36 *De con. di.iii*, [*c. 28*] *Venerabiles*: See 90/20 above.

108/47 *cros*: Lyndwood's *Provinciale* (1433) summarizing the distinction between *latria* and *dulia*, citing Aquinas, leaves open the question of adoration of the actual material cross on which Christ died. The believer must, with some mental agility, separate in his mind the material from which the cross is made and the image brought to mind by the sight of it:

> Si autem [imago Christi] consideretur ut Imago, tunc quia idem motus est in Imagem, inquantum est Imago et Imaginatem, unus honor debetur Imagini et Imaginato. Et ideo cum Christus Latria adoretur

ejus Imago debet similiter Latria adorari (Bk. III, ti. 27, rubrics, p. 252b; 1679 edn.).

John of Damascus is uncompromising: 'Adoremus autem et typum pretiosae crucis, etsi ex alia materia facta est, non materiam honorantes; absit!' (*De Fide*, ed. E. M. Buytaert (1955), pp. 92–3). Pauper strikes an uncertain note, seeming to say that the wood of the original cross may be venerated with *hyperdulia*—though the cross as image of Christ may be given *latria*: authorities disagree; he claims that he is merely doing his best to disambiguate the English word 'worship' so that the wider range of Latin terms for the same word can be understood by Dives in the vernacular (cf. *Chastising of God's Children*, late fourteenth century: 'it passiþ fer my wit to shewe ȝou in any maner vulgare [in English] þe termes of diuinite' (ed. Bazire and Colledge, p. 95). Pauper's views should not be confused with those he is trying to correct. Compare Sawtre's (1401) replies to his inquisitors' questions about the worship of the cross, McNiven (1987), pp. 83–5; see also *Speculum Christiani* (1360's-1370's), ed. Holmstedt (EETS, 182), pp. 186–90; *Speculum Sacerdotale* (early fifteenth century), ed. Weatherly (EETS, 200), p. 1; *TWT*, pp. 56–61; *WLP*, p. 229/2831–42.

110/20 *Seynt Austyn*: The sense indicates that the passage is in Augustine's *De civ. dei*, 10.4: 'Multa denique de cultu divino usurpata sunt quae honoribus deferrentur humanis, sive humilitate nimia sive adulatione pestifera', etc. (*CCL* xlvii, p. 276/3–5; *PL* 41: 281).

110–13/1–74 *Thuryficacioun*: The Christian symbolism of the rite of censing is spelled out by Durandus (*Rationale*, *CCCM* cxl, 4.10–11, pp. 291/15–20; 292/1–6). See Rock 1: 161–4, especially his notes on thuribles.

111/28 *Dirigatur . . .* : In the Mass, an antiphon sung or recited after the Epistle. In the Sarum rite, this is the Gradual (*gradale*) for Feria iii, Dominica xix after Holy Trinity, and the fourth Sunday of September (*Sarum Missal*, ed. Legg, pp. 58, 190, 200). Also see Durandus, *Rationale* (*CCCM* cxl, 4.19; pp. var.–30).

112/46–7 *þe wyse man*: Ecclus. 35: 21: 'Oratio humiliantis se nubes penetrabit, et donec propinquet non consolabitur, et non discedet donec aspiciat Altissimum.' The GO: 'Ad superiora respicit affirmans quia dominus orationem humilium misericorditer exaudit, qui non cessant donec consolationem accipiant' (2: 780). Cited below, 199/16–17.

112/47 *missal . . . gospel*: Two of the liturgical books for the conduct of the Mass; the Missal contains the Antiphonary, the Gradual, the Epistolary, the Evangeliary, the Ordo, and the Sacramentary. The Gospel here would be the book containing the lections for the Mass.

113/1–116/76 *est*: Augustine says: '. . . cum ad orationem stamus, ad orientem conuertimur, unde caelum surgit; non tamquam ibi habitet deus . . .

sed ut admoneatur animus ad naturam excellentiorem se conuertere, id est
ad deum . . .' *De Ser. Dom. in Mon.* II, 5,18 (*CCL* xxxv, p. 108). John of
Damascus makes the same arguments (*De fide*, Bk. 4, c. 12; ed. Buytaert,
pp. 304–6). Honorius Augustodunensis (early twelfth century) lists three
reasons why the Christian worshipper should face east: (1) Paradise is in the
east, (2) Christ means 'sun', (3) the sun rises in the east, and Christ, the sun
of justice, will reappear in the east (*PL* 172: 575). Durandus says a church
must be built 'ut caput recte inspiciatur uersus orientem' *Rationale*, *CCCM*
cxl, 1.8; p. 15/107–14. Rock, 2: 380 & note. Cf. 114/21–2 below.

114/8 *Di. xi, Ecclesiasticarum*: The canon 'Ecclesiasticarum' occurs in a
section of Gratian's *Decretum* containing a list of customs handed down by
the Church which are not contained in the Bible. The answer to the
question, 'Que orientem uersus nos orare litterum forma docuit?' is given in
the chapter heading: 'Inuiolabilis est consuetudo, que nec humanis legibus
nec sacris canonibus obuiare monstratur' (D. 1 c. 11; Friedberg 1: 24). An
English translation of this passage, with the Ordinary Gloss, can be found in
Gratian, tr. Thompson (1993), p. 39.

114/21–2 *Crist deyid westward . . . [Io. 19: 30]*: The cardinal points, north,
south, east and west, were invested with Christian symbolism. As the east
symbolised the reappearance of Christ at the Second Coming, so the west
symbolized the crucifixion and the descent of Christ into the darkness of the
tomb. The nearest the GO comes to a mention of east and west is (on Matt.
27: 46): 'Cum inclinata est dies ad vesperam & tepefactus est sol a feruore,
passionem consummat, ostendens se mori propter peccata nostra quibus a
diuina luce et dilectione in hanc noctem cecidimus. Mane surrexit dominus
docens resuscitatos in anima se esse perducturum in lucem aeternae
felicitatis' (4: 86). See 113/1–116/76 above.

115/36 *[Mt. 27: 40]*: ' " . . . et in triduo illud reaedificat, salva temet
ipsum" '. GO: 'Praedictum erat in libro sapientiae, "morte turpissima
condemnemus eum". . . .quia ergo crucifigebatur & non liberabantur,
credebant illum non esse dei filium, propterea pendenti a ligno insultant
& caput agitant' [Sap. 2: 20]' (4: 85).

115/57 *Oriens*: Zech. 6: 12: 'Ecce vir Oriens nomen eius, et subter eum
orietur, et aedificabit templum Domino.' There is no foundation for the
etymology (if it is one) given here; Isidore of Seville (c560–636), says that
'Crist' comes from the same root as 'Chrisma' (*Etym.*, Bk. VI, c. 19: 50); cf.
Augustine: 'Messias hebraice, Christus graece est, latine Vnctus. Ab
unctione enim dicitur Christus. Crisma unctio est graece; ergo Christus,
unctus', *In Ioh.*, 7.14 (*CCL* xxxvi, p. 74/6–8; *PL* 35: 1444)

116/75 *an hundryd disciplys and twenty*: Acts 1: 15: '. . . erat autem turba
hominum simul fere centum viginti'; the number 120 is (apocryphally)
connected with the Ascension described in Acts 1: 9. The GO explains the

number 120, the age of Moses at his death, as a sign that Jesus was the successor of Moses and the one who would lead his people into the Promised Land (4: 453). Nicolaus de Lyra says the number 120 merely stands for 'many' persons (*Postilla* 4).

116/79 *Ezechielis viii* [*16*]: '. . . et ecce in ostio templi Domini inter vestibulum et altare quasi viginti quinque viri dorsa habentes contra templum Domini et facies ad orientem et adorabant ad ortum solis'. The GO: 'Signat xxv viros qui in quadrum solida statione fundati sunt, et a quinque sensibus, per quinquies quinque figuram efficiunt quadranguli, non solum templum habere post tergum sed instar ydolorus applicare ad nares suas ramum palmarum . . . vt per hoc eos ydola adora significet' (3: 240). The passage is part of a sixth-century BC vision of the destruction of the Jerusalem temple.

116/87 [*Ps. 112: 3*]: Applied by Augustine to the imperative of preaching, with humility and without vainglory: 'Deum decet, Dominum decet et semper et ubique praedicare' (*Enarr. in Ps.*, CCL xl, p. 1630/33–4; PL 37: 1471).

117/91 *Leo Papa*: Pope Leo the Great (d. 461) in a Nativity sermon deplores sun worship:

De talibus institutis etiam illa generatur impietas, ut sol in inchoatione diurnae lucis exsurgens a quibusdam insipientioribus de locis eminentioribus adoretur; quod non nulli etiam Christiani adeo se religiose facere putant. . . . (*PL* 54: 218–219).

See also F. J. Doelger, *Sol salutis* (1920), pp. 1–20. See 113/1–116/76, 114/ 21–2 and 115/57 above.

117/3–43 *þe craft of astronomy*: Isidore of Seville defined the difference between 'astronomy' and 'astrology':

Inter Astronomiam autem et Astrologiam aliquid differt. Nam Astronomia caeli conversionem, ortus, obitus motusque siderum continet, vel qua ex causa ita vocentur. Astrologia vero partim naturalis, partim superstitiosa est. Naturalis, dum exequitur solis et lunae cursus, vel stellarum certas temporum stationes. Superstitiosa vero est illa quam mathematici [astrologers] sequuntur, qui in stellis auguriantur, quique etiam duodecim caeli signa per singula animae vel corporis membra disponunt, siderumque cursu nativitates hominum et mores praedicare conantur (*Etym.* 2: 3.27.6–15).

Augustine had set the tone in Bk. 4 of the *Confessions*: 'These imposters therefore whom they style astrologers . . .' (LCL 26, 1: 152–3). He attacks astrology at greater length in *De civ. dei.*, 5.1–11 (CCL xlvii, pp. 128–42; PL 41: 139–54). Aquinas says that 'if anyone observes the stars in order to prognosticate casual or fortuitous events, or indeed to know for certain about the future activities of men, he acts on false and vain premisses and involves himself with demons and in illicit superstition; if he uses observation of the stars to predict events caused by the stars, such as drought, rain and the like, this will not constitute illicit or superstitious divination' (*ST* II–II.95.5). John Gower's *Confessio Amantis* (1390) reflects the opposition of the Church (ed. Macaulay, 2: 251/646–54). Lydgate's 1426 translation of Deguileville's *The Pilgrimage of the Life of Man* (*c*.1355) has a debate between 'Astrology' and 'Pilgrim' on this issue which marshals all the familiar arguments (ed. Furnivall, EETS es 77, 83, 92, pp. 534–551). On astrology and Gower, Chaucer and their contemporaries, see Wedel (1920), pp. 100–156. On Chaucer and astrology, Wood (1970), *passim*. On Wycliffite hostility to astronomy, *English Works*, ed. F. D. Matthew (EETS os 74), p. 225.

119/1 *Genesis i* [*14–19*]: Genesis 1: 14: 'Et sint in signa et tempora et dies et annos'. The time-keeping function of the heavenly bodies is insisted on in the commentaries: they are not deities in their own right. The GO says: 'De sole quippe certum est que circuitum compleat trecentis, lxv diebus et quadrante, qui est annus solaris' etc. (1: 12).

119/19 *Ecclesiastes iii* [*22*]: For [22] read [1]: 'Omnia tempus habent et suis spatiis transeunt universa sub caelo.' GO: 'incertum et fluctuantem statum conditionis humanae superdocuit, nunc omnia in mundo esse contraria, & nihil stare perpetuum eorum, sci., quae sub sole fiunt, & intra tempus quia substantiae spirituales nec loco nec tempore continentur' (2: 697). Cited below 144/16.

120/32 *lawe*: 'Non liceat Christianis tenere traditiones gentilium et obser-uare uel colere elementa, aut lunae aut stellarum cursus aut inanem signorum fallaciam . . .' (C. 26 q. 5 c. 3; Friedberg 1: 1027). The canon 'Non liceat' is more a list of forbidden superstitions than a distinction between signs and causes. Cited below 159/49–59.

120/34–41 *horlege . . . clokke*: When *D&P* was written, weight-driven clocks (as distinguished from earlier water-driven clocks) had been used in England for a little more than a century but were far from commonplace. They were evidently first used in monastic communities in which monks or friars kept a regular schedule of prayers. A clockwork mechanism for ringing the bells in church towers preceded clocks with dials. *The Westminster Chronicle* records that in 1390 in a period of scarcity 'the mayor of London caused a proclamation to be made throughout the city that no stranger should make, or stand ready to make, any sale in the city after the clock had struck eleven [ultra pulsacionem xj. in signo]', ed. Hector and Harvey (1982), pp. 452–3. On the etymology and history of clock, bell and orloge, see A. G. Rigg (1983), pp. 255–74); Mooney (1993), pp. 191–9.

120/47–73 *instrumentys of God's gouernaunce*: In Pauper's comparison with
the blacksmith, there is an implied balance between God's ordinate and His
absolute power: just as a blacksmith has control over the edge of the knife or
axe he is sharpening and over the motion of the grindstone but is
constrained by the nature of the materials and the limits of his skill and
strength, so God is constrained by the nature of His creation once He has
set it in motion. God, the instrument-maker, is said to have 'ordeynyd' the
heavenly bodies to move 'in on certeyn cours . . . queche cours þey schullyn
kepyn into þe day of doom' (121/60 below); this is a God whose power is
'ordinate', keeping to the rules laid down at the beginning. Mainly, this
seems to be Pauper's view. At the end of the chapter, however, Pauper
appears to fall into a contradiction: 'þe planetys . . . alwey þey been redy to
fulfellyn þe wyl of God' (121/71–3 below). This evokes a God who is
always poised to alter the machinery, a God of 'absolute', arbitrary power;
cf. Peter Lombard, for whom the power of God was limited; He, for
example, could not will evil (*Sentences* I.42. cc. 1–3); and Thomas Aquinas,
ST I.25.1–6. See 121/1–7, 178/25–7 below.

121/1–7 *God may doon . . . qhat he wele*: Dives seems to ignore Pauper's
comparison between God and a blacksmith of Cap. xviii (God's ordinate
power) and to react only to his final, loosely-phrased reference to God's
absolute power (see above 120/47–73). Cf.Chaucer's 'necessitee condicioneel' in his 'Nun's Priests's Tale' (*CT*, 258–9/3243–50. Pauper likewise opts
for 'necessitee condicioneel', a view consistent with Robert Holcot's position
on future contingents (see his 'Quodlibet III' in *Robert Holcot: Seeing the
Future Clearly*, ed. Streveler and Tachau (1995), p. 76 and *passim*). Cf. Leff
(1957), pp. 23–34; Delatorre (1987), pp. 57–60 and *passim*.

122/27–32 *Ionas*: God's repentance is found in the Book of Jonah 3: 10: 'Et
vidit Deus opera eorum quia conversi sunt a via sua mala et misertus est
Deus super malitiam quam locutus fuerat ut faceret eis et non fecit'. The
GO: 'Videns mutata opera libenter mutat sententiam . Potius dicamus que
perseuerauit in proposito suo, *a principio volens miseri . . .*' (3: 402). This
interpretation remains consistent with Augustine, *De civ. dei*, 5.10 (*CCL*
xlvii, pp. 140–1; *PL* 41: 152) and Aquinas (*ST* I.9.1). Cf. *EWS* 1, Ep. Serm.
4/126.

122/33 *ferthe . . . Kynggys [20: 1–7]*: 2 Kgs. 20: 2–3, 6: Hezekiah 'convertit
faciem suam ad parietem et oravit Dominum dicens,/ Obsecro Domine
memento quomodo ambulaverim coram te in veritate et in corde perfecto et
quod placitum est coram te fecerim, flevit itaque Ezechias fletu magno'.
Isaiah then says to Hezekiah: '. . . et addam diebus tuis quindecim annos'.
The GO (addressing the question of foreknowledge): 'Nec praefixum in
praescientia dei temporis vitae prolongatum est, sed illud quod peccando
amiserat ex largitate dei redditum' (2: 171).

123/44–5 *þe sonne chaungede his cours*: 4 Kgs. 20: 11: Isaiah the Prophet invoked the Lord 'et reduxit umbram per lineas quibus iam descenderat in horologio Ahaz retrorsum decem gradibus'. The GO, after some speculations about the behaviour of the sun's shadow in outlying parts of the world, interprets the ten steps of the sun's shadow as ten stages in world history, from the fall of Lucifer to the Passion and Resurrection of Christ, when the sun of justice ascended again, '& omnem illam vmbram legis veritatis radiis illustrauit' (2: 172).

123/53–56 *De penitencia, di. i, Sufficiat*: The correct reference would seem to be to c. 64, which consists of a brief citation from St Ambrose: 'Nouit Deus mutare sentenciam, si tu noueris emendare delictum' (De poen. D. 1 c. 64; Friedberg 1: 1177). See Ambrose, *In Lucam*, II.33; *PL* 15: 1645.

124/67–70 *Pouyl . . . [Rom. 11: 34]*: The GO says (in summary) that while the Father may be incomprehensible, the Son rational, it is the Spirit that addresses itself to man: 'Si aliquod bonum in aliquo videmus, per spiritum ei datum a patre & filio credimus' (4: 299). Nicolaus de Lyra: 'O altituda': non enim sensus hominis attingit ad discutiendam iusticiam iudiciorum dei seu ad discutiendam gratias gratuitam nullis meritur precedentibus redditam (*Postilla* 4).

124/77–8 *Ps. 24: 10*: Cited in LL4: '[A]ll þe weyys of oure lord arn mercy & trewþe & al his mercy is medlid with trewþe & ry3tfulnesse; he wolde sauyn mankende be swych proces of ry3tfulnesse, be which proces of falsnesse & of þe fendis malice mankende was lost' (fo. 119rb). Augustine on the two ways says: 'Et ideo uniuersae uiae Domini, duo aduentus Filii Dei, unus miserantis, alter iudicantis. Peruenit ergo dum tenens uias eius qui nullis meritis suis se liberatum uidens, deponit superbiam, et deinceps cauet examinantis seueritatem, qui clementiam subuenientis expertus est' (*Enarr.*, 24.10; *CCL* xxxviii, p. 138/4–9; *PL* 36: 185). Cited below 2–26/70–5 and 2–226/45.

125/5–6 *Ptolomenus*: Ptolomy's second-century *Almagest*, with additions by Arabic astronomers, was carried to Spain in the ninth century. Its translation into Latin in 1252 signalized the reemergence of European science, see Thorndike, *The Sphere of Sacrobosco* (1949), pp. 15–16 and *passim*; and Grant, *Planets* (1996), pp. 37–8). The sun, moon and five planets made up seven spheres; an eighth sphere, divided into the primum mobile and the 'fyrmament' (125/26 below), moved with the planets around the earth daily, each sphere moving at its own speed and at the same time moving through the zodiac. It was the function of the astrolabe to provide a model of all these motions, see Wood, *Chaucer* (1970), pp. 298–301; Grant, op. cit., pp. 99; 100–3. Dives here expresses an enlightened view when he says that 'the werkyngge of þe bodyis abouyn' inclines the individual to behave in a certain way but does not necessitate any particular action or actions.

125/6–7 *vir sapiens*: Lydgate's *Pilgrimage* has a version of the supposed Ptolemaic saying 'vir sapiens dominatur astris':

> And in hys Centyloge a-ryht,
> The grete clerk, kyng Tholome,
> Affermeth ther (who lyst to se);
> He seyth (As I reherse kan)
> That in erthe A wyse man
> Haueth domynacioun
> Above ech constellacioun.
>
> (ed. Furnivall (EETS es 77, 83, 92),
> p. 550/20615–20621)

Nicholas Oresme's version is: 'dit Ptholomee que un homme sage a seignourie sur les estoilles' (p. 68); the saying does not in fact appear in the known manuscripts of Ptolemy's *Centiloquium*, and G. W. Coopland says the sentence, 'quoted on every hand from the thirteenth century onwards, presents one of the minor mysteries of history', *Nicholas Oresme* (1952), p. 175.

125/24 *fiue planetys*: See Trevisa's Bartholomaeus 8.11 (*Properties* 1: 475/6–26); cf. E. Grant, *Planets*, pp. 310–23.

125/28–9 *a day naturel . . . noon*: In *c.*1405 there was no single way to set the beginning of a day. Depending on one's purpose, the day could begin at sunrise, noon, or sunset. The 'natural' day, or common day, referred to here comprised the whole period of sunlight—dawn to dusk—and the whole night from dusk to dawn. The 'day artificial' ran 'fro sonne arisyng tyl it go to reste', explained Chaucer's *Astrolabe* (Pt. II: 7/1–22, *CT*, p. 672). Compare William of Conches (d. *c.*1154): 'Naturalis vero dies, viginti quatuor horarum spatium continet' (*PL* 194: 70), and Pseudo-Bede (relying on Isidore of Seville): 'Isidorus diffinivit, dicens: Dies legitimus [naturalis] est viginti quatuor horarum usque dies et nox spatia sui cursus ab oriente in occidentem, solis sui volubilitate concludat', whereas the artificial day was 'ab ortu solis usque ad occasum' and was divided into three parts, 'mane, meridies et suprema' (*De divionibus temporum, PL* 90: 656). The astronomer's day ran from noon of one day to noon of the next, since the meridian provided a fixed point for making calculations: 'To knowe the degre of the sonne . . . . Sek besily with thy rule the highest of the sonne in mydde of the day' (Chaucer, *Astrolabe* 14, *CT*, p. 673). See *The Kalendarium* (1386) of Nicholas of Lynn, ed. and tr. S. Eisner, pp. 58–9/24–26; Lyndwood, *Provinciale* IV, ti. 1 & 2: note, 'De die', to 'De Desponsatione impuberum' (1679 edn., p. 271a). The 'Christian' day, for the purpose of celebrating saints' days, began at dusk, see Trevisa's Bartholomaeus, 9.3 (*Properties*, 1: 520/13–29). For a broad overview of the meaning of time in the Middle Ages, Burrow, *Essays* (1984), pp. 55–94. The clarity of *D&P*, line 29, would be improved by the addition of 'or' before 'from'.

126/34 constellacioun, coniunccioun, respect: An astrological 'constellation' is 'the position of a planet or the moon in relation to the ascendent sign of the zodiac' (*MED* s.v. 'constellacioun'). An astrological 'conjunction' is: 'The apparent proximity of two or more planets or other heavenly bodies; the position of these when they are in the same or two adjoining signs of the zodiac' (*MED* s.v. 'conjunccioun'). Astrological 'respect' or aspect is defined as: 'The relative positions of the heavenly bodies as they appear to an observer on the earth's surface at a given time' (*OED* s.v. 'aspect' II 4). The *MED* (s.v. 'respect(e') cites only this instance in *D&P*; cf. Trevisa's Bartholomaeus 8.9 (*Properties*, 1: 464/28 ff).

127/55–62 Esau and Iacob: See Gen. 25: 21–3. Augustine uses this argument against astrology several times; it appears in *De gen. ad lit.*, Bk. 2, cap. 17: 'Quid ergo vanus quam ut illas constellationes intuens mathematicus, ad eundem horoscopum, ad eandem lunam diceret unum eorum a matre dilectum, alterum non dilectum?' (*PL* 34: 273). See 117/3–43 above.

127/4–6 Genesis 8: 21: The GO cites Gregory's *Moralia* 28.19 (*CCL* cxliiiB, p. 1430/19–25; *PL* 76: 474), which in turn cites Job 38.8 and 1 Cor.3: 7.

127/7 Prouerb. xx [9]: 'Quis potest dicere, Mundum est cor meum, purus sum a peccato?' GO: 'Non dicit, Quis habet, quia dicitur, Beate mundo corde. Et innocens manibus & mundo corde. Sed qui potest dicere quia temeratum est se laudere, et quia sunt qui sua quasi fortia laudant, proximorum quasi vilia despicunt, subdit, "Pondus & pondus" . . .' (2: 677).

128/13 Prouerb. xxix [15]: 'Virga atque correptio tribuit sapientiam; puer autem qui dimittitur voluntati suae confundet matrem suam.' Cited below 324/3.

128/17 Prouerb. xxii [6]: 'Proverbium est adolescens iuxta viam suam; etiam cum senuerit non recedet ab ea.' The GO cites the Horation proverb: 'Quo semel est imbuta, recens seruabit odorem testa diu', adding 'Et graeca narrat historia alexandrum magnum et moribus et incessu leonidis pedagogi sui non potuisse carere et viciis quibus paruus infectus fuerat' (2: 680). See 128/24–5 below.

128/19 ʒong seynt: See Whiting S19 (p. 500). *ME Serm.* (fourth quarter of the fourteenth century: 'Itt is a comond [*sic*] prouerbe bothe of clerkes and of laye men, "ʒounge seynt, old dewell"' (ed. Ross, EETS, 209, p. 159/37–39). J. A. Burrow (1984). citing its use in *D&P*, studies the proverb's sources and wide use (*Essays*, pp. 177–91).

128/22 Trenorum iii [27]: LL4: '& þerfore Jeremye seyth þat yt ys good to a man whenne he hath born þe ʒok of our lord from hys ʒougthe' (fo. 68ʳᵃ).

GO: 'scilicet, solitarium sedere et tacere, haec omnia bona excludo est ut sederat solus cum deo qui se sentit portare graue iugum a iuuentute sua. . . . Hoc iugum propter austeritatem correctionis graue est, sed spe remunerationis suaue, qui hoc iugum tulerit cum deo solitarius sedebit non mixtus negociorum uel disideriorum turbis: tacebit ab omno strepito saeculi uel excusatio peccati non erit necessaria illi' (3: 202).

128/24–5 *Quod noua testa capit*: Pauper uses a much-cited old saw to answer Dives' old saw in 128/17 above. 'Quod semel est imbuta recens, servabit odorem testa diu' derives from Horace (Ep. I, 2/69–70; *Horace, Satires*, ed. Fairclough, LCL 194, p. 266). It is cited by Augustine in *De civ. dei*, 1.3 (*CCL* xlvii, p. 3/10–11; *PL* 41: 16). It is cited in the GO without attribution in reference to Prov. 22: 6 (2: 680; see 128/17 above); by John of Wales, *Communiloquium* (2.2.1); in Arundel's 1408 *Constitutions*, (Lyndwood, 66a, at end (1679 edn.) on instructing the young in orthodox doctrine and ruling out public or private disputations on such matters. Whiting (S240) cites Osbern Bokenham, who says: 'For, as longe to-forne be a poete was tolde,/ What newe shelle taketh it sauouryth olde (*Legendys*, ed. Sergeantson, EETS, 206, p. 45/1649–50). See 128/17 above.

129/36–47 *þe husbonde and þe wyf moun synnyn togedere*: This excursus on the conceiving and upbringing of children fits better into the discussion in *D&P*'s sixth Precept, especially cap. i; see note 2–58/18. Here Pauper gives a hint of the unusually sympathetic view of the position of women he will develop later when he says: 'Neuertheles þe synne is in the askere nought in þe 3eldere' (129/41). The possibility of sinful behaviour between licitly married couples is a standard part of the penitential manual. Thomas of Chobham's *Summa* opens the section on 'coitu coniugali' by warning that a man can sin mortally with his own wife and goes on to discuss 'impetuosus coitus':

. . . coitus propter saturandam libidinem per meretricias blanditias: quidam autem fit in membro mulieris non ad hoc concesso; quidam autem coitus fit in tempore prohibito; quidam etiam coitus impetuosis est cum muliere pregnanti vicina partui, vel cum menstruata, vel cum decubante in puerperio . . . (ed. Broomfield, pp. 333–5).

Cf. John of Wales, *Communiloquium*: 'Sapiens vir amare debet uxorem casto iudicio non affectu meretricio' (2.4.5); See 2–58/18, 2–62/6–22 below.

129/51–62 *synne . . . sekenesse*: The NT unequivocally links sin and physical illness. John 9: 41: 'Dixit eis Iesus: Si caeci essetis, non haberitis peccatum'. Jas. 5: 14–15: 'Infirmatur quis in vobis? inducat presbyters Ecclesiae, et orent super eum . . . et oratio fidei salvabit infirmum et alleviabit eum Dominus: et si in peccatis sit, remittentur ei'. The author of *D&P* is less conventional when he adds a comment on preventive medicine. Trevisa's Bartholomaeus 6.4 says the mother-to-be 'schal be reuled in good diete',

(*Properties*, 1: 299/14]). St Bridget's *Liber* says: 'All þe strenghe þat a child hase in þe wombe is of þe kynde of þe fadir and modir. And some tyme þat matir þat is consayued, for some indispocicioun of sekenes in þe *fadir or modir*, is febill and noȝt so stronge þat it may abide, wherefor it is hasti to dede' (italics added; ed. Ellis (EETS, 291), 1: 371/19–22).

130/64 *Ion ix* [*39*]: For [39] read [3]: 'Respondit Iesus, 'Neque hic peccavit neque parentes eius, sed ut manifestetur opera Dei in illo'. Chrysostom, *In Ioanem* (Hom. 56): 'Non autem ex hoc ostendit quod alii caeci facti sunt propter peccata parentum: neque enim contingit uno peccante alium puniri' (*CA*, 2: 464; *PG* 59: 306–7 has the sense but not the exact words). Augustine comments that neither the blind man nor his parents were free of original sin, but the blind man was not born blind because of any sin he or his parents had committed (*CA*, 2: 464; *In Ioh.*, 44.3; *CCL* xxxvi, pp. 382–3; *PL* 35: 1714–15).

130/1–2 *vndir dyuers sygnys*: The 'signs' are the twelve segments of the zodiac. According to 'judicial astronomy', or astrology, each of the 'signs' is further correlated with the planets, the sun and moon, the four elements, the calendar, and human destiny. See, e.g., the 'Tabula' in the *Kalendarium* of Nicholas of Lynn (1386), ed. & tr. S. Eisner (1980), pp. 180–1. See also Trevisa's Bartholomaeus 8.9–17 (*Properties*, 1: 460–94). See 117/3–43, 125/ 5–6 and 126/34 above.

131/8 *sexe hundryd myle on lengthe*: The 'mile' did not become a standard-ized distance until modern times, Compare Bede: 'Quae per milia passum octingenta in boream longa, latitudinis habet milia ducenta' (*Ecclesias. Hist.*, ed. Colgrave and Mynors (1969), pp. 1–2; tr. *Opera*, LCL 246, 1: 10–11). Since it is the realm and not the entire island that is referred to, perhaps *D&P*'s 600 miles is approximately right. It is more accurate than Trevisa's Bartholomeus 15.15, which gives the size of 'Anglia' (citing Pliny, Orosius and Isidore) as 'aboute eyght and fourty syþes fyue and seuentie myle' (*Properties*, 2: 734). On the other hand, 'mile' and 'statute mile' are not the same; in this period 'mile' may mean modern 1 1/2 miles, see *William Worcestre Itineraries*, ed. J. H. Harvey (1969), p. xv. See also 'The Shires and Hundreds of England' (Jesus Coll. MS 29, fo. 267^r: 'Engle lond is. eyhte hundred Myle long. from penwyþ steorte . . . þe breade of Engle londe is. þreo hundred myle brod', *Old English Miscellany*, ed. Morris (EETS os 49), p. 145.

131/12 *make monye*: Counterfeiting was as much an underworld activity in early fifteenth-century England as in all prior and subsequent money-using societies. See *Calendar of Inquisitions* Vol. 7, ¶s 28, 537, 539, 570, 572–3, for prosecutions in this period. Cf. J. G. Bellamy, *Crime and Public Order* (1973), pp. 64–5, on 'one of the most skilful and daring of medieval criminals . . . the seal counterfeiter'.

132/4 *Seynt Gregory*: Gregory's Homily X on Matt. 2: 1–12, replying to the heretical Priscillianists, who claimed that the star of the Magi was created to guide the earthly life of Christ, says 'non puer ad stellam, sed stella ad puerum cucurrit . . . non stella fatum pueri, sed fatum stellae is qui apparuit puer fuit' (*PL* 76(2): 1112).

133/29–34 *For it was noo planete ne sterre of þe firmament*: The star of the Magi—as a true prognostication of the time and place of the birth of Christ—was sometimes used as an argument in favour of judicial astronomy (modern astrology), as Dives' speech (132/12–17 above) illustrates. Against this, Pauper makes the scientifically well–informed argument that the smallest star in the firmament is larger than the earth; hence the 'star' of the Magi was not a natural star but a special creation. The early Church generally opposed astrological divination, its opposition culminating in Augustine's unequivocal Book 5 of *De civ. dei* (see above 117/3–43). But for all such condemnations the star of the Magi remained a 'stumbling-block': one response to the star was that astrology had been permitted until the coming of Christ. Another was Chrysostom's more influential argument that the star was not a real star but a pro tem creation, a miracle (*Hom. in Mt.*, Hom. 6, *PG* 56: 61 ff.; and Ps.-Chrysostom *Op. imperf.*, Hom. 2, *PG* 56: 636–8). William Herebert (d. 1333), in an Epiphany sermon, follows these predecessors and Peter Comestor in saying the star was a special creation, not a star or comet (*Works*, ed. S. R. Reimer (1987), p. 50). This view is echoed in a 1413 sermon: 'þis stere was no fix stere in heven, noþur no planete . . . but it was a comete, stella comata, new made by þe myghty powre of almyȝthy God' (*ME Sermons*, ed. Ross (EETS, 209), p. 227/8–11). See *CA* 1: 31–5, citing commentary on the star of the Magi from Remigius (d. *c*.533) to Augustine. On 'stumbling-block' see Wedel (1920), p. 17. See 134/68 and 135/10 below.

133/37 *vmbre*: The shadow of the earth causing an eclipse of sun or moon. Tables showing the times of such eclipses from 1387 to 1462 are given, with uneven accuracy, in Nicholas of Lynn's *Kalendarium* (1386), ed. & tr. S. Eisner (1980), pp. 142–63. For the use of the 'umbre' of a man to tell the hours of the day, see idem, pp. 189–193.

133/45 *firmament*: In the Ptolemaic system, refers to the eighth sphere containing the fixed stars. Trevisa's Bartholomaeus, 8.2: 'þe meuynge [of þe firmament] is kyndeliche rounde about [and aslonte, and rounde aboute] fro þe est to þe west, and bereþ aboute and drawiþ wiþ him be symple meuynge and iliche swift, in the space of a nyȝt and a day, al þat is þervndir anon to þe place of þe fuyre' (*Properties* 1: 449–50/36–3).

134/64 *Iacebat in presepio*: In Drèves, *Analecta* 45, No. 7 (in 'I Cantiones Variae'), pp. 22–3: the first line: 'Lumen patris resplendit', and Stanza 3 is:

Virgo, parens mitissima,
Infantem lactans Deum
Qui iacet in praesepio
Maerendo plasma reum
Vilis locus praesaepium,
sed puer ille dives
Cui cantant in gloria
Caelorum summi cives.

In the same volume of Drèves, No. 23, a hymn attributed to Hilary (315–67), contains the line in Stanza 3; the first line is, 'Nascitur ex virgine'; Stanza 3:

Iacet in praesaepio
Cuius natalitio
Mundus floret gaudio.

In Drèves, *Analecta* 34, the second stanza of hymn No. 9, first line 'Lucis orto sidere', has:

Iacet in praesepio
Spreto regum solio
Degens in infantia

Cf. F. J. Mone, *Lateinische hymnen*: 'vili jacet praesepio' in Hymn 28, 1: 39/29.

134/4 *Seynt Austyn*: See 133/29–34 above.

134/68 *þe materye þat it cam fro*: So says Peter Comestor: the star fulfilled its function and vanished, 'revertens in praejacentem materiam unde sumpta fuerat' (*PL* 198: 1542). See 133/29–34 above, 135/10 below.

135/10 *Seynt Ion wyt þe Gyldene Mouthe*: St John Chrysostom (347–407) argues that the star of Bethlehem was neither a natural star nor a validation of astrology: 'this star was not . . . a star at all . . . but some invisible power transformed into this appearance, which was intended to wean the world from old authorities and teach it to obey a new law' (*Homily VI*, tr. P. Schaff, p. 37; *PG* 56: 61 ff.). Ps.-Chrysostom (?fifth century) brings Balaam's prophecy into the story and fleshes out the personalities of the Magi (*PG* 56: 637 ff.). On Ps.-Chrysostom, see the first volume of the projected *CCL* edition of the *Opus Imperfectum in Matthaeum*, whose editor, J. van Banning, attributes the work to a fifth-century Arian bishop from an area south of the Danube (*CCL* lxxxviiB, pp. v–vi). The work, judging from the nearly 200 surviving manuscripts, was immensely popular; until the time of Erasmus, it was believed to have been written by St Chrysostom. For the scepticism of the Wycliffite sermon writers about such legends, upon which 'men muson ydully' (*EWS* 1, Ep. Serm. 7/78–9). On the growth of the legend of the

Magi, see Thorndike (1923), 1: 474, ff.. See further 133/29–34 and 134/68 above and 135/11 below.

135/11 *Balaamys prophecye*: Num. 24: 17: 'Orietur stella ex Iacob,/ Et consurget virga de Israel'. Cited in LL4, fos. 13ra, 13rb, 121ra. Balaam had a medieval reputation as both a false and a true prophet; his cloudy prophecy of a star that would come forth from Jacob was later applied to King David and, by extension, to the birth of Christ and the coming of the Magi; see further below 2–34/19–35, 2–262/1–263/26, 2–266/10–267/53. Nicolaus de Lyra's *additio* to Num. 24 links Balaam's prophecy to Daniel and the Magi, as well as to the destruction of Jerusalem and the dispersion of the Jews (*Postilla* 1). A sermon of 1413 posits that: '. . . too thyngus meved hem [the Magi]: oon, þe vndirstondyng of þe pleyn prophecie of Balaam . . . [and] þe wondirfull gouernaunce of þis stere' (*ME Sermons*, ed. Ross, EETS, 209, pp. 226/36–7; 227/7–8; 40). *The Stanzaic Life of Christ* makes the connection with Balaam by asserting that the Magi 'weren of Balaams blode' (ed. F. A. Foster, EETS, 166, p. 59/1750; cf. P. Comestor *Historia*, *PL* 198: 1541). The Vintners' 'Play of the Magi' in the Chester Mystery Cycle opens with Balaam's prophecy:

> that ilke starre that I may see
> that Balaham sayd should ryse and bee
> in his prophecye.

(ed. R. M. Luniansky and D. Mills (EETS ss 3), 1: 156–7, ll. 1–8, 17–18). See 2–34/19–35 below.

135/15 *Seynt Austyn*: See 117/3–43 above.

135/18 *xxvi, q. iv, Igitur*: Here Dives cites canon law against Pauper. The canon 'Igitur' is descriptive rather than proscriptive, but its list of demons includes the Magi, whose 'mathematical' arts were legitimate until the time of the birth of Christ ('cuius artis scientia usque ad Christum fuit concessa') (C.26 q.3 & 4 c.1; Friedberg 1: 1025). The source of the canon 'Igitur' is alleged to be Augustine's 'De divinatione daemonium' (*PL* 40: 581–92; cf. 152/3 below). At the beginning of cap. xxv, the author of *D&P* rather inconsistently makes Dives ask Pauper for his own (Dives') source for this opinion; compare the passage in the text, 135/14–19 above, with that in 136/2 below.

135/32–3 *Di. xxxvii, Qui de mensa*: The canon 'Qui de mensa' is among a group of canons dealing with secular learning, classed by Gratian among the 'palea'. The canon holds that the example of the prophet Daniel demonstrates that it is not sinful to acquire secular learning and that it is indeed even useful (D. 37 c.11: Friedberg 1: 138–9); on source, see below 139/85–6.

136/2 *Exodi xx [4]*: For Exod. 20: 4, see 81/7 above.

136/12–13 *xxvi q. iv, Igitur*: Cited above 135/18.

136/21 *Ysaie xiv [12–15]*: Isa. 14: 13–15: 'Qui dicebas in corde tuo, /In caelum conscendam super astra Dei exaltabo solium meum;/ sedebo in monte testamenti, in lateribus aquilonis;/ ascendam super altitudinem nubium, ero similis Altissimo./ Verumtamen ad infernum detraheris in profundum laci.' LL4 interprets and paraphrases: 'Lucifer coueytid for to ben euene with god & seyde, "I schal settin myn sete abouyn þe sterris & wendin vp into heuene & ben lyk to hym þat is heyest." But onon for his pride he fel doun into helle with alle his cursede aungelis þat assented unto hym' (fo. 134ʳᵇ). The diatribe against the fallen Nebuchadnezzar in Isaiah was early interpreted as a description of the fall of Satan. The GO on 'Lucifer': 'Diabolus in exordio mundi creatus vel inter angelos gloriosus sed corruit secundum illud, "Videbam sathan sicut fulgur de caelo cadentem [Luke 10: 18]", qui prius cogitabat in caelum conscendum . . . post lapsum quoque arrogat idem sibi, vnde & gloriatur ascendere super angelos in caelum, vel super nubes corda, sci., electorum, & a sedere in monte testamenti in ecclesia' (3: 26).

137/47 *Deutero. xviii [10–12]*: '. . . aut qui ariolos scisitetur et observet somnia atque auguria nec sit maleficus, nec incantator ne pythones consulat nec divinos et quaerat a mortuis veritatem. /Omnia enim haec abominatur Dominus . . .'. The GO on 'ariolos': 'Qui circumeunt aras nefandis precibus, & diuinationem in extis animalium quaerunt'; on 'auguria': 'Quasi augeria quae in vocabis auium geruntur' (1: 998). Cited below 177/6–178/15.

137/53–138/73 *We fyndyn . . . Isaie xlvii [13] . . . helpyn þe*: The author of *D&P* supplies a somewhat abbreviated translation of the Latin text, selecting v. 9, the first and third lines of v. 10, vv. 11–13, and the last line of v. 15. The GO on 'diuynourys of heuene' (Lat. 'augures caeli') recalls the Magi and the prophet Balaam: 'Astrologi qui stellis arbitrantur omnia regi, "Quasi quare non prouiderunt omnia tibi?" Hi vulgo appellantur mathematici qui cursu astrorum res mundanas putant regi, vnde, "Ab oriente venerunt magi dicentes, 'Videmus stellam . . .'"'. Vel a vaticinio balaam prouocati, qui ait, "Orietur stella ex iacob . . ."' (3: 71–2).

138/73 *Pouyl . . . Act. 5: 38–9*: The sense can be found in Acts: '. . . si est ex hominibus consillium hoc, aut opus, dissolvetur:/si vero ex Deo est, non poteritis dissolvere illud . . .'; the exact words can be found in Prov. 21: 30: 'Non est consilium contra Dominum.'

138/74 *Sapien. xiii*: Wisd. 13: 1–2: 'Vani autem sunt omnes homines . . . [qui] solem et lunam, / Rectores orbis terrarum deos putaverunt.' The GO reproves proto-scientists who ignore the immutability of the Creator and worship him in his creatures; it continues with a list of 'sciences': 'Alii ignem colebant quem vulcanun vocabant; alii etherem vel aerem, quem iouem vel iunonem dicebant; alii nimiam aquam, i.e., neptunum; alii girum stellarum, qui diuersis figuris animalium, positiones et cursum distribuebant astrorum; alii solem quem phebum vocabant; alii lunam, i.e., dianam' (2: 735–6).

139/85–6 *lawe of holy cherche*: For the canon 'Igitur' see above, 135/18. The two canons 'Legimus' and 'Qui de mensa' are among a group of canons dealing with secular learning. Both cap. 7 and cap. 9 are headed 'Legimus' and both uphold the value of secular learning; cap. 7 refers to St Jerome's story that he was rebuked by an angel for reading Cicero (Ep. 22, *Select Letter of St Jerome*, ed. F. A. Wright, LCL 262, p. 127). Gratian's *post dict.* gives a list of OT examples, from Moses to Daniel, of the positive value of pagan learning. C. 9 is attributed to St Ambrose: 'Seculares litterae legendae sunt, ut non ignorentur. Legimus aliqua, ne legantur; legimus, ne ignoremus; legimus, non ut teneamus, sed ut repudiemus' (D. 37 c. 9: Friedberg 1: 137–8). 'Qui de mensa' is cited above 135/32–3.

139/87 *ad Galatas iv*: Gal. 4: 10–11: 'Dies observatis, et menses, et tempora, et annos. / Timeo vos, ne forte sine causa laboraverim in vobis.' The GO cites Jerome on OT observances of 'times' (4: 363). Nicolaus de Lyra: '. . . celebrant iudei neomensis et tempera, vt temporas egressionis de egypto mense primo, & temporas liberationis ysaac mense septimo, etc, et annos, scilicet, septimum annum qui dicebatur remissionis & quinquegesimum qui dicitur iubiles, & que tal obseruantia erat illis illicita ideo subditur (*Postilla* 4). Burchard of Worms (c.965–1025), in his *Decretum*, citing Paul and Ambrose, says: 'Those who "observe days" say: "I think tomorrow is not going to be beneficial; indeed nothing should be started the day after." . . . Those who cultivate "months" observe the phases of the moon, saying: "In the seventh moon documents should not be prepared, in the ninth moon servants should not be brought into the household". . . . "Times" are observed by those who say: "Today is good for beginning something, and so it will be a holiday." And again: "Tomorrow it will be forbidden to leave the house." Those who observe "years" say, "It is the kalends of January, a new year", as if a year were not accumulated day by day' (*PL* 140: 835). See 182/2–183/36 and 184/2–3 below.

139/92 *I ad Corinth. i*: 1 Cor. 1: 19–20: 'Perdam sapientiam sapientium, et prudentiam prudentium reprobabo. / Ubi sapiens? ubi scriba? ubi conquisitor huius saeculi? Nonne stultam fecit Deus sapientiam huius mundi?' Pauper translates 'scriba' and 'conquisitor huius saeculi' into the more topical 'man of law' and 'seeker of nature'; that by the latter he means the purely theoretical scientist rather than the observer is indicated by his praise of 'þe shepperd in þe feld, þe shipman in þe see' who read the weather better than 'alle þe astronomyenys of þis lond' (141/48–50 below). The GO on 'sapientiam huius mundi': 'Ubi stultum & infirmum dei contemnitur, quam est secundum rationes mundi quam impossibile iudicat quod in naturis rerum non videt. . . . quia sapientia mundi ante nesciuit deum per sapientiam dei, i.e., per hanc magnificantiam mundi, ac tam sapienter instituti opificii ornatum, creatoris sui non est venerata sapientum' (4: 308).

139/97–8 *sekere . . . of þis word*: See 2–129/71 below.

140/29 *Actus Apostolorum i* [*7*]: The GO on 'Non est vestrum nosce': 'Non ait, Non erit, sed 'Non est', notans adhoc esse infirmos & ideo ad secretum non esse idoneos' (4: 452). Nicolaus de Lyra: '. . . sicut & petitionem filiorum zebedei repulit [i.e., Christ] vt stultam, dicens "Nescitis quod petatur, sed illud quod sequitur ad vos pertinet"' (*Postilla* 4). The reference is to Matt. 20: 20–22.

140/32 *Ysaie xxiv* [*16*]: Cited twice in LL4: ' "Myn priuyte I kepe to me", for þoʒw man or womman haue a priue special grace of god he schulde nout schewyn it out but as it nedith to helpe of his euene cristene & to þe worschepe of god, þat god be worschepid in alle þinge' fo. 88vb; fo. 30va. GO: 'In hebraeo alis terrae; alae autem vel fines terrae prophete sunt & apostoli qui de terrenis ad celestia volent & quibusdam preceptorum finibus uiuendi modum terminant' (3: 41).

141/40–1, 143/50–1 *As I seyde ferst*: See above 120/47–73, 121/1–7.

141/2–53 *Fallyng of soot*: An early observer of natural phenomena, William of Conches (c1080–c1154), discussed the causes of rain (*De philosophia mundi, PL* 172: 76). John of Salisbury's *Policraticus* first grants the value of natural signs, such as wind and weather, then attacks all varieties of occult forecasting (Bk. II, cc. 2–29 (*CCCM* cxviii, pp. 74–171). See Thorndike (1934), 3: 141–6.

141/48–50 *And so knowyt . . . lond*: Though Pauper's comment sounds like a harbinger of the renaissance, the view that hands-on experience is more valuable than auguries was expressed long ago by Origen: 'Sic medici, quam libet malis moribus, quaedam arte sua praenoscunt. Item gubernatores experientia quadam et observationibus docti signa habant, ex quibus ventorum impetus variasque aeris mutationes praevideant' ('Contra Celsum', *PG* 11: 1174–5).

142/14 *borow*: Variant readings of this rare word are 'borw' and 'borough'; listed in the *OED* s.v. 'brough'; in *MED* s.v. burwe'. *D&P* manuscripts BYL understand it as 'sercle'; the variant spelling 'borough' may be an attempt to understand it as meaning something circular, see below. The word 'borewes' is used in *Vices and Virtues* (tr. fourteenth century) in reference to women's hair: 'þilke þat maken borewes and hornes of heer', (ed. W. N. Frances, EETS, 217, p. 179); the editor relates the words to OE 'beorg', a walled town, op. cit., p. 346, as do the *OED* and *MED*. Other spellings of the same word: 'burr', 'burrow'.

143/1 *þe mone*: There were two schools of thought about the cause of tides. One was that underwater currents created by mountains or whirlpools made the ocean flood and recede; the other, that they were caused by the influence of the moon. For the first kind of explanatiion, see Macrobius's *Commentary* (tr. W. H. Stahl), pp. 214–216; William of Conches, *De philosophia mundi*, *PL* 172: 80–1. For the second, Grosseteste (c1170–1253), who says that the moon causes tides: '. . . luna est causa fluxus maris' (*De impressionibus*, ed. L. Baur, p. 48). Trevisa's Bartholomaeus, 8.17 also opts for lunar causation (*Properties* 1: 490), as does Gerald of Wales (*Topographia Hibernica, Opera* V, 77–80).

144/16 *Eccles. iii* [*1 et seq.*]: Cited above 119/19.

144/20 *Ieremie viii* [*7*]: 'Milvus [puttok] in caelo cognovit tempus suum;/ Turtur [dove], et hirundo [swallow], et ciconia [stork] custodierunt tempus adventus sui;/ Populus autem meus non cognovit iudicium Domini.' In the translation, 'et ciconia' is omitted. Cited in LL4, fo. 84vb. The GO: 'Quasi etiam aues sua norunt tempora, ut sciant quando ad calida festinantes loca rigorem hyenis declinare debeant, & veris principio ad solitas redire rigiones' (3: 114).

144/28 *þe Philosophre*: The idea may be derived from Aristotle's discussion of 'measure' in *Metaphysics* Bk. X (*Oxford Aristotle*, 2: 1662 ff.), or from his discussion of 'the motion of the heavens' and the regularity of time in Bk. II.6 (op. cit. 1: 476).

144/30 [*Ps. 104: 20–3*]: For [Ps.104: 20–3] read [Ps.103: 20–3]: 'Posuisti tenebras et facta est nox, in ipsa pertransibunt omnes bestiae silvae, / catuli leonum rugientes ut rapiant, et quaerant a Deo escam sibi; / ortus est sol et congregati sunt, et in cubilibus suis collocabuntur, / exhibit homo ad opus suum et ad operationem suam usque ad vesperum.' The psalm is here read as a hymn to God's creation, cf. v. 24: 'Quam magnificata sunt opera tua, Domine'. Augustine interprets the lion and other beasts of the woods as demons and the rising sun as Christ, who dispels fear and initiates the peace of the Church (*Enarr.* 103.3.22–4; *CCL* xl, pp. 1517–20; *PL* 37: 1374–8).

145/37–42 *In þe dawnyng and sprynggyng of þe day*: Compare earlier hymns to light in *D&P* HP-A, cap. i, 52/41–7 and 119/19 above.

145/45 *Genesis i* [*12*]: Gen. 1: 12: 'Et protulit terra herbam virentem, et adferentem semen iuxta genus suum, lignumque faciens fructum, et habens unumquodque sementem secundum speciem suam.' The GO (Gregory) interprets figuratively: 'Terra enim est ecclesia, quae verbi pabulo nos reficat & patrociniis vmbraculo custodit, loquendo pascit opitulando protegit, ut non solum herbam refectionis proferat sed etiam arborem protectionis', adding a figurative interpretation of 'lignum', which 'secundum speciem suam semen producit cum mens nostra ex sui consideratione quod in alterum faciat colligit & recti operis germen parit' (1: 12).

146/59 *as lorer, box, hul and yuy . . .saffron*: trees added in MS Y; a colophon to this manuscript states that *D&P* was copied in Lisbon in 1465, see 'The *Manuscripts*' above. See text 2–326/note.

146/73–147/81 *moreyn*: The passage apparently reflects the still living memory of the Black Death of the mid fourteenth century. Henry Knighton opens his account of the years 1348–1349 with the words: 'Isto anno et anno sequenti erat generalis mortalitas hominum in universo mundo' (*Chronicle*, ed. G. H. Martin, pp. 94–5). In England, he says, the plague arrived first in the port cities Southampton and Bristol (98–9). He describes the ensuing scarcities of goods and labourers (100–1) and the mortality among the clergy, a result of which was the hiring of illiterate or semi–literate replacements (102–3). Thomas Walsingham's early fifteenth-century chronicle says that for the year 1349: 'fuit tanta mortalitas hominum, ut multi periti putarent decimam partem humani generis relictam fuisse superstitem. . . . Saeviente, ut praefertur, in Anglia tanta peste hominem, Dominus Clemens Papa concessit plenam remissionem omnibus vere confessis et contritis, morientibus in hac epidemia, per totum regnum'. Like Knighton, he mentions the sheep dying in the fields at the same time as the populations of towns and villages (*Ypodigma*, ed. H. T. Riley, p. 292). The fifteenth-century *Brut*: '. . . so gret a pestilences of men fro þe Est into þe west, & namely þoruȝ bocches [bubos], þat he þat siked þis day, deid on þe iij. day after . . . in þes dayes was deþ wiþoute sorwe, weddyng wiþoute frendship, wilfull penaunce, and derþe wiþout scarste, and fleyng wiþoute refute or socour' (ed. F. W. D. Brie, EETS os 136, p. 303). *PP* refers to parishes 'pore siþþe pestilence tyme' (A-Text, Prol./ 81). See also Walter le Baker's *Chronicon* (*c.*1400), ed. J. A. Giles, pp. 189–91. Ziegler, *Black Death* (1969): 'England [before the Black Death] was a thriving country . . . [in the course of the epidemic], taking a conservative view, between a third and half the people must have died . . . To appreciate the full impact of so fearful a calamity on an ignorant and credulous people calls for an intense effort of historical imagination' (pp. 118; 128; 129).

147/5–20 *wondrys . . . comete*: The comet of 1402, which provides a *terminus a quo* for the date of composition of *D&P* (see Introduction, p. xviii) was not a phantasm; it was seen and recorded by many on the continent. In February, 1402, the chronicler Adam of Usk, travelling from Cologne to Pisa, 'beheld a dreadful comet which went before the sun, a terror to the world—to the clergy which is the sun therof, and to the knighthood which is its moon—which forecast the death of the duke of Milan, as it soon after came to pass. His dreaded arms too, a serpent azure swallowing a naked man

gules on a field argent, were then oftimes seen in the air' (*Chronicle*, ed.
C. Given-Wilson, pp. 154–6). In England, the *Brut* records: 'a sterre seyne
in þe firmament, þat schewed hym-self þrouȝ alle þe worlde, for dyuers
tokenns þat schulde befalle sone after; þe which sterre was named & called
be clergie "Stella comata"' (ed. Brie, EETS os 136, p. 363/20–2). See
Henry Knighton, *Chronicle* (for 1355), ed. Martin, pp. 128–9; and Thomas
Walsingham, *Ypodigma*, ed. Given-Wilson, pp. 397–8. Bishop Robert
Grosseteste (who bequeathed his scientific writings to the Oxford Franciscans) wrote a short book on the comets (*c.*1197) which combined an
apparently original idea of comets as made of pure fire with the more
traditional idea that they were ominous portents because of their location in
the spheres of the planets (R. Southern, *Grosseteste* (1986), pp. 147–50; text
in *Werke*, ed. L. Baur, pp. 36–41). See also Wylie (1898), 1: 274–5; 4: 280;
and Thorndike (1934), 4: 78–80;83–4.

148/44 *a comoun lawe*: The law of 1401 contained two novelties, first,
making heresy a capital offence, and, second, execution by burning. *D&P*
for no very evident reason refers here only to the first of these. Treason
might be punished by beheading or by hanging, depending on the rank of
the convicted person. Lollardy, e.g., could, especially after the Oldcastle
Rising of 1413–4, be seen as heresy or treason and sometimes both. On more
than one occasion, those convicted were hanged, beheaded and burned (cf.
M. Aston, 'Lollardy and Sedition' in *Peasants, Knights and Heretics*, ed.
Hilton (1976), pp. 273–218). Adam Usk, chronicaling the death of Archbishop Arundel in 1414, praises him for equating heresy and high treason
and advocating the double punishment of hanging and burning (*The
Chronicle of Adam of Usk*, ed. Given-Wilson, pp. 248–9). Penalties short
of execution for unorthodox preaching were not new in 1401. Parliament, in
1382, had empowered sheriffs to imprison those who preached the errors
condemned by the Blackfriars Council of 1382; see Wilkins, iii: 254–5;
Wylie, *History*, 1: 189–90.
   The reference in *D&P* to 'a comoun lawe' enjoining burning for heretics
and hanging and beheading for persons who 'speke with the trewthe' may
possibly be intended to remind certain well–informed readers of the case in
1402 of a Franciscan of Aylesbury convent, who was betrayed by a fellow
friar for having spoken against Henry IV. The chronicler reports in direct
speech a colloquy between the accused friar and the King, in which the friar
fearlessly asserts his continuing loyalty to Richard II. For his outspokenness,
the friar is hanged and beheaded. The chronicle continues with an account
of what seems to have been a more widespread loyalty to Richard among
friars in other parts of the country (*Eulogium* (*continuatio*), ed. F. S. Haydon,
3: 389–94). For another perhaps deliberately blurred reference to current
politics see 209/21–7 below.

149/53–4 *Werre, hunger, tempest and moreyn*: The fear of foreign invasion, with explicit mention of the Bretons (258/61 below) seems to echo the prediction of Sawtre, the heretic condemned and executed in 1401: 'I who am sent by God say to you [the archbishop of Canterbury] that you and all your clergy and the king too will shortly succumb to an evil death, and that a people's foreign tongue will soon conquer and rule over this kingdom; and that these things are on the very threshold of coming to pass' (*Chronicle of Adam of Usk*, ed. Given-Wilson, pp. 122–3; further on Sawtre, McNiven (1987), pp. 81–9).

149/56 *shert*: 'short', see *Corrigenda*.

149/57 *þe kyng . . . shal ben chaunged*: When *D&P* was written, such a prediction about the king still fell outside the provisions of the statute of 1352 on treason. But increasingly in the period between 1381 and 1485 'compassing or imagining' the death of the king was equated with waging war against the crown (Bellamy (1970), p. 103). In 1402, the crimes for which certain anti-Lancastrian Franciscan friars were arrested consisted of words, spoken or written, in some cases only alleged; a number of these friars were sentenced to death (*Eulogium (continuatio)*), ed. Haydon, 3: 390–94; E. F. Jacob, *Fifteenth Century* (1961), pp. 27–9; Bellamy (1970), p. 116, citing I. D. Thornley, 'Treason by Words in the Fifteenth Century', *EHR* 32 (1917), 556–7; cf. 250/18–251/58 below). See 148/44 above. Referring to this, *Mum and the Sothsegger* (1403–6) says:

> . . . þaire lesingz haue lad þaym to lolle by þe necke;
> At Tibourne for traison y-twyght vp þay were
>   (ed. M. Day and R. Steele, EETS, 199, p. 39/419–20)

149/60 *Eccli. 10: 8*: Ecclus. 10: 8: 'Regnum a gente in gentem transfertur propter iniustitias et iniurias et contumelias et diversos dolos.' The GO invokes the *translatio* theme: 'Hoc fere omnes gentium testantur historie chaldeorum, persarum, grecorum, & romanorum. Ad hoc propter pervaricationum translatum ad gentes euangelium' (2: 754). Cited 253/32–3 below.

VOL. 1: 1, COMMANDMENT I, CONT., CAP. 30–64, pp. 149–220

149/1 *iudicial of astronomye*: See 117/3–43 above.

149/3 *may*: For 'may' read 'many'.

149/5 *as the blynde man casteth his staf*: The sense of the saying is that astrologers conjecturing about future events sometimes happen to hit upon the truth. Whiting, M 36, cites the saying from the Wynkyn de Worde printing of *D&P* of 1496. Cf. *EWS* 1, Ep. Serm. 3/70.

149/6 *astronomye*: Astrology; see 117/3–43 above.

150/17 *falsen the kynges seel or . . . monye*: 'A category of treason clearly delineated in the legal writings of the late thirteenth century was the counterfeiting or clipping of coin or the forging of the king's seal'; the Great Statute of Treasons of 1352 equated forging, either of coin or of the king's seal, with treason, punishable by the same sentence (J. G. Bellamy, *Law of Treason* (1970), pp. 17; 85; 93; see also J. G. Bellamy, *Crime* (1973), p. 64; Pollock & Maitland, 2: 502–3). Cf. Thomas Hoccleve's 'Dialogue':

> had I be / for an homicide yknowe,
> or an extorcioner / or a robbour,
> or for a coyn clippere . . .
> > (ed. Burrow, EETS, 313: p. 37/64–6;
> > see also 'Excursus III', pp. 120–4).

150/21 *comoun clamour of þe people*: Cf. 209/21–7 below.

151/41 *nedy noteles men*: The MED overlooked the word 'noteles' ('little known', or 'obscure'); the first citation in the *OED* is dated 1616. The 'nedy noteles men' or 'faytours' seems to refer to the lay vagrants ('gyrovagues') that are complained of in *PP* (see Scase (1989), pp. 125–8). William Taylor's 1406 sermon alludes to persons who seem to be lay imitators of the friars: 'a new vnfoundid sect of beggeris, walkinge in greete noumbre in habite of seculer preestis, þat prechen for wynnyng, and merueilously wiþ her fablis bimadden þe puple' (*TWT*, p. 19); see also M. Mollat, *The Poor*, tr. A. Goldhammer (1986), pp. 247–50; J. Misraki, 'Criminalité', in *Etudes . . . pauvreté*, ed. M. Mollat (1974), 2: 535–6. Cf. 57/20–1 above.

151/51 *nigromauncye*: see 164/64–71 below.

152/3 *Austyn . . . xxvi, q. iv, Sciendum*: The canon 'Sciendum' is cited from Augustine's 'De divinatione demonum' (*PL* 40: 584–5), in which he says demons have swift aerial bodies that make it possible for them to predict future events (C.26 q.4 c.2; Friedberg 1: 1025–6). In his 'Retractions', however, Augustine appears to think he overestimated the powers of demons (*CCL* lvii, p. 114; *PL* 34: 467). In Pauper's paraphrase, the list of ills caused by those who act as agents of 'þe proude spryt'—'moreyn and syknesse, hunger and droughte, dissencioun and werre' brought about by 'wycches, faytours, astronomyenes'—is more specific than its source. Peter Brown discusses some reasons why patristic writers spent so much time denouncing sorcerers, fortunetellers, diviners and other magicians; transmitted to the middle ages via canon law, these denunciations, at least in part, shaped clerical expectations about folk beliefs ('Sorcery' in his *Religion and Society* (1972), pp. 119–46).

153/11 *Mathei viii [23–34]*: For [23–34] read [31–2]. Matt. 8: 31–2: 'Daemones autem rogabant eum dicentes, Si eicis nos, mitte nos in gregem porcorum. / Et ait illis, Ite'. Both the GO and Nicolaus de Lyra stress that the power of the 'fend' is less than that of God: 'Nisi quis more porci vixerit, dyabolus in eius potestatem non accipit, nisi forte ad probandum' (GO 4: 34). Nicolaus de Lyra: 'Non que demoniaci possint nisi quantum permittit eius deus' (*Postilla* 4). Chrysostom is cited by the *CA*: 'Per hoc autem manifestum est quoniam nullus est qui non potiatur divina providentia' (1: 146). Chrysostom, 'In Matt.', Hom. 28.3, says: 'Inde liquet, neminem esse quin Dei providentia fruatur' (*PG* 57: 354).

153/14 *Iob i [12] & ii [6]*: 'Dixit ergo Dominus ad Satan, Ecce universa quae habet in manu tua sunt; tantum in eum ne extendas manum tuam. . . ./ Dixit ergo Dominus ad Satan, Ecce in manu tua est; verumtamen animam illius serva.' The GO allegorizes the conversation between God and Satan as an image of the good and bad angels who watch over humans and stresses the greater power of God, even his foreknowledge that temptation will be resisted: '. . . per prescientiam certitudine retributionis' (2: 376). The 'hand' given to the Devil is interpreted as a power less than absolute: under 'manum tuam' the interlinear gloss adds: 'frenat hic diabolum' (2: 377). The point about the 'graunt of God' is made in Chrysostom's 'In Matt.', Hom. 28.4 (*PG* 57/353–4); see 153/11 above. St Gregory's discussion of these passages also stresses the limits of the powers given to Satan; Job will not be tempted beyond his power to resist; his physical life will be spared; he will not be abandonned by God: 'Manu itaque aduersarii [Satan] sanctus uir [Job] traditur sed tamen in intimis adiutoris sui manu retinetur' (*Moralia*, 2.19–20; 3.6–7; *CCL* cxliii, pp. 71–2; 117–18; *PL* 75: 564–5; 602–3).

153/18 *III Regum xxii*: 1 Kgs. 22: 22: 'Et ille ait: Egrediar et ero spiritus mendax in ore omnium prophetarium eius. Et dixit Dominus: Decipies et praevalebis: egredere et fac ita.' The GO cites Paul (perhaps referring to the passages cited below, 154/27–30): 'Contra spiritualia nequitiae in caelestibus: omnis exercitus assistit deo, quia et voluntas electorus spirituum diuinae deseruit potestati . . .' (2: 140). Cited below 155/71, and at greater length 2–11/30–1.

154/27–30 [*Iac. 1: 12*] . . . [*1 Cor. 10: 13*]: Jas. 1: 12: 'Beatus vir qui suffert tentationem: quoniam cum probatus fuerit, accipiet coronam vitae, quam repromisit Deus diligentibus se'; in *D&P* translated as a rhyming couplet. The GO (interlin.): 'Quia per exercicium tentationum probatur in fide perfectus propter quod etiam tentatur' (4: 512). 1 Cor. 10: 13: 'Tentatio vos non apprehendat nisi humana: fidelis autem Deus est, qui non patietur vos tentari supra id quod potestis, sed faciet etiam cum tentatione proventium ut possitis sustinere.' The GO: 'Humana enim tentatio est ut in necesssitate vel pressura non diffidat homo deo, auxilium humanum requirendo. Propter

christum ergo pati, humana temtatio est per quam perficitur apud deum';
Augustine's gloss on the same text ends: 'Si non est in nobis perfectio
angeli, non sit presumptio dyaboli' (4: 322). These two texts are the basis of
Pauper's theodicy: evil is subordinate to God's purposes.

154/31 *penance*: The Lateran Council of 1215 enjoined confession at least
yearly for all Christians, with penance to be carried out according to the
instructions of the priest of one's own parish. See the canon 'Omnis
utriusque', citing the Fourth Lateran Council (De poen. D.5 c.12; Friedberg 2: 887–8). On penance, see Hugh of St Victor, *De sacramentis*, Bk.
2.14.2 (*PL* 176: 554–5); P. Lombard, *Sent.*, Bk. 4, di. 20–1 (2: 371–86).

154/39–43 *And perfor Crist . . . Io. viii [44]*: John 8: 44: 'Vos ex patre diabolo
estis: et desideria patris vestri vultis facere. Ille homicida erat ab initio, et in
veritate non stetit: quia non est veritas in eo: cum loquitur mendacium, ex
propriis loquitur, quia mendax est, et pater eius.' This is a favourite text,
cited six times in *D&P* and four times in LL4. In each case it is cited in
part: 'your father, the fend' (163/37–8, 2–82/66 below; LL4, fos. 42vb, 56ra,
58va, 83ra); 'the fend, a manqueller' (2–21/4–5 below); 'the fend, a liar'
(154/42 and 2–231/48 below); or 'the fend, a manqueller and liar' (161/40–
2 below). The GO: 'Ecce iam determinat quis sit pater eorum cuius filii sunt
non nascendo, vt manichei dicunt, sed imitando' (4: 246). *D&P* does not
follow the lead of the gloss and derive the message that men are the sons of
two fathers, God and the Devil, with Christ as the mediator between them,
cf. *EWS* 3, Serm. 150/44–73, citing John 8. Rather, Pauper views the 'fend'
as an antagonist worthy of man's best 'wil to withstonde'; cf. 98/51 above.
Augustine uses the text as a basis for a theodicy: God is the perfect creator,
but His materials are not as perfect as He is, just as an architect is superior
to the wood he uses; hence evil: 'faber si scammum fecit, lignum ipse non
creauit' (*In Ioh.*, 42.9–11; *CCL* xxxvi, pp. 369–73; *PL* 35: 1703–4).

155/50 *xxii, q. ii, Homines, et Is autem*: The canon 'Homines' holds that men
swear falsely both when they deceive and when they are deceived (C.22 q.2
c.3; Friedberg 1: 867); the source is Augustine's Sermon 100 (*PL* 38: 973).
The canon 'Is autem' holds that it is always a lie if the motive is to lie, even
in a good cause or even if what is said happens to be true (C.22 q.2 c.4;
Friedberg 1: 867–8). The source is Augustine's *Enchiridion*, c. 22 (*PL*
40: 243).

155/65 *Mathei viii; Marci i; Luce iv, and [8: 28]*: Matt. 8: 29: 'Et ecce
clamaverunt dicentes, Quid nobis, et tibi Iesu Fili Dei? Venisti huc ante
tempus torquere nos?' Mark 1: 24: 'Dicens, Quid nobis et tibi Iesu Nazarene
venisti perdere nos? scio qui sis, Sanctus Dei'. Luke 4: 34, 8: 28: 'Dicens,
Sine quid nobis et tibi Iesu Nazarene venisti perdere nos? Scio te qui sis
Sanctus Dei. . . . obsecro te, ne me torqueas.' The GO on Matt. 8: 29 cites
Mark and Luke: 'Marcus dicit quod nullus iam daemoniacum poterat ligare.

Lucas, ruptus cathenis in deserto agi quia gentes nullo vinculo ligum poterant cohibere, vnde deterius saeuiebant in se uel in aliis' (4: 34). The gloss on Mark 1: 25 ('Obmutesce', 'putte hem to silence', referred to below, 155/73) is Bede's: 'Ideo contra ipsum mortis auctorem primo debuit medicina salutis operari: primo lingua serpentina, ne ultra virus spargeret, occludi' (*PL* 92: 141; cited also in the GO, 4: 92). More to the point perhaps is Nicolaus de Lyra's gloss: 'Si enim cognouissent demones ipsum esse deum, nunque induxissent iudeos ad ipsum crucifigendum (*Postilla* 4).

155/71 3 *Reg. 22: 22; 2 Par. 18: 21*: 1 Kgs. 22: 22 is cited above, 153/18, and 2–11/30–1 below. 2 Par. (Chr.) 18: 21: 'Egrediar, et ero spiritus mendax in ore omnium prophetarum eius', referring to the story of Ahab. The gloss justifies the license given by God to the 'spiritus mendax': 'Juste datur licentia malignis spiritibus, vt quos volentes in peccati laqueo strangulant in peccati poenam etiam nolentes trahant' (GO, 2: 242).

156/11 *Contra . . . clerkys closyn hem in ryngys*: Reflecting popular belief, Caesarius of Heisterbach's (*c.*1180–1250) 'The Demons and the Knight' is a tale about a clerk who instructs a knight in how to summon the Devil to a circle (tr. Scott and Bland, 1929; see J. B. Russell (1972), pp. 38–43; and cf. Chaucer's 'Parson's Tale': '. . . nigromanciens in bacyns ful of water, or in a bright swerd, in a circle, or in a fir [fire], or in a shulderboon of a sheep' (*CT*, p. 307/600–5). On such 'circles', see *Fasciculus morum*, ed. Wenzel, pp. 578–9. Cf. Duffy (1992): 'humanity . . . beleagured by hostile troops of Devils . . . is not a construct of the folk imagination. Such ideas were built into the very structure of the liturgy' (p. 279). See also R. Kieckhefer, *Magic* (1989), pp. 159–61; 172–4, and bibliography pp. 202–13. On demons, V. I. J. Flint, *Rise of Magic* (1991), pp. 101–8.

156/31 *Marci v* [9]: Mark 5: 9: 'Quod tibi nomen est? Et dicit ei: Legio mihi nomen est, quia multi summus'; Bede refers to exorcism in his gloss: 'Sed et nostri temporis sacerdotes, qui per exorcismi gratiam daemones ejicere norunt, solent dicere patientes non aliter curari, nisi quantum sapere possunt, omne quod ab immundis spiritibus visu, auditu, gustu, tactu, vel alis quolibet corporis, aut animi sensu vigilantes dormientesve pertulerint, confitendo patenter exponant' (*PL* 92: 177; GO, 4: 101; *CA* 1: 467).

157/1 *xxvi, q. vii, Non obseruetis*: The canon 'Non obseruetis' comprises a list of superstitions from an untraced Augustinian text. It includes auguries based on 'menses, aut tempora, aut dies, et annos, aut lunae' (see 157/5 below), auguries of birds (see 157/10 below), of 'Pithagorus' (see 157/12 below), and the Apostles Lots (see 157/14 below). It does not include 'Al-holde' (see 157/6–7 below): C.26 q.7 c.16; Friedberg 1: 1045–6. Cf Burchard of Worms *Decretum* (*PL* 140: 835–6).

157/5 *dysmole dayis*: Dismal days are unlucky days ('dies mali'), also called Egyptian days ('dies aegyptiaci'): Du Cange s.v. 'dies' 7; see also *MED* s.v 'dismal'. Strictly, the word 'days' is pleonastic, and the scribe of MS G was more correct to omit it. In Chaucer's 'Book of the Duchess', e.g., 'dismal' is used without the added 'days': 'I trowe hyt was in the dismal' (*CT*, p. 345/ 1206–9). Cf. Peter Comestor: 'Notandum quia plures fuerunt in Aegypto plagae quam decem, quas Exodus non enumerat . . . Unde quidem dies Aegyptiaci dicuntur, quia in his passa est Aegyptus, quorum duos tamen in singulis mensibus notamus ad memoriam, cum plures forte fuerint' (*Historia*, *PL* 198: 1152–3). Raymond of Peñafort warns: 'non obseruetis dies, quos dicunt Aegyptiaci . . .' (*Summa*, Bk. 1, 'De sortilegis', p. 103). See Durandus, *Rationale* 8.6.3 (*CCCM* cxlB, p. 157); *An Apology for Lollard Doctrines* (*c*.1420), 'þeis Egipcian daies, þat we call dysmal', ed. Todd, p. 93; Thorndike (1923), 1: 695–6, listing manuscripts with references to 'Egyptian days'; John C. Hirsh, 'Fate, Faith and Paradox: Medieval Unlucky Days as a Context for 'Wytte hath Wondyr', *MÆ* 66, No. 2 (1997), 288–92.

157/6–7 *settynge of mete . . . Al-holde*: Pauper seems to refer to a spirit or goblin who is to be propitiated with a food offering on the night before All-Souls day, Halloween. The etymology of the word 'holde' is double-sided, having meanings associated with kindness and fear: in Middle English, 'hold' can mean 'kind', or 'gracious' but in Old English can also mean 'carcase' or 'dead body'. 'Al-Holde' would thus be a benign night spirit embodying the fear of the dead. For the Halloween connection with the dead, see Ginsburg (1991), p. 184; cf. Hutton (1996), pp. 379–80, on English records of such practises. The fifteenth-century *Speculum Sacerdotale* claims that All Hallows is a Christianized version of an ancient Roman festival, which under the Christian dispensation is to be devoted to prayers for the release of souls from Purgatory, for whom the Church prescribes 'oblacions, prayingis, and doyingis of almes deedes' (ed. Weatherly, EETS, 200, pp. 218–25). The same account of origins appears in Voragine's *Legenda aurea* (Graesse, No. 162; *GL*, 2: 272–80). Cf. John of Salisbury's *Policraticus*, Bk. II, c. 17, *CCCM* cxviii, pp. 105–6; H. C. Lea, *Inquisition* (1888), 3: 492–500; *Handbooks of Penance* (ed. McNeill and Gamer, 1938), pp. 323; 331; J. B. Russell, *Witchcraft* (1972), p. 49 note; A. Gurevich, *Medieval Popular Culture* (1988)—who discerns a popular belief in a benign Holda as against a clerical demonization of her, p. 84.

157/7 *ledyng of þe plow*: R. Chambers gives a mid-nineteenth-century account of a rural festival, 'Plough Monday', on 'the first Monday after Twelfth Day' which seems by then to have become mixed up with mumming and morris-dancing but also to have included door-to-door begging (*The Book of Days*, ed. R. Chambers (1883), 1: 94–6). On the connection with folk drama, see E. K. Chambers, *Medieval Stage* (1903; repr. 1954), 1: 208–10. According to Duffy (1992), the 'plough ceremonies held on the first working day after Christmas, were fertility rites, when the young men of the village harnessed themselves to a plough which they dragged round the parish, ploughing up the ground before the door of any household which refused to pay a token' (p. 13). Hutton (1996), referring to *D&P*, cites a wide variety of English customs associated with the beginning of the ploughing season (pp. 124–33).

157/9 *þe iudicial of astronomye*: See 117/3–43.

157/10 *chiteringe of bryddis*: Cf. Lev. 19: 26: 'non augurabimini'. Origen (c.185-c.254), citing Leviticus, says that 'verus Deus ad significandas res futuras non brutis animantibus utitur, ne hominibus quidem e vulgo; eligit ad hanc rem sanctissimas purissimasque animas, quas afflat sue nomine et fatidicas reddit' (*Contra Celsum* Bk. IV, 95; tr. O. Chadwick (repr. 1965), p. 259; *PG* 11: 1174). In patristic times, divination by birds was put on the list of forms of prognostication to be avoided by Christians. Aquinas classifies augury from 'avium garritu' as sinful only when demons are expressly invoked at the same time (*ST*, II–II.95.3). The fourteenth-century *Memoriale* says that 'rustici confidunt in auguriis et garritu avium' (ed. Haren, 1975, p. 85). Cf. Chaucer's 'The Parson's Tale': '. . . divynailes, as by flight or by noyse of briddes' (*CT*, p. 307/600–5). The Lollard *Apology* (c.1420): 'be war þat þu wil not folow þe abhominacoun of þe folk þat . . . askiþ ariolers, nor dremis, ne chitering of briddis' (ed. J. H. Todd, repr. 1968, p. 92). Carpenter's *Destructorium* (1428; ed. G. R. Owst, 1952) refers to auguries of 'pies chiterynge' (p. 35, note 6). See Flint (1991), pp. 116–118; 196–9.

157/12 *þe sper of Pittagoras*: *MED* cites this as the earliest example, s.v. 'spere' 3. The 'sphere of Pythagoras' does not refer to the spheres or globes used in astronomy but to a method of divination using the symbolism of numbers: the day on which an illness occurred might be combined with a numerical interpretation of the letters of the patient's name and the result looked up in a chart giving recommended treatments, see Thorndike (1923), 1: 370; 682–5; 692–4, listing manuscripts, including Harl. 1735, containing 'the medical notebook . . . of John Crophill, who practiced medicine in Suffolk under Henry IV', largely, it seems, by means of astrology. John of Salisbury's *Policraticus* refers to a Pythagorean table (Bk. I, c. 12; *CCCM* cxviii, ed. Keats-Rohan, p. 60). K. Thomas (1972), gives further sources (pp. 238–9); see also Flint (1991), p. 134; *OCD*, s.v. 'Pythagoreanism'.

157/13 *songewarie, þe book of dremys*: The *MED* cites *D&P*'s use of the word 'songewarie' and also that of *PP*: 'Ac I haue no sauour in songewarie for I se it ofte faille' (B-Text, VII/154). Cf. *An Apology for Lollard Doctrines*, ed. Todd, p. 95. Albertus Magnus notes the poor record of success among diviners and says that 'si dicamus Deum mittentem hanc scientiam fatuis et melancholis et aliis amentiam patientibus, et quod non intermitteret eam prudentissimis et optimis viris, et quod immittat eam quibus libet indifferenter et idiotis hominibus, magnum videbitur esse inconveniens' (*Opera*, Bk

2, 9: 202). Aquinas avers that most dreams have natural causes but that some few are inspired by God or by demons; divination by the latter is, of course, unlawful (*ST* II–II.95.6). Trevisa's Bartholomaeus, 6.27, taking note of Aristotle, Macrobius, Gregory, and Augustine, has an equally balanced view: some dreams are sent by angels, some by demons, and some result from bodily conditions, and in general 'eueriche man metiþ sweuenes acordinge to his complexioun, witt, and age' (*Properties*, 1: 337/32–3). John of Salisbury's *Policraticus* condemns dream interpretation, while leaving open the possibility of visions genuinely inspired by God (Bk. II, c. 15; *CCCM* cxviii, pp. 94–9). Thorndike (1923) points out that dream books 'are found in Latin manuscripts at least as early as the tenth century' (2: 294). See Flint (1991) on the roots in classical culture of medieval beliefs about dreams, and on the 'lunaria de somnis' connecting dream interpretation with the phases of the moon (pp. 193–6). S. F. Kruger, *Dreaming* (1992), thoroughly canvasses the subject; on dreambooks, see esp. pp. 7–16. The G manuscript of *D&P* contains a tale centred on a prognosticating dream. See 194/1 ff., and 2–193/25–194/61 below.

157/14 *þe Apostolis Lottis*: *Sortes apostolorum*, a method of forecasting by throwing dice. As the name indicates, it claimed a certain legitimacy from the Biblical account of how Matthias was chosen as the replacement for Judas (Acts 1: 26; see below 167/7). Bede argued, however, that this occurred before Pentecost: 'Inde est quod Matthias, qui ante Pentecosten ordinatur, sorte quaeritur' (*Super Act. Apost.*, *PL* 92: 945). Aquinas, after surveying the views of Augustine and Bede, says that 'si vero necessitas imminat, licitum est cum debita reverentia sortibus divinum judicium implorare' (*ST* II–II, 95.8). Thomas de Chobham, citing Jerome, says the same (*Summa* D.5, Q.2a; ed. Broomfield, pp. 468–9), as does Raymond of Peñafort, *Summa*, Bk. I, p. 102. See also Carpenter's *Destructorium* (1428; ed. G. R. Owst, 1952, p. 35); Thorndike (1923), 1: 727, 2: 606–7; see Flint (1991), pp. 221–4; 273–89, on St Augustine's influence on the 'Christianizing' of lots.

158/15 *gaderyng of herbis*: Conditionally forbidden by canon law: 'Nec in collectionibus herbarum que medicinales sunt aliquas obseruationes aut incantationes liceat attendere, nisi tantum cum symbolo diuino aut oratione dominica. . .' (C. 26 q. 5 c. 3: Friedberg 1: 1028); see also, idem, q. 7, c. 18 (Friedberg 1: 1046). Raymond of Peñafort finds it licit to combine herbs with the Creed and prayers (*Summa*, Bk. I, pp. 104–5). In the early thirteenth century, Thomas de Chobham follows canon law in warning against mixing heathen incantations with Christian medical treatment but says that if psalms are sung while herbs are gathered 'ad laudandum et exorandum deum ut per ipsum habeant prosperitatem in opere suo, bene facit et non peccat' (*Summa*, 5, Q. VIIIIa, ed. Broomfield, pp. 480–1). Flint (1991) refers to a passage in Augustine's *De doctrina christiana* Bk. II, as a 'loophole' in the prohibitions against herbal magic, namely, that the intentions of the user are to be taken into account (pp. 301–3; ref. to Augustine: *CCL*, xxxii, p. 64/19–21; *PL* 34: 56–7). In an illness, it was often difficult for the healer to distinguish between the orthodox use of prayer and unorthodox magical incantations intended to strengthen the curative powers of medicinal herbs: see Kieckhefer (1989; repr. 1992), pp. 64–9; 83–5 and *passim*; F. M. Getz, ed. (1991), *passim*. See also Duffy (1992), pp. 267–298.

158/15–19 *hanging of scrowis*: Pauper follows Aquinas's warning 'ne cum verbis sacris contineantur aliqua vana, puta aliqui characteres inscripti praeter signum crucis' (*ST* II–II.96.4). Thomas de Chobham's (1216) penitential *Summa* makes the same distinction, recounting a story about a man who attempts to enter a brothel while wearing a gospel text around his neck and is sent away by the indignant 'meretrix', cured of his sins (ed. Broomfield, 1968, pp. 479–80). C. F. Bühler, 'Prayers and Charms', discusses surviving manuscripts comprising scrolls, or rotuli, on which are promises that the wearers will come to no harm (*Speculum* 39 (1964), 270–8). W. R. Jones discusses the late sixth-century 'Christ-letter' sent by the Archangel Michael, showing that such credulity was by no means limited to the simple and ignorant; the 'letter' was copied and translated throughout Europe, east and west, and survived numerous attempts to discredit it. It appears in BL, Add. MS. 15236 (s.xiii-s.xiv) along with herbal recipes, charms, and the like ('The Heavenly Letter in Medieval England', *Medievalia et Humanistica* 6 (1975), 163–78). On charms, Duffy (1992), pp. 266–287.

158/26 *he*: Should probably also be editorially emended to read [þey].

158/27–39 *xxvi, q. v, Episcopi . . . paynym*: The canon 'Episcopi' urges clerics to eradicate the practise of certain women said to be ensnared by Satan, who serve the pagan goddess Diana, or Herodias, and ride about the world at night on 'quasdam bestias' (C.26 q.5 c.12; Friedberg 1: 1030–1). It was evidently Burchard of Worms (d. 1025) who standardized the reference to 'Diana' and 'Herodias':

. . . quaedam sceleratae mulieres retro post Satanam conversae, daemonum illusionibus, et phantasmatibus seductae, credunt se et profitentur nocturnis horis, cum Diana paganorum dea, vel cum Herodiade et innumera multitudine mulierum equitare super quasdam bestias, et multa terrarum spatia intempestae noctis silentio pertransire ejusque jussionibus velut dominae obedire et certis noctibus ad ejus servitium evocare. (*PL* 140: 831–2)

A twelfth-century penitential:

Qui daemonis illusione decepti creduntur et profitentur se in famulatu ipsius quam vulgus insipiens Herodiadem vel Dianam vocant, et cum innumera multitudine ire vel equitare, et ejus jussis obedire. *Reliquae Antiquae*,ed. T. Wright and J. O. Halliwell, 1: 285.

Thomas de Chobham's *Summa* (1216) has the same, nearly word for word (D.5, Q.IIIa; ed. Broomfield, p. 472]). Raymond of Peñafort refers to the same deluded women and their nocturnal rides (*Summa*, Bk. I, pp. 106–7). Cf. Lea (1887), 3: 448–9; 494–500; Kittredge (1929), p. 244; J. B. Russell (1972), pp. 75–100; Flint (1991), pp. 122–6. See 157/6–7 above.

158/39 *he þo*: see 61/3–4 above.

158–9/39–49 *And he þo . . . but þey woldyn amendyn hem:* A parody of the mass intended to elicit the aid of the Devil for nefarious purposes. As early as 694, the seventeenth Council of Toledo prohibited this, under pain of degradation for the officiating priest and perpetual exile for him and for his employer (Mansi, 12: 99); it was still being prohibited in 1274, in Constitution 17 of the Council of Lyons, which speaks of a 'detestabilem abusum' by those who similarly misuse the cross and holy images (idem, 24: 92). Raymond of Peñafort refers to priests who shroud the altar in black, remove altar lights and surround the crucifix with thorns before saying Mass for the Dead for a living person (*Summa*, Bk. I, p. 106). Kittredge (1929) cites Gerald of Wales's (1147-c.1223) story of 'wicked priests who pervert the sacrament of the altar to black magic, celebrating masses over waxen images for the sake of cursing some victim, or singing the 'missa fidelium' ten times or more, with an imprecation, in order that the person may die before the tenth day or soon after and be buried with the dead' (p.147). The story is from Gerald's *Gemma Ecclesiastica* D. I, c. 49, and his source in turn is Peter the Chanter (d. 1197), whom he copies word for word: 'Item (quod flens dico): Hoc tantum sacramentum quidam in artem magicam verterunt, celebrando missas super imagines cereas ad imprecandum alicui, etiam alicui imprecantes, missam fidelium decies vel pluries decantant, ut ante decimum diem vel post in brevi moriatur, et cum mortuis sepeliatur' (*PL* 205: 106). See Lea (1887), 3: 447; K. Thomas (1971), who cites this passage from *D&P*, p. 34.

159/49–59 *as þe lawe seyth . . . diuinaciones*: The canon law citations comprise C. 26 q. 5 c. 12 ('in þat same place and in þe neste chapitele . . . & Si quis' (see 120/32, 158/27–39 above), and C. 26 q. 5 cc. 2, 5, 9, 10, and 3 (Friedberg 1: 1027–32). These canons list the many kinds of witchcraft and prescribe suspension from office, perpetual penance, retirement to a monastery, or excommunication for members of the clergy who are implicated in such practices.

159/54 *lawe imperial . . . et 1. Culpa:* From Justinian's code: 'De Maleficis et Mathematicis et Ceteris Similibus . . . 5. Nemo haruspicem consulat aut mathematicum, nemo hariolum. augurum et vatum prava confessio concescat. Chaldaei ac magi et ceteri, quos maleficos ob facinorum magnitudinem vulgus appellat, nec ad hanc partem aliquid moliantur. sileat omnibus perpetuo divinandi curiositas. etenim supplicium capitis feret gladio ultore prostratus, quicumque iussis obsequium denegaverit . . . 8. Culpa similis est prohibita discere quam dicere', *Corpus iuris civilis*, C.9.18 (2: 379–80).

159/61 *Also it is defendyd . . . Extra, lib. v, ti. xxvi, c. i & ii*: This canon law citation, to which there are no manuscript or early printed textual variants in *D&P*, is probably a mistake. But canon X 5.21.2 ('De sortilegiis') states: 'Presbyter, qui per inspectionem astrolabii furta requirit, ad tempus suspenditur ab altaris ministerio' (Friedberg 2: 822). Raymond of Peñafort: 'What of priests or religious from whom vessels or church ornaments are stolen; or lay persons from whom things are stolen—are they never to search for them by using an astrolobe, or similar instrument? To this you reply, following all authorities, that it is by no means allowed if it is accompanied by the invocation of demons or some other supersitious act; indeed whoever does this sins gravely' (*Summa*, Bk. I, pp. 105–6). See also the fourteenth-century *Memoriale* on the confessor's penalty for such a use of witchcraft (quoted in part from canon law): 'Si quis in tabulis vel in libris pro rebus furatis detegendis . . . demones invocaverit, si laicus fuerit a communione ecclesie debet privari' (ed. Heren, p. 139).

A case before the London courts in October 1382 illustrates common-place belief in sorcery:

> Robert Berewold of London promised Alan, a water carrier, that he would find out who had stolen a mazer from the house of Matilda of Eye. Thereupon he took a loaf, fixed a wooden peg in the top, placed four knives on each side in the form of a cross, and then 'did soothsaying and art magic' over them. Having completed the ritual he then named the culprit as one Johanna Wolsy. Johanna for this took him to court, which decided that by such soothsaying and magic arts people might have their good name tarnished, and that furthermore such sorcery was manifestly opposed to Christian doctrine. Alan was sentenced to the pillory. . . . (Bellamy, 1973, p. 63)

160/11–15 *kyngis lawe . . . holy chyrche lawis*: The references in *D&P* to the several authorities of the 'lyche lord', 'kyngys lawe and londis lawe' reflec* the continuing decentralized character of the enforcement of English civi* law: '[T]he group of professional lawyers which had [in the thirteenth century] formed itself round the king's court was small; the king's perman-ent justices were few, the serjeants were few, and some seven scor* apprentices and attorneys seemed enough. A great deal of legal busines* was still being transacted, a great deal of justice done, by those who were no* professional experts. The knight, the active country gentleman, would a* times be employed as a justice of assize or of gaol delivery, besides makin* the judgments in the county court. . . . In one way or another the commo*

folk were constantly receiving lessons in law; the routine of their lives often
took them into the courts, even into courts presided over by a Pateshull, a
Raleigh, a Bracton' (Pollock & Maitland, 1: 220). Henry de Bracton's *De
legibus et Consuetudinibus Angliae* was an early attempt to unify and system-
atize English law. By contrast, canon law provided a unified code of written
law and a university-trained body of ecclesiastics to administer it. Since the
justices who administered both kinds of law were often clerics, the effect of
canon law on English common law was far-reaching. Some effects were
beneficent: 'English law, more especially the English law of civil procedure,
was rationalized under the influence of the canon law' (Pollock & Maitland,
2: 134). Other outcomes were such conflicts as the quarrel between Henry II
and Thomas Becket over the Constitutions of Clarendon (of 1164), which
attempted to set limits to the jurisdiction of the Church courts (idem,
1: 439–57; see Smalley (1973). See 209/221–7 and 2–52/26 below.

161/42 *Io. 8: 44*: See 154/39–43 above.

162/1–92 *Swyche craftis . . . holy preyeris . . .* : Dives continues to point to
the difficulty of distinguishing between rites that are 'holy' or legitimate and
rites that are strategems of 'þe fendis craft' and Pauper to insist that the
distinction must be made. In this connection, Duffy (1992) refers to the
'accessibility of the daily celebration to the laity. . . . the laity controlled,
often indeed owned these altars. They provided the draperies . . . the images
and ornaments and lights. . . . they specified the times and seasons at which
the appearance and worship of the altar was to be varied' (et seq., pp. 113–
116, citing *The Doctrinale of Sapience*, ed. William Caxton (1489), fo. 673ᵛ.
Cf. 168/9–31 below.

162/19–20 *holy candel . . . feet roddyd of*: Pauper's example of the use of a
holy candle as a weapon against an enemy is not attested elsewhere; Thomas
(1971), p. 51, cites this example alone. The symbolic power of candles is also
(or mainly) connected with their use in church services; candles blessed at
Candlemas (February 2) were carried away from the ceremony 'to be lit
during thunderstorms or in times of sickness, and . . . placed in the hands of
the dying' (Duffy (1992), pp. 16–17).

163/37–38 *Vos facitis . . . Io. viii [44]*: See above 154/39–43.

163/45–7 *somtyme þey cuttyn hemself . . . III Regum xviii [28]*: 1 Kgs. 18: 28:
'Clamabant ergo voce magna et incidebant se iuxta ritum suum cultris et
lanceolis donec perfunderentur sanguine.' Refers to Elijah's taunting of the
priests of Baal, whose rites and bloodletting fail to elicit a response from
their god.

164/61 *ferste commandement*: See 81/7 above.

164/63–4 *iudicial of astronomye*: see 117/3–43 above.

164/64–71 *pyromancye, aeromancye, geomancye, ydromancie, nygromancie*: This list of supposed occult practises is a regular feature of the penitentials, taking its cue from canon law, in part derived from Augustine's *De divinatione demonum* (*PL* 40: 581–92; C. 26, q. 3 & 4, c. i: Friedberg 1: 1024). Rather than being schools of divination, however, the first four are a categorization of the materials used in divination on the basis of the four elements: 'pyro-' includes divination by lighted candles, 'aero-' by the winds, or by birds, 'geo-' by magic stones or metallic objects, and 'ydro-' by holy wells or basins of water. 'Nygromancie' is a catch-all term with a confused etymology. The VL word is 'nigromantia', which suggests black magic (DuCange s.v.); but Isidore of Seville explained to the Middle Ages that the origin was really Greek νεκρος, dead body, and thus had to do with bringing dead bodies to life by sprinkling them with blood; in the sixteenth century, this explanation carried the day, hence the modern spelling of the word (*Etym.* VIII ix [1: 8: 9/11–12]); cited by Aquinas (*ST* II–II.95.3). Cf. Burchard of Worms: '. . . verro autem dicit divintionis quatuor esse genera: terram, aquam, aerum, et ignem' (*PL* 140: 840). See Kieckhefer (1989; repr. 1992), pp. 151–75; Flint (1991), pp. 52–3; 120; 214–16. See 151/51 above.

165/88 *zongrir*: Read 'zongere': young people.

165–6/6–7 *And perfor Iob . . . Iob 41: 25*: 'Ipse est rex super universos filios superbiae.' Cited in LL4: 'he is kyng abouyn alle chyldryn of pryde', fo. 62ʳᵃ. The 'Behemoth' of the VL Bible is glossed as the 'fend' outwitted by the crucifixion of Christ: 'Iste est titulus dyabolis; sic humilitas christi qui signo utrius que exercitus secernitur. . . . per hoc quid in imo ponitur viciorum radix esse monstratur, sicut enim inferius radix tegitur, sed ab illa rami exterius panduntur, ita se superbia intrinsecus celat, inde fiunt aperta mala' (GO, 2: 454). St Gregory on Leviathan: 'Quia enim originem perditionis nostrae se praebuit superbia diaboli, instrumentum redemptionis nostrae inuenta est humilitas Dei' (*Moralia*, 34.54; *CCL* cxliiiB, p. 1771/176–8; *PL* 76: 748).

166/8–9 *Antecrist . . . 2 Thess. 2: 3–4*: '. . . filius perditionis /qui adversatur et extollitur supra omne quod dicitur Deus aut quod colitur, ita ut in templo Dei sedeat ostendens se quia sit Deus.' The identification with Antichrist is in the glosses: '. . . diaboli qui perdidit homines . . . vnde antichristus dicitur' (GO, interlin., 4: 402); cf. Nicolaus de Lyra: '. . . loquitur enim de antichristo prophetice' (*Postilla* 4). See 213/44–55 below.

166/12–13 *Sent Powil . . . [Col. 3: 5]*: '. . . avaritiam, quae est simulacrorum servitus', cited 100/33 above and 2–78/60, 2–264/57 below.

166/13–14 *Sent Ierom . . . god*: St Jerome, in *Commentariurum in Epistolam ad Ephesios Libri tres*, c. 5, says the avaricious man is an idolator (*PL* 26: 554).

166/19 *Sent Powil . . . Phil. 3: 19*: '. . . quorum Deus venter'. GO: 'Vt gloria eorum temporalis perducet eos confusionem aeternum' (4: 386).

166/20–2 *Inasmychil . . . synne in general*: That the first Commandment comprises all is a commonplace, which recurs in *D&P*, see below 2–28/43–7, 2–28/47–8;52–7 and 2–29/71.

166/1 *lottys*: See 157/14 above.

167/7 *Act. 1: 26*: 'Et dederunt sortes eis et cecidit sors super Mathiam, et adnumeratus cum undecim apostolis.' See 157/14 above, where Bede's argument that lots were allowable before Pentecost is cited. The GO cites this same text (4: 454).

167/8 *Genesis xxiv* [*14*]: 'Igitur puella cui ego dixero, Inclina hydriam tuam ut bibam, et illa responderit, Bibe, quin et camelis tuis dabo potum, ipsa est quam praeparasti servo tuo Isaac, et per hoc intelligam quod feceris misericordiam cum domino meo.' Nicolaus de Lyra's postil stresses that 'Eliezer non quesiunt signum per modum augurii vel diuinationis quod est illictum' (*Postilla* 1). The GO (Augustine) says it is very like augury: 'Quaerundum est quid differat illicitae augurationes a petitione hac qua petit seruus ut sibi ostenderet deus ipsam futurum uxorem ysaac . . .', but finds it excusable in this case, as in other OT episodes. Gregory adds a gloss allegorizing the water (the words of the preachers) and the camels as the 'stulti' who, along with the 'prudentes', hear the words of the preachers (1: 63).

167/9 *Prouerb. xvi* [*33*]: 'Sortes mittuntur in sinum sed a Domino temperantur.' The moral of which, says the gloss, is that man's hidden merits are subject to the deferred judgement of God (GO, 2: 674).

167/25–7 *D.xxxv, Episcopus, et Extra . . . gamys*: The canon 'Episcopus' provides that deacons, presbiters and bishops who are inebriates or dicers shall be deposed (Gratian; C.35 c.1; Friedberg 1: 131). The canon 'Clerici' (in a section of the corpus juris dealing with the 'vita et honestate clericorum') warns clerics against mimes and actors as well as against gaudy attire and games of chance (Innocent III; X 3.1.15; Friedberg 2: 454).

168/9–31 *only to blend þe peple . . . mankende*: Wyclif, in *c.*1381, warned of the tendency of sacramental ritual to produce a mystique, in his *De Euch.*, p. 323. Cf. 162/1–92 above.

168/32–4 *To helyn mennys woundys . . . shewyth wel*: The thirteenth-century *Ancrene Riwle* mentions the use of oil and wine for wounds (EETS, 252, ed. Mack and Zettersten, p. 159/28–9]). A thirteenth-century Franciscan manuscript gives a prescription to stop bleeding: the application of wool and olive oil, accompanied by a prayer, see Reichl (1995), p. 312. Guy de Chauliac's *Cyrugie* (1363) gives a recipe for treating wounds, citing Galen and Avicenna: 'emplastrum nigrum (i. a blak emplastre)', and 'vnguentum de lino, i. an oynement made of þe rede poudre incoporede (i. medled wiþ waschen terebentyne' (ed. Ogden, EETS, 265, p. 210). On the theory and teaching of medicine in late medieval Oxford, see F. M. Getz, *HUO*, 2: 373–405.

169/5 *holynesse . . . ypocrysye . . . wychecraft*: A threefold distinction is made among: (1) prayer directed to God (and seen to be directed to God), which is praiseworthy; (2) prayer that pretends to achieve a miracle, which is both hypocritical and sinful, and (3) prayer that is directed to the Devil, which is witchcraft. To make Pauper prove his argument, Dives concocts some test cases involving snake-charming and revenants.

169/16–18 *in nedderys and serpentis . . . Genesis iii [1 et seq.]*: Gen. 3: 1 ff.: 'Sed et serpens erat callidior cunctis animantibus terrae quae fecerat Dominus Deus.' Augustine says the serpent is unique among beasts since it contains the spirit of the Devil; in Paradise before the Fall, God allowed this, just as Christ allowed the demons to enter the bodies of pigs; thus snake charmers have power over the Devil, *De gen. ad lit.* XI, cc. 2, 12, 28 (*PL* 34: 431). In St Gregory's *Dialogues*, St Benedict's power over snakes is exemplified when he uses a 'draco' to frighten a monk back into his monastery (Bk. II, c. 25; *PL* 66: 182).

169/19–21 *Is it ony peryl . . . how he faryth?*: Stories of pacts to return from death with a report on the state of the deceased proliferated as, especially from the thirteenth century on, the idea of purgatory became a settled dogma. Augustine's *De civ. dei* had opened the door to the possibility by asserting that those dead who were predestined for salvation could be helped by prayer, and by his speculations about the 'first death' preceding the final judgement (e,g. Bk. 21.13–14; 16; *CCL* xlviii, pp. 778–80; 782–3; *PL* 41: 727–9; 730–1). St Gregory's 'Dialogues' refer to purgatorial fire (Bk. IV, c. 39, *PL* 77: 396), as does Bede's 'De tabernaculo' (*CCL* 119A: 128). Honorius' *Elucidarium* (early twelfth century) was influential (*PL* 172: 1158–9). After Aquinas' death (1274), the continuators of his *Summa* added a supplement filling out the doctrine of purgatory, including the idea of returning souls, or ghosts (*ST* Suppl. QQ. 69–71); Alan of Lille, Alexander of Hales, Albertus Magnus, St Bernard, and Bonaventure (among others) elaborated on the theme. Peter Cantor's *Verbum Abbreviatum* helped to popularize the idea (*PL* 205: 30–1). The second Council of Lyons (1274) apparently confirmed the doctrine in extra-Constitutional correspondance between Gregory X and Emperor Michael VIII: 'Eos, qui post baptismum in peccata labuntur non rebaptizandos . . . eorum animas poenis purgatoriis, seu catharteriis . . . post mortem eis fidelium vivorum suffragia, Missarum scilicet sacrificia, orationis, et eleemosynas, & alia pietatis officia, quae a fidelibus pro aliis fidelibus fieri consueverunt secundum ecclesiae instituta . . . illas . . . sunt purgatae, mox in coelum recipi' (Mansi, 24: 70–1). See A. Michel, *DTC* xiii, 1: 1163–1326, s.v. 'purgatoire'; for a recent view,

LeGoff (1981; tr. 1984); on LeGoff's translation, see Edwards, 'Purgatory: Birth or Evolution' (1985), *JEH* 36, 634–46.

169/22 *Sent Powyl . . . [2 Cor. 11: 14]*: '. . . ipse enim Satanas transfigurat se in angelum lucis'. The GO: 'In his diebus malignis, ubi ista sollicitudo non est inutilis, ne cum sathanas transfigurat se fallendo ad aliqua perniciosa seducat. Nam cum sensus corporis fallit, mentem vero non movet a vera recta quod sententia qua quibus fidelem vitam gerit, nullam est in religione periculum. Vel cum se fingens bonum ea vel facit vel dicit quae congruunt bonis angelis etiam si credatur bonus, non est error periculosus, aut morbidus . . . opus est magna vigilantia' (4: 351). Cited below 2–118/8.

170/48–50 *Sent Powil . . . vnpunchyd*: Col. 3: 24 has the sense: 'Scientes quod a Domino accipietis retributionem hereditatis Domino Christ servite/ qui enim iniuriam facit recipiet id quod inique gessit', but other texts (Rom. 2: 6, 2 Cor. 5: 10, and Heb. 2: 2) are similar. Innocent III's *De Miseria* (1195) is a possible source: 'Sicut dicit Apostolus . . . nullum malum preterit impunitum, nullum bonum irremuneratur relinquit', ed. Lewis (1978), p. 229/33–9. See also *Old English Miscellany* (1244–50): 'Ne schal non vuel beon vn-bouht . ne no god [good] vn-vorgulde' (ed. Morris, EETS, os 49, p. 60/60); and *The Book of the Knight of La Tour Landry* (1372): 'Ther shall nor good dede nor good lyff [go] vnrewarded, nor no wickednesse vnponisshed' (ed. Wright, EETS os 33, p. 165/16–17).

171/58–61 *þe Philosophre*: The first sentence of Aristotle's *Metaphysics* (*Oxford Aristotle*, 2: 1552); Latin translation by William of Moerbeke c1260.

172/1–70 *fastyngis newly foundyn*: Margery Kempe (in the early fifteenth century) 'mad a vow to fastyn o day in þe weke for worschep of owr Lady whyl sche had leuyd, whech vow sche kept many 3erys' until dissuaded by her confessor on grounds of health (ed. Meech and Allen, EETS, 212), p. 163. H. E. Allen's explanatory note refers to H. G. Richardson (*NQ*, 11 (1911), 4: 321, 527; 5: 54, and *The Library* 15 (1934), 32), who had noted the *D&P* reference to the Lady Fast but was unable to supply supporting evidence for it. Duffy (1992) says: 'A custom like the Lady fast, in which the devotee noted which day of the week Lady Day in Lent (the feast of the Annunciation, 25 March) fell on, and observed that day throughout the year as a fast in honour of the Virgin, was established by 1410, much to the disgust of the author of *Dives and Pauper*' (pp. 41–2). Duffy (idem, Pl.14) points to the element of chance brought in by the use of a kind of roulette wheel, spun in order to set the day of the fast for the ensuing year; the wheel, with yarns attached, might perhaps have been thought of as symbolizing one of Mary's iconographic attributes as a spinster; on such 'wheels' see G. McM. Gibson, *Theater of Devotion* (1989), p. 152, and Fig. 6.7; W. H. Sewell, 'The Sexton's Wheel and the Lady Fast', *Norfolk Archaeology* 9 (1884), 201–14. A reference to the Fast (though not to the element of chance in its observance) is in Walter Hilton's *The Scale of Perfection* (ed. Underhill, p. 282).

173/29–33 *Salomon . . . don our deuyr*: Eccles. 9: 1. perhaps cited from memory, cf. Vulgate: 'et tamen nescit homo utrum . . .' (1: 993).

173/41 *De con., di.iii, Ieiunia, et c. Sabato*: The canons 'Ieunia' and 'Sabato' refer to the correctness of observing fast days on the fourth and sixth days of the week: on the fourth day, Judas betrayed Christ; on the sixth day, Christ was crucified (De cons. D.3 c.16 and De cons. D.3 c.13; Friedberg 1: 1356–7 and 1355–6). Referred to below, 275/19.

174/54–61 *Friday . . . angelys gretynge*: Peter Comestor: 'Creditur autem conceptus octo Kalendas Aprilis, et, revolutis triginti tribus annis, eadem die mortuus' (*PL* 198: 1537). The late fourteenth-century *Stanzaic Life of Christ*: 'Vpon a Friday oure lady / Conceyued Crist with al mekenesse / ffor on a Friday, bi trewe story,/ Adam both wroȝt & wayuet wesse' (ed. Foster, EETS, 166, pp. 3/65–70, 72–4).

174/1 ff. *Is it leful . . . dremys*: See 157/13 above for discussion of dreams as prognostication. Chapters 43–5 of Commandment I return to the topic but begin instead with the physical causes of dreams. For the history of dreaming and dream theory, from Aristotle to the end of the Middle Ages, Kruger (1992), pp. 17–122.

175/6–7 *Salomon . . . Ecclesiastes v [6]*: Eccles. 5: 6; 'Ubi multa sunt somnia plurimae vanitates et sermones innumeri tu vero Deum time'.

175/22 *þe Filosofre, De sompno & vigilia*: Aristotle, 'On Divination in Sleep': 'Even scientific physicians tell us that one should pay diligent attention to dreams', *Oxford Aristotle*, 1: 736; Gallop (1991), p. 105/6–7; the introduction stresses Aristotle's physicalist view of dreams, pp. 1–54. Cf. 157/13 above.

175/27–8 *þe kyng Pharao and Nabugodonosor*: Pharaoh's dreams are found in Gen. 41: 15–36; Nebuchadnezzar's in Daniel 2: 1–45.

175/29–31 *Sent Powil . . . Daniel in hese prophecye*: St Paul's 'dream' is found in 2 Cor. 12: 1–4; Balaam's visions are found in Num. 23: 9 and 24: 17 *passim*; St John's visions in the Book of Revelations, *passim*; Daniel's prophecies in Dan. 1: 17, 2 *passim*; 4 *passim*, 5: 17, 7: 1–28, and 8: 1–27.

176/38–40 *And perfor Salomon . . . wakyn*: Eccles. 5: 2: 'Multas curas sequuntur somnia et in multis sermonibus invenitur stultitia.' GO: 'Quasi sicut qui multa cogitat, ipsa frequenter somniat, sic in stulticiam recidit qui vltra se de deo disputat. Vel quia modo videmus per speculum & in aegnimate et quasi per somnum extimamus nos tenere quod non habemus, et tamen nihil habemus' (2: 700).

177/65–6 *Sent Gregorie . . . sompnia*: St Gregory's *Moralia in Job*, 8.43 (on Job 7: 14): 'Saepe namque malignus spiritus his quos amore vitae praesentis vigilantes intercipit prospera etiam dormientibus promittit; et quos formidare adversa considerat, eis haec durius somnii imaginibus intentat, quatenus indiscretam mentem diversa qualitate afficiat, eamque aut spe sublevans, aut deprimens timore, confundat.' etc. (*CCL* cxliii, p. 414/88–93; *PL* 75: 827). *Moralia* 8.41–2 deals with the causes of dreams. Cf. *Chastising of God's Children* (late fourteenth century), on how 'þei shul be examyned þat han visions and reuelacions, to knowe whether þei comen of a goode aungel or of a wicked spirit', ed. Bazire and Colledge (1957), pp. 175–82. *Moralia* 8 is cited 2–212/44 below. See 157/13 above.

177/2 *Leuitici xix* [26] . . . *feyth perynne*: *D&P* emphasizes its source by adding 'witchcraft' to the translation. The GO condemns all such superstitions as defiance of God's creation ('deum videtur infamare') and as the practices of 'barbari' and 'pagani' (1: 254). Gregory's *Moralia* 8 (see 177/65–6 above) cites this passage (*CCL* cxliii, p. 413/68; *PL* 75: 827).

177/6–178/15 *Deutronomii xviii* [*10–11*] . . . *xiii* [*1–3*] . . . *nouȝt*: Deut. 18: 10–11: 'Nec inveniatur in te . . . qui ariolos sciscitetur et observet somnia atque auguria, ne sit maleficus ne incantator ne pythones consulat ne divinos et quaerat a mortuis veritatem'. The GO on 'ariolos': 'Qui circumeunt aras nefandis precibus & diuinationem in extis animalium quaerunt'; on 'auguria': 'Quasi auiguria in vocibus auium geruntur. Vel auigaria ab auium garritu'; on 'phitones': 'Ventriloquos, de quorum ventre daemones loquuntur a phitio sic dictos, i.e., apolline quem deum diuinatoris credebunt esse' (GO 1: 398). Deut. 13: 1–3; 5: 'Si surrexerit in medio tui prophetes aut qui somnium vidisse se dicat et praedixerit signum atque portentum/ et evenerit quod locutus est et dixerit tibi, Eamus et sequamur deos alienos quos ignoras et serviamus eis;/ non audies verba prophetae illius aut somniatoris, quia temptat vos Dominus Deus vester, ut palam fiat utrum diligatis eum an non in toto corde et in tota anima vestra.' The GO: 'Vult intelligi ea quae a diuinis non secundum deum dicuntur, etiam si euenerint non esse sic accipienda vt fiant quae ab eis praedicuntur, nec praeter potestatem suam ostendit esse quae ita contingant. Sed quare permittat supponit ad cognoscendum, sci., quantum diligant deum, seruientes ipsis, non illi qui omnia nouit' (1: 391). To his translation of Deut. 13 the author of *D&P* adds: 'sothsawere', 'ȝif he steryth þe to mametrie or to ony wychecraft' and 'þey he were þin owyn broþir be fadyr and be moodyr þu schuldyst nouȝt sparyn hym in þat cas'. Cf. 157/10 (birds) and 158–9/39–40 (altars) above.

178/20 *Ecclesiastici xxxiv* [*7*]: Ecclus. 34: 7: 'Multos enim errare fecerunt somnia et exciderunt sperantes in illis.' The GO comments that dreams are caused by illusions of the Devil, by overeating, and by special revelations of

God (e.g., Joseph and Daniel). But dreams should not be used as auguries: 'ualde enim detestbilia somnia ostenduntur quam auguriis coniunguntur' (2: 779).

178/25–7 *God . . . may changyn and letyn þe werkyng of kende*: See 120/47–73 and 121/1–7 above.

179/44–5 *kyng Pharao . . . kyng Nabugodonosor*: Gen. 41: 1–38 and Dan. 2: 1–49; 4: 8–27.

181/1–11 *frowde*: Popular belief tends towards the lucky toad; clerical opinion towards the evil toad: in a *Gesta Romanorum* story, a toad is allegorized as the Devil (ed. S. J. H. Herrtage, EETS, es 33), pp. 17–19; Kittredge (1934) cites an Odo of Cheriton story (*Cat. of Rom.*, No. 122, 3: 70) about a peasant who finds a gigantic toad guarding his treasure hoard (p. 204, note p. 517). *Jacob's Well* retells a 'Caesarius of Heisterbach' story about a usurer whose hoard of ill-gotten wealth is turned into 'frowdys', which then devour the usurer himself (ed. A. Brandeis, EETS, os 115, 1: 209; cf. Tale 785 in *Alphabet of Tales*, ed. Banks (EETS os 126), p. 523. On the other hand, John of Salisbury's *Policraticus* (1159) says: 'Meeting a toad augurs future success, but to me the mere sight is unpleasant' (Bk. I, c. 13; *CCCM* cxviii, p. 66/150–9).

181/6: *he þo*: See 61/3–4 above.

182/14 *þe puttok*: The European kite, 'milvus milvus', see *MED* s.v. 'puttok'. The *Gesta Romanorum* has a fable in which the kite is moralised as the 'fende': 'Therefore fle we the puttok of helle vnto the wynges of *criste*' (ed. S. J. H. Herrtage, EETS, es 33), pp. 370–1. The account in Trevisa's *Bartholomaeus* 12.27 does not use the term 'puttok' but paints a picture of a cruel and cowardly 'kyte' (*Properties*, 1: 634–5]).

182/2–183/26 *þe kalendis of Ienuer . . . Sattyrday*: 'Kalendis' in reference to days of the month is used in two ways: (1) the 'kalendis' of a month may simply refer to the first day of the month, or (2) after the thirteenth of any month (in eight months of the year; after the fifteenth in the other four months), the expression used may be 'so many days before the "kalendis" of the next month'; that is, reckoned inclusively, 30 January would be 'three days before the "kalendis" of February'; see R. D. Ware, 'Medieval Chronology', in *Medieval Studies*, 2nd edn., ed. James M. Powell (Syracuse, N.Y., 1992), pp. 252–77. A twelfth-century penitential refers to lore about the first day of the year: 'Qui kalendas Januarii ritu paganorum futura maleficiis inquirendo obstruant, vel ipsa die opera incipit ut quasi malius nullo anno prosperentur': *Reliquae Antiquae*, ed. T. Wright and J. O. Halliwell, 1: 285. Mirk's *Festial* (fl. 1400) says that a sin is greater if committed on a holiday, fast day, or day in Lent rather than on a week day (ed. Erbe, EETS, os 31), p. 46/1490–8). Cf. Burchard of Worms' *Decretum*, which warns against superstition about 'times' (*PL* 140: 835). Cf. Lindström (1974b).

183/14–20 *M CCCC . . . þis ȝer*: 'This year' would appear to be 1405, based on the day on which 1 January fell in 1400, an important indication of the date of writing of *D&P*. See H. G. Richardson, 'Dives and Pauper' in *NQ* 11 (1911), 321–3; see *D&P* Introduction, pp. xviii–xix.

183/27–8 *Som dyuynyn be þondryng*: The twelfth-century manuscript, Cotton Vesp.D.XIV, No. 34, contains a short table of predictions about thunder, one for each month of the year. Thunder in January leads 'toweard mycele windes, & wel gewænde eorþe wæstme, & gefiht'; thunder in February forbodes the deaths of many, and the forecast is poor until July, when things improve through the month of December, a 'god gear [year] on tilþe, & sibb, & sehte [peacemaking]' (*Early English Homilies* (ed. Warner, EETS, os 152), p. 91/9–22; noted by B. Lindström (1974, a/b). This scheme may have originated in another climate than England's, however, because it does not quite agree with Pauper's explanation; cf. the list in the Thornton manuscript, fo. 50 (*Religious Pieces*, ed. Perry, EETS, os 26, p. 114). See also the fourteenth-century chart for divination by thunder in Kieckhefer (1989), pp. 86–7. A Wycliffite sermon (1390s) blames 'feendes' for thunder (*EWS* 1, Ep. Serm. 51/38–42); but another, set going by Luke 10: 18 ('Videbam Satanam sicut fulgur de caelo cadentem'), omits demons and refers to the natural reasons why the light of a thunderclap reaches us sooner than the sound (*EWS* 2, Serm. 62/29–38). See Flint (1991), pp. 108–116.

184/1 *amongys gentylis*: On gentility in this period see N. Saul, 'Chaucer and Gentility', in *Chaucer's England*, ed. B. Hanawalt (1992), pp. 41–55; cf. 52/21, 53/22–3 above.

184/2–3 *twelue dayys in Christemesse*: On calendar magic or prognostication, see 139/87, 182–3/2–26 and 183/27–8 above. Cf.'Christmas Day Prognostications' from MS. Digby 88, in *Secular Lyrics*, ed. Robbins (1952), pp. 63–7. These, however, forecast according to the day of the week on which Christmas falls.

184–5/20–24 *þat was to connyn . . . þat is, to conne*: Manuscripts DTYBL make a different reading of the first passage, possibly based on the attraction of the common phrase 'good and evil that was to come'; and manuscripts YH make a reading of the second passage based on the attraction of 'knowing weal and woe that is to come'. In the first case, manuscripts GRH unambiguously have 'connyn', and in the second case manuscripts GRDTB clearly have 'conne'. The first phrase would read nearly as well if written as 'þe fend hyȝte Adam and Eue þat þey schuldyn ben as goddis knowing good and wykkyd þat was to *comyn* ȝif þey woldyn etyn of þe tre aȝens Goddis precept.' The second phrase would not, however, make as

good sense if 'comyn' were substituted. I chose the more difficult reading for
both. A translation of the two phrases might read: 'At the beginning of the
world, the Devil promised Adam and Eve that they should be like gods,
knowing good and evil. This was to find out whether, against God's
command, they would eat from the tree. . . . Nowadays he promises men
in the same way that they will be like gods, knowing future weal and woe—
that is, know the future by the fantasies he puts into their heads—until he
brings them into real woe. . . .'

185/1–2 *to makyn metal gold and syluyr*: Dives makes a glancing allusion to
an enormous subject; as J. W. Spargo says in regard to Chaucer's 'Canon's
Yeoman's Tale', 'anyone interested in alchemy will speedily learn that the
subject is thus far as the sands of the sea unnumbered'. Spargo provides a
bibliography and general introduction (*Sources and Analogues*, pp. 685–98).
See also *CT*, C-Y Prol., p. 271/623–638). See further, Thorndike (1934) for
the medieval history of alchemy; a series of appendices give extracts from
alchemical writings (3:*passim*). See also R. P. Multhauf, 'Science of Matter'
in Lindberg (1978), pp. 372–82; and J. D. North, 'Natural Philosophy', in
HUO, 2: 74–5.

186/24 *xxvi, q. v, Episcopus*: The canon law reference as it stands is
incorrect. The intended reference may be to the canon 'Episcopi' cited
above (158/27–39) dealing mainly with the Diana/Herodias beliefs or
practices; at the end there occurs, without the word alchemy, the following:
'Quisquis ergo credit fieri posse, aliquam creaturam aut in melius aut in
deterius inmutari, aut transformari in aliam speciem vel in aliam similitu-
tinem . . .infidelis est, et pagano deterior' (C.26 q.5 c.11; Friedberg 1: 1030–
1), which might be imagined to cover the case.

186/1–12 *What seyst þu . . . Vident*: Two themes are intertwined here: the
unluckiness of meeting clerics, and an objection to clerics who hunt. On the
first, John of Salisbury's *Policraticus* (1159) says wryly: 'To meet a priest,
they say, is unlucky—I myself think it is just as unlucky to meet a wise man'
(Bk. I, c. 13; *CCCM* cxviii, p. 67). On hunting clerics, Robert of Brunne's
early fourteenth-century *Handlyng Synne* says:

> 3yf þou delyte þe oftyn stoundes,
> yn horsys, haukys, or yn houndes;
> 3yf þou clerk auaunsed be,
> Swyche game ys nat graunted to þe
> (ed. Furnivall, EETS, os 119, 123), p. 108/3083–6.

Cf. the fourteenth-century *Memoriale Presbytorum*: 'Omnis venacio clericis
regulariter est interdicta' (ed. Heren, 1975), pp. 112–13; section a:liii).
Chaucer's critical portrait of a hunting monk is well known (*CT*, Prol., 26/
165–207). The canon law references are to (1) 'Ne clerici' against involvement of monks in secular business, including hunting (X 3.50.1; Friedberg

2: 657); (2) 'De clerico venatore', which applies the same prohibition to bishops, priests or deacons (X 5.24.1–2; Friedberg 2: 825); (3) 'Quorundum', warning that bishops should not be unduly familiar with members of their households, including joining with them in the hunting of beasts and birds (D.34 c.1; Friedberg 1: 125); and (4) 'Vident', attributed to Augustine, which warns those who take pleasure in hunting: 'Qui enim uident uenatorem et delectantur, uidebunt Saluatorem et contristabuntur' (D.86 c.10; Friedberg 1: 300).

186/12–16 *What seyst þu . . . riȝth hond*: The unluckiness of the left hand is writ large in the iconography of the tympanums above the west portals of cathedrals where Christ, with outstretched arms, receives the saved on his right hand and rejects the damned on his left, cf. Matt. 25: 41: 'Tunc dicet et his qui a sinistris erunt: Discedite a me maledicti in ignem aeternum.' Pauper makes an ill-tempered leap from the trivial to the eschatalogical when he refers the 'proud getter's' arrogant 'On the lyft hond, frere!' (187/ 25–6) to the Last Judgement; compare, e.g., St. Jerome's 'Adversus Jovinianum': 'Qui in terrano fuit, a sinistris est et peribit. / Qui in coelesti, a dextra est, et salvabitur' (*PL* 23: 328); Burchard of Worms: 'quod dextera Dei, sit pars angelorum electa, sinistra autem ejus, pars angelorum reproba' (*PL* 140: 1030–1); Aelred of Rivaulx, 'De Institutione Inclusarum' (1160–2): 'Beholde stondynge on the lift syde a wrecched companye with gret stenche, gret drede and gret sorwe' (ed. Barratt, EETS, 287), p. 24/957–8; cf. *EWS* 3, Serm. 197/69–70: 'þe left syde of þe Fadir, on whiche Crist shal not sitte'. For the persistance of the superstition, see Opie (1989), pp. 230–1. See 187/34–43 below.

187/34–43 *God at þe dom . . . angelys*: Matt. 25: 33–41. LL4: 'Comyth ȝe myn fadrys blyssyd chyldryn & takith þe kyngdam & þe blysse þat was ordeynyd to ȝow from þe settynge of þe world' (fo. 68vb); 'For as he seyth in þe gospel, þat we don to þe leste of hese we don it to hym' (fo. 127vb); 'Goth fro me cursyd wrechis into þe fyr of helle wiþouten ende þat is ordeynyd to þe fend & hese aungelis' (fo. 81ra–b). The *CA* cites Augustine on the awesome nature of the Judgement scene: '[Q]uando uidebitur illud quod erat in principio Verbum, Deus apud Deum, per quod facta sunt omnia? quando uidebitur illa forma Dei, de qua dicit apostolus, "Cum in forma Dei esset . . ." [Phil.2: 6]? Magna enim illa forma ubi adhuc aequalitas Patris et Filii cognoscitur: ineffabilis, incomprehensibilis, maxime paruulis. Quando uidebitur? Ecce ad dexteram sunt iusti, ad sinistram sunt iniusti . . .' (*In Ioh.*, 21.14; *CCL* xxxvi, pp. 220–1/9–15; *PL* 35: 1572; cf. *CA* 1: 370). On 'lyft syde' see 186/12–16 above. Matt. 25 is cited six more times below: 2–242/29–38, 2–246/31, 2–249/28, 2–287/25, 2–315/39, 2–317/25–6.

188/14–45 *so manye fayre chirchys*: Pauper attempts to throw cold water on Dives' patriotic enthusiasm for English church architecture, but the architectural flowering of the fourteenth century in England stands as evidence of the accuracy of Dives' judgment. In her history of the development of Perpendicular, Joan Evans stresses the continuity of building through a period of wars, plagues, and shortages: 'To the men of the fourteenth and fifteenth centuries building was in itself a good act; if ecclesiastical, it glorified God, if secular, it was a part of good administration. In times of stress and shortage, to build might, indeed be a doubly virtuous act' (*Oxford History of English Art*, 5: 74). On Westminster Abbey and the Plantagenets, see Binski (1995). In this exchange, Dives and Pauper appear to change places: until now, Dives has been critical of church images, elaborate funeral rites and the like, and it would have been more consistent for him to be the one to attack beauty and ornament in church buildings, cf. *EWW* (1978), p. 85/75–8; Aston (1988), p. 113). A. D. Brown (1995) cites this passage in *D&P*, pp. 110–31.

188/16 *Sent Gregorie*: St Gregory's sermon on the talents (Matt. 24: 14–30), cited above (64/10–12), carries the general sense of Pauper's words: 'Sed Dominus, qui talenta contulit, rationem posituris redit, quia is qui nunc pie spititalia dona tribuit districte in judicio merita exquirit, quid quisque accepit considerat, et quod lucrum de acceptis reportet pensat . . . . Quisquis charitatem non habet etiam dona quae percepisse videbtur amittit' (*Homilia* IX, *PL* 76 [2]: 1107–8). See 2–251/5 below.

189/32–45 *For þe peple . . . wickyd þewys*: Sermons and penitentials complain repeatedly about layfolks' behaviour in church: parishioners come reluctantly; they are inattentive; the women overdress and preen themselves, distracting the men, etc. The author of *D&P* in his later sermon cycle complains that: 'þese dayys mochyl folk wyl nout lowyn hem to syttyn doun at þe sermoun, ne welyn heryn it wiþ meek herte, but þei welyn stondyn þat þey moun redely gon awey 3if þe prechour plese hem nout' (LL4, fo. 41ᵛᵇ). *Jacob's Well* attacks 'rounyng & ianglyng in cherch' and inveighs against women's elaborate hairdos (MS Salisbury 174, fos. 190ᵃ; 196ᵃ–97ᵃ). In the same period, Mirk enjoins:

> 3et þow [parish priest] moste teche hem mare
> þat whenne þey doth to chyrche fare,
> þenne bydde hem leue here mony wordes,
> Here ydel speche, and nyce bordes . . .
> (*Instructions*, ed. Peacock, EETS, os 31), p. 9/264–67)

On sermon audiences, see Owst (1926), pp. 200–21; Spencer (1993), pp. 64–77.

189/40 *Robyn Hood*: The legend may have arisen from a real Robin Hood tried in 1354 'for trespass of vert and venison in the forest of Rockinghem in Northants' (E. K. Chambers (1945), pp. 130; 129–37). Perhaps the earliest

reference to Robin Hood appears in *PP*, also in connection with what not to
do in church; Sloth says:

> I kan noȝt parfitly my Paternoster as þe preest it syngeþ,
> But I kan rymes of Robyn hood and Randolf Erl of Chestre,
>
> .   .   .   .
>
> I am ocupied eche day, halyday and ooþer,
> Wiþ ydel tales at þe Ale and ouþerwhile in chirches
> > (B-Text, V/394–5; 402–3, ed. brackets om.)

Another early reference, 'Friar Daw's Reply' (1420): 'many men speken of
Robyn Hood & shotte neuere in his bowe' (*Jack Upland*, ed. Heyworth,
p. 80/233). For manuscripts containing Robin Hood tales, see *Catalogue of
Romances*, 1: 517–22; see also Wilson (*Lost Literature*, 1952), pp. 128–31
(who refers to this instance in *D&P* on p. 130).

190/4–5 *heye chyrchis . . . grete bellys*: Dives' complaint does not directly
address the question of image worship (see 81/9, 82/42–4, 85/54–5, and
102/17–21 above) but rather 'the social injustice of images', cf. Aston
(1988), p. 124. This is a theme prominent in Lollard polemic, and (as Aston
points out) it is expressed in the General Prologue to the LV of the
Wycliffite Bible: 'Whanne men ȝeue not almes to pore nedy men, but to
dede ymagis, either riche clerkis, thei robbyn pore men of her due porcoun,
and needful sustenaunce assingned to hem of God himself' (FM, 1: 34; cf.
EWW, p. 84/59–63; *PR*, pp. 321–2). 'Jack Upland' says: 'Frere . . . [w]hi
make ȝe so costli housis to dwelle ynne, siþ Crist dide not so . . . [and] alle is
pilage of pore men' (ed. Heyworth, p. 61/165–9); cf. John Audelay's later
complaint against the friars (second quarter of the fifteenth century):

> Behold, syrus, apon here chyrche, now I ȝou pray,
> Apon here bellys, on here bokys, and here byldyng
> > (*Poems*, ed. Whiting, EETS, 184, 1931), p. 27/460–1.

190/11–15 *Salomon*: On Solomon's temple, see 1 Kgs. 6 & 7: often cited in
defence of elaborate church building.

190/18 [*Mc. 12: 41–4*] . . . *a pore wydue*: The GO, after explaining
'gazofilacium' (temple treasury) and 'quadrans' ('ex tribus consistit, cogitato,
verbo, facto'), sums up the moral of the story: 'Nec perpendit quantum
offeras eius sacrificio, sed ex quanto'. Jerome is cited: 'Vnisquisque
quadratum potest offerre. Haec est tota panis in leuitico, quae est voluntas
prompto' (4: 123). Bede allegorizes: '. . . diuites . . . Judeos de justitiae legis
elatos, porro vidua pauper Ecclesiae simplicitatem designat . . . Vidua vero,
quia vir eius pro ea mortem pertulit' PL 92: 258; cf *CA* 1: 529; *EWS* 3,
Serm. 235/12–20.

190/21–191/40 *Exodi xxx* [*11–16*] . . . *pouert*: In Nicolaus de Lyra's gloss is
found the interpretation that the rich and poor should give equally: '. . . et

equaliter in hoc expendebant diuites et pauperes ne diuites sanctiores se pauperibus reputarent, vel magis participare de diuinis, per hoc etiam que equaliter ponebant singuli' etc. (*Postilla* 1). Bede allegorizes: 'Mystice autem summa filiorum israel summam omnium electorum significat quorum nomina scripta sunt in caelo' (GO, 1: 189). See 192/54–193/75 below.

192/54–193/75 *II Regum* [*7: 13–14; 3 Reg. 5: 3*] . . . *kyng dauyd . . . doynge*: 2 Sam. 7: 13–14, 8: 1–18; 1 Kgs. 5: 3: the author of *D&P*, paraphrasing the passages from 2 Sam. and 1 Kgs., imports the phrase 'man of blood-schadynge' (*D&P* 192/71) from 2 Sam. 16: 8: 'quoniam vir sanguinum es'. Intentionally or not, he underlines the contrast between the warlike King David and the peaceful King Solomon. This would seem relevant to the circumstances in which *D&P* was written; see Introduction, pp. xviii ff. On the earlier reign of Henry IV and the minority of Prince Henry, see Wylie (1898), 3: 323–36; A. L. Brown (1964), 1–30; Allmand (1992), pp. 39–58; Pearsall (1994), 386–410. For a list of references to the story of the biblical King David in *D&P*, see 2–85/19ff. below.

193/2–19 *Io. xii* [*3–5*]: John 12: 3–5: the fact that in this gospel Judas is openly called a thief (v. 6) is usually glossed to mean that Christ admonishes Christians to tolerate the failings of their fellow Christians: 'Nouit furem, sed non prodit, docens tolerare malos' (GO, 4: 253). Augustine: 'Videamus quod ad ista Dominus respondeat. . . . Furem noverat, nec prodebat, sed potius tolerabat, et ad perferendas malos in ecclesia nobis exemplem patientiae demonstrabant' (*In Ioh.*, 50.11; *CCL* xxxvii, p. 437/6–10; *PL* 35: 1762). In *Jacob's Well*, Judas is depicted more specifically as a systematic stealer of tithes: 'Iudas grucchyd, & seyde: "Why is þis oynement þus wastyd? it myȝt a be sold for iij. hundred pens, & haue be ȝouyn to pore folk"' (ed. Brandeis, EETS os 115, p. 43/14–16). In the Wycliffite sermons, a covetous Judas is a type of the covetous priest (*EWS* 3, Serm. 177/15–16). In Franciscan polemic, mendicancy is defended on the ground that Judas was the only disciple to carry a purse, i.e., purse-carrying though not inherently wrong was perilous to moral life, as signified by the fact that Judas was the only wicked apostle (Bonaventure, *Apologia pauperum* VII, 35–7, X, 1–3; *Opera* VIII, pp. 284; 304). In *D&P*, Judas is made to signify those who hypocritically decry expenditure on churches in the name of charity to the poor—and who then skimp on alms and support of the clergy. On 'ypocrysie' see 212/3–213/9 below.

194/32 [*Lc. 10: 7*]: Luke 10: 7: '. . . dignus est enim operarius mercede sua'. The GO cites a homily of St Gregory (*In Evang.* 17), commenting that the 'workman' earns both an earthly and a heavenly reward (GO, 4: 198): '. . . duae mercedes debentur, una in via altera in patria; una quae nos in labore sustentat, alia quae nos in resurrectione remunerat' (*PL* 76: 1075); Gregory ends with a caveat, however: 'Sal etenim terrae non summis si corda audientum non condimus' (idem, col. 1143); cf. *CA*, 2: 145.

194/33 [*I Cor. 9: 1–14*]: The key passages are: 'Numquid non habemus potestatem manducandi et bibendi?. . . . Quis militat suis stipendiis unquam?. . . . Si nos vobis spiritualia seminavimus, magnum est si nos carnalia vestra metamus?. . . . Ita et Dominus ordinavit iis qui Evangelium annuntiant, de Evangelio vivere' (vv. 4, 7, 11, 14). Verse 7 is cited 2–155/76 below; v. 11, 65/56 above and 2–291/37–8 below; v. 14, 2–177/21–4 below, and in LL4, fo. 41vb. The word 'prechynge' does not appear in the biblical text, but the interlinear GO on v. 9 is: 'Non prohibebis predicatorem viuere de predicatione' (4: 320).

194/37 *Austyn . . . super Psalmum 103: 14*: The phrase 'Godys kny3this', suggested by 'Quis militat' (1 Cor. 9: 7; see 194/33 above), does not appear in Ps. 103: 14, but Augustine's gloss on Ps. 103 says: 'Accipis spiritualia, redde carnalia: debita sunt militi, militi reddis; provincialis Christi es' (*Enarr.*, 103.3.91; *CCL*, xl, p. 1507/32–3; *PL* 37: 1365). See below 2–177/26–7, 2–290/23–5.

195/1 *Mathei vi* [6]: Matt. 6: 6: 'Tu autem cum oraveris, intra in cubiculum tuum, et clauso ostio, ora Patrem tuum in abscondito: et Pater tuus, qui videt in abscondito, reddet tibi.' Pauper's allegorical interpretation of 'cubiculum' and 'ostium' is traditional. The GO says the text teaches simplicity of mind and flight from the vainglory of the world; the 'cubiculum' is the heart; the 'clauso ostio' shuts out idle fancies so that the mind may direct its attention to God (4: 24). Augustine says: 'Quae sunt ista cubicula nisi ipsa corda . . . [c]laudendum est ergo ostium, id est carnali sensui resistendum est' (*De Serm. Dom.*, 2.3.11; *CCL* xxxv, pp. 101/234–102/243–4; *PL* 34: 1274). The Wycliffite view is the same: 'Crist biddiþ not men preye algatis in bed or in couche for he wole þat men preyen in chirche' (*EWS* 3, Serm. 145/84–5). On private chapels, see 195/16–19 below.

195/16–19 *chambre or . . . oratorie*: The practise of constructing places for prayer in private dwellings began to be popular in the thirteenth century (see J. R. H. Moorman (1955), p. 15). A licence was required, the earliest record of which in an episcopal register was in 1277, 'when the Archbishop of York gave permission for the rector of Tuxford (Notts.) to have a private chapel' (idem, Regist. W. Gray, p. 16). Permits included restrictions, such as that the offerings collected must be given to the parish church, that marriages and baptisms not be celebrated there, and that on important holidays patrons attend services in the parish church (idem; see Wilkins, ii, 9; Lyndwood, *Provinciale*, 'Constitutio domini Othobonis' (1222), p. 6, and 'Constitutions of Stratford' (1342), p. 49a (edn. 1679). The practice was controversial: Trevisa's translation of FitzRalph's sermon 'Defensio Curatorum' (1357) has a 'conclusion' against such oratories: 'for parischons . . .

to schryue hem . . . þe parische chirche is more worþi to be chosen þan oratory oþer chirche of freres' (*Dialogus*, ed. Perry, EETS, 167), p. 40. *PP* comments unfavourably on the new desire for privacy (B-Text, X/99–103). The Pastons, in the fifteenth century, had a private chapel and private chaplain, a sign of privilege and good breeding (Bennett (1968), p. 205). See McFarlane's assessment of 'private chapels in the houses of the laity' as an aspect of English *devotio moderna* (1972), p. 225. Compare Pantin (1976) on the increased desire, in this period, for privacy in religious observance and in daily life ('Instructions', in Alexander and Gibson (1976), pp. 405–6). See also Andrew D. Brown (1995), pp. 76–7; 203–8. See 196/26–7, 196/34–8 and 353/50 below.

196/26–7 *De conse., di. i, Si quis* [*etiam*]: The canon 'Si quis etiam' provides that even those clerics who have permission to hold services in private chapels or oratories shall nonetheless officiate at major feasts in their parish churches (De cons. C.1 c.35; Friedberg 1: 1302–3).

196/34–8 *Mathei xviii* [*19–20*]: 'Ubi enim sunt duo uel tres congregati in nomine meo, ibi sum in medio eorum'. Matt. 18: 20 is cited in LL4: 'Wher two or þre ben gadryd togedere in myn name þat is charite þer am I in þe myddis of hem' (fo. 23^(rb)); *D&P* 'be' (196/38) should read 'ben', as in the LL4 translation. The GO interprets the 'duo' less literally as the body and spirit of a single person: 'Quia si corpus vult quam spiritus vult tamen boniarum [*sic*] rerum est petitio' (4: 60). The *CA* cites Origen: 'Sicut enim in musicis nisi fuerit conventa vocum, non delectat audientam, sic in Ecclesia, nisi consensum habuerit, non delectatur Deus in ea, nec audit voces eorum' (1: 275) See 195/16–19 above.

196/39–42 *Ambrose . . . ad Romanos* [*15: 30*]: 'Multi enim minimi dum congregantur unanimes, fiunt magni et multorum preces impossibile est ut non impetrent' (Ps.-Ambrose, 'Commentaria in XII Ep. Pauli', *PL* 17: 186–7). Cited in GO, 4: 305.

196/43 *Ioel ii* [*16*]: Joel 2: 15–16: 'Sanctificate ieiunium, vocate coetum, / congregate populum, sanctificate ecclesiam, coadunate senes, congregate parvulos et sugentes ubera.' GO: 'Praedicatores & prophetas hortatur sermo diuinus ut praedicent penitentiam antequam veniat hostilis gladius, quasi superius vos monui de penitentiam & per commemorationem crudelitatis hostium & per commemorationem mecum clementiae, nunc autem iterum & iterum praecipio cauite' (3: 377).

197/50 *Laudate . . . Ps. 116: 1*: The word 'gentes' ('folc' in *D&P*) is glossed 'gentiles' (GO, interlin., 2: 605); it is translated 'gentiles' in the EV: 'Preise ȝee the Lord, alle Jentilis' and 'Alle hethen men' in the LV (FM 2: 858ab). The translation in *EWS* 1, closer to the LV, stresses the coming together of 'alle maner men' (Ep. Serm. 2/92). Augustine: 'Audiant magis illi qui huius ciuitatis filii esse noluerunt, cum se ab omnium gentium communione praeciderunt' (*Enarr.* 116.1; *CCL* xl, p. 1657/3–5; *PL* 37: 1494).

197/53 *Sent Powyl, ad Colocenses iv* [2]: Col. 4: 2–3: 'Orationi instate, vigilantes in ea in gratiarum actione, / orantes simul et pronobis ut Deus aperiat nobis ostium sermonis . . .'. On 'ostium' the GO: 'Id est, os meam faciat apertum quod ad hoc datum est ut inde prodeat verbum. Apertum est quando multa & magna dicit' (4: 394).

197/1–4 *many general processionys*: 'During the Rogation, or, as they were then better called, the gang-days, and whenever any swart evil had betided this land, our clergy and people went in procession through the streets of the town, and about the fields of the country parishes, with Christ's holy rood and banners wrought with the figures of His saints, borne before them' (Rock, 3: 181–2). The *Sarum Missal*, 'Feria secunda in rogacionibus', directs: 'Preparatis omnibus que ad processionem pertinent. In principio processionis deferatur Draco. secunde, Leo. tercio, uexilla cetera. Deinde sequatur processio suo ordine, sicut solet in ceteris diebus', going on to prescribe the antiphons to be sung, some for rain, some for calm weather, some against death or the depredations of enemies (ed. Legg, pp. 150–4). See Lyndwood, *Provinciale*, 'Constitutions of Ottobon', headed: 'In toto Regno Angliae, Scotiae, & Hiberniae, fiat quotannis Processio publica & Solemnis ab omnibus Christi fidelibus in Crastino Octave Pentecostes pro Pace jam obtentam semper conservandam, & terram Sanctam recuperandam' (Part 2, tit. 35, pp. 137–40; edn. 1679). Owst (1926; repr. 1965) richly documents Rogationtide and other intercessary processions (pp. 200–221). See also Duffy (1992), pp. 136–9, 427; Hutton (1996), pp. 277–87. Rubin (1991) describes the widespread fourteenth-century Corpus Christi processions (the Thursday after Trinity Sunday) as an expression both of communal pride and intercivic rivalry (pp. 243–71).

199/1–2 *a comoun sawe . . . þirlyth heuene*: See Whiting, P357, pp. 469–70, citing this instance. *MED*, s.v. 'thirlen' 2, cites *D&P*'s non-proverbial use (112/47, text, above), but not the proverbial use here, nor the instance (cited by Whiting) in the play *Mankind* (1465–70), spoken by Tytyvillus: 'A schorte preyere thyrlyth hewyn' (ed. Eccles, EETS, 262), p. 172/559–60. Cf. *WLP*, 136/2890–1; 298/note 2890–1. See Glossary.

199/3–15 *Mathei vi* [7] . . . *þe schortere is his preyere*: Matt. 6: 7: 'Orantes autem, nolite multum loqui, sicut ethnici, putant enim quod in multiloquio suo exaudiantur'. Augustine comments on this text in *De Serm. Dom.*, 2.3.14, where his 'Fit ergo in oratione conversio corporis ad Deum et purgatio interioris oculi, cum ea quae cupiebantur, temporaliter excluduntur, ut acies cordis simplicis ferre possit simplicem lucem, et in ea manere cum gaudio, quo beata vita perficitur' comes closest to *D&P*'s 'steynge up of manys herte to God' (*CCL* xxxv, p. 104/290–7; *PL* 34: 1275). Cited in

CA, but with wrong reference (1: 103). The GO leans towards Dives: 'Sicut hypocritarum est ostendi et placere hominibus, ita gentilium est multi-loquium a quibus & coepit. Hi enim exercendae linguae magis operam dant quam menti mundandae, vt hoc, nugatorii officii genus esse ad eum prece flectendum transferunt, putantes quod sicut orator iudicam, ita & ipsi deum flectere queant' (4: 24). Cited again below, 200/6,

199/16–17 *holy writ . . . skyys*: Ecclus. 35: 21, cited above 112/46–7.

199/21 [*Lc. 18: 14*]: Luke 18: 14: '. . . quia omnis qui se exaltat, humiliabitur, et qui se humiliat, exaltabitur'; 'in his preyere' here amplifies the translation. Cited in LL4, fos. 36rb and 113rb; fo. 113rb: 'for euery man þat loȝwith hym for god schal ben heyyd in blisse'. GO: 'Posita pharisei & publicani contrauersia, ponitur iudicis sententiae ut caueatur superbia' (4: 203).

200/22 [*Iac. 4: 6*]: Jas. 4: 6: 'Deus superbis resistit, humilibus autem dat gratiam.' Cited in LL4, fo. 122va. Cf. 195/1 above, in which the argument is that externals are not efficacious; but here, *how* the suppliant prays decidedly affects his state of inner devotion. The relevant gloss: 'Malos omnes punit deus, sed superbis specialiter resistere dicitur, quia maiori poena plectuntur, qui deo subdi poenitendo negligunt. Sed humilibus dat gratiam, qui in suorum plagis vitiorum manibus ueri medici se subdunt' (GO 4: 577).

200/6 *Mt. 6: 7*: See 199/3–15 above.

200–1/8–14 *Luce xx* [*47*] . . . *and þe glose also*: Luke 20: 47: 'Qui devorant domos viduarum simulantes longam orationem, hii accipient damnationem maiorem.' The GO: 'Sub obtentu prolixae orationis, qui vt religiosiores appareant, prolixius orant, vbi ab infirmis quibuslibet, & peccatorum suorum conscientia turbatis, quasi patroni laudes et pecunias accipiant, quorum oratio sit in peccatum, vt non solum pro aliis non possint intercedere; sed nec sibi ad salutem proficere, immo pro ipsis oratio magis damnabuntur' (4: 210). Cf. Bede, 'In Lucae evangelium' 5.20 (*PL* 92: 582–3).

201/15–17 *Marci vii* [*6*] . . . *in erde*: 'Populus hic labiis me honorat, cor autem eorum longe est a me'; cf. Isa. 29: 13. In *D&P*, 'for God . . . in erde' is added to the biblical verse. GO (Jerome): 'Latratum phariseorum reprimit furca rationis, i.e., moysi & ysaiae increpatione, ut & nos haereticos verbis scripturae vincere possimus' (4: 1–7).

201/18 *a comoun prouerbe*: This is the only instance of the saying found by Whiting, S585, p. 540b.

201/23–5 *And perfor þe Pharisen . . . boþyn*: The references may be to Matt. 23: 1–7 (cf. Matt. 6: 7 on Peter) and Matt. 16: 23, Mark 8: 29–30, Luke 9: 20–1.

201/31 *Ecclesiastici vii* [*15*]: Ecclus. 7: 15: 'Noli verbosus esse in multitudine presbyterorum,/ et non iteres verbum in tua oratione'. GO: 'Noli sensum tuum docere, audi sapientiam seniorum. Tutius est enim audire quam loqui . . .' (2: 751).

202/42–3 *And perfor . . . placis of preyere . . . skyllys*: Pauper gives scrupulously utilitarian reasons for church buildings and communal services, avoiding any implication that the places or times possess sacred or numinous qualities in their own right: it is convenient, he says, to have a building to worship in, and the society of others helps prevent the mental aberrations fostered by solitude. He does not go as far as the Wycliffite sermon writer who says that prayer is better done in the open air, conceding that 'often tyme, in reyny wedur, chirches don good on haly day' (*EWS* 2, Serm. 73/23–4).

202/47 *iapyys*: Read 'iaperyys'.

202/57–8 *Sent Powil . . .* [*Iac. 2: 14–26*]: It now seems to me to be less likely that the author of *D&P* attributed St James's 'et fides sine operibus mortua est' to Paul; rather the allusion may be to Rom. 10: 10, cited below, 203/15–18.

202/1–3 *Werto schul we preyyn . . . ʒeuyn us?*: Pauper's reply to Dives' query about God follows Aquinas: '. . . there is a first being, which we call God; this first being is necessarily pure act without admixture of any potentiality, since potentiality is posterior to act. Everything that is subject to change is in some measure potential. From which it follows that it is impossible that God be moved' (*ST* I, 9.1); thus 'men necessarily act, not to change the divine disposition but so that by their actions they may fulfill God's ordinances. . . .our prayer is not designed to alter God's disposition but to obtain the rewards which God has ordained' (idem, II–II, 83. 2). Pauper appropriately stresses the effect of prayer on the suppliant, 'to excityn his herte to mor deuocioun', but also its effect on 'þe fend', to whom it causes 'confusion' and 'peyne'; cf. d'Avray (1995), p. 263.

203/15–18 *Sent Powil . . . Rom. 10: 10*: The GO: 'Quod est in corde debet esse in ore. . . . peccatum fuit petro, ore negare cum crederet corde' (4: 296). On 'corde': 'Cetera potest nolens sed credere non potest nisi volens' (GO 4: 296). In this connection, St Peter's denial of Christ always comes up; the GO: 'Peccatum fuit petro, ore negare, cum crederet corde. Cum enim lacrimis diluit quod ore negauerat, si saluti faciebat quod corde tenebat, veritas & credenda est & loquenda' (idem). Cf. 202/57–8 above.

203/19–20 *preyere . . . singuler*: Aquinas: 'Duplex est oratio: communis et singularis,' etc. (*ST* II–II, 83.12).

204/36–8 *I Regum* [*1: 10–13*] *. . . herde no man here voys*: 1 Sam. 1: 10–31: '. . . cum esset Anna amaro animo, oravit ad Dominum, flens largiter . . .'.

The gloss comments on Hannah's 'singuler' prayer: 'Homo videt in facie, deus in corde . . . Dominus autem respexit ad orationem eius, qui videbit cor eius' (GO 2: 4).

204/42 *Os, lingua, mens, sensus, vigor*: The first line of the second stanza of a hymn beginning: 'Nunc sancte nobis spiritus', which is doubtfully attributed to St Ambrose, see Raby (1953), p. 34 note 1; on Ambrose, idem, pp. 32–41. The hymn appears in the *Canterbury Hymnal*, ed. Wieland (1982), p. 30, and in Drèves, *Analecta*, 43, No. 16, as stanza 6 (of 7) of a hymn beginning 'Omnipotenti Domino,/ Digna demus praeconia':

> Os, lingua, mens, sensus, vigor,
> Confessionem personent,
> Flammescat igne caritas,
> Nec a laude se temperet.

Julian (*Dictionary of Hymnology*, 1892) says the stanza is found in English manuscripts from the eleventh century on and in most medieval breviaries, Roman and Sarum rites (1: 823).

204/45–50 *As Crist seyth . . . [Lc. 6: 45]*: GO: 'Per oris locutionem vniversa quae actu vel cogitu de corde proferuntur, dominus significat, non & verbum pro facto solet poni. Vnde non fuit verbum quod non ostenderet eis' (4: 164).

204/50–2 *And perfor pe prophete . . . [Ps. 15: 9]*: Augustine: 'Propter hoc et in cogitationibus meis iucunditas, et in uerbis exsultatio' (*Enarr.* 15.91; *CCL* xxxviii, p. 91/8–10; *PL* 36: 145).

204/57–8 *faytouris, heretikys, ypocritys*: For the inclusion of 'ypocritys' in this list, see below 212/3–213/9.

205/60–1 *Peccator . . . [Ps. 111: 10]*: The LXX αμαρτωλος becomes VL 'peccator' and *D&P* 'fend of helle'; cf. LL4: 'þe synful man schal sen þis & he schal ben wroth . he schal gronchin with hys teeth & feyntyn for woo' (fo. 69ᵛᵇ). For Augustine, the 'peccator' is the sinner who does not repent in time (*Ennar.*, 111.8; *CCL* xl, p. 1629/1–14; *PL* 37: 1470).

205/1–12 *And perfor we redyn . . . Sent Clement*: St Clement (d. *c.*100), Bishop of Rome and martyr, Feast 23 November. As the story of his exile on the 'ylde of Cersone' is told in *The South English Legendary*, Clement goes to the 'wylþernisse' and there finds two thousand Christians. After he has miraculously produced a source of water for them, he builds sixty-five churches (ed. D'Evelyn and Mill, EETS, 236), 2: 530–3/461–552. The story in the *Legenda Aurea* closes with Pope Leo's mission to 'Tersona' (Ryan tr.: 'Chersoneus'), where the remains of the saint are found and returned to the church of Saint Clement in Rome. In this version, Clement builds seventy-five churches for the two thousand inhabitants (Graesse, No.170; *GL* 2: 323–32); cf. *Speculum Sacerdotale*, drawn from the *Legenda* (ed. Weatherly, EETS, 200), p. 241/28. Cf. *ODS*, pp. 83–4. See 216/61–2 below.

205/13 *Sent Jerom . . . Actus Apostolorum*: St Jerome's second Prologue to Acts concludes: 'Actus apostolorum nudam quidem sonare uidentur historiam et nascentis ecclesiae infantiam texere' (*Novum Testamentum*,ed. Wordsworth, Pt. 3, Fasc. 1, p. 1). The version in the GO has 'videtur habere vel sonare' for 'quidem sonare uidentur' (4: 451). It is also to be found in St Jerome's *Epistula LII ad Paulinum, PL* 22: 540–49. FM translates Jerome's first Prologue, in which no mention is made of the infancy of the Church (1: 61–78).

206/19–20 *after a certeyn forme . . . kepyng her ourys*: In the later Middle Ages, the usual sequence of 'hours' of the (monastic) liturgical day was: Nocturnes, Lauds and Matins, Prime, Terce, Sext, Nones, Vespers, and Compline ('Completorio'). Compare an earlier discussion of the daily offices by Praepositanus (c. 1150–1210), *Tractatus de officiis*, Bk. 4 (ed. J. A. Corbett (1969), pp. 217–281). So-called 'cathedral' hours were simpler, usually observing three only and omitting the chanting of the psalms. See C. Jones. (1975; rev. edn. 1992); Vogel (1986); Pfaff (1982).

206/28–33 *without note*: Dives expresses a Lollard-leaning preference for plainchant—or perhaps no music at all ('without note')—over the newer polyphony. It was the Lollard view that 'bi song þe fend lettiþ men to studie and preche þe gospel' ('Of Feigned Contemplative Life', *English Works* (ed. Matthew, EETS, os 74), pp. 191–2, 206). Objections to church bells appear in the testimony in heresy trials (Tanner,1977), pp. 49, 61, 81). Chichele's *Register* (1415) reports John Claydon's heretical views on music: 'non licet sacerdotibus occupari in ecclesiis circa cantum set in studio legis Christi et predicacione sedula sui verbi' (ed. Jacob, 4: 137). See *PR* (1988), p. 322; F. Ll. Harrison, 'Music at Oxford', *HUO*, 2: 359–61. See 206/30 below.

206/30 *hackyn þe wordis and þe silablis*: See *MED* s.v. 'hakken' 3a: 'to break (a musical note) into a number of smaller notes'; *D&P* is not cited. The modern term is 'hocket' (VL 'hoketus'), a word derived from OF 'hoquet', or hiccup. It is a contrapuntal device, the simplest form of which 'alternated single notes and rests, usually in the two upper voices of a motet. The notes and rests may be of the same or different values, but the notes of each voice fill in the rests of the other'; for examples in musical notation, see Hoppin, (1978), pp. 344–5. The Lollards opposed such 'hacking' or 'knacking' in church music. *The Lanterne of Light* (c1410) attacks 'feyned syngyng', saying that the 'syngars in þe fendis chirche breken curiouse nootis'(ed. Swinburn, EETS, os 151), pp. 58–9. For other examples of hostility to 'knacking', see *English Works* (ed. Matthew, EETS, os 74), pp. 76, 91, 118, 169, 191–2; *EWW* (1978), pp. 86; 181–2; *PR* (1988), p. 322. Even the orthodox *Jacob's Well* is censorious about those who 'stodye more in voys-brekyng in cherche

þan in deuoute syngynge' (ed. Brandeis, EETS, os 115, p. 295/12–13). See
Robbins, *Secular Lyrics*, p. 221, No. 27, line 14. See 206/28–33 above and
208/74–9note below.

207/48–55 And perfor Dauid . . . [Ps. 97: 4] . . . [Ps. 99: 2]: Augustine, on
Ps. 97: 4: 'Gaudete et loquimini. Si quod gaudetis loqui non potestis,
iubilate . . .' (*Enarr.* 97.4; *CCL* xxxix, p. 1374/2–3; *PL* 36: 1254). On Ps.
99: 2, Augustine has a long peroration on the joyous spirit in which God
should be worshipped (*Enarr.* 99.4–14); when not expressible in words,
delight in God's creation can be sung: '. . . et inter cantica quae uerbis
enuntiant, inserunt uoces quasdam sine uerbis in elatione exsultantis animi,
et haec uocatur iubilatio' *Enarr.* 99.4; *CCL* xxxix, p. 1304/17–19; *PL*
36: 2372). Ps. 99.2 is cited 298/53–9 below.

207/57 Sent Bernard: In his first sermon on the Song of Songs, St Bernard
(1090–1153) says that song is not 'strepitus oris, sed jubilus cordis; non
sonus labiorum, sed motus gaudiorum; voluntatum, non vocum consonantia.
. . . Est quippe nuptiale carmen, exprimens castos iucundosque complexus
animorum, morum concordiam, affectuumque consentaneam ad alterutrum
caritatem' (*Opera*, ed. Leclerq *et al.* (1957–77), 1: 7/30–8/1–5; *PL* 183: 789).

207/59–67 And perfor Godis offys . . . De conse., di. v, Non mediocriter: Pauper
agrees with the canon 'Non mediocriter' that in church music it is
'gladnesse' that counts most: 'Quapropter melior est quinque psalmorum
cantatio cum cordis puritate, ac serenitate, et spirituali ylaritate, quam
psalterii modulatio cum anxietate cordis atque tristicia' (De cons. D. 5 c. 24:
Friedberg 1: 1418). The canon may have originated in St Jerome's (or Ps.-
Jerome's) 'Regula monachorum', in which cap. 33 describes how to say the
office, 'Sic semper moderatus, attentus, quietus et suavis sonus in vocibus,
ut nulla pompa nullaque carnalis delectatio habeat locum in praeconiis', etc.
(*PL* 30: 431–2).

207/70 Apocalyps: The reference is probably to Rev. 5: 9 ('et cantant novum
canticum') and 15: 3 ('et cantant canticum Mosi . . .').

208/71–2 Dauid . . . [Ps. 149: 1]: Augustine interprets 'nouum' in light of
the two Testaments: 'Vetus Testamentum, uetus canticum: Nouum Testamentum, nouum canticum' (*Enarr.* 149.1; *CCL* xl, p. 2178/5–6/4–6; *PL*
37: 1949).

208/74–9note þey þat . . . many oþer: The objection to 'knakking', especially
in 'grete ryche chyrches', in the other manuscripts of *D&P* directly
contradicts the defence of church music that concludes cap. lix in MS G,
a defence more consistent with the rest of the text and more likely to have
been the Franciscan author's own view. See 206/30 and 'Relationships
Among the Manuscripts' above.

208/9–10 *martir in Latyn*: Isidore of Seville: 'Martyres Graeca lingua, Latine testes dicuntur . . .' *Etym.* 7.11.1 ff.

208/12–17 *þe Iewis*: The popularity of Thomas of Monmouth's 'Life and Miracles of St. William of Norwich', it is said, helped to create the climate for the expulsion of the Jews from England in 1290 (ed. Jessopp and James (1896), pp. ix–lxxxviii). More recent views: Langmuir (1984); J. M. McCulloh (1997), 'Jewish Ritual Murder. . ', *Speculum* 72: 3, 698–740. On anti-Jewish tales, see Rubin (1999), *passim*. For general background: Cohen (1999). See 222/26–36, 236/13, 2–144/107, 2–150/1–2, and 2–197/64–5 below.

208–9/17–21 *Romaynys. . . .acursyd*: Part of the scenario for the coming of Antichrist, as worked out in the late Middle Ages, was a decline in the power of Rome and its subordination to the French. See, e.g., *Cursor Mundi* (*c.*1300), Pt. 4 (ed. Morris, EETS, os 66), pp. 1273–7. From a peak of authority and prestige in the mid thirteenth century, the city of Rome had by the last quarter of the fourteenth century fallen into decay. The departure of the papacy for Avignon was followed by a sharp decline in population, much of which, for sheer survival, decamped for the country-side. Rival clans who remained in the city staked out their claims and built private fortifications. When the papacy attempted to reestablish itself, they faced a hostile population, ruins, and schism. On the history from 400–1534, see Gregorovius (1971), pp. 259–68; 345–65. On the architectural history, to 1308, Krautheimer (1980).

209/21–7 *And now Englych nacioun . . . martyris*: If 'Here owyn kyng' refers, as it logically should, to Richard II's obscure death in 1400, it is likely that 'her buschopys' refers both to the killing of Thomas Becket in the distant past and to the killing of Archbishop Scrope in the more recent past. On the immediate 'popular canonization' of Scrope, see McKenna (1970), 608–73 (citing also Josiah C. Russell's article (1929), on p. 609). A ballad dated 1405 begins:

> The bysshop Scrope that was so wyse,
> nowe is he dede, and lowe he lyse;
> To hevyns blys yhit may he ryse,
> Thurghe helpe of Marie, that mylde may.
> (*Historical Poems*, ed. Robbins, p. 90)

Cf. *Political Poems*, ed. T. Wright, 2: 114–18. See also Walsingham *Ypodigma*, pp. 414–5; Wylie (1884) 2: 339–46. See 148/44 above.

210/30 [*2 Thes. 2: 9–12*]: See 213/44–55 below.

210/31–3 *Sent Gregorie*: St Gregory (c.540–604), using the metaphor of a young sapling (cf. *D&P* 210/16 ff.), claimed that miracles were necessary for the infant Church: 'Ut enim fides cresceret, miraculis fuerat nutrienda, quia et nos cum arbusta plantamus, tamdiu eis aquam infundimus, quousque ea in terra jam convaluisse videamus; et si semel radicem fixerint, in rigando cessamus. . . . Nolite . . . amare signa quae possunt cum reprobis haberi communia; sed haec quae modo diximus charitatis atque pietatis miracula amate, quae tanto securiora sunt . . . et de quibus apud Dominum eo major sit retributio' ('XL Homilarium in Evangelia', Lib. II, Hom. 29: *PL* 76[2]: 1215–16).

212/11–14 *þe glose, Mathei vii* [*22*] . . . *Mathei vii* [*23*]: The GO, interlin., specifies Balaam and Caiphas as examples of false prophets (see 135/11 above), and the marginal gloss warns: 'Sicut cauendi sunt qui habent speciem bonae vitae propter dogma nequiciae, sic & hi econtrario qui cum integrae fidei & doctrinae sint turpiter viuunt. Utrumque enim necesse est vt & opus sermone & sermo operibus comprobetur' (4: 31; biblical references to Judas: Matt. 10: 1, Mark 6: 7, Luke 9: 1; to Balaam: Num. 23 and 24; to Caiaphas: John 11: 49). Ps-Chrysostom: 'Sed considera, quia *In nomine* dicunt, non *In spiritu*; prophetant enim in nomine Christi, sed in spiritu diaboli; quales sunt divinatores. Sed sic discernuntur: quoniam diabolus interdum falsa dicit, Spiritus sanctus nunquam. . . . Daemonia autem eiiciunt in nomine Christi habentes spiritum inimici; magi autem non eiciunt, sed eicere videntur, colludentibus sibi daemonibus' (*Op. Imperf.*, Hom. 19: *CA* 2: 130; cf. Augustine, *De serm. Dom.* Bk. II, c. 25; *CCL* xxxv, pp. 184–5). Pauper returns to the theme of deceiving outward appearances and the supreme importance of inward 'charite', cf. 162/1–92, 168/9–31, 169/5 above and 212–3/32–9 below. Matt. 7: 22–3 is cited in LL4, fos. 63va, 65ra.

212/3–213/9 *Ypocritys & heretikys* . . . *raueyn*: Matt. 7: 15: 'Attendite a falsis prophetis, qui veniunt ad vos in vestimentis ovium, intrinsecus autem sunt lupi rapaces.' Note that 'a fructibus eorum cogniscetis eos' (Matt. 7: 16) must here be reinterpreted to cover the case of those whose outward appearance *and deeds* are good, but who are inwardly 'ypocritys & heretikys'. Behind good appearance and good works, some 'don and techyn pryuely' things that are 'wol wyckyd' (213/41–2), says Pauper. These 'hypocrites' are now added to comets, monstrous births, and fiery appearances in the air as evil signs of the times (cf. Knighton, *Chronicle*, ed. Martin, pp. 300–1). The Lollards flung the accusation back: 'þer is no werse synne' than 'þe malis of ypocrisye. . . . furst and moste religiows and clerkys . . . frerys [who] seyn þat þei beggon for charite' (*EWS* 1, Serm. 23/30–59). Hypocrisy is a main theme of Wyclif's last work: 'Radix autem tocius huius malicie est ypocrisis tam in hiis sectis quatuor [the mendicants] quam in populo per ipsas seducto' etc. (*Op. Evan.*, 2: 36/36–9); his late, unfinished *De antichristo* (1384) is a diatribe against hypocrisy in the Church, which concludes by identifying the Pope (Clement VIII) as Antichrist (Bk. I, c. 9; pp. 35 and *passim*; 'hec papa vel Antichristus', p. 229). At the other extreme, Margery Kempe's over-demonstrative piety was attacked in these terms: '. . . þe pepyl thorw entysyng of owyr gostly enmy & be þe sufferawns of owyr Lord spak a-geyn þis creatur for sche wept so sor, & seyd sche was a fals ypocryte & falsly deceyued þe pepyl, & thretyd hir to be brent' (ed. Meech and Allen, EETS, 212), p. 33. See Szittya (1986), pp. 61, 170–1, 180. See 193/2–19 above, 213/44–55 below.

213/44–55 *so many wondris . . . errouris*: 2 Thes. 2: 8–11, along with passages in 1 and 2 John and Revelations, is an important proof text for predictions about the Antichrist. 'Ille iniquus' is so interpreted: he is to be a force undermining the Church through false seeming and hypocrisy; he will mimic genuine Christian behaviour in order to destroy Christianity from within. The GO refers to Augustine's commentary on 2 Thes. 2: 1–12: '. . . those men will be led astray by these signs and portents who shall deserve to be led astray, "because", as the Apostle said, "they received not the love of truth for their salvation"' (*De civ. dei*, 20.19; *CCL* xlviii, p. 733/1113–5; *PL* 41: 687); cf. GO, 4: 402. Burchard of Worm's *Decretum* gives a broad definition of the Antichrist: 'Omnis qui secundum professionis suae normam, aut non vivit aut aliter docet, Antichristus est' (*PL* 140: 1052). Citing Gregory's *Moralia*, Burchard refers to open signs of the coming of Doom and says that, unlike these, Antichrist will appear cloaked in sanctity (idem, col. 1053; cf. *Moralia*, 32.15: 'uero etiam iustos fallat, signis sanctitatem simulat. Illis enim suadet elatione magnitudinis, istos decipit ostensione sanctitatis' (*CCL* cxliiiB, p. 1648/88–90; *PL* 76: 651). Langland links Antichrist to clergy corrupted by the temporalities of the Church (*PP*, B-Text, XX/127–8; cf. Kerby-Fulton (1990), pp. 279–84). The Lollard *Lanterne of Light* calls those who distribute indulgences, those who forbid the Bible in the mother tongue and those who burn heretics, among others, Antichrists (ed. Swinburn, EETS, os 151), pp. 14–21. On Joachimism and Antichrist, see Reeves (1969) *passim*; on Adso's tenth century 'Letter' and on the influence of Bonaventure, McGinn (1979), pp. 82–7, 196–241; Emmerson (1981) *passim*; on the Ps.-Pauline tradition, Forsyth (1986), pp. 279–84 and *passim*. See 166/8–9, 210/30, 212/3–213/9 above.

213/1–3 *no solempnyte . . . in her beryynge*: Dives enunciates a view that was shared by the Lollards: 'men letyn it a gret perfeccion þese dayys' to avoid all display in burial rites. Johannes Reve, e.g., at his heresy trial in 1430, renounced a belief 'that it is as meritorie and as medful and as profitable to all Cristis peple to be byryed in myddynges, medues or in the wilde feldes as it is to be byryed in churches or churcheyerdes' (Tanner, *Heresy*, p. 112). See also *PR* (1988), p. 343. McFarlane (in 1972) assessed the burial provisions of the wills of the 'Lollard knights' for evidence of Lollard sympathies (p. 211). Cf. the suggestiion by J. A. F. Thomson (in *Lollardy and the Gentry*, ed. Aston and Richmond, (1997), pp. 95–111) that, among the gentry, fashion may have been as much of an influence on such wills as Lollardy.

J. R. H. Moorman (1955), pp. 391–3, has noted that the secular clergy counted on burials as an important source of income, but 'with the advent of the friars all this was changed'. Not until 1300 and the bull, *Super cathedram*, was there an agreement that 'the friars might bury whom they liked in their churches, but must give one quarter of all offerings and legacies to the parish priest'. Manuscript G (see *D&P* 214/13–14note) does not include (or omits) a passage which stresses the importance to the poor of the alms provided at burials.

214/18 *zilden . . . dette of her body*: The phrase, in mnuscript G only, is elsewhere applied to sexual relations between husband and wife, see 129/ 36–47 above, 250/88, 2–61/36 below.

214/19–22 *soulys in purgatorie*: On purgatory, see 169/19–21 above. St Bernard speaks of purgatory as a region not of destruction but of instruction; after the torments of fire or extreme cold, the dead would be purged of sin. Therefore, he says: 'Interpellabo gemitibus, implorabo suspiriis, orationibus intercedam, satisfaciam sacrificio singuilari: ut si forte videat Dominus, et judicet laborem convertat in requiem, miseriam in gloriam, verbera in coronam' (Serm. 42: *PL* 183: 663–4; *Opera*, ed. J. Leclercq *et al.*, v. 6(1), p. 259). In respect to intercessory prayers, Peter Lombard (c.1100–60) attempts to adjudicate between the rich man and the poor man, 'pariter sed mediocriter bonis', who do not receive the same prayers and offerings from the living (*Sententiae* IV, d. 45, c. 4 (II, p. 526)). William of Auxerre addresses the question of *how* the dead in purgatory can be aided and concludes: 'sciendum est que non euolat qui est in purgatorio pro suffragiis futuris; sed dum suffragia fiunt vel facta sunt non euacuatur iusticis divina, si tota demitur per suffragia ecclesiae, homo enim dicitur se punire si alius puniat se pro ipso: sicut si frater meus soluat debitum quod debeo absolutus sum. Eodem modo si ecclesia satisfaciat pro illo qui est in purgatorio pro absoluto habet eum deus: omnis enim fratres summus' (*Summa aurea*, facs. edn., 4, fo. 305ra). Cf. the fifteenth-century *Speculum Sacerdotale* (ed. Weatherly, EETS, 200), p. 225/15–17.

214/26–215/30 *For þe body . . . bryzter þan þe sonne*: Cf. Matt. 13: 43: 'Tunc iusti fulgebunt sicut sol in regno Patris eorum', referred to again below 286/ 26. St Bernard speaks of the 'locus splendoris, ubi justi fulgent sicut splendor firmamenti' (*Serm.* 42: *PL* 183: 664; *Opera*, ed. J. Leclercq *et al.*, v. 6(1), p. 260). Honorius, *Elucidarium*: 'D. . . . qualia corpora habebunt sancti? —M. Septies quam sol splendidiora' (*PL* 140: 1168). Aquinas says bodies will then be like glass because what is in them will appear outwardly, and to the glory of such bodies will be added the splendour of the soul, just as natural color is enhanced by sunlight (*ST*, Supp., 85.1: my paraphrase).

Henry of Sawtre's twelfth-century *Tractatus* includes a similar light-filled vision of heaven: 'Tanta uero lucis erat illa patria claritate lustrata ut sicut lumen lucerne solis obcecatur splendore, ita solis claritas meridiana posse uideretur obtenebrari lucis illius patrie mirabili fulgore' (*St Patrick's Purgatory*, ed. Easting, EETS, 298), p. 142/788–90. Cf. *D&P* 2–319/27 below.

215/36–44 *Ecclesiastici vii [37]* . . . *Ecclesiastici xxxviii [16–18]*: On Ecclus. 7: 37, the GO: 'Ad eleemosynam pertinet sepultura mortuorum . . .' (2: 752). On Ecclus. 38: 16–18: 'Admonitio honorum patrum vt filii proparant sibi viaticum honorum. . . . Quia qualis eris talis ante iudicem stabis vt recipias secundum opera tua' (2: 783).

215/47–52 *In þe lawe of kende* . . . *Genesis l [7–13]* . . . *worchypful*: Out of this list, only Jacob (Gen. 50: 7–13) can be said to have had a grand funeral. The death of Abraham is recorded in Gen. 49: 38, 50: 13; the death of Isaac, Gen. 35: 28; the death of Jacob, Gen. 49: 33, 50: 1–14; the death of Samuel, 1 Sam. 25: 1, 28: 3; the death of David, 1 Kgs. 2: 10; the death of Solomon, 1 Kgs. 11: 43; the death of Joshua, Josh. 24: 29, Judges 2: 8; the death of Tobit, Tobit 14: 11. The deaths of Joshaphat and Ezekiel are not recorded; the death of one of the Maccabees is alluded to, 1 Macc. 22: 21.

216/56–8 *Io. xix [39–42]*: GO: 'Non frustra ait, sicut mos est iudaeis, sed admonet in huismodi officiis morem cuisque gentis esse secundum' (4: 268). Augustine comments briefly that it seems to him that it wasn't the 'custom of the Jews' but the custom of all people that was being observed in the burial of Christ (*In Ioh.*, 120.4; *CCL* xxxvi, p. 662/18–21; *PL* 35: 1954). Bede says of 'linteis' here that because the body of Christ was wrapped in a fine cotton cloth ('in sudone munda'), the body of Christ (or the eucharist) is not wrapped in silk or cloth of gold but in a fine cotton fabric (*CA*, 2: 575–6). For the commendation of Mary, see Matt. 26: 10–13.

216/61–2 *And many seyntys* . . . *Sent Agas & many opere*: According to the *Legenda aurea*, Saint Clement's body was retrieved from the sea and reburied in St Clement's in Rome (Graesse, No.170; *GL* 2: 331–2). St Katherine's body was carried by angels to Mount Sinai (Graesse, No. 172; *GL* 2: 339; see also Osbert Bokenham, *Legendys* (ed. Sergeantson, EETS, 206), p. 200/7346–52). St Agnes had a basilica built over her grave in Rome (Graesse, No. 24; *GL* 1: 103; Bokenham, op. cit., 128/4687–93; see 349/70 below). The grave of St Paul the Hermit was dug (as Pauper recounts) by two lions under the supervision of St Anthony (Graesse, No. 15; *GL* 1: 85). On Clement, see 205/1–12 above.

216/77–9 *Extra, De regulis iuris, lib. vi*: The legal maxim is found in the collection 'De regula iuris' of Pope Boniface VIII (Sext. 5.12.5; Friedberg 2: 1123).

217/88 *Extra, De sepulturis, c. Fraternitatem*: The canon 'Fraternitatem' is
taken from the correspondance of Pope Innocent III; at issue is the request
of a monk to be buried in a certain ancient monastery, formerly a church.
The Pope takes account of the limitations of space in such sites and directs
that the body of the monk be returned instead to the burial place of his
forefathers (X 3.28.3; Friedberg 2: 549–50).

217/91–8 *Di. xxi, Nunc autem [diuina]* . . . *Sent Peter's feet*: The canon
'Nunc autem diuina' is from the correspondence of Pope Nicholas I (d. 867).
In his letter, the Pope upholds the principle that inferiors are not allowed to
pass judgement on their superiors: 'Prima sedes non iudicabitur a quo-
quam'. He illustrates his point by telling the story of an early Bishop of
Rome, Marcellus, who was judged severely by his bishops after he had been
forced by the pagans to place a grain of incense on the alter fire (D.21 c.7;
Friedberg 1: 71). The story of his death and miraculous burial by St Peter
appears in the *Legenda aurea* (Graesse, No. 60; *GL* 1: 248–9).

217/107–9 *Salamon* . . . *[Eccli. 19: 23]*: LL4: 'þe wyckyd man loȝwyth hym
schrewedelyche & for a wyckyd ende for hys herte & hys þouȝt is ful of gyle
& of malyce' (fo. 67ᵛᵇ). The GO is more explicit, naming such men heretics
and hypocrites: 'Sic heretici & hypocritae ostendunt virtutum speciem sed
veritatem eius non habunt' (2: 763).

217/1 *marketys and feyris*: Dives and Pauper concur with the Lollards: 'And
þus don men today: prestis sufferen hem to make þer chaffere in þe chirche
for litil of hern. . . . And þus [the] ende wherfore þe chirche was ordeyned is
turnyd fro preyour into synne', *EWS* 3, Serm. 148/28–32. John Audeley
(ante 1450) complains against the churches: 'ȝe schul make no marketys ne
no marchandyse, . . . / Hit chasis away charyte, ȝour couetyse', (*Poems*, ed.
Whiting, EETS, 184), p. 37/1–3. Yet from at least as early as the twelfth
century precincts in which to hold markets and fairs were leased to
merchants by abbey churches. In 1245, Henry III chartered a fair to
Westminster Abbey; such licences were sources of income both to churches
and to lay gentry and burgesses of towns, and it was England's network of
fairs that enabled her to participate in the international trade in cloth, wool,
wine and other goods. See Thrupp (1966), pp. 272–92; Moore (1985), pp. 1–
23 and *passim*. Nightingale (1995) points out that 'fairs developed generally
from the patronal feast-days of the great churches and abbeys which
attracted itinerant traders to sell their goods to the crowds of worshippers',
p. 35; also pp. 368–9, 557 and *passim*. See also Masschaele (1997). See 217/
4–218/23, and 217/5–218/15 below.

217/4–218/23 *For we fyndyn* . . . *secularte*: Clerical objections to markets
and fairs held on church property were based on the gospel accounts of
Christ's cleansing of the temple and occasioned by the rowdy or immoral
behaviour that was a feature of such gatherings of lay people (cf. *D&P* 219/

47–7 below). The GO: 'Si in figurali templo quod est domus orationis prohibet negociationem quod honesta putatur cum sit de his quod in templo offeruntur quanto magis prohibet potationes & cetera grauiora' (4: 228–9). On this topic, Raymund of Peñafort, citing scripture, says that some kinds of business ('negotia') are made dishonest by the places where it is carried on, specifically within church precincts (*Summa*, Bk. II, p. 247). In the eyes of the Lollards, the den of thieves pericope prefigures the symony and worldliness of the contemporary clergy, see *EWS* 3, Serm. 148/13–36, Serm. 165/1–49. John 2: 13–17 is cited in LL4, with an attack on 'rekeles buschipis' who 'for coueytyse procurin to han merchauntis & chapmen stondynge in here cherchys & sellyn hem þe lond of þe sanctuarie for þe monye as balyys don in þe merket place', with a cross reference to this passage in *D&P*, where (says the friar) 'of þis materye & how goddys hous is maad a dene of þeuys I seyde mor opinly' (fos. 84rb-84va). See 217/5–218/15, 2–193/12 below.

217/5–218/15 *Io. ii [13–17]* . . . *a dene of þeuys*: '. . . nolite facere domum Patris mei domum negotationis'. In his sermons, the author of *D&P* makes John 2: 13–17 the occasion for an attack on the commercial activities he sees in the churches of his own time, and he refers to what he has said in his earlier work: 'But of þis materye & how goddys hous is maad a dene of þeuys I seyde mor opinly in *diues & pauper* in þe fyrste precept' (LL4, fo. 84va). The GO allegorizes the animals bought and sold in the temple and allegorizes the temple itself as the human body (4: 228–9). Augustine, *In Ioh.* 10.4–9, remarks that even worse crimes are committed in churches than buying and selling; 'Qui sunt qui oues uendunt et columbas? Ipsi sunt qui sua quaereunt in ecclesia, non quae Iesu Christi' (*CCL* xxxvi, p. 102/3; *PL* 35: 1469). A Wycliffite sermonizer finds in Io. 2: 13–17 a warning against simony: 'And heere Crist shewide . . . and tauȝt hou lordis shulden chastise symonye and oþer synnes þat ben usid in þe chirche' (*EWS* 3, Serm. 165/5–7). Cf. *CA*, 1: 305–6. Cited below 276/39.

218/15–18 *[Mt. 21: 12]* . . . *[Mc. 11: 15; Luc. 19: 45]* . . . *[Mc. 11: 16]*: The synoptic accounts of the Cleansing of the Temple; see above 217/5–218/15.

218/28–9 *rybaudye* . . . *in holy chirche*: See 189/32–45 above.

218/29 *Sent Austyn*: I have not found Augustine's alleged statement that he would have chased the buyers and sellers in the temple to the pit of hell. His gloss on Matt. 21: 12 connects the expulsion from the temple with simony: 'Sic et mystice quotidie de ecclesia eijicit. Et habet unius criminis reos vendentes et ementes ecclesiastica officia' (GO 4: 66).

218/33–219/35 *For as þe glose . . . fleddyn aweye*: The gloss on Matt. 21: 12: 'Igneum et sidereum aliquid radiat ex eius oculis; lucet in facie maiestas deitatis' (GO, 4: 66).

219/36–8 *in þe tyme of his passioun* . . . [*Io. 18: 6*]: 'Ut ergo dixit eis, Ego sum, abierunt retrorsum et ceciderunt in terram'. GO: 'Hac vna voce tot feroces & fortes moriturus prostrauit, virtute latentis deitatis que volebat quidem compraehendi, sed non nisi quando voluit' (4: 205). Augustine, *In Ioh.*, 112.3: '"Ego sum", dicit Christus; et a Iudaeis exspectatur Antichristus, ut retro redeant, et in terram cadant, quoniam deserentes caelestia, terrene desiderant' (*CCL* xxxvi, p. 634/16–18; *PL* 35: 1931).

219/39 *a dene of þeuys*: Matt. 21: 13: 'Vos autem facistis eam speluncam latronum'. See 217/5–218/15 above, 2–193/12–19 below.

219/50–4 *And 3if ony man* . . . *De conse., di.i, Si motum, et c. Significasti*: The canon 'Si motum' provides that if homicide or adultery has polluted a church, the church must be reconsecrated (De cons. D.1 c.19; Friedberg 1: 1299). The canon 'Significasti' from the correspondance of Pope Alexander III (d. 1181) specifies the punishment of adulterous priests and orders the aspersion with holy water of the church where the adultery occured (X 5.16.5; Friedberg 2: 806). Durandus specifies the reasons for reconsecration ('reconcilianda') of a church: if on the premises sexual acts have been performed, blood has been shed, thefts or other crimes have been committed, or infidels or excommunicates have been buried (*Rationale* 1.6.38–46; *CCCM* cxl, pp. 78–84). The fourteenth-century *Memoriale* enjoins penance for those who by committing sexual acts pollute churches or churchyards (ed. Haren, 1975), pp. 140–2. See 219/56 below.

219/55 *Ioannes in Summa sua, lib. iv, ti. ii, q. xliii, Vtrum liceat*: John of Freiburg's *Summa confessorum*: 'Vtrum liceat debitum reddere . . . quia locus polluti peccati indigeat reconciliacione . . . dicit que debitum reddendum sit omni tempore et omni hora salua cum debita honestate que in talibus exigitur . . . in loco sacro . si non petitur alius locus hii . tunc reddit cum dolore cordis . . . non credo que peccet moraliter . concordat & hiis sacra glossa' (Bk. 4, t. 2, q. 43: MS Bodley 299, fo. 252ᵛ).

219/56 *Durandus, Summa sua, lib. iv, ti.ii, q.xxxiii*: The reference is to William Durandus's legal *glossa*, his *Speculum iudiciale* (Bale, 1574; repr. Aalen 1975). for which in his lifetime he was best known. It is referred to four times in *D&P*; I have not had access to this work. On Durandus as a legist, see Gy (1992); Brundage (1995), pp. 146–7; 228–9. The other references in *D&P*: 237/9, 2–184/5, 2–184/27–8 below.

219/61–2 *xiii, q. ii, Questa, et c. sequenti*: The canon 'Questa' holds that no fee may be exacted for burial. The source is a letter of Pope Gregory in reply to a query from the Bishop of Sardinia about the request of 'Nereida clarissima femina' that she be allowed to buy a burial plot from his church. Gregory denies the request, citing the biblical story of Ephron and Abraham (Gen. 23: 3–20), indicating that even the 'pagan' Ephron had compunctions about accepting money for a burial place. Though a burial plot could not be sold, a gift might be accepted on the occasion of a burial (C.13 q.2 c.12; Friedberg 1: 724–5). As for 'sequenti', all 32 canons in Causa XIII deal with burial customs and regulations. See 2–193/3–8 below.

220/64 *xvi, q. vii, Et hec diximus, [c. 9]*: The canon 'Et hec diximus' against buying and selling in churches is taken from Origen's Homily 15, referring to Matt. 21: 13 'Vos autem fecistis illam speluncam latronum'; it severely criticizes the worldly people who attend church in his own time, as well as the clergy which tolerates their behaviour ('In Matt.', Tom. 16, *PG* 13: 1450–1) (C.16 q.7 c.9; Friedberg 1: 802).

220/72–4 *I Regum ii [30] . . . despyt*: 'Sed quicumque glorificaverit me glorificabo eum; qui autem contemnunt me erunt ignobiles'. LL4: 'Whoso worschepe me I schal worschepe hym & þey þat dyspisin me schul ben vyleynys & wiþouten worschepe' (fo. 84vb).

220/86 *Wyckyd costum . . . ben do away*: As *D&P* MS H indicates (see variant to line 86), the phrase comes from the canon law. Titulus IV, 'De consuetudine', deals with customary law, and all of its chapters contain warnings against upholding custom against natural or divine law. The *dict. ante* c. x states: 'Non valet consuetudo, per quam quis inducitur ad peccandum vel bona propria dissipandum' (X 1.4.1–11; Friedberg 2: 41).

VOL. I: 1, COMMANDMENT II, pp. 221–62

221/1–4 *secunde comandement . . . his name in veyn*: Exod. 20: 7: 'non assumes nomen Domini Dei tui in vanum nec enim habebit insontem Dominus eum qui assumpserit nomen Domini Dei sui frustra'. For the division between the first and second Commandments see 81/7 above.

221/7 *christenyd*: Baptism, in a broad sense, is a solemn ceremonial oath to renounce the Devil, and it is this aspect of the sacrament to which Pauper refers ('þe vouh þat we makyn in bapteme to forsakyn þe fend', 249/62–4 below). The Latin literature of religious instruction less often brings baptism into the discussion of the second Commandment than does the vernacular, which usually reminds the lay man or woman that baptism is an oath, and to break an oath is to take the name of God in vain. *The Lay Folks' Catechism*, mid fourteenth century:

> Here alle men or wymmen þat turne to grete synnes aftyr here cristyndom [baptism] in þat þey taken þe name of god in vayn. For at here cristyndom þey forsake þe fynd [Devil] and alle his pompis. hys pride. and alle hys werkys . . .and bynde hem wyl-fully to goddys hestys (ed. Simmons and Nolloth, EETS, os 118, p. 37/559–64)

In the Sarum rite, the promise to renounce the Devil was preceded by a rite of exorcism, using prayer, salt and saliva, performed at the door of the church. At the baptismal font, the priest placed his right hand on the infant and asked, 'Do you renounce Satan?' The godparent replied, 'I do renounce ["Abrenuncio"].' In the name of the child, the 'abrenuncio' and the 'credo' were pronounced three times in response to the priest's questions. This was followed by the triple immersion of the infant, and by the injunction, 'Serua mandata' (*Sarum Missal*, ed. Legg, pp. 123–31).

For William of Auxerre (d. 1231), the rite was not a true exorcism but merely symbolised the expulsion of the Devil; it was, however, productive of grace for the person baptised (*Summa*, Bk. 4; facs. edn., fo. 253^v). Of the seven sacraments, baptism was regarded as the most essential; *Jacob's Well*: 'baptem is ground of alle oþere sacramentis' (MS Salisbury 174, fo. 163^b). On the full, late medieval understanding of baptism, see Aquinas, *ST* III 66.1–12. See also Burchard of Worms, *Decretum*, *PL* 140: 727–50; Hugh of St Victor, *De sacramentis*, Bk. II, Pt. 6.4–15; tr. R. J. Deferrari (1951), pp. 290–302; Durandus, *Rationale*, 6.83; *CCCM* cxiA, pp. 413–29; Thomas de Chobham, *Summa*, ed. Broomfield, pp. 91–9.

222/26–36 *Sent Powil . . . þe name of Crist is schamyd*: Rom. 2: 24 cites the text of Isa. 52: 5. The biblical sense here is that just as sinful Christians tarnish the name 'Christian' so (according to Isaiah) God's name was tarnished by the oppressors of the Jews. Like St Paul, however, the Gloss suggests that it is the Jews who tarnish the name of God: 'Inter gentes blasphematur nomen Dei per Judaeos' etc. (4: 274). In *D&P*, all reference to the Jews has disappeared. Cf. 208/12–17 above.

222/29 *ypocritys*: See above 212–3/32–9. There may be an implied reference to 2 Cor. 13: 'Nam eiusmodi pseudoapostoli sunt operarii subdoli, transfigurantes se in apostolos Christi.'

222/36–7 *preyere . . . Sanctificetur*: Matt. 6: 9–13.

222/5–12 *iaperys . . . ne for þe worchepe of God*: A sermon of *c.*1413 reminds hearers that breaking the second Commandment by habitual swearing is also a breach of the oath that made them Christians (*ME Sermons*, ed. Ross, EETS, 209, pp. 108/21–6). Pauper's examples of how God's name is taken in vain skip without explanation from the trivial (the oaths of 'iaperys') to the serious (the teaching and preaching of heresy) and back again (words spoken in 'nyce merthe').

223/13–15 *þe prophete . . . [Ps. 49: 16]*: Cited and tr. in LL4, fo. 73rb. Augustine's exposition of this passage exhorts preachers of Christ's word to conform their behavior to their words (*Enarr.*, 49.23; *CCL* xxxviii, p. 593/14–42; *PL* 36: 580).

223/25–7 *holy wryt . . . [Ps. 75: 12]*: Cited above 103/60.

224/5–225/39 *Iudicum xi [30–40]* . . . *Iepte* . . . *synne*: Jephthah and his daughter, Judg. 11: 30–40, is the archetypal story of the consequences of an unwise oath. Cited also in LL4, fos. 122$^{rb–va}$. See 225/50–1 below.

225/50–1 *Maystir of Storijs* . . . *Josephus*: On Jephthah, Peter Comestor cites Josephus: 'Arguit Josephus Jephthe, quia obtulit holocaustum non legitimum, nec Deo charum. Quid si canem obvium habuisset, immolasset eum Domino? Fuit ergo in vovendo stultus, in solvendo impius' (*Historia*, *PL* 198: 1284). Josephus is cited from the *Antiquitatis Iudaicae*, Bk. V, c. 7, ed. F. Blatt (1958), p. 340/19–21; tr. in *Josephus*, V, ed. Thackeray and Marcus, LCL 281, 5: 117–21). On Jephthah, see *ABD* 3: 680–2. See below 225/53–6.

225/53–6 *Ysodorus* . . . *xxii, q. iv, In malis promissis*: The canon 'In malis' (C 22.q 3.c 5; Friedberg 1: 876) is cited from its source, Isidore of Seville, *Synonyma de Lamentatione Animae Peccatricis* (*PL* 83: 858). Cf. Ps.-Augustine's gloss on Judg. 11: 30–40, which denounces Jephthah, from his deplorable parentage to his foolish vow, and his foolish carrying-out of the foolish vow; no mention is made of his repentence (*Questiones Veteris et Novi Testimenti*, 43 (*PL* 35: 2239–40). Aquinas argues, as Pauper does, that vows entailing evil acts are not to be fulfilled but points to Jephtha's repentence (*ST*, II–II, 88.20).

226/2 *blasfemye*: Aquinas defines blasphemy as disparagement of the goodness of God (*ST*, II–II, 13.1).

226/14 *othis swerynge*: Casual swearing, as a mode of speaking, is condemned in Matt. 5: 37 (cited below, 231/45–232/86), and this condemnation is repeated by the patristic writers and the penitentials; cf. Jonas of Orleans (d. 843), *De institutione laicali*, citing Jerome:

> Inter stultiloquium et scurrilitatem hoc interest, quod stultiloquium in se nihil sapienter habet, scurrilitas vero de prudenti mente descendit, et consulto appetit quaedam urbana verba, vel rustica, vel faceta, quam nos jocularitatem possemus alio verbo appellare, ut risum moveat audientibus. (*PL* 106: 250–1)

Thomas de Chobham's *Summa* (citing Matt. 5: 37) advises the penitent (or his confessor) that the biblical warning applies to those who swear by their boots or their knife (ed. Broomfield, p. 554). *Jacob's Well* claims that 'manye folk han browȝt into swiche a perlyous custom þat vnethys kun þei speke ony woord but ȝif þei sweryn be god in veyn or be summe of his creaturys' (MS Salisbury 174, fo. 186^b).

226/25–6 *excusyth* . . . *accusyth & agrechyth*: The same combination of words is repeated on p. 227/5–6 and may be a rendering of Latin 'considerent se ipsos redargutorie accusantes' used by Wyclif in the same context (*De mand.*, p. 204/14).

227/29 *Ecclesiastici xxiii* [9]: Verses 9, 10 and 12 are translated in the text of *D&P*: 'Multus enim casus in illa/ nominatio vero Dei non sit adsidua in ore tuo/ et nominibus sanctorum non admiscearis/ quoniam non erit immunis ab eis./ . . . ./ vir multum iurans implebitur iniquitate/ et non discedet a domo illius plaga.' The GO: 'Vetat iuramentum ne fiat periuriam, vnde, "Nolite iurare neque per caelum, necque per terram" [Matt. 5: 34]', etc. (2: 767).

227/40 [*Ecclus. 27: 15*]: 'Loquella multum iurans horripilationem capiti statuet, et inreverentia ipsius obturatio aurium'. GO: 'Quia sicut actio eorum bonis contraria, ita & loquela ad mala dicendum prona ad audiendum grauis (2: 773). Cited again below 258/5–7.

227/1 *swearynge*: Several passages in this chapter of *D&P* (lines 4–6, 12–21) are paralleled in 'Pore Caitif''s tract on the second Commandment:

> And summe seien . but if I swere no man wol leue me . . . if þi seruant dide a þing þat þou haddist him forfendid, euer þe oftir þat he did it þe wors þou woldist ben apaied, & more ʒit if he scorned þee þerto and seide þat he did so for þi loue to haue þee in mynde . . . & nemeli if þou were his lord eþer hys kyng, þen myche more wol god þat is lord of al . . . lest he be putte out of mynde among þe chosen of god . . . (MS Bodley 938, fos. 126ᵛ-127ʳ; cf. MS Bodley 3, fos. 35ᵛ-36ʳ).

There is a looser parallel in a fifteenth-century sermon (*ME Sermons*, ed. Ross, EETS, 209, p. 109/20–30). The common source may perhaps be the Ps.-Chrysostom *Opus imperfectum*:

> Sed forte dicis, Quid faciam? Non mihi credit, nec vult credere nisi juravero. Acquiesce magis pecuniam perdere quam salutem. Pretiosior tibi videateatur anima tua, quam res tua. Si rem aliquam perdideris, vivere potes: si Deum perdideris, quomodo vives? (*PG* 56: 697–8)

Wyclif's *De mand.* in its discussion of the second Commandment, has a similar (but not identical) list of three 'sophistical' excuses for swearing: 'triplex fictum responsum sophisticum' (p. 203/18). Cf. de Chobham *Summa*, ed. Broomfield, p. 418; the *Book of Vices and Virtues* (ed. Francis, EETS, 217), p. 2/4–6.

D&P contains four other passages from which 'Pore Caitif' may have borrowed wording, see (235/37–42, 2–18/67–19/85, 2–304–12/cap. v–vi, 2–314/1–315/32) and three briefer passages with somewhat similar phrasing (2–253/18–19), 2–255/1–256/34, 2–317/1–22). On the dating and manuscripts of 'Pore Caitif' see Hartung *Manual* 9: 3135–6; B3470–1). The pioneering work on the manuscripts of 'Pore Caitif' was done by Sister M. T. Brady; see Brady (1954), (1958), (1989). See 2–304–12/cap. v–vi below.,

228/21–34 *Christ pleynyyth . . . Ps. lxviii*: The remainder of verses 27–9 is: 'Et super dolorem vulnerum meorum addiderunt/ adpone iniquitatem super iniquitatem eorum/ et non intrent in iustitia tua/ deleantur de libro viventium/ et cum iustis non scribantur'. The psalm is traditionally linked to the crucifixion; cf. Augustine's commentary (*Enarr.*, 68.11–13; *CCL* xxxix, pp. 925–7; *PL* 36: 861–3).

229/40 *Tomas, De ueritate*: Thomas Aquinas: '. . . swearing an oath is not beneficial except to the person swearing; two things are required for the proper use of oaths, first that one swear discretely not frivolously and for a necessary cause; for this, judgement and discretion on the part of the swearer are required; second, in what is to be confirmed by an oath there must be nothing false or illicit; and this requires that what is sworn to be true and that it be just: a rash oath lacks good judgement, a lying oath lacks truth, a wicked or illicit oath lacks justice' (*ST* II–II, 89. 3; OP edn., Rome (1894), 3: 642).

229/10 *Extra, lib. i, De eleccione, Significasti*: The canon 'Significasti' from a papal letter of Gregory III (d. 741) justifies the taking of an oath upon receiving the archepiscopal pallium. Oath-taking in this case is viewed as an expedient, 'pro fide, pro obedientia, pro unitate', in the administration of the Church (X 1.6.4: Friedberg 2: 49–50). The injunction to Peter, 'Feed my sheep', takes precedence over the 'Do not swear' of Matt. 15: 34 (see below 230/22, 231/45–232/86). 'Assoylyyng from a cours' is, however, not found in the text of this canon. Compare Constitution 43 of the Fourth Lateran Council (1215), which placed restrictions on oaths taken by clerics to lay persons (Title: 'Ne sine causa clericus fidelitatem laico faciat', Mansi, 22: 1027–8).

229/12 *Ieremye . . . iv* [2]: Jer. 4: 2: 'et iurabis: Vivit Dominus in veritate et in iudicio et in iustitia'. The GO (Jerome): 'In sugillationem, sci., mortuorum deorum, per quos iurat omnis ydolatria' (3: 106).

230/22 *Extra, lib. ii, De iureiurando, Etsi Christus*: The canon 'Etsi Christus' holds: 'Licite ex causa necessaria etiam per religiosus iuratur.' The text of the canon directly confronts the conflict between the biblical injunction 'Sit sermo vester, *est est, et non non*' (Matt. 5: 34) and the felt need of the administrators of the Church for formal oaths. Matt. 5: 34 is shown to be qualified by words and deeds recorded in other parts of the Bible (Jas. 5: 12, Rom. 1: 9, 1 Cor. 15: 31, Ps. 109: 3, 131: 11, Lev. 19: 12, Eccles. 23: 12, 1 Tim. 5: 23, Matt. 5: 23). Christ himself used the phrase, 'Amen dico vobis' as a way of swearing to the truth, and many other instances are cited from the Old and New Testaments. A comparison is made between swearing and wine: good in moderation, evil in excess (X 2.24.26; Friedberg 2: 369–71). See 231/45–232/86 below.

231/45–232/86 [*Mt. 5: 34*]: The entire passage, verses 34–7, is: 'Ego autem dico vobis, non iurare omnino, neque per caelum, quia thronus Dei est/ neque per terram, quia scabillum est pedum eius, neque per Hierosolymam, quia civitas est magni Regis/ neque per caput tuum iuraveris, quia non potes unum capillum album facere aut nigrum/ Sit autem sermo vester *est est, non non* quod autem his abundantius est a malo est'. The GO rephrases the passage and adds: 'Ideo bis dicit ut quod ore dicit operibus probes, quod verbis negas factis non comprobes vel confirmes' (4: 22).

Aquinas poses Dives' question: 'Doesn't *a malo* mean swearing is unlawful?' (*ST*, II–II, 89.2), and he uses Augustine to answer it:

> Si iurare cogeris, scias de necessitate uenire infirmitatis eorum quibus aliquid suades. Quae infirmitas utique malum est, unde nos cotidie liberari deprecamur, cum dicimus: 'Libera nos a malo.' Itaque non dixit: Quod autem amplius est malum est; tu enim non malum facis, qui bene uteris iuratione, quae etsi non bona tamen necessaria est, ut alteri persuadeas quod utiliter suades; sed a malo est illius, cuius infirmitate iurare cogeris (*De serm. Dom.*, I, 17; *CCL* xxxv, p. 59).

The early fifteenth-century 'Testimony' of the Lollard, William Thorpe, makes the same Augustinian point:

> 'Ser, siþ I mai not now oþir wise be trowid no but bi swerynge, and I perseyue, as Austin seiþ, þat it is not spedeful þat ȝe þat schule be my breþeren bileuen me not, þerfore I am redi bi þe word of God, as þe Lord comaundide me bi his word for to swere' (*TWT*, p. 78/1759–62; ed. brackets om.)

231/65 *Iacobi v* [*12*]: The rest of verse 12 is: '. . . neque per caelum, neque per terram, neque aliud quodcumque iuramentum; sit autem vestrum Est est, Non, non, uti non sub iudicio decidatis'. The GO warns that each idle word will be answered for at the Judgement ('omne ociosum verbum quod locuti fuerint homines reddent rationem de eo in die iudicii') (4: 519).

232/71–2 *a malo . . . of euyl*: The phrase *a malo* in Matt. 5: 37 was discussed by Augustine in his reading of this passage, see 231/45–232/86 above. The GO draws on the same source; affirming that the evil is done by the one who forces another to swear (4: 22). Matt. 5: 37 is cited in Com. VIII below, 2–218/10–11.

232/81 *Mathei v* [*33*]: Cited 103/54 above, 233/17–18 below.

232/84 *Deutronomii vi* [*13*]: 'Dominum Deum tuum timebis, et illi soli servies, ac per nomen illius iurabis.' Cited twice in LL4 (fos. 34vb and 102va) and above, 101/4.

232/5–16 *Sent Powil . . . Hebreos vi* [*16*]: Heb. 6: 16 is cited again 242/23 and 252/2 below. The EV also using the word 'more', translates: 'Forsothe men swere by the more of hem' (FM 4: 488a). Aquinas cites Heb. 6: 16 in arguing that 'when a man swears by God, he acknowledges ['profitetur'] God to be more powerful in respect to His unfailing truth and His universal knowledge. . . . thus it is clear that an oath is a religious act and constitutes latria' (*ST*, II–II, 89.4: Rome edn., 1894, 3: 643).

233/17–18 *glose . . . Mathei v [33]*: GO: 'Hoc enim per quod jurat quilibet veneratur: hoc amat, hoc timet; ideo lex praecipit ut non juretur nisi per deum' (4: 22). Cited above 103/54, 232/81.

233/27 *Sent Thomas*: The reference may be to *ST*, II–II, 89.6: '*Contra*: . . . it is customary to swear by the gospels, by relics, and by the saints. *I answer that*: . . . an oath is principally referred to that same God whose testimony is invoked; secondarily the oath of any creature is not considered in itself but as a manifestation of divine truth. Thus we swear by the gospels, that is, by the God whose truth is manifested in the gospels, and by the saints, who believed and acted on this truth' (OP edn., Rome, 1894, 3: 645). The reference to Aquinas is found only in *D&P* MS G.

234/5 *Sent Austyn*: Augustine, in *Sermo* 180: 'Cum ergo filios suos, vel caput suum, vel salutem suam quisque in juratione nominans, quidquid nominat obligat Deo' (*PL* 38: 975). The *MED* s.v. 'þedom' (the *D&P* translation of 'salutem') cites Chaucer's 'Shipman's Tale': 'Yuel thedam on his monkes snowte!' (*CT*, B 1595, p. 208/405) and *PP*: 'Ne men þat conne manye craftis, clergie it telliþ, /Thrift oþer þedom with þo is selde yseiȝe' (A-Text, X/107–8).

235/37–42 *he forsakyth . . . his mouth*: Phrases in this passage are echoed by 'Pore Caitif':

> . . . he forsakiþ þe help of al good werk þat euer he wrouȝt wiþ hise hondis, and when he kissiþ þe book wityngly sweryng fals he forsakiþ þe help of alle þe goode preiers and of alle \þe goode wordis þat euer he beed [*sic*] eþer seide wiþ his mouþ . . . (MS Bodley 938, fo. 143ᵛ)

On 'Pore Caitif', see 227/1 above and 2–304/12/cap. v–vi and 2–317/1–22 below.

235/44–5 *Crist . . . vndyr forme of bred*: One of a very few references to the eucharist in *D&P*, cf. 87/37 above, 2–38/37 below.

235/6 *Ysodorus, xxii, q. v, Quacumque*: The canon 'Quacumque' holds that an oath consists of what the other party to the oath understands it to be. The source is Isidore of Seville's *Sentenciarum*, Bk. II, c. 31: 'Quacumque arte uerborum quis iuret, Deus tamen, qui conscientiae testis est, ita hoc accipit, sicut ille, cui iuratur, intelligit. Dupliciter autem reus fit, qui et nomen Dei in uanum assumit, et proximum dolo capit' (*PL* 83: 634; C. 22 q. 5 c. 9; Friedberg 1: 885).

236/13 *þe lyf of Sent Nicholas*: The tale of the Jew and the defaulting Christian is probably derived from the version in Gerald of Wales's (1127–

c.1243) *Gemma ecclesiastica* (*Opera*, RS 21, 2: 156–7). In the *D&P* version, the setting is transferred from the altar of St Nicholas to a law court and expanded and made more dramatic by the use of direct dialogue. A vernacular analogue to the story in *D&P* is found in the late thirteenth-century *South English Legendary*. The concluding lines:

> Her ȝe seoþ hou hit goþ bi men, þat wiþ gyle swerieþ iwis
> þeȝ he þurf gyle swerie soþ, iwis forswore he is
> (ed. D'Evelyn and Mill, EETS, 235, p. 561/351–2),

point up the same moral lesson Pauper wishes to teach, that it is possible to lie by swearing to what is true. The writer of *D&P* omits the line, 'The other, because he was a Jew, was not believed' (idem, p. 561/330). Another vernacular English version of the story is found in Mirk's *Festial*, ed. Erbe, EETS, es 96, pp. 11–15. Cf. 208/12–17 above.

237/50 *xxii, q. ii, c. 1*: The canon 'In dolo iurat' holds that perjury is committed if one intends to do other than one swears one will do. The *dict. ante* cites Augustine's *Enarr.* on Ps. 23: 4: 'innocens . . . non iuravit dolose' (*CCL* xxxviii, p. 136/6–9; *PL* 36: 183). The canon cites Cassiodorus' interlinear gloss: 'In dolo iurat qui aliter facturus est quam promittit, cum periurium sit nequiter decipere credentem' (GO 2: 481; C. 22 q.2 c.1; Friedberg 1: 866).

237/9 *Durandus, Summa, Extra, De iureiurando, c. Sicut, et c. Tua*: Two canon law references derived from the epistles of Pope Alexander III (d.1181): (1) the canon 'Sicut ex literis' states that a monk may not abjure his vows (X.2.24.13; Friedberg 2: 363); (2) the canon 'Tua nos' is about judging a cleric who has sworn contradictory oaths: the second oath must prevail, but the cleric must be expelled from office (X.2.24.11; Friedberg 2: 362). The reference to Durandus is here to his legal *Summa*, the *Speculum iudicale*, see 219/56 above.

238/14 *xxii, q. iv, Inter cetera*: The canon 'Inter cetera' is derived from Augustine's reply to a query from a bishop, Severus Milevitanus, about the predicament of a certain Hubald. Hubald had been forced by the relatives of a concubine ('pelicis') to swear he would marry her and would no longer care for his mother and brothers. Augustine replied that he had consulted Ambrose about the matter and would advise the bishop to inform Hubald that an oath ('iuramentum') was not intended to be a chain of iniquity, nor to result in matricide or fratricide. Let Hubald continue to care for his mother and brothers. Those who forced him to swear are the ones guilty of perjury (C. 22 q. 4 c. 22; Friedberg 1: 880–1). Gratian's *post dict.* adduces the story in Josh. 9, which is retold in *D&P*, 260/17–48 below.

238/4–7 *be þe lawe . . . peyne*: The legal maxim, 'Agentes et consencientes pari pena puniantur', is cited in Latin below, 2–57/76–7. It is cited in *PP*, B-Text, XIII/427; and in Robert of Brunne's *Handling Synne*:

Noþeles, þe consentour
Shal be holde for a lechour;
Euene peyne shul þey bere,
þe toon þe touþer shal answere.
(ed. Furnivall, EETS, 119,123, pp. 243/7619–22)

238/7 *be Godis body, bonys, herte, blood*: See 240/49–66 below.

238/15 *Sent Austyn*: 'Fuit hic homo quidam simplex, innocens, bene fidelis, a multis vestris, id est, Hipponensibus, imo ab omnibus cognitus, Tutus-lymeni vocatus. Tutu[s]lymeni quis vestrum non novit, qui cives estis? Ab illo audivi quod dico. Nescio quis negavit ei, vel quod commendaverat, vel quod ei debebatur; et hominis fidei se commisit. Commotus provocavit eum ad jusjurandum. Juravit ille, iste perdidit: sed isto perdente, ille penitus periit. Dicebat ergo iste Tutuslymeni homo gravis et fidelis, ipsa nocte exhibitum se fuisse ad judicem, et cum magno impetu atque terrore se pervenisse ad praesidentem excelsum quemdam et admirabilem virum, cui parebat officium similiter excelsorum, jussum fuisse perturbatum retro revocari, et interrogatum fuisse his verbis: Quare provocasti hominem ad jurationem, quem sciebas falsum esse juraturum? Respondit ille: Negavit mihi rem meam. Responsum est illi: Et nonne melius erat, ut rem tuam quam exigebas perderes, quam animam hominis istius falsa juratione perimeres?' (*Sermo* 308, c. 5; *PL* 38: 1409–1410).

239/13 *xxii, q. i, Si quis per capillum*: The canon 'Si quis per capillum': 'If anyone swears by the head or hair of God or is in the habit of blaspheming in this way, he shall be deposed if he has clerical status; if he is a lay person, he shall be anathematized. And if anyone swears by creatures he shall be sharply reprimanded and in addition he shall do penance, as the synod has decreed. ¶ 1. If anyone has not exposed such a man, no doubt he will be punished by Divine condemnation. ¶ 2. And if a bishop has neglected to correct him he shall be sharply rebuked' (C. 22 q. 1 c. 10; Friedberg 1: 863).

239/20 *þe lawe imperial . . . glose*: Roman law; the gloss could have been any one of a number, the most popular being that of Accursius (d. 1263); his *Glossa ordinaria* was published in Lyon in 1584; a more modern edition of the *Corpus iuris civilis* is that of P. Krueger *et al.*, see *OCL* s.v.

239/22 *in Almanye . . . 3o & Nen*: Pauper adds verisimilitude to his reference to Germany by translating '3a' and 'Nay' into 'Ja' and 'Nein'.

239/31 *ad Hebreos vi [6]*: Pauper makes a skewed use of Heb. 6: 6, the context of which is St Paul's attack on those who have fallen away after baptism: these crucify Christ a second time. The GO: 'Quia in baptismo sumus conformes morti eius & sepulturae. Qui putat secundo baptizari, secundo christum quantum ad se crucifigit, quod est eum habere ostentui &

derisioni, vt semel mortuum est, ita nos in baptismo semel morimur peccatis, non secundo vel tercio' (4: 421).

240/49–66 *þe myraclys of our lady . . . helle withoutyn ende*: The tale is known as the 'Tale of the Bloody Child'. In an early fourteenth-century version, the swearer is 'a ryche man' (*Handlyng Synne*, ed. Furnivall, EETS, os 119, 123, pp. 25–9); in the *Fasciculus morum* he is 'quidam Lumbardus nomine Hubertus de Lorgo' (ed. Wenzel, pp. 166–7). In the English *Gesta Romanorum*, 'a man' (ed. Herrtage, EETS, es 33, pp. 409–11). In two of Thomas Brinton's sermons, the story is told of 'quodam maledicto' (*Sermons*, ed. Devlin, 1: 191, 2: 367). The tale also appears in John Bromyard's fourteenth-century handbook for preachers, *Summa praedicantium* (Tübach *Index*, No. 5103). The tale is used as an exemplum against swearing, usually in an exposition of the second Commandment. It is difficult to know how much social observation lies behind the formulaic claim that

> Gentyl men, for grete gentry,
> wene þat grete oþys beyn curteysy;
> Noþeles, blode, fete, & yȝen,
> þey scorne Ihesu, and vpbreyde hys pyn
> (*Handlyng Synne*, ed. Furnivall, p. 25/669–72),

since all the tales repeat it and since it is the point of the story that follows. Compare Chaucer's 'Parson's Tale': 'What seye we eek of hem that deliten hem in sweryng, and holden it a gentrie or a manly dede to swere grete othes?' (*CT*, p. 307/601–3). Another formula, with patristic sources, usually included is: 'þou doost more dyspyȝt & more blasphemye to god þan þe iewys þat nayled hym on þe cros' (e.g., *Jacob's Well*, MS Salisbury 187, fo. 187ʳ; idem, ed. Brandeis, EETS os 115, p. 153/26–7).

241/1 ff. *What seist þu*: Compare the contemporary *Jacob's Well*:

> . . . men swere, be it for ouȝt or for nouȝt, be . . . his hevyd, or his hood, or ony swich oþere oth. . . . þei sweryn be god . . . be his soule, his body, his herte, his flesch, his bonys, his peyne, his deth, his feet, his nayles, or be ony of his oþer lymes. þanne þei rende god iche lyme fro oþer . . .
> (ed. Brandeis, EETS, 115, p. 153/15–27)

The euphemism 'koc' for 'God' is attested from Chaucer onwards (see *CT*, Mcp, prol., p. 282/9), but in the combination 'cokkes bones' or 'kokkis blood' rather than 'cockis body'. In the late fourteenth-century *Gawain*, it is used as an oath but not as an imprecation: 'And I schal swere bi God and alle his gode halȝez,/ As help me God and þe halydam . . .' (ed. Davis, 2nd edn. 1967. p. 58/2122–3); see also *TWT*, p. 74/1648. The euphemism, 'be our lakyn' for 'by Our Lady' is not attested elsewhere before the sixteenth century, see *OED* s.v. 'lakyn 2', where the word is said to be a contraction of 'lady + kin'; cf. Shakespeare's *Tempest* 3.3.1. See above 239/13, 240/49–66.

242/23 *as Sent Powil seith*: The reference is to Heb. 6: 16: 'Homines enim per maiorem sui iurant'; see above 232/5–16; cited again below 252/2.

243/45 *3a, 3a, Nay, nay*: Matt. 5: 37; see 226/14 and 230/22 above.

243/4 *þe lawe*: See 244/14 below.

244/14 *xxii, q. i, Mouet te*: The canon 'Mouet te' holds that it is better to swear truthfully by false gods than to swear falsely by God. The source is St Augustine's second letter to Publicolus: '. . . considerare, utrum si quispiam per Deos falsos iurauerit se fidem seruaturum, et eam non seruauerit, non tibi uidetur bis pecasse?. . . .Verumtamen sine ulla dubitatione minus malum est per Deos falsos iurare ueraciter, quam per Deum uerum fallaciter' (Ep. 47.2, *PL* 33: 184; C. 22 q. i c. 16; Friedberg 1: 865).

244/19 *Genesis xxxi [52–53]*: 'Deus Abraham, et Deus Nachor iudicet inter nos, Deus patris eorum. Iurauit ergo Iacob per timorem patris sui Isaac.' GO: 'Per timorem, sci., quo timebat deum quem commendauit supra, dicens '& timor patris mei [Gen. 31: 42]', etc. (1: 82).

245/41–2 *xxxv, q. vi, Episcopus in synodo, & ii, q. i, Si Peccauerit, & q. vii, Plerique, & vi, q. ii, Si tantum*: The four canons cited are (1) 'Episcopus', which provides for the appointment of a committee of seven or more upstanding men of the parish to investigate any derelictions or backslidings (C. 35 q. 6 c. 7; Friedberg 1: 1279); (2) 'Si peccauerit', an extract from Augustine's sermon 82.10, in which he says that if your brother sins against you, try to settle it between you, citing the behaviour of Joseph when he learned of Mary's pregnancy (*PL* 39: 506–14). When crimes are committed against all and are known by all, settle matters publicly (C. 2 q. i c. 19; Friedberg 1: 447); (3) 'Plerique', which excerpts the same sermon of Augustine's, where he says that many good men suffer from others' sins because they lack the documents to prove others' guilt; a commentary by Gratian follows, citing biblical examples beginning with the quarrel between Noah and his sons (C. 2 q. 7 c. 27; Friedberg 1: 489–91); and (4) 'Si tantum', which says that if a bishop knows of a person's crime but has no way to prove it he should keep silent but try privately to correct the miscreant (C. 6 q. 2 c. 2; Friedberg 1: 561). All of the foregoing apply to Church administration; Pauper has applied them to the behaviour of secular lords and their household servants.

245/1 *college*: Here not necessarily a collegiate church but a body of scholars or students living in an endowed establishment, as at Oxford or Cambridge. Cf. 353/49 and 2–136/50 below.

245/8 *Extra,[lib. ii, ti. xxiv]*: The canon 'Veritatis' is taken from an exchange between Pope Clement III (d. 1191) and Vasallus, in which Vasallus asks whether he is obliged to swear an oath to the successor of his former prelate. Clement answers that, all other things being equal, he is not obliged to do so (X 2.24.14; Friedberg 2: 363–4).

245/8–9 *Raymundus, lib. i, ti. De periurio, ¶ xvi, Item pone*: Raymond of Peñafort, in a chapter on perjury, puts the question whether a hostage who is compelled to swear an oath is obliged to keep it. Raymond says, citing Augustine and others, that on the face of it the answer would seem to be no. But oaths are of two kinds, assertive and promissory. Fear excuses the breaking of promissory oaths but not, under all circumstances, assertive oaths: some assertive oaths should not be made under any kind of compulsion (*Summa*, Bk. I, pp. 87–9).

246/26–7 *Iohannes, in Summa confessorum, lib. i, ti. ix, q. xiv, Quero*: The reference is to John of Freiburg's *Summa confessorum*, found in MS Bodley 299, fo. 30^v.

246/31–4 *wheþer his synne is forȝouyn*: Pauper passes lightly over an important issue: does God alone forgive sins, or has the power of forgiveness been wholly delegated to the Church, or are the powers shared? Dives assumes the second; Pauper implicitly assumes the third. Compare Aquinas: 'God alone directly remits sin, acting instrumentally through baptism as an inanimate means and through the priest as an animate means. . . . and thus it would appear that the power of the keys is not ordained as a cause of the remission of sin but as a disposition toward the remission of sin' (*ST*, Supple., 18.1; OP edn., Rome, 1894, 5: 99).

246/36 *Summa confessorum . . . Quid de uxore*: The reference is to John of Freiburg's *Summa confessorum*, Bk. I, ti. 9, q. 12, found in MS Bodley 299, fo. 30^r, citing the case of a woman accused of adultery.

246/36–7 *Extra, lib. v, De purgacione canonica, Accepimus*: The canon 'Accepimus' takes up the case of a prelate who wishes to swear that he was free from a sin for which he had formally atoned. He is told that absolution does not confer immunity from any particular sin; he is directed to swear instead that after his promotion he will not sin in the same way, and his co-swearers are directed to swear only that they believed that he had sworn to the truth (X 5.34.16; Friedberg 2: 877).

246/39 *Hostiensis*: The reference is to Hostiensis' *Summa aurea*. Henry of Segusa (Henricus de Segusio, c. 1200–1271), called Hostiensis, was 'Cardinal (of Ostia), canonist and diplomat. He taught possibly at Bologna and certainly at Paris. His *Summa*, 'sometimes called *Summa Copiosa* (1253) . . . was a synthesis of Roman and canon law and [was] in constant use until the seventeenth century' (edn. Venice 1570; see *OCL* s.v.). During the later Middle Ages, to study canon law was 'Hostiensem segui' (Van de Wiel, *History of Canon Law* (1991), pp. 121–2). He is mentioned, disparagingly, in Dante's *Paradiso*, as 'him of Ostia' (12: 83). See Gallagher (1978), with valuable bibliography on pp. 9–13; and, in brief, Brundage (1995), pp. 155–7, 214. See 'Non-scriptural Index' below for further references in *D&P*.

246/43–4 *Summa confessorum, ti. viii, q. lxxxiii*: Refers to John of Freiburg's *Summa*, Bk. I, ti. 8, q. 83, found in MS Bodley 299, fo. 29^r, Quid si.

247/2 *Reymund*: Raymond of Peñafort; 'Votum est alicuius boni cum deliberatione facta promissio: si enim fiat de re mala, vel de bona, sed sine deliberatione non obligat. Isidorus. 22.q.4. in malis promissis rescinde fidem; in turpi voto muta decretum. & ext. eo. litteraturam' (*Summa*, Bk. I, 'De transgressione voti', p. 54). Impediments to the taking of vows, such as are discussed in the rest of the chapter, are detailed in idem, Bk. 4, pp. 530–3.

248/33 *quia est actus latrie*: Aquinas: 'votum est actus latriae, sive religionis' (*ST*, II–II, 88.5). The following Article (88.6) answers Dives' question (l. 30) about vows; 'For three reasons it is better and more meritorious to do something with a vow rather than without a vow. First because a vow . . . is an act of *latria*, which is preeminent among the moral virtues. . . . Second, because one who vows to do something and does it subjects himself to God more than one who merely does it. . . .Third, because a vow fixes the will firmly towards the good . . .' (OP edn., Rome, 1894, 3: 628–9). Dispensations from vows are discussed in *ST*, II–II, 88.10–12. On *latria*, see 102/17–21 above.

248/45 *Sent Iamys*: See below 249/66–72.

249/66–72 *pilgrimage . . . holy lond . . . Sent Iamys*: Compare Chaucer's fictional pilgrim, the Wife of Bath (*CT*, Prol., p. 31/463–6). After Rome and Jerusalem, Santiago de Compostela was the most important destination for the devout pilgrim of the later Middle Ages. English pilgrims sailed to the port of La Coruña, a much more expeditious means of travel than the overland walk, which consumed, at a minimum, a toilsome four months' time. Though Wyclif himself says little about pilgrimages, 'Lollard sources are predictably hostile' (*PR*, p. 307); Lollard William Thorpe is dismissive: pilgrims, he says, 'now gon hidir and þider on pilgrymage . . . more for þe helþe of her bodies þan for þe helþe of her soulis' (*TWT*, p. 63/1289–90). On general background, see Sumption (1975), *passim*.

249/70 *Reymond*: Raymond of Peñafort's *Summa* says that when vows to make pilgrimages, and other such vows, are changed into something better the vows are not broken (Bk. I, 'De transgressione voti', ¶ 15, p. 75).

249/70 *Extra, [lib. iii, ti. xxxiv] c. i*: The canon 'De peregrinationis' states that vows to go on pilgrimage may be converted into a greater vow and, with the consent of one's prelate, be carried out by giving alms. The prelate must, however, take into account the person and his circumstances when dispensing from such a vow. The source is a letter from Pope Alexander III to the bishop of Exeter (X.3.34.1; Friedberg 2: 589). The canon 'Magnae devotionis' (c. 7 in the same Title) solves the problem of what to do if a vow to go on pilgrimage becomes moot for any reason: the money equivalent of the expense of the pilgrimage may be sent as a subsidy to the Holy Land. Cf. de Chobham, *Summa* (ed. Broomfield), pp. 564–5. See above 249/66–72.

250/88 *dette of her body*: Cf. 129/36–47 above, 2–61/36 below.

249/80 *Sent Tomays . . . Kent*: When Archbishop Thomas Becket was cut down in Canterbury Cathedral in 1170 by knights of Henry II, his death caused an immediate public outcry, and his tomb became the object of pilgrimages. Miraculous cures were attributed to the Saint (canonized in 1173). With Our Lady of Walsingham, the shrine of Becket was one of the two most popular pilgrimage destinations in England. See 209/21–7 above.

250/88 *dette of his body*: Cf. 129/36–47, 214/18 above, 2–61/36 below.

250/92 *Extra, lib. v, De regulis iuris, Quod non est licitum*: The canon 'Quod non est licitum' holds that in cases of necessity what is normally forbidden may be done, as in the case of illness a fast may be broken, or in the case of war, battle may be continued (X 5.40.4; Friedberg 2: 927). The text is a summary of Bede's gloss on Mark 2: 27 (GO 4: 96; PL 92: 154–5): 'What is unlawful is made licit by necessity. The Maccabees fought on the Sabbath; today, breaking a fast because of illness is not breaking a vow'. Cf. Aquinas (*ST*, II–II, 88.10 and 11) and de Chobham (*Summa*, ed. Broomfield, p. 560). The canon is cited again below, 287/22.

250/15–6 *þe wif to þe housebond & þe child to þe fadir*: Aquinas says that 'a vow is a promise made to God', hence 'no vow of a girl living in the household without the consent of her father nor of a wife without the consent of her husband' may stand (*ST*, II–II, 88.8), and 'if boys or girls before the age of puberty have not reached the age of reason they cannot obligate themselves by a vow; such a vow may be negated by their parents' (idem, Art 9; OP edn., Rome, 1894, 3: 631; 633). Cf. de Chobham, *Summa*, ed. Broomfield, p. 560.

250/18–251/58 *a confessour*: That this passage on confession appears only in manuscript G, may attest to the controversial nature of the topic. What is controversial is, however, not the nature of confession itself, as part of the sacrament of penance, but the abuse of confession by powerful lay persons. The probable reference is to the attack on Franciscan friars who (*c.*1399–1405) remained loyal to Richard II and were implicated—reportedly by breach of confessional secrecy—in conspiracies aimed at restoring him to power. On confession, Aquinas says: 'In any confession, sin is disclosed to the priest and hidden from others by the seal of confession ('confessionis sigillo')' (*ST*, Suppl., 7.1; OP edn., Rome 1894, 5: 44). See 2–3/36, 2–241/89 below.

252/1 *periurie*: The dual system of ecclesiastical and lay courts was productive of great confusion about witnesses, oaths, and evidence. To encourage true testimony, ecclesiastical courts relied on a theological definition of perjury; according to Aquinas: 'What is ipso facto contempt of God is a mortal sin; perjury implies contempt of God . . . hence it is clear that perjury, by its very nature, is a mortal sin' (*ST*, II–II, 98.3; OP edn., Rome, 1894, 3: 699). In this period, the lay system of justice was still reverting to trial by battle or the duel to establish guilt or innocence. Trial by jury, in the fourteenth century, could be only slightly less a trial of strength than a pitched battle: when each side produced a gang of compurgators, their numbers and reputations tended to count more than the facts of the case. A jury more closely resembled a group of sworn witnesses than a modern jury sworn to *hear* witnesses (Pollock and Maitland, 2: 598–674). The Lollard opposition to oaths seemed to undercut the effort of the Church to supplant trials by ordeal or battle with trials based on sworn testimony. Note, in cap. 18, Pauper's remark that penitent sinners 'arn be þe lawe restoryd aȝeyn to her fame *so þat þey mon ben witnessis in doom*, and her oth owyth ben receyuyd' (256/16–19 below). McNiven (1987), in his discussion of the confrontation between Archbishop Arundel and William Thorpe on the taking of oaths, comments: 'The question of oath-taking was intimately bound up with the central theme of the true source of authority. The administration of oaths was a key aspect of the enforcement of obedience to the Church's decrees' (p. 111); for Thorpe's Testimony, *TWT*, pp. 72–9. See also Bartlett (1986), pp. 29–33. See above 160/11–15 (on English law), and below, 255/86–96, on the tale of the Scot who preferred death to perjury.

252/2 *Sent Powil . . . ad Hebreos vi [16]*: See 232/5–16 and 242/23 above.

252/15–16 *þe Philosofre*: Aristotle says that the ancients 'made Ocean and Tethys the parents of creation, and described the oath of the gods as being by water . . . for what is oldest is most honourable, and the most honourable thing is that by which one swears' *Metaphysics*, Bk. I, c. 4 (*Oxford Aristotle* 2: 1556/29–33).

252/23 *Sent Thomas . . . In questione de quodlibet*: 'Frustra autem in causa homicidii controversiae finis esset juramentum, si homicidium esset gravius peccatum quam perjurium: praesumeretur enim quod qui majorem culpam homicidii commisisset, non videtur minorem perjurii incurrere. Unde ex hoc ipso quod in causa cujuslibet peccati defertur juramentum, manifeste ostenditur quod perjurium pro maximo peccato debet habere; nec immerito, quia perjurare nomen Dei, videtur quaedam divini hominiis denegatio: unde secundum locum post idolatriam peccatum perjurii tenet, ut ex ordine praeceptorum apparet' (*Quodlibet*. I, Art 18; *Opera omnia*, Parma edn., 1859, 9: 470).

252/23–4 *Ioannes in Summa confessorum, lib. i, ti. ix, q. xxiv, Vtrum*: John of Freiburg's *Summa*, MS Bodley 299, fo. 31ᵛ.

253/32–3 *Ecclesiastici x* [*13 et seq.*]: Ecclus. 10 [8], cited above, 149/60.

253/47–8 *þis lond . . . changid to anoþer nacion*; See above 149/53–4 and 257/43–51 below.

253/53 *questemongeris*: A species of petty criminal making an income from giving false testimony in court trials. They are noted by Langland (c1377): (*PP*, B-Text, XIX/366–9, ed. W. W. Skeat; 1: 570; 572). The *MED* cites *D&P*, s.v. 'quest(e' 1b, and the Royal 18 B.xxiii sermons of about the same date: 'þise false questmongers þat for a litill money or els for a good dyner will saue a theffe and dampne a trewe man' (*ME Sermons*, ed. Ross, EETS, 209, p. 174/17–19). A. Williams (1948), 200–4, gives further citations and concludes that the usual definition in this period was 'bribed juror'.

254/61 *Ysaie, xxviii* [*15*]: 'Flagellum inundans cum transierit non veniet super nos, quia posuimus mendacium spem nostram et mendacio protecti sumus.' GO (interlin.) on 'mendacio': 'Diabolo qui est pater mendacii' (3: 46).

254/67 *Exodi xxiii* [*7*]: Read 'Exod. 23:[1]'. The text in *D&P* omits 'tuam' after 'manum' and for 'pro' has 'per'. Cited below 2–50/28–34.

254/70–1 *Maleficos . . . Exodi xxii* [*18*]: The GO defines 'maleficos' as those: 'qui prestigiis magice artis & dyabolicis signentis agunt, vel hereticos, quia consortio fidelium qui vere viuunt excommunicandi sunt, donec maleficium erroris in eis moriatur' (1: 158). Nicolaus de Lyra's postil: 'In hebreo habet, Sortilegam non patieris viuere, et licet exprimat mulierem tamen mihi intelligitur de homini sortilego, sicut exprimit translatio nostra, sed scriptura exprimit illud quod communius accidit, scilicet, que mulieres sint sortilege. Ex hoc etiam patet que cum dicitur Maleficos etc., intelligitur spiritualiter de maleficio quod consistit in sortilegiis. Ponitur autem ista lex inter eas qui reprimunt concupiscentiam carnalem, quia sortilegia frequenter fiunt in his qui pertinens ad actum carnis' (*Postilla* 1). Cited below, 2–13/10, 2–144/114.

254/78 *Barraban*: Usually Barabbas. See Matt. 27: 16, Mark 15: 6–7, Luke 23: 18, and John 18: 40. See also *ABD*, 1: 607.

255/86–96 *a Scot apelyd an Englychman*: The *Vita Ricardi Secundi* has, for 1398: 'Sub hiis diebus iussit rex fieri unum theatrum, Anglice "lystes", apud Bristolliam, pro duello habendo inter unum armigerum Anglicum appellantem, et unum militem, Scoticum origine sed Anglicum iuratur defendentem. Qui appellans, in theatro renuncians appellacioni sue, tractus fuit et suspensus' (p. 149/3489–93). The more circumstantial account of this event in *D&P* might appear to have been based on personal knowledge, especially given the direct dialogue and the suggestion of a Scottish accent in 'Lard' (255/89), except for the fact that in the *Historia* the English appellant is hanged and the Scot is freed, while in *D&P* it is the Scot who refuses to swear and is hanged. For laws then governing duels in cases of appellancy, see Glanvill's *Treatise*, ed. Hall, pp. 171–3.

255/2–3 *xxii, q. i, Predicandum*: The canon 'Predicandum' directs that the faithful should be instructed that perjury is as grave a sin as adultery, homicide or fornication, and the same penalty should be imposed. Those who refuse to confess to and repent this sin are to be ejected from the fellowship of the Church. The source is Pope Eutychian (275–83) (C.22 q.1 c.17; Friedberg 1: 866).

256/15–16 *xi, q. i, Conspiracionum & Coniuracionum*: These two canons are cc. 21 and 22, in reverse order. The first (21) is from the Council of Chalcedon (451): (1) 'Coniurationum': Intrigue and criminal conspiracy, called by the Greeks 'fratria', are to be inhibited by public law. Even more they should be prohibited in the holy Church of God. If clerics and monks are found to be conspiring or plotting, or joining factions or 'fratrias' against their bishops or others, they are to lose their rank (C.11 q.1 c.21; Friedberg 1: 632). The second canon (22) is from an epistle of Pope Calistus (d. 1124) to the bishops of France: (2) 'Conspirationum': The Pope has heard that people are conspiring against their bishops. Such conspiracies are abominable not only among Christians but among pagans ['ethnicos']; such conspirators and their followers are condemned by Church and secular law. Those with clerical rank are to be deprived of it and others are to be deprived of communion with the Church (C.11 q.1. c.23; Friedberg 1: 632; cf. Burchard of Worms, *PL* 140: 853).

256/21 *Hostiensis*: From Hostiensis' *Summa aurea* on Roman and canon law; see 246/39 above.

256/22 *Extra, lib. lii, De testibus, c. Ex parte, & vi, q. i, Quicumque*: For 'lii' read 'ii'. Two canons: (1) 'Ex parte' involves a legal case that was a tangle of lay and clerical claims: A., a priest who had canonically received and peacefully held the church of Clunoden for thirty years or more, was attacked by a certain H., a soldier, who claimed a hereditary right to the Church property. Using suborned witnesses, the soldier won his case in the local court. The Pope urges that the priest be restored to his church and that the corrupt witnesses against him be solemnly warned of the peril to their immortal souls of the sin of perjury (X 2.20.7; Friedberg 2: 317). The canon is derived from a letter of Pope Eugenius III, 'an ardent reformer of the morals of the clergy' (*ODCC*, p. 472), to the Bishop of Hereford. (2) The canon 'Quicunque' directs that whoever gives a licence to anyone to kill or despoil the goods of anyone who pronounces a sentence of excommunication against kings, princes, barons, nobles, bailiffs ('ballivos') or any of their ministers or others or aids those who give such orders, or knows of such orders is to incur a like sentence of excommunication. Whoever remains under the sentence of excommunication for two months cannot thereafter obtain a benefice without apostolic absolution. The source is a decretal of Pope Gregory X (d. 1275), issued at the Council of Lyons (Sext. 5.11.11; Friedberg 2: 1102).

256/26 note *for perjury, as in Portugale*: The Lisbon copyist of *D&P* planted evidence of his work both in his colophon and in the body of the text, see *D&P* 1:xiv and 146/59 above. The marriage of John of Gaunt's daughter, Philippa of Lancaster, to the king of Portugal in 1387 led to closer cultural ties between the two countries, see P. E. Russell (1955). For comments on the kind of street show described by the Lisbon scribe, see Flynn (1994), pp. 153–68. See 2–236/final note.

257/31 *Hostiensis*: The 'same place' refers to the *Summa aurea* cited 256/21 above. See 246/39 above.

257/32 *Ysaye lix [14]*: For [14] read [13–15]. In this citation of verses 13 through 15, some phrases are added to the translation in *D&P*, producing a somewhat macaronic result; the bracketed phrases are additions. Verse 13: 'Concepimus [false contruyingis] et locuti sumus de corde verba mendacii.'/ Verse 14: 'Et conversum est retrorsum iudicium et iustitia longe stetit', [he dorst no3t put forth his hed], 'quia coruit in platea veritas', [he was born doun opynly & no man wolde helpyn hym up], 'et aequitas' [seith he, ne efnehed in schiftyng and in demyng] 'non potuit ingredi',/ Verse 15: 'et facta est veritas in oblivionem, et qui recessit a malo praedae patuit'. See below, 2–225/11–28, for a variant translation.

257/43–51 *þe rewme of Engelond for periurie*: Charges of perjury were rife on both sides during the years 1399–1400 when Henry of Lancaster took over the throne and public order was reduced to the force of arms. The pro-Lancastrian chronicler, Adam of Usk, writes for the year 1399:

> Item, per certos doctores, episcopos, et alios, quorum presencium notator unus extiterat, deponendi regem Ricardum et Henricum, Lancastrie ducem, subrogandi in regem materia, et qualiter et ex quibus causis, juridice committebatur disputanda. Per quos determinatum fuit quod perjuria, sacrilegia, sodomidica, subditorum exinnanicio, populi in servitutem reduccio, vecordia, et ad regendum imbecilitas, quibus rex Ricardus notorie fuit infectus, per capitulum "Ad apostolice" . . . deponendi Ricardum cause fuerant sufficientes

about which charges King Richard himself is unreliably reported by Usk to have replied in kind. (Usk, *Chronicon*, ed. Thompson, p. 29; now see *The Chronicle . . . Usk*, ed. and tr. Given-Wilson (1997), pp. 62–5. On Usk as eyewitness and historian, see Gransden (1982), 2: 183–4; 186. On the fear of a French invasion expressed at the end of the chapter, see above 149/53–4.

258/5–7 *as Salamon seith*: Ecclus. 27: 15, cited above 227/40.

259/1 *breakyng of comenant*: When strong civil institutions are absent, nothing stands between the individual and the force of arms except sworn oaths backed by powerful religious faith; it is difficult for the modern mind to gain a real sense of the scope and importance of the crime of perjury for a Dives and a Pauper. See above 252/1.

260/17–48 *Iosue ix [1–27]*: Josh. 9: 1–27. Pauper's account closely follows Peter Comestor's version (*Historia.*, *PL* 198: 1266).

261/55–262/79 *secunde book of Kyngis, xxi [1–9]* . . . *Mastir of Storyys*: 2 Reg. 21: 1–9 (2 Sam. 21). Pauper's account closely follows Peter Comestor's version: in the Bible, the famine is caused by blood guilt; in Comestor it is inflicted by God because of the false oath ('irritum juramentum') made to the Gibeonites (*Historia*, *PL* 198: 1342).

262/90 *Ezechielis xvi [52]*: 'Ergo et tu porta confusionem tuam . . . ergo et tu confundere, et porta ignominiam tuam, quae iustificasti sorores tuas.' The GO (Jerome): 'Vt propria, sci., torquearis conscientia, et nunc voluntate propria sustine cruciatum ne sustineas in perpetuum'; in a second gloss, Jerome applies the text to priests who corrupt lay persons by their example ('sacerdos male vivens . . . exemplo laicos currumpat') (3: 252–3).

262/94 *Malachie ii [2–3]*: 'Si nolueritis audire, et si nolueritis ponere super cor, ut detis gloriam nomini meo, ait Dominus exercituum, mittam in vos egestatem, et maledicam benedictionibus vestris, et maledicam illis, quoniam non posuistis super cor. / Ecce ego proiiciam vobis brachium, et dispergam super vultum vestrum stercus solemnitatum vestrarum, et assumet vos secum.' The GO applies the text to priests: 'Proprie sacerdotis dicitur quod si non dederint gloriam nomini domini per suam bonam conversationem, patientur egestatem omnium honorum, hi quia non benedicunt sanctis ex vero corde, sed per dulces sermones seducunt corda innocentium, non merentur dei benedictionem' (3: 454). This citation ends Commandment II with a malediction, or 'clamour'; see below 324/27–325/31 and Com. X, cap. 7 and 8, for further examples in this text; cf. Lester Little (1993), pp. 59–85.

VOL. I: 1, COMMANDMENT III, pp. 263–303

263/4–6 *thredde comandement* . . . *haly day*: Exod. 20: 8: 'Memento ut diem sabbati sanctifices.' Exod. 23: 12: 'Sex diebus operaberis: septimo die cessabis, ut requiescat bos et asinus tuus: et refigeretur filius ancillae tuae, et aduena.' The interlinear gloss points out the correspondence between the third precept of the first Table and the third member of the Trinity:

'Tercium mandatum pertinens ad spiritum sanctum cuius dono requies eterna promittitur & sanctificatio perficitur' (cf. 265/68 below). The 'six days' of work are figuratively six thousand years: 'Sex milibus annorum quibus laboratur'. In respect to the sabbath of the seventh day: 'de sabbato iudeorum dicitur, 'Sabbata vestra odit anima mea'. 'Sabbath' refers to the life after death: 'que post hanc vitam vera requies, carnalis & spiritualis'. The number seven also signifies perfection: 'Significans que in perfectione senarii sunt nobis opera facienda vt postea fruamur requie eterna' (GO, 1: 153). On the numbering of the Commandments see 81/7 above.

263/19–21 *Sent Austin . . . Genesis i* [*37*]: For [37] read [3]: '. . . dixitque Deus, fiat lux et facta est lux'. The GO: 'Non laborauit deus in operando: qui solo verbo fecit omnia, dicendo 'fiat' (1: 17). Augustine says: 'God rested from all the works that He made in the sense that from then on He did not produce what He had made. Hence it is true that God rested on the seventh day, and it is also true that He works even until now' (*De Gen. ad Lit.* Bk. 4, c. 12, *PL* 34: 304–5). See 264/29 below.

264/29 *God . . . was neuer in trauayl*: Augustine says that anthropomorphic conceptions of God's 'work' must be eschewed; God neither worked nor needed to rest, 'for the power and might of the Creator, who rules and embraces all, makes every creature abide; and if this power ever ceased to govern creatures, their essences would pass away and all nature would perish. . . . God made the creatures that were to be in the future in such a way that without Himself being subject to time He made them subject to time'. His 'rest' must be understood symbolically to mean that on the seventh day He ceased to create new forms and specified that day as a day of rest for mankind (*De Gen. ad Lit.* Bk. 4, cc. 8–17; 35: *PL* 34: 301–8; 320).

264/36 *Io. 5: 17*: The beginning of the gospel of John is usually identified with the beginning of the book of Genesis. In the Longleat sermons, the writer of *D&P* makes the customary identification (fos. 136rb-137ra). Augustine (on John 5: 17) makes Pauper's distinction between the work of creation and the work of governance: 'Per me regitur mundus in istis operibus. Pater meus et tunc operatur est cum fecit mundus, et usque nunc operatur cum regit mundum; ergo et per me fecit cum fecit, et per me regit cum regit' (*In Ioh.*, 17.15; *CCL* xxxvi, p. 178/24–7; *PL* 35: 1534). The Wycliffite sermon writer makes the same distinction in other words: 'But fro þat Crist was man, Crist worchiþ by his double kynde, by his godhed and by his manhed. . . . . by þis he wold not mene þat þe Fadir leeueþ nou to worche, but þat Crist haþ newe kynde by which he reuliþ þis world' (*EWS* 3, Serm. 168/8–13).

264/48–53 *þorw þe Rede Se . . . Deutronomii* [*11: 4*] *. . . lond of lyf*: The crossing of the Red Sea is linked typologically to the baptism of Christ (and of Christians), beginning with 1 Cor. 10: 1–2: 'patres nostri omnes . . . mare transierunt/ et omnes in Mose baptizati sunt'. The GO, on Exod. 14: 'Mare rubrum baptismus christi sanguine consecratum significat' (1: 139, giving Isidore of Seville as source). Cf. Peter of Riga's *Aurora*:

> Moysi uirga Rubrum tangit Mare, transit Hebreus,
> Expirat Pharao cum legione sua:
> Virga crucem notat hic, baptismum sanguine Christi
> Perfusum Rubri denotat unda Maris.
>
> (ed. Beichner, 1: 100/219–22)

In this passage, the cross is linked to the Red Sea crossing by way of Moses' rod, perhaps not too great a step since Moses' rod is a traditional prefiguration of the cross. Mirk's *Festial*, like *D&P*, links the Red Sea, baptism, and crucifixion: '. . . þe font, þat is now þe Red See. . . . For þe watyr yn þe fonte betokenyþ þe red blod and watyr þat ran down of þe wondys of Cristis syde in þe wheche . . . þe veray fend ys drowned, and all hys myȝt lorne, and all cristen pepull sauet' (ed. Erbe, EETS, es 96, p. 127/ 23–7).

265/62 *Ysaye i [17]*: For [17] read [16–17]. The GO is perhaps responsible for the reference to the Apocalypse below (265/68): '. . . peccata quae prius in modum coccini sanguinea fuerunt dimittentur & opera sanguinis investe domini mutabuntur, quae de agni vellere confecta est quem sequuntur in apocalipsi qui splendent candore virginitatis' (3: 4).

265/68 *Apocalpys, xiv [13]* . . . *holy gost*: LL4 cites and expands on Rev. 14: 13: 'And þerfore seynt Ion seyth þat þe holy gost byddyth þat alle men & wommen in heuene restin from here trauaylys . Hyr ys hate & enuye . þer ys endeles charite . for þer euery man & womman ys glad of oþeris welfare . Hyr ys seknesse . þer ys endeles helþe . Hyr ys dred þer ys alwey sekyrnesse', etc. (fo. 53^(va)). The first three Commandments (or the first Table of the Commandments) concern man's relation to God. The alignment of the first three Commandments with the Trinity is usually referred to Augustine's Sermon 9 ('De decem chordis'): 'Quae decem praecepta sic sunt distributa, ut tria pertineant ad deum. . . .Unus est deus noster. . . . Quia uero ipse unus deus, pater est et filius et spiritus sanctus, in spiritu sancto hoc est, in dono dei, requies nobis sempiterna promittur' (*CCL* xli, p. 118/222–231; *PL* 38: 80). Compare Grosseteste: '. . . primum de istis tribus mandatis pertinet ad Patrem, secundum ad Filium, tertium ad Spiritum Sanctum', *De Decem Mand.*, p. 36/1–2. See also Peter Lombard, *Sentences*, Bk. III, d. 37, c. 3 (2: 209). The idea is repeated in the text below, 300/60–71.

265/4 *cerimonial*, . . . *iudicial* . . . *moral*: Aquinas discusses the degree to which the precepts contained in the Old Testament are binding upon Christians, concluding: 'Three kinds of precepts of the old law must be posited, that is, *moral* precepts, which are dictated by nature, *ceremonial* precepts, which govern religious ordinances ['cultus divini'], and *judicial* precepts, which determine the rules of justice among men' (*ST*, I–II, 99.2– 5; OP edn., Rome 1894, 2: 708). Grosseteste observes that under the old law, the Commandment was observed 'ad litteram'; under the new law, 'cessat hec legalis observancia, sicut in multis locis veteris testamenti est predicta cessatura' (*De decem mand.*, ed. Dales and King, p.30).

266/22 *Why is it . . . Sonday*: Wyclif lists five reasons why the Sabbath was changed to Sunday: (1) Creation began on Sunday, (2) the Resurrection occurred on Sunday, (3) Pentecost was on Sunday, (4) the Last Judgment will be on Sunday, and (5) the Easter vigil (like other vigils) had necessarily to fall on a Sunday, and this vigil symbolises the advent of the eighth and last age of the world (*De mand*, pp. 209–12). See above 265/4.

266/32 *Dockynge, super Deutronomyum*: Thomas de Docking (d. *c.*1270) was seventh Lector to the Friars Minor at Oxford. His works comprise commentaries on the Bible in which his method was to establish the literal meaning of the text before putting forward allegorical interpretations, a method followed later by the better-known Nicolaus de Lyra. His comment- ary on Deuteronomy is referred to five times in *D&P* (see Non-scriptural Index). The references to Docking in *D&P* are a strong indication that the author read in the Franciscan *studium* at Oxford, see Introduction, p. xxv. See A. G. Little (1926), pp. 46–52; A. G. Little (1943), pp. 98–121; J. I. Catto, 'New Light on . . . Docking', MRS, 6 (1968), 135–49; *BRUO* 1: 580. Docking's remark that the day of doom will fall on a Sunday ('hec die iudicatimus est mundum') can be found in MS Balliol 28, fo. 37rb. On manuscripts, see Rouse and Rouse, *Authentic Witnesses* (1991), pp. 422–3. See 2–162/75–7, 2–164/137, 2–220/13 below.

267/41 *Reymund, lib. i, ti. De ferijs*: Raymond of Peñafort: 'Item, tanta est excellentia huiusmodi diei quod in nullo alio die potest Episcopus con- secrari' (*Summa*, Bk I, p. 110b).

267/53–5 [*Lc. 18: 12*] . . . *Marci xvi* [2], *& Mathei xxviii* [*1*]*1:* The verse from Luke reports the words of the Pharisee who says that he fasts twice on the sabbath ['in sabato', tr.'in the week', i.e., the 'sabbath' of the old law] and gives tithes of all he gets; the verses from Mark and Matthew tell of the two Marys who rose early on Sunday—the new sabbath—to go to the tomb of Jesus.

268/74 *Ieremie . . . xxxi* [*11–13*]: For [11–13] read [11; 13]: 'Redemit enim Dominus Iacob [*D&P* 'populum suum'], et liberavit eum de manu potentioris. . . . /Tunc laetabitur virgo in choro, iuvenes et senes simul, et convertam luctum eorum in gaudium, et consolabor eos et laetificabo a dolore suo'. On Jer. 31: 11, the GO has: 'Aduersariae partes quae natura fortior aut fide sorciores, si tamen liberantur ab eo qui alligat fortem & domum eius diripit' (3: 148). Jer. 31: 13 is cited 298/50 below.

268/81 *Osee ii* [*11*]: Hos. 2: 11: 'Et cessare faciam omne gaudium eius, solemnitatem eius, neomeniam eius, sabbatum eius, et omnia festa tempora eius'. In historical context, the prophet Hosea, in the eighth century BC, was attacking Israel for imitating Canaanite cultic practises, see *ABD*, 3: 291–7. The GO refers to the idols of the Chaldeans and Assyrians as the cause of the wrath of Yahweh. Cited below, 283/12.

268/13–17 *Exodi xxxiv & xxxv . . . as it haddyn ben to hornys*: The reference to the 'horns' of Moses is found in Exod. 34: 29–30, 35: 'Cumque descenderet Moyses de monte Sinae, tenebat duas tabulas testimonii, et ignorabat quod cornuta esset facies sua ex consortio sermonis Domini.' 'Cornuta' is Jerome's translation of Hebrew 'qeren', meaning either 'horns' or 'rays of light'. Ruth Mellinkoff (1970), in her study of the 'horns of Moses' tradition, points out that Jerome's version is not, as has sometimes been claimed, a mistranslation, and that 'qeren' should be, as it was in the past, interpreted as a sign of power and kingship (pp. 1–9, 138–40 and *passim*). The GO does not comment at length on Moses' horns, but, citing Isidore of Seville, suggests that they symbolize the two testaments, armed against false teachings ('cornua duorum testamentorum quibus contra dogmata falsitatis incedit armata'), 1: 198. On the mitre, see 2–228/46 below.

269/34–5 *þe veyl of þe Iewys temple*: Matt. 27: 51, Mark 15: 38, Luke 23: 45. The GO: Velum quod dicebatur exterius que nunc ex parte videmus, cum autem venerit quod perfectum est, tunc velum interius disrumpetur' (4: 86).

270/46 *recreacion*: The *MED* cites only *D&P* and *The Orchard of Syon* for this sense of the word: '. . . þe first creacioun and . . . þe secounde recreacyoun þat a man resceyueþ in þe blood of my sone, whereynne I haue refoormyd hym by grace' (ed. Hodgson and Liegey, EETS, 258, p. 327/13–15).

270/48 *Sent Austyn*: See above 264/29.

270/55 *al power in heuene & erde*: Matt. 28: 18: 'Et accedens Iesus locutus est eis, dicens: Data est mihi omnis potestas in caelo et in terra.' GO: 'Et ideo pius magister & illos ad fidem confortat, & dubios ad fidem vocat, intimans ad quantam pervenerit gloriam' (4: 88).

270/1–4 *Leuitici xxiii* [*33–6*]: 'Et locutus est Dominus ad Moysen dicens, / Loquere filiis Israhel, a quintodecimo die mensis huius septimi erunt feriae tabernaculorum septem diebus Domino. / Dies primus vocabitur celeberrimus atque sanctissimus, omne opus servile non facietis, / et septem diebus offeretis holocausta Domino. Dies quoque octavus erit celeberrimus atque sanctissimus, et offeretis holocaustum Domino: est enim coetus atque collectae, omne opus servile non facietis in eo.' See further vv. 39–43. Aquinas alludes to 'the feast of Scenopoegiae, or of tabernacles, which was kept for seven days to commemorate the blessing of divine protection when God led them [the Jews] through the desert, where they lived in tabernacles (or tents). Hence during this feast they had to take *the fruits of the fairest tree*, i.e., the citron, *and trees of dense foliage*, i.e., the myrtle, which is fragrant, *and branches of palm-trees and willows of the brook*, which retain their greenness a long time; and these are found in the Land of promise; to signify that God had brought them through the arid land of the wilderness to a delightful land.' (*ST*, I–II, 102.4; OP edn., Rome, 1894, 2: 755; tr. Dom. Fathers 2: 1067). The Jewish Feast of Tabernacles prefigures the Christian Feast of the Church Dedication (idem, 103.3; OP edn., 2: 780). Cited below, 296/3.

271/18–19 *tabernacle . . . Ps. 18: 6*: St Augustine says that 'in sole' symbolizes the luster of the earthly Church, which ought to challenge heretics and timid Christians: 'Quid tu, haeretice, fugis in tenebras? Christianus es? audi Christum. Seruus es? audi dominum. Filius es? audi patrem: emendare, reuiuisce' (*Enarr.*, 18.6; *CCL*, xxxviii, p. 109/7–10; *PL* 36: 160). He glosses 'de thalamo suo': '. . . ille tamquam sponsus, cum Verbum caro factum est, in utero uirginali thalamum inuenit' (idem, p. 109/27–9). Compare *Ancrene Wisse*: 'Maries wombe . . . weren hise ancre huses' (ed. Tolkien, EETS, 249, p. 193/4–5). Among other figurative uses, 'tabernacle' is applied both to the body of Christ (as it is here) and to his sepulchre. 'Tabernacle' also names the receptacle for holding the eucharistic wafer in its pyx.

272/42–4 *in þe gospel . . . endeles tabernaculys*: Luke 16: 9; see 54/11 above, 2–156/14 below, and LL4, fo. 64vb.

272/44–6 *tabernaculys . . . Ps. 83: 2–3*: The *D&P* translation is a poetic one. Augustine seizes on the contrast between the 'tabernacula' and the 'torcularia' of the previous verse: in this life, we are (as Christ figuratively was) in a wine press, but we desire other tabernacles, where we will no longer be pressed down (*Enarr.*, 83.5; *CCL*, xxxix, p. 1150/28–35; *PL* 36: 1059).

272/57–8 *firste day & . . . eyȝte day*: The first day of the week is the eighth day of the preceding week, thus both are applicable, figuratively, to the endless Sunday of the eighth, and final, age. Augustine established the medieval view that world time comprised six ages. These were to be followed by two more periods, one of rest following the Second Coming, and the other (for the elect) an endless age of heavenly bliss (*De civ. Dei*, 22: 30; *CCL* xlviii, p. 866/141–5; *PL* 41: 804). Cf. Grosseteste: 'Talem quippe accionem significat dies octavus, qui et primus, quia non aufert illam requiem sed glorificat. . . . ut postquam facta est talis resurreccio in Domini corpore . . . quod corpus ecclesie speraret in finem, iam dies dominicus, id est octavus, qui et primus, inciperet celebrari' (*De decem mand.*, ed. Dales and King, p. 38/1–2, 13–15). Wyclif cites Grosseteste, repeating that the sixth age is 'a Christo usque ad finem mundi, septima quiescencium incomplete in purgatorio et octava beatorum perpetuo quiescencium in celo' (*De mand.*, p. 212/1–3; 15–26). Cf. Ps.-Bede (*De temporum ratione*, *PL* 90: 520–1). See also Burrow (1988), pp. 79–92.

272/2 *thre maner of Sabatis*: Wyclif: 'Triplex enim ponitur sabbati observancia. Prima generalis, preservando nos a viciis, secunda specialis, preservando nos ab operibus servilibus, et tertia specialissima, preservando nos a mundi solicitudinibus' (*De mand.*, pp. 212/31–2, 213/1–2).

273/13 *Mathei xv* [*19*]: 'De corde enim exeunt cogitationes malae, homicidia, adulteria, fornicationes, furta, falsa testimonia, blasphemiae:/ haec sunt quae coinquinant hominem.' LL4: 'out of þe herte gon wickid þouȝtis manslauȝte . auouterie . fornycacioun . þefte . fals witnesse . blasfemye', fo. 117vb. The GO says that the Devil is not the origin of sin but only fosters the sins that arise in the human heart: 'Non enim a dyabolo immittuntur, sed et propria voluntate nascuntur. Dyabolus enim incentor est non auctor, quia nec interora nisi per habitus & gestus nouit' (4: 53). Cited below 2–98/72, 2–253/13.

273/20 *Mt. 5: 24*: 'Relinque ibi munus tuum ante altare, et vade prius reconciliari fratri tuo: et tunc veniens offeres munus tuum'. LL4: 'ʒif þu offre þi ʒifte at þe auter be it of preyer or of offerynge & þu haue in mende þat þi broþir hath onyþyng aʒens þe go fyrst & be reconcylyd to þi broþer & þan come & offre þi ʒifte' (fo. 38vb; also cited fo. 93ra). the GO restates the verse and offers an 'Vnde versus':

> Prius caritatem proximo exsoluat
> Qui munus suum deo placere optat.
>
> (4: 20)

274/1 *Origines super Leuiticum xxviii*: *D&P* 274/2–10 is an English version of a passage also cited by Wyclif: 'Relinquentes iudaicum sabbatum, qualis debeat esse christiano sabbati observacio videamus. Ergo si in sabbato nihil mundani geras, spiritualibus vaces, ad Ecclesiam veniens verbo Dei aurem prebeas, celestia cogites, de futura spe solicitudinem geras, venturum iudicium pre oculis habeas: hec est observacio sabbati christiana' (*De mand.*, p. 228/13–19). Both Wyclif and the author of *D&P* cite Origen on Lev. 28 as the source (though there are only twenty-seven books of Leviticus). The actual source is Origen on Numbers, Homily 23 (*PG* 12: 749–50). In Wyclif's citation, however, the text has been shortened slightly and the phrase 'non respicias ad praesentis et visibilis, sed ad invisibilia et futura' has been omitted; in *D&P*, 'ne to þingis visible but . . . to þingis þat . . . ben invisible' seems to incorporate the missing phrase. A common source for the text of Origen may account for both mis-citations. Origen is cited above 81/7, 157/10, 220/64.

275/15 *Extra, lib. ii, ti. De ferijs, Omnes dies dominicos*: The canon 'Omnes dies dominicos' enjoins keeping the sabbath from vespers to vespers as a day on which no legal or commercial business, licit or illicit, is done (X 2.9.1; Friedberg 2: 270). Cited below 287/3, 290/32–3, 291/29.

275/19 *De con., di. iii, Ieiunia*: De cons. D.3 c.16; Friedberg 1: 1356. Cited above 173/41.

275/24–5 *Trenorum i* [7]: The already figurative meaning of the passage has been transferred to still another figurative meaning: in the biblical lament for the fall of Jerusalem in 587 BC, the city is personified as a widow whose enemies mock her downfall (there is no mention of 'sabbaths'). In *D&P*, the 'city' has become the human soul, and the 'enemies' are the 'fendys'. Wyclif, in citing this text, applies it to non-Christians' derision of Christians who perform servile tasks on the sabbath (*De mand.*, p. 224/2–9).

275/36 *paruys*: The word derives from 'paradisus', which was the name given to a grove of trees surrounding the portico of a temple. In the shortened form 'parvis' it named the atrium or porch of a cathedral, originally the entrance to St Peter's in Rome, subsequently also Notre Dame in Paris and St Paul's in London. Since it was a place where secular business could be transacted, 'to hold a parvis' came to mean simply to hold a meeting or talk business. Compare Chaucer's 'A sergeant of the lawe, war and wys,/ That often hadde been at the Parvys' (*CT*, Prol., p. 28/309–10).

276/39 *dene of peuys*: Matt. 21: 13: 'Scriptum est: Domus mea domus orationis vocabitur: vos autem fecistis illam speluncam latronum'; see also Mark 11: 17, Luke 19: 46. See 217/5–218/15 above.

276/41 *Ysaye, i* [*13*]: For [13] read [14–15; 13]: 'Kalendas vestras et sollemnitates vestras odivit anima mea, facta sunt mihi molesta, laboravi sustinens,/ et cum extenderitis manus vestras, avertam oculos meos a vobis, et cum multiplicaveritis orationem non audiam, manus vestrae sanguine plenae sunt./. . . ./Iniqui sunt coetus vestri.' LL4 cites Isa. 1: 15: 'God seyth to swyche cruel folk whan ȝe schul leftyn up ȝoure hondys to me I schal turnyn myn eyyn from ȝou and when ȝe schul multyplyyn preyerys to me I schal nouȝt heryn ȝou for ȝoure hondys ben ful of blood', fo. 36rb. The GO restates the warning, citing Hosea 13: 9 and suggesting: 'Vtendum est hoc testimonio contra eos qui cum quotidianis operibus sanguineas manus habeant in oratione dies noctesque inuigilant' (3: 4). Cited below 283/12, 2–18/66.

276/15 *Numeri xv* [*32*]: For [32] read [32–5]: 'Factum est autem, cum essent filii Israel in solitudine, et invenissent hominem colligentem ligna in die sabbati. . . .Dixitque Dominus ad Moysen: Morte moriatur homo iste, obruat eum lapidibus omnis turba extra castra.' The GO recognizes that the punishment of the man gathering sticks on the sabbath appears extreme and explains that the story is figurative (1: 311). 'Pore Caitif' (see 227/1 above) parallels *D&P*'s connection of the story with hell fire:

> . . . a man was stonyd to þe deeþ bi þe comaundemet of god for he gaderide stickis in þe sabot day, and dide no gretter trespas, as it is writun in þe book of goddis lawe. For siche folk gaderen manye brondis of coueitise & oþere grete synnes to brenne her soulis in peyne' (MS Bodley 3, fo. 40^{r-v})

277/28 *seruyle werkys*: The definition of 'servile works' is far more sweeping in the OT than in the NT. Broadly, the NT interpretation is that sin is a 'servile work'; hence activity that is necessary or useful is permitted so long as it does not become an occasion for sin (cf. Augustine, *Sermo* IX (*CCL* xli, pp, 110–1; *PL* 38: 77). Wyclif: 'Preservacio igitur a peccato est necessarissima et perfectissima sabbatizacio, quia alia non valet nisi virtute illius; nec opus inficit sabbatizantem nisi de quanto peccatum prius inficit' (*De mand.*, p. 222/26–9). Wyclif, however, concurs with Grosseteste, who envisages the sabbath as ideally devoted to quiet and contemplation—a prefiguration of the rest in heaven (*De decem mand.*, ed. Dales and King, p. 35). Pauper draws the line between work for profit and work for need (*D&P* 278/41–5 below); what this means in practice is spelled out in greater detail in the next eleven chapters.

277/31 [*Io. 8: 34*]: Cited three times in LL4: '. . . for as cryst seyth he þat doth synne is seruaunt of synne & seruyth þe fend' (fo. 34vb; also fos. 67va, 95vb). The *CA* cites Augustine, 'Omnis, inquit [Jesus], iudaeus, graecus, dives, pauper, imperator et mendicus, si facit peccatum, servus est peccati' (2: 453). The general sense is found in Augustine's *In Ioh.* 41.3–8; *CCL* xxxvi, pp. 359–62; *PL* 35: 1693–7). Cited also in the Wycliffite sermons (*EWS* 3, Serm. 150/10–15).

278/2–3 *Sapiente vi* [*7*] *& xi* [*20–6*]: For [7] read [8]; for [20–6] read [25]. 'Quoniam pusillum et magnum ipse fecit, et aequaliter cura est illi de omnibus/. . . . Diligis enim omnia quae sunt, et nihil odisti horum quae fecisti, nec enim odiens aliquid constituisti'. Compare LV: '. . . for he made the litil man and the greet man, and charge [Nicolaus de Lyra sidenote: "puruyaunce"] is to hym euenli of alle men. . . . For thou louest alle thingis that ben, and thou hatist no thing of tho, that thou madist' (FM 3: 94b;104b). The GO stresses the beneficence of the deity, the 'bonus opifex', who makes the sun shine on good and evil alike (2: 734).

279/23 *Genesis ii* [*2–3*]: 'Complevitque Deus die septimo opus suum quod fecerat, et requievit die septimo ab universo opere quod patrarat,/ et benedixit diei septimo et sanctificavit illum, quia in ipso cessaverat ab omni opere suo quod creavit Deus ut faceret.' Augustine reiterates that it is mistaken to think that God needed rest after six days of creation; rather He set aside the seventh day for man to find rest in Him (*De gen. ad lit.*, 4.16; *PL* 34: 306–7). Cf. 284/8, 284/22 below.

279/30 *Ps. 144: 9*: The GO cites Augustine: 'Miseratio eius [God's] reddita est operibus eius; seueritas eius est non in opera sua, sed in opera tua' (2: 645; *Enarr.*, 144.12; *CCL* xl, p. 2097/13–15; *PL* 37: 1877).

279/32 *Iac. 2: 13*: Jas. 2: 13: 'Iudicium enim sine misericordia illi qui non fecit misericordiam, superexaltat autem misericordia iudicio'. LL4: 'Mercy enhaunsith ri3tful doom' (fo. 26va; also cited in LL4 fos. 58vb, 66ra and 112ra). The gloss, attributed to Bede: 'Sicut in iudicio dolebit, qui non fecit misericordiam, ita qui fecit remuneratus exultabit atque gaudebit' (GO, 4: 515). Cited below 2–235/34.

279/41 *Marci ii [27]*: 'Et dicebat eis: Sabbatum propter hominem factum est, et non homo propter sabbatum.' The GO cites Bede: 'Ita sabbatum custodiri preceptum est, vt si necessitas fuerit non sit reus qui violaverit' (4: 96).

280/1 *four maner of Sabatis*: In Leviticus, Moses prescribes the sabbath of days in Lev. 23: 1–3; the sabbath of months in 23: 23–36; the sabbath of years in 25: 1–7; and the sabbath of sabbaths (year of jubilee), 25: 8–17.

280/17–19 *lyf actyf . . . lyf contemplatyf*: See 68/43–5 above.

281/2 *ouyr a pousant pas*: The limitation on the distance that could be covered on foot on the sabbath is based on Josh. 3: 4; cf. Acts 1: 12.

281/5 *Sabat . . . Sonday*: The change from sabbath observance to Sunday observance took place gradually as the membership of the early Church changed from Jews to gentiles. St Paul said tolerantly: 'Nam alius iudicat diem inter diem: alius autem iudicat omnem diem: unuquisque in suo sensu abundet' (Rom. 14: 5). Wyclif (in 1377–8) mentions the toleration of the apostles, who showed 'se esse liberos quoad illud, omiserunt sabbatizacionem ferie septime' (*De veritate*, 3: 118). Pauper's argument is that Sunday is symbolic of many 'grete dedis and wondris þat God dede' on that day (and on other days 'translated' to Sunday), while the Jewish sabbath is primarily a memorial of the Creation.

282/36–40 *The porsday . . . of hem alle*: The biblical basis for the Ascension Day feast is found in Mark 16: 19, Luke 24: 51, Acts 1: 1–12. The feast is celebrated liturgically forty days after Easter. Pauper's suggestion that the procession marking the Feast of the Ascension took place on the Sunday after Ascension Day (*D&P* 282/43–6) is borne out by the fact that the Sarum missal provides for services on the vigil of the Ascension, on the Day of the Ascension and on the Sunday following Ascension Day (*Sarum Missal*, ed. Legg, pp. 154–8).

283/7 *Mathei xii [8]*: The translation of 'filius hominis' here, and below, 2–226/65, by 'þe maydonys sone' may perhaps be a Franciscan-inspired evasion of the problematic phrase, 'Son of Man', with its messianic overtones. The intention of the Franciscan author of *D&P* may have been to stress the orthodox belief that Jesus was not in fact the son of a human father. By contrast, the LV translates: 'For mannus Sone is lord, ȝhe, of the sabat' (4: 29b). A history of the use of the term can be found in the *ABD*, 6: 137–50.

283/12 *Ysaye i* [*13*] *& Osee ii* [*11*]: Isa. 1: 13: 'Ne adferatis ultra sacrificium frustra, incensum abominatio est mihi, neomeniam et sabbatum et festivi-tates alias non feram; iniqui sunt coetus vestri' (see 276/41 above). Hos. 2: 11: 'Et cessare faciam omne gaudium eius, solemnitatem eius, neomeniam eius, sabbatum eius, et omnia festa tempora eius' (see 268/81 above). The GO defines 'neomeniam': 'Festum nonae lunae quod celebrabant in prin-cipio mensium. Neos nonum mene lune, unde Buccinate domino in neomenia tuba' (3: 40).

283/20–1 *Colossences ii* [*16–17*]: 'Nemo ergo vos iudicet in cibo aut in potu aut in parte diei festi aut neomeniae aut sabbatorum/ quae sunt umbra futuorum: corpus autem Christi'. *D&P* touches on the fundamental assumption of Christian exegetes that the Jewish Bible was a prefiguration of the NT. Origen, in *First Principles*: 'The splendour of Christ's advent has, therefore, by illuminating the law of Moses with the brightness of the truth, withdrawn the veil which had covered the letter of the law and has disclosed, for every one who believes in him, all those "good things" which lay concealed within' (Bk. 4, Ch. 1; *PG* 11: 343; tr. G. W. Butter-worth (1973), p. 265b; see 274/1 above). Augustine: 'Vetus enim testamen-tum est promissio figurata. Nouum testamentum est promissio spiritaliter intellecta' (*Sermo* 4.9: *CCL* xli, p. 25; *PL* 38: 37). Wyclif (in 1377–8): 'multis talibus testimoniis [which have been listed] utitur apostolus Heb. nono et decimo ad probandum, quod dacio noue legis prophetate impleta est in Jesu Cristo', *De veritate*, 3: 113/20–2.

283/25 *Sent Gregori . . . Antichrist*: St Gregory's Epistle to the Romans: 'Pervenit ad me quosdam perversi spiritus homines, prava inter vos aliqua et sanctae fidei adversa seminasse, ita ut in die Sabbati aliquid operari prohiberent. Quos quid aliud nisi Antichristi praedicatores dixerim?' ('Registri epistolarum', 13, Ep. 1; *PL* 77: 1253–5). See 284/31 below.

284/31 *De con., di. iii, Peruenit*: The canon 'Pervenit' is from St Gregory's letter, cited in note 283/25 above: 'I have heard that certain men of perverse disposition have sown certain ideas among you that are contrary to the holy faith, namely that no one is to work on the sabbath. What are these but the preachers of Antichrist? . . . . Because he pretends to restore respect for Sunday, and because he compels the people to judaize so as to restore external laws and attract the perfidious Jews, he wants the sabbath to be observed. It has also been reported to me that perverse men have preached to you that no one should wash on the Lord's Day. And indeed if someone wants to wash for pleasure ['pro luxuria et pro uoluptate'], we grant that this may be done on other days. But if for bodily necessity, we do not prohibit that it be done on Sunday' (De cons. D.3 c.12; Friedberg 1: 1355; in the Friedberg edition, the reference to Gregory is incorrect). Cf. Raymond of Peñafort's *Summa*, Bk. I, ¶ 3 (p. 110), which cites the same epistle.

284/3 *Solomon seith*: The reference is to Wisd. 11: 21: 'Sed omnia mensura et numero et pondere disposuisti'. For the GO, this points to God's governance of Creation: 'In mensura qualitas, in numero quantitas, in pondere ratio. In his constituit deus mundum & gubernat & iudicaturus est. In his iustus iudex conprehendi non potuit nec reprehendi, omnis in claustro horum trium abscondita latet' (2: 734). For the enormous influence of this citation from the Book of Wisdom, see E. R. Curtius (1948; tr. 1953), pp. 503–9. Number symbolism seems to have entered the patristic tradition via Plotinus. Augustine frequently comments on the meanings of numbers. See Hopper (1938) on 'perfect numbers' (p. 37), and on patristic views (pp. 69–88). See 284/8, 284/22 and 2–249/20 below.

284/8 *þe numbre of sexe*: Pauper's explanation of the perfection of the number six—that it is the sum of its aliquot parts—is taken from Augustine's *De Gen. ad Lit.*, Bk. 4, c. 2 (*PL* 34: 296–7). Cf. Isidore of Seville: 'Senarius namque [numerus] qui partibus suis perfectus est, perfectionem mundi quadam numeri [sui] significatione declarat' (*Etym.* Lib. III, iv/2–3; *PL* 82: 156). Trevisa's Bartholomaeus 19.116: 'For þe nombre of sixe, þat is parfite and ymade of his owne parties, tokneþ þe parfitnesse of þe worlde' (*Properties*, 2: 1353/32–3). See 284/3 above, 284/ 22 below.

284/22 *Genesis ii [1]*: 'Igitur perfecti sunt caeli et terra, et omnis ornatus eorum.' In *De Gen. ad Lit.*, Augustine points to the sixth day and the sixth hour in which Christ finished the work of redemption: 'Posteaquam sexto die . . . quam dicunt sextam sabbati, consummavit omnia opera sua' (Bk. 4, c. 11; *PL* 34: 304). The GO also ties the six days of creation to the human life span (1: 16).

284/1 *Why bad God reste on þe seueþe day*: Cap. xiii begins with a summing up of what has been said earlier about the sabbath. See above 263/19–21, 264/29, 266/22, 279/23, 281/5. The end of the chapter looks ahead to the description of heaven that will be elaborated in Commandment X, cap. 9 and 10 below.

285/13 *four elementis*: A reference to the three 'powers' of the soul, vegetable, sensible and rational (see Trevisa's Bartholomaeus 3.7; *Properties*, 1: 96/14–16), and four 'humours' of the body, 'blood, flewme, colera, and melencolia' (idem, 4.6, 1: 147/32–3).

286/22 *seuene blyssis*: Eadmer (c1055–c1124), biographer of St Anselm, appears to have been responsible for the enumeration of blessings to be given the resurrected body. He lists seven for the body and seven for the soul in his 'Liber de beatitudine coelestis patriae' (*PL* 159: 587–600). On Eadmer see Antonia Gransden, *Historical Writing* (1974–82), 1: 129–42. See 286/24 below.

286/24 *four blissis*: Wyclif deduces the four blessings of the resurrected body from 1 Cor.15: 42–4:

> *Seminatur*, inquit, *in corrupcione, surget in incorrupcione*: ecce inmortalitas, *seminatur in ignobilitate, surget in gloria*: ecce post opacitatem dos claritatis vel pulcritudinis, *seminatur in infirmitate, resurget in virtute*: ecce tercio post ponderositatem dos agilitatis, *seminatur corpus animale, resurget corpus spirituale*: ecce quarto post grossiciem dos subtilitatis (*De mand.*, p. 150/16–23).

286/26–7 *as bryȝt as þe sonne . . . inpassiblete*: Matt. 13: 43: '. . . tunc iusti fulgebunt sicut sol'; see above 214–15/26–30, below 2–319/27. Aquinas (or his continuator) takes up 'impassibility' and speculates that 'the human body and all that is in it will be perfectly subject to the rational soul, just as the soul will be perfectly subject to God; hence it will be impossible for the glorified body to undergo any change contrary to that disposition by which it is perfected by the soul; and so those bodies will be impassible' (*ST*, Suppl., 82.1; OP edn., Rome, 1894, 5: 492–3). For speculation about the speed with which glorified bodies will be able to move from place to place see idem, 84.3. Wyclif speculates in the *Trialogus* (of 1382–3) that 'after the day of judgement no body will make sudden local movements but instead will be moved successively with a speed imperceptible to us' and, in effect, the distinction between large and small, fast and slow will no longer exist (Bk. 4, cap. 41). The Wycliffite *Lanterne*: 'þe firste doweri [of heaven] is impassibilite' (ed. Swinburn, EETS os 151, p. 26/22). On the joys of heaven, see further below, Com. X, cap. 9 and 10.

287/2 *Reymond*: Raymond of Peñafort: 'Tempora feriandi per annum, id est, omnem diem dominicam a vespera usque ad vesperam' *Summa*, Bk. I, ¶ 3 (p. 111).

287/3 *Extra, li. ii, ti. De ferijs, c. Omnes dies dominicos*: X 2.7.9; Friedberg 2: 270. Cited above, 275/15 and below, 291/29.

287/4–7 *Leuitici xxiii [32] . . . Extra, [De ferijs] Quoniam*: The canon 'Quoniam' states that the rules for sabbath keeping prevail from vespers to vespers. Between Easter and Pentecost, genuflection should not be performed; the rest of the year, local custom should dictate. Other injunctions follow that are not relevant to this context (X 2.9.2, Friedberg 2: 271).

287/22 *Extra, lib. v, De regulis iuris*: The canon 'Quod non est licitum' summarizes Bede's gloss on Mark 2: 27: 'Quod non est licitum lege, necessitas facit licitum', etc. (X 5.41.4; Friedberg 2: 927; 'In Marci', *PL* 92: 154–5). Cited above 250/92. See 287/24 below.

287/24 *De con, di. i, Sicut, & di. v, Discipulos*: Two canons: (1) 'Sicut': Masses are not to be sung except in properly consecrated places unless extreme necessity compels otherwise, citing the legal maxim, 'Quoniam necessitas legem non habet' (De cons. D.1 c.11; Friedberg 1: 1297). The maxim is cited 60/50 above and 2–141/13–14 below. (2) 'Discipulus': The canon adduces the example of the disciples, whom Christ excused for eating kernels of grain from the fields on the sabbath (De cons. D. 5 c. 26; Friedberg 1: 1419; the biblical references are to Matt. 12: 1, Mark 2: 23, and Luke 6: 1).

On the maxim, 'Need has no law', see Alford (1988), pp. 102–3; Alford cites this passage in *D&P* and refers to Szittya (1986) on the maxim 'as a Franciscan principle' used to justify mendicancy (p. 278). Gradon (1980), in discussing the character of 'Need' in *PP*, refers to the use of the principle, if not the maxim itself, in the argument for mendicancy in the Bull 'Exiit qui seminat', where the argument runs: 'ab omni lege extreme necessitas sit exempta' (cf. Sext 5.12.3; Friedberg 2: 1113): in 'Langland and the Ideology of Dissent', repr. in *Middle English Literature*, ed. J. A Burrow (1989), pp. 195–221.

287/25 *Extra, De furtis, Si quis propter necessitatem*: The canon 'Si quis' appears to hold that anyone who steals out of moderate necessity should be allowed to do penance (theft in utter need did not require penance; theft in lesser need required a severer punishment). The source of the canon is given as 'Theodore', presumably St Theodore of Tarsus (d. 690), though the Penitential attributed to him is of later date: 'Si quis propter necesssitatem famis aut nuditatis furatus fuerit cibaria, vestem vel pecus, poeniteat hebdomadas tres, et, si reddiderit, non cogatur ieiunare' (X 5.18.3: Friedberg 2: 810). On Theodore, *ODCC*, p. 1360.

288/28 *Extra, De ferijs, c. Licet*: The canon 'Licet' provides that 'servile work' such as fishing may be done on the sabbath when need for food requires it. The editor's note suggests that the addressee of Pope Alexander III's epistle is uncertain ('quippe Hiberniae episcopatus'). The Pope's reply answers a query about allowable activity on the sabbath with the tolerant opinion that, in 'your region, where fruit does not abound and where the people derive most of their sustenance from the sea', regulations about holiday work may be relaxed, providing always that the Church and the poor are given some of the gain. (X 2.9.3: Friedberg 2: 271).

288/35 *Ion in Summa confesssorum, lib. i, ti. xii, q. vii*: Refers to John of Freiburg, who cites the example of the Maccabees (*Sum. Confess.*, MS

Bodley 299, fo. 38^{r-v}). The same passage can be read as a gloss on Raymond of Peñafort's *Summa*, Bk. I, 'De feriis', ¶ 7 (pp. 113–5). Necessity, says the glossator, excuses many categories of work on the sabbath: 'propter periculum hostium', it is allowable to till fields or pick crops. It is also allowable to build churches, continue a journey, get a haircut, arm for defence, and even (if employed by a scholar) take notes and correct texts, but with restrictions: 'Scholaribus etiam non credo quod liceat grande aliquod transcribere de quaterno in quaternum diebus huiusmodi; lectiones tamen suas, quas fine scriptura non possent memoriae commendare, vel sermones, quos stylo, vel plumbo notauerunt, scribere credo permittitur; & lectiones librorum, quos audiunt corrigere: locare autem, & conducere operas suas, vel alienas, propter libros huismodi diebus corrigendos, non debent' (p. 114). See below 289/10–32.

288/40 *Io. vii* [*23*]: John 7: 23: 'Si circumcisionem accipit homo in sabbato . . . mihi indignamini quia totum hominem sanum feci in sabbato?' The GO: '. . . sed non est contra legem quod totum hominem sanum feci in sabbato: ego dominus sabbat' (4: 242). Augustine comments: 'Manducatis siquidem et bibitis sabbato, quia pertinet ad salutem; per quod ostenditis, opera salutis nullo modo esse die sabbati omittenda' (*CA*, 2: 436, from *In Ioh.*, 30.4; *CCL* xxxvi, p. 292/19–24; *PL* 35: 1635).

288/45 *Mathei xii* [*11–12*]: 'Quis erit ex vobis homo, qui habeat ovem unam, et si ceciderit haec sabbatis in foveam, nonne tenebit et levabit eam?/ Quanto magis melior est homo ove? Itaque licet sabbatis benefacere'. The GO terms this an exemplum which teaches the duty of charity: 'Homo ante adventum christi dextera habuit languidam, quia ab elemosinis torpebat; sinistram sanam, quia suae utilitati intendebat; sed, vieniente christo, dextra sanatur vt sinistra quia quod congregauerat auide modo distribuit caritate' (4: 43).

288/45–55 *Crist helede a woman*: Luke 13: 11–17: healing of a crippled woman. The GO connects the story with the Commandments: 'Haec mulier non nisi post decenocto annos erigi potuit quia humana natura hanc corruptionem deponere & ad induendam incorruptionem aeternae beatitu-dinis erigi non poterit nisi prius impleuerit legem; ergo in decem praeceptis continetur & gratiam in qua christi resurrectio facta est & nostra expectatur' (4: 190).

289/61 *Mathei xii* [*1–4*]: The GO allegorizes: '*Spicas* vellunt, dum singulos homines a terrena intentione retrahunt. *Fricant*: dum exemplis virtutum etiam a concupiscentia carnis mentes exuunt. *Grana* comedunt, dum emundatos in corpus ecclesiae traiiciunt. Vnde hoc agunt discipuli ante dominum quia necesse est praecedat sermo doctoris et sic gratia cor illustrabit auditoris. *Sabbato* quia hoc agunt spe quietis aeternae ad quam & alios inuitant' (4: 42). The Wycliffite sermon writer uses the passage to attack the 'new orders' of clerics: 'And pharisees chargen today þer customs þat þey han founden, but maundementis þat God haþ bedun þey putten bihynde as untrewe men' (*EWS* 3, Serm. 213/36–8). Cited below 2–141/23.

289/5 *Deutronomii v [12–14]*: 'Observa diem sabbati, ut sanctifices eum, sicut praecepit tibi Dominus Deus tuus. . . .'. The Commandments of Exod. 20 are elaborated in Deuteronomy.

289/9 *Exodi xxxi [14] . . . Leuitici xxvi [2] & xix [3]*: Exod. 31: 14: 'Custodite sabbatum meum, sanctum est enim vobis: qui polluerit illud, morte morietur.' Lev. 26: 2: 'Custodite sabbata mea, et pavete ad sanctuarium meum.' Lev. 19: 3: 'Sabbata mea custodite.'

289/9–10 *Ieremie xvii [21–4] . . . Ezechielis xx & xxii & xxiii*: Jer. 17: 22: 'Sanctificate diem sabbati.' Ezek. 20: 20: 'Et sabbata mea sanctificate, ut sint signum inter me et vos.' Ezek. 22: 26 'Sacerdotes eius . . . a sabbatis meis averterunt oculos suos.' Ezek. 23: 38: 'Polluerunt sanctuarium meum in die illa, et sabbata mea profanaverunt.'

289/10–32 *Be þe lawe, bocheris . . .* : Most of these permitted exceptions to strict sabbath-keeping can be found in Raymond of Peñafort's *Summa* (Bk. I, *De ferijs*, ¶ 5, pp. 114–5) See above 288/35.

290/32–3 *Ion, Summa confessorum, lib. i, ti. xii, De ferijs*: Found in John of Freiburg's *Summa*, 'De feriis' (MS Bodley 299, fos. 37ᵛ-40ᵛ); 'tabula iuris' here refers to the section of canon law entitled 'De feriis', X 2.9 (Friedberg 2: 270–3). Cited above 275/15, 287/3 and below 291/29.

290/7 *Prechouris*: Boniface VIII's papal bull of 1300, *Super cathedram*, strengthened the legal position of the Friars Preachers and Friars Minor, without, of course, ending their rivalry with the secular clergy. The bull referred to the conflicts over preaching, confessions, and burials and provided for licensing (X.3.7.2; Friedberg 2: 1162). Spencer (1993) discusses preaching in England in the aftermath of *Super cathedram* (1300), through the Oxford crisis over Wycliffism in the 1380's and the promulgation of Arundel's Constitutions in 1407–9, pp. 167–182.

290/21 *hors and carte or schyp*: See 249/66–72 above.

291/12 *makyng of holy chirche*: Referred to in the chapter of Raymond of Peñafort's *Summa* cited above (Bk. I, *De ferijs*, ¶ 5, p. 114). See 288/35, 289/10–32 above.

291/29 *Extra, De ferijs, Omnes dies dominicos*: Cited above 275/15, 287/3, 290/32–3.

293/7 *holy writ*: 1 Sam. (1 Reg.) 15: 22: 'Melior est enim obedientia quam victimae: et auscultare magis quam offerre adipem arietum.' The GO points out that the tree of knowledge in Eden was not prohibited because it was bad but because God wanted to teach obedience. The GO also instances

Paul, who announced that he was not bound by the rules of Jerusalem but was prepared to abide by local customs (1: 25).

293/12–20 *Steraclis, pleyys and dauncis*: The *MED* suggests that the word 'steraclis' is a noun formation from the verb 'stiren' after the pattern of 'miracle' and 'spectacle'. In manuscripts BY, the word 'miraclis' is twice substituted, indicating that the word was unusual. Pauper here expresses an attitude towards miracle plays that harks back to the views of the writer of *Handlyng Synne* (1303): gatherings for entertainment are occasions for sin, he wrote, but plays depicting the birth or Resurrection of Christ help to strengthen religious belief (ed. Furnivall, EETS, os 119, 123. p. 155/4636–59). The two kinds of plays Pauper gives as examples, the Herod plays and the Easter plays, range from those containing the much-loved boisterous role of the raging Herod—'honest merthe'—to the harrowing 'crucifixio Christi' play of Easter—'deuocioun'. Attitudes towards the religious plays in the vernacular seem, in this period, to have remained uncertain. Hudson (1988) argues that the divide between Lollard and anti-Lollard views was never clear-cut (*PR*, pp. 387–9). The author of *D&P* in his later sermons, seems more opposed to 'steraclis' than he is here: 'But now men ȝeuyn hem more on þe halyday to seruyn þe fend . . . & raþere wyl gon to markettis feyrys steraclis & vanytes þan to goddis seruyse . . .' (LL4, fo. 16ʳᵃ).

293/21–2 *De con, di.iii, Irreligiosa, & Extra, li. iii, ti. i [Quum] decorum . . . glose*: Two canons: (1) 'Irreligiosa' forbids popular singing and dancing ('irreligosa consuetudo est') during church services (De cons. D.3 c.2; Friedberg 1: 1353). The source is the fourth Council of Toledo (633), which proclaimed that it was an irreligious custom ('Irreligiosa consuetudo est') for the people to participate in what should be solemn religious rites. Instead of hearing the divine office, it goes on, they are treated to ribald songs and disgraceful performances; this must cease. (2) 'Quum decorum' declares that theatrical performances by clergy in the church building, even though sanctioned by custom, are forbidden (X 3.1.12; Friedberg 2: 452). The text of the canon is from a decretal of Pope Innocent III, who, in 1207, inveighed against theatrical shows put on in churches at Christmastime. In such shows, he says, deacons, priests, and subdeacons appear masked and perform obscene actions and gesticulations in full view of the congregation; this cheapens clerical dignity at the very time when the word of God should be preached with particular solemnity. It is clear that both of Pauper's citations fall far short of a defence of 'steracles, pleyys & dauncis þat arn don principaly for deuocioun', cf. Woolf (1972), p. 365, note 30.

294/34–5 *Ps. 117: 24*: The GO: 'Hic est annus iubileus figuraliter . . . quia tunc serui manumittebantur, possessiones dominis restitebantur, et nos hac die a seruitute peccati redempti summus, quibus est hereditas restitura aeterna' (2: 606).

294/35 *Sent Austyn*: From Augustine's often-cited 'De decem cordis', *Sermo* IX, 3: 'Melius enim faceret iudaeus in agro suo aliquid utile quam in theatro seditiosus exsisteret. Et melius feminae eorum die sabbati lanam facerent quam toto die in maenianis suis impudice saltarent [dancing shamelessly on their balconies]' (*CCL* xli, p. 110/94–7; *PL* 38: 77). An excellent example of the misapplication of a fifth-century observation to different circumstances in the fifteenth.

294/54 *Leuitici xxiii* [*27;29*]: The biblical text refers to the annual Day of Atonement, which occurs on the tenth day of the seventh month. It is the only fast day of the Jewish year. See also Lev. 16 and Num. 29/7–11; cf. Heb. 9 and 10.

294/57 *Prouer. xiii* [*12*]: The GO: 'Quia nimirum quam diu differtur spes aeternorum affligitur anima fidelium, vel pro dilatione bonorum vel illatione malorum. At verbi venerit quod desiderat, facile obliuiscitur quod sustinuerat quia in aeternum vivere incipit cum suo redemtore quod tota intentione quaerebat' (2: 670).

295/75 *feste of clensynge*: The Day of Atonement, see 294/54 above.

295/80 *þe Rede See drye foot*: Exod. 14: 21–3. See 264/48–53 above.

296/3 *Leuitici xxiii* [*40–3*]: On the Feast of Tabernacles, or Succoth, see 270/1–4 above.

296/16 *Neemie viii* [*10*]: GO on Neh. 8: 10: 'Doctores qui mentes auditorium sacris lectionibus ad lacrima excitant et idem consolantur, dum gaudia secutura promittunt' (2: 295).

296/17 *Di. xxx, Si quis tanquam, & Si quis presbiter*: Two canons: (1) 'Si quis tamquam' condemns unauthorized fasting. Promulgated by the Council of Gangra (c345), which was concerned with false asceticism. 'Si quis, tanquam hoc continentiae conuenire iudicans, die dominico ieiunauerit in eiusdem diei contemptum, anathema sit' (D.30 c.7; Friedberg 1: 108). (2) 'Si quis presbiter' also condemns unauthorized fasting; the source is a synod called to the Lateran in 649 by Pope Martin I. 'Si quis presbiter propter publicam penitentiam a sacerdote acceptam absque aliqua necessitate die dominica pro quadam religione ieiunauerit, sicut Manichei, anathema sit . . .' (D.30 c.17; Friedberg 1: 110).

296/20–1 *Di.lxxvi, Ieiunium, & De con., di.iii, Ieiunium*: Two canons: (1) 'Ieiunium' allows four instead of three fasts per year; the source is a letter of Pope Callistus (d. c222): 'Ieiunium, quod ter in anno apud nos celebrare didicisti, conuenientis nunc per quatuor tempora fieri decernimus, ut, sicut annus per quatuor uoluitur tempora, sic et nos solempne quaternium agamus ieiunium per quatuor anni tempora' (D.76 c.1; Friedberg 1: 267). (2) 'Ieiunium' forbids fasting on Sundays and the fifth ferial week: 'Ieiunium dominici diei, et quintae feriae nemo celebrare debet . . .'. The source is a

letter of Pope Miltiades (d. 314). (De cons. D.3 c.14; Friedberg 1: 1356). On
Popes Callistus and Miltiades, *ODP*, pp. 13–14; 26–7.

297/28 Marye þe sustir of Aaron: Exod. 15: 20–1. The GO allegorizes: 'Quia
ergo in choro aequaliter omnes voces resonant, per eum charitas significetur,
qua omnes in christo vnum summus' (1: 142). On Miriam and her song, see
ABD 4: 869–70.

297/32 2 Kyngis, þe sexte chapitle [14–23]: 2 Sam. 6: 14–23. In the
interpretation of the story of David dancing before the ark, it is the contrast
between the behaviour of David and the behaviour of Michal that is seized
upon. Predictably, Michal prefigures the scoffing Jews: '. . . et christus cum
testamentum nouum in ecclesiam suam transferret, iudeis in cruce ludi-
brium [object of scorn] fuit, nudus apparuit dominus potentiam, illis
abscondens carnis infirmitatem quasi ephot lineum ostendit. . . . gloriosior
ancillis apparet quae in typo sinagogae sterilis permansit' (GO 2: 58). St
Gregory's commentary, cited in the GO, emphasises the humility of David:
'Pugnando quippe hostes subdidit, saltando autem coram Domino semetipsum uicit' (*Moralia*, 27.77; *CCL* cxliiiB, p. 1391/70–2). For a list of the
many references to King David in *D&P* see 2–85/19 below.

298/50 Ieremie xxxi [13]: 'Tunc laetabitur virgo in choro, iuvenes et senes
simul, et convertam luctum eorum in gaudium, et consolabor eos et
laetificabo a dolore suo'. GO (interlin.): '. . . vt quos crux terruit lenificet
resurrectio' (3: 148). cited above 268/74.

298/53–4 Ps. 99: 2: See 207/48–55 above.

298/59–60 saddith . . . baddith: The two words are apparently neologisms,
the sense of which must be derived from the context. The *MED* does not
pick up 'bad' as a verb and for 'sad' (s.v. 'saden' v.) cites this instance in
D&P, with the meaning 'become steadfast . . . serious of purpose'. Another
translation might be: 'Be devout, but not grim; joyous, but not frivolous.'

298/2 firste table: Compare Wyclif: 'Sicut ergo primum mandatum prime
tabule est maximum quoad dileccionem Dei, cum refertur ad honorificenciam Dei patris, sic et istud primum mandatum secunde tabule est
maximum quoad dileccionem proximi, cum refertur ad honorificenciam
hominis patris' (*De mand.*, p. 293/10–14)

298/12 two preceptis of charite: The biblical reference is to Matt. 22: 37–40,
Mark 12: 29–31, and Luke 10: 27.

299/26 Sent Austyn: This may be a reference to *Sermo IX*: 9, 'De decem
chordis': 'Cum coeperis et tu odisse te talem qualis es, sicut te talem odit
deus, incipis iam ipsum diligere deum qualis est' (*CCL* xli, p. 126/362–4;
PL 38: 82).

299/40 Qui est: The biblical reference is to Exod. 3: 13–14: 'Si dixerint
mihi, Quod est nomen eius? quid dicam eis? /Dixit Deus ad Mosen: *Ego*

sum qui sum. Ait: Sic dices filiis Israel: *Qui est* misit me ad vos.' The GO (Jerome): 'Deus autem tantum est qui non nouit fuisse vel futurum esse. Solus autem pater cum filio & spiritusancto vere est. Cuius essentiae comparatum nostrum esse, non est. Vnde & dicimus, Vivit deus, quia essentia diuina vita vivit, quam mors non habet' (1: 117).

300/45 [*Io. 14: 6*]: 'Dicit ei Iesus: Ego sum via et veritas et vita; nemo venit ad Patrem nisi per me.' Cited below 2–191/64, and in LL4, fo. 56vb, fo. 137ra: 'I am weye, I am trewþe, I am liif', and fo. 137va: 'No man ne woman comyth to þe fadyr but be me'. Pauper's application of this text to 'stodie to knowyn þe trewþe' echoes a sermon of Augustine's on the same text: 'Question the world, the furniture of the heavens, the brightness and arrangement of the stars, the sun providing for the day, the moon which comforts the night; question the earth bearing its yield of herbs and trees, full of animals. . . . question the sea . . . question the air . . . question them all and see if they don't answer you, after a fashion in their own way, "God made us". Serious and great-minded philosophers have inquired into these things, and have come to a knowledge of the artist through the works of art' (Sermon 141: tr. E. Hill (1992), 4: 410; *PL* 38: 776–8). Augustine's *In Ioh.*, 69.1–3, stresses the difficulty of knowing Christ, even for the apostles themselves: 'Thomas apostolus ut te interrogaret, habuit te ante se, nec tamen intellegeret te . . .' (*CCL* xxxvi, pp. 499–502; *PL* 35: 1816–8). Cited below 2–191/64.

300/60–7 *The firste precept*: See 263/4–6 and 265/68 above.

300/59 *Sent Powil*: The reference is probably to 1 Cor. 2: 13: '. . . quae et loquimur non in doctis humanae sapientiae verbis, sed in doctrina Spiritus, spiritualibus spiritualia comparantes'.

300/66 *paraclitus*: The biblical references are to John 14: 15–17, 14: 25–26, 15: 26, 16: 4–11, and 16: 12–15, the only one of the gospels in which the term appears. The root meaning of 'paraclete' is unclear, and etymology gives little guidance. Du Cange, s.v. 'paracletus', says that the meaning 'advocatus' relates to the use in John 14: 16. Augustine, *In Ioh.* 74.4, says that 'paracletus' is Latin 'aduocatus' (*CCL* xxxvi, p. 514/2–4; *PL* 35: 1828). Augustine connects the Paraclete with the Commandments, though not specifically with the third: '. . . sine Spiritu sancto Christum nos diligere et mandata eius seruare non posse' (idem, pp. 513–5/26–7).

300/73 *Ps. 75: 11*: Augustine's comment on this verse is that it is a reminder that sins have been left behind in baptism; this is a cause for rejoicing: 'et facti sumus noui homines, in spe quidem gaudentes' (*Enarr.*, 75.15; *CCL* xxxix; p. 1047/11–12; *PL* 36: 966).

301/77 *Ps. 93: 19*: Augustine: 'Multi dolores, sed multae consolationes; amara uulnera, sed suauia medicamenta' (*Enarr.*, 93.22; *CCL* xxxix, p. 1323/35–6; *PL* 36: 1210).

301/1 *Marci xii* [*30*]: '. . . et diliges Dominum Deum tuum ex toto corde tuo, et ex tota anima tua, et ex tota mente tua, et ex tota virtute tua'. GO, citing Bede: 'Ostendit scriba in hac responsione inter scribas & pharisaeos grauem questionem diu versatam esse, quod esset primum mandatum & maximum in lege. Alii hostias & sacrificia laudabant, alii fidei & dilectionis opera praeferebant, quia plurimi patrum ante legem absque omni sacrificiorum consuetudine ex fide tamen que per dilectionem operatur deo placuerant nemo autem absque fide & dilectione. In qua sententia scriba iste dederat se fuisse' (4: 123).

301/3 *Sent Bernard*: The reference is to Bernard's *Sermones in cantica*: 'Disce, O Christiane, a Christo, quemadmodum diligas Christum. Disce amare dulciter, amare prudenter, amare fortiter. Dulciter, ne illecti; prudenter, ne decepti; fortiter, ne oppressi ab amore Domini avertamur' ('Serm. super cant.' 20, *Opera*, ed. J. Leclercq *et al.*, 1: 116/17–19; *Sermo* 20, *PL* 183: 868).

301/12 *Rom. 8: 35*: 'Quis ergo non separabit a charitate Christi? tribulatio? an angustia? an fames? an nuditas/ an periculum? an persecutio? an gladius?' LL4: '. . . who schal departyn vs from þe charite of crist' (fo. 101^{vb1}). At the end of Rom. 8, the GO cites Prov. 30: 8, in the variant form, 'Diuitias & paupertatas ne dederis mihi', cf. 59/3–9 above.

302/26–7 *Ps 90: 14*: Augustine: 'Noli timere quando tribularis. . . . Fluctus sunt maris, turbaris in nauigio, quia dormit Christus. Dormiebat in naui Christus, peribant homines. Si fides tua dormit in corde tuo, tamquam in naui tua dormit Christus; quia Christus per fidem in te habitat' *Enarr.*, 90.11; *CCL* xxxix, p. 1276/2–7; *PL* 36: 1169).

302/30 *Psal. xxxix* [*5*]: LL4: 'Also hope makith vs blessid & þerfore dauid sayth blissid is þat man whose hope is þe name of oure lord god' (fo. 133ra). The second phrase of the verse is not translated in LL4; the *D&P* translation of 'insanias falsas' by 'false witnesses' may be a slip caused by the attraction of the stock phrase 'false witness'. The variant in MS G, 'widnessys' may, however, be a scribal error for 'wodnessys': the Wycliffite bible translates 'insanias' by 'woodnesses' (LV 2: 776; cf. the LXX: μανιας ψευδεις). In his commentary on the verse, Augustine appears to interpret 'insanias falsas' as the 'circissarius' [lover of circuses] and the 'amator et laudator illius uenatoris, illius histrionis', all of whom may be redeemed for Christ (*In Ioh.*, 39.8; *CCL* xxxviii, p. 431/30–1; *PL* 36: 439).

302/32–3 *Sent Powil*: 1 Cor. 6: 11: '. . . sed iustificati estis in nomine nostri Iesu Christi, et in Spiritu Dei nostri'. GO: (Augustine): 'Nota "sed", repetitam conunctionem non paruum pondus dare sententiae' (4: 315). Cf. Acts 4: 12: 'Nec enim aliud nomen est sub caelo datum hominibus, in quo oporteat nos salvos fieri.'

303/67 *Ysaye lxvi* [*23*]: Isa. 66: 23: 'Et erit mensis ex mense, et sabbatum ex sabbato; veniet omnis caro ut adoret coram facie mea, dicit Dominus'. The GO gives a quasi-scientific explanation of 'mensis ex mense': 'Mene graece, latine luna, vnde "neomenia", quasi "noua luna". A mene mensis apud illos qui initium kalendarum non secundum solis cursum et diuersa spacia mensium sed secundum lunae circumitum et terminant & incipiunt, quod hebraei faciunt. Per mensem ergo lunam, per lunam, quae modo crescit modo decrescit, &, sicut aiunt physica et phylosofi, a sole quod non habet lumen recipit, ecclesia intelligitur de qua. Permanebit cum sole & ante lunam & alibi. Pulcra vt luna electa vt sol, et hoc est "erit mensis ex mense"' (3: 98).

VOL. I: 1. COMMANDMENT IV, pp. 304–359

304/17–18 *Honora patrem tuum*: Exod. 20: 12: 'Honora patrem tuum et matrem tuam, ut sis longaevus super terram, quam Dominus Deus tuus dabit tibi.' The Gloss explains that the first three Commandments, or first table, pertain to God, the seven following Commandments, or second table, pertain to one's neighbor ('ad proximum'). Of the seven Commandments of the second table, the first three pertain to the soul, 'quae est irascibilis, concupiscibilis, rationalis', and the final four pertain to the body, 'quaternarius corpori' (GO 1: 153). On the numbering of the Commandments, 81/7 above.

305/31 *age . . . vnclenesse . . . wanwyt*: Grosseteste, also in the context of the fourth Commandment, is even more explicit about old age: 'Sunt autem quidam qui . . . despiciunt parentum paupertatem et eorundem senectutem et senectutis incommoda utpote sensuum defeccionem, virium inbecillitatem, rugose contraccionis in cute deformitatem, dorsi incuruitatem, membrorum tremorem, gressum titubacionem, linguam iterum pueriliter balbucientem', etc. (*De decem mandatis*, ed. Dales and King, p. 47/5–10)

305/35–50 *Genesis ix* [*20–25*] *. . . confermyd of God*: Noah was the first to plant 'wyne trees':

> be-tidde a day he was for squonkin
> and or he wiste of wyne was dronkin.
>
> (*Cursor Mundi*, ed. Morris, EETS os 57,
> Pt. I, p. 124/2017–18).

Compare Peter Comestor: '*bibensque vinum*, sed ignorans vim ejus' (*Historia*, PL 198: 1087). The event that followed, the scorning of Noah by his son Ham, is interpreted as a prefiguration of the crucifixion. Augustine comments: '. . . passionem quippe Christi, quae illius hominis nuditate

significata. . . . *In domo sua* eleganter ostendit quod a suae carnis gente et
domesticis sanguinis sui utique Iudaeis, fuerat crucem mortemque passurus'
(*De civ. dei*, 16.2; *CCL* xlviii, pp. 499/26; 500/63–5; *PL* 41: 478) The GO
(from Isidore of Seville) interprets the nakedness of Noah and the scorning
of his son Ham as a pre-enactment of the crucifixion: 'Passio enim est
transacta non expectatur futura' (1: 41). Like *D&P*, in its discussion of the
fourth Commandment, *Jacob's Well* cites the scorning of Noah (Salisbury
MS 174, fos. 191^b-192^b). On Noah and the Flood traditions, see *ABD*,
4: 1122–31.

305/51–3 *Syth Cam . . . þe childys fadir?*: Dives' query could have been
suggested by the *Historia Scholastica*; Comestor replies: 'Maledixit autem
non filio, sed filio filii, quia sciebat in spiritu filium non serviturum fratribus,
sed semen ejus, nec omnes de semine, sed eos qui de Chanaan descenderat.
Peccata quidem patrum saepe vindicantur in filios temporaliter' (*PL*
198: 1087).

306/63 *Prouerbiorum xxx* [*17*]: GO: 'Qui diuina iudicia reprehendunt
subsannant patrem, et haeretici dum praedicatores sanctae ecclesiae irrident
partum matris despicunt . . . 'Corui' dicuntur doctores qui peccati
nigredinem humiliter confitentur. 'Filii aquilae' quia per gratiam eius sunt
renati, qui in carne ad caelum transuolauit, qui alibi filii sponsi dicuntur'
(2: 689). Cited in the context of the fourth Commandment in *Jacob's Well*
(Salsbury MS 174, fo. 191^b).

306/68–9 *Ecclesisatici vii* [*29–30*]: To his translation, Pauper adds the
phrase: 'ne what peyne she hadde whan she bar þe of hir body' (ll. 70–1
below). Grosseteste cites the same text, in the same context: 'Cum itaque a
nullo tantum quantum a parentibus accepimus cum nisi per illos non
fuissemus, nulli alii ad tantam beneficiorum retribucionem tam arte
astringimur quam nostris parentibus (*De decem mand*, ed. Dales and King,
p. 42/17–26).

306/74 *Leuitici xx* [*9*]: 'Qui maledixerit patri suo, aut matri, morte moriatur:
patri, matrique maledixit, sanguis eius sit super eum.' Origen (c185-c254)
interprets the literal death sentence of Leviticus figuratively: the person who
cuts himself off from God the father, from the Heavenly Jerusalem (the
mother of all), from the prophets, and from the teachings of the Church
condemns himself to eternal fire ('Hom. in Leviticum', XI, *PG* 12: 534–5).
The GO also cites Origen on this text, summing up: 'Quid igitur
expectandum est illis qui negant deum esse auctorem mundi & quae caelesti
hierusalem dicuntur ad aliquam terrenam civitatem invertunt sensibus
deprauatis' (1: 256).

307/12 *Prouer. xx* [*20*]: 'Qui maledicit patri suo et matri extinguetur lucerna
eius in mediis tenebris.'

307/15 *Prouer. xxviii* [*24*]: 'Qui subtrahit aliquid a patre suo et matre et dicit hoc non est peccatum particeps homicidae est.'

307/17–31 *Absolon . . . & hys lyf*: 2 Kings [2 Sam.] 16: 15–18: 33. Nicolaus de Lyra's gloss stresses the fact that Absolom's rebellion against his father is a mortal sin; it is for this reason that David's grief is so intense: 'Plangebat [David] enim mortem eius spiritualem quia mortuus erat in peccato mortali actualiter persequando patrem'. The three spears with which Absalom is killed are also symbolic: 'Moraliter exponendo, absalom persequens dauid & viros eius tyrannum significat simplicium oppressorem, cuius caput adheret quercui mundi sublimia appetendo. Tribus lanceis configitur triplii con-cupiscentiae assentiendo, in foueam proiecitur, ad inferos descendendo' (*Postilla* 1). The GO, citing Isidore of Seville, sees Absalom as a parricide (1: 74); other glossators stress the parallel between Absalom and Judas (1: 73). Peter of Riga's retelling of the story of Absalom suggests that Absalom hanging in the branches of the oak tree prefigured Judas, who hanged himself after the crucifixion of Jesus (*Aurora*, ed. Beichner, 1: 281/ 265–6). For other references to the story of David in *D&P*, see 2–85/19 below.

307/33–5 *Salomon . . . Adonye*: 3 Reg. (1 Kgs.) 1: 5–53 and 3 Reg. [1 Kgs.] 2: 17–25. GO: Adonijah, as the elder brother of Solomon and would-be 'dominator dominus', symbolises the Jewish people and the Old Law; when the younger son, 'rex pacis', is preferred as the successor, the result is the perfidious behaviour of the Jews (1: 88). On Adonijah, *ABD* 1: 75–6. For other references to the story of David in *D&P*, see 2–85/19 below.

307/35–6 *Deutronomii xxi* [*18–21*]: The GO: 'Inobedientem ergo filium & viciosum moyses obrui lapidibus; euangelium quoque duris increpatonibus, quasi lapidibus, tales arguit, [cf.] "Genimina viperarum . . ."' (Luke 3: 7). (1: 402). The same passage is cited by Grosseteste, who comments that such a punishment is right in principle even though in the time of grace such a penalty is not observed literally (*De decem mand*, ed. Dales and King, p. 45). Cited below 322/25–6.

308/49–50 *Mathei xv* [*4–6*] *. . . ypocrysye*: For [4–6] read [4–7]. The GO: 'Impietatem sub nomine pietatis inducunt qui docent quod oblatio domini qui verus est pater obsequiis parentum praeferatur, et hoc pro lucris suis, vnde & patres ne sacrilegii crimen incurrant, deo consecrata deuitant & egestate conficiuntur' (4: 52–3). The Wycliffite sermon writer uses this text to attack the friars, the 'new orders':

And þus þes pharisees don today, for 3if þes ordris geten neuere so myche good þei seyn þat al is þer ordris, and it were a dedly synne to scatere þes godis in þe world, but in þer ordre shal þey be dispendid. . . . And 3if þey 3yuen ou3t to þer pore kyn, oþere seyen þat þei ben cursid . . . (*EWS* 3, Serm. 161/19–25).

On hypocrisy, see 169/5, 212–3/32–9, 222/29 above.

308/3 *Mayster of Propyrtes . . . storc*: Trevisa's translation of Bartholomaeus 16.9 on the stork: 'In elde here briddes [the storks' offspring] fediþ hem, and þerfore as longe tyme as þey spendeþ in reringe of hire briddes, as longe þey beþ ifedde by hire briddes' (*Properties* 1: 620/7–9). Compare Alexander Neckam (copied from Cassiodorus): 'Nam cum parentes eorum pennas senio coquente laxaverint, nec ad proprios cibos quaerendos idonei potuerint inveniri, plumis suis genitorum frigida membra refoventes, escis corpora lassa reficiunt, et, donec in pristinum vigorem ala grandaeva redierit, pia vicissitudine juvenes reddunt quod a parentibus parvuli susceperunt' (*De naturis rerum*, ed. Wright, Bk. I, c. 75, p. 113). For the same story and an etymology connecting the Greek word for 'stork' with the idea of gratitude, see Ambrose, *Hexameron*, Bk. 5, c. 16 (*PL* 14: 243–4).

309/14–15 *pellicanus*: Patristic interpretations of the psalmist's 'Similis factus sum pellicano solitudinis' (Ps. 101: 7) are responsible for the identification of the pelican with Christ. In his discussion of this psalm, Augustine elaborates an allegory in which the three birds, the pelican, the night owl ('nycticorax') and the sparrow ('passer'), represent three aspects of, or stages in, the earthly life of Christ. The pelican represents his solitary birth and upbringing, the night owl his agony before and during the crucifixion, and the sparrow his resurrection. The pelican is further likened to Christ because it killed its young, who then lay in the nest for three days before being revived by blood from the mother bird's breast ('Christi, cuius sanguine uiuificati sumus'), *Enarr.*, 101.8 (*CCL* xl, pp. 1431–2/1–60; *PL* 31: 1299–1300). Trevisa's Bartholomaeus 12.30, the source for the account in *D&P*, gives two accounts of how the pelican chicks are killed; the first is parallel to Augustine's, but the second is the one selected here, no doubt because it is the one applicable to the fourth Commandment. In this version an adder (not the mother bird) kills the chicks, thus muting the parallel with the Redemption; and it is the second version which tells the relevant story of the grateful and ungrateful chicks (*Properties*, 1: 636–7). That the actual bird was prized but not well known in England is indicated by the Christmas gift to Queen Anne in 1393 of 'a large and remarkable bird with an enormously wide gullet'—which the editors of the *Westminster Chronicle* think must have been a pelican (ed. Hector and Harvey, pp. 510–11). See below 2–300/ 20–34.

310/9–19 *Tymotheum v [3–5; 17]*: 1 Tim. 5: 3–5; 17: 'Viduas honora, quae vere viduae sunt. . . . Qui bene praesunt presbyteri duplici honore digni habeantur, maxime qui laborant in verbo et doctrina'. One of the glosses on the meaning of 'duble worchepe' is attributed to Augustine (GO 4: 410; cf. *De bono viduitatis*, cc. 8, 9, 10; *PL* 40: 436–8).

311/30–40 *Salomon. . . . childryn for helpe*: Ecclus. 33: 19; 22. Cf. Robert of Brunne's *Handlyng Synne* (ed. Furnivall, EETS, os 119,123, p. 32/1174–6).

311/40–53 *an elde man. . . . from þe cold*: The tale of the undutiful son is told in Robert of Brunne's *Handlyng Synne* (ed. Furnivall, EETS, os 119,123), pp. 40–2; cf.ed. Sullens (1983), pp. 31–2; Appendix II, p. 381–7. The tale is No.6 in William of Waddington's 'Manuel des péchés' (Herbert, *Catalogue of Romances*, 3: 286). It is found in Jacques de Vitry, *Exempla*, ed. T. F. Crane (1890), 210, and retold in Peter Idley's *Instructions* (1445–50), ed. C. D'Evelyn (1935), pp. 126–8. In Tübach's *Index* it is Tale No. 2001.

311/53–313/81 *þis cas in Colcester*: In spite of the circumstantial 'Colcester', the tale is attested elsewhere. *IMEV* lists sources, p. 674 (No. 4202). A slightly different version of the verses that conclude the tale is found in *ME Sermons* (ed. Ross, EETS, 209, p.98/35–8):

> With þis betull be he smytte,
> þat all þe world well it witt,
> þat ʒeveþ þe vnkeend all is þinge,
> And goyþ hym-selfe on beggynge.

Two more versions, one in French, are given in the edition of the Latin text of the story, 'De divite qui dedit omnia filio suo', *Latin Stories*, ed. Wright, pp. 28–9.

313/3 *Lc.* [*14: 26*]: Pauper follows the gloss in his reply to Dives: love the person, hate the sin (GO 4: 194). St Gregory considers Dives' question: 'Quomodo parentes et carnaliter propinquos praecipimur odisse, qui iubemur et inimicos diligere?' His interpretation is figurative rather than (like Pauper's) historical: Your devotion to Christ must be so much stronger than to your parents that, in comparison, your love of parents is hatred ('In Evang.', Hom. 37, *PL* 76: 1275–6; *CA*, 1: 209a-b).

313/19 *Mathei x* [*35*]: The GO suggests that 'patrem' may here be interpreted as the Devil ('Vos ex patre dyabolo estis'), from whom Christ wishes to separate us. 'Mater' may be interpreted as the synagogue, from which the primitive Church separated itself (1: 40). This interpretation follows Augustine, who adds that by sword is meant the separation of the people of God from worldly society, 'nunc Babylonia, nunc Aegypto, nunc Sodoma', as well as the division between Church and synagogue ('Quaest. Evang.', App. 3, *CCL* xlivB, p. 120/1–13).

314/27–8 *þe same place*: Matt. 10: 37: 'Qui amat patrem aut matrem plus quam me non est me dignus, et qui amat filium aut filiam super me non est me dignus.' The GO: Post deum amandi sunt, sed si utrumque non potest seruari, odium in suos pietas est in deum' (4: 40).

314/36 *II ad Corinthios* [*12–14*]: The gloss interprets the passage differently from Pauper, distinguishing between worldly and spiritual goods: 'Carnales patres filiis nam spirituales dignum est vt a filiis sumptus accipiant; hic autem in tantum probat se nolle accipere vt transferat causam carnali patris ad spiritualem & dicit non solum se pro salute eorum impendere sed et mori paratum' (GO 4: 353). Pauper concludes the discussion of this subject with an argument based on nature rather than on biblical texts: 'be weye of kende', he says, parents must care more for children than children for parents.

315/16–7 *Sent Austyn*: St Augustine's letter concerns the profession of religion in which Mother Church substitutes for one's carnal parents: 'Quo etiam tibi nunc quaedam mulier mater est, hoc ipse utique non est et mihi' (Ep. 243; *PL* 33: 1056).

316/40 *Summa confessorum, lib. iii, ti. xxxiv, q. ccxlix*: The passage may be found in John of Freiberg's *Summa*, MS Bodley. 299, fo. 242vb; it allows for aid to indigent parents from those professed in religion, with cautions against fraud and excess.

317/52–3 *Sent Powil . . . I Tim. 5: 8*: 'Si quis autem suorum et maxime domesticorum curam non habet, fidem negavit, et est infideli deterior.' The gloss refers to Jesus' entrusting the care of his mother to St John (GO 4: 410).

317/6 *xvi, q. i, Decime, et Quoniam*: Two canons: (1) 'Decime' holds that tithes are payable to the clergy and failure to pay defrauds one's fellow Christians. Tithes are a debt owed to the poor (C.16 q.1 c.66; Friedberg 1: 784). (2) 'Quoniam' points out that the clergy hold property in trust for the poor; clerics who have property of their own should not expect to be supported by the Church (C.16 q.1 c.68; Friedberg 1: 784–5). The canon is taken from an epistle of Jerome to Pope Damasus (d. 384). Cited five more times below (see Canon Law Index) and by Raymond of Peñafort, *Summa*, Bk.I, p. 131b.

317/18 *gret richesse*: The wealth of the clergy was at this period a highly controversial matter. The popular view is reflected by *PP*:

> Ac now is Religion a rydere, a rennere by stretes,
> A ledere of louedayes and a lond buggere,
> A prikere on a palfrey fro place to Manere . . .
> (B Text, X/311–14, p. 425).

In 1404, according to Walsingham, 'milites Parliamentales' petitioned the King for a general seizure of the supposed excesssive holdings of the Church (*Historia*, 2: 265–6). The attempt was easily brushed aside, but the Church was not, in fact, of one mind about its possessions or its right to them. The mendicant orders had reopened the question of the legitimacy of Church ownership of property, and their position remained at odds with that of the seculars and the monastic possessioners. On the wealth of the English

Church, Workman (1926), 2: 112–115; Dom D. Knowles (2nd edn., 1966), pp. 685–7. On Ullerston's unpublished 1401 tract 'Defensorium dotationis ecclesiae', see J. I. Catto, 'Wyclif and Wycliffism in Oxford', *HUO*, 2: 238–40. For a brief summary of the issues, Pantin (1955), pp. 126–30. See below 2–161/59–64.

317/20–1 *purchasyn*: The word can have an invidious sense in Middle English, see *MED* s.v. 'purchasen' 2(c), citing *D&P* 1/43, TABLE B, viii cap. Cf. 2–254/42–52 below. See Glossary.

317/23 *Sent Benet*: The story about the poor man asking St Benedict for 12 shillings is from St Gregory's *Dialogues*, Bk. II, c. 27 (*PL* 66: 134). The story about Agapitus and the unbroken oil jar is from Bk II, c. 28 (*PL* 66: 136).

318/48 *wyndounne*: A spelling of 'window' found only in MS G (first scribe only) and said to be characteristic of Norfolk; see A. McIntosh and M. Laing, 'Middle English *wyndown*', *Neuphil.* 97 (1998), 295–300 (ref. p. 296). See Glossary.

319/37–8 *þe lyf of Sent Gregory*: The story is found in the *Legenda aurea* (Graesse, No. 46; *GL*, 1: 172).

319/71 *Sent Franceys*: The story is from Thomas Celano's 'Second Life of St Francis', written *c*.1246–7. At a time when the church of St Francis at Portiuncula was besieged with visitors, a friar asked whether the goods of entering novices could be stored to provide for their needs. St Francis refused and said: 'Strip the altar of the Blessed Virgin and take away its many ornaments. . . . Believe me, she would be more pleased to have the Gospel of her son kept and her altar stripped than that the altar should be ornamented and her son despised. The Lord will send someone who will give back to our mother the ornaments he has lent to us' (*St Francis of Assisi, Writings and Early Biographies*, ed. M. A. Habig, *et al.* (3rd edn. 1973), p. 419).

319/4–5 *Quod omnes tangit ab omnibus approbari debet*: The principle that what touches all must be approved by all derives from Roman law. It is found in the *Corpus iuris canonici*, listed among the 'regulae' of Pope Boniface VIII (Reg. 29, X 5.12.5; Friedberg 2: 1121–4). For the history of the translation of the maxim from Roman to canon law see G. Post, 'A Romano-canonical maxim', *Traditio* iv (1946), 197–251. See below 320/6–7.

320/6–7 *Nemo potest plus iuris transferre in alium quam sibi competere dinoscitur*: The maxim is found in the *Corpus iuris*, listed among the 'regulae' of Pope Boniface VIII (Reg. 79, X 5.12.5: Friedberg 2: 1121–4). Like the above maxim (see 319/4–5 above), this one seems to be about general principles of ownership that might be written into the charter of a corporate body. But it is broader, in that the laws of ownership and possession are

more far-reaching than the laws of corporations. Under the heading of
'seisin' an historical introduction to the subject can be found in Pollock and
Maitland, dealing with such matters as proprietary rights, conveyances, and
gages (2: 29–183).

320/12–13 *Quia quicquid adquiritur monacho adquritur monasterio*: At the
beginning of this argument, Dives and Pauper talk past each other. Dives
makes the sophistical point that if charity is individual and the goods of a
religious order are held in common, then no goods can be dispensed to the
poor. Pauper replies with a denunciation of those religious orders which
forget that the goods of the Church are the property of the poor and fail to
dispense their wealth. Against Dives' false principle, Pauper refers to the
natural law that all things are common for those in need. Gratian: 'Iure
divino omnia sunt communia omnibus; iure uero constitutionis hoc meum,
illud alterius est' (D. 8 c. 1; Friedberg 1: 11). Cf. *EWS* 3, Serm 161/12–14.
See 320/29 above, 2–136/47 below.

320/29 *xii, q. i, Dilectissimus*: The canon 'Dilectissimus' urges clerics to
embrace a common life and discipline. The source is a Clementine epistle,
in which is found Pauper's reference to the air and the sun: '. . . the air, he
said, is not divided, nor is the splendour of the sun; so should it be with
other things . . . The Apostles and their disciples kept this custom and led a
common life . . . all who had houses or fields sold them and placed the
proceeds at the feet of the Apostles . . . wherefore [fearing the example of
Ananias and Saphira] we command you to obey the teaching and practice of
the Apostles . . .' (C. 12 q. 1 c. 2; Friedberg 1: 676–7). See 2–136/48,
2–137/60, 2–158/78 below.

321/37 *Actus Apostolorum iv [32]*: 'Multitudinis autem credentium erat cor
unum et anima una, nec quisquam eorum quae possidebat aliquid suum esse
dicebat, sed erant illis omnia communia'. The GO interprets this passage
more narrowly as a form of cenobitism among the early Christians intended
to imitate a future heavenly state (4: 462–3). The canon law citation that
follows was cited above, 320/29. Both citations are repeated by Dives, with
the same phrase about the air and the light of the sun, below, 2–137/54.

321/42 *a man of religion . . . on an hors*: Compare Chaucer's monk (*CT*, Prol.
p. 26a/167–71).

321/50 *Act. 5: 29*: The GO: 'Non nouus nec a nobis nuper inuentus, vt
eorum inobedientia sit inexcusabilis' (4: 465). LL4: 'it behouith in þis cas
more to obey3in to god þanne to men' (fo. 1rb). In the Longleat sermons, the
citation bolsters the writer's argument in favour of preaching the gospel in
English—against 'somme prelatis' who 'han defendyt me to techin þe gospel
& to writin it in englych'. Cited below 338/12–15.

321/56 *Mathei xv* [*3*]: The GO: 'Si vos mandata dei contemptitis propter traditiones hominum, quare arguistis discipulos qui mandata hominum dimittunt, vt scita dei custodiant? (4: 52). Cf. 308/49–50 above,

321/6 *Prouer. xxiii* [*22*]: The GO interprest 'mater tua' as the Church (2: 681).

322/9–24 *Ecclesiastici iii* [*2*]: Verses 2, 5–11 and 18 are translated in the text. The GO underlines verse 11 ('Benedictio patris firmat domos filiorum') with a list of OT figures (Ham, Abraham, Iaphet, Noah, Isaac, Jacob, Absalom) who illustrate the consequences of incurring a father's wrath or blessing (2: 747).

322/25–6 *Deutero. xxi* [*18–21*]: See 307/35–6 above.

322/26–35 *Ieremie xxxv* [*6–19*]: For [6–19] read [6–7; 18–19; 16–17]. The GO understands the story of Jonadab as a comment on perfectionism and links it to the gospel injunction, 'Si vis perfectus esse, vade & vende omnia quae habes': 'Mystice autem rechabite significatur eos qui desiderio perfectionis transcenderunt mandata legis' etc. (3: 156).

322/35–323/42 *Sent Powil . . . Ephes. vi* [*1–4*]: The GO adds a reminder that the second table of the Commandments relates to man; thus what God is to the first three Commandments, fathers are to the remaining seven Commandments (4: 378).

323/46–8 *And Salomon . . . Prouer. i* [*8*]: The GO allegorizes the 'father' and 'mother': 'Potest ex persona dei patris dei mater ecclesia, quam tunc sinagoga vocabitur, vel ipse gratia apud hebraeos enim spiritus qui gratiam praestat, 'femine ruba' [*sic*] dicitur' (2: 654). Cited below, 330/5–8. Note that in *D&P* 323/46 the reading should be: 'her þe lore of þin fadir'; see corrigenda to Vol. I: 1.

323/50 *he is a fool . . . Prouer. xv* [*5*]: 'Stultus irridet disciplinam patris sui; qui autem custodit increpationes astutior fiet'; the GO: 'Stultus est omnis peccator qui terrenis actibus deditus in futuorum nihil praeuidet is disciplinam irridet dum derogat diuinae correctioni' (2: 672).

323/53 *Salomon . . . Prov. 19: 13*: The GO comments that though God is 'impassible' he sorrows when he sees the beings he created serving the Devil (2: 676–7).

323/53–9 *Confusio patris . . . Ecclesiastici xxii* [*3–4*]: Ecclus. 22: 3–4: The remainder of the passage is: '. . . in filia autem in deminoratione fiet; /filia prudens hereditas viro suo, nam quae confundit in contumeliam fit genitoris'.

323/60 *Prouer. x* [*1*]: 'Filius sapiens laetificat patrem, Filius vero stultus maestitia est matris suae.' GO: 'Qui accepta fidei misteria bene seruat, laetificat deum patrem. Qui vero haec actione male vel haeresi commaculat matrem contristat ecclesiam' (2: 666).

323/61 *Prouer. xvii* [*25*]: The GO comments that the foolish, in spite of good examples set before them, prefer to seek out sensual pleasures (2: 675).

324/3 *Prou. xxix* [*15*]: This 'Spare the rod . . .' proverb is cited above 128/13.

324/6 *firste booc of Kyngis*: The story of Eli and his sons Hophni and Phinehas is found in 1 Sam. (1 Kgs.) 1: 3, 2: 12, 4: 4–11. Examplars of unfilial and irreligious behavior ('filii Belial, nescientes Dominum'). they were lost, along with the ark of God, in battle with the Philistines. The biblical text says that Hophni and Phinehas are 'worthless men' but does not blame their father, Eli, for their behaviour. The GO, however, interprets the name Eli as 'extraneus, a Deo enim alienus . . . qui subditos non corrigit' and says that the leniency and tolerance of the father led to the downfall of both father and sons (2: 6). Peter of Riga expands on the paternal negligence of Eli and on his death as a prefiguration of the 'death' of the synagogu (*Aurora*, ed. Beichner, 1: 253/161–4). The *Cursor Mundi* stresses the moral lesson that the sins of the fathers will be visited upon the *fathers*, 'for oft on þe fader fallis þe wrake/ þat sende is for þe childe sake' (ed. Morris, EETS, os 59, Pt. II, p. 420b/7281–2). In LL4, the death of Eli by falling backwards out of his chair is seen as a symbol of 'fallinge into dedly synne' and Eli is described as 'þe synful prest' (fo. 94va).

324/17 *leue frendys & goode childryn alle*: This form of address occurs unexpectedly and is inconsistent with the conventions of the dialogue up to this point. This was noted by Richardson (1934) p. 37, who used it to support the view that *D&P* was begun as a sermon cycle and recast as a dialogue. Cf. 1/1a and 51/2 above.

324/24 *Ecclesiastici iii* [*6*]: The GO on 'in filiis': 'In sobole vel in discipulis quorum nutrimento gaudent quia magistris vel parentibus suis obediunt, vel melius filios fructum honorem operum accipiunt' (2: 747). Cited by Grosseteste (*De decem mand,,* ed. Dales and King, p. 40/28 ff).

324/27–325/31 *he is acursyd . . . Deut. xxvii* [*16*]: This malediction occurs in a passage containing a much longer list of curses which is translated at greater length in Commandment X (2–313/20–6). A comparable passage, citing Deut. 27: 16, occurs in a sermon by the Franciscan William Herebert (Serm. 2, in *Works*, ed. Reimer, p. 53/214–33). See 262/94 above, 2–313/20–314/53 below.

325/39 *Ecclesiastici iii* [*2*]: For [2] read [3]: 'Deus enim honoravit patrem in filiis.' GO: 'Cui deus honorem constituit non debet a filiis inhonorari, quia deus iudicio suo exquiret qualiter praeceptum suum seruetur' (2: 747).

325/41–6 *Salomon . . . Ecclesiastici xvi* [*1–4*]: For [1–4] read [1; 3–4]: 'et ne iucunderis in filiis impiis si multiplicentur, non oblecteris super ipsos si non est timor Dei in illis /. . . /melior est enim unus timens Deum quam mille filii impii,/ et utile est mori sine filiis quam relinquere filios impios.' The gloss defines 'impiis' as: 'qui cogitatione, locutione, opere seipsos seques-trant a societate honorum' (GO 2: 759).

325/46 *Sapien. iv* [*6*]: Wisd. 4: 6: 'Ex iniquis enim somnis filii qui nascuntur, testes sunt nequitiae adversus parentes in interrogatione sua.' In *D&P*, the translation of 'in interrogatione sua' is 'at þe dom': this may derive from the comment on 'testes' in the gloss: 'probatione, sci., et argumentum quia merito damnandi sunt, sci., hereticos vel quoslibet malos' (GO, interlinear, 2: 727).

325/52–5 *Salomon . . . Ecclesiastici vii* [*26*]: Ecclus. 7: 25–6: 'Filii tibi sunt? erudi illos, et curva illos a pueritia illorum./ Filiae tibi sunt? serva corpus illarum et non ostendas hilarem faciem tuam ad illas.' The GO: 'Sicut bonos seruos affectu filiorum habendos, sic ancillas quam si filias habendas esse docet, sed cum disciplina. Vnde lacta filium & pauentem te faciet, lude cum eo & contristabit te: non arrideas illi ne doleas & in nouissimo obstubescant [*sic*] dentes tui [Ecclus. 30: 10]' (2: 752). That these admonitions were taken very seriously is indicated by Bennett (1968), see Ch. 6, 'Parents and Children'.

326/60–4 *Salomon . . . Prouer. xiii* [*24*]: The GO: 'Nam et bonus pater filium et discipulum magister catholicus ne ad iniquitatem deflectat, sollicitus erudit' (2: 670). The proverbial saying is attested in English c1000, and this instance (with the old dating of 1470) is listed in Whiting, P251 and Y1. Cited again below, 2–146/43–6.

326/64–74 *þe egle*: The ultimate source of the tale about the eagle and its young is Aristotle's *Historia animalium*, Bk. 9, 34, which says that: '. . . the sea-eagle is very keen-sighted, and before its young are fledged tries to make them stare at the sun, and beats the one that refuses to do so, and twists him back in the sun's direction; and if one of them gets watery eyes in the process, it kills him, and rears the other' (*Oxford Aristotle*, 1: 965/3–6). The tale is also found in Ambrose's *Hexameron*, Bk. 5, 18.60 (*PL* 14: 246). and in Alexander Neckam's *De natura rerum*, Cap. 23 (ed. Wright, p. 71). In English, it is found (citing Ambrose) in Trevisa's Bartholomaeus, 12.2 (*Properties*, 1: 603/7–23).

326/76–9 *Tobie iv* [*5*]: For [5] read [6]: 'Omnibus autem diebus vitae tuae Deum in mente habe, et cave ne aliquando peccato consentias, praetermittas praecepta Dei nostri.'

326/79–82 *Salomon . . . Ecclesiastes vi* [*3–5*]: Eccles. 6: 4: '. . . non videt solem neque cognovit distantiam boni et mali'. The GO comments on the sin of avarice: 'Adeo auarus ut nec de sepultura cogitet vel sepe pro diuitiis occisus obiicitur insepultus, vel quia nullam sui memoriam relinquat cum omnibus bonis affluat' (2: 701).

326/82–5 *in þe neste chapitele*: Eccles. 7: 12: 'Utilior est sapientia cum divitiis, et magis prodest videntibus solem.'

327/88 [*Eccl. 2: 14*]: See 91/37 above.

327/88–94 *Dauyd . . . [Ps. 122: 2]*: On Ps. 122: 2, Augustine: 'Et serui sumus et ancilla sumus; ille et dominus est, et domina est. Aut quid sibi uolunt ista uerba? et quid sibi uolunt istae similitudines rerum? Adtendat aliquantum Caritas uestra. Non mirum si serui sumus, et ille dominus est; sed mirum si ancilla sumus, et ille domina est. Sed neque hoc mirum quia ancilla sumus; ecclesia enim sumus; nec illud mirum, quia et ipse domina est; uirtus enim est et sapientia Dei' (*Enarr.*, 122.5; *CCL* xl, pp. 1817–18/6–13; *PL* 37: 1653).

327/4 *no lewyd folc*: A reference to the Arundel Constitutions of 1407–9; for texts, see Lyndwood, *Provinciale*, Bk. 5, Title 5; (1679 edn., pp. 288–305); Wilkins, iii, 314–19. *D&P*'s response to Arundel is an attempt to place the essential theology contained in the Latin instruments of the Church ('Godis lawe' 327/7–8) at the disposal of the devout, educated lay person. Compare Peter Heath's comment on the 'deep irony that some of the efforts to expunge heresy were in the end the more injurious to the church' (1988), p. 256. For an account of the impact of the Constitutions on the mendicants and other preachers, see Spencer (1993), pp. 163–88. For evidence that the author of *D&P* contributed a sermon to the debate, see 327/10 below.

327/10 *Erunt verba . . . takyn of God*: A closely similar passage is found in 'Tracts in Favour of Scriptural Translation', 2 vols., ed. Simon Hunt (D.Phil. thesis, 1994); *D&P* passage: 1: 257–8/24–59. The passage is part of a longer (*c.*7500 word) tract, the first of twelve, assembled from a variety of sources and adapted by a Lollard editor to support the case for distributing the scriptures in English. The tracts are dated, conjecturally, before 1407, when the first of the Arundel Constitutions was promulgated in Oxford. The first tract makes a strong argument for the distribution of vernacular scriptures especially to members of the lay upper class. It deals with counter-arguments in a manner comparable to Ullerston's tract of around the same time, see Hudson (1985), pp. 74–83. A guess can be made that a sermon by the author of *D&P*—not now extant—was written first; a Lollard extract, or extracts, from this sermon came second; and, third, the author of *D&P* reworked a passage from his earlier sermon for Commandment IV xi. In his redaction, the author replaced full Latin quotations with 'etc.' and omitted a citation of 'Seneca' after 'comoun þingis' (328/24–5). The Lollard version of the original sermon was then revised to obscure the *D&P* author's nuanced attitude to religious images in favour of categorical rejection. In the mid-nineteenth century, the twelve tracts were quoted and commented on in the Preface to the Wycliffite Bible (then attributed to Wyclif; see FM, 1: xiv). See Introduction, p. xx.

328/20 *Deutero. vi* [6–9]: 'Eruntque verba haec quae ego praecipio tibi hodie, in corde tuo, /et narrabis ea filiis tuis et meditaberis sedens in domo tua et ambulans in itinere, dormiens atque consurgens, /et ligabis ea quasi signum manu tua, eruntque et movebuntur inter oculos tuos, /scribesque ea in limine et ostiis domus tuae.' The GO, referring to Matt. 23: 5, says the Pharisees use phylacteries and fringes because they have misread the texts of the ten Commandments ('mali interpretantes in membranulis decalogum'), 1: 381–2.

328/23–31 *Sent Austyn . . . xxiii, q. iv, Duo, et q. v, Non putes*: Two canons: (1) 'Duo' is about the balance between justice and mercy. It warns against exacerbating the sinfulness of sinful paupers by giving them excessive alms (C.23 q.4 c.35; Friedberg 1: 915–6). The source is Augustine's exegesis of Ps. 32.5, briefly cited in the GO (2: 491–2; *Enarr.*, 32.12, *CCL* xxxviii, pp. 256–7/1–43; *PL* 36: 285–6). (2) 'Non putes' states that failure to discipline a servant or a son is not love (C.23 q.5 c.41; Friedberg 1: 940). The canon is attributed to Augustine's *In Ioh.* (tract. 7), but the exact wording is not found there; cf. 7.7 (*CCL* xxxvi, pp. 70–1/19 ff.; *PL* 35: 1440–1).

328/33 *I Petri* [*4: 10*]: 'Unusquisque, sicut accepit gratiam, in alterutrum illam administrantes, sicut boni dispensatores multiformis gratiae Dei.' The GO (interlinear): 'Quodlibet donum spiritusancti ad seruendum aliis, tam secularibus quam spiritalibus' (4: 526).

328/36 *helpyn her soulys with holy preyere*: On purgatory, see 169/19–20, 214/19–21 above; 2–190/37–192/103 below.

328/38–45 *Salomon . . . Ecclesiastici xxx* [*4*]: For [4] read [2–5]. 'Qui docet filium suum laudabitur in illo et in medio domesticorum in illo gloriabitur;/ qui docet filium suum in zelum mittit inimicum, et in medio amicorum gloriabitur in illo;/ mortuus est pater illius et quasi non est mortuus, similem enim reliquit sibi post se;/ in vita ipsius vidit et laetatus est in illo, in obitu illius non est contristatus nec confusus est coram inimicis.'

329/4 [*2 Cor. 1: 3*]: LL4: 'Also god is a name of souereyn pytee & þerfore he is clepid fadyr of mercyes & god of al comfort' (fo. 87rb). GO: 'Paterne dans veniam peccatorum, & bona opera & in tribulatione constantiam' (4: 327).

329/12–18 *But he may say . . . Malachie i* [*6*]: In *D&P*, 'timebit' is added after 'dominum suum'. The rest of the verse is: 'Si ergo pater ego sum, ubi est honor meus? et si dominus ego sum, ubi est timor meus, dicit Dominus exercituum. Ad vos, o sacerdotes, qui despicitis nomen meum, et dixistis in quo despeximus nomen tuum?' The translation in LL4 adds 'schal dredydn': 'þe sone, seyth he, worchypyth his fadyr, & þe seruaunt schal dredyn his lord; syth þan I am ȝoure fadyr, wher is my worchype, & syth I am lord of al where is my dred þat ȝe schuldyn schewyn to me?' (punctuation added, fo. 43^{rb–va}). The GO points to the historical background of the Book of Malachi, the struggle of the returnees from Babylon to rebuild the Jerusalem temple (3: 453).

329/22 *Malachie ii* [*10*]: The rest of the verse is: 'Quare ergo despicit unusquisque nostrum fratrem suum, violans pactum patrum nostrorum?' After 'fratrum suum' *D&P* adds 'be pryde & ouer-ledyng'. See 329/12–18 above.

329/22–7 *Also for tender loue . . . Ysa. xlix* [*15*]: 'Numquid oblivisci potest mulier infantem suum, ut non misereatur filio uteri sui, et si illa oblita fuerit, ego tamen non obliviscar tui.' LL4: 'þerfore he seyth be þe prophete . whor þe womman may forȝetyn here ȝonge chyld þat sche schal not han rewþe on þe chyld of here wombe & þey sche forȝete here chyld I schal nout forȝetyn þee but I schal schewyn mercy & pyte to þee' (fo. 58ra; cited again in LL4, fo. 134vb). The GO refers to the historical context, the prophet's expression of the love of God for Jerusalem (3: 74).

329/28–31 *And þerfor . . . Ecclesiastici xxiv* [*24–5*]: The rest of the passage: '. . . et timoris et agnitionis et sanctae spei;/in me gratia omnis vitae et veritatis; in me omnis spes vitae et virtutis.'

330/5–8 *Salomon . . . Prouer. i* [*8*]: Cited above 323/46–8. In this second translation, 'patris' becomes 'gostly fadir' and 'matris' becomes 'holy chirche'.

330/8–10 *Of þis maner fadrys . . . II Machaborum i* [*25*]: 'Domine Deus. . . ./ qui fecisti patres electos et sanctificasti eos . . .'.

330/13–14 *Sent Powil . . . I Cor. 4: 15*]: '. . . nam in Christo Iesu per evangelium ego vos genui'. The gloss warns against interpreting Paul's words as a claim to the status of a god: 'unus est enim pater deus' (4: 313).

330/18–9 *Sent Powil . . . I ad Thimotheum v* [*18*]: 'Dignus est operarius mercede sua.' The gloss quotes Augustine: 'Accipiant ergo sustentationem necessitatis a popolo, mercedem dispensationis a domino; non enim a popolo redditur quia merces illis qui sibi in charitate euangelii seruiunt, sed tamen dispendium datur in quo vt possint laborare pascantur' (4: 411).

330/20 *Os. 8: 4*: 'Ipsi regnaverunt et non ex me; principes exstiterunt et non cognovi.' The GO: 'Contra meam voluntatem petierunt sibi regem; sicut ceterae gentes habent a qua stulticia vt reuocaret eos samuel exponebat eis legem regni, et filios et filias eorum regibus seruituras praedicebat, vt reuerterentur ad deum regem dementissimum' (3: 364).

330/22–331/26 *Sent Powil . . .* [*Phil. 2: 21*]: The reference to 'ten þousant maystris' derives from 1 Cor. 4: 15: 'Nam si decem milia pedagogorum

habeatis in Christo, sed non multos patres'. The verse from Phil. 2: 21:
'Omnes enim . . .', is glossed: 'His sunt mercenarii qui sunt tolerandi, quia
eadem habent in ore, quae et pastores qui utique sunt diligendi. Fures vero
qui falsa praedicant & latrones qui occidunt sunt cauendi' (GO, 4: 383–4).

331/27–8 *Ps. 13: 4*: 'Nonne cognoscent omnes qui operantur iniquitatem,
qui devorant plebem meam sicut escam panis?' In this translation, 'omnes'
are 'woluys of raueyn'; in the second translation in *D&P* they become
'tyrantis, extorcioneris & false men', see 2–14/14 below. Augustine:
'Deuorant autem populum, qui sua commoda ex illo capiunt, non referentes
ministerium suum ad gloriam Dei, et ad eorum quibus praesunt salutem'
(*Enarr.*, 13.5; *CCL* xxxviii, p. 87/4–6; *PL* 36: 142).

331/28–33 *Ysaye . . . Ysa. lvi* [*11*]: The rest of verse 11 is: 'Omnes in viam
suam declinaverunt, unusquisque ad avaritiam suam, a summo usque ad
novissimum'. In the Longleat sermons, the author of *D&P* expands on the
beginning of the verse: 'et canes inpudentissimi nescierunt saturitatem': '&
þerfore þe prophete seyth þat swyche folk [the uncharitable] ben houndis
withoutyn schame and wenyn neuere to han inow . . . also houndis louyn
wel ese & slep & þat þey betokenyn vnlusti folk & ydyl folk & slow to
goodnesse þat slepyn in here synne & wyl nout wendyn to schryfte & to
amendement swyche ben domme houndis þat mowe nouȝt berkyn & þerfore
prelatys & prechourys þat wyl nouȝt spekyn ne cryyn aȝens synne ben
lykenyd to dowme houndys' (LL4, fo. 37ᵛᵃ). The GO, on 'canes': Sicut
canes gregem, sic praelati debent custodire plebem. . . . Quod est, sicut
canes sine discretione, etiam bonos saepe persequitur, sic & iudaei
impudenter clamauerunt . . .' (3: 83).

331/33–8 *schepherdis, prelatis . . . Ieremie x* [*21*]: 'Quia stulte egerunt
pastores et Dominum non quaesierunt, propterea non intellexerunt, et
omnis grex eorum dispersus est.' For 'pastores' *D&P* has 'prelatis & curatis
of holy chirche'. To 'dispersus est' the translator adds: 'be heresye, be debat,
diuysioun, & dissencioun'. The interlinear gloss explains 'pastores' as
'principes quorum culpa populus dispergitur' (3: 118).

331/38–40 *Wo, seith God . . . Ieremye xxiii* [*1*]: 'Vae pastoribus qui
disperdunt et dilacerant gregem pascuae mea, dicit Dominus.' LL4: 'Wo
be to þe schepperdys þat dyscateryn & forrendin þe flok of myn lesue . ȝe
han seyth he dyscateryd myn flok & ȝe han chachyd hem out & ȝe vysytyd
hem not but I schal gadryn hem togedere & turnyn hem aȝen into here lond
& to her lesue þat ys þe lond of lyf & heuene blysse' (fo. 52ʳᵇ). The gloss
interprets the passage as a warning to the Jews: 'Quia omnis spes iudaici
regni defecit transit a principes ecclesie & synagoga cum suis pastoribus
derelicta atque damnata ad apostolos sermo fit, de quibus dicitur, Super eos
suscitabo pastores', (3: 136). Cited below, 2–18/59–60.

331/40–9 *Sent Gregory . . . þe mark of þe offys*: Homily 17, 'Designavit dominus', on the sending forth of the disciples (Luke 10: 1–9): 'Ecce mundum sacerdotibus plenus est, sed tamen in messe Dei rarus valde invenitur operator, quia officium quidem sacerdotale suscepimus, sed opus officii non implemus' (*PL* 76: 1139).

332/2–6 *And perfor God . . . Leuitici xix [32]*: The rest of the verse: '. . . et honora personam senis et time Deum tuum; ego sum Dominus.' GO: 'In senibus est sapientia & in multo tempore prudentia hinc paulus ait. Presbiter duplici honore digni habeantur, maxime qui laborant in verbo & doctrina.' Cited below 347/17.

332/7–11 *Sent Powil . . . I ad Tymotheum [5: 1–2]*: 'Seniorem ne increpaveris, sed obsecra ut patrem, iuvenes ut fratres,/ anus ut matres, iuvenculas ut sorores in omni castitate.' The GO: 'ne indigne ferens se a minore correctum magis exasperetur quam proficiat' (4: 410).

332/11–16 *Oftyn tyme eld folc . . . Ysa. [65: 20]*: 'Non erit ibi amplius infans dierum et senex qui non impleat dies suos, quoniam puer centum annorum morietur, et peccator centum annorum maledictus erit.' LL4: 'God seyþ þat þe chyld of an hondryd ȝeer schal ben cursid & þe synnere of an hondryd ȝer schal deye', fo. 16ra. Cited below 2–27/13–14. This passage suggests the *puer senex* topos, which derives from late pagan Antiquity but which has analogues in the Bible, cf. Tob. 1: 4 and Wisd. 4: 8 (cited below, 347/11–15). Curtius (1948) says that the topos 'was impressed on the memory of the West by a much-read text of Gregory the Great, who began his life of St. Benedict with the words: "Fuit vir vitae venerablis . . . ab ipso suae pueritiae tempore cor gerens senile"' (tr. 1953, pp. 98–105; cited from p. 100).

332/22–3 *Sent Gregory*: Cited in Gregory's *Moralia in Job*, 17.6, where he says that a boy has a long life in which to be corrected; an old sinner should be treated severely, 'ne ex clementia iudicis crescat supplicium peccatoris' (*CCL*, cxliiiA, p. 855/14–27; *PL* 76: 14).

333/6–7 *And perfor Naaman . . . IV Regum v [13]*: 2 Kgs. 5: 13: '. . . accesserunt ad eum [Naaman] servi sui, et locuti sunt ei: Pater, et si rem grandem dixisset tibi propheta, certe facere debueras? quanto magis quia nunc dixit tibi lavare et mundaberis?' The fact that his servants addressed Naaman as 'father' has little to do with the story of the encounter between Naaman and Elisha. The gloss points out that it was his servants who advised the unwilling Naaman to wash himself in the Jordan as Elisha had commanded. His doing so and the resultant cure of his leprosy are interpreted as a prefiguration of the baptism of Jesus by John (GO 2: 148). The healing is referred to in the NT, Luke 4: 27. On Elisha, see 348/31–48 below; see also 2–174/35–42.

333/7–9 *Iob . . . xxix* [*16*]: Job 29: 16: 'Pater eram pauperum, Et causam quam nesciebam diligentissime investigabam.' LL4: 'I was fader of þe pore & þe cause þat I knew not I souȝte it vp wol besylyche' (fo. 15ᵛᵃ). St Gregory interprets this passage to mean that charity given in fear is insufficient; the donor must act from the motives of a father: 'Quia igitur aliud est bonum opus ex praecepto, aliud uero etiam ex affectu facere' *Moralia* 19.24 (*CCL*, cxliiiA, p. 989/8–10; *PL* 76: 124).

333/10–27 *Sent Powil . . . ad Ephesios vi* [*5–9*]: Eph. 6: 5–9: the GO: 'Seruitus coepit ex peccato, prima enim seruiturus causa peccatum ut homo homini condicionis vinculo subderetur, quod non fuit nisi deo indicante, apud quem non est iniquitas, & nouit diuersas poenas meritis distribuere delinquentium' (4: 379) The source of the gloss is Augustine's *In Ioh.*41.3–13, in which the sense is found, though not the exact words (*CCL* xxxvi, pp. 359–65; *PL* 35: 1694–1700).

334/37–60 *Sent Petir . . . fyrste pystel, ii* [*18–25*]: 1 Pet.2: for [18–25] read [13–22]. The translation in *D&P* is a free one; only part of verse 18 is cited in Latin. The gloss echoes the biblical text; on verse 13: 'Et ut conversatio vestra omnibus placeat, non resistans alicui dignitati hominum, alicui personae, alicui principatui cui deus vos subdi voluit, quia non est potestas nisi a deo, & qui potestati resistit dei ordinatione resistit' (GO 4: 523). Verse 17 ('Subiecti estote') is cited at 106/55 above, and at 347/20, 354/16–18 below. Verse 18 ('Serui subditi') is cited at 102/11 above. Verse 22 ('qui peccatum non fecit') is referred to below, 2–301/59. Verses 13–14 are freely translated in LL4, fo. 34ᵛᵇ.

334/60–335/82 *Sent Powyl . . . ad Romanos xiii* [*1–6*]: Like *D&P*, LL4 cites Rom. 13 at length, verses 1–8: 'And þerfore seynt poul biddith þat euery man & womman schulde ben soget & meke to his emperour & to his kyng & to his temperel lordys for þey ben goddis ministris & han takin þe swerd to meyntenyn þe gode & to punschin schrewis & þerfore seyth he ȝe payyn tribuȝt to hem for þei seruyn god þerfore ȝeldith þanne seyth he to alle men here dette . to hym þat ȝe owin tribuȝt payyth tribuȝt . and to hym þat ȝe owyn custom or rente payyth custom & rente . & to whom ȝe owyn dred & worschepe ȝeldith dred & worschepe & nameli to god for he owith to be dred & worschepid & louyd abouyn alle þinge . owe ȝe nout to ony man but onli þat ȝe louyn ȝow togedere for charite is a dette þat may neuere ben ful payd in þis world' (fo. 113ᵛᵇ). The gloss to verse 3 ('nam principes') is attributed to Augustine: 'Si iubeat quod non licet, hic sane contemne potestatem, timendo potestatem maiorem, ergo si aliud imperatur aliud deus iubeat contempto illo obtemperandum est deo' (GO 4: 301). The frequency with which Rom. 13: 1–6 is cited in *D&P* reflects the author's pervasive anxiety about social unrest; cf. Bammel (1984), pp. 365–83. Cited below, 2–13/19 (v. 4), 2–33/65 (vv. 3–6), 2–138/13–14 (v. 1).

335/5–336/15 *Sent Austyn . . . schrewys*: Ps. 63: 2; Augustine: 'Non timeam eum qui corpus et animam occidit; sed timeam eam qui habet potestatem et corpus et animam occidere in gehenna ignis' (*Enarr.*, 63.2; *CCL* xxxix, p. 809/32–4]; *PL* 36: 761–2).

336/15–9 *And perfor God seyde . . . Ieremie xxv [8–9]*: Jer. 25: 8: 'Propterea haec dicit Dominus exercituum pro eo quod non audistis verba mea/ ecce ego mittam et adsumam universas cognitationes aquilonis ait Dominus et ad Nabuchodonosor regem Babylonis servum meum et adducam eos super terram istam et super habitationes eius et super omnes nationes quae in circuitu illius sunt et interficiam eos et ponam eos in stuporem et in sibilum et in solitudines sempiternas'. Cited below 2–177/29–30, 2–264/60–265/67.

336/29–36 *And perfor he seith . . . Ysa. x [5]*: For [5] read [5–7]. 'Assur' refers to the ancient kingdom of Assyria, during the first millennium BC, a predominant power in southwestern Asia. In the eighth century BC, Assyria destroyed Israel as an independent kingdom. Isaiah envisions Assyria as God's instrument to punish the sins of his people and, in his more hopeful passages, predicts the birth of a saviour from the line of David. The gloss on verse 7 ('ipse autem non sic arbitrabitur'): 'Sic philosophi, sic haeretici, sic persecutores xtiani nominis, cum deus aliquos eis verberandos permittit in omnes saeuiunt, nec verberare sed occidere cupiunt, & paucis superatis in omnes audaciam sumunt' (GO 3: 20).

336/1 *lordchepe*: St Augustine, citing biblical precedents, says that God, to serve just ends, grants power to the just and unjust: 'regnum vero terrenum et piis et impiis, sicut ei placet cui nihil iniuste placet', *De civ. dei*, 5.21 (*Augustine*, LCL 412, 2: 250–1). Wyclif dissents: 'dominium civile est dominium occasione peccati humanitus institutum' (*De civ. dom.*, 1: 127/ 17–18). Though God may sometimes, he says, give evil rulers grace to rule, he does not give their ownership legitimacy. This view, taken up by the Lollards, was among the views condemned as heretical by Pope Gregory XI in 1377 (*FZ*, p. 495). The Oxford Franciscan, William Woodford, attacked Wyclif's views on this subject (*Fasciculus rerum*, ed. E. Brown, 1: 190–265). Cf. Walsh (1981), pp. 160–4; 176–405. See 63/17, 72/17–30, 160/11–15 above, and 2–138/1–2 below.

337/9–11 *Iob xxxiv [30]*: Gregory's *Moralia* 15.16 on this verse says that the 'ypocritam' can be identified as Antichrist: '[P]otest ipsum omnium hypocritarum caput antichristus designari' (*CCL* cxliiiB, p. 1259/30–1; *PL* 76: 343).

337/11–14 *And perfor . . . Osee xiii [11]*: Hos. 13: 11: 'Dabo tibi regem in furore meo, Et augeram in indignatione mea.' The GO assumes the 'regem' is Jeroboam (3: 372), but, according to the *ABD*, Hos. 13: 11 is commonly thought to be an allusion 'to the punishment of [King] Hosea by the Assyrians'. (3: 294).

337/14–18 *þe Philosofre*: Aristotle's 'Nicomachean Ethics' (4: 3: 15–16): '. . . if he were bad, he would not be worthy of honour, since honour is the prize of virtue, and the tribute that we pay to the good': (ed. Rackham, LCL 73, p. 217/13–16); *Oxford Aristotle* (1984), 2: 1774/1–2). Cited above, 107/9.

337/28–32 *Sent Powil . . . ad Ebreos xiii [17]*: LL4:'Obey3ith to 3oure prelatis & to 3oure souereynys & be 3e soget & meke to hem for þey wakin in gret besinesse as þey schul 3euyn answere for 3oure soulis' (fo. 9vb). Like Dives, the gloss cautions against blind obedience: 'Obediendum est utique prelatis & predicatioribus in quantum doctrina & mores illorum sanctae et pie exisunt. Si autem a via rectitudinis deuiauerint, non faciamus qualia agunt sed qualia dicunt nisi forte & in doctrina aberrent . . . non ad vitam eorum sed ad mores intendite' (4: 449).

338/12–15 *Sent Petir . . . Actus Apos. [5: 29]*: See 321/50 above.

339/19 *xi, q. iii, Non semper*: 'Non semper' is summarized from Ambrose, 'Liber de paradiso', cap. 6: 'Non semper malum est non obedire precepto; cum enim dominus iubet ea, que Deo sunt contraria, tunc ei obediendum non est' (C.11 q.3 c.92; Friedberg 1: 669; *PL* 14: 304).

339/28–9 *a gret clerk . . . Seneca, lib. iii, De beneficijs*: 'It is a mistake for anyone to believe that the condition of slavery penetrates into the whole being of a man. The better part of him is exempt. Only the body is at the mercy and disposition of a master; but the mind is its own master, and is so free and unshackled that not even this prison of the body, in which it is confined, can restrain it from using its own powers, following mighty aims and escaping into the infinite to keep company with the stars. It is, therefore the body that Fortune hands over to a master . . . that inner part cannot be delivered into bondage' (*Seneca, Moral Essays* 3, LCL 310: 'On Benefits', 3.19, pp. 164–5). John of Wales, though echoing the Augustinian view that slavery resulted from sin (*De civ. dei* 19.15), also cites Sececa: '[Q]ui est seruus conditione liber est virtuali libertate mente' (*Communiloquium* 2.1.1).

341/16–8 *Som clerkys . . . Petrus, super ii Sent., d. ult*: Peter Lombard cites Rom. 13: 2 on obedience, but, like Pauper, qualifies: 'Si vero princeps aliquis vel diabolus aliquid iusserit vel suaserit contra Deum, tunc resistendum est.' In support, he cites Augustine: 'Potestati ergo diaboli vel hominis tunc resistamus, cum, aliquid contra Deum suggesserit' (*Sentences*, 1: 579–80/21–2; 30–1; Augustine, Serm. 62.13; *PL* 38: 420–1 (wording differs from Peter Lombard).

341/18–19 *Summa confessorum, lib. iii, ti. xxxiii, q. v*: The reference is to John of Freiburg's *Summa* (MS Bodley 299, fo. 179^{r–v}). Q. 5 opens with the question, 'quero utrum subditi teneantur prelatis suis in omnibus obedire', and the answer is, Not in matters contrary to the articles of faith. The section goes on to specify a number of categories of obedience. Like *D&P*, John cites Seneca's 'De beneficiis'; cf. 339/28–9 above.

341/26–32 *Danielys prophecie . . . Daniel iv*: Dan. 4: 1–37. The glossator says the story speaks for itself but suggests that Nebuchadnezzar is a type of the Devil: 'significetur dyabolus, quod nos non recipimus ne omnia quae legimus vmbra et fabulae vidantur'. Such a tale, like the classical myths about chimeras and centaurs, is intended to show the power of God (GO 3: 330). On Nebuchadnezzar, *ABD* 4: 1058–9.

341/32–43 *Sedechie . . . Ierem. xxvii [5–9]*: On Zedekiah, King of Judah, see *ABD* 6: 1058–71. The glossator also wishes to allegorize this tale (see above, 341/26–32), finding a parallel between the fall of Nebuchadnezzar and the fall of Lucifer, who left the heavenly Jerusalem and descended to the earthly Babylon (GO 3: 143).

341/43–342/46 *And God . . . [Mt. 22: 21]*: LL4: 'And þanne he seyde to hem ȝeldith þanne to þe emperour þingis þat ben þe emperouris & to god þingis þat ben goddis' (fo. 112vb). GO: 'Vel sicut caesar exgit impressionem suae imaginis, sic & deus animam lumine sui vultus signatum' (4: 69).

342/49 *cursyn a man*: Aquinas (or his continuators) says that the Church practises two levels of excommunication, major and minor. Major excommunication separates the Christian from the Church ('a communione fidelium') and minor excommunication separates the Christian from the sacraments ('a suffragiis et aliis spiritualibus') (*ST*, Suppl., 21.1; OP edn., Rome (1894), 5: 118). The preachers' manuals contemporary with *D&P* grappled with the kinds of arguments made here. Thomas of Chobham's *Summa* deals with such questions as whether a priest may excommunicate a bishop, and whether a priest may excommunicate himself (ed. Broomfield, pp. 211–2). The power of excommuniction is linked with the power to bind and loose, or the power of the keys, referred to above (92/13–15). On major and minor excommunication, see Logan (1968), pp. 13–14.

342/67 *schertlyche*: Read 'streytlyche'.

342/69–70 *Summa confessorum, lib. iii, ti. xxxiii, q. vi, Quid si episcopus*: The reference is to John of Freiburg's *Summa* (MS. Bodley 299, fo. 179^v). The opening question is, What if a bishop orders a priest to excommunicate a man he knows is innocent? The answer is 'Numquid in hoc tenetur obedire sacerdos.'

343/8–9 *Reymond, lib. i, ti. ix, De iuramento et periurio, c. xiv, Quid de iudice*: Raymond of Peñafort's *Summa* discusses such cases at length, e.g.: 'What of a judge who knows an accused man arrested for a capital crime is other than the one who is guilty of the crime . . . and who sees witnesses prepared to swear falsely, [shall he] on that account knowingly condemn an innocent man? . . . I advise that he delegate the matter to someone else, if possible to a superior, if he will take the case, and so relieve his conscience, positing that the other will judge in the case with the utmost seriousness' (paraphrased; Bk. I, pp. 90–2).

343/21 *Deutero. xvii* [*12*]: The gloss relates this OT text to the NT: 'Christi qui est sacerdos in aeternum secundum ordinem melchisedech, qui vicarius sibi substituit quibus ait, "Qui vos audit me audit, et qui vos spernit me spernit" etc. (Luke 10: 16). Iure ergo damnationis sustinet sententiam, qui contemnit diuinitatis potentiam' (GO 1: 396).

343/25 *Prov. 21: 1*: The GO: 'Omnium hominum non solum regis cor in manu domini "quia in manu eius sunt omnes fines terrae" (Ps. 94: 4). Sed regem sanctum quemque vocat qui viciorum bella in se vincere, virgulta maliciae novit extirpare. Sicut enim dominus aquarum diuisionibus terrarum fines simul & aeris implet, tegit quoque aquis superiora caelorum, "ita cor regis quocumque voluerit" inclinat (Prov. 21: 1). Quia sicut diuisiones gratiarum secundum voluntatem suam, et angelis & hominibus tribuit, ita corda sanctorum quibus cumque voluerit digna donationibus reddit. Et taceat pelagianus, quia absque gratia dei nullus est locus saluti' (2: 678).

344/33–4 *Rom. 14/23*: 'Omne autem, quod non est ex fide, peccatum est.' Pauper adds '& of good conscience' to his translation of 'ex fide' possibly with an eye to the gloss, which seems to recognize that faith can be based on ignorance: 'Non tamen omne quid sit cum fide bonum est, quia ignorantia quae est ex culpa nocet' and 'Omnis vita infidelium peccatum est' and further 'Fides vestra vult vt bono agat hoc quod bene intelligit esse agendum, & peccatum est quod aliter sit quam probatum est' (GO 4: 303).

345/1 *bookys*: In late medieval Oxford, books were the cause of acrimony between friars and other scholars. The friars were accused of hoarding:

> Frere, what charite is it to gadere vp þe bokis of Goddis lawe, many mo
> þanne nediþ ȝou, & putte hem in tresorie, & do prisone hem fro seculer
> preestis & curatis, wher bi þei ben lettid of kunnynge of Goddis lawe to
> preche þe gospel freli? (*Jack Upland*, ed. Heyworth, p. 70/373–6)

The controversy has been studied by R. H. and M. A. Rouse, with particular attention to Wycliffite writings on the subject (1987), pp. 369–84. See further, Catto (1968), 146–8. The library of the Franciscan convent at Oxford owed its early preeminence to the legacy of Bishop Grosseteste, see R. W. Hunt (1955, repr. 1969), pp. 121–45.

346/20 *xxxiii, q. v, Noluit*: The canon 'Noluit' holds that wives should follow the dictates of their husbands in all matters (C.33 q.5 c.16; Friedberg 1: 1255). The source is Augustine's 'Quaest. de numeris', 59, which begins: 'Manifestum est ita uoluisse legem feminam esse sub uiro, ut nulla uota eius . . . reddantur ab ea nisi auctor uir fuerit permittendo' (*CSEL* xxviii, pp. 363–6).

346/22 *Bernard, in a pystyl*: Bernard of Clairvaux, Epistola VIII.4, ad Adam monachum: 'Sane hoc advertendum, quod quaedam sunt pura bona:

quaedam pura mala, et in his nullam deberi hominibus oboedientiam, quoniam nec illa omittenda sunt, etiam cum prohibentur, nec ista, vel cum iubentur, committenda. Porro inter haec sunt media quaedam, quae pro modo, loco, tempore vel persona, et mala possunt esse, et bona, et in his lex posita est oboedientiae, tanquam in ligno scientiae boni et mali, quod erat in medio paradisi' (*Opera*, ed. J. Leclerq *et al.*, 7: 33/22–7; *PL* 182: 95).

346/5–6 *Frensch tunge*: Cf. 239/22 above.

347/11–15 *Salomon . . . Sapien. iv [8]*: Wisd. 4: 8; for comment on the *puer senex* topos, see 332/11–16 above.

347/17 *Leuitici xix [32]*: Cited 332/2–6 above.

347/18–26 *And in þe newe lawe . . . I Petri ii [17]*: Cited above 102/11, 106/55, and below, 354/16–18.

347/26–8 *Sent Powyl . . . I ad Corinth. xiv [40]*: The gloss summarizes St Paul's plea for the orderly management of those in the congregation who wish to 'speak in tongues', repeating that the women must keep silent (GO, 4: 342).

347/6–348/10 *Sent Powil . . . ad Ephes. iii [15]*: The gloss is mainly concerned with distinguishing sonship from adoption: 'Et nota quod christus dei unigenitus per naturam, adoptionis beneficio patrem se esse significat, dicens. . . . similiter et spiritus sanctus, per quem justi adoptuntur in filios. Homo autem dicitur pater per natura, vel auctoritate exempli, vel ratione beneficii . . .'. Angels are, however, alluded to: 'Ab illo enim qui est pater omnium & angeli in caelo & homines in terra acceperunt ut patres alios vocarent' (GO 4: 373).

348/15–20 *two angels . . . in þe gospel*: Matt. 18: 10: '. . . dico enim vobis, quia angeli eorum in caelis semper vident faciem Patris mei, qui in caelis est.' GO: 'Cur non sunt contemnenditur [little children] quia pro eius quotidie mittuntur angeli' (4: 59). Cf. the second century *Shepherd of Hermas*: 'There are two angels with man, one of righteousness and one of wickedness. . . . Now see also the works of the angel of wickedness. First of all, he is ill tempered, and bitter and foolish, and his deeds are evil, casting down the servants of God' ('The Shepherd of Hermas' 6.2.1–4, *Apostolic Fathers*, LCL 24, pp. 96–7).

348/22 *Sent Ierom*: Jerome's comment on Matt. 18: 10 (see 348/15–20 above) can be found in the *CA*: 'Magna enim dignitas animarum ut unaquaeque habeat ab ortu nativitatis in custodiam sui Angelum delegatum' (*CA* 1: 271; *PL* 26: 135).

348/24–31 *þe angel Raphael . . . Tobie [12: 12–13]*: The first mention of Raphael occurs in the Book of Tobit; he is mentioned again in Enoch 1.20 (*OT Pseudepigrapha*, ed. J. H. Charlesworth (1983), 1: 23). On Tobit, see

ABD, 6: 585–94. In the Longleat sermons, the author cites this text in praising the salvific roles of angels and the Virgin: 'And be here [the Virgin] as be a leddre aungelis comyn doun to vs for at here biddinge & at here comaundement þey comyn doun to vs for to kepin vs & for to defendin vs from þe fendis & to wissin vs & to techin vs & to comfortin vs & at here comaundement þey gon vp & berin vp oure preyeris & oure gode dedis & presentin hem to god & spekin for vs & preyȝin for vs' (fo. 126ra).

348/31–48 *þe ferde book of Kyngis* . . . [*6: 8–23*]: The focal point of the story of the prophet Elisha is his host of angelic helpers: on these, Nicolaus de Lyra's gloss: 'Plures enim nobiscum sunt sanctebat enim per spiritum sanctum protectionem angelicam in sui auxilium aduenisse, cuius potestas quasi incomparabiliter maior est quam humana' (*Postilla* 1). The GO draws a NT parallel, pointing out that Elisha did not kill his enemies but fed them and let them go in peace, just as Saul, before his conversion, had been tolerated by God; Jesus said: 'Diligite inimicos vestros et benefacite his qui oderunt vos [Matt 5: 44]', (2: 150).

349/48–52 *Dauyd* . . . *Ps. 124: 2*: Augustine expands on the theme of mountains, rejecting the notion that mountains are invariably protective. Some indeed evoke angelic presences, but others evoke evil forces, such as the great heretics Donatus, Maximianus, Photinus or Arius. The true Christian's mountain should be Mount Zion: 'ut qui confidunt in Domino sicut mons Sion, non commoueantur in aeternum' (*Enarr.*, 124.4–6; *CCL* xl, pp. 1837–40; *PL* 37: 1652–3).

349/52 *Sent Cecilie*: The legend of St Cecilia, a third-century Roman martyr, is told in Jacobus de Voragine's *Legenda aurea* (Graesse, No. 169; *GL*, 2: 318–23). Chaucer's 'Second Nun's Tale' retells her story (*CT*, pp. 262–9; on his sources, see Gerould in *Sources and Analogues*, pp. 664–84. In the mid fifteenth century, Osbern Bokenham produced another metrical version (*Legendys*, ed. Sergeantson, EETS, 206, pp. 201–25). See *ODS*, pp. 72–3. See 2–91/28 below.

349/70 *Sent Agnes*: The legend of St Agnes, a fourth-century Roman martyr, is told in Jacobus de Voragine's *Legenda aurea* (Graesse, No. 24; *GL*, 1: 101–4). The story is retold in Osbern Bokenham's *Legendys* (ed. Sergeantson, EETS, 206, pp. 110–29). See *ODS*, pp. 5–6. See 216/61–2 above.

350/91–5 *Also* . . . *Sent Kateryne*: The legend of St Katherine of Alexandria is set in the fourth century but not attested until the ninth. The first English version dates from the thirteenth century (*The Life of Saint Katherine*, ed. Einenkel, EETS, os 80). A metrical version appears in Osbern Bokenham's *Legendys* (ed. Sergeantson, EETS, 206, pp. 172–201). See *ODS*, pp. 69–70. See 216/61–2 above.

351/106 *Dauyd . . . [Ps. 31: 6]*: Augustine: 'Inde orabit ad te omnis sanctus, quia dimisisti peccata. Nam si non dimitteres peccata, non esset sanctus qui ad te oraret, "Pro hac . . ." etc.' (*Enarr.* 31.17; *CCL* xxxviii, p. 237/3–7; *PL* 36: 269).

351/14 *Angele qui meus es, etc.*: The author of this hymn, Reginald (d. c1109), by birth French, was a monk of Canterbury in the late eleventh century to early twelfth century. His major literary work is an epic in verse on the life of St Malchus, of which this hymn, 'Angele qui meus es' forms a part. The hymn is listed in H. Walther, *Initia Carminum*, 973; and in Drèves, *Analecta* 1, No. 293, pp. 379. A collection of Reginald's shorter poems is preserved in MS Bodley Laud misc. 40. The hymn appears in MS Ashmole 750, fos. 102^v-103^r, which also contains a fragment of the text of *D&P*. See Rigg (1992), pp. 24–30; and brief mention in Raby (1953), p. 333.

351/4 *patronys*: J. R. H. Moorman (1963) says, 'The parish priest was . . . a small freeholder living upon his glebe which he normally tilled himself. As a member of the manorial community he owed allegiance to his lord, while as a servant of the Church he also took his oath to the bishop' (p. 28). The inevitable conflict of interest is reflected in the sections of the *Corpus iuris*, Causa 16, q. 7 and 'de iure patronatus', upon which the following chapter draws. On the entire subject, see Heath (1969), pp. 27–48.

351/6 *xvi, q. vii, Pie, in glosa*: The canon 'Piae mentis' declares that the builder of a church does not retain special privileges (C.16 q.7 c.26; Friedberg 1: 807–8). The source is a pastoral letter of Pope Gelasius (d. 1119) Cited 352/38–40 below.

352/25 *xvi, q. vii, Filijs*: The canon 'Filiis' extends the above prohibition (351/6) to the heirs of those who constructed the church building; but it also suggests that such an heir may report abuses to the king: '. . . regis hec auribus intimare non differant' (C.16 q.7 c.21; Friedberg 1: 809). Cited below 353/53.

352/33 *xvi, q. vii, Quicunque*: The canon 'Quicunque' holds that patrons (or founders of churches) have the right of providing, consulting, and finding incumbents but do not have the right to sell, give or use Church property. The penalty of a year's excommunication may be imposed (C.16 q.7 c.30; Friedberg 1: 808). The source is an Edict of the fourth Council of Toledo (633).

352/34 *Extra, lib. iii, De iure patronatus, c. Nobis fuit*: The canon 'Nobis fuit' holds that a patron derives from his construction of a church a limited right of election of an incumbent, the right to a ceremonial place of honour, and the right to provision of food if he should become needy (X 3.38.25; Friedberg 2: 617). The source is a decretal of Pope Clement III (d. 1191) The canon is cited below, 353/52–3, 353/58.

352/35 *xii. q. [ii], Apostolicos, et c. Sacrorum, et ibidem, q. ii, Aurum*: Three canons from Causa 12: (1) 'Apostolicos' states that sacred vessels which are the property of a church are not to be sold except to redeem captives (C.12 q.2 c.13; Friedberg 1: 690); (2) 'Sacrorum' holds the Church property may legitimately be used for the redemptions of captives (C.12 q.2 c.13; Friedberg 1: 691); (3) 'Aurum' holds that sacred vessels belonging to a church may be sold to redeem captives, build churches and bury the dead. The canon is excerpted from Ambrose, who asks, 'Quid est opus custodire quod nihil adiuuat?' ('De officiis' 2.28; *PL* 16: 140). (C.12 q.2 c.70; Friedberg 1: 710–11).

352/38–40 *xvi, q. vii, Pie mentis*: See 351/6 above.

352/41 *Extra, lib. iii, De celebracione missarum, consuluisti*: The canon 'Consuluisti' holds that a priest must normally celebrate mass only once a day, except in an emergency ('nisi causa necessitatis suadeat') or at Christmas time (X 3.41.3; Friedberg 2: 636). The source is an epistle of Pope Innocent III, whose *De miseria humnae conditionis* is cited above (170/48–50).

352/45 *xvi, q. vii, Monasterium*: The canon 'Monasterium' holds that a patron who is responsible for building a church may present a candidate for preferment, provided he is of good character; the provision for a lay subsidy, however, does not appear in this canon. The source is a Roman synod held under Popes Eugenius II (d. 827) and Leo IV (d. 855) (C.16 q.7 c.33; Friedberg 1: 809–10).

352/48 *Extra, De iure patronatus, c. Preterea*: The canon 'Preterea' enjoins excommunication for lay patrons who install clerics and fail to support them, and minor excommunication for priests who receive such preferment. Decreed by Lateran III, in 1179 (X 3.38.4; Friedberg 2: 610). See 352/48–9 below.

352/48–9 *Hostiensis, Summa, lib. iii, e. ti.*: The reference is to Hostiensis' *Summa aurea*; on Hostiensis, see 246/39 above. It is possible that his gloss on X 3.38.4 suggested that a patron might reserve an annual rent from Church property, which provision is not in the canon but stated here by the author of *D&P*.

353/49 *chirche collegiat*: Collegiate churches were so-called because they were under the direction of a group of canons, varying in number from four to several tens. Though the oldest of these churches go back to Anglo-Saxon times, many were founded by lay patrons in the thirteenth century; see J. R. H. Moorman (1955), pp. 19–23. Cf. 245/1 above.

353/50 *chanterie*: Chantries were privately-endowed masses, sung for the souls of benefactors and their families. The practice originated very early in the history of the Church but was greatly expanded in the fourteenth and fifteenth centuries. J. R. H. Moorman (1953) points out that the chantry system was related to the formation of collegiate churches (see 353/49 above): 'In some instances a parish church was turned into a collegiate church served by a number of clergy each of whom was in a sense, a chantry-priest' (p. 144). The foundational study of English chantries is by K. L. Wood-Legh (1965).

353/52–3 *Extra, De iure patronatus, c. Nobis fuit*: See above 352/34.

353/53 *xvi, q. vii, Filijs*: See above 352/25.

353/57 *Hostiensis, lib. iii, ru. De iure patronatus*: The reference is to Hostiensis' *Summa aurea*. On Hostiensis, see 246/39 above.

353/58 *Extra, de iure patronatus, Nobis fuit, in glosa*: See 352/34 above.

353/61 *Ysa. i* [2]: The glosses to this verse compare men unfavourably with dogs, who, for little sustenance, defend the household. The gloss goes on to list the first-born of Israel who were passed over for younger siblings: Cain, Ishmael, and Esau. The later arrivals, the apostles and Christians, have succeeded to the title of sons of God: 'Nos secundi & cauda dicti versi eis potestatem filios dei fieri' (GO 3: 2). Cited twice in LL4: 'I haue auaunsyd chyldryn & brout hem forth of nout & þey han dispysyd me' (fo. 43rb); 'I haue brouȝt forth chyȝldryn & vaunsid hem wol heyliche & þey han dispisid me' (fo. 139ra).

353/66 *Is. 1: 4*: GO: 'In tytulo personem causam tempusque commemorat. Secundo attentos facit. Tercio narrat quid locutus sit dominus. Quarto in excessibus gentem increpat peccatricem' (3: 2–3).

354/81 *Extra, De eleccione, [Quum] in cunctis*: The canon 'Quum in cunctis' sought to raise the standard both of age (at least 30) and of learning of those proposed for the office of bishop, as well as the age (at least 25) and other qualifications for lesser offices; those proposing candidates should inquire into 'et aetatis maturitas, et gravitas morum, et literarum scientia' (X 1.6.7; Friedberg 2: 51–2). It was promulgated by the third Lateran council (1179) under Pope Alexander III (d. 1181); text in Mansi, 22, 1.3, p. 218.

354/91 *Hostiensis, lib. iii, De iure patronatus*: The reference is to Hostiensis' *Summa aurea*. On Hostiensis, see 246/39 above.

354/16–18 *Sent Petir . . . Sent Powil*: For 1 Pet. 2: 17, see 106/55 and 347/18–26 above. For Rom. 12: 10, see 106/56 above.

355/35–7 *Sent Powil . . . ad Philiipenses ii* [3]: The gloss is Augustine's: 'Vere hoc existimandum, quia potest esse in alio aliquid occultum quo superior sit etiam si bonum nostrum que illo videmur superiores esse non sit occultum' (GO 4: 382).

355/3–356/5 *Worchepe þin fadir . . . Deutero. vi* [1]: For vi [1] read [5: 16]; the error here is Dives'. The passage referred to is: 'Honora patrem tuum et matrem sicut praecepit tibi Dominus Deus tuus ut longo vivas tempore et bene sit tibi in terra quam Dominus Deus tuus daturus est tibi'. The interlinear gloss on 'patrem' is 'carnalem vel spiritualem; ad litteram, vel deum et ecclesiam'; and the interlinear gloss on 'vivas' is: 'vita eterna pro qua laborandum est'. The marginal gloss spells out Pauper's comment (356/13–16) that this precept is the first of the second table and that, properly interpreted, includes the next six precepts (GO 1: 380). Cf. 304/17–18 above.

356/13 *Iob 10: 22*: 'Terram miseriae et tenebrarum ubi umbra mortis et nullus ordo, sed sempiternus horror inhabitat.' The gloss is an abbreviated version of St Gregory's explication of this text. The 'terram miseriae' is a foretaste of hell. The gloss on 'nullus ordo' says that, on the contrary, there is an order in this hell: God torments sinners according to the deserts of each individual. Both accounts conclude with a reference to Lazarus in the bosom of Abraham; the worst torment of all, say Gregory and the gloss, will be the sight of the suffering of those we loved in life (GO 2: 398; *Moralia*, 9.66.101–2; *CCL* cxliii, pp. 528–9/32–57; *PL* 75: 915).

357/10–40 *whan þei wiln rebellyn*: This vehement protest against social unrest may be an echo of the Peasants' Revolt of 1381. Other echoes may be found in the text: 2–57/83–8, 2–209/88–95, and 2–262/91 below. On the history of the Revolt, see *Knighton's Chronicle*, ed. Martin (1995), pp. 209–43; Thomas Walsingham, *Historia*, ed. Riley (1876), 1: 454–84; *The Westminster Chronicle*, ed. Hector and Harvey (1982), pp. 2–19; Oman (1906); R. B. Dobson (1970).

358/52–7 *Mayster of Kendis . . . crisolitus*: Trevisa's Bartholomaeus 16.28 says of the chrysolite: 'a litel stoon of Ethiopia, schynyng as gold and spranklyng [*sic*] as fyre, and is liche to þe see in colour and somdel grene' (*Properties*, 2: 840). One variety of chrysolite called the *crisolentus* changes colour: 'As þe day passeþ his colour wexeþ dym. And þis stoon takeþ most soone [fire]. And if it is yset by þe fire anon it wexeþ alie [*sic*], as Isider seiþ libro xv, *de gemmis aureis*' (2: 841); the reference is to Isidore of Seville's *Etym*, Bk. 16.15 (2: 16.15/21–5). Cf. Alexander Neckam, 'De Laudibus Divinæ Sapientiæ', in *De natura rerum*: 'Nomen chrysolito color aureus indidit, arcet/ Compescitque metus degeneremque fugam', ed. Wright, p. 467/179–80.

VOL. 1: 2, COMMANDMENT V, pp. 2–1–57

2–1/2 *pur charite*: See 52/35–6 above.

2–1/5 *Non occides* [*Ex. 20: 13*]: Expositions of the fifth Commandment normally comprise discussion of extended senses of 'kill' under the rubric

'killing in thought, word, and deed'. Thus the fifth Commandment forbids
hatred, slander and backbiting as well as murder; but the prohibition
against killing is relaxed to allow just wars, the judicial execution of the
guilty, and the slaughter of animals. Cf.Aquinas, *ST*, I–II.100.8, Reply to
Obj. 3 (OP edn., Rome, 2: 725). Like Aquinas, Wyclif says 'occides'
means 'inuiste occidere' and goes on to consider the implications of
'Omnis qui odit fratrem suum homicida est' (1 Io. 3: 15; *De mand*,
pp. 329–46; see below 2–1/9). *Jacob's Well* includes under the heading
'gostly mansleȝt' failure to rescue those in peril, withholding of wages,
withholding of alms, slander, flattery and hatred (Salisbury MS 174, fos.
194ʳ-195ʳ). On the numbering of the Commandments see 81/7 above.

2–1/9 [*1 Io. 3: 15*]: Augustine: 'You have killed the person you hate.
Amend your ways . . .' (Serm. 58.8, *PL* 38: 397). The GO: 'Qui ex odio
insequitur fratrum prouocat ad iram & discordiam & sic quantum ad se
occidit eum anima' (4: 538). To the objection that murder is worse than
hate, Wyclif replies that body and soul are a unity and whoever kills the
soul is guilty of a graver sin than one who kills the body. Clerics who fail
to preach the gospel are guilty of this sin (*De mand.*, pp. 334/25–8-335/
1–8).

2–1/19–21 *Ecclesiastici xxviii* [*22*]: Ecclus. 28: 22: 'Multi ceciderunt in ore
gladii, sed non sic quasi qui interierunt per linguam suam.' The GO
connects this passage with heretical teaching (2: 776).

2–1/21–2 *Prouer. xviii* [*21*]: 'Mors et vita in manu linguae; qui diligunt eam
comedent fructus eius.'

2–1/24–2/33 *Dauyd . . .* [*Ps. 56: 5*]. *. . . Sent Austyn*: Augustine interprets
Ps. 56: 5 as a prefiguration of the crucifixion: 'Noli adtendere inermes
manus sed os armatum; inde gladius processit quo Christus occideretur,
quomodo et de ore Christi, unde et Iudaei occiderentur. Habet enim ille
gladium bis acutum, et resurgens percussit eos, et diuisit ab eis quo faceret
fideles suos. Illi malum gladium, ille bonus: illi sagittas malas, ille bonas.
Nam habet et ipse sagittas bonas, uerba bona, unde sagittat cor fidele, ut
armetur. Ergo aliae istorum sagittae, et alius istorum gladius . . .' (*Enarr.*,
56.12; *CCL* xxxix, 702/28–33; *PL* 36: 669). See 208/12–17 above.

2–2/35–6 *De pen., di. i, Homicidiorum*: The canon 'Homicidiorum' rules that
homicide, detraction, and hatred are equivalent sins (C. 33 q.3 c.24;
Friedberg 1: 1164). The source is an epistle of Pope Clement I (c.91-c.101).

2–2/42–4 *Salomon . . . Ecclesiastes x* [*11*]: 'Si mordeat serpens in silentio
nihil eo minus habet qui occulte detrahit'. The GO connects this passage
with the obligation to confess one's sins (2: 705).

2–2/45–8 *Salomon . . . Sap. i* [*11*]: Wisd. 1: 11: 'Custodite ergo vos a
murmuratione quae nihil prodest, et a detractione parcite linguae, quoniam

responsum obscuram in vacuum non ibit, os autem quod mentitur occidit animam'. The GO refers to the OT story of the Egyptian midwives, Shiprah and Puah, who lied to save newborns; it points out that they were rewarded for their good deeds, not for their lies (2: 724), see 2–215/ 58–60 below.

2–3/10–13 *Dauyd* . . . [*Ps. 9B: 3*]: Augustine: 'Adulantium linguae alligant animas in peccatis. Delectat enim ea facere, in quibus non solum non metuitur reprehensor, sed etiam laudator auditur' (*Enarr.*, 9.21; *CCL* xxxviii, p. 68/4–7; *PL* 36: 126).

2–3/17–8 *Sent Powil* . . . [*Gal. 1: 10*]: 'Modo enim hominibus suadeo aut Deo? Aut quaero hominibus placere, si adhuc hominibus placerem, Christi servus non essem'.

2–3/26–31 *Dauyd* . . . [*Ps. 140: 5*] . . . *Sent Austyn*: Augustine's interlinear gloss: 'falsa laus adulatoris . . . non crescit caput meum de adulatione, non me delectat oleum peccatoris' (GO 2: 640). In his *Enarrationes*, 140.113, Augustine connects the 'oleum peccatoris' with the parable of the wise and foolish virgins (Matt. 25: 1–13; *CCL* xl, pp. 2035–6/20–9; *PL* 37: 1824). See 2–6/51–74 and 2–6/65–6 below. Augustine's 'þe swerd of þe enmy pursuynge' may refer back to the passage from the *Enarr.* on Ps. 56: 5 cited above, 2–1/24–2/33.

2–3/32–3 *Salomon* . . . *Ecclesiastes vii* [*6*]: 'Melius est a sapiente corripi quam stultorum adulatione decipi'. The GO: Better the wounds of a friend than the false kisses of an enemy (2: 702).

2–3/36 *tellere of schrifte*: The crime of betraying the confessional is not specified in the canon cited below, 2–3/36–7. See 250/18–251/58 above.

2–3/36–7 *Di. xlvi, Clericus* [*qui adulat.*]: The canon 'Clericus qui adulationibus' states simply that the cleric who is a flatterer ('adulator') or a traitor ('proditor') is to be deprived of his office (D.45 c.3; Friedberg 1: 168). The source is the fourth Council of Carthage (see *ODCC*, s.v. Carthage). The previous canon (c. 2, 'Sunt nonnulli') quotes the passage in St Gregory's *Moralia* cited below, 2–4/38–50.

2–4/38–50 *Ve qui* . . . *Ezechielis xiii* [*18–19*]: The interlinear gloss explains the small, soft pillows as a metaphor for 'suauem adulationem' and refers to Epicurus, 'quorum vox est, Manducemus et bibamus' (GO 3: 246). Gregory's *Moralia*, 18.4.8, cites Ezek. 13: 18 in connection with Job 27: 5: 'Ad hoc quippe puluillus ponitur, ut molliter quiescatur. Quisquis ergo male agentibus adulatur, puluillum sub capite uel cubito iacentis ponit, ut qui corripi ex culpa debuerat, in ea fultus laudibus molliter quiescat' (*CCL* cxliiiA, p. 890/10–13; *PL* 76: 42). See 2–3/36–7 above and 2–4/11–5/19 below.

2–4/1–10 *flaterye . . . Ysa. iii* [*12*]: The chapter opens with a general complaint about the state of England, whose rulers 'flatter' the people, telling them they are blessed and well off when they are not. The modern word has tended to lose the Middle English sense of general, especially political, dishonesty; cf. *MED* s.v. 'flateren' (b). The writer of *D&P* here as elsewhere shores up his complaints with biblical citations, either to emphasise or conceal his true beliefs on sensitive issues. Cf. 2–209/97 below.

2–4/11–5/19 *þo pilwys . . . Sent Gregory . . . Iob xxvii* [*5*]: For 'þo pilwys' (Ezek. 13: 18), see 2–4/38–50 above, where Gregory's *Moralia* 18.4 (*CCL* cxliiiA, p. 890; *PL* 76: 41) on Job 27: 5 is also cited.

2–5/19–22 *Salomon . . . Prouer. xvii* [*15*]: 'et qui iustificat impium et qui condemnat iustum abominabilis est uterque apud Dominum'.

2–5/22–7 *þerfor God lykenyth flatereris . . . Ezechielis xiii* [*10*]: 'Eo quod deceperint populum meum dicentes pax, et non est pax, et ipse aedificabat parietem, illi autem liniebant eum luto absque paleis'.

2–5/27–36 *flatereris . . . neddere . . . Maystir of Kende, libro xviii*: Trevisa's translation of Bartholomaeus 18.37 says of the 'dipsa': 'And suche addres beþ so litel and smale þat vnneþe þey beþ yseye whanne me[n?] tredeþ þeron. The venyme of hem sleeþ ar it be feled so þat vneþe he feeleþ sore þat schal deye' (*Properties*, 2: 1184/9–12). His source is Isidore of Seville, who says: 'Dipsas, genus aspidis, qui Latine situla dicitur, quia quem momorderit siti perit' (*Etym.* 12.4.13). Bartholomaeus 18.9 refers to the 'tyrus' under the heading of serpents ('De angue'), citing Aristotle on how the 'tyrus' manages to swallow (*Properties*, 2: 1133/13–18). The connection between serpents and flattery is not made in either text.

2–6/42–5 *Sent Iamys . . . Iacob. iii* [*5*]: Jas. 3: 5: 'Ita et lingua modicum quidem membrum est, et magna exaltat; ecce quantus ignis quam magnam silvam incendit'. LL4: '[O]ure tunge is but a lytyl party of þe body & it defylyth al þe body whanne it is flammyd with þe fyr of helle' (fo. 63ʳᵇ). Cf. 2–1/21–2 above.

2–6/45–8 *Dauyd . . . Ps. 139: 4*: Augustine draws a parallel with 'serpentes': 'In serpente maxime adstutia est et dolus nocendi; propterea etiam serpit. Non enim uel pedes habet, ut eius uestigia cum uenit audiantur. In eius itinere uelut lenis et tractus, sed non est rectus. Ita ergo repunt et serpunt ad nocendum, habentes occultum uenenum et sub leni contactu' (*Enarr.*, 139.6; *CCL* xl, p. 2015/2–7; *PL* 37: 1806).

2–6/51–74 *as þe gospel seith . . . þe fyue maydenys folys*: Matt. 25: 1–13, the parable of the Wise and Foolish Maidens: 'Tunc simile erit regnum caelorum decem virginibus quae accipientes lampades suas exierunt obviam sponso et sponsae . . .'. The figurative meaning of the oil, or

the lack of oil, in the lamps of the maidens is somewhat elusive here, and
it is necessary to distinguish between the 'lamps' and the 'oil'. The 'lamps'
are good deeds performed solely for 'preysynge & flatrye of þe peple'; the
'oil' is delight in good deeds, 'gostly merþe & ioye in conscience'. In the
Longleat sermons, the 'oil' is unequivocally delight in good works: '[þ]ey
[the foolish maidens] haddyn non oylee in here lampys, þat is to seye þey
haddyn non charite in here hertis & in here conscyencys. But þe fyue
wyse maydenys haddyn olee in here lampys & þerfore þey wern receyuyd
onon into heuene blysse' (LL4, fo. 81rb). This is also the view of Nicolaus
de Lyra, who says that the oil represents 'spirituale gaudium, quod oritur
ex operibus bonis factis propter deum' (*Postilla* 4). In his history of the
interpretations of the parable, from Origen to Ludolph of Saxony,
S. Wailes (1987) sees as unresolved two main lines of interpretation, the
first linking 'oil' with good works and the second linking 'oil' with the
love of God and neighbor that should accompany good works (p. 177–84).
See 2–6/65–6 below.

2–6/65–6 *Sent Austyn . . . sermon*: Augustine's Sermon 93.10 seems to be
responsible for some of the ambiguity in what *D&P* says about the oil in the
lamps of the wise and foolish maidens. The lamps of the wise maidens 'were
burning from the oil inside them, from the assurance of their consciences,
from their inner boast, from their deepest charity. But those of the foolish
ones were also burning. . . .[b]ecause there was no dearth of admiration from
other people'. The foolish maidens beg for oil from the wise maidens
because, for them, it represents the flattery they crave, 'other people's
admiration'. Hence, as *D&P* somewhat confusingly says here, the 'oil'
represents a positive value when in the lamps of the wise maidens and a
negative value when in the lamps of the foolish maidens, thus *both* 'gostly
preysing' *and* 'wordely preysynge' (tr. E. Hill (1991), 3: 473; *PL* 38: 578).
See above 2–6/51–74.

2–7/75–6 *Dauyd . . . [Ps. 52: 6]*: Augustine: 'filius hominum, non filiis Dei
maluit displicere. Inde disipata sunt ossa eorum, illius ossa nemo confregit'
(*Enarr.*, 52.9; *CCL* xxxix, p. 644/34–6; *PL* 36: 618).

2–7/80–4 *Salomon . . . [Eccli. 28: 15] . . . mustrere*: Ecclus. 28: 15–16:
'Susurro et bilinguis maledictus, multos enim turbavit pacem habentes. /
Lingua tertia multos commovit et dispersit illos a gente in gentem'. On
'lingua tertia' the gloss: 'Haeretica doctrina quam nec veteri nec nouo
testamento concordent & auditorum corda conturbat & de gentem per gens
seditionem excitat' (GO 2: 776). Referred to again below 2–8/33–4, 2–9/
68–9.

2–7/1 *mustrere*: Pauper uses the word 'rounere' as a gloss for the rare word
'mustrere' (note the gloss in MS H, 7/81n above). See *Prompt. Parv.* (ed.
Mayhew, EETS, es 102) svv. 'musteryn' and 'rownyn'; the word 'mustrere'

is not attested for the fourteenth century, but the word 'rounere' appears in *PP*, B-Text, 4/13; and in *CT*, FrT, p. 126/1550.

2–7/6–7 *Romanos i [29–30]*: Rom. 1: 29–30: '. . . repletos omni iniquitate, malitia, fornicatione, avaritia, nequitia, plenos invidia, homicidio, contentione, dolo, malignitate, sussurones,/ detractores. Deo odibiles, contumeliosos, superbos, elatos, inventores malorum, parentibus non oboedientes'. The gloss on 'Deo odibiles': 'Ne leuis putetur susurratio vel detractio quia in verbis sunt addit de eis deo odibiles vt intelligant se per solam susurrationem & detractionem aeternam incurrere posse damnatorum' (GO 4: 277).

2–7/9–11 *Salomon . . . Prouer. vi [19]*: 'Proferentem mendacia testem fallacem et eum qui seminat inter fratres discordias'. The gloss cites Donatus (fourth-century schismatic) and Arius (fourth-century heresiarch) as examples of those who sow discord among brothers (GO 2: 662). Cited below 2–237/47–8.

2–7/11–14 *Salomon . . . Ecclesiastici xxi [30–1]*: Ecclus. 21: 30–1: 'Dum maledicit impius diabolum, maledicit ipse animam suam. / Susurro coinquinabit animam suam et in omnibus odietur, et qui manserit odiosus erit; tacitus et sensatus honorabitur'.

2–7/14–8/18 *Leuitici xix [16]*: 'Non eris criminator nec susurro in populo, non stabis contra sanguinem proximi tui; ego Dominus'. Nicolaus de Lyra appends a note to his postil on Lev. 19 stressing that the Commandments were first promulgated in Exodus as laws about actions, but in Leviticus were reinterpreted as based on the command to love one's neighbor as oneself: 'Diliges proximum tuum sicut teipsum'. Thus the fifth Commandment is rightly interpreted as forbidding a hate-filled attitude (*Postilla* 1).

2–8/22–5 *Salomon . . . Prouer. xxvi [20]*: 'Cum defecerint ligna extinguetur ignis et susurrone subtracto iurgia conquiescent'.

2–8/31–2 *Of swiche God . . . Prouer. viii [13]*: 'Timor Domini odit malum arrogantiam et superbiam et viam pravam, et os bilingue detestor'. On 'arrogantiam' the gloss says: 'Arrogantiam et superbiam in eis qui ceteris se meliores existimant. Viam pravam in eis qui aperte male faciunt, os bilingue in eis qui in bonis quae loquuntur stabile quippiam non habent. Sed iuxta auditorum libitum sua verba commutant' (GO 2: 664).

2–8/33–4 *Salomon þe þredde tunge*: Ecclus. 28: 16; 19: 'Lingua tertia multos commovit . . . lingua tertia mulieres viritas [*sic*] eiecit et privavit illas laboribus suis'. Nicolaus de Lyra's postil: 'Lingua ter, qui seminat discordias, est enim tertia seu media inter linguas illorum quos discordat' (*Postilla* 3). Cf. 2–7/81 above; cited below, 2–9/68–9.

2–9/49 *Seneca*: The saying can be found in one of the prose versions of the
Secreta Secretorum, but without the attribution to Seneca: '[T]how shalte
Preyse *and com*mende scarsly *and* seldewannes, but thou shalte blame more
scarsly, more a-vysely, and more selde' (ed. Steele and Henderson, EETS
es, 74), p. 157/18–20. John Alford (1992) says the saying, doubtfully
attributed to Seneca, is cited as Senecan by Hugh of St Cher, Alan of
Lille, and Vincent of Beauvais. He cites *D&P* as an additional vernacular
source; cf. *PP*, B-Text, XI/107: '*Parum lauda; vitupera parcius*' (1992),
pp. 72–3.

2–9/68–9 *Salomon . . . Ecclesiastici xxviii [19–20]*: See 2–7/80–4, 2–8/33–4
above.

2–10/4–18 *ferde booc of Kyngis . . . Ieremye*: The story of Zedikiah
('Sedechye'), 597–586 BC, the last king of Judah, is found in 1 Kgs.
22: 11; 24, 2 Kgs. 24: 18–25: 7; 2 Chron. 36: 11–14; Jer. 21: 1–7; 24: 1–10;
32: 1–5; 34: 1–3; 37: 6–10. LL4 refers to Zedikiah as a type of the Devil: 'þe
fend is lykenyd to a fals prophete whos name was sedechye whyche made
hym two hornys of yryn in tokene of gret strencthe . . .' (fo. 80ᵛᵃ).

2–11/25–30 *þe grete synne*: In identifying the 'great sin' several possibilities
present themselves. One is the deposition of King Richard II in 1399, an
event of which it might have been dangerous, even as late as *c.*1405, to
express a criticism. A more likely possibility is the sin of sodomy. This sin is
commonly alluded to as the sin the speaker or writer cannot name or
describe. In the fourteenth-century translation of the *Somme le roi*: 'þe last
[sin of lechery] is so foule and so hidous þat [it] scholde not be nempned,
þat is synne aȝens kynde. . . . þis synne is so myslykyng to God, þat he
made reyne fier and stynkynge brymston vpon þe citees of Sodom and
Gomorre', *Book of Vices and Virtues*, ed. Francis (EETS, 217), p. 46/4–16.
Mirk's *Instructions*: '. . . of synne aȝenes kynde/ Thow schalt thy paresch no
þynge teche,/ Ny of that synne ne thynge preche' (ed. Peacock, EETS, os
31, p. 7/223–5). The author of the *Fasciculus morum* says: 'I leave others to
describe it' (ed. Wenzel, pp. 686–9). See 2–63/51, 2–64/68–9, and 2–96/
19–20 below.

2–11/30–1 *þe predde book of Kyngys*: 1 Kgs. 16/29–34; 17/1–24; 18/1–46;
19/1–21; 20/13–43; 21/1–29; 22/1–54. King 'Acab' (VL 'Achab', KJV
Ahab') ruled Israel from *c.*873–851 BC; though a powerful and successful
king, he was given a negative portrait by the Deuteronomic historians who
dealt with his reign. Nicolaus de Lyra's postil refers to Ahab's introduction
of 'open idolatry' and to his marriage to Jezebel, 'que erat nutrita in
ydolatria' (*Postilla* 1). In *D&P*, the emphasis is on his priestly advisers,
especially 'Mychee' (VL 'Michaeas', KJV 'Micah'), as 'false, flatrynge
prophetis'. Referred to above 153/18, 155/71 and below 2–14/22–3.

2–12/63–5 *Dauid . . . in his book*: Ps. 51: 6: 'Dilexisti omnia verba praecipitationis linguam dolosam'; Ps. 108: 2: 'Deus laudabilis mihi ne taceas quia os impii et os dolosi contra me apertum est'; Ps. 119: 2–3: 'Domine, libera animam mean a labiis iniquis, a lingua dolosa./Quid detur tibi et quid adponatur tibi ad linguam dolosam?' Augustine: 'Quid est lingua dolosa? Ministra fallaciae est lingua dolosa, aliud in corde gestantium, aliud in ore promentium. Sed in his subuersio, in his submersio' (*Enarr.*, 51.11; *CCL* xxxix, p. 631/8–10; *PL* 36: 607; cf. idem, 108.2; *CCL* xl, pp. 1585–6/ 1 ff.; *PL* 37: 1452; idem, 119.4: 'Quae est lingua dolosa? Subdola, habens imaginem consulendi, et perniciem nocendi . . .', p. 1780/3–13; *PL* 37: 1599–1500).

2–12/70–1 *þe deuelys hooc. . . . Adam & Eue*: An early theory of the Redemption was that the Devil had to be lured into shedding the blood of Christ so that the price of man's redemption could thus be paid and mankind set free. This was expressed metaphorically as angling, with Christ on the cross as the baited hook—prefigured by Job 41: 1, 'Canst thou draw out Leviathan with a hook?' St Gregory: 'In hamo igitur captus est [i.e., the Devil], quia inde interiit unde deuorauit. Et quidem Behemoth iste Filium Dei incarnatum nouerat, sed redemptionis nostrae ordinem nesciebat' (*Moralia* 33.14, *CCL* clxxxB, p. 1685/28–31; *PL* 76: 680). The *Legenda aurea*: 'Christ had hidden the hook of his godhead under the bait of his humanity, and the Devil, wanting to swallow the bait of his flesh, was caught by the hook of his divinity' (*GL*, 1: 210; Graesse, No. 53). Cf. *PP*: 'So shal grace that bigan al make a good ende/ And bigile þe gilour, and þat is good sleighte' (B-Text, XVIII/158–62).

2–12/76–7 *secunde book of Kyngis xx [8–9]*: 2 Sam. 20: 8–9 recounts the killing of Amasa (captain of Absalom's army) by Joab. Earlier, against King David's command, Joab had killed Absalom (2 Sam 18: 10). After David's death, Joab was executed by Solomon.

2–12/82–4 *Judas trayhyd Crist*: Matt. 26: 49. On Judas, 193/2–19 above.

2–13/10 *Exodi xxii [18]*: Cited above 254/70–1, and below 2–144/113–4.

2–13/12 *Exodi xxiii [7]*: The Latin text is: 'insontem et iustum non occides'; 'innocentem' may have been borrowed from Dan. 13: 53: 'Innocentem et iustum non interfices', cited above (in Com. II, cap. iii) 225/46–7.

2–13/19 *ad Romanos xiii [4]*: Rom. 13: 4: 'Dei enim minister est tibi in bonum, si autem malum feceris, time; non enim sine causa gladium portat, Dei enim minister est, vindex in iram ei qui malum agit'. See 334/60–335/ 82 above. Cited 2–33/65 below.

2–14/5–6 *Pasce fame morientem . . . Di. lxxxvi*: The canon 'Pasce fame morientem' warns that failure to feed the starving is equivalent to murder (D. 86 c. 21; Friedberg 1: 302). The canon is attributed to Ambrose, *De officiis*, but (according to editor's note) is not found there. Cited below, 2–291/52.

2–14/14 *Ps. 13: 4*: Cited above 331/27–8.

2–14/21 *He þese*: See 61/3–4, 158/39 above.

2–14/22–3 *Michee iii [1–3]*: Mic. 3: 1–3 carries out the theme of Ps. 13: 4 cited above, 2–14/14. Wicked rulers, says the prophet, are equivalent to cannibals: 'Et dixi, Audite principes Iacob et duces domus Israhel [lordis & lederis of þe peple], numquid non vestrum est scire iudicium? [to demyn what is good & what is wyckyd, what is trewe & what is fals],/ qui odio habetis bonum et diligitis malum [& loþin goodnesse & louyn schrewyd-nesse], qui violenter tollitis pelles eorum desuper eos et carnem eorum desuper ossibus eorum,/ qui comederunt carnem populi mei et pellem eorum desuper excoriaverunt, et ossa eorum confregerunt'. Explanatory phrases added by the author of *D&P* are in brackets. GO (interlinear): 'Qui annunciaui deum qua si regem et dominum ante suos processurum, adnuncio etiam malos propter crudelitatem suam non exauditurum' (3: 406). On Micah, *ABD* 4: 807–10. See 2–11/30–1 above.

2–15/44–60 *3 Reg. 21. . . . IV Regum x [7, and 4 Reg. 9: 24; 33–7]*: The GO gives the story of Naboth's vineyard a Christological interpretation: Ahab, one of the ancestors of Christ, by acquiring the vineyard symbolizes Christ, the true vine ('ubi vinum spirituale germinare debuit'). Naboth's reluctance to sell prefigures Christ's resistance to the Pharisees. Jezebel's death prefigures the death of the synagogue (2: 138). The story of Naboth's vineyard (3 Kgs. 21) is repeated below, 2–255/1–256/34.

2–16/2–8 *Ecclesiastici xxxiv [27]*: Ecclus. 34: 26–7: 'Qui aufert in sudore panem quasi qui occidit proximum suum./Qui effundit sanguinem et qui fraudem facit mercedem mercenario'. *D&P* translates an alternate text for 'mercenario': 'fratres sunt' (Vulgate; 2: 1072, 27n). The GO: 'In sudore vultus sui pauper acquirit panem. Qui hunc violenter tollit quasi interficit' (2: 279–80).

2–16/12 *Iac. v [4]*: Jas. 5: 4: GO (interlinear): 'Ecce merces operariorum qui messuerunt regiones vestras qui fraudatus est a vobis clamat, et clamor ipsorum in aures Domini Sabaoth introiit' (4: 518). LL4: 'for þe hyre of ȝoure werkman þat han repin ȝoure feldys in þe countre whyche is fraudyd & with heldyn be ȝow cryyth to god, & þe cris of hem is entrid into þe eris of þe lord of hostis' (fo. 81vb).

2–16/12–15 *Salomon . . . Ecclesiastici xxxiv [25]*: Ecclus. 34: 24–25: 'Qui offert sacrificium ex substantia pauperum, quasi qui victimat filium in conspectu patris sui./Panis egentium vita pauperis est; qui defraudat illum homo sanguinis'.

2–16/17–22 *typis . . . xvi, q. i, Decime, et Quoniam quicquid*: See 317/6 above.

2–16/27 *Io. 21: 15–17*: Exegesis of this passage usually deals with the triple injunction to feed (which cancels Peter's triple denial of Christ) and with the essence of Christian charity as service to others. The point made in *D&P*, however, is the difference between lambs and sheep: the lambs are the poor, the sheep the rich. In the *CA*, only Theophylact (eleventh century) comments on this difference: 'Agni sunt qui introducuntur, oves vero perfecti' (2: 590; *PG* 124: 311). Nicolaus de Lyra makes a similar distinction: 'Dicit ei pasce oues meas ante bis dixerat, Pasce agnos meos, quia infidelibus tres sunt gradus, scilicet, incipientium, proficientium, et perfectorum, illi qui sunt in duobis primus gradibus dicuntur agni, et illi qui sunt in tertio oues nominantur' (*Postilla* 4). Augustine does not make the distinction (*In Ioh.* 123.4: CCL xxxvi, pp. 677–8; *PL* 35: 1966–8]).

2–17/42–57 *Ezechiel . . . xxxiv [3–8]*: For [3–8] read [2–6]. To the translation of the biblical text *D&P* adds the phrases: 'þat is to seye, to þe prelatis & curatis of holy chirche, whyche schuldyn ben schepperdis of Goddis schep & of þo soulys þat he bou3te so dere. Wo be to þese chepherdis'; '& of þe pore peple 3euyn þei no tale'; 'withoutyn pyte 3e comandedyn to hem many grete þingis & greuous & regnedyn amongis hem'; 'þat 3euyt ony tale of hem'. Nicolaus de Lyra's postil likewise interprets the passage as aimed against unworthy pastors of the Church: 'Gregem autem meum non pascebatis exemplo bone vite et verbo sane doctrine' (*Postilla* 2). The GO, after citing the historical addressees of Ezechial's words, lists: 'episcopos, presbiteras, dyaconos' (3: 285). Jerome, 'Commentariorum in Ezech.' 11.34 (*PL* 25: 341–8; ref. to 'supercilium episcoparum' is in col. 345).

2–18/59–60 *Ieremie xxiii [1]*: See 331/38–40 above. Note that *D&P* (all manuscripts) here adds an explanatory '& of my pasture' to 'Iesue'.

2–18/66 *Ysa. i [15]*: 'Et cum extenderitis manus vestras, avertam oculos meos a vobis; et cum multiplicaveritis orationem, non audiam, manus enim vestrae sanguine plenae sunt'. LL4: 'And god seyth to swyche cruel folk when 3e schul leftyn up 3oure hondys to me I schal turnyn myn eyyn from 3ou and when 3e schul multyplyyn preyerys to me I schal nou3t heryn 3ou for 3oure hondys ben ful of blood' (fo. 36rb). Cited above 276/41, 283/12.

2–18/67 *Grosthed, Dicto. xiii*: Grosseteste's *Dicta* comprise 147 short lectures and sermons 'collected and arranged by Grosseteste himself from sermons and lectures of his earlier years in Oxford (and perhaps Paris)' (S. H. Thomson (1940), p. 214). Some of the *Dicta* were printed by E. Brown in *Fasciculus rerum* (1690; repr. 1967), but not *Dictum* 13, which can be found in manuscripts that contain the entire collection. The manuscripts compared for the Explanatory Notes are Bodley 830 and 798, and Laud misc. 374. The *incipit* of *Dictum* 13 in Bodley 830, fo. 16^v is: 'Manus vestre pollute sunt sanguine & digiti vestri pleni iniquitate, Isaye 59 . . .'; the *explicit*: '. . . & in sanguinem pauperum iacet suorum fundamenta domorum & edificorum'; *D&P* provides a fairly close translation. *Jacob's Well* cites *Dictum* 13 more briefly (Salisbury MS 174, fo. 194^r).

2–18/67–19/85 *An vniust schader.* . . . *pore men*: A very similar passage appears in 'Pore Caitif': 'An vniust scheder out of mannes blood : is seid to haue blody hondis / ffor blood sched out is in þe hondis of þe scheder out : as effect þat her werkis in þe cause / ffor þe hond of þe scheder is cause of blood sched so siþen bodily fode is cause of blood of mannes body . bi whiche þis transitorie lif is sustened . he þat wiþdraweþ sustenance fro a make pore man in myscheef : wiþdrawiþ fro þe same pore man his blood in þe sustenyng of his lif / þerfor þe blood of pore men is preued to be in þe hondis of þo men : in whos hondis þo þinges ben wiþholden vniustly bi whiche oþer bi þe priis of whiche þinges : nedy men ouȝten to be norischid / And he þat weldiþ bi violence eþer bi þeefte eþer bi any fraude eþer disseit þat þing wherby pore men ouȝten to be sustened haþ hondis defoulid wiþ blood of pore men / And he þat etiþ & drynkiþ of siche possession & cloþiþ himsilf and bildeþ housis & wallis of sich possession : etiþ & drynkiþ þe blood of pore men & is cloþid in þe blood of pore men . and makiþ þe foundement of his bilding in þe blood of pore men' (MS Bodley 938, fos. 136^v-137^r; also found in MS Bodley 3, fo. 51^{r-v}). On 'Pore Caitif', 227/1 above.

2–19/3–6 *Sent Gregory*: The passage referred to is probably one attributed to Gregory in the *CA* under the heading of Mark 9: 41: 'Qui ergo ad sanctitatis speciem deductus, vel verbo ceteros destruit, vel exemplo, melius profecto erat ut hunc ad mortem sub exteriore habitu terrena acta constringerent quam sacra officis in culpa ceteris imitabilem demonstrarent, quia nimirum si solus caderet, utcumque hunc tolerabilior inferni poena cruciaret' (1: 503; the passage is, however, not found in Gregory's 'Regulae Pastoralis'). See 2–19/9 below.

2–19/9 *Mc. 9: 41*: Mark 9: 41: 'Et quisquis scandalizaverit unum ex his pusillis credentibus in me bonum est ei magis si circumdaretur mola asinaria collo eius et in mare mitteretur'. The commentary on Mark 9: 41 in the *CA* does not apply it specifically to 'men of holy chirche' (1: 503–4). In the gloss, Bede says that in a conflict between scandal and truth, scandal must be accepted (GO 4: 114).

2–19/15 *ad Romanos xiv* [*13*]: The gloss: 'Non autem dico offendiculum vel scandalum, eo quod cibus sit immundus, quia scio per hoc quod fiducia est in hiesu, qui postquam venit absolvit a lege. Commune ponit per immundo, tractum a vasis quae ante omnibus vsibus erant communia post sacrificijs dedicata, iam non communia, sed sancta dicebantur, vel ipsi iudaei dicebantur proprie prius populus dei, alii vero omnes communes & immundi' (GO 4: 303).

2–19/15–23 *And perfor þe lawe . . . x, q. iii, Cauendum*: The canon
'Cauendum' directs that bishops, in their visitations, shall not levy excessive
costs upon their parishioners (C.10 q.3 c.7; Friedberg 1: 624–5). It was
promulgated in 813 (canon 14, Mansi: 14: 96). J. R. H. Moorman (1955)
describes a bishop's entourage: '. . . the legal officers, the penitentiaries,
apparitors, proctor, advocates, attorneys and sequestrators, each with his
clerk or secretary. . . . chaplains and clerks of the chapel. . . . accountants
and auditors, stewards and bailiffs, foresters, fowlers, parkkeepers and
huntsmen. . . . squires, valets, servants and pages' and sometimes 'a
personal bodyguard of soldiers' (pp. 175–9).

2–19/27–20/29 *Sent Ierom . . . I, q. i, Hii quoscumque*: The canon 'Hii
quoscumque', is summed up in Gratian's *post dict.*: those who are pre-
eminent in dignity ought to be pre-eminent in holiness (C.1 q.1 c.44;
Friedberg 1: 375–6). The source is St Jerome's 'Commentariorum in
Michaeam', *PL* 25: 1207–90, referred to below, 2–181/21–5.

2–20/30 *ad Romanos xiv [21] et [I] ad Corinth viii [9–13]*:: Rom. 14: 221:
'Bonum est non manducare carnem et non bibere vinum, neque in quo
frater tuus offenditur aut scandalizatur aut infirmatur'. On 'offenditur', the
GO: 'Perturbatus nesciens quid teneat . . . qui a fide recta discedit' (4: 203).
1 Cor. 8: 9–13: 'Quapropter si esca scandalizat fratrem meum, non
manducabo carnem in aeternum, ne fratrem meum scandalizem'. For the
translation of Latin 'scandalizo, -are' as 'slaundryn', see *Prompt. Parv.* (ed.
Mayhew, EETS, es 102), which, s.v. 'slawnderyn', gives Lat. 'scandalizo'.

2–20/31–9 *Osee v [I]*: Hos. 5: 1–: '. . . quoniam laqueus facti estis
speculationi et rete expansum super Thabor,/ et victimas declinastis in
profundum'. The sense is that men of Holy Church, who should be
watchtowers against sin, have themselves become causes of sin. As *Jacob's
Well*, citing the same passage, puts it: '. . . ȝe þat owyn to be *ware lokerys* to
werke wel & to ȝeuyn oþere good exaumple to werke weel beeth made a
gryn [*sic*] & a nett in holy cherche. (MS Salisbury 174, fo. 194ʳ; ital. add.).
Augustine uses 'speculatores' to refer to bishops: 'Ad hoc enim speculatores,
hoc est populorum praepositi, constituti sunt in ecclesiis, ut non parcant
obiurgando peccata' (*De civ. dei*, I.9; *CCL* xlvii, p.10/79–81; *PL* 41: 23).
The RSV translates 'ye have been a snare on Mizpah', see *ABD* 4: 879–81.
'Pore Caitif' seems to have drawn on the *D&P* translation of Hos. 5: 1: cf.
MS Bodley 3, fo. 52ʳ; MS Bodley 938, fo. 137ʳ⁻ᵛ; see 227/1 above. Cited
below 2–81/20.

2–20/44–5 *þe prophete . . . Rom. I: 17*: Rom. 1: 17 cites Hab. 2: 4: 'Ecce qui
incredulus est, non erit recta anima eius in semet ipso; iustus autem in fide
sua vivet'. Rom. 1: 17 has 'ex' for 'in', and the GO, for both texts, points out
a difference between the Hebrew and Greek texts, saying that 'apostolus
[Paul] vtitur his testimoniis quae a gamaliele doctore legis didicerat' (3: 420–

1; 4: 275). The *ABD*: 'In the NT, Hab. 2: 4 serves as the major textual basis for the doctrine of "justification by faith" in Rom. 1: 17 . . .' (3: 1–6). LL4 cites Rom. 1: 17: 'þe ry3tful man lyuyth be feyth' (fo. 59ʳᵃ).

2–20/47 *Iac. 2: 17*: Jas. 2: 17: 'Sic et fides si non habeat opera, mortua est in semet ipsam'. LL4: 'Feyth withouten dedys of charite ys a ded feyth' (fo. 58ʳᵃ); also cited and tr. in fos. 81ʳᵇ and 115ʳᵃ. GO: 'Sicut sola verba pietatis nudum vel esurientem non recreat, si non & cibus praebeatur & vestis, ita fides verbotenus seruata non saluat' (4: 515). Here Pauper expresses his tolerant 'Do your best' philosophy, cf. Introduction, p. liii.

2–21/4–5 *Crist seith . . . a manqweller*: John 8: 44: 'Ille homicida erat ab initio'; cited six times in *D&P* and four times in LL4, but usually only in part. See 154/39–43 above.

2–21/17–19 *Crist seith . . . Mt. 4: 4*: GO: 'Persuasio tua tentatio est quia agis de cibo corporis & non de cibo mentis. Inferior pars hominis pane sustentatur, alia verbo dei reficitur, quia vero agis de inferiori, patet quod tentator sis' (4: 14). Cf. LL4: 'Man & womman lyuyth nout only in bodyly bred but he lyuyth in euery word þat comyth out of goddys mouth' (fo. 69ʳᵃ). See ref. to St Martin in 51/1–2 above.

2–22/24 *Ieremie xv [19]*: The GO cites St Gregory: 'Vilis quippe est deo praesens mundus, preciosa est ei munda anima [anima humana]. Qui ergo preciosum a vili separat, quasi os domini vocatur, quia per eum dominus verba sua exserit, qui ab amore praesentis seculi loquendo quae potest, humanam animam euellit' (3: 126; *Moralia*, 18.38.59; *CCL* cxliiiA, p. 925/20–5; *PL* 76: 71). Cf. LL4 '3if þu departe precious þyng from þyng of no value, þat is to seye vertue from vycys, chesynge vertu & forsakynge vicis, þu schal ben as my mouth' (fo. 33ᵛᵃ).

2–22/32–4 *Dauyd . . . [Ps. 106: 20]*: Augustine, on 'delyueryd hem': 'Vnde? Non de errore, non de fame, non de difficultate uincendi peccata, sed *de corruptela eorum*' (*Enarr.*, 106.11; *CCL* xl, p. 1577/19–21; *PL* 37: 1425). LL4: 'God sente his word & made hem hool & delyueryd hem from here deyyngis' (fo. 137ᵛᵃ).

2–22/38 *[Io. 8: 51]*: John 8: 51: 'Si quis sermonem meum servaverit, mortem non videbit in aeternum'. Augustine comments on the kind of 'death' spoken of here: 'aliam mortem . . . mortem secundam, mortem aeternam, mortem gehennarum, mortem damnationis cum diabolo et angelis' (*In Ioh.*, 43.11; *CCL* xxxvi, p. 377/6–8; *PL* 35: 1710).

2–22/39–47 *alle þo þat lettyn Godis word*: An indirect reference—presumably after 1407—to the efforts of Archbishop Arundel to control unlicensed preaching; see above 148/44, 327/4.

2–23/54 *I, q. i, Interrogo vos*: The canon 'Interrogo vos' enjoins that Christ's word and Christ's body in the eucharist are to be given equal reverence:

'Non sit minus verbum Dei quam corpus Christi'. The source is a sermon of Ps.-Augustine, *PL* 39: 2319 (C.1 q.1 c.94; Friedberg 1: 391–2).

2–23/56–7 *And rather a man schulde forberyn his messe þan his sermon*: The evidence from late medieval England suggests that much routine preaching was greeted with inattention or rudeness but that excellent content and delivery immediately attracted an enthusiastic following, see *Margery Kempe*, ed. Meech and Allen (EETS, 212), pp. 98, 166, 185, and *passim;*. Owst (1926), pp. 144–94; Spencer (1993), pp. 78–133; Duffy (1992), pp. 57–8. See 54/46–52, 189/32–45, and 290/7 above.

2–23/71–24/73 *Dauid . . . Ps. 106: 18*: LL4: 'Here soule hath loþid al maner mete & fedinge of goddys word' (fo. 69ᵗᵃ). Augustine: 'Vt quod te delectat uerbum Dei, non tibi tribuas, neque hinc aliqua infleris arrogantia, et auidus cibi, in eos qui fastidio periclitantur superbe insilias. Intellege etiam tibi praestitum esse hoc, non a te tibi esse. Quid enim habes quod non accepisti?' (*Enarr.*, 106.11; *CCL* xl, p. 1576/8–12; *PL* 37: 1425).

2–24/3 *Di. xliii, Ephesiis [c.4]*: The canon 'Ephesiis' holds that those clerics who fail to preach the word of God incur blood guilt (D.43 c.4l; Friedberg 1: 156). The source is an epistle of St Gregory, who cites Acts 20: 26–7, where Paul says, 'I testify to you this day that I am innocent of the blood of all of you/ for I did not shrink from declaring to you the whole counsel of God [RSV]': Ep. 34, to a Syracusan monk, *PL* 77: 48 7.

2–24/3–12 *Ezechielis iii [17–18]*: Ezec. 3: 17: 'Fili hominis, speculatorem dedi te domni Israel . . .': *D&P* here translates 'speculatorem' as 'daye-wayte'; the Wycliffite bible (EV) translates: 'a biholder, *or a spier*' (3: 506ᵃ). The word (as at 2–20/31–9 above) refers to the cleric, who is obligated to preach God's word; cf. the gloss: 'Predicatorem speculatorem vocat' (GO, 3: 230). Cited again below 2–134/18–27. See Glossary.

2–24/14 *xi, q. ii, Qui Cristi, et Qui abstulerit*: Two canons: both state that thieves who despoil the Church are murderers. The first, 'Qui Cristi' (c. 1), is from an epistle of Stephan I (d. 257). His two surviving letters are in *PL* 3: 1033–44. The second canon, 'Qui abstulerit' (c. 6) is attributed to Anacletus, a first-century bishop of Rome, none of whose writings survive (C.12 q.2 cc. 1, 6; Friedberg 1: 687–8).

2–24/20–5 *Example of þe þef*: Luke 23: 42–3.

2–25/26 *xxvi, q. vi, Si presbiter, et c. Agnouimus*: Two canons: both state that denial of absolution to a dying person is equivalent to murder. The first, 'Presbiter' (c. 12), is attributed to Pope Julius (d. 352), and the second (c. 13) to Pope Celestine I (d. 432) (C.26 q.6 cc.12, 13; Friedberg 1: 1039–40). The latter canon refers to Luke 23: 42–31 alluded to above, 2–24/20–5.

2–25/34 *Ezechiel, xxxiii [12 et seq.]*: '. . . et impietas impii non nocebit ei in quacumque die conversus fuerit ab impietate sua . . .'. GO (interlinear):

'Penitenti et bene agenti dominus enim in vtroque non preterita secundum presentia iudicat' (3: 284).

2–25/42–6 *Sent Austyn . . . Sermone de innocentibus*: Augustine's Sermon 3, 'De innocentibus', is an excerpt from a sermon by the Venerable Bede on Gal. 4: 24, an exegesis of the story of Hagar and Ishmael (Gen. 16). It appears in the Maurist edition of Augustine's sermons and will appear in an appendix to the final volume of the *CCL* edition of Augustine's sermons, according to an editorial note in *Sermones de vetere testamento*, *CCL* xli, p. 17.

2–25/46–56 *As fel in Englond . . . 'Ore auant a deblys!'*: In spite of the circumstantial 'As fel in Englond', the story is attested in four manuscripts listed in J. A. Herbert, *Catalogue*: (1) Royal 7 C.i, fo. 116ᵛ: 'Convertimini', a collection of *exempla* for the use of preachers, perhaps by Robert Holcot (d. 1349), manuscript of the late fourteenth century; (2) Harl. 5369, fo. 247, early fifteenth century; (3) Harl. 5396, fo. 185, mid fifteenth century; and (4) Arundel 384, fo. 62, mid fifteenth century (3: 130–1, 116–8, 43–6, 106–18). The four manuscripts have variant spellings of the tyrant's expletive.

2–26/56–66 *Salomon . . . Ecclesiastici v [5–9]*: In the somewhat free translation of this text the author substitutes 'þin' for 'meorum' (26/60) and adds 'þat nout wiln amendyn hem, & his mercy to hem þat wiln amendyn hem' (lines 26/62–3 below).

2–26/70–5 *Dauid . . . [Ps. 24: 10]*: Cited above 124/77–8, and below 2–226/45.

2–26/5 *xxii, q. v, Ille*: The canon 'Ille' equates forcing someone to swear falsely to murdering him. The text was formerly attributed to Augustine but is now uncertain (C.22 q.5 c.5; cf. editorial note in Friedberg 1: 883–4).

2–27/7–8 *Salomon . . . Prouer i [32]*: GO: 'Auersio et prosperitas perdit cum a timore conditeris auersus animus, ira eiusdem conditeris in his quae peccat, nihil sustinere videtur aduersi sed ut Iob [21: 13] ait, 'Dicunt in bonis dies suos, et in puncto ad infernum descendunt' (2: 656).

2–27/13–4 *Isa. lxv [20]*: See 332/11–16 above.

2–27/16–17 *Salomon . . . Prouer. xxi [25]*: Cf. the translation in LV: 'Desiris sleen a slow man; for hise hondis nolden worche ony thing' (3: 34). Cf. 2–27/18–9 below.

2–27/18–19 *Dauid . . . Ps. 136: 9*: Nicolaus de Lyra interprets 'paruulus' more literally: 'Intelligitur de paruulis babylonis, quos crudeliter interfecerunt medi et persei babyloniis destructione suum, que dicit Esa. xiii de babyloniis, "Suscitabo super vos medos qui argentum non quaerant nec aurum velint, sed sagitis paruulos interficient et lactantibus ubero vteris non miserebuntur et super filios non parcet oculus eorum"' (*Postilla* 3). Augustine interprets 'paruulus' as the nascent evil desires ('nascentes malae cupiditates') which must be cast down on the stone ('ad petram') interpreted as Christ (1 Cor. 10: 4; *Enarr.*, 136.21; *CCL* xl, pp. 1978; *PL* 37: 1773–4). Cf. the interpretation of St Jerome, 2–27/23–4 below.

2–27/23–4 *Sent Ierom . . . ad Paulam et Eustochium*: St Jerome wrote Letter XXII to Eustochium in *c*.384. After citing Ps. 136: 9, he said: 'It is impossible that the body's natural heat should not sometimes assail a man and kindle sensual desire; but he is praised and accounted blessed, who, when thoughts begin to rise, gives them no quarter, but dashes them straightway against the rock: "And the Rock is Christ" ' (*Select Letters of Jerome*, tr. J. A. Wright, LCL 262, pp. 66–7; *PL* 22: 398).

2–27/30–1 *Al þe law . . . in þe gospel*: Matt. 22: 36–40, cited above 67/56.

2–28/40 *ten is a numbre perfyth*: The Pythagoreans, according to Aristotle, were the first to study numbers and to believe that everything in the universe was numerically expressible; in their view, 'the number 10 is thought to be perfect' (Aristotle, 'Metaphysics', A, 5, *Oxford Aristotle*, 2: 1559). See Hopper (1938), pp. 44–5. Cf. 284/3, and 284/8 above.

2–28/43–7 *Sent Iamys . . . Iac. [2: 10–11]*: In his Serm. 179A, Augustine tries to soften the rigor of St James's 'Quicumque autem totam legem servaverit offendat autem in uno, factus est omnium reus'. His argument is that charity is the root of the Commandments; hence a sin against charity is a violation of all the Commandments (179A.5), but (as his translator says) it is an argument that cannot be pressed too far (*Sermons*, tr. E. Hill (1992), 5: 306–13; *PL* Suppl. 2: 708–15). The GO puts it that an offense against charity is an offense against all the Commandments: 'Qui in vno, i.e., charitate offendit (quae est radix omnium praeceptorum) ab omnibus praeceptis quae sunt quasi filii charitatis accusatur' (4: 514). Cited below 2–29/71, 2–31/37.

2–28/47–8; 52–7 *Sent Austyn . . . De decem cordis*: '[T]ota lex in duobus praeceptis est, in dilectione dei et dilectione proximi. Ad duo itaque praecepta, id est, ad dilectionem dei et proximi pertinet decalogus' *Serm.* 9.7 (*CCL* xli, p. 120/263–5; also pp. 135–6/520–2, 139/175–7; *PL* 38: 75–91). Cf. Peter Lombard, *Sent.*, Di. 37, c. 1 (2: 206). Cited in the *Fasciculus morum*, ed. Wenzel, p. 182. See 2–31/5–16 below.

2–28/50–1 *Tobie iv [16]*: 'Quod ab alio odis fieri tibi, vide ne alteri tu aliquando facias'. See 215/47–52 above, 2–62/6–22, 2–78/55–8 below.

2–28/55–60 *Dauid & Sent Austyn . . . Ps. 32: 2*: Augustine: 'Putate me cytharoedum esse, quid uobis possem amplius canere? Ecce psalterium fero, decem chordas habet' (*Sermones*, *CCL* xli, p. 117/114–5; *PL* 38: 79). In his *Enarr*. 32.5, Augustine distinguishes between the cithera (lyre) and the psaltery (harp) and allegorizes the two parts of the cithera, the concave wood and the strings, the wood corresponding to the earthly nature of man and the strings to his heart and mind (*CCL* xxxviii, pp. 250–1).

2–29/64 *Mayster of Kende, lib. xviii*: Trevisa's translation of Bartholomaeus, 18.71: 'I haue yradde in a booke þat a strenge ymade of a wolues gutte ydo among harpestrenges ymade of þe guttes of scheep destroyeþ and corrumpeþ hem' (*Properties*, 2: 1224/36–8).

2–29/71 *Iac. 2: 10*: Jas. 2: 10: 'Quicumque autem totam legem servaverit, offendat autem in uno, factus omnium reus.' See Augustine's Sermon 179A (tr. E. Hill (1992), 5: 306–12; *PL* Supp. 2: 708–15) on this text; see above 2–28/43–7. Cited below 2–31/37.

2–30/26–35 *Sent Ion . . . Apoc. xvii* [*3*]: Rev. 17: 3: 'Et vidi mulierem sedentem super bestiam coccineam, plenam nominibus blasphemiae, habentem capita septem, et cornua decem.' The GO on 'mulierem': 'illos molles qui euae, a qua peccatum incepit, conformantur, qui habent diabolum fundamentum . . .' etc.; on 'capita septem': 'sensus [the five]; & postea errorem; & tandem antichristum per quae septem diabolus ducit homines ad peccatum'; on 'cornua': 'decem regna quae erunt tempore antichristi, per quam alia intelliguntur' (4: 569). Nicolaus de Lyra, noting the 'in spiritu' in the first phrase of verse 3, warns that this vision 'non fuit corporalis sed imaginatia et intellectualis' (*Postilla* 4).

2–31/37 *Iac. ii* [*10*]: See 2–28/43–7 and 2–29/71 above.

2–31/3 *For we mon don to God neyþer good ne euel*: Aquinas, on the impassibility of God: '[P]rimum ens oportet esse purum actum absque permixtione alicujus potentiae, eo quod potentia simpliciter est posterior actu . . . Ex quo patet quod impossibile est Deum aliquo modo mutari' (*ST* I.9.1). Peter Lombard: 'Deus autem nec loco nec affectione mutari potest' (*Sent.* 1: 97/23). Exod. 3: 14 'Dixit Deus ad Moysen: *Ego sum qui sum*' was so interpreted by the earliest Christian exegetes, cf. Augustine, 'Est uocor? Quia maneo in aeternum, quia mutari non possum. . . . Ergo incommutabilitas dei isto uocabulo se dignata est intimare: *Ego sum qui sum*' (Serm. 6.4: *CCL* xli, p. 64/73–8). The dogma dates back at least as far as the Council of Chalcedon (451), and St Anselm based his theory of the Redemption on it (*Cur Deus homo, Opera* 2: 59). Cf. 120/47–73, 202/1–3, 203/29–30 above, 2–32/21, 2–190/37–192/103 below.

2–31/5–16 *Sent Austyn in þe same book*: Augustine's sermon, 'De decem chordis': 'Seruum si haberes, uelles ut seruiret tibi seruus tuus. Serui tu meliori domino deo tuo. . . . [N]am si quis interrogetur, dicit, Nolo ut uxor mea tale aliquid faciat—si concupisco uxorem proximi mei, nolo quisquam concupiscat meam. . . . Non uis corrumpi domum tuam, quare corrumpis domum dei?' (*Sermones* 9.15–16: *CCL* xli, pp. 138–9/570–1, 136/527–9, 138/562; *PL* 38: 86–7). See 2–28/47–8; 52–7 above.

2–31/17–18 *Sent Powil . . .* [*1 Cor. 3: 17*]: 'Si quis autem templum Dei violaverit disperdet illum Deus. Templum enim Dei sanctum est quod estis vos'. Cited in *Jacob's Well*: 'Whoso dyffoule his body and soule þat is þe temple of god with leccherye god schal dampnyn hym' (Salisbury MS 174, fo. 197^r). The gloss cites Augustine at length on the meaning of 'templum', concluding that while even baptised infants belong to the 'templum dei', those persons who are conscious of the indwelling of the Trinity are 'beatissimi' (GO 4: 311–2).

2–32/21 *þin ymage peyntyd on a bord*: From Augustine's sermon, 'De decem chordis': 'Vnde tibi facit inuriam, qui uolerit forte lapidare tabulam tuam pictam, in qua tabula imago tua est in domo tua inaniter posita ad uanum honorem tuum, nec sentiens, nec loquens, nec uidens. Si quis illam lapidet, nonne in te it contumelia?' (*Sermones* 9.15; *CCL* xli, p. 137/541–5; *PL* 38: 86). Pauper does not want to make the argument that the Christian ought not to sin because his sin will be displeasing to God; he makes the more circumspect argument that the Christian ought to show respect to the image of God—to himself as well as to the images in a church building—by obeying 'alle hese hestis'. Note the careful wording of what follows: you do wrong to God '*in þiself*; þu dost wrong *to his grace, to his ʒifte*' (ital. added, 32/25–6). Cf. 2–31/3 above.

2–32/29 *I Io. iv* [*20*]: 1 John 4: 20: 'Si quis dixerit quoniam diligo Deum, et fratrem suum oderit, mendax est'. LL4 cites the remainder of verse 20: '[H]e þat louith nout his broþer whom he seth at eyʒe, how may he louyn god whom he saʒw neuere? (fo. 102vb). Cited below, 2–231/41–2.

2–32/31–5 *Genesis ix* [*6*]: 'Quicumque effuderit humanum sanguinem [tr. adds: wrongfullyche], fundetur sanguis illius: ad imaginem quippe Dei factus est homo' [tr. adds: 'for why, seith he . . . despysyd & distryyd'].

2–32/35–43 *Therfor God . . . Genesis iv* [*10–12*]: 'Dixitque ad eum, Quid fecisti? vox sanguinis fratris tui clamat ad me de terra./ Nunc igitur maledictus eris super terram quae aperuit os suum et suscepit sanguinem fratris tui de manu tua./ Cum operatus fueris eam non dabit tibi fructus suos; vagus et profugus eris super terram'. The GO interprets the 'vox sanguinis fratris' as the 'vocem sanguis christi'; 'maledictus' as a prefigura-tion of the Church's penalty of excommunication; and the unfruitfulness of the earth and the condemnation of Cain and his descendants to wandering as a prefiguration of the Jews' denial of Christ, the destruction of Jerusalem, and the Jews' dispersion among other peoples (1: 32).

2–33/50–1 *fledde to Goddis auter . . . Exodi xxi* [*14*]: 'Si quis de industriam occiderit proximum suum et per insidias, ab altari meo evelles eum ut moriatur'. The GO refers to the OT account of the six cities of refuge for homicides. In light of the NT, the passage is interpreted to refer to those called homicides 'qui scandalizauerit vnum de pusillis istis qui in me credunt [Matt. 18: 6]' or 'qui odit fratrem suum [Matt. 5: 23]'; for others, who injure someone else ignorantly, the Church is the city of refuge. Augustine further glosses Exod. 21: 14 as a reference to the

Redemption: God gave up his own son for us; hence Judas acted justly, cf. Rom. 8: 32 (GO 1: 155). Though no topical allusion may be intended here, the right of sanctuary still existed in the England of this period. The Tresilian case of 1388 tested whether treason was a crime for which sanctuary could not be resorted to (see *Westminster Chronicle*, ed. Hector and Harvey, pp. 310–13; Aston (1967), pp. 346–7). In this case, the right of sanctuary was not denied.

2–33/51–3 *Sent Iohn . . . Apoc. xiii* [*10*]: Rev. 13: 10, part of verse 10 only: '[Q]ui in gladio occiderit, oportet eum gladio occidi'. GO: Antichristus & sui occidunt gladio materiali & persuasionis & peribunt gladio aeterni iudicii' (4: 565).

2–33/55 *Mt. 7: 2*: Part of verse 2 only: '. . . et in qua mensura mensi fueritis remetietur vobis'. GO: 'Potest in hac mensura in qua aliud mensuratum est, ut triticum aliud mensurari, ut ordeum & alia quantitas, ut si unus modius de uno centum de alio. Ita facit deus, et non inique ut illi in aeternum' (4: 29). Cited again below 2–249/45(2).

2–33/56 *Io. 18: 11*: John 18: 11: 'Mitte gladium in vaginam' (cf. Matt. 26: 52). The GO allegorizes this as an admonition to preachers: 'verbum praedicationis converte ad gentes' (4: 265).

2–33/60–1 *Apoc. i* [*16*]: Rev. 1: 16, part of verse only: '. . . et de ore eius gladius utraque parte acutus exibat'. The GO again links the sword with the word of the preacher: ' "De ore", id est, de insinuatione exiuit praedicatio quae vtrumque secat in veteri testamento carnalia opera in nouo concupiscentias' (4: 551).

2–33/65 *Sent Powil . . . ad Romanos xiii* [*3–6*]: For [3–6] read [4]; cited above 2–13/19. See 334/60–335/82 and 2–13/19 above.

2–33/3–4 *pis word* occides *in Latyn*: Augustine argues that the prohibition 'non occides' applies to human beings only (not to plants or animals) and not to those humans who are justly condemned to die or who are killed in just wars (*De civ. dei*, 1.20–1; *CCL* xlvii, pp. 22–3; *PL* 41: 34–5). Aquinas, citing Augustine and Aristotle, says that 'non occides' does not forbid the killing of animals, which are devoid of reason and intended for man's use (*ST*, II–II, 64.1). Cf. 2–34/19–35 below.

2–34/16–17 *Genesis ix* [*2–3*]: Gen. 9: 3, part of verse 3: 'Et omne quod movetur et vivit, erit vobis in cibum.' See 2–33/3–4 above, 2–35/41–6 below.

2–34/19–35 *Balaam . . . Numeri xxii* [*22–33*]: The use of the Balaam story to argue for the view that animals are included in the fifth Commandment prohibition of killing is, in Dives' mouth, perhaps intended as mildly humorous or at least as an illustration of lay misreading of scripture. In *D&P*, two further references to Num. 22 interpret Balaam as a personification of covetousness (2–262/1–263/26) and his ass as a figure for the instability of worldly wealth (2–266–7/32–53). On Balaam and the Magi, 135/11 above. See also Ps.-Augustine, 'De Balaam et Belac', *PL* 39: 1809–10; Comestor, *Historia*, *PL* 198: 1230.

2–35/41–6 *God seyde to Noe . . . Genesis ix [2–5]*: 'Omnes pisces mari manui vestrae traditi sunt/ et omne quod movetur et vivit erit vobis in cibum quasi holera virentia tradidi vobis omnia,/ excepto quod carnem cum sanguine non comedetis'. The gloss gives as a reason why meat-eating was allowed: 'propter infecunditatem terrae & hominis fragilitatem' (GO 1: 40; see also GO on Gen. 6: 13, 1: 35). Cited above 2–34/16–7 and below 2–35/57.

2–35/46–8 *Deutero. xii [23–5]*: For [23–5] read [23]. Deut. 12: 23: 'Hoc solum cave ne sanguinem comedas; sanguis enim eorum pro anima est, et idcirco non debes animam comedere cum carnibus'. The GO suggests that, 'mystice', the prohibition was intended to elevate the moral life of 'carnales homines' (1: 390).

2–35/57 *Genesis ix [4]*: See 2–34/16–7, 2–35/41–6 above.

2–35/59–61 *Salomon . . . Sap. v [18]*: GO (Rabanus Maurus): 'Creator omnium cuius arma sunt veritas, iusticia & iudicium per creaturam sibi subiectam corripit delinquantes' (2: 728).

2–36/7 *iuge ordenarie*: 'In canon law, any cleric having ordinary jurisdiction, i.e. jurisdiction following automatically from an office that he holds, as distinguished from delegated jurisdiction . . . [such jurisdiction] belongs to the Pope, bishops, and certain lesser ranks of clergy. In English ecclesiastical law, it is applied to a bishop when exercising the jurisdiction belonging to his office as *iudex ordinarius* of the diocese, and to an official of a bishop having judicial power' (*OCL*, p. 906).

2–36/15–16 *Sent Austyn . . . lib. i, De libero arbitrio*: 'Si homicidium est hominem occidere, potest accidere aliquando sine peccato. Nam et miles hostem et iudex uel minister eius nocentem, et cui forte inuito atque imprudenti telum manu fugit, non mihi uidentur peccare, cum hominem occidunt' (*De libero arbitrio* I, iv, 25; *CCL* xxix, p. 216/27–31; *PL* 32: 1226).

2–37/30 *Mathei xix [6]*: 'Quod ergo Deus coniunxit, homo non separet', a text usually applied to the union between spouses (cf. *CA*, 1: 281; GO 4: 61). A Lollard preacher, in the last quarter of the fourteenth century, applied it to the union between the gospel text and its right interpretation, which union (he said) ought not to be adulterated by 'an hoore witt' (*EWS* 3, Serm. 239/43).

2–37/40–1 *[xxiii], q. v, Si homicidium, et in questionibus Leuitici*: The canon 'Si homicidium' holds that official execution is not homicide. The citation is from Augustine, *De libero arbitrio* I, iv, 25 cited above, 2–36/15–16. The canon also cites Augustine's 'In quest. Levitici', which is Augustine's 'In quest. Heptateuch.', Q. 2.71 (*PL* 34: 622) (C.23 q.5 c.41; Friedberg 1: 941).

2–37/2–3 *why mon nout prelatys . . . slen swyche trespasourys*: Official prohibitions against the participation of priests in judicial processes involving the spilling of blood go back to the earliest Church councils. Canon law cites from the eleventh Council of Toledo (675): 'His a quibus Domini sacramenta tractanda sunt, iudicium sanguinis agitare non licet' (C. 23, q. 8, c. 30; Friedberg 1: 964; cf. Mansi, 2.6, p. 141). Aquinas says that clerics are forbidden to put convicted criminals to death for two reasons: because they represent Christ, who when he was struck did not strike, and because they are ministers of the New Law, which did not prescribe punishment by death or maiming (*ST*, II–II, 64.4). See 2–38/20–1 below.

2–37/7–38/10 *Exodi xxxii [27 et seq.] . . . Numeri [25: 5 et seq.] . . . I Regum xv [32–3] . . . III Regum xviii [40]*: Dives has drawn this list of OT references from the canon law chapter cited below (2–38/11), and from the one immediately preceding it. (1) Exod. 32: 27–8: 'Ponat vir gladium super femur suum: ite, et redite de porta usque ad portam per medium castrorum, et occidat unusquisque fratrem, et amicum, et proximum suum./ Fecerunt filii Levi iuxta sermonem Mosi, cedideruntque in die illo quasi tria milia hominum.' (2) Num. 25: 7–8: '. . . Finees filius Eleazari filii Aaron sacerdotis . . . perfodit ambos simul virum scilicet et mulierem in locis genitalibus'. (3) 1 Sam. 15: 33: 'Et in frusta concidit Samuhel Agag coram Domino in Galgalis.' (4) 1 Kgs. 18: 40: 'Duxit eos Helias ad torrentem Cison et interfecit eos ibi.'

2–38/11 *xxiii, q. viii, Occidit*: The canon 'Occidit' says that times and circumstances must be considered in applying OT texts to present-day life (C.23 q.8 c.14; Friedberg 1: 956). The source is a sermon of St Chrysostom citing the story of Phineas (Num. 25: 7–8), the story of Abraham and Isaac (Gen. 22), and of Ananias and Saphira (Acts 5): see Homily 17.5, tr. Schaff, in *Chrysostom, Homilies* (NAPF, 1978), 10: 121; *PG* 57: 262–3.

2–38/16–18 *Conuerte gladium . . . Io. 18: 11*: John 18: 11 and Matt. 26: 52 are conflated, see 2–33/56 above, 2–57/81 below. For Matt. 26/52, see 2–48/66 below.

2–38/20 *xxiii, q. viii, De episcopis*: Gratian's *dict. ante*, beginning 'De episcopis', opens the canon-law argument against the bearing of arms by Christian clerics with a reference to 'Conuerte gladium' (John 10: 11) cited above, 2–38/16–18 (C.23 q. 8 c.1; Friedberg 1: 953). Subsequent chapters in Questio 8 argue that the weapons of a Christian are sorrow, tears and prayers, that clerics who die in battle should not be given Christian burial, and that clerics who bear arms are to be demoted in grade.

2–38/24–5 *Mathei xi [29]*: LL4: '[L]erith of me, for I am meke & loȝw of herte' (fo. 101rb). GO: 'Humiles ut neminem contemnant, mites ut nullam laedant; corde ut idem extra in opera sit et in corde ne latent serpens in specie columbae' (4: 42). The *CA* cites Augustine, Sermon 69.2 (*c*.413): 'Magnus esse vis? A minimo incipe. Cogitas magnam fabricam constituere celsitudinis? De fundamento prius cogita humilitatis' (1: 188b; *PL* 38: 440–2).

2–38/30 *Mathei v [44]*: '. . . diligite inimicos vestros, benefacite his qui oderunt vos'. GO: 'Contra ecclesiam pugnatur tribi modis, odio verbis, cruciatu corporis; ecclesia econtra diligit, benefacit, orat. Hoc est nouum mandatum, hoc de filiis irae facit filios dei, vnde sequitur vt sitis filii Adoptio filiorum sola caritate acquiritur' (4: 22). The *CA* cites Augustine, Ps.-Chrysostom, Gregory and the GO (1: 95).

2–38/37 *þe sacrament of þe auter*: The longest passage on the eucharist in *D&P* (cf. 87/37 and 235/44–5 above). Here Pauper deals only with the symbolism of the rite. The predominant Aquinian teaching (*ST*, III, 74–7) had been questioned by Franciscans, including John Pecham, Richard of Middleton and Duns Scotus, see Burr (1984), pp. 32–107; Macy (1994), 11–41.

2–39/44–5 *Nam sicut . . . Cristus*: The Sarum rite has, among the 'prefaciones' of the Mass: 'Eterne deus. Qui cum unigenito filio tuo et spiritu sancto unus es deus . unus es dominus. Non in unius singularitate persone . set in unius trinitate substancie' (*Sarum Missal*, ed. Legg, p. 214).

2–40/70 *in figure of cristis passion*: Shedding of blood in the OT, from the slaying of Abel onwards, is routinely interpreted as a prefiguration of the crucifixion, cf. Heb. 13: 11–12: 'Quorum enim animalium infertur sanguis pro peccato in sancta per pontificem, horum corpora cremantur extra castra./ Propter quod et Iesus ut sanctificaret per suum sanguinem populum extra portam passus est'. The idea is found in Bede: 'Therefore, all the sacrifices and victims that were burnt on the altar indicated figuratively either the passion of the Lord or the devotion of his saints, which was burning with the flame of charity' (*Bede: on the Tabernacle*, tr. A. G. Holder (1994), p. 87; *CCL* cxixA, p. 78; *PL* 91: 451).

2–40/1–8 *Schadyng of blood . . . xxiii, q. viii, Quicumque clericus*: The canon 'Quicumque clericus' says that no solemnities shall be provided for clerics killed in war, fights or tournaments ('gentilium ludis'); Christian burial is, however, permissable (C.23 q.8 c.4; Friedberg 1: 954). *Jacob's Well* has a list of violent games similar to the one in *D&P*: 'pleying at þe two hande swerd, at swerd & bokelere, & at two pyked staf, at þe hurlebatte' (ed. Brandeis, EETS, os 115, p. 105/29–30).

2–40/11 *xv, q. i, Si quis insaniens*: The canon 'Si quis insaniens' provides that if a person kills another person in a fit of insanity but later returns to sanity, only a light penance shall be imposed (C.15 q.1 c.12; Friedberg 1: 749). The source is an edict of the Council of Worms, 1122.

2–40/15 *Also 3if . . . xv, q. i, Si quis non iratus*: The canon 'Si quis non iratus' states that in a case in which a sane person inflicts accidental death as a result of physical punishment, a lighter penance shall be imposed (C.15 q.1 c.13; Friedberg 1: 749). The canon is attributed to Jerome, but the editor notes that it is found in Ps.-Chrysostom, 'Opus imperfectum' 28.11; I have not found it there, however.

2–40/15–41/16 *Extra, lib. v, . . . Presbiterum*: The canon 'Presbiterum' holds that a priest who inadvertently causes death by applying physical punishment is guilty of homicide and must be removed from his sacerdotal office (X 5.12.7; Friedberg 2: 796). The source is an epistle of Pope Alexander III, d. 1181.

2–41/17–18 *Extra . . . Ad audienciam*: The canon 'Ad audienciam' holds that it is homicide to impose a task on another which is likely to cause death (X 5.12.12; Friedberg 2: 797–8). The source is a decretal of Clement III (d. 1191) and is based on the case history of a priest who inadvertently caused a death in the course of meting out discipline; he has been removed from office, but now, having performed penance, seeks to return to his duties. The decision is left to the discretion of his superior.

2–41/19 *Extra . . . Significasti*: The canon 'Significasti' is derived from the case history of a priest who in attempting to stop a robbery in his church strikes the thief a non-mortal blow. Lay persons, arriving on the scene, kill the thief. It is held that the priest, having performed penance, may resume his duties (X 5.12.18; Friedberg 2: 800–1). From an epistle of Innocent III to the bishop of Padua. See 2–55/38–9 below.

2–41/20–3 *Also 3if clerkys . . . Extra . . . Peticio*: The canon 'Peticio' states that those clerics who fight, even against enemies of the faith, and cause death may no longer perform the sacraments (X 5.12.24; Friedberg 2: 803–4). From an epistle of Honorius III (d. 1227) to a priest, Pelagius.

2–41/23–42/71 *Also þe iuge . . . Reymond, lib. ii, ti. 1*: The passage is extracted and translated from Raymond of Peñafort's *Summa*, Bk. II, 'De homicidia', pp. 151–5. On 'assessour' see 2–239/42 below.

2–43/75 *Summa confessorum, lib. ii, ti. i, q. xxv, Quid de illis*: From John of Freiburg's *Summa confessorum* (MS Bodley 299, fo. 59ᵛ).

2–43/75–80 *3if a prest . . . ibidem, q. xxvii*: From John of Freiburg's *Summa confessorum* (MS Bodley 299, fo. 59ᵛ).

2–43/79–80 *Hostiensis, lib. v, rubrica De homicidio, Quid de presbitero*: From Henry of Segusa's *Summa aurea*; see above 246/39.

2–43/5 *xxiii, q. viii, Igitur*: The canon 'Igitur' holds that a pope may order the people to assemble to fight against the Saracens (C.23 q.8 c.7; Friedberg 1: 954–5). The canon is from an epistle of Pope Leo IV (d. 855).

2–44/9–10 *Hostiensis, lib. v, rubrica De homicidio, q. Quid si quis*: From Henry of Segusa's *Summa aurea*; see above 246/39.

2–44/13 *Extra . . . Postulasti . . . Tua nos*: Both canons are from epistles of Pope Innocent III. 'Postulasti' (c.21) assures a bishop that the cleric who cooperates with civil authority in the punishment of a malefactor is not guilty of any resulting bloodshed (X 5.12.21; Friedberg 2: 802–3). 'Tua nos' (c.19) tells a story about a *scolaris* who was struck down by a thief. The following day, the scholar's fellow students found the thief and turned him over to the authorities. When these officials had determined the truth of the charge, they punished the malefactor by castration and blinding. Was the said *scolaris* then to be allowed to proceed to holy orders? The answer is that nothing should prevent his doing so (X 5.12.19; Friedberg 2: 801–2).

2–44/22–46/67 *3if a clerk . . . Summa confesssorum, lib. ii, ti. i*: From John of Freiburg's *Summa confessorum* (Bodley MS 299, fos. 57ʳ-62ᵛ). See 219/55 above.

2–46/5 *Luce xxii [36]*: Nicolaus de Lyra interprets literally: '. . . per hoc innuens quod licita esset eis defensio moderata tempore persecutionis' (*Postilla* 4). LL4, as in *D&P*, interprets the words 'Qui non habet' as aimed at Judas: 'Whyche wordys he seyde only for Iudas, not byddyng hym don so but be weye of prophecye þat he schulde don so & so vndyrnemynge hym preuelyche of his euyl purpos, so shewynge þat he knew hys wyckyd purpos; & þerfore cryst seyde þo wordys nout in þe plurer numbre but in þe synguler numbre as to on alone þat was Iudas, wych selde his cloth & bou3te hym a swerd to comyn with oþere schrewys to takyn cryst' (fo. 48ʳᵇ). The GO adds prefigurative interpretations to its literal one: 'mystice', Christ enjoins the Christian to 'sell' his patrimony and 'buy' the word of God; with the 'sword' of suffering ('passionis'), a martyr's crown is won (4: 214; cf. 2–48/69 below). A Wycliffite sermon accuses the friars of using this text to justify fighting with material arms. But, says the preacher, by 'swords', 'Crist mente swerde of þe Holy Gost' (*EWS* 3, Serm. 145/117). See 2–47/ 25–7 below.

2–47/25–37 *'Domine, ecce duo gladii hic' . . . [Lc. 22: 38–9]*: Luke 22: 38 is the major scriptural basis for the 'two swords' doctrine (or doctrines) relating the spiritual and temporal powers of the Church to secular authority. The general belief that the spiritual 'sword' of the Church was superior to the material sword of the lay power, enunciated by Ambrose and Augustine and by a series of popes, was restated by St Bernard (1090–1153) in *De consideratione*, c. 3: 'Alioquin si nullo modo ad te pertineret et is, dicentibus Apostolis, "Ecce gladii duo hic" non respondisset Dominus "Satis est" sed "Nimis est." Uterque ergo Ecclesiae et spiritualis scilicet gladius, et materialis; sed is quidem pro Ecclesia, ille vero et ab Ecclesia exserendus: ille sacerdotis, is militis manu, sed sane ad nutum sacerdotis, et

Jussum imperatoris' (*PL* 182: 776). Boniface VIII in the Bull 'Unam sanctam' (1302) strongly, and controversially, restated the doctrine that the authority of the spiritual sword wielded by the Church was greater than that of the temporal powers: 'Oportet autem gladium esse sub gladio, et temporalem auctoritatem spirituali subiici potestate' (Extra. 1.8.7; Friedberg 2: 1245–6; tr. in Tierney (1964), p. 189; Latin text also in *Les régistres de Boniface VIII*, ed. G. Digard *et al.* (1921), No. 5582: 888–90. In *D&P*, Pauper argues against Dives' reading of Luke 22: 38 as granting both 'swords' to the Church. Properly understood, in line with the gloss (GO 2: 214), the meaning of the gospel text is that the Church's only sword is 'þe swerd of Godis word'. In LL4. he writes: 'Cryst made an ende of here foly speche with þis word, It is inow, *Satis est*. . . . And þerfore no men of holy chyrche schuldyn autorysyn hem be þese wordys for to fytyn with þe swerd ne to slen men (fo. 48rb).

2–47/37–40 *On the same maner . . . Deutero. iii* [*26*]: As the gloss points out, Moses is figuratively the Old Law, and it is Joshua who prefugures the New Law and is a type of Christ: 'Iosue autem typus christi qui saluator interpretatur' (GO, 1: 377).

2–47/40–2 *Also God . . .* [*2 Reg. 24: 16*]: 2 Sam. 24: 16: '. . . et ait angelo percutienti populum, Sufficit, nunc contine manum tuam. Erat autem angelus Domini iuxta aream Areuna Iebusei'. The biblical text refers to Araunah the Jebusite, from whom David purchased the threshing floor that became the site of the temple of Solomon, see *ABD*, 1: 353.

2–47/45 [*Mc. 14: 41*]: Mark 14: 41: 'Et venit tertio et ait illis, Dormite iam et requiescite. Sufficit, venit hora ecce tradetur Filius hominis in manus peccatorum'. St Jerome interprets 'tertio' to signalize that we should ask for past, present and future grace in our prayers (*CA*, 1: 546).

2–48/51–2 *Iudas . . .* [*Io. 13: 27*]: GO: 'Non praecipit, sed praeicit iudae malum, nobis bonum, quia hoc vult cito fieri, non tam festinando in illius poenam quam in salutem fidelium' (4: 256). Augustine, *In Ioh.*, 62.1–6, expands on this theme (*CCL* xxxvi, pp. 483–5; *PL* 35: 1801–3). Nicolaus de Lyra: 'Non dicit hoc percipiendo vel consulendo que perceptum diuinum vel consilium non potest esse de malo sed tamen [mortaliter?] permittendo ratione dicta tersi verba cristi fuerunt aliis apostolis obscura' (*Postilla* 4). See *CA*, 2: 509b–510a.

2–48/60 [*Lc. 22: 38*]: See above 2–47/25–37.

2–48/66 '*hoso smyte with þe swerd*': Matt. 26: 52: 'Omnes enim qui acceperint gladium, gladio peribunt.' Cited above 2–38/16–18, and below 2–57/81. Nicolaus de Lyra: 'Gladium non accipit que eo vtitur ad vindictam propria auctoritate, hoc est illicitum; gladio autem vtitur sibi tradito que eo vtitur ad punitorem malorum zelo iusticie, sicut principes qui auctoritatem habunt a deo, que in hoc princeps minister dei est, ut dic paulus apotolis, et similiter ministri ad hoc a principibus constituti . . .' etc., (*Postilla* 4).

2–48/69 *Sent Ambrose*: St Ambrose, 'In Lucam' 10.54 and 10.90: 'Est etiam gladius spiritalis, ut uendas patrimonium, emas uerbum, quo mentis penetralia uestiuntur. Est etiam gladius passionis, ut exuas corpus et immolatae carnis exuuiis ematur tibi sacri corona martyrii. . . . Et tu si ueniam uis mereri, dilue culpam lacrimis tuam; eodem momento, eodem tempore respicit te Christus' (*PL* 15: 1607;1944; *Traité . . . S. Luc*, 2: 174;186). Cf. 2–46/5 above.

2–48/71–3 *Non veni pacem . . . Mathei x [34]*: LL4: 'Therfore crist seyth þat he cam not to sendin swyche pes in erþe but swerd & dyuycioun for to destruyȝyn swych synful pes' (fo. 62rb). GO: 'Missum est bellum bonum ut rumperetur pax mala' (4: 40). See 2–311/148 below.

2–49/79–80 *Ananyam & Safiram . . . Act. v [1–10]*: Peter Comestor retells the story of Ananias and Saphira, suggesting that the severity of their punishment (death) had a parallel in the punishment of the man who gathered sticks on the Sabbath (Num. 15: 32–6; *Historia: PL* 198: 1659). Peter Lombard tells the story as an illustration of the fact that men can be invaded by demons (*Sentences* 2.8.3–4 [1: 370]). *Handlyng Synne* tells the Ananias story as a warning against lying to a confessor (ed. Furnivall, EETS, os 119, 123), pp. 365–6. Cf. *ABD* 1: 224. Cited again 2–49/80–3, 2–259/12–15 below.

2–49/80–3 *xxiii, q. viii, Petrus . . . Act. ix [40–1]*: The canon 'Petrus' cites the stories of the healing of Tabitha and the deaths of Ananias and his wife, taken from Gregory's *Dialogues*, II.30 (*PL* 66: 188). While Tabitha was restored to life by prayer, Ananias and his wife died as a result of their own guilt. The point here seems somewhat more subtle than Pauper's assertion that the 'word & þe cursyng' of clerics is greatly to be feared; rather, St Gregory distinguishes between the power of prayer to restore life and the effect of a rebuke upon a guilty person (C.23 q.8 c.16; Friedberg 1: 956–7).

2–49/87–9 *Sent Powil . . . Heb. 4: 12*: 'Vivus est enim Dei sermo, et efficax et penetrabilior omni gladio ancipiti et pertingens usque ad divisionem animae ac spiritus'. Cited in part in LL4: 'Also þat he is þe word of god he is liif & þerfore seynt poul seyth *Vivus est sermo dei* etc. þe word of god is lyuynge & of gret doynge' (fo. 137va). Again, the text appears to be pressed for a meaning it does not have in context. According to St Paul, the 'sword' of the word of God acts not as a lethal weapon but on the conscience. Cf. 2–49/80–3 above and the gloss (GO, 4: 429). Cited below, 2–308/39.

2–49/2;7 *xxiii, q. v, Si non*: The canon 'Si non' holds that killing in a just war is not homicide (C.23 q.5 c.9; Friedberg 1: 933). The body of the canon is a lengthy citation from Augustine's *De civ. dei*, Bk. I, cc. 17, 20, 21, 26, dealing largely with the question of suicide. Only the first half sentence seems pertinent: 'Si non licet priuata potestate alicui hominem occidere innocentem, cuius occidendi licentiam lex nulla concedit . . .' (*CCL* xlviii, pp. 18–27; *PL* 41: 30–40; *City of God*, LCL 411, 1: 76–112). Aquinas cites *De civ. dei*, Bk. 1, c. 20 in his article on suicide (*ST*, II–II, 64.5). See 2–51/ 16 and 2–52/38–46 below.

2–50/28–34 *God seith . . . Exo. xxiii* [2]: Exod. 23: 1–2: 'Non suscipies vocem mendacii nec iunges manum tuam ut pro impio dicas falsum testimonium. /Non sequeris turbam ad faciendum malum nec in iudicio plurimorum adquiesces sententiae ut a vero devies'. Exod. 23: 1 is cited above, 254/67.

2–50/36–7 *Di. lxxxvi, Si quid, et xi, q. iii, Quamuis, et [xv], q. vii, Si quid*: Three canons: (1) 'Si quid' urges that an accusation should be received cautiously and the facts of the matter thoroughly investigated (D.86 c.33; Friedberg 1: 303). The text is attributed to a pastoral letter of St Gregory to the bishop of Corinth. (2) 'Quamuis' states that in legal judgements facts are not to be admitted without evidence (C.11 q.3 c.75; Friedberg 1: 664). The source is Augustine's Serm. 351, 'De pen.' 3, where he says: 'Nam si nominatio sufficit, multi damnandi sunt innocentes' (*PL* 39: 1537–49; see esp. 351.10, col. 1547 ; (3) 'Si quid' warns that when accusations are made, the facts of the case are to be carefully scrutinized and ecclesiastical superiors are to be consulted (C.15 q.7 c.2; Friedberg 1: 757). The canon is essentially identical to (1) above, but the recipient of Gregory's epistle is here said to be the Bishop of Palermo.

2–50/40 *Extra, De verborum significacione, c. Forus, in glosa*: Title XI is a collection of definitions of legal terms. 'Forus' is cited from Isidore of Seville's *Etym.* Bk. 8.15, defining the word 'forum' in the sense of court of law (see *DML* s.v. 'forum' (1), 6 & 7). Only a few sentences are relevant to the context in *D&P*: 'Argumentum nunquam testibus, nunquam tabulis dat probationem sed sola investigatione invenit veritatem . . . Iure autem disceptare est iuste iudicare. Non est ergo iudex si non est in eo iustitia' (X 5.40.10; Friedberg 2: 914).

2–51/49–50 *xxiii, q. ii, Iustum*: The canon 'Iustum' defines the just war and the just judge. The latter definition is relevant here, and *D&P* cites the last sentence in the text of the canon (C.23 q.2 c.1; Friedberg 1: 894). The source is Isidore of Seville's *Etym.* (see preceding note), which begins with a sentence from his Bk. 18, 1.2 and concludes with three sentences from Bk. 18, 15.6: 'Iudex dictus est, quia ius dictat populo, siue quod iure disceptet. Iure autem disceptare est iuste iudicare. Non enim est iudex, si non est iusticia in eo'.

2–51/8–9 *comonte of mankende . . . þe Philosofre . . . v Ethicorum*: The comparison between the state and the body is not found in Aristotle's *Nicomachaean Ethics* but is found in Bk. I of the *Politics* (*Oxford Aristotle*,

2: 1988/19–22). The comparison between the Church and the human body,
derived from the classical comparison between the body and the community, is found in St Paul (1 Cor. 12: 12–17); it is a commonplace throughout
the Middle Ages. See Augustine (*De civ. dei* Bk. 22, c. 18; *CCL* xlviii,
p. 837/17 ff.; *PL* 41: 779–80); Aquinas (*ST*, III, 8.1); John of Salisbury,
Policraticus V, c. 2.

2–51/16 *xxiii, q. v, Si non licet*: Cited 2–49/2;7 above.

2–52/28 *Senta Lucie . . . Pascasius*: 'Lucia: non inquinatur corpus nisi de
consensu mentis' (*Legenda Aurea*, Graesse, No.4; *GL*, 1: 28). On the
historicity of St Lucy, see *ODS*, pp. 250–1. Aquinas cites the dictum of
St Lucy in his Reply to Obj. 3 in the Article of the *ST* cited above, 2–49/
2;7. Cf. the 'metrical life of St Lucy' in Osbern Bokenham's *Legendys* (ed.
Sergeantson, EETS, 206), pp. 243–57. Cited below 2–278/43–50.

2–52/38–46 *Samson . . . Sent Austyn . . . [Iud. 16: 30]*: The reference to
Samson occurs in the canon law citation from Augustine above, 2–49/2;7
and 2–51/16: 'Nec Samson aliter excusatur, quod se ipsum cum hostibus
ruina domus obpressit, nisi quia Spiritus latenter hoc iusserat, qui per illum
miracula faciebat' (C.23 q.5 c.9; Friedberg 1: 934). The biblical reference is
to Judg. 16: 28–30 (see 2–84/4–19 below). Aquinas refers to Samson in the
same connection, *ST*, II–II, 64. 5, Reply to Obj. 4. See 2–84/4–19 below.

2–53/9 *[Lc. 10: 16]*: 'Qui vos audit me audit, et qui vos spernit me spernit'.
GO: In audiendo vel spernendo euangelii praedicatorem quisque sciat se
non uiles personas sed ipsum saluatorem spernere vel audire, quia in
discipulo magister auditur & in filio pater honoratur' (4: 178).

2–53/13 *I ad Corinth. iii [8]*: 'Qui plantat autem et qui rigat unum sunt;
unusquisque autem propriam mercedem accipiet secundum suum laborem'.
Again Pauper rejects an external criterion of value in favour of a subjective
one: the intrinsic moral worth of the individual.

2–53/28 *to slen hyr þe lawe cyuyle*: Pauper here acknowledges a distinct
difference between canon law and civil law, notwithstanding the general
principle that the two should supplement one another. Chobham's penitential (1216), while recognizing that there are many men who hate their
wives, states that 'adulterium nunquam est morte puniendum in ecclesia dei
sed sola penitentia purgandum' (*Summa*, ed. Broomfield, 7.9a.11, p. 459),
citing the canon 'Inter haec', which states that no one is permitted to kill an
adulterous wife (C.33 q.2, c.6; Friedberg 1: 1152). See 160/11–15 above.

2–54/43 *[Eph. 5: 33]*: For [33] read [28]: 'Ita et viri debent diligere uxores
suas ut corpora sua'. GO: 'Una caro christus & ecclesia, quia deus apud
deum per carnem particeps noster factus est. Unius christus caput & corpus
quasi integer vir quia & femina de viro facta est, & ad virum pertinet'
(4: 378). See 2–62/64 below.

2–54/50 *Summa confessorum, lib. iv, t. ix, q. x*: John of Freiberg's *Summa confessorum*, Q. 10 asks: 'Utrum magis peccet qui occidit uxorem utrum qui occidit parentem?' and his answer is that it is a greater sin to kill a parent 'quia magis repugnat nature' (MS Bodley 299, fo. 263ʳ).

2–55/13 *dominus Deus . . . sabaoth*: The phrase 'Dominus deus exercitum' is found most often in Isaiah, see 6: 3 for one example. The phrase 'Dominus Deus sabaoth' is found in the OT in Jer. 1: 20 and in the NT in Rom. 9: 29 and Jas. 5: 4.

2–55/15–21 *þat batalye be ryȝtful . . . xxiii, q. i, [Noli]*: The canon 'Noli' commends the just war, which is a war waged in order to establish peace ('ut pax queritur') (C.23 q.1 c.3; Friedberg 1: 892). The source is St Augustine's letter to Pope Boniface I (d. 422). Pauper cites Aquinas' three criteria for a just war: the command of a legitimate sovereign, a just cause, and a rightful intention (*ST*, II–II, 40.1). Cf. Brundage (1969), pp. 19–29; F. H. Russell (1975), *passim*; bibliog. pp. 19–29. See below 2–144/94–114.

2–55/30 *For þei a persone gadere to hym rebellis*: On sedition, Aquinas says that though sedition is usually sinful, against a tyranical ruler or government it may be justified (*ST*, II–II, 42). On rebels in London in the early fifteenth century, see M. McKisack in *Studies Presented to F. M. Powicke*, ed. Hunt, Pantin and Southern (1969), pp. 84–5.

2–55/38–9 *licitum est vim vi repellere*: This legal maxim is adduced in the canon law citation above (2–41/19): 'Si vero, quem, admodum perhibetur, sacerdos iste prius ab illo percussus sacrilego, mox eum cum ligone in capite repercussit, quamvis vim vi repellere omnes leges et omnia iura permittant' (X 5.12.18; Friedberg 2: 801). Aquinas cites it in *ST*, II–II, 64.7, also in respect to the moral status of self-defence.

2–56/69–70 *Summa confessorum, lib. ii, ti. v, q. xlv et xlvi*: John of Freiburg's *Summa confessorum*, MS Bodley 299, fos. 73ʳ ('Que exiguntur ad bellum iustum') -74ʳ ('Sibi').

2–57/72 *ȝoure persone be nout able to fyȝtyn ne to slen*: The sense of 'persone' here is physical condition or status: your *person* is not such that you can fight physically; see *MED*, s.v. 'persoun(e, (1)2 and (2)1'. Pauper's remark (if not a commonplace; it is used, e.g., in the 'Tretyse of Gostly Batayle') may cast some light on the author's representation of Dives' age and condition, indicating that he is depicted as a man of middle age.

2–57/76–7 *Agentes et consencientes pari pena puniantur*: Legal maxim, cited 238/4–7 above.

2–57/81 *Mt. 26/52*: See 2–38/16–18 and 2–48/66 above.

2–57/82–3 *Ve qui predaris! . . . Ysa. xxxiii [1]*: '. . . nonne et ipse praedaberis? et qui spernis nonne et ipse sperneris?' The GO: 'Contra

Senacherib, possunt haec etiam referri ad quemlibet raptorem & adipsum diabolum' (3: 52). On Sennacherib, King of Assyria (704–68 BC), see Isaiah, 36–7.

2–57/83 Al day ʒe mon sen what venchance fallith: See 257/43–51 above.

VOL. 1: 2, COMMANDMENT VI, pp. 2–58–129

2–58/3–4 Ex. 20: 14: While the biblical sixth Commandment forbids only adultery, Christian exegetes have included many other kinds of sexual misbehaviour. Wyclif's list of offences against the sixth Commandment is similar to the list in lines 8–17 of the text (*De mand.*, pp. 346–9). On the numbering of the Commandments see 81/7 above.

2–58/18 synnyn medlyng with his wif: Aquinas (or his continuator) maintains that pleasure in sex is natural and is at most a venial sin (*ST*, Suppl. 49.6). Peter Lombard compares coitus to rest after labour and food after hunger, saying that sexual pleasure is not sinful unless it is immoderate ('nisi sit immoderata'). He admits, however, that St Gregory disagrees, asserting that coitus without sin is impossible. *Sententiae*, 4.31.8 (2: 450/8–9; 450/11–31). Thomas de Chobham (1216) agrees that it is possible for a man to sin mortally with his own wife, and his list of how this may occur parallels Pauper's (*Summa*, ed. Broomfield, pp. 333–90; cf. canon law, C.32 q.4 c.5; Friedberg 1: 1128–9, on this point). On early penitentials dealing with married heterosexual relations see Payer (1984), pp. 19–36; for decretist theories, see Brundage (1987), pp. 278–88; and for the period 1348–1517, idem, pp. 487–509. See 129/36–47 above.

2–59/32 [1 Petr. 3: 7; 1 Cor. 7: 5]: 1 Pet. 3: 7: 'Viri similiter cohabitantes secundum scientiam, quasi infirmiori vascuo muliebri inpertientes honorem, tanquam et coheredibus gratiae vitae uti non impediantur orationes vestrae'. The GO stresses that the purpose of marriage is the production of children, and exhorts husbands to be considerate of their wives as co-heirs of the grace of God (4: 524). 1 Cor. 7: 5: 'Nolite fraudare invicem nisi forte ex consensu ad tempus ut vacetis orationi, et iterum revertimini in id ipsum, ne temptet vos Satanas propter incontinentiam vestram'. The GO (interlinear), reiterates that neither spouse has power over his or her own body, but each has power over the other's body (4: 316). See 2–61/36 and 2–66/25 below. 1 Pet. 3: 7 is referred to below (where the verse reference [: 3–5] should read [: 7], 2–91/20–2.

2–59/32–7 Genesis vii . . . Noe & his pre sonys keptyn hem chast: The tradition that Noah and his sons were continent during the Flood is extra biblical. It appears in John of Damascus (c675–c749): 'He separated them from their wives so that with the help of chastity they might escape the deep' (*De fide*, Bk. 4.24; *PG* 94: 1207–8). It is allegorized in Ps.-Augustine, 'Dialogus quaestionum lxv, Orosii', which is referred to below in another connection, see 2–112/20 (*PL* 40: 750). Comestor explains: 'Tempore afflictionis vacandum est ab amplexibus mulierum' (*Historia*, *PL* 198: 1083). See Mirk's *Festial*: 'God bade Noye and his þre sonnes goo ynto þe schyppe by homself; and Noyeys wyfe and hys sonnes wyues by homselfe; for encheson þat, yn tyme of afflicyon, men schuld absten hom from coupull of woymen' (ed. Erbe, EETS, es 96), p. 72/24–7).

2–59/51–3 *Sent Powil . . . ad Ebreos xiii [4] . . . Haymo*: The Haymo referred to was probably Haymo of Faversham (d. 1244), a Franciscan who was a leader in the early years of the Order. His commentary on the Pauline epistles survives, in part, in Balliol MS 183. On Heb. 13: 4, Haymo writes: 'Honorabile enim conubium est . amore filiorum legitime uxorem ducere . temporibus que certius ab ea abstinere . . . conubii torus immaculatus est . hoc est legitimum concubitus . . . & immaculatus lectus' (fo. 204ra). Heb. 13: 4 is cited again 2–77/25 below.

2–60/1 ff. *Matrimonye*: The Pauline foundations of the laws of marriage are stated in 1 Cor. 7: 2–7, 36–40 and Eph. 5: 22–33. Peter Lombard gives the two 'causis': 'Coniugii autem institutio duplex est. Una ante peccatum ad officium facta est in paradiso, ubi esset *thorus immaculatus* [Heb. 13: 4, see above, 2–59/51–3] et nuptiae honorabiles . . . altera post peccatum ad remedium facta extra paradisum, propter illicitum motum devitandum. Prima ut natura multiplicaretur, secunda ut natura exciperetur et vitium cohiberetur': *Sentences*, Bk. 4, d. 26, c. 2 (2: 417/2–7), as does Hugh of St Victor, *De sacramentis* II, xi (*PL* 176: 481), who begins: 'Institutio conjugii duplex est, una ante peccatum ad officium; altera post peccatum ad remedium'. Both go on to say that, as a sacrament, marriage represents the union between Christ and the Church.

2–60/19–20 *a ryng on hyr fyngir*: The *Sarum Missal* sets forth the rite at the church door: 'Statuantur vir et mulier ad hostium ecclesie coram presbitero et dicatur a uiro dos mulieris et ponatur super scutum uel super aliud siue aurum siue argentum seu cetera. Deinde detur femina a patre suo uel ab amicis aperta manu si puella est, tecta si uidua, quam uir recipiat in dei fide et sua seruandam sanam et infirmam et teneat eam per dexteram manum in sua manu dextera, post hec dicatur . . . [After the ring is blessed by the priest], '[h]ic accipiat sponsus annulum et incipiens a pollice sponse dicat dicente presbitero, "In nomine patris", ad secundum digitum, "Et filii", Ad tercium, "Et spiritus sancti amen'. Ibique dimittatur. Postea dicat sponsus, "De isto anulo te sponso" ' (pp. 413–4). The custom of saying a blessing on the thumb and first two fingers (i.e., in the name of the Father, Son and Holy Ghost) has been given as a possible explanation for the placing of the wedding ring on the fourth finger; cf. Kraus (1975), Plate 6, showing a fifteenth-century French carving of the hands of bride and groom in which the groom's thumb bears a wedding ring. Mirk's *Festial* says the wedding ring is placed on the 'fyngur þat haþe a veyne to hure [the bride's] herte' (ed. Erbe, EETS, es 96), p. 291/8–9. See 2–61/45–7 below.

2–61/36 *þe dette of her bodyys*: The doctrine rests on 1 Cor. 7: 3–4: 'The husband should give to his wife her conjugal rights, and likewise the wife to her husband./ For the wife does not rule over her own body, but the husband does; likewise the husband does not rule over his own body, but the wife does' (RSV). In considering marriage, Aquinas puts in first place the mutual obligation of husband and wife to pay the debt (*ST*, IIIa, 64.1–9). Cf. Peter Lombard: 'Absque consensu alterius, neuter [spouse] continentiam profiteri potest' (*Sentences*, 2: 422/9). See note 129/36–47 and text 250/88 above.

2–61/41 *Deutero. vi* [*5*]: 'Diliges Dominum Deum tuum ex toto corde tuo et ex tota anima tua et ex tota fortitudine tua.' LL4: 'Thu schalt louyn þin lord god with al þin herte, with al þin soule & with al þin my3tis & with al þin meende & þin þou3t, & þu schalt louyn þin ney3hebore as þinself' (fo. 90vb). The GO (Gregory): 'Per amorem dei gignitur amor proximi & per amorem proximi nutritur amor dei' (1: 381).

2–61/45–7 *Thre ornamentis*: Rock cites this passage in *D&P* as evidence for the use of ring, brooch and garland in the medieval wedding ceremony (4: 202). For her wedding, Chaucer's Griselda was adorned with 'a corone on hire heed' (*CT*, CT, p. 142/381). See 2–60/19–20 above.

2–61/52–5 *Sent Powyl . . . Eph. 5: 25*: Cited twice in LL4: '& þerfore seynt powyl seyþ, 3e men louyþ 3oure wyfuys as crist louyth holy cherche' (fo. 18vb); '& þerfore, seyth he, 3e husbondis louith 3oure wiifins [*sic*] as crist louede his spouse holi cherche' (fo. 106rb). GO: 'Ita faciat vir de uxore quae caro eius quia sic et christus nutrit ecclesiam cibo corporis sui & fouet spiritualibus in iumentis praeceptorum virtutum & bonorum operum' (4: 378).

2–62/64 *Ephes. v* [*26–9; 22–4*]: For [26–9] read [28]: v. 28: 'Ita et viri debent diligere uxores suas ut corpora sua. Qui suam uxorem diligit, seipsum diligit' (see 2–54/43 above); vv. 22–4: 'Mulieres viris suis subditae sint, sicut Domino, /quoniam vir caput est mulieris, sicut Christus caput est ecclesiae, ipse, salvator corporis,/ sed ut ecclesia subiecta est Christo, ita et mulieres viris suis in omnibus'. GO (Ambrose): It is worthier to serve than to obey, but either should be done in chaste fear of Christ, who mandated humility (4: 378).

2–62/6–22 *Tobye vi* [*10–22*]: The motif of the dangerous bride, or of the husband killed on his wedding night, can be followed in S. Thompson's *Motif-Index*, see T172.0.1 (5: 361). In *D&P* the story serves as an object lesson in sexual moderation. Bede gives the story a Christological exegesis (*PL* 91: 930). Cf. *The Book of Vices and Virtues* (ed. Francis, EETS, 217), pp. 247–8; and *Jacob's Well* (Salisbury MS 174, fo. 196ᵛ). In Peter of Riga's heavily allegorized version, the story of Tobias and Sarah prefigures the Redemption (*Aurora*, ed. Beichner, 1: 316–338). John of Wales uses the story to show that a husband who is too ardent a lover of his wife is an adulterer (*Communiloquium* 2.4.5). John Gower's metrical version derives the moral that, in matrimony, reason must temper the laws of nature, *Confessio Amantis*, ed. Macaulay (EETS, os 82), 2: 383–4/5351–83. 'Pore Caitif's retelling of the story is closely similar to *D&P* but is aimed against sexual excess in married women (MS Bodley 938, fos. 138ᵛ-139ʳ; and MS Bodley 3, fos. 53ᵛ-54ʳ).

2–63/25 *Deutero. xxii* [*22*]: 'Si dormierit vir cum uxore alterius, uterque morietur, id est, adulter et adultera, et auferes malum de Israhel'. The GO interprets the punishment less literally: the impenitent adulterers are condemned to eternal torment, 'eterno deputabitur tormento' (1: 404).

2–63/27–32 *Salomon . . . Prouer. vi* [*30–3*] *. . . Bede*: Vv. 32–3: 'Qui autem adulter est propter cordis inopiam perdet animam suam;/ turpitudinem et ignominiam congregat sibi et obprobrium illius non delebitur'. Vv. 30–1: 'Non grandis est culpae cum quis furatus fuerit, furatur enim ut esurientem impleat animam;/ deprehensus quoque reddet septuplum et omnem substantiam domus suae tradet'. Bede, 'Super parabolas salomonis': 'Furtum non ex sui aestimatione, sed ex comparatione peccati majoris, i.e., adulteriis, non grandis esse culpae perhibetur; sicut Hierusalem gravius peccanti dicitur, *Justificata est Sodoma ex te*, non quia Sodoma nulla vel pauca, sed quia Hierusalem plura peccauit' (*PL* 91: 962; cf. GO, 2: 662).

2–63/38–44 *Salomon . . . Sapien. iii* [*16–19*]: 'Filii autem adulterorum inconsummati erunt, et ab iniquo toto semen exterminabitur,/ et si quidem longae vitae erunt in nihilum conputabuntur, et sine honore erit novissima senectus illorum,/ et si celerius defuncti fuerint non habebunt spem, nec in die agnitionis adlocutionem; / nationis enim iniquae dirae sunt consummationes.'

2–63/50 *Sapien. iv* [*3–5*]: 'Multigena autem impiorum multitudo non erit utilis, et spuria vitulamina non dabunt radices altas, nec stabile firmamentum conlocabunt,/ et si in ramis in tempore germinaverint, infirmiter posita a vento commovebuntur, et a nimietate ventorum eradicabuntur,/ confringentur rami inconsummati, et fructus illorum inutilis et acerbi ad manducandum et ad nihilum apti'. The GO: 'Alternati de catholicis et haereticis loquitur, ut horum laudabilem sapientiam illorum vituperabilem demonstret versutiam' (2: 726).

2–63/51–64/63 *pope Boneface þe predde . . . d. lvi, Si gens Anglorum*: The writer of the letter is St Boniface (*c*.675–754), an English saint and martyr but not a pope. The paragraph cited in canon law is extracted from a much longer letter to King Ethelbald of Mercia (746–7). It complains of the self-indulgent and 'Sodomitical' sexual habits of the English people (D. 56 c.10; Friedberg 1: 222; *PL* 89: 760–1; ed. and tr. E. Emerton as 'Letter lxxii' (1940), pp. 124–30). *Jacob's Well* cites what is apparently a version of the same letter but one that suppresses the accusation of sodomy (ed. Brandeis, EETS, os 115, p. 161/6–16). The letter is cited in the *Fasciculus morum*, ed. Wenzel, pp. 686–9. It is used by Bishop Brinton in 1375 in a sermon deploring the evils of the time (*Sermons*, ed. Devlin, 1: 216). On the career of St Boniface, see Duckett (1947), pp. 339–455; *ODS*, pp. 46–8. See 2–64/ 68–9, 2–96/19–20 below.

2–64/68–9 *Godis lawe . . . moder tunge*: Archbishop Arundel's Constitutions of 1407–9 include: 'Periculosa quoque res est, testante Beato *Hieronymo*, Textum Sacrae Scripturae de uno in aliud Idioma transferre, eo quod in ipsis translationibus non de facili idem in omnibus sensus retinetur, prout idem Beatus *Hieronymous*, etsi inspiratus fuisset, se in hoc saepius fatetur errasse. Statuimus igitur, & Ordinamus, ut nemo deinceps aliquem Textum Sacrae Scripturae auctoritate sua in linguam *Anglicanum*, vel aliam, transferat per viam Libri, Libelli, aut Tractatus: nec legatur aliquis hujusmodi Liber, Libellus, aut Tractatus jam noviter tempore dicti *Johannis Wickliff*, sive citra compositus, sive componendus in posterum, in parte vel in toto, publice vel occulte, sub poena Excommunicationis majoris, quosque per loci Dioecesanum, seu (si res exegerit) per Concilium Provinciale ipsa translatio recognita & approbata fuerit. Qui contra fecerit, ut fautor Haeresis & erroris similiter puniatur', Lyndwood's *Provinciale*, s.v. 'Constitutiones Provinciales Concili Oxoniensis', p. 66 (1679 edn.). For other references to laws restricting translation of the Bible see 148/44, 327/4, 327/10 above.

2–64/75–6 *þe secunde booc of Kyngis, xii [9]*: The story of David and Bathsheba is here very briefly told, and solely to make the point that sexual misbehaviour will be followed by social and personal misfortune; MS G omits three sentences that drive home the point. For a list of references to the story of David in *D&P*, see 2–85/19 ff. below.

2–65/92 *Iudicum xx [1–48]*: The story begins in Judg. 19: 1: a runaway wife is reclaimed by her husband, but on their journey home, at Gibeah in Benjamin, the wife is raped and murdered by local hooligans. The husband carves her corpse into twelve pieces and sends them to the twelve tribes as a call to arms. In the resulting internecine warfare, the tribes are nearly wiped out. Pauper's 65,000 seems to be an underestimate of the biblical casualty figures. LL4 cites the same passage, giving the same figure: 'Also for auouterie & lecherie þat was don with a mannys wiif þer wern slayn at goddys byddinge sexty þousand & fyue þousand & alle a cuntre destruyȝyd' (fo. 94ra). Cited below 2–105/27.

2–65/94–5 *a comoun prouerbe*: An analogue appears in Chaucer's 'Merchant's Tale': 'On brotel ground they buylde, and brotelnesse/ They fynde whan they wene sikernesse' (*CT*, p. 154/1279–80). Whiting, W649, lists an analogue from *Cursor mundi*: '. . . na werk may stande/ wit-out grounde wel to be lastande' (ed. Morris, EETS os 57, p. 14/124–6).

2–65/6–66/9 *This bon . . . Genesis ii [24]*: 'Quam ob rem relinquet homo patrem suum et matrem et adherebit uxori suae, et erunt duo in carne una'. In his commentary on this verse, Augustine points to the narrative discrepancy between Gen. 2: 23 and Gen. 2: 24: in the first, Adam speaks of what has just occured, the creation of Eve ('bone of my bone'). In the second, the voice of a commentator appears to intervene, predicting marriage and commenting on the couple's state of naked innocence. Augustine's solution follows Tertullian in suggesting that Adam spoke the words 'filled with a spirit of prophecy' ('ecstasis Adae'); he also follows Matt. 19: 4 and Eph. 5: 31–2 in attributing the words to Adam (*De gen. ad Lit.* 9.19; *PL* 34: 408). Tertullian (c160–225), *De anima* 11.4 (ed. Waszink (1947), p. 15/16–22; notes, pp. 198–8.

2–66/25 *power ouyr operis body*: Cf. 250/88, 2–59/32, 2–61/36 above.

2–66/27 *þe rybbe of Adam*: In *De gen. ad Lit.* 9.5, Augustine, in a rather Shavian passage, ponders the question why God made Eve as a helper for Adam rather than a servant: 'How much more agreeably could two male friends, rather than a man and woman, enjoy companionship and conversation in a life shared together.' He concludes that this proves that woman's only 'help' to a man is the bearing of children (*PL* 34: 397; *CSEL* 28–1: 275). Peter Lombard, however, like *D&P*, thinks that the use of the rib bone was intended to show that woman was meant to provide conjugal companionship ('ob coniugalem societatem'): *Sentences* 4.28.4 (2: 435). Cf. *Jacob's Well*: 'God made eue noȝt of Adamys hed ne of his fote but of his myd rybbe in signe þat þou man schuldyst kepe þe in myddes . þat is in temperure in mene mesure' (Salisbury MS 174, fo. 132ʳ).

2–67/10–71/113 *Sent Austyn, libro De decem cordis*: Most of *D&P* cap. v is translated from sections 3, 4, 11 and 12 of Augustine's *Sermo* IX ('De decem cordis') of *c*.411 (*CCL* xli, pp. 111–2/110–126; pp. 114–5/163–6; p. 115/167–71; pp. 130–32/438–61; pp. 115–6/171–83; p. 116/183–95; p. 128/394–407; pp. 128–9/407–19; p. 130/425–32; *PL* 38: 77–8; 83–4). See below 2–71/5–14.

2–71/5–14 *Sent Austyn in þe same booc*: Augustine, *Sermo* IX.12 ('De decem cordis'), *c*.411 (*CCL* xli, pp. 130–1/435–41; *PL* 38: 84). *D&P* 71–2/14–34 paraphrases rather than translating the rest of Serm. 9.12 (idem, pp. 131–2/441–61). See 2–67/10–71/113 above, 2–71/13 below.

2–71/13 *god principal*: Is the sense 'good principle' or 'God above all'? Comparison with the Latin original solves what might otherwise be a crux in

the Middle English: 'Et deus super te, tantum deus' (*CCL* xli, p. 131/441);
see above 2–71/5–14.

2–72/38–83 *Io. viii* [*2–11*]: On the story of the woman taken in adultery,
Augustine says that a sharp line cannot be drawn between justice and mercy;
God is merciful to the sinner who repents, but the sinner cannot know how
much time he has for repentance; justice is not only law in itself but also the
administration of law, and the guilty are not fit to administer legal punishment: 'Puniatur peccatrix, sed non a peccatoribus' (*In Ioh*, 33.4–7; *CCL*
xxxvi, pp. 307–10; *PL* 35: 1648–51). The Wycliffite sermon writer, like
D&P, applies the text to the administration of the law: '[I]ustisis of ech law
shulden be riȝtwes and clene of lif, for God mut reule men of þe lawe, hou
þey shulen iuge in ech caas'; unlike *D&P*, he refuses to speculate on what
Jesus wrote on the ground: 'Muse we not what Crist wroot . . . siche veyn
curiouste were a temptyng of God' (*EWS* 3, Serm. 164/31–3; 55; 61).

2–74/91–2 *iii, q. v, Constituimus, et vi, q. i, Qui crimen*: The first of the two
canons, 'Constituimus', states that persons of ill repute or those who consult
fortune tellers may not be accusers or witnesses in legal trials (C.3 q.5 c.9;
Friedberg 1: 516). The source is a papal epistle of Eusebius (d.310) The
second canon, 'Qui crimen', warns that persons who accuse others of crimes
must themselves bear scrutiny (C.3 q.6 c.18; Friedberg 1: 524). The canon
is attributed to a decretal of 'Pope Hadrian', probably Hadrian I (d. 795).

2–74/92–5 *Sent Ambrose . . . iii, q. vii, Iudicet*: The canon 'Iudicet' warns
that only those who do not have a criminal past may be permitted to judge
others (C.3 q.7 c.4; Friedberg 1: 527). The source is said to be a sermon of
St Ambrose, but editorial notes give conflicting views on which is the
particular sermon. The *dict. ante* is pithy: 'Ille de uita alterius iudicet, qui
non habet in se ipso quod puniat'.

2–74/97 *xxxii, q. vi, Nichil iniquius*: The canon 'Nichil iniquius' states that
an adulterer may not dismiss ('dimittere') his wife because of her adultery
(C.32 q.7 c.1; Friedberg 1: 1139). The text is an extract from Augustine, *De
serm. dom. in monte*, I, 16, 46 (*CCL* xxxv, p. 53/1127–33), citing Rom. 2: 1:
'In quo enim alterum iudicas, te ipsum condemnas; eadem enim agis quae
iudicas'.

2–74/99 *xxvii, q. ii, Si tu*: The canon 'Si tu' warns that a husband who
abstains from sexual intercourse without his wife's consent may be accused
of causing her to commit adultery (C.27 q.2 c.24; Friedberg 1: 1070). The
source is Augustine's 'De coniugiis adulterinis', 1.8.4, but according to the
editor's note this passage has the sense but not the exact wording; cf. *PL*
40: 455–6.

2–74/100 *xxxii, q. v, Ita ne*: The canon 'Ita ne' holds that violation of the
body does not entail violation of the soul ('pudicitia sit virtus animi') (C.32

q.5 c.3; Friedberg 1: 1132). It is an extract from Augustine's *De civ. dei*, 1.18 (*CCL*, xlvii, pp. 18–19/1–9; *PL* 41: 31).

2–74/101–2 *xxxiv, q. i* [*Cum*] *per bellicam*: The canon 'Cum per bellicam' holds, in summary, that whoever marries again, believing his spouse to be dead, must be made to return to the first spouse if she reappears (C.34 qq.1 & 2 c.1; Friedberg 1: 1256). The source is an epistle of Pope Leo I to Bishop Aquileia of Nice (*c.*458), see *PL* 54: 1136B–37B, Ep. 159, cc. 1–4. It is cited in the same connection in Peter Lombard, *Sentences* 4.38.3 (2: 482).

2–74/108 *xxxiv, q. ii, In lectum*: The canon 'In lectum' holds that a man cannot be forced to abandon his legitimate wife if he has unknowingly slept with her sister (C.34 q.1&2 c.6; Friedberg 1: 1259). The citation is said to be from the Council of Triburiensi, but the editor of Peter Lombard's *Sentences*, citing the same canon, notes that it is not found in the records of this council (4.36.3; 2: 474, see n. 3).

2–75/112 *xxii, q. i, Si quis vxorem*: The canon 'Si quis uxorem' holds that the one who sleeps with an adulterous spouse must render three years of penance (C.32 qq. 1 & 2 c.6; Friedberg 1: 1117). It is cited from a penitential attributed to Theodore of Tarsus, c.602–90, but is of later date. The text may be found in *Councils and Ecclesiastical Documents*, ed. W. Haddon and W. Stubbs, 3: 173–213.

2–75/113 *Extra, lib. iii, ti. xiii, Discrecion*[*em*]: The canon 'Discrecionem' states that an 'affinity' is not grounds for dissolving an existing marriage: 'Affinitas superveniens non dissolvit sponsalia de praesenti' (X 4.13.6; Friedberg 2: 698). The text is from an epistle of Innocent III.

2–75/118–9 *Extra, lib. iv, De diuorciis,* [*ti. 19*] *c. Gaudemus, et Si ergo*: The canon 'Gaudemus' comprises 'Si ergo'; both are in c. 8. 'Gaudemus' holds that non-Christians who are married within the prohibited degrees are not to be separated after their conversions. If the non-Christian has plural wives, he must retain only the first after his conversion, even if he has previously dismissed her and married another (X 4.19.8; Friedberg 2: 723–4). The source is an epistle of Innocent III.

2–75/10–11 *Summa confessorum, lib. iv, ti. xxii, q. vi, Quero, etc.*: From John of Freiburg's *Summa confessorum*, Bodley MS 299, fo. 273ʳ.

2–75/19–20 *Summa confessorum, lib. iv, ti. xxii, q. vii, Vtrum vir*: John of Freiburg's *Summa confessorum*, Bodley MS 299, fo. 273ʳ.

2–76/1–5 *simple fornicacion*: Aquinas answers Dives' objection by saying that fornication is a mortal sin (*ST*, II–II, 154.2). The penitentials lean toward the view that the offence is a serious and, depending on circumstances, a mortal sin, cf. de Chobham, *Summa*, ed. Broomfield, p. 344. In canon law, fornication is held to be only slightly less criminal than adultery, see Brundage (1987), pp. 72; 247;342; 380–5; 459–63. In everyday life,

however, the view persisted that simple fornication was a minor offence, and
there were differing views among legists. In the later Middle Ages, efforts to
regulate fornication by law greatly increased, see *Councils and Synods* 1: 385–
86, 411; Lyndwood, *Provinciale*, s.v. 'Constitutiones' of Archbishop Sudbury (1381): 'Quod omnis conjunctio maris & foeminae extra matrimonium
est mortale peccatum', p. 59^a (1679 edn.).

2–77/13–14 *I ad Corinth. vi [9–10]*: 1 Cor. 6: 9–10: 'An nescitis quia iniqui
regnum Dei non possidebunt? Nolite errare, neque fornicarii, neque idolis
servientes, neque adulteri, /neque molles, neque masculorum concubitores,
neque fures, neque avari, neque ebriosi, neque maledici, neque rapaces
regnum Dei possidebunt'.

2–77/14 *in þe chapitele nexst aforn*: 1 Cor. 5: 11: 'Si is qui frater nominatur
est fornicator, aut avarus, aut idolis serviens, aut maledicus, aut ebriosus, aut
rapax, cum eiusmodi nec cibum sumere'. LL4: 'Seynt powyl . . . seyþ þere .
ȝif þer be ony fals coueytous man nyggard or drunkelew or raueynour or
ȝouyn to ydolatrie or to lecherie . I bydde ȝow þat ȝe etyn ne drinkin wiþ
non swych' (fo. 24vb). The gloss, from Ps.-Augustine, 'De vera et falsa
poenitentia', warns that care should be taken to avoid condemning the
innocent (GO, 4: 314).

2–77/23 *ad Ephes. v [3]*: 'Fornicatio autem et omnis immunditia aut avaritia
nec nominetur in vobis, sicut decet sanctos.' In the gloss, Ambrose notes on
'avaritia' that: 'avarus est adulter qui sibi res alienas vsurpat, i.e., alienam
uxorem' (GO 4: 377).

2–77/25 *Ad Ebreos xiii [4]*: '. . . Fornicatores enim, et adulteros iudicabit
Deus'; the first portion of v. 13 is cited at 2–59/51–3 above.

2–77/28–32 *Sent Ion . . . Apoc. xxi [8]*: '. . . et homicidis et fornicatoribus et
veneficis et idolotris et omnibus mendacibus pars illorum erit in stagno
ardenti igne et sulphure, quod est mors secunda'. The GO says that those
persons will be damned who 'timore poenarum fidem accipere fugiunt vel
acceptam relinquunt' (4: 575).

2–77/32–6 *Salomon . . . Ecclesiastici ix [6;10]*: 'Ne des fornicariis animam
tuam in ullo, ne perdas te et haereditatem tuam . . . / Omnis mulier quae est
fornicaria quasi stercus in via conculcabitur'.

2–77/38–40 *whan a sengle man medelyth*: See 2–76/1–5 above.

2–78/47 *Crescite et multiplicamini*: Gen. 1: 28 is a text often cited, more or
less seriously, to justify fornication. Augustine says, however, that in context
it is to be understood figuratively, 'provectu mentis et copia virtutis
intelligatur', citing Ps. 137: 3, 'Multiplicabis me in anima mea virtute'
('De bono conjugali', *PL* 40: 374). Augustine is cited approvingly by
Grosseteste against those who obstinately deny that fornication is a mortal
sin (*De decem mand.*, ed. Dales and King, p. 67/27–8). Grosseteste says

Gen. 1: 28 may be interpreted figuratively as a mandate to teach: '. . . qua quisque bonus satagit et nititur generare bonum in alio quale est in se ipso' (*Hexaemeron*, ed. Dales and Green, p. 197/20–1). Cited 63/10, 72/10 above. See 2–76/1–5 above.

2–78/55–8 *Tobie . . . iv [13]*: See 2–62/6–22 above.

2–78/60 [*Colos. 3: 5*]: Cited 100/33–4, 166/12–13 above, 2–264/57 below.

2–78/64–9 *Leuitici xxi [9] . . . Deutero. xxii [13–21]*: Lev. 21: 9: 'Sacerdotis filia si deprehensa fuerit in stupro, et violaverit nomen patris sui, flammis exuretur'; the GO allegorizes the 'filia' as the synagogue, which is the daughter of God: 'vnde relinquetur filia syon sicut umbraculum in vinea' (1: 258). Deut. 22: 20–1: 'Quod si verum est quod obiicit, et non est in puella inventa virginitas,/ eicient eam extra fores domus patris sui, et lapidibus oburent viri civitatis eius et morietur'.

2–79/79 *Mathei v [28]*: 'Ego autem dico vobis: quia omnis qui viderit mulierem ad concupiscendum eam, iam moechatus est eam in corde suo.' Bede comments: '. . . non secundum quod quisque potuit & non licuit sed secundum quod voluit & proposuit ex conscientia accusatur vel defenditur' (GO 4: 21). Cf. *CA*, 1: 87. Cited 2–85/39, 2–87/77, 2–299/6 below.

2–79/19 *I ad Corinth. vi [16]*:'An nescitis quoniam qui adhaeret meretrici, unum corpus efficitur? Erunt enim (inquit) duo in carne una.' On 'unum corpus', the GO refers (interlin.) to Genesis ('mulier de viro facta') and to medical science: 'tradunt phisici quod adeo veniuntur, quia si sanguis eorum commisceretur omnio coniungeretur' (4: 315).

2–80/24–32 *Salomon . . . Ecclesiastici [23: 32–6] . . . glose*: 'Sic et mulier omnis relinquens virum suum et statuens hereditatem ex alieno matrimo-nio,/ primo enim in lege Altissimi incredibilis fuit, et secundo virum suum dereliquit, tertio in adulterio fornicata est, et ex alio viro filios statuit sibi;/ [v. 34 om.]/non tradent filii eius radices et rami eius non dabunt fructum;/ derelinquent in maledictum memoriam illius, et dedecus illius non delebi-tur'. The gloss says that adultery in men is as damnable as in women: 'Equaliter & in viro et in faemina damnatur adulterium'; it goes on to interpret the passage as an allegory of heresy and apostasy (GO 2: 768).

2–80/5–6 *Adam . . . erit?*: The Latin lines are referred to below (2–85/20) as 'þin vers'. The list is a commonplace in sermons, used when the preacher required *exempla* of the perils posed by women. Cf. *Sir Gawain and þe Green Knight*, ed. Tolkien and Gordon, rev. edn. Davis, p. 66/2416–9. Also found in legal texts: 'Vnde versus: Adam, Sampsonem, sic David, sic Salomonem, foemina decepit: quis modo tutus erit?' (in a section on clerical concubinage, 'Constitutio Domini Othonis', Lyndwood, *Provinciale* (edn. 1679), p. 42a)

2–80/10 *many mo women han ben deceyuyd*: See 2–81/29–40 below.

2–80/13–81/17 *Ecclesiastes vii* [27]: 'Et inveni amariorem morte mulierem, quae laqueus venatorum est et sagena cor eius vincula sunt manus illius, qui placet Deo effugiet eam qui autem peccator est capietur ab illa'. The gloss on 'venatorum': 'Demonum qui venantur animas nostras, quorum mulieres retia et sagene heretici' (GO 2: 702).

2–81/20 *Osee v* [*1*]: See above, 2–20/31–9, where Hos. 5: 1 is given a different translation and interpretation.

2–81/29–40 *þis fals excusacioun . . . woman in defaute*: The popular view was that Eve caused the Fall, as illustrated by the *Book of the Knight of La Tour-Landry* (1372), in which Eve's nine pre-lapsarian sins are described and Adam is not mentioned (ed. Wright, EETS, os 33, pp. 54–62). Augustine asks: How could the woman have fallen first if she had not already been 'proud'? (*De Gen. ad Lit.*, PL 34: 245–80). Ambrose concurs: 'It seems to me, however, that the initial violation and deceit was due to the woman . . . we can discern the sex which was liable first to do wrong' ('Paradise' 12.56, tr. Savage (1961), pp. 336- 7; 'Paradiso', PL 14: 319–21; CSEL 32.1: 267–336). Bede finds the answer in the punishment meted out by God: '. . . et maritus habere dominium meruit mulieris non natura, sed culpa' ('Hexaemeron' Bk. I; PL 91: 59). Augustine's view is echoed by Nicolaus de Lyra, who points to Eve's 'amor proprie' and pride (*Postilla* 1). In Robert Mannyng of Brunne's *Handlyng Synne*, however, Adam's excuse is cited under the heading of what not to do in shrift:

> 'Lord,' he seyde, 'my wyff made me begynne,
> 'þat yche wyff þat þou me wro3t,
> 'She synnede fyrst & y no3t.'
> (ed. Morris, EETS, os 119,123, p. 387/12346–8)

Few sympathetic views of Eve's temptation are on record, but Peter Comestor may have contributed to Pauper's stance in attempting a psychological explanation: Eve was overcome by involuntary sexual feelings aroused by the tempter—though he later says that Eve sinned less than the serpent but more than Adam (*Historia*, PL 198: 1072–3). A contributing cause of the blaming of Eve was the growing popularity of the idea that Eve was an antitype of Mary; the 'Ave' addressed to Mary reverses the spelling of Eve's name; Justin Martyr (d. 165) was the first to draw the parallel (J. Quasten, *Patrology*, 1: 211–12). In the end, Dives is not swayed by Pauper's arguments, and the subject is taken up again below, 2–83/77–8, 2–84/109–24, 2–121/2–3, 2–126/82–4, 2–127/9, 2–126/1–129/92.

2–81/44–5 *þe neddere . . . a face lyk a woman*: The ultimate Latin source of this extra-biblical notion may be the *Vita* of Adam and Eve (dating from 100 B.C.- 200 A.D.), in which Eve describes her tempter as an angel of light: ' "then Satan came in the form of an angel and sang hymns to God as the angels" ' (J. H. Charlesworth, *OT Pseudepigrapha* (1985), 2: 277). In the *ME*

Sermons (*c*.1413) there appears: 'To the foule fende such folke be lykened, that appered to Adam and Eve in Paradyse and shewed a fayre womans face hym to be-gyle, and vnder that fayre face there was hydde a foule fynde [fiend]' (ed. Ross, EETS, 209, p. 294/35–9). See also the metrical version of Grosseteste's 'Castle of Love': 'Then he come in neddir liknesse to eue with a wommans face' (*Minor Poems of the Vernon MS*, ed. Horstmann, EETS, os 98, p. 409/53); cf. Comestor (*PL* 198: 1072). The mystery plays adopt the theme: see *The Chester Mystery Cycle* (ed. Lumiansky and Mills, EETS ss 3), 1: 21/193–5; *The N-Town Play* (ed. Spector, EETS ss 11, 12), 1: 28/156. Cf. *The Holkham Bible Picture Book*, ed. W. O. Hassall, fo. 4 (London, 1954).

2–81/45 *Bede & þe Maystyr of Storiis*: Bede, 'Hexaemeron', Bk. I, describes the serpent as a blend of animal and angelic being: 'quantumlibet enim praevaricatores angeli de supernis sedibus suae perversitatis et superbiae merito dejecti sint' and 'semen diaboli praevaricatores sunt angeli' (*PL* 91: 53; 58). Peter Comestor: 'Eligit etiam quoddam genus serpentis, ut ait Beda, virginum vultum habens' (*Historia*, *PL* 198: 1072).

2–82/66 *Io. viii* [*44*]: Cited above 154/39–43, 161/42, 163/37–8, 2–231/ 43–8.

2–82/74–5 *Sent Powil . . . 2 Cor. 6: 15*: 'Quae autem conventio Christi ad Belial?' GO: 'Item, nihil habet templum dei cum ydolis & vos estis templum dei. Ideo non debetis communicare cum his qui sunt templum dyaboli' (4: 345).

2–83/77–8 *I ad Tymotheum ii* [*14*]: 'Et Adam non est seductus, mulier autem seducta in praevaricatione fuit'. A long gloss from Augustine (similar to a passage in *De civ. dei* 14.11) maintains that Eve was seduced by the promises of the serpent but Adam, wanting to avoid offending his 'friend', Eve, counted on God's forgiveness; Adam's sin was therefore less than Eve's. An interlinear gloss points to the moral weakness of Eve as the reason why women may not teach in the churches, though they may instruct their children daily in matters of faith (GO 4: 407). Nicolaus de Lyra's gloss is similar to Augustine's: 'In hoc que crederet esse verus serpentis dictum, "Eritis sic dii", fuit tamen seductus in hoc que ad exhortationem mulieris comedit de ligno vetito ne contristaret eam, et que credit illam transgressionem non sic esse puniendam' (*Postilla* 4). See 2–126/1–128/92, 2–126/ 6–7. 2–127/9 below.

2–83/87–90 *Sent Austyn, De civitate . . . Eccli. 10: 15*: 'In occulto autem mali esse coeperunt ut in apertam inoboedientiam laberentur. Non enim ad malum opus perveniretur nisi praecessisset voluntas mala. Porro, malae voluntatis initium quae potuit esse nisi superbia? *Initium* enim *omnis peccati superbia est*' (*De civ. dei* 14.13: *CCL* xlviii, p. 434/23–5; *PL* 41: 421). Ecclus. 10: 15 is cited in LL4: 'þe begynnyng of euery synne ys pride, for it makyth manys herte & womannys fyrst to gon awey from god þat made hym of nouȝt' (fo. 67va).

2–83/92–4 *Salomon . . . Prouer. xvi [18]*: Another translation of Prov. 16: 18 is given in LL4: 'Lowȝnesse folwith þe proude & joye & blisse schal takin hym þat is loȝw & meke in spyryȝt' (fo. 87va).

2–83/95–103 *Sent Austyn*: That Adam and Eve were proud and altogether too pleased with themselves before they tasted the apple is repeated several times in the rest of *De civ. dei* 14.13, most succinctly: 'Non ergo malum opus factum est, id est illa transgressio, ut cibo prohibito vescerentur, nisi ab eis qui iam mali erant' (*CCL* xlviii, p. 434/18–20; *PL* 41: 421). See 2–83/87–90 above.

2–83/104 *þerfor Sent Powil seith*: Probably a reference to 1 Cor. 15: 22: 'Et sicut in Adam omnes moriuntur, ita et in Christo omnes vivificabuntur'.

2–84/107–8 *to Adam alone he seyde*: Gen. 3: 17: 'Adae vero dixit . . . maledicta terra in opere tuo.'

2–84/109–24 *Ambrose, super Lucam*: In his 'In Lucam', Ambrose consistently and often refers to Eve's sin as the first and greater sin. In his 'De paradiso', 12.56, he does, however, refer to the mitigating circumstance that Eve confesses her sin—for which she receives a lighter punishment. There he also refers to 'the fact that she was the one destined to bring forth redemption' (tr. J. J. Savage, pp. 336–7; 350; *PL* 14: 319–21; 328). In neither work is there found the statement that Eve's sin was less than Adam's; Ambrose is cited in 2–81/29–40 above. *Jacob's Well* refers to Adam's attempt to shift the blame: 'Adam seyde, lord, þe womman which þou ȝaue me to be my felawe ded me etyn of þe appyl . . . As who seyth, þou [God] & sche were cause of my synne' (ed. Brandeis, EETS, os 115, p. 261/1–4). Cf. Blamires (1997), pp. 112–19.

2–84/4–19 *Sampson . . . [Iud. 16: 4–31]*: The story of Samson, in its OT setting a powerful lesson on the dangers of exogamy, has been reinterpreted in Christian terms as a prefiguration of the story of the Redemption (see *ABD*, 5: 950–4). Dives and Pauper respond to it chiefly as good fiction: Dives connects it with popular mysogyny; Pauper draws from it an object lesson in sexual morality. Another reference, 2–52/38–46 above.

2–85/19 ff. *Dauyd . . . Kyngis, xi [2–17]*: 2 Sam. 11: 2–17. In *D&P*, the stories about King David are frequently retold: the story of David and Abigail (2–142/53–144/89), of David's feigned madness (2–218/26–30), of David dancing before the Ark of the Covenant (297/32), of David and Bathsheba (2–64/75–6, 2–85/19, 2–105/30, 2–122/28, 2–297/56–62), of David's mourning for his infant son (2–261/68–73), of David's son, Absalom (307/17–31, 2–105/42), of Amnon and Tamar (2–88/107–116), of David's death and the building of Solomon's temple in Jerusalem (192/54–193/75).

2–85/20 *as þu seydyst in þin vers*: See above, 2–80/5–6.

2–85/39 [*Mt. 5: 28*]: See 2–79/79 above; cited 2–87/77, 2–299/6 below.

2–86/47–58 *Sent Gregory . . . Mathei xxvi [69–75] et Marci xiv [66–72]*: St Gregory first says the serving maid ('ancilla') was tempted by curiosity, but corrects himself, saying she was just doing her job ('sed ab ostiaria est ancilla requisitus'): *Moralia* 17.31.48 (*CCL* cxliiiA, pp. 879–80/15–19; *PL* 76: 34). On Matt. 26: 69–75, the GO accounts for the prominence of women in the temptation of Peter and the discovery of the resurrection by alluding to the fact that Eve was the first to be tempted (4: 83). On Mark 14: 66–72, the GO comments that since a woman was foremost in the Fall, so it was fitting that she should appear foremost in the Redemption in being first to attest the resurrection (4: 131).

2–86/58–66 *Salomon . . . Deutero. xvii [17]*: 'Non habebit uxores plurimas quae inliciant animum eius, neque argenti et auri immensa pondera.' Middle Engliish 'hors' in this context could be taken to mean 'whore', but if so the plural would normally be spellt 'ho(o)res', see *MED*, s.v. 'hor(e (2)'; the word probably refers back to 'equos' in the previous verse: 'non multiplicabit sibi equos'. The gloss (from Augustine) makes a distinction between 'many' ('plures') wives—a privilege granted to kings—and the 'multiplication' ('multiplicatio') of wives, especially those of foreign birth (GO 1: 397).

2–87/77 [*Mt. 5: 28*]: See 2–79/79, 2–85/39 above and 2–299/6 below.

2–87/82 *Men lechourys*: Brothels were established as a defensive measure against such sexual freebooting: 'Municipal authorities licensed or sponsored the brothels not to protect the prostitutes or their customers but to maintain social order', Karras (1996), p. 32; cf. J. Rossiaud, *Medieval Prostitution*, tr. L. G. Cochrane (N.Y., 1988, repr. 1995), pp. 11–26. Pauper's 'Men comounly ben . . . begynnerys of lecherie' echoes 'De decem cordis', a sermon in which St Augustine castigates male pride in virility: 'Si quis uolutatus fuerit cum ancillis suis, amatur, blande accipitur. . . . Si quis autem existat qui dicat se castum, . . . ne insultent, ne irrideant, ne dicant non esse uirum' (9.12, *CCL* xli, p. 131/452–6; *PL* 38: 84]).

2–87/96–107 *Daniel, xiii [1–64] . . . Susanne*: The story of Susannah and the Elders has, down the millennia, clung to its association with the biblical text despite frequent relegation to apocryphal status. Among early Christian exegetes, Hippolytus, Bishop of Rome in 230, saw Susannah as 'a type prefiguring the Church; Joachim her husband prefigures Christ. The garden is the election of the saints, who like trees that bear fruit are planted in the Church. Babylon is the world; the two elders are typical of the two nations who plot against the Church' (Charles, *Apocrypha* (1913), 1: 645). For the use of Daniel 13 in the Sarum rite, on the 'Sabbato post oculi', where it is paired with the story of the woman taken in adultery (John 8: 3–11), see *Sarum Missal*, ed. Legg, p. 78. A Middle English version of the story of Susannah in alliterative verse dating from *c.*1350 has been edited from five manuscripts by A. Miskimin (1969); a 'History of the Legend to 1400' is given in her App. I, pp. 189–99; cf. the earlier edition, *The Minor Poems of the Vernon MS, II*, ed. Furnivall (EETS, os 117), 2: 626–36. See below 2–222/15.

2–88/107–116 *þe secunde book of kyngis, Regum xiii [1–19*: The firstborn son of King David, Amnon, is known only for the rape of his half-sister, Tamar, as recounted in 2 Sam. 13; see *ABD*, 1: 196–7. For other references to the story of David, see above, 2–85/19 ff.

2–88/5 *þu excusist mychil women & accusist men*: Pauper has been pursuing an Augustinian line, drawing on Augustine's sermon, 'De decem cordis', the relevant portions of which are translated in the text of *D&P* above, 2–67/10–71/113.

2–89/14 *Mulier . . . [Prov. 31: 30]*: 'Fallax gratia et vana est pulchritudo; mulier timens Dominum ipsa laudabitur'. The GO cites the example of Job, who praised God in prosperity and adversity, and alludes to the wise virgins who with 'burning lamps of virtue' enter the heavenly kingdom with the bridegroom (2: 693). Cf. 2–6/51–74 and 2–6/65–6 above.

2–89/16–18 *Salomon . . . Ecclesiastici xxv [17; 26]*: 'Omnis plaga tristia cordis est, et omnis malitia nequitia mulieris est,/. . . Brevis malitia super malitiam muleris'. The glosses on 'omnis plaga' and 'brevis malitia' are similar; on 'brevis': 'Parua est omnis malicia ad comparationem ydolatrie & prauitatis haereticae quia peccant, non per fragilitatem carnis sed per superbiam mentis' (2: 771).

2–89/22–37 *Salomon . . . Ecclesiastici xxvi [1–3; 16–17; 19; 21; 23–4]*: In his translation of the biblical text of Ecclus. 26: 1–24, the writer of *D&P* has extracted a paean to good women by omitting fifteen lines which are largely in dispraise of women (e.g., v. 8: 'A jealous woman is the grief and mourning of the heart', Douai). Cf. Introduction, p. xxxii.

2–89/37–8 *Salomon . . . Ecclesiastici xix [2]*: The GO: 'Fornicatio qua derelicta veritate fide, iunguntur demoniis' (2: 762).

2–90/55 *flyȝt is best fyȝth*: This instance is the only listing of the saying in Whiting, F281, p. 189.

2–90/1 *Womanys aray*: An age-old complaint against women. The Pauline epistles transmitted the theme to Christian moralists, see below 2–91/17–20, 2–91/20–2.

2–91/17–20 *Sent Powil . . . I ad Tymo ii* [*9–10*]: 'Similiter et mulieres in habitu ornato cum verecundia et sobrietate ornantes se, et non in tortis crinibus, aut auro aut margaritis, vel veste pretiosa,/ sed quod decet mulieres promittentes pietatem per opera bona.' The gloss (interlin.) advises that women should adorn themselves in the virtues of modesty and sobriety. They should studiously avoid moving men to concupiscence; good works should be the outward sign of their piety (GO, 4: 407). *Jacob's Well* cites St Gregory as its authority for saying that 'wommen þat arayin hem nycely to be seyn of folys synnyn grevously þow3 þei haue no wyll to do þe synne in dede' and goes on to denounce women who 'setyn all here stodye in pride of aray of here heed & of here body to lokyn in myrrourys in kemmyng here heed, in here hornys, in peerlys, in oþer ryche aray abowte the heed . in ryngis, in brochys, in bedys, in longe trayles' (Salisbury MS 174, fos. 196ʳ, 197ʳ). Cf. Richard Rolle's *Fire of Love* (ed. Harvey, EETS, os 106), pp. 94–5/37 ff..

2–91/20–2 *Sent Petyr . . . fyrste pystyl iii* [*3–5*]: For [: 3–5] read [: 7]: 'Viri similiter cohabitatntes secundum scientiam, quasi infirmiori vaso muliebri inpertientes honorem'. See 2–59/32 above.

2–91/28 *Sent Cecilie*: '. . . illa subtus ad carmen cilicio erat induta et desuper deauratis vestibus tegebatur'. See 349/52 above.

2–91/31–2 *embyrdayys, gangdayys . . . vygilyys*: Ember days are the Wednesday, Friday and Saturday after the feast of St Lucy (13 December), after Ash Wednesday, after Whitsunday (50th day after Easter) and Holy Cross day (14 September). Gang days are the three Rogation days (Monday, Tuesday, Wednesday) before Ascension Day (the fortieth day after Easter). Vigils were originally night-time services, as before Easter, but in the later Middle Ages were generally kept on the day preceding a major feast day.

2–92/53–4 *ankerys & incluhs*: On the seventh state of chastity, see, e.g., *The Book of Virtues and Vices*, ed. Francis (EETS, 217), pp. 264–72; the *Ayenbite of Inwit*, ed. Gradon (EETS, os 23), pp. 238–45. On Richard Rolle and the 'perfect life', see Watson (1991), pp. 7–18. See 2–93/87–91 and 2–188/68 below.

2–92/58 *Man, be weye of kende*: Dives expresses what is undoubtedly a popular view of the greater moral stability of women in sexual matters, but he also sees that this view conflicts with the theology of the Fall (see 2–81/29–40 above). In reply, Pauper distinguishes between natural moral stability and moral stability imparted by grace: women, 'knowynge her frelte', seek and receive God's help.

2–93/67 *Ps. 110: 10; Eccli. 1: 16; Prov. 9: 10*: The text is the same in each, except that Prov. 9: 10 has 'principium' for 'inicium'. Augustine on Ps. 110: 10 asks, Who would disagree? But, he warns, to understand and not to act on the understanding is perilous (*Enarr.* 110.9; *CCL* xl, p. 1625/8–9; *PL* 37: 1466).

2–93/87–91 *But women [oftyn] takyn þat stat*: Margery Kempe's *Book* records her consultation (early in the second decade of the fifteenth century) with Julian of Norwich about her own visions and revelations, because 'þe ankres [anchoress] was expert in swech thyngys & good cownsel cowd ȝeuyn'. Margery Kempe's 'most dred was þat sche xuld turnyn & not kepyn hir perfeccyon' (ed. Meech and Allen, EETS, 212, pp. 42/16–17; 43/271). See Clay (1914) on the 'oracular office' of hermits and anchorites, pp. 146–66; more generally, Bynum (1982), pp. 110–262.

2–93-4/91–109 *Genesis xii [13] & xx [2] . . . Abraham . . .de Lyra*: It is unusual for the story of Abraham and his family and descendents to be used to illustrate the thesis that women are readier than men to call upon God's help. Nicolaus de Lyra first gives a practical reason why Abraham instructed his wife to call herself his sister—he had to act in self-defence—but he derives from the Hebrew text that at the same time Sarah knew she was under the protection of an angel (*Postilla* 1).

2–94/109–23 *Abraham . . . Ysmael . . . & Isaac . . . Gen. 21: 9–14*: Again (see 2–93/91–94/109 above) the story of Isaac and Ishmael is given a very narrow interpretation: a woman knew the mind of God better than her husband. *D&P*'s 'not goodly' (text 2–94/113) is not supported by the Vulgate text. Nicolaus de Lyra says the Vulgate's 'ludentem' is a mistranslation of the Hebrew, which means 'playing at idol-worship' (*Postilla* 1). Cf. LV, FM 1:116var. Early modern translations: 'a-mocking' (Tyndale) and 'mocking' (KJ).

2–95/123–134 *Esau & Iacob . . . [Gen. 27: 33]*: All elements of the story of the twins, Esau and Jacob, are ignored in this interpretation except Rebecca's superior knowledge of the intentions of God. This is the aspect singled out by St Paul: 'Non ex operibus sed ex vocante dictum est ei [Rebecca],/quia maior serviet minori, sicut scriptum est' (Rom. 9: 12–13). The GO repeats that Rebecca acted through no merit of her own 'sed sola gratia' (4: 293).

2–95/11–13 *[Eccli. 33: 29]*: The GO: 'Describitur ergo qualis debeant esse seruilis nutritura & disciplina vt habeant . . . victum & vestitum non vagandi ocium' (2: 778–9). Cited, with a different translation, below 2–310/111–12.

2–95/13–6 *Ecclesiastici xxxiii [25]*: 'Cibaria et virga et onus asino, panis et disciplina et opus servo.' GO: Necesse est ut iniqui serui seueritat dominorum conprimantur, ne illicita fruantur libertate. In quibus non natura despicienda sed improbitur coercenda, aut sciant se subditos esse. Recte autem serui sunt qui viciis seruiunt' (2: 778–9).

2–96/19–20 *Ezechielis xvi* [*passim*]: The particular accusation of sodomy is part of a sermon in which 'Jerusalem' is personified as a beautiful young woman who has become a harlot. In Ezek. 16: 49, sodomy is personified as the sister of 'Jerusalem': 'Ecce haec fuit iniquitas Sodomae, sororis tuae; superbia, saturitas panis et abundantia et otium ipsius, et filiarum eius, et manum egeno et pauperi non porrigebant', which last phrase is followed by the instruction to give alms as a remedy against lechery, leading to the citation of Luke 11: 41 below (2–96/26). LL4: 'And þerfore god seyth þat pryde & plente of mete & habundaunce of rychesse & ydylschepe & for þey wolden nout helpin þe pore folk wern þe wyckydnesse of sodom & gomor & cause of here synne & of here destruccioun (fo. 62rb); '. . . & fille of bred & plente of rychesse & eese wern cause of þe wickidnesse of sodomy & also for þei wolden nout helpin þe pore folk' (fo. 109rb). See 2–11/25–30, 2–63/51–64/63, 2–64/68–9 above.

2–96/26 [*Lc. 11: 41*]: LL4: 'Зeuyth elmesse of зoure relef & of зoure superfluite & alle þingis ben clene to зow' (fo. 117va). GO: 'Iam bonus doctor quomodo contagium corporis mundari debeat docet. . . . Totus enim hic locus ad hoc dirigitur, ut nos ad studium simplicitatis invitet & superflua iudaeorum & terrena condemnet, qui secundum corpus intelligendo legem, vitro & catino propter fragilitatem comparantur. . . . Prima elemosina est mederi animabus vestris credendo in me qui corda mundo, & per fidem mundatis cordibus omnia etiam exteriora erunt munda' (4: 183–4).

2–96/27–8 *a man to han mende of hys deth*: On the Latin *momento mori* poem, see Rigg (1992), pp. 39, 120–7, 237–8, 304–12; Patterson (1911; repr. 1966, pp. 13–15; 47–155). See 2–247/10 below.

2–96/35–8 *Salomon . . . Ecclesiastici vii* [*40*]: Interlinear gloss on 'memorare': 'ad mortem, vnde omnis qui natus est ex deo non peccat' (GO 2: 752). LL4: 'þink indyrly of þi laste þingis & of þin ende & schalt þu neuere synnyn dedlyche' (fo. 22ra). Cited again below, 2–273/98 and 2–303/4–7.

2–96/38–97/55 *We redyn . . . þat whylum smellyd so swote*: The story of Fair Rosamund is based on a historical personage, Rosamund Clifford (d. 1176), mistress of Henry II. In 1191, Hugh, bishop of Lincoln, discovered her tomb occupying a place of honour in Godstow nunnery; he ordered a reburial outside the church and is said to have been responsible for the inscription on her tomb cited in *D&P*, extant until the Reformation. By the late thirteenth century, her story had become a popular legend, embellished with fictions about her labyrinthine bower reachable only by following a silken thread, about her two sons by Henry II, and about her poisoning by Queen Eleanor. Cf. Thomas Deloney's ballad, 'Fair Rosamond', in Thomas Percy's *Reliques* (1840), pp. 124–7. A likely source of the version in *D&P* is Trevisa's translation of Ranulf Higden's *Polychronicon*, 8: 53–4.

2–97/59–60 *Sent Powyl . . . I ad Corinth. xv [33]*: 'Nolite seduci corrumpunt mores bonos conloquia mala.' GO: 'A pseudo qui de medicina quaerunt vulnus & descripturis conantur torquere vinculum, vnde laqueum mortis inijciant' (4: 334).

2–97/62–4 *[Iob 31: 1]*: 'Pepigi foedus cum oculis meis ut ne cogitarem quidem de virgine.' On this verse, St Gregory sermonizes at length on the importance of disciplining one's thoughts against fleshly temptation (*Moralia*, 21.2.4–7; *CCL*, cxiiiA, pp. 1065–9; *PL* 76: 189–93). *D&P* follows him in citing Jer. 9: 21 (see below 2–97/68).

2–97/64–6 *Ieremye . . . Treno. iii [51]*: Lam. 3: 51: 'Oculus meus depraedatus est animam meam in cunctis filiabus urbis meae.' The verse is taken from the portion of Lamentations in which the speaker is a male alternate to the principal speaker, a female personification of the fallen city of Jerusalem, destroyed in 586 BC. There is no obvious reason why the verse should here be interpreted as a warning against the seductions of 'þe women of his cyte'. Nicolaus de Lyra sheds no light; in his gloss, he says the Hebrew text has been mis-transcribed: 'Sic ordinatur iste versus pro precedentem prout in hebreo habere, quamuis in aliquibus libris nostris sit econuerso; dicit ergo, "Oculus meus afflictus est a magnitudine fletus"' (*Postilla* 2). The GO allegorizes the passage as a prefiguration of the Passion, but it also has a passage referring the 'oculus' to the temptations presented by women, which may have influenced the reading in *D&P*: 'Oculus temtationis dicitur quia per eum temptamur, vnde qui viderit mulierem ad concupiscendum', etc. (3: 204).

2–97/68 *Ieremie ix [21]*: 'Quia ascendit mors per fenestras nostras, ingressa est domos nostras disperdere parvulos de foris, iuvenes de plateis.' GO: 'Quia tanta erit fortitudo et velocitas hostium, ut non expectent hostium sed per fenestras & tecta conscendant' (3: 146).

2–98/72 *Mathei xv [19]*: Cited above, 273/13 (with the LL4 translation), and below, 2–253/13, where the Latin text is given.

2–98/72–4 *Salomon . . . Prouer. iv [23]*: LL4: 'Keep þyn herte with al maner kepyng for þens comyth lyf & deth' (fo. 49ʳᵇ); 'With al maner keping kepe we þin herte . for why from þe herte goth boþin liif & deeth' (fo. 99ʳᵃ). GO: 'Sunt qui recte vivere videntur hominibus sed quia recta intentione non faciunt, a deo qui cor respicit pravam, & vita reprobatur quae credebatur bona; omni ergo diligentia cordis mundiciam serua, quia ad eius examen modus extimatur vitae' (2: 660).

2–98/75 *Maystir of Kendys, lib. xviii*: The Trevisa translation of Bartholomaeus, 18.103: '. . . þe fox . . . feyneþ him as þough he were seke and ouercome and fleeþ away. And while þe brok [bauseyn] goþ oute and geteþ his pray þe fox comeþ into his denne and defouleþ his chambre wiþ vryne and oþer vnclennesse. And þe brok [bauseyn] is scoymous of suche foule þynges and forsakeþ his hous þat is so defouled and geteþ needefulliche anoþer wonyng place' (*Properties*, 2: 1254/9–15). On the words 'brok' and 'bauseyn', see 94/29–32 above. For other examples of the tale, see J. A. Herbert, *Catalogue of Romances* 3: 13, No. 82; 3: 25, No. 214; 3: 555, No. 184; 3: 578, No. 41.

2–99/2–4 *Sent Gregorie . . . passion*: On recourse to meditation on the Passion as a remedy for sexual temptation, see 84/39 above.

2–99/5–101/60 *gestis . . . a gret kyngis sone*: The core of the 'tale of the bloody shirt', probably older than the Christian tradition, was adapted in the early centuries as an allegory of the Redemption. It appears in the Latin *Gesta Romanorum*—cf. *D&P* 'we fyndyn in gestis' (ed. Herrtage, EETS, es 33, pp. 23–6). In the *Fasciculus morum* (ed. Wenzel), the knight is Virgil's Aeneas, and the couplet 'Cerne cicatrices' is attributed to Ovid (see 2–100/18–21 below), pp. 204–5. The tale is among the extensions of the fables of Odo of Cheriton (d. 1247), see J. A. Herbert, *Catalogue of Romances*, No.104, p. 55. Middle English versions of the tale are found in the *Ancrene Riwle* (EETS, 249, pp. 198–9), on which see Dobson (1975), pp. 173–6); and in *The Book of the Knight of La Tour-Landry* (ed. Wright, EETS, os 33, pp. 142–3). See 2–100/18–21 and 2–100/29–32 below.

2–100/18–21 *Cerne cicatrices . . . Beheld myn wondys*: The Middle English translation of 'Cerne cicatrices' ('Beheld myn wondys') is listed in *IMEV*, No.498; *D&P* is not cited. S. Wenzel, *Verses in Sermons* (1978), points out (pp. 161–3), that the Latin lines are from Ovid's *Amores*:

> cerne cicatrices, veteris vestigia pugnae—
> quaesitum est illi corpore, quidquid habet.
>   (III, viii/19–20; LCL 41, *Heroides and Amores*,
>   1: 482/19–20)

2–100/29–32 *Whyl Y haue his blood in mende*: *IMEV* Supp. No.'s 3568.5 and 4074.5, citing the 'Gesta Romanorum' (but not *D&P*). Two prose versions of 'the bloody shirt tale' are found in the *Gesta Romanorum* (ed. Herrtage, EETS es 33), pp. 23–6. See 2–99/5–101/60 above.

2–100/43 [*Phil. 2: 7–8*]: 'Sed semet ipsum exinanivit formam servi accipiens, in similitudinem hominum factus et habitu inventus ut homo,/ humiliavit semet ipsum factus oboediens usque ad mortem, mortem autem crucis.' LL4: 'Whanne he was in þe forme of god he anynteschid hymself, þat is to seye, he lowid hymself so mechil þat he took þe forme & þe schap of his seruaunt & was maad into þe liknesse of men & was foundin as man in cloþinge of oure manhod' (fo. 139ra; a briefer reference on fo. 56rb). The translation of VL 'semet ipsum exinanivit' by 'anynteschid hymself' is unusual; the *MED* does not cite *D&P* but does cite the *Pauline Epistles* (ed.

Powell, EETS, es, 116) and Nicholas Love's *Mirror* 43 (ed. Sargent). Referred to, with the same translation, below 2–301/30.

2–101/58–9 *Isaye i* [6]: 'A planta pedis usque ad verticem non est in eo sanitas, vulnus et livor et plaga tumens non est circumligata nec curata medicamine neque fota oleo.' The GO links Isaiah 1: 6 to the story of the good Samaritan and to the dispersion of the Jews (3: 3).

2–102/71–91 *Reminiscens . . . To wynnyn mannys loue*: The Latin lines could be (and ought to have been) set out as verse:

> Reminiscens sacrati sanguinis
> Quem effudit amator hominis
> Effundo lacrimas.
>
> Non est locus ingratitudinis
> Ubi torrens tante dulcedinis
> Attingit animas.

The entire Latin poem appears in Horstman. *Yorkshire Writers*, 1: 435, from BL MS Arundel 507, fo. 107^r (see also Drèves, *Analecta*, 8: 2). The 'Victorine' stanza form is common in Latin hymns, appearing most notably in the 'Stabat mater dolorosa' (F. J. Mone, ed., *Lat. Hymn.*, No. 446, 2: 147; and see Raby (1953), pp. 436–40). There are close similarities between this poem and stanza 35 and the first half of stanza 36 of 'An ABC Poem on the Passion of Christ' (BL MS Harley 3954, fo. 87^r), in *Political, Religious and Love Poems*, ed. Furnivall (EETS, os 15), p. 278.

2–102/93 *Sent Ierom*: Cited from St Jerome's letter written in 411 to Rusticus about the requirements of the monastic life. Rusticus became Bishop of Narbonne in 430 (tr. LCL 262, Ep. CXXV.11, pp. 416; *PL* 22: 1072–85). See 2–202/48–52 below.

2–102/97 *Exodi xxxiii* [20]: 'Rursumque ait non poteris videre faciem meam, non enim videbit me homo et vivet'. The gloss by St Gregory explains that in OT times God was not to be identified with any image, but after the Incarnation, the image of God was visible in Christ (GO, 1: 195). Cited below 2–325/69.

2–103/101 *Sent Thomas, De ueritate teologye*: Aquinas's continuator devotes Q. 97 to the punishment of the damned. In Article 1, he says the damned will pass from the most intense heat to the most intense cold. In Article 3, a kind of non-corporeal weeping will occur. In Article 4, there will be darkness. In Articles 5 and 6, the fire of hell will be corporeal. In Article 7, hell is located in the bowels of the earth (*ST*, Supp. 37.1–7; OP edn. (1894), 5: 622–30).

2–103/110–11 *Sent Bernard . . . Meditacionys*: The Ps.-Bernard 'Meditationes': '[N]ihil aliud ibi audietur nisi fletus et planctus, gemitus et ululatus, moerores atque stridores dentium: nihilque ibi videbitur, nisi vermes, et larvales facies tortorum, at teterima monstra daemonum. "Vermes crudeles mordebunt intima cordis:/ Hinc dolor, inde pavor, gemitus, stupor, et timor horrens". Ardebuntque miseri in igne aeterno in aeternum et ultra. In carne cruciabuntur per ignem, in spiritu per conscientiae vermem. Ibi erit dolor intolerabilis, timor horribilis, fetor incomparabilis, mors animae et corporis sine spe veniae et misericordiae. Sic tamen morientur, ut semper vivant; et sic vivent, ut semper moriantur. . . . Bonum siquidem et malum, vita et mors, ante nos sunt posita, ut ad quod voluerimus manum extendamus. Si tormentis non terrent nos, saltem invitent praemia' (*PL* 184: 491–2). A Middle English translation of Grosseteste's early-thirteenth-century 'Castle of Love' has a parallel list of torments: 'filth', 'stynk', 'brennand fire', 'gret cold', 'gnasting of teth', 'And euer in the hert a sorowe souerayne/ That thai haue lost for a litil lykyng of synne/ the ioye of the siȝt of god that al godenes is Inne', 'Of the paynes of hell', *Minor Poems of the Vernon MS* (ed. Horstmann, EETS os 98, p.438/1095–1110).

2–104/4 *Genesis xxxiv* [*1–31*]: The story of the rape of Dinah is here told as a warning against lechery. In its biblical context, it bears on the question of exogamy: Shechem was a Canaanite, and the war leading to the destruction of his city was caused by the refusal of Dinah's brothers to countenance her marriage to a non-Israelite (see *ABD*, 2: 200). The GO censures Dinah's carelessness—'quia sponte negligens, vagatur mox a dyabolo corrumpatur' (1: 84), and Nicolaus de Lyra her 'curiositas' (*Postilla* 1). Cf. 2–104/11 below.

2–104/11 *Numeri xxv* [*1–15*]: As in the story of the rape of Dinah (2–104/4 above), the story of Phinehas is essentially about exogamy, not lechery. The man and woman were slain by Phinehas not for fornication but because the woman was a Midianite. The GO makes the story the occasion of a long sermon on the temptations of the flesh ('Ipsa historia nos aedificat, docens quia aduersus nos militat fornicatio'), in which figure Balaam, Jezebel, St Paul (on 'meretrices'), and even 'amatores philosophiae' who study old tales instead of the scriptures (1: 341–2). Brief references in LL4, fo. 80vb, and 2–264/41 below.

2–105/25 *Genesis vi* [*17–18*]: For [17–18] read [11–13]: 'Corrupta est autem terra coram Deo et repleta est iniquitate . . . /et ego disperdam eos cum terra.' The sins prevalent before the Flood are not specified in Genesis. Exegetes, from Philo of Alexandria onwards, have speculated about what these sins might have been.

2–105/27 *Iudicum xix et xx*: See above, 2–65/92.

2–105/30 *II Regum xi & xii*: 2 Sam. 11 & 12. The penalty for adulterers is found in Lev. 21: 10. For the story of David and Bathsheba and a list of references to the David story in *D&P*, see above, 2–85/19 ff.

2–105/37 *Genesis xxxviii* [*7–10*]: The story of Onan has been associated with the practice of masturbation, but it is more properly coitus interruptus of which Onan was guilty; see *ABD* on this and on levirate marriage, 5: 20–1.

2–105/39 *Tobie vi* [*13*]: See above, 2–62/6–22.

2–105/42 [*2 Sam. 13: 32*] Tamar, daughter of King David and Maacah, sister of Absalom, and half-sister of Amnon, was raped by Amnon and avenged by Absalom See above, 307/17–31; for other references in *D&P* to the story of David, see 2–85/19 above.

2–105/45–6 [*Gen. 19: 30–8*]: Lot, a nephew of the patriarch Abraham, escapes from the destruction of Sodom and Gomorrah, losing his wife but taking refuge with his daughters in a cave, where, perhaps believing they were the earth's sole survivors, the daughters conceive sons by their father, Moab and Ben-ammi, see *ABD* 4: 372–4.

2–105/47 [*Gen. 35: 22*]: '. . . abiit Ruben et dormivit cum Bala, concubina patris sui quod illum minime latuit; erant autem filii Iacob duodecim.' Reuben was the first-born son of Jacob and Leah, who lost his birthright as a result of his seduction of Bilhah, who had been Rachel's slave as well as Jacob's concubine; cf. 1 Chr. 1: 5. Cited below, 2–316/59.

2–106/60–1 *Genesis xix* [*17–28*]: Pauper expresses the received idea that Sodom and Gomorrah were located near the Dead Sea and that their crime was sodomy. Josephus, claiming to have seen the pillar of salt himself (Gen. 19: 26), first describes the Sodomites as merely 'overweeningly proud of their numbers and the extent of their wealth' but goes on to note that the Sodomites, at the sight of the angels who, in the guise of beautiful young men, warned Abraham, 'were bent only on violence and outrage to their youthful beauty', *Jewish Antiquities* 1.1–4 (LCL 186, 1: 94–9; see also Comestor, *Historia, PL* 198: 1101).

2–106/73 *þe Maystir of Storyys*: Peter Comestor: 'Licet enim illi mensuram excederent delicti, tamen quasi naturaliter peccabant, et universos subvertit etiam parvulos pro peccatis parentum, in quo provisum est illis, ne diu viventes, sequerentur exempla patrum, et est aliquod bonum reum non esse, qui gloriosus non est' (*Historia, PL* 198: 1101).

2–107/2–3 *þe secunde booc of Kyngys, vi* [*6–7*] . . . *Maystir of Storyys*: 2 Sam. 6: 6–7: Uzzah (here and in Comestor 'Oza') is one of five OT figures who bear this name. The Uzzah mentioned here is known only because of the death that resulted from his effort to keep the ark from falling from the wagon bearing it to Jerusalem. In the biblical account, the emphasis is on the numinous quality of the ark; it is not suggested that Uzzah's death resulted from sexual impurity. Comestor gives three alternate explanations: according to Josephus, because he was not a priest, Uzzah should not have touched the ark; the ark should have been borne on men's shoulders; or Uzzah had

had intercourse with his wife on the previous night (*Historia*, *PL* 198: 1330); cf. Josephus, *Jewish Antiquities* 7.2 (LCL 281, 5: 408).

2–107/16 *Di. xxxii, Nullus, et c. Preter hoc*: Two canons: (1) 'Nullus' forbids parishioners to hear the mass of a priest who has a concubine or a 'subintroductam mulierem' (D. 32 c.5; Friedberg 1: 117). The source is a papal letter of Nicholas II (d. 1061). (2) The canon 'Preter hoc' is a decree of Pope Alexander II (d. 1073) which says the same as 'Nullus' but which continues with the citation of the opposing views of Jerome, Augustine and others, turning on the question whether the sacrament itself is altered by the prior conduct of the priest. The conclusion is that only in the case of baptism (which in an emergency a lay person may perform) can the requirement of celibacy be waived (D.32 c.6; Friedberg 1: 117–9).

2–107/23 *Di. xxviii, Decernimus*: The canon 'Decernimus' declares that clerics who are ranked as subdeacons or above who have wives or concubines must not occupy ecclesiastical office or benefice (D.28 c.2; Friedberg 1: 101). The source is a decretal of Pope Innocent II (d. 1143).

2–108/25–9 *Di. lxxxi, Clericus . . . Cum omnibus*: Two canons: (1) 'Clericus' orders the suspension of clerics who frequent women's domiciles ('matronarum domicilia') (D.81 c.20; Friedberg 1: 286). The source is a decretal of Pope Lucius III (d. 1185). (2) 'Cum omnibus' directs that women living in the same households as priests must be close relatives, such as mothers, grandmothers, aunts and the like (D.81 c.27; Friedberg 1: 288). The decree was issued by the third Council of Carthage (on these Councils, see *ODCC*, s.v. Carthage).

2–108/32–7 *Extra, De cohabitacione . . . Vestra*: Two canons: (1) 'Inhibendum' provides that any women suspected of incontinence, however closely related she may be, must be ejected from the households of clergy (X 3.2.1; Friedberg 2: 454). (2) 'Vestra' is a papal reply to a query about how long a fornicating cleric may be allowed to administer the sacraments. Much depends on whether the sin is openly known; if the fornication is known, the cleric should not administer the sacraments; if not, he may continue. The sacraments themselves are not, in any case, impaired (X 3.2.7; Friedberg 2: 455–6). The epistle derives from the papacy of Lucius III (d. 1185).

2–108/46 *Extra, eodem, c. Vestra, et c. Quesitum*: For the canon 'Vestra' see 2–108/32–7 above. The canon 'Quesitum' is cited from Pope Gregory IX (d. 1241). It provides that a 'clericus concubinarius' is not to be shunned or suspended from his office unless his sin becomes notorious (X 3.2.10; Friedberg 2: 457).

2–109/51–2 *Di. lxxxi, Si quis amodo*: The canon 'Si quis amodo' is from a letter of Pope Alexander II (d. 1073) to the bishop and king of Dalmatia answering a query about the penalty for clerical fornication ('Si . . . feminam acceperit'). Whether he is bishop, priest or deacon, he shall not appear in the church during services nor shall he have any portion of the goods of the Church (D.81 c.16; Friedberg 1: 285). Cited below, 2–169/39–43.

2–109/52–60 *Sent Gregorie . . . Di. lxxxi, Si qui sunt*: The canon 'Si qui sunt' holds that priests, deacons or subdeacons who are persistent fornicators ('qui in crimine fornicationis iacent') shall not be allowed to enter the church until they have become penitent and changed their behaviour (D.81 c.15; Friedberg 1: 284–5). The source is an epistle of St Gregory VII (Hildebrand), who was Pope from 1073–1085. Cited below, 2–169/49–50.

2–109/61–3 *But ȝe wil heryn . . . Malachie ii [1–2]*: 'Et nunc ad vos mandatum hoc, o sacerdotes,/ si nolueritis audire et si nolueritis ponere super cor ut detis gloriam nomini meo, ait Dominus exercituum, mittam in vos egestatem et maledicam benedictionibus vestris et maledicam illis quoniam non posuistis super cor'. The gloss reiterates the threat (GO, 3: 454).

2–109/7–8 *Summa confessorum, lib. iii, ti. xxxiv, q. CCi, Quero, etc.*: John of Freiburg's *Summa*, MS Bodley 299, fo. 238ᵛ.

2–110/16–17 *xxvii, q. i, Nupciarum . . . Impudicas, et Sciendum*: Three canons: 'Nuptiarum' (from the Palea) is a long discussion of the indissolubility of marriage vows summed up in the *dict. ante*: conjugal vows are not to be dissolved (C.27 q.1 c.41; Friedberg 1: 1060). The second canon 'Impudicas' is from a conciliar decree which orders that immodest or lascivious persons are to be ejected from monasteries or workhouses (C.27 q. 1 c.11; Friedberg 1: 1051). The third canon 'Sciendum', also from a conciliar decree, states that those who violate the persons of women vowed to chastity are sacrilegious and sons of perdition ('filii perditionis') (C.27 q.1 c.37; Friedberg 1: 1059).

2–110/20–1 *xvii, q. iv, Sunt qui*: The canon 'Sunt qui' (from the Palea) appears to concern changes of mind in cases of repentance. In the case of those who repent a vow to give their possessions to the poor, St Ambrose says, all such persons have to fear is failure to carry out the penance for their sin—whether or not it is a sin of sacrilege (C.17 q.4 c.3; Friedberg 1: 815). The source is Ambrose's 'De penitencia' 2.9.

2–110/22 *xxxii, q. vii, Quid in omnibus . . . glose*: The rather confused wording of the canon 'Quid in omnibus' is clarified by Gratian's *post dict.*, which says that whoever has divorced a wife because of fornication may not marry another while the first is living (C.32 q.7 c.16; Friedberg 1: 1144).

2–111/39 *[Lc. 12: 47]*: 'Ille autem servus qui cognovit voluntatem domini sui et non praeparavit et non fecit secundum voluntatem eius vapulabit multas [severely flogged]'. Ambrose glosses 'vapulabit': 'Multi existimantes se minus vapulaturos si nesciant quid operari debeant auertunt ne audiant veritatem. Sed cum possent scire vellent studium adhibere, non nescientes, sed contemtores iudicantur' (GO 4: 188).

2–111/40 [*Sap. 6: 7*]: Wisd. 6: 7: 'Exiguo enim conceditur misericordia, potentes autem potenter tormenta patientur'. The GO glosses 'exiguo' as 'His qui per ignorantium uel fragilitatem vel necessitatem peccauerunt et humili penitentia deleuerunt'; the gloss on 'potentes': 'Qui, sci., mandata dei contemnendo, grauia peccata commiserunt, nec penituerunt. Sicut enim potentiores fuerunt in impietate, fortiora sustinebant tormenta gehennae' (2: 728).

2–111/46–51 *Sent Gregorie*: St Gregory says: 'Et tunc ad ueram cognitionem redeunt subditi, cum ad aeterna supplicia peruniunt hi qui male fuerant praelati, apte subiungitur' (*Moralia* 18.14.22; *CCL* cxliiiA, p. 898/8–10; *PL* 76: 49).

2–111/58–9 *Summa confessorum, lib. iii, ti. xxxiv, q. CCii*: John of Freiburg's *Summa confessorum*, MS Bodley 299, 'Post hoc', fo. 238ᵛ.

2–111/59–64 *For þese skyllys . . . di. 32, c. Omnium sacerdotum*: The canon appears to be 'Cum sacerdotum'; it enjoins the celibacy of all men in sacred orders. Clerics who were married before their promotions must become celibate; those who have wives must live thenceforward as if they were unmarried; those who are unmarried must remain so (D.32 c.1; Friedberg 1: 116). The source is a papal letter of Leo IV (d.855), a saint and fervent reformer of Church discipline.

2–111/1–4 *bygamye . . . Di. lxxxii, Proposuisti*: 'Bigamy' here has both the literal sense of having two wives and the figurative sense of compromising the unity between Christ and the Church. Distinction 82 is not about bigamy but about the responsibility of bishops to give to the poor. The canon 'Proposuisti' is, however, about setting an example by disciplining concupiscent clerics (D. 82 c.2; Friedberg 1: 290). Bigamy is mentioned in the preamble to Distinction 35, but what follows is mostly about drunkenness. Distinctions 33 and 34 contain the most material relevant to clerical 'bigamy', see Friedberg 1: 122–30, and 'De bigamis', Friedberg 2: 146–8. Burchard of Worms has a relevant Decretum, headed: 'Ut non laici, nec bigami, nec viduorum mariti, sed irreprehensibiles ordinentur episcopi' (*Decretum, PL* 140: 551). See 2–116/128, 2–116/130–1 below.

2–112/12 [*Eph. 5: 23 et seq.*]: 'Quoniam vir caput est mulieris sicut Christus caput est ecclesiae ipse salvator corporis, /sed ut ecclesia subiecta est Christo, ita et mulieres viris suis in omnibus./ Viri diligite uxores sicut et Christus dilexit ecclesiam et se ipsum tradidit pro ea.' The GO: '. . . christus nutrit ecclesiam cibo corporis sui & fouet spiritualibus indumentis praeceptorum virtutum & bono operum'. Augustine's gloss refers to the creation of Eve: 'Sicut eua de adam facta traxit ab eo carnem & ossa, ita nos a christo instituti, alii sumus vt ossa robusti, alii vt caro infirmi . . .' (4: 378).

D&P's Marian interpretation of the passage is not found in the gloss. See 2–114/88 below.

2–112/20 *Sent Austyn, In questionibus Orosii*: From Ps.-Augustine, 'Dialogus quaestionum lxv, Orosii': '*Quaest. xlv.* Numquid quia opus erat Adae ut ei conjux fieret, aliter non poterat fieri, nisi ut dormienti costa detraheretur, ex qua conjux aedificaretur? *Resp.* Poterat Deus etiam aliter facere, sed ideo congruentius judicavit ut sic faceret, unde aliquid significaretur. Sicut enim dormienti Adae costa detrabitur ut conjunx efficiatur, ita et Christo morienti de latere sanguis effunditur, ut Ecclesia construatur. Communicando nempe corpori et sanguini Christi efficitur Ecclesia Christi conjunx' (*PL* 40: 747–8). For a previous implicit reference to Christ 'slepynge upon þe cros' see 2–66/27 above.

2–114/88 [*Eph. 5: 27*]: '. . . ut exhiberet ipse sibi gloriosam ecclesiam, non habentem maculam aut rugam aut aliquid eiusmodi sed ut sit sancta et inmaculata'. The gloss provides wedding imagery: 'Fit enim ex duobus quasi una quaedam persona, sci., et capite & corpore ex sponso & sponsa . . .' (4: 378), but, again, not the Marian imagery invoked by Pauper. Cf. 2–112/ 12, 2–112/20 above.

2–115/99 [*1*] *ad Tymo. iii* [*2*]: 'Oportet ergo episcopum inreprehensibilem esse, unius uxoris virum. . . .'. GO: 'Id ist, monogamum post baptis[mum]. Si enim & ante coniungem habuit quae obierit, non ei inputatur, cui prorsus nouo nec stupra nec alia quae ante fuerunt, iam obsunt' (4: 408). In answering Dives, Pauper makes a post-biblical interpretation of the text: a priest must have been married only once before becoming a priest.

2–116/128 *Summa confessorum, lib. iii, ti. De bygamis*: John of Freiburg's *Summa confessorum*, 3.3.1–13: MS Bodley 299, fos.114ʳ-115ᵛ (the heading 'De bigamis' appears on fo. 114ʳᵃ). See also Raymond of Peñafort's *Summa*, Bk. 3, 'De Bigamijs', pp. 259–64, in which the marginal gloss is by John of Freiburg. See 2–111/1–4 above.

2–116/130–1 *Extra, lib. i, ti. De bygamis, c. Quia*: The canon is from an epistle of Innocent III answering a query from an English archbishop who was a papal legate. The Pope advises that priests who have concubines, whether successively or several at one time, are not guilty of bigamy (X 1.21.6; Friedberg 2: 148). See 2–111/1–4 above.

2–116/6 *Extra, lib. iii, ti. De [purificatione] post partum*: The canon 'Volens' is from an epistle of Innocent III answering a query from the Archbishop of Armagh. The Pope assures the Archbishop that women may attend Church services as soon after childbirth as they wish; the shadow ('umbra') of OT restrictions has long been dispelled (X 3.47.1; Friedberg 2: 652).

2–116/13–14 *Genesis xvi* [*1–3*]: In contrast to Dives' literal reading, the figurative interpretation of the story of Abraham, Sarah, Hagar and Ishmael dates from the earliest times. For patristic typology (referring to Gal. 4: 22–6), Sarah and Hagar and their sons foreshadow the division between the two testaments and between the earthly and heavenly Jerusalem: 'Vmbra sane quaedam ciuitatis huius et imago prophetica ei significandae . . .' (Augustine, *De civ. dei* 15.2–3; *CCL* xlviii, p. 454/1–2; *PL* 41: 438). The GO, citing Rabanus Maurus, answers Dives' question, saying 'Non est adulter Abram . . . quia nondum promulgata erat lex euangelii unius uxoris, & genus suum multiplicandum'. The gloss continues, however, with a series of typological interpretations: Hagar is the 'terrenam hierusalem . . . in qua vetus lex carnaliter et seruiliter exercebatur'; Sarah is 'vero gratia'; Sarah and Hagar foreshadow the two testaments and the division between 'sinagoga' and 'ecclesia'. The Saracens are foreshadowed by the 'desert' (1: 49–50). In Comestor's *Historia*, Ishmael is said to be the progenitor of the Saracens: 'Tamen de genere ipsius hoc praedictum est, quia Sarraceni vagi sedibus incertis gentes, quibus desertum ex latere jungitur impugnant, et ab omnibus impugnantur' (*PL* 198: 1096).

2–117/30–1 *Priuilegium . . . xxv, q. i, c. vltimo* [*16*]: The canon 'Ideo permittento' is from an edict of Pope Leo IV (d, 855) and says that laws received from the Fathers should be obeyed without exception (C.25 q.1 c.16; Friedberg 1: 1010–12). The canon is, however, followed by Gratian's long *post dict.* setting forth the difference between law and equity and concluding with the ringing pronouncement that equity is a fundamental principle of law, and the Church may make exceptions to rules in the interest of justice. The maxim 'Priuilegia singulorum non possunt legem facere communem' is cited by Gratian, attributed (doubtfully) to Jerome, 'In expositione Ionae', c. 1.

2–117/34 *Sent Austyn*: In his *De civ. dei*, 5.4–5, Augustine makes the story of Esau and Jacob (Gen. 25: 24–6) the basis of his argument against astrology (*CCL* xlvii, pp. 131–3; *PL* 41: 144–6); cf. *De doct. christ.*, 2.22.33 (*CCL* xxxii, p.57/13–9).

2–118/5 *saddyn þe eyr*: Aquinas: '. . . cum enim ipse [the Devil] *possit formare corpus ex aere* cujuscumque formae, et figurae, ut illud assumens in eo visibiliter appareat, potest eadem ratione circumponere cuicumque rei corporeae quamcumque formam corpoream, ut in ejus specie videatur' (*ST*, Ia, 114.4; OP edn., Rome, 1884, 1: 850).

2–118/8 [*2 Cor. 11: 14*]: Cited 169/22 above.

2–118/14–15 *incubi . . . succuby*: The biblical starting point for beliefs in demons who consort with women is Gen. 6: 1–4, where the 'sons of God' and the 'daughters of men' together breed the 'mighty men that were of old'. This passage, combined with later ones telling of the visitations of angels in human form, gave rise to much speculation (cf. Num. 13: 32–3). Josephus (c. 37-c. 97) expands on the passage: 'For many angels of God . . .

now consorted with women and begat sons who were overbearing and disdainful of every virtue, such confidence had they in their strength' (*Jewish Antiquities*, 1: 73; LCL 242, 4: 34–5); see ed. note on 'sons of God'). Augustine—against a background of pagan belief in the possibility of sexual relations between gods and humans—speculated that 'Siluanos et Panes, quos uulgo incubos vocant, inprobos saepe extitisse mulieribus et earum appetisse ac peregisse concubitum' (*De civ. dei*, 15.23, CCL xlviii, p. 489/ 16–18; *PL* 41: 468–71). Nicolaus de Lyra notes that there are several explanations of 'filii dei': 'nomen hebraicus quod ibi ponitur, scilicet, 'eloym', aliquando accipitur pro deo, aliquando pro diis in plurali, aliquam pro iudicibus . . .' etc., and concurs that the 'filii dei' are the descendents of Seth, and that the 'filias hominum' are descendents of Cain ('qui erant curiose dissolute et lubrice'). He adds that God's wrath, and the Flood, was provoked by the exogamy practised by the sons of Seth (*Postilla* 1). By the time of Peter Comestor, the word 'incubus'was firmly associated with Gen. 6: 1–4 and its 'giants': 'Potuit etiam esse, ut incubi daemones genuissent gigantes . . . quia incubi vel daemones solent in nocte opprimere mulieres' (*Historia*, PL 198: 1081). The explanatory note on Chaucer's reference to 'incubus' in the Wife of Bath's Tale refers to this passage in *D&P* (*CT*, p. 117/880; n. p. 873).

2–119/17 [*Ps. 105: 39*]: '. . . et fornicati sunt in adinventionibus suis'. The gloss (attributed to Augustine) on 'adinventionibus' (LL, 'devices'): 'Non quia primi invenissent sed quia alios imitati sunt. Quid in graeco aptius et hic et supra, vnde et alii transferunt studio, vel affectiones vel voluntates' (GO, 2: 593). This is somewhat clarified in the source, Augustine's *Enarr.* 105.31, where he understands 'adinventiones' as those things which 'non a seipsis excogitauerunt sed alios imitati sunt' (*CCL*, xl, p. 1565/29; *PL* 37: 1415). Hence *D&P*'s 'her owyn fyndyngis'.

2–120/25–7 *Sent Powil . . . II ad Corinth. iv* [2]: 'Sed abdicamus occulta dedecoris, non ambulantes in astutia neque adulterantes verbum Dei, sed in manifestatione veritatis commendantes nosmet ipsos ad omnem conscientiam hominum coram Deo.' The interlinear gloss: 'Non solum aperta mala sed etiam cogitationes. . . . vt pseudo qui videntur humiles' (GO, 4: 341).

2–120/31–4 *Sent Iamys . . . Iac. iv* [4]: The Vulgate gives 'Deo' as an alternate reading for 'Dei' (2: 1862, note). The gloss stresses that it is not the powerful oppressors or blasphemers who are to be feared so much as the worldly ('amatores mundi'). These include adulterers, who love the world more than the word of God (GO, 4: 517).

2–120/36–9 *Babilonie . . . Apoc. 17: 1–2, 5*: In the writings of the early Church, 'Babylon' was a symbolic name for pagan Rome. In later periods, 'Babylon' was used (as it is here) as a general symbol for corrupt worldly power, the antitype of the Heavenly Jerusalem. It was also applied to the papacy by its critics, who often contrasted the worldly Church and the Church as the Bride of Christ. In *Hali Meiðhad* (1190–1220), 'þe hehe tur of Ierusalem', or 'Syon', represents the high ideal of maidenhood, while 'Babilones folc, þe deofles here of helle' represent 'flesches lustes and feondes eggunge' (ed. Millett, EETS, 284, p. 2/4–16).

2–120/40–1 [*1 Tim. 6: 10*]: Text cited above, 58/34, 78/32, below, 2–253/ 14, 2–296/37–8, and in LL4, fos. 34vb, 95va.

2–121/52 *Apoc. xvii et xviii* [*4; 8–10*]: Rev. 17: 1–2, 5 is cited above, 2–120/ 36–9. LL4 cites Rev. 18: 4: 'My peple, go ȝe out of babilonye, þat is to seyȝe, out of schenschepe and schenful companye & takyth no part of here synnys' (fo. 14rb). The gloss at the beginning of Rev. 18 describes the chapter as a vision of the punishments that are to follow the Last Judgement: 'In haec sexta visione agit de ultimis paenis quas patientur impii in inferno pro singulis peccatis & primum de babilone ostendit, post ex de bestia & pseudo prophetis, tandem de ipso diabolis in quo finis patet. In quo damnato erit finis istam damnationem executurus a christo praedicatem esse dicit vt maior ei fides habeatur' (GO, 4: 570).

2–121/2–3 *þe synne of Adam . . . þe synne of Eue*: In cap. x, Pauper argued that Adam 'was mor in defaute þan woman' (2–81/39–40 above) because it was to him God gave the command not to eat of the tree, and because Adam compounded his disobedience by excusing himself to God. That Adam's sin was greater than Eve's is also shown by the fact that God chose to be incarnated as a man and suffer as a man Here Pauper argues that worse sins may be more lightly punished on earth while greater sins will be punished more severely in purgatory or hell (2–122/40–2 below); but in the following chapter, he asserts that in fact Eve's punishment was *less* than Adam's, hence, by the previous logic, her sin was greater than Adam's. The author appears not to see the inconsistency. But by the end of Commandment VI the argument has become more atmospheric than logical or theological. See 2–81/29–40, 2–83/77–8, 2–84/109–24 above; and a recapitulation 2–126/ 1–129/92 below.

2–121/22–3 *periurie . . . in þe secunde comandement*: See 252/1 above.

2–122/28 *Dauyd dede auouterie*: For references to the story of David and Bathsheba see 2–64/75–6, 2–85/19 ff., 2–105/30 above, 2–297/56–62 below. For a list of all the references to the story of David, see 2–85/19 above.

2–122/32–3 *Moyses . . . Salomon, Ieroboam, Acaz*: Moses: see Num. 15: 32– 6; Salomon: 1 Kgs. 11; Ieroboam: 1 Kgs. 12 and 13; and Acaz (Ahaz): 2 Chron. 28: 2.

2–122/43 *contricion*: The essential first step in the sacrament of penance. Contrition is to be followed by confession and satisfaction, see Aquinas, *ST*, Supp., 1.1.

2–123/58 *þe lyon is chastysyd*: Trevisa's translation of Bartholomaeus, 18.65, says: 'þe leoun dredeþ whanne he seeþ or hiereþ a whelpe ybete', giving Solinus (early second century) as a source (*Properties*, 2: 1216/18–19; on Solinus, *Collectanea rerum memorabilium*, ed. Mommsen (2nd edn., Berlin, 1895), pp. 119–20. See Whiting, W211, for references to the saying, including this one in *D&P*. The story is alluded to in Chaucer's 'Squire's Tale': 'And for to maken othere be war by me/ As by the whelp chasted [*sic*] is the leon' (*CT*, p. 175/490–1), on which see C. S. Brown and R. H. West, 'As by the Whelp Chastised is the Leon', *MLN* 55 (1940), 209–10.

2–123/61–9 *Therfor Crist . . . Luce xiii [1–5]*: Pauper's list of precedents for the punishment of Eve now includes Sodom and Gomorrah (Gen. 19: 24–5), the lion and the whelp (2–123/58 above), and two groups of innocent Galileans (2–123/61–6). The gloss on Luke 13: 1–5 instructs that the deaths of these innocents are a prefiguration of the Last Judgement and suggests further that the eighteen (eighteen is the Hebrew letter corresponding to the first letter of 'Jesus') killed by the Tower of Siloam are a prefiguration of Christ's death (GO 4: 189).

2–125/52 *Sent Austyn, super Genesim, lib. xi, cap. xiv*: 'For we must believe that even before her sin woman had been made to be ruled by her husband and to be submissive and subject to him' (*The Literal Meaning of Genesis*, tr. J. H. Taylor, 2: 171; *De gen. ad lit.*, *PL* 34: 450). See 2–66/27 above.

2–125/66–7 *þe Maystir of Storiis*: Comestor's *Historia*: 'Et elata mulier [Eve] volens similari Deo, acquievit' (*PL* 198: 1072). There is a similar application of 'elata' in Peter Lombard's *Sentences*: 'Et talis quidem elatio in mente mulieris pro certo fuit, qua credidit et voluit habere similitudinem Dei . . . putant esse verum quod diabolus dicebat', Bk. II, cap. 2 (1: 441/2–4).

2–126/82–4 *And so boþin lordchep in þis world & subieccion ben punchyng of Adamys synne*: '. . . the servitude by which men later began to be slaves to other men obviously has its origin in punishment for sin' (*The Literal Meaning of Genesis*, tr. J. H. Taylor, 2: 171; *De gen. ad lit.*, *PL* 34: 436; 450).

2–126/1–128/92 *Ʒet clerkys arguyn . . . skylfolyche*: A summary of the disjointed argument about the guilt of Eve carried on in chapters 10, 23, 24 and 25 may clarify the issues. Dives complains that women, beginning with Eve, are the snares and deceivers of men. Pauper retorts that Adam was more at fault than Eve (81/41). While both Eve and Adam were filled with pride (83/92), Eve was the weaker partner (83/83), so Adam should have known better. Dives argues that men are in fact weaker psychologically than women, as proved by the 'fact' that male anchorites more often go mad (92/

53–8). Pauper replies that, on the contrary, men are more stable, but women, knowing their weakness, are more apt to ask for and receive God's grace (93/87–91). Dives has heard 'clerkys' say that Eve incurred the harder punishment, ergo her sin was greater than Adam's (121/3–7). Pauper (rashly) counters by asserting that God often punishes smaller sins more severely than greater ones, reserving full punishment for the afterlife (121/10–16). That Eve's punishment was lighter is shown by her not having been cursed, as Adam was (123/3–7). Furthermore, part of Adam's punishment was having to care for a weaker, enfeebled Eve (126/88–91). Likewise, after the Fall, Adam's sovereignty was more of a burden than a privilege—so much so that men sometimes find themselves in a subordinate position to a woman (129/76–80). In the end, Dives fails to pick up the implication that, if Adam has been more severely punished as a result of the Fall his guilt is less and he can expect lighter punishment in the next world—and the guiltier Eve can expect a harsher one.

2–126/6–7 *Sent Austyn, De civ. dei, lib. xiv, cap. xi*: Augustine: 'Ac per hoc in eo quidem quo mulier seducta est non est ille seductus' (*De civ. dei* 14.11; *CCL* xlviii, p. 433/91–2; *PL* 41: 410).

2–127/9 [*1 Tim. 2: 14*]: See 2–83/77–8 above, 2–127/26–9 below.

2–127/26–9 *Sent Austyn . . . Ysodorus, De summo bono, lib. ii*: Augustine: 'Non enim frustra dixit apostolus: "Et Adam non est seductus . . .", nisi quia illa quod ei serpens locutus est tamquam uerum esset accepit, ille autem ab unico noluit consortio dirimi nec in communione pecacati nec ideo minus reus, si sciens prudensque peccauit' (*De civ. dei*, 14.11; *CCL* xlviii, p. 433/74–84; *PL* 41: 419). Isidore of Seville, *Sententiarum* II.c.17 (*PL* 83;620), also citing 1 Tim. 2: 14.

2–127/28–9 *Adam . . . Sent Austyn . . . þe Maystir of Sentence, lib. ii, d. xxii*: Augustine: 'Sed inexpertus divinae severitatis in eo falli potuit, ut veniale crederet esse commissum. Ac per hoc in eo quidem quo mulier seducta est non est ille seductus, sed eum fefellit quo modo fuerat iudicandum quod erat dicturus. . . . Etsi credendo non sunt ambo decepti, peccando, tamen ambo sunt capti et diaboli laqueis inplicati' ['For the Apostle was not speaking idly when he said: "And Adam was not deceived. . . .". He must have meant that Eve had accepted what the serpent said to her as though it were true, while Adam refused to be separated from his sole companion even in a partnership of sin. Yet he was no less guilty if he sinned with knowledge and forethought'] (tr. from LCL 414, *City of God*, 4: 331; *De civ. dei* 14.11: *CCL* xlviii, p. 433/89–96; *PL* 41: 420). Peter Lombard: 'Adam vero nec illud credidit, et de poenitentia et Dei misericordia cogitavit . . .' (*Sententiae*, Bk. II, di. 22, c. 4; 1: 442/21–2).

2–127/31 *Mathei xii [32]*: The gloss is drawn largely from Augustine's 'De sermone domini', 1.22.75, and Chrysostom's Sermon 41 on Matthew; both stress the difference between ignorance and knowledge. On Matt. 12: 32, Augustine says that what can be forgiven before conversion to Christianity cannot be forgiven afterwards (*CCL* xxxv, p. 85/1847–52; *PL* 34: 1267). Chrysostom says Christ's answer to the disciples' questions about blasphemy against the Holy Spirit is: '. . . of this surely you are not ignorant, that to cast out Devils and to do cures is a work of the Holy Ghost. It is not then I only whom ye are insulting but the Holy Ghost also. Wherefore your punishment can be averted by no prayers, neither here nor there' (Hom. 41.5, tr. P. Schaff, p. 267; *PG* 57: 417–9).

2–129/71 *so lowe in ordre of kende*: At the close of Commandment VI, the place of Adam and Eve in the natural order has been altered by the Fall; the natural order has lost its original perfection; thus there is a certain dissonance between the natural order and God's will. The problem is neatly summarized in the *Cursor Mundi*:

> He that made kynd may fulle-fille
> Ayen kynd what is his wille.
> (ed. Morris, EETS, os 59, Pt. II), p. 626/10899–900)

2–129/90 *þe doom of oþir clerkis*: The scribe who revised the *D&P* Table (Table B) was on Dives' side of the controversy over Eve. The summary of Commandment VI, caps. 24 and 25, in Table A is: 'þe synne of Adam was mor greuous . . . God punchid hardere Adam þan he dede Eue, for hys synne was more' (17/65–9 above). In Table B, the scribal comment has been added: 'For that was þe opynyen of hym þat drewe þis boke' (42/cap. xxv above).

VOL. 1: 2, COMMANDMENT VII (1),
pp. 2–130–173

2–130/3 [*Ex. 20: 15*]: The GO (citing Isidore of Seville) asks the question whether 'non furtum facies' differs from the ninth Commandment, 'non concupisces'; Isidore answers that the ninth is broader in scope and contains the seventh (1: 153). Nicolaus de Lyra defines 'non furtum facies' as 'omnis contractio rei aliene, vel retentio iniusta', citing Raymond of Peñafort's *Summa* (see 2–130/16–17 below), *Postilla* 1. Grosseteste (*c.*1230) sums up the seventh Commandment: '. . . prohibetur omnis usurpacio rei aliene, sive vi, sive clam, sive fraude aliqua' (*De decem mand.*, ed. Dales and King, p. 75/8–9). From which it follows, says Wyclif: 'quod omnis rapina, omnis iniusta exacio vel iniuriacio in bonis fortune sub furti nomine continetur', *De mand.*, p. 365/5–7. On the numbering of the Commandments see 81/7 above.

2–130/16–17 *Reymund, lib. ii, ti. De furtis*: Raymond of Peñafort: 'Furtum est contrectatio rei alienae, mobilis, corporalis, fraudulosa, inuito Domino, lucri faciendi gratia, vel ipsius rei, vel etiam vsus eius,' etc. (*Summa*, Bk. II, 6.1, p. 219a).

2–131/31 *xiv, q. v, Penale, et xxxii, q. iv, Meretrices*: Two canons: (1) 'Penale': Gratian's *dict. ante* states that the penalty should be more severe for the violent seizure of something than for mere theft (C.14 q.5 c.13; Friedberg 1: 738). The source is said to be Augustine's 'In lib quest. Exod.' Q. 71, but it is found in his 'In Heptateuch.', Bk. 2, q. 71, on Exod. 20 (PL 34: 620). (2) 'Meretrices' defines the word 'moechia' as illicit coitus and illicit use of the sexual organs. It claims that prostitution and fornication are both forms of theft, hence both are forbidden by the seventh Commandment. *D&P* singles out the parenthetical phrase: 'non enim rapinam permisit qui furtum prohibuit'. The source is Augustine's 'In quest. Heptateuch.', Q. 71 (C.32 q.4 c.11; Friedberg 1: 1130; *PL* 34: 621).

2–131/4–9 *Salomon . . . Ecclesiastici v [16–17]*: '. . . et lingua tua capiaris et confundaris,/super furem enim est confusio et paenitentia et denotatio pessima super bilinguem'. The interlinear gloss on 'furem': 'Vnde fur non venit nisi vt furetur, & mactet et praedat' (GO 2: 749). *D&P* adds '& woman' to the translation of 'bilinguem'.

2–132/11–15 *Salomon . . . Prouer. xxii [1]*: GO: 'Nam si quis mundum universum lucuretur merito totum contemneret, vt eius nomen scriberetur in celis eiusque memoria inter sanctos atque angelos figeretur aeterna' (2: 679).

2–132/27 *vi, q. i, Deteriores*: The canon 'Deteriores' holds that theft of a good reputation is worse than theft of material possessions (C.6 q. 1 c.15; Friedberg 1: 557). The 'nexte chapitele' probably refers to the canon 'Summa iniquitas', which holds that detraction of brothers ('fratres') is equivalent to murder, citing 1 John 3: 15: 'Omnes qui fratrem suam odit homicida est'. Gratian's *post dict.* states that from this it would appear that the carnal ('carnales') are prohibited from criticizing the spiritual ('spirituales') but not the other way around (C.6 q.1 c.16; Friedberg 1: 558).

2–132/30–4 *De con., d. v, Nichil enim prodest*: It does not help to fast and pray unless the mind is free of sin and the tongue from detraction. The canon is atributed to Pope Pius I (d. c155), about whom nothing certain is known. The editor's note refers to Gregory's *Moralia* 25.16, a passage on correcting subordinates, but no close parallel is found there (De cons. D.5 c.23; Friedberg 1: 1417–8).

2–132/37–8 *vi, q. i, Ex merito, et xi,d q. iii, Non solum*: Two canons: (1) 'Ex merito' holds that subordinates ('subditos') must not criticize their clerical superiors ('prelatos'). The canon is attributed to Pope Anterus (d.236), about whom little is known. The editor's note casts doubt on this attribution, however (C.6 q.1 c.13; Friedberg 1: 557). (2) The canon 'Non solum' holds that to deny being a Christian is to deny Christ, citing the example of St Peter's denial of Christ (C.11 q.3 c.85; Friedberg 1: 666–7). The source (but not the exact wording) is Augustine's *In Ioh.*, 66.1, on John 13: 36–8 (*CCL* xxxvi, pp. 493–5; *PL* 35: 1810–11).

2–132/38–40 *Salomon . . . Prouer. iv [24]*: 'Remove a te os pravum et detrahentia labia sint procul a te'. GO: 'Duobus modis sciendum vt os tuum ne prauum loquatur aliquid tua labia ne detractionibus assuescant custodias, et alius quam quod huic vicio subditos nosti, ne te corrumpant, fugas' (2: 660).

2–132/42 *Ecclesiastici xxviii [28]*: 'Sepi aures tuas spinis et noli audire linguam nequam, et ori tuo facito ostia et seras'. GO: 'Postquam malum linguae extirpauit ad doctrinam auditoris se conuertit' (2: 774).

2–133/47–50 *Salomon . . . Prouer. xxv [23]*: 'Ventus aquilo dissipat pluvias et facies tristis linguam detrahentem'. GO: 'Si hilari vultu audieris detrahentem, tu illidas fomitem [strike a spark] detrahendi. Si verbo tristi vt ait quidam discit non libenter dicere, quod didicerit non libenter audiri' (2: 684).

2–133/50–8 *The childryn . . . Numeri xiv [1–45]*: The Book of Numbers, chaps. 11–14, 16–17, 20–21, tells the story of the murmuring of the Israelites during the Exodus; of the first generation in the wilderness of Sinai, only Caleb and Joshua survived, Num. 26: 64–5. The GO glosses the hesitation of the people in the face of the 'giants' and other terrors of the unknown in the land of Canaan reported by Joshua and Caleb as a prefiguration of the obstacles to Christian faith (1: 306–7). Numbers contains the story of Balaam referred to above, 2–34/19–35.

2–133/59–61 *Marie . . . Numeri xii [1–16]*: Num. 12: 1: 'Locutaque est Maria et Aaron contra Mosen propter uxorem eius aethiopissam.' Miriam was temporarily punished with leprosy for criticizing Moses' exogamous marriage to an Ethiopian or 'Midianite' or 'Cushite' woman. In the GO, the complaint against Miriam is interpreted on a literal level as a warning against detraction, in particular by 'heretics' ('lepra enim consequitur detractantes & cacologos'). Miriam's leprosy and cure are interpreted as prophetic of the eventual conversion of the Jews (1: 303–5).

2–133/2 *Ieremye xxiii [30–2]*: The translation in *D&P* expands on the biblical verses, stresssing 'fenydyn miraclys of ymagis' which gull the simple folk ('. . . prophetas somniantes mendacium . . . qui narraverunt ea et seduxerunt populum meum in mendacio suo et in miraculis suis'), and alludes again to the newly-enacted restrictions on preaching (see 2–133/3–134/18 below). The GO: 'Semper enim mendacium imitatur veritatem, aliter enim non potuit decipere' (3: 137).

2–133/3–134/18 *false prechourys* . . . *þefte of Goddis word*: For those with
ears to hear (and to identify 'þei' in line 10), this is another allusion to
Archbishop Arundel's Constitutions (1407–9) restricting the activities of
preachers. See above 148/44, 327/4, 2–64/68–9 and 2–133/2.

2–134/18–27 *Speculatorem* . . . *Ezech iii [17–20]*: For 'speculatorem' and
Ezek. 3: 17–18, see 2–20/31–9, 2–24/3–12 above. The gloss (Gregory) on
'sanguinem' ('þe blood', 2–134/1–135/9 below): 'Sanguine peccatum
designatur quod culpae praepositi si tacuerit imputatur, vnde libera me de
sanguinibus peccatis, sci., carnis' (GO 3: 230).

2–134/1–135/1–9 *Iob* . . . *xxiv [6–14]*: Verses 6, 7, 9, 14 and the end of 12
of the Vulgate text of Job 24, in that order, are translated in *D&P*. The
author has chosen to cite a portion of the Book of Job long known for its
difficulty in the Hebrew, see *ABD*, 3: 866. Read in context, the end of verse
12 would be expected to continue the negative theodicy of the speeches of
Job/Elihu, but the Vulgate instead follows the LXX in changing the signs to
positive and attributing final justice to God (cf. RSV: 'God pays no
attention to their prayer'). Also by reversing the order of verses 12 and
14, *D&P*'s author allows himself to import 'fur' from verse 14 and add it to
'inultum' in verse 12, making the words more relevant to Commandment
VII ('God . . . suffrith nout swyche *a þef* pasyn vnpunchyd'). St Gregory's
Moralia, 16.49.62–72, interprets the fields and vines of verse 6 as the
universal Church, despoiled by false preachers ('peruersi praedicatores');
heretics, he says, use good works as a protective clothing for heresy. The
poor are the uninstructed, who are misled by heretics ('Vulgus autem
pauper est populus indoctus'). God, however, does not finally abandon
justice ('aeterna iustitia ferire non neglegit'). The 'mane' of verse 14 alludes
both to the Last Judgement and to the oblivious prosperity of the present
time; the 'thief' is the preacher who fails to give warning, thus the one who
injures secretly ('per iniqua consilia latenter laedit'): *CCL* cxliiiA, pp. 834–
41; *PL* 76: 1150–7.

2–135/15 *rapina* . . . *raueyn*: *Catholicon* (1483), ed. Herrtage (EETS os 75),
s.v. Ravyn: '*rapina*, *rapt*us; versus: ¶ Rerum rapina sed raptus fit mulierum'
(p. 300). See also *MED*, s.v. 'ravin(e'.

2–135/18–19 *vusura* . . . *gowyl & usure*: See *MED*, s.v. 'gavel, 2'. John of
Wales denounces usury, citing the Bible, Ambrose, Augustine, Chrysostom,
and Cicero, concluding: 'Magna ergo dementia est ab aliquibus vsuram
querere, quia hoc est contra legem nature et scripture euangelice et contra
innatam bonitatem et conditiones creature omnibus creatis se com-
municantis, vt patet in luce, igne, terra, aqua' (*Communiloquium* 2.6.4).
See Nelson (2nd edn. 1969), pp. xix–28. See further below, Com. VII, caps.
24–28.

2–135/22–136/27 *Sent Austyn . . . Epistula ad Macedonium*: Augustine to Macedonius: 'Hoc enim certe alienum non est, quod jure possidetur; hoc autem jure quod juste, et hoc juste quod bene. Omne igitur quod male possidetur, alienum est; male autem possidet, qui male utitur', Ep. 153.26 (*PL* 33: 665). See 2–157/39–40, 2–162/77 below.

2–136/27–8 *withholdynge of elmesse from þe pore*: Wyclif includes this among the sins against the seventh Commandment: 'Et patet quod non per se in ablacione temporalium civiliter dominantis a carente tali titulo consistit vetacio [interdiction] huius furti, sed per se in consumpcione iniusta bonorum Dei . . .' (*De mand.*, p. 367/30–3).

2–136/31–45 *Salomon . . . Ecclesiastici iv [1–8]*: See 52/23–32 above, where Ecclus. 4: 2–6 is translated. Ecclus. 4: 1 'Fili elemosynam pauperis ne fraudes, et oculos tuos ne transvertas a paupere'. . . . Ecclus. 4: 7–8: 'Congregationi pauperum affabilem te facito, et presbytero humilia animam tuam et magnato humilia caput tuum; /declina pauperi aurem tuam et redde debitum tuum, et responde pacifica in mansuetudine'. In v. 7, successive translations have moved from the Greek συναγωγη [lit. 'synagogue'] to the Latin 'congregationi pauperum' to Middle English 'congregacioun of pore folc'; the second clause of the verse appears to have been independently altered by the author of *D&P*, from an injunction to pay respect to the priest ('presbytero') and the great man ('magnato') to an injunction to pay respect to the poor folk in the congregation (text 136/42).

2–136/45–6 *Sent Powil . . . [2 Cor. 9: 7]*: See 52/32 above.

2–136/47 *Be lawe of kende . . . alle þing is comoun*: Gratian's *dict. ante* to D.8 c.1 (Friedberg 1: 12–13): 'Nam iure naturae sunt omnia communia omnibus'; he distinguishes natural law from customary law and statute law, citing Augustine's *In Ioh.* 6.25–6, in which Augustine says: 'Diuinum ius in scripturis habemus, humanum ius in legibus regum', concluding, 'fratres . . . ueniant ad catholicam, et nobiscum habebunt non solum terram, sed etiam illum qui facit caelum et terram' (*CCL* xxxvi, pp. 66–7; *PL* 35: 1436–7). For a discussion of the issues involved, see d'Entrèves (1951; repr. 1972), *passim*; Chodorow (1972), pp. 99–111. A translation of D.8 c.1 with the Ordinary Gloss can be found in *Gratian* (1993), pp. 24–5. See 63/13–18, 63/17, 320/12–13, and 320/29 above.

2–136/48 *xii, q. i, Dilectissimis*: C.12 q.1 c.2; Friedberg 1: 676–7. Cited and tr. above, 320/29; cited below, 2–137/60–1, 2–158/78.

2–136/50 *college*: See 245/1 and 353/49 above.

2–137/54 *Act. iv [32]*: See 321/37 above.

2–137/56 *Di. xiii, ¶ 1*: The canon 'duo mala' holds that in choosing between two evils one must use pure reason ('purae ratione acumine investigemus') to decide which is the less culpable choice (D.13 c.1; Friedberg 1: 31). The canon is derived from the eighth Council of Toledo (seventh century). For a translation of the text and the Ordinary Gloss, *Gratian* (1993), p. 49.

2–137/59–60 *Sent Austyn: Omnia sunt iustorum*: On Matt. 5: 5, Augustine says: 'You will only in very truth possess the earth when you stick closely to the one who made heaven and earth' (Sermon 53.2; tr. E. Hill (1991), 3: 67; *PL* 38: 365).

2–137/60–1 *xii, q. i, Dilectissimus*: For 'Dilectissimus' read '. . . issimis'. The passage referred to is: 'Communis enim usus omnium, que sunt in hoc mundo, omnibus hominibus esse debuit. Sed per iniquitatem alius hoc dixit esse suum, et alius istud, et sic inter mortales facta est diuisio' (C.12 q.1 c.2; Friedberg 1: 676). Cited 320/29, 2–136/48 above, and 2–158/78 below.

2–137/67 [*Lc. 16: 2*]: Cited in LL4: 'Ʒeld acountis of þin balyschepe. Thanne he schul askyn how þu hast spent þin soule & þe vertues & þe gracis þat he sente þee & how þu hast spent þin body & þin fyue wyttis & oþere bodyly vertues & how þu hast spent þin tyme & temperel goddis whyche þu hast left whanne þu schuldyst a don it & for euery wyckyd dede þat þu hast don' (fo. 82ʳᵃ). On the parable of the unjust steward (Luke 16: 1–8), 2–157/42–158/54 below.

2–137/71–2 [*1 Tim. 6: 8*]: Cited 71/50 above. For 'alimenta et quibus tegamur' *D&P* has 'victum et vistitum'; the Vulgate does not give variants.

2–138/1–2 *Godis lawe . . . lawe of kende*: See 63/17, 160/11–15 and 2–136/47 above. Earlier in Commandment VII, the canon law background of 'natural law' and 'God's law' has been discussed. In this chapter, the contrasted notion of civil law is taken up.

2–138/6 *Ioseph . . . Genesis xlv* [*9*]: 'Deus me fecit dominum universae terrae Aegypti'.

2–138/1 ff.*Sith alle þing is comoun*; Pauper here sums up his social philosophy: yes, natural law gives all persons dominion over their own souls and bodies; yes, theft of property is a great sin; but some persons hold and administer property by 'dispencacioun' (a word repeated eleven times in this chapter) of God. God's purpose, says Pauper, is to keep the temptations of wealth far from the mass of people. Thus Pauper frees one kind of property-holding—that received by 'dispencioun'—from all taint of sin. Cf. Wyclif: 'Dominium civile est dominium occasione peccati humanitatem institutum (*De civ. dom.* 1: 127/7–8). See above 51/6, 51/8, 63/3–16, 63/17, 72/17–30, 160/11–15, 336/1, 342/47, 2–136/47.

2–138/13–14 *Sent Powil . . .* [*Rom. 13: 1*]: See 334/60–335/82 above.

2–138/19 *Sent Austyn*: 'Deus verus . . . in cuius potestate sunt regna omnia': *De civ. dei*, 1.36 (*CCL* xlvii, p. 34/10–11; *PL* 41: 47).

EXPLANATORY NOTES 231

2–139/38–9 *Sent Powil* . . . [*1 Cor. 4: 2*]: 'Hic iam quaeritur inter dispensatores ut fidelis quis inveniatur.' LL4: 'But now, seyth he, it is asayd who is foundyn trewe amongis þese spenderis & dyspensouris & balyis' (fo. 81vb). The GO: 'Iam in praesenti cum expectandum esset donec deus iudicet' (4: 312).

2–140/79–82 *Sent Powyl* . . . *ad Galatas iv* [*1–2*]: GO: 'Modo vos gentiles & nos iudei sumus christi, & semen abraae & haeredes, sed olim nos iudaei sub lege sicut haeres futurus & a patre substitutus. Ecce iterum quare lex non est tenenda' (4: 362).

2–141/2–3 *soundyth* . . . *sondyth*: The sense is: 'Stealth often bespeaks (or indicates) theft and robbery, and sometimes it bespeaks secret pilfering . . .'; see *MED* s.v. 'sounen 6.'. For the verbs 'sounden' (sink in, penetrate) and 'sounden' (heal) with which 'sounen' (bespeak) can easily be confused, see *MED* s.v. 'sounden' v. (1) and v. (2). Cf. 55/36 above.

2–141/13–14 *in gret nede alle þing is comoun*: The legal maxim 'Necessitas legem non habet' is cited in a canon which seeks to place limits on places where mass may be celebrated—the rule to be observed except in cases of utter need (De cons. D.1 c.11; Friedberg 1: 1297). See 60/50 and 287/24 above.

2–141/23 *Mathei xii* [*1–4*]: Cited above 289/61. Nicolaus de Lyra's gloss also refers to the example of David (1 Sam. 21) and cites Hosea 6: 6: 'Misericordiam volo et non sacrificium'; Matt. 12: 1–4 shows, he says, that 'in nouo testamento autoritate eius mutata est' (*Postilla* 4). The commentary in *CA* stresses the superiority of the authority of Christ to that of the Pharisees and priests of the temple, and the contrast between the letter and spirit of the law. None of these exegetes suggests that the story turns on the legal maxim, 'necessitas legem non habet', the rationale found in Raymond of Peñafort's *Summa*, which also cites Matt. 12: 1–4 and 1 Sam. 21 (Bk. II, p. 224b). See 60/50, 287/24 and 289/61 above.

2–142/28 *be weye of elmesse þe wyf*: *D&P* continues to follow Raymond's *Summa* (see 2–141/23 above), giving an almost word-for-word translation (Bk. II, pp. 252a–253a).

2–142/44–5 *bona parafernalia*: Common law in medieval England provided that all of a wife's movable property, or chattels, should become the property of her husband at the time of the marriage, with the exception of her 'necessary clothes' and her 'jewels, trinkets and ornaments of the person, under the name of *paraphernalia*' (Pollack & Maitland, 2: 404–5). While the husband was alive, his power over the property his wife brought to the marriage was nearly absolute; during the later medieval centuries, however, it became more usual for (propertied) wives to make valid wills disposing of, at least, personal property. It is more likely that the source is Raymond of Peñafort's *Summa*: at the end of the section on theft, ¶ 12, he asks: 'Quid de vxore, quae furatur viro suo pecuniam, vel alia, vt inde faciat eleemosynam?' The reply is given in the section on business (cited in the previous note): 'Si uxor habet res paraphernales, id est proprias praeter dotem, sic dictas a para, quod est dos, quasi iuxta dotem, potest de illis etiam inuito viro facere eleemosynam' (Bk. II, p. 252a).

2–142/53–144/89 *firste . . . Kyngis, xxv [1–44] . . . [1 Sam. 25: 1–42]*: Another chapter in the story of King David is given here; cf. 2–85/19 above for list of references in *D&P*. For an early retelling of the story, see Josephus (c. 37–c. 100), *Jewish Antiquities*, Bk. VI, 291–310 (LCL 490, Vol. 5, pp. 313–21). The gloss, predictably, interprets Nabal as the Jews who resist the Holy Spirit and follow carnal law ('legem carnaliter sequentes'). Abigail represents those who are converted to Christ (GO, 2: 40). Nicolaus de Lyra comments on David's numerous wives, including Abigail: '. . . dicitur que rex constitutus de israel non debeat sibi multiplicare vxores. Dicendum que illud intellegitur de vxoribus alieni genis inclinantibus animam viri ad idolatriam' (*Postilla* 1).

2–144/94–114 *ry3tful bataylye*: The theory of the 'just war' was touched on above (2–55/15–21). Here, the topic is more narrowly defined as property damage resulting from war. Isidore of Seville's definition of the just war makes property an issue: a just war is waged to recover property ('geritur de rebus repetitis') as well as to repel enemies (*Etym.*, 18.1). Canon law, citing Ambrose, holds that failure to defend oneself against an injury is tantamount to inflicting an injury ('Non in inferenda': C.23 q.3 c.7; Friedberg 1: 897; 'De officis', 1.36). But canon law also firmly holds that the purpose of a just war is to establish peace. Defeated enemies and war captives are to be treated with mercy ('Noli': C.23 q.1 c.3; Friedberg 1: 892). See F. H. Russell, *The Just War* (1975). See 2–55/15–21 above.

2–144/107 *[Ps. 58: 12]*: Augustine identifies 'eos' in this verse with the Jews: 'Nam ecce inimici Iudaei, quos uidetur significare psalmus iste, legem Dei tenent'; not all are guilty, says Augustine, 'quia multi eorum conuersi ad eum quem occiderunt, et in eum credendo, ueniam et de effuso ipsius sanguine meruerunt, exemplum, que praebuerunt hominibus . . .' (*Enarr.*, 58.2.2 (*CCL* xxxix, p. 746/14–5;31–4; *PL* 36: 706–7). The GO cites both Augustine and Cassiodorus to the same effect; both stress keeping the Jews alive as memorials to the Old Law and to the death of Christ: 'Ideo ne occidas, ne populi et si non modo obliuiscantur mei si non sint testes legis et mortis christi' (2: 525b). Cited for the same purpose in de Chobham's *Summa*: 'Verumtamen ideo ita sustenentur precipue iudei quia capsarii [reliquaries] nostri sunt et portant testimonium legis contra se pro nobis' (ed. Broomfield, p. 434). Note that this rather bloodthirsty passage appears only in MS G. Cf. 208/12 above. See Cohen (1999), pp. 23–65 and *passim*.

2–144/114 *Exodi xxii* [*18*]: See 254/70–1 above, where 'maleficos' includes witches, magicians, excommunicates, heretics and felons; cf. 2–13/10 above, where 'maleficos' refers to those who commit manslaughter.

2–145/1 *Ʒif a cristene man be takyn presoner*: Raymond of Peñafort's *Summa* puts the question, Is it theft to steal Christians held captive by pagans? The answer, elaborated in John of Freiburg's gloss, is that it is not theft, provided that terms of a truce are not violated, and not only may 'Christianos' be stolen from such an enemy but also munitions and castles (Bk. II, p. 225a). Raymond cites St Augustine: 'Cum quis mouet iustum bellum, vtrum aperte pugnet, an ex insidius nihil ad iustitiam interest' (Bk. II, p. 225ab), referring to Augustine's *Quest. in Heptateuch.* 6, q. 10 (*PL* 34: 781), and St Gregory: 'Contra hoste fidei, non solum aperte, sed a dorso est etiam laborandum', from Gregory's Ep. 3 ('ad Velocem') in Bk. II (PL 77: 510). Both citations are also found in canon law: (1) 'Dominus deus', C.23 q.2 c.2 9 (Friedberg 1: 894), and (2) 'Et pridem', C.23 q.8 c.17 (Friedberg 1: 957).

2–145/8 *þe feyth þat he hotyth nout*: The sense is: in weighing faith to one's enemy, which one has not promised, against faith to God, which one has promised, one must choose the latter.

2–145/14 *Ʒif a þing be lost*: Raymond of Peñafort acknowledges a difference of opinion about found items: 'Multi sine peccato putant esse, si alienum, quod inuenerint, teneant', but says that found money must be returned if it is possible to find the owner, offering a reward or taking the money to a church; all else failing, the money may be given to the poor (*Summa*, Bk. II, p. 224a).

2–145/20 *pentancer*: The word appears in MS G only. The *MED*, s.v. 'penitencere': 'A priest appointed by a pope or bishop to administer the sacrament of penance, especially in cases reserved to the bishop or pope.' Cf. *PP* (B-Text, XX, p. 677/318–20); and Chaucer's 'Parson's Tale', in which the division of labour between the local priest and the 'penitauncer' is clearly shown (*CT*, p. 324b/1005–10).

2–145/23 *Sent Austyn . . . Sent Gregori*: The propositions, 'Si quid inuenisti, quod non reddidisti, rapuisti' and 'Deus cor interrogat, non manum', attributed to Augustine and Gregory, are found in canon law, but there attributed (doubtfully) to Ambrose ('Si quid', C.14 q.5 c.6; Friedberg 1: 739). They are also cited by Raymond of Peñafort (*Summa*, Bk. II, p. 224).

2–146/31–2 *þe Philosofre . . . principiis obsta*: Ovid, not Aristotle, is the source of the saying. See *The Art of Love and Other Poems*, 'Remedia amoris', pp. 184–5/91 (LCL 253, *Ovid II*, tr. J. H. Mozley, 2nd rev. edn. 1979).

2-146/38-43 *whan a þef schulde ben hangyd*: The story of the thief who bites off his father's nose appears in many collections of *exempla*: Jacques de Vitry, *Exempla*, ed. Crane, No. 209, p. 287; Ps.-Boethius, 'De disciplina scholarium', c. 2 (*PL* 64: 1227); *Fasciculus morum*, ed. Wenzel, pp. 99-3; *An Alphabet of Tales* (ed. Banks, EETS, os 126, 127), p. 152; the Tübach *Index*, No. 3488; John of Wales *Communiloquium*, 2.2.1. Other manuscript sources are listed in Herbert, *Catalogue of Romances*, Vol. 3: 73 (No.153), 97 (No.48), 169 (No.29), 265 (No.52), 391 (No.296, No.297), 432 (No.29), 461 (No.83), 469 (No.30), 486 (No.91), 536 (No.5), 592 (No.113), 616 (No.146), 648 (No.1).

2-146/45-6 *Salomon . . . Prouer. xiii [24]*: Cited above 326/62.

2-146/46-58 *a pore man louyd wel goos flesch*: I have not traced an analogue to this story; it is in the class of tales about bargains with the Devil, see Stith Thompson *Index*, 5: 39: M210.

2-147/5-6 *Reymund, lib. ii, ti. De furtis*: Raymond of Peñafort: 'Rei alienae ideo apponitur, quia non committitur furtum in re plenissime propria, plenissime dico, qui si alius haberet in re illa ius, puta creditor, cui res est pignori obligata, vel commodatarius, vel socius, vel similis alia persona, dominus furtiue surripiens alicui tali personae committeret furtum' (*Summa*, Bk. II, p. 219b).

2-148/27-30 *anoþir mannys seruant . . . selle or bye man or woman*: Raymond of Peñafort: 'dicitur furtum hominis, cum, quis liberum hominem scienter vendit, donat, vel accipit, vel permutat . . . si ancillam, vel seruum alienum solicitauerit, & exportauerit' (*Summa*, Bk. II, p. 220a).

2-148/33-4 *3yf a man haue hyryd or borwyd an hors*: Raymond of Peñafort: 'Qui accepit equum, vel aliam rem commodatam vsque ad certum locum, & ipse vltra locum illum procedat cum illa re, committit furtum (John of Freiburg's gloss: 'Quando scilicet credebat Dominum inuitum, non forte si sciret'), *Summa*, Bk. II, p. 221b.

2-148/43-5 *lende awey anoþir mannys good*: Raymond of Peñafort: 'Credo committit furtum si pignori sibi obligato vtatur' (*Summa*, Bk. II, p. 222b). Cf. 2-148/33-4 above.

2-149/53 *3yf a þing stoln perche*: Raymond of Peñafort: 'Item quid si res furtiua pereat casu fortuito, numquid tenebitur ad restitutionem postea fur? . . . non liberatur fur rem deteriorem reddendo; item tenetur restituere rem cum omnibus fructibus: & si meliorauit eam, pascendo forte equum, vel porcum furtiuum, vel simile, non potest petere, vel retinere expensas' (*Summa*, Bk. II, p. 222a).

2-149/62 *3yf þe þef profryd þe lord*: Raymond of Peñafort: '. . . est tamen casus, in quo non tenetur fur de casu fortuito, si obtulit rem domino loco, &

tempore congruo, & dominus noluit accipere: iam enim purgauit moram'
(*Summa*, Bk. II, p. 222b).

2–149/68–70 *Ʒif a man . . . þe value of þe vhs*: Raymond of Peñafort: 'Item
cum furtum est commissum in vsu rei tantum, & non in ipsa re, tenetur
etiam post restitutionem rei ad aestimationem illius vsus; aliter enim non
esset purgatum furtum' (*Summa*, bk. II, p. 222b).

2–149–50/70–92 *Y suppose þat man . . . bye . . . a þing stolyn*: Raymond of
Peñafort: 'Item quid si aliquis emit rem furtiuam ignoranter, & bona fide, &
in foro publico, & publice, numquid potest saltem pretium, quod numer-
auit, petere a domino cum deprehendit rem esse furtiuam, vel numquid
poterit retinere rem, donec pretium sit ei solutum? Non . . . Item circa eum
dico que poterit retinere expensas, quas existens bone fidei ratione facit circa
rem conseruandam, vel meliorandam; & non tenetur de fructibus perceptis
durante bona fide' (*Summa*, Bk. II, 222b–223a).

2–150/92–4 *Ʒyf a man stele from a ryche nygard*: Raymond of Peñafort: 'Item
quid si aliquis furatur, vel rapit rem ab vsurario, vt inde faciat eleemosynam
. . . in his committitur furtum? Solutio, ad primum dico furtum, siue
rapinam committi; non enim facienda sunt mala, vt veniant quaecumque
bona . . . si totum tribuat, quod abstulerat, addit potius peccatum, quam
minuat; qua aufert sibi copiam restituendi' (*Summa*, Bk. II, p. 223b). The
reference to Augustine is 'ad Claudium contra Iulianum', lib. v, 182b (found
in *PL* 44: 803–5, but with differing text). See 2–150/94–5 below.

2–150/94–5 *xxxii, q. iv, Sic non sunt*: The canon 'Sic non sunt' is brought in
rather oddly here; the subject is adultery, but the canon states that adultery
for the purpose of acquiring sons is no better than theft in order to feed the
poor; hence there is some relevance to the topic of theft (C.22 q.4 c.10;
Friedberg 1: 1130. The source is Augustine, 'Ad Claudium contra
Iulianum', 5.16 (*PL* 44: 803–5). See 2–150/92–4 above.

2–150/1–2 *Mon nout cristene men stelyn ȝunge chyldryn of Iewys*: John of
Freiburg's gloss on Raymond of Peñafort's *Summa*: 'Sed numquid possunt
auferri eis filij eorum ad baptizandum? Respondeo: adulti non debent, nisi
consenserint sponte, baptizari . . . dum tamen non facerent propter
compellendos hoc modo parentes ad fidem, sed propter saluandos pueros
per fidei sacramentum; ad cuius susceptionem sufficit, quod non inueniat
obicem contrariae voluntatis' (Bk. I, p. 33a). Thomas Aquinas says that it
was never the custom of the Church to baptize the children of Jews against
the wishes of their parents, and if it were done it would be a violation of
natural law (*ST*, III.68.10). See 208/12–17 above and 2–151/13–17 below.

2–151/13–17 *Sent Siluestre . . . questione de quolibet*: In his argument against
forcible baptism of Jewish children, Thomas Aquinas refers to St Silvester's
(d. 335) friendship with the Emperor Constantine and St Ambrose's
friendship with the Emperor Theodosius (*Quodl.* 2.7, *Opera*, 9: 478,

Parma edn., 1859; tr. S. Edwards (1983), p. 92). On St Sylvester, see *ODS*, p. 366.

2–151/18 *Summa confessorum, libro i, ti. iv, Utrum pueri*: John of Freiburg's *Summa*, MS Bodley 299, fos. 13^r-13^v.

2–151/19 *3if a woman stele*: John of Freiburg's gloss on Raymond of Peñaforte's *Summa* is, in summary: I believe that a wife with the consent of her husband may restore items to her master which were stolen from him before her marriage; but if the items were consumed or if the husband alone was the thief and the wife participated and consented and the consumption was not intended but spontaneous and the husband did not oppose it, she may, without his consent, restore secretly from their common property what was stolen; this will not be considered theft, nor mortal sin nor requiring penitence (Bk. II, p. 226b).

2–152/39 *Summa confessorum, lib. ii, ti. vi, Quid de illa*: 'Quid de illa muliere que fecit furtum' (c.12) is found in John of Freiburg's *Summa*, MS Bodley 299, fo. 98^r. It is to the same effect as John of Freiburg's gloss cited above, 2–151/19.

2–152/40–153/62 *Summa confessorum, lib. ii, ti. vltimo, In quibus*: 'In quibus', c. 37 of Bk. 2, ti. 8 of John of Freiburg's *Summa*, is found in MS Bodley 299, fos. 113^r-113^v.

2–153/1–154/35 *Summa confessorum, lib. ii, ti. viii, q. i et qu. ix*: John of Freiburg's *Summa*, MS Bodley 299, fos. 107^v-108^r (q. 1) and fos. 108^v-109^r (q. 9).

2–154/41–2 *Isaie i [22]*: The GO reads the verse morally: 'Vinum tuum mystum' is 'aqua quia praecepta sanctae scripturae, quibus corrigere debet auditores ad illorum voluntatem . . . enolit, sensu suo admixto vinum corrumpit'; and figuratively: 'Haeretici quoque euangelium corrumpunt, pessimi caupones [innkeepers], de vino aquam facientes cum aquam in vinum verterit dominus quod miratur architriclinus [governor of the feast]; et regina saba [Sheba] in convivio salomonis collaudans pincernas [wine mixers] et ministros vini' (3: 4–5). Nicolaus de Lyra'a postil connects this verse rather to the Jews' reversion to idol worship than to false business practices (*Postilla* 2).

2–154/44–50 *Deutero. xxv [13–16]*: 'Non habebis in sacculo diversa pondera maius et minus. . . . Abominatur enim Dominus eum qui facit haec et aversatur omnem iniustitiam'. The GO, first pointing out that this passage repeats the one in Lev. 19: 35–6, interprets morally: '. . . studendum est ne diversa pondera in corde habeamus, i.e., districtionis regulam nobis mollientes, eos quibus verbum dei praedicamus districtioribus praeceptis quasi grauioribus ponderibus obruamus' (1: 409).

2–155/55 *þe same clerc . . . q. xi*: John of Freiburg's *Summa*, lib. ii, ti. viii, q. xi: MS Bodley 299, 'Vtrum vendicatio', fo. 109^r.

2–155/76 [*I Cor. 9: 7*]: 'Quis militat suis stipendiis umquam? Quis plantat vineam et fructum eius non edit? Quis pascit gregem et de lacte gregis non manducat?' Note that *D&P* changes the soldier, farmer, and shepherd into knight, trader, and craftsman. The GO applies the verse to preachers (4: 320). See 194/33 above.

2–156/89–90 *Hostiensis in Summa, lib. iii, rubrica, De deposito*: The reference is to Henry of Segusio, author of an important commentary on canon law, the *Summa aurea*, of 1253, referred to eleven times in *D&P*. See 246/39 above.

2–156/2–7 *Salomon . . . Ecclesiastici [34: 21–4]*: Verses 21, 24, and 23 are cited, in that order: 'Immolans ex iniquo oblatio est maculata, et non sunt beneplacitae subsannationes iniustorum. . . . /Qui offert sacrificium ex substantia pauperum quasi qui victimat filium in conspectu patris sui./ . . . Dona iniquorum non probat Altissimus in oblationibus iniquorum, nec in multitudine sacrificiorum eorum propitiabitur peccatis.' The Vulg. gives 'Immolantis' as a variant reading for 'Immolans'. LL4 (translating verses 21, 23, and 24): 'Ʒyf ony man make sacrifice of euyl gotyn good, hys offeringe is foul in goddys syʒte, & god approuyth nout þe ʒyftis of schrewys ne takith heed to here offeringis; & he þat offerith sacrifice of þe pore mannys good is lyk hym þat braynith þe sone in syʒte of hys fadyr' (fo. 76va). The GO equates the offering of ill-gotten goods with putting money into a sack with holes in it ('in saccum pertusum'), GO 2: 779).

2–156/8–10 *Salomon . . . Prouer. iii [9]*: LL4: 'Worschepe þu oure lord god of þin owyn good & nout of oþer mennys good' (fo. 76va). *D&P* and LL4 add 'not of other men's goods' to the translationn. The GO glosses 'Honora': 'vt, sci., homines qui eius plasma sunt, qui ad eius imaginem facti sunt recreentur' (2: 657).

2–156/10–11 *Tobie . . . iv [7]*: 'Ex substantia tua fac elemosynam', is the first clause of verse 7. LL4 refers to the same text but does not translate it: '& þerfore tobie seyth þat almesse delyueryth þe soule from euery synne & fro deth' (fo. 38ra). On 'ex substantia', the interlinear gloss is: 'Non de rapina' (GO, 2: 334). Cited below 2–284/75.

2–156/14 [*Lc. 16: 9*]: See 54/11, 75/10, 272/42–4 above.

2–157/35 *Deutero. xxiii [18]*: 'Non offeres mercedem prostibuli nec pretium canis in domum Domini Dei tui quicquid illud est quod voverint, quia abominatio est utrumque apud Dominum Deum tuum.' LL4: 'þu schal nouʒt offeryn þe mede of lecherye ne þe prys of þe hound in þe hous of þy lord god' (fo. 377vb). The gloss, from Augustine, comments on the reason for the prohibitions against dogs and other animals as well as against the profits of prostitution. Such animals as horses and pigs and donkeys are prohibited as offerings because they are useful to man. The proceeds of prostitution were prohibited because prostitution itself was prohibited and profits from it should not be used to expiate the sin (GO, 1: 405).

2–157/39–40 *xiv, q. v, Non sane*: The canon 'Non sane' holds that ill-gotten gains may be used to help those in need (C.14 q.6 c.15; Friedberg 1: 742). The source is a letter of Augustine's (Ep. 153.24, ad Macedonium, *PL* 33: 664), in which it is made clear that such charity does not excuse the means by which the money was acquired, such as bribes: '. . . facilius ea quae hoc modo acquisierunt, tanquam sua pauperibus largiuntur, quam eis a quibus accepta sunt, tanquam aliena resistunt'. See 2–135/22–136/27 above, 2–162/77 below.

2–157/42–158/54 *þe false baylye . . . rychesse of þis world*: The parable of the false steward (Luke 16: 1–8) has always presented difficulties to interpreters. The story, on the face of it, seems to commend a kind of fraud. The author of *D&P* makes a characteristically Franciscan and Bonaventuran interpretation of the parable as, primarily, an injunction to give alms. Bonaventure sees the parable as a lesson in a higher form of prudence: 'Est tamen *prudentia spiritus*, quae est in filius lucis excellentior quam prudentia carnis, quae est in viris carnalibus . . . Habet tamen aliquid prudentia ista mundana, quod excitat et instruit ad prudentiam diuinam' (*Opera*, 7.407). See also extracts from Augustine, Ambrose, Gregory, Theophylact and others in *CA*, 2: 222–5. Wailes (1987) summarizes the medieval exegeses of the parable (pp. 245–253). Flusser (1982), in light of the Dead Sea Scrolls, sees the parable as Jesus' attack on the perfectionism of the Essenes, pp. 176–97.

2–158/54–5 *rychesse of wyckydnesse*: Luke 16: 9: 'Facite vobis amicos de mamona iniquitatis ut cum defeceritis recipiant vos in aeterna tabernacula.' The author of *D&P* 'forgets' that this verse has been discussed earlier; see 54/11 above.

2–158/59–60 *Sent Powyl . . . [1 Tim. 6: 9]*: For 1 Tim. 6: 9–10 see 71/31–6 above. 2–265/76–82, 2–274/21 below.

2–158/60–2 *Salomon . . . [Eccli. 11: 10]*: 'Fili ne in multis sint actus tui et si dives fueris non eris immunis a delicto si enim secutus fueris non adprehendes et non effugies si praecucurreris.' LL4: 'And þerfore salomon seyth 3yf þu be riche þu schalt nout ben vngylty of senne' (fo. 83rb).

2–158/69–70 *Diues diuicias*: Found in Hans Walther, No. 6059. The verse appears in the *Fasciculus morum*, ed. Wenzel, p. 314. It is also cited in Lyndwood's *Provinciale*, from the Council of London (1236/7), s.v. 'Constitutions of Ottobon', in a section on clerical absentees (p. 31b; 1679 edn.). See below 2–274/11.

2–158/73–4 *Salomon . . . [Eccl. 5: 9]*: See 58/39 above. Eccles. 5: 9 is also cited 59/18–19, 78/37 and 80/36 above.

2–158/78 *xii, q. i, Dilectissimis*: Cited above 320/29, 2–136/48, 2–137/60–1 (C.12 q.1 c.2; Friedberg 1: 676–7). The frequency with which the canon 'Dilectissimis' is cited underlines the importance, especially for Franciscans, of the distinction between the commonality of natural law and the dubious origins of the civil laws governing private possession.

2–159/97 *þat balye*: See 2–157/42–158/54 above.

2–160/11–22 *Sent Ambrose*: Cf. Ambrose, 'In Lucam' 7.245: 'Non reprehenditur uilicus in quo discimus non ipsi esse domini, sed potius alienarum uilici facultatum' (*PL* 15: 1854).

2–160/31–2 *an emperour . . . Qui omnibus preest omnibus indiget*: The Latin saying sums up an argument made by Pauper in the HP Prologue: 'the ryche man haþ more nede þanne the pore'. He explains: the poor man has enough if he has food and clothing; but the rich man must support his station in life and care for the needs of his household and retainers (see 58/41 above).

2–161/44 *Sent Ierom*: The sense is found in Jerome's letter: 'When you have received money to be spent on the poor, to be cautious and timid with it while crowds are hungry, or—what is most manifest villainy—to take any of it for yourself, is to surpass the cruelty of the worst robber' (Ep. LII.16, 'Ad Nepotianum'; LCL 262, *Select Letters . . . Jerome*, pp. 226–7; *PL* 22: 539).

2–161/49–50 *Sent Bernhard, in Epistula ad Eugenium*: Bernard writes to Pope Eugenius (d. 1153): 'Ad hunc ergo clamant pauperes a finibus terrae. Sanctitas vestra liberet fratres suos de manibus quaerentium animas eorum nec Ismaelitis negotiatoribus eos venundari potiatur' (Ep. 239, *Opera*, ed. J. Leclercq *et al.*, 8: 121). As to 'anoþer pistel . . . to a chanoun', Bernard's letters to Canon Oger remonstrate with him for having given up the post of abbot to return to the cloister; Bernard is sympathetic but reproachful. But I have not found a passage in the four letters to Oger that is closely similar to 161/55–9 in *D&P* (cf. Ep. 87–90, Bernard, op. cit., 7: 224–58).

2–161/59–64 *þese men of holy chirche . . . rydyn on heye hors*: The Wycliffite 'Of prelates' complains: 'O lord! what tokene of mekenesse . . . is þis; a prelat as an abott or a priour, þat is ded to þe world . . . to ride wiþ foure score hors, wiþ harneis of siluer & gold' (ed. Matthew, EETS, os 74), p. 60. A Wycliffite sermon: 'As ȝif bischopis fiȝten nou and ben arayed in horss [*sic*] and meyne, or ben greet in houshold and oþer þingis to fede þe world, þei ben enemyes to Crist' (*EWS*, 3, Serm. 165/16–18). Cf. 317/18 above.

2–162/75–7 *Dockynge, super Deutero. v cap: quia non dimittitur*: The passage on restitution is found in Docking's 'Super Deutero.', Balliol MS 28, fo. 46ᵛᵇ. On Thomas Docking see 266/32 above. See 2–162/95, 2–164/137 and 2–220/13 below.

2–162/77 *Sent Austyn, in Epistula ad Macedonium*: Augustine to Macedonius: 'Si enim res aliena, propter quam peccatum est, cum reddi posit non redditur, non agitur poenitentia, sed fingitur: si autem veraciter agitur, non remittetur peccatum, nisi restituatur ablatum; sed, ut dixi, cum restitui potest . . .', in Ep. 153.20 (*PL* 33: 662). Cited in Docking's 'Super Deutero', see 2–162/75–7 above. Referred to above 2–135/22–136/27, 2–157/39–40.

2–162/95 *Dockynge*: See 2–162/75–7 above, with further references.

2–163/101–2 *Sent Powil* . . . [*2 Thess. 3: 10*]: 'Nam et cum essemus apud vos hoc denuntiabamus vobis, quoniam si quis non vult operari nec manducet.' LL4: 'He þat nout trauaylith whanne he may, eete he nout, þat is to seye, he is nout worþi his mete þat wyl nout trauaylyn whanne he may' (fo. 96ʳᵃ); 'He þat trauaylith nout whanne he may, eete he nout' (fo. 129ʳᵃ). The GO (Augustine) says that this means that the servants of God should work in order not to be compelled to beg for necessities (4: 403).

2–163/107–9 *Sent Powil . . . I ad Tymo. iii [1] . . . glose*: The gloss is from a letter of Jerome to Oceanus and begins: 'Opus non dignitatem, laborem non delicias, non crescere fastigio sed humilitate decrescere, vt fiat seruus & minister hominum propter christum'. The obedience of Jacob, Leah, and Moses is cited. The etymology of 'episcopus' is discussed and the Latin equivalent is said to be 'superintendens'. Finally: 'Ociam sanctum quaerit charitas veritatis, negocium iustum suscipit necessitas charitatis' (GO 4: 408; Ep. 69.8, *PL* 22: 662). Nicolaus de Lyra comments that the dignity of office is less important than the duty to serve God and one's neighbour (*Postilla* 4).

2–163/116–7 *her vykerys & her parys prestis*: The division of England into parishes predates Christianization. Parishes were gradually incorporated into the diocesan system, but, in the medieval period, lay patrons retained ancient and heritable rights to present candidates for parish posts. Lay patrons were also responsible for the establishment of vicarages: '[I]nstead of appointing a man as rector' of a parish, the lay patron 'would hand over all his rights to a monastery which thereupon became rector, making itself responsible for collecting the income and seeing that the church was served. . . . By the end of the thirteenth century there is no doubt that at least half the parish churches of England had been thus appropriated, by far the majority having gone to the religious houses'. The result of this system was often that the monastery retained much of the income from parish tithes and spent as little as possible on the salaries of the vicars who served the people of the parish (J. R. H. Moorman (1955), pp. 38; 42; 51). On vicarages and tithes, A. G. Little, 'Personal tithes', *EHR* 60 (1945), pp. 70–5. See also H. Thompson (1947), pp. 40–71; 101–31; J. R. H. Moorman (1953; repr. 1980), pp. 28–9, 97–100; Constable (1964), pp. 9–19; 99–197); Heath (1969), pp. 27–48. See 2–183/86–9 below.

2–164/129 *as for lernynge*: For an account of the transformation of the Friars Minor, after the death of St Francis, into 'one of the most learned institutions in the world', see J. Moorman (1968), pp. 123–39. Cf. 51/ HOLY POUERT above.

2–164/137 *Dockynge*: Thomas Docking's 'Super Deutero' 5, Balliol MS 28, fo. 47ʳ. On Docking, see 2–162/75–7 above with further references.

2–164/139–40 *Sent Ierom, ad Nepocianum*: Jerome's letter was written in 394 to Nepotianus, nephew of his life-long friend, Heliodorus: 'Qui autem vel ipse pars domini est vel dominum partem habet, talem se exhibere debet, ut et possideat dominum et ipse possideatur a domino. . . . habens victum et vestitum his contentus ero et nudam crucem nudus sequar' (Ep. 52.5; *Select Letters of St Jerome*, LCL 262, pp. 198;200; *PL* 22: 531); the *D&P* citation is, however, probably from canon law, see 2–164/150–9 below.

2–164/150–9 *xii, q. i, Clericus*: The canon 'Clericus' asserts the principle that the cleric should not own secular property (C.12 q.1 c.5; Friedberg 1: 677). Pauper's etymology of 'clerk' is quoted from the text of the canon. The source is Jerome's letter to Nepotianus cited above, 2–164/139–40.

2–165/162 *þe lawe . . . Res ecclesie*: The canon 'Res ecclesie' states that it is the bishop who dispenses the common property of the Church (C.12 q.1 c.26; Friedberg 1: 686). The source is a letter of Pope Urban II (d. 1099).

2–165/166 *Di. xlvii, Sicut*: The canon 'Sicut' denounces avarice in churchmen (C.47 c.8; Friedberg 1: 171–2). The text is attributed to a sermon of Ambrose on Luke 12: 16, 'hominis cuisdam divitis uberes fructus ager adtulit', referred to below, 2–275/50–1. The reference here is, however, a false one. Gratian's long *post dict.* deals with clerical celibacy and the dangers to clerical morality posed by wives and children.

2–165/69–70 *xvi, q. i, Quoniam, in fine*: Pauper's summary of the canon refers to a clause at the end, which says that clergy who have sufficient funds to live on must not defraud the Church and the poor by subsisting on tithes (C.16 q.1 c.68; Friedberg 1: 784–5). The first part of this canon was cited above (317/6). The source is a letter of Jerome to Pope Damasus (d. 384). Raymond of Peñafort cites 'Quoniam', adding a citation of Prosper of Aquitaine (d.c463), 'De contemplatiua vita', lib. 2, c. 9 & 10, in which the accusation is homicide ('ipse est reus homicidij') if tithes are withdrawn from the poor to support well-off clergy (*Summa*, Bk. I, 'De decimis', ¶ 18, p. 131b).

2–165/1 *sacrilege*: In classical Latin, the meaning of 'sacrilege' had already been extended from meaning theft of sacred things to meaning profanation of any kind (*OLD* s.v. 'sacrilegus'). *D&P*'s false etymology (deriving 'sacrilege' from 'sacra' + 'laedo') is taken from Balbus's *Catholicon* (1460), s.v. 'Sacrilegium' (facs. edn. 1971), as is the reference to the pollution of a churchyard as a sacrilege. Cf. Raymond of Peñafort, whose etymology is the same (*Summa*, 'De sacrilegiis', Blc. 1, p. 115a); *Fasciculus morum*, ed. Wenzel, pp. 306–7; *Jacob's Well*, which uses the Middle English word in the extended sense: '. . . sacrilege, þat is, brekyng of þe sacrament of holy cherche' (ed. Brandeis, EETS, os 115, p. 160/26–7).

2–165/13 *xvii, q. iv, Quisquis*: The canon 'Quisquis' discusses the kinds of sacrilege and penalties for each (C.17 q.4 c.21; Friedberg 1: 820). The source is a letter attributed to Pope John VIII (d. 882): 'Sacrilegium committitur, si quis infregerit ecclesiam, uel triginta passus ecclesiasticos qui in circuitu ecclesiae sunt. . . . Similiter sacrilegium committitur auferendo sacrum de sacro, uel non sacrum de sacro, siue sacrum de non sacro' etc.

2–165/15 *xvi, q. vii, Decimas*: There are two canons 'Decimas' (both from the Palea). The first, 'Decimas Deo', cites OT precedent for tithing. The second, 'Decimas, quas', prohibits any quid pro quo agreement with a bishop on tithes. Theft is, however, not specifically mentioned (C.16 q.7 cc.6 and 7; Friedberg 1: 802).

2–166/18–28 *xvi, q. i, Quia iuxta, et Decime . . . Reuertimini*: Three canons: (1) 'Quia iuxta' appears to be an imperial rescript prohibiting distribution ('distribui') of Church property without the authority of the ruler; Gratian's *post dict.* says that the canon seems to conflict with earlier conciliar decrees (C.16 q.1 c.59; Friedberg 1: 780–1). (2) The canon 'Decime' is cited above (317/6). (3) The canon 'Reuertimini' states that non-payment of tithes defrauds the poor. The source cited (St Jerome, 'Super Malachiam', 3) is a false lead (C.16 q.1 c.65; Friedberg 1: 783–4).

2–166/28–9 *Reymundus in Summa sua, lib. i, ti. De decimis*: Raymond of Peñafort: 'In summa nota quod ille qui bene & fideliter dat decimam, quadrupliciter remuneratur a Deo . . . abundantia fructuum . . . sanitas corporis . . . indulgentia peccatorum . . . caeleste regnum' (*Summa*, Bk. I, p. 137b).

2–166/29–34 *þe lawe . . . Decime*: The canon 'Decime' is cited above, 317/6 and 2–166/18–28, but here a different portion is referred to: If it is a sin to be late in payment of tithes it is a worse sin not to pay at all; 'Deus enim noster, qui dignatus est totum dare, decimam a nobis dignatus est accipere, non sibi, sed nobis sine dubio profuturam. Sed si tardius dare peccatum est, quanto magis peius est peccatum non dedisse?' (C.16 q.1 c.66; Friedberg 1: 784).

2–166/37–8 *xvi, q. vii, Quicumque . . . Extra, lib. iii, ti. xxx, Pastoralis*: Two canons: (1) 'Quicumque' holds that tithes must be paid from all kinds of increase: '. . . de grano, aut de uino, aut de fructibus arborum, aut de pecoribus, aut de horto, aut de negocio, aut de ipsa uenatione sua' (C.16 q.7 c.4; Friedberg 1: 801). The source is a Quadragesima sermon of St Ambrose

(*PL* 17: 625 ff.). (2) 'Pastoralis', from an epistle of Pope Innocent III, answers a query from a bishop about whether expenses of production can be deducted before the amount to be tithed is calculated; the response is positive: expenses involved in manufacture or in buying and selling of goods may be deducted from the amount owed (X 3.30.28; Friedberg 2: 565–6). Cited 2–167/61–2 and 2–167/72 below.

2–166/39–44 *Reymundus . . . lib. i, ti. xii*: Raymond of Peñafort: 'Item, debent dari decimae de omnibus fructibus terrarum, pomis arborum, herbis hortorum, nutrimentis animalium, lana, lacte, foeno, lignis, fictis, piscationibus, venationibus, pensionibus, molendinis, etiam de vento, balneis, fullonicis, argentarijs, metallarijs, lapidicinis. Item de negotijs, & artificijs, & caeteris bonis, etiam de tempore' (*Summa*, Bk. I, p. 124ab).

2–166/44–5 *Hostiense, lib. iii, eodem ti.*: The reference is to Henricus of Segusa's *Summa aurea*, a commentary on the Decretals. On Hostiensis, see 246/39 above.

2–167/61–2 *Extra, lib. iii . . . Pastoralis et Cum homines*: Two canons: (1) 'Pastoralis' is cited above, 2–166/37–8; it goes on to say 'Nec pro restaurando detrimento quarumlibet rerum, ex quibus decimae persolvuntur, credimus deducendas expensas de proventibus decimandis, quia penes dominum res permanent restauratae, ut si pars aliqua moriatur armenti deterioretur vinea, portio mercis depereat, vel totus clibanus destruatur' (X 3.30.28; Friedberg 2: 566). (2) 'Cum homines' directs that tithes be paid without deduction of expenses if they are praedial tithes. The canon is cited from an epistle of Pope Alexander III (d. 1181) to the Bishop of Exeter (X 3.30.7; Friedberg 2: 558). The general rule was that praedial tithes were to be paid without deduction of expenses, and personal tithes were to be paid after the deduction of expenses; see A. G. Little, 'Personal Tithes' (1945), 57–88.

2–167/64–5 *alle þing þat newith*: The reference is to Deut. 15: 22: 'Decimam partem separabis de cunctis frugibus tuis quae nascuntur in terra per annos singulos'. See 2–163/116–7 above, 2–168/1–6 below.

2–167/72 *Extra . . . Pastoralis, in glosa*: X 3.30.28; Friedberg 2: 565–6. See 2–166/37–8, 2–167/61–2 above.

2–168/1–6 *To what chirche . . . Summa confessorum*: Pauper's reply to Dives' question, 'To what church shall tithes be paid?' glosses over a host of questions about who should pay tithes, to whom tithes should be paid, who should receive (and not pay) tithes, and to what body of law (canon or civil) or custom appeal should be made in disputed cases. In late medieval England, a large proportion of parish churches had long been farmed out to monasteries, which controlled the collection and dispensing of tithes. See A. G. Little, 'Personal Tithes' (1945), 67–88; Knowles (2nd edn. 1966), pp. 597–600; Constable (1964), pp. 47–56. On 'chopping of churches',

2–183/86–9 below. John of Freiburg on tithes: *Summa confessorum*, Bk. I, ti. 15 (MS Bodley 299. fos. 44^r–50^v.

2–168/13 *xii, q. ii, Quatuor . . . glose*: The canon 'Quatuor' prescribes a quadripartite division of tithes: '. . . conuenit fieri portiones, quarum una sit pontificis, altera clericorum, tertia pauperum, quarta fabricis est applicanda' (C.12 q.2 c.27; Friedberg 1: 696). The source is an epistle of Pope Gelasius I (d. 496). On the quadripartition of tithes, see Constable (1964), pp. 47–56.

2–168/15–16 *x, q., Decreuimus*: The canon 'Decreuimus' is from a conciliar decree which prescribes annual visits by bishops or their deputies and the application of funds for the repair of churches, a third to be contributed by the bishops: 'Decreuimus . . . si qua forte basilica fuerit reperta destituta, ordinatori eius reparari precipiatur, ab episcopis autem tertia pars ex omnibus accipiatur sicuti antiqua traditione nouimus esse statutum' (C.10 q.1 q.10; Friedberg 1: 615).

2–168/16 *Guido in Rosario*: Guido di Baysio (d. 1313), an Italian canonist, wrote a commentary on the *Decretum* of Gratian called the *Rosarium* (ed. Lyons 1512), which has been called 'indispensable for knowledge of older canonical writings' (*OCL*, pp. 543–4). See Ullmann (1975), p. 180; Brundage (1995), pp. 212–3. Cited below 2–169/49–50.

2–168/19 *þe chapel beryth awey*: H. Thompson (1947): 'In large parishes there were scattered hamlets from which access to the mother church was difficult, especially in winter. . . .The provision of local chapels for such outlying areas no doubt began at an early date. In Leicestershire, for example, early in the thirteenth century, there were in a little over two hundred parishes more than a hundred dependent chapels' (p. 123). The rivalry between parish church and chapel is alluded to in *Margery Kempe*: '. . . in a worshepful town wher was o parysch cherch & tweyn chapelys annexid . . . fel gret ple & gret heuynes be-twen þe Priowr whech was her person & curat & þe forseyd paryschenys þat desyred to haue fvntys [baptismal founts] & purificacyons in þe chapelys lych as weryn in þe parysch cherch' (ed. Meech and Allen, EETS, 212, pp. 58–9/29–31; 1–5).

2–168/20 *þe curat*: The term 'curate' is sometimes loosely applied, but here, following the mention of chapels, it probably refers to the class of assistant priests hired to perform clerical functions in churches in outlying areas. Their frequent inadequacy is assumed in Chaucer's 'Summoner's Tale', which also depicts their rivalry with the friars, who are, however, criticized for even more serious faults. See the fictional friar's comment in *CT*, p. 130/ 1816–9. Cf. Chaucer's 'Parsons's Tale': 'By swiche undigne preestes and curates han lewed men the lasse reverence of the sacramentz of hooly chirche' (*CT*, p. 315/790).

2–168/24 *Hostiense*: On Hostiensis, see 246/39 above. On the canon law with which Hostiensis disagrees, see 2–169/30 below. In view of the excommunication of William Russell, OFM, in 1425 for preaching that tithes should be given directly to the poor, note that MS G omits 'or of þe pore pareschynys' (168/29); on Russell, see A. G. Little (1892), pp. 257–8; idem, *EHR* 60 (1945), pp. 67–8. The Wycliffite 'De officio pastorali' agrees with Pauper that sinful curates should not receive tithes, 'for al þer lif is wlappid wiþ synne . . . & þus men shulden not ȝyue hem offeringis ne oþere tiþis, þe while þey lyuen þus' (ed. Matthew, EETS, os 74, p. 435).

2–169/30 *Extra, li. iii, ti. De decimis, c. Tua [nobis]*: The canon 'Tua nobis' holds that (praedial) tithes are to be paid to the Church without deduction for seed or other expenses ('sumptum'). The decretal on which it is based (of Innocent III) responds to a report that there has been resistance by some to paying tithes ('Nonnulli etiam vitam clericorum tanquam abominabilem destestantes, decimas eis ob hoc subtrahere non verentur'); but, says the Pope, allegations of clerical bad behaviour must not be allowed to excuse nonpayment (X 3.30.26; Friedberg 2: 564–5). For Hostiensis' opposing view, see below 2–169/36–7 and further, to the end of Com. VII, xiv. See 2–170/70–2 below. The author of *D&P* here deals with a legal conflict by splitting the argument between 'Dives' and 'Pauper' such that Gratian's *Decretum* is cited against the later Decretals (Extravagantes, Dives' 'Extra'). Unlike later papal decrees, the *Decretum* had never been promulgated as binding law. It was left to the commentators, notably Hostiensis (whom Pauper invokes on his side of the argument), to attempt to harmonize differences. For the handling of discrepancies between the *Decretum* of Gratian and the additions to canon law comprising the *Decretals*, *Sexts*, and *Clementines*, and the question of the promulgation of canon law, see Kuttner, *Medieval Councils* (1949; Variorum repr. 1980), I: 305–12.

2–169/36–7 *Hostiense in Summa sua, lib. iii . . . De decimis, ¶ Et quare*: On Hostiensis and the *Summa aurea*, see above 246/39. See 2–169/30 above.

2–169/39–43 *Gracianus . . . Di. lxxxi, Si quis amodo, cum aliis capitulis sequentibus*: The canons 'Si quis amodo', 'Si qui sunt presbiteri', and 'Clericus' relating to the sexual misbehaviour of clerics are cited above, 2–10 8/25–9, 2–109/51–2, 2–109/52–60 (D.81 cc.16, 15, 20; Friedberg 1: 285, 284, 286). Other citations of similar content are also found in the Notes to Com. VI, c. xviii: 2–107/16, 2–107/23, 2–108/32–7, 2–108/46, 2–110/16–17, 2–116/130–1. This is the only mention by name of Gratian (d. *c.*1160), the father of canon law; see 63/17 above.

2–169/49–50 *Gwydo in Rosario on 'Si qui sunt'*: The canon 'Si qui sunt' (D.81 c.15; Friedberg 1: 284) on the removal of clerics who are fornicators, or otherwise deviant, is cited above, 2–109/52–60. On Guido di Baysio, see 2–168/16 above.

2–170/70–2 *Extra, lib. iii, ti. De decimis, c. Tua nobis*: The canon 'Tua nobis' is cited above, 2–169/30 (X 3.30.26; Friedberg 2: 564–5). The *Decretum* appears to hold that tithes may be withdrawn from sinning clerics, and the *Decretals* indicate that they may not. Pauper, using *divisio*, makes the argument that tithes may be withdrawn from *open* malefactors, but not from clerics whose sins are hidden from general view.

2–171/98 *Extra, lib. iii, De prebendis, c. Extirpande*: The canon 'Extirpande' holds that the priest of a parish must have sufficient to live on; in some areas, where stipends have become fractional, it is difficult to find qualified priests: '[S]tatuimus, ut, consuetudine qualibet episcopi vel patroni, seu cuislibet alterius non obstante, portio presbyteris ipsis sufficient assignetur' (X 3.5.30; Friedberg 2: 478–9). The source is Innocent III's Fourth Lateran Council of 1215. Raymond of Peñafort cites the fourth Lateran Council to the same effect (*Summa*, Bk. I, pp. 127–8).

2–171/1 *typis personalys of Iewys*: Pauper's reply is unsupported, though it was generally asssumed that tithes were to be paid by Christians only. John of Freiburg's gloss on Raymond of Peñafort's *Summa* suggests that in certain cases, tithes *praediales* (i.e., gains derived from crops or animals) might be sought from Jews (Bk. I, p. 126). In certain other special cases, where Jews have come to occupy houses in which Christians formerly lived, tithes *personales* might be sought (Bk. I, pp. 37–8). A. G. Little, in his study of personal tithes, notes 'that Jews, though liable to praedial tithes, were exempt from personal tithes' ('Personal Tithes' (1945), p. 80).

2–172/22 *Reymundus, li. i, ti. De decimis*: See ¶ 14–15 in the section on tithes: '[S]i emptor fuit bonae fidei & soluit decimam, tenetur ei venditor; si fuerit male fidei, non tenetur, nisi expresse dictum, & cautum fuerit: debet tamen vterque agere penitentiam de dolo, & quasi furto. . . . si aliquis furtiue, vel etiam violenter armata manu rapuit totum aceruum, vel partem de area rustici ante solutionem decimarum . . . Dominium decimae residet iuxta ecclesiam, etiam ante separationem . . . [but if] violenter sibi ablatum est ab extraneo, cui non potuit prohibere, non tenetur, sed aget ecclesia contra raptorem' (*Summa*, Bk. I, pp. 136–7).

2–172/24–5 *Reymund . . . Innocent . . . Extra, [III, 30], In aliquibus*: The canon 'In aliquibus' states that tithes are enjoined by both God's law and custom: 'Illae quippe decimae necessario solvendae sunt, quae debentur ex lege divina vel loci consuetudine approbata' (X 3.30.32; Friedberg 2: 568). The source is Pope Innocent III's fourth Lateran Council (1215). Cf. Constable (1964): 'These tithes were the property of God, not a voluntary offering by man' (p. 18). Raymond of Peñafort says: 'Decima est omnium bonorum iuste quaesitorum aequalis pars Deo debita' (*Summa*, Bk. I, p. 123a).

2–172/27 *Leuitici . . . [27: 30]*: 'Omnes decimae terrae sive de frugibus sive de pomis arborum Domini sunt et illi sanctificantur'. GO: 'Eius enim qui terrena sapit, decima quidem sancta est' (1: 274).

2–172/29 *lawe posityf* . . . *mannys lawe*: See above, 160/11–15. Note that *D&P* is careful to rank customary law ('consuetude') below God's law and natural law.

2–172/31 *Extra, li. i, ti. iv, Cum dilectus*: The canon 'Quum dilectus' upholds the right, by ancient custom, of a church to appoint a prelate (X 1.4.8; Friedberg 2: 39–41). The canon is from an epistle of Pope Innocent III to several Church officials in 1209. They inquire whether local 'consuetude' should be observed, which would result in the election of one of the two candidates, or whether a recent statute allowing the patron to appoint the abbot (resulting in the election of the other candidate) should prevail? Innocent opts for 'consuetude'. In *D&P*, part of the *dict. ante* is quoted.

2–172/34 *þe tente part*: One of the sources of such number symbolism available to the author of *D&P* was Robert Grosseteste's *De luce*: 'Grosseteste states that form is represented by the number one, matter by two, and composition by three, "since there is patent in it formed matter and materialized form and the property of composition itself." The compound besides these three things has its own nature and so is represented by four. Now $1 + 2 + 3 + 4 = 10$. "Wherefore every whole and perfect thing is ten"' (Thorndike (1923), 2: 444, citing *De luce* from the Baur edn. (1912; repr. 1993), p. 58). Cf. Hopper (1938), p. 117. Another available source was Trevisa's translation of Bartholomaeus, 19.123: 'The nombre of ten passeþ nyne by oon, and is ende, bounde and mere of alle simple nombres, and first of alle þe compouned, and is worþy to presente oure lord Crist God, þat is *alpha et oo* . . . þe ioye and blisse of aungels and men' (*Properties*, 2: 1359/27–32).

2–173/48 *firste frws*: The payment of praedial tithes from first fruits has been alluded to (see 2–167/64–5 above). Pauper's reply mentioning hundredth parts, sixtieth parts, etc., seems to open the way to a discussion of the infeudation of tithes, but the complications of this subject may have daunted the author, who goes on to another chapter and topic. Constable cites as an instance of infeudation: 'The bishop of Grenoble paid three hundred and forty-nine shillings of Valence to Bernard the Lombard and his family for one-sixth of one half of the tithes of St Ismier and for the entire other half, of which Bernard held two-thirds as an allod and the other third as a fief from three brothers . . . who in turn held it from three other brothers, who held it from the bishop and surrendered it to him in return for a mule worth a hundred shillings and a grant of some lands illegally usurped by their father' (1964, p. 113). For a more recent discussion of tithes at the parish level, see R. N. Swanson (1989), pp. 209–228.

VOL. 1: 2, COMMANDMENT VII (2),
pp. 2–173–210

2–173/5 *Io. x* [*1*]: A text cited routinely in discussions of simony. Augustine specifies three groups which do not enter the sheepfold by the door: those who scrupulously follow the Commandments but do not follow Christ, philosophers who argue subtly about vice and virtue but do not follow Christ, and heretics (Arians, Sabellians and others) who are nominal but not doctrinal Christians ('Nomen habes, rem non habes'), in *In Ioh.* 45.1–5 (*CCL* xxxvi, pp. 389–90; *PL* 35: 1720–1).

2–173/10 *What is symonye?*: Pauper answers the question with a word-for-word translation of Raymond of Peñafort's definition: 'Simonia est studiosa cupiditas, vel voluntas emendi, vel vendendi aliquod spirituale: nec oportet addi, vel spirituali annexum: nam spirituali annexum spirituale est' (*Summa*, Bk. I, p. 3). Found in *Fasciculus morum*, ed. Wenzel, from the same source, pp. 354–5.

2–173/12 *þe Philosofre*: In the *Nicomachean Ethics*, Aristotle stresses that moral excellence is a state, not merely a calculus of actions, cf. II, 4, where he says, 'Actions, then, are called just and temperate when they are such as the just or the temperate man would do; but it is not the man who does these that is just and temperate, but the man who also does them *as* just and temperate men do them' (*Oxford Aristotle*, 2: 1746/5–7).

2–174/27–34 *Simon Magus, a gret wyche . . . Act.* [*8: 18–20*]: 'Cum vidisset autem Simon quia per inpositionem manus apostolorum daretur Spiritus Sanctus, obtulit eis pecuniam dicens, "Date et mihi hanc potestatem ut cuicumque inposuero manus accipiat Spiritum Sanctum." Petrus autem dixit ad eum, "Pecunia tua tecum sit in perditionem, quoniam donum Dei existimasti pecunia possideri."' Historically, Simon Magus was 'the last representative of pre-Christian Gnosticism' (Quasten, *Patrology*, 1: 255). Irenaeus (d. c200) early identified Simon Magus as the source of all heresies: 'Simon, the father of all heretics' (*Early Christian Fathers*, LCC I, p. 369. Isidore of Seville cites Simon Magus first in his catalogue of heretics (*Etym.*, 8.5.2).

2–174/35–42 *Giesy . . . IV Regum v*: For Gehazi, see 2 Kgs. 5: 19–27. LL4 summarizes: 'The meselrie of fals coueytyse is betokenyd be þe meselrie of Gyesy whyche for fals coueytyse took mede for þe helþe & þe cure þat god hadde don be his mayster Helysen & Naaman, prince of Surie; for Helysen helid hym & maad hym clene & wolde non meede takin. But whanne þis prince was hool & gon forth in his weye, Gyesy þe seruaunt of Helysen ran after hym & askyd 3yftis in his maystris name falsly & took of hym two besauntis of syluyr & many cloþis & went & hidde is. But his mayster

Helysen knewe his falshed be reuelacioun of þe holy gost & seyde to hym: "For þu hast þus takin syluer & cloþis to makin þee ryche, þe meselrie of Naaman schal cleuyn to þee & to al þin kyn after þee." And onon he wax a foul mesel' (fo. 93vb). By the later Middle Ages, Gehazi had become a type of the simonist. The story is briefly referred to above, 333/6–7, and below, 2–259/4–5. *ABD* 2: 926.

2–174/46 *symonye*. . . . *In þre maner*: *D&P* follows Raymond of Peñafort: 'Committitur simonia tribus modis . . . aliud enim est munus a manu; aliud ab obsequio; aliud a lingua. Munus a manu pecunia est. Munus ab obsequio est seruitus indebite impensa. Munus a lingua fauor' (*Summa*, Bk. I, p. 6a). Wyclif classifies spiritual theft ('furtum sacerdotum') as simony, the buying or selling of what is sacred, and defrauding the poor (*De mand.*, p. 379/20–9).

2–175/53–65 *in receyuyng of holy ordre is don symonye*: *D&P* continues to follow Raymond of Peñafort: 'Item nota, que simoniaca dicitur ordinatio, alia ex parte ordinatoris tantum, alia ex parte ordinandi tantum, alia ex parte vtriusque; alia ex neutrius parte, quae est, cum vtroque ignorante, amicus ordinandi dat, vel promittit consiliario Episcopi' (*Summa*, Bk. I, p. 6a).

2–175/73–4 *Extra, li. [v], ti. De Symonya, c. Sicut tuis literis*: The canon 'Sicut tuis literis' is derived from a papal letter to an abbot about a complicated case of simoniacal bribes offered, refused, and denied for the post of abbot. Innocent III (in 1199) concludes that the election is not tainted by simony if the bribery was unknown to the prospective abbot (X 5.3.33; Friedberg 2: 762–3).

2–176/86 *Summa confessorum, lib. i, ti. i*: John of Freiburg's *Summa* deals with simony in Bk. I, ti. 1 (MS Bodley. 299, fos. 2^v–11^r). Q. 47 (fo. 8^v), 'Quid de eo qui scit episcopum suum symonicum', appears to be the closest to the topic referred to here.

2–176/4 *Reymund*: Raymond of Peñafort asks, When are such gifts justified? He answers that they are justified in five cases: first, when offered with no conditions attached; second, if given for spiritual gifts or services; third, if given as thanks for spiritual services performed; fourth, if given for charity; fifth, as a remedy for a previous injustice (*Summa*, Bk. I, pp. 6b–7a).

2–177/21–4 *Powyl . . . I ad Corinth. ix [14]*: 'Ita et Dominus ordinavit his qui evangelium adnuntiant de evangelio vivere.' See 194/33 above.

2–177/26–7 *Sent Austyn . . . [Ps. 103: 14]*: 'Producens faenum iumentis et herbam servituti hominum ut educas panem de terra.' See 194/37 above, 2–290/23–5 below.

2–177/29–30 *Danyel . . . Danieli iv [:24]*: For [: 24] read [: 27]. 'Quam ob rem rex consilium meum placeat tibi et peccata tua elemosynis redime et iniquitates tuas misericordiis pauperum, forsitan ignoscat delictis tuis.' God, says the gloss, intends to punish sin and to save mankind ('Intendit enim peccata punire, homines saluare'), GO, 3: 331.

2–177/36 *Extra, De symonia, c. Dilect[us] fili[us]*: The canon 'Dilectus filius' is derived from a letter of Pope Innocent III to the Archbishop of Canterbury, who had inquired whether punishment for simony might be lessened in cases where ancient custom had been followed. Innocent replies that all such prelates must be suspended from their offices until penance has been performed. As a whole, the canon does not appear quite relevant to Pauper's argument, but the final sentence may be what he has in mind: 'Illud tamen gratanter recipi poterit, quod fuerit sine taxatione gratia oblatum' (X 5.3.30; Friedberg 2: 759–60).

2–177/39 *to gon to Rome*: In *D&P*, 'going to Rome' comes under the heading of honest service to a bishop, cf. Raymond of Peñafort, *Summa*, Bk. I, p. 7b. In the Wycliffite sermon cited above, however, it is part and parcel of simony: 'And þus men seien þat many clerkis traueilen in þe court of Rome and han many beneficis, al if þei don neuere good in hem' (*EWS* 3, Appendix, p. 320/46–8).

2–177/55 *Reymundus, li. i, ti. i*: Raymond of Peñafort says: 'Beneficium vero simplex, si indiget, & sentis se dignum, potest petere absque metu peccati, & simoniae . . . Si vero non indiget, peccat, vt patet per illam ad aures' (*Summa*, Bk. I, p. 9a).

2–178/21 *i, q. i, Reperiuntur*: The canon 'Reperiuntur' deals with penalties for symony. Knowingly taking money for Church office is cause for excommunication (C.1 q.1 c.7; Friedberg 1: 359). The source is the eighth Council of Toledo (?seventh century; the date of this council is uncertain; see Mansi, Vol. 10, pp. 775–8). The same material is found in Raymond of Peñafort's *Summa*, (Bk. I, p. 10a), which *D&P* continues to parallel.

2–179/29–30 *Sent Powil . . . [1 Thess. 5: 22]*: 'Ab omni specie mala abstinete vos'. GO: 'Solent enim spiritus immundi fallaciter dicere bona & inter haec subinducere praua, vt per haec quam bona sunt accipiantur & mala (4: 400).

2–179/35 *Reymund*: Raymond of Peñafort gives the argument for allowing money payment for marriage rites as follows: 'Propter matrimonium, in quo, vt est tantum officium naturae, & contractus naturalis, non confertur gratia, & ideo pro eo, vt sic, dari pecunia potest' citing Extra, 'De sponsalibus', (X 4.1.1–32; Friedberg 2: 661–72). He adds that if lay persons 'ex pia consuetudine' give gifts at burials or weddings it is allowable so long as these are not solicited by the priest (*Summa*, Bk. I, p. 18ab).

2–179/40–3 *Also vestimentis & chalys*: Raymond of Peñafort: 'Hoc etiam dico pro calice consecrato, vel similibus, que possunt vendi absque periculo simoniae, etiam in eadem forma, alijs Ecclesius in casibus necessitatis' etc.

John of Freiburg's gloss adds: 'conflata autem possunt vendi laicis' (*Summa*, Bk. I, p. 18a).

2–179/49–54 *3if a preste* . . . *Reymund*: Raymond of Peñafort: '[D]ico, quod si tenetur ex officio ad hanc Missam, vel exequias, vel simile, exigere propter hoc aliquid, simoniacum est . . . Si vero non tenetur, & desunt ei sumptus, potest licite recipere' (*Summa*, Bk. I, p. 19a).

2–179/54–5 *Extra, Ne prelati vices suas, etc., c. vltimo*: The canon 'Querelam' directs that a certain cleric, wrongly accused of simony, be restored to his church (X 5.4.4; Friedberg 2: 768). The source is a papal letter from Pope Alexander III (d.1181) to the Bishop of Exeter.

2–179/60 *De con, di, i, Sufficit*: The canon 'Sufficit' says that one mass per day should be sufficient. If a priest is persuaded or bribed to celebrate more, he endangers his salvation (De cons. D.1 c.53; Friedberg 1: 1308). The source is a decree of Pope Alexander II (d. 1073), issued at the Lateran synod of 1063.

2–179/60–180/92 *3yf mounkys* . . . *Reymundus, ubi supra*: The four examples of simony in the rest of this chapter are drawn from the section on simony in Raymond of Peñafort's *Summa*: (1) the making of processions or the singing of dirges may not be done for a stipulated fee, but contributions may be received without simony (pp. 19b–20a). (2) As for guilds and fraternities, Raymond says: If the money is given for relieving the poor or redeeming captives, it is not simony (p. 20b). John of Freiburg's gloss cites Luke 16: 9 (see 54/11 above) to show the difficulty of drawing the line between symony and charity and concludes that gifts are illicit if they are intended to bring a corresponding action on the part of the cleric but allowable if intended to maintain the clerical office (p. 20b); see also idem, ¶ 22, p. 23. (3) Raymond asks: If a layman tries to interfere in an election and asks for money on condition that he will desist from such efforts, Is it simony? Answer, Yes (idem, p. 21b). But in two similar cases simony is not committed: If my friend gives money in order to procure my election, or if someone gives money in order to prevent my election (idem, p. 15b). (4) The cleric may not receive orders from a simoniacal bishop; indeed, says Raymond, 'cum enim ille [the bishop] non habeat executionem, non posset illi [the cleric] dare' (idem, p. 22a; see 2–180/85–92 below).

2–180/85–92 *dispensacioun, i, q. i, Si [qui] a symoniacis*: The canon 'Si qui a symoniacis' enjoins that ordination by a simonaical bishop may stand unless the candidate knowingly allowed such an ordination (C.1 q.1 c.108; Friedberg 1: 400–1). The source is a conciliar decree by Urban II (d. 1099), concluding: '. . . Qui uero scienter se a symoniacis consecrari (imo execrari) permisserint, eorum consecrationem omnino irritam esse decernimus' (Mansi, Vol. 20, p. 805). Cf. Raymond of Peñafort, *Summa*. Bk. I, p. 22a.

2–180/1–181/8 *ʒif religious . . . i, q. ii, Quam pio*: Dives' question is from
Raymond of Peñafort, whose answer is that all such pacts are simony ('absit
omnis pactio'), *Summa*, Bk. I, pp. 24b–25a. The canon 'Quam pio' is from a
letter of Boniface VIII (d. 1303) to the effect that converts are not to be
asked for money (C.1 q.2 c.2; Friedberg 1: 408).

2–181/13–21 *ʒif a clerk . . . Extra, eodem, Si quis ordinauerit*: The canon 'Si
quis ordinauerit' declares that ordainers, presenters (of candidates) and
ordinands who collude in an ordination conditional on future provision are
to be suspended, pending papal dispensation (X 5.3.45; Friedberg 2: 767).
The source is a papal letter of Gregory IX (d. 1241). Before ordination, a
cleric was required to have a 'title', or a guaranteed source of maintenance.
Canonically, this was the responsibility of the ordaining bishop (*Decretum*
1.70.2; modified in X.3.5.2 & 16 (Lateran III, of 1179), but in the period of
D&P, it was often the practice for ordinands to offer a religious house as
their title, a practise that lent itself to abuse; see Heath (1969), pp. 17–18).

2–181/21–5 *ʒif ony man . . . i, q. i, [Duces, inquit]*: The canons in Quest. I
deal with particular cases of symony. 'Duces inquit' warns that good
prophets do not expect payment for their prophecies (C.1 q.1 c.23;
Friedberg 1: 367–8). This and the following canon, 'Numquam', are
based on St Jerome's 'Commentariorum in Michaeam' (*PL* 25: 1207–90),
in which Jerome cites biblical examples, from St Peter to Saul, Samuel,
Jeroboam, Elisha and Nehemiah, of the sale of spiritual goods. In a *post dict.*
to the following canon, 'Numquid', Gratian qualifies by pointing out that
God's gifts may follow suspect actions, as in the case of Jacob, who received
his father's blessing through chicanery. Cf. 2–19/27–20/29 above.

2–181/27–30 *Holy watyr . . . symonye*: The specific prohibitions are in John
of Freiburg's gloss to Raymond of Peñafort's *Summa*: 'Vnde nec panis
benedictus, nec aqua benedicta, cum per eius aspersionem dimittantur
venialia, vendi non debent . . . pro chrismate, vel baptismo nihil exigatur'
(Bk. I, p. 8b).

2–181/30–2 *Also þey . . . Extra, eodem, In tantum*: The canon 'In tantum' is
summed up in the *dict. ante* as a flat prohibition of any payments demanded
as the price of an anointing or an investiture (X 5.3.36; Friedberg 2: 764).
The source is a papal letter of Innocent III to the Archbishop of Canterbury
(in 1190) about a report of payments exacted for the administration of the
eucharist. He orders such practices among the suffragans and others
('suffraganeos tuos, et officiales eorum') to be stopped immediately.

2–181/32–5 *ʒif þe curat . . . Extra, eodem, Audiuimus*: The canon
'Audivimus' forbids bishops to exact payment for installing clergy, monastic
confessions, or burials, setting a penalty of double indemnity (X 5.3.41;
Friedberg 2: 766). The source is a papal decree of Innocent III. Cited again
below, 2–184/9–19.

2–181/36–182/44 *3if þe curat . . . Extra, eodem, Ad apostolicum*: The canon 'Ad apostolicum' orders clerics not to try to exact money for burials and weddings by putting up false objections ('impedimenta fictitia fraudulenter opponunt'); the particular bribe of a 'bed' or 'beste cloþ' is not mentioned. The decree goes on to condemn lay heretics who pretend piety in order to avoid customary contributions. This is not alluded to directly but may be the basis for the otherwise odd passage in the text suggesting that payment may 'aftirward' be compelled in order to keep to old custom (X 5.3.42; Friedberg 2: 766). The source is a papal decree of Innocent III.

2–182/44–183/79 *þou a clerk . . . he doth symonye*: The examples of simony in this portion of the text continue to be drawn from Raymond of Peñafort's *Summa*. The example of a tip given a porter or janitor ('portatio', 'ianitori') is not simoniacal 'quia recipere in sumptus, & stipes tabernaculi, non est simonia'; John of Freiburg's gloss agrees, providing the tip is given without ulterior motive (p. 16a). In respect to the weddings or confessions of members of different parishes, John of Freiburg's gloss on Raymond of Peñafort's *Summa* rules that it is not simony if a gift is shared between the two parishes (Bk. I, p. 17b–18a). On baptisms, when a fee is demanded by the priest, John of Freiburg's gloss holds that in such a case the lay man or woman should baptise the infant—unless he or she does not know the proper words to use; in which case it is better to pay the priest simoniacially in order to save the infant (idem, pp. 21b–22a). What if a justly interdicted, suspended or excommunicated cleric pays money to be reinstated? John of Freiburg's gloss says it is simony. But if an unjustly accused cleric gives money in order to be reinstated it is simony only on the part of the recipient and not on the part of the giver (idem, p. 22a).

2–183/79–81 *3if ony patron . . . Extra, eodem, Nemo*: The canon 'Nemo' says that grace or favor ('gratia vel favore') are simoniacal when used to conceal sin or soften penitence (X 5.3.14; Friedberg 2: 754). The source is a papal letter of Alexander III. The same is found in Raymond of Peñafort's *Summa*, which also cites the canon (Bk. I, p. 18a).

2–183/83–6 *3if a patron . . . Petrus Tarentinus, super iv. Sentenciarum, d. xxv*: Found in 'In lib. ii-14 Sententiarum', see Balliol MS 61, fos. 272$^{\text{va–vb}}$ (*Catalogue*, ed. R. A. B. Mynors (1963), pp. 41–2). Peter of Tarantaise (Pope Innocent V) wrote a major commentary on Peter Lombard's *Sentences* edited in the seventeenth century by T. Turco & G. B. de Marinus).

2–183/86–9 *choppyng of chirchis*: The brokering of benefices was a growth industry from the thirteenth to the end of the fifteenth century and arose from the need to fit clerics to suitable or desired posts. Exchange of information about available livings ranged from informal communication between incumbents to use (and abuse) of the services of 'chopchurch' traders in benefices; see Dahmus (1964), pp. 214–5; 261–5; Heath (1969), pp. 44–8; Swanson (1989), pp. 55–6. Buying and selling of the right of patronage was a practise that more often involved simony. The advowson, or right to present a cleric to a vacant post, was considered to be a saleable as well as heritable object (cf. *Fifty Earliest English Wills*, in which 'þe londes and rentes . . . with a-vowsoune of þe chirche' are willed in 1411 (ed. Furnivall, EETS, os 78, p. 20/9–10); though productive of much litigation, the practice continued to the end of the Middle Ages (cf.'Constitutions' of John Stratford (1342): in which it is proclaimed that, 'Nos hunc abusum abolere volentes', a limit of twelve denarios is to be set on the fee for writing letters of inquisition, institution, or collation & commission for inducting clerics, etc. (Lyndwood, *Provinciale* (1679 edn.), pp. 49b-50a; 53a-54a).

2–183/89–91 *3if a man . . . symonye*: This sentence strays into the realm of usury but may have been suggested by a passage from the opening of Raymond of Peñafort's *Summa* on simony: 'Videtur tamen quod sola intentio, vel voluntas non etiam studiosa, vel declarata, faciat simoniacum, sicut & vsurarium' (Bk. I, p. 4a). John of Freiburg's gloss: '. . . intentio percipiendi aliquid ex mutuo vltra sortem [the principal loaned], licet non sit in pactum deducta, reum facit accipientem, & debet induci ad restituendum' (idem).

2–183/91–3 *3if þe lewyd man withhelde . . . symonye*: Unlike the possibility that the sale of advowsons by lay patrons may be allowable under some circumstances (see 2–183/86–9, 2–183/89–91 above), the withholding of tithes by the layman is illicit: '. . . ius percipiendi decimas, vel oblationes non competit ei [the layman], sed illi soli, qui habet ordinem ecclesiasticum' (Raymond of Peñafort's *Summa*, Bk. I, p. 4a: John of Freiburg's gloss). On tithes, which from the seventh to the eleventh centuries were in the hands of laymen, see Constable (1964), pp. 63 ff.

2–183/93–100 *3if prechours or pardonystrys . . . restitucion*: To some extent, wandering preachers (among them, the Franciscans), were in competition with wandering pardoners, or questors; the friar-author of *D&P* points to the unfair competition offered the friars by unscrupulous mendicants who would turn begging for the needy into a profit-sharing plan in collusion with the parish priest. In a poor parish, or one in need of funds for church building, there was a strong temptation to license a pardoner to collect money for purposes other than alms (see Chichele *Register* of 1424 on the licensing of such collectors for the purpose of raising funds for building, ed. Jacob, 4: 256–62; Clay (1909), pp. 188–90). Because of Chaucer's vivid portrait of a Pardoner in the *CT* (pp. 193–202), there is a large modern literature on the subject. On Chaucer's Pardoner, see A. L. Kellogg and L. A. Haselmayer, 'Chaucer's Satire of the Pardoner', *PMLA* 66 (1951), 251–77; Mann (1973), pp. 145–52, and Scase (1989), who discusses the association of pardoners and mendicant friars, pp. 142–3.

2–183/1–184/4 *3if man or woman . . . spytilhous of leprousis . . . ambrye*: The
text refers to John of Freiburg's gloss on Raymond of Peñafort's *Summa*,
which distinguishes between payment to be admitted to a hospital or
leprosarium (not simony) and money given for spiritual services, which is
deemed to be simony (Bk. I, p. 27b).

2–184/4–6 *a monkis ry3t*: The sale by a religious house of an annuity giving
the right to life-time maintenance. A caution against buying 'a monkis ry3t'
is contained in John of Freiburg's gloss on Peñafort's *Summa*: 'Item quid de
illis, qui emerunt victum vnius Monachi ad totam vitam suam: numquid est
simonia?' It is not simony but 'non est tamen securum emere'; see 2–183/1–
184/4 above. On 'corrodies' and the legal complications that might result
from them, see Pollock and Maitland, 2: 134–5. See below 2–194/63. See
also J. R. H. Moorman (1955), pp. 269–71; Heath (1969), pp. 185–6; Rubin
(1987), pp. 161, 165–6, 171–3.

2–184/5–9 *Durandus . . . in Summa, in lib. ii eodem ti*: The reference to
Durandus's 'booc' is here either to his *Speculum iudiciale* or to his
Repertorium aureum iuris canonici. On William Durandus of Mende
(d.1296) as a legist, see Gy (1992), pp. 47–133; Brundage (1995), pp. 146–
7, pp. 228–9.

2–184/9–19 *3if priour or abot . . . Extra, eodem, c. Sicut pro certo et c. In
tantum, c. Veniens, c. Audiuimus et c. Iacobus*: Five canons: (1) 'Sicut pro
certo' derives from a general council of Pope Innocent III and states that it
is simoniacal to exact any payment for the consecration of a bishop or the
blessing of an abbot or the ordination of a cleric, custom notwithstanding (X
5.3.39; Friedberg 2: 765). (2) For the canon 'In tantum' see 2–181/30–2
above. (3) The canon 'Veniens' is derived from a papal letter of Alexander
III (d. 1181) concerning a monk who had given payment to be admitted to a
monastery 'de consuetudine monasterii'. If the report is true, the monks are
to be held to restitution and also suspended from their offices and
transferred to other monasteries (X 5.3.19; Friedberg 2: 755–6). (4) For
the canon 'Audiuimus' see 2–181/32–5 above. (5) The canon 'Iacobus' is
derived from a papal letter of Gregory IX (d. 1241) in reply to an accusation
that Canon Jacob was refused acceptance as a canon on the pretext that it
was customary to provide a dinner for the canons and prebendaries; the
prior is advised that the canon is to be received without the observance of
such a custom (X 5.3.44; Friedberg 2: 767).

2–184/22–3 *3if man or woman . . . trentel, for anuel, for 3erday*: A 'trental' was
a series of thirty masses, sung on thirty consecutive days or thirty days
during the year; an 'annual' or 'yearday' was a mass sung on the anniversary
of a death; a mass of the Holy Ghost was a votive mass (*Sarum Missal*, ed.
Legg, pp. 385–6). The general rule was that masses must be sung gratis,
assuming that the priest subsisted on the tithes of his parish, and allowing

that it was customary to give an offering (see 2–179/49–54 above). To the question, what about annuals, triennials, anniversaries, masses of the Holy Spirit, or other special masses? John of Freiburg's gloss on Raymond of Peñafort is: 'Respondeo in omnibus talibus casibus dare, vel accipere temporale pro spirituali simoniacum est' (*Summa*, Bk. I, p. 20a). See Wilkins, 1: 506, 581, 635–40, 650, etc.; Lyndwood, *Provinciale*, Second Council of Oxford, 1236, 'De prohibita missarum venditione', where it is strictly forbidden to sell annuals or trentals (1679 edn., p. 12a). Cf. the will of Lady Alice West (1395) leaving money 'for to synge and seye MMMM and CCCC [4400] Masses for my lord sir Thomas West-is [*sic*] soule, and for myn, and for alle cristene soules, in the most hast that it may be do, withynne xiiij nyght next after my deces' (ed. Furnivall, EETS, os 78, p. 6/24–8). Cf. *Margery Kempe*, 'Appendix', for record of payment to the Friars Minor for trentals for three deceased members of the Corpus Christi Guild of Lynn (ed. Meech and Allen, EETS, 212, p. 365).

2–184/27–8 *Williami . . . Summa confessorum, lib. i, ti. i q. xlii*: The question 'Quid si nullum' dealing with colleges and the sale of masses, along with Williams's gloss, is found in John of Freiburg's *Summa confessorum* (MS Bodley 299, fo. 8ʳ). William's gloss is probably that of William Durandus, Bishop of Mende (d. 1296), found either in his *Repertorium* or his *Speculum iudiciale*; referred to above 2–184/5–9.

2–184/31,33 *college*: The Wycliffite view of such arrangements was negative: 'þer ben þre maner of collegies þat vsen þis craft of appropring . . . cathedral chirches . . . chapels of prinsis . . . collegies [*sic*] of studies . . . alle acorden in þis, þat þey han almes of pariȝschens & ȝit dwellen not on þe parijs [parish] as herdis [pastors] for to teche hem; & þey blasfemes in god' ('De officio pastorali' (ed. Matthew, EETS, os 74, p. 419). See above 245/1, 353/49, 2–136/50.

2–185/41–8 *Sent Austyn . . . receyuyd into blisse*: The biblical reference is to the 'mamona iniquitatis' of Luke 16: 9, see 54/11 and 2–156/14 above.

2–185/48–52 *And þus . . . Extra, Ne prelati vices suas, c. Quoniam enormys*: The canon 'Quoniam enormys' forbids the sale by clergy of annual services (X 5.4.3; Friedberg 2: 768). The canon was promulgated at the Council of Turin convened by Pope Alexander III.

2–185/53 *statuȝt synodal*: Dives' objection points to the difficulty of disentangling payments to a priest or parish intended for maintenance from those intended as direct payments for such spiritual benefits as masses. The reference could well be to Archbishop Sudbury's constitution, 'De salariis presbyterorum', of 1378, which does spell out fees for annuals, but in an effort to limit them, as Pauper retorts. It begins by denouncing farmed-out or inflated payments; Sudbury goes on to say that his predecesssor, Archbishop Islip, had set payment of five marks to chaplains for singing annuals and six for higher-ranking clerics. He now sets the lowest payment at seven marks (or three marks and board) and eight marks (or four marks and board) for higher ranks (Lyndwood's *Provinciale*, 'Constitutiones Provinciales in Concilio Oxon.', pp. 58b–59a (1679 edn.)). Cf. *D&P*'s 'ten marc' (text, 2–188/74 below). On payments for masses, Pfaff (1974), 75–90. The denunciatory passage cited seems to have been quoted word for word from Simon Islip's (1349–66) Constitutions of 1362 (see Lyndwood, op. cit., p. 56a; *Councils & Synods* ii, s. v. Islip, does not have this.

2–186/1–2 *þe gyldene trental*: On trentals, see 2–184/22–3 above. The 'golden trental' is attacked by 'Jack Upland' (*c.*1390) and defended by 'Friar Daw' (ca 1420): 'Whi make 3e men bileue þat 3oure golden trentale, soold for a certeyn summe of money—as fyue schylingis or more—may brynge a soule out of helle or of purgatorie?' asks Jack. Friar Daw replies:

> And so þat gilden trentel þat þou spekist of,
> þat now is purchasid of preestis out of freris hondis,
> Delyueriþ noo soule out of þe peyne of helle,
> Ne purgen may of purgatory but as it is deserued,
> For charite is þe mesure þat demeþ þat meyne.
> (ed. Heyworth, pp. 62/199; 89/519–22)

An Apology for Lollard Doctrines of about the same period, makes the same point, 'þat prestis to sing may not first mak couenaunt wiþ out symonie', citing canon law, as well as Hostiensis and Peter Cantor (ed. Todd, p. 52). See 2–185/53 above and 2–186/20, 2–187/36–42, 2–188/76–189/77, 2–190/37–192/103 below.

2–186/20 *salerye*: An early use of the word for the annual stipend of a priest; cf. 'Jack Upland' (*c.*1390): 'Frere, if þou þinkist it a good dede to begge for þin idil briþeren at hoom, þere eche oon of 3ou haþ an annuel salarie eþer two . . .' (*Jack Upland*, ed. Heyworth, p. 66/285–7).

2–186/23–187/29 *Reymund . . . Extra, li. iii, De celebracione missarum, c. ii . . . swyche messys*: Raymond of Peñafort gives as an example of an *obsequium* that might go with a benefice the daily singing of a mass of the BVM; John of Freiburg's gloss puts the question whether a mass can serve specified individuals and answers that it cannot be tailored to individual needs; masses which are combined owing to constraints of time and place are as valuable as separate masses (*Summa*, Bk. I, p. 8a). The *dict. ante* to the canon 'Quidam' (c. 2) states that special masses are not to pre-empt ferial masses. The text gives the example of certain lay persons, 'maxime matronae', who are in the habit of hearing special masses on John the Evangelist, the Holy Trinity or St Michael. They may hear such masses only in addition to regular masses (X 3.41.2; Friedberg 2: 635–6).

2–187/36–42 *Synodalys of Englond. . . .Constituciouns of Lamethe*: The Constitutions of Lambeth (1281), under the auspices of Archbishop John

Pecham, strictly forbade special masses (Lyndwood, 'Constitutiones Provinciales in Concilio Oxon.', *Provinciale* (1679 edn.), p. 27a). The text is also
found in *Councils and Synods*, 2: 895. Stipends are taken up in the
Constitutions of Islip (1362); Islip, after denouncing the insatiable avarice
of some ('insatiabilis avaritia ab aliis operariis') who say many masses to
increase their incomes, admonishes priests to be content with their customary stipends and chaplains to limit themselves to one gold mark beyond
their usual stipends (Lyndwood, *Provinciale*, 'Constitutiones Simoni Islepe',
pp. 56b-57a (1679 edn.). In 1391, Archbishop Winchelsey was still
inveighing against profiteering in chantries and advises that priests who
sing special masses must first be licensed and then strictly limited in the
prices they can charge (Lyndwood, idem, pp. 61a-62a). Pauper's complaint
about prices and working conditions and his vignette of bargaining sound
very much as if drawn from observation of the harried life of the chantry
priest and support the view that public demand for special masses was as
motivating as clerical greed. See Wood-Legh (1965); Heath (1969), pp. 22–6.

2–188/63 *our ladyys day*: The Feast of the Annunciation 25 March. William
Durandus gives directions for changing the day of the Feast in years when it
falls on or near Easter (*Rationale*, 7.9, *CCCM* cxlB, pp. 46–7). Rubrics for
the mass are given in the *Sarum Missal*, ed. Legg, pp. 259–60.

2–188/68 *weryn þe hayre*: Refers to the practice of wearing a shirt made of
cloth woven from hair next to the skin as a form of penance. Though the
practice is associated with monastic austerities, the *Ancrene Wisse* twice
deprecates it as extreme for women anchorites: 'Me is leouere þ[at] ȝe þolien
wel an heard word, þen an heard hére [hair]' (ed. Tolkien, EETS, 249,
pp. 214–5/17–18).

2–188/75 *Sent Gregory . . . purgatorie*: The connection between Gregory and
the early liturgy appears largely based on comments on music in some of his
letters and on legend, as purveyed by the stories in the 'Dialogues' and in
the *Legenda aurea*: 'Gregory remodelled the Church's offices and chant, and
founded a school for the chanters' (Graesse, No. 46; *GL*, 1: 180). Gregory's
use of a musical metaphor in his *Moralia*, 30.3.12, helped to associate his
name with Church music: the preacher, he says, should touch the minds of
his hearers with the skill of the musician touching the strings of his harp
('cithara': *CCL* cxliiiB, p. 1499/100–5). Vogel (1986), p. 31, points out:
'The ancient Christian era was one in which churches freely created their
own liturgical *formulae* . . . Even at the time of Gregory the Great (590–
604), there was no *liber sacramentorum* except for local use'. The development of the connection between the mass and assistance to souls in
purgatory is also an indirect one; it is traced by Pfaff (1974), pp. 76–7,
who begins his discussion: '[I]t is necessary to understand . . . that St

Gregory's Trental has nothing to do with Gregory the Great . . .'. See 2–188/76–189/77; 2–189/80–190/97 below.

2–188/76–189/77 *Sent Gregoryys trentel*: A popular ballad preserved in several manuscripts begins:

> A nobull story wryte y fynde,
> A pope hit wrote to haue yn mynde
> Of his modur, (& of her lyf)
> That holden was an holy wyfe
>> (*Political, Religious and Love Poems*, ed. Furnivall,
>> EETS, os 15, pp. 114–22)

Also edited in *Minor Poems of the Vernon MS*, I (ed. Horstmann, EETS, os 98, pp. 260–8). Manuscripts are listed in *IMEV*, Nos. 83, 1653, 3184. See Hartung *Manual*, 6: 1771; 1799. On purgatory, see 169/19–21, 214/19–20, 328/36 above, 2–190/37–192/103 below.

2–189/80–190/97 *lib. iv Dialogorum . . . pretty dayys*: Dialogues, Bk 4 (*PL* 77: 424–5).

2–189/1–190/29 *þe lyf of Sent Tebaut . . . þe soule stille in his peyne*: The story of St Theobald is retold in the *Legenda aurea* (Grasse, No. 163; *GL*, 2: 282–3)).

2–190/31–7 *Sent Gregory . . . Legende of Sentis . . . Soulynmesse day*: Refers to Gregory's *Dialogues*, see above 2–188/75, 2–188/76–189/77; 2–189/80–190/97; 2–189/1–190/29, and to the *Legenda aurea* (Graesse, No.163; *GL*, 2: 280–90).

2–190/37–192/103 *But þe peple . . . soulys þat he syngyth for*: This passage seems to skitter between a jocular approach to bargaining for votive masses (eighty successive masses are surely a better bargain than thirty if the price for either is twenty shillings!) and a more serious reiteration of the often-repeated message of *D&P* that all prayers are intended to change the attitude of the believer, not God's acts: what money will *not* do is stressed in a series of 'ne ȝe schul nout's on p. 192/85–103. The final injunction is: give freely to the priest 'to excytyn hys deuocious to preyyn for ȝou'. On purgatory, see 169/19–20, 214/19–22, 328/36 above.

2–191/64 *Io. 14: 6*: See above 300/45.

2–192/80 *Mc. 12: 42–4*: See above 190/18.

2–192/81 *a peny meteles*: Refers to the difference in payment depending on whether or not board is included; see above 2–185/53.

2–192/94–5 *artyd be þe lawe of his takyng*: The sense is: the priest is governed by Church law in the amount he may receive from the lay public for special prayers, but he is not governed except by his conscience in how or for whom he offers prayers.

2–193/3–8 *3if religious . . . xiii, q. ii, Questa, et c. Postquam*: The canon 'Questa' (C.13 q.2 c.12) is cited 219/61–2 above. The canon 'Postquam' states that no payment is to be required for burial; see Gratian's *dict. ante*: 'Etiam coacti de sepultura precium accipere non debemus' (C.13 q.2 c.13; Friedberg 1: 724–5). The text of Gregory's papal letter cites the example of Abraham, who bought a burial place for his wife from a Hittite, who refused at first to take payment (Gen. 23: 8–17, 25: 9, 49: 29–30, 50: 13; cf. GO 1: 62).

2–193/8 *Summa confessorum, li, i, ti. xvi, q. i*: In John of Freiburg's *Summa confessorum* the question, 'Quid sit sepultura' is found in MS Bodley 299, Bk. I, fos. 52^v-53^r.

2–193/12 [*Mt. 21: 13*]: 'Scriptum est, domus mea domus orationis vacabitur; vos autem fecistis eam speluncam latronum'. See above 217/5– 218/15.

2–193/12–19 *And 3if collegis . . . ringynge of her bellys . . . Summa confessorum, li. i, ti. i*: John of Freiburg's gloss on Raymond of Peñafort's *Summa*: 'Quid de monasteriis, vel sonatorijs, id est, officio pulsandarum campanarum . . . ? Respondeo . . . simonia est talia vendere.' A proviso adds, however, that, if it is the local custom to do so, the office of bell ringer may be bestowed, rented or inherited without incurring simony (Bk. I, p. 28a).

2–193/20 *þe vyce of symonye*: As Swanson (1989) points out, simony was an inevitable result of the way in which the Church in this period was structured: 'with the absence of any impersonal system to secure promotion for the worthy within the church . . . a patron was unlikely to grant a benefice to a particular individual for purely altruistic motives' (p. 66); see the section 'Career pressures and patronage', pp. 50–82. In this connection, Swanson cites *D&P*'s story of the two priests discussed below, 2–193/25– 194/61, idem, p. 65.

2–193/25–194/61 *Fel in Engelond . . . pore frere menour*: No source or exact analogue for the story has been found. In *D&P*, the story appears only in MS G. It is unusual for its dated and placed reference to the Friars Minor. The locale, 'Coventry', and the year, '1350', may, of course, have been added, cf. the tale 'Ore au deble' above, 2–25/46–56.

The two priests in the tale clearly commit simony in two of the ways detailed above: to acquire their benefices, one gives money, the other service. The less-sinning vicar has merely failed to divide his tithes into the canonical four parts, apparently by omitting the portion for the bishop— though how this would *decrease* the portion for the poor is not arithmetically clear. The point of the story thus turns on the attitude of the judge. If the judge's criticism of the vicar's tripartition of his tithes is considered on its own and not in relation to quadripartition, the judge must be urging *more* than a third for the Church and the poor respectively and *less* than a third—

or perhaps nothing—for the vicar. The vicar, no doubt noting the Franciscan leanings of the judge, opts for joining an Order in which money will not be his to apportion, and the responsibility for dividing between Church and poor will fall to his superiors. The tale can, in short, be read as a criticism of the canonical directives on tithes from a Franciscan perspective; or it can be read as a story whose main point is either so unclear or so explicit in its Franciscan perfectionism that subsequent scribes chose to omit it altogether.

On the quadripartition of tithes, see Constable (1964), pp. 43–56, et seq., who points to great differences over time in practice and theory. Burchard of Worms (d. 1025) on quadripartition: citing an epistle of Pope Gelasius: 'una pontificis, altera clericorum, tertia pauperum, quarta fabricis applicanda'; and again, from the Council of Nantes: 'pauperum et hospitum et peregrinorum esse stipendia. . . quatuor partes inde fiant, una ad fabricam ecclesiae relevandam, altera pauperibus distribuenda, tertia presbytero cum suis clericis habenda, quarta episcopo reservanda' (*PL* 140: 70).

2–194/63 *leueresonys*: An agreement for a stipulated sum to provide board and lodging for life, see *MED*, s.v. 'livere' 3.3. John of Freiburg's gloss on Raymond of Peñafort's *Summa* puts the question about those who buy lifetime board and room ('victum') from a monk: it is not simony, he says, if no spiritual services are purchased at the same time, but 'non est tamen securum emere, nisi probabiliter dubiteter, cuius melior sit conditio, ementis, aut vendentis' (Bk. I, pp.27b–28a). Cf. the Provincial Constitutions of the Council of Oxford, 1222: 'De corrodiis non vendendis', which says corrodies are not to be sold except in cases of urgent need and with the consent of the diocese (Lyndwood, *Provinciale* (1679 edn.), p. 5b). On corrodies, see 2–184/4–6 above.

2–195/86–8 *lyuerysonys . . . Constitucionibus Octoboniensis, c. Volentes*: On 'lyuerysonys' see 2–194/63 above. The Constitutions of Ottobuono, the papal legate and cardinal, afterwards Pope Adrian V (1276), were promulgated in England in 1268. The text appears in Lyndwood's *Provinciale* ('Constitutio Domini Othoboni', Tit. 48, pp. 150–1 (1679 edn.); cf. *Councils & Synods* (1964), 2: 788).

2–195/1–4 *usure . . . Reymund, lib. ii, eodem ti.*: The inclusion of usury among the prohibitions of the seventh Commandment is traced to St Ambrose ('De Tobia': *PL* 14: 797–832; see *Patrology*, Vol.IV, ed. Berardino (1994), p. 161, and St Jerome ('In Ezech.', 6.18: *PL* 25: 176) and remains essentially unmodified to the end of the Middle Ages. On 'De Tobia', see T. P. McLaughlin on the 'embarrassing' text of Ambrose ('Canonists on Usury' in *Medieval Studies*, 1 (1939), 81–147, p. 137). In the twelfth century, Gratian cites the authority of Pope Gelasius (d. 496) and others against usury: 'Quod uero nec clericis, nec laicis liceat usuras exigere,

probatur auctoritate Gelasii et aliorum' (C.14 q.4; Friedberg 1: 736). Peter
Cantor (d. 1197) campaigned against usury (*Verbum abbreviatum*, *PL*
205: 156–9); 255; see J. W. Baldwin (1970), 1: 296–311). Peter Lombard
cites Augustine (*Enarr.*, *CCL* xxxix/667; *PL* 37: 1400) when listing usury
under 'furtum' (*Sentences*, 3.37.5 (2: 211/7–9). Constitution 67 of the
Fourth Lateran Council (1215) forbade usury (Mansi, 22: 1054–5).
Thomas Aquinas states that usury is unjust because it involves buying
and selling something intangible, the *use* of money—admitting, however,
that the sale of the use of other things, such as houses, is lawful (*ST* II–II,
78,1–4). Wyclif (in *c.*1374) says that usury may reasonably be called theft
and, like *D&P*, distinguishes worldly from spiritual usury (*De mand.*
pp. 370/7; 375/12 ff.). See also Noonon (1957); Nelson (2nd edn. 1969),
with extensive bibliography.

2–195/8 *Reymund . . . usure*: Raymond of Peñafort: 'Species vsurae sunt
duae, alia spiritualis . . . Alia vero corporalis' (*Summa*, Bk. II, p. 227b).

2–195/10–196/17 *Luce xix [23] . . . mede in heuene*: The text continues: '. . .
et ego veniens cum usuris utique exegissem illud.' The parable of 'the
Talents' (Luke 19: 12–27, Matt. 25: 14–30) was the scriptural basis of the
concept of spiritual usury. St Ambrose allegorizes the uses of the talents as
the duty to preach the gospel of Christ ('Expo. . . . secundum Lucam' VIII,
PL 15: 1854). St Gregory allegorizes the talents as three different individual
gifts—the five senses, spiritual understanding, and (mere) intellect (Hom. 9,
PL 76: 1105–9). In Bede's view, the servant earning ten talents represents
the teachers sent to the Jews, the servant earning five talents represents the
teachers sent to the gentiles, and the servant earning nothing represents the
teacher who fails to do his evangelical duty. 'Usury' is interpreted as the
reward for preaching, which should greatly exceed the effort expended ('In
Lucam', *CCL* cxx, pp. 336–41; *PL* 102: 563–6). The GO interprets the two
faithful servants as 'doctores populi' and the bad servant as 'malos
catholicos' (4: 206). Nicolaus de Lyra's interpretation is that the rich man
is Christ; the servants are the Jews, who for the most part reject Christ; the
talents are rewards in heaven for good works on earth (*Postilla* 4). See
2–202/36–8 below.

2–196/19 *comenant of lendynge*: This refers to the 'mutuum' or contract
between lender and borrower, as differentiated from a 'societas', or partnership, contract. Without a written contract, a lender could not enforce the
terms of the loan; with a contract, a lender risked violating the canon or civil
laws regulating usury.

2–196/28–9 *Luce vi [35]*: The text 'Date mutuum' had a long afterlife as a
justification for opposing money-lending at interest. According to Noonan
(1957), 'St Anselm of Canterbury (1033–1199) . . . is the first medieval
author to suggest the similarity of usury and robbery' and his 'still

undeveloped comparison is then given real force by his disciple, Anselm of Lucca' as 'specifically a sin against the Seventh Commandment', p. 17. Luke 6: 35 was cited in the thirteenth-century Decretals of Pope Gregory IX (X 5.19.10; Friedberg 2: 814) as the basic authority for condemning usury, see 2–199/33–9 below.

2–196/38–197/55 *For þe usurer . . . þe hous*: The argument is taken from Thomas Aquinas (*ST*, II–II, 78.1).

2–197/56 *þe Philosofre . . . Ethicorum . . . Polliticorum*: Aristotle's *Nicomachean Ethics* 5.2 (*Oxford Aristotle*, 2: 1784) points to the 'injustice' of one person's making a gain in a transaction between two persons; the *Politics* 1.10 (idem, 2: 1997) more specifically says: 'The most hated sort [of exchange of money] . . . is usury, which makes a gain out of money itself, and not from the natural object of it.' The reference here to Bk. 3 of the *Politics* is an error. In the later Middle Ages, Aristotle was cited, with little justification, as providing the basis in natural law for the prohibition of usury; cf. Noonan (1957), pp. 12, 21–2.

2–197/64–5 *Contra . . . þe Iewys*: A reference to Deut. 23: 19–20, see below 2–207/14.

2–198/6–7 *Summa confessorum, lib. ii, ti. vii, q. iv*: John of Freiburg's *Summa confessorum*; see MS Bodley 299, fo. 99ᵛ, for ti. 'Utrum concedere peccuniam signatum'.

2–198/10–11 *Extra, lib. v, ti. De usurys, c. Conquestus, in glosa*: The canon 'Conquestus' is extracted from a letter of Pope Alexander III (d. 1181) to an abbot who has (on the evidence of a plaintiff) retained the proceeds of land pledged to him for a loan. He is directed to deduct the returns from the debt owed, unless the land happens to be infeuded to his monastery. Gratian's *dict. ante* is: 'Fructus rei pignoratae computari debent in sortem [at interest], et excipit unum casum [i.e. infeudation]' (X 5.19.8); Friedberg 2: 813). The glossators commented at length on the canons in Title 19, 'De usuris'; see McLaughlin (1940), 1–22. Pauper does not allude to the difference between the treatment of Church and lay property; see comments on the glosses on this canon, including those of Raymond of Peñafort, Alexander of Hales and Hostiensis, by Noonan (1957), pp. 102–3.

2–198/11–17 *Ʒif þe intencion . . . þe ʒifte*: Raymond of Peñafort puts the question whether a payment to ensure the fulfilment of a contract is usury. The reply is that it is not, provided that the payment is judicially imposed ('a Iudice proposita') or is a one-time contract mutually agreed ('de comuni consensu partium'), *Summa*, Bk. II, p. 231a.

2–198/17–23 *Ʒif a man do vsure . . . symonye*: Raymond of Peñafort asks whether usury is allowable if *civil* laws permit it. The reply is that it is not allowable, because it is against natural law against which there is no dispensation: 'contra tale ius [natural law] nulla lex, nulla dispensatio potest admitti' (*Summa*, Bk. II, p. 236b; cf. *Decretum*, Di. 8 c. 2, citing Augustine's *Confessions* 3.8; LCL 26, 1: 127–8). On Aristotle, natural law and usury see above 2–197/56.

2–198/23–199/33 *ʒif lordys of myllys. . . .harmyd & hyndryd*: Specific mention of contracts between mill owners and bakers does not appear in Raymond of Peñafort's 'De usuris', from which the above examples are drawn. Mills may be referred to in his question, What about those who buy or otherwise receive the usufruct of the mills ['molarium'] of a castle or village which also contains churches and monasteries? Raymond replies that, if some 'Aduocatus' [administrator?] freely serves the monastery or church, giving his advice gratis, he may receive fees from this usufruct (*Summa*, Bk. II, p. 233).

2–199/33–9 *ʒif þe lendere . . . Extra, lib. v, eodem ti. Consuluit*: The canon 'Consulit' is drawn from a letter of Pope Urban III (d. 1187) replying to a query about restitution of clerical profits from usury and other aspects of exchange when there is no written contract or 'mutuum', only the intention to receive interest. The *dict. ante*: 'Mutuans ea mente, ut ultra sortem aliquid recipiat, tenetur *in foro animae* ad illud restituendum, si ex hoc aliquid consecutus est. Idem in non dante parabolam iuramenti, nisi aliquid inde recipiat. Et idem in vendente rem plus quam valeat, quia differt solutionem' (ital. added; X 5.19.10; Friedberg 2: 814). The difference between matters to be settled in courts of law and matters for the 'internal forum' is frequently at issue. Cf. McLaughlin (1939), 106, n. 203. See 2–196/28–9 above.

2–199/45–51 *ʒif a man . . . Extra, lib. iii, De fideiussoribus, c. Peruenit, et c. Constitutus*: The Title 'De fideiussoribus' is about fiduciaries— executors, trustees, or those who stand security. Alexander III (1159–1181) at the Council of Carthage laid down the principle that 'Clericus fideiussionibus inserviens abiiciatur' (X 3.22.1). The canon 'Peruenit' (1) is drawn from a letter of Pope Lucius III (d. 1185) to the bishop of Ely. Clerics of St Albans had stood surety for two other clerics, and when the two defaulted on their loan their backers were forced to pay up, with interest. The papal reply is that the fiduciary clerics are to be repaid, with the interest, and the defaulting clerics are to be suspended from office (X 3.22.2; Friedberg 2: 530). The canon 'Constitutus' (2), drawn from a letter of Lucius III to the Archbishop of Canterbury, concerns a certain Stephen, who is being pursued by creditors for the debt of one Chancellor P., a debt contracted at the time of the second Lateran Council, unpaid and still accumulating interest. The papal letter directs that Stephen be relieved of this obligation. If the said Chancellor P. refuses to stand judgement, he is to be relieved of his benefice (X 3.22.3; Friedberg 2: 530–1). Cf. McLaughlin (1939), 130.

The canon law reference does not seem to have a direct bearing on the text of *D&P*.

2–199/51–8 *3if a man. . . .Extra . . . Nauiganti*: The important canon 'Nauiganti' is from a letter of Gregory IX (papacy 1227–1241) to Frater R. The subject is money paid to a lender beyond the stipulated interest to compensate for perils sustained in travelling to market, in this case the perils of sea travel. A hypothetical case is a trader who buys grain, wine or oil from X in order to sell them later to Y at a higher price, assuming the risk. This is to be considered usurious (X 5.19.19; Friedberg 2: 816). This doctrinally very conservative position on loans was, however, controverted by many other canonists and theologians over a period of two hundred and fifty years. The controversy turns on the difference between a loan ('mutuum') and a partnership ('societas'). The first is considered usurious if anything beyond 'sortem' (interest, variously defined) were paid to the lender; the second was allowable so long as the partners shared all risk. Compare Raymond of Peñafort, 'De usuris' ¶ 7, in which he says it is not usurious to receive something in compensation for peril incurred by the seller, though others (he adds) may disagree (*Summa*, 2.7.5, Bk. II, p.232b-233a). For the comments of other glossators on 'Naviganti', see Noonan (1957), pp. 114; 137–9; 148–9; 151–2. Aquinas's view was opposed to 'Naviganti', though, as Noonan points out, his views on usury were inconsistent (idem, p. 145; *ST*, II–II, 78.2, Reply to Obj. 5). On the scholastic treatment of usury, McLaughlin (1939) is foundational, though narrower in scope than Noonan (1957).

2–199/58–200/62 *Summa confessorum, lib. ii, ti. vii*: John of Freiburg's *Summa confessorum*, q. 16, 'Usura sit permissa', cites the canon 'Naviganti' (MS Bodley 299, fo. 100^v-101^r). 'Naviganti' is also cited in q. 28 (fo. 101^v), and q. 38 (fo. 103^r). See above 2–199/51–8.

2–200/62–83 *3if a man lende syluer . . . usure*: The six instances of buying cheap and selling dear given here are related to the canon 'Naviganti' cited above (X 5.19.19; Friedberg 2: 816). All have to do with price fluctuation and the assumption of risk. Gain resulting from either of these was considered usurious.

2–201/14–24 *3if a man betake . . . neuere dye*: The joke about 'immortal sheep' is cited in de Chobham's *Summa*: 'Item, alicubi consuetudo est quod aliqui liberant ad firmam *oves immortales* quo nunquam scilicet morientur ei cuius sunt,' etc. (ital. added, ed. Broomfield, pp. 516–7; the editor, Broomfield, cites the source as Peter Cantor's *Summa*, fo. 109^{r-v}). John of Freiburg's gloss on Raymond of Peñafort also says that such contracts are usurious and that 'hoc est enim quasi tradere oues immortales' (*Summa*, Bk. II, p. 235a). See also, without the joke, reference to giving sheep to the poor man and making him assume all the risk (*Fasciculus morum*, ed. Wenzel, pp. 348–9). In the vernacular, such a borrowing practice seemed particularly odious to the writer of 'Pore Caitif': 'Also whanne ony man takiþ his beest to a pore man up sich condicioun, þat if it dieþ it schal die to þe pore man & not to hym; siche ben þe deuyls charmes . . .' (MS Bodley 3, fos. 59ᵛ-60ʳ). See 227/1 above.

2–201/24–30 *Ʒif men in tyme of plente . . . Genesis xlvii*: Gen. 47: 13–22 was customarily cited to justify buying supplies, such as grain, to store in case of dearth. Joseph was seen as a type of ideal ruler who administered grain reserves for all his people without fear or favour or profiteering. John of Freiberg's gloss on Raymond of Peñafort's *Summa* (followed by *D&P*) excuses Joseph: he did not hoard in order to profit; he hoarded in order to prevent famine (Bk. II, p. 236a).

2–202/36–8 *Salomon . . . Prouer. xi* [*26*]: *D&P* adds 'domini' to the Vulgate text. The interlinear gloss refers to the bad and lazy servant who hid his talent (2–195/10–196/17 above), and allegorizes the withholder of grain as the preacher who fails to preach (GO 2: 668).

2–202/48–52 *Ʒif a clerk . . . xiv, q. iv, Canonum, in glosa, et De con., d. v, Numquam*: Two canons: (1) 'Canonum' states that whoever wishes to be a member of the clergy must not study the art of buying cheap and selling dear. The source is a sixth-century conciliar decree (C.14 q.4 c.3; Friedberg 1: 736). (2) The canon 'Numquam', extracted from an epistle of St Jerome to the monk Rusticus, recomends the reading of scriptures and otherwise keeping the hands busy with farming, planting, irrigation, bee-keeping, and the like (De cons. D.5 c.33; Friedberg 1: 1420–1). The second ccanon is of little relevance to the text of *D&P* here (see Letter 125, *Jerome, Select Letters*, LCL 262, pp. 416–19). Cited above, 2–102/93.

2–202/52–8 *Ʒif a man lende . . . Reymund et Summa confessorum*: Raymond of Peñafort: 'Item, qui annonam veterem mutuuant, vt recuperent nouam, vsuram committunt, quia meliorem rem recuperare volunt' (*Summa*, Bk. II, p.236a). John of Freiburg's gloss says, however, that he, John, is reluctant to condemn such sales ('istos non audeo condemnare') if they are beneficial to those concerned (idem).

2–202/58–203/77 *Be Goddis lawe. . . . very God*: 'Goddis lawe' refers to the canon law of the Church. 'Emperor's law' refers to Roman or civil law (Justinian's code), one of the bases of Gratian's *Decretum* (1140) and, until the Reformation, one of the Oxford faculties (see J. L. Barton, 'The Study of Civil Law' (*HUO*, 1: 519–64). Study of civil law was regarded as foundational for the study of canon law. 'Mannys lawe' refers to the common law of England, based on customary law and administered by the itinerant justices of the King's courts. Canon law forbade usury, but civil law allowed exceptions in cases where the borrowing or lending was mutually beneficial or was a matter of need on the part of the borrower.

2–203/77–87 *Also þe notorijs . . . in Summa confessorum*: In John of Freiburg's *Summa confessorum*, the question, 'Quid de notariis' is found in Bk. II, 7.45; the question 'Quid de prelatis subscribentibus' follows it, Bk. II, 7.46 (MS Bodley 299, fo. 104ʳ).

2–203/1–204/10 *What þyne . . . Extra, eodem ti.[19], Quia in omnibus*: The canon 'Quia in omnibus' declares that open usurers are excluded from communion and Christian burial; clerics contravening this decree are to be punished (X 5.19.3; Friedberg 2: 812). The source is the third Lateran Council (1179) under Pope Alexander III. On penalties for usury, McLughlin (1940), 1–12.

2–204/10–14 *Ʒif þe usurer . . . Extra, eodem ti. [19], Tua nos*: The canon 'Tua nos' rules that heirs of usurers are bound to restitution to those from whom their forebear extorted usurious payments (X 5.19.9; Friedberg 2: 813–4). The source is a papal letter from Alexander III (d. 1181) answering a bishop's query about the obligations of such heirs.

2–204/14–17 *Ʒif þe usurer . . . Extra, eodem [ti. 19], Quia frustra*: The canon 'Quia frustra' declares that a usurer may not be given a hearing until he has restored his usurious gains with interest (X 5.19.14; Friedberg 2: 815). The source is a papal letter of Innocent III to a bishop, dated 1205.

2–204/18–26 *Ʒif he kepe . . . Extra, li. ii, ti. De iudiciis, c. Cum non ab homine*: The canon 'Cum non ab homine' directs that a cleric who has been convicted under Church law of theft, perjury, homicide or other serious crime and who proves incorrigible must first be excommunicated then turned over to the secular arm for punishment (X 2.1.10; Friedberg 2: 242). The source is a papal letter of Pope Celestine III (d. 1198).

2–205/43–6 *Ʒif þe usurer . . . Extra, eodem [19], Cum tu*: The canon 'Quum tu' declares that usurers are bound to restore all their usurious profits to their clients or their heirs, including profits made before the Lateran Council of 1174. If the clients cannot be found, such gains are to be given to the poor. Until this is done, reconciliation with the Church cannot be achieved (X 5.19.5; Friedberg 2: 812–3). The source is a papal letter of Alexander III to the Archbishop of Salerno.

2–205/56–8 *Ʒif a Iew . . . Extra, eodem, Post miserabilem*: The canon 'Post miserabilem' directs that Jews shall be forced to restore usurious gains by the withdrawal of Christians from all association with them and by the power of secular princes and potentates (X 5.19.12; Friedberg 2: 814–5). The source is a papal letter of Innocent III to the Archbishop of Narbon, dated 1198.

2–205/60–206/73 *No lord, no colege . . . Gregorium X, et Concilium Lugdunense, ti. De usuris, c. Usurarum, hec in Summa confessorum, li. ii, ti. eodem*: The canon 'Usurarum' bans the establishment of usury as a business and directs that usurers are to be expelled after three months' warning. The penalty for clerics, including colleges and universities, is excommunication; lay persons are also to be censured by the Church (Sext 5.5.1; Friedberg 2: 1081). The source is a decree by Gregory X (papacy 1271–6) at the second general Council of Lyon in 1274; see Mansi, 24: 119 (c.26). Cf. Kuttner, 'Conciliar law in the making: the Lyonese constitutions (1274) of Gregory X in a Manuscript of Washington', (in *Medieval Councils*, Variorum reprint, 1980: XII: 39–81); *Councils & Synods* (1964), 2: 809–16; John of Freiburg's *Summa confessorum*, Bk. II, ti. 7, q.60, 'Qum collegium accipit usuram' (MS Bodley 299, fo. 105ʳ).

2–206/73–80 *Also . . . payde fyrst*: What is described here, without the name, is pawnbroking. The pawnbroker is the 'buyer' who buys an article at less than its full value and sells it back to the seller for its full value, making a profit on the transaction. Cf. Lyndwood, *Provinciale*, Second Oxford Council, 1236, 'De pignore': 'Inhibeatur frequenter, ne pignus retinere quispiam contendat, postquam de fructibus sortem percepit, deductis expensis, quoniam iusura est', p. 13a (1679 edn.).

2–206/5–207/6 *Exodi xxii [25]*: 'Si pecuniam mutuam dederis populo meo pauperi qui habitat tecum, non urgues eum quasi exactor nec usuris opprimes.' Nicolaus de Lyra's comment is that this biblical text allows for lending in case of great need, noting that nothing is said excluding gentiles or the rich, merely that the poor must be succoured first, especially the poor who are one's neighbours. He notes that the Hebrew is literally 'Nec morsus pones super eum', comparing usury to a snake bite ('sicut serpens mordens in silentio') that is not painful at first but later kills. He cites Deut. 33, which seems to permit usury with gentiles, but, he says, only to avoid greater evils: 'permissio minoris mali ad maius euitandum' (*Postilla* 1).

2–207/6–10 *Leuitici xxv [35–7]*: 'Si adtenuatus fuerit frater tuus et infirmus manu et susceperis eum quasi advenam et peregrinum et vixerit tecum,/ ne accipias usuras ab eo nec amplius quam dedisti, time Deum tuum ut vivere possit frater tuus apud te; pecuniam tuam non dabis ei ad usuram, et frugum superabundantiam non exiges.' On 'adtenuatus [thin, weak]', GO: 'Mirare legislatoris sapientiam & pietatem in humilibus enim sublimia exponit, secundum litteram vero dat regulam pietatis' (1: 268).

2–207/14 *Deutero. xxiii [19–20]*: 'Non fenerabis fratri tuo ad usuram pecuniam, nec fruges nec quam libet aliam rem, sed alieno, fratri autem tuo absque usura id quod indiget commodabis, ut benedicat tibi dominus Deus tuus in omni opere tuo, in terra ad quam ingredieris possidendam.' GO: 'Usuram & auariciam remouet, & charitatem impendere iubet' (1: 405). Nicolaus de Lyra: 'Istud est permissio non liciti sed minus mali ad euitandum maius, scilicet ne fratres suos iudeos grauarent vsuris' (*Postilla* 1), cf. 2–206/5–207/6 above.

2–207/22 [*Ps. 54: 11–12*]: Augustine urges the Christian to condemn usury in light of the 'Dimitte nobis debita nostra' of the Lord's Prayer (*Enarr.* 54.13–15; *CCL* xxxix, pp. 666–7). The GO cites this interpretation (2: 520).

2–207/23–34 *he say a booc . . . wrong þat it is ryȝt*: 'Pore Caitif' borrowed some of the wording of this passage: '. . . he seiþ þat he saw a book fleinge in þe eir þat was twenti cubitis long & ten of brede, and he axide þe aungel of god, what it miȝte be, and the aungel seide to hym, it is þe curs of god þat goþ to þeuis housis & to alle mennes housis þat forsweren hem silf bi þe name of god . . . Wo be to ȝou he seiþ þat bynden hous to hous & couplen feld to feld & seyen þat riȝt is wrong & wrong is riȝt' (MS Bodley 3, fo. 58ᵛ; MS Bodley 938, fo. 142ʳ). On 'Pore Caitif' see 227/1 above.

2–207/27–8 *Zacharie v [1–3]*: The prophet Zechariah's fifth vision, The Flying Scroll: 'Et conversus sum et levavi oculos meos et vidi, et ecce volumen volans,/ et dixit ad me, "Quid tu vides?" et dixi ego, "Video volumen volans; longitudo eius viginti cubitorum et latitudo eius decem cubitorum"./ Et dixit ad me, "Haec est maledictio quae egreditur super faciem omnis terrae, quia omnis fur sicut ibi scriptum est iudicabitur, et omnis iurans ex hoc similiter iudicabitur."' Nicolaus de Lyra comments that the book flew from the temple: 'hec est maledictio, id est, pena pro peccatis inflicta, sicut Ezech. ii vidit librum in quo erant scripte lamentationes'; the flying book prefigured the scattering of the Jews as punishments for the sins of theft and perjury (*Postilla* 2). The GO is divided, interpreting the book as a record of sins and as a book containing the scriptures. It also prefigures the dispersion of the Jews as a result of the sins of theft and idolatry (2: 439).

2–207/28–32 *Salomon . . . Prouer. xxi [6–7]*: 'Qui congregat thesauros lingua mendacii vanus est et inpingetur ad laqueos mortis./ Rapinae impiorum detrahent eos quia noluerunt facere iudicium'.

2–207/32–6 *To smyche God . . . Ysa. v [8; 20]*: 'Vae qui coniungitis domum ad domum et agrum agro copulatis usque ad terminum loci/. . . .qui dicitis malum bonum et bonum malum, ponentes tenebras lucem et lucem tenebras, ponentes amarum in dulce et dulce in amarum.' The GO, on v. 8, predictably interprets the verse as aimed at the avaricious ('auarissimi') Jews. It is also aimed at heretics who join dogma to dogma ('dogmata dogmatibus coniungunt'). In v. 20, the GO sees a reference to the Jews who chose Barrabas rather than Christ. Allegorically, the 'bitter' and the 'sweet' signify truth and falsehood, but it is difficult to distinguish between them; 'difficile autem vitamus hoc maledictum, cum et malus adulemur propter potentiam & bonos despiciamus propter inopiam' (3: 11–12). Cited again below, (v. 20) 2–223/30, (v. 8) 2–255/52–60.

2–208/53–60 *Iosue, vi et vii . . . ony oþir iurne*: Achan (Achar) stole cloth, silver and gold from the war booty of Jericho, and his crime, after he was forced to confess it, was punished by stoning (Josh. 7: 1; 6–26). His story is often linked with the story of Ananias and Saphira in Acts 5: 1–10 (2–49/ 79–80 above) and the parable of the talents in Luke 19: 11–27 and Matt. 24: 14–30 (2–195/10–196/17 above), see *ABD* 1: 54. In exegesis, stress is usually put upon the collective nature of the guilt; God holds the entire community responsible for Achan's misdeed. The GO denies the collective nature of guilt but says that the tale is a caution against the infectious nature of sin and a warning to preachers: 'Ex una enim ouem morbida grex universus inficitur', citing Matt. 5: 30: 'Si manus tua scandalizat te abcide eam' (1: 439). Referred to again, 2–259/15–16 below.

2–209/67–9 *Salomon . . . Sapientia ii* [*21*]: 'Haec cogitaverunt et erraverunt, excaecavit enim illos malitia eorum.' The Vulgate does not list 'obcecauyt' as a variant of 'excaecavit'. On the background of 'The Wisdom of Solomon' see *ABD*, 6: 120–7.

2–209/69–70 *Selynus, De mirabilibus mundi*: Gaius Julius Solinus' *Collectanea Rerum Memorabilium* was written soon after A.D. 200; it is a geographical miscellany based largely on Pliny. Solinus' comment on the Well of Sardinia may have reached the author of *D&P* via an alphabetical compilation for preachers under the heading of 'perjury'. Solinus reports that the well is salubrious for strengthening broken bones, easing the bite of a poisonous ant ('solifugis') and afflictions of the eyes, and for providing a test for perjury: 'Nam quisquis sacramento raptum negat, lumina aquis adtrectat: ubi periurium non est, cernit clarius, si perfidia abnuit, detegitur facinus caecitate et captus oculis admissum fatetur' (*Collectanea*, ed. T. Mommsen (1895), p. 47/14–16). Solinus is cited above, 2–123/58.

2–209/82–6 *Sent Ambrose, super Lucam*: 'In Lucam' 8.13 (*PL* 15: 1859); cited above, 57/10.

2–209/87 *al our nacioun*: Compare with similar laments about the state of England, 149/53–4, 149/53–4, 257/43–51, 357/10–40, 2–4/1–10, and 2–57/83 above and 2–262/91 below.

2–210/95–101 *þerfor God . . . Ieremie viii* [*10*]: In translation, *D&P* alters the order of v. 10 and adds 'et ideo corruent' after 'mendacium': 'Propterea dabo mulieres eorum exteris, agros eorum heredibus, quia a minimo usque ad maximum omnes avaritiam sequuntur, a propheta usque ad sacerdotem, cuncti faciunt mendacium.' GO: 'Receperunt mercedem suam & qui verbum domini abiecerunt ipsi abiecti sunt' (3: 114).

2–210/102–7 *Ysaye . . . Ysaie i* [*23*]: 'Principes tui infideles socii furum, omnes diligunt munera sequuntur retributiones; pupillo non iudicant et causa viduae non ingreditur ad eos.' Cf. LL4: 'Thin princis & þin lederis ben nout trewe, & þey ben þeuys felawys. Alle þey louyn ȝyftys & folwyn ȝeldingis aȝen & don non ryȝtful dom to þe wyduys & to fadyrles chyldryn þat nout moun ȝeuyn hem ȝyftys.' And he adds: 'But almyȝty god haue þu mercy on engelond & sende vs grace to knowe þee & þin goodnesse & to knowyn oureself & to amendin vs of oure wyckydnesse' (fos. 85va, 91vb). the GO cites Jerome: 'Nos quoque debemus cauere ne ab illis accipiamus munera qui de lacrimis pauperum congregant diuitias, ne simus socii furum ne dicatur de nobis, 'Si videbas furem', etc. (Ps. 49: 18, see below 2–210/107–11).

2–210/107–11 *Si uidebas . . . [Ps. 49: 18] . . . þese dayys*: The translation of Ps. 49: 18 adds the phrases: 'to helpyn hym as false iugis in temporelte don þese dayys' and 'as iugis in þe spirituelte don þese dayys'; it is notable that the author of *D&P* evenhandedly denounces the judges in the courts of civil law as well as those in the ecclesiastical courts—who could of course be one and the same person. Augustine on this verse suggests that praise of a thief is collusion with his theft (*Enarr.*, 49.26; *CCL* xxxviii, p. 594/1–10).

VOL. 1: 2, COMMANDMENT VIII, pp. 2–211–252

2–211/7 *Non loqueris . . . [Ex . 20: 16]*: 'Non loqueris contra proximum tuum falsum testimonium.' The meaning of 'witness' in this Commandment comprises the individual conscience, the role of a legal witness in a trial, and the Christian facing the Last Judgement. Nicolaus de Lyra: 'Et secundum doctores nostros non solum intelligitur prohibitum falsum testimonium in iudicio, vt dicunt hebrei, sed etiam extra iudicium, et omnis detractio, vt mendacium contra proximum et quocumque nocumentum quod potest inferri proximo verbo dum tamen sit contra caritatem' (*Postilla* i). On the numbering of the Commandments see 81/7 above.

2–211/9 *Sent Austyn*: Augustine says that in light of the injunction to love one's neighbour as oneself (Matt. 22: 39), the Commandment forbids bearing false witness against oneself (*De civ. dei*, 1.20; *CCL* xlvii, p. 22/8–18).

2–211/9–10 *Sent Thomas, De ueritate teologie, libro v*: Thomas Aquinas' *Questiones de veritate* Bk. 5 is about Providence and the influence of the stars on human life; it does not touch on truth-telling. Bk. I is about Truth, but in an abstract sense: a true proposition can be about both what is and what is not, etc. (see 'Quid est veritas', etc., in *Opera*, 9.1.1–2 (Parma edn., 1859, pp. 5–22).

2–211/11 *qui tacet consentire uidetur*: A legal maxim. In the canon law, the *liber sextus* (published in 1298), which follows the decretals of Gregory IX, concludes with Boniface VIII's (papacy 1294–1303) list of legal maxims, of which this is Regula 43 (VI 5.12.5; Friedberg 2: 1123). See Whiting, No.

S733, p. 550; cf. *Mum and the Sothsegger* (ed. Day and Steele, EETS, 199), p. 49/752–7.

2–211/17–21 *Sent Austyn . . . Epistula ad Cassulanum*: Casulanus asks Augustine whether there is a scriptural basis for fasting on Sunday. Augustine says no, and, after discussion, goes along with Ambrose, who, when asked, says that in Rome he fasts on Sunday because it is the Roman custom, but in Milan he does not, because it is not the Milanese custom (c. 14, col. 151). Augustine points to the hypocrisy of those who overeat and drink when not fasting: it is preferable not to fast at all and to be moderate all the time. He only touches on what Pauper says about harming or helping one's fellow Christian with words when he says (in c. 2, col. 137): 'et videbis eum pene universam Ecclesiam Christi, ab ortu solis usque ad occasum, verbis injuriosissimis nequaquam lacerare timuisse' ('Ep. 36', *PL* 33: 136–151).

2–211/24 *Ion . . . Crisostomus*: The reference is probably to Ps.-Chrysostom (see 135/10 above), whose *Opus Imperfectum* is referred to 135/10 above and 2–248/15–249/18 below. The passage: 'Nemo potest alterius esse testis idoneus nisi qui ipse fuerit testificatus ab altero' seems relevant to both contexts (*PG* 56: 673). A later homily in the *Opus Imperfectum*, dealing with the parable of the talents, has a passage that also seems to parallel the criticism here of those who know the truth but keep silent. The third servant, who hid his talent, is chastised for not increasing it by 'spiritual usury': only if the message of the faith is circulated from hand to hand ('de manu in manum') by preaching will it increase and spread (*PG* 56: 938). On the talents, see 2–195/10–196/17 above.

2–212/44 *Sent Gregory, lib. viii Moralium*: The Latin sentence in *D&P* (212/48–49) seems more like a summary than a quotation from the *Moralia*, Bk. 8, in which several passages express the idea that telling one's troubles relieves the mind. See especially chapters 20–22 and in particular the comments on Job 7: 11, 'Loquar in tribulatione spiritus mei', beginning 'Tribulatio quippe spiritus linguam commouet ut reatum praui operis vox confessionis impugnet' (*CCL* cxliii, p. 409/1–3; *PL* 75: 822–4). *Moralia* 8 is cited above, 177/65–6.

2–213/2 *Sent Austyn, libro De mendacio*: Augustine's *De mendacio*, c. 14, says there are *eight* kinds of lies: 1. Lying about 'doctrina religionis', which nothing excuses. 2. Harming someone unjustly and benefiting no one. 3. Harming someone to help someone else ('quod ita prodest alteri, ut obsit alteri'). 4. Lying for the sake of lying. 5. Lying to please or flatter ('quod fit placendi cupiditate de suauiloquio'). 6. Lying to help someone, without harming anyone ('quod et nulli obest, et prodest alicui'). 7. Lying without harming anyone but helping someone, as in an interrogation by a judge (7. would seem to be identical to 6., and Migne's note says it is omitted in some manuscripts). 8. Lying which harms no one and may protect someone (*PL* 40: 505). Augustine's *Enarr.* on Ps. 5, cites Sap. 1: 11 (see 2–215/58–60 below) and discusses the gradations of lying, including harmless lies (*CCL* xxxviii, p. 22/34–6; *PL* 36: 86).

2–214/46 [*Mt. 12: 36*]: 'Dico autem vobis quoniam omne verbum otiosum quod locuti fuerint homines reddent rationem de eo in die iudicii.' LL4: 'Thanne þu schalt ȝelden answere boþin for þe grete & for þe smale insomechyl þat as crist seyth men schul ȝeuyn rekenynge at þe dom of euery ydyl word þat þey han spokyn' (fos. 82^{ra–rb}). GO: 'Si deo ocioso verbo reddet homo rationem in die iudicii, quanto magis vos qui opera sanctiis spiritus dicitis esse belzebub' (4: 45). Cited below, 2–249/38.

2–214/51–2 *Maystyr of Sentence, lib. iii, d. xxxviii*: Peter Lombard: 'His videtur innui mendacia illa quae fiunt ioco vel pro salute alicuius, imperfectis esse venialia peccata' (*Sentences* 2: 213/15–16).

2–215/54–5 *Sent Austyn, libro Contra mendacium*: In c. 1 of *Contra mendacium*, Augustine cites Rom. 3: 8: 'Faciamus mala ut veniant bona', commenting: 'Quid est enim aliud, Mentiamur, ut hereticos mendaces ad veritatem adducamus . . . an aliquando bonum est mendacium, vel aliquando mendacium non est malum? . . . non dubitantes addere etiam ipsum Dominum Christum, nec se aliter arbitrantes veracem suam ostendere falsitatem, nisi Veritatem dicant esse mendacem' (*PL* 40: 519). Cited twice in Grosseteste's 'De octavo mandato' (*De decem mand.*, ed. Dales and King, p. 82).

2–215/58–60 *Sent Gregory, libro xviii Moralium . . . [Sap. 1: 11]*: Sap. 1: 11 is cited above 2–2/45–8. In Bk. 18 of the *Moralia*, Sap. 1: 11 is cited to support the view that some degree of sin attaches to all lying (*CCL* cxliiiA, p. 888/18). It is cited by Grosseteste, 'De octavo mandato' (*De decem mand.*, ed. Dales and King, p. 83/21–2). See 2–2/45–8 above.

2–215/61 [*Ps. 5: 7*]: 'Odisti omnes operantes iniquitatem, perdes loquentes mendacium, virum sanguinum et dolosum abominabitur Dominus.' The GO derives its gloss from Augustine's *Enarr. in Ps.* 5.7 (*CCL* xxxviii, pp. 22–3), citing as examples of allowable lying the madman who should not be given a sword and the Egyptian midwives, Shiprah and Puah (GO 2: 461; see 2–215/1–8 below).

2–215/65–7 *Non menciemini . . . Leuitici xix [11]*: GO: 'Cognitionem ostendit, multa putamus parua quam sunt maxima, ut mendacium, periurium, quam furto sunt coniuncta, & recte quia hoc furto cooperantur' (1: 253).

2–215/1–8 *Exodi i [15–21] . . . hous & lond*: Dives cites one of the standard OT instances of lying, the story of the Egyptian midwives, Shiphrah and Puah, so that Pauper can give the standard justification (cf. Augustine, note

2–215/61 above); Augustine cites the Egyptian midwives in his 'De mendacio' and 'Contra mendicitatem', *PL* 40: 491, 510–1, 541–2). Cf. Comestor (*Historia*, *PL* 198: 1142–3). Nicolaus de Lyra says the lying of the midwives was a light sin ('officiosum et veniale peccatum'), *Postilla* 1.

2–216/16–20 *Cleophas & Amaon* . . . [*Lc. 24: 13–35*]: On the question whether Christ deceived or lied to Cleophas ('Finxit se longius ire', Luke 24: 28), the *CA* cites Augustine's *De quaest. evan.*, who says the episode did not involve lying but was symbolic, 'figura veritatis' (*CCL* xlivB, p. 116/1–9; *CA*, 2: 314a). The author of *D&P* may have derived the name of Cleophas's companion on the road to Emmaus from Peter Comestor (*Historia*, *PL* 198: 1639) or from his source, Ambrose, *Super Lucam* (*PL* 15: 1941. He is not named in the gospel of Luke, but in the Latin liturgical drama and the later vernacular 'Peregrinus' plays Cleophas' companion is called 'Luke' (Young (1933), 1: 688); cf. the 'Sadlers Play' in the Chester mystery cycle, in which he is 'Lucas' (ed. Lumiansky and Mills, EETS ss 3, pp. 356 ff.). Referred to 2–285/36 below.

2–216/30 *Genesis xxvii* [*1–29*]: Pauper's figurative interpretation of the story of Jacob and Esau is found in Peter Comestor, who also notes that Jacob does not lie to Isaac: 'Nec mentitur, sicut nec Christus dicens Joanem esse Eliam, non personaliter, sed in similitudine, ut dicit Gregorius in Homilia', referring to Matt. 11: 14 (*Historia*, *PL* 198: 1114). On recent criticism of the Jacob narrative, see *ABD*, 3: 598–609.

2–217/53 [*Mc. 13: 11*]: 'Et cum dixerint vos tradentes nolite praecogitare quid loquamini sed quod datum vobis fuerit in illa hora id loquimini; non enim estis vos loquentes sed Spiritus Sanctus.'

2–217/1–7 *Sent Austyn. . as he wil*: In his 'De mendacio' Augustine deals with tacit lying in only one passage, where he says the desire to slander another person is a sin which is not hidden from God: 'Fit autem ista detractio per malevolentiam . . . sed etiam tacitus talem vult credit; quod est utique ore cordis detrahere: quod dicit obscurum et occultum Deo esse non posse' (*PL* 40: 509).

2–217/7 *þe Philosofre . . . i Peryarmanyas*: Aristotle's *De interpretatione*: 'Now spoken sounds are symbols of affections in the soul' (*Oxford Aristotle*, 1: 25/4).

2–218/10–11 [*Mt. 5: 37*]: Cited above, 231/45–232/86 and 232/71–2.

2–218/15 *Sent Austyn, in libro Contra mendacium*: The sense is found in ¶ 13–14 of Augustine's 'Contra mendacium': . . . 'cur loquens in corde suo veritatem, tam amaro fletu punivit mendacium quod ore deprompsit'; and, citing Ps. 14: 3, 'Qua propter illud quod scriptum est, "Qui loquitur veritatem in corde suo", non sic accipiendum est, quasi retenta in corde veritate, loquendum sit in ore mendacium' etc. (*PL* 40: 526).

2–218/26–30 *Dauyd . . . I Regum xxi* [*13*]: I Sam. 21: 13: 'Et inmutavit os suum coram eis et conlabebatur inter manus eorum, et inpingebat in ostia portae, defluebantque salivae eius in barbam.' The GO interprets this passage not in light of David's 'deception' but as a prefiguration of the humiliation of Christ at the crucifixion (2: 35). For a list of other references to the story of David in *D&P* see 2–85/19 above.

2–219/37 *þe ferde booc of Kyngis* [*10: 18–28*]: 2 Kgs. 18–28 tells the story of Jehu's surprise attack on King Joram and his founding of the city of Samaria on the site of his victory. Further on Jehu, see *ABD*, s.v. Jehu (1), 3: 670–3.

2–219/44–6 *Iosue . . . Iosue viii*: Guided by 'the Lord', Joshua instructs his besieging army to pretend flight in order to draw the opposing forces from the city of Ai, a plan that was successful (Josh. 8: 4–8). A gloss attributed to Augustine asks whether such intended deception is the same as lying, and whether there is such a thing as justified lying ('ut secundum aliquam significationem hoc quod insidiis factum est ad veritatem referatur'): GO, 1: 442.

2–219/30 *Iacob . . . Esau*: Gen. 27: 1–29, see 2–216/30 above.

2–220/13 *Dockynge, super Deuteronomium*: On Docking, see 266/32 above for further references in *D&P*. Docking's 'Super Deuteronomium' is found in Balliol MS 28. The reference to lying occurs in the section on Deut. 19, numbered 19 in the manuscript.

2–220/15–18 *Salomon . . . Ecclesiastici xix* [*4*] *. . . ibidem*: Ecclus. 19: 4: 'Qui credit cito levis corde minorabitur, et qui delinquit in animam suam insuper habebitur'. Ecclus. 19: 16: 'Et non omni verbo credas, est labitur lingua sed non ex animo.' Both verses are cited below, 2–262/82–3.

2–220/18–22 *The fool . . . Prouer. xiv* [*15*]: 'Innocens credit omni verbo; astutus considerat gressus suos.'

2–220/22–3 *Ecclesiastici xxxiii* [*3*]: 'Homo sensatus credit legi Dei et lex illi fidelis.'

2–220/26–7 *Catoun . . . Non te collaudes nec te uituperes ipse*: This may be derived from an authentic distich of 'Cato':

> Nec te conlaudes nec te culpaveris ipse:
> hoc faciunt stulti, quos gloria vexat inanis.
> (*Disticha Catonis* II, 16, ed. M. Boas, pp. 117–8)

The same text is given in *Minor Latin Poets* (LCL 434, p. 606), which also provides a brief introduction to the medieval 'Cato' and a sketch of the textual transmission of the *Disticha* (pp. 585–9). The verses are also found in *Minor Poems of the Vernon MS*, II, with essentially the same Latin text and the English translation: 'Preise no mon him-seluen, /Ne blame him-self also' (ed. Furnivall, EETS, os 117, p. 581/345–6).

2–220/28–30 *Salomon . . . Prouer. xxvii* [*2*]: LL4: 'Leet anoþer preysin þee & nout þin owene mouth, a straunger & nout þin lyppis' (fo. 86ᵛᵃ). Cf. 2–220/26–7 above.

2–220/36 [*Ps. 115: 11*]: 'Ego dixi in excessu meo, omnis homo mendax.' Augustine also points to the gain in humility resulting from the knowledge that it is human to lie under the pressure of fear, citing the example of St Peter: 'si enim omnis homo mendax, in tantum non erunt mendaces, in quantum non erunt homines; quoniam dii erunt, et filii Altissimi' (*Enarr. in Ps.* 115.3; *CCL* xl, p. 1654/25–7).

2–221/41–3 *þe Philosofre, iv Eticorum,* [*vii*] *c. . . . quam eyron*: Aristotle's *Nicomachean Ethics*: 'Both forms of untruthful man [the boaster and the self-deprecator] are culpable, and particularly the boastful man' (*Oxford Aristotle*, 2: 1779/31–2).

2–221/43–4 *Ricardus de Media Villa, super Sentencias, lib. iii, d. xxviii, q. iv*: Richard of Middleton, on Matt. 5: 43: 'Nemo carnem suam vnquam odio habuit, non, sci., per se: per accidens autem aliqui odiunt carnem suam, sicut illi qui se interimunt, eo que in vita ista detinentur in aliquo statu odibili' etc. ('Super iv libros Sententiarum Petri Lombardi quaestiones', 3.4.28 (Brixiae, 1591; facs. *Manuscripta*), pp. 336 ff.). See above 104/9–10.

2–221/52 *Sent Austyn . . . Matthei* [*26: 15*]: St Augustine on Matt. 26: 15: 'Et ait illis, "Quid vultis mihi dare et ego vobis eum tradam?" At illi constituerunt ei triginta argenteos.' Augustine says the verse 'significauit per Iudam Iudeos iniquos, qui sequentes carnalia et temporalia quae ad quinque sensus pertinent corporis, Christum habere noluerunt. Quod quia sexta aetate mundi fecerunt, sexies quinos tamquam pretium uenditi domini accepisse significatum est' (*Quaest. evang*, I, xli; *CCL* xlivB, p. 32/1–7; cited in *CA*, 1: 381a).

2–221/66 *cristene men, fals witnessys*; This closing comment looks back to the Coventry story, a dream vision of a purgatorial trial (2–193/25–194/61 above), forward to *D&P* chapters 6–12 on the laws governing witnesses, and further ahead to the Last Judgement, *D&P* chapters 13–18.

2–222/4–5 *iv, q. iii,* [*Item*] *in criminali, vide Item serui*: *D&P* refers to Item 36. The canon 'Serui' holds that servants can be interrogated for their own actions, not as witnesses for or against their masters: 'Serui neque pro domino, neque aduersus dominium, sed pro facto suo interrogari possunt' (C.4 qq.2–3 (c.3); Friedberg 1: 537–41). Gratian's long *dict. ante* summarizes the questions to be taken up in QQ. 1–3, all having to do with the conditions under which witnesses may testify in cases involving excommunication. 'Item 36, "Serui"' appears in Part IV, which comprises a list of requirements for witnesses cross-referenced to the *Institutes of Justinian* (Roman law—in which, however, the subject is witnesses to wills, not witnesses in trials). The Roman law referred to states more generally: 'In testibus autem non debet esse qui in potestaste testatoris est' (*Inst.* 2.10.9, p. 170). Various parts of the same canon are cited six times below, 2–235/ 40, 2–235/42–6, 2–236/48–50, 2–236/51–2, 2–236/53–4, 2–236/54–5.

2–222/13–14 *Condicio . . . require*: On mnemonic verses, see 2–58/15–17 above. A similar verse is found in *Fasciculus morum*, ed. Wenzel, pp 477–8; this verse is listed in Walther, No.719.

2–222/15 *Sent Stefene . . . Crist . . . Nabot . . . Susanne*: On the martyrdom of St Stephen, Acts 7: 57–60; on false witnesses against Christ, Matt. 26: 48, 26: 59–61, 27: 12–13; on Naboth, 3 Reg. 21, and above, 2–15/44 ff.; on Susannah, 'The Book of Susanna', *Apocrypha*, ed. R. H. Charles, 1: 638–51; and see above 2–87/96–107.

2–223/30 *Ysa. v [20]*: Cited above, 2–207/32–6.

2–223/37–224/62 *camelyon . . . Maystyr of Kende*: Trevisa's translation of Bartholomaeus 18.221 refers to the chameleon's changes of colour and says: 'His face is as it were a beste compouned of a swyne and of an ape' (*Properties*, 2: 1159–60/2;7). Trevisa also says the chameleon is 'foul of colour in his deþ' (idem, 2: 1160/20). Alexander Neckam, referring to Solinus, says the chameleon imitates all colours easily except red and white and suggests a figurative interpretation parallel to the more extended one in *D&P* (*De Natura Rerum*, ed. Wright, pp. 68–9). A negative signification of the chameleon is also found in the *Ayenbite of Inwyt*, where he is, like the Devil, a type of the liar: 'he [the Devil] is ase þe gamelos þet leueþ by þe eyr and naȝt ne heþ ine his roppes [entrails] bote wynd' (ed. Gradon, EETS, os 23, p. 62/30–1). The *Fasciculus morum* compares the flatterer ('adulator') to the chameleon (ed. Wenzel, pp. 172–3).

2–224/69–71 *Sent Powyl . . . [Tit. 1: 16]*: LL4: 'Of swyche wyckyd lyueris seynt poul seyth . . . "þey feyn þat þey knowin god, but with here wyckede dedys þey forsakin god"' (fo. 58ra). The GO: 'Si negatio non tantum lingua fit, sed etiam factis certe multos inuenimus anti christos qui ore confitentur christum & moribus dissentiunt ab eo', etc. (4: 419).

2–224/75 *[Mt. 23: 3]*: Augustine in his sermons frequently cited this text, especially to cap an argument; see sermons 74.2, 99.13, 101.10, 11, 137.6 and 179.10. Sermon 101.10–11 (preached in 397) advises hearers to do as the preacher preaches, not as the preacher does: 'A good man preaches to you; pick the grapes from the vine. A bad man preaches to you; pick the grapes hanging in the hedge' (*Sermons*, tr. E. Hill, 4: 70; *PL* 38: 605–11).

2–224/4 *fortetyn*: Misprinted for 'forgetyn'.

2–224/5 *two men of lawe*: I have not found an analogue to this tale.

2–225/11–28 *Ysaye . . . [59: 13]*: For [13] read [13–15; 12–13]. Isa. 59: 13–15 is cited and translated, with interpolations, above 257/32. A different interpolated translation appears here (*D&P*, lines 13–20). The translation, with the interpolations in brackets: 'We han conceyuyd [be studie and be good information, knowing of þe trewþe &] of our own herte, and [of our owyn contrewynge we han] spokyn wordis of lesyngis [and of falshed, & þerfor] ry3tful doom is turnyd bacward and ry3tfulnesse stood from far [& my3the nout neyhyn;] trewþe fel doun in þe strete, and equite my3te nout entryn; þe trewþe is al for3etyn, and he þat wente away from wyckyd þing [& wolde a lyfyd in pees and trewþe, he] was opyn pray [to false men]'.

2–226/45 [*Ps. 24: 10*]: See 124/77–8, 2–26/70–5 above.

2–226/46 [*Ps. 114: 5*]: 'Clemens Dominus et iustus et Deus noster misericors'. The *D&P* translation adds: 'to alle þat wil amendyn hem'. Augustine comments: 'Non enim poenalis, sed salutatis dolor est quem secando medicus facit' (*Enarr.*, 114.5–7; *CCL* xl, p. 1650/13–4; *PL* 37: 1488–9).

2–226/52 *Actus Apostolorum i* [*8*]: 'Eritis mihi testes in Hierusalem et in omni Iudaea et Samaria et usque ad ultimum terrae.' The first part of the verse is cited in LL4, fo. 124ra.

2–226/61 *3if he reproue pouert*: On poverty, see 51/HOLY POVERT1, 53/ 14–19, 59/3–9 above.

2–226/65 *Mathei viii* [*20*]: 'Et dicit ei Iesus, "Vulpes foveas habent et volucres caeli tabernacula; filius autem hominis non habet ubi caput reclinet."' For the translation of 'filius hominis' by 'þe maydenys sone' see 283/7 above.

2–226/66–9 *Sent Powyl . . . II ad Corinth. viii* [*9*]: Cited above 1/8a. Augustine's gloss points out that Christ assumed poverty while not losing his riches ('paupertatem enim assumpsit & diuitias non amisit'); a second gloss to the same verse comments that, with Christ's poverty, we put off the rags of iniquity and put on the garments of immortality (GO 4: 341).

2–227/4 *Galaad*: Galahad, the ideal knight of Arthurian legend, was seen as an analogue of the figure of Christ. In the later, Christianized versions of the legend, it was Galahad who was destined to achieve the quest for the Holy Grail. Frappier (1959), p. 305, points out that his name corresponds to Gilead in the RSV translation, and is 'one of the mystic appellations of Christ'; cf. Gen. 31: 48: 'Dixitque Laban, "Tumulus iste testis erit inter me et te hodie", et idcirco appellatum est nomen eius Galaad, id est, tumulus Testis', where the word is said to mean 'witness cairn'. Loomis (1963) traces the derivation to a sermon by Gilbert of Holland on Cant. 6: 1 (pp. 106–7; 179–80).

2–227/27 *Sent Gregory*: This citation of Gregory was probably drawn from the Latin text in *Speculum Christiani*, where it appears in a section on preaching (ed. Holmstedt, EETS, 182, p. 173/8–9).

2–228/32 *amyte*: The amice is a vestment covering the head and shoulders, put on by the priest after the sandals. Before saying mass, priests and bishops put on six vestments, the amice, alb, belt, stole, maniple, and chasuble. Durandus says of the amice that it symbolizes strength ('operum fortitudo designatur'). The two cords attached to the amice and hanging down in front symbolize the purpose of the priest, which must be pure ('in azymis sinceritatis et ueritatis'). The vestment closely surrounds the neck, symbolizing that deceptive words must not arise from the throat. It covers the head to symbolize the descent of the Bride of the Lamb from the clouds, clothed in fine linen (Apoc. 19: 7–8). The detail about the mocking of Christ also comes from Durandus, who says the amice recalls the blindfolding of Christ when Herod's soldiers beat him and ordered him to prophecy (Matt. 26: 67: *Rationale*, 3.2; *CCCM*, cxl, pp. 184–6). The liturgy included blessings of the vestments. The *Speculum Christiani*:

> Firste the preste *that* es to synge masse wasche3 his hondes . . . he doo3
> ouer aftyrwarde halowede vestimentes, of which firste es the amyte, for
> it heyle3 or couere3 the hede, and it be-tokennes feyth, *that* owe to be
> hadde by-for al thynges to couere the hede [or] vndyrstandynge . . .
> veryly to leue of hool doctrine of the chirch. (ed. Holmstedt, EETS,
> 182, p. 180/10–18)

For blessings of 'amitum, album, zonam, manipulum, stolam et casulum' see the *Sarum Missal*, ed. Legg, p. 216.

2–228/36 *aube*: After the amice, the priest puts on the alb, a long white linen tunic with sleeves. According to Durandus, its spareness ('nichil superfluum') and whiteness are symbolic: the whiteness of the fabric is achieved by art, not nature, just as human morality is achieved not by nature but by good works and by grace. The opening for the head symbolizes chastity, and its lacing ('ligula') symbolizes the tongue of the priest, which absolves penitents. The belt of the alb symbolizes the restraint of sensuality. The length and coverage of the garment symbolise enduring faith, as well as renewal of life and hope after baptism. The pure white of the alb recalls the appearance of Christ at the Transfiguration ('Nam in transfiguratione resplenduit facies eius sicut sol'). Finally, the alb represents the white garment in which the 'Herodians' clothed Christ; the detail about the fool's costume (228/37–8) is not in Durandus, however (*Rationale*, 3.3; *CCCM* cxl, pp. 186–8). Cf. the *Speculum Christiani*: 'The aube *that* es nest do on be-tokene3 nuynge of lyfe *that* Criste had *and* taught to be folowede' (ed. Holmstedt, EETS, 182), p. 180/18–20. Cf. Rock (1: 347–57).

2–228/38(1) *fanon*: The fanon, also called a maniple and a 'sudareum', is a covering for the lower part of the left arm (originating in a linen handkerchief carried in the left hand during celebration of the mass). Durandus says the maniple symbolizes good works and penitence. It also symbolizes the rope by which Christ was bound (*Rationale*, 3.6: *CCCM* cxl, pp. 193–4). The *Speculum Christiani*: 'The maniple or phanone in the lefte hande be-token3 pacyence in aduersite, *that* es betokende by the lyfte syde' (ed. Holmstedt, EETS, 182, p. 180/23–5). Cf. Rock (1: 344–7).

2–228/38(2) *stole . . . gyrdil*: The stole, worn over the alb, covers the shoulders; it may be embroidered with a cross. The girdle is a belt of leather or fabric, also worn over the alb (A. Durandus says that it symbolizes the yoke of the Commandments and of the command to teach (cf. Matt. 11: 29–30). Other meanings include perseverance, prudence, temperance and obedience. The stole also represents the ligatures which bound Christ to the pillar (*Rationale*, 3.5; *CCCM* cxl, pp. 191–2]). The *Speculum Christiani*: 'The stoole strenynge the breste in maner of the cros be-token3 *that* he owe3 not to be schamede of the cros of Criste, bot to be redy to suffre maliciose wrongys for hys loue, or elles the stole *that* es putte in the necke be-token3 obedyence, for Criste was made obeynge vn-to the deth' (ed. Holmstedt, EETS, 182, p. 180/15–9). Cf. Rock (1: 357–63).

Of the girdle ('zona seu cingulo'), Durandus says that it symbolizes continence and chastity of mind and body. The two hanging ends symbolize prayer and fasting. The girdle also symbolizes justice, the two poles of which are avoidance of evil and doing of good. The girdle also recalls the flagellation of Jesus (*Rationale*, 3.4; *CCCM* cxl, pp. 188–90). The *Speculum Christiani*: 'The gyrdel be-token3 conscience *that* Criste commande3 prestes seynge: Tucke3 vp 3oure reynes, or ellys 3oure reyne3 musten be tuckede vp, wher lechery reyne3 moste, in token of chastite *and* clene lyuynge' (ed. Holmstedt, EETS, 182, p. 180/20–3).

2–228/43 *chesyple*: The chasuble originated from a heavy cloak worn as an outdoor covering. It is also called a 'planeta' 'paenula' 'casula' 'casubula' or 'amphibolus'. As a vestment, it is a full-length covering, open at the sides and donned last The chasuble, Durandus says, symbolizes charity, without which the priest is as sounding brass. The two portions of the chasuble, front and back, symbolize love of God and of neighbor. Its seamless construction represents the unity of the Church. Finally, it represents the purple robe in which the soldiers dressed Christ (John 19: 1), *Rationale*, 3.7 (*CCCM* cxl, pp. 195–6). The *Speculum Christiani*: 'The chesipule or planete callyde, *that* es a-bouen othyr vestimentes be-token3 charite, *that* es excellente aboune [*sic*] othyr vertuys' (ed. Holmstedt, EETS, 182, p. 180/29–31). Cf.Rock (1: 257–301).

2–228/46 *mitre*: The episcopal hat originated as white and cone-shaped. Durandus says the mitre, put on after the chasuble, signifies the two testaments, the anterior the NT and the posterior the OT. The two 'horns' of the mitre recall the 'horns' of Moses after his descent from Sinai with the two tables of the Commandments (see 268/13–17 above).

The two horns also represent the spirit and the letter of interpretation and recall the crown of thorns of Christ's Passion. In such seasons as Easter to Advent, or the Nativity to Septuagesima, a gold-fringed ('aurifrisiata') mitre is worn, because the mitre also symbolizes the divinity of Christ (*Rationale*, 3.13; *CCCM* cxl, pp. 209–12). Cf. Rock (2: 75–101).

2–228/51–4 *þe croos þat þe buschop berith . . . þe archebuschopys croos*: According to Rock, by the end of the eleventh century it was customary for an archbishop to have carried before him a straight staff topped with a cross (crosier). Contrasted with an archbishop's crosier, a bishop's staff had a bend, like a shepherd's crook (2: 184–93). Durandus says the 'baculo pastorali' signifies 'correctionem pastoralem'; it is also a reminder of Moses' rod. The bone and wood of which it is made symbolize severity and mercy; the curvature of the top likewise symbolizes the bending of God from severity to mercy; the staff is a 'baculus' rather than a 'virga' because it is intended for support more than for correction ('non solum corripit, sed etiam sustentat'): *Rationale*, 13.15; *CCCM* cxl, pp. 214–17). See 2–230/2–231/27 below.

2–228/55 *The buschopys glouys*: Gloves, or 'chirotheca', worn at mass symbolize purity. Durandus also invokes the use of 'gloves' by Jacob to hide his hands, at the prompting of the Holy Spirit, as well as Christ's 'deception' of the Devil in his incarnation (*Rationale*, 3.12; *CCCM* cxl, pp. 207–8). On bishops' gloves and the use of small metal balls as hand-warmers, see Rock, 2: 132–6).

2–228/56 *sandalyys*: Durandus says that clerical sandals symbolize the role of the preacher; the solid soles protect him from the pollution of the earth, while the open tops signify a heart and mind always open to God. The contrasting closed and open surfaces of the sandals show that the preacher must be neither too clear nor too obscure; he must not cast pearls before swine. The lacing ('lingula') symbolizes the preacher's tongue. In his preaching, he must not seek the blessing of the earthly Esau but that of the heavenly Jacob. Finally, the preacher's shoes (and stockings) symbolize the union of soul and body (*Rationale*, 3.8; *CCCM* cxl, pp. 197–201). Cf. the *Speculum Christiani*: 'The couerynge of feete represente3 incarnacion of Cryste' (ed. Holmstedt, EETS, 182), p. 180/31–2. John of Wales' *Communiloquium* drawing on Hugh of St Victor, *De Sacramentis*, II, 4.14, also makes the closed sole and openwork top of clerical sandals ('ex coreo [leather] perforato') symbolize the preacher's medias res between earthiness and sublimity (4.5.3). Rock describes and illustrates shapes, colours and ornaments of sandals from the time of Bede to the late Middle Ages (2: 194–204). See 93/4–5, 93/6 above.

2–230/88 *Beda, De officio diuino*: The reference is to Honorius Augustodunensis' *Gemma animae*, Bk. I. Of the 'alba', he says: 'Lingula [tongues], quae in caputio [collar] nunc innectitur, nunc resolvitur, est potestas linguae sacerdotalis, quae nunc ligat peccantes, nunc solvit poenitentes' (*PL* 172: 605). The 'collar' of the alb may also be called an 'apparel', see King (1954), pp. 118–9; 2–228/36 above..

2–230/91–2 *prestys coroune . . . schauynge*: Durandus says that the tonsure of the priest is a reminder that Christ on the cross wore a crown of thorns. The shaving of the crown symbolizes detachment from worldly possessions (*Rationale*, 2.1; *CCCM* cxl, pp. 130–3).

2–230/2–231/27 *Bede, lib. i, De diuino officio*: The reference is to Honorius Augustodunensis (see 2–230/88 above). Honorius says the shape of the cross originated in the shepherd's staff ('baculus pastoralis'), curved at one end to catch the feet of lambs and sheep (*PL* 172: 609–10). The rest of *D&P*'s description of the bishop's cross is found in Durandus (*Rationale* 3.15; *CCCM* cxl, pp. 214–17). A shorter version is found in John of Wales' *Communiloquium*, 4.5.3. See 2–228/51–4 above.

2–231/38–40 *Sent Ion . . . I Io. ii* [*4*]; 'Qui dicit se nosse eum et mandata eius non custodit, mendax est in hoc veritas non est.' GO: 'Non est magnum unum Deum nosse, cum et demones credant & contremiscant' (4: 535).

2–231/41–2 [*I*] *Io. iv* [*20*]: 'Si quis dixerit quoniam diligo Deum et fratrem suum oderit mendax est', cited above, 2–32/29.

2–231/43–8 *Ambrose . . . Ion viii* [*44*]: For this much-cited verse, see above 154/39–43, 161/42, 163/37–8, 2–80/5–6, 2–82/66. The passage on lies is not found in Ambrose's 'In Luc'; I have not found it in his sermons.

2–232/8 *xiv, q. v, Non sane*: The *dict. ante* sums up the canon 'Non sane': what is badly acquired may sometimes be well spent. The body of the text refers to the bribing of judges ('Sed non ideo debet iudex uendere iustum iudicium, aut testis uerum testimonium'), the right of judges and other officials to payment other than bribes, and the use of such ill-gotten gains either for restitution to the injured or for alms (C.14 q.5 c.15; Friedberg 1: 742). The source is Augustine's Epistle to Macedonius (No.153), cited above, 2–135/22–136/27, 2–157/39–40.

2–233/31 *Reymund, lib. ii, ti. De testibus*: Raymond of Peñafort: 'Testis debet', opens with the Latin text of Pauper's speech in *D&P*, ll. 1–6: 'Testis debet esse communis persona sicut & iudex, & pro vtraque parte dicere debet puram, & meram veritatem, quam scit de facto, super quo inducitur, non adiecta aliqua falsitate' (*Summa*, Bk. II, ¶ 40, p. 213a). Raymond (l. 8) also cites the canon 'Non sane' (C. 14, q. 5) cited above (2–232/8), and he goes on to say that witnesses may receive expenses (ll. 8–10), must bear witness on behalf of their neighbours, or sin gravely if they fail to do so (ll. 10–14), and that clerics must not bear witness in trials that could result in a death penalty (ll. 15–16). If a witness takes a bribe, he is bound to make restitution to those he has injured; he is not bound to return the bribe to the person he took it from (idem, p. 214a; further on restitution, idem, p. 209ab).

2–233/31–234/67 *How many witnesses . . . Hostiensis in Summa, lib. ii*: The source is Hostiensis' *Summa aurea*, Bk. 2, 'De testibus', which argues that more witnesses are needed for persons of higher status. This seems to be related to the canon 'Nullus' (C. 4, q.4 c.1; Friedberg 1: 541–2), which says that at least four persons are needed in any case, the judge, accuser, defender, and witnesses, etc.; or to 'Si testes', Gratian's long extract from the Digest and Code (C.4 q.2–3 c.3; Friedberg 1: 538–41), which says that witnesses must have 'fides, dignitas, mores, grauitas', must be free, unbribed, not close family members of the accused, and be two or more in number. On Hostiensis, see 246/39 above.

2–234/2–3 *be schrifte*: On the seal of the confessional, see 250/18–251/58 above.

2–235/17–18 *Salomon . . . Ecclesiastici xxvii [17]*: 'Qui denudat arcana amici perdet fidem et non inveniet amicum ad animum suum.' GO: 'Ostendit in quo maxime leditur amicicia, in malo, sci., proditionis, quam fidem, sci., perdit, & amiciciae equitatem non custodit, & ideo dissipat caritatem' (2: 773).

2–235/20–1 *Salomon . . . Ecclesiastici vi [9]*: 'Et est amicus qui egreditur ad inimicitiam, et est amicus qui odium et rixam et convicia denudabit.'

2–235/34 *Sent Iamys [2: 13]*: Cited above, 279/32.

2–235/35–6 *Summa confesorum, li. ii, ti. De testibus*: The section on witnesses in John of Freiburg's *Summa confessorum* 2.5, has no passage directly bearing on Jas. 2: 13, but a long discussion of the need for concordance of witnesses, illustrated by Daniel's judgement in the case of Susannah falsely accused by the elders (Dan. 13), implies that judgement should be tempered with mercy (MS Bodley 299, fos. 93^r-94^r).

2–235/36–8 *Also þer is witnesse . . . Di. xxviii, Priusquam*: The canon 'Priusquam' holds that no man lacking a longstanding habit of continence is to be elected to a bishopric (D. 28 c. 4; Friedberg 1: 101). The source is a letter of St Gregory, which says that John, a deacon, who has a small daughter, should not expect to be made a bishop. Gratian's *dict. ante* c. 4: 'Qui longam sui corporis continentiam non habet in episcopum eligi non debet'. St Gregory's letter is found in *Epistolas*, Bk. 10, No.62 (*PL* 77: 1114–5).

2–235/40 *þer may no man . . . iv, q. iv, Nullus vmquam . . . ibidem*: The canon 'Nullus umquam' holds that no one may be accuser, witness and judge at the same time (C.4 q.4 c.1; Friedberg 1: 541). the source is a letter of Pope Fabian (d. 250), in which he says that at a minimum there must be four persons involved in any legal trial: judge, accuser, defendant and witness, and the trial procedure must be equitable.

2–235/42–6 *In cause of felonye . . . iv, q. iii, Testes . . . ibidem*: The first reference is to part 2 of the canon 'Placuit'. On repeat witnesses, Gratian's *dict. post* c. 2 (palea) is: 'Item in criminali causa: "Produci testis non potest, qui ante in eum reum testimonium dixit", sicut in 22. lib. Dig. tit. de testibus [lege 23] inuenitur'. The second reference is to the following canon, c. 3, ¶ 1, a *dictum* of Gratian's: 'In testibus fides, dignitas, mores, grauitas moderanda est' (C.4 qq.2–3 cc.2–3; Friedberg 1: 538). For the reference to the Justinian code, see 2–222/4–5 above.

2–236/46–237/48 *Swyche folc . . . xxxv, q. vi, c. 1*: The canon 'Consanguineos' specifies which degrees of consanguinity should count in ascertaining consanguinity. If blood relatives are not available, close friends of longstanding may be consulted (C.35 q.6 c.1; Friedberg 1: 1277). Gratian's *dict. ante*: 'Consanguinei tantum, uel, si progenies defecerit, antiqui et ueraces propinquitatem in sinodo conputent'. The source is a decretal of Pope Fabian (d. 250).

2–236/48–50 *Be witnesse of on . . . [iv], q. iii, Testes*: Gratian's *dictum*, in 'Si testes', c.3, ¶ 38: 'Unius uero testimonium nemo iudicum in quacumque causa facile admiti; imo unius testis responsio omnia non audiatur, etiamsi presidiali curiae honore prefulgeat' (C.4 qq.2–3 c. 3; Friedberg 1: 540–1). *D&P*'s textual notes point out that all manuscripts read 'iii, q. iii, Testes', but Causa 3 (about the time that may elapse between presenting and hearing a case, and related matters) is not about the 'witnesse of on'. In the same Question (3), however, ¶ 26 begins: 'Ubi numerus testium non adicitur, etiam duo sufficient' (idem, 1: 540). See 2–222/4–5 above.

2–236/50 *Deutero. xix [15]*: 'Non stabit testis unus contra aliquem quicquid illud peccati et facinoris fuerit, sed in ore duorum aut trium testium stabit omne verbum.' GO: 'Et contra impius et haereticos cum testimoniis scripturarum indigenus, duos testes, i.e., vetus & nouum testimentum adhibemus, vel tres, i.e., euangelium prophetas, apostolum & sic stat verbum' (1: 399). Nicolaus de Lyra says that in homicide cases there must be at least two or three carefully examined witnesses; a lying witness should receive the same punishment as the one guilty of the crime (*Postilla* 1).

2–236/50 *Numeri xxxv [30]*: 'Homicida sub testibus punietur; ad unius testimonium nullus condemnabitur.'

2–236/51–2 *No man . . . xv, q. iii, Sane, in fine . . . post me*: The canon 'Sane' holds that those accused of such offences as lèse majesté or simony (i.e., against either civil or canon law) shall not give testimony. Gratian's *post dict.*: '. . . tociens legibus inperatorum in ecclesiasticis negociis utendum est'. 'In fine' Gratian says: '. . . dum de se confitetur, super alienum crimen ei credi non oportet' (C.15 q.3 c.5; Friedberg 1: 752). That no man is a sufficient witness in his own case appears in a *dictum* of Gratian's beginning 'Si testes', c.3, ¶ 24: 'Nullus idoneus testes in re sua intelligitur' (C.4 qq.2–3 c.3; Friedberg 1: 540). See 2–236/54–5 below.

In line 52 of *D&P*, the paragraph sign before 'Item in criminali' should instead be a conventional symbol for 'capitulum'; this phrase appears in part two of the canon 'Placuit', in which Gratian refers to the Justinian code: 'Produci testis non potest, qui ante in eum reum testimonium dixit', sicut in 22 lib. Dig. tit. de testibus [lege 23] inuenitur' (C.4 qq.2–3 c.2; Friedberg 1: 538).

2–236/53–4 *Euery man . . . iv, q. ii.[c.]i*: The canon 'Testes' (c.1) holds that witnesses from the household of the accuser or those under fourteen years of age cannot be allowed to testify. In line 54 of *D&P*, the paragraph sign before 'i' should be a conventional symbol for 'capitulum' (C.4 qq.2–3 c.1; Friedberg 1: 538) See 2–222/4–5 above.

2–236/54–5 *þe defendour . . . iv, q. iii, Testes . . . ibidem*: The reference is not to the canon 'Testes' but to a *dictum* of Gratian's, beginning 'Si testes', c.3. In ¶ 18, Gratian says: 'Testes, quos accusator de domo produxerit, interrogari non placuit' (C.4 qq.2– 3 c.3; Friedberg 1: 539). See 2–222/4–5 above.

2–236/57–60 *An heretyk . . . xxiv, q. i, Miramur*: The canon 'Miramur' holds that a person who is excommunicated cannot serve as a witness. The canon itself does not mention heretics and heathens, but Gratian's *dict. post* c. 37 contains the following: 'Si enim quos diuina testimonia non secuntur, *quia extra ecclesiam sunt*, pondus humani testimonii perdiderunt aduersus eos, qui in ecclesia esse uidentur, nec aduersus eosdem ecclesiasticae auctoritatis pondus habere poterunt qui ab eius fide discessisse probati sunt . . .'. The source of the canon is an epistle of Pope Nicholas I (858–67); (C. 24 q. 1 c. 37; Friedberg 1: 981).

2–236/1–3 *He þat is vnable . . . ii, q. vii, Ipsi apostoli*: The canon 'Ipsi apostoli' holds that those who are not, or who are not qualified to be, in holy orders may not testify against priests: 'Ipsi apostoli, et eorum successores statuerunt, ut sacerdotes Domini non accusent, nec in eos testificentur, qui sui ordinis non sunt nec esse possunt'. The source is an epistle of Pope Fabian (236–50); (C. 2 q. 7 c. 38; Friedberg 1: 495).

2–236/4 *He þat beryth . . . xi, q. iii, Abiit*: The canon 'Abiit' states that a person who testifies falsely or denies the truth for a bribe makes himself one with the perfidious Jews: 'Qui falsum testimonium dicunt, et ueritatem pro pecunia negant, sceleris Iudae participes fiunt' (C.11 q.3 c.83; Friedberg 1: 666). The source is Bede's 'Super Marcum' 3.14 (*PL* 92: 269–70).

2–236/4–6 *ȝif prestis . . . v, q. vi [Si quis]*: For [Si quis] read 'Quia in finem': The canon 'Quia' holds that priests or deacons who give false testimony in cases involving money must be suspended from office for twelve years; in criminal cases, appropriate penalties must be imposed. The editor notes, however, that the text here is uncertain (C.5, q.6, c.3; Friedberg 1: 552). It is also possible that the author of *D&P* may have had in mind another canon, 'Si quis coactus', which holds that a cleric coerced into perjury shall do penance for 120 days. If coercion was not involved, the penalty is one year on bread and water and two additional years of penance. The source is the 'Penitential of Theodore' (C.22 q.5 c.3; Friedberg 1: 883).

2–236/7–237/16 *Euery fals witnesse . . . xxii, q. v, Si quis . . . ibidem*: For the canon 'Si quis coactus', see 2–236/4–6 above (C.22 q.5 c.3; Friedberg 1: 883). The canon 'Si quis se' holds that the cleric who perjures himself or knowingly induces another cleric to perjure himself shall do penance for forty days on bread and water, and others, if they were parties to the crime, must do similar penance. The source is Pope Gelasius I (492–6); (C.22, q.5, c.4; Friedberg 1: 883).

2–237/16–18 *þe wordis of witnesse . . . Extra, lib. ii, ti. De testibus, c. Cum tu*: The canon 'Quum tu' deals with legal appeals ('appellationes'). The relevant phrase here is: 'nos dicta testium benigne interpretari' (X 2.22.16; Friedberg 2: 320). The source is a decretal of Alexander III.

2–237/19–20 *þe witnesse . . . Extra, li. ii, ti. De probacionibus, c. Licet*: The canon 'Licet' does not deal directly with suborned witnesses, but the underlying case was a long-drawn-out jurisdictional struggle between a Ravenna church and a commune, in which the commune put forward many witnesses who contradicted one another, making it easy to decide the case in favour of the Ravenna church (X 2.19.9; Friedberg 2: 311–12). The source is a papal letter of Innocent III.

2–237/20–2 *Men schul . . . eod. ti., Per tuas*: The canon 'Per tuas' involves a question of paternity: if the mother of R. (the mistress of T.) has long claimed T. as the father of R., can she be believed if she now wishes to swear publicly that T. was not the father—her motive being to legitimize the illicit relationship between her son R. and his putative first cousin, S.? The *dict. ante*: 'Si qui nominent aliquem filium, et ita communiter reputatur, non creditur postea alteri eorum iuranti contrarium' (X 2.19.10; Friedberg 2: 313). The source is a papal letter of Innocent III.

2–237/25–6 *Ʒif þe witnesse . . . Extra, li. ii, ti. De testibus cogendis, c. Preterea*: The canon 'Preterea' has as point 3 in its *dict. ante*: 'Potest tamen, si erraverit [the witness], in continenti, non ex intervallo, dictum suum corrigere' (X 2.22.7; Friedberg 2: 343). The source is a decretal of Celestine III (d. 1198).

2–237/28–9 *Witnessis . . . Extra, De testibus et attestacionibus, c. ii . . . In omni*: The *dict. ante* of the first canon 'In nomine': 'Nulla est receptio testium facta contra non citatum' (X 2.20.2; Friedberg 2: 315). The *dict. ante* of the second canon, 'In omni': 'Ubi agitur ad correctionem de peccato

impediendo, principalis persona admittitur in testem' (X 2.20.4; Friedberg
2: 316).

2–237/30–3 *ȝif a man . . . eod. ti.*, *Intimauit*: The canon 'Intimauit' holds
that those who swear not to testify may be compelled to do so (X 2.20.18;
Friedberg 2: 321). The case was brought to the attention of Pope Alexander
III by the bishop of Exeter. A priest, R., informed the bishop that G., a
cleric, his chaplain and many others have sworn that they will not testify
against him. The pope warns that such testimony must nonetheless be
produced immediately.

2–237/33–7 *No man . . . eod. ti.*, *Personas*: The canon 'Personas' forbids
collusion in giving false testimony: 'a testimonio repellitur simili morbo
laborans' (X 2.20.20; Friedberg 2: 321–2). The source is a papal letter of
Alexander III.

2–237/37–9 *No mannys . . . eod. ti.*, *Nuper*: The canon 'Nuper' rests on the
case of A., who entered the Order of Friars Minor but left without making
profession. The custodians of the Order refuse to swear that A. had left *after*
making profession, claiming that simple affirmation was sufficient. But the
pope replies that only a sworn deposition can be received as testimony when
the testimony is prejudicial to any person (X 2.20.51; Friedberg 2: 339). The
source is a decretal of Honorius III.

2–237/39–41 *þe honeste . . . eod. ti.*, *In nostra*: The canon 'In nostra' derives
from a case involving a dispute about a benefice between an archdeacon and
an abbot and his monks. One side produced sixteen witnesses, the other
twenty five witnesses; the recipient of the papal letter is directed to pay
attention to the quality, not the quantity, of the witnesses (X 2.20.32;
Friedberg 2:var.–7). The source is a letter of Innocent III.

2–237/41–3 *For discussyn . . . eod. ti.*, *Tam literis*: The canon 'Tam literis'
involves a dispute over the fitness of a candidate for a benefice. On the
evidence of 'laici et feminae', the candidate had contracted a marriage with a
widow and was thus disqualified. Such evidence was to be received as valid
(X 2.20.33; Friedberg 2: 327). The source is a papal letter of Innocent III to
the Prior of Saint Fridan of Lucca and master G., canon of Pisa, dated 1203.
The *dict. ante* c. 33: 'Ad probanda impedimenta electi, laici et feminae
admittuntur'.

2–237/43–6 *Sek folc . . . eod. ti.*, *Si qui*: The canon 'Si qui' holds that a
judge may send discreet examiners to witnesses who are unable to appear
before him (X 2.20.8; Friedberg 2: 318). The source is a papal letter of
Eugenius III to the bishop of Exeter and others.

2–237/47–8 *Salomon . . . Prouer. vi* [*19*]: Cited above 2–7/9–11.

2–237/48–238/51 *euery lyere . . . Prouer. xii* [*17; 19*]: Only the second
halves of verses 17 and 19 are translated: 'Qui autem mentitur testis est

fraudulentus./ . . . Qui autem testis est repentinus concinnat linguam mendacii.'

2–238/53 *Salomon . . . Prouer. xix* [*9*]: 'Testis falsus non erit inpunitus et qui loquitur mendacia peribit.'

2–238/4–6 *Ego sum . . . Ier. xxix* [*23*]: The end of verse 23: 'Ego sum iudex et testis, dicit Dominus.' LL4: 'For god þat is souereyn iuge & souereyn trewþe & knowyth al schal ben oure domysman & witnesse aȝens vs, & þerfore he seyth, I am domysman & I am witnesse' (fo. 108ʳᵃ. A 'domysman' is both a judge in a court of law and in an extended sense Christ as judge on Judgement Day, see *MED*, s.v. 'domes-man, 1 and 2'.

2–238/6–7 *Iob . . .* [*Iob 16: 19*]: For [19] read [20]: 'Ecce enim in caelo testis meus et conscius meus in excelsis.' St Gregory gives a Christological interpretation to the verse: the Son testifies to the Father; Christ's Resurrection testifies to eternal life (*Moralia*, 13.24; *CCL* cxliiiA, pp. 683–4).

2–238/8–9 *Sent Powil . . .* [*2 Cor. 1: 12*]: 'Nam gloria nostra haec est testimonium conscientiae nostrae, quod in simplicitate et sinceritate Dei, et non in sapientia carnali, sed in gratia Dei conversati sumus in mundo abundantius autem ad vos.' GO: 'Testimonia sunt bona opera, quae testantur exterius quid sit in conscientia' (4: 338).

2–238/13–16 *Moyses . . . Deutero. iv* [*26*]: 'Testes invoco hodie caelum et terram, cito perituros vos esse de terra quam transito Iordane possessuri estis, non habitabitis in ea longo tempore sed delebit vos Dominus atque disperget in omnes gentes . . .'.

2–238/16–24 *Y clepe heuene . . . Deutero. xxx* [*19–20; 17*]: 'Testes invoco hodie caelum et terram quod proposuerim vobis vitam et mortem, bonum et malum, benedictionem et maledictionem; elige ergo vitam ut et tu vivas et semen tuum;/ et diligas Dominum Deum tuum atque oboedias voci eius et illi adhereas; ipse est enim vita tua et longitudo dierum tuorum . . . Sin autem aversum fuerit cor tuum et audire nolueris atque errore deceptus adoraveris deos alienos et servieris eis, [v. 18] praedico tibi hodie quod pereas.'

2–239/26–8 *Sent Powil . . . I ad Corinth. xi* [*31*]: 'Quod si nosmet ipsos diiudicaremus, non utique iudicaremur.'

2–239/39–40 *Ideo . . . I ad Corinth. xi* [*30*]: 'Ideo inter vos multi infirmes et inbecilles et dormiunt multi'; 'per mortem' is added.

2–239/42 *assessouris*: Legal officials who advise the judge in a trial on matters of law (cf. use of word 2–41/24 above). Margery Kempe was examined on her eucharistic opinions before the Abbot of Leicester '& his assessowrys syttyng at þe awter, the whiche dedyn hir sweryn on a boke þat sche xulde answeryn trewly to þe Artyculys of þe Feyth lych as sche felt in hem' (ed. Meech and Allen, EETS, 212, p. 115/5–8).

2–239/50 *And feyth seith*: See below (text 2–264/43–58) for a personification of 'Coueytyse'.

2–239/50–2 *And feyth* . . . [*Iac. 2: 26*]: 'Sicut enim corpus sine spiritu emortuum est, ita et fides sine operibus mortua est.'

2–240/59–60 *Anima* . . . [*Ez. 18: 4 & 20*]: The last phrase of Ezek. 18: 4 and the first phrase of Ezek. 18: 20 are: 'Anima quae peccaverit, ipsa morietur.' The GO cites the NT promises of eternal life and refers to the example of Balaam (Num. 22–4) as one who died to sin in order to live with the souls of the just (3: 255).

2–240/61 *bigamus*: See above 2–111/1–4, 2–116/130–1.

2–240/72 *fourty trewe witnessis*: The Council of Lambeth, 1281, prescribed that 'quilibet Sacerdos plebi praesidens quater in anno, hoc est, semel in qualibet quarta anni, une die solenni vel pluribus, per se vel per alium, exponat populo vulgariter absque cujuslibet subtilitatis textura fantastica xiiii. Fidei Articulos; x. Mandata Decalogi; duo Praecepta Evangelii, scilicet geminae Charitatis; & vii. etiam Opera Misericordiae; vii. Capitalia Peccata, cum sua progenie; vii. Virtutes Principales; ac etiam vii. Gratiae Sacramenta' (Lyndwood, *Provinciale*, 'Constitutiones Provinciales Concilia Lambethensis', p. 28a (1679 edn.)). *The Lay Folks' Catechism*, Archbishop Thoresby's instruction book, issued in English and Latin in 1357, is an example that closely follows the guidelines (ed. Simmons and Nolloth, EETS, os 118).

2–240/78 *Sent Gregori in his omelye*: Source not found.

2–241/89 *þin confessour*: See 250/18–251/58 above.

2–241/1 *at þe dredful dom*: Chapters 14–18 of Commandment VIII are chiefly about the Doom, or Last Judgement. The biblical sources of the tradition are NT references to Christ's reappearance as judge (e.g., Matt. 25: 31–46, Mark 13: 26–7, Luke 21: 25–8) and the imagery of the Book of Revelations. The synoptic gospels are less specific about who will be judged, but other NT texts imply that all persons will be judged (Rom. 2: 2–16, I Cor. 6: 2). The patristic writers assumed that the present, or sixth, age would end with a final judgement of humankind.

2–241/3–7 *Sent Powil* . . . [*cf. I Thess. 4: 15–16*]: '. . . non praeveniemus eos qui dormierunt,/ quoniam ipse Dominus in iussu et in voce archangeli et in tuba Dei descendet de caelo, et mortui qui in Christo sunt resurgent primi.' Cf. Eph. 5: 14: 'Propter quod dicit, surge qui dormis et exsurge a mortuis et inluminabit tibi Christus.' Neither text has the same wording; the source may instead be one of the vernacular Doomsday plays, see 2–241/7 ff. below. The gloss, attributed to Haymo: 'Tuba erit magna vox angelorum. Vel in tuba, quia manifeste. Vnde, videbit omnis caro salutare domini. Vel sicut tuba in bellis quia tunc inimicos debellabit, & sicut tuba in festis, amicos ad festiuitatem aeternae gloriae inuitabit' (GO, 4: 398). Aquinas on this passage, 'Ep. I ad Thess.', *Opera*, Vol. 13, p. 567 (Parma edn., 1862). Cf. 2–242/28–9 below.

2–241/7 ff. *And anon in þe twynk of an eye*: The N-Town Judgement Play begins with the speech of the archangel Michael:

> Syrgite, Alle men aryse!
> Venite Ad Judicium
> For now is sett þe hye justyce
> And hath assygnyd þe Day of Dom.
> Rape ȝow redyly to þis grett assyse,

and continues with the archangel Gabriel's

> Bothe pope prynce and prysste with crowne,
> Kynge and caysere and kyghtys kene,
>
> .   .   .   .
>
> Nowther pore ne ryche of grett renowne
>
> .   .   .   .
>
> For alle ȝoure dedys here xal be sene
> Opynly in syght.
>
> (ed. Lumiansky and Mills, EETS ss 11),
> pp. 409/1–5; 410/14–5; 18; 21–2

On the Doomsday or Judgement Plays of the mystery cycles see Owst (1933), pp. 516–26, stresing the close ties between the plays and contemporary sermons. See also D. J. Leigh, 'The Doomsday Mystery Play' in *Med. Engl. Drama*, ed. Taylor and Nelson (1972), pp. 260–78.

2–241/17 *And as þe lyon*: See the first reference to the legend of the lion and his cubs above, 97/23.

2–242/28–9 *Sent Powil* [*I Thess. 4: 16*]: For [16 read [16–17]: 'Et mortui qui in Christo sunt resurgent primi, /deinde nos qui vivimus qui relinquimur, simul rapiemur cum illis in nubibus obviam Domino in aera, et sic semper cum Domino erimus.' Aquinas' commentary on this passage deals with the question of the order in which the dead will rise. There are two opinions, he says, but he finds the better of the two the belief that at the second coming the living will die and rise again, along with the deserving dead (Ep. I ad Thess., c.4., Lectio 2, in *Opera*, Vol. 13, p. 568; Parma edn., 1859). On I Thess., cf. *ABD* 6: 515–17.

2–242/29–38 *Venite . . .* [*Mt. 25: 34; 41*]: 'Tunc dicet rex his qui a dextris eius erunt, "Venite benedicti Patris mei, possidete paratum vobis regnum a constitutione mundi". . . .Tunc dicet et his qui a sinistris erunt, "Discedite a me maledicti in ignem aeternum qui paratus est diabolo et angelis eius"'. The GO (v. 34) interprets hungering and thirsting figuratively as hunger and thirst for justice satisfied by the 'bread' of the word and the 'drink' of wisdom ('pane verbi' and 'potu sapientiae') (4: 78). Cf. 187/34–43 above. Cited below, 2–246/31, 2–317/25–6.

2–242/42–9 *And perfor deme wel þinself*: The passage makes explicit the implicit message of the 'Coventry' story (2–193/25–194/61 above), which recounts a dream rehearsal of the Last Judgement.

2–242/49 ff. *Ion-with-þe-gyldene-mouth . . . [Apoc. 1: 7]*: Rev. 1: 7: 'Ecce venit cum nubibus et videbit eum omnis oculus et qui eum pupugerunt et plangent se super eum omnes tribus terrae . . .'; cited twice in LL4: 'þe maydenys sone schal comyn with þe sky3is, þat is to sey3e, with þe nyne ordrys of aungelys & with alle seyntis gloryfiyd & with al þe court of heuene' (fo. 4ʳᵃ); 'Euery ey3e schal sen hym at þe doom & alle þat prekede hym with pynys in hys pascioun & with þe prykelys of synne in here myslyuynge' (fo. 50ᵛᵇ). St Chrysostom and Ps.-Chrysostom discuss the Judgement scene in homilies on Matt. 25: 34, the first in his 'In Matth.', Hom. 79 (*PG* 58: 718–9), and the second in the 'Opus Imperfectum', Hom. 54, *PG* 56: 213–16. Neither describes a scene in which angels present the instruments of the Passion. The author of *D&P* seems rather to have drawn on the Last Judgement plays of the mystery cycles; see the Judgement Play of the Chester Mystery Cycle (ed. Lumiansky and Mills, EETS ss. 3), 1: 439/13–20.

2–243/53–80 *Than Crist . . . angelys*: The complaint of Christ is part of several of the mystery cycle Doomsday (or Judgement) plays. In the Towneley 'Judgement', the complaint begins, 'Here may ye se my woundys wide/ That I sufered for youre mysdeed' and ends, 'Say, man, what suffered thou for me?' (ed. Stevens and Cawley, EETS ss 13), 417–18/ 576–7; 697). Owst (1933), p. 521, points out that such a 'complaint' was a standard component of the Lenten sermon, see 2–249/28 below.

2–243/80 *Sent Gregory*: I have not located this phrase, though an analogue may be Gregory's homily IX on Mt. 25 (*PL* 76: 1105–9).

2–244/92 *Salomon . . . Sapien. v [18]*: For [18] read [21]: 'Et pugnabit cum illo orbis terrarum contra insensatos'. Nicolaus de Lyra says of 'Et pugnabit': 'Nam omnibus creaturis vtetur ad afflictionem reproborum, sicut econuerso omnes creature cedent ad gloriam electorum' (*Postilla* 3).

2–244/92–6 *Crisostomus*: A similar passage, attributed to Chrysostom, appears in the *Speculum Christiani*: 'Vertues of heuen schal be mouede: the synnes accusynge schal be on the ryght syde, inumerable fendes schal be on the lefte syde, the gastful cloude of helle schal be vnderneth, the iuge excitede to wreth schal be a-boue, the gylty conscience schal brenne wyth-in, wher vnneth a ryghtful man schal be sauede' (ed. Holmstedt, EETS, 182), pp. 54–5/2–6. Cf. Ps-Chrysostom, who expands on Matt. 31–46 in his 'Opus imperfectum' (*PG* 56: 211–216).

2–244/96–120 *Sent Austyn* . . . [*Eph. 4: 32*] . . . [*Sap. 5: 8*]: Eph. 4: 32: 'Estote autem invicem benigni, misericordes . . .'; but the intended reference may be Luke 6: 36: 'Estote ergo misericordes sicut et Pater vester misericors est'. Wisd. 5: 8–9: 'Quid nobis profuit superbia, aut quid divitiarum iactatio contulit nobis?/ Transierunt omnia illa tamquam umbra'. Cited in LL4: 'What halp vs oure pride, what halp vs oure richesse & oure avauntinge? Al þis is pasid as þe schadue' (fo. 117vb). Cited again below, 2–271/41–272/65. It is not clear which sermon of Augustine's begins 'Bretheryn, takyth hed . . .' and includes references to Eph. 4: 32 (or Luke 6: 36) and Wisd. 5: 8. Sermon 58.7 (*c.*410–12) for catechumens, in discussing the Lord's Prayer, urges forgiveness and cites Wisd. 5: 8 as a warning that some will repent too late (*PL* 38: 393–400); cf. Serm. 114.3 (*PL* 38: 652–4).

2–245/2–9 *Defecit gaudium* . . . *Trenorum* [*5: 15–16*]: Various forms of this rhymed translation of Lam. 5: 15–16 are listed in the *IMEV*, Nos. 221 (which gives the source as Lam. 5: 15–16), 3311, 3397 and 3398. The specimen printed in *Political, Religious and Love Poems* under the title, 'The Sinners' Lament', is almost different enough in wording to be an independent translation:

> al þe ioȝe of oure herte nou is went a-wey:
> for into serwe [*sic*] & into wo, tornid is al oure pley.
> þe coroune of oure heued is felle to gronde:
> þat euere we sennede, weylawey þe stonde!
>
> (ed. Wright, EETS, os 15, p. 261)

Another version is found in the same collection from MS Harley 7322, (perh. late fourteenth century), p. 268/7–12. This manuscript is described in the catalogue as showing signs of having been used as a resource for preaching ('in usum forte praedicantium'), containing excerpts from the Bible, the Church Fathers, Cicero, Pliny, Solinus, Gelius, Boethius, Bede, Isidore, William of Malmsbury, Alexander Neckam and others—including, here and there, 'versus rudiores Anglici et Gallici' (*Catalogue of the Harleian MSS*, 3: 525). The fourteenth-century 'Charter of the Abbey of the Holy Ghost' has a version of the second couplet:

> þe fairest flour of al oure garlond is fallen away;
> alas, alas & weloway, þat euere we dede synne.
>
> (Horstman, *Yorkshire Writers* 1: 348, cited from
MS Bodley Laud misc. 210).

For other manuscripts and editions see *IPMEP*, No. 590.

2–245/13–246/39 *þe doom of God* . . . *þe bowe*: The archer and his bow as a symbol of the Last Judgement is suggested by Ps. 7: 13–14 (see 2–246/32 below). Augustine's discourse on Ps. 7: 'This bow, then, I would readily assume to be the Holy Scriptures, in which the strength of the NT, like a bowstring, has bent and overcome the rigidity of the Old. This bow has shot forth the apostles like arrows ('Hinc tamquam sagittae emittuntur apostoli')'. Augustine notes that 'burning arrows' *per se* are not found in the Greek text of the psalm but rather 'arrows for those who will burn' ('Sed siue ipsae sagittae ardeant, siue ardere faciant'), and he goes on to connect these burning arrows with the Last Judgement (*Enarr.* 7.14–15; *CCL* xxxviii, pp. 45–6; *PL* 36: 106–7) as does Ps. 59: 6, See 2–246/36–9 below.

2–246/31 [*Mt. 25: 34; 41*]: See 187/34–43, 2–242/29–38 above.

2–246/32 [*Ps. 7: 13–14*]: On the 'burning arrows', see above, 2–245–6/13–39. The GO (citing Cassiodorus): 'Sicut enim qui tedendit arcum minatur. Ita per sacram scripturam minatur malis ne remissa putetur dei patientia. Et 'parauit' qui mox missurus sagittam putetur, sicut quid arcum parat ut sagittam mittat'(2: 464). The GO also cites the gloss by Augustine referred to below, 2–246/36–9.

2–246/36–9 *Dauyd . . .* [*Ps. 59: 6*]: *D&P* interprets the archer and bow as a sign of the Last Judgement, as does Augustine in his discourse on Ps. 59: 'Per tribulationes . . . temporales, significasti tuis fugere ab ira ignis sempiterni'; Augustine cites 1 Pet. 4: 17–18: 'Tempus est ut iudicium incipiat a domo Dei', and goes on to say that the farther the string of the bow is drawn back the more impetus is given to the arrow; thus the longer God withholds his Judgement, the more severe his punishment ('Quanto magis differtur iudicium, tanto maiore impetu uenturum est'). For the faithful, however, the longer the time allowed for repentance the more deserving they will be (*Enarr.* 59.6–7, *CCL* xxxix, pp. 758–9; *PL* 36: 717–8). In the vernacular, a parallel image is found in the fourteenth-century translation of the *Somme le roi*:

> . . . as þe archer, þe depper þat he [God] draweþ his bowe, þe grettere stroke he ȝeuyþ . . . And certeyn God haþ y-bent his bowe and bigynneþ to drawe, as þe Sauter seiþ, for to slee synful men and wommen but þei be ware. (*The Book of Vices and Virtues*, ed. Francis, EETS, 217, p. 176/1–5)

The same imagery is used in the Middle English 'The Three Arrows on Doomsday': 'þe first arow es when he sal bide þaim rise & come til þe dome. . . . þe tothir arowe es þat sal smert þaim ful sare. . . . þe threde arowe þat he sal schote, sal be when he sal say þat Mathew says in þe gospell: *Ite maledicti in ignem eternum*' (from the anonymous 'Holy Boke Gratia Dei', see Hartung *Manual* 9: 3055; 3133; text cited from Horstman, *Yorkshire Writers*, 1: 117–20. See above 2–245/13–246/39.

2–246/1–2 *dom in special and dom in general*: This refers to the two phases of the final judgement on the individual soul. A Particular ('special') Judgement occurs at death, and the soul is admitted either to a vision of God, to purgatory, or to hell. The General Judgement occurs after the destruction of the earth (preceded by the fifteen signs of the Doom) and follows the resurrection of the body. The NT parable of Dives and Lazarus (Luke 16: 19) and Christ's words to the penitent thief (Luke 23: 43) are the chief scriptural reference points for the belief in an immediate Particular Judgement. Loosely conceived in the patristic period, the belief became controversial during the papacy of John XXII (1316–1334), when the Pope advanced the opinion that souls upon death would not enjoy a vision of God but would have to wait for the general resurrection and General Judgement. His view was condemned by the university of Paris in 1333, and the succeeding pope, Benedict XII, in 1336, issued a Bull, *Benedictus deus*, ruling that souls destined to be among the blessed have 'an intuitive, face-to-face vision of the divine essence' (*ODP*, p. 218). Augustine says of the first and second resurrections, citing John 5: 25–6: 'Nondum de secunda resurrectione, id est corporum, loquitur [i.e., John], quae in fine futura est, sed de prima, quae nunc est' (*De civ. dei* XX 6; *PL* 41: 665). Note that in ll. 5–6 the author of *D&P* stresses that 'onon as þu art ded' a judgement on your soul will be carried out. Cf. 2–242/28–9 above.

2–246/4 [*Io. 12: 31*]: LL4: 'Now ys þe doom of þis world; now þe prince of þys world schal ben cast out' (fo. 54vb). Augustine's exegesis of this verse stresses that the ultimate fate of the Devil was settled at the time of the Passion, but that his power to tempt will continue until the Last Judgement ('In Ioh', 52.6–11; *CCL* xxxvi, pp. 448–50; *PL* 35: 1771–3). The GO on 'Nunc iudicium': 'Discretionis, sci., quod est ante vltimum damnationis, quia nunc per passionem iure dyaboli destructo multi liberabuntur. Vnde exponendo subiungit . . .' (4: 254).

2–246/6 *Salomon* . . . [*Eccli. 38: 23*]: '. . . sic enim erit et tuum; mihi heri et tibi hodie.'

2–247/10 *many tokenys of warnynge*: 'Signs of Death' were a common theme in medieval Latin and English verse; cf. *Fasciculus morum*, ed. Wenzel, pp. 718–21; *Political, Religious and Love Poems*, ed. Wright (EETS, os 15), pp. 249–50; 253; *The Pricke of Conscience*, ed. R. Morris (Berlin, 1863), pp. 22–3; *English Lyrics of the XIIIth Century*, ed. C. Brown, p. 130, and notes on the genre, pp. 220–2. Cf. 2–96/27–8 above.

2–247/13–44 *fyuetene sondry tokenys* . . . *Sent Austyn, De ciuitate, li. xviii*: The legend of the Fifteen Signs before the Doom is ancient and widespread. Luke 22: 25–8 provided a gospel text for sermonizing on Signs of the End. Biblical and inter-testamental apocalypses, such as Daniel, Enoch and Revelations, provided a stock of images. The 'Apocalypse of Thomas' may be the earliest extant text (eighth-century manuscript) to give a numbered list (seven) of Signs (see *The Apocryphal New Testament*, ed. Charles, pp. 555–62). Petrus Damianus (d. 1070) has a version in his 'De novissimis et Antichristo' (*PL* 145: 840), as does Radulphus Ardens (*c.*1100) in a homily on the second coming (*PL* 155: 1678).Peter Comestor (*Historia, PL* 198: 1611) appears to have followed a twelfth-century version of Ps.-Bede ('Opera paraenetica', *PL* 94: 54). Comestor in turn is the closest analogue to the vernacular versions in *D&P*, *Jacob's Well*, the Northern Homily Cycle, Bromyard's *Summa praedicantia*, and the *Pricke of Conscience*. Jacobus de Voragine's *Legenda aurea* (Graesse, No. 1; *GL* 1: 8) has a nearly identical list of Signs, which (in English) is followed by Mirk's *Festial*, John Lydgate's 'The fifftene toknys aforn the doom', David Lyndesay's 'The Buke of the Monarche' and by Play XXII ('Antichrist') in the Chester Mystery Cycle. As in *D&P*, St Jerome's 'Hebrew Annals' and St Augustine's *De civ. dei* are conventionally cited as sources for the Fifteen Signs, but Jerome's 'Hebrew Annals' are not extant, and Augustine does not provide a comparable list of Signs. The fullest modern study of the origins of the Signs is by Heist (1952), pp. 1–21; 197–9; and *passim*.

2–247/42 *þe vale of Iosaphat*: Joel 3: 2: 'Congregabo omnes gentes et deducam eas in vale Iosaphat, et disceptabo cum eis ibi super populo meo et hereditate mea Israhel quos disperserunt in nationibus, et terram meam diviserunt.' The Valley of Jehoshaphat, thought to be in the Kidron valley east of Jerusalem, has been associated with the Last Judgement by Jews, Muslims and Christians. A fifth-century church located there was rebuilt by the crusaders, who also founded a monastery. The *Legenda aurea* refers to the valley of Johoshaphat (Graesse, No.1; *GL*, 1: 9), as does Peter Comestor (*Historia, PL* 198: 1611).

2–247/45 [*Mt. 24: 36; Mc. 13: 32*]: Matt. 24: 36–7: 'De die autem illa et hora nemo scit, neque angeli caelorum nisi Pater solus./ Sicut autem in diebus Noe ita erit et adventus Filii hominis.' V. 36 raised Trinitarian questions for the commentators: Jerome notes that 'neque Filius' is added after 'Pater solus' in some codices, *CA*, 1: 357–8. Mark 13: 32: 'De die autem illo vel hora nemo scit neque angeli in caelo, neque Filius, nisi Pater.' With the addition of 'neque Filius' in this verse, the commentators raise questions about the human and divine natures of Christ, *CA*, pp. 535–6.

2–248/1–2 *xi, q. iii, Quatuor*: The canon 'Quatuor' lists four ways in which human judgement may be corrupted: fear, cupidity, hate and love (C.11 q.3 c. 78; Friedberg 1: 665). The canon is wrongly atributed to Gregory, and, according to the editor, it is found in Burchard of Worms (c.965–1025), who cites Isidore of Seville (*Decretum, PL* 140: 914). The reference to Isidore is found in his *Sententiarum*, Bk. 3, cap. 54 (*PL* 83: 726–7).

2–248/15–249/15–16 *Sent Ion . . . super Matheum, Opere inperfecto, Omelia vi*: Ps.-Chrysostom: '. . . quia nemo potest alterius esse testis idoneus, nisi qui ipse fuerit testificatus ab altero' (Hom. 6, *PG* 56: 673). See 2–211/24 above.

2–249/20 *in numbre, in whyȝte, in mesure*: Sap. 11: 21: 'Sed omnia mensura et numero et pondere disposuisti.' See 284/3 above.

2–249/24–6 *goodis of kende . . . of fortune . . . of grace*: In penitentials and confessionals, these 'goods' are linked to discussion of the sin of pride. Compare the *Ayenbite of Inwyt*: 'þe ilke þri manere guodes / þet men heþ of god. byeþ / þe guodes of kende. þe guodes of hap. þe guodes of grace' (ed. Gradon, EETS, os 23, I: 23–4); *The Book of Vices and Virtues*: '. . . þer beþ þre manere of goodes þat a man haþ of God . . . þe goodes of kynde . . . þe goodes of fortune . . . þe goodes of grace' (ed. Francis, EETS, 217, pp. 19–20); Chaucer's 'Parson's Tale': 'Now myghte men axe wherof that Pride sourdeth and spryngeth, and I seye, somtyme it spryngeth of the goodes of nature, and somtyme of the godes of fortune, and somtyme of the goodes of grace' (*CT*, p. 302/446–50).

2–249/28 [*Mt. 25: 42*]: Matt. 25: 42–3: 'Esurivi enim et non dedistis mihi manducare, sitive et non dedistis mihi potum./ Hospes eram et non collexistis me, nudus et non operuistis me, infirmus et in carcere et non visitastis me.' For references to Matt. 25, see 187/34–43 above. Cf. 2–243/53–80 above on the complaint of Christ. St Chrysostom's Homily 58, the complaint of Christ is found in Homily 79, *PG* 58: 718–9. Ps.-Chrysostom's Homily 56, on the same theme is found in *PG* 56: 213–6. See above 2–243/53–80.

2–249/38 [*Mt. 12: 36*]: Cited above, 2–214/46.

2–249/38–41 *Sent Bernard . . . vessel*: I have not found the Latin source for the statement that the rich man will answer for every thread of his garment, etc.. Bernard says of clothing: 'Si curiosas vestes requiris, pro ornata vestium subter te sternetur tinea, et operimentum tuum erunt vermes' ('Medit. de Humana Conditione', *PL* 184: 491).

2–249/43 [*Mt. 5: 26*]: 'Amen dico tibi non exies inde donec reddas novissimum quadrantem.' The GO on 'nouissimum quadrantem': 'Id est, minuta peccata, quia nichil erit impunitum, vel per quadrantem nouissimum significatur terrena peccata, quia prima pars mundi caelum, secunda aer, tertia aqua, quarta nouissima terra. Ergo donec reddas nouissimum quadrantem, i.e., donec luas peccata quae terra contraxisti' (4: 20).

2–249/45 *netyn*: Misprint for 'metyn'.

2–249/45 [*Mt. 7: 2*]: Cited above, 2–33/55.

2–250/53 *Daniel v*: Dan. 5: 25–8: 'Haec est autem scriptura quae digesta est, "mane, thecel, fares", et haec interpretatio sermonis, "mane" numeravit Deus regnum tuum et conplevit illud;/ "thecel" adpensus es in statera et inventus es minus habens;/ "fares" divisum est regnum tuum et datum est Medis et Persis.' 5: 27 is cited twice in LL4: 'þu art peysid in a balaunce & þu art foundin hauynge to lytyl' (fo. 87va; same tr. in fo. 114ra). The dream

vision, interpreted as a divine judgement on an erring king, makes Dan.
5: 25–8 appropriate to this portion of *D&P*. The GO: 'Primum pertinet ad
terminationem regni, secundum ad terminationem vitae regis, tercium ad
translationem regni' (3: 334).

2–250/65 [*Mt. 20/14*]: 'Tolle quod tuum est et vade; volo autem et huic
novissimo dare sicut et tibi.' Remigius of Auxerre (d. 908): 'Recipe
mercedem tuum et vade in gloriam' (*CA*, 1: 294).

2–250/74 [*Mt. 19: 28*]: Cited above 54/8 (where it is cited as Matt. 18: 28
and corrected to Mt. 19: 28); 75/7–8.

2–251/5 *Sent Gregory*: 'Quanto dona . . .' cited twice above, 64/10–12, and
cf. 188/16.

2–251/7–15 *Sent Iamys . . . Iac. v [1–3]*: 'Agite nunc divites, plorate
ululantes in miseriis quae advenient vobis. /Divitiae vestrae putrefactae
sunt, et vestimenta vestra a tineis comesta sunt;/ aurum et argentum
vestrum eruginavit, et erugo eorum in testimonium vobis erit, et mandu-
cabit carnes vestras sicut ignis thesaurizastis in novissimis diebus.' LL4 (tr.
vv. 1–4): 'ȝe ryche men, now doth what ȝe moun & wepith & cryyth for
ȝoure myscheuys þat schul comyn to ȝow. /ȝoure richesse is rotyn & ȝoure
cloþis ben mothyeetyn;/ ȝoure gold & ȝoure syluer þat is mowlyd & rustyd
schul ben wytnesse aȝens ȝou; ȝe tresoryn to ȝow wrethye in þe laste dayys,/
for þe hyre of ȝoure werkm[e]n þat han repin ȝoure feldys in þe countre
whyche is fraudyd & with heldyn be ȝow cryyth to god, & þe cris of hem is
entrid into þe eris of þe lord of hostis' (fo. 81vb). GO: 'Non solum
immisericordes diuites visibilis gehennae ignis cruciabit, sed etiam memoria
inanium diuitiarum quibus suos culpas redimere potuerint & ante iudicium
animas eorum & post resurrectionem etiam carnes exuret, cum sibi irasci
coeperint quare culpas elemosinis non redemerint' (4: 518).

2–251/17 *Sent Austyn*: This tag is cited in the *Speculum Christiani*: 'He may
not dye euyle *that* has lyuede wel, and he vnnethis dyeȝ wel *that* has lyuede
euyle': 'Non potest male mori, qui bene vixit, & vix bene moritur, qui male
vixit' (ed. Holmstedt, EETS, 182, pp. 208–9/1–2).

2–251/19 *Salomon . . . Prouer. xiv [25]*: 'Liberat animas testis fidelis et
profert mendacio versipellis.' GO: 'Catholicus praedicator, qui testimonia
scripturarum fidelita praedicat et profert haereticus mendacia'. On 'versipellis': 'id est diabolus . . .' (2: 671).

2–251/23 [*Is. 55: 6*]: 'Quaerite Dominum dum inveniri potest, invocate eum
dum prope est.' GO on 'Querite': Gentes suscipiunt misericordias Dauid, et
vos dediganimi, sed agite poenitentiam, et convertimini dum tempus
habetis'; on 'dum prope': 'Ne vestris vitiis recedat, qui appropinquat
appropinquantibus sibi, et filio reuertenti laetus occurrit' (3: 81).

2–251/29 [*Gal. 6: 10*]: LL4: 'Whyl we han tyme do we good to alle, but princepaly to hem þat ben ney3 vs in þe same feyth' (fo. 91vb). GO: 'Tempus seminandi est praesens vita qua currimus. In hac licet nobis quod volumus seminare. Cum vero transierit tempus operandi aufertur. Vnde operamini dum dies est, veniet nox quando iam nullus poterit operari' (4: 367).

2–252/30 *Salomon . . . Ecclesiastes ix* [*10*]: 'Quodcumque potest manus tua facere, instanter operare, quia nec opus nec ratio nec scientia nec sapientia erunt apud inferos quo tu properas.' LL4: 'What goodnesse þin hond may don, do it besyly, for after þin deth schal ben non wark ne connynge ne wysdam to moryn þin mede ne to helpyn þee 3yf þu goo to helle' (fo. 82rb).

2–252/35 [*Io. 9: 4*]: 'Me oportet operari opera eius qui misit me donec dies est; venit nox quando nemo potest operari.' Augustine maintains that what is meant by 'nox quando nemo potest operari' is the 'night' of the damned who at the Last Judgement are relegated to the Devil and his minions. For those who are saved, however, the 'day' of Christ is unending: '. . . dies praesentiae Christi usque in consummationem saeculi extenditur' ('In Ioh.', 44.5–6; *CCL* xxxvi, p. 384/15–17; *PL* 35: 1716).

VOL. 1: 2, COMMANDMENT IX,
pp. 2–253–294

2–253/4–5 *Non concupisces . . . Exodi xx* [*17*]: 'Non concupisces domum proximi tui, nec desiderabis uxorem eius, non servum, non ancillam, non bovem, non asinum nec omnia quae illius sunt.' *D&P* follows the tradition of the western Church in dividing Exod. 20: 17 into two precepts. This view would appear to go back to Augustine, who saw Exod. 20: 17 as an interiorizing of two earlier Commandments, the sixth against adultery and the seventh against theft, to which the prohibition of wrongful desire for a woman and wrongful coveting of material things, respectively, should be made to correspond. The fact that the 'ninth' and 'tenth' Commandments rest on slightly differing biblical texts, Deutero. 5: 21 and Exod. 20: 17, led to a further problem in ordering: in Exod., 'domum' precedes 'uxorem'; in Deutero., the order is reversed. The patristic and scholastic tendency— when not treating the 'ninth' and 'tenth' as a single Commandment—was to follow the Deuteronomic order (cf. Peter Lombard, *Sentences*, 3.40.1 (*Sententiae*, 2: 228); Hugh of St Victor, *De sacramentis* I, 12.20 (*PL* 176: 358c–359b). Wyclif treats the last two Commandments together, but under the heading of the ninth Ccommandment he discusses sexual temptation, and on the tenth Commandment (which he divides into three topics) he says that having already discussed sexual temptation he will now

take up the broader meaning of concupiscence, citing (like *D&P*) 1 Tim. 6: 10 (*De mand.*, pp. 434/29–31; 455–6). Cf.Reginald Pecock's summary of the whole matter in his *The Donet* (ed. Hitchcock, EETS, 156, p. 157/21–31). See above 81/7.

2–253/13 *Mathei xv [18–19]*: Matt. 15: 19 is cited above 273/13, 2–98/72, and in LL4, fo. 117vb.

2–253/14 *[1 Tim. 6: 10]*: 1 Tim. 6: 10 is cited above 58/34, 78/32, 2–120/40–1, and below 2–296/38, and in LL4, fos. 34vb, 95va.

2–253/18–19 *And ryȝt as . . . drawyn away*: Phrasing borrowed by 'Pore Caitif': '. . . as a weed is wel clensid out of a lond whanne þe rote is drawen awey . . .' MS Bodley 3, fo. 64^r; MS Bodley 938, fo. 145^v. On 'Pore Caitif', 227/1 above.

2–254/40 *false purchasouris*: The tenor of the discussion of the ninth Commandment shifts here from inner motivation, or disposition of the will, to one particular outcome of 'myscoueytise' in relation to property. The Middle English 'purchasouris' by itself and without the addition of 'false' had an invidious sense, see 317/20–1 above, where a rapacious concentration on acquiring lands and rents to the exclusion of other values is the meaning of 'to purchasyn'. On similar use in Chaucer, see *A Chaucer Glossary*, ed. N. Davis *et al.* (1979), s.vv. 'purchas' and 'purchasour'. See also Robert of Brunne's *Handlyng Synne*, where the suspicions attaching to a 'purchasoure' are clearly expressed (ed. Furnivall, EETS, os 119, 123), p. 296/9453–68. Cf. the use of 'purchasyd' in 'The Castle of Perseverance' (*The Macro Plays*, ed. Eccles, EETS, 262), p. 90/2971–81. See 2–254/42–52 below.

2–254/42–52 *To swyche false purchasouris . . . Michee ii [1–2]*: Mic. 2: 1–2: '. . . in luce matutina faciunt illud, quoniam contra Deum est manus eorum,/ et concupierunt agros et violenter tulerunt et domos rapuerunt, et calumniabantur virum et domum eius virum et hereditatem eius.' A modern English translation of 'calumniabantur' might be 'accuse falsely'; the Middle English translation 'chalanchedyn' has a range of meanings, from 'accuse falsely' to 'dispute' and 'lay (legal) claim to', the last being the sense in this context, see *DML*, s.v. 'calumniare' 3; cf. Alford (1988), s.v. 'chalengen' 2; and cf. Chaucer's 'Physicians's Tale': 'The peple anon had suspect in this thyng,/By manere of the cherles chalangyng' (*CT*, p. 193/263–4). See above 2–254/40.

2–255/52–60 *Ysaye v [8–9]*: Isa. 5: 8 is cited above, 2–207/32–6. Isa. 5: 9: 'In auribus meis sunt haec Domini exercitum, "Nisi domus multae desertae fuerint grandes et pulchrae absque habitatore."' The GO explains 'in auribus meis' as the inspiration by God of the prophets. The deserted houses are interpreted figuratively as the verbal presumptions of the heretics

('pompa & structura haereticorum verborum & diale[c]tica argumenta'),
3: 11.

2–255/60–5 *Salomon . . . Prouer. xxiii* [*10–11*]: 'Ne adtingas terminos
parvulorum et agrum pupillorum ne introeas;/ propinquus enim eorum
Fortis est, et ipse iudicabit contra te causam illorum.' the GO restates the
verses and adds: 'Possimus per pupillos et paruulos illos accipere, de quibus
dicitur, "Videte ne contemnatis unum de pusillis istis qui in me credunt
. . ."' etc., Matt. 18: 10 (3: 681).

2–255/1–256/34 *Acab . . . Nabot . . . kyngdam*: The story of Naboth's
vineyard (1 Kgs. 21) is summarized above, 2–15/44–60 (see also 155/71
above). Here more of the biblical account is given, including some of the
direct dialogue, the details about the writing of the false document, and the
warnings of the prophet Elijah. In Commandment V, the tale was fitted to
an extended sense of 'Thou shalt not kill'; here the tale illustrates the
particular sin—false purchase—against 'Thou shalt not covet' which the
author of *D&P* wants to stress. 'Pore Caitif' borrowed wording from the
D&P translation of 'Naboth's Vineyard', see MS Bodley 3, fos. 65ᵛ-67ʳ; MS
Bodley 938, fos. 146ᵛ-147ʳ. On 'Pore Caitif' see 227/1 above.

2–256/35–257/52 *We redyn . . . Sent Beatrice . . . to helle*: The source of this
version of the legend is Voragine's *Legenda aurea* (Graesse, No. 104; *GL*
2: 22–3). The tale also appears in Robert of Brunne's *Handlyng Synne*
(EETS, os 119,123), pp. 194–5/6001–6038. See also *ODS*, pp. 358–9.

2–257/56–8 *a comoun prouerbe . . . no ioye*: Whiting, G 333 (p. 245), lists this
instance. The Latin proverb is listed in Walther, I, 620.5081. Cited again
below, 2–268/73–5.

2–258/14–259/46 *Y rede. . . . heuene blysse withoutyn ende*: The tale of the
three gallows, which I have not found elsewhere, belongs to a large class of
tales presenting a vision of punishment after death for specific sins; the
Coventry tale (2–193/25–194/61 above) is one such.

2–259/4–5 *Naaman . . . IV Regum v* [*1–27*]: Referred to above, 333/6–7 and
2–174/35–42, where the summary of the tale in LL4 (fo. 93ᵛᵇ) is given.
Peter Comestor's retelling of the tale of Gehazi concludes with the
observation that it is not recorded that Gehazi's descendents were lepers,
but the 'leprosy' of simony spread from him (*Historia*, PL 198: 1392).

2–259/5–11 *Iudas . . . 'Heyl, Maystyr'*: The betrayal of Jesus by Judas
Iscariot is recounted in Matt. 26: 14–16, 47–9; 27: 3–10; Mark 14: 10, 43–6;
Luke 22: 3–6, 47–8; John 14: 26; 18: 5, and his death most graphically in
Acts 1: 18. Peter Comestor gives the detail about the flight of his spirit from
his viscera: '. . . delatum est ori, quo osculatus erat Dominum, ne per os
spiritus effunderetur' (*Historia*, PL 198;1625).

2–259/12–15 *Ananye . . . [Act. 5: 1–11]*: Cited above, 2–49/79–50/80.

2–259/15–16 *Nakor . . . Iosue vii [16–26]*: Nakor is biblical Achan (Achar, Achor), whose punishment for theft is often cited in conjunction with the punishment of Ananias and Saphira (Acts 5: 1–11). Cf. Peter Comestor's account, which discusses the punishment of Achan (Achar) and his family by both fire and stoning (*Historia*, PL 198: 1264–5). See *ABD* 1: 54 and 2–208/53–60 above.

2–259/17–260/40 *We fyndyn yn þe lyf of Sent Barlaam . . . nout half so mychil*: *D&P* follows the Middle English translation of *Barlaam and Josaphat* almost word for word, with some abbreviations (ed. Hirsh, EETS, 290), pp. 41–2. The 'archer' in *D&P* is 'a man' in the source; the verse, 'Perdita ne plangas . . .' is omitted; *D&P*'s pearl the size of an ostrich's egg is a precious stone the size of a raven's egg in the source; *D&P*'s moral at the end of the tale is more succinctly expressed. For other manuscript sources, Herbert, *Catalogue of Romances*, 3: 264 No.36; 556 No.202; 586 No.149; 650 No.39; 692 No.62. The tale appears in translation in *The Fables of Odo of Cheriton*, ed. J. C. Jacobs, No.113, pp. 160–1. See 2–281/2–282/26 below.

2–260/43–4 *nyȝtyngale . . . Catholicon*: The story of Philomela is found in Ovid's *Metamorphoses*, Bk. 6 (*Ovid*, LCL 42, pp. 316 ff.). Later tradition reversed the names of the two birds, identifying Procne with the swallow and her sister Philomela with the nightingale. The Franciscan Archbishop, John Pecham's poem, 'Philomena', identifies, at least implicitly, the sufferings of the legendary Philomela with the sufferings of Christ. In *D&P*, the identification is stated flatly, but by reference only to the Latin etymology of the word and the sweet song of the bird. For Pecham's 'Philomena', Drèves, *Analecta*, 50, No.398; further on Pecham's poem, see Raby (1953), pp. 425–9; Rigg (1992), pp. 222–3; a tr. from Old Georgian, Lang (1966), pp. 96–8.

2–261/49 *Hoc solum . . . possimus*: This dubious maxim is not found in the canonical list of Benedict VIII (Friedberg 2: 1122–4), and not found in the *Speculum Christiani*.

2–261/53–63 *Salomon . . . [Prov. 23: 4] . . . Prov. xxiii [5]*: 'Noli laborare ut diteris sed prudentiae tuae pone modum; /ne erigas oculos tuos ad opes quas habere non potes, quia facient sibi pinnas quasi aquilae et avolabunt in caelum.' *D&P* glosses Latin 'habere': 'scilicet, de iure' and 'ryȝtfullych'. The GO allegorizes 'setting bounds to prudence' as setting bounds to the faith received from the Fathers of the Church ('terminos fidei et veritatis datae a patribus'), 3: 681).

2–261/68–73 *Dauyd . . . II Regum xii [15–23]*: Another chapter in the story of David (see 2–85/19 above). David's quick recovery from mourning the death of his son is here made an exemplum against the sin of covetousness; the death is usually interpreted as the price paid for David's sins of adultery and murder ('percussitque Dominus parvulum quem pepererat uxor

Uriae'). Peter Comestor explains David's reaction as an effort to console Bathsheba: 'Hoc autem aiebat David, ut consolaretur Bethsabee, quia diligebat eam' (*Historia*, *PL* 198: 1334).

2–261/75–262/76 *þing þat is mychil desyrid . . . Maystir of Storiis*: It is not clear where Peter Comestor makes this proverbial observation.

2–262/82–3 *Qui cito . . .* [*Eccli. 19: 4*]: Cited above, 2–220/15–18.

2–262/91 *Engelond on byttyr balys*: Cf. earlier complaints about the state of England: 149/53–4, 357/10–40, 2–4/1–10, 2–57/83, 2–209/87.

2–262/92 *Salomon . . . Ecclesiastici* [*19: 16*]: 'Et non omni verbo credas est qui labitur lingua sed non ex animo'.

2–262/94–6 *Seneca . . . lyȝtlyche*: The sense is found in Seneca's Epistle 13: 'Ita est, mi Lucili; cito accedimus opinioni. Non coarguimus illa, quae nos in metum adducunt . . .' et seq. (LCL 75, *Seneca* IV, *Epistolae morales* I, 13.8, pp. 76–91).

2–262/1–263/26 *Numeri xxii* [*1–41*]: The story of Balaam and his ass was recounted above (by Dives), 2–34/19–35, to make a possibly ironical point about the killing of animals. Here the story is recounted by Pauper to illustrate the poor results of covetousness. Cited above 2–34/9–35 and 2–266/10–267/53 below.

2–264/31–4 *a philosofre . . . in pees*: A version of the saying is found in *The Minor Poems of the Vernon MS II*: 'Quietissime viuerent homines si tollerent ista duo verba: meum et tuum' (ed. Furnivall, EETS, os 117, p. 540/*ante* 277). See Whiting, M571 (p. 404), citing this example. Another example appears in *Political Poems and Songs Relating to English History*, ed. Wright, 1: 252.

2–264/41 [*Numeri 25: 1–9*]: Num. 25: 4: 'Et iratus Dominus ait ad Mosen, "Tolle cunctos principes populi et suspende eos contra solem in patibulis ut avertatur furor meus ab Israhel"'. The story of Phineas, which follows, is referred to above, 2–104/11.

2–264/46–9 *'Se,' seith Coueityse*: The personified abstraction in this passage, like those above, 2–239/50, is reminiscent of those in the morality plays contemporary with the writing of *D&P*. *The Castle of Perseverance* (*c.*1400–25) contains a character, 'Syr Couetyse', whose sin is property-grabbing:

> Now am I sory of my lyf.
> I haue purchasyd many a day
> Londys and rentys wyth mekyl stryf.
> I haue purchasyd holt and hay,
> Parkys and ponndys and bourys blyfe,
> Goode gardeynys wyth gryffys gay . . .

The Macro Plays (ed. Eccles, EETS, 262), pp. 28/841–2; 90/2970–5; on date, p. x. On 'purchasyd', see above 2–254/40.

2–264/52 *Balaam*: Num. 22: 22–33; see 2–34/19–35 above.

2–264/54–5 *Sent Ierom*: See 166/13–14 above.

2–264/57 [*Col. 3: 5*]: Cited above, 2–78/10, 100/33, 166/12–13 (followed by the reference in the previous note to Jerome).

2–264/60–265/67 *Nabugodonosor . . . [Dan. 3: 1–6]*: On Nebuchadnezzar, see *ABD* 4: 1058–9. For earlier references to Nebuchadnezzar see above 336/15–19, 2–177/29–30.

2–265/69 [*2 Tim. 3: 12*]: 'Et omnes qui volunt pie vivere in Christo Iesu persecutionem patientur.'

2–265/69 *Sent Gregory*: Gregory frequently expressed the view that the world is a moral testing ground. He is cited three times to this effect in the *Speculum Christiani*, though without use of the imagery of furnace and oven: 'Tribulacio porta est regni celorum' (ed. Holmstedt, EETS, 182, p. 193/20–1; also pp. 195/9–12 and 199/30–2).

2–265/76–82 *Sent Powil . . . I ad Tymo, vi [9–10]*: Cited above (v. 9) 2–158/59–60, and (v. 10) 58/34, 78/32, 2–120/40–1, 2–253/14; below (v. 9) 2–274/21, and (v. 10) 2–296/38.

2–266/7–9 *Sent Austyn . . . I ad Tessalo. iv [12]*: For [12] read [13]. 1 Thess. 4: 13: 'Nolumus autem vos ignorare fratres de dormientibus ut non contristemini sicut et ceteri qui spem non habent.' Augustine's sermons, Nos.172 (n.d.) and 173 (of 412), are on this theme. In the first, he says that such things as funeral processions and monuments console the living, who feel a natural grief; prayers and works of mercy performed for the sake of the dead may help those who were deserving before their deaths; finally, human sorrow will be assuaged by divine promise: 'Inde dolet humana condicio, hinc sanat diuina promissio' (*PL* 38: 935–9). The GO draws on these sermons (4: 398). Nicolaus de Lyra's gloss contrasts the hopeless grief of the pagans with the hope-filled joy of Christians (*Postilla* 4).

2–266/10–267/53 *Balaam*: Balaam (Num. 22–4) has been referred to in several connections above: 135/11 (the prophecy of the Magi), 2–34/19–35 (meat-eating), and 2–262/1–263/26 (covetousness). Here Balaam's ass is allegorized as worldly wealth.

2–267/53–63 *Rychesse . . . iugolouris hors . . . maystir*: The tale is found in Jacques de Vitry (*Exempla*, ed. Crane, p. 258). Manuscripts are listed in Herbert, *Catalogue of Romances*: Harley 463 (No.178, fo. 21, col. 2, p. 21; Harley 206 (No.20, fo. 109, pp. 699–700).

2–268/73–5 *comoun prouerbe . . . þe þredde eyr*: See above, 2–257/56–8.

2–268/15–16 [*Mt. 13: 22*]: 'Qui autem est seminatus in spinis hic est qui verbum audit et sollicitudo saeculi istius et fallacia divitiarum suffocat verbum et sine fructu efficitur.' The *CA* cites Jerome, who cites Gen.

3: 17–19: 'Inter spinas et tribulos panem tuum manducabis', commenting on the mystical significance that whoever devotes himself to carnal and worldly affairs eats true heavenly food among thorns (1: 214b).

2–269/37 *Tullius, lib. ii De officijs*: Cicero's *De officiis*, Bk. II, 24: 'Nec enim ulla res vehementius rem publicam continet quam fides, quae esse nulla potest, nisi erit necessaria solutio rerum creditarum' (*Cicero*, LCL 30, Vol. 21, pp. 260–1/90–3).

2–269/39–40 *þe predde booc, De officijs*: Cicero's *De officiis*, Bk. III, 5: 'Detrahere igitur alteri aliquid et hominem hominis incommodo suum commodum augere magis est contra naturam quam mors, quam paupertas, quam dolor, quam cetera, quae possunt aut corpori accidere aut rebus externis' (*Cicero*, LCL 30, Vol. 21, pp. 288–9/21–5).

2–270/4–7 *to a whel . . . stounde*: Cf. *Fasciculus morum*, ed. Wenzel: 'Sicut umbra cum declinat, ablatus est homo de medio; et sicut navis pertransit aquam fluctuantem, cuius cum preterit non est invenire eius vestigium', pp. 98–9; 'Similiter sicut folium' (idem, pp. 52–3); 'Nam pellis avari est varia mundi fortuna, sicut per rotam Fortune . . .' (idem, pp. 372–3). 'A Luue Ron' by the Franciscan Thomas of Hales (c.1170–1245):

> þus is þes world as þu mayht seo.
> al so þe schadewe þat glyt away.
> (*Old English Miscellany*, ed. Morris, EETS, os 49, p. 94/31–2; not found in *IMEV*)

On the wheel of fortune, see 2–270/10–29 below.

2–270/10–29 *þe whel of fortune . . . aduersarie*: See Whiting, F506 (pp. 203–5). Bishop Brinton's Sermon 6 (undated) uses the image: 'Quo ad nostrum progressum in mundo, si videamus qualiter *rota fortune* mirabiliter se vertente nunc sumus diuites, nunc pauperes, nunc sani, nunc egri, nunc iuuenes, nunc senes, nunc viui et lasciui, nunc mortui et sepulti' (ital. added; 1: 10). The editor notes that 'a picture of the wheel of fortune is still to be seen in the Rochester Cathedral'; another reference to 'ista rota fortune' appears in a later sermon of 1373 (*Sermons*, ed. Devlin, 1: 99). For the tag 'regnabo, regno, regnaui, sum sine regno', see Patch (1927), p. 164 and note 2.

2–270/30 [*Ps. 11: 9*]: 'In circuitu impii ambulabunt, cum exultati fuerint vilissimi filiorum hominum.' Augustine: 'Id est, in temporalium rerum cupiditate, quae septem dierum repetito circuitu, tamquam rota uoluitur; et ideo non perueniaunt in octauum, id est in aeternum, pro quo iste psalmus titulatus est' (*Enarr.* 11.9; *CCL* xxxviii, p. 84/1–4; *PL* 36: 139).

2–271/32 [*Ps. 82: 14*]: 'Deus meus, pone eos ut rotam, quasi stipulam ante faciem venti.' Cf. RSV, 'Make them like whirling dust'(Ps. 83: 13). Augustine answers the question, Why 'put them as a wheel': '. . . quod rota ex his quae retro sunt extollitur, ex his quae ante sunt deicitur; sic fiunt omnes inimici populi Dei. Non enim haec optatio, sed prophetatio est' (*Enarr.* 82.11; *CCL* xxxix, p. 1144/2–7; *PL* 36: 1054).

2–271/41–272/65 *lykenyd to a schip . . . Sapien. v [8–10]*: The passage is based loosely on Wisd. 8–10: 'Quid nobis profuit superbia, aut quid divitiarum iactatio contulit nobis; /transierunt omnia illa tamquam umbra, et tamquam nuntius percurrens,/ et tamquam navis quae pertransit fluctuantem aquam, cuius cum praeterierit non est vestigium invenire, neque semitam carinae illius in fluctibus.' the LV: 'What profitide pride to vs, ethir what brouȝte the boost of richessis to vs? All tho thingis passiden as schadewe, and as a messanger bifore rennynge. And as a schip, that passith thorou the flowynge watir, of which whanne it hath passid, it is not to fynde a step, nethir the path of the botme therof in wawys' (FM, 3: 92–3b). LL4 cites Wisd. 5: 8–9, see above 2–244/96–120. See 2–272/65–273/95 below.

2–271/57–272/60 *Alle þese grete kyngis*: *D&P*'s prose version of the 'ubi sunt' theme. A medieval Latin progenitor is the 'De contemptu mundi' of the Franciscan poet, Jacopone da Todi (d. 1306). stanzas 8 and 9 of 10:

> dic, ubi Salomon, olim tam nobilis,
> vel ubi Samson est, dux invincibilis,
> vel pulcher Absalon, vultu mirabilis,
> vel dulcis Jonathas, multam amabilis?
>
> quo Caesar abiit, celsus imperio,
> vel Dives splendidus, totus in prandio?
> dic, ubi Tullius, clarus eloquio,
> vel Aristoteles, summus ingenio?

(ed. Raby (1953), pp. 434–6)

An early Middle English use of the theme is entitled 'Ubi Sount Qui Ante Nos Fuerount' but lacks the 'Ubi Salomon' passage (*English Lyrics of the Thirteenth Century*, No.48, ed. C. Brown, pp. 85–7). John Lydgate's 'As a Mydsomer Rose', in stanzas 9–12 of 15 uses the theme, beginning 'Wher is now Dauid, the moost worthy kyng' (*The Minor Poems* II, ed. MacCracken, EETS, 192, pp. 780–5). See *IMEV* Supp., Nos 1865, 2087, 3310 and 4160 for manuscripts and editions of poems using the 'ubi sunt' theme.

2–272/65–273/95 *Mannys lyf . . . a schip*: See above, 2–271/41–272/65. LL4, in a sermon for the fourth Sunday after Epiphany, on Matt. 8: 23, giving a spiritual interpretation of the verse ('gostly to spekin'), repeats this passage in *D&P* almost word-for-word: 'Be þis boot or þys schyp I vnderstonde mannys lyf vpon erþe . for as a schyp is at boþin endys streyȝt & narw & large in þe myddys . so þe fyrste begynnyng of mannys lyf is wol streyȝt & narw' [here the reference to Job 1: 21 is given] 'But þe myddys of hys age is somdel wyd & large . for at twenti ȝeer he hath hys

bewte . at þrytty hys ful myȝt & hys meste helþe be comoun cours of kende .
at forty he is mest wys . & at fyfty man hath comounly hys meste rychesse .
But þis wydnesse of welþe lestyth no whyle, but onon it drawyth to anoþer
streyȝt ende, for onon eelde, febylnesse, seknesse & pouert comyn on . & at
þe laste deth makyth a wol streyȝt eende' [another reference to Job 1: 21,
followed by a verse translation of Job 14: 1–2 and references to Eccles. 2: 1
and Prov. 6: 3–4] 'Also þe helm of þe schyp wherby it is steryd may ben
vnderstondin deth . for he þat wyl sterin weel a schyp or a boot he stant not
in þe myddys of þe schyp but in þe laste ende . ryȝt so he þat wyle gouernyn
weel þe schip of hys lyf in þe see of þis world he may not stondin in þe
myddys of hys schyp, for he may not settyn hys herte, hys lykinge & hys
trost in þe welþe & in þe helþe þat he hath in hys myddyl age . but he muste
stondin in þe laste ende of hys schyp & þinkin of hys deth & of hys laste
ende & þinkin hoȝw vncerteyn it is, how byttyr, how dredful, how peynful
whanne þe herte schal breste, þe eyȝin ouyrturnyn, al þe body fatyn &
chaunchin into dolful hew . Therfore salomon seyþ' etc. (fos. 21vb-22ra).
The sermon continues with an allegorization of all parts of the ship, from
oars to sail, mast and anchor.

2–273/98 *Ecclesiastes vii [40]*: Read 'Ecclesiasticus': the error is in the
manuscript; the same error appears in the manuscript of LL4, fo. 22ra. Cited
above, 2–96/35–8, and below, 2–303/4–7.

2–274/11 *Diues diuicias*: The same couplet was cited above, 2–158/69–70.

2–274/21 [*1 Tim. 6: 9*]: Cited above 2–158/59–60, 2–265/76–82, and in
LL4, fos. 34vb, 95va.

2–274/21–6 *Sent Iamys . . . Iacobi i [10–11]*: 'Dives autem in humilitate sua
quoniam sicut flos faeni transibit,/ exortus est enim sol cum ardore et
arefecit faenum, et flos eius decidit, et decor vultus eius deperiit; ita et dives
in itineribus suis marcescet.' The GO comments that riches in themselves
are not evil; love of riches is. On 'flos faeni': 'Justus vt palma floret, injustus
et faenum, quia ille manet, hic cito transit. Flos iusti spes quae fructum
expectat, radix iusti charitas quare immobilis manet; mali radix cupiditas,
flos debetatio temporalium'. On 'dives in itineribus', the GO reminds the
rich man that the heat of the sun foreshadows the severity of final
judgement; only the 'just' or fruitful tree will survive (4: 512).

2–274/27 *þe schadwe alwey pasynge*: See above 2–270/4–7.

2–275/38–9 *sledyr weye*: Cf. *EWS*, 1 (Ep. Serm. 51/75): 'And þes þre ben
nedeful to men þat fiȝten in slydir wey, cley and vnknowen'.

2–275/50–1 *Luce xii [16–21]*: The parable of the Rich Fool. The GO calls it
an 'exemplum ad declinandam auaritiam temporalium'; the rich man is not
condemned for labouring but for putting his trust in labour instead of giving
to the poor 'vt ab eis reciperetur in aeternis tabernaculis'. Cf. Ambrose on

Luke (*PL* 15: 1818–9). Wailes (1987) cites the medieval commentators (from Ambrose to Ludolph of Saxony) and remarks that the 'sources contain no thorough allegory for this parable' (p. 220).

2–276/1–5 *þe fox in wyntyr*: The source of this tale appears to be Robert Holcot's (d. 1349) unedited 'Wisdom Commentary'. Smalley (1960) cites the Latin passage: 'Vulpecula, transitura glaciem, apponit aurem ad glaciem et audit aquam currentem et fluentem fortiter sub glacie nullo modo confidit de illa glacie, quia est nimis tenuis ad supportandum eam' (Sap. lect. xvii, C, fos.209vb-30va; pp. 169–70). Holcot is also the source of the 'Ore a deblys' tale (2–25/46–56 above) and at least part of the story of Fair Rosamond (2–96/38–97/55 above).

2–277/18 *II Regum xiv* [*14*]: 2 Sam. 14: 14: 'Omnes morimur, et quasi aquae delabimur in terram quae non revertuntur, nec vult perire Deus animam, sed retractat cogitans ne penitus pereat qui abiectus est.'

2–277/19–38 *Sent Bernard . . . tempora fuerunt*: Ps.-Bernard's 'Meditationes de humana conditione' 3.9: 'Ubi sunt amatores mundi, qui ante pauca tempora nobiscum erant? Nihil ex eis remansit, nisi cineres et vermes. Attende diligenter quid sunt, vel quid fuerunt. Homines fuerunt sicut tu: comederunt, biberunt, riserunt, duxerunt in bonis dies suos; et in puncto ad inferna descenderunt. . . . Hic caro eorum vermibus, et illic anima ignibus deputatur. . . . Quid profuit illis inanis gloria, brevis laetitia, mundi potentia, carnis voluptas, falsae divitiae, magna familia, et mala concupiscentia? Ubi risus, ubi jocus, ubi jactantia, ubi arrogantia? De tanta laetitia, quanta tristitia! post tantillam voluptatem, quam gravis miseria!' (*PL* 184: 491).

2–278/43–50 *Sent Lucye*: The conversation beteen St Lucy and her mother appears in Jacobus da Voragine's *Legenda aurea* (Graesse, No. 4; *GL*, I: 27–9). The story of St Lucy's martyrdom is referred to above, 2–52/28.

2–278/5–279/24 *two foolys . . . in þe ouene*: I have not found a direct source for this tale. It is a type of folk tale listed by Stith Thompson under the heading of 'Deceptions', K955, 'Murder by burning' (*Index* 4: 356).

2–278/9 *Whor* [MS G]: The meaning is 'whether' or 'can it be that?'; This spelling is not found in the *MED* sv. 'whether'. The other manuscripts of *D&P* substitute 'wher', 'wheþer' and 'For'. The word is used twice in LL4: 'Or ȝyf he aske hym an ey whor he schal takin to hym a scorpyoun' (fo. 57rb; cf. fo. 134vb). See *LALME*, Map 570, I: 447. See 'Manuscripts of *D&P*' above.

2–280/41 *Iob xix* [*21*]: On this verse, St Gregory makes his often-repeated observation that God tests good men by allowing Satan to strike at them: 'Sciabat quippe uir sanctus quia et per hoc ipsum quod peruersa uoluntate contra se satan egerat, potestatem non a semetipso, sed a Domino habebat' (*Moralia*, 14.51; *CCL* cxliiiA, p. 734/20–3; *PL* 76: 1070).

2–280/45–281/71 *Turpinus . . . þe same man*: The 'Pseudo-Turpin Chron-icle', a twelfth-century Latin prose miscellany of unknown authorship, comprises stories of the death of Roland connecting it loosely to the *Chanson de Roland*. It also contains saints' legends, *exempla*, and other homiletic material. In *D&P*, the uncle, 'Romericus', and his 'relative' of the Latin text become 'a knight' and his 'nephew', and some of the place names of the original are eliminated. The concluding detail that the nephew's body was recognized by its coat-armour is not found in the Latin original. Editions of the Latin text are found in C. Meredith-Jones, *Historia Karoli Magni et Rotholandi ou Chronique du Pseudo-Turpin* (1936), and in Ferdinand Castets, *Turpini Historia Karoli Magni* (1880). An expanded version of the tale is found in a thirteenth-century Anglo-Norman translation, edited by Iam Short, *The Anglo-Norman 'Pseudo-Turpin Chronicle' of William de Briane* (1973). The tale of the faithless executor is also told in Thomas of Chobham's *Summa*, ed. Broomfield, pp. 499–50, and in John of Wales' *Communiloquium* 7.3.4. It is listed in *An Alphabet of Tales* (ed. Banks, EETS, os 126,7), No. 314, pp. 216–7. See Hartung *Manual, 1: 88–100; 256–66*.

2–281/2–282/26 *Vita Barlaam*: The story of 'The Three Friends', or what was later known as the 'Everyman' story, has its ultimate origin in a christianized version of the life of the Buddha, dating from the sixth century B.C.. Latin versions of the tale are found in the *Legenda aurea* (Graesse, No. 180; *GL*, 2: 255–66); in the *Exempla* of Jacques de Vitry, No. 120, ed. Crane; in Bromyard, *Summa Praedicantium*, s.v. *amicitia* I. 52^v, col. 2; in the *Gesta Romanorum*, No. 83 (ed. Herrtage, EETS, es 33), pp. 127–32; in Vincent of Beauvais, 'Parabola de tribus amicis contra eosdem', *Speculum Historiale* 15, 16; 'De utilitate passionis domini', *Speculum Morale*, I. iv. 19; and briefly in John of Wales's *Communiloquium*, 3.2.3. An overview of the origins and history of the legend is given by Hirsh in his edition of *Barlaam and Iosaphat* (EETS, 290), pp. xv–xxviii. For a translation from Old Georgan, see D. M. Lang (1966), pp. 78–9. See 2–259/17–260/40 above.

2–282/30–4 *Tempore felici*: Cf. Prov. 19: 4: 'Divitiae addunt amicos plurimos; a paupere autem et hii quos habuit separantur.' The saying occurs in Chaucer's 'Monk's Tale' (*CT*, p. 245/2244–6), and in his translation of Boethius (*CT*, 'Boece', p. 426/66–8). It is listed in Whiting, F 667. The Vernon MS, item 49, 'Proverbs', attributes to Seneca a proverb with the same sense, giving Latin, French and English versions (ed. Furnivall, EETS, os 117, p. 539).

2–283/62–284/67 *Salomon . . . Ecclesiastici xxix [15]*: GO (interlinear): 'Bene monendo consulendo, in corde enim absconditur elemosina' (2: 774).

2–284/75 *Tobie iv [7–11]*: Cited above 2–156/10–11.

2–284/3 *Luce vi [30]*: '. . . et qui aufert quae tua sunt ne repetas'. Augustine: 'Omni petenti, inquit, non: omnia petenti, ut id des quod dare honeste et iuste potes. Quid si enim pecuniam petat, qua innocentem conetur opprimere' etc. (*De serm. dom.*, I, 20, 66–7; *CCL* xxxv, p. 76/1670–3; *PL* 34: 1263–4; *CA*, 2: 90b).

2–284/3 *Luce xiv [12–14]*: 'Dicebat autem et ei qui se invitaverat, "Cum facis prandium aut cenam noli vocare amicos tuos neque fratres tuos neque cognatos neque vicinos divites, ne forte et ipsi te reinvitent et fiat tibi retributio; sed cum facis convivium, voca pauperes, debiles, claudos, caecos, et beatus eris, quia non habent retribuere tibi; retribuetur enim tibi in resurrectione iustorum." ' The *CA* gives Origen's figurative interpretation: 'Mystice vero qui vanam gloriam vitat, vocat ad spirituale convivium pauperes, idest imperitos, ut ditet; debiles, hoc est laesam conscientiam habentes, ut sanet; claudos, idest declinantes a ratione, ut rectas semitas faciant; caecos, idest qui carent contemplatione veritatis, ut veram lucem videant' (2: 206b). The Wycliffite sermons would extend the teaching to curates, who ought to be poor: such curates give spiritual alms in return for material gifts (*EWS*, 3, Serm. 225/14–16).

2–285/15 *ȝeldynge aȝen hyr in hirde*: The sense is, 'In expectation of a material reward'. The phrase is found only in MS G. Compare the LV translation of Luke 14: 12: 'fiat tibi retributio': 'it be ȝolde aȝen to thee' (FM 4: 196b). Cf. 'De officio pastorali' in *English Works* (ed. Matthew, EETS, os 74), p. 436: 'noon herdis offis'. *EWS*, 3: 319/15: 'herdis office'. See 2–284/3 above.

2–285/22–4 *Cana. . Marie Maudeleyn*: For Cana, see John 2: 1–10; for Mary Magdalene and Martha, perhaps Luke 8: 2, 10: 38–42, though the latter Mary is not thought to be Mary Magdalene (see *ABD*, 4: 573–4, 579–82); for Zacheus, Luke 19: 2–9 (for Zachaeus as a type of the rich man who makes proper use of his wealth, see *ABD*, 6: 1032–3).

2–285/33–4 *Luce ix [11]*, & *Mathei xiv [14]*: Luke 9: 11: '. . . et eos qui cura indigebant sanabat'; Matt. 14: 14: '. . . et misertus est eius et curavit languidos eorum'.

2–285/36 *[Lc. 24: 13ff.]*: See 2–216/16 above.

2–285/37 *Abraham & Loot*: Abraham entertains angels, Gen. 18: 1 ff.; on Lot, Gen. 19: 1 ff.

2–286/42 *Act. x [1–48]*: Cornelius was the first non-Jewish convert to Christianity; see *ABD* 1: 1156.

2–286/46 *[Rom. 12: 20]*: 'Sed si esurierit inimicus tuus, ciba illum; si sitit potum da illi; hoc enim faciens carbones ignis congeres super caput eius.'

2–286/65 note *Extra, De religiosis*: The reference in MS H of *D&P* is to X 3.36.1–9, but the canons in this section of the decretals of Gregory IX concern episcopal jurisdiction over monasteries rather than the allocation of alms (Friedberg 2: 602–7).

2–287/25 [*Mt. 25: 36; 40*]: '. . . in carcere eram et venistis ad me. . . . quamdiu fecistis uni de his fratribus meis minimis, mihi fecistis'. The GO: 'Fratres mei & mater sunt qui faciunt voluntatem patris mei [Matt. 12: 50; Mark 3: 35] . . . qui esurientem et sitientem iusticiam pane verbi reficit, vel potu sapientiae refrigerat'. Other comments in *CA*, 1: 371. Matt. 25 is cited seven times in *D&P* and three times in LL4, citations listed above, 187/34–43.

2–287/25–6 *Sent Austyn, De verbis domini, sermone xxxv*: St Augustine on Matt. 5: 3: 'Incipit enim beatitudo ab humilitate: Beati pauperes spiritu, id est non inflati, dum se diuinae auctoritati subdit anima timens post hanc vitam ne pergat ad poenas, etiamsi forte in hac uita sibi beata esse uideatur' (*De serm. dom.*, 1.3.10; *CCL* xxxv, pp. 7–8/149–52; *PL* 38: 1233). Citations of Matt. 5: 3 above: 54/2–3, 56/79, 77/21–2; below, 2–289/85; and LL4, fo. 133ra.

2–287/27 *hem þat pore*: Read 'hem þat ben pore'.

2–288/42 [*Mt. 5: 19*]: 'Qui ergo solverit unum de mandatis istis minimis et docuerit sic homines, minimus vocabitur in regno caelorum.' Augustine: 'Mandata ergo minima significantur per unum iota et unum apicem. Qui ergo soluerit et docuerit sic, id est secundum id quod soluit, non secundum id quod inuenit et legit, minimum uocabitur in regno caelorum; et fortasse ideo non erit in regno caelorum, ubi nisi magni esse non possunt' (*De serm. dom.*, 1.8.20; *CCL* xxxv, p. 21/445–50; *PL* 34: 1239).

2–289/85 [*Mt. 5: 3*]: 'Beati pauperes spiritu, quoniam ipsorum est regnum caelorum.' See 54/2–3 and 2–287/25–6 above.

2–290/11 *Sent Austyn*: Cf. 2–284/3 above. In his *De serm. dom.*, Augustine says that a poor servant of God ('seruum dei') should not be judged to be acting contrary to the injunction to take no care for the morrow if he tries to provide for his material needs; Christ, he says, was ministered to by angels (2.17.57; *CCL* xxxv, p. 150/1265–75; *PL* 34: 1294–5).

2–290/16 *Cristis knyth*: Cf. 1 Cor. 9: 7. See above, 88/24, 98/51, 194/37, below 2–290/23–5.

2–290/19 *Ʒeue þu euery man þat askyth*: Luke 6: 30; see above, 2–284/3, below 2–290/23–5.

2–290/23–5 *Augustinus . . . Psalmi* [*103: 14*]: Augustine brings Luke 6: 30 and 2 Cor. 9 into his lengthy discussion of 'Producens fenum iumentis et herbam servituti hominem'. *D&P*'s 'Christ's knight' is suggested by Augustine's 'milites Christi' (p. 1509/27); his 'pore prechour' by Augustine's 'Ergo praedicatores uerba, et iumenta et serui sunt' (p. 1508/1); and his 'Leet þin elmesse swetyn in þin hond' by Augustine's 'Sudet eleemosyna in manu tua, donec inuenias iustum cui eam tradas' (p. 1509/36–7; also found on p. 1462/10–11). Augustine ends with an exhortation to seek out needy preachers: 'Itaque curios estote ad ista, fratres mei; inuenietis multorum Dei seruorum indigentiam, tantum ut uelitis inuenire . . .' (p. 1509/49–52); *Enarr.*, 103. 3.10; *CCL* xl, pp. 1506–9; *PL* 37: 1364–7). Cited above, 194/37 and 2–177/26–7.

2–290/27–8 *xvi, q. 1, Apostolicis*: The canon 'Apostolicis' condemns those who are unwilling to contribute to the needs of 'apostolic men' and evangelists of Christ (C.26 q.1 c.67; Friedberg 1: 784). The source is said to be St Jerome, but the exact reference is uncertain.

2–290/30 *Reymund, De hospitalitate ordinandorum*: Raymond of Peñafort: 'Sed circa hanc hospitalitatem modus & discretio adhibenda est: eorum namque, qui petunt eleemosynam, alij petunt quasi ex debito, vt praedicatores, & praelati; alij simpliciter pro corporis sustentatione' etc., *Summa*, Bk. 3, p. 272.

2–291/37–8 *Sent Powil* [*1 Cor. 9: 11*]: See above 65/56–7.

2–291/38 [*Di. xlii*], *Quiescamus*: The canon 'Quiescamus' states that no distinctions should be made among persons given hospitality. The text cites Abraham's reception of the angels, Gen. 18: 1–16 (D.42 c.2; Friedberg 1: 152). The source is the homily of St Chrysostom cited below, 2–291/46.

2–291/42–4 *Abraham . . . [Gen. 18 & 19]*: Referred to above 2–285/37. 2–291/38.

2–291/46 *Ion-with-þe-gyldene-mouth, super Epistulam ad Ebreos*: St John Chrysostom's 'Enarratio in Epistolam ad Hebraeos', Hom. 11, c. 6 (*PG* 63: 89–91).

2–291/52 *xi, q. iii, Quoniam multos, et Di. lxxxvi, Pasce, et Non satis*: Three canons: (1) 'Quoniam' is from a decretal of Gregory VII; the *dict. ante*: 'De his qui sine culpa excommunicatis communicant'; Gregory says that the innocent who suffer because of their close relations with the excommunicated, such as wives, children or servants, and those who unknowingly consort with excommunicates, should be treated with leniency, as well as those who give to excommunicates out of compassion (C.11 q.3 c.103; Friedberg 1: 672–3). (2) 'Pasce' is cited above, 2–14/5–6. (3) 'Non satis' enjoins unstinting and immediate aid to those in direst need, above all to those who suffer unjustly: 'Nam etsi omnibus debetur misericordia, iusto amplius' (D.86 c.14; Friedberg 1: 300–1). The source is St Ambrose, *De officiis*, Bk. I, c. 30, no. 147 (*PL* 16: 66).

2–291/56–7 *Sent Austyn . . . v, q. v, Non omnis . . . Di. lxxxvi, Pasche*: (1) The canon 'Non omnis' can be extended to mean that alms should in some cases be withheld: 'Nec qui parcit est amicus, nec qui verberat inimicus', or sometimes punishment may be the best form of compassion (C.5 q.5 c.2; Friedberg 1: 549–50). The source is a letter of St Augustine. (2) For the canon 'Pasche' (D.86 c.21; Friedberg 1: 302–3), see 2–14/5–6 above.

2–292/25–8 *Di. lxxxvi, Non satis . . . Ambrose, De officiis* [*unde . . . teneris*]: For the canon 'Non satis' (D.86 c.14; Friedberg 1: 300–1), see 2–291/52 above.

2–293/29–30 *Sent Austyn . . . þe booc of cristene lore, lib. i, c.x*: Augustine's comment on alms-giving appears in chapter 29 of *De doctrina Christiana*: 'Omnes autem aeque diligendi sunt, sed cum omnibus prodesse non possis, his potissimum consulendum est, qui pro locorum et temporum uel quarumlibet rerum opportunitatibus constrictius tibi quasi quadam sorte iunguntur' (*CCL* xxxii, p. 22/1–4; *PL* 34: 300).

2–293/47–8 *Di. xxv, Vnum,* ¶ *Multi, et Di. xli, Non cogantur*: (1) The paragraph 'Multi' is found in ¶ 5 of Gratian's *post dict.* to the canon 'Vnum'. It warns against over confidence in the power of purgatory to cleanse from mortal sin and is not relevant to the point being made here by Pauper. A later passage, in ¶ 7, listing minor sins, includes the minor sin of indulging paupers: 'si, pauperibus esurientibus, nimium deliciosa uel sumptuosa conuiuia preparauerit' (D.25 c.3; Friedberg 1: 93). The source is the fourth Council of Toledo (Tolletano IV, of 633), which, under Isidore of Seville, issued important liturgical regulations. (2) The canon 'Non cogantur' is taken from Augustine's Sermon 61.12 (*c.*412–16), on Matt. 7: 7–11. It is also about alms-giving (D.41 c.3; Friedberg 1: 149). Augustine says: 'Let your superfluities provide the poor with their necesssities' (tr. E. Hill, 3: 147; *PL* 38: 414).

2–293/48–53 *Sent Austyn . . . xiii, q. ii, Si quis irascitur*: The canon 'Si quis irascitur' directs testators to bequeath to the Church a portion of their wealth equal to that of one of their heirs: 'Unum filium habet: putet Christum alterum; duos habet: putet Christum tertium; decem habet: faciat Christum undecimum' (C.13 q.2 c.8; Friedberg 1: 723). The source is Augustine's sermon on clerical life, No.355, dated 425–6; it is found in *PL* 39: 1568–1575 (quotation from cols. 1571–2).

2–294/59–60 *Sent Austyn . . . lib. xxi, c. xxvi*: Augustine in *De civ. dei*, 21.27: '. . . elemosynae faciendae sunt, ut, cum de praeteritis peccatis deprecamur, exaudiamur; non ut in eis perseverantes licentiam malefaciendi nos per elemosynas comparare credamus' (*CCL* xlviii, p. 801/59–62; *PL* 41: 747).

VOL. 1: 2, COMMANDMENT X, pp. 2–295–326.

2–295/7 *Exodi xx* [*17*]: *D&P* here gives conflicting explanations for the ordering of the ninth and tenth Commandments. The first explanation is that Moses' people while in the desert were more inclined to sins of property; later, in the Promised Land, more inclined to sins of lechery. But the second explanation is that youth is more inclined to lechery, age to covetousness (see below 2–298/20 on the scribal error in this passage). Without explaining his choice, the author selects the first alternative. In this, he follows Isidore of Seville's gloss: 'Nonum [Commandment] mundi cupiditatem, decimum adulterii cognitionem' (GO 1: 153). See 2–253/4–5 above on the division of the prohibition in Exod. 20: 17 into two Commandments. On the numbering of the Commandments generally, see 81/7 above.

2–295/14–20 *Sent Austyn*: Contrary to what Dives says, St Augustine, in his eighth sermon on the OT, makes the ninth Commandment refer to the coveting of a neighbour's wife and the tenth to the coveting of a neighbour's property, from maidservant to ox and ass (*Serm.* 8.12–13; *CCL* xli, pp. 89–91/261–314). Augustine's explanation thus favours the order of Deuteronomy 5: 6–21 rather than that of Exod. 20: 17. Thomas Aquinas credits Augustine with the separation of Exod. 20: 17 into two precepts, one prohibiting the coveting of goods, the other prohibiting the coveting of another's wife, but does not allude to the ordering (*ST*, I–II.100.5). Hugh of St Victor (*De sacramentis* I, 12.20–21; *PL* 176: 358c–359b) lists the ninth Precept as 'Non desiderabis vxorem proximi tui' and the tenth as 'Non concupisces domum proximi tui'; his commentary includes the NT reference to Matt. 5: 27–8 (cf. *D&P*, 2–299/6), which widens the prohibition to include all concupiscence, including the persons and things of one's own household. In ordering the ninth and tenth Commandments, *D&P* may not be referring to any patristic or scholastic text, however, but simply relying on the vernacular conventions of his own period: see for example Robert of Brunne's *Handlyng Synne*, ed. Furnivall, EETS, os 119,123, p. 103/2903–24; *The Lay Folks Catechism* (ed. Simmons and Nolloth, EETS, os 118, pp. 54–5); and *Jacob's Well* (Salisbury MS 174, fos. 200ᵛ–201ʳ).

2–296/28–9 *Sent Powyl . . . [Gal. 5: 17]*: 'Caro enim concupiscit adversus spiritum, spiritus autem adversus carnem; haec enim invicem adversantur ut non quaecumque vultis illa faciatis.' LL4: 'þe flesch fyȝtith aȝenis þe spyryȝt & þe spyryȝt aȝenis þe flesch' (fo. 95ʳᵃ). Augustine's gloss: 'Ipsius enim carnali concupiscentiae causa non est in anima sola, nec in carne sola, ex vtroque enim fit quia sine vtroque delectatio nulla sentitur' (GO, 4: 366). Cited below 2–304/1–2.

2–296/37–8 *Sent Powil . . . [1 Tim. 6: 10]*: Cited above 58/34, 78/32, 2–120/40–1, 2–253/14; LL4 fos. 34ᵛᵇ, 95ᵛᵃ.

2–297/56–62 *kyng Dauyd*: See 2–85/19 ff. above for a list of *D&P* references to the story of David. The story of David and Bathsheba is found in 2 Reg. [2 Sam.], chapters 11, 13, 15, 18.

2–298/1–6 *Whan God . . . Deutero. v* [*6–21*]: The difference referred to is between the 'non concupisces domum proximi tui nec desiderabis uxorem eius' of Exod. 20: 17 and 'non concupisces uxorem proximi tui, non domum non agrum . . .' of Deutero. 5: 21, see 2–295/7 above.

2–298/20 *of þe eye . . . coueytyse*: This phrase should be omitted as a scribal error, seemingly caused by eyeskip, which makes nonsense of the passage. Though there is no sign of correction in MS G, MS T (and only MS T) cancels 'eye' and inserts 'flech'; MS T unfortunately spoils this correction by cancelling 'flesch' in 298/21 and writing 'ey' above it. The eyeskip is, however, important for manuscript relationships, see 'Relationships among the Manuscripts of *D&P*' above.

2–299/6 *Mathei v* [*28*]: Cited above 2–79/79, 2–85/39, 2–87/77. This text is the standard NT authorization for strengthening and broadening the OT prohibitions of adultery and concupisence. Aquinas, on this topic, points to the greater emphasis in the New Law on inner attitudes, or 'interior acts' (*ST*, I–II.107.4). Hence the prescription of meditation on the Passion as a remedy for sexual temptation.

2–300/20–34 *Mayster of Kende . . . a pellycan . . .* [*Ps. 101: 7*]: This is a repetition of the pelican tale recounted above (309/14–15); see above for Augustine's commentary on Ps. 101: 7. Isidore of Seville cites the Augustinian version without the comparison to Christ (*Etym.* 12.7.26). Albertus Magnus tells the story of the pelican parents reviving their young with their own blood, after which the parents are so enfeebled that the chicks have to feed them. But Albertus is sceptical: 'Haec autem potius in hystoriis leguntur quam sunt experimento probata per physicam' ('De animalibus', Bk. 23.90; *Beitrage*, 16: 150–6). Alexander Neckam, invoking Medea, also has the pelican killing its young before reviving them with its blood (*De naturis rerum,,* ed. Wright, pp. 118–9). On the history of the bestiary pelican, see McCulloch (1960), pp. 155–7; Portier summarizes the biblical pelican (1984), pp. 35–91. See 309/14–15 above.

2–301/30 [*Phil. 2: 7*]: See 2–100/43 above.

2–301/59 [*1 Pet. 2: 22*]: 'Qui peccatum non fecit, nec inventus est dolus in ore ipsius'. Augustine: '. . . Iesus Christus, qui nullum peccatum fecit, portauit aliena peccata. Et dedignatur portare aliena peccata, cui peccata dimissa sunt?' (*Serm.* IV.16; *CCL* xli, p. 32/375–8). 1 Pet. 2: 13–22 is cited above, 334/37–60.

2–301/64–302/67 *Sent Iohn . . . Apocalypsis i* [*5*]: LL4: 'He louede vs & wech vs from oure synnys with hys precious blood' (fo. 20^(va)).

2–302/79–83 *Salomon . . . Canti. viii* [*6*]: LL4: 'þe loue of god is strong as deth, & his brondis ben brondis of fyr & of flammys' (fo. 91^(ra)). Standard medieval interpretation viewed the Song of Songs as lyrical praise of the love of God; Bede is frequently cited as an early authority: 'Sicut mors corpus intermitit sic ab amore rerum corporalium aeternae vitae charitas occiditur', in 'In cantica canticorum' (*PL* 91 (2), p. 1235). In the later Middle Ages, St Bernard's sermons on the Canticles were widely influential and have been judged responsible for making the Song of Songs the most commented-on book of the OT. The author of *D&P* prefaces his three citations of Canticles here (LL4, fo. 91ʳᵃ, a sermon for Trinity 13) with a reference to St Bernard. For a survey of the history of commentary on the Song of Songs, from Origen to the thirteenth century, see E. Ann Matter (1990). See 2–303/92–4 below.

2–303/92–4 *Canti. viii* [*6*]: A Christological interpretation of 'signaculum' is given by St Gregory (*Super canticorum* 8.6: *PL* 79: 541–2), who is cited by Bede ('In cantica canticorum allegorica exposito', *CCL* cxvixB, pp. 269–71; *PL* 91 (2), p. 1235). The Canticles are cited only twice in *D&P*, but in his later sermons, the friar cites what he calls 'þe book of loue' twenty eight times. He uses the imagery of lilies, of newly shorn and washed lambs and, above all, the physical beauty of women to illustrate what the love of God ought to entail: 'The touchinge & felinge of man & woman schal ben fild & fed in þe touchinge of crist oure beste frend & mest belouyd' (*Cant.* 3: 4; LL4, fo. 118ᵛᵃ). The GO on the Song of Songs has been edited and translated by Mary Dove (*In canticum canticorum*, *CCL* clxx, pars 22; on Cant. 8: 6, see p. 393; on medieval interpretations of the Canticles, see pp. 40–9). See above 2–302/79–83.

2–303/94–7 *Sent Powil . . . ad Galathas v* [*16*]: In *D&P*, 'Wel of lyf and gostly fyr' is added to the translation: the phrase 'fons vitae' occurs in, e.g., Ps. 35: 10, Prov. 13: 14, 14: 27, 16: 22; the phrase 'ministros suos flammam ignis' in Heb. 1: 7, 'linguae . . . ignis' in Acts 2: 3. But the English phrase may have been suggested by the 'lampades ignis' of Cant. 8: 6 just cited, 2–303/92–4 above.

2–303/4–7 *Salomon . . . Ecclesiastici vii* [*40*]: Cited above, 2–96/35–8, 2–273/98.

2–303/13–304/29 *Vitis patrum . . . Alexander*: 'Malui me vivam in hoc monimentum inferre, quam offendere animam quae facta est ad Dei imaginem'; the tale is found in *De vitis patrum* 8.5 (*PL* 73: 1095–6).

2–304/22–9 *þe lyf of Sent Bryd*: The tale of St Brigid of Ireland (d. *c*.525, feast day 1 Feb.) is told in metrical form in the late thirteenth century *South English Legendary* (ed. d'Evelyn, EETS, 235), 1: 45–6/221–52. See also *Supplementary Lives* (ed. Hamer and Russell, EETS, 315), 345–6/108–70. See *ODS*, pp. 56–7.

2–304/1–312/187 *Thre þingis ben nedful to þe knyȝt*: 'A Tretyse of Gostly Batayle' is a short prose tract of religious instruction, derived, according to Bloomfield (1952), pp. 220–2, from 'Pore Caitif' (see 227/1 above). In

Raymo's view, 'Its main sources are *Dives and Pauper* and 'Pore Caitif'
(Hartung *Manual*, 7: 2331). It was printed by Horstman (*Yorkshire Writers*,
2: 420–30), who (unkindly) attributed it to Richard Rolle. The manuscripts
date from the mid to late fifteenth century (see Hartung *Manual*, 7: 2540,
and see Note 83/1–84/38 above). On the Christ/knight theme, see 98/51
above.

The parallel passages from 'A Tretyse' are too lengthy to cite in full in
these notes, but a representative passage in the text of 'A Tretyse'
(Horstman, 2;423) corresponding to *D&P* X, v (2–305/45–306/65) will
suffice to show how close the wording of the two texts is. An elipsis marks
substantial variants from, omissions from or additions to *D&P*: 'Off thys
sadylle . . . spake to Cayne whan he was wroth with hys brothere Abelle:
Why seyde . . . art thow wroth and why ys thy face and thy chere so
fallene? . . . for he was fallen owte of the sadylle of pacience . . . for yeff
thow doo welle, thow shalt reseeue off me goode mede, and yeff thou do
euylle, anone thy synne cometh to the yate to be punysshede, but the
desyre off synne shall be vnder the and . . . thy powere as the horse vnder
. . . ande thow shalt be lorde therof yif thou wylle, *Genes* 4 . . . Cayne be
mysgournaunce of hys horse felle owte off the sadylle and off pacience into
manslawghter off hys brothere . . . [5 lines] . . . But sytte . . . as Iob dyde,
and sey as he seyde when he had lost alle hys goode, and alle hys
chyldrene were slayne and hym-self smytene with . . . sekenes . . .
horryble, than he seyde, Yeff we haue take goode thingis of goddis . . .
why shull nat we suffre . . . painfulle thyngis off hys . . . blessyde by [*sic*]
oure lordis name, *Iob 1 & 2 capit.*'

For the verbal parallels between 'A Tretyse' and the passion meditation
in Commandment I, ii, see 83/1–84/38 above. For the parallels with the
'child born in prison' *exemplum* in Commandment X, xiii, see 2–323/4–
324/37 below. For the two versions of the 'bernac' story, see 2–306/1–6
below.

2–304/1–2 *Sent Powil . . .* [*Gal. 5: 17*]: See 2–296/28–9 above.

2–304/6–7 *kny3thod . . . Iob vii* [*1*]: 'Militia est vita hominis super terram, et
sicut dies mercennarii dies eius.' St Gregory's commentary on this verse
reiterates the sense of it: 'Omnes ergo qui spe caelestium praediti, exercitio
uitae praesentis atterimur, in alieno laboramus. Nam saepe et reprobis
seruire cogimur, mundo quae mundi sunt reddere coartamur; et alieno
quidem labore fatigamur, sed tamen praemia nostra percipimus . . .'
(*Moralia* 8.12; *CCL* cxliii, p. 389/10–15; *PL* 75: 808). Cited below
2–307/20–3.

2–305/39 [*Lc. 21: 19*]: LL4: '. . . in pacience 3e schul sauyn & kepyn 3oure
soulis' (fo. 101va). On this verse, the *CA* (2: 275) cites Gregory's *Moralia*,
5.16; *CCL* cxliii, p. 241/33–41; *PL* 75698), cf. Job 4: 5.

2–305/45–306/56 *Cayn . . . Genesis iv [6–7]*: 'Dixitque Dominus ad eum, 'Quare maestus [var. iratus] es et cur concidit facies tua?/ Nonne si bene egeris recipies sin autem male statim in foribus peccatum aderit, sed sub te erit, appetitus eius et tu dominaberis illius'. Both Jerome and Nicolaus de Lyra comment that the Hebrew text does not say what angry words Cain spoke to Abel (GO 1: 31; *Postilla* 1). The commentary in the GO on these difficult and puzzling verses appears to reach back as far as Philo (d. *c.*50) for its explanation of why Cain's offering was not acceptable to God. One explanation is that Abel correctly 'divided' the first-born from his flock and 'divided' the blood from the flesh, while Cain merely gave produce from his fields but did not 'divide' the best produce as his offering (Philo, 'Questions and Answers on Genesis', LCL 380, *Philo, Supp. I*, pp. 39–40).

2–306/65 *Iob i [21] et ii [10]*: Job 1: 21 is cited above 56/68, 71/45, 77/12, 2–272/82; LL4, fos. 8rb, 21vb. Job 2: 10: 'Si bona suscepimus de manu Domini quare mala non suscipiamus?' St Gregory draws the lesson of patience: 'Sancti viri tribulationum bello deprehensi, cum uno eodemque tempore alios ferientes, atque alios suadentes ferunt, illis opponunt scutum patientiae, istis iacula intorquent doctrinae' (*Moralia*, 3.21; *CCL* cxliii, p, 140.3–6; *PL* 75: 619).

2–306/1–6 *Mayster of Kende, liv. iv*: The story is found in Trevisa's translation of Bartholomaeus, 4.2 (*Properties*, 1: 135/35–6-136/1–9). 'A Tretyse of Gostly Batayle' (see above 2–304/1–312/187) has the tale in very much the same words as in (and possibly derived from) *D&P*:

> The master off kynde telleth *libro 4 de qualitate elementorum*, that there ys a byrde callede a barnake. Thys byrde vexeth [*sic*] owte of a tree ouer the watir, and als longe as it hongith one the tre hit ys dede, but assone as hit loseth frome the tree and falleth into the water, anone hit ys quycke and swymmeth forth. Thys byrde hath lytylle flessh and lasse blood. By thys tree I vnderstande mankynde that came off Adam ande Eue; by thys byrde I vnderstande euery crystene mane and womane; the whyche whane they be furst borne off here modere, be dede by orygynalle synne and nat able to the lyff off grace ne to blysse . . . (*Yorkshire Writers*, ed. Horstman, 2: 423–4).

2–307/13 *[Eph. 2: 3]*: '. . . et eramus natura filii irae sicut et ceteri'. LL4: 'We wern somtyme chyldryn of wretthe be corupcioun of adammys synne' (fo. 63va). On 'filii irae' the GO (citing Augustine): 'Cum ira Dei nascuntur mortales, quia peccante Adam, vicium pro natura inolevit. Tenebatur enim iusta damnatione genus humanum et erant omnes natura filii irae'; Augustine corrects the view that 'nature' is the source of man's evil. Rather it was man's evil which necessitated the sacrifice of Christ (4: 371; cf. Augustine's *Retractiones*, 1.10; *CCL* lvii, pp. 32–3/74–80).

2–307/18–19 *I Petri ii* [*11*]: The GO comments that restraint of fleshly desires is a preparation for heaven; the unregenerate have a homeland on earth ('reprobi hic habent patriam'), where their desires may be satisfied (4: 523).

2–307/20–3 *Iob . . . vii* [*1*]: See above 2–304/6–7.

2–307/26 [*Eph. 6: 11*]: Omit; see 2–307/27–308/38 below.

2–307/27–308/38 *Sent Powil . . . ad Ephesios vi* [*12–17*]: For [12–17] read [11–17]. This passage is the scriptural basis for allegorizations of the knight and his armour of the sort exemplified above, 2–304–12/cap. v–vi. Eph. 6: 11–17: 'Induite vos arma Dei ut possitis stare adversus insidias diaboli . . . /et induti loricam iustitiae/ et calciati pedes in praeparatione evangelii pacis;/ in omnibus sumentes scutum fidei . . . /et galeam salutis adsumite et gladium Spiritus quod est verbum Dei'.

2–307/33–7 *haubirchoun . . . swerd*: A haubergeon, or hauberk, was a coat of mail (Latin 'lorica') made by sewing metal rings on a leather garment (Broughton, *Dictionary of Knighthood* (1986), pp. 234–5). On the knight's sword, 'the knight's most treasured possession', see idem, pp. 436–7; 171.

2–308/39 *ad Hebreos iv* [*12*]: '. . . penetrabilior omni gladio ancipiti'. See above 2–49/87–9.

2–309/77–91 *scheld of feith . . . gostly enmyys*: *Jacob's Well* compares the Christian faith to a shield with three corners: the Godhead of Christ, the manhood of Christ, and the Church (Salisbury MS 174, fo. 215^b). On the history of shield design see Broughton (1986), pp. 419–20.

2–309/92 *basenet*: In this period, a metal helmet: 'a tall pointed covering which came well down the neck and sides to protect the ears and back of the head' (Broughton (1986), pp. 50; 238).

2–310/103–7 *Ieremie xvii* [*5;7*]: 'Haec dicit Dominus maledictus homo qui confidit in homine et ponit carnem brachium suum et a Domino recedit cor eius. . . ./Benedictus vir qui confidit in Domino'. LL4: 'And Ieremie seyth, Blissid be he þat trostith in oure lord god' (fo. 133ra).

2–310/107–8 *Sent Powil . . . rerebras and vaumbras*: A reference to Eph. 6: 14–17, see above 2–307/27–308/38. Rerebraces were metal defenses for the upper arm; the term vambrace referred to the whole defensive armour of the arm (Broughton (1986), pp. 398; 135).

2–310/110 [*Tit. 3: 8*]: '. . . ut curent bonis operibus praeesse qui credunt Deo, haec sunt bona et utilia hominibus'. GO: 'Id est, magis proficere & seipsis meliores fieri' (4: 420).

2–310/111–12 *Ecclesiastici xxxiii* [*29*]: See above 2–95/11–13.

2–310/116 *iacke or þe aketone*: A knee-length quilted coat with sleeves worn under armour; a term with many variants: acton, auqueton, gambeson, hacketon, haqueton, wambais, wambesium, wambs, see Broughton (1986), pp. 10; 273.

2–310/119–122 *Sent Powil . . . I ad Corinth.* [*13: 7*]: 'Omnia suffert, omnia credit, omnia sperat, omnia sustinet'. The GO on 'omnia credit': 'Sed domini, non dictur omnibus credit'; on 'omni sperat': 'Sic in praeoribus, i.e., in populo israelis apparuit, qui sperabant habere quod promittebat deus'; on 'omnia sustinet': 'In capite, i.e., in christo, qui patienter expectauit gloriam resurrectionis & ascensionis' (4: 329).

2–311/133 *as seith Sent Austyn*: *De civ. dei*, 19.12: 'Pacis igitur intentione geruntur et bella, ab his etiam qui uirtutem bellicam student exercere imperando atque pugnando. Vnde pacem constat belli esse optabilem finem' (*CCL* xlviii, p. 675/7–10; *PL* 41: 637).

2–311/148 [*Mt. 10: 34*]: 'Nolite arbitrari quia venerim mittere pacem in terram, non veni pacem mittere sed gladium.' Cited above, 2–48/71–3.

2–312/163 [*Eph. 6: 14*]: Cited above 2–307/27–308/38.

2–312/167 [*Phil. 3: 20*]: LL4: 'Oure lyuynge is in heuenys' (fo. 23va). Cited also LL4, fos. 96vb, 106ra, and 106va.

2–312/169 [*2 Tim. 3: 17*]: Emend reference to [Eph. 6: 13]: '. . . ut possitis resistere in die malo et omnibus perfectis stare', cited above 2–307/27–308/ 28.

2–312/173 [*I Thess. 5: 17*]: 'Sine intermissione orate.' GO (Augustine): 'Iustus enim nunquam desinit orare, nisi desinat iustus esse. Semper orat qui semper bene agit. Ipsum enim desiderium bonum oratio est. Et si continuum est desiderium, continua est oratio' (4: 400).

2–312/182 [*Ps. 7: 10*]: '. . . et scrutans corda et renes Deus'. Augustine: 'Opera enim nostra, quae factis et dictis operamur, possunt esse nota hominibus; sed quo animo fiant et quo per illa peruenire cupiamus, solus ille nouit, qui scrutatur corda et renes Deus' (*Enarr.*, 7.9; *CCL* xxxviii, p. 43/42–5; *PL* 36: 104).

2–313/5 *Mathei xix* [*17*]: Cited above 54/18–55/28, 75/18, below 2–322/ 10. LL4: 'ʒif þu wilt entrin into þe liif wiþouten ende, kepe þe comaundementis' (fo. 113rb).

2–313/7 [*Eccl. 12: 13*]: Eccles. 12: 13. LL4: 'Dred þin god & kep hese comaundementis; þis is euery man . þat is to seyʒe, þis ys þe perfeccioun of euery man' (fo. 69vb). Also cited in LL4, fo. 92rb.

2–313/12–17 *Sent Austyn . . . De civitate, libro xx, c. iv*: The passage is found in Augustine's *De civ. dei*, 20.3, which cites Eccles. 12: 13 (cited above 2–313/7): 'Quicumque enim est, hoc est, custos utique mandatorum Dei, quoniam qui hoc non est, nihil est, non enim ad veritatis imaginem reformatur, remanens in similitudine vanitatis' (*CCL* xlviii, p. 702/34–40; *PL* 41: 661).

2–313/17–18 *Dauyd* . . . [*Ps. 118: 21*]: Augustine says that it is one thing to break the Commandments through ignorance or weakness and quite another to break them because of pride, as did Adam and Eve (*Enarr.*, 118.9.2; *CCL* xl, pp. 1689–90/9–28; *PL* 37: 1522–3).

2–313/20–314/53 *Deutero xxvii* [*11–26*]: Liturgical 'Clamours' were ordinarily to be performed four times a year, (1) on St Michael's Day or the first Sunday of Advent, (2) the first or third Sunday in Lent, (3) Whitsunday, and (4) Lamentations Day (see Wilkins, 1: 438; 585; 'De Accusatoribus Excommunicandis': Lyndwood, *Provinciale*, 'Oxon. Const.' (1222), p. 16 (1679 edn.); Powicke & Cheney, *Councils & Synods* II: 1, p. 125). The *Fasciculus morum*, ed. Wenzel, says that believers in witchcraft are 'cursed by God and his holy Church' four times a year (pp. 500–1, citing canon law ('Episcipi': C.26 q.5 c.12; Friedberg 1: 1030, referred to above, 158/27 and 186/24). *Jacob's Well* refers to the 'great curse', which is to be performed four times a year 'solemnely, þat is, wyth cros standyng, wyth bellys ryngynge, wyth candelys brennynge' (ed. Brandeis, EETS, os 115, pp. 13–22; ed. note 5, p. 18, refers to the Constitutions of Oxford, of Mepham, and Stratford, as well as to Raymond of Peñafort's *Summa*). See Lester Little (1993), esp. pp. 72–85.

2–314/1–315/32 *Ʒif þu wil* . . . *þin fadris aforn þe*: A translation of Deut. 28: 15–34. The GO interprets 'venemous eyr' (315/12) as sinful living; the 'brazen air' (315/13) as a prefiguration of the hardness of the people whose laws were engraved on stone ('sicut duro popolo lex in lapide dabatur'); 'flen aweye be seuene weyys' (315/18) as God's threat to punish the people as fulfilled in the dispersion of the Jews; 'seknesse' (315/26) as heresies; 'þin wif' as a prefiguration of the conversion of Jewish scriptures to the uses of the Church and the removal of the sterility of merely ceremonial laws (1: 412–13). 'Pore Caitif' picks and chooses passages from the first half of this translation in its much shorter treatment of Deut. 28: 15–34; cf. 2–317/1–22 below (MS Bodley 938, fo. 150ʳ). On 'Pore Caitif' see 227/1 above.

2–315/39 [*Mt. 25: 41*]: Cited above, 187/34–43, 2–242/29–38, 2–246/31.

2–316/59 [*Gen. 35: 22*]: Cited above 2–105/47.

2–316/68–9 [*Rom. 12: 14*]: Augustine, in his comment on Ps.103: 35 ('Deficiant peccatores a terra'), cites 'Benedicite et nolite maledicere' against the seeming severity of the psalm. Who is not a sinner ('Quid non sint, nisi iniqui?'), he asks, and answers that 'deficiant' points rather to the absence of goodness in the sinners than to God's curse on them. At this point in his text, the author of *D&P* appears to have similar qualms about the cursing of sinners (*Enarr.*, 103.4.19; *CCL* xl, pp. 1534–5; *PL* 37: 1389–90).

2–317/1–22 [*Deut. 28: 1–13*]: A translation of the verses in Deuteronomy. The GO begins by emphasising that it is the obedient who are to be blessed; 'frut' (317/6) is interpreted to mean that those with different gifts to offer are to be equally blessed; 'comyng yn & goyng out' (317/9) refers to the 'ostium' of the Church, which is the 'door' by which all must come to Christ (John 10: 1); 'tresour abouyn from heuene' (317/17) is interpreted as the prophets and apostles sent from heaven; 'lend ['fenerabis'] to oþir nacionys' is interpreted as the fruitful spread of Church doctrine to all nations (1: 411–12). 'Pore Caitif' draws some phrases from the *D&P* translation, cf. MS Bodley 938, fo. 150ᵛ. On 'Pore Caitif', see 227/1 above.

2–317/25–6 *Mathei xxv [34]*: Cited above 187/40, 2–242/36, 2–246/31.

2–318/29–46 *Sent Austyn*: Augustine in the final chapters of *The City of God* hints at the blessings he anticipates in the Heavenly City but does not provide an extended description. He expects the deserving to be at peace, to be able to see God face to face, and to live with transfigured bodies in a realm of light. Mortal life will be at at end but there will be life ('plane certeque uitalis, hic corpus animale . . . adgrauat animam, sed spiritale sine ulla indigentia ex omni parte subditum uoluntate'), *De civ. dei*, 19.17; *CCL* xlviii, p. 685/63–70; *PL* 41: 646). In the Heavenly City, everything will be lovely in form and motion: 'Omnes quippe illi . . . harmoniae corporalis numeri non latebunt, intrinsecus et extrinsecus per corporis cuncta dispositi . . . rationales mentes in tanti artificis laudem rationalibis pulchritudinis delectatione succendent' (idem, 22.30; *CCL*, xlviii, p. 802/10–15; *PL* 41: 801). God as the source of light is referred to in an earlier passage in the *City of God* (*De civ. dei*, ll.21; *CCL* xlviii, 11.21, p. 340/37–49; *PL* 41: 334–5).

2–318/1 [*Mt. 5: 14*]: '. . . non potest civitas abscondi supra montem posita'. LL4 cites the first line of the verse: 'Vos estis lux mundi' (fo. 1387ʳᵇ). The verse refers to the Apostles, and perhaps more broadly to the Church, not directly to the Kingdom of Heaven. But as part of the Sermon on the Mount it is of course related to the idea of the Kingdom of Heaven as the goal of Christian preaching. Cf. 59/63–4 above.

2–318/7–8 *Ysaye . . . lx [18–21]*: '. . . et occupabit salus muros tuos et portas tuas laudatio,/ non erit tibi amplius sed ad lucendum per diem nec splendor lunae inluminabit te, sed erit tibi Dominus in lucem sempiternam et Deus tuus in gloriam tuam;/ non occidet ultra sol tuus et luna tua non minuetur, quia Dominus erit in lucem sempiternam et complebuntur dies luctus tui./ Populus autem tuus omnes iusti in perpetuum hereditabunt terram, germen plantationis meae opus manus meae ad glorificandum'. The translation in *D&P* is loose and interpolated, and the hymn to light continues to the end of the chapter, drawing upon the imagery of Revelation, cf. Rev. 21: 4, 6–8, 22: 5. The GO notes that the passage as a whole refers to the last days ('ad ultimum tempus'); the 'germen' of v. 21 refers to angels and the elect, seeds planted by God, who by their good works further the glory of creation (3: 89).

2–319/27 [*Io. 8: 12*]: GO: 'Quae nube carnis tegitur, et sic tolleranda hominibus efficitur, vnde & peccata possum dimittere & etiam hominem illuminare' (4: 245). The comment in the GO appears to have been extracted from Augustine's longer commentary on the verse in *In Ioh.* 34.1–10. Christ, he says, is figuratively the 'sun'. In his incarnation, he hides his 'sun' under the cloud of flesh. His is the light which lights the way to the fountain of eternal life. To follow his light is to abandon external conflicts and gain the hope of transcending the internal conflicts inherent in the human condition (*CCL* xxxvi, pp. 311–17; *PL* 35: 1652–7). Cited below 2–320/8.

2–320/2 [*Apoc.*] *xxi* [*10–11*]: Read [10–27]. *D&P* cap. xi is a glossed translation of Rev. 21: 10–27 with interpolations from Matthew and the Book of Tobit. *D&P*'s additions to and other deviations from Rev. 21: 10–27 are: 'whyche ston . . . gospel', citing John 8: 12 (320/6–7); 'redy porterys . . . goode soulys' (320/10); 'þat is to seye . . . square & it hadde' (320/11–321/17); 'in tokene . . . & baranye', om. Rev. 21: 14–18 (321/18–24); 'and in þo stonys . . . Goddis lomb', cf. Rev. 21: 14, and inserting a paraphrase of Tob. 13: 16–18 (321/29–30); '& al þe wal . . . smaragdys' (321/30–31); 'And as Tobye . . . wel declaryn' (321/34–7); 'but alwey day . . . wynter', omitting Rev. 21: 26 (323/48–9); 'Crist . . . blod' (322/52–3).

2–320/8 [*Io. 8: 12*]: See above 2–319/27.

2–322/1–16 *Doctor de Lira* [*on Apoc. 21: 14*] . . . *ȝatis of heuene*: On Rev. 21: 14, Nicolaus de Lyra says the foundations are: 'xii articlos fidei, nam secundum que dicit apostolus, Heb. xi, fides est substantia sperandorum, id est, bonorum celestium que sunt res sperande, & in hac diffinitione fidei accipitur substantia per inchoatione siue fundamento, eo que fundamentum est inchoatio domus per fidem vero formatam inchoatam beatitudo celestis in nobis sicut plenius fuit dictum Hebreorum xi' (*Postilla* 4). About the twelve gates (Rev. 21: 12) Nicolaus de Lyra says they are: 'obseruationes mandatorum, per quos habetur ingressus ad beatitudinis statum, Matth. xix. . . . Nam obseruatio decem preceptorum decalogi cum duobus preceptis caritatis fac ad vitam ingredi' (idem).

2–322/6–7 *Sent Powil* . . . [*2 Cor. 1: 23*]: For 'statis' the Vulgate reads 'stetistis' (2: 1790 note).

2–322/10 [*Mt. 19: 17*]: Cited above 54/18–55/28, 75/18, 2–313/5 and LL4, fo. 113rb. Here, *D&P* amplifies 'vitam', adding 'of þis blysful cite þer no man deyyth'.

2–322/16–18 *Dauyd* . . . [*Ps. 118: 32*]: LL4: 'Lord, sey3t he, I haue ronnyn be þe wey3e of þin comaundementis whanne þu hast maid myn herte large be charite & be dedys of elmesse' (fo. 32va). VL 'dilatasti' in both *D&P* and LL4 has been interpreted as the infusion of 'charite', perhaps influenced by Augustine's commentary: 'Cordis dilatatio, iustitiae est delectatio. Haec munus est Dei, ut in praeceptis eius non timore poenae angustemur, sed dilectione et delectatione iustitia dilatemur' (*Enarr.*, 118.10.6; *CCL* xl, p. 1695/22–6; *PL* 37: 1327). This interpretation fits the citation of the psalm to a context in which the promise of heaven is the motive and reward for keeping the Commandments.

2–323/23–8 *Dauyd* . . . [*Ps. 118: 35–6*]: 'domine' and 'Deus' are added to the VL text. This citation of Ps. 118 is the third of a series, see 2–313/17– 18, and 2–322/16–18 above. Augustine, continuing his commentary on Ps. 118, expands upon the sin of avarice as the chief obstacle standing in the way of obedience to the Commandments (*Enarr.* 118.11.6; *CCL* xl, pp. 1698–9; *PL* 37: 1530).

2–323/4–324/37 *a child born in . . . prisoun*: The *exemplum* of the child born in prison can be traced to St Gregory's *Dialogues*, where it is used to the same effect as in *D&P*; it begins: 'Ac si enim praegnans mulier mittatur in carcerem' (*PL* 77: 320). The tract, 'A Tretyse of Gostly Batayle' (*Yorkshire Writers*, ed. Horstman, 2: 434–5) borrowed the tale and much of the wording of the tale from *D&P*, lines 5–67 in cap. xiii. On the 'Tretyse' see 2–304–12/cap.v–vi above. LL4 also repeats the tale, in shorter form, in its sermon for the third Sunday after Easter (*c.*440 words in *D&P*, *c.*220 words in LL4). LL4, fo. 53vb.

2–325/57 *Luce ix* [*28–33*]: Luke 9: 33: '. . . bonum est nos hic esse, et faciamus tria tabernacula, unum tibi et unum Mosi et unum Heliae, nesciens quid diceret'. St Ambrose: 'Sed non capit humana condicio in hoc corruptibili, in hoc mortali corpore facere tabernaculum deo' ('In Luc', 7.18; *PL* 15: 1791–2).

2–325/62 [*Rom. 7: 24*]: GO: 'Infelix non in mente sed in carne, "Quis me liberat?" Liberabitur cum mortale hoc induet immortalitatem, ubi nulla concupiscentia permanebit' (4: 289).

2–325/69 [*Ex. 24: 18; 33: 20*]: 'Ingressusque Moses medium nebule ascendit in montem, et fuit ibi quadraginta diebus et quadraginta noctibus. . . . / Rursumque ait non poteris videre faciem mean, non enim videbit me homo et vivet'. The GO (Bede), on Exod. 24: 18, compares Moses' ascent of Mount Sinai to the preacher's study of divine law. 'Quadraginta' symbolises multiples of the Decalogue, which must be preached to all peoples in all four quarters of the globe (1: 162). For the gloss on Exod. 33: 20, see 2–102/ 97 above.

324   EXPLANATORY NOTES

2–325/75 [*1 Cor. 2: 9*]: '. . . quod oculus non vidit nec auris audivit nec in
cor hominis ascendit quae praeparavit Deus his qui diligunt illum'.

2–var./78–80 *To which . . . Amen*: Cf. the chapter endings in *Jacob's Well*,
sometimes abbreviated 'To whiche blysse, etc.', sometimes given in full (ed.
Brandeis, EETS, os 115, e.g., p. 76/3–6). Cf. *ME Sermons* (ed. Ross, EETS,
209, pp. 8, 12, 15, 19, etc.). The Latin form, from which this is derived, is
'Ad quod perducat'; see e.g. Bishop Brinton, 'Serm. 19' (c.1377), in
Sermons, ed. Devlin, 1: 79.

2–326/80 var. *Deo gracias . . . scribes of MS Y*: The colophon to MS Y offers
the only placed and dated manuscript copy of the text of *D&P*, see Plate of
Yale MS 228, fo. 199ʳ (misprinted fo. 210ᵛ) opposite p. 2–325 (see
'Manuscripts' above). The colophon is written in the hand of the second
scribe, who also made two additions to the body of the text, adding tropical
varieties to a list of trees (see 146/59 above) and commenting on the harsh
punishment of perjurors he had witnessed in the streets of Lisbon (see 256/
26note above). The fact that an English manuscript was being copied in
fifteenth-century Lisbon points to the close diplomatic, military and trading
relations between England and Portugal during the late-medieval period.
B. A. Shailor, who wrote the catalogue description of the Yale MS
(Beinecke Library), notes the business accounts on the reverse side of the
colophon page and speculates that the manuscript 'was owned by a cloth
dealer, possibly an English merchant trading with Portugal' (*Catalogue of
Medieval and Renaissance Manuscripts, Beinecke Library, Yale*, MRTS 34
(1984), 1: 321). Unfortunately, no trace of the church or monastery of
Sancta Katherina remains in present-day Lisbon.

I am grateful to Anne Hudson for the correct interpretation of the end of
the colophon. In the edition (I: 2), in the final note on p. 326, '5 4 lebir'
should read 'iiᵈ x lebis', translatable as either '204' or '210' leaves'. The 'x'
in the colophon—written with a loop—can be read either as an arabic '4' or
as a Roman 'x' (see further on the problematic foliation of MS Y in
'Manuscripts' above).

GLOSSARY

The words included in the glossary have been chosen from the text of *Dives and Pauper* on the grounds that (1) they are unrecorded elsewhere, that (2) they are used in obsolete senses, or (3) that they are spelled or inflected in ways that might make it unduly difficult for a reader to identify them with their modern forms. The bulk of the glossary falls into the latter two categories.

The glossary is alphabetized in the normal way except that 3 (yogh) and þ (thorn) are treated as separate letters in alphabetizing; words beginning with 3 and þ are listed after words beginning with G and T respectively. 3 and G, þ and TH, I and Y and U and V are otherwise treated as interchangeable. Letters enclosed in parentheses, indicating alternate spellings, are not taken into account in alphabetizing. Parenthesized letters are scribal variants that do not change the meanings, e.g. al(l)echyn. A swung dash is used to avoid repetition of the head word in an entry.

A few verbs having many senses and forms are given a divided listing. The separate senses are given first, with page/line references, and, after a paragraph indentation, the forms are given, again followed by page/line references.

Head words are followed by abbreviated and italicized grammatical information; abbreviations are listed below. Definitions are given after the grammatical information. My intention has been to supply definitions that are good translations in the contexts in which the words appear. When there are words closely associated with glossed words, normally prepositions, those that are the same in the text and in the translation are not repeated. If the associated words are not the same, the modern English equivalent is supplied in parentheses, e.g. *maystre of* may be translated as 'authority (over)', or *sekyn up* as 'search (out)'. Definitions are not repeated where they are identical for subsequent citations of forms of words except for changes of number or tense. In cases where a word is a translation of the Vulgate Latin and the Latin word sheds light on the Middle English word, I supply the Latin. I have tried to limit the number of alternative definitions given for a single form of a word; where two defining terms appear, they are to be considered equivalent to one another, the choice being left to the reader of the text. Explanatory material is enclosed in parentheses and follows the definitions.

Page/line references follow the definitions and are usually given in numerical order. Page/line references for a single form of a word are limited to three; additional references may be given for spelling variants. An asterisk above a page/line reference indicates that the editor has corrected or emended this instance of the word in the text; the correction or emendation will be found in the list of errata and corrigenda. Page/line references to the second volume of the text, *D&P* I:2, are preceded by '2-'. An *a* or *b* after a line number means that on that page two or more lines with the same number occur; *a* refers to the first, *b* to the second; (1) and (2) refer to the first and second occurrences of a word in a line of text.

ABBREVIATIONS

absol. absolute form of possessive pronoun
adj. adjective
adv. adverb
al. other manuscripts
aux. auxiliary
card. num. cardinal numeral
cf. compare

comp. comparative
conj. conjunction
demons. demonstrative
explet. expletive
fig. figurative sense
imp. imperative
inf. infinitive

interject. interjection
interr. interrogative
intr. intransitive
n. noun
ord. num. ordinal numeral
pass. passive
pa.t. past tense
pl. plural
possess. possessive
pp. past participle
ppl. adj. participial adjective
pr. present tense
pr.p. present participle
pron. pronoun
propr. n. proper noun
refl. reflexive
sg. singular

subj. subjunctive
tr. transitive
trs. translation
v. (following the head word) the infinitive
form of the transitive verb
var. entry is found in the variants to the
text of *D&P*; the sigla of the manuscripts in which the variant reading
appears are listed in *D&P* Vol. 1:1, xi–
xii.
vbl. n. verbal noun
MED: *Middle English Dictionary* (Ann
Arbor, Michigan)
OED: *Oxford English Dictionary*
VL: Vulgate Latin (*Biblia Sacra* ed.
Colunga & Turrado, 4th edn., Sala-
manca, 1965)

A

a(n see **han**
abach *adv.* back 2–245/19, 21.
abaschith *pr.3 sg.* terrifies 2–241/17.
abas(s)(c)hyd *ppl.adj.* abashed 99/72–73,
205/63 (cf. V.L. *tabescet*), 252/21, afraid
2–40/75, terrified 2–247/21.
abeyyst *pr.2 sg.* endure 2–102/84 (cf.
MED abeien).
abydyn *v. intr.* stay 85/48, delay 354/82,
2–45/61, remain 288/28, wait 2–278/44;
tr. await 132/31, 2–169/52, 2–241/23; ~
pr.1 pl. 53/8; **abydyth** *pr. 3 sg. intr.*
delays 2–45/58, 2–245/20, ~ *of* holds
back 2–244/102, ~ *of his pay* delays
repayment 2–200/59; **abydyn** *pr.3 pl.*
dwell 175/21; **abyde** *subj.3 sg.* should
delay 2–237/24; **abydyn** *subj.2 pl.*
should reach 358/51; **abide** *imp. sg.*
wait! 71/2; **abood** *pa.t.3.sg.* ~ *of* delayed
2–128/38.
abydyngge *ppl.adj.* in expectation of 53/5.
able *adj.* liable (to) 357/16, 17.
abood see **abydyn**
abouten, -tyn, abowtyn *adv.* around 94/
19, 121/59, 349/50, ~ *to perfourne* in the
course of doing 150/25.
abouteward *adv. al* ~ everywhere else
183/23–24.
abrod(e *adv.* widely apart 83/10, 84/41,
abroad 156/15, wide 2–20/32, 2–81/19,
20.
abstynyn *v. intr. refl.* refrain 117/93, 2–

38/31, 2–179/29; **abstinen** *pr.3 pl. refl.*
275/12.
abusyo(u)n *n.* abuse 36/viii, 321/42.
acardyng *adj.* suitable 2–91/11.
acceptyn *v.* approve 216/71; **acceptyd**
pa.t.3 sg. 216/68.
accioun *n.* cause for (legal) complaint 2–
76/37, 2–156/84, 86.
accusacionys *n.pl.* disclosures 227/5–6.
accusyth *pr.3 sg.* discloses 226/26.
achetyd *pp.* escheated (made to revert to
the king) 159/56, 2–281/5 (cf. chetyd).
achu *adj.* reluctant, afraid 160/14; cf.
MED s.v. **acheuen**; cp. **escheu**, adj.
acordyn *v. intr.* harmonize 2–29/67, agree
2–153/18, 2–235/21; **ac(c)ordiγ** *pr.3 sg.*
71/36, 334/60, 2–170/68; **a)cordyn**
pr.3 pl. 186/18, 2–80/23, 2–262/79;
acurs- see **curs-**
ady3tyn *v.* dress 289/11, *refl.* 2–91/17;
ady3t, adyth *pp.* prepared 2–246/33,
2–276/63, adorned 271/15, dressed 2–
90/4, 2–91/29.
admytte *v.* allow, permit 72/8.
adryd *ppl.adj.* afraid 269/18.
aduoket *n.* advocate, supporter 352/16,
legal advocate 2–41/24.
aeromancye *n.* aeromancy (divination by
air or weather) 164/65.
afer(id, af(f)erd *adj.* afraid 57/1, 77/1,
170/26, 219/35.
afer *adv. 3e ben maad snare to lokynge* ~
your neglect of clerical duty has made

you a snare to your parishioners (as *trs.* of V.L. *speculationi*; see Notes) 2–20/32.

afesyn *v.* daunt, scare off 2–44/23 (cf. **fesyng**).

aforn *adv.* previously, earlier 80/56, 123/47, 219/59, beforehand 117/12.

af(f)orn *prep.* in front of, in the presence of 2/3, 85/54, 55, 2–8/28, at the head of 91/29, ahead of 2–67/15.

after *prep.* according to 151/50, 2–53/14.

ageynsey *subj.pr.3 sg.* should oppose 2–151/22.

aȝen(y)(s, aȝenst, aȝenus, ageyn, ayen *prep.* at var./68, 69/71, contrary to 81/12, against 49/56, 224/21, before 224/16, 310/3, 2–34/31, in anticipation of 224/16.

aȝen *adv.* see **ledyn**

agrechyn *v.* increase 344/47; **agrechith** *pr.3 sg.* 220/84, 226/26; **agrechyn** *pr.3 pl.* 2–127/21.

agrechynge *vbl.n.* augmenting 227/6.

agreuyth *pr.3 sg.* offends 252/13, 2–53/21; **agreuyn** *pr.3 pl.* 158/22, 214/14; **agreuyd** *pp.* 223/35, injured 2–296/51.

ayenward, aȝen- *adv.* conversely, vice versa 30/lii, 2–122/48–49ᵛᵃr.

aketone *n.* stuffed jacket worn under coat of mail 2–310/116.

aknowyn, aknow(e *adj. be(n/was/is ~* confess 198/28, make known, disclose 251/34, 2–234/11, acknowledge 2–108/45, 2–204/19.

al *adv. or adj. (as intensifier) ~ in gyle* guilefully 61/25, *~ forbled* blood-covered 2–99/17, *~ in erde* altogether worldly 201/17, *~ forbetyn* severely beaten, 238/28, *~ aloud* in a loud voice 2–257/45.

aldris *possess. pron.* of all, everyone's 319/2, 2–324/33.

al(l)echyn *v.* (1) allege 342/63, cite 2–134/31, 2–171/89; **al(l)eg(g)ist** *pr.2 sg.* cite 60/28, 78/38, 232/81; **alechyth** *pr.3 sg.* 2–169/38, 39; **aleggen** *pr.2 pl.* 73/26; **alechyn** *pr.3 pl.* 2–170/67, claim 2–178/24; **alechynge** *pr.p.* claiming 317/15; **alechid** *pa.t.3 sg.* alleged 319/63; **alleggide** *pa.t.2 pl.* cited 72/20;

alechith *pr.3 sg.* (v.2) alleviates 300/70.

alethyn *v.* decrease 2–152/50.

algatis *adv.* nonetheless, notwithstanding 187/28.

al-holde *n.* a pagan spirit or goblin associated with All Hallows eve 157/7.

alya(u)nce *n.* relatives by marriage 2–15/56, 2–236/57, 2–256/33.

alienyd *pp.* alienated, unlawfully removed 317/2.

Almanye *propr. n.* Germany 239/22.

ambrye *n.* almonry (residence of almoner) 2–184/3.

amende, -dyn *v.* repair 63/25, 123/56, change 314/33, *refl.* reform 67/53, 85/46, 123/50; **amendith** *pr.3 sg.* improves 2–108/35; *refl.* reform 2–26/62, 63; **amende** *subj.pr.3 sg.* should repair 74/8, should recover 248/52; **ament** *imp. sg.refl.* reform! 241/64, 2–267/45; **amendyddyn** *pa.t.3 pl. refl.* reformed 122/29; **amendit(h** *pp.* improved 309/27, 2–149/58, benefitted 2–150/92, 2–154/27, 30;

amendement *n.* (moral) reform 122/32.

amendynge* *n.* repair 190/18.

amis see **omys**

amyte *n.* amice (white vestment). See notes 2–228/32, 2–229/62.

amountyn *v. intr.* signify 135/6.

and *conj.* if 52/37.

anemys(t, anentis *prep.* (preceded by *as*) regarding, in respect to 55/33, 76/33, 227/6; (without *as*) 286/24, 315/2, 2–269/24, 26.

anggwysshe *imp.sg.* distress! 52/24.

anguych, -wich *n.* distress 2–136/35, 2–265/70.

anyntechyd *pa.t.3 sg. refl.* abased, lowered 2–100/39, 2–301/50 (cf. V.L. *semetipsum exinanivit*; see Notes, 2–100/43).

anker(y)s, ancrys *n.pl.* hermits, anchorites 41/xiii, 2–92/53, 56, 2–93/72, 78.

annexit *ppl.adj.* connected 2–173/12; trs. from Lat. *annexum*, see Notes.

anow(e *adj.* enough 2–281/10, 2–282/35, 2–320/49 (cf. **inowȝ**).

anowe *adv.* enough 2–208/42 (cf. **inow**).

antiphene *n.* antiphon (responsive singing in Church service) 89/40.

an(n)uel *n.* a mass said once a year or on the anniversary of a death 45/xx, 2–184/23, 2–188/63, money for annual mass 2–187/38.

an(n)uel(l)er(e *n.* priest who celebrates anniversary masses for the dead 45/xx, 2–185/54; **anuelerys** *pl.* 2–179/54.

apeyryn v. damage 2–224/57; **apeyrith** pr.3 sg. tr. impairs 2–108/35; **apeyre** subj.3 sg. intr. should be impaired 2–200/2; **apeyryd** pp. harmed 2–154/31.

apel n. accusation (legal) 255/92, 95.

apelyd pa.t.3 sg. accused (legally) 255/86.

Aperyl propr. n. April 148/23.

ap(p)eryn v. intr. appear 170/36, 2–118/11, 2–119/29; **apperyth** pr.3 sg. 28/xxix; **apperyn** pr.3 pl. 28/xxix, 147/15; **apere** subj.2 sg. should appear 2–243/82; **ap(p)erid** pa.t.3 sg. 132/14, 147/17, 238/28; **apperyddyn** pa.t.3 pl. 2–325/50.

aperseyuyn pr.3 pl. perceive 242/35.

apert adj. open 2–178/5, in ~ openly 212/34.

apert adv. openly 169/2.

applyyd ppl. adj. applicable 10/47, 265/69, 299/24.

appose v. accost 151/47.

aproprychyn v. assign 2–191/52; **ap(p)ropirchyd** pp. 320/27, 31, 34, 2–136/49, 52.

aray n. clothing 94/28, 260/32, 2–90/2, decoration 100/20, aray 285/23, 2–19/19.

arayyd ppl. adj. adorned 271/15, armed 349/42.

arayyn v. decorate, furbish 191/42, arm 288/34, refl. dress 2–91/23.

arblast n. crossbow 2–44/28.

areynyng vbl.n. arraigning 2–193/32.

ares-, arys- see **rys-**

arestyn v. stop 2–241/22.

arettyd pp. attributed 54/51, 130/76, 2–173/41, directed 82/30, credited 130/73.

arlys n.pl. earls 317/18, 320/15.

arn see **ben**

arnyst n. in ~ in earnest 241/8.

aroutyn v. rebuke 2–136/43.

artyn v. compell, constrain 172/17, 2–192/87; ~ hym of restrain from 2–192/95; **artyd** pp. controlled 121/4, 122/24, 182/9, limited 2–192/93.

arwe n. arrow 2–246/26; -**wys** pl. 2–246/34.

as conj. ~ for in furtherance of 157/7, ~ þis tyme as of this time 2–129/91 (see Notes).

asay n. trial 344/52.

asay(ȝ)yn v. try, try it out 129/56, 2–278/

10, 12; **asayyth** pr.3 sg. tests 178/14; **asayȝit** imp. pl. 61/19; **assayyd** pp. sampled 2–324/43 (cf. **vnasayd**).

asayȝyngge vbl.n. testing 61/8.

aschyn n.pl. ashes 2–277/25, 2–315/15.

ashlandryd, aslaundryt pp. offended (by), scandalized (by) 2–141/18, 2–214/48.

ask- see **ax-**

askyngys n.pl. prayers 173/24.

asolyyn see **assouleyn**

asondre adv. apart 197/58.

aspyen pr.3 pl. ~ after spy out 151/42.

assent n. of theuys ~ in collusion with thieves 150/34, of the ~ to a party to 150/30.

assentant adj. in assent 2–104/14.

assessour n. assessor (legal official, adviser to a judge in matters of law) 2–41/24; **assessouris** pl. 2–239/42.

assyth n. penance, atonement 246/43, 255/105.

assoylyyng vbl.n. releasing 229/10.

assouleyn, asolyyn v. absolve 14/30, 245/13, 2–24/16; **assoylyd, asolyyd** pp. 2–132/21, 2–182/72.

astat(e n. circumstances 29/xl, high station 37/xxii, station in life 2–91/28, sauyng her ~ taking their position into account 248/30 (cf. **stat**).

astrolabye n. astrolabe (model of the Ptolemaic universe) 159/61.

astronomye n. astrology, astronomy (in invidious sense) 3/50, 137/55.

astronomyen n. astrologer, astronomer (in invidious sense) 139/4; **astronomyenys, -es, -myeres** pl. 3/43, 28/xxx, 150/32.

atastyn v. taste 2–22/37.

at prep. at the level of 51/3, present at 154/34, by prompting of 160/8.

ateyntyn v. accuse a witness of giving false evidence 2–235/30 (cf. **teynt**).

atyr(e n. dress, attire 16/45, 2–91/10, 30 (cf. **tyr**).

atret adv. slowly, deliberately 200/33, 34 (cf. **trete**).

atteyntyng vbl. n. attainting (accusing a witness of giving false evidence) 47/xi (cf. **teynt**).

attestacyoun n. testimony 32/vii.

aturne n. per ~ by deputy 2–241/15;

attornes, atturnes *pl.* attorneys 2–269/
19, 2–277/38, 2–278/2.

atwoxsyn, -wyxin, -wexsyn, -wexe,
-wuxsyn, atwyn *prep.* between 15/22,
111/24, 26, 187/29, 309/15, 314/25, 2–
152/56.

avalyyn *v.* ~ *hem to* gain for them 174/63.

auanceys *n. pl.* those who have been
installed in office by a patron 353/59.

auansement *n. in* ~ *of* in hope
of promoting 2–180/1, promotion 2–
181/5.

auansynge *vbl.n.* promotion 2–180/3.

auarous *adj.* avaricious 166/13.

avauncyn *v.* promote to (ecclesiastical)
office 352/43; **auaunsyd** *pp.* promoted
352/26, 353/61, 2–176/80.

auauntement *n.* boasting, self-glorifica-
tion 2–220/32, 33.

auauntere *n.* boaster (about) 2–221/41.

aube *n.* alb (vestment of white cloth), see
Notes 2–228/36, 2–229/63.

Aue *n.* Ave (devotional prayer to the
Virgin Mary) 158/17, 162/13; **Aueis**
pl. 240/52.

auenture *n.* accident, chance event 143/
45, 167/15; **auentur(ys** *pl. here* ~ what
will happen to them 140/12, events 143/
53, 281/19.

auere *n.* property, possessions 2–135/21.

aught- see au(gh)t-

au3t see owe

auysely *adv.* wisely, judiciously 258/8.

avisement *n.* deliberation, counsel 7/4,
31/iii, 223/36; *be* ~ advisedly 2–213/15.

auysyn *v. refl.* consider prudently 250/4,
2–226/53; **auyse** *imp.pl.* warn 291/33;
auysedyn *pa.t.3 pl. refl.* considered 261/
51; **avysyd** *pp.* has considered the matter
2–238/50, *refl.* 250/2.

aumener *n.* almoner (cleric in charge of
alms giving) 319/61.

auntyr *n.* danger 2–43/78.

avohwyn *v.* avow, admit 2–7/5; **avoh-
wyd, avouhyd** *pp.* vowed 225/60, 2–
58/9 (cf. **vouh-, vow**).

auoydyd *pp.* refuted, turned aside 109/3.

auoydyn, auoyde *v.* escape 126/46, do
away with 205/17.

avouh see vouh

auout(e)rye, auowt(e)rye *n.* adultery 14/
57, 40/xxiii, 68/19, 256/4, 2–53/27;
auouterys *pl.* 2–210/110.

auowtress *n.* adultress 41/ix.

au(gh)te(e)r(e *n.* altar 39/xvii, 86/25,
111/11, 319/72, altar (as sanctuary) 2–
33/50.

awondred *adj.* surprised 1/7, astonished
(by) 2–259/23.

axe *v.* ask 80/54, 56; **axist** *pr.2 sg.* 80/61,
62; **axiþ, asky3t** *pr.3 sg.* 80/62, requires
58/52, 131/21; **axen** *pr.1 pl.* ask 80/58;
axide *pa.t.3 sg.* 75/19.

B

baas *n.pl.* bases (of pillars) 2–89/33.

bac *adj.* ~ *hous* bake-house 2–278/7.

bacbyte *pr.3 sg.* slander 2–132/28; **bac-
bytedyn** *pa.t.3 pl.* spoke spitefully 2–
133/50.

bacbyter *n.* slanderer, defamer 2–131/6;
-erys, -eres *pl.* 46/vi, 2–131/9, 2–132/
18.

bacbytynge *vbl.n.* defaming, slandering 2–
132/24.

backys *n.pl.* bats 279/46.

baddith *imp. pl.* misbehave (perh. a nonce
word) 298/60.

bale *n. bote of euery* ~ remedy for every ill
300/69; **balys** *pl.* troubles 2–64/67, 2–
262/91.

ba(y)l(l)y(e *n.* bailiff 18/32, 43/xi, 2–157/
43; stewardship 2–137/68; **balyys
bailiffs** *pl.* 2–137/69, 2–159/96.

banchid *pp.* banished 251/45–6.

banchynge *vbl.n.* banishment 1/2b, 2–1/
12.

bannyn *v.* curse 305/30; ~ *pr.3 pl.* 325/
40; **bannyd** *pa.t.3 sg.* 306/73.

bannyng(e *vbl. n.* cursing 31/ii, 223/19.

bar- see ber-

baranye *adj.* barren 2–315/14, 2–321/24.

bara[yn]hed *n.* barrenness 138/58.

baratour *n.* quarrelsome person 127/63;
-tourys *pl.* 2–287/13–14.

baratous *adj.* quarrelsome 244/25 *var.*
rdtbyl.

bare *adv.* barely, at minimum 73/39; ~
adj. naked 305/40.

baret *n.* fighting, strife 2–287/14.

barlech *n.* barley 2–4/45.

barnag see bernak

bas(s)(e)net *n.* basinet (helmet with visor)
24/15 *var.* H, 2–229/62, 2–308/37.

batterys *n.pl.* injurers (?) 2–225/10 (perh.

aphetic form of MED **debatour**; cf. line 10 *var.*: *bachyteris* RDH).

baudekyn *n.* brocade (silk cloth woven with gold or silver thread) 100/37.

baume *n.* balm 2–181/29.

baus(e)yn *n.* badger 42/xiv, 2–98/76; **bauseynis** *possess.sg.*; ~ *pl.* 94/30 (see Notes).

baxtere *n.* baker 63/23; **baxteris** *pl.* 2–198/23.

be *prep.* by 1/2a, 3/48, 3/50; through 7/1, 129/52; according to 132/3, 140/31, 144/20; in regard to 199/10, 241/1; with 316/49, 50, 352/30; beside 144/8; at (the time of) 157/6; ~ *wey(e of kende* naturally 11/13, 144/17, 167/6; ~ *his liif* in his lifetime 80/40; ~ *bryge* in quarrelling 354/84; ~ *olde tyme* in days of old 216/69.

be *v.* see **ben**

becomyn *pp. wher þeı se is* ~ where the sea has gone 2–247/18, *wher ben þey* ~ where have they gone 2–272/60.

bedes see **byddyng(e**

befalle *v.* happen 125/13.

begylyn *v.* cheat 185/9, 17, 219/40, 235/5, deceive 31/lxii, 241/6; **begyle** *subj.3 sg.* should deceive 2–154/38; **begylid** *pp.* beguiled 186/20.

begylyng *vbl.n.* deceiving 43/x.

begon *pp.* decked, adorned 321/44.

beȝoundyn *prep.* across 2–153/5.

behaluyd *pa.t.3 sg.* wrapped 350/78.

behest, byhe(e)ste *n.* promise, vow 12/62, 38/xxvi, 123/57, word, contract 48/14, *lond of* ~ Canaan (the promised land) 260/18, 2–133/55; **behestes** *pl.* promises 31/iii, 153/16, 2–9/66.

behyȝte *pa.t.3 sg.* promised 2–175/70; **behyȝt** *pp.* 49/75 (cf. **hotyn**).

behouely *adj.* appropriate 351/107 (cf. **bihofful**).

beho(o)uy(þ)t(h, bihoueþ *pr.3 sg.* needs 58/55–56, 74/26, behooves one 338/13, 2–115/99–100.

beyȝȝyn see **byyn**

beyng(g)(e *vbl.n.* being, life 95/7, 355/20, 21, 22.

belappyd *pp.* covered, enfolded 350/78 *var. al.*

belaunce *n.* scales 2–250/58.

beldamys *n.pl.* grandmothers 2–108/27.

belokyn *pp.* contained 298/11 (cf. MED **bilouken**).

ben, been, be *v. intr.* be 6/134, 52/31, 148/35, *tr.* make 251/34, 255/93; **am** *pr.1 sg. intr.* am 53/12; **art** *pr.2 sg.* art 53/14, 35; **is** *pr.3 sg.* is 18/43, 2–187/50; **be(e)n, arn** *pr.1 pl.* are 53/7, 60/59, 61, 80/64, 260/30; **ben** *pr.2 pl.* are 296/15, 358/48; **be(e)n, ar(n** *pr.3 pl.* are 66/35, 149/46, 294/46, 328/34; **be** *pr. subj. 1, 2, 3 sg.* may be 59/4, 76/52, 150/21, 2–56/49; ~ *pr. subj. 3 pl.* may be 143/58; **be(th** *imp. sg.* be 52/21, 56/60; **be(e)th** *imp.pl.* be 41/viii, 106/56, 296/13, 298/60; **was** *pa.t.3 sg.* was 16/28, 54/47, 255/95; **wer(e, weryn, wer(e)n** *pa.t.3 pl.* were 41/viii, 170/51, 251/38; **wer(e, wher** *pa.t.subj.3 sg.* if there were 100/34, was 119/11, 151/45, were 132/8, 251/34; **would be** 206/28; **wer(e)n, weryn** *pa.t.subj.3 pl.* were 74/2, 124/85, 211/3; BE(N *pp.* been 2–159/87, 88.

benaylyd *pp.* nailed 2–243/65.

benefyce, -FYS *n.* benefice (an ecclesiastical living) 2–164/132, 2–182/71; **-fycis** *pl.* 44/xii, 2–162/97, 100, benefactions 265/55, 274/38, 2–119/7.

benethyn *adv.* below 119/4, 120/33.

benygnyte *propr.n.* Ȝoure ~ Your benignity (as title of respect) 71/7.

bequoþin *pp.* bequeathed 345/10.

bere, beryn *v.* bear 46/ix, 159/40, 2–218/21, carry 2–266/13; **berist** *pr.2 sg.* 2–30/15; **berith, -yȝt** *pr.3 sg.* holds 92/22, carries 335/74, 2–230/6, bears 2–266/15; **beryn** *pr.1 pl.* 2–221/16; ~ *pr.3 pl.* carry 171/8, 348/23, bear 2–221/54, wear 2–164/158, *fig.* 2–33/64; **bere** *subj.2, 3 sg.* should bear 66/32, should carry 2–42/71; **beryng(e** *pr.p.* bearing 47/xii, 2–220/23; **bar** *pa.t.3 sg.* carried 193/13, 2–259/8, bore (child) 306/70, 329/25, ~ *heuy of* disapproved 193/5, took hard 2–94/116, 2–99/9; **boryn** *pa.t.3 pl.* carried 350/94, 2–189/3; **born** *pp.* borne 128/23, 209/32, 257/37, 2–117/47, carried 218/19.

beryelys *n.pl.* burials 112/55 (cf. **byryyn**).

beryyd see **byry-**

beryn *pr.3 pl.* bare (by shaving) 2–164/158.

berynge *vbl.n.* carrying 2–181/35, behaviour, conduct 324/20, 325/33.

bernak, bernac, barnag *n.* barnacle goose 23/13–14 *var.* H, 49/61, 2–306/2.

berne *n.* barn 2–314/4, 2–317/7; bernys *pl.* 2–275/57.

beschadewith *pr.3 sg.* shades 315/56.

besegyd, besechyd, besechit *pp.* besieged 348/33, 2–189/17, 2–207/18.

beseyn *pp.* mistreated, abused 240/57.

besemyth *pr.3 sg.* befits 2–77/23.

besettyn *pr.3 pl.* decorate 159/42.

besy- see bisi-

besy, bisi *adj.* anxious, concerned 52/39, 79/9, 337/30, active 2–162/99.

besydyn *adv.* there ~ nearby 153/12 (cf. V.L. *non longe ab illis*).

besyly(che, bysiliche, -selyche *adv.* actively, diligently 276/11, *var.*/64, 2–49/14, 2–299/9.

besynesse *n.* eagerness 68/45, activity 69/50, business 2–129/84, *don his* ~ do his utmost 36/xi, 327/7, 2–50/24, 2–104/8.

besottyd *ppl. adj.* infatuated 186/21, 2–85/12.

besottyn *v.* confuse 2–315/21.

bespadlyd, bespatelyd *pp.* (condition of being) spat upon 2–101/67, 2–243/65.

b(e)st(e *n.* beast (collectively) 115/54, 120/43, an animal 127/61, domesticated animal 278/1, 10; bestys *pl.* animals 98/43, 46, domestic animals 278/9, 16.

bestayle *n.* domestic animals 2–166/36, 2–167/51.

bestongyn *pp.* pierced 2–243/66.

betakyn *pr.3 pl.* entrust 310/22, entrust to 2–155/79; bet(o)ok(e, betooc *pa.t.3 sg.* 92/12, 311/40, 2–23/48; betake *subj.3 sg.* should entrust with 2–147/6, should entrust 2–201/14; betakyn, bytaken *pp.* entrusted 18/30, 2–71/11, entrusted to 43/x, 321/39, conferred upon 268/8, 2–38/15.

betymys, betyme *adv.* early 2–153/8, in good time 2–238/12.

beþynke, -kyn *v. refl.* take careful thought 263/5, 274/35; beþink *imp. sg. refl.* 273/17; beou(3)te *pa.t.3 sg. refl.* 277/21, plotted 236/19.

betokenyn *v. intr.* symbolise 265/56, 59; betokenyth, -keny3t *pr.3 sg.* 15/5, 93/1, 99/12, portends 147/7; betok(e)nyn *pr.3 pl.* signify, symbolise 2/8, 9, 94/20, 179/43, portend 147/5–6; betokenede

pa.t.3 sg. 147/20; betoknyde *pa.t.3 pl.* 176/32 (cf. token-).

betrachyn, -trayhyn *v.* betray 2–46/10, 16, 2–221/61; betraythyd *pa.t.3 sg.* 2–259/6.

bettyl *n.* club, mallet 312/75, 313/78.

bewreyyn *v.* betray 2–205/40.

byd(d)(yth, -dyt3, byt *pr.3 sg.* enjoins 195/1, commands 221/3, 299/28, 300/48, 2–96/24–25; byddyn *pr.3 pl.* request 213/3; bydde *subj.3 sg.* should request 217/90, 345/12, command 2–45/54, 55; bad(de *pa.t.3 sg.* 81/18, 123/35, 217/96; bedyn, bad- *pa.t.3 pl.* 2–11/36, 2–228/35; bod(d)yn, boden *pp.* enjoined 30/lii, 35/xvii, 303/62, 2–47/30.

byddyng(e *vbl.n.* order 35/xvii, 338/4, *bedys* ~ reciting prayers 162/3, 170/45, 204/45.

byere, beyer *n.* buyer 217/2, 2–153/16.

biforn, be- *prep.* before 21/38 *var.* DT, 123/47, 59 *var.* byl (cf. aforn).

bigge see byyn

byheeste see behest

bihofful *adj.* needful 71/35 (cf. behouely).

by(h)yn, beyen, bey3yn, bigge *v.* buy 54/13, 75/12, 2–154/45, ransom 352/33, redeem 2–243/67; byyth *pr.3 sg.* buys 2–153/20, 2–171/7, 2–177/34; byyn *pr.3 pl.* 2–174/34; bye *subj.3 sg.* should buy 2–148/28, 2–149/71; beye *imp.sg.* buy! 2–177/30; bou3te *pa.t.1 sg.* redeemed 2–243/69; ~, bou(h)te, boughte *pa.t.3 sg.* 51/5, 189/2, 329/5, bought 2–155/69; boww3t *pp.* 43/viii.

byynge, bigging *vbl.n.* buying 80/60, 2–149/77, 2–177/33.

billyth *pr.3 sg.* pecks (out, with beak) 309/29, *var.*/72, 2–268/8.

byndyn *v.* control 156/30, *refl.* commit 245/43, 247/6; bynt *pr.3 sg.* enslaves 156/8, binds 245/45, 4, 246/22; bynden, -dyn *pr.3 pl.* control 156/7, 26, *refl.* commit 2–279/26; boundyn *pa.t.3 pl. refl.* committed 245/7, *tr.* bound 2–17/51 (cf. bo(u)ndyn).

byr *n.* violent emotion, passion 2–67/16.

byrdene *n.* burden 2–95/14.

byryyn *v.* bury 2–181/36; berydyst *pa.t.2 sg.* 348/28, 29; byryyd, beryid *pp.* 112/55, 164/69, 2–181/37.

byryyng, beryyng(e *vbl.n.* burial 19/70,

31/lxiii, 213/2, 3; **bery3ynggys** *pl.* 112/ 52, 213/5 (cf. **beryelys**).

birþuns *n.pl.* burdens 76/40.

bisie *v. refl.* strive 71/4, 72/15; **besyyst** *pr.2 sg. refl.* busy 2–261/52; **besy** *imp.sg. refl.* strive 2–260/25 (cf. **besy**).

byt *n. to han þe bettir* ~ to have better grazing 2–268/5.

bytaken see **betakyn**

blak, blac, bleyk *adj.* black 142/26, 168/ 33, 238/28.

blasyngge *pr.p.* emblazoning, rendering illustrious 98/52.

bledyng *vbl.n.* bleeding 309/23 (cf. **blod-**).

blemchynge *vbl.n.* blemishing 2–304/24.

blenchin *pr.3 pl.* blink var./71.

blenchyng(e *vbl.n.* blinking var./67, 69.

blend(ith, blent *ppl. adj.* blinded 158/33, 165/84, 188/4, 220/82, 83.

blendyn *v.* blind, deceive 168/9; **blen-dith, blynd-** *pr.3 sg.* 168/15, 2–8/38; **blendyn** *pr.3 pl.* 185/17, 2–10/72; **blentyn** *pa.t. subj. 3 pl.* had blinded 2–11/23.

bletlyche *adv.* gladly, cheerfully 224/27.

blew, blo *adj.* blue 142/15, 26, 238/29, 2–223/39.

blyndhed *n.* blindness 2–247/11, 2–315/21.

blys(s)ful(le *adj.* blessed 2/17a, 63/3, 193/3, 271/24.

blisse *n.* happiness 77/28, 2–318/41, *heuene* ~ beatitude 55/49, *to þe same* ~ with the same joy 67/49.

blissyd *ppl.adj.* blessed (by priest) 113/64.

blyssyn *v.* bless 2–313/24; **blissyd** *pa.t.3 sg.* 93/39; ~ *pp.* 2–317/7, 8.

blo see **blew**

blo(o)d(e *n.* blood 84/28, 264/51, 276/46.

blody *adj.* bloody 2–101/55.

blont *adj.* blunt 2–231/23, *gryndyn* ~ *& pleyn* grind without an edge and even 120/55, 56.

blosmys *n.pl.* blossoms 145/55.

bobetyd *pa.t.3 pl.* cuffed, struck with fists 2–228/35.

bocheris *n.pl.* butchers 289/10.

bokeler *n.* buckler, small shield 2–40/4.

bole *n.* bull 2–119/29.

bolle *n.* bowl, vessel 2–278/13, 2–279/16.

bolt *n. folis* ~ *is soone yschott* a fool shoots too soon 71/1–2.

bo(o)n *n.* bone 38/vii, 2–65/6; **bonys, -es** *pl.* 38/vii, 240/45.

bo(u)ndache *n.* bondage (as state of obligation) 2–125/55, 2–126/73.

bonde *n. chalangyn men for* ~ pledge to repay a debt using land as security 2–254/50.

bonde *adj.* in condition of servitude 53/14, 65/49, 333/21.

bo(u)ndyn, bownden *ppl.adj.* obligated 15/23, 44/xii, 73/10, enslaved 162/60, constrained 65/49, 67/14, 156/13, in bonds 289/54 (cf. **byndyn**).

bone *n.* boon 174/67, 224/28, 32.

bonere *adj.* kind, gentle 2–251/25.

boodys see **boþis**

boot *pa.t.3 sg.* bit 2–146/40.

bord *n.* (dining) table 312/58, altar table 2–181/31, 2–195/11, 2–239/36.

bordful see **bourd-**

bordyngys *n.pl.* burdens 76/40 *note*.

bor(o)w, borough *n.* the circle of light around a candle flame 142/14 (see Notes).

borw(e, borw3 *n.* person who acts as surety for another's debt 236/15, 32, 2–199/41, 42, 43.

borwere *n.* borrower 2–199/41; **borwerys, -es** *pl.* 22/15, 48/11.

borwyn *v.* borrow 2–199/45; **borwith** *pr.3 sg.* 2–199/40, 2–205/52; **borweyn** *pr.3 pl.* 2–268/16; **borwe** *subj.3 sg.* should borrow 2–205/49, 50, 51; **borwyd** *pp.* 2–147/1, 2–148/34.

borwyng *vbl.n.* borrowing 17/14.

bost *n.* bombast 187/25.

bote *n.* remedy 300/69, deliverance 2–211/2, *soule* ~ salvation 53/17.

boþis, boodys *n.pl.* booths 218/17, 2–193/10.

bound- see **bond-**

boundys *n.pl.* (1) bonds, fetters 2–103/107, 2–228/38, 2–160/18.

boundys *n.pl.* (2) boundaries (cf. V.L. *terminos*) 2–255/61.

bourde *n.* jest 46/ii, 2–219/6.

bourdeful, bord- *adj.* joking, unserious 2–213/9, 2–214/39, 41, 46.

bourys *n.pl.* bowers, small apartments 2–247/26.

bowyn *pr.3 pl.* turn (*fig.*) 2–313/18 (cf. V.L. *declinant a*); **bowe** *imp.sg.* bend, train 325/53, 2–323/27 (cf. V.L.

inclina); **bowedyn** *pa.t.3 pl.* turned 331/31; **bowyd** *pp.* bent 84/40, 325/56, 57, pressed 2–20/37.

bowys, -wis *n.pl.* boughs, branches 271/16, 296/4, 307/24.

boxsedyn *pa.t.3 pl.* beat with fists 2–228/35.

brasene *adj.* brazen, made of brass 2–315/13.

brede *n.* breadth 131/8, 2–207/24, 2–264/59.

bredskepe *n.* bread basket 2–249/40.

breyd *n. as for a* ~ once in a while 291/13, 21.

brekerys *n.pl.* breakers (of law) 24/19.

brekyn *v.* break 2–128/54, fail to observe 9/10, put an end to 166/2; **brekyst** *pr.2 sg.* break 2–28/47; **brekyt(h** *3 sg.* severs 41/vii, breaks 204/47; **breke** *2 pl.* disobey 321/55; **brekyn** *pr.3 pl.* break 2–15/43; **breke** *subj.3 sg.* should break 250/91, 2–29/70; **brak, brac** *pa.t.3 sg.* broke (to pieces) 236/38, 312/74, 350/92, broke 2–25/53, disobeyed 2–127/24; **brokyn** *pp.* broken 237/40.

brekyng(e, brakynge *vbl. n.* breaking (in sense of disobeying) 33/xv, 259/1, 356/16, 2–124/20.

breme *adj.* raging, fierce 68/41, 2–298/25.

brennyn, brenne *v.* burn 107/15, 108/35, 277/27, 2–279/18, (*fig.*) 234/18, 2–246/35; **brenne** *pr.1 sg.* am burning (to death) 2–279/21; **brenne** *subj.3 sg.* should burn 2–190/24; **brennyng** *pr.p.* 349/42, 2–77/31; **brenne** *imp.sg.* burn! 2–279/22(1); **brente** *pa.t.3 sg.* burnt 2–279/23; **brent, brend** *pp.* 82/37, 159/56, (*fig.*) 2–246/35.

brennyng(g)(e *ppl. adj.* burning 147/10, 286/37, 2–77/31, 2–246/34.

brennyng *ppl. adv.* ~ *hoot* burning hot 2–278/8.

brenston(e *n.* brimstone 2–77/31, 2–258/20.

brestyn *v. intr.* burst (into) 2–247/28; **brast** *pa.t.3 sg.* burst 83/7, 93/40, 2–259/7; **brostyn** *pa.t.3 pl.* broke, shattered 2–52/43.

brydale *n.* wedding 2–285/22.

bryd *n.* bird 49/60, (collectively) 120/44; **bryd(d)ys** *pl.* 25/ii, 63/11, baby birds, chicks 308/4, 309/6 et seq..

bryge *n.* strife 354/84; **brygis** *pl.* quarrels 2–262/88.

brygour *n.* contentious person, wrangler 2–319/23.

brymbelys *n.pl.* brambles 2–124/29, 2–268/5, 6.

bryngyn *v.* bring (forth) 2–124/29; **brou(3)t(e** *pa.t.3 sg.* brought 240/48, 2–85/11, brought back 348/26; **brow3-tyn** *pa.t.1 pl.* carried 260/37; **broughtyn** *pa.t.3 pl.* brought 145/46; **brou(3)t, browth** *pp.* 24/26–7 *note*, 308/4, 2–195/73; ~ *in* habituated to 226/22.

brocke *n.* badger or beaver 94/32–4 *var.* BYL.

brockyn *pr.3 pl.* bargain, haggle 2–186/10.

brod *n.* brood 2–98/84.

broydyn *pp.* reproached 2–63/53.

broydyng *vbl.n.* braiding (of hair) 2–91/18.

brokys *n.pl.* brooks 306/64, 65.

brondys *n.pl.* firebrands (*fig.*) 277/26, 2–302/83, 84, 90.

brosyn *v.* bruise 210/18; **brosyd** *pa.t.3 sg.* injured 2–34/22.

brostyn *ppl.adj.* burst 260/36 (cf. **brest-**).

brosure *n.* injury 2–83/94.

broustere *n.* brewer 63/24; **brewsteris** *pl.* 151/41.

bunchyn *pr.1 pl.* beat, strike with hands 105/19; ~ *pr.3 pl.* 86/5.

bunchyngge *vbl.n.* beating, striking 104/7.

buschel *n.* vessel used as a bushel measure 312/61, 64, 67.

buschements *n.pl.* ambushes 2–307/31.

buschop *n.* bishop 21/21, 195/21; **bucho-pys** *possess.sg.* 21/23; **buschopys** *pl.* 209/22.

buschopryche *n.* bishopric 2–163/108, 110.

buskys *n.pl.* bushes, low shrubs 2–268/5.

bux(s)um *adj.* obedient lo2/12, 305/28, 357/6.

buxumnesse *n.* humble obedience, meekness 358/44.

C

caas see **cas**

cachith *pr.3 sg.* drives 309/29, var./72, 2–266/26, compels 2–26/3; **cac(c)hyn** *pr.3 pl.* 145/35, 2–80/1, drive 156/21, 23;

cache *pr.subj.3 sg.* may compel 2–316/
70; **keche(e, kechyd** *pa.t.3 sg.* drove 7/
147, 307/17, 2–297/63; **keche** *pa.t.
subj.3 sg.* may have compelled 247/5*,
2–171/100; **cachyd, -chith, c(h)achid**
pp. driven 4/69, 218/30, 2–105/28,
compelled 170/34, 278/14, 2–41/29.

cayser *n.* emperor 2–241/9.

caitif *n.* poor man, wretch 70/19, 72/8a
(see Notes).

calculyn *pr.3 pl.* calculate (astrologically)
138/70 (cf. **cast**).

calfryn *n.pl.* calves 2–201/19.

camalion, camelyon *n.* chameleon 21/
15, 46/vi, 2–223/37, 47.

can, kan see **conn-**

canoun *adj. lawe* ~ canon law (ecclesiastical law) 28/xxxiv.

carectys *n.pl.* written letters or words
158/17.

carful *adj.* anxious 300/70.

cariage *n.* carting (of materials) 291/12,
20; **cariagis** *pl.* 291/17.

carpe *v. intr.* quibble, argue 72/8.

carteweye *n. comyn as þe* ~ common as the
public road 71/38.

cartynge *n.* work of a carter 278/42.

ca(a)s, case *n.* (*sg.* and *pl.* forms are
indistinguishable) instance 178/18;
event, occurrence 311/53, 2–40/11, 2–
148/38; cause, reason 287/12; circumstances, cases, instances 7/8, 14/49, 50,
15/17; specifically 40/ix; *in* ~ in the
circumstances 64/18, 73/19, 2–36/65,
in some circum-stances, perhaps even
170/25, 249/75, 344/65, 2–3/16; *per-
forme þat* ~ carry out that obligation 2–
148/40.

castyn, caste *v.* throw 71/49, 336/29, 2–
305/36, devise (against) 2–45/49; ~ *pr.3
pl.* calculate (astrologically) 138/71,
scheme, calculate 219/43, plot 275/35;
cast(e *imp.sg.* throw! 52/26, 2–278/14,
2–279/18; **cast, kest** *pa.t.3 sg.* threw 2–
189/18, 2–267/62; **kestyn** *pa.t.3 pl.*
305/44; **cast** *pp.* thrown (*fig.*) 2–9/61.

castyngge *ppl.adj.* ~ *out of þe peple* outcast
53/34 (cf. **reprof**, see Notes).

cat(t)el *n.* property 61/5, 118/40, 2–132/
26.

cause *n.* legal case 236/18, 2–232/16, 2–
233/32, cause 249/67; **causys** *pl.* legal

cases 2–222/2, 6, 8; reasons 248/48,
conditions 248/43.

censeer *n.* container for incense 111/13,
16.

censyn *v.* cense (burn incense in religious
service) 3/30, 113/65; ~ *pr.3 pl.* 112/52,
113/70; **censyd** *pp.* 3/31, 112/39, 48
(cf. **encen-, sens-**).

censyng(g)e *vbl.n.* offering incense 3/29,
110/6, 113/62.

certeyn(e *n. set in som* ~ based on some
assurance 344/52–3, *sey in* ~ testify with
certainty 47/x.

chach- see **cach-**

chaffar(e *n.* wares, merchandise 234/9, 10,
2–153/9; trade, business 2–130/10, 2–
167/49 (cf. **schafar-**).

chalanch *n.* challenge, legal summons
255/90, 91.

chalangyn *v.* claim 2–145/19; **chalangist**
pr.2 sg. 236/28; **chalangyn** *pr.3 pl.* 2–
139/45, lay claim against 2–254/50;
chalange *subj.3 sg.* should claim 2–
145/19; **chalangyd** *pa.t.3 sg.* 236/16;
chalanchedyn *pa.t.3 pl.* laid claims
against 2–254/49; **chalangyd** (*of*) *pp.*
confronted by 325/49.

chamel *n.* camel 55/30; **chamaliis** *pos-
sess.sg.* 92/ 25; ~ *pl.* 1/6b, 55/40.

chanchyn, chaungyn *v.* change 122/20,
123/55, 223/31; **chanchith, chaun-
gith, -gyȝt** *pr.3 sg.* 3/41, 27/xix–xx,
123/51; **chanchyn, chaungen, -gyn**
pr.3 pl. 3/41, 27/xx; **chanche** *imp.sg.*
change! 225/59; **chanchyth** *imp.pl.* 2–
70/106; **chanchyd, chaungede, -yd**
pa.t.3 sg. 122/29, exchanged 2–197/59;
chanchydyn, -edyn *pa.t.3 pl.* altered
122/31, 123/43, 174/64; **chaungyd,
changith** *pp.* changed 149/55, 57,
altered 249/71.

chanchynge, chaungyng *vbl.n.* change of
rule 149/51, 52, exchanging 2–176/8, 2–
197/57, 58, altering 249/67.

chancis *n.pl.* accidents 2–41/39.

chanoun *n.* canon (cleric attached to a
cathedral or collegiate church) 2–161/
55, ~ *reguler* regular canon (cleric under
quasi-monastic rule) 2–184/11; **cha-
no(u)nys** *pl.* 2–161/62, 2–179/61.

chanterie *n.* chantry (endowment allowing
a priest to sing daily masses for the soul
of the donor) 353/50.

chapel *n.* oratory (not a parish church or cathedral) 2–168/19 (cf. MED **chapel** 2.).

chapit(e)le *n.* chapter (in a treatise or book) 1/3a, 159/49, 297/32; **chapitelis** *pl.* 1/2a.

chapman *n.* merchant 2–155/72–73; -mennys *possess.pl.* 18/25; -men *pl.* 19/71, 34/xvi, 219/49.

chapmanhod *n.* trading, business activity 2–155/76.

charch(e, charge, iarge *n.* load 55/47, 76/45, 51, importance, substance 7/5, 103/51, 224/5, 226/15.

charchyn, chargyn *v.* urge, obligate 4/83, 169/19, give more weight to 235/32, 321/48; **charchist** *pr.2 sg.* take seriously 262/88; **charchit(h, chargyth, iargyȝt** *pr.3 sg.* obligates 65/53, 170/38, values highly 309/28 (cf. *var.*), weighs 2–145/27; **charchyn** *pr.3 pl.* weigh heavily 2–193/20; **charchyt, -yd, chargiddyn** *pa.t.3 sg.* 252/25, 2–145/27; **charchyd** *pp.* obligated 253/41, taken seriously 2–193/21.

chargyd, -gyt, i(ch)argyd *ppl.adj.* loaded 55/40, 76/39, burdened 55/47, 65/49, weighed, valued 188/6, 2–23/68.

charl see cherl

charm *n.* sorcery, magic 168/35, 36; **charmys** *pl.* 168/9/10, 13, 20.

charmour *n.* sorcerer 168/12; **charmour(i)s** *pl.* 138/59, 156/3, 2–201/23.

charnel *adj.* carnal 334/35, 2–177/48, worldly 23/13, 2–226/60, intemperate 2–306/72.

charnelte *n.* carnality 2–307/16.

chastysyn *v.* punish 118/39.

chaunchabilte *n.* changeableness 2–84/110.

chaunchouris *n.pl.* money changers 218/9.

chauniable, cha(u)nchable, *adj.* changeable 122/17, 202/2, 248/39.

chaunsel *n.* chancel (part of church containing altar and choir) 2–109/50.

chees- see ches-

chenchepe see shenchepe

chep *n. þe betere* ~ for a lower price 2–155/63, *sellyn gret* ~ sell cheaply 2–153/5.

cher *adj.* fond, attentive 2–300/22.

cherchit *pr.3 sg.* cherishes var./70.

cher(e *n.* countenance, facial expression 2–

133/45, 46, 2–306/47, countenance 298/56, 2–214/51, *glad* ~ smiling face 325/55.

cherl, charl *n.* bondman, servant 90/11, 2–129/82; **cherlys** *pl.* 162/61.

cherte *n.* devotion 349/54 *note.*

cheser *n.* one who chooses 2–177/51.

chesyn *v.* choose 2–22/27, 2–311/158; **che(e)s** *pr.3 sg.* 1/3b, 53/39, 54/41, 42; **chese** *imp.pl.* choose! 2–238/18; **ches** *pa.t.1 sg.* 330/22; *pa.t.3 sg.* 2–316/71; **chosyn** *pp.* 2–177/46, 2–316/63.

chesyng *vbl.n.* choosing 166–7/5–7.

chesyple *n.* chasuble (ecclesiastical vestment, sleeveless mantle worn over the alb and stole by celebrant at mass) 2–228/43, 2–229/67. See Note to 2–228/43.

chetyd *pa.t.3 sg.* escheated, confiscated 2–15/49 (cf. **achet-**).

chettyn see shettyn

cheualrie *n.* nobility (as a class) 257/50, chivalry 2–54/5.

cheueteyn *n.* lord, notable 256/26*, military leader, chieftain 307/25–6, 339/41, 2–111/50.

chydyng *vbl.n.* quarelling 2–8/24, 2–13/5.

childynge *vbl.n.* childbirth 247/10.

chiteringe *vbl.n.* chirping 157/10.

chopping *vbl.n.* ~ *of chirchis* buying, selling or brokering of benefices 2–183/86.

chosyn *ppl.adj.* singled out for merit 330/9 (cf. **ches-**).

citeseyn *n.* ~ *of heuene* denizen of heaven 274/41.

clad *ppl.adj. so* ~ so provided for 2–184/20 (cf. MED **clothen**).

clamour *n. comoun* ~ general outcry of the people 150/21.

cleir, cler(e *adj.* intelligible 115/31, clear, translucent 133/48, unarguable 2–208/39, ~ *of* unsmirched by 227/34.

clene *adj.* pure 224/23, 271/28, clean 295/85; **clenyst** *comp. adj.* purest 271/27.

clene *adv.* completely 8/34, 32/xiv, 2–253/18.

clenesse *n.* purity 197/5.

clepyn, clepe *v.* call for, summon 2–44/17, name, designate 48/30; **clepe** *pr.1 sg.* call 2–238/14; **clepith, -pyȝt** *pr.3 sg.* 108/34, calls upon 233/30, summons 2–251/24; **clep(p)yn** *pr.3 pl.* 234/24, 2–251/23, call 2–188/76, *refl.* style 136/13; **clepyth** *imp.pl.* summon! 196/43; **cle-**

pynge *pr.p.* invoking 169/38; clepydyn *pa.t.3 pl.* designated 295/78; CLEPYD, -IT *pp.* named, designated 88/22, 192/62, 2–15/46, called 13/6, 95/18, 221/16, 351/7, summoned 156/16.

clerc *n.* cleric (general term for member of the clergy) 3/53, 12/50, 19/63; clerkes, -ys *pl.* 39/xviii, 102/15, 110/4.

clerere *comp.adj.* clearer, more translucent 215/29.

cleuyn *v.*(1) split in two 2–247/31; clef *pa.t.3 sg.* split 269/35, 2–302/75; clouyn, clofyn *pp.* 85/44, 2–299/16, 2–311/154.

cleuyn *v.*(2) cling 2–65/8, 2–66/10, 2–238/20; cleuyth *pr.3 sg.* 2–298/26; cleuyn *pa.t.3 pl.* clung 94/17.

clyftis *n.pl.* crevices 312/64, 67.

clippe *v.* embrace 85/42 *var.* byl.

clyps *n.* eclipse 147/11.

clokke *n.* clock 120/41, 42, 43.

clo(o)þlees *adj.* unclothed 63/26, 74/9.

closyn *v. pr.3 pl.* enclose 156/11; -syd *pp.* 156/15.

cloþ *n.* garment 2–46/6, 2–229/68, 2–249/39; cloþis *pl.* ~ *of þe auter* altar cloths 159/41, 319/72.

clotte *ppl. adj.* patched, clouted 260/20.

cloutys *n.pl.* rags 2–302/70.

cockis *n.possess.* be ~ *body* a veiled form of 'God's' 241/3 (cf. koc).

cohwyd *pa.t.3 sg.* coughed 311/44 (cf. rohwyd).

col(l)ege *n.* college (a resident body of clerics supported by an endowment) 245/1, 354/83, 2–136/50; collegis *pl.* 45/xx, 2–180/72, 2–184/33.

colysyons *n.pl.* conspiratorial groups 308/47 *var. al.*.

collegiat *adj. chirche* ~ a church to which is attached an endowed body of clerics 353/49, 54.

colligaciouns *n.pl.* conspiratorial groups 308/47.

colour *n. vndyr* ~ *of* under pretext of 180/16, 291/10, 308/51, 320/14.

comely *adv.* commonly 182/13a, 293/11.

comelyng *n.* newcomer, stranger 53/12 (cf. V.L. *advena*), 2–314/40.

com(m)ena(u)nt, cum-, comenawnt, comonaunt, couenawnt *n.* covenant 329/22, 259/6, contract 2–147/3, agreement 2–155/80, 2–174/19, 2–184/15;

comenantis *pl.* covenants 259/8–9, contracts 2–152/56.

comynge, komyng *ppl.adj.* approaching 179/38, future, to come 150/14.

comynyng *vbl.n.* fellowship 72/8–9 (cf. comunyn).

com(e)n(e, com(m)e, comyn *v. intr.* come 138/72, 149/3, 150/20, 152/12, 155/56, ~ *at on wyt the* embrace thee 84/40; comyth, -y3t *pr.3 sg.* comes 97/27, 179/40, 41; comyn *pr.3 pl.* 179/43; kome, come *subj.3 sg.* may come 179/37, should come 114/20; comyth *imp.pl.* come! 288/49; cam *pa.t.3 sg.* 236/19; comyn, kemyn *pa.t.3 pl.* 261/43, 2–42/535, 56, ~ *to age* came of age 2–151/4.

comoun *adj.* in common 6/129, communal 49/68, *in* ~ in general 91/4, 93/1.

como(u)nte(e, comunte *n.* community (in general sense) 49/69, 117/13; religious community 245/1, congregation assembled in church 196/30; comontes *pl.* religious communities 2–206/67*.

com(o)un(yn *v. intr.* ~ *togedere fleschly* have sexual intercourse 16/30, be physically affectionate 130/75; comounyn, comyn *pr.3 pl. tr.* share (out) 2–196/15, 2–269/43, *intr.* commune (share in the sacrament) 2–39/61; comowne *subj.3 sg.* should have intercourse 219/50–1; comoun *subj.3 pl.* 129/38.

comounys *n.pl.* the common people 2–209/92.

companyyn *v.* associate 2–86/67.

compellynge *vbl.n.* compulsion 292/1.

co(u)nceyl, -seyl, -sell *n.* advice, counsel 16/47, 41/xiii, 118/43, 157/2, 340/60, 61, 349/58, secret 2–64/65, 2–234/15, 16(1), secrets 184/41, private confidences 21/31, 150/28, 29, 2–234/13(2, 3), secrecy 2–131/28, 2–234/11, mind 139/6, 7, 150/30.

conceyl *adj.* secret 2–234/13(1), 16(2).

concludid *pp.* Now þou art ~ Now I have proved the point to you 72/6 (cf. *nunc tibi concluditur*).

confermyn *v.* establish 252/4; confermyd *pp.* endorsed, approved 10/40, 262/77, 305/50.

confyderatoures *n.pl.* accomplices, conspirators 45/xix.

conformyd *ppl. adj.* submissive 299/28.

conformyn *v. refl.* imitate 207/68; conforme *imp.sg.* submit! 299/30.

confortable *adj.* comforting 2–26/1.

confusioun *n.* downfall 150/14.

coniectyn, coniecte *v.* conjecture 150/13, 152/4, 12; coniectyn *pr.3 pl.* 136/15.

coniectyng *vbl.n.* guessing (about) 150/20, conjecturing 176/57.

coniecture *n.* guesswork (about) 150/11.

coniunccioun *n.* conjunction (in astrological parlance, apparent proximity of planets of the same or adjoining signs of the zodiac) 121/72.

coniuryn, -iuren *v.* conjure up 4/67, 28/xxxiii; coniuryd *pp.* 155/1.

coniurysonys *n.pl. holy* ~ holy exorcisms 28/xxxiv, 156/20, 24.

connyn, conne *v.* know 135/29, 327/5, be able to 278/8, learn 339/22; canst *pr.2 sg.* 123/56; can, kan *pr.3 sg.* 87/35, 185/6, can do 131/26; connyn, conne, kunnen *pr.3 pl.* know how to 78/10, 117/12, 139/84, 185/1, 226/23; ~ *non skyl* have no special knowledge 2–93/82; conne, konne, kunne *subj.2 sg.* should be able to 55/38, 76/36, 253/32; connyng(g)e *pr.p.* knowing 137/44, 2–12/75; coude *pa.t.1, 3 sg.* was able 65/5, 134/2, 153/15, 185/4; ~ *þank* was grateful 192/65; cowdyn *pa.t.2 pl.* could 305/34; ~, coudyn *pa.t.3 pl.* were able to 123/58, 185/6, 14, 2–215/6.

connyn(g)g(e *vbl.n.* knowledge, learning 139/95, 168/28, 2–110/34, 2–229/70, 71, perusal 2–102/95.

conscience *n.* judgement 343/16, conscience 345/75.

co(u)nseil see conceyl

consentant *ppl.adj.* ~ *to* a party to 2–151/27, 2–152/36.

consuetude, conswetude *n.* tradition, custom 116/73, 2–171/94–95, 97, 2–172/29, 32.

contynance *n. be nyce* ~ with suggestive manner or facial expression 2–303/8 (cf. nyce).

cont(e)ynyn *n. intr.* be sexually continent 2–66/26, 2–79/6; contynyd *pp. tr.* contained 10/45.

contra *adv.* on the contrary (in clerical disputation) 59/1, 354/9.

contra *prep.* (in clerical disputation, followed by *te*) against (thee), contrary to (what you have just said) 61/1, 63/1, 313/1.

contraryyn *pr.3 pl.* disagree 2–235/25.

contrarious *adj.* antagonistic 2–29/74.

contre see cuntre

contrect *n.* agreement, bargain 2–153/12.

contrewynge *vbl.n.* devising 2–225/15.

contryt *adj.* contrite 246/28.

conuenient *adj.* appropriate, suitable 109/53, 150/16, 356/20, accurate 60/29, 79/32.

conuersacioun *n.* conduct 2–29/72–73.

conuycte *pa.t.3 sg.* convicted 2–88/106; conuyct *pp.* 255/93, 2–36/23, 2–130/23.

copable *adj.* guilty 2–127/27.

cope *n.* canopy, vault 2–265/75; COPYS *n. pl.* cowls, hoods (of monks or friars) 2–161/63.

coplyn *v.* join, couple 241/7; ~ *pr.2 pl.* 2–207/33, 2–255/55.

cord- see acord-

corde *n.* string (of harp or other musical instrument) 2–28/61; cordis *pl.* 2–28/57.

cordyng *vbl.n.* reconciling 275/23.

coroune *n.* crown (of head) 2–164/158; crownes *pl.* 44/xii.

cosynys *n.pl.* relatives 2–284/6.

cost(e *n.* expenditure, outlay 193/18, 216/69, expense 310/2, own expense 353/69, *don swyche* ~ spend so much 189/93; costis *pl.* expenses 2–19/18, 2–155/71, 2–232/9.

costful *adj.* costly 190/11, 12, 215/46.

costum- see custum-

couent *n.* convent (organized group of friars, monks, canons or nuns) 317/9, 15; convent (in general sense, group or congregation) 2–318/34; couentis *possess.sg.* 317/24.

coueyte *pr.1 sg.* want 2–227/17, long 2–325/63; coueytith *pr.3 sg.* covets, desires illicitly 2–296/28; coueyte *subj.pr.3 sg.* should covet 2–295/23.

couenawnt *n.* contract 45/xxi.

coue(y)tyse, coueitise *n.* covetousness 10/5, 22/1, 45/xxviii, 75/15.

coun- see conc-

counable *adj.* appropriate 2–149/63.

cour- see cur-

craft *n.* skill 135/7, 13, 20 (cf. science), craftiness 146/56, 151/56, trade, handwork 290/28, 2–167/49, *men of* ~ skilled

workmen 58/48, ~ of astronomye
astrology 139/87, 91; **craftis** pl. sleights
156/4.
craftely adj. artful, skilfully made 52/44.
craftylyche, craftely adv. artfully, skilfully 207/50, 2–12/78.
crakyddyn pa.t.3 pl. broke 83/11.
crauas n.pl. crevices 312/64.
craue v. desire 59/15, 80/36.
creature n. man 70/17, 82/30, 102/17;
creaturys pl. living things (other than
man) 119/22.
creaunce n. sellyn to ~ sell on credit 2–
198/30.
creme n. consecrated oil, chrism 2–179/32
var. al.
crepyng vbl.n. moving forward on the
knees, or prone 26/iv.
crepit pr.3 sg. crawls 309/17; **crepyn** pr.1
pl. approach on the knees, or prone 2/5,
87/3; ~ pr.3 pl. 26/iv, 87/2.
cresyd ppl.adj. increased in wealth 2–167/
57.
cresy3t pr.3 sg. increases 68/39.
crisme n. consecrated oil 162/15, 2–179/
32 (cf. **creme**).
crisolitus n. chrysolite (semi-precious
stone) 358/54, 2–321/27.
crisopassus n. chrysoprase (semi-precious
stone) 2–321/28.
cristen(yn v. baptise 18/21, 43/ix, 2–151/
11; **cristenyd** pp. 2–151/9.
crystyndam, -tendom, -tendam n.
christendom 133/40, 148/29, 158/21.
crist(e)ne adj. Christian 8/25, 18/21, 43/
ix, 112/55.
croce, cro(o)s n. bishop's crosier 46/ix, 2–
230/1, 15.
crop(p n. crop (all parts of a tree except for
the roots) 36/v, 314/51, 357/24.
croschyn v. gnash 205/62.
cuntre(e, contre n. local district or
(loosely) realm 122/15, 144/6, 148/37,
328/30, 2–25/47; **cuntres, contre(i)s**
pl. 144/9, 149/54, 206/19, 239/23,
260/31.
cure n. cure (clerical office) 44/xii, 2–163/
113, 121, 2–171/99, 100, responsibility
278/3, 2–293/40, care 316/36, 347/3,
351/109, clerical concern (for) 330/2,
17, 355/25, 2–17/35, tutelage 2–151/7,
cure (medical treatment) 2–296/47.
curyous, cory- adj. elaborate 190/4, over-

ingenious or over-ornamented 208/74–9
var. al..
c(o)uriouste n. occult practice 158/18,
idle curiosity 179/10, elaborateness, sho-
winess 2–225/36.
curl adj. curly 95/11.
curs, co(u)rs n. ecclesiastical interdict
229/10, curse, condemnation (by
parent) 315/16, 322/20, condemnation
(by God), anathema 353/64, 2–4/37, 2–
315/37; **cursys** pl. 2–314/2, 2–315/32.
(a)cursyd ppl.adj. excommunicated 342/
51, 52, 53, anathematized 2–313/18, 2–
314/35, 38.
(a)cursyn, corsyn, curs v. excommunicate 24/21, 37/xix, 342/49, 52, 60, 66,
pronounce anathema upon 262/93, 2–
313/27, 2–316/65; **cursyd** pp. excommunicated 342/57.
cursyng(e vbl.n. excommunication 217/
94, 2–316/70.
custom, costum n. custom 216/58, habit
220/84, 223/36.
customyd ppl.adj. habituated (to) 36/xiv.
custumable adj. habitual (of an act) 31/iv,
358/31, 2–68/34, habituated (of a
person) 46/ii, 332/17, 18, 20, 2–3/35.
custumably, -ablelyche, costumablye
adv. habitually 226/15, 27, 231/49, 2–
214/42.

D

daye-wayte n. watchman (trs. Lat. speculatorem); this instance cited in OED
from Wynkyn de Worde ed., s.v. 'Day
24'; MED cites only 'dai-wacche' s.v.
'dai 13' (p. 8236).
dalya(u)nce n. conversation 2–90/52, 53,
dealings 2–93/78, serious discussion 2–
102/92.
dalyyn v. converse, chat 303/55.
dampnyn, dampne v. condemn legally
14/53, 40/xxi, send to hell 2–26/73;
dampne subj.3 sg. should condemn
14/54; **dampnyd** pa.t.3 sg. condemned
2–2/31; **dampnyd** pp. condemned legally 342/2, 2–52/37, sent to hell 106/51,
201/13–14.
dar pr.1 sg. venture to (as verbal auxiliary)
217/112, dare 2–25/36, 2–269/47; ~ pr.3
sg. 58/34, 2–7/4; **dorn, dur** pr.3 pl. 2–
15/42, 2–68/33, 2–269/43; **dur(ste**
subj.3 sg. should dare 2–59/39, 2–142/

42; ~, **dorst** *pa.t.3 sg.* 257/36, 350/79, 2–95/130; **dorstyn, durs-** *pa.t.3 pl.* 205/4, 269/18, 2–296/33.

daswyng *vbl.n.* dimming 2–247/11.

daunge(e)r *n.* control, power 53/37, 311/30, state of indebtedness 2–281/5, 2–282/26.

debat(e *n.* dissension 2–8/25, 2–9/57, *makyt* ~ causes dissension 2–7/9.

deceyu- see **deseyu-**

deceyuable *adj.* deceptive 155/70, 2–82/50, 2–87/92.

declaracioun *n.* clarifying explanation 109/1, 5.

declaryn, -clare *v.* explain 304/4, 2–321/37, make clear 2–27/29; **declare** *imp.sg.* explain (to) 55/37; **declaryd** *pa.t.2 sg.* expounded 2–13/1; ~ *pa.t.3 sg.* promulgated 2–28/36, explained 2–128/38.

declaryng *vbl.n.* exposition 33/iii, 35/xix.

decollacion *n.* beheading 238/15.

dede *n. stonyn to* ~ stone to death 2–122/32, 2–208/56, *brenne to þe* ~ burn to death 2–279/21.

defau(gh)te, defawte *n.* lack 62/60, error, failing 2–24/10, 2–152/59, 2–290/17, (a) defect 2–154/36 et seq., *be* ~ *of* because of a defect in 356/25, *in* ~ at fault 41/xi, 16/37, *in* ~ *of* at fault for 16/39, *for* ~ from neglect 192/52; **defautys** *pl.* sins 14/28, 352/23, defects 18/27, 43/x, petty misdeeds 244/37.

defendant *n.* defendant, transgressor 160/21.

defendyt *ppl.adj.* forbidden 2–27/25, 2–86/67, 2–213/26.

defendyn *v.* protect 302/27, *refl.* 2–56/44; **defendith, -dy3t** *pr.3 sg.* forbids 7/10, 12, 61/25, 81/13, 82/22, 23; **defendyn, -den** *pr.3 pl.* watch over 12/56, 37/xxiii, defend 96/31; **defendede, def(f)endyd(de** *pa.t.3 sg.* forbad 81/7, 83/46, 49, 136/1, 177/1, 2–33/4; **defendyd** *pp.* forbidden 228/12.

defendourys *n.pl.* defenders (military, as one of the estates of the Church Militant) 2–92/43.

defensyn *v.* fortify 288/33.

defhed *n.* deafness 2–247/11.

degradyd *pp.* deposed, reduced to lay status 239/17–18.

degre(e *n.* status, station in life 1/3b, 53/

23, 86/21, 131/27, relative status 90/25, extent, degree 355/18, 19, 2–137/65.

dey3ngge, deyynge *vbl.n.* dying 112/53, 169/20, 2–103/119; **deyyngis** *pl.* deaths 2–22/35.

dey(3)in, deye *v. intr.* die 68/29, 132/31, 2–24/8; **deyyst** *pr.2 sg.* 2–102/83; **dey(3)yn** *pr.3 pl.* 146/77; **deye** *subj.3 sg.* should die 328/43, 2–240/57; **deyid(de** *pa.t.3 sg.* died 52/36, 88/18, 111/20; **deyedyn** *pa.t.3 pl.* 2–259/13; **deyid(de** *pp.* 2–22/36.

deylyn *v.* have dealings with 2–111/56, 2–208/44.

deynte *adj.* delicate, luxurious 58/51, 52, 2–95/7.

del *n. euery* ~ every bit 2–274/17.

delys *n.* luxury, worldly pleasure 308/56, 315/60, 2–121/50, 2–275/49; **delices** *pl.* 70/16.

delyuer *adj.* agile, active 152/5.

delyuerhed, -eryd *n.* agility, nimbleness 95/21, 286/29.

deluerys *n.pl.* diggers of ditches or furrows 181/12.

deluyn *v.* gouge 306/65; **dolfyn** *pp.* dug 2–9/54 (cf. **dolu-**).

demyn, deme *v.* judge 21/37, 65/42, 43, 171/6, 2–239/26; **demyth, -y3t** *pr.3 sg.* 124/63, 182/11; ~ *imp.pl.* judge! 338/15; **dempte** *pa.t.3 sg.* condemned 122/27, judged 171/5; **demyd** *pa.t.3 pl.* 2–210/106; **demptyn** *pa.t. subj.1 pl.* were to judge 2–239/27; **dempte** *pa.t. subj.3 pl.* 171/5; **dempt(e** *pp.* 54/9, 65/43.

demyng(e *vbl.n.* judging 171/4, 240/50, 257/38.

denye *v. intr.* make a denial 79/22, **denyyd** *pa.t.3 sg. tr.* refused 2–100/27.

departyn *v.* separate 301/20, 2–76/30, 32, oppose 313/19–20, break, sever 2–37/31; **departyth -teth** *pr.3 sg.* severs 15/25, 41/vii, 2–39/48; **departe** *subj.3 sg.* may separate 301/9, separate 2–22/24; **departyd** *pp.* divided 166/3, 320/27, 343/26, separated 2–250/62.

departyng *vbl.n.* division 2–39/58.

depnesse *n. a mechil* ~ unfathomable (cf. V.L. *abyssus multa*) 124/79.

depo(o)s(e *n.* deposit, something taken for safe keeping 18/30, 43/x.

deprauyn *pr.3 pl.* vilify 325/40.

deputat *ppl.adj.* deputized 2–164/155.

dere *adj.* ~ *on a farþinge* valued at a farthing 2–192/78–9.

dere *adv.* dearly 51/6, 2–153/10, at higher cost 2–183/85, 2–201/25; **der(r)ere** *comp.adv.* more dearly 2–153/7, 2–155/69.

deryn, dere *v.* harm 153/22, 217/112, 286/28, 2–85/16; **deryd** *pa.t.3 sg.* 2–84/117.

derk, derc see þerk-

derworþi *adj.* precious 191/33.

derworþilyche *adv.* tenderly, lovingly 210/8–9.

deseyt, -ceyt *n.* deceit 20/8, 46/iv, 155/58, 235/10.

deseyuably *adv.* deceitfully, falsely 243/50.

deseyuyn *v.* deceive 103/45; **deseyuyth, deceyu-** *pr.3 sg.* 234/28, undermines 2–65/95 (cf. V.L. *fallit*); **deseyuyd** *pp.* deluded 89/41, deceived 103/45, 138/61.

deseyuyth *ppl.adj.* deceived 343/12.

despar- see dispar-

despites see dis-

desteneye *n.* destiny 132/16, predestining (by) 3/47, predestination 132/2, 3, 5, 8.

dethward *adv.* *disposicion to* ~ tendency to result in death 2–1/13.

dette *n.* duty 200/32, 214/18, debt (of money) 2–183/91; ~ *of here body* sexual intercourse (as debt married couples owe one another) 129/36–47, 250/88, 2–61/76; **dettys** *pl.* debts (of money) 280/15.

dette *ppl. adj.* owed 2–170/75.

dettour *n.* ower of debt 2–183/90.

deu, dew(e, dw *adj.* appropriate, fitting 57/12, 78/11, 146/68, 196/28, 202/39.

deuelschip *n.* false god, idol 25/v; cf. **deuelshene.**

deuelshene *n.* devilishness (illusory gifts of the devil) 54/11, 14, 75/10 (see *MED* sv. 'deuel' n. 5; see Notes).

deuer, deuyr *n.* *don her/our* ~ do their/our duty 36/xiii, 173/33, 251/48, 290/19.

deuicion *n.* division 2–310/131.

deuyn- see dyuyn-

devys *n.* devising 190/11, 2–192/88.

deuors, dyuors *n.* divorce 15/22*, 2–106/69.

dyckyn *v.* entrench (defend with dikes or embankments) 288/33.

difformite *n.* diversity, deviance (in rites) 114/5.

dyghtyn, dyȝtyn *v.* dress, prepare (meat) 63/24, 281/3, 296/12; **dyȝt** *pp.* prepared for harvest, cured (hay) 287/17.

dyghtyng(e, dyȝt- *vbl.n.* preparing, decorating 107/25, clothing, garments 2–308/34.

dignete *n.* respect 109/55, social status 110/19.

dykerys *n.pl.* ditch diggers 181/12.

dylapidacion *n.* wasteful expenditure 317/15, deterioration 351/15.

diligence *n.* *don his/her* ~ do his/their best 2–43/85, 2–79/4.

dyntys *n.pl.* blows 2–307/26, 2–310/119.

dirige *n.* dirge (in church service, the Office for the Dead) 2–179/50, 56, 61; **dirigeis, -ygees** *pl.* 2–179/32, 2–193/14, (memorial services for the dead by special arrangement with a cleric) 2–184/25.

dy(y)s(e *n.pl.* dice 4/79, 29/xxxviii, 167/14, 2–203/68.

discateryth *pr.3 sg.* scatters, disperses 2–133/48; **discateryn** *pr.3 pl.* 2–18/58; **discateryd** *pp.* 2–17/56.

discheuele *adj.* bare-headed 307/22.

dysconfyt(h, dyscunfytyd *pp.* defeated 99/74, 192/64, 2–12/63.

disconfortedyn *pa.t.2 pl.* disheartened, discouraged 2–4/49.

dyscret *adj.* discreet, wise 230/17, 345/72.

discury(y)n, descuren *v.* disclose, reveal 153/7, 157/36, 2–234/15; betray 2–46/20, 2–47/23; **descuren** *pr.3 pl.* 151/45; **discure** *subj.3 sg.* should reveal 2–235/17.

discuryng *vbl.n.* revealing 150/28.

discussyn *v.* investigate (legally) 2–50/26, 2–237/41; **discussedyn** *pa.t.subj.1 pl.* were to examine 2–239/27.

dys(h)ese *n.* affliction, trouble 56/66, 94/31, 148/38, 180/27, 247/19, *in* ~ *of* to the harm of 2–13/9.

disesy *adj.* difficult 302/39.

disgradit, -dyd *pp.* demoted, removed from office 159/45, 256/14–15, 2–3/35.

disheryth *pp.* disinherited 256/8.

dishesyd *ppl.adj.* troubled, afflicted 318/25, 2–70/94.

dishesyn *v.* trouble, worry 189/34, harm, injure (bodily) 2–45/43; ~ *pr.2 pl.*

52/20; **dyshese** *imp.sg.* afflict 52/25; **dishesyd** *pa.t.3 sg.* injured (in body) 2–267/41.

dysiargyd, -chargid *ppl.adj.* unburdened, free 65/49, 51, 73/40.

dysiargy3t *pr.3 sg.* unburdens, relieves 65/53 (cf. **iarg-**).

dismettyn, -mytte *v. refl.* divest 11/9, 36/iv, 11/9, 310/28, 2–286/58.

dysmole *adj.* unlucky, unpropitious 157/5.

dysour *n.* jester, story teller 2–267/64; **dysouris** *pl.* 222/7, 2–214/50.

disparachyd *pa.t.3 sg.refl.* degraded 2–100/39; **desparachyd** *pp.* 2–99/9.

dispendynge *vbl.n.* expenditure 320/33.

dispensacio(u)n *n.* dispensation (rights over property) 2–138/21, 2–139/29–30, power of dispensation 2–142/29, dispensation (in sense of exemption from) 2–137/56, *in his* ~ at his disposal 2–139/30.

dispensatour(e *n.* proprietor 43/v, 2–139/55; **dispensouris** *pl.* 2–139/39, 2–140/78, 85.

dispensyn *v. intr.* give dispensation (to or for) 20/78, 344/58, 345/72, 76, 79, 2–198/20.

disperplyyn *pr.3 pl.* scatter, disperse 331/39; **disperplyyd, -parplyyd, -plyyt** *pp.* 331/37, 2–7/84, 2–9/53, 2–10/15 (cf. **sparplyyd**).

dispyght, -pyt(h, despyt(h *n.* scorn 53/21, 68/21, 208/14, *han* ~ *of* scorn 68/21, insult 90/7, 162/9, 220/70, 222/31, in scorn 116/86, *in* ~ *of* in contempt of 160/29, ignominy 216/82, 262/89, *in* ~ in disgrace 220/71, 74, *had sweryng in* ~ taken swearing lightly 262/88, in contempt 302/36, 214/25; **despites** *pl.* insults 149/59 (cf. **spyth**).

dyspyghtful *adj.* pitiful, miserable 172/14.

dyspisyd *pp.* scorned 88/13, 115/32.

dispit(t)ous *adj.* spiteful, cruel 115/35, disgraceful, shameful 307/28, 2–243/67, 2–259/13.

dispit(t)ously *adv.* cruelly 187/39, 255/98, shamefully 226/16, 238/8, 262/75.

displesance *n.* displeasure 206/41.

disposyt(h *pr.3 sg.* inclines towards 2–238/49, *refl.* is inclined 2–238/51; **dis-**

posith *pr.imp. pl. refl.* prepare 2–312/174.

disseyuably *adv.* deceitfully 226/16.

disseyuen *v.* deceive 151/57, 153/15.

distinccioun *n.* analytical definition 109/1.

distret *adj.* distracted 2–20/50, 2–21/64.

distry(3)yn, destruyyn, dystroy3e *v.* destroy 83/7, 336/19, 33–34, 2–29/82; **distr(u)yyth** *pr.3 sg.* 322/20, 2–133/48; **distryyn** *pr.3 pl.* 2–4/9; **dystr(u)yyd** *pa.t.3 sg.* 13/8, 336/22; ~, **destryyd** *pp.* 2–7/76, 2–105/24, 2–253/22.

ditement *n.* indictment 2–41/27.

dyuers(se *adj.* several, various 3/24, 19/58, 146/63.

dyuerste *n.* diversity 146/62.

dyuyn(e *adj.* divine (addressed to God) 2/16b, 102/18, 26, 27, 232/11.

dyuynyn, deuynyn *v. intr.* prognosticate 3/50, 121/7, 139/1, 141/38; **deuynyn** *pr.3 pl.tr.* foretell 29/xlvii.

diuynys, -nourys *n.pl.* diviners, soothsayers 136/13, 137/51.

diuision *n.* allotment (of property) 2–137/61 (cf. **propryte**).

do see **don**

doere *vbl.n.* doer 167/6; **doerys** *pl.* 14/45, 334/42, 2–13/9.

doyng(g)e *vbl.n.* activity 96/28, performance 167/7; **doynggys** *pl.* activities 144/13.

do(o)lful *adj.* ~ *clopyng* fabrics suited to mourning 149/61, 159/41.

dolys *n.pl.* (1) gifts, alms (dispensed at burials) 213/5, 6.

dolys *n.pl.* (2) boundary markers 2–314/37.

doluyn *ppl.adj.* buried 2–283/52 (cf. **deluyn**).

dom- see **doom-**

do(o)m(e *n.* Last Judgement 7/14, 21/36, 38, 2–241/1, legal judgement 20/14, 21/32, 253/41, 43, decision 225/60, discretion 230/17, power of judgement 2–248/1, *in* ~ in a court of law 46/vi; **domes, -mys** *pl.* judgements 27/xix, 70/26, 117/7, 122/23, 253/36.

domysman *n.* chief judge 2–37/5, 2–74/93, God 2–243/84.

do(o)n(e, doun *v.* be done 4/61, do, accomplish, perform 18/43, 26/iii, 31/lxii, 52/20, 61/9, 85/50, cause,

bring about, make 39/xii, 153/16, 253/
43, 327/10, 2–86/51, place, put (on,
away, to death) 76/40, 92/18, 93/8,
260/20, give, offer 82/29, 30, 87/41
90/12, 13, 16, 2–284/1, *pro-verb* 6/137,
17/68, 73/22, 79/29, 316/45, *intr.* try
36/xi, act 45/xxviii, 61/7(2), 66/27, put
(out of doubt) 71/5, behave 81/11; *aux.*
to *v.* 81/8; ~ *his diligence* try his best 2–
43/84–85 (cf. **besynesse**), ~ *dyspyght*
offers insult 90/7, ~ *on þe cros* placed
on the cross 2–2/29, *hat noȝt to ~ of* has
no such power over 2–139/31, ~ *swyche
cost* spend so much money 189/43, ~
made had made 48/6.

   do(o)n(e *inf.* 2/3, 4/61, 18/31, 31/
lxii, 36/xi, 85/50, *passive inf.* 250/87;
do(o *pr.1 sg.* 71/5, 81/12; **do(i)st** *pr.2
sg.* 54/41, 61/7, 2–32/25; **do(o)th, doiþ**
pr.3 sg. 79/29, 87/35, 41, 102/28, 30;
doo(n *pr.1, 2 pl.* 52/20, 62/47, 90/16;
do(o)(n, doen *pr.3 pl.* 18/41, 45/xxviii,
79/14, 81/11(2), 190/7; **do(o** *imp.sg.*
66/27, 225/60; **do(th** *imp.pl.* 54/9, 55/
21, 75/9; **doo** *subj. 1 sg.* 81/11(2); **do**
subj.3 sg. 168/17, 346/16; **don** *subj.3 pl.*
2–278/2; **dede** *pa.t.1, 3 sg.* 48/6, 92/18,
21, 2–86/46, 2–243/71; **dedist** *pa.t.2 sg.*
238/22; **dedyn, dide(n** *pa.t.pl.* 68/34,
73/22, 24, 2–288/46; **do(o)n(e** *pp.* 61/9,
134/67, 151/42, 43, 188/24, 220/86.

do(o)un *adv.* down 114/24.

dortour *n.* monastic dormitory 120/39.

dotacion *n.* endowment of a religious
foundation 351/8, 353/73.

douk, dwc, dhuk *n.* (a) duke 256/26, 2–
276/14, Duke (title) 257/49; **d(o)ukys**
pl. 317/18, 334/40.

doute, dowte, dou(g)hte, dohute *n.*
doubt 47/x, 109/4, 64, 339/20, 342/
67, *þingis of* ~ doubtful matters 292/
52; **doutis, dowtes, doughtys** *pl.* 27/
xiii, 69/79, 343/10.

doutyr, do(u)wȝ(h)tir *n.* daughter 224/13
et seq., 311/33–34, 2–78/65; **douȝtrys**
pl. 2–105/43.

dowys *n.pl.* doves 218/8.

drauȝt *n.* pulling in harness (of draught
animals) 290/31.

drawyn *v.* draw 125/20, drag 2–244/86,
attract 284/30, 2–230/12, disembowell
(as part of process of execution) 118/23;
drawyt(h *pr.3 sg.* pulls 89/43, lures 2–

12/70, holds 2–245/20; **drawyn** *pr.3 pl.*
tempt 57/23, lure 2–19/2, 5, misappropriate 2–137/63; **drowe** *subj.3
sg.refl.* should withdraw 202/45;
drewe, drow *pa.t.3 sg.* wrote (book)
42/xxv, attracted, drew 134/62, 2–
302/67, pulled 218/16; **drewyn,
drowyn** *pa.t.3 pl.* 187/32, attracted 2–
122/33; **drawyn, -wen, -wun** *pp.*
tempted 79/21, disembowelled 150/19,
252/26, 255/93, ~ *doun* demolished
256/8.

drawyn *ppl.adj.* disembowelled 118/23.

dred *n.* reverence, respect 329/16, 334/45,
47, 2–247/34, *loue* ~ state of God-fear-
ingness 329/29, respectful love 334/49
(see Notes), fear 2–40/68, 2–50/18, 2–
69/60.

dred(e)ful(l *adj.* awe inspiring, terrifying
21/36, 47/xiv, fearful 170/41.

dredyn *v.* fear 329/15; ~ *pass. inf.* to be
feared 226/26; **drede** *pr.1 sg. refl. I* ~ *me*
I fear 117/90, 189/26; ~ *pr.2 pl.* fear
329/17; **dred** *subj.3 sg.* should fear 2–
62/60; ~ *imp.sg. refl.* be afraid! 335/74,
348/38; **dredith** *imp.pl.* fear 334/46.

dreye *adj.* dry 142/14.

dreyin *pr.3 pl.* dry 146/60.

drem *n.* dream 176/52, 179/1; **dremys** *pl.*
174/1 *et seq.*

dremere *n.* dreamer 178/13; **dremeris** *pl.*
178/16.

dremyth *pr.3 sg.* dreams 176/51, 179/42;
dremyn *pr.3 pl.* 175/10, 13, 19;
drempte *pa.t.3 sg.* 2–193/29.

drenchen *v.* cause to perish by drowning
153/12; **drynchyn** *pr.3 pl.* 2–265/80;
drynche *subj.3 sg.* should drown 2–43/
77; **drenchid** *pa.t.3 sg.* 295/80, 2–248/
51; ~ *pp.* 251/46, 297/25.

drery *adj.* glum, downcast 2–146/49.

dryefoot *adv.* with dry feet 295/80, 297/
24.

dryhed *n.* dryness 2–103/106.

drynch- see **drench-**

drynkyn *v.* drink, imbibe 305/38; **drynke**
subj.2 sg. should imbibe 2–90/43.

dryt *n.* dirt 2–77/35.

dronke(s)chep(e *n.* drunkenness 218/28,
2–105/43.

dro(u)nk(yn *ppl.adj.* drunken 305/37, 39,
2–90/43, 2–143/85.

dublehed *n.* duplicity 2–219/53.

duellyn, dwellyn *v.intr.* remain 85/48, continue 2–294/63; **dwellyn** *pr.3 pl.* remain 265/10; **dwellyd** *pa.t.3 sg.* 283/4.
duellyng *vbl.n.* stopping place 126/31.
duellyng *ppl.adj.* abiding 53/9, 10.
dulhed *n.* dullness 2–27/28.
dur see **dar-**
durande *ppl.adj.* enduring 98/61.
du(y)te *n.* duty 44/xii, 18/41; **du(y)te(e)s** *pl.* 101/7, 2–171/86.
dutynge *ppl. adj.* doubting, hesitant 2–12/73.

E

eex *n.* axe 120/50, 52.
3)efne, euen(e, euyn *adj.* equal 1/16, 30/liv, 63/17, 340/54, 63, 2–57/76, equal (to) 154/37, 285/33, similar 126/50, even (number) 284/6, 10, 285/34, level 2–247/32, ~ *cristene* fellow Christian 68/22, 84/26, 181/10, 275/22.
efnehed *n.* impartiality, equity 257/38, moderation, the golden mean 285/32.
eft *adv.* a second time 239/28.
eftsonys *adv.* a second time 2–72/53, 2–86/53, 2–263/14.
eggyn *pr.3 pl.* incite 2–21/3 (cf. **myseggyn**).
ey *n.* egg 2–260/31, 39; **eyryn** *pl.* 309/8.
ey(3)e, yih, i3e *n.* eye (human) 86/5, 6, 91/33, eye (of needle) 1/7b, 25/v, 76/30; *þu seist at* ~ you can plainly see 120/51, 357/17, 358/37, *open atte* ~ plain to see 149/47, *han* ~ *to* keep in mind 91/33, 114/12; **eyne** *pl.* 52/28, 240/40, 53, var./86.
ey3tetene, eytene *card.num.* eighteen 288/46, 2–123/65.
eylede *pa.t.3 sg.* ailed, troubled 2–255/12.
ey(i)r, heyir *n.* air 52/43, 141/49, 5, 7, 147/11, 175/18.
eyr(e *n.* heir 274/41, 307/9, 2–140/66, 67; **h)eyris** *pl.* 22/3, 90/18, 329/8.
eyþer *pron.* each 25/iv, *euer-* ~ each of them 70/5.
eyþir, -ER *adj.* either 349/62, 2–42/58.
eyþir *adv.* either 193/21.
eld(e *n.* old age 128/17, 146/77, 312/54, agedness 68/40, 260/37.
eld(e, held *adj.* old 4/76, 68/38, 312/54, decayed, worn 260/21, 22, *be* ~ *tyme* long ago 6/137, 110/1, *3er* ~ years old

307/33; **eldre** *compar. adj.* elder 2–105/33; **eldist** *compar. adj.* eldest 2–73/56.
eldere(s *n.pl.* elders in age 11/32, 68/21, 150/27.
eldyn *pr.3 pl.* age, grow old 95/9, 359/60.
eleccioun *n.* choice 122/20.
eleuete *ord.num.* eleventh 2–247/35.
ellis, elles *adj./adv.* otherwise 17/13, 45/xxi, 288/30; *God forbede* ~ God forbid that it should be otherwise 293/26.
elmesse *n.* alms 18/19, 23/29, 34, 213/5, *do* ~ give alms 2–150/99, ~ *doynge* almsgiving 170/45.
embyrdayys *n.pl.* ember-days (four periods of fasting and prayer, of three days' duration, following the first Sunday in Lent, Whitsun-day, Holy Cross Day and St. Lucy's Day) 2–91/31–32.
empyrys *n.pl.* empires 98/55.
en)cens *n.* incense 111/16, 27, 30.
encensyn *v.* cense (use incense in religious rite) 110/3 (cf. **censyn**).
encensynge *vbl.n.* censing (use of incense in religious rite) 110/1 (cf. **sensyng**).
enclynyn *v.* direct, bend 343/28.
encres *n.* profit 2–167/58.
endi3t *pp.* indicted, prosecuted 253/38.
endyrlych(e, ynderly, interly, enterelyche *adv.* sincerely, devoutly 2–99/4, 2–101/62, 62 *var.* rdtbylh, 68, 2–102/79, inwardly 2–273/97, heartily 2–279/19, 19 *var. al.*
endued, -yd, induyd, -duyt *ppl.adj.* endowed 44/xii, 316/51, 2–161/47, endowed with 317/7.
enhauncyd *ppl.adj.* puffed up 2–83/95.
enhaunsyth *pr.3 sg.* enhances, improves 168/31, 2–235/35.
enlumynyd *pp.* enlightened, instructed 2–23/59.
enmy, -myte *n.* enmity 2–120/33, 2–158/72, enemy 2–145/7.
enmy *adj.* inimical, hostile 2–128/48.
enmychepe *n.* enmity 2–235/19.
ensa(u)mple *n.* example 26/vi, 35/iii, 79/11, exemplary tale 42/xiv, 48/19–20; **ensamples** *pl.* 48/22.
entyrmete, -mettyn *v. refl.* meddle (in) 38/xxvi, 327/4*, 358/32; **entermetyn** *pr.3 pl. refl.* concern (themselves with) 124/82, 147/3.
entyrual *n.* interval 2–237/24.

entre(e *n.* entrance 41/vii, 55/46, 250/90.

entrikyd *ppl.adj.* deceived 188/4, ensnared 2–11/26 (cf. **intryk-**).

er, or *adv.* before (in time) 16/28, 41/viii, 92/18, 206/40.

erde, herthe *n.* earth 15/11, 100/36, 164/69, *fig.* 281/25.

erdely, erþeli *adj.* earthly 70/16, 166/11, 206/38, 2–30/20.

ere *n.* ear 2–276/3; h)erys, -yn *pl.* 258/7, 2–16/12, 2–97/58, 2–276/9, (of corn) 289/60, 2–141/17.

eryin *v. intr.* plough 119/18.

h)eryyng *vbl.n.* ploughing 277/37, 278/42.

ern(e)de *n.* errand 311/49, 2–43/81.

ernyn *n.* earn 101/55.

erryn *pr.3 pl.* err 2–48/61; **erre** *subj.3 sg.* should err 2–44/31, 33.

errowrys *n.pl.* errors 148/26.

h)ese *n.* comfort 295/60, 302/23, 2–158/75, convenience 352/40, relief 44/xiv.

eselyche *adv.* easily 2–99/3, 2–310/121.

esement *n.* relief 218/25, 291/32.

h)esy *adj.* easy 25/v, 55/30, 302/38, low (in price) 101/53.

Estryn *propr.n.* ~ *day* Easter 97/31, 148/22, 195/22, 293/24.

etyn *v.* eat 2–81/42, 2–141/23; ~ *pr.3 pl.* 2–15/37; **ete** *subj.2 sg.* so þat þu ~ provided that you eat 2–35/48; **ete** *imp.sg.* eat! 2–35/47; **etyth** *imp.pl.* 2–35/53; **e(e)t** *pa.t.3 sg.* 289/58, 2–81/36, 2–261/71; **etyn** *pa.t.3 pl.* 137/45, 289/61, 2–15/52; **etyn** *pp.* 289/59.

etyng *vbl.n.* eating 279/19.

e(i)þer *conj.* or, alternatively 42/xx, 75/10, 14.

euele, euyl *n.* evil 21/17, 2–31/3, 4.

euele, euyl *adj.* evil 223/21, 22, ~ *-goten* ill-gotten 43/xi.

euele, euyl, yuel *adv.* poorly, badly 80/61, 283/9, 317/13, 2–34/23.

euene see **efne**

euenely *adv.* equally 126/30, 2–159/88.

euere *adj.* every 333/20.

euerychon *pron.* every one 82/37, 2–133/54.

euerydel *n.* everything 125/11.

Euesong *n.* Evensong (vesper service held at sixth canonical hour) 10/32, 34/xvi, 206/21, 291/34–35.

euyn *n.* evening 34/xvi, 206/21, 274/11, *up* ~ towards evening 2–216/18 (cf. **up**).

excusacioun *n.* excuse, apology 41/x, 228/11, 229/36, explanation 42/xx; **excusacio(u)nys** *pl.* 3/43*, 15/14, 27/xx.

excusyn *v. intr.* make excuses 2–69/76.

executour(i)s *n.pl.* executors (of estates, agents) 2–269/19, 2–278/2, 3, 4, 2–279/25–26.

executrye *n.* executorship 2–268/72.

exposicioun *n.* interpretation 25/v, vi, 40/xx, 77/24.

expositour *n.* (legal) interpreter 2–172/29 (cf. **termyn-our**); **-tourys** *pl.* expounders 76/37.

expowneþ *pr.3 sg.* expounds 77/27.

expownyng *vbl.n.* interpretation (scriptural) 50/80–81 (MSS BL).

F

fadirchepe *n.* fatherhood 348/9.

faylyn *v. intr.* weaken 2–111/49; **faylyth** *pr.3 sg.* 2–111/48; **fayle** *subj.3 sg.* ~ *of* should be delinquent in 2–199/40.

fayn, feyn *adv.* gladly 69/78, 125/21, 149/8, 230/23.

fayr *adv.* politely 187/27.

faytour *n.* trickster, cheat 151/37; **faytoures, -tour(i)s, -towres** *pl.* 28/xxx, 29/xlix, 150/31, 194/41, 2–187/55.

fayterye, -tourye *n.* trickery, deception 45/xxii, 125/18, 136/14, 168/19.

fall(yn *v. intr.* happen 5/99, 29/xlvii, 117/12, occur 125/9, 160/17, lapse (into) 170/26, fall 358/34, falter 2–232/11, *it schuld* ~ *hym* to he would be led into 176/54; **fallyt(h, fallyσt, falleth** *pr.3 sg.* falls 58/30, 78/28, befalls 177/75, happens 140/14, 150/19, occurs 125/12, 2–69/56, 57, comes 245/51; **fallyn** *pr.3 pl.* occur 6/137, 28/xxix, 147/9, 14; **falle(n, felle** *subj.3 sg.* may fall 174/52, should fall 76/3, 125/11, 182/3, should occur 169/15, 248/42, 43, 44, should turn 2–223/42, befall 2–40/12; **fallen** *subj.1 pl.* should succumb 154/30; **fel** *pa.t.3 sg.* happened 170/26, 174/53, there fell 236/34, it happened 2–97/42, chanced 2–143/70, ~ *slep on hym* he fell asleep 236/34, ~ *out* resulted 2–107/1; **fall)yn** *pp.* ~ *for* resulted from 16/50, 22/5, 33/xviii.

falsen *v.* counterfeit 150/17.

falshed(e *n.* falseness, duplicity 20/86, 46/v, 148/42.

fame *n.* reputation 229/9, 256/20, 2–131/29.

fangyn *v.* receive 85/42 (cf. MED **fongen**).

fanoun *n.* maniple (embroidered band attached to the wrist of the priest at mass) 2–228/38/40, 2–229/64. See Note to 2–228/38/40.

fantasye *n.* delusion 174/65, 189/31, idea 2–45/44; **fantasyys** *pl.* 177/71.

fare *n.* state of being 356/11, *gret* ~, *lusty* ~ riotous living 308/41, 317/23, 324/15.

fare, -yn *v. intr.* fare 63/19, 2–280/57, ~ *wel(e* dine well 35/xviii, 296/2; **fare** *pr.1 sg.* 2–280/57; **faryth, -y3t** *pr.3 sg. it* ~ *be* it happens with 120/48, 210/15; **faryth** *pr.3 sg. so it* ~ so it goes 2–282/26; **faryn** *pr.3 pl.* fare 180/19, 181/41, 42 252/26, 2–18/81; **farende** *pr.ppl.* faring 2–96/30; **ferde** *pa.t.3 sg.* fared 2–94/103, 2–280/56.

faste *adv.* close 236/36; *farwel* ~ be gone! get lost! 2–281/10.

fatyn *v. intr.* fade 349/68, 2–274/14; **fatyth** *pr.3 sg.* 358/56, 2–270/5, 2–274/24; **fatyn** *pr.3 pl.* 359/61.

fatyng *vbl.n.* fading 2–247/12.

faute *n.* fault 78/10.

fautoures, -tourys *n.pl.* adherents, followers 28/xxxiv, 159/56.

febyl, feble *adj.* poor, scanty 51/9, 2–227/15, unexemplary, poor (in moral sense) 337/34.

feblyn *pr.3 pl.* grow feeble (with age) 95/9.

feblyschid *ppl. adj.* enfeebled, weakened 258/57.

federys *n.pl.* feathers 52/43, 349/61.

fedryd *ppl.adj.* with feathers 95/21.

feer *adj.* afraid 254/59.

feers *adj.* warlike 98/57.

fey3t *n.* faith 61/10, 13.

fey3t see **fy3t-**

feyne see **fenyyn**

feyneres *n.pl.* feigners 43/iii.

feynt *adj.* physically weak 2–27/11, small amount of 2–130/10.

feyntyth, fen- *pr.3 sg. intr.* faints 272/50, *tr.* weakens, cushions 2–310/118.

feir, fe(e)r(e, fyr *n.* fire 107/16, 111/14, 18, 157/7, 164/58, 63, 277/24, 2–247/39.

feyre *n.* fair, market 18/17; **feyris, -res** *pl.* 31/lxiv, 219/45, 48, 277/38, 290/16.

fel *adj.* cruel, savage 244/24, 2–101/45, 2–230/14.

felaw(e *n.* companion (on equal terms) 2–66/29, 34, 37, 2–81/37, 2–129/82; **felawys, -es** *pl.* fellows 48/12, equals 124/85, co-conspirators 2–74/91, business associates 2–153/8.

felawchepe, felaughshipe *n.* co-conspiracy 151/56, friendship 2–193/27, 2–282/16.

feld *pp.* cut down 287/17.

fele *adj.* many 130/66, 2–282/36.

felyn *v.* experience 234/29; **felyst** *pr.2 sg. refl.* feel 2–90/51; **felyt** *pr.3 sg.* 2–217/9; **felyn** *pr.1 pl.* experience 147/19; ~ *pr.3 pl.* sense 144/27; **fele** *subj.1 sg.* should feel 2–278/14; ~ *subj.3 sg.* should deem 247/13, 2–177/53; **feltyn** *pa.t.3 pl. refl.* felt 2–296/50.

felyng(ge *vbl.n.* bodily appetite 100/26, sense of touch 157/35, 2–103/122.

femel *n.* female (bird) 309/8, female sex 2–215/5.

fe(e)nd(e *n.* the Devil 4/62, 96/36, 128/21, 153/2; **fendys, feendes** *pl.* devils, evil spirits 4/69, 28/xxxi, 96/31.

fenyyd, feyn- *ppl.adj.* deceptive 20/7, 46/iv, 2–217/2.

fenyyn, feyne *v. refl.* feign 29/xxxix, 284/29; **fenyyth** *pr.3 sg.* 2–162/79, *refl.* pretends 156/13; **fenyyn** *pr.3 pl.* counterfeit 4/81, 17/3, *refl.* pretend 2–212/29; **feynyn** *pr.p.* feigning 29/xli; **fenyyd** *pa.t.3 sg.* pretended 2–280/55, 2–216/23, *refl.* pretended to be 2–88/109; ~ *hym to go* made a pretence of going 2–216/19; **fenyedyn** *pa.t.3 pl.* feigned 2–133/7; **fenyyd** *pp.* pretended 2–216/22.

fenyyng, feyn- *vbl.n.* feigning 29/xxxix, 46/iv, pretence 20/9, 200/9, 2–219/49, 52, 54.

fent- see **feynt-**

fer *n.* fear 258/6.

fer(re *adj.* distant 144/9, 218/25, lengthy 290/2.

fer *adv.* far 131/18, 178/31, 201/16.

ferde, ferthe *ord.num.* fourth 10/50, 122/33.

fere *n.* accomplice 151/38.

fereful *adj.* frightening 47/iii.

ferie *n.* holiday 267/51.

feryyn *v. intr.* keep holiday, rest 267/52.

ferme *n.* farm (property leased for agricultural use) 18/24, 43/ix; **fermys** *pl.* 2–166/41.

fermour *n.* farmer (one who leases land) 18/24, 43/ix, 2–152/41.

fe(e)rs *adj.* fierce 98/57, 2–230/14, 2–251/26.

ferst(e *adv.* first 101/55, 106/57, 141/41.

ferste, firste *adj.* first 102/21, 81/1.

fesyng *vbl.n.* intimidation 2–44/25 (cf. **afesyn**).

fest *adj.* tight, snug 93/12.

feste *n.* feast day 173/43, 174/51; **festys** *pl.* feasts 58/53.

festyn *v.* fasten 2–161/63; **festyth** *imp.pl.* fix, implant 2–311/150; **festede** *pa.t.3 sg. intr.* caught fast 307/24.

festyng *vbl.n.* fastening 93/5.

fet(te *adj.* fatted, covered with fat 2–17/48, 2–89/28.

fettyn *v.* fetch 297/32; ~ *pr.3 pl.* 309/11; ~ *pa.t.2 pl.* 2–17/52.

fettynge *vbl.n.* fetching 309/9.

feuerys *n.pl.* fevers 2–315/12.

fewte *n.* fealty 101/8.

fyftyd, fyuetyde *ord.num.* fiftieth 280/12, 281/26.

figure *n.* statue 102/30, prefiguration, foreshadowing 270/1, 265/5, 279/39, 2–216/35, 2–117/26, 40; **figuris** *pl.* representations (in sculpture or painting) 91/9, figurations 269/31, 33.

figurede *v. pa.t.3 sg.* prefigured 266/17; **figuryd** *pp.* prefigured 303/66.

fyȝt(h *n.* fight 2–90/55, battle 2–99/14, 2–311/136.

fyȝtyn, fytyn, fyȝthe, feyȝt *v. intr.* fight, do battle 154/32, 224/8, 255/87, 89, 90, 2–55/41, 2–56/63; **fyȝtyn** *pr.3 pl.* 2–42/52; **fyȝtynge** *pr.p.* 2–36/9; **fauȝt** *pa.t.3 sg.* 2–100/42.

fyndyn, -ith *v.* provide 310/19, find 2–282/35, 36; ~ *pr.1 sg.* 174/69; **fynt** *pr.3 sg.* provides 303/59, finds 2–282/29; **fond** *pa.t.3 sg.* found 174/68, 218/8, 305/40; **fo(u)ndyn** *pa.t.3 pl.* founded, established 251/56, established (by) 63/15, found 2–281/69, ~ *up* devised 2–190/29 (cf. MED **finden** 23b); ~ *pp.*

discovered 218/26, 27, 2–78/70, 2–318/46.

fyndyngis *n.pl.* willful behaviour 2–119/14, 17.

fyrmament *n.* sphere of the fixed stars (Ptolemaic eighth sphere) 125/26, 133/29, 33, 45.

fyrshed *n.* severity, cruelty 2–17/54.

fyshere *n.* fisherman 131/4.

fyue *card.num.* five 174/67.

fyuete *ord.num.* fifth 13/1, 265/59, 2–1/3.

fyuetene *card.num.* fifteen 2–247/14.

fyuetente *ord.num.* fifteenth 2–247/40.

fleyyng *vbl.n.* flight 157/10.

fleynge *vbl.n.* fleeing 340/4.

flemd(e *adj.* outlawed 53/5, 280/14, 2–32/43.

flen *pr.2 pl.* flay, skin 2–14/20, 22.

fle(i)n, fle(e *v.* escape 59/8, 122/20, 160/11, 2–267/48, shun, avoid 67/7, 195/14, 300/45, 2–27/30, flee 85/48, 114/5, 2–261/61, fly (from the nest: the form is that of the verb **fle(i)n**, sense is borrowed from verb **flyyn**, cf. MED) 309/11; **fleth** *pr.3 sg.* avoids, eschews 252/17, 2–71/14, escapes 2–199/44; **flein** *pr.1 pl.* eschew 103/51; **flen** *subj.3 pl.* should avoid 217/111; **fle** *imp.pl.* shun! 2–231/43; **fledde** *pa.t.3 sg.* avoided 2–41/30, fled 2–263/8, 12; **fled** *pp.* avoided 217/99, 2–41/31.

flyyn *v. intr.* fly 182/16, 2–259/21, 24, 2–260/28; **fleit** *pr.3 sg.* 96/9; **flye** *subj.3 sg.* should fly 182/14; **fl(e)yynge** *pr.p.* flying 182/19, 21; **fleyy** *pa.t.3 sg.* 2–259/8; **flown** *pa.t.3 pl.* 2–281/67 (cf. **fle(i)n**).

fly(ȝ)t(h *n.* flight 309/5, 2–90/55, escape 2–56/46.

flyttyth *pr.3 sg.* transfers, moves 2–314/36; **flyttid** *pp.* 253/33.

flod *n. in* ~ in the sea 52/42.

flour *n.* flower 22/18, 2–270/5, (*fig.*) 91/7, 2–98/85; **flourys** *pl.* 107/18, 2–323/15; *in hys* ~ in the prime of life- 2–270/12.

foysoun *n.* abundance, increase 2–63/35.

folc *n.* people 1/13, 13/15, 178/19.

foly(e *n.* foolish doctrine 29/xlvi, 125/18, 132/18, sinful act 55/21, 66/31, 132/18, foolish act 2–127/15, *lete gret* ~ consider it very foolish 147/3, *do noo* ~ *be noo womman* do not sin with any woman 55/

21, 66/31; **folyis** *pl.* foolish words 132/18.

foly(e, fol(lych *adj.* foolish 53/39, 227/34, 323/62, 2–188/72.

folylyche, -leche *adv.* foolishly 225/49, 246/34, 331/34.

folwyn, folwe *v.* follow 29/xlv, 5/91, 2–50/32; ~ *subj.3 sg.* should follow 2–44/22, 2–68/29, 30; **folwyn** *subj.3 pl.* 340/60; **fol(e)we** *imp.sg.* follow! 55/26, 75/25; **folwyd(e** *pa.t.3 sg.* 2–12/61, 2–50/19.

folwyng(e *ppl.adj.* subsequent 5/100, 101, following 132/16.

fond- see **find-**

fondyng(e *vbl.n.* temptation 2–21/7, 2–127/23, 2–146/53.

foo *n.* foe 2–286/45; **fo(o)n** *pl.* 62/37, 2–282/37.

fool *n.* fool 71/1, 4 ~ *sage* professional fool 2–278/6, *naturel* ~ simpleton 2–278/7, *as* ~ *hardy* like a reckless fool 350/80, ~ *symple man* simpleton 2–220/18; **folis** *possess. sg.* fool's; **fo(o)lys** *n.pl.* foolish persons 5/103, 124/71, 140/36, professional fools 2–278/5, 2–279/24.

for why, for qhy, for þe þat *conj.* because 65/52, 186/15, 199/8, 285/12, 357/5.

forasmechil *conj.* ~ *as* since 115/38.

forberyn, -bere *v.* do without 73/34, 2–23/56, give up, relinquish 2–23/49, 56, 2–153/21, 23.

forbetyn *ppl.adj.* severely beaten 238/28.

forbled *ppl.adj.* blood-stained 2–99/17.

forbode *n.* prohibition 83/14, 137/45, 228/18, 279/19.

forboden *ppl.adj.* forbidden 47/i, 2–117/19.

forbodyn *pp.* 160/29, 2–125/63.

fordryfen *ppl.adj.* driven out 2–17/52.

forfare *intr. subj.3 sg.* should perish or decay 2–149/65.

forfendyd *ppl.adj.* forbidden 13/1.

forfendynge *vbl.n.* prohibition 2–296/41.

forfendyth *pr.3 sg.* forbids 2–295/13, 2–299/3; **forfendit** *pa.t.(or perh.pr.)3 sg.* 2–299/2.

forfeth *n.* sin, transgression 52/3.

forfetyn *v.* transgress 67/16, 252/22; **forfetist** *pr.2 sg.* 2–30/22; **forfetyth** *pr.3 sg.* 160/21, 2–85/38; **forfetyn** *pr.3 pl.* 2–222/23, 2–224/67; **forfete** *subj.3 sg.* should transgress 67/52; **forfetyn**

subj.3 pl. 327/19; **forfetyd** *pa.t.3 sg.* 225/49.

for3ete *ppl.adj.* forgotten 257/39.

for3euenesse, -3ifnesse *n.* forgiveness 351/104, 107.

for3euere *n.* forgiver 104/4.

for3euyn *v.* forgive 85/45, 103/48; **for3eue** *imp.sg.* 84/26; **for3af** *pa.t.3 sg.* 84/27.

for3it *pr.3 sg.* forgets 2–244/104; **for3at** *pa.t.3 sg.* 2–325/55.

forme *n.* statue 102/30, 31 (cf. V.L. *idolum*), outward appearance 87/37, 235/45.

forme *adj.* foremost 2–272/84, 2–273/88.

formir *(-fadirys)*, **forme** *(-fadrys) adj.* fore (-fathers) 329/22, 2–257/2.

forneys *n.* furnace 2–265/70.

fornicarie *n.* lecherous or unchaste person 2–77/19, 35; **fornicariis** *pl.* 2–76/10, 2–77/15, 29, 33.

forrendyn *pr.3 pl.* tear apart, rend 239/32, 331/39, 2–18/59; **forrente** *pa.t.3 sg.* 2–257/51.

forrent(e *ppl.adj.* torn to pieces 84/31, 2–101/66, 2–281/69.

forsakyn, -sake *v.* renounce 15/19, forgo 63/12, 77/16, escape 79/11; **forsaky3t** *pr.3 sg.* forgoes 61/3, renounces 64/27; **forsakyn** *pr.1, 3 pl.* 61/5, 62, 45; **forsake** *subj.3 sg.* should forsake 2–75/15; **forsoke** *pa.t.3 sg.* sacrificed 61/33, rejected 79/13, lost 238/17–18; **forsakyn** *pp.* forgone 100/29.

forsakyngge *vbl.n.* renouncing 61/31.

forshewyn *v.* show forth, demonstrate 143/47.

forspatlyd *ppl.adj.* spat upon 2–301/53.

forth *adv. seye* ~ continue speaking! 68/42, *han his* ~ carry the day, triumph 2–224/3, *lyuyn* ~ *in pride* live overconfidently 2–4/3.

forthere, farþ- *comp.adj.* farther away 152/4, 199/9.

fortorn *ppl.adj.* badly torn 240/55, 2–101/66.

fortrauaylyd *pa.t.3 sg.* wearied 2–257/50–51.

forþ(in *v.* advance 2–4/9 (cf. MED **forthen** 4), carry forth 2–309/71.

foruty *card.num.* forty 82/21.

forwondyth *ppl.adj.* severely wounded 2–101/46.

foule *adj.* muddy, fouled 187/24.

foul(y)s *n.pl.* birds (collectively) 52/41, 96/9, 98/48, 157/10.

foundyn *ppl.adj.* established 172/1.

fourtyde *ord.num.* fortieth 2–173/51.

fraternyte *n.* fraternity (a body of men associated for lay or religious purposes) 2–180/69, 71, 73; **fraternytes** *pl.* 2–180/67, 68.

fraudyn *pr.3 pl.* defraud 2–183/98; **fraudyt** *pp.* defrauded 2–195/74.

frawde *n.* fraud 43/xi.

fredam *n.* rights, prerogatives 117/5, authority 118/20.

frele *adj.* frail 248/38, 2–71/111, 8, 2–95/4.

frel(e)te *n.* frailty 61/33, 223/29, 2–84/110.

frentyk *adj.* mad, deranged 2–56/61.

frere *n.* friar (member of a mendicant order) 186/14, 187/26, ~ *menour* Franciscan friar 2–194/61; **freres, -rys** *pl.* 30/1, 187/23, 29, 30.

fretyn *v.* chafe, fray 2–29/68; **fretyth** *pr.3 sg. refl.* 2–212/40; **fretynge** *pr.p.* chafing 2–244/90.

froude, frowde *n.* toad or frog 5/94, 181/2, 4, 2–97/45; **frowdis** *possess.sg.* 181/7; **froudys** *n.pl.* 2–103/113.

frut(h, frwt *n.* fruit (literal) 107/18, 145/47, fruit (*fig.*) 212/31, 248/36, harvest 2–32/42, reward 2–245/115; **frws, frutys** *pl.* (first) fruits 19/55, 2–173/48, crops 2–166/39.

ful *adj.* complete 280/22.

ful *adv. intensifier* very, quite 48/16, 70/15, entirely 2–41/31.

fullynge *ppl.adj.* ~ *placis* fulling places (where cloth is beaten to thicken it) 2–166/42.

fundacion *n.* foundation 351/7, 352/46.

furbuschyd *ppl.adj.* polished, burnished 2–309/97.

G

gaderyng *vbl.n.* process of collecting 158/15, 291/13; **gad(e)ryngis** *pl.* gatherings (of people) 197/1, 276/47.

gad(e)ryn *v.* collect 195/7, harvest 280/7, gather 287/13, 14; **gaderyth** *pr.3 sg.* 2–63/29; **gadryn** *pr.3 pl.* 2–27/14; **gadere** *subj.3 sg.* should assemble, recruit 2–55/30; **gaderyd** *pa.t.3 sg.* collected 277/16;

gad(e)ryd *pp.* assembled 196/34, 41, 2–52/44, joined, united 271/27, gathered 287/17.

gay see **gon**

gayn *adj.* ~ *path* near path, shortcut 2–267/58.

gallochis *n.pl.* sandals fastened with thongs (V.L. *sandaliis*) 93/5, 6, 8.

galwys *n.pl.* gallows 2–146/54, 2–258/22.

game *n. in* ~ in jest 241/8.

gamyn *n.* game of chance 167/15, 16, play, playfulness 2–72/27, sports 2–277/31, 32; **gamys** *pl.* games of chance 167/27, jokes 2–72/27.

gangdayys *n.pl.* Rogation Days (three days preceding Ascension Day or Holy Thursday) 2–91/32.

gase *subj.3 sg.* may gaze 2–275/39.

gastely *adj.* ghastly, terrifying 359/62.

gebet(t)is *n.pl.* gibbets 262/74, 2–264/40.

geynseyn *v.* contradict, dispute 2–84/1; **geynseith** *pr.3 sg.* 2–237/19; **geynseye** *subj.1 sg.* should refuse 2–175/67.

gendryn *v.* engender (*fig.*) 330/11, conceive 2–78/73, 2–118/4; **gendryd** *pp.* engendered 264/28.

gentyl *adj.* noble (in rank) 2–316/59.

gentylis *n.pl.* gentlefolk, gentry 90/15, 184/1, 2–10/12.

geomancye *n.* geomancy (divination by signs derived from the earth or by the use of dotted paper) 164/67.

gerdelys *n.pl.* belts 2–161/61.

gernere, garne(e)r *n.* building or structure for storing grain 61/18, 2–314/4, 2–317/7; **garneris** *pl.* 2–275/57.

gestis *n.pl.* (1) chivalric tales or romances 2–99/5.

gestis *n.pl.* (2) invited guests 2–257/49.

getyn, gete *v.* earn 73/31, get, obtain 131/23, 2–87/82, 2–217/55, seize 2–17/40; **gete** *pr.1 sg.* 53/19; **gety3t, -iþ** *pr.3 sg.* accumulates 60/27, receives 197/50, *refl.* gets (for himself; cf. V.L. *sibi adquirent*) 53/32; **getyn** *pr.3 pl.* acquire 2–166/47; **gete** *subj.3 sg.* should receive 2–292/10; **gat** *pa.t.3 sg.* received 345/9, 2–24/22, obtained (for) 2–84/2; **gotyn, getyn** *pp.* 2–151/14, earned 2–16/3, begotten 2–65/87, acquired 2–157/24, 26, recovered 2–260/26.

getynges *vbl.n.pl.* acquisitions 43/iv.

getter(e, iettere *n.* swaggerer, bully 187/
23, 24, 2–267/54; ietterys *pl.* 2–277/22.

gyesytes, gyeȝitas *n.pl.* symoniacs (sellers
of spiritual goods) 44/xvi, 2–174/36.

gyhyȝt *pr.3 sg.* guides 118/35, 132/9;
gyhyd *pa.t.3 sg.* 132/21.

gyldene *adj.* golden 19/69, 135/10, 2–
186/1 (cf. **trentel**).

gyle *n.* guile 149/58, 2–12/66, sleight 180/
22, deception 236/24, 2–130/9; gyles *pl.*
sleights 71/37.

gylous *adj.* duplicitous, deceptive 13/9,
235/5, 2–12/64, 65, 67.

gylouslyche *adv.* treacherously, guilefully
237/41, 2–12/77.

gynnynge *vbl.n.* beginning, origin 356/24.

gynnyth, gynnyȝt *pr.3 sg.* begins 145/39,
357/21, 2–27/22; gynne, gynnyn *pr.3
pl.* 114/29, 145/37, 2–25/40; gynne
subj.3 sg. should begin 2–282/29.

gyrdyl *n.* girdle (ecclesiastical vestment)
2–228/38.

gyrdyn *v.* gird 2–308/44.

glad(e *adj.* cheerful 52/33, joyous 294/35.

gladyn, glade *v.* ~ *of* assuage 268/78,
297/49, *intr.* rejoice 145/39; gladith
pr.3 sg. tr. gladdens 323/59, 2–5/15;
gladyd *pa.t.3 sg.* 297/46; gladyt *pp.*
301/78.

glaryynge *ppl.adj.* glowing, brilliant 269/
17.

gle *n.* pleasures 2–277/31.

glede *n.* bird of prey, kite 182/14 *var.*
RDT (cf. **puttok**).

glemerid *pa.t.3 sg.* glistened 349/62.

glose *n.* gloss (the Glossa Ordinaria of the
Bible) 80/54, 139/90, 155/73.

glotoun *n. þe* ~ *þerof* the one who is greedy
for 41/xii.

gnodd(ed)yn *pa.t.3 pl.* forced kernels of
grain out of the ear by rubbing 289/60,
2–141/17.

go see go(o)n

gobet *n.* morsel 2–4/46.

godisbrede *n.* affinity, kinship (as between
godparent and godchild) 2–58/11.

Godward *adv.* (directed towards) God
201/34, 295/71.

goynge *vbl.n.* walking 352/37.

golyardeys *n.pl.* minstrels 88/27.

golys *n.pl.* sluices 61/19 (cf. V.L. *cataractas*; see Notes).

go(o)n *v. intr.* go 53/37, 63/26, 27, 186/5,

~ *on feer* catch fire 178/32; gost *pr.2 sg.*
goest 327/13; goȝt, goth *pr.3 sg.* turns
120/52, goes 121/59, ~ *abouten* surrounds 144/7, lives 328/46; goon *pr.2
pl.* go, travel 137/52; go(o)n *pr.3 pl.* go
away, stray 48/12, 121/61, 150/11, 171/
8, walk, travel 171/2; ~ *so gay* make a
display of finery 151/41–42; gon *subj.3
pl.* should go 161/36; goth *imp.pl.* go! 2–
315/39; goynge *pr.p.* extending 2–309/
99; wente *pa.t.3 sg.* went 55/27, 236/33,
37, 312/68; wentyn *pa.t.3 pl.* went
about 93/3, 297/30, 33; *pp.* go(ne,
agon gone 2–267/35, ~ *longe sith* too
long a time 321/1, cf. *var.* RDTBYLH.

good *n.* worldly goods 52/39, 41, 60/35,
merchandise 60/44, *haue* ~ *of his* ~ have
the joy of his possessions 80/40.

goot *n.* goat 94/32–34 *var.* Y; gotys, geet
possess.pl. 94/29, 94/32 *var.* BL.

go(o)stly *adj.* spiritual 11/31, 36/xiii, 65/
54, 251/38, spiritually understood 49/
59.

gostly, -lyche *adv.* spiritually 60/59, 60,
285/11, 2–209/88, 2–274/19.

gouernyn *v. refl.* discipline 179/35.

gouernance *n.* authority to rule 340/6, *in
his* ~ under his authority 2–139/31.

goweler *n.* usurer 2–150/93.

gowyl *n.* usury 2–135/19, 2–195/1.

graunt *n.* permission 153/10, 13, 156/6.

grenehed *n.* greenness 146/58–59.

gres *n.* grass 115/54, 144/12, 145/46.

gret(t)e *pa.t.3 sg.* greeted 174/54, 240/51.

grete *adv.* lavishly 151/42, 161/57.

gretynge *vbl.n.* greeting 174/61.

greuaunse *n.* ~ *of* causing resentment
among 2–86/64.

greuous *adj.* irksome 282/44.

greuoushed *n.* gravity, seriousness 2–122/
46.

greuously *adv.* gravely 213/50.

gryckyshe *adj.* Greek 144/9.

gronchyng *vbl.n.* gnashing 2–103/102.

gro(u)ndyn *pr.3 pl.* establish, base 2–19/
84, *refl.* 173/35, 2–93/84, 2–138/18;
grownded *pp.* established 35/xviii,
based (on) 2–138/28.

grongynge *vbl.n.* gnashing or grinding of
teeth (perh. a nonce form of **gronchyng**,
itself a blend of *crengen* and *grinten*) 2–
103/111.

Grosthed *propr.n.* Robert Grosseteste,

Bishop of Lincoln (c1170–1253) 2–18/67.

grount, gro(u)nd(e *n.* plot of ground 219/60, tract of land 353/72, floor 2–23/54, foundation (*fig.*) 2–65/97.

grucche *v. intr.* complain 70/21; **grochyth** *pr.3 sg.* 2–69/64; **grochin, -chen** *pr.3 pl.* 6/115, 30/liii, 193/17, 226/3; **groche** *subj.2 sg.* should complain 259/24; **grochede, grucchid** *pa.t.3 sg.* 30/liii, 193/6.

grutchyng *vbl.n.* grumbling, resentment 25/i; **grochyngis** *pl.* 2–305/30.

3

3a see **3e**

3a, 3a *adv.* expression of mild derision 101/45.

3arde see **3erd(e**

3arne, 3erne *adv.* hurriedly 200/33, quickly 2–271/44.

3ate *n.* gate 55/39, 263/10, 2–56/47; **3atys** *pl.* 24/24, 2–23/71, 2–318/10.

3e, 3a *n.* 'yea', 'yes' affirmative 32/xii, 230/37, 41, 2–218/12, 13.

3e *pron.2 sg./pl.* you (singular, in formal address) 1/3a, 51/10, 52/21, you (plural) 51/19, 52/20, 54/5 (cf. þou).

3e, 3a *adv.* indeed 124/79, 353/69, ~ *forsoþe* yea 283/2, 346/15, 2–302/80.

3efne see EFNE

3el *n.* health 222/12, *with gret* ~ in great safety 349/54 (cf. **heyl-**).

3eldere *n.* the one who submits 129/41.

3eldyn *v.* render 103/47, 57, yield, pay 129/44, 2–50/39, accede to 2–67/15, acknowledge 2–240/86; **3eldith** *pr.3 sg.* yields 2–115/122; **3ilden** *pr.3 pl.* 214/18; **3elde** *subj.3 sg.* should yield 2–115/113; **3eld(e** *imp.sg.* repay 306/71, give in return! 2–69/67, give! 2–137/68; **3eldyth, -dy3t** *imp.pl.* offer! 103/60, 223/27; **3ald** *pa.t.3 sg. refl.* conceded 2–82/55, 56; **30ldyn** *pp.* repaid 2–149/78, returned 2–149/78, 2–156/17.

3eldynge, 3yldyng *vbl.n.* repaying 204/39, 2–285/15, ~ *a3en* bribes, kickbacks 2–210/105.

3eldys *n.pl.* guilds 2–180/67.

3el(o)w *adj.* yellow 142/26, 2–223/40.

3eman *n.* yeoman 118/20.

3e(e)r(e *n.* year 119/12, 157/8, 9, 352/47, *be* ~ per year 45/xx, 2–180/69, ~ *day*

day on which services of commemoration are held for a deceased person 45/xx, 2–184/23, 33; **3er(ys** *pl.* 2–151/8, 2–181/20.

3erd *n.* yard (enclosure for storing hay, cattle or poultry) 2–166/36.

3erde, 3arde *n.* rod 324/3, var./62, 336/24, 26, 2–95/14.

3erne see **3arne**

3esilff *pron. refl.* yourself 74/2.

3euere *n.* bestower 99/63, almsgiver 2–136/46.

3euyn, 3eue(n, 3yue, 3if *v.* give 17/61, 19/49, 53/19, give alms 72/3, *refl.* devote 197/54, 274/2, render 64/10, bestow 65/44; **3euy3t, 3euith, 3yueþ** *pr.3 sg.* gives 12/35, 64/27, 30, 73/17, 2–175/55, *refl.* 64/29; **3euyn, 3yuen** *pr.2 pl.* give 64/8, 72/8; **3euyn** *pr.3 pl.* 64/7, 8, *refl.* devote 4/76, 131/15; **3eue, 3if, 3yue** *subj.3 sg.* should give 224/9, 318/46, 2–176/78, 81, may (God) give 223/21; *refl.* should give 150/12; **3eue, 3yue** *imp.sg.* give! 55/25, 59/12, 13, 80/46; **3af** *pa.t.3 sg.* established 15/9, gave 64/26, 92/13, 307/20, pronounced 2–124/8; **30uyn** *pa.t.3 pl. refl.* devoted 138/56; **30uyn, 30uen, 30uun, 3euyn** *pp.* given 43/viii, 73/19, 84/20, 168/29, 30, promulgated 12/62, 38/xxvi, given over to 149/48, imposed 2–124/17.

3euyng(e *vbl.n.* almsgiving 23/28, giving 166/2.

3if, 3ef *conj.* if 8/36, 55/24, 150/12.

3ifte *n.* benefaction 60/62, gift 64/26, bribe 2–175/56; **3iftys** *pl.* gifts 64/12, 300/50.

3yl- see **3el-**

3is *adv.* yes (in answer to a question containing a negative) 243/11, 247/5, 2–43/84 (cf. 3A).

3it, 3et *adv.* still 116/87, 123/42, 169/18, *ben* ~ *to done* are still to be done 151/43.

3it, 3et *conj.* but, nevertheless 8/34, 61/1, 92/13, 144/6.

3yuynge *ppl.adj.* almsgiving 73/17.

30ng(g)(e, yong, 3unge *adj.* young 26/xi, 43/vii, 81/15, 350/87, 2–150/1.

30nge *n.pl.* young people 165/90.

30nger(r)e *n.pl.* juniors 165/88* (misprinted in text; should be read as **30ngere**), 355/31.

30ok *n.* yoke (*fig.*) 128/23.

ȝotyn *pp.* cast (metal) 2–179/43.

ȝotyn *ppl.adj.* cast (metal) 2–313/29.

ȝou, ȝow *pron.sg./pl.* you (formal *sg.*) 1/6a, 52/35, you (*pl.*) 55/42, 43, 187/36; ȝour(e *pron.sg./pl.possess.* your 51/3, 74/3, 4, 5, 276/42; ȝouris *pron.sg./pl.absolute* yours 75/4. (cf. ȝe).

ȝougþe, ȝuugthe *n.* youth 11/21, 53/35, 55/24.

H

habirgeon *n.* hauberk (jacket of mail) 24/15 *var.* H (cf. haubirchon).

hackyn *v.* hack (to break words into syllables in order to sing them to a series of musical notes) 206/30 (see Notes).

hackyngys *vbl.n.pl.* (figurative use of hackyn, q.v., applied to overlong or tedious anecdotes) 206/32.

halyday *n.* holy day 9/7, 10, 34/xiv, 66/30; halydayys, -dayes, holy- *pl.* 34/xvi, 35/xvii, xviii, 283/1.

halle *n.* house 140/22.

halledam *n. explet.* holy doom 241/2.

halsyn *v.* embrace 85/42.

halue *n. on othir* ~ from another source 130/77, 150/10, 178/29.

haluyndel *n.* half 2–157/45, 2–189/11.

halwyd, halowed *ppl.adj.* celebrated 9/1, 15, 23, 270/57, consecrated 27/xv, 111/11, 2–233/61, hallowed 163/34, 263/11.

halwyn, halwe *v.* celebrate 9/7, 263/6, 272/1, 287/9; halwist *pr.2 sg.* 273/28, *þu* ~ *nout from synne* you do not seek absolution from sin 2–30/6; halwe, -with *pr.3 sg.* celebrates 9/19, 274/9; halwyn *pr.3 pl.* 9/3, 272/39, 284/26; halwe *imp.sg.* hallow! 66/30, halwyth *imp.pl.* 196/43; halwe *subj.2 sg.* should hallow 289/4, 5; halwyde *pa.t.3 sg.* sanctified 263/15.

halwyng *vbl.n.* celebration 273/23, consecrating 352/46.

han *v.* experience 1/9b, 94/20, 24, 118/26, behave (selves) 25/vi, 39/ix, 2–232/1, have, possess 52/38, 56/73, 63/4, 90/22, feel, obtain 54/19, 189/27, 2–17/40, hold (more dear, in contempt, in reverence) 66/29, 101/52, 350/95, train (eyes on) 91/33, receive 99/70, 103/39, 216/65, direct (up to) 112/54, reach (end, person) 115/51, 292/47, have (children,

young, servants) 131/22, 209/3, 7, 240/60, 309/16, put (forth) 137/31, harbor (envy, scorn) 189/28, 358/49, experience, undergo 198/13, 270/45, 46, get (the better of) 255/96, *as aux.* 152/11, ~ *her lust* satisfy their desires 16/41, ~ *forth here domys* hold sway 137/31, ~ *forth* exercise 165/5, ~ *hym* hold himself (to be) 166/8, ~ *more haste to* hurry more towards 199/5, ~ *up his part* get back his share 2–201/16, *refl.* ~ *hem to* conduct themselves in respect to 25/vi. ~, haue *inf.* 80/43, 81/2, 157/4, *refl.* 25/vi, 46/ix; han, a(n, hatþ, haue *aux.* 55/23, 56/64, 57/21, 64/24, 25, 65/57, 100/39, 40; haue *pr.1 sg.* 52/38; hast *pr.2 sg.* 55/25, 59/68, 64/14; hat(3, haþ *pr.3 sg.* 1/9b, 55/52, 70/16; han *pr.1 pl.* 53/9, 99/70; ha *pr.2 pl.* 329/19; han, hauen *pr.3 pl.* 57/17, 152/11, 14; hauyȝt *imp.pl.* 52/34; haue, ha *subj.2 sg.* 259/22, 24; haue *subj.3 sg.* 58/31, 74/16, 329/26; hadde *pa.t.3 sg.* 51/12, 112/54, 270/45; haddyn *pa.t.3 pl.* 69/65; haddist *pa.t.subj. 2 sg.* 63/28, 228/12; hadde *pa.t. aux.* 83/48; had(e, A *pp.* 100/39, 2–176/83.

handele *subj.3 sg.* should touch 2–87/77.

hangyn *v.* hang 240/58, 2–104/13; hangith, hongyth *pr.3 sg.* 2–68/23, 2–258/26; hangit *imp.pl.* 2–101/60; hyng, heng *pa.t.3 sg.* hung (upon) 84/37, 87/6, 89/31, hung 240/54, 307/25, 2–100/23, was hanged 2–24/20, 2–164/149, *refl.* hanged 2–259/7; hyngyn *pa.t.3 pl.* hung 240/53; hangyn *pp.* (be) hanged 160/31, 240/58, 241/65.

hangyn *ppl. adj. doon hym* ~ have him hanged 118/23, 160/31.

hap *n.* accident, chance 2–141/5, good fortune 2–282/36; happis *pl.* mishaps, ill luck 227/31.

happely(che *adv.* perhaps 170/27, 255/96, 311/35.

happyd *pa.t.3 sg.* happened 305/36, 2–143/65.

harachous *adj.* cruel, violent 244/25 (cf. baratous).

hard(e *adj.* severe 19/72, 279/45, difficult 81/11.

harde *adv.* harshly 51/18, with difficulty 55/36, 76/34, severely 139/91, 2–146/31, cruelly 2–251/14.

hardenesse *n.* boldness 138/59.

hardhed *n.* hardship, difficulty 344/47.

hardy *adj.* bold 2–72/28, 2–109/56, *as fool* ~ in a foolhardy way 350/80.

harmys *n.pl.* injuries done 2–178/16, *his* ~ injuries done him 244/22.

harneys *n.sg./pl.* harness (for horse) 44/ xii, 2–280/49, harness (leg armour) 2– 308/61, harnesses (for decorative sword belts) 2–161/60.

harneysyd *pp.* decorated, adorned 2–161/ 64.

hartyn *pr.3 pl.* harden 2–223/36.

hartyth *adj. euyl-* ~ evil-hearted 2–207/29 (mis-*trs.* of V.L. *excors?* see Notes).

hasty *adj.* sudden 290/25.

hastyn *pr.3 pl.* hasten 307/11, bring on 2– 14/11, 24; hastyd *pp.* 2–42/73.

hastinesse *n.* haste 33/xvi.

hastlyche *adv.* quickly, speedily 2–26/61.

hattere *comp.adj.* hotter 2–279/29 (cf. hoot).

haubircho(u)n *n.* hauberk (jacket of mail) 2–307/33, 2–308/45, 52–53, 58 (cf. habirgeon).

haunsyn *v.* glorify, exalt 2–8/42.

haunsyng *vbl.n.* promoting 2–183/83.

hauntyd *pa.t.3 sg.* frequented 2–108/24.

hauntyd *ppl.adj.* practised 257/28.

he *pron.3 sg.masc.* he (referring to male person, God, or abstract personification as grammatical subject of sentence) 1/9a, 8/26, 51/5; (in appositional construction) ~ *þat* . . . ~ *þat* he who . . . it was he who 61/3–4; it is he who . . . it is he who 2–72/26; hym him (direct object) 5/92, 83/49, (indirect object) 4/64, 84, 52/29, (in dative constructions: *he hatȝ al þat hym nedyt*) 58/43, 62, 59/22; *refl.* 8/23; he *þat emphatic* it is he who 61/4, 168/21; þei, he, it *pron.3 pl. masc./fem.* they 5/91, 6/137, 15/6, 36/xiii, 57/14, 186/4, 223/2; hem, (h)ys *oblique cases* them 3/50, 14/28, 290/17, 289/13, 312/63; þe(m)self, hem(self, -silf(f *refl.* 4/76, 37/xxi, 51/4, 11, 66/38, 346/23, 24; he þo, he þese, þey þoo *emphatic* they, it is they who 61/7, 27, 62/38, 104/67, 158/39, 181/6, 7, 251/56, 2–14/21, 2– 181/6 (cf. hern, her(e, his, hese, self).

he(i)d see hefd

hedows, hedous, hydous *adj.* hideous 152/15, 164/48, 2–103/112.

heer see her

hefd, hed *n.* head 83/5, 227/41, 231/54, leader, chief 91/34, 37, 2–70/97, 2–82/ 64; hefdis, hedys *pl.* 94/20, 2–30/27, *lesyn her* ~ grow dazed, lose their wits 118/32, 2–25/39.

hefdyn *pr.3 pl.* behead 2–35/64; he(f)dyd, hefdit, heueded *pp.* 92/16, 149/46, 159/55, 2–15/58.

hefne *n.* heaven 207/68, 2–76/7.

heȝge *imp.sg.* ~ *þin erys* hedge thine ears about (cf. V.L. *s(a)epi . . . spinis*) 2–132/ 40.

hey *n.* (1) hay 2–166/41, heyys *pl. gadryn ynne* . . . ~ gather in hay 287/13, 14.

hey *n.* (2) *in* ~ on high, in heaven 2–238/7.

hey(e, hiȝ *adj.* high, highly serious 83/7, 160/29, 255/86, solemn 88/16, 110/2, very valuable 2–51/10, highly intellectual 2–225/36, grave 217/109, elevated 78/7, high in rank 2–238/12, loud 203/ 25, 207/69.

heid, hed(e *n.* heed, notice 60/52, 64/32, 157/9, 188/17, 18, 19.

heyer *comp.adj.* higher (in rank or status) 346/2, 347/22, 2–41/34.

heyest, heyhist *comp.adj.* highest 96/9, most solemn 87/32, highest (in rank) 324/6.

heyghte, heyȝte, heiȝe, hight, heite, heyȝe *n.* height 136/24, 256/9, 2–89/ 31, *var.* YH, 2–264/59.

heyyd *pp.* raised, elevated 199/20.

heyir see eyr-

heyl(e *adj.* healthy, sound 93/40, 117/10, 296/15, recovered, healed 2–174/29, ~- *sum* wholesome 121/67–8.

heyly, -liche, hyely *adv.* proudly 53/14, fervently 87/4, gravely, seriously 86/8, 188/5, greatly 218/10.

heyrys see eyr

heylsum *adj.* wholesome 121/67–68.

heyuyȝt *pr.3 sg.* raises, elevates 53/27.

held see eld-

helde *ppl.adj.* ~ *be it!* agreed! 2–278/10.

heldyn, hold-, holde *v.* adhere to, believe in 2/21b, 107/5, 2–27/19, hold (plow, a cross) 63/21, 88/17, 19, maintain 66/26, 2–107/15, hold (something up) 86/5, 87/33, 105/14, support 105/13, 2– 107/4, consider (to be) 149/8, 162/2,

230/40, hold onto, hold up, retain 162/
60, 289/54, 2–44/17, 18, 2–305/23,
keep (in error) 213/55, embrace (sexually) 2–64/71, bind (*fig.*) 250/88, hold
(*fig.*) 217/1, 242/34; *intr.* hold (with or
against in argument) 107/5, 313/22, 2–
121/2, 2–129/87, 2–278/10, beholden
(to) 2–278/3.
~ *inf.* 37/xxv, 236/23, 242/34, 2–27/
19, 2–44/17, 2–107/4; **holdist** *pr.2 sg.*
refl. 75/37; **heldyȝt**, halt *pr.3 sg.* 86/14,
162/60, 250/88; **heldyn** *pr.1 pl.* 105/14;
~ *pr.3 pl.* 86/5, 107/5, 217/1, 2–121/2;
helde *subj.3 sg.* 105/13; **hold, held**
imp.sg. 2–44/18, 2–305/23; **heldyn,**
holdyn, holde *pp.* 149/8, 162/2, 289/
54, 2–44/32.
helede, helyd *pa.t.3 sg.* healed 288/45, 2–
22/34; **heledyn** *pa.t.3 pl.* 2–17/51;
helyd *pp.* 2–5/38, 2–22/34, 2–69/71.
helpe *n.* helper 351/112, helpmeet 2–128/
51, 59, 60, aid 2–282/18, 23, *for ~ of* to
help 170/46.
helpely *adj.* helpful 98/47, 2–225/37.
helpyn *v.* help, aid 310/15, 2–128/61;
halp *pa.t.3 sg.* 2–15/51, 2–272/62, 2–
283/56; **holpyn** *pa.t.3 pl.* 310/15; ~
subj.pa.t.3 pl. 96/32; ~, **holpe** *pp.* benefitted 22/10, 23/33, 48/7, 170/31.
helpyng *vbl.n. of the ~* among those helping 150/31.
hem, her(e see **he**
hem *n.* uncle 2–280/56.
hendir *comp.adv.* nearer 358/56.
hen(nu)s, henys *adv.* hence, to death 51/
13, 70/13, 2–138/10, ago 65/3, 66/23,
far away 212/18,
hentyn *pa.t.3 pl.* snatched, seized 2–281/
66.
her(e, hyr(e, hir, hyr see **s(c)he, he**
he(e)r, heyre, hayre *n.* hair 92/26, 95/11,
307/23, 350/75, *weryn þe ~* wear a hair
shirt 2–91/30, 2–188/66.
her(e *adj.* their 18/39, 23/27, 43/ii, 54/41
(cf. **he**).
here *pron.* see **hern**
hereaforn *adv.* in times past 61/11.
heraunttys *adj.* errant, wandering 98/52.
herawdys *n.pl.* heralds 88/27.
herberwe, herbarwe *n.* shelter 2–243/77,
2–249/31, 2–285/35.
heremyte *n.* hermit, eremite 216/63.

herere *n.* listener 2–133/49; **hereris** *pl.*
207/62.
heresie *n.* heresy 148/27, 331/37, 2–20/
41, 2–23/60; **eresyys** *pl.* 222/10, 2–92/
55.
heretyk, -tyc *n.* heretic 2–42/72, 2–43/74,
2–236/57; **heretykys** *pl.* 17/3-4, 194/
41, 204/57, 58.
heryn, here *v.* hear 90/5, 152/9, 198/16,
2–119/10, listen to 338/14; **heere** *pr.1*
sg. learn 79/1; **heryȝt** *pr.3 sg.* hears 85/
56; **heryn, heren** *pr.1 pl.* 147/19; **heren**
pr.3 pl. overhear 150/27; **here** *subj.2 sg.*
should hear 258/21, should listen to 2–
97/58; **her(e** *imp.sg.* hear! 330/6, 2–
132/40, 2–257/46; **herith** *imp.pl.* 322/
10; **harde** *pa.t.1 sg.* 321/1; **hardist**
pa.t.2 sg. 2–315/34; **herd(e, harde**
pa.t.3 sg. 55/26, 204/38, 224/13, 2–
106/54; **herd, hard** *pp.* 107/4, 123/39,
251/42, 2–68/37.
heryng(e *vbl.n.* hearing (attending) 2–23/
68, (sense of) hearing 2–320/54.
h)eritage *n.* inheritance 118/24, 2–213/
22, heritage 307/10, 30.
heris see **ere**
hern, her(e *pron. absol.* theirs 77/23, 320/
18, 2–195/71 (cf. **he**).
herte, harte *n.* heart 32/xi, 240/41, 54,
fig. 6/122, 2–1/8, will 61/9, 10, inner
moral sense 2–227/5, 2–253/9, 10,
aȝenys ~ against (his) wishes 2–94/121,
with gret ~ emphatically 2–25/54; **hertis**
pl. thoughts 2–254/29.
herth(e see **erde**
hertly, -lyche *adv.* heartily 207/52, 351/
108.
hese see **his**
hesy see **esy**
hesyd *pp.* relieved 279/46.
hest(e *n.* law set forth by God 2–33/8, 2–
208/51, 54, promise 2–217/40, 243/13;
hestys *pl.* vows 225/56, 57, 243/13,
God's laws 67/11, 356/17, the Commandments 2–28/39, 41.
hetnesse *n.* heathendom 133/40.
heuenes *n. possess.sg.* heaven's 76/29, 31,
77/32.
heuy *adj.* sorrowful 149/61, 276/42, dis-
approving 2–133/49, reluctant 208/76,
weighed down (*fig.*) 353/66.
heuy *adv. bar ~ (þer)of* took it hard 193/5,

2–94/116, were so distressed by 2–99/ 9–10.

heuylyche *adv.* ponderously, solemnly 207/61.

heuynesse, heue- *n.* foreboding 177/70, torpor 207/57, 63, 236/34, melancholy 2–19/15, 2–318/30, 36, reluctance 2– 136/42.

hew *n.* hue, colour 145/55.

hye, hiʒ *adv.* much, highly 124/82, 147/3, high 78/7.

hyʒt- see hot-

hyʒte *pa.t.3 sg.* was called 2–62/6, 8, 2– 85/10, 33.

hijlden *pr.2 pl.* strip skin from, flay 2–14/ 20 *var.* BYL (cf. MED **hildinge**).

hyyn *v. refl.* hasten 2–306/70; **hyʒe** *imp.sg.* 84/30.

hilyng, helyng *vbl.n.* clothing 71/51, 2– 14/27 *var.al.*

hyllyth *pr.3 sg.* covers 2–228/32; **hyl** *imper.sg.* shroud 215/42; **hilde** *pa.t.2 pl.* clothed 2–243/76; ~ *pa.t.3 sg.* hid, covered 350/76; **hyldyn** *pa.t.3 pl.* 2– 228/34; **hyl(ly)d** *pp.* 26/xb, 2–228/34.

hymselfward *pron.3 sg.refl.* for his own advantage 185/7.

hynderyng(e *vbl.n.* detriment 247/21, 320/16, 357/16.

hynd(e)ryn *v.* harm 2–159/101, mistreat 10/4; **hynderith** *pr.3 sg.* harms 2–8/42; **hinderyn** *pr.3 pl.* pester 35/ii; **hynder- ynge** *pr.p.* harming 2–1/16.

hyng- see hang-

hyr(e *n.* wages 38/viii, 182/13a, 2–16/9, payment 53/18, 2–285/15, *let to* ~ rent out 290/21, 2–179/53, *~-seruyce* service done as a bribe 2–175/50; **hyrys** *pl.* wages 13/13, 2–16/2, 2–130/12.

hyr, her(e *adj.* her 73/37, 224/14, 25, 346/20 (cf. SCHE).

hyr *adv.* ~ *benepe* here on earth 3/55, 2– 302/71, now, at this time 2–159/2, 2– 173/14.

hirde *n. hyr in* ~ payment to one's own household 2–285/15 (cf. **hyr(e**; cf. *D&P* I:I, xv). See Note, 2–285/15.

hyrene see **yrn**

hyryd *ppl.adj.* hired 2–16/5.

his, hese *adj. possess.* his 3/41, 14/29, 58, 17/68, 85/46 (cf. **hern**).

hyuys *n.pl.* bee hives 2–166/37.

ho *pron.* who (before direct question) 55/

33, 2–11/52, 2–325/62, who (before indirect question) 2–139/38, *as ~ seye* as if one said, as much as to say 2–81/36 (cf. **qhoo**).

Hoche *n.* Ark of God 297/33, 2–107/4, chest 312/70, 318/32.

hokyr *n.* contempt, scorn 222/5.

ho(o)l *adj.* complete 79/16, in one piece 93/40, 2–310/127, full 2–249/41, intact 349/56, whole (of body) 288/40.

holy *adv. ringyn* ~ ring church bells for or before church services 287/8–9.

holde *ppl.adj.* attached, beholden 2–278/3 (cf. **heldyn**).

holwe *adj.* hollow 236/21.

homely, -lyche *adj.* familiar 90/15, 325/ 55.

homlyche *adv.* familiarly 351/112.

hond *n.* (1) hand (as part of body) 92/27, 187/19, power, authority 2–204/25, hand (*fig.*) 77/9, 2–175/48, 49; **hondys, -des** *pl.* hands (as parts of body) 104/6, 235/39, power, authority 27/xiv, 311/40, 2–18/75.

hond *n.* (2) hound 2–123/58; **houndys** *pl.* 2–15/52, 2–256/29.

honeste *n.* decorum, respectability 293/30, 316/39, 2–152/52.

h)onestly *adv.* properly, respectably 190/9.

hong- see hang-

honoracioun *n.* honouring 109/53.

honterys *n.pl.* hunters 5/105.

hontynge, hunt- *vbl.n.* hunting 186/6, 11, 13.

hoo *interj. seie* ~ say 'enough!' 71/42 (see Notes).

hool *adv. al* ~ entirely 146/76 (cf. **hol**).

horyd, hored *ppl.adj.* (preceded by *whyt-*) having greyish-white hair 332/3, mouldy 260/21, 23, 35 *var.* BYL

h)orlege, -loge *n.* clock 119/24, 120/34, 39, 122/6.

horleger *n.* clock maker or clock tender 120/50; **horlegerys** *possess.sg.* 122/10.

horriblete *n.* horror 2–82/69.

ho(u)s(e)bo(u)nd(e *n.* husband 15/13, 17, 41/vii, 345/12, 2–70/92, 94.

hoso *indef.pron.* whoever 170/47, 219/40, 2–16/12.

hospital *n.* almshouse (charitable founda- tion for care of the poor) 2–183/1.

hostelerys *n.pl.* inn keepers 151/41.

ho(o)t *n.* promise 2–175/68, 2–234/15.

ho(o)t(e *adj.* hot 143/37, 38, 280/8. 2–278/8.

hotyn *v.* promise 2–25/36; hotyth *pr.3 sg.* 177/66, 185/22, 234/8; hotyn *pr.3 pl.* 185/11, 234/15, 2–180/69; hote *subj.3 sg.* should promise 2–175/62, 72; hyȝte, hyghte *pa.t.3 sg.* 137/43, 184/18, 2–87/89, assured 2–280/50; hyȝtyn *pa.t.3 pl.* 2–10/8 (cf. behyȝt).

hotyng *vbl.n.* promising, vow 247/1.

houyn *v. intr.* rise (to surface) 2–247/19.

houselyd *pp.* given communion 172/9, 2–203/4.

houselyng *vbl.n.* the communion rite 2–181/31.

housyn *v. intr.* build (houses or barns) 2–18/83, 2–275/47, 2–315/22.

housynge *vbl.n.* house building 291/20, 21, barns 2–275/56.

hout see ouȝt

how(e, howȝ, howgh, hou(gh *adv.* how, in what way (as *interrog.adv.*) 76/1, 83/1, 2–81/40, in what way (as *conjunct.adv.*) 2/2, 83/5, 2–16/9, to what extent 77/36, that 28/xxxiv.

hul *n.* holly 146/59.

hurlebat *n.* weapon, or game using weapons, perh. wooden bats 2–40/5.

I/J/Y

I, Y *pers.pron. 1 sg.* 52/38, 40, 81/11, 159/1, 264/36 (cf. ME).

iacinctus *n.* jacinth (gem of blue colour) 2–321/28–29.

iacke *n.* jack (stuffed jacket worn under mail 24/15 *var.* H 2–310/116, 125, 130 (cf. aketone).

iangelyng *vbl.n.* din, noisy altercation 275/35.

iape *n.* laughing stock 53/38, jest, mocking speech 115/35, 2–281/64.

iaperye *n.* trickery 158/35, 168/18, 2–157/26, mockery 222/3; iaperyys *pl.* tricks 202/47*.

iaperys *n.pl.* tricksters 4/67, 28/xxxiii, 151/39, 156/3.

iapyn *v.* mock, tease 2–72/30; iapinge *pr.p.* 305/42.

iarg- see charch-, charg-

iaspis *n.* jasper (a variety of chalcedony) 2–321/25.

ich(e, eche *adj.* each 25/vi, 34/x, 120/38, 348/15, ~ *dayis bred* daily bread 62/4.

iche, ech *pron.* each 37/xviii, 63/32, 145/47.

ydyl *adj.* idle, frivolous 103/51, 2–98/69, 2–214/44, 45, slothful 2–310/112.

ydylshepe, -chep(e, -schyp *n.* idleness, sloth 207/65, 294/44, 2–96/18, idle pursuits 308/44, *take in* ~ take in vain 66/30, 222/9, 229/45.

ydromancie *n.* hydromancy (witchcraft by means of water, such as tides or wells) 164/71.

Ieneuer, Ianyuere *n.* January 5/99, 29/xlvii, 182/2.

iestourrys *n.pl.* jesters 88/27–28.

iettere see getter

Iewerye *n.* Jewry 2–226/51.

yhs *n.* piece of ice 2–189/2, 6, 9, ice 2–276/3.

yih, iȝe see eye

ike, eke *conj.* ~ *þan* therefore, ergo (preceding conclusion of an argument) 264/37, 294/54, 313/5, 2–216/21.

ylde *n.* island 205/9.

ymaged *ppl.adj.* sculpted or painted 26/iv.

ymagery *n.* sculptured, painted, embroidered (etc.) representations of saints and other religious figures 26/i, 82/43, 91/1, 3.

imperial *adj.* ~ *lawe* Roman law 28/xxxiv.

immedyat(lyche *adv.* directly, without intermediary 152/28, 2–110/18, 2–121/20.

in(ne *prep.* in 1/4a, 81/1, 99/68, on 18/39, 40, in a state of 52/30, in respect to 81/11, held in 88/23, at 99/8(1), 135/27, 142/30(2), in scope or power of 131/29, 132/1, 139/2, during 144/13, 181/8, into 158/22, 170/26, 177/67, against 262/92, of 2–230/93,

inclynaccioun *n.* disposition 126/50, 127/64.

incluhs *n.pl.* anchorites (cloistered persons) 2–92/54, 56.

incluhs *adj.* cloistered, enclosed 2–92/56.

inconuenient *adj.* improper 252/18.

indepartabiliche *adv.* inseparably 2–79/74.

yndyr- *adj.* ~ *herte* inmost heart's 2–301/62, ~ *sorwe* inward sorrow 2–212/43, ~ *wyȝt* conscience 104/74, ~ *wyttis* common sense 195/7 (cf. endyr-).

induy- see endu-

infect *adj.* stained, corrupted 2–84/118.

information, -cioun *n.* instruction 71/50, 275/22, 314/34.

inhibicions *n.pl.* prohibitions 2–142/34.

inhonest *adj.* indecent, shameful 2–128/62.

inhonesteis *n.pl.* shameful actions 2–223/55.

ynnyn *v.* harvest, reap 2–315/24.

ynow(3)(e *n.* enough, sufficient 58/38, 71/42, 186/19, 291/22.

inow(e *adv.* sufficiently 90/21, 2–99/4, 2–129/88 (cf. anow(e).

ynow(3)(e *adj.* enough 71/42, 80/42, 90/21, 2–282/27 (cf. anow-).

inpassiblete *n.* impassibility (the freedom from death, sickness, pain or other bodily afflictions of angels) 286/27.

inpertinent *adj.* irrelevant 344/44.

interdyt *n.* interdict, excommunication 2–206/67, 68.

in(n)(e)to *prep.* unto 71/29, 339/39, facing towards 113/1, 2, 114/9, 11, until 65/5, 135/16, as 2–60/2.

intrykyn *v.* involve, enmesh 2–265/72 (cf. entrik-).

iocund *adj.* joyous, insouciant 2–257/43.

ioy(e *n.* joy 49/75, 145/39, 207/52.

iogulourys see iugulourys

ioyyn *v. intr.* rejoice 209/33; ioyyt *pr.3 sg.* rejoices (in) 2–268/74.

ionyyn *v.* (1) impose on 2–54/38; enionyid *pp.* enjoined 256/3.

ionyyn *v.* (2) join, clasp 254/69, 2–50/29; ~ *pr.2 pl.* link, annex 2–207/33, 2–255/55.

iorne, iurne *n.* journey 10/27, 155/54, 290/20, expedition, campaign 2–208/60; iornyes *pl.* 34/xvi, 290/1.

iowel *n.* jewel 2–53/6, 7, 2–132/15.

yrn, hyrene *n.* iron 2–230/20, 2–315/14.

irregular, -ler *adj.* irregular (in violation of canon law) 14/49, 2–39/53, 55, 2–111/1.

irreguler(y)te, -lar(y)te(e *n.* irregularity (a violation of canon law) 14/50, 40/xix, 2–114/66.

irresonnable, vnreson- *adj.* ~ *bestis* irrational animals 98/42, 2–119/28, 2–314/45.

is *v.* see ben

is *demons. pron. pl.* these 152/21 (cf. þei, he).

it (they) see he

iudicial *n.* predictions (of astrology) 3/49, 135/16, 137/49.

iudicial *adj.* ~ *astronomye* astrology 28/xxv, 139/84.

yuel see euel

iuge *n.* judge 12/47, 236/18, 343/7, 31; iugis, -gys *pl.* 343/20, 2–88/98, 2–233/44.

iugolour *n.* minstrel, entertainer, magician 2–267/64; iugolourys iogulourys, -lowres *possess.sg.* 22/14, 48/10, 2–267/54; iugulouris *possess.pl.* 2–157/27; ~ *pl.* 2–74/86.

yuy *n.* ivy 146/60.

iulie *n.* July 183/30.

iunie *n.* June 183/30.

iurerys *n.pl.* swearers (in law court), witnesses 234/29.

iurne see iorne

iustis *n.pl.* jousts 2–40/5.

iustyse, -tice *n.* judge in court of law 2–36/22, 2–49/3, 4, 6.

K

kalender, calander *n.* calendar (the ecclesiastical listing of feast days, saints' days, fast days, etc. 173/47), (the year, as divided into days and months) 182/10, (table of contents) 2–var./80 *var.*Y; kalendyrs *pl.* books, guidebooks 108/29 *var.* H. See Notes.

kalendis *n.sg./pl.* kalends (first day of a month) 182/2, 13, 183/14, 22. See Notes.

karyn *v. intr.* be concerned 52/46.

kech- see cach-

keen, kenne *n.* relationship, kinship 90/18, 2–109/4, 2–293/38; keen *pl.* kin, relatives 128/14.

kelyn *v.* cool 2–189/4, 2–279/33.

kende, kynde *n.* essential human nature 1/1b, 51/6, 63/14, nature (the natural order external to man) 3/55, 56, 28/xxix, 90/8, 10, 2–129/71, species 95/5, 266/25, human form 215/33, 35, feminine nature or gender 2–88/8, 2–89/9, *of* ~ by nature 175/10, *in his* ~ in his essential nature 95/3, *comoun cours of* ~ the order of nature 123/60, 125/9, 139/98, *be* ~ by natural means 168/14, *han not be* ~ have no natural way 2–96/22, *don her* ~ perform according to natural laws 3/55, 28/xxviii, 144/19, *precept of* ~ precept of natural law 2–28/50; **kendys** *pl.* natural attributes (of celestial bodies) 138/82.

kende(ly, kynd(e)ly *adj.* natural (guided by the laws of human nature) 36/v, 72/18, 171/58, (guided by the laws of earthly or celestial nature) 145/36, 183/29, 32, 184/6, humanly kind, loving 310/27, 2–128/55.

kendely, kynd- *adv.* naturally, on account of one's human nature 72/21, 299/19.

kenrede, kyn- *n.* kin, relatives 262/69, 70, 71, 73, 322/31, 32, 328/40; **kenredys, kyn-** *pl.* tribes (of Israel) 54/8, 2–316/59.

kepyn *v.* care for 63/21, 2–88/110, watch over 348/19, 2–20/39, maintain 2–16/21; **kepy3t, -iþ** *pr.3 sg.* preserves (for) 59/26, 80/44; **kepte** *pa.t.subj.3 sg.* watched over 129/59.

kepynge *vbl.n.* maintenance 264/40.

kest- see **cast-**

kyln *v.* kill 161/49.

kyne *n.pl.* kine, cows 2–119/29.

kynde see **kend-**

kyþin *pr.3 pl.* inform 151/40; **kyd** *pp.* made known, revealed to the world 88/25.

knakkyng *ppl.adj.* elaborately trilled 208/73 *var.al.*.

knaue *n.* common person, uncouth person 297/38; **knauys** *pl.* 90/15.

kny3t, knyth *n.* knight 181/2, 339/40, 2–36/9; **kny3this** *pl.* 194/37.

kny3tchepe *n.* knighthood 2–166/46.

kny3thod *n.* knighthood 2–304/6, 2–307/21.

knyttyn *v. refl.* unite 2–79/74; **knyttith** *pr.3 sg.* adjoins 356/15, *refl.* joins 221/10.

knyttynge *vbl.n.* uniting 2–112/13.

knockys *n.pl.* blows 2–46/17.

knowynge *vbl.n.* knowledge 170/52.

knowith *pr.3 sg.* knows physically, has sexual intercourse with 2–115/115; **knowe** *subj.3 sg.* ~ *togedyr fleschly* should have intercourse with 2–115/116, 120; **knowyng** *pr.p.* having intercourse with 41/vii; **knewyn** *pa.t.3 pl.* knew (in both sexual and non-sexual senses) 2–87/73; **knowyn** *pp.* known (sexually by) 2–75/117, 2–115/108.

knowlechyn *v.* acknowledge 203/16, 2–81/39; ~ *pr.1 pl.* 105/11, 15; ~ *pr.3 pl. refl.* 2–224/69; ~ *subj.pr.1 pl.* should acknowledge 203/8, 12, 13; **knowlechid** *pa.t.3 sg.* 2–24/21, 2–82/57, 58, 60.

knowlechyng(ge *vbl.n.* acknowledgement 99/69, 103/36, 203/14.

koc, cok *n.* euphemism for 'God' in an oath 241/1, slang word for penis in oaths 7/21, 32/xii, 242/20, 26, 243/53, 10 (cf. **cockis**).

kom- see **com-**

L

labbe *n.* tattletale, gossip 2–8/16.

lacchyn *v.* catch, ensnare 125/19.

lachesse *n.* slackness, laziness 2–290/17.

lackere *n.* blamer 2–221/42; **lackeris** *pl.* 2–9/47 (cf. **lakk-**).

lackyn, lakke *v.* blame, criticize 20/12, 46/v, 2–6/41, 2–90/47; **lackith** *pr.3 sg.* 2–8/41, *what* ~ *me 3it* what do I lack still 75/23; **lac(ke** *imp.sg.* blame! 2–9/50, 2–220/27; **lackyng** *pr.p.* blaming 2–220/25, 2–222/26; **lackedyn** *pa.t.3 pl.* criticized 2–133/51; **lakkyd** *pp.* blamed 25/vii, 57/9, 78/8.

ladyd *pa.t.3 sg.* loaded 2–143/67.

lady *propr.n.* *our(e* ~ the Blessed Virgin Mary 108/43, 174/54, 240, 51; **ladyys** *possess.sg.* 4/86.

layfe *n.* laity 256/25, 353/77, 354/82.

lakyn *n.* in oaths, euphemism for (Our) Lady 32/xii, 241/3. See Notes.

lakk- see **lack-**

lakkyng *vbl.n.* reproaching 25/vii, 41/xii, blaming 2–220/34.

lamb- see **lomb-**

langouryn *v. intr.* languish, suffer for protracted period 2–189/92, *tr.* cause to languish 2–190/30, 39.

large *adj.* spacious 2–272/67, 72.

largesse *n.* generosity 59/20.

lastyd see **lestyn**

late *adv.* recently 187/22, tardily, slowly 306/5, *now* ~ just now 172/3, 237/8.

latoun *n.* metal (alloy of copper, tin and other metals) 2–155/57, 2–161/69.

lawe *n.* *þe* ~ canon law 90/20, 114/8, *elde* ~ Old Testament 98/40, *newe* ~ New

Testament 114/20, ~ *imperial* Roman law 159/53, *kyngys* ~ common law 160/11, *londis* ~ customary or local law 160/11, ~ *cyuyle* state law (as opposed to Church law) 2–53/28, ~ *posityf* statute law 2–172/29,

law(3)hyn *v. intr.* laugh 2–138/23, 2–279/35; **lahwe** *pr.1 sg.* 2–279/23; **lawhyn** *pr.3 pl.* 2–279/35; **low(h** *pa.t.3 sg.* 2–279/19, *tr.* 305/41.

lawhynge *vbl.n.* laughing 2–277/32.

leche *n.* doctor 68/27, 175/11, 2–42/60; **lechys** *pl.* 175/23, 288/33.

lechecraft *n.* healing, arts of medicine 2–296/47.

lechinge *vbl.n.* relieving, alleviating 2–23/64 (cf. **alech-**).

lechour *n.* lecher 2–107/15; **lec(-c)(h)ouris, -owres** *pl.* 40/vi, 2–44/36, 2–74/87, 2–210/110.

ledere *n.* leader, chieftain 91/34, 339/41; **-erys** *n.pl.* 350/101.

led(d)yn *v.* lead 139/5, 294/37, 2–70/98, transport 290/17; ~ *pr.3 pl.* 289/15; **ledde** *pa.t.3 sg.* led 137/48; **leddyn** *pa.t.2 pl.* ~ *it . . . a3en* fetched it . . . back 2–17/52; **led** *pp.* led away 2–94/102.

leet see **let-**

lefght *adj.* left 91/5.

lefne *n.* lightning 295/82, 2–281/65 (cf. **leuen-**).

leful(l, leueful *adj.* lawful 2/1, 26/i, 61/11, 261/52.

lefullyche, -fuly, -foly *adv.* lawfully 8/25, 229/2, 250/18, 316/30.

leggeharneys *n.* leg armour 24/15 *var.* H.

ley(y)n, leie, ligge *v.* lay 76/52, lay (bet) 71/2, lay (hands on) 236/22, lay (covering on) 311/50, put (in pledge) 2–198/2, store (grain) 2–275/53, 56; **leyt(h** *pr.3 sg.* lays (hand) 7/14, 235/32, lays (ear to) 2–276/3; **ley** *pr.3 pl.* lay (hand) 235/30; **ley** *imp.sg.* hear! (lay ear to) 274/3; **leyde** *pa.t.3 sg.* laid 236/25, 36, 2–302/70, laid (on), beat 2–263/17, *refl.* lay 236/35, 2–255/10; **leydyn** *pa.t.3 pl.* laid (ear to) 2–276/9; **leyd** *pp.* put to bed 311/43.

leyynge, liggyng *vbl.n.* *wed(de* ~ pawning, giving security for repayment 17/15, 43/viii.

leman *n.* paramour 219/51; **lemanys** *pl.* 219/50.

lendyn *v.* lend 2–196/31; **lende** *subj.3 sg.* should lend 2–148/43; **lendyth** *imp.pl.* lend! 2–196/27; **lente** *pa.t.3 sg.* lent 2–147/1, 2–199/56.

lendyng(e, lenyng *vbl.n.* money lending 43/viii, lending (of goods) 2–147/3, 2–195/3.

lendys *n.pl.* loins 2–307/32, 2–308/43, 44, 2–312/182.

leneþe *n.* length 2–238/21.

lenynge *pr.p.* leaning 236/19.

Lentoun, -tyn, Lente *n.* Lent (the forty days before Easter) 2/14, 99/1, 173/43–44, 2–58/24.

leon, lyon *n.* lion 97/23, 341/29; **leonys** *pl.* 216/64.

leonesse *n.* lioness 97/25.

lepre *n.* leprosy 2–174/38.

leprousis *n.pl.* lepers 2–184/3.

leryn *v.* learn 265/55, 310/14; ~ *pr.3 pl.* 209/7; **leryth** *imp.pl.* learn! (cf. V.L. *discite*) 265/62; **leryd** *pp.* 81/1.

le(e)syn, lese *v.* lose 52/39, 40, 94/16, 2–2/38, cause to be damned 96/32, 348/18, confound 139/93, destroy 323/55; **leesiþ, lesith** *pr.3 sg.* loses 78/37, 353/73; **lesyn** *pr.3 pl.* 2–290/4; **le(e)s** *pa.t.3 sg.* 92/21, 238/20, 2–316/57, damned 137/42; **lost, lorn** *pp.* lost 238/25, destroyed 251/57, 287/17, damned 265/58.

lesyng(e *vbl.n.* (1) lie, falsehood 125/17, 2–30/15, 2–213/18, lying 20/8, 148/27, 2–219/54; **lesyng(g)ys, -es** *pl.* lies 151/36, 154/41, 2–4/47, 48, lyings, telling of lies 20/4, 153/3, 2–211/10.

lesynge, leesyng *vbl.n.* (2) losing 229/4, destruction 257/42.

lesyngmongeres, -ys *n.pl.* spreaders of lies 46/i (space after **lesyng** in text should be omitted), 2–132/18.

lesse *adj.* lesser 42/xxiii.

lessyn *v.* diminish 2–159/101; **lessith** *pr.3 sg.* 2–127/10, *intr.* grows less 183/22; **lessyd** *tr. pp.* decreased 347/4.

lessynge *vbl.n.* lessening 2–23/65.

lest(e *adj.* least 153/22, 2–69/58, smallest 2–5/34.

lestyn *v. intr.* continue, endure 54/20, 170/23, 272/50; **lestyth** *pr.3 sg.* 2–106/58; **lestyd, last-** *pa.t.3 sg.* lasted, persisted 134/54, *tr.* kept his promise (to) 2–280/51.

lestyng *vbl.n.* endurance 273/4.

lestyngge *ppl.adj.* enduring 134/54.

lesue *n.* pasture 331/39, 2–18/59.

let(yn, lat(yn, lete *v.* let (go past) 5/106, consider, deem 12/61, 139/3, 354/5, allow, permit 61/23, 2–224/3, 2–189/95, grant 313/79, leave (untouched) 348/28, leave (naked) 2–135/4, *refl.* consider (self) 5/112, 59/67, 328/34, let (to hire) 220/62, 2–152/40, 2–201/6, (with preposition 'by') have high (or low) regard for, esteem 53/40, 139/96, 2–288/28, be poorly regarded 2–63/41, delay 2–26/64.

    letyn, lat-, lete *inf.* 61/23, 191/27, 313/79, 2–86/49, 2–189/92; **lete** *pr.1 sg.* 100/27, 159/1, 328/34, 2–257/1; **letyst, leet** *pr.2 sg.* 59/67; **letyth, -yȝt, lat(yth, leet** *pr.3 sg.* 54/44, 139/96, 342/49, 2–201/6; **letyn** *pr.3 pl.* 5/106, 53/40, 2–288/28; **lete** *subj.3 sg.* 2–189/95; **lete, le(e)t, lat** *imp.sg.* 227/30, 250/4, 2–3/28, 29, 2–53/31; **letyth** *imp.pl.* 2–244/112; **lete** *pa.t.2 sg.* 348/28; **leet** *pa.t.3 sg.* 261/59, 2–152/44, 46, 48, 2–188/83, 2–260/28; **letyn** *pp.* 324/4, 2–63/41, 2–196/38; **ket** *imper.* 2–26/64.

lete *ppl.adj.* *wern wel* ~ *of hemself* had an overly high opinion of themselves 2–83/97.

leteryd, lettrid *ppl.adj.* literate 79/1, 312/54, 2–44/33.

letynge *vbl.n.* (a) letting (to hire) 2–198/8.

lettere *n.* impediment (to) 2–254/30.

lett(yn *v.* check, hinder 22/20, 48/19, 114/13, keep 100/28, 340/61, prevent 178/26, 2–86/43, 2–142/35, hold back 314/27, harm 2–42/48, 50, deprive 2–291/36; **lettyth, letteþe** *pr.3 sg.* prevents 33/xv, checks 152/26, hinders 2–191/75, holds back 2–205/55, 2–23/51; **lettyn** *pr.3 pl.* impair, override 315/18; **let** *imp. sg.* delay! 2–26/64; **lettyng(e** *pr.p.* checking, thwarting 96/33; **lettyd** *pa.t.3 sg.* prevented 2–102/90; **lettedyn** *pa.t.3 pl.* deprived 2–198/29; **lettyd** *pp.* kept 293/16, hindered 2–187/44.

lettyng(e *vbl.n.* hindrance 56/75, 57/19, 77/19, impediment 286/30, 35, omitting 2–190/34; *for* ~ *of lucre* in order not to

decrease profits 100/31; **lettyngys** *pl.* preventatives 178/28.

leue *n.* permission 118/21, 29, 152/14, 340/56, 2–75/22.

leue *adj.* dear 1/1, 51/2, 346/21.

leueful *adj.* proper, permissable 113/3.

leuen(e *n.* lightning 142/21, 2–103/106, 2–319/35 (cf. **lefne**).

leuer *comp.adj.* *is* ~ is more willing 30/lv (cf. MED **lef**).

leuer(e, leuyr *comp.adv.* *han* ~ more gladly 101/52, would rather 168/25, 189/38, 39, *han* ~ *to* would more gladly 5/93, 279/43 (cf. MED **lef**).

leuyn *v.* (1) fail to do 137/37, let pass 186/15, remain 318/47, leave (behind) 325/45, eschew 137/37, 2–71/19, 2–91/34; **le(e)uyst** *pr.2 sg.* leave 79/15, renounce 2–71/17; **leuyth, -yȝt** *pr.3 sg.* abandons 100/17, 2–119/14, *þat* ~ *þe ouyr þer* what remains to thee at the end of the year (V.L. *reliquiae tuae*; cf. **ouyr**) 2–314/5; **leuyn** *pr.2 pl.* eschew 2–290/9; **leuyn** *pr.3 pl.* omit 202/40, ~ *ben* abandon 187/33; **leue** *imp.sg.* depart from var./78; **lefte, -tyn** *pa.t.3 sg./pl.* remained 2–10/14, 2–73/57; **leftyn** *pa.t.subj.3 pl.* should abandon 62/41.

leuyn, lyuyn *v.* (2) believe 20/10, 87/43, 151/36, 2–83/82, *intr.* 87/43, 2–50/36; **leuyth** *pr.3 sg. tr.* 2–324/19, 22; **leuen** *pr.3 pl.* 151/54; **leuyȝt** *imp.sg.* believe 52/33; **leue** *subj.3 sg.* should believe 2–198/15, 2–324/39; **leuyngge** *pr.p.* believing 62/35; **leuedist** *pa.t.2 sg.* believed 2–11/29; **leuedyn** *pa.t.3 pl.* 2–125/66, 2–216/27; **leuyd** *pp.* 2–125/67, 2–261/75.

leuyngis *n.pl.* leftovers, winter-stored foods 2–317/8 (cf. V.L. *reliquiae*; cf. **ouyr**).

leuys *n.pl.* leaves 107/18, 145/54.

lewyd *adj.* lay, non-clerical 167/25, 239/18, 327/4, illiterate 2/1b, 82/43, 86/18, 90/23, ignorant 87/39, 338/39, 2–19/7.

lewydnesse *n.* ignorance 89/41, 107/3.

lych(e *adj.* liege (owing service to) 118/19, 25, 26, 160/5, 228/16, liege (service owed by) 2–86/41.

lyche *n.* lord, person owed service 333/3.

lyer(e *n.* liar 154/42, 44; **lyerys** *pl.* 2–212/30, 2–214/43.

lyf- see **lyu-**

lyflyche *adv.* in lively fashion 207/60.

ly(j)flod(e *n.* livelihood, sustenance 51/17, 71/51, 2–96/23.

lyft, lefght *adj.* left 91/5, 187/25, 29, 2–243/56.

ligg- see **ley-**

lyghter *comp.adj.* lighter 152/6 (cf. **lyʒt-**).

lyghtheid, lyʒthed *n.* lightness 95/21, 286/29.

lyghtly, ly(ʒ)thlych(e, -ly, lyt(h)ly *adv.* easily, with small effort 58/29, 93/13, 343/26, 2–12/78, quickly, casually 78/27, 170/24, 343/26, 2–9/44, 45, carelessly 200/33, 223/36, less ceremonially 278/44, speedily 2–52/34.

lyʒt(h *n.* light 169/22, 218/33, 2–274/28.

lyʒt(h, lyth *adj.* light 152/5, 286/30, easy 302/38, easily swayed 2–50/35.

liʒter *comp.adv.* simpler 77/37.

lyhtyn *v. intr.* alight 2–174/30; **lyʒtyn** *pr.3 pl. tr.* light 163/29; **lyʒtyd** *pa.t.3 sg.* alit 266/31.

lyyn, lye(n *v. intr.* tell a lie 132/18, 154/35, 45, 229/37; **lyyst** *pr.2 sg.* lie 2–30/15; **lyhit, lyyth** *pr.3 sg.* 154/46, 155/52, 58, 2–212/25; **lyyn** *pr.3 pl.* 20/1, 234/26; **lye** *imp.sg.* 2–239/45; **lyyth** *imp.pl.* 2–215/66; **lyede** *pa.t.1 sg.* 155/55; **lown** *pa.t.3 pl.* 260/38.

lyyng *vbl.n.* lying 2–217/1.

lyke, lijk *adj.* similar 70/10, 328/43, 2–320/5, likely, credible 149/56, alike 127/58.

lykened *v.* (1) *pp.* compared 39/xii.

lykyʒt *v.* (2) *pr.3 sg. refl.* pleases 118/37, 41; **lyke** *subj.3 sg.* should please 41/ix, 71/7.

lykyng *vbl.n.* (1) appearance 95/10.

lykyn(g)g(e *vbl.n.* (2) pleasure 100/24, 279/43, 298/52, 62, 2–6/51, 2–320/56, desire, concupiscence 84/34, 100/24, 279/43, *han mor* ~ have more desire 207/58.

lykyng(e *adj.* pleasing 52/45, 272/47, 2–96/31.

lykkedyn *pa.t.3 pl.* licked 2–15/53.

lyme *n. lyf & ~* life and limb 251/50, 2–13/18; **lymys, lemys** *pl.* offspring 179/7, 2–21/5, 14, 2–82/68.

lymyt *ppl.adj.* limited 173/46.

ly(y)(n *v. intr.* lie (dead, sick) 97/26, 197/55, lie (naked) 305/40, lie in bed, sleep 311/40, 2–59/35, 39, lie (in sin, lechery,

hell) 2–25/30, 2–68/18, 2–101/54, lie (in wait, in ambush) 2–33/49, lie (with), have sexual intercourse (with) 2–68/37, 2–104/18, 2–118/2, lie (in, in childbirth) 2–116/8, lie (bound, in prison) 2–289/66.

~ *inf.* 2–25/30, 2–59/39, 2–304/36; **lyʒth** *pr.3 sg.* 2–314/42; **lyn, lyth** *pr.3 pl.* 97/26, 197/55, 2–116/8; **lychyng(e** *pr.p.* 305/40, 2–33/49, 2–68/37; **lay** *pa.t.3 sg.* 2–68/39, 2–316/58; **leyyn** *pa.t.3 pl.* 2–59/35; **leyn** *pp.* 2–101/54, 2–118/2.

lynage *n.* lineage 2–96/32.

list(e *pr.2 sg.* like, choose 79/14, 15, in *impers.constr. me* ~ *to* I want to 188/1.

lyth- see **light-**

lyth *n.* ~ *fro(m)* ~ limb from limb 92/33–4, 2–281/69–70.

lythlyere *comp.adv.* more easily 2–71/10 (cf. **lyʒt-**).

lityl, lytele *adj.* few 213/5, small 2–27/8, small (price) 2–176/13.

lytyl, litel *adv.* somewhat 91/2, ~ *and* ~ little by little 148/34, 2–272/71.

litle *n.* little things 148/34.

lytteris *n.pl.* letters (in sense of affidavits) 2–249/23.

lyue, lyf *n.* life 113/60, *be her* ~ in their lifetime 22/22, ~ *actyf* secular life 69/54, 59, ~ *contemplatif* life of a monk or recluse 69/49, 53; **lyuys** *pl.* ways of life 68/43.

lyuerysonys, -souns, leueresonys *n.pl.* liveries (payments in the form of living expenses) 19/74, 45/xxiii, 2–194/63.

lyuer(y)s *n.pl.* persons 156/22, 23, 162/2, 212/13.

lyuyn, leue *v. intr.* live 41/ix, 2–71/20, live (by), subsist 61/6, 2–164/134; **lyueþ, lyuyth, lifn** *pr.3 sg.* lives, exists 70/17, lives (after death) 171/14; **leuyn** *pr.2 pl.* are alive 2–278/50; **lyuen, lifn, leuyn** *pr.3 pl.* live (on earth) 72/12, 252/26, 2–4/3, live (after death) 171/13; **lyfde** *pa.t.3 sg.* dwelt 2–143/57; **leued, lyfyd** *pp.* lived 152/11, 153/17, 2–225/19.

lyuyng(e, leuyng *vbl.n.* life 1/26, behavior 36/ix, 328/38, 48, conduct 2–56/57, 58, circumstances of life 1/1b, 51/15, livelihood 53/37, 62/44, 98/58; **lyuyngis** *pl.* circumstances of life 70/14.

lofte *n. on* ~ upright 2–275/42.
loggys *n.pl.* lodges, huts 270/6, 8 (cf. V.L. *umbraculis*).
lokeris *n.pl.* watchmen 2–20/34.
lokyn *v. intr.* look 288/47, look (to, for aid) 311/39; **lokyth** *pr.3 sg.* looks var./79, ~ *to* searches out 2–26/62; **loke** *subj.3 sg.* should look 2–85/37, 2–275/41; **lok(e** *imp.sg.* take care 299/35, 327/19, 2–194/53; **lokyd** *pa.t.3 sg.* searched 312/65, looked 2–85/39.
lomb *n.* lamb 92/26, 28, 30; **lambryn** *n.pl.* 281/3, 2–201, 18, (*fig.*) 2–16/26, 2–38/28.
lond *n.* plot of ground, tract of land 19/70, 2–168/5, nation, England 6/136, 148/40, 2–211/2, land (*fig.*) 356/11, 12; **londis** *possess. sg.* ~ *lawe* law of the land 20/81, 45/xxvi, 160/5; ~ *pl.* countries 2–99/10.
lone *n.* loan 2–196/28 *var.* RDTBYL.
longe see **go(o)n**
longynge *ppl.adj.* belonging 218/19.
longit(h, longgy3t *pr.3 sg.* is appropriate (for, to) 2/23b, 21/33, 232/11, (is the prerogative of) 12/60, 352/22, belongs (by right) 54/4, pertains 218/22, 340/3, 2–31/1, belongs 2–95/13, 15; **longyn** *pr.3 pl.* are appropriate (for, to) 15/6, 215/39, 40, are enjoyed (by) 42/xix, pertain 340/10, 12; **longe** *subj.3 sg.* should pertain 2–42/70; **longede** *pa.t.3 sg.* belonged 2–197/70, 71, 82/19; **longgedyn** *pa.t.3 pl.* were appropriate 110/23.
lordchep(e, -chipe, -shepe *n.* proprietorship 17/7, 58/49, 63/13, 2–138/3, 4, rulership 149/55.
lore *n.* doctrine (Christian) 1/8a, 231/62, 241/12, (private or parental) teaching 321/4, 330/6, doctrine 323/41, (false) teaching 321/56, 323/41, 2–19/3.
lorer *n.* laurel (tree) 146/59.
lorn see **lesyn**
losyd *ppl.adj.* famed, known (for) 2–222/10 (cf. *MED* **losen** *v.*(1)).
losyn, lowse *v.* unload 55/53, 56/56, 76/51, unloosen 57/90; **losyth** *pr.3 sg.* releases 2–245/20, *refl.* separates 2–307/4; **losyd** *pp.* released (from) 289/57 (cf. *MED* **losen** *v.*(2)).
lot *n.* chance 167/15; **lottys** *pl.* lots (some-

thing used for the purpose of deciding by chance) 166/1, 4.
loth *adj.* reluctant 189/35, 36, loathsome 358/51.
lothyn *v.* hate 99/11; **loþe** *pr.1 sg.* 2–8/32; **loþith** *pr.3 sg.* displeases 207/62; **loþin** *pr.2 pl.* hate 2–14/19; **loþith** *pr.3 pl.* 2–23/69.
lothynge *vbl.n.* loathing 200/36.
louer *n.* louvre (opening in roof to let out smoke or let in light) 178/31.
louys *n.pl.* loaves 289/59, 2–141/22.
lounesse, low(e)nesse *n.* humility 54/50, 110/21, 197/5, 217/106.
loutyn *v. intr.* bow 112/40; **lowty3t** *pr.3 sg.* 87/34; **loutyn** *pr.1 pl.* 105/27.
loutyng(ge, lowtyngge *vbl.n.* bowing 104/6, 108/51, 112/43, 204/33.
low(e *adj.* humble 322/8, var./58.
lowyr *comp.adj.* ~ *degre* lower social status 355/40.
low(e)liche, lowly *adv.* humbly 51/17, 333/30, 342/58.
lowyn *v.* humble var./60, *refl.* 90/4, 2–128/43; **lowy3t, lowyth** *pr.3 sg.* humbles 53/27, *refl.* 112/46, 199/17, 18, 20, 217/108; **lowyn** *pr.3 pl. refl.* 2–4/4; **lowyd** *pa.t.3 sg. refl.* humbled 2–82/59.
lucre *n.* profit (in pejorative sense) 277/36, 290/24, 2–7/73, 2–20/59.
lunacioun *n.* lunation (a synodic month) 142/30, 33.
lust *n.* desire, longing 2–312/183, sexual desire 2–62/3, 2–86/60, 2–87/93; **lustis** *n.pl.* 2–62/17.
lusty *adj.* vigorous, flourishing 359/59, 2–96/31.
lustles *adj.* lazy, spiritless 2–310/112.

M

magnefyist, -nifiest *pr.2 sg.* praise, glorify 54/1, 75/1; **magnifyyd** *pa.t.3 sg.* made much of 210/10.
may see **moun**
maigtenen see **ment-**
mayn *n.* mutilation 2–42/63, 68.
maynyn, maim- *v.* wound 2–39/63, *refl.* mutilate 2–52/32; ~ *pr.3 pl.* wound 2–15/43, *intr.* 2–39/63, *refl.* mutilate 2–42/64; **maynyd, main-** *pp.* 2–42/65, 2–44/30.
maynynge *vbl.n.* mutilation 2–1/12, 2–63/36.

mayster *n.* master 132/20, ~ *of Storijs propr.n.* Peter Comestor 225/50; ~ *of Kende* Bartholomaeus Anglicus 2–5/28, ~ *of Propyrtes* 308/3; **maystrys** *possess.pl.* employers' 292/2, 3; ~ *pl.* 151/40.

maystr(y)(e *n.* authority (over) 132/19, mastery (over) 224/9, 12–13, victory (over) 2–12/59, 2–309/93, 96, victory 2–101/44.

makyn *v.* make 164/61; **makist** *pr. 2 sg.* 2–260/35; **maky3t** *pr.3 sg.* 97/27, 247/3; **makyn** *pr.1 pl.* ; ~ *pr.3 pl.* 164/59; **mac** *imp.sg.* 2–132/41; **make** *subj. 3 sg.* should make necessary 2–44/27; MA(A)D *pp.* compelled 152/19, *do it* ~ have it built 353/68, ~ *perfyt* perfected 2–112/19, ~ *hem with child* got them with child 2–118/2.

makyng *vbl.n.* building 30/li.

malt *pp.* melted 2–190/26.

malefesoures *n.pl.* evildoers 44/xiv.

mamet, maument *n.* idol 81/3, 164/59, 2–219/38; **mam(m)etis** *pl.* 166/12, 217/93, 243/5.

mam(m)etrye *n.* idol worship 166/23, 178/12, 2–264/56; **mametrerys** *pl.* practice of worshipping idols 2–76/11–12 *var. al.*

manchour *n.* manger, feeding trough for animals 288/51.

maner *n.* manor house 2–183/84.

maner(e *n.* kind of, sort of 11/8, way, fashion 11/11, 177/62(2), kinds of 20/3, 4, *on þis* ~ in this way 105/26, *mesure and* ~ limits of moderation 129/38; **maner(e)(ys** *pl.* ways 12/58, 13/10, 37/xxiv.

manqweller, -queller *n.* murderer 254/77, 307/14, 2–21/6; **manqweller(y)s, -quellerys** *pl.* 13/12, 39/xviii, 161/37, 251/52.

manslaut(h)e *n.* manslaughter 13/1, 2, 2–1/5, 11, 2–32/34.

mansleer(e *n.* murderer 2–1/10, 2–32/36, 2–42/51; **mansleer(y)s** *pl.* 38/vii, 2–2/35, 2–37/39.

marc *n.pl.* marks (coins worth 160 pennies) 2–188/74, 2–224/7.

margery(e *n.* pearl 2–260/30, 2–321/33.

massa- see **messa-**

mateynys *n.pl.* matins (one of the canon-

ical hours, here a service before the mass) 206/20.

mater(y)e *n.* material 113/66, 2–42/72, (physical) matter 134/68, (subject) matter 19/67, 321/1, 2–47/34, cause 2–78/46, 2–288/58, *takyn mest* ~ taken most pains 239/34, *takyn gret* ~ *of lownesse* make it a cause of humility 2–67/46; **materys** *pl.* (intellectual) matters 2–225/36.

maugre *n.* ill will, blame 53/22.

maument see **mamet**

Mawdeleyn *propr. n.* (Mary) Magdelene 30/liii.

me *pron.dir. obj.* me 53/13, 297/40, 2–260/37; ~ *indir. obj.* to me 52/47, 55/37, 66/22; **me, mysilff** *refl.* myself 53/16, 70/25; *impersonal construction* ~ *nedy3t* what I need 52/47, 60/52, ~ *thinky3t* I think 57/22, ~ *meruayly3t* I marvel 67/1.

mechil see **mich-**

mede *n.* reward 12/52, 63, 60/48, 49, 103/47, of reward 137/38, state of rewardedness 53/30, bribe 21/26, 46/x, 2–221/54, earnings 2–157/33, credit 292/57; **medys** *pl.* rewards 356/17, bribes 2–210/105.

med(e)ful *adj.* praiseworthy 5/110, 62/52, 113/3, 200/27, 248/30.

medfullych(e *adv.* praiseworthily 2–37/1, 6, 2–218/27, 2–220/34–35.

mediat *adv.* indirectly, by way of intermediaries 152/28.

medicinable *adj.* healing 168/33.

medyl *adj.* middle 146/77.

medyn *v.* reward 107/10, 2–288/44; **medith** *pr.3 sg.* 329/7; **medyd** *pp.* 137/36, 2–289/70.

med(e)lyd *ppl.adj.* mixed 178/30, 182/11, 259/27.

med(d)(e)lyn, medle *v. refl.* use 227/33, have sexual intercourse 2–58/25; **medely3t, -lith** *pr.3 sg.* mixes 130/79, has intercourse 2–59/58; **medle** *subj.3 sg.* should have intercourse 15/20, 2–58/19, 22, 2–59/37; **medlyn** *subj.3 pl.* 2–59/43, 45, 47; **medlyng** *pr.p.* having sexual intercourse 2–58/18; **medelyd** *pa.t.3 sg.* 2–63/26; **medelydyn** *pa.t.3 pl.* 2–62/9; **med(e)lyd** *pp.* mixed 124/75, 286/40, 293/15, 2–12/66.

medlyng *vbl.n.* sexual intercourse 2–58/14.

medue *n.* meadow, pasture 2–166/36.

meyntenyngge *vbl.n.* persistence (in) 125/17.

menbre *n.* member (tongue) 2–6/43, bodily member (inclusive) 2- 51/9; **menbris** *pl. synful/pryue* ~ sexual organs 2–78/60, 2–91/15, 2–104–105/19–20.

mende, mynde *n.* mind (all mental faculties) 10/49, 67/47, 82/38, recollection, reminder 22/20, 48/19, 49/52, *haue* ~ *to* remember to 33/v, 34/vii, ~ *-makyngge* reminder 86/28, 111/22, *more fresh* ~ livelier reminder 87/30, *makyn* ~ *of* reminds us of 100/16; **mendis** *pl.* reminders 281/19, .

mendynant *n.* mendicant (begging friar) 316/44.

mene, meen *n.*(1) means 171/64, step towards 2–95/8, intermediary 111/23, 25, 143/49, moderation, mean between extremes 94/32–4 *var.* BYLH, 285/32, *made* ~ *perfor* used a middle man 2–194/44; **menys, -nes** *pl.* means 42/i, 143/44, intermediaries 350/101, instruments 143/44, means 2–130/7, ~ *& motyuys* means and motives 2–13/6.

mene, meynee *n.*(2) household, entourage 58/45, 74/20, 327/13.

mene *adj.* intermediary 316/26.

menour *adj.* Franciscan friar 2–194/61.

menstral *n.* minstrel 2–267/57, 61, 63, 64; **mynstralys** *possess.sg.* 2–267/55; **menstralys** *pl.* 2–157/27.

menstrasie *n.* music, musical entertainment 297/34.

me(y)ntenance *n.* maintenance, repair and upkeep 190/16, 191/41.

me(y)nteþin, -tenen, **maigtenen, mayntene** *v.* maintain 5/108, 190/25, 351/14, persist in 78/33, 148/32, 43, 2–69/51, support 356/24, 2–55/19; **me(y)nteþin** *pr.3 pl.* persist in 194/43, sponsor 159/57, 217/3; **meynteþid** *pa.t.3 sg.* upheld 257/30; **meynteþith, -id** *pp.* supported 254/62, maintained 300/65. Spelling with medial thorn is found only in the hand of the first of the three scribes of MS G; it is not listed in *MED*.

mentyl *n.* mantle (loose tunic) 93/12; **menttelys** *pl.* 93/9.

mercha(u)ndye *n.* goods, merchandise 218/13, 220/63(1), 289/15, trading, merchandising 218/14, 220/63(2), 2–155/70.

mercyabelyche *adv.* mercifully 2–73/83.

merciable, mercyabyll *adj.* merciful 226/6, 337/8.

mery(e, myrye *adj.* merry 204/51, 297/26, 2–213/10, 2–319/37.

meritorie *adj.* meritorious 2–289/83.

merþe *n.* joy 94/23 (V.L. *laeticia*), 100/17, 2–6/56, mirth 145/40, 207/49, 2–321/38, merrymaking 10/38, 158/32, 293/14, *makyn* ~ make merry 10/39; **merþis** *pl.* merrymaking 2–193/28, 2–281/11.

merueyly3t, -uelyyth, -aylyth, maruaylyyth *v. pr.3 sg. impersonal construction* wonder, marvel 107/1, 154/35, 336/2.

meselrye *n.* leprosy 2–259/3.

messageris, massage(ris- *n.pl.* deputies 204/58, emissaries 260/20, 290/17, 2–143/66, functionaries 2–85/26, *on* ~ as emissaries 2–286/40–41,

messe, mysse *n.* celebration of the Eucharist 13/25, 2–108/47, 2–187/32, 33; **messys** *possess.pl.* 162/15; ~ , **myssis** *pl.* 45/xxii, 2–108/41, 2–187/29, 30, 31.

meste *adj.* greatest 166/18.

mes(o)ur(e *n. out of* ~ immoderately 150/15, *in* ~ *and maner* moderately and properly 173/33, 2–60/59.

mesuryn *v.* restrain 2–90/45.

mete *n.* food 53/18, 157/6, 182/21, a meal 2–285/21, 2–286/40, bait 2–12/69, 74; **metys** *pl.* foods 296/11.

mete *adj.* becoming 350/78.

meteles *adj.* without food 63/27, 74/9, 2–247/25, *a peny* ~ (the sense perh. may be) a penny (as wages) without added bread 2–192/81, 84.

metyn *v.*(1) measure 312/59, 60; ~ *pr.3 pl.* complete the measure of 284/9, 11, measure out 2–33/54(1), 2–249/44; ~ *pp.* meted out 2–33/54(2).

metyn *v.*(2) *intr.* dream 180/17 et seq.; ~ *pr.3 pl.* 180/18, 19, 181/39, 43. Found in MS G only.

metyn, mete *v.*(3) ~ *with* encounter 29/xlvi, 181/1, 182/19; **metyn** *pr.3 pl.* ~

with 91/30, 181/8, 12, 182/20; METTE *subj.3 sg.* should meet 224/10; ~ *pa.t.3 sg.* met up 187/23; **mettyn, metten** *pa.t.3 pl. refl.* met 51/4, 70/4 (cf. V.L. *obviaverunt sibi*).

meuable *adj. good* ~ moveable goods 2–131/30, 2–254/33, 2–295/12.

meuen *pr.3 pl.* move 95/25.

mychere *n.* thief 2–135/7, 2–173/8, 13, 14; **mycher(y)is** *pl.* 219/47, 244/22, 2–173/9.

mycherye, mecherye, *n.* thievery 17/12, 153/3, 2–135/12; **mycheryis** *pl.* 244/22.

mychyd *pp.* stolen 193/13.

mych(il, mechil *n.* much 51/3, 70/3, 165/84, *þus* ~ as much as 51/3.

mych(il, mechil, muche *adj.* much 10/34, 33/xvii, 53/22, 153/18.

mych(il, mechil, moch, muchil *adv.* much 5/113, 165/74, greatly 107/1, 294/39.

myddys *n.* center 96/28, 2–309/79, midst 196/35, middle 2–272/83, 2–274/30.

mydmorwe *n.* midmorning 2–280/61.

mydouernon, -ouyrnon *n.* mid-afternoon 10/32, 292/38, 39–40.

myght, my(3)th *n.* power 104/63, 155/63, 341/22, strength, physical or moral force 204/40, 41, 301/3, 17, 2–55/38; **my3tys** *pl.* powers 301/18, 2–61/40.

my3t see MOUN

my3ty *adj.* powerful 209/31, **my3tyere** *comp. adj.* stronger 196/47; **my3thyest** *comp. adj.* most powerful var./65.

my3telyche *adv.* mightily, fervently 301/5, 21, 2–61/40.

mylleward *n.* miller 74/5, 290/28 *var.* Y; **mullewardis** *pl.* 290/28 *var.* BL.

mynde see **mende**

ministre *n.* minister, agent 335/73, agency 2–287/21; MINISTRIS *pl.* agents 335/80.

mynystryn *v.* administer 2–39/65, 2–112/7, officiate 2–107/11; **mynystryth** *pr.3 sg.* administers 2–108/34; **mynystre** *subj.3 sg.* should minister (to) 328/32–33.

minourrys *n.pl.* miners 131/20.

myracles *n.pl.* miracle plays 293/12, 13, 18 *var.* Y (cf. **steraclis**).

myrie *adj.* merry, happy 2–213/10, 2–257/43.

myrys *n.pl.* mires, swamps 2–311/159.

mysanswer *n.* wrong answer 2–44/31.

mysbedyn *v.* ill use 2–206/4; **mysbodyn** *pp.* abused 2–165/6.

mysberyn *subj.3 pl. refl.* should misbehave 352/29.

mysche(e)f *n.* harm 13/4, 15/7, 2–13/1, trouble 57/16, 58/61, ill fortune 59/9, 78/14, 129/60, wrong-doing 198/28, wickedness 58/39, *at* ~ in hardship 318/39; **myscheuys** *pl.* misfortunes 24/19, 356/18, 2–126/89.

mysche(f)uous *adj.* wretched, miserable 59/69, 75/38, 2–126/91.

mysco(u)nseyl(l *n.* bad advice 38/ix, 2–20/40.

mysconsuetude *n.* evil customs 220/81.

myscoueyte *subj.3 sg.* should desire sinfully 2–295/20.

myscoueytyse *n.* sinful desire 2–137/78.

myscraft *n.* sinful or dangerous medical practice 2–42/50; **myscraftes** *pl.* 39/xviii.

mysdemyn, -deme *v.* ~ *of* misjudge, think ill of 179/11, 2–56/57.

mysdyetyngge *vbl.n.* improper eating 129/52.

mys(h)eggynge *vbl.n.* bad advice 2–20/40, 2–21/7, 2–151/5 (cf. **eggyn**).

mysentytysyng(e *n.* enticing to sin 38/ix, 2–19/2.

mysfare *n.* need, privation 2–298/14, 2–306/72.

mysfaryn *v. intr.* fare badly 2–207/17.

myshad *ppl.adj.* wrongly possessed 2–135/26.

myshappyn *v. intr.* come to grief 2–32/45, ~ *pr.3 pl.* 140/13, 161/58.

myshegge *n.* enticement 2–148/27 (cf. **eggyn**).

mysheryng *n.* sin committed through sense of hearing 2–97/58.

myshusynge *pr.p.* abusing 352/19.

myslykynge *n.* a dislike 176/42.

misloue *n.* illicit or immoral love 179/11, 2–84/8.

myslust *n.* evil desire 2–85/19, 2–299/13; **myslustis** *pl.* 2–119/14.

mysmedicinys *n.pl.* medicines wrongly given 2–42/61.

myspay(y)d *ppl.adj.* displeased, offended 258/4, 15, 283/11, 2–141/13.

myspryde *n.* overweening pride 148/26, 152/17.

mysspeche *n.* misspeaking, abuse of speech 31/ii.

mysspedyn *v. intr.* suffer misfortune 2–166/23–24.

myssuffr(r)a(w)nce *n.* misguided indulgence 36/x, 324/9.

mystakynge *n.* theft 2-130/5–6.

mystechers *n.pl.* misinformers, misleaders 39/x.

mystechys *n.pl.* bad traits 325/31 (cf. techis).

mystyhed *n.* obscurity 269/33.

mystretyn *pr.3 pl.* misappropriate 2–195/83.

mystretyng *vbl.n.* misappropriating 2–240/75 (cf. tretyn).

mysu(h)s(e *n.* abuse 15/7, 129/37, 2–135/20, mistreatment 128/16, misuse 228/10, evil behavior 188/10, var./59, 2–287/7.

myswil *n.* evil intention 2–296/50, 51.

mytis *n.pl.* mites (small coins, half farthings) 64/21, 190/19, 2–192/78.

mytre *n.* mitre (headdress of bishop) 2–228/48, 2–229/69.

mo(o, more *n.pl.* additional number 57/7, 24, 58/44, 284/15, 17, more, larger amount 2/18a, 58/61, 62, 59/22, greater 17/67, *sweryn be his* ~ swear by his superior 242/24.

mo(o)dir, -der *n.* mother 10/3, 4, 11/8, 20, 23, 35/i, 209/7; **mod(e)ris** *possess.sg.* 56/63, 2–324/37; **moodrys** *pl.* 313/8, 327/8, 2–108/27.

mon see **moun**

mone *n.*(1) *makyth* ~ makes complaint 331/41, 2–300/28.

mone *n.*(2) moon 3/34, 28/xxviii, 142/25.

monestith *pr.3 sg.* admonishes 2–244/105.

mony3t, monyth *n.* month 119/13, 183/28, 280/20; **moneþis, monythis** *pl.* 134/55, 183/31, 224/30.

monyour *n.* minter of coins 131/4; **monyourrys** *pl.* 131/6, 7, 9.

mont *n.* mountain 268/14, 295/82; **montys** *pl.* 224/30, 2–281/68.

mor(e, mo(o *comp.adj.* more 1/9b, 57/24, 59/63, 79/12, greater 320/11, 2–235/25.

mor(e *comp.adv.* more 5/110, 17/65, 52/40, rather 2–66/27.

mo(o)rd(r)e, m(o)urd(r)e *n.* murder 39/xiv, 148/26, 41, 153/3, 161/33, 257/52, 2–32/44.

mordryth *pr.3 sg.* murders 2–314/47*.

more *n.* her ~ their betters (cf. V.L. *per maiorem suum*) 232/6, 242/24.

mor(e)yn *n.* plague 117/14, 192/58, 341/40.

moryn *v.* enhance, make more of 191/43, 47, increase 2–67/41; **moryth** *pr.3 sg. intr.* 183/21; **more** *imp.sg. tr.* increase! 88/9; **moredyn** *pa.t.3 pl.* enhanced 205/6.

moryng *vbl.n.* increase, enhancement 154/26, 170/47, 2–23/64.

mornyn *v. intr.* repent 10/39, *tr.* mourn the loss of 224/29.

mornyng(e *vbl.n.* mourning 100/21, 215/43, 294/51, 55.

morwyn, morwe, morne *n.* morning 206/20, 270/52, 2–143/85.

mosel *n.* muzzle 2–223/50.

mote, motyn *v. pr.t.forms*, **must(e, most(e)(n** *pa.t.forms, with pr.t. or fut. senses* must (expressing necessity) 75/2, 101/6, 242/28, 334/62, 2–70/100, 101; may (expressing a wish or hope) 82/35, 186/4, 2–70/96.

muste *pr.1 sg. intr.* must 101/6; ~, **mostist** *pr.2 sg.* 55/53, 63/27, 76/51; **mote, muste, moste** *pr.3 sg.* 56/72, 74, 76, 74/27, 113/71, 242/28, 334/62, may 2–70/96; **muste** *pr.1 pl. impers.* vs ~ we must 56/82; **mote, motyn, most(en, must(en** *pr.2/3 pl.* 54/13, 64/10, 82/35, 157/32, 197/61, 352/26, 2–62/60, 63, may 186/4.

motynge *vbl.n.* disputing, in legal cases 277/38.

moulyd *ppl.adj.* mouldy 260/21, 35.

moun, mon, may, mow(e, my3t *v. intr.* (as complete verb) be able (to) 51/11, 73/34, 98/58 (see Notes), 106/57, 328/37, 2–269/31, (as *aux.*) be able (to) 65/43, 262/94, 259/31, have power (to), be enabled (to) 1/3a, 58/36, 65/44, 328/37, 345/69, 70, ought, should 43/ix, 104/66, 2–272/83, (in sense of purpose or expectation) may 90/22, 355/3, be allowed to 354/82, 83, 86.

mo(u)n *infin.* 1/3a, 65/43, 44, 2–248/54, 56; **mow** *pr.2 sg.* 355/3; **may, mai** *pr.3 sg.* 54/2, 55/33, 72/7, 78/33,

90/22; **mo(u)n, mai** *pr.1 pl.* 71/49, 103/40, 104/66, 173/27, 2–292/9; ~ *pr.2 pl.* 55/43, 61/6, 2–70/108, 2–71/ 112; **mo(u)n, mow(e)(n, may** *pr.3 pl.* 6/123, 8/38, 14/43, 27/xix, 41/ix, 51/ 11, 352/29; **mowe** *subj.1 sg.* 304/5, 318/ 30; ~ *subj.2 sg.* 2–292/8; **mow(e** *subj.3 sg.* 114/7, 177/70, 352/21; **moun** *subj.3 pl.* 138/69; **myȝt-, myght-** *pa.t.* (forms with past, present and future meanings) **myght** *pa.t.1 sg.* 101/4; **myghte, -tist** *pa.t.2 sg.* 52/37, 138/63, 328/37, 2–71/ 10, 2–147/58, 2–269/30; **myȝt(h)(e, myght(e** *pa.t.3 sg.* 154/37, 217/111, 220/79, 259/34; **myȝ(h)te, -tyn** *pa.t.3 pl.* 61/6, 2–187/44.

mowys *n.pl.* grimaces 115/35.

muc *n.* muck, dung 2–243/73.

multyplyyn *v.* increase alchemically 5/ 103, 185/2, 6, increase the number of 276/45, *refl.* accumulate, amass 2–86/ 64.

murde see **mordre**

murdour *n.* murderer 2–32/45.

must *v.* see **mote**

mustrere, musterer *n.* tattletale, gossip 13/5, 38/iv, 2–7/81; **must(e)rerys** *pl.* 2–7/7, 12, 2–8/18, 24, 2–131/9. Cf. 'rounere'; see Notes 2–71.

N

nacio(u)n *n.* nation (a people, not a king-dom or polity) 188/2, 253/34, 48, 2–7/ 84; **nacionys** *pl.* 188/3, 2–197/68.

nakydhed *n.* nakedness 2–124/21, 2–310/ 114.

name *n.* reputation 328/27, 2–63/35.

narw(e *adj.* narrow 2–267/47, 2–272/66, 68.

ne *conj.* nor 18/18, 23/9, 51/15, (in corre-lative construction) ~. . . ~ neither . . . nor 103/40.

nede *n.* neediness 58/37, 59/15, 78/35, *helpe at* ~ aid to those in need 36/iv, v.

nedele *n.* needle 55/39; **ned(e)lys** *pos-sess.sg.* 25/v, 55/31, 77/38.

ned(d)ere, -dre *n.* snake 92/19, 309/15, 16, 17, serpent (Satan) 2–81/44, 2–127/ 25; **ne(d)d(e)rys** *pl.* serpents 4/82, 169/ 9, 2–103/113.

nedfulhed *n.* what is necessary (for) 2–220/9, 11.

nedhed *n.* neediness, want 262/92.

nedys *adv.* necessarily 2–28/54.

nediþ *pr.3 sg.*(impers. constr.) *it* ~ *him* he has to 80/57; **nedyde, nedede** *pa.t.3 sg. it* ~ *to* it was necessary to 2–27/28; **nedyd** *pp.* necessitated 122/24, 137/40.

ned(e)ly(ch *adv.* necessarily 352/26, 2–101/47, 2–291/34, compulsorily 2–110/15.

nedr- see **neddr-**

neeth *n.* net 125/19.

negard- see **nygard-**

neyhand *adv.* nearly 2–92/46.

neyhyn *v. intr.* approach, draw near 2–225/17, 2–318/4.

neyþer *pron. her* ~ neither of them 2–76/ 27, 2–156/22.

neyþir, -þer, neþre *conj.* nor 41/xii, (followed by *ne*) neither 51/15, 79/5, 90/5.

nemelyn *v.* utter 259/22; **nemelyst** *pr.2 sg.* 223/17; **nemelyth** *pr.3 sg.* invokes 229/43, enumerates 265/67; **nemelyn** *pr.3 pl.* utter 222/7–8; **nemele** *imp.sg.* use (in speaking) 227/31; **nemelyd** *pp.* spoken 222/4, attributed (to) 2–77/22, enumerated 2–242/44.

nemelynge *vbl.n.* uttering 222/2.

nere *comp.adj.* nearer (to) 149/8.

nesche *adj.* soft cushioning 2–310/117.

neschhed *n.* softness 2–310/117.

nest(e *n.* nearest kin 317/53, 2–64/82, 2–128/51, nearest and dearest 2–128/51, 2–218/20.

ne(x)st(e *adv.* next 261/61, 269/42, 285/ 2, next to 252/10, nearest 351/108, 2–66/28, 30, 31.

nest(e *adj.* next, following 159/49, var./ 82, closest 2–66/37.

neue *n.* nephew 345/2, 354/87, 2–174/20.

newe, -ly *adv.* newly, recently 4/86, 172/ 1, anew 165/83.

newith *pr.3 sg.* renews itself 2–167/64, 65; **newyn** *pr.3 pl.* 2–209/75.

nyce, nyse *adj.* simple, foolish 151/35, 174/65, 223/20, shameful 7/21, 176/ 51, 241/4, 17, seductive, enticing 2–303/8, superstitious, suspect 157/5, 11, 165/89, 173/24, 35.

nyg(g)ard, negard *n.* miser 43/viii, 59/ 16, 2–142/54; **nyggardys, -des** *pl.* 13/ 11, 38/vii, 44/xii.

nygardschip, -chepe, negardshepe,

-chepe *n.* niggardliness, miserliness 59/
14, 79/34, 318/45, 2-322/20.

nigroma(u)nsy, -cie *n.* necromancy (divination by communication with the dead)
151/51, 164/68.

ny3h(y, nyh(3, nhey, nihi *adv.* nearly
129/56, 148/38, 150/27, 153/1, 335/2,
close to 2-59/42, 2-255/4, close (in
kinship) 90/2, 18, close to, nigh
(person, God's presence, hell) 96/29,
125/22, 2-23/70, adjacent 144/8.

ny3(h)er(e *comp.adv.* nearer 199/13, 2-
274/33.

ny3hit *pr.3 sg.* grows near 199/18; nyhyn
pr.3 pl. 2-299/31; ny3hyd *pp.* brought
near to 2-24/75.

ny(3)hed *n.* closeness, relatedness 2-292/
2, 18, 2-293/35.

nihi see ny3h

nyl- see wyl-

nyne *card.num.* nine 15/1.

nyn(e)te *ord.num.* ninth 166/26, 2-30/18,
2-247/30.

no(o, no(o)n(e *adj.* no, not any (*no(o)n(e*
forms are used before vowels and *h* but
also frequently before consonants) 23/9,
81/2, 3, 131/9, 172/18.

nobelye, nobyleye *n.* social rank 2-292/3,
23, excellence, nobility 2-321/46.

noble *n.* a gold coin 2-162/71, 2-186/8.

noyance *n.* danger 2-35/40.

noyyt *pr.3 sg.* harms 2-53/3.

noy(o)us(e *adj.* harmful, injurious 71/34,
256/11, 2-35/41.

non-residenseres *n.pl.* clerics not living in
their own parishes 44/xii.

norchyn *v.* indulge 315/59–60, bring up,
nurture 330/12, promote 2-285/16;
norchit *imp.pl.* nurture 323/41;
norchyd *pp.* nourished 2-14/32.

norchynge *vbl.n.* bringing up, nurturing
2-60/8.

norture *n.* breeding, upbringing 90/16,
339/44, 2-71/13, 19.

note *n.* musical note 207/43, *be / withoutyn ~* with/without singing 206/29;
NOTIS *pl.* musical notes 206/32.

noteles *adj.* obscure, unnoted 151/41.

notory(e *adj.* notorious 42/xvii, 2-107/20,
2-168/23.

notorijs, notaryes *n.pl.* notories 20/81,
45/xxvi, 2-203/77, 79.

nouche *n.* brooch 2-162/71; nouchis *pl.*
2-161/62.

nouycerye *n.* novitiate (period of proba-
tion) 344/46, 54.

nou(gh)t, nou3t *n.* nothing 60/56, 132/9,
156/6, 2-318/5, *is ~* amounts to nothing
24/16, 62/51, *seruyn of ~* serve no
purpose 137/34, *þing of ~* a trifle 226/
15.

nout(h, nought, nowt, no3t, n(au)3t *adv.*
not 6/137, 45/xx, 156/7, 191/38, 210/
34, 258/17, *ryght ~* in no way 57/11,
nothing at all 73/15–16 (cf. ryght).

O

o, o(o)n *prep.* in 69/72, 84/18, 106/36, on
2-148/37, *~ massage* on an errand 2-
286/40, *dere ~ a farþinge* at the value of
a farthing 2-192/78, *~ a tyme* once 238/
16.

occupyed *pp.* possessed 37/xix.

occupyyng *vbl.n.* possession 43/iv.

ochyr *n.* usher 2-86/47.

of *adv.* off 93/36, 162/20, 342/54.

of *prep.* by 80/67, 115/38, 135/31, 149/2,
part of 117/6, from 249/81, 276/7, for
100/22, 130/81, concerning 109/1, *~
offys* by virtue of his office 2-42/70, *~
myne* one of mine 212/19.

offens *n.* offence 162/9, 295/72, 301/8,
offence (to) 182/8, displeasure 295/72,
301/8.

offycerys *n.pl.* officials 2-140/68, 2-157/
35.

offys *n.* function 106/53, 107/12, service
134/68, 2-60/2, office 200/31, 328/25,
331/48, 49, 2-42/70, church rite 207/
59, 214/23, 2-108/41, office quarters 2-
140/68.

ofne, ouene *n.* oven 2-278/8, 9, 11, 13, 2-
279/20, 24.

oftyn *adj.* frequent 161/57, 2-299/30.

olee, olye *n.* oil 168/33, 280/7, 318/41.

o(n)lyue *adj.* alive 159/44, 170/24, 171/
12.

omelye *n.* homily, sermon 132/5, 188/16,
2-19/4.

omys, amis *adv.* amiss, dishonestly 13/
14, 38/viii, *don ~* behave sinfully 170/
41, 171/54, 254/80.

o(o)n *pron.* one 3/44, 30/liv, 48/40, someone 170/27, *many ~* many a one 254/73.

o(o)n, o(o) *adj.* one 14/35, 39, 48/39, 64/ 21, 196/31, 2–2/44.

onbydyn see unbydyn

on(n)eþis, -eþe, vn(n)eþis, *adv.* scarcely, hardly 148/38, 226/23, 232/78, 2–69/ 53.

onhed *n.* unity 2–39/38, 2–113/56.

ony(e *adj.* any 8/23, 90/19, 20.

onys *adv.* once, on one occasion 180/32, 223/2, 282/28, one time 42/xx, 161/54, 2–2/36, once before 101/45, once again 63/1.

onlefull *adj.* unlawful 39/xviii.

onlusthed *n.* slothfulness 2–194/68.

onon *adv.* soon 89/33, 123/44, at once, immediately 97/28, 123/36, 204/52.

opynly *adv.* clearly 96/7, 97/14.

oppresyn *v.* overpower 2–304/35.

onsondre *adv.* asunder 2–39/48, 2–246/ 24.

or *adv.* see er

or *conj.* ~...~ either . . . or 54/13, 129/37, 342/50–51.

oratorie *n.* oratory, private chapel 195/16, 196/29, 32; oratoriis *pl.* 17/59, 195/20.

orchod *n.* irksomeness 2–92/55.

ordeynyn *v.* care, manage 11/13, 172/20, 2–137/69, provide 62/48, 2–256/18; ordeynyd *pa.t.3 sg.* ordered 92/33, designated 192/73; ordeynyd *pp.* provided 2–258/37.

ordenance *n.* provisions 202/5.

ordenarie *n. judge* ~ presiding judge (in a non-ecclesiastical court) 2–36/7.

ord(e)re *n.* order (of priority) 48/26, religious rule 200/31, 2–56/52, ordination 2–175/53; ordrys *pl.* orders (religious rules) 2–41/33, 34, rites of ordination 2–175/54.

ordryd *pp.* ordained 2–175/55, 56, 2–177/ 46.

ordinel *adj.* regular, orderly 229/7.

ordynour *n.* ordainer 2–177/51.

orygynal *n.* etymology, derivation 93/6–7.

original *adj.* derived from the beginning 2–307/10.

oryson *n.* prayer (part of the mass) 2–188/ 70.

orlege see horlege

h)ost *n.* army 295/81, 297/25.

o(o)th *n.* oath 8/25, 28, 31, 32/xiv; oþis, o(o)thes *pl.* 7/6, 31/v, 32/xiii, 103/51.

oþ(e)r(e *pron.* (the) other, another 25/iv, 37/xxv, 202/55; oþeris *possess.sg.* 340/ 63; othere *pl.* others 53/15, to others 113/74.

oþ(e)re, oþir *adj.* other 1/4b, 269/23, 2–10/17.

ouer- see ouyr-

oueral *adv.* everywhere 87/1, 113/3, 183/ 24, 25, 26, 201/37.

ouerest *adv.* on top 312/76.

ouer-ledyng, ouyr- *vbl.n.* oppression, tyranny 329/21*, 2–14/9.

ouȝt, h)out *n./pron.* anything 131/26, 185/8, 319/2, 2–150/80, something 2–283/45.

ouȝt, hout *adv.* at all, in any way 138/66, 274/36, 2–53/32.

ouyr *adv.* across 2–11/29, ~ ȝer at the end of the year 2–314/5 (cf. leuyngis; cf. V.L. *reliquiae tuae*).

ouyrdon *adv.* excessively 186/22, 217/98, 99, 225/52.

ouyrdo(u)n, ouer- *adj.* excessive 110/21, 148/26, 176/40, 2–103/102.

ouyr-gylt *adj.* gilded 2–161/57.

ouyr-ledyn *v.* oppress 2–9/59.

ouyr-ledyng *vbl.n.* oppression 2–14/9.

ouyrmor(e, ouer- *conj.* furthermore 62/ 38, 65/53, 160/31, 295/73.

ouyrpressyn *v.* oppress 2–206/5 (cf. V.L. *opprimes*).

ouyrscyppe *v. intr.* skip over something 200/34.

ouyrset *pp.* overcome 209/31.

(h)our(e *adj.* our 53/5, 187/38, 200/7, (cf. we, lady).

outragyn *pr.3 pl. intr.* break out of bounds 2–268/12.

outtakyn* *ppl. adj.* excepted 339/31.

outtakyn *prep.* excepting 133/35, except 2–35/45.

outtakith *pr.3 sg.* excepts 2–286/47.

outwending *n.* departure 70/10.

owe, h)ou(ȝt-, h)auȝt- *v.* own, possess 2–145/18, 21, 23, owe 236/21, 318/26, 2–170/57, (in impersonal construction) ought 107/10, 220/78, (in present and past forms, as modal verb expressing obligation) ought 5/112, 12/61, 87/30, 226/19; *refl.* ~ hyr chaste ought to keep herself chaste 2–70/102, 107.

   owe *pr.1 sg.* 2–69/67; owyst *pr.2 sg.* 2–69/67, 2–291/41; owyt(h, h)owy(ȝ)t *pr.3 sg.* 11/11, 87/30, 108/47, 217/99,

304/23; **owyn** *pr.1 pl.* 229/38, 304/24;
~, **-en** *pr.3 pl.* 12/59, 36/xv, 37/xxii;
auȝtyst *pa.t.2 sg.* 258/5, 2–67/15;
h)**aughte, auȝte, owȝte** *pa.t.3 sg.* 110/
7, 214/16, 236/21, 318/26; **ouȝtyn,
auȝtyn** *pa.t.1 pl.* 209/36, 2–302/85;
houtyn, auȝtyn *pa.t.3 pl.* 105/35,
239/34.
owene *adj.* own 61/26, 64/37, *out of oure*
~ far from our home 53/7.

P

payyd *ppl.adj.* satisfied 186/20, 357/8, 2–
137/72, pleased 210/29, 228/13.
pay(y)n *v.* pay 190/22, 246/24, 2–268/17;
paien *pr.1 pl.* 80/58; ~ *pr.2 pl.* 80/61;
paye *subj.2 sg.* 2–269/30; **pay** *imp.sg.*
please 66/31.
paynym *n.* pagan, non-Christian 158/39,
194/42, 252/17; **paynynys** *possess.pl.* 2–
52/42; ~ *pl.* 2–2/28, 2–144/111.
paleys *n.* palace 2–15/45, 2–85/23, 2–
190/22.
pardonystre *n.* pardoner 2–183/99; **par-
doneres, -ystrys** *n.pl.* 45/xix, 2–183/
93–94.
parychen *n.* parishoner 2–179/45, 2–234/
64; **parisshens, parychenys, pareschynys** *pl.* 44/xiv, 2–169/29, 2–182/
56.
parys(che *adj.* parish 19/50, 194/46, 2–
163/117, 118.
part(y *n.* part 204/45, 239/15, 2–301/61,
location 115/59, 2–77/30, agency 2–84/
119, 121, 2–114/90, *in* ~ , *a* ~ in part,
partially 16/31, 175/11, 2–135/16, *in* ~
of partly for 100/22, *to han* ~ *þerof* to
partake thereof 59/25–26, 80/43, *þe
beter* ~ the better alternative 72/6; **par-
tyys, -ties** *pl.* portions 2/12b, 26/ix,
regions 98/55.
partyd *ppl.adj.* forked, venomous 2–2/45.
partyn *v.* divide 119/7 (cf. **depart-**).
partyng *vbl.n.* dividing up 166/2.
paruys *n. holdyn her* ~ *of . . . wrongs þei
þinke to don* hold their meetings to plot
wrongdoing 275/36 (see Notes).
pa(a)s *n.pl.* paces 281/2, routes 2–44/23,
takith heed to hys ~ watches his step 2–
220/20.
pasyn *v.* pass 1/6b, 114/17, escape 221/5,
227/38, surpass 136/28, 2–110/34,
travel 158/29, depart 227/37, 2–64/80,

cross 2–266/25; **pasyth, -syȝt** *pr.3 sg.*
passes 114/18, 142/11, 358/55, sur-
passes 285/5, 8; **pasen, pasyn** *pr.3 pl.*
exceed 124/67, 130/67, surpass 152/13,
2–61/30, 2–227/19, travel 186/13, 2–
44/23; **pase** *subj.3 sg.* should go
beyond and exceed 2–148/35, should
exceed (*fig.*) 2–58/21, 2–92/36, 2–235/
26, may be passed 2–287/20; ~ *imp.sg.*
go (on to another subject) 321/1; **paste,
pasyd(den** *pa.t.3 sg.* passed 115/34,
surpassed 271/17, 2–96/41; **pastyn**
pa.t.3 pl. 2–123/66; **pasyd** *pa.t.subj.3
sg.* should have surpassed 189/25.
pasyng *vbl.n.* by-passing, avoidance 2–
225/27, *steryng and* ~ manoeuvering
and flying 152/6.
pas(s)yng *ppl.adj.* surpassingly great 66/
14, 162/61, travelling 91/27, 290/22,
exceeding 190/20, 281/4, excessive
2–92/46, ~ *synne* extremely grave sin
252/8.
pasyng *ppl.adv.* more than 156/9, 202/42,
2–61/32, 2–160/9.
Pask *n.* Easter 35/xviii.
paþyd *pp.* paved 2–321/35.
patro(u)n *n.* patron (founder or benefactor
of a religious institution) 351/11, 353/51;
patronys *pl.* 37/xxiv, 351/4.
pecible *adj.* peaceful 192/62.
pees see **pe(e)s**
peyne, pyne *n.* punishment 4/70, 137/40,
255/1, 2–16/6, pain 147/78, 279/42, 2–
24/21, torment (of hell) 16/49, 240/44,
2–22/36, sorrow 2–128/52, 55;
p(e)ynys, -nes *pl.* punishments 28/
xxxiv, pains 240/43, torments (of hell)
2–103/123.
peyntyd *pp.* painted 2/126, 96/1.
peyntyd *ppl.adj.* painted 82/34, 2–32/21.
peyntour *n.* painter 89/47.
peynture *n.* painting 2/10, 26/vi, 82/44.
pelfre *n.* booty, spoil 2–130/23, 2–208/56.
pellure *n.* fur used for trimming or lining
a garment 58/51.
pellycan(e *n.* pellican 23/7, 35/iii, 2–300/
21, 24.
pentancer *n.* penitencer (a priest empowered to administer the sacrament of
penance) 2–145/20.
pepyll *n.pl.* persons 48/31.
per, pur *prep.* ~ *charite* for charity's sake

52/36, 2–1/2, ~ *aturne* by attorney 2–241/15.

perauenture *adv.* perhaps, perchance 223/34, 2–2/39, 2–21/65.

perchyn, pershyn *v. intr.* perish 129/59, 205/64, 288/31; **perchyn** *pr.3 pl.* 2–111/47; **perche** *subj.3 sg.* should perish 2–16/23, 2–149/53; **perchid** *pa.t.3 sg.* perished 2–150/88; ~, **-chedyn** *pa.t.3 pl.* 261/62, 2–106/72; **perchyd** *pa.t.-subj.3 sg.* should have perished 191/31, 192/52; **perchyd** *pp.* 2–17/53, 2–152/44.

perchynge *vbl.n.* perishing 2–19/14, 2–122/52.

perfeccio(u)n *n.* rule of life 65/4, 9, 66/11 et seq., 285/6, *in* ~ in a life of renunciation 2–250/73, 76, *men of* ~ men who follow a religious rule 2–250/73–4.

perfy(3)t(h, perfyght, parfijt *adj.* perfect (complete) 34/xii, 279/35, 2–28/40, 41, 284/5, perfect (morally perfected) 55/25, 66/16, 75/24, 2–215/54, pure 2–317/72.

perfythly *adv.* perfectly, without fault 2–113/59.

perfythnesse *n.* perfection (natural completeness) 284/5–6.

perfourne, -forme, -myn *v.* carry out 150/25–26, perform 2–148/40, carry on 304/3; **performyd** *pp.* carried out 2–30/12.

perys *n.pl.* companions 186/17, 2–318/41.

perlyous, -lews *adj.* perilous 29/xl, 177/64, 217/102, 2–42/62.

perre *n.* precious stones, jewelry 58/51, 2–91/19.

personalys *adj.* of all property except land 2–168/2.

perso(u)n(n)e *n.* (man's, God's, king's) person 333/25, 337/23, 343/22, 2–57/72, parson, cleric 330/3, 351/12, 352/42, 43; **personys** *pl.* (men's) persons 337/24, 2–88/8, parsons, clerics 203/21, 2–163/124, 2–193/26.

perteyneþ *pr.3 sg.* belongs 72/14, 25.

peruert *adj.* corrupted 2–229/83, 2–248/1.

peruertyd *pp.* turned away 2–151/5.

pe(e)s *n.* peace 30/lv, 153/17, 182/6.

pesybyleche, -ly, -bely(che *adv.* peaceably 244/33, 37, 304/6, 2–212/46.

pyc *n.*(1) pitch 2–258/20.

pyc *n.*(2) point (of iron; spike on the end of a staff) 2–230/20.

pye *n.* magpie 2–268/7.

pyler, peler *n.* pillar 2–228/42, 2–301/54; **pylerys** *n.pl.* 2–52/42, 2–89/32.

pylyn *v. intr.* pillage 2–208/62, *tr.* rob 2–17/39; ~ *pr.3 pl.* 2–15/38.

pylynge *vbl.n.* pillaging 2–18/62.

pylouris *n.pl.* pillagers 2–249/35.

pilwe *n.* pillow 2–5/15, 16; **pilwys** *n.pl.* 2–4/41.

pyromancye *n.* pyromancy (divination by fire) 164/64.

pystyl, -tel *n.* epistle (of apostles or church fathers) 283/25, 310/8, 334/60, 61, epistle (as lection in Church service) 2–107/19.

pyte *n.* compassion (for) 2–25/47, compassion 2–38/23, 2–215/4, 2–288/42.

Pittagoras *propr.n. spere of* ~ sphere of Pythagoras (instrument used for divining) 157/12.

pytty *adj.* pitted (ground) 2–311/160.

place *n.* dwelling place 2–256/37, 38, 2–257/41, 42.

ple *n.* legal suit 275/13, 306/4, 2–158/57; **pley(y)s** *pl.* litigation 2–9/57, 2–262/88.

plech *n.* pledge 234/6.

pley *n.* play 167/16, 2–267/60; **pleyys** *pl.* stage plays 293/12, 294/38, 41, 48, games 2–40/3.

pleyyn *v.* play 2–203/68, *refl.* enjoy 2–163/115; **pleyth** *pr.3 sg. intr.* plays 2–267/63; **pleyydyn, pleyyd** *pa.t.3 pl.* 297/34, *tr.* 2–268/70.

pley(3)yng(e *vbl.n.* acting in stage plays 293/22, 294/42, playing (in games) 2–40/4.

pleyferys *n.pl.* playmates 224/29.

pleyn *adj. blont & ~* without an edge and even 120/55–56, *~ and smothe* even and smooth 121/67, level 2–311/158, full, plenary 2–49/9, 11, *in ~ pasture* in open pasture (on a level with neighbours) 2–268/10.

plenyyn *v. intr.refl.* complain (about) 2–68/33, 2–212/38, 41; **plenyyth** *pr.3 sg.* complains 228/21; **plenyyn** *pr.3 pl. refl.* 2–161/51; **plenye** *subj.3 sg.refl.* should complain 2–44/10; **plenyyth** *imp.pl.refl.* make your complaint 351/111; **plenyynge** *pr.p. refl.* making a complaint 228/33.

plent *n.* accusation 245/51 (MS G only); pleyntis *pl.* 2–68/32; see MED sv. 'pleint(e'.

plenteuous *adj.* plentiful 2–275/52, bountiful 2–298/12, bountifully supplied, rich 2–317/16.

plentevouslyche *adv.* bountifully 280/11.

plesa(u)nce, -auns *n.* pleasure 154/47, 162/8, 248/29, in/to ~ of in order to please 339/47, 2–120/29.

pletyn *v. intr.* litigate 2–275/37, 2–308/64; plete *subj.3 sg.* should go to court 2–266/26.

pletynge *vbl.n.* litigating 277/38, 2–287/6, 2–320/51.

plyth *n.* plight 206/23.

plurer *adj.* plural 2–81/23, 2–249/28.

poynt *n.* point 2–310/100, topic, matter 2–16/16, time, stage (of life) 2–267/51, in ~ to on the point of 2–14/6, 2–189/13.

poluht, poll(o)ut *adj.* profaned 219/52, 2–59/40, 41, 2–165/8.

pond *n.pl.* pounds sterling 185/2, 3, 242/31.

por- see pur-

possessioner *n.* an endowed cleric 316/49, 317/11; -erys *pl.* 317/7.

potestatys *n.pl.* heavenly powers 2–318/42 (V.L. *potestates*, cf. Eph.6:12).

poþel *n.* puddle 2–106/58.

potyn, puttyn *v.* put 2–205/63, put, place 112/52, 355/17, put away 187/18, *refl.* put 53/36; pote, putte *pr.1 sg. refl.* 187/36, entrust (self to) 2–194/52; potist *pr.2 sg.* ~ *ʒin part* throw in your lot 2–210/110; potith *pr.3 sg.* posits 2–213/2, puts 2–298/5; puttyn *pr.1 pl.* 187/38, *refl.* put (ourselves) 62/54, 105/17; ~ *pr.2 pl.* put 187/36; potyn *pr.3 pl.* 292/45, 2–62/16; pote, putte *subj.3 sg.* may be put 2–299/11, *refl.*should put 62/51.

poudyr *n.* dust 2–277/25, 2–315/15.

pouert(ee *n.* poverty 1/4a, 70/(title), 1, 7, 2–230/93.

powalyys *n.pl.* poles 210/17.

power *n.* be(e)n of ~ are able 17/59, 42/xx.

prechyn *v. intr.* preach 1/3b, 112/50, 2–22/40; prechyth, preche *pr.3 sg.* 2–11/27, 2–177/25; prechydyn *pa.t.3 pl. tr.* preached to 2–25/48.

prechyng(e *vbl.n.* preaching 2–23/57, 2–24/74, 2–60/63.

prechour *n.* preacher 2–22/21, 22, 26, 2–

69/73; prechour(y)s *pl.* 17/3, 331/44, 2–10/19.

precious *adj.* expensive 2–227/14.

preciously *adv.* expensively 216/59.

predialys *adj.* tithes (based on produce from real property) 2–167/58, 2–168/4.

preef, prof *n.* demonstration 31/lxii, legal proof 342/64.

preyyd *pa.t.3 sg.* asked 187/26, 236/25; preyynge *pr.p.* 236/23.

preyshable *adj.* praiseworthy 2–167/63.

preiudys *n.* harm 173/38, 247/18, 2–190/45.

prelat(h *n.* prelate (ecclesiatic of high rank) 188/8, 246/43, 344/40; prelatis *pl.* 348/12.

prelatye, prelacye *n.* clerics of high rank, collectively 37/xix, 257/51, 341/13, 20, 24.

presentacyo(u)n *n.* presentation (naming of a cleric to a bishop for institution to a benefice) 37/xxiv, 353/78, 79, 354/81, 83.

presentyn *v.* present (recommend a cleric to a bishop for a benefice) 351/12, 354/86; presentith *pr.3 sg.* 352/42; presente *subj.3 sg.* should present 353/77, 78; presentynge *pr.p.* 353/75.

presyd *pa.t.3 sg.* pressed 187/29.

pre(e)st(e, preist *n.* priest 3/28, 88/17, 159/45, 219/53; pre(e)stys, -tes *pl.* 27/xiv, 98/39, 156/19–20, 2–88/99.

presumyn *v.* ~ *of hemself* be presumptuous 130/80–1.

pretendyth *pr.3 sg.* depicts falsely 177/68–69, pretendyn *pr.3 pl.* 177/73, claim 2–291/41.

pretense *adj. lordschip* ~ usurped authority 72/19, 29; see Notes.

preu- see prou-

preuy, pryue(i *adj.* private 55/39, 124/85, secret 70/26, 148/28, 149/4, 150/32, personal 60/58, ~ *menbrys* sexual organs 2–91/15, 2–104/19–20.

pryckyd *ppl.adj.* inscribed 133/33.

principal *n.* model 2-67/48, rule of conduct 2–71/13 (see Notes).

principal, -cepal *adj.* chief, preeminent 105/30, 2–70/103, 2–163/122.

pryorie *n.* priory 353/50; pryoryys *pl.* 2–184/13.

pryour *n.* prior (head of monastery or

house of mendicants) 256/26, 2–184/10; **pryouris** *pl.* 2–194/62.

prys *n.* (sales) price 18/26, 101/53, value 2–18/77, 2–22/25, 2–149/73, payment 191/33, 2–198/3, 2–320/46.

prysyn *v.* set a value on 2–192/81.

pryuelyche *adv.* secretly 165/86, 213/42, 219/43, privately 2–7/2, 4, 2–31/34.

pryuyn *v.* dispossess (from) 352/29; **pryuyth** *pr.3 sg.* deprives 2–53/5; **priuyn** *pr.3 pl.* 214/25; **pryuyd** *pa.t.3 sg.* dispossessed 307/32, 2–9/62; ~ *pp.* deprived 167/22, 2–107/22, 2–182/71, dispossessed 2–9/62, 2–183/74, 78.

pryuyte *n.* private affairs 140/33; **priue-te(i)s** *pl.* secrets 2–235/17, 20, *book of God(d)is* ~ N. T. Book of Revelations 2–33/52, 2–77/28.

proces(se *n.* reasoned argument (in a sermon) 40/v, legal trial 21/35, (legal) rules or procedures 160/5, 23, 2–13/16, story, narrative 293/23, 2–48/67.

procession *n.* **gon** ~ make a religious procession 6/119, 197–8/9–10; -YS *pl.* 197/8–9, 198/25.

procuracye *n.* advocacy (in pejorative sense; lobbying for ecclesiastical office) 354/90.

procuratour *n.* business manager of a convent 319/64.

procuryn *n.* *pr.3 pl.* bring down (upon them) 2–87/95.

prof *n.* *witnesse of* ~ witness in a legal trial 2–222/5, 7.

prof(e)re *n.* *of his owyn* ~ on his own initiative 246/35, 2–59/46.

profes(s *adj.* ~ *in religion* professed, having made religious vows 316/32, 2–113/44.

profession *n.* religious vows 316/35.

profyght, -fyth *n.* benefit 112/51, 331/24, 337/28.

profytabilhed *n.* usefulness, productiveness 2–293/35.

profythabelyche *adv.* profitably 304/2.

profytyth *pr.3 sg.* benefits, is of use 2–260/35; **profyghtyn** *pr.3 pl.* 112/48.

profre *n.* initiative 246/35, 2–59/46, offer 2–157/37.

propyrchyn *pr.3 pl.* appropriate 138/27, 2–138/27, 2–164/136.

propirhed *n.* proprietorship (of personal property) 2–138/22, 2–139/44.

propirte *n.* property 138/22, ownership

17/7, 2–137/61, 2–138/22, attribute 115/60, definition 2–34/15; **propyrteys** *pl.* proprietorships 43/v.

propre *n.* *in* ~ in private possession 2–142/44, *as* ~ as private property 2–165/163.

propre *adj.* private, individual 139/42, 50, 321/41, 2–139/42, 43, 46.

propryetarye *n.* cleric who violates vow of poverty 2–188/82.

proprietarye, -aryys *adj.* (clerics) owning goods in violation of clerical vows 18/42, 44/xii.

protestacyoun *n.* affirmation 102/35, 103/42.

proudelych *adj.* haughtily 332/8–9.

provendre *n.* prebendary (holder of a prebend) 2–177/43.

prouyn, preue *v.* prove to, demonstrate to 71/3, prove (legally) 342/64; **preue** *pr.1 sg.* prove, demonstrate 80/52; **preuest** *pr.2 sg.* 74/16; **prouyth, -yȝt, preueþ** *pr.3 sg.* 69/61, 72/32, tests 2–312/182; **prouyd** *pp.* 229/5.

prowde *adj.* ostentatious 44/xii.

punshyn, punchyn, punych *v.* punish 41/vi, 122/22, 26, 2–13/18, *refl.* 2–240/87; **punyssheth, punchyth** *pr.3 sg.* 39/xviii, 2–121/11, 13, 15; **punchyd** *pa.t.3 sg.* 14/48, 217/5, 2–128/40, 42; **pun(i)shyd, -chyd** *pp.* 32/xi, 137/35, 159/52, 2–121/16.

punching(e *vbl.n.* punishment 161/59, 180/33, 277/39.

purchas *n.* acquisition of property 2–276/7.

purchasyn *v.* *intr.* acquire property, see 'purchasourys' 317/20–21, 2–150/99.

purchasour(y)s, -sowrs *n.pl.* buyers, with invidious connotation, see *MED* sv. 2 c, citing *D&P* Table, 22/1–2, 47/i, ii, 2–254/40.

purgacioun *n.* clearing 229/8–9.

puryfyed *pp.* churched (ritual of purification after childbirth) 2–116/1.

purpo(o)s, por- *n.* *more to* ~ more to the point 101/60, 321/2, *hadde not hese* ~ failed in his aim 193/14, *be* ~ purposely 2–33/49, *what is þis to* ~ ? what is the point of this? 2–260/40.

purposyn *v.* plan 2–275/48; **purpose** *pr.1 sg.* intend 71/51, 139/5; **purposen** *pr.3 pl.* 150/29, 152/19.

purpure *n.* purple 2–228/43.

pursueris *n.pl.* prosecutors (those who bring legal action) 2–37/24.

pursuyn *v.* persecute 251/37, 57, prosecute 2–73/74; **pursuyn** *pr.3 pl.* persecute 2–15/41.

put *ppl.adj.* fixed 122/18.

puttyn, potyn *v.* subject 172/18, put 342/54, 355/17, submit (to) 2–191/53, *refl.* attempt 345/70; **potist** *pr.2 sg.* throw (in your lot) 2–210/110; **pottyth, putty3t** *pr.3 sg.* assigns 131/23, places 131/26, proposes 2–213/2; **puttyn, pottyn** *pr.3 pl.* train 131/24, put 292/45, put away 2–62/16; **put** *subj.3 sg.* should put (her) up to 2–75/112; ~ *imp.sg.* ~ *up* put away 2–33/56; ~ *pa.t.3 sg.* added 2–12/73; ~ *pp.* ~ *awey* sent away 2–291/44, 45.

puttok *n.* European kite 5/96, 29/xlvi, 144/21.

Q

qhan(ne, whenne, whan(ne *conj.* when 55/40, 115/33, 150/22, 184/39, 195/15.

qhat, what *pron.* what 52/21, 93/1, 154/34.

qhat, what *adj.* what 63/22, 24, 25, 144/19, 2–51/45.

qheel *n.* wheel 92/32, 96/27; **qheelys** *pl.* 95/24.

qhelpys *n.pl.* whelps 97/25.

qhens *adv.* whence 52/2.

qher- see **wher-**

qhereso *adv.* wherever 118/27.

qherof *adj.* what purpose 82/36.

qhy *conj.* why 65/2, *for* ~ because 65/52.

qhyght *adj.* white 142/26.

qhyl(e *conj.* while 62/46, 99/5.

qhyle *n.* while 147/18, *adv. phr. a* ~ awhile 66/24.

qhoo *pron.* who 63/20, 21, 22, 124/69; **qhom** *oblique cases* whom 65/9, 86/16 (cf. HO).

qhoos(e, w(h)os(e *adj.* whose 53/8, 62/36, 91/8, 189/2, 2–96/39.

qhooso *pron.* whosoever 53/31, 56/76, 62/42 (cf. hoso).

quarrerys *n.pl.* quarries 2–166/43.

queche, qheche *adj.* which 65/7, 93/6, 100/13.

queche, qheche, wheche, whych(e *pron.* which, who 55/39, 62/39, 73/30, 131/17, 151/35, 208/15, 2–238/3.

queer *n.* choir 112/40.

queke see **qwyk-**

quekyn *v. intr.* come to life 112/56; **qwy(c)kyth** *pr.3 sg.* 2–307/5, *tr.* gives life to 2–39/41, 42; **quekyn, qwykyn** *pr.3 pl. intr.* revive, quicken 97/28, 2–300/33; **qwykedyn, quyk-** *pa.t.3 pl. tr.* revived, brought to life 2–4/42, 47; **quekyd** *pp.* enlivened, warmed 111/18.

quemyn *v.* make recompense (for) 116/61, gratify, please 331/35, 350/102, 2–244/111.

quest(e, qwest *n.* legal trial, inquest 14/54, 40/xxi, 344/36, 37, 2–240/85; **questis** *pl.* 253/39.

questemongeris *n.pl.* shady persons who profit from inquests or trials 253/53.

qwene *n.* queen 2–61/51.

qwere *conj.* where 151/39 (cf. w(h)er).

qwychyn *v. intr.* complain 2–271/49.

qwyk(e, qwyc *adj.* alive 2–4/43, 2–41/43, 2–303/20.

qwy(c)ke, quycke, queke *n.pl.* the living, living persons 54/9, 75/8, 216/72, 272/38, 2–221/64.

R

rafne *n.* raven 2–268/7; **rafnys, -nes** *pl.* 306/64, 2–281/66.

rankour *n.* rancour 273/23.

raþer(e *adv.* rather 169/8, 210/35, 254/81.

raþere *adj.* quicker 161/33.

rauechid *pp.* snatched up 2–325/58.

raue(y)nour *n.* robber, malefactor 127/62, 2–160/20; **-nouris, -owres** *pl.* 20/84, 45/xxviii, 2–74/86.

rau(e)yn(e *n.* rapine 213/39, 331/27, 2–29/80 (cf. V.L. *rapina*), *bestys of* ~ beasts of prey 145/31.

raunsom, -son *n.* ransom 84/21, 2–165/16, 2–179/42.

real *adj.* royal 251/50.

rebel(l *adj.* rebellious 337/7, 2–128/48, 2–305/17.

rebellys *n.pl.* rebels 2–40/73, 2–55/30, 31.

rebellyn *v.* rebel against 357/10, *intr.* rebel 2–55/39.

recles- see **rekeles-**

reconcyled *pp.* reconsecrated 219/54.

recreacion *n.* re-creation, spiritual regeneration 270/46, 48, 61 (cf. MED).

recuryd *pp.* recovered 2–260/26.

red *n.* advice 2–315/22.

red *ppl.adj.* deprived 14/31.

redely *adv.* readily 142/13.

redy *adj.* ~ *to* on hand, available 151/57.

redyn, rede *v.* guess 2–228/35 (MS H var. is 'gessyn'; cf. MED sv. 'reden' v. 7); *intr.* read 82/43, 83/1; ~ *pr.3 pl. tr.* 109/65; **rede** *imp.sg.tr.* 85/49; ~ *pa.t. 1 sg.* 2–224/5; **redde** *pa.t.3 sg.* 2–100/22; **red** *pp.* 97/31, 251/42.

redyng(g)(e *vbl.n.* reading 82/42, 109/64, 2–102/92.

referryn *v.* be directed (towards) 112/51; **referryd** *pp.* applied 89/37, directed 233/29, 31.

reformation *n.* restoration 266/19.

reformyn *v.* redeem 265/58; **reformyd** *pp.* restored 2–313/14.

refreynyn *v.* restrain 2–159/83, 2–306/55; ~ *pr.3 pl. refl.* 2–62/4; **refreynyd** *pp.* 2–304/15.

refreschyn *v.* refresh (cf. V.L. *refrigerabit*) 322/15.

refusiþ *pr.3 sg.* rejects 79/28.

regne *n.* reign 2–250/57, 2–270/25.

regnyn *v. intr.* are the rule 275/33, flourish 2–245/11; **regne** *pr.1 sg.* rule 2–270/20; **regny3t, -nyth** *pr.3 sg.* predominates 68/38, 275/31, flourishes 165/85, 2–4/1, rules 215/33; **reg(y)nyn** *pr.3 pl.* 84/24, 35, 2–81/29; **regnynge** *pr.p.* flourishing 172/16; **regnedyn** *pa.t.2 pl.* reigned 2–17/55; **regnede** *pa.t.3 pl.* predominated 98/59–60; **regnyd** *pp.* flourished 2–64/65.

rehersid *ppl.adj.* cited 70/23, 71/45.

rehersynge *vbl.n.* repetition 2–299/30.

rehersist *pr.2 sg.* cite, repeat 79/31; **rehersith** *pr.3 sg.* 25/ix; **rehersid** *pa.t.3 sg.* repeated 2–298/3, 11.

reioysyn *v. intr. refl.* rejoice (in) 209/35, *tr.* enjoy 2–221/61.

a)reysyn *v.* raise, arouse 2–64/81, resurrect 2–241/20, 2–301/62; **resyd** *pa.t.3 sg.* raised 2–264/60 (cf. **risyn**; cf. MED reisen, arisen).

reyuyn *v.* rob 2–255/62; **reyuyd** *pp.* 2–165/9.

rekeles *adj.* careless 172/9, 2–46/62.

rekeleshed(e, recles- *n.* carelessness 260/12, 274/36, 324/16.

rekeleslyche *adv.* carelessly 223/29, 2–23/52.

rekenyng(g)(e *vbl.n.* reckoning, account

21/40, 64/10, 2–137/66; **rekenyng(g)ys** *pl.* 64/13, 73/13, 2–251/6.

relef *n.* leftovers 2–293/45.

releuynge *vbl.n.* relief 293/27.

relygioun *n.* religious orders 33/xv, 249/71, 73, 344/48.

religious *n. sg.pl.* person(s under religious rule 11/17, 12/49, 315/8, 320/30, 31, 344/53.

remelaunt *n.* remainder 110/14; **remnantis** *pl.* 301/74.

rem, remys see **rew-**

remeuyd *pp.* related 22/8, 48/4.

remouyng *vbl.n.* avoidance 49/56.

ren *n.* run, gallop 307/25.

rendyn *v.* tear 92/33; **rentist** *pa.t.2 sg.* 241/63, *intr.* was torn 269/35.

renegat *adj.* renegade, unfaithful 2–229/83, 84.

reneyyn *pr.3 pl.* deny, abjure 2–261/66.

rennyn *v. intr.* run 185/10, 2–247/33, follow 2–322/21; **ronne** *pr.2 sg.* run, associate 2–210/108; **rennen** *pr.3 pl.* come quickly 70/22, rush 291/10; **rennyng** *pr.p.* running, flowing 2–276/13; **ronnyn** *pa.t.3 pl.* ran 236/39, streamed 2–228/50.

repreuyn, reprou- *v.* refute 135/24 (see Notes), condemn 135/30, 32, 343/14; **repreuyth, reprouy3t** *pr.3 sg.* 3/49, rebukes 52/22; **repreuen, reprou-** *pr.3 pl.* rebuke (for) 39/xi, condemn 194/38; **reproue** *subj.3 sg.* should condemn 2–226/61; **reprof** *imp.sg.* condemn! 258/20; **reprouyng** *pr.p.* ~ *of* condemning 2–225/32; **reprouyd** *pa.t.3 sg.* rebuked 201/25, 2–263/22, blamed 2–125/43, 44; **repreuid, reprou-** *pp.* condemned 28/xxv, 2–67/9, rebuked 36/xiv, disapproved 2–188/71.

reprof, -pref *n.* reproach 90/15, 224/30, 2–86/54, 55, shame 208/14, 2–64/58, ~ *and castynge out of þe peple* an object of scorn and an outcast 53/34 (cf. V.L. *opprobrium . . . et abiectio plebis*; see Notes).

repugne *v.* oppose 343/13; **repugnyth** *pr.3 sg. intr.* ~ *to* is more out of keeping (with) 2–111/43.

rerebras *n.* armour for the upper arm 24/15 *var.* H 2–310/107–108.

respect(e, respecth *n.* aspect of planets

(in astrology) 118/28, 121/72, 126/34, 41; **respectys** *pl.* 126/36.

reste *n.* tranquillity 121/68.

restith *imp. pl. refl.* cease! 265/62 (cf. V.L. *Quiescite*).

restituȝt *pp.* reinstated 2–182/72, 2–183/75.

reuerence *n. of mor* ~ more highly esteemed 232/7.

reueryys *n.pl.* states of madness 2–92/54.

reuful *adj.* pitiful 2–106/54.

reuys *n.pl.* reeves (overseers of a landlord's tenants) 2–137/69, 2–159/96.

reule *n.* conduct 68/47, 339/38, 44, guidance 96/38, rule (of law) 319/3, religious rule 344/41, 42.

reulyng, rew- *vbl.n.* conduct, self-rule 68/33, guidance 95/19.

reward *n. takyn* ~ *þat* have regard for the fact that 2–35/63.

rewyn *v.* regret 2–257/11.

rewler *n.* manager 319/65; **rewlour(y)s** *pl.* officials 308/38, 343/27.

rewlyn, rewle, reulyn *v.* govern 23/11, 49/58, 117/7, *refl.* regulate 120/35 et seq.; **rewlyȝt, reulith** *pr.3 sg.* governs 118/35, 132/9, 145/42, 43, regulates 120/42, 43; **rewlyn, reulyn** *pr.3 pl.* 95/25, 120/45; **rewlyd** *pp.* governed (by) 248/27.

rewme, reme *n.* kingdom 77/32, 37, rulership 149/52 et seq.; **re(w)mes, -mys** *pl.* kingdoms 38/xxvi, 57/5, 98/55.

rewþe, reuþe *n.* compassion 329/25, 356/20, 2–35/62.

rybaudye *n.* ribaldry, bawdiness 189/40, 218/28, 293/15, 16, 298/59.

rychesse *n.* riches, wealth 1/5b, 18/34, 249/75; **richesse, richessis, -es** *pl.* 25/viii, 79/5, 8.

rydour *n.* severity, harshness 251/51 (cf. MED reddour).

ryght, ri(ȝ)t(h) *adv. intensifier* very 312/70, 2–11/37, ~ *nouȝt* not at all 156/5, nothing at all 249/76, ~ *now* just now 211/5, ~ *so,* ~ *þus* likewise 2–5/36, 2–272/67, 85, 2–274/25, 30, 34, ~ *up* upright, vertical 297/24, 2–81/44, 2–247/16; *hadde* ~ *mychil trauayle* worked hard 2–224/8; (in *conj. phr.*) ~ *as . . . so* just as . . . so 57/13–14, 78/11–12, 96/35, 115/44 (cf. nout(h)).

ryȝt *n.* rights, just legal claim 2–232/11, 27.

ryȝt *adj.* straight 2–245/15, 2–246/23.

ryȝtwys *adj.* righteous 40/xxiii.

ryȝt(h)wysne(se, ryght- *n.* righteousness 88/9–10, 132/10, 228/30.

rymplyng *vbl.n.* wrinkling 2–247/11.

ryngyn see holy

ryot *n.* riotous living 308/40, 44, 2–287/7.

ryseris *n.pl.* rebels 251/52.

risyn, rise, a)reysyn *v. intr.* rise 115/49, 357/21, arise 120/35, stand up 310/3, *fig.* 154/31, rebel 2–44/36; **risith** *pr.3 sg.* rises 357/20; **rysyn** *pr.3 pl.* arise 97/29, 2–60/59; **a)rysyn** *subj.pr.3 pl.* should rise 357/26, should rise up 358/30; **roos** *pa.t.3 sg.* rose 97/25, 115/45, 267/61; **areysyn** *pa.t.3 pl.* rose up 358/38 (cf. **areysyn**; cf. *MED* risen, arisen).

rysynge *vbl.n.* rebellion 308/47.

ryue *v. intr.* split 2–241/13; **roof** *pa.t.3 sg. tr.* impaled 2–104/19.

ro(o)d(e *n.* rood (cross on which Christ died) 264/52, 2–102/75, 2–164/150, ~ *tree* 174/57, (a representation of the) cross 26/iv, 89/43.

roddyd *pp. han don hese feet* ~ *of* caused his feet to rot off 162/20 (cf. rotyn).

rody *adj.* ruddy 359/59.

rofe *n.* roof 140/22.

rohwyd *pa.t.3 sg.* coughed 311/44 (cf. cohwyd).

rokys *n.pl.* rooks, crows 2–281/66.

Romaynys *propr.n.pl.* Romans 208/17, 2–286/57.

rombyd *pa.t.3 sg.* paced, walked 2–85/23, 2–258/16.

rotyn *ppl.adj.* rotten 2–251/11 (cf. roddyd).

rounere, rowner *n.* whisperer (spreader of gossip, tale-bearer) 38/iv, 2–7/2; **rounerys** *pl.* 2–7/12. See Note 2–7/1. Cf. 'mustrere'.

S

saaf *ppl.adj.* saved 76/32.

sabot, sabat *n.* sabbath 34/x, 263/7, 281/1; **sabotes, sab(b)atis** *pl.* 9/14, 34/ix, 280/1.

sacrid *pp.* consecrated (to clerical office) 266/40, 2–178/23.

sacring *vbl.n.* consecrating of persons to clerical office 2–178/22.

sad(de *adj.* sober, serious 24/26, 50/82, 347/14.

saddyn *v.* thicken 2–118/5; **saddith** *imp.pl.intr.* be sober 298/59.

sadly *adv.* seriously, soberly 171/14, 258/8, 2–305/34.

sadnesse *n.* seriousness, sobriety 298/56, 57, 347/9, 2–227/8, 9.

sage see **fool**

saif *quasi prep.* except 73/39, ~ *þi pacience* without offence to your patience 79/30.

salerye, -arye *n.* stipend of a priest 2–186/20, 2–187/36 et seq..

sanct- see **seyn-**

saphirus n. sapphire 2–321/26.

sardius *n.* precious stone, 'sard' 2–321/27.

sarsyn, -cyn *propr.n.* Saracen (in general sense: a non-Christian) 194/41, 252/17, 317/53.

Sauteer *n.* Psalter, the book of Psalms 106/50; **sauterys** *pl.* psalms 2–184/25.

sauterye, sawtree *n.* psaltery 39/xii, 2–28/56, 58, 61.

saw(e *n.* saying 64/6, 199/1, advice, instruction 71/36, 311/32, 2–242/44, prediction 152/30, explanation 358/36, song, lament 2–245/1; **sawys, -wes** *pl.* predictions 125/14, explanations 149/46.

schadue, schad(e)we *n.* shadow 22/18, 48/17, foreshadowing 265/5, 269/25, 283/22.

schadyn *v.* shed (blood) 198/13; **schadith** *pr.3 sg.* 2–16/4, 2–32/32; **schadde** *pa.t.3 sg.* 264/52, 270/51, 2–311/155; **schad, schat** *pp.* 192/70, 208/16, 240/41.

schafaryn *v.intr.* conduct trade or business 2–149/76 (cf. **chaffar-**).

schal(l, shal, s(c)hul(l-, s(c)huld-, scholde *aux.v.* (with sense of obligation or intention to act) ought to, must 2/19b, 36/xii, 56/56, 75/19, 81/2, 3, 106/50, 52, 204/44, 337/19, (conveying future sense to the main verb) shall, will 1/3a, 75/6, 19, 205/61, 62, 318/29, (conveying future conditional sense to the main verb) would, should 63/20, 72/27, 74/8.

s(c)hal, schul *pr.1 sg.* 56/64, 2–100/31, 2–284/1; **s(c)halt, schul** *pr.2 sg.* 1/11b, 75/19, **schal(l, schul** *pr.3 sg.* 46/x, 75/19, 2–319/33; **s(c)hul(len, shulle**

pr.1 pl. 2/19b, 36/xii, 106/50; **schul(en** *pr.2 pl.* 1/3a, 75/6, 2–311/157; **s(c)hul-len, shullyn** *pr.3 pl.* 6/125, 65/42, 75/8; **shulde** *pa.t.1 sg.* 83/1; **shuldist** *pa.t.2 sg.* 63/18; **s(c)hulde** *pa.t.3 sg.* 74/3, 86/18; **shulde, schuldyn** *pa.t.1 pl.* 240/39, 241/14; **schulde, -den** *pa.t.2 pl.* 74/2, 8; **schuldyn, -den, sholde** *pa.t.3 pl.* 36/v, 43/ix, 44/xiv, 204/44.

schamefast *adj.* ashamed 2–292/25.

schamefastnesse *n.* modesty 2–71/13, 2–91/18.

schamfoly *adv.* ignominiously 239/22.

schapyn *ppl.adj.* shaped 2–118/22, 23.

scharpit *pp.* sharpened 2-6/47.

schauyn *v.refl. don hem* ~ have themselves shaved 290/25.

schauynge *vbl.n.* tonsure 2–230/92.

sche, she *pron.3 sg.fem.* she 33/xv, 63/28, 309/21; **hyr, her(e** her (direct or indirect object) 224/19, 346/18, 2–58/19; **hyr** *refl.* herself 2–100/33 (cf. **hyr** *adj.*).

schede *n.* sheath 2–12/79, 2–38/17, 2–48/65.

scheld, sheld *n.* shield 24/15 *var.* H, 96/30, 2–309/77, 78, 85.

schen(t)chep(e, shenship *n.* disgrace, ignominy 6/135, 11/21, 306/58, 2–120/36.

schendyn, shende *v.* confound 53/40, 54/42, injure 308/45, 2–119/24–25, damage 2–29/81; **schent, schendyth** *pr.3 sg.* injures 323/57, 324/5, *refl.* 2–212/43; **s(c)hent** *pp.* defeated and confused (cf.V.L. *confundantur confusione*) 82/35, ruined (by) 165/84, 2–126/5, disgraced 2–131/6. lost 2–243/83.

scheryn *pp.* clipped 290/26.

schetyn *v. intr.* shoot 2–38/27, 2–45/49; **schetynge** *pr.p.* tr. 2–245/18; **yschott** *pp.* 71/2 (cf. **bolt**).

schetynge *vbl.n.* shooting 2–246/22.

schettyn, shett-, s)chett- *v.* shut 152/9, 195/3, 9, 2–88/115, *refl.* 2–303/20; **shettist** *pr.2 sg.* ~ *up* store up, hoard 2–160/15; **schet** *imp.sg.* enclose (cf. V.L. *conclude*) 2–283/64; ~ *pa.t.3 sg.* shut 312/62; **schet(tyn** *pp.* shut 2-6/59, closed 2–97/48, barred 2–99/103.

schettyng *vbl.n.* shutting 2–56/46.

schew- see **shew-**

schew *n. makyn a* ~ show off 2–198/2.

schiftyng *vbl.n.* judging 257/38; in a

doublet with 'demyng', *MED* sv. schif-ting(e c., gives this as the only instance of this sense.

schof *pa.t.3 sg.* shoved 187/30.

schoy3yn, schoyen *v.* put shoes on 2–309/68; **shooyn** *pr.3 pl.* 101/54; **scho3yth** *imp.pl.* shoe (your feet) 2–308/34; **shoodde, shoyd, schoyen, schoe** *pp.* shod 101/43, 47, 290/26 *var.* RDTH.

schortlyche *adv.* briefly 2–318/44.

schrewe, shrewe *n.* a wicked person 14/56, 127/59, 357/71; **s(c)hrewys** *pl.* 6/141, 57/20, 212/12.

schrewyd, shrewyd(de *adj.* wicked 225/57, 259/27, 325/45, hurtful, cruel 51/19, 53/20, 2–132/37.

schrewydlyche *adv.* wickedly 217/109.

schrewydnesse, shrew- *n.* wickedness 3/44, 127/60, 2–3/9, cruelty 2–35/53.

schryf(y)n, schryuen, schrifen, schreuyn *pp.* shriven, confessed 8/34, 52, 157/33, 172/9, 181/37, 2–182/56.

schrifte *n.* confession 8/52, 99/6, 109/10, *in ~* in the confession box 251/30.

schuld- see **schal**

science *n.* knowledge (as opposed to skill) 135/17, 22 (cf. **craft**), pseudo-learning 139/1.

sckepedyn *pa.t.3 pl.* leapt 297/35 (cf. V.L. *saltabat*).

sckyppynge *vbl.n.* leaping (cf. V.L. *saltantem*) 297/37.

sclaundre see **s(ch)la(u)n-**

scoom *n.* dross, slag 2–154/40 (cf. V.L. *scoriam*).

scorge *n.* whip 218/10, 335/12 (*fig.*); **scorgis** *pl.* 2–242/52.

scorn(e, skorne *n.* object of scorn 53/38, mockery 228/11, *lowh to ~* jeered at 305/41; **scornys** *pl.* jeers 115/34.

scornyng *vbl.n.* mocking 31/ii, mockery 305/49.

scouryd *pp.* cleansed (*fig.*) 336/27.

scrippis *n.pl.* sacks, baggage 260/22.

scrowe *n.* paper or parchment (containing writing) 312/76; **scrowis** *pl.* 158/15.

seculer *n.* person not under religious rule 315/8; **seculerys, -es** *pl.* laymen, the laity 16/55, 42/xviii, secular clerics 320/31.

seculerte *n.* the secular world, the laity 218/23.

sed *n.* seed (*fig.*), children 353/67.

seer *adj.* withered 107/14, 22.

seent see **sent**

sege, seche *n.* siege 2–85/33, 2–189/19.

seyl *n.* sail 2–271/43.

seylynge *pr.p.* sailing 2–270/5, 2–271/42.

seyn(e, seie(n, sey *v.* say 4/64, 150/13, 299/31, tell 149/4, *~ his bedys* tell his beads 200/31; **seie** *pr.1 sg.* say 78/30; **sey(i)st** *pr.2 sg.* 90/21, 213/1, 2–159/2; **seiþ, seyt(h, sey3t,** *pr.3 sg.* 1/8a, 80/40, 81/1, 2, 307/13; **seyyn, seien** *pr.3 pl.* 71/42, 201/28; **seye, saye** *subj.3 sg.* should speak 4/66, 200/33, 34, should say 155/2, should express 249/78; **sey** *imp.sg.* say! 251/58, reply! 320/22; **seiynge** *pr.p.* saying 80/46; **seidist** *pa.t.2 sg.* said 79/33, 90/23, have said 2–13/7; **seide** *pa.t.3 sg.* 79/32; **seyd, saide, seyn** *pp.* spoken 155/72, 2–2/40, 2–192/2, said 71/48, 206/18, 2–276/13.

sey(y)nge *vbl.n.* utterance 201/27, 207/64.

seyntuary, sanctuary(e *n.* church precincts 31/lxiv, 291/28, 2–193/4.

se(e)k(e *adj.* in ill health 117/10, sick 150/16, ailing 197/56.

sekyn, sechyn *v.* search (out) 124/80, 331/34, seek 2–24/11; **sekyn** *pr.3 pl.* 331/24; **souhte** *pa.t.1 sg.* 333/9; **sou3te** *pa.t.3 sg.* pursued 2–86/60; **soutyn** *pa.t.2 pl.* searched for 2–17/53; **sou3te** *pa.t.3 pl.* pursued 2–86/61; **sou3t** *pp.* pursued (by) 2–214/36.

sekyr, sykyr *adj.* safe 53/10, 107/24 *var. al.*, 302/35, 322/20, 341/23, steady 2–89/33 (cf. V.L. *pedes firmi*), certain 62/55, 101/58, 230/14, 15, sure 6/140, 31/lxii, 212/21, 23, 302/35, solid 2–89/34.

sekyrly, sykerly, -lyche *adv.* firmly 173/45, safely 2–45/39, securely 107/24 (perh. scribal error), for certain 8/35, 32/xiv, 62/36, 173/45.

sekyrnesse *n.* surety, pledge (for a loan) 236/14, security, safety 2–142/26, 2–158/71.

self, silf *pron 3 sg. refl. in ̃ ~* in itself 226/17, 233/15, itself 174/53, intrinsically 241/13, *of þe- ~* in themselves 37/

xxi, 346/23, 24, *be þe(m)-* ~ separately 66/38, 2–183/84.

semely *adj.* appropriate 116/69, easily believable 162/5, likely 244/30, 252/20, 2–45/47, 2–261/74, suitable, preferable 310/25, in accord (with) 2–235/27, apparent 2–44/19, seemly, attractive 2–305/41.

se(e)n *v.* see 52/45, 186/10, 348/40, understand 2–29/1; **se(e)ist** *pr.2 sg.* see 86/12, 2–159/2; **se(e)(i)th, syȝth** *pr.3 sg.* 85/56, 180/23, 2–224/58; **seen** *pr.1 pl.* 147/20; ~ *pr.3 pl.* 99/71; **se** *subj.3 sg.* should see 244/31; **seeyt** *imp.pl.* behold! 92/30, 31; **sauȝ** *pa.t.1 sg.* saw 2–11/46, 50; **say(ȝ, sauhȝ, saw(ȝ** *pa.t.3 sg.* 174/57, 348/35, 349/41, 2–12/73, 2–73/63; **sey(ȝ)yn** *pa.t.3 pl.* 116/71, 76, 175/31; **seye** *pa.t.subj.3 sg.* 2–45/41; **seyn** *pp.* 251/42, 2–69/52, 2–73/60.

sensyng *vbl.n.* incensing 27/xv (cf. **encens-**).

se(e)nt *n.* (aphetic form of descent) *be* ~ *of heritage* by inheritance, by lineage 52/1, 2–257/6.

sentence *n.* opinion 134/66, 2–192/2, pronouncement 2–314/52.

senuys *n.pl.* sinews 83/11.

sepulturis *n.pl.* burial rites 2–179/32.

serchaunt *n.* sergeant (officer of the court, charged with duty to arrest or summon before the court) 2–194/36.

seryn *v. intr.* dry 356/26; ~ *pr.3 pl.* 146/60; **seryd** *pa.t.3 sg.* withered 2–107/5.

seruage *n.* bondage, servitude 264/48, 339/27, 29, 2–125/69, service 156/8, service (to) 166/12.

seruyle *adj.* ~ *werkes* secular work (done for subsistence or profit) 34/vii, 277/28, 32, 35.

seruyn *pr.3 pl.* are serviceable 176/36; **seruyd** *pa.t.1 sg.* treated 2–263/20.

ses- see **ces-**

setis *n.pl.* seats, benches 218/17.

settyn *v.* put 77/28, 125/15, 179/39, plant 119/17, 322/28, set 122/10, establish 136/22, establish themselves in 2–63/46, incline 2–109/61, ~ *feith to* put faith in 180/30; **set(tyȝt, -ith** *pr.3 sg.* puts 77/31, *refl.* broods 309/20; **settyn** *pr.3 pl.* put 82/35, 136/27, value 2–277/36; **sette** *subj.2 sg.* should place 299/22; **sette** *pa.t.3 sg.* placed 119/3, ~ *nought by*

little valued 54/49; **set(t)(h** *pp.* set 95/12, ~ *by* valued 70/19, 100/34, 2–288/38, ~ *in* invested in 100/49, grounded 2–61/34.

seuene *card.num.* seven 2–319/29.

seuynth, seue(ne)te, seueþe *ord.num.* seventh 34/xi, 166/26, 263/7, 2–247/27.

sewyng see **suynge**

sewirte *n.* safety 280/15.

sexe, syxe *card.num.* six 9/20, 21, 34/xii.

sexte, syxte *ord.num.* sixth 34/xii, 2–130/1.

sextyde *ord.num.* sixtieth 2–173/51.

shal see **schal**

s(c)hap(p)ere *n.* creator 89/49, 103/38, 104/65, 330/37.

shapyn, schape *v.* make, tailor 63/22, 74/4.

s(c)harp *adj.* rough 92/26, 2–321/24.

shend- see **schend-**

shene *adj.* shining 52/43.

shenship see **schen-**

sherd *n.* shard (fragment of earthenware) 128/25.

s(c)hete *n.* winding sheet, shroud 2–281/12, 2–282/39.

shett- see **schett-**

shewyn *v. intr.* appear 146/68; **schewit(h** *pr.3 sg.* shows 89/51, 149/2, 356/7, 9; **shewyt(h** *pr.3 sg. it* ~ there is 142/36, manifests 142/25, 30, shows forth 143/39, 40, shows 155/50, 210/35, *refl.* is shown 83/8; ~ *pr.3 pl.* 63/17; **schewe** *subj.3 sg.refl.* should appear 184/11; **schew** *imp.sg.* show! 160/20, 165/79; **shewyngge** *pr.p.* 98/41; **s(c)hewyd(d)(e, schewit** *pa.t.3 sg.* 89/51, 261/54, revealed 92/28; **schewyd** *pa.t.-subj.3 sg. refl.* should have appeared 184/12; **schewyt, -wyd** *pp.* showed 2/18b, 2–30/23, manifested 210/12–13, 23.

sholes *adj.* shoeless 63/26.

sho(o)n, schon *n.pl.* shoes 100/37, 260/21, 33, 2–228/57.

shoo- see **schoy-**

shrew- see **schrew-**

sicle *n.* shekel. small coin 190/23.

syde *adj.* large, ample 2–91/12.

syȝ(h)t(he *n.* sense of sight 157/35, 195/11, sight (of God) 164/49, 227/39, 286/36; **syȝthis** *pl.* visions 175/31.

syhyn *v. intr.* sigh 2–288/58; **syȝhe** *subj.3 sg.* may sigh 2–25/35.

syhyng *vbl.n.* sighing, sadness 94/25; sy3hyngis *pl.* sorrowings 306/69–70.

symony(e *n.* simony (buying or selling of church offices or services) 44/xvi, 2–173/9.

symonyac *adj.* simoniacal 2–173/15, 2–174/21.

symonyakis, -yentes *n.pl.* simoniacs 44/xvi, 2–174/35.

sing(u)ler(e *adj.* solitary 30/lviii, 203/26, 27, 203/27, singular 2–46/15, 2–66/20.

syngulerlyche *adv.* solely, exclusively 2–60/24.

sysys *n.pl.* assizes 2–224/6.

syth(yn *adv.* ever since 183/19, 251/40, *first on & ~ anoþer* first one then another 353/75.

syth(in, sethe, syn *conj.* since 53/35, 69/68, 149/56, 172/17, 218/20, 230/34.

sithys *n.pl.* times 267/62, *be ~* by turns 309/8, *sexe ~ on* six times one 284/11, *seuene ~ bry3tere* seven times brighter 2–319/29.

sittyn *v. intr.* sit (as judge in legal cases) 236/18, 2–37/4; syt(ty3t *pr.3 sg.* 120/53, 2–270/19.

skye *n.* cloud 115/52, 2–281/64, sky 133/48; skyys *pl.* 2–319/36, heavens 112/47, 136/24, 199/17.

s(c)kyl *n.* reason 285/24, 2–38/36, argument, reasoning 87/31, 2–34/12, 14, common sense 90/1; s(c)kyllys *pl.* reasons 30/lviii, 114/9, arguments 3/43, 220/79, 320/22.

skyl *adj.* reasonable 2–240/57.

skyl(ful, -fol *adj.* reasonable 56/88, 244/39, 332/1.

s(c)kylfully, -folyche *adv.* reasonably 163/36, 292/53, cogently 2–129/92.

slakyd *pa.t.3 sg.* softened 279/21, 34.

s(ch)la(u)ndre, sclaundre, sklaunder *n.* open scandal 148, 29, 246/29, 341/17, 2–19/24, 2–78/46, *3euyn occasyoun of ~* give occasion of scandal 38/ix, 2–19/25, 27–28.

s(k)la(u)ndryn *v.* discredit, bring into disrepute 171/3, cause to sin (by scandalizing) 2–19/7; slaundryn *pr.3 pl.* 2–19/22; slaundryt *pp.* offended, angered 2–142/36; MED sv. sclaundren cites *D&P*..

slaundrous *adj.* scandalous 2–201/12.

slau(3)the, slaughthe, slouthe *n.* sloth 84/29, 188/10, 202/48, 285/31, 294/44.

slaw *adj.* slow 2–244/105.

sle(n *v.* slay 28/xxxv, 160/8, 199/34; slest *pr.2 sg.* 2–14/7, 2–30/17; sle(e)t(h *pr.3 sg.* 31/lx, 309/18, 2–2/44, 47, 2; slen, slee(n *pr.3 pl.* 13/20, 39/xvi, 2–21/15; sle *subj.3 sg.* should slay 160/20, 2–51/19; *~ imp.sg.* slay! 75/20; slow *pa.t.3 sg.* slew 92/34, 257/50, 350/81, *refl.* 2–21/8; slowyn *pa.t.3 pl.* 160/19, 198/19, 209/18; slayn *pp.* slain 31/lx, 309/19, 2–37/2.

slederyt *pr.3 sg. intr.* slides, slips 2–275/45; sledryn *pr.1 pl.* slip 2–277/18.

sledyr, slyder *adj.* slippery 22/19, 48/18, 2–275/38.

sleer *n.* slayer 2–53/3, 16, 18; sleerys *pl.* 2–42/57.

sley, sly(e *adj.* prudent 323/50, sly 7/17, 151/46, 189/30, 235/2, spiteful 2–223/56.

sleyghte, slet3e, sleyþe, sleeþe *n.* prudence (cf. V.L. *prudentiam*) 139/94, sleight, trick 235/7, 348/24, 2–248/7, guile 2–12/67, 69; sleyghtys, sley(3)þis *pl.* knowledge, skills 139/97, sleights 2–87/79, 2–206/1, 2–307/31.

sleyng(e *vbl.n.* slaughter 39/xv, murder 2–53/12.

sly3e *n.pl.* prudent, worldly wise 139/94 (cf. sleyghte).

slyleche, -lyche, sley- *adv.* slyly 151/47, 2–12/71, covertly 2–45/39.

slow3 *n.* mire 2–223/52.

smaragdus *n.* emerald 2–321/26.

smytyn, smyte *v. intr.* do battle, fight 2–44/24, 2–230/8; smyt(h *pr.3 sg. tr.* strikes 129/60, 148/33, *refl.* 309/21, 2–300/31; smytyn *pr.3 pl. intr.* strike blows 2–42/54, *tr.* afflicts 130/63; smetist *pa.t.2 sg.tr.* smote 228/25; smette, smot *pa.t.3 sg.* 307/26, 2–228/36, *intr.* struck (or, was caught) 307/23; smettyn *pa.t.3 pl. intr.* did battle 2–42/53; smet *pp. tr.* struck 93/36, 2–165/7, smitten 2–306/61.

smytynge *vbl.n.* battling, striking blows 2–13/5.

smoþere *n.* smoke 2–121/49.

smoþerynge *ppl.adj.* smouldering, smoking 2–258/20.

snybbe *subj.2 sg.* should rebuke 259/23.

so *conj.* (in correlative clauses) ~ *þat* provided that 2–35/48, so long as 2–56/56.

so *adv.* thus 130/83, ~ *to* in order to 2–190/28.

sodeyn *adj.* unanticipated 47/xvi, over-eager 2–238/49 (cf. V.L. *repentinus*).

sodekene *n.* subdeacon 2–107/19, 2–109/49; **sodekenys** *pl.* 2–169/46.

softhed *n.* softness 2–310/117.

softyth *pr.3 sg.* softens, buffers 2–310/117.

soget *n.* subject (of a king; not a bondman) 12/39, 108/49, 109/54, person owing obedience to a religious superior 345/72, 79, subordinate 108/49, 109/54, 323/43; **soget(t)is, sug(g)ettis, -es** *pl.* subjects (of a king) 37/xv, 113/71, 229/7, clerics owing obedience 14/28, 345/66, 2–20/40, dependants 278/9, subordinates 334/38 et seq..

soget *adj.* subordinate 334/49, 62, 339/39, 2–125/50, subject 2–56/67.

sok- see **souk-**

solacious *adj.* restorative 293/30, 294/31.

solas *n.* recreation 300/70, 2–281/11, consolation 2–66/37.

solemply *adv.* deliberately 2–55/34.

solempne *adj.* formal, rich 2–91/30, solemn, serious 34/x, 250/86, 2–314/52, imposing (architecturally) 30/li, 2–324/18.

solemp(ne)te, -nyte(e *n.* ceremonial, ritual 6/131, 31/lxiii, 189/3, 213/1, 2–219/39.

soler(e *n.* upper room or apartment 2–15/55, 2–85/23.

solyid *pp.* sullied 101/44.

somdel, sum- *adv.* in some degree, somewhat 133/35, 240/51, 312/54.

somdel *adj.* a certain amount of 2–142/27.

sompnearie *n.* divination by dreams 157/13 *var.* BYL.

somtyme *adv.* ~. . . ~ once . . . another time 2–285/29–30.

somwhat *n.* something 149/61.

sonde *n.* sending, dispensation 179/37, 2–306/64.

sondry, sun- *adj.* various 96/3, 4, 114/9, 152/7, 8, *on* ~ separately 2–197/46.

sonere *adv þe* ~ as soon as possible 158/23.

songewarie *n.* dream interpretation 157/13.

soothsyggers *n.pl.* soothsayers 28/xxx.

sor(y *adj.* unhappy, glum 296/13, 2–146/49, suffering 2–17/50, unfortunate 318/33, unpleasant 2–242/38.

sore *adv.* sorely 105/24, 123/36, 217/94.

sorgerye *n.* surgery 2–42/63.

sorynesse *n.* vexation, distress 298/57.

sorwe *n.* sorrow 51/14, 94/25, 147/19.

sot *n.* fool 2–85/13; **sottis** *pl.* 2–265/72.

soted *pp.* pursued (? perh. form of the verb *suit*; not in MED) 256/26 *var.* Y.

sotel *adj.* subtle, crafty 32/ix, 152/4, ethereal 152/8.

sotelte *n.* trickery 2–261/57; **sotiltees** *pl.* 71/37.

soth(e *n.* the truth 4/66, 7/17, 28/xxxii, *seyn þe* ~ tell (or speak) the truth 2–10/74, 2–221/47; **sothis, -es** *pl.* (tell) truths 149/5, 151/55, 229/38, 2–225/32.

so(o)th(e *adj.* true 63/5, 68/38, 94/27.

soþin *ppl.adj.* boiled, cooked 2–143/68.

sothly *adv.* truly 178/25, 2–227/18.

sothsawe *n.* truth 155/52; **-sawys** *pl.* truth telling 155/57 et seq..

sothsawere *n.* prophet 178/10; **sothsaweres** *pl.* soothsayers 150/32.

sothsawyn *v. intr.* tell the truth 161/53/54.

sotilhed *n.* transparency 286/31.

soudyouris, sowdyoures *n.pl.* soldiers 40/xxiv, 2–56/66.

souereyn(e *n.* master 12/39, 35/xvii, superior 108/50, 109/54, 335/65, 338/2 et seq.; **souereyn(y)s** *pl.* 11/33, 12/65, 333/11, masters 333/22.

soukynge, sokande *ppl.adj.* suckling 196/46, 2–257/44.

Soulynmesse (*day*) *n.* All Souls' Day, November 2, 2–190/36–37.

soundyn *v.*(1) *intr.* reflect (poorly upon) 259/34; **so(u)ndith** *pr.3 sg. tr.* bespeaks 259/32, 2–141/2, 3, *intr.* resounds 2–255/58; **soundyn** *pr.3 pl. tr.* bespeak 2–220/14 (cf. MED *sounen* 6.)

soundyn, sowen *v.* (2) ~ *wol/ful harde to myn vnderstondyng* penetrate my mind with great difficulty 55/36, 76/34 (cf. MED *sounden* *v.* (1).

soundynge *vbl.n.* pronouncing 201/27.

so(u)wyn, sewe *v.* sew 63/22, 74/5; **souwyn** *pr.3 pl.* 2–4/40.

sowles *n.pl.* souls 29/xli, 171/52.

sparyn *v. intr.* show mercy 122/22, refrain

129/40, hold back 315/16, hoard 317/
20, *tr.* be considerate of, show mercy to
13/18, 99/74, 332/19, 2–230/21; **spar**
imp.sg. show mercy! 2–230/21; **sparyng**
pr.p. saving 276/9, 2–149/51.

sparyng *vbl.n.* saving 276/9, 2–149/51.

sparunlyche *adv.* sparingly 2–9/50.

spece, spyce *n.* kind 2–122/39, 2–182/41;
specys, spycys, -es *pl.* 15/1, 17/5, 2–
58/6, 2–195/7.

special *n. in* ~ in particular 91/3, 167/2,
245/48.

speckyd *ppl.adj.* patched, mended 260/21.

sped(e *n.* success, luck 20/89, 45/xxviii,
112/51, 2–208/60.

spedful *adj.* profitable, expedient 124/65,
173/28, 195/15.

spedyn, sped(e *v. intr.* fare 186/3, 2–11/
36, 37, prosper 6/119, 140/15, 18, suc-
ceed 196/42, *refl.* conduct 287/10, *tr.*
advance (cause) 2–237/34; **spedy3t** *pr.3
sg.* (impersonal construction) *the* ~ is
beneficial to you 60/53; **spedyn** *pr.3
pl. intr.* fare 140/15, 2–208/61, 63.

speer *n.* wooden screen for blocking
draughts 311/44.

spekyn *v.* speak 200/1, 4, ~ *hym good*
speak well of him 302/49; **speki(3)t(h**
pr.3 sg. speaks 201/15, 19, ~ *a3en*
answers 51/18, ~ *hym euyl* speaks evil
of him 2–8/29; **spec** *imp.sg.* speak! 2–
47/39; **speke** *subj.3 sg.* should speak
200/25, 201/18, 22; **spak, spac** *pa.t.3
sg.* spoke 97/33, 201/23, 24, 204/37,
295/81; **spokyn** *pa.t.3 pl.* 200/5–6.

sper *n.* ~ *of Pittagoras* sphere of Pythagoras (a globe modelling the cosmos) 157/
12.

spere, spyr *n.* spear 2–228/52, 2–301/57;
sperys *pl.* 163/46.

sperplyyd *ppl.adj.* dispersed, scattered 2–
11/47 (cf. **disparplyyd**).

spices see **spec-**

spilt *pp.* destroyed, slain 2–102/81.

spyrytualytee, -uelte *n. matere of* ~ spiritual matters 44/xvii, the clergy, the
Church in general 2–210/103.

spyrytuell *adj.* holy 45/xxiii

spytful *adj.* humiliating 215/54.

spytfully *adv.* pitilessly 277/21, 23.

spyth *n.* insult 283/11, ~ *to* insult to 262/
83 (cf. **dispyght**).

spytilhous *n.* an asylum for lepers 2–
183/2.

spittously *adv.* contemptuously 2–88/114.

spolyyn *v.* rob, despoil 2–144/103, 105; ~
pr.3 pl. 2–135/5; **spolyyd** *pp.* 2–144/
104, 112.

spousebreche *n.* adultery 2–64/57, 2–73/
59, 2–299/2–3, 4.

spret, sprad *ppl.adj.* spread 2–20/32, 2–
81/19, 20.

spryng *n.* shoot 325/56.

spryngyn, spryngge *v. intr.* spring up
114/26, 145/38, 146/61, spread 2–99/
13; **spryngith, spryngge3t** *pr.3 sg.*
dawns 114/27, spreads 260/25, *tr.* sprin-
kles 309/22; **spryngge yn** *pr.3 pl. intr.*
grow, flourish 145/38; **sprynge** *subj.3
sg.* should spread 2–271/47; **spro(u)n-
gyn** *pp.* sprung up 205/14, 210/25.

sprynggyng *vbl.n.* arising 145/37.

sp(y)ryt(h, spyry3t, spirt *n.* spirit 56/77,
95/3, 2–320/2, *þe proude* ~ the devil
152/27, ~ *lyer* a lying spirit, a devil
155/70, 2–12/57, spiritual being 2–
118/3; **sp(i)rytis, -tes** *pl.* spirits 95/2,
99/71, 156/21, ghosts 4/85, 29/xli,
171/1.

sqwyer, sqweer *n.* squire 181/2, 2–276/
15.

staant see **stond-**

stablyd *pp.* established, rooted 205/15,
210/26, 248/37.

stacioun *n.* booth (as place to sell goods)
2–204/18.

staf *n.* stave, club (used as weapon or in
games) 2–38/26, 2–40/4, staff 149/5, 2–
230/4, 8, 9; **stauys** *pl.* staves 2–46/11.

stary3t *pr.3 sg. intr.* gazes steadily 86/14.

sta(a)t *n.* condition, state of being 4/84,
170/43, rank, social status 58/43, 45,
94/33, 149/47, stage 206/27, 28, *in
perfyth* ~ following a religious rule of
life 2–214/53, 2–215/54; **statys** *n.pl.*
statuses 130/3, estates (of the church,
clerics, knights, commons) 293/19.

stede *n.* ~ *& tyme* (sufficient) place and
time in order to 2–25/37, *for* ~ *& tyme*
on that one occasion 2–291/40.

stey(3)yn *v. intr.* rise 116/76, 136/22,
142/13; **steyit(h** *pr.3 sg.* 111/33, 112/
58; **stey** *pa.t.3 sg.* 116/65, 271/35, 282/
37.

stey(ʒ)ynge *vbl.n.* rising, ascension 199/ 12, 2–191/61.

stelyn, stele *v. intr.* steal 17/13, 79/27, 2– 34/11; **stelyt(h** *pr.3 sg.* 2–145/10, 2– 173/13; **stelen** *pr.3 pl.* 43/vii; **stele** *subj.3 sg.* should steal 2–144/90; **stal** *pa.t.3 sg.* 2–146/51, 2–208/58, 2–259/ 16; **stole** *pa.t.subj.3 sg.* should (not) have stolen 2–146/51; **stoln** *pp.* 2–145/25.

stemys *n.pl.* shafts 269/16.

steraclis *n.pl.* miracle plays 293/12, 13, 18 (see Notes).

steryn *v.(1) refl.* move 2–254/39; **steryʒt, -yth** *pr.3 sg. intr.* 63/11, 2–35/43; **sterynge** *pr.p.* alive, moving (cf. V.L. *movebuntur*) 327/16; (cf. MED steren *v.(1)*; **steren** and **stiren** are not clearly separable verbs, cf. **steryn** *v.(2)* below).

steryn, styrn, styre *v.(2)* urge, prompt 8/ 26, 32/xiii, 82/38, 40, 90/24, 2–47/24; **steryʒt, steryth** *pr.3 sg.* 112/44; **steryn** *pr.3 pl.* inspire 5/92; **steryth** *subj.3 sg.* should urge 178/12; **steryth** *imp.pl.* incite! 323/40; **styrde** *pa.t.3 sg.* incited 159/46; **ster(y)d, stired** *pp.* attracted 41/xii, stirred, moved (*fig.*) 70/21, 82/ 41, 169/7, 203/30, 2–11/31, (cf. *MED* stiren *v.* and **steryn** *v.* (1) above).

steryng(ge *vbl.n.*(1) manoeuvring, steering 152/5, movement, course 120/30, 37, 122/18, 19 (cf. **pasyng**).

steryng(ge *vbl.n.*(2) stirring 111/31, 112/ 42, inciting 174/4, 2–189/12; **styrynges** *pl.* (sexual) impulses 29/xlv, 2–305/30.

sterre *n.* star 27/xxiii; **sterrys** *pl.* 88/11, 117/2, 213/45.

stif *adj.* firm 2-100/26.

stilhed(e *n.* silence 20/3, 2–2/43, 2–211/ 13.

stille *adj.* silent 2–211/12, 2–232/25.

styllyn *pr.2 pl.* subdue, check 334/44.

stynckande *ppl.adj.* stinking 2–299/18.

styngyth *pr.3 sg.* bites 2–300/26; **stang** *pa.t.3 sg.* 2–300/43; **stonge, stoungyn** *pp.* pierced 240/40, 2–301/56.

stodyyn, studyyn *v.* prepare 276/11, study, search 284/17; **stodie** *pr.2 sg.* 300/44; **stodyyn** *pr.2 pl.* endeavour 301/7; **studyyn** *pr.3 pl.* prepare 276/ 12; **studye** *imp.sg.* try! 300/45, *refl.* make an effort 2–284/72.

stoffyn *v.* stuff 2–275/58.

stok, stoc *n.* block of wood 85/52, 107/13,

2–119/8; **stockys** *pl.* 90/19, 105/32, 110/3, stumps 256/10.

stole *n.* stole (liturgical) 2–228/38, 40, see Note.

stol(e)n, -yn *ppl.adj.* stolen 43/viii, ix, 150/33, 2–145/25, 27.

ston *adj.* made of stone 86/26.

stondyn *v. intr.* stand fast 105/11, stand 138/69, hold good 2–153/12, stand up in court 2–208/38, ~ *to* obey 343/16, 345/74, 346/30, assume 2–200/2, rely on the evidence of 2–233/58; **sta(a)nt, stondeth, -iþ** *pr.3 sg.* depends (on) 68/ 45, 47, 127/64, 143/40, 211/7, 8, stands 74/33, is constituted (by) 107/24, 2– 297/76, is included (among) 346/29, 31, remains 2–139/52; **stondyn** *pr.3 pl.* stand 1/6a, 49/47, depend on 139/2, abide (by) 208/9; **stonde** *subj.3 sg.* should rest (on) 249/82, is consistent with 346/33; ~ *imp.sg.* stand (by) 138/ 63 (V.L. *sta*); **sto(o)d** *pa.t.3 sg.* abided (by) 154/40, 161/40; **stod** *pp.* ~ *fro far* made to stand at a distance 257/35–36 (cf. V.L. *longe stetit*).

stondyng *ppl.adj.* so ~ with such an attitude (or posture) 25/iii.

storblyth *pr.3 sg.* disturbs 2–7/82, 2–263/ 30.

storblour *n.* disturber 2–263/27.

stounde *n.* hour (in indefinite sense) 2– 245/8, 2–270/7; **stoundys** *pl.* appointed hours 140/30.

stout *adj.* arrogantly unruly 308/39 (cf. V.L. *protervus*).

straunge *adj.* alien 81/2.

streyt(e *adj.* strict 21/39, 47/xvii, 274/6, narrow 2–34/20, 2–263/10, 15, tight 2– 227/13, confined 2–272/66, 68, stingy 2–322/19.

streyte *adv.* tightly 83/10, 2–322/22, strictly 2–20/54.

streythed *n.* narrowness 55/39, 76/38, meanness, stinginess 59/14, 79/34–35.

st(h)reytlyche *adv.* strictly, severely 342/ 67*, 2–46/2, 2–106/56.

stubby *adj.* stubbly 2–311/160.

stud- see **stod-**

studious *adj.* continual, incessant 2–111/ 60 (cf. V.L. *studiosa*), disposed to learn 2–244/107.

subieccion *n.* subordination 229/7.

subuersyoun *n.* destruction 42/xvi.

sueche see **swyche**

suffrable *adj.* endurable 110/25–6, 2–138/13.

suffragis *n.pl.* intercessory prayers 191/35, 214/17, 216/74, the intercessions 2–180/73.

suffra(u)nce *n.* permission 153/19, 317/4, 348/17, indulgence 128/11.

suffryn *v.* allow 218/20, 2–205/61, tolerate 283/13, 2–22/45; **suff(y)r(r)yth, -it, -yȝt, -eþ** *pr.3 sg.* allows 15/59, 128/31, 154/25, 161/52, 186/20; **suff(y)r(r)yn** *pr.3 pl.* 45/xxvii, experience 158/35, endure 335/10; **suffre** *subj.3 sg.* should allow 151/57, 2–45/46; **suffre** *imp.pl.* allow 164/49; **suffyr(ry)d** *pa.t.3 sg.* 45/xxiv, 161/53; **suffrid** *pp.* 128/13, 135/31, 161/46.

suhyn, suwe *v.* follow 114/14, 2–68/25; **suen** *pr.3 pl.* 73/29; **suhyngge** *pr.p.* 116/67.

suynge, sewyng *ppl.adj.* ensuing 1/1a, 29/xlvii.

suyngli *adv.* consequently 72/14.

sum, som *adj.* some 25/iii, 106/48, 235/12, (in correlative clauses) one . . . another 130–131/3–5.

summe, somme *pron.* some 21/41, 131/19, 20, 21, 2–213/18.

sumptous *adj.* sumptuous 217/99.

sumqhat, somwhat *n.* something 101/60, 149/61.

sumqhat *adv.* (in correlative construction) in part . . . in part 91/3, 4.

sumtyme *adv.* once 110/23.

superalterie *n.* portable altar 111/12.

sustre, -ter *n.* sister 2–64/72, 2–65/90; **sustrys** *pl.* 332/10.

swalwe *n.* swallow 144/22.

swatte *pa.t.3 sg.* sweated 270/50.

swerd *n.* sword 2–33/56, 57, 61, use of the sword 14/46, (God's) wrath 148/37, sword (*fig.*) 335/74, 2–2/26.

swete, swote *adj.* sweet 111/33, 349/63, 2–97/54–55.

swetyn *v.* sweat, 2–290/20 (from Lat. 'sudet').

swetelyche *adv.* sweetly 302/23.

swych(e, sueche, sweche *adj.* such 7/21, 24/26, 52/33, 95/6, 7, 149/4, 358/50, 2–220/12.

swyche, sueche, sweche *pron.* such (persons) 136/17, 150/34, 156/28, such (matters) 339/38, 40.

swync, swynk *n.* toil 2–16/3, 2–124/32.

swolwyn *v.* swallow 2–244/88.

T

take *ppl.adj.* undertaken 58/30.

takere *n.* recipient 65/53.

takyl *n.* apparatus 2–246/33.

takyn, take *v.* take (in vain, heed) 31/i, 134/59, take (bribe) 21/27, receive 65/46, 48, 72/3, 2–205/47, 2–275/43, steal 83/14, take on, assume (flesh, name) 90/9, take (away) 146/76, 2–147/7, 221/12, taken (as) 151/38, seize 160/17, 2–53/27, resort 185/8, take (as a pattern) 208/79, give (something to) 236/22, 312/60, 2–200/62, bring 236/29, follow (example) 337/35, give away 2–30/13, 2–163/121, recoup (expenses) 2–155/70, take (back) 2–197/54.

~ *inf.* 63/3, 72/3, 221/3; **take** *pr.1 sg.* 224/27, 2–164/146; **takist** *pr.2 sg.* 2–30/13; **takyȝt, takiþ** *pr.3 sg.* 64/17, 73/17, 221/12; **takyn, taken** *pr.1, 2 pl.* 62/6, 64/8, 73/9; ~ *pr.3 pl.* 64/7, 72/8(2); **tak(e** *subj.3 sg.* 2–43/82, 2–53/27, 2–147/7; **takyn** *subj.3 pl.* 2–163/103, *refl.* 161/44; **tak, tac** *imp.sg.* 337/35, 2–104/2, 2–207/6, 7; **takit(h** *imp.pl.* 2–244/98, 113; **to(o)c, to(o)k** *pa.t.3 sg.* 21/27, 90/9, 311/49; **tokyn** *pa.t.3 pl.* 83/14, 134/59; ~ *pa.t.subj.3 pl.* 160/17; **take, -kyn** *pp.* 151/38, 236/29, 2–148/31.

takyng(e *vbl. n.* receiving 65/52.

takinge *ppl.adj.* receiving 64/16, 73/16.

tale *n.* ȝeuyn no ~ *of/to* take no account of 148/37, 172/10, think little of 230/35, 2–25/30.

taliagis *n.pl.* taxes, duties 185/14.

talyys *n.pl.* tallies, accounts 2–249/23.

taskyd *pp.* taxed 2–167/64, 2–172/26, 2–173/50.

taskynge *vbl.n.* taxation 2–185/60.

t(a)ast *n.* sense of taste 50/84 (MS L), 2–103/121.

tauernerys *n.pl.* tavern keepers 151/41, 289/11.

tawȝt *pa.t.3 sg.* taught 47/iv.

taxkys, taskys *n.pl.* taxes 185/13, 198/21.

techyd *ppl.adj.* euyl ~ badly trained 2–304/9, wel ~ well trained 2–304/11.

techis *n.pl.* traits, qualities 11/24, 324/9, 27, 2–305/16.

te(y)nt *ppl.adj.* attainted, convicted (as traitor, perjuror) 255/93, 256/6, 2–222/10 (cf. **ateyntyn**).

tek *n.* tap, light blow 2–316/47.

tel *imp.sg.* tell 167/2; **telde** *pa.t.3 sg.* 305/42; **teldyn** *pa.t.3 pl.* 2–11/37, 2–133/4; **teld(e, told** *pp.* 88/27, 155/74, 167/2, counted 2–195/6.

temperyn *v.* moderate 2–142/35, 37; **temperyth** *pr.3 sg.* regulates 167/10 (cf. V.L. *temperantur*).

temporelte *n.* laymen (all persons not members of the clergy) 2–210/103, 109.

tene *n. treye & ~* vexation and trial 323/62, 324/27 (cf. V.L. *ira*; cf. *var.* BYL *wraþþe*).

> **tene** *imp.sg.* vex, trouble 2–136/34.

> **tent** see **teynt**

> **tent** *n. ȝeuyn ~ to* give free rein to 2–62/16.

tente *ord.num.* tenth 19/54, 166/25, 2–30/18.

tentesum *n.* a party of about ten persons 321/42–43.

tepet, typ(p)et(e *n.* part of hood or sleeve, scarf 7/21, 32/xii, 241/4.

terys *n.pl.* tears 215/42, 348/27, 2–102/76.

termynyn *v.* decide, determine 358/33; **termyn(y)d** *pp.* determined, settled 252/6, 8.

termynour *n.* determiner, source of definitive legal judgement 2–172/30 (cf. **expositour**).

testament *n.* testimony 137/32.

therkyn *v.* darken 115/30 (cf. **þerk-**).

thyrl- see **þirl-**

thral *adj.* enthralled 118/18 (cf. **þral**).

thretynggis *vbl.n.pl.* threatenings 333/23.

thuryficacioun *n.* incense offering (burning of incense in church ritual) 110/1, 111/30.

thuryfyingge *vbl.n.* incense offering 111/25.

tilþe *n.* cultivation 131/19, 2–32/41, 2–152/57.

tylþin, tyl(yy)n, *v.* till, cultivate 63/20, 2–315/23, till (*fig.*) 331/45; **tylyyst** *pr.2 sg.* produce from the soil 2–315/24.

tymere, tymbre *n.* tambourine 224/14, 297/28; **tymbrys** *pl.* 297/29.

tyr *n.* dress, attire 2–90/2, 2–104/5 (cf. **atyr**).

tyrantrye *n.* oppression 205/4, *don non ~* not be overbearing 2–19/17.

tysyng *vbl.n.* enticing 153/2.

titele *n.* title (certificate of presentment to a benefice required by bishop from a candidate for ordination) 2–181/13, 15; see Notes 2–181/13–22; MED sv. 'title' *n.* 7.

tyþe *n.* tithe 2–167/75, 2–171/7, 11; **tyþis** *pl.* 18/46, 110/13, 2–166/19.

tyþin *v. intr* pay tithes (on) 18/45, *tr.* impose tithe on 2–167/67; **tyþid** *pa.t.3 sg.* tithed (tithes were paid) 2–172/18 tithed (paid tithes on) 2–172/20; ~, -IT; *pp.* 2–168/76, 2–171/5.

tyþing *vbl.n.* paying of (a) tithe 2–172/18, 21.

tyxt *n.* text 269/37.

to *adv.* too, excessively 52/46, 226/6, 8, 2–168/76.

to *prep.* (used in modern senses for the most part but occasionally meaning 'for', 'with', 'in' or 'as') *he bout it ~* he bought it for 18/29, *metten ~ hemsilff* met with one another 70/4, *~ raunsom of* for ransom of 84/21, *~ Godys ymage* in God's image 106/45, *~ hys concubine* as concubine 2–85/10, *betere ~ hem* better for them 2–106/76.

to(n *adj.* one (of two) 175/25, 199/10, *wyt þe ~ kne* with the one knee 106/40, 110/20, *þe ~ syde* the one side 146/75.

to(o, two *card.num.* two 66/36, 203/19, 284/12.

tobrestyn *pr.3 pl. intr.* split, shatter 357/18.

tok(e)ne *n.* symbol (object or act bearing religious significance) 82/42, 89/30, 98/44, emblem 88/24, sign 101/51, 176/43, 212/21, portent 142/15, seal (cf. V.L. *signaculum*) 2–303/93; **tokenys** *pl.* portents 21/38, signs 61/12, 119/8, 9, 142/16, symbolic acts 104/5, symptoms 176/45,

tokenyd *pp.* symbolised 303/64.

tokenyng(g)(e *vbl.n.* symbolism 110/9, 111/31, symbolic warning 2–246/38.

tollyn *v.* entice 101/56.

tollyng *vbl.n.* enticing (to) 101/50.

to(u)nge, townge, tunge *n.* tongue, mode of speech 38/iv, act of speaking 204/43,

257/53, 2–1/16, language 109/62, 253/
49, 346/5; **tungis** *pl.* acts of speaking 2–
2/27, (*fig.*) strips of cloth (part of vestment) 2–228/49.
tonne *n.* cask, barrel 319/56.
torent *pp.* torn to pieces 241/64, 260/34
(cf. **rent-**).
toþer(e, tothyr *adj.* other 49/71, 66/41,
93/36, 118/42.
tothir, -þer *pron.* other 146/75, 191/44.
totorn *pp.* badly torn 84/32, 260/21, 34.
towalyis *n.pl.* tools 95/16.
toward *adj.* advancing, going forward
314/44, 2–270/17.
tracede *pa.t.1 sg.* searched for 333/9.
trayhyd *pa.t.3 sg.* betrayed 2–12/82.
translatid *pp.* transferred 257/44, 48,
258/60, 281/5.
trauayl(e, traueil *n.* work, labor 10/36,
53/21, 80/59, affliction, trouble 53/21,
267/60, 2–207/19, endeavour 154/39;
trauaylys *pl.* household tasks 2–9/63.
trauaylyn, traueyle *v. intr.* work, labor
10/29, 34/xvi, 119/16, *tr.* torment,
harass 2–206/4; **trauaylyst** *pr.2 sg.
intr.* try 2–260/37; **trauaylyth** *pr.3 sg.*
endeavors 180/29; **trauaylyn, traueilen** *pr.3 pl.* work 10/26, 73/31, 292/1,
3; **traualyd** *pa.t.3 sg.* 263/19, 2–49/14;
trauaylid *pp.* 139/89, 2–9/64, *tr.* tor-
mented (by) 157/32.
traualyouris *n.pl.* workers, labourers 194/
32.
tre(e *n.* the cross 52/36, tree 210/16; **treis**
pl. 256/9, 296/4.
tree *adj.* wooden 86/26.
treye *n.* vexation 323/62, 324/27 (cf.
tene).
tremelyd *pa.t.3 sg. intr.* trembled 2–106/
50.
tremelynge *vbl.n.* trembling, fear 333/13.
trendelys *n.pl.* orbs 95/24.
trentel, -tal *n.* requiem mass 2–184/23,
money for saying requiem masses 2–
187/38, *þe gyldene* ~ the Golden Trental, a set of thirty requiem masses 19/69,
45/xxii, 2–184/23, 2–186/1–2, 2–190/
30 (see *Notes*).
treschwald *n.* threshold 327/17.
treso(u)r *n.* treasure 322/12, 2–260/30, 2–
317/17.
tresoryn *v.* treasure, cherish 314/37, 38
(cf. V.L. *thesaurizare*); **tresoryst** *pr.2 sg.*

refl. store up 2–284/72; **tresoryd** *pp.
refl.* stored up 2–251/14.
trespas *n.* misdeed, sin 85/45, 116/61,
123/56.
trespasist *pr.2 sg. intr.* sin 2–29/3; **tres-
pasyn** *pr.3 pl.* 136/17; **trespase** *subj.2
sg.* should sin 2–29/2; ~, **trespace** *subj.3
sg.* 118/22, 38, 2–76/36; **trespasyd** *pp.*
sinned 274/36.
trespasouris *n.pl.* sinners 2–33/63, 2–37/
1, 3.
tretable *adj.* tractable 2–305/19.
trete *adv.* slowly 30/lvi (shortened form of
atret; *MED* sv. 'tret(e').
tretyys *n.* treatise 1/1a.
tretynge *vbl.n.* appropriating 2–130/17.
tretith *pr.3 sg.* misappropriates 2–173/2;
tretyn *pr.3 pl.* 2–161/42; *intr.* write
(about) 2–276/1; **trete** *subj.3 sg.* should
associate 176/50; **tretyd** *pp.* dealt (with),
discussed 1/4a, 5a.
tretour *n.* traitor 131/13, 160/23, 193/2.
tretouslyche *adv.* traitorously 2–64/77–
78, 2–85/34.
tret(o)urye, tret(h)(e)rye *n.* treason 52/3,
118/23, 148/25, 253/37, treachery 2–
297/59.
trewe *adj.* faithful 53/20, honest 238/18,
253/45, ~ *folc* honest men 2–233/39.
tryyn *v.* try (determine by legal trial) 252/
19, try (purify by fire) 2–265/70; **tryid**
pp. tested 237/42.
trewthe, *n.* truth, in legal context 229/43;
God 154/36; *pl.* true facts 154/34.
trone *n.* throne 231/52; **tronys** *pl.* 54/7.
trost, trist *n.* trust 36/v, 174/1, 299/19,
22.
trostyn, trust- *v. intr.* trust 5/88, 22/22,
140/16; **trostit(h** *pr.3 sg.* 299/19, 20;
trostith *imp.pl.* 351/110.
trowe *pr.1 sg.* believe, suppose 147/18,
189/25, 211/1; **trowyt** *pr.3 sg.* opines
218/30.
truantys *n.pl.* truants (those who absent
themselves from church) 199/5.
truauntyn *v. intr.* play truant (stay away
from church) 202/51–52.
trumpe *n.* trumpet 295/83, 2–241/4.
trupth *interject.* exclamation expressing
contempt (cf. V.L. *vah*) 115/36.
turnys *n.pl.* stratagems 2–275/48.
turtyl *n.* turtle dove 144/21.
twey(ne *adj.* two 26/vii, 315/6, 2–193/26.

tweyys, twyys *adv.* twice 180/32, 219/37, 2–197/48.

twentydsum *n.* party of about twenty persons 321/43 (cf. tente-).

twynk, twync *n.* ~ *of an eye* twinkling of an eye 95/22, 286/31, 2–277/28.

þ

þan(ne *adv.* then, at that time 66/23, 89/51, consequently 76/32, 228/16, *as for* ~ at that time 190/24.

þan(ne *conj.* than 1/5b, 3/32, 25/iii, 41/x.

þat *demonstr. pron.* that 117/1, that which 147/7, that respect 81/11, such that 2–177/43; þo(o *pl.* those 39/11, 69/75, 144/9, 302/35.

þat *rel.pron.* who 14/33, 34, 52/25, which 83/7, that 89/36; þat *pl.* who 39/xi, 61/27, 82/35, 104/67; (he þat see he).

þat *conj.* that 1/6b, 147/14, 150/16, what 52/47, *for* ~ because 97/20.

þat *demonstr. adj.* that 134/52, 97/18, 142/33; þo(o)(e *pl.* those 57/8, 84/32, 193/16.

þe *pron.* see þu

þe *def.art.* the 1/3, 51/15, 18, 52/22.

þedam *n.* thriving, prosperity 234/5, 6.

þedyr *adv.* thither 189/36, 248/48, 2–68/27, 30, ~. . . ~ whither . . . thither 2–68/27.

þef *n.* thief 151/38, 159/1, 193/9; theuys *possess.pl.* 151/38; ~ *pl.* 17/4, 218/15, 2–44/19.

þefte *n.* theft 17/1, 159/1.

þey see he

þey(3 *conj.* see þou(3.

þen(y)s *adv.* thence 142/31, 2–140/69.

þer(e *conj.* where 140/25, 212/22, 234/16, when 153/16 (cf. w(h)er).

þera3en(y)s *adv.* contrariwise 115/39, thereagainst 160/14.

þerfore *prep.* for it 2–150/79.

þerk(e, derk, derc *adj.* dark 115/30, 2–208/39, 40, 2–323/4.

þerk(nesse, þerc-, derk- *n.* darkness 24/26–27 var. H, 59/17, 307/8–9, 2–82/75 (cf. therk-).

þertoward *adv.* pointing towards it 92/27–8.

þeself see self

þewys *n.pl.* habits, customs 189/45, 2–97/61, 2–132/25, personal qualities 271/16.

þin(ne *adj.* thy 52/28, 65/1, 76/51, 193/75, 222/39 (cf. þU).

þirlith, thyrly3t *pr.3 sg.* pierces 6/120, 30/lvi, 112/47, 199/1, 16, 17.

þis *demonstr.adj.* this 1/1a, 86/23, 109/1, 150/23, þese, þise *pl.* these 51/2, 98/54, 150/24.

þis *demonstr.pron.sg.* this 81/7, 136/11, that 81/11; þese *pl.* these 52/31, 142/16 (cf. he).

þolyde *pa.t.1 sg.* endured 228/27; þolde *pa.t.3 sg.* 334/57, 2–243/53.

þondyr *n.* thunder 183/32, 295/82, 2–103/106.

þondryn *v. intr.* thunder 183/30; þondrith *pr.3 sg.* 183/28.

þondryng *vbl.n.* thundering 5/99, 183/27.

þornys *n.pl.* thorns 159/42, 2–124/29.

þorw, þorou3 *prep.* through 77/30, 295/80*, by 92/20, 2–100/36, on account of 100/18, 353/66.

þou(3, þow, þey(3, though *conj.* yet 6/141, 57/3, 86/11, 243/12, though 15/21, 32/ix, 124/85, 152/10, 243/11, 249/78, ~. . . 3it though . . . yet 8/34, 12/43–44.

þou3t, þout(h *n.* thought (of something) 157/36, thought (in general) 286/30, mind 273/5, 6, 300/52, sorrowful thought, worry 2–14/11; þOU3TIS *pl.* thoughts 273/12, 2–91/17.

þousant, -and *card.num.* thousand 197/58, 284/14, 16; þousontis *pl.* 2–52/44.

þral *n.* slave 277/30, 305/48, 2–66/32; þrallys *pl.* 156/9, 162/61 (cf. thral).

þraldam *n.* slavery 305/50, 2–129/78, 2–144/109.

þre(e *card.num.* three 10/47, 25/ii, 221/5.

þredde, thrydde *ord.num.* third 13/6, 32/vi, 81/17.

þrest, thryst *n.* thirst 53/21, 62/59, 301/10.

thresty *adj.* thirsty 69/64.

threttene *card.num.* thirteen 318/31.

þrettenete *ord.num.* thirteenth 2–247/38.

þretty *card.num.* thirty 174/55, 193/15, 16, 217/96.

þrettyd *ord.num.* thirtieth 2–280/52.

þryys *adv.* thrice 89/44, 2–16/25.

þryuyn *v. intr.* thrive 306/5.

þ(o)u *pron.2 sg.* thou 52/37, 71/1, 2–314/7; þe(e *oblique cases* thee 52/41, 71/6, 79/10, to thee 71/3, *more þan* ~ *nedy3t*

GLOSSARY 387

more than needful for thee 60/53, *wo* ~
be woe be to thee 2–147/56; **þi(n)self**
refl. thyself 55/23, 67/48 (cf. **þin**).

U/V

vanchid *pa.t.3 sg. intr.* vanished 265/7(2),
2–189/19; ~ *pa.t.3 pl.* 265/7(1).
varie *subj.3 sg. intr.* should vary or change
353/74.
vaumbras, vaun- *n.pl.* armour for fore-
arm 24/15 *var.*H, 2–310/108.
vauntagys *n.pl.* perquisites 2–187/39.
veil(le *n.* veil 26/iv, 89/43, 269/21 et seq..
veyn(e *adj.* worldly, frivolous 46/vii, 128/
31, 2–214/51, empty 2–2/5, *in* ~ use-
lessly 139/90.
veynly, -lyche *adv.* frivolously 201/18, 2–
161/54.
venchable *adj.* vengeful 2–242/34.
**ven(ȝ)cha(u)nce, venȝance, vengeauns,
veniaunce** *n.* punishment (in sense of
retributory misfortune) 16/51, 148/33,
198/26, 208/17, vengeance (in sense of
retaliatory action) 42/xvi, 2–13/20;
venchancys *pl.* misfortunes 16/50.
venchyn *v.* inflict, wreak 335/75, *refl.*
avenge 2–143/77, 82; **venchyd** *pp.* 2–
55/24.
venerye *n.* hunting, the chase 2–166/36.
venymyn *v. refl.* poison 129/58.
ver(e)y *adj.* true, veritable 88/7, 165/89,
2–203/77.
verylyche *adv.* truly, accurately 2–312/
184.
vers *n.* tale, account 2–85/20; ~ *pl.* lines of
poetry 2–97/49.
vertu(e *n.* strength 314/51, power 4/69,
90/22, 107/11, 17, value 107/15, goodness 107/10, 21, 22, 152/22, 2–9/62, 2–
290/6; **vertuys** *pl.* (healing) powers
107/20.
vhs *n.* possession 317/2, usage, custom
287/7, use 2–130/20, 2–140/74, 2–
146/53, purpose 2–165/163, 165, *in* ~
customary 2–69/58.
vygyles, -gilyys *n.pl.* eve of a holy day 34/
xvi, 2–91/32.
vy(c)kir *n.* vicar (priest of parish in which
the tithes are appropriated to a monastery) 330/3, 352/18, 2–187/37; **vycar-
yes, vykerys** *pl.* 44/xii, 2–163/116.
vyleyn *adj.* base, servile 339/46, 2–66/38,
2–129/82.

vyleny(e, vylonye, velony, vylanye *n.*
shame, disgrace 11/22, 152/30, 242/
21, 2–9/68, harm 171/9, slander 2–87/
92; **velanyys** *pl.* shameful actions 176/
54, 244/23.
vyndache, -deche *n.* harvest 2–135/3, 2–
166/35.
vynourrys *n.pl.* vine growers 131/21.
vysyd *pp.* warned 2–152/47 (cf. **auys-**).
visitacioun *n.* visitation (periodic inspection of parish, diocese or religious institution by bishop, archbishop or other
clerical authorities) 13/19; **visitacyones**
pl. 39/ix.
vitailleres, -ieris *n.pl.* food sellers 34/xvi,
289/11, 291/24.
vyta(i)li(i)s *n.pl.* foods 58/47, 74/22, 2–
240/84, foodstuffs 121/68, 260/24, 289/
13.
vmbre *n.* shadow 133/37.
vnable *adj.* physically unfit 2–64/60, pro-
fessionally unqualified 352/45, 353/79,
2–39/55, morally unfit 235/44.
vn(h)ablyd *pp.* disqualified (for) 167/23–
24, 2–178/6.
vnasayd *ppl.adj.* untested 344/54.
vnauyselyche *adv.* injudiciously 250/5.
vnbydyn *v. intr.* delay 290/27; **onbydyn**
pr.3 pl. 276/9.
unboundyn, -bunden *ppl.adj.* released
(from) 33/xv, unconstrained 65/49 (cf.
boundyn, byndyn).
vnbuxum *adj.* disobedient 35/ii, 307/36,
322/25.
vnbuxumnesse, -somnesse *n.* disobedience 12/64, 38/xxvi, 166/25.
vnconnyng *ppl.adj.* ignorant 2–47/46.
vnconnyng(e, -konnyng *vbl.n.* ignorance
202/53, 334/44, 2–42/60, 2–127/14.
vndirnemyn *v.* rebuke 14/27, 332/8;
vndirnemyth *pr.3 sg.* 2–14/15, 2–133/
2, 2–210/102; **vndirneme** *subj.2 sg.*
should rebuke 259/24; **vndirnam**
pa.t.3 sg. rebuked 319/53, 324/8, 2–
34/25; **vndirnomyn** *pp.* 332/14, 23,
2–3/32, 2–128/39.
vndirnemynge *vbl.n.* chastising, discipline 323/41, 49, 324/3, 2–212/36.
vnderset *ppl.adj.* supported, sustained 68/
23.
vndirsette *pa.t.3 sg.* supported, strengthened 210/22–23.

vndirstondyn *ppl.adj.* made understood 165/2, 166/10.

vndon *v.* undo, betray 150/23, reveal 2–10/21, destroy 2–211/2.

vn(n)eþis see on(n)eþis

vneuene *adj.* unequal 2–158/80, 2–159/88, 92.

vneuenehed *n.* inequality 2–159/90, 92, 94.

vngentyl *adj.* uncouth, uncivil 2–64/58, 2–316/55.

vngyltelych *adv.* innocently 334/56, without just cause 342/2.

vngilthed *n.* innocence 342/61, 62.

vnʒoldyn *ppl.adj.* unrewarded 170/49.

vnkende *adj.* uncharitable 329/13, 340/51, 2–111/39, 42, 2–302/78.

vnkendnesse *n.* uncharitableness 300/53, 2–110/37.

vnkunnynge *n.* imprudence (cf. V.L. *imprudentium*).

vnleueful, -leful *adj.* unlawful 135/31, 184/38, 2–27/15.

vnlykyng *adj.* unpleasing 2–28/63.

vnlysty *adj.* slothful 208/76.

vnlose *pr.2 sg.* unburden 56/68 (cf. losyn).

vnlothfulnesse *n.* beauty, attractiveness 2–102/82.

vnlusthed *n.* sloth, unwillingness 207/57.

vnorne *adj.* unlovely, repellent 358/51, 359/62.

vnpacience *n.* ~ *of* impatience caused by 79/27.

vnpes *n.* dissension 2–38/32.

vnpytous *adj.* uncharitable (towards) 248/28.

vnpower *n.* incapacity 245/14, 248/54.

vnryʒth *n.* injustice 2–207/19.

vnsekyr *adj.* uncertain 2–194/64.

vnsely *adj.* unhappy 2–325/62.

vnskylful *adj.* unintelligent 216/80, 239/31, unreasonable 2–142/37.

vnskylfuly, -fulyche, -folyche *adv.* foolishly, ignorantly 323/41, 354/13–14, 2–89/9.

vnteyyth *pr.3 sg.* unties 288/51.

vnthende *adj.* of poor quality 88/19, 146/71.

vnthryfty *adj.* unwholesome 129/57, unprosperous 2–65/99.

vntyme *n.* unsuitable or unlawful time 129/39.

vnwarly *adv.* unawares 2–53/11.

vnwyʒtty *adj.* lacking wisdom or reason 51/10, 138/78, 81.

vnworshepist *pr.2 sg.* lack respect for 2–29/3; vnworchepyth *pr.3 sg.* 325/30–31, 2–54/47; vnworchepyd *pa.t.3 pl.* lost (him) respect 324/12; ~ *pp.* unrespected 328/46.

voyde *adj.* empty 319/56.

voydit *pp.* emptied 2–99/103.

vouhyt *pa.t.3 sg. refl.* vowed 8/46; vohwyd *pp.* 2–109/5, 2–110/10 (cf. avoh-).

vo(h)w, vohu, a)vouh *n.* vow 8/40, 45, 223/23, 246/23, 2–110/26; a)vo(h)wys *possess.pl.* 103/56, 223/22, 24; a)vowis, a)vouhis *pl.* 7/4, 103/58, 60, 250/10, 11.

vp(pyn *prep.* upon 217/94, 2–45/58, 2–115/126, to the extent of 38/xxv, 352/18, 2–162/80, as 45/xxvi, on (the topic of) 106/50, 335/5, 348/22, 2–169/49, against 2–208/61, ~ *tyme of* until the time of 2–188/82, ~ *usure* at usury 2–199/40, 2–203/66, ~ *euyn* toward evening 2–216/18, han ~ *his part* get back his share 2–201/16.

vpsodoun *adv.* upside down 147/12.

vs see WE

vsa(u)nt *adj.* habituated 227/30, 33, 237/52, 239/10, habitual 230/32.

vsantly *adv.* habitually 237/10.

vsyd *ppl.adj.* practiced 161/34, 296/19.

vsyn *v.* make use of 167/10, 16; usist *pr.2 sg.* use 235/7; vsith *pr.3 sg.* 162/7; vsyn *pr.3 pl.* make use of 157/14, 158/19, 162/12, practise 185/8, (in *aux.* sense) are accustomed 287/8; VSE *subj.2 sg. refl.* should be accustomed 230/28, 37; ~ *subj.3 sg.* should frequent; vsyd *pa.t.3 sg.* engaged in 167/22.

vsure(e *n.* usury 45/xxiv.

usurere *n.* usurer 45/xxvii; usureres *n.pl.* 45/xxviii.

ut(t)(e)ryst(e, -est *comp.adj.* most utter 216/81, utmost 239/21, 2–129/90, 2–321/37.

vttyrly *adv.* overall, in the main 83/49.

W

waan- see wan-

waar- see war-

waast *adj.* wasteful 30/liii.

wacchyn *pr.3 pl. intr.* stay awake, watch 118/31.

wach *n.* wakefulness 2–95/10.

wachyn *v.* hire, pay wages to 2–160/29, 30.

waching *pr.p.refl.* washing 2–85/24 (cf. **wasch-**).

waiouris *n.pl.* bets, wagers 71/7.

wayte *n. daye-* ~ watchman 2–24/5, 2–134/19–20 (cf. V.L. *speculatorem*), *lychyng in* ~ lying in wait 2–33/49.

waytyn, wayte *v.*(1) expect, hope for 177/5, 180/12; **waytedyn** *pa.t.3 pl.* lay in wait 2–88/99.

waytyn *v.*(2) ~ *hym good torn* return the favour 254/75.

wakyn *v. intr.* be active, be diligent 197/54, 2–310/110; **wook** *pa.t.3 sg.* awoke 238/28, 305/45, 2–194/55.

wakyng *vbl.n.* lying awake, wakefulness 294/44.

wallyn *v. intr.* build walls 288/33.

wa(a)nbeleue *n.* (religious) disbelief 62/35, 170/26, 182/17, lack of trust 232/76, *of* ~ distrustful 230/29.

wanbeleuynge *ppl.adj.* disbelieving 2–80/26.

wanhope *n.* despair 31/iv, 226/7, 2–212/43.

wanyen *v. intr.* wane 2–319/16.

wanyynge *vbl.n.* waning 2–319/32.

wansynge *vbl.n.* wasting away 2–63/34.

wantyn *pr.3 pl.* lack 108/46, 207/67, 307/11.

wantyng(ge *vbl.n.* lack 60/35, 80/50, 2–103/107.

wanwyt *n.* foolishness 305/31.

wappid *pp.* enveloped 240/55.

war *imp.sg.* ~ *þe souereyn þat* let the ruler beware lest 293/7, ~ *hym of* let him recall 2–148/33; *imp.pl.* ~ *hem þat* let them be cautious who 290/9,

wa(a)r *adj.* warned 140/10, 148/35, 150/23, 2–128/41, wary 213/37, 2–265/71, careful 52/21, 179/8, 2–56/49, alert 2–20/34.

warchyn *v. intr.* watch (perh. error for *wacchyn* through confusion with forms of *warkyn*? cf. *var.*H *werkyn*) 2–20/34.

warcmanchepe *n.* craftsmanship 2–167/53–4.

wardly see **word-**

wardlychhed *n.* worldliness 2–164/146.

wary- see **weryng**

wark, warc *n.* labor, work 9/2, 263/9, 2–95/16, 2–123/4, life's work 2–163/108, deed 302/40; **warkys** *pl.* activities (of angels, devils) 95/22, 221/8, acts 213/40, works 221/8, 302/44, 2–20/46, tasks 263/7.

warkeris *n.pl.* instigators 2–87/85.

warkyn, werk- *v. intr.* labour, work 9/21, 120/31, 263/7, 2–252/34, function 121/64, *tr.* to work 2–231/34; **warkyth** *pr.3 sg.* performs 168/14; **warke** *pr.1 pl.* let us do 2–251/29; **worchen** *pr.3 pl.* work 71/29; **warc** *pa.t.3 sg.* worked (*fig.*), moved 2–217/51, 2–219/52.

warkynge *vbl.n.* agency 168/10, 216/63.

warly, -lyche *adv.* circumspectly 29/xlv, 180/15.

wars- see **wers-**

warse *n.* a worse state of affairs 183/21.

warse *comp.adj.* worse 211/42, 2–108/34 (cf. **wers-**).

waschyn *v. refl.* wash 2–88/100.

waste *n.* consumption 2–197/43, 59.

wastyn *v.* consume 2–302/89, 2–315/11; **wastyth** *pr.3 sg.* 2–302/87; **wastyn** *pr.3 pl.* 2–165/168, dissipate 2–287/5; **waste** *subj.3 sg.* should destroy 2–152/53, 2–168/20; **wastyd** *pp.* destroyed 2–151/24.

waueryt *pr.3 sg. intr.* flutters 2–271/34; **waueryn** *pr.3 pl.* flutter (*fig.*), fluctuate 2–271/36.

wawys *n.pl.* waves 2–272/64.

wawyth *pr.3 sg.* swings 2–262/94.

wax- see **wex-**

we, vs *pers.pron.1 pl.* we 52/4, 56/82, 206/34, 35, 265/59; **vs** *oblique cases* us 52/45, 195/5; **our** *absolute* ours 2–161/53; **oureself** *refl.* ourselves 67/44, 90/17.

wed(de *n.* bet, wager 17/15, 43/viii, pledge, security for loan 2–148/49, 2–198/2.

wede *n.* clothing 51/9, 52/44.

wedyr *n.* weather 3/53, 121/67, 142/17.

wedlac *n.* wedlock 15/7, 2–62/1, 23, 2–65/101.

wed(d)ryng(e *n.* weather conditions 183/35, 184/3.

wedue, wydue, wydwe *n.* widow 64/20, 190/18, 2–115/118; **wyduys** *possess.pl.* 200/9; ~ *pl.* 310/10, 2–135/5.

weduhed *n.* widowhood 138/57.

wey(e *n.* journey 133/41, 47, path, road 182/15, 187/24, course 133/46, 2–271/38, *be* ~ *of* as a way of 113/69, *be oþer* ~ otherwise 149/6, 7, *in þe* ~ anywhere, somewhere 181/2, *be þe* ~ on the road 186/13, 2–43/6; **weyis** *pl.* course of action 124/74.

weyefaryng *ppl.adj.* travelling 290/18.

weylith *imp.pl.* lament! 2–251/9.

weyst *pr.2 sg. intr.* weigh 2–250/58; **weyn** *pr.3 pl.* 2–250/48; **weyn, wown** *pp. tr.* 2–195/6, 2–250/47, 58.

wel(e *n.* well-being 56/58, 140/17, weal, good fortune 191/46, 301/9, 2–103/109.

wel *adj.* well off 2–277/37.

welaway, -wey *interject.* alas! 148/35, 44, 2–245/8.

weldyȝt *pr.3 sg.* controls 118/35.

welfar(e *n.* well-being, good fortune 12/62, 355/2, 2–323/6, pleasure 294/56, 295/61, luxurious living, extravagance 308/44, 2–306/72.

welkyn *v. intr.* wither 349/67, 2–274/14; **welkyt(h** *pr.3 sg.* 2–274/24, 25.

wellynge *ppl. adj.* boiling 2–77/30.

wendyn, wende *v. intr.* go 56/64, 112/36, 136/24, 356/12, return 2–74/104; **wendyn, -en** *pr.3 pl.* go 51/13, 70/13, 290/4, return 145/33; **wende** *imp.sg.* go (back) 2–266/32; **wendyth** *imp.pl.* go! 187/42, 212/17, return 2–101/64.

wenyn *v.* believe 173/24, 2–147/21; **wenyst** *pr.2 sg.* 86/16, 329/24, 2–69/70; **wenyth, -yȝt** *pr.3 sg.* 85/3, 151/53, 2–47/29, supposes himself 237/46, 230/15; **wene** *pr.2 pl.* suppose 2–255/57; **wenyn, wenen** *pr.3 pl.* expect 5/96, 29/xlvi, suppose 89/38, believe 168/35; **wene** *subj.3 sg.* should believe, should deem 343/31, 2–198/14; **wenist** *imp.sg.* believe! 329/24; **wenynge** *pr.p.* supposing 167/7, 237/48, 2–147/14; **wende** *pa.t.1 sg.* believed 188/2; ~ *pa.t.3 sg.* 170/32, 192/67, 312/67, supposed himself 341/29; **wendyn** *pa.t.3 pl.* believed 138/76, 151/45, 2–47/29, expected 2–9/46.

went- see **gon**

wepene *n.* weapon 2–33/61, 2–44/23.

w(h)er, qher(e, qwere *conj.* where 83/45, 139/95, 151/39, 236/36, 2–12/77, 2–15/44 (cf. **þer(e, qher-**).

weredyn *pa.t.3 pl.* wore 2–91/29.

wery *adj.* weary 70/22, 199/5, 201/30.

weryng, waryynge *vbl.n.* cursing 31/ii, 223/20.

werk- see **wark-**

werkyngge *vbl.n.* operation 117/16, 125/3 (cf. **wark-**).

werkys *n.pl.* actions 83/15, 17 (cf. **wark-**).

werre, warre *n.* war 30/lv, 117/15, 183/17.

wers(e, warse *comp.adv.* worse 63/20, 148/36, 159/45, 186/3.

werst, warste *comp.adj.* worst 2–7/79, 2–132/20.

werto *conj.* for what purpose 202/1.

wete see **wyt**

w(h)eþir, -er *conj.* (emphasising interrog. sense in a question posing alternatives; cf. *utrum*) 2–52/1, 2–67/1, 2–109/1, whether 2–56/54.

wetyn, wit(yn, -ten *v.* believe 258/18, learn 165/91, 2–11/40, 2–237/45, find out 312/66, 2–145/16; **woot** *pr.1 sg.* know 53/31, 55/35, 144/3; **wost** *pr.2 sg.* 338/9; **wite, w(h)o(o)t(h, wete** *pr.3 sg.* 12/46, 154/34, 173/30, 230/14, 344/59, 60, learns of 15/20; **wetyn** *pr.1 pl.* know 106/48; **wytyn, wetyn** *pr.3 pl.* 213/8, 342/1; **wete** *imp.sg.* 2–64/56, 2–160/19; **wetith** *imp.pl.* 333/19; **wetynge** *pr.p.* 226/15, 238/13, believing 2–45/42; **wuste** *pa.t.1 sg.* knew 172/13; **wystist** *pa.t.2 sg.* 238/23; **wyste, wuste** *pa.t.3 sg.* 202/2, 2–50/15, 21, 2–86/41, 61; **wystyn, wustyn** *pa.t.3 pl.* 349/46, 2–47/49; **wyste** *pa.t.subj.3 sg.* 2–205/45; **wystyn** *pa.t.subj.3 pl.* 165/81, 170/50; **wyst, wust** *pp.* known 172/13, 2–68/37.

wetyng- see **wityng-**

wetyngly, wit(t)yngly, witynge *adv.* knowingly 155/59, 237/3, 2–3/24, 2–26/3.

wexsyn, waxsyn *v. intr.* grow 107/17, become 2–209/73, 2–247/32; **wexsyȝt, waxsyȝt, waxsith** *pr.3 sg.* 141/5, grows 309/23, 2–273/5, 7; **wexsyn, wax(s)yn** *pr.3 pl.* 68/39, 182/5, 308/43, 2–8/39; **waxsyþ** *imp.pl.* increase! 2–78/47; **wex, wax** *pa.t.3 sg.* grew 107/16, 350/75, became 224/18, 2–144/87; **wox(s)yn, waxsyn** *pp.* grown 309/5, var./68, 2–17/32, matured 205/14, 210/19, 309/11.

whansyn *v. intr.* vanish 2–166/24.

what *adv.* at whatever 42/xx, 172/6 (cf. qhat).

when- see qhan-

whet(e *n.* wet (weather), rain 141/45, 47, 142/18.

whych- see wych-, queche

whidir, whedir *adv.* whichever way 343/ 28, whither 349/46, 2–273/93, ~ *oweye/ of weye* where are you off to? 2–147/55, 56.

whilys *adv. þer* ~ meanwhile 2–279/38.

whylum *adv.* at one time, once 2–97/55.

whisterer *n.* tattletale 38/iv.

why(ʒ)te *n.* weight 284/3, 2–154/47, 2– 195/5; w(h)yʒtis, weyʒtis *pl.* 2–86/65, 2–130/8, 2–154/44, 45.

whor *intrrog.conj.* can it be that . . . ? 2– 278/9 (a form of 'whether'; not in MED but cf. LALME 1:447 Map 570; see Notes).

wyche *n.* witch 2–174/27; w(h)ychis, wycches, -ys *pl.* 4/60, 73, 28/xxxiii, 124/70, 2–157/27.

wycke *adj.* wicked 294/36, evil 3/42, 2– 12/75.

wickid *n.* evil 257/40 (cf. V.L. *a malo*).

wycket *n.* door, gate 2–303/19; wycketys *pl.* 2–97/68.

wyde *adj.* loose, ample 2–91/12.

wyghʒt, wyʒt(h, wyth *n.* man, person 131/12, 220/80, 244/31*, 2–147/57.

wyʒt see wyt

wil *n. be in* ~ *to* be willing to 2–142/42.

wil(e, wele, welyn, wol(l)(e *v. tr.* and *intr.* will 27/xviii, 154/30, 32, 299/31, wish (to) 42/xx, 217/114, desire (to) 55/24; *aux.v.* (giving sense of willing, wanting or desiring to the main verb) 41/xi, 53/ 19, 56/71, 73, 60/56, 152/26, (convey-ing future sense to the main verb) 32/x, 2–313/4, (conveying sense of future contingency to the main verb in respect to habitual or expected actions) 17/13, 87/39, 150/13, 278/13.

welyn *infin.* 63/30; wole, woll, wele, wil(e *1, 3 sg.* 27/xviii, 32/x, 87/39, 140/20, 270/59, 341/32; wyl(t *2 sg.* 53/36, 55/52, 66/20, 299/31; wil(n, wyl(l)(en, welyn, wol(l)en *1, 2, 3 pl.* 41/xi, 47/iii, 53/19, 54/13, 150/13, 152/26, 163/39, 180/30; wolt, wyle *subj.2 sg.* 56/71, 75/24; wele *subj.3 sg.* 56/73, 121/64; wyl(e)n *subj.pl.* 154/30,

32, 351/109; wold(e *pa.t.1, 3 sg.* 16/27, 56/67, 66/26, 270/53, 57; woldyst *pa.t.2 sg.* 52/37, 228/13, 2–31/12; woldyn, -de(n *pa.t.3 pl.* 61/24, 170/ 51, 270/57, 345/69; woldyn *pa.t.subj.3 pl.* 184/20, 185/6; *wyl . . . nyl* will . . . will not 117/7, 137/31, 165/6.

wyl(l *n.* intention 49/48, 92/23, choice 92/25, *is in* ~ wills 123/53.

wilfulle *adj.* voluntary 48/36, ~ *man* man of good will 25/iii.

wilfully *adv.* voluntarily 58/29, 64/35, 78/28.

wilynge *adv.* willingly 155/59.

w(h)ilys *n.pl.* wiles 2–87/78, 84.

wyllyn *v. intr.* wander, stray 2–314/38.

wyl(le)ward-going *n.* wearing wool next to the skin as penance 162/16, 346/14.

wyn *n.* wine 2–90/43, grapes 280/7, 2– 166/35; wynys *pl.* grapevines 2–135/3.

wyndounne, -downe *n.* window 318/48, 2–15/55; -dowys *pl.* 190/40. See Note 318/48.

wynnyn *v.* profit 2–200/68, 72, 2–266/23; wynnyth *pr.3 sg.* 2–199/44.

wynnyng(e *vbl.n.* profit 56/70, 2–135/17– 18, 2–203/86, profit-making 277/36, 38.

wynsyn *v. intr.* kick (*fig.*) 2–305/16.

wyrynesse *n.* weariness 291/15.

wisdammys *n.pl.* bits of lore, pieces of advice 2–259/22, 24.

wise *n.* way, maner 32/xiii, 187/35, 229/4, ways 222/2; wyses, -ys *pl.* 26/vii, 2– 58/18, 19.

wys(s)e *adj. maken hem* ~ pretend to know (about) 29/xlvii, 136/8, 151/50, 177/4, 183/27.

wyskid *ppl.adj.* beaten with twigs or branches 2–268/6.

wyssyn *v.* guide 133/41, 47; wisse *subj.3 sg.* should guide 2–45/42; wyssyd *pp.* 2– 209/65.

wyssyng *vbl.n.* guidance 120/28.

wyst-, wytyn see wet-

wy(ʒ)t *n.* intellect, mind 119/27, 124/67, 2–27/28, judgement 54/41, 292/57, *stondyn to her* ~ defer to their views 346/30; wi(ʒ)ttis *pl.* senses 104/73, 129/50, minds 117/8, 12, wits 347/14.

wyt, wete *pr.3 sg.* attributes, imputes 336/ 35; *it is to* ~ *þat* those are to be reproached (who swear . . .) 226/26

var. in MSS RDT; cf. *MED* sv. 'witen'
v. 3, 1b.

wyt-, wys- see **wet-**

wyth see **wyȝht-**

wytdrawe, -drawyȝt *pr.3 sg.* withholds
from 62/42, withholds 62/44; **withdra-**
wen *pr.3 pl.* hold back, restrain 43/iii,
2–134/13; **wytdrawe** *subj.3 sg.* should
keep back from 62/42.

withdrawynge *n.* taking 2–130/6.

withheldyn *pr.3 pl.* withhold from 13/13,
withhold 13/23.

wit(t)ynge *vbl.n.* knowledge 17/9*, 43/vi,
299/32 (see **wetyn-**).

wytsonday *n.* Whitsunday (seventh
Sunday after Easter, Pentecost) 282/25.

wyt(h)stondyn, -stonde *v. intr.* stand fast,
persevere 96/34, 258/59, resist 154/30,
33; **witstondith** *pr.3 pl.* oppose 313/14;
withstondyn *pp.* 308/45.

wy(ȝ)tty *adj.* intelligent 138/79, 2–96/31,
wise 300/46, 48, 2–309/88.

wlatyn *v.* hate 2–110/24; **wlate** *pr.1 sg.* 2–
8/32; ~ *pr.2 sg.* 258/3; **wlatyth** *pr.3 sg.*
2–154/49; **wlatyn** *pr.3 pl.* 2–82/69;
wlate *subj.2 sg.* should hate 258/3.

wo(o *n.* harm 13/7, 38/iv, misfortune
147/9, 148/39, misery 88/21, sadness
286/39.

wo(o)d(e *adj.* angry 2–69/72, insane 2–
144/90, 2–218/27, ~ *in* mad with 2–
64/59, 71.

wode *n.* wood 2–8/22, 2–42/71, wood-
lands 141/50; **wodis** *pl.* 256/9.

wodnesse *n.* madness 2–40/9, 10, 12, 2–
315/20.

wofyn *ppl.adj.* woven 2–310/126.

woke *n.* week 267/50, 274/36, 278/14;
wokys *pl.* 148/22.

wo(c)keday *n.* weekday 9/9, 274/31, 276/
3.

wol, wel *adv.* very 22/17, 51/6, 9, 16, 63/
5, 169/5.

wold see **wile**

wolle, wulle *n.* wool 131/20, 146/71, 2–
17/48.

wombe *n.* stomach 166/18, 19, 2–17/49,
2–259/20.

wondirfolyche *adv.* miraculously 2–81/
44.

wondyrful *adj.* astonishing 54/17, 2–140/
65, 2–170/55, extraordinary 149/53, 2–
186/2.

wondis *n.pl.* wounds 237/51, 238/28,
240/43.

wondryly *adv.* wondrously 216/63.

wone *adj.* wont, accustomed 208/1, 319/
67, 2–11/34, 2–34/29.

woot see **wetyn**

worch- see **wark-**

worchepe, -chipe, wurshepe *n.* status,
rank 12/53, 58/53, 2–99/12, homage
12/59, (religious) worship 87/37,
honour 88/23, 124/65, 208/10, 328/
41, credit 153/31, respect 189/29, 332/
21, 2–64/61; **wurshepys** *pl.* states of
dignity 59/66.

worchepfully *adv.* worthily 190/9.

worchepyn, wurshepyn *v.* honor 12/53,
54, 55, 106/52, 346/2, pay respect to
347/23; **worchepe** *imp.sg.* honor! 347/
17; **worchepith, wurshepyȝt** *imp.pl.*
106/55, 347/19, 25; **worchepyd** *pp.*
honored 328/39–40, 347/7a.

worchere *n.* creator 70/4 (cf. **warkyn**).

worchipful *adj.* creditable 6/138, 209/28.

wor(l)d, war(l)d *n.* world 12/36, 51/8,
54/42, 2–292/16, 2–302/69.

word(de)ly, ward(e)ly *adj.* worldly 1/11a,
65/51, 274/2, 2–6/68.

worm *n.* ~ *of conscience* torments of conscience 2–103/107, 118; **wormys** *pl.*
reptiles 2–103/113.

worþ(i, wurthy *adj.* deserving of 112/39,
116/81, 137/35, 337/15, of any value
168/35, 320/23, 2–123/71.

wos(e *rel.pron. possess.* whose 189/2, 254/
64, 338/42, 2–96/39.

wostlyche *adv.* truly 236/30–31.

wow(e *n.* wall 2–250/52, 2–270/15;
wowys *pl.* 140/22, 2–5/23.

wraw *adj.* angry, wrathful 307/36.

wreche *n.* punishment, retribution 148/
24, 209/24, 34, 2–244/102, revenge 2–
13/5, 2–105/40.

wretthe *n.* wrath 68/17, 84/23, 160/9.

wryȝt(h)e *n.* wright, skilled workman 120/
49, 121/8.

wry(y)n *v.* cover 100/28, 305/41, 311/52;
wryhyt *pr.3 sg.* 2–14/28; **wryyn** *pr.3 pl.*
refl. conceal 212/36; **wryynge** *pr.p.* 269/
31; **wryedyin** *pa.t.3 pl.* covered 305/45;
wry(h)yd *pp.* 2/14b, 99/1, sheltered 2–
14/30.

writ(h, wryȝt *n.* writing 353/56, *holy* ~

scripture, the Bible 20/5, 87, 88/29, 169/10.

writen *v.* write 257/54; **wrytith** *pr.3 sg.* 2–41/26; **write** *subj.3 sg.* should write, draw up (document) 2–44/15; **wro(o)t** *pa.t.3 sg.* wrote 96/5, 7, 2–63/52; **wretyn** *pp.* 112/48.

writer *n.* scribe in legal proceding 2–41/25.

wrytyn *ppl.adj.* written (law) 2–208/49.

wrong(e *ppl.adj.* bent 2–230/10, 2–231/25, 2–245/15, bent (*fig.*) 2–245/16, 2–246/24, 27, 29.

wrong(g)e *n.* evil intention 66/33, 2–254/34.

wroth *adj.* angry 1/7a, 205/62, 305/46, 2–143/63.

wrotyn *v.* root, dig 2–223/56.

wrotynge *vbl.n.* rooting, digging 2–223/53.

wur- see **wor-**

INDEX OF BIBLICAL REFERENCES

[Citations in square brackets are supplied by the editor. Citations followed by an asterisk have been emended; see 'Errata and Corrigenda' lists.]

Genesis

1 [:3] 263/21*
1 [:12] 145/45
1 [:14–19] 119/1
[1:28] 63/10
[1:28] 72/10
[1:28] 2–78/48
[1:28] 2–79/2
2 [:1] 284/22
2 [:2–3] 279/23
2 [:21–4] 2–66/9*
3 [:1 et seq.] 169/17
4 [:6–7] 2–306/52
4 [:10–12] 2–32/43
6 [:11–13] 2–105/25*
7 [:1–24] 2–59/32
8 [:21] 127/4
9 [:2–3] 2–34/16
9 [:2–5] 2–35/46*
9 [:6] 2–32/31
9 [:20–5] 305/35
12 [:11–20] 2–93/91*
16 [:1–3] 2–116/13
[18 & 19] 2–291/44
19 [:17–28] 2–106/60
[19:30–8] 2–105/45
20 [:2] 2–94/92
[21:9–14] 2–95/123
24 [:14] 167/8
27 [:1–29] 2–216/30
[27:33] 2–95/133
31 [:52] 244/19
34 [:1–31] 2–104/4
[35:22] 2–105/47
[35:22] 2–316/59
38 [:7–10] 2–105/37
45 [:9] 2–138/6
47 2–201/30
50 [:7–13] 215/49

Exodus

1 [:15–21] 2–215/1
15 [:1–20] 297/22
20 [;3–5] 81/7

20 [:4] 136/2
[20:13] 2–1/4
[20:14] 2–58/3–4
[20:15] 2–130/3
[20:16] 2–211/7
20 [:17] 2–253/5
20 [:17] 2–295/7
[20:17] 2–297/72*
21 [:14] 2–33/51
22 [:18] 2–144/114
22 [:18] 254/71
22 [:18] 2–13/10
22 [:25] 2–206/5
23 [:1] 254/67
23 [:1–2] 2–50/34*
23 [:7] 2–13/12
[24:18] 82/21*
[24:18;33;20] 2–325/69
30 [:11–16] 190/21
31 [:15] 289/9*
32 [:27 et seq.] 2–37/7
33 [:20] 2–102/97
34 & 35 268/13
37 [:7–9] 81/15

Leviticus

19 [:11] 2–215/67
19 [:16] 2–8/18
19 [:26] 177/2
19 [:32] 332/6
19 [:32] 347/17
20 [:9] 306/74
21 [:9] 2–78/66
23 [:27; 29] 294/54
23 [:32] 287/4
23 [:33–6] 270/1
23 [:40–3] 296/3
25 [:35–7] 2–207/10
26 [:2] & 19:[3] 289/9
[27:30] 2–172/27

Numbers

12 [:1–6] 2–133/61
14 [:1–45] 2–133/58
15 [:32] 276/15

22 [:1–4] 2–262/1
22 [:22–33] 2–34/35
[24:17] 135/12*
[25:1–9] 2–264/41
25 [:1–15] 2–104/11
[25:5] 2–37/8
35 [:30] 2–236/50

Deuteronomy
3 [:26] 2–47/40
4 [:9] 328/22
4 [:26] 2–238/16
5 [:6–21] 2–298/6
5 [:12–14] 289/5
5 [:16] 356/5*
6 [:5] 2–61/41
6 [:13–14] 101/4
6 [:6–9] 328/20
6 [:13] 232/84
[11:4] 264/50
12 [:23–5] 2–35/48
[13:1–3] 177/8
17 [:12] 343/21
17 [:16–17] 2–86/66*
18 [:10–11] 177/6
18 [:10–12] 137/47
18 [:13] 66/15
19 [:15] 2–236/50
21 [:18–21] 307/35–6
21 [:18–21] 322/25–6
22 [:20–1] 2–78/68–9*
22 [:22] 2–63/25*
23 [:18] 2–157/35
23 [:19–20] 2–197/65*
23 [:19–20] 2–207/14
25 [:13–16] 2–154/50
27 [:11–26] 2–313/20
[28:1–13] 2–317/22
30 [:19–20; 17] 2–238/23

Joshua
7 [:16–26] 2–259/16

Judges
11 [:30–49] 224/6
[16:4–31] 2–85/19
[16:30] 2–52/46
19 & 20 2–105/27
20 [:1–48] 2–65/92

1 Kings (1 Samuel)
I, [1:10–13] 204/36
I, 2 [:30] 220/72
[I, 4] 324/14
[I, 15:22] 293/7*

I, 15 [:32–3] 2–37–8/8–9
I, 21 [:13] 2–218/30
[I, 25:1–42] 2–144/89
I, 25 [:1–44] 2–142/53

2 Kings (2 Samuel)
II, 6 [:6–7] 2–107/2
II, 6 [:14–23] 297/32
II, 7 [:13], 8 [:1–18] 192/69
II, [7:13–14] 192/54
II, 8 [:1–18] 192/69
II, 11 [:12–17] 2–85/21
II, 11 & 12 2–105/30
II, 12 [:9] 2–64/75
II, 12 [:15–23] 2–261/73
II, 13 [:1–19] 2–88/108
[II, [3:32] 2–105/42
II, 14 [:14] 2–277/18
[II, 18] 307/35*
II, 20 [:8–9] 2–12/76
II, 21 [:1–9] 261/55
[II, 24 [:6] 2–47/42

3 Kings
III, 5 [:3] 192/54
III, 7 [:29;36] 81/18
III, 18 [:28] 163/47
III, 18 [:40] 2–38/10
III, 21 2–255/1
[III, 21] 2–15/44
III, 22 [:22] 153/18
III, 22 [:22] 155/71
[III, 22:2;6] 2–11/31*

4 Kings
IV, 5 [:1–27] 2–259/5
IV, 5 [:13] 333/7
IV, 5 2–174/42
IV, 6 [:8–23 348/32
[IV, 9:24;33–7] 2–15/59
IV, 10 [:7] 2–15/59
IV, [10:18–28] 2–219/37
IV, 20 [:1–7] 122/33
IV, [25:1–7] 2–10/18*

Nehemiah
8 [:10] 296/16

Job
1 [:12] 153/14
1 [:21] 2–306/65
[1:21] 56/68
[1:21] 71/45
[1:21] 77/12
[1:21] 2–272/82

2 [;6] 153/14
2 [:]9] 2–306/65
5 [:6] 70/25
7 [:1] 2–304/7
7 [:1] 2–307/22
[7;14] 177/65ᵛᵃr.
[10:22] 356/13
[16:20] 2–238/7*
19 [:21] 2–280/41
24 [:6–14] 2–135/9
27 [:5] 2–4/13
29 [:16] 333/9
[31:1] 2–97/64
34 [:30] 337/11
[41:25] 166/7

Psalms
[5:7] 2–215/61
[7:10] 2–312/182
[7:13–14] 2–246/32
[9:3] 2–3/11
[11:9] 2–270/30
[13:4] 331/28
[13:4] 2–14/14
[15:9] 204/51
[18:6] 271/19
[24:10] 124/77
[24:10] 2–226/45
[24:10] 2–26/71
[31:6] 351/106
[32:2] 2–28/60
[33:11] 62/58
[35:7] 124/79
[38:13] 53/12
39 [:5] 302/30
[39:18] 80/53*
[39:18] 60/38
[49:16] 223/15
[49:18] 2–210/108
[52:6] 2–7/76
[54:11–12] 2–207/22
[56:5] 2–2/25
[58:12] 2–144/107
[59:6] 2–246/37
[61:11] 56/58
[61;11] 76/2
[63:2] 335/5–6
68 [:27–9] 228/34
[75:11] 300/73
[75:12] 103/60
[75:12] 223/26
[82:14] 2–271/32
[83:2–3] 272/46

[90:14] 302/26
[93:19] 301/77
[97:4] 207/49
[99:2] 207/51
[99:2] 298/53
[101:7] 2–300/38
[103:14] 194/37
[103:14] 2–290/24
[103:14] 2–177/27
[103:20–3] 144/30*
[105:39] 2–119/17
[106:18] 2–24/73
[106:20] 2–22/34
[110:10] 2–93/67
[111:10] 205/61
[112:3] 116/83
[114:5] 2–226/46
[115:111] 2–220/36
[116:1] 197/51
[117:24] 294/34
[118:21] 2–313/18
[118:32] 2–322/18
[118:35–6] 2–323/23–8
[122:2] 327/91
[124:2] 349/52
[136:9] 2–27/19
[139:4] 2–6/46
[140:5] 2–3/27
[144:9] 279/30
[149:1] 208/72

Proverbs
1 [;8] 323/48
1 [:8] 330/8
1 [:32] 2–27/8
3 [:9] 2–156/10
4 [:23] 2–98/73
4 [:24] 2–132/40
6 [:19] 2–237/48
6 [:19] 2–7/10
6 [:30–3] 2–63/30
8 [:13] 2–8/32
9 [:10] 2–93/67
10 [:1] 323/60
11 [:26] 2–202/38
12 [:17;19] 2–238/51
13 [:12] 294/57
13 [:24] 2–146/45
13 [:24] var./62
14 [:15] 2–220/22
14 [:25] 2–251/21
15 [:5] 323/50
16 [:18] 2–83/93

16 [:33] 167/9
[17:5] 52/23
17 [:15] 2–5/21
17 [:25] 323/61
18 [:21] 2–1/21
19 [:9] 2–238/53
[19:13] 323/53
20 [:9] 127/7
20 [:20] 307/12
[21:1] 343/25
21 [:6–7] 2–207/32
21 [:25] 2–27/16
21 [:30] 138/73–4*
22 [:1] 2–132/15
22 [:2] 51/2
22 [:2] 70/2
22 [:6] 128/17
[23:4] 2–261/54
23 [:5] 2–261/63
23 [:10–11] 2–255/65
23 [:22] 321/6
25 [:23] 2–133/50
26 [:20] 2–8/25
27 [:2] 2–220/30
28 [:24] 307/15
29 [:15] 128/13
29 [:15] 324/3
30 [:8–9] 59/3
30 [:8–9] 79/2
30 [:17] 306/63
31 [:30] 2–89/14

Ecclesiastes
[2:14] 91/37
[2:14] 327/88
3 [:1 et seq.] 144/16
3 [:1] 119/19*
[5:2] 176/40*
5 [:6] 175/6–7
[5:9] 58/39
[5:9–16] 59/18–9*
[5:9] 78/37
[5:9] 80/36
[5:9] 2–158/74
6 [:2] 59/23
6 [:2] 80/40–1
6 [:3–5] var./81–2
7 [:6] 2–3/33
7 [:27] 2–81/17
9 [:1] 173/30
9 [;10] 2–252/32–3
9 [:15] 1/11
10 [:11] 2–2/43

12 [:13] 2–313/7

Ecclesiasticus
[1:16] 2–93/67
3 [:2] 322/9
3 [:3] 325/39
3 [:4–11] 322/24
3 [:6] 324/24
4 [:1–6] 52/32
4 [:1–8] 2–136/45
[5:5–9] 2–26/66
5 [:16–17] 2–131/9
6 [:9] 2–235/21
7 [:15] 201/31–2
7 [:26] 325/55
7 [:29–30] 306/68
7 [:37] 215/36–7
7 [:40] 2–96/37
7 [:40] 2–273/98*
7 [:40] 2–303/6–7
9 [:6; 10] 2–77/36
[10:8] 149/60
10 [:8] 253/32–3*
[10:15] 2–83/92
[11:10] 2–158/62
[12:13] 2–313/7
16 [:1–4] 325/46
19 [:2] 2–89/38
19 [:4] 2–220/17
[19:4] 2–262/83
[19:16] 2–262/92
[19:23] 217/108
21 [:30–1] 2–7/13
22 [:3–4] 323/58–9
23 [:9] 227/29
[23:32–6] 2–80/32–3
24 [:24–5] 329/31
25 [:17–26] 2–89/18
26 [:1–3;16–17;19–21;23–4] 2–89/36
[27:1] 57/25–6
[27:1] 78/24
27 [;15] 227/40
[27:15] 258/7*
27 [:17] 2–235/18
[28:15] 2–7/81
28 [:19–20] 2–9/68–9
28 [:22] 2–1/21
28 [:28] 2–132/42
29 [:15] 2–284/67
30 [:2;4] 328/45*
33 [:3] 2–220/22
33 [:19–22] 311/38
33 [:25] 2–95/16

[33:29] 2–95/13
33 [:29] 2–310/111
34 [:7] 178/18–20
[34:21;24] 2–156/7*
34 [:25] 2–16/15–16
34 [:26–7] 2–16/2–7*
[35:21] 112/44–7*
[35:21] 199/17*
38 [:16–18 215/44
[38:23] 2–246/7–9

Song of Soloman (Canticles)
8 [:6] 2–302/83
8 [:6] 2–303/93

Isaiah
1 [:2] 353/61
[1:4] 353/66
1 [:6] 2–101/58
1 [:14–15;13] 276/41*
1 [:13] 283/12
1 [:15] 2–18/66
1 [:16–17] 265/62*
1 [:22] 2–154/41
1 [:23] 2–210/107
3 [:12] 2–4/10
5 [:8–9] 2–255/60
5 [:18–20] 2–207/36
5 [:20] 2–223/30
10 [:5–7] 336/36*
14 [:12–15] 136/21
24 [:16] 140/32
28 [:15] 254/61
33 [:11] 2–57/83
41 [:23] 136/10
42 [:8] 82/32
47 [:9–15] 137/54
49 [:15] 329/27
51 [:11] 94/22
52 [:5] 222/33
[55:6] 2–251/23
56 [:11] 331/32
59 [:13–15] 2–225/11–13;21
59 [:13–15] 257/32*
60 [:18–21] 2–318/7
[65:20] 332/16
65 [:20] 2–27/13
66 [:23] 303/67

Jeremiah
4 [:2] 229/12
8 [:7] 144/20
8 [:10] 2–210/101
9 [:21] 2–97/68

10 [:2] 331/37
14 [:9] 221/19
15 [:19] 2–22/24
17 [:5;7] 2–310/106
17 [:21] 289/9
23 [:1] 331/40
23 [:1] 2–18/59
23 [:30–2] 2–133/2
25 [:8–9] 336/19
27 [:5–9] 341/43
29 [:23] 2–238/5
31 [:11;13] 268/74
31 [:13] 298/50
35 [:6–19] 322/26
[38:39] 2–10/18*

Lamentations
1 [:7] 275/24
3 [:27] 128/22
3 [:51] 2–97/65
[5:15–16] 2–245/9

Ezekiel
3 [:17–18] 2–24/12
3 [:17–20] 2–134/27
8 [:16] 116/79
13 [:10] 2–5/27
[13:17] 2–5/16*
13 [:18–19] 2–4/50
16 [:52] 262/90
16 passim 2–96/19–20
[18:4; 20] 2–240/60
20 [:20] 2–268/2
20, 22, 23 289/10
33 [:12 et seq.] 2–25/34
34 [:2–6] 2–18/57*

Daniel
[3:1–6] 2–265/66–7
4 [:27] 2–177/30*
4 [:1–37 341/32
5 2–250/53
13 [:1–64] 2–87/96–7
[13:53] 225/47

Hosea
2 [:11] 268/81
2 [:11] 2–20/39
5 [:11] 2–81/20
[8:4] 330/20
[13:11] 337/13

Joel
2 [:16] 196/43

Jonah
[3:10] 122/30*

Micah
2 [:1–2] 2–254/52
3 [:1–3] 2–14/22

Zechariah
5 [:1–3] 2–207/27
[6:12] 115/57*

Malachi
1 [:6] 329/17
2 [:1–2] 2–109/63
2 [:2–3] 262/94
2 [:10] 329/22
3 [:10] 61/20

Maccabees
II, 1 [:25] 330/10

Tobit
4 [:6] var./79*
4 [:7–11] 2–284/75
4 [:7] 2–156/11
4 [:13] 2–78/58
4 [:16] 2–28/51
6 [:10–22] 2–62/6
6 [:13] 2–105/39
[12:12–13] 348/31
13 [:21] 2–321/32
[13:22] 2–321/36

The Wisdom of Solomon
[1:11] 2–215/60
1 [:11] 2–2/48
2 [:21] 2–209/68
3 [:16–19] 2–63/44
4 [:3–5] 2–63/50
4 [:6] 325/46
4 [:8] 347/15
[5:8] 2–245/117
5 [:8–10] 2–272/65
5 [:18] 2–35/61
5 [:21] 2–244/92*
[6:7] 2–111/40
6 [:8] 278/2–3*
7 [:5] 51/12
7 [:5] 70/9
11 [:25] 278/2–3*
13 [:1–3] 138/74

Matthew
[4:4] 2–21/19
[4:7] 61/2
[4:7] 61/29

4 [:10] 101/2
4 [:10] 102/24
[5:2–3] 54/3*
[5:3] 56/79
[5:3] 77/22*
[5:3] 2–289/85
[5:14] 59/66*
[5:14] 2–318/1
[5:19] 2–288/42
[5:24] 273/20
[5:26] 2–249/43
5 [:28] 2–79/79
5 [:28] 2–85/39
[5:28] 2–87/77
5 [:28] 2–299/6
[5:33] 103/54
5 [:33] 232/81
5 [:33] 233/17
[5:34] 231/46
[5:37] 2–218/11
5 [:37] 231/55
5 [:37] 231/69
5 [:44] 2–38/30
6 [:6] 195/1
6 [:7] 199/3
[6:7] 200/6
[6:28–30] 52/47
7 [:2] 2–249/45
[7;2] 2–33/55
7 [:13–14] 56/87
[7 :15] 213/37
7 [:22] 212/11
7 [:22–3] 212/14
8 [:20] 2–226/65
8 [:29] 155/64
8 [:31–2] 153/11*
[10:34] 2–311/148
10 [:34] 2–48/73
10 [:35] 313/19
11 [:29] 2–38/25
12 [:1–4] 2–141/23
12 [:1–4] 289/61
12 [:18] 283/7
12 [:11–12] 288/45
12 [:32] 2–127/31
[12:36] 2–214/46
[12:36] 2–249/38
[13:22] 2–268/15
[13:43] 286/27*
14 [:14] 2–285/34
15 [:3] 321/56
15 [:4–6] 308/49
15 [:18–19] 2–253/13

15 [:19] 2–98/72
15 [:19] 273/13
[18:10] 348/20*
18 [:18] 92/14
18 [:19–20] 196/38
19 [:6] 2–37/30
19 [:16–26] 54/18*
19 [:16–26] 75/18
19 [:17] 2–313/5
19 [:17] 2–322/10
[19:21] 66/20
[19:28] 54/8*
[19:28] 75/7
[19:28] 2–250/74
[20:14] 2–250/65
[21:12] 218/15
[21:13] 2–193/12
[22:21] 342/45
[22:37–40] 2–27/33*
[22:40] 67/56
[23:3] 2–224/75
[24:36] 2–247/45
[25:1–13] 2–6/65*
[25:34] 187/40
[25:34;41] 2–242/36
[25:34; 41] 2–246/31
25 [34] 2–317/25
[25:36; 40] 2–287/25
[25:40; 41] 187/40
[25:41] 187/40–1
[25:41] 2–242/36
[25:41] 2–246/31
[25:41] 2–315/39
[25:42–3] 2–249/28
[26:15] 2–221/56
[26:52] 2–38/18*
[26:52] 2–57/81
26 [:69–75] 2–86/57
[27:40] 115/36
28 [:1] 267/55

Mark
1 [:24] 155/65
2 [:27] 279/41
5 [:9] 156/31
[6:9] 93/5
7 [:6] 201/15
[9:41] 2–19/9
10 [:24–5] 77/35
[11:15] 218/16
[11:16] 218/18
12 [:30] 301/1
[12:41–4] 190/18

[12:42]4] 2–192/80
[13:11] 2–217/53
[13:32] 2–247/45
[14:41] 2–47/45
[14:66–72] 2–86/58
16 [:2] 267/54

Luke
4 [:34] 155/65
6 [:20] 75/3
6 [:30] 2–284/3
6 [:35] 2–196/28
[6:45] 204/48
[8:28] 155/65
9 [:11] 2–285/33
9 [:28–33] 2–325/57
[10:7] 194/32
[10:16] 2–53/9
[11:3] 62/3
[11:41] 2–96/26
12 [:16–21] 2–275/50
[12:47] 2–111/39
[13:1–5] 2–123/68
14 [:12–14] 2–284/4
[14:26] 313/3
[14:33] 55/51*
[14:33] 76/49
[16:1–8] 2–157/43
[16:2] 2–137/67
[16:9] 54/12*
[16:9] 75/12
[16:9] 272/44*
[16;9] 2–156/14
[18:12] 267/53
[18:14] 199/21
[18:18] 68/26
19 [:23] 2–195/10
19 [:45] 218/16
20 [:47] 200/8
21 [:1–4] 64/20
21 [:1–4] 73/20
[21:19] 2–305/39
[22:36–40] 2–27/33*
[22:38–91] 2–47/37
[22:38] 2–48/60
[24:13–35] 2–216/20
[24:13 et seq.] 2–285/36

John
[1:29] 92/30
2 [:13–17] 217–18/6–7
[5:17] 264/36
7 [:23] 288/40
8 [:2–11] 2–72/38

[8:12] 2–319/27
[8:12] 2–320/8
[8:34] 277/31
8 [:41; 44] 163/38*
8 [:44] 2–82/66
8 [:44] 154/42
8 [:44] 161/42
8 [:44] 2–231/8
[8:51] 2–22/38
[9:4] 2–252/35
10 [:1] 2–173/5
12 [:3–5] 193/2
[12:31] 2–246/4
[13:27] 2–48/51
[14:6] 2–191/64
[14:6] 300/45
[18:6] 219/38
[18:11] 2–38/18
[18:11] 2–33/56
[19:30] 114/22
19 [:39–42] 216/56
20 [:23] 92/15
[21:15–17] 2–16/27

Acts

1 [:7] 140/29
1 [:8] 2–226/52
4 [:32] 2–137/54
4 [:32] 321/37
5 [:1–10] 2–49/80–2
[5:1–11] 2–259/15
[5:29] 321/50
[5:29] 338/13
[8:18–29] 2–174/33
9 [:40–1] 2–49/83
10 [:1–48] 2–286/42
[12:8] 93/8*
20 [:35] 63/2
20 [:35] 72/2*
20 [:35] 73/27*

Romans

[1:17] 2–20/45
1 [:29–30] 2–7/7
2 [:24] 222/34
[7:24] 2–325/62
8 [:28] 71/28
[8:35] 301/12
[10:10] 203/18
[11:33–4] 124/68
[12:10] 106/56
[12:14] 2–316/68
[12:20] 2–286/46
13 [:1–6] 334/61

[13:1] 2–138/14
13 [:3–6] 2–33/65
13 [:4] 2–13/19
14 [:13] 2–19/15
14 [:21] 2–20/30
[14:23] 344/34
[15:30] 196/39

1 Corinthians

1 [:19–20] 139/92
[1:27–8] 53/39*
[2:9] 2–325/75
2 [:13] 300/60*
3 [:8] 2–53/13
[3:17] 2–31/18
[3:19] 54/45
[4:2] 2–139/39
[4:7] 64/15
[4:7] 73/14–15
[4:15] 330/13
[5:11] 2–77/14*
6 [:9–10] 2–77/13–14
[6:11] 302/34*
6 [:16] 2–79/19
[7:5] 2–59/32
8 [:9–13] 2–20/30
[9:7] 2–155/76
9 [:11] 65/57
[9:11] 2–291/38
9 [:14] 2–177/24
[9:1–14] 194/33
[10:13] 154/30
11 [:30] 2–239/40
11 [:31] 2–239/28
[13:7] 2–310/122
14 [:40] 347/28
15 [:33] 2–97/60

2 Corinthians

[1:3] 329/4
[1:12] 2–238/9
[1:23] 2–322/7
4 [:2] 2–120/27
5 [:8] 53/8
6 [:15] 2–82/75
8 [:9] 1/8
8 [:9] 2–226/68–9
[9:7] 52/33*
[9:7] 2–136/46
[11:14] 2–118/8
[11:14] 169/22
[12:14] 314/36

Galatians
[1:10] 2–3/18
4 [:1–2] 2–140/82
4 [:10–11] 139/87
5 [:13] 102/9
[5:14] 67/57
5 [:16] 2–303/97
[5:17] 2–296/29
[5:17] 2–304/2
[6:10] 2–251/29

Ephesians
[2:3] 2–307/13
3 [:15] 348/10
[4:32] 2–244/97
5 [:3] 2–77/23
[5:14] 2–241/7*
[5:23 et seq.] 2–112/12
5 [:25;28;22–4] 2–62/64*
[5:27] 2–114/88
[5:28] 2–54/43*
5 [:28;22–4] 2–62/64*
6 [:1–4] 323/42
6 [:5–9] 333/26
6 [:11–18] 2–307/27*
[6:13] 2–312/169*
[6:14] 2–312/163
[6:14–17] 2–310/109*

Philippians
2 [:3] 355/37
[2:7–8] 2–301/50
[2:7–8] 2–100/43
[2:10] 99/67*
[2:21] 331/25
[3:19] 166/19
[3:20] 2–312/167

Colossians
2 [:16–17] 283/20–1
[3:5] 2–78/60
3 [:5] 100/33–4
[3:5] 166/13
[3:5] 2–264/57
[3:24–5] 170/50ᵛᵃr.
4 [:2] 197/53

1 Thessalonians
4 [:13] 2–266/8*
[4:16–17] 2–242/29*
[5:17] 2–312/173
[5:22] 2–179/30

2 Thessalonians
[2:4] 166/9

2 [:9] 213/51
[2:9–12] 210/30
[3:10] 2–163/102

1 Timothy
2 [:9–10] 2–91/20
2 [:14] 2–83/77
2 [:14] 2–127/9
3 [:1] 2–163/109
3 [:2] 2–115/99
3 [:13] 53/32
[5:1–2] 332/11
5 [:3–5] 310/9
[5:8] 317/53
[5:17] 310/16*
5 [:18] 330/19
[6:8] 71/50
[6:8] 2–137/71
6 [:9–10] 2–265/82
6 [:9–10] 71/31*
[6:9] 2–158/60
[6:9] 2–274/21
[6:10] 2–120/40
[6:10] 2–253/14
[6:10] 2–296/38
6 [:10] 58/34
6 [:10] 78/32

2 Timothy
[3:12] 2–265/69
[4:5] 2–310/110*

Titus
[1:16] 2–224/71

Hebrews
1 [:14] 95/18
4 [:12] 2–308/39
4 [:12] 2–49/89
6 [:6] 239/31
6 [:16] 232/5
[6:16] 242/24*
6 [:16] 252/2
[11:37] 94/32
13 [:4] 2–59/53
13 [:4] 2–77/25
[13:14] 53/10*
13 [:17] 337/29

James
1 [:10–11] 2–274/26
[1:12] 154/27
[2:10–11] 2–28/47
2 [:10] 2–31/37
[2:13] 2–235/34

[2;13] 279/32
[2:14–26] 202/58
[2:17] 2–20/47
[2:26] 2–239/52
3 [:5] 2–6/44
4 [:4] 2–120/32
[4:6] 200/22
5 [:1–3] 2–251/15
5 [:4] 2–16/12
5 [:12] 231/65

1 Peter
2 [:11] 2–307/19
2 [:13–22] 334/60*
[2:17] 106/55
2 [:17] 347/20
2 [:17] 354/16ᵛᵃr.
[2:8] 102/11
[2:22] 2–301/59
[3:7] 2–91/21*
[3:7] 2–59/32
[4:10] 328/33

1 John
2 [:4] 2–231/40
[3:15] 2–1/9
4 [:20] 2–32/29
4 [:20] 2–231/41

Revelation
1 [:5] 2–302/67
[1:7] 2–242/51
1 [:16] 2–33/60–1
3 [:17] 59/70
3 [:17] 75/39
13 [:10] 2–33/53–1
14 [:13] 265/68
[17:1–2;5] 2–120/39
17 [:3] 2–30/28
17 & 18 [:4; 8–10] 2–121/52
21 [:8] 2–77/32
[21:10–11] 2–320/2
[21:12–20] 2–321/32
[21:21] 2–321/34
[21:22–7] 2–322/53

INDEX OF NON-BIBLICAL
REFERENCES

List includes only names cited in the text; it does not include sources cited in the Explanatory Notes.

Ambrose
'De officiis' 2–292/25–8
'In Lucam' 7.245 2–48/69, 2–84/109–24, 2–160/11–22, 2–209/82
'De paradiso' 12.56 2–84/115–18

Ps.-Ambrose
'Commentaria in xii Ep. Pauli' 196/39

Aquinas
'Summa theologiae' 229/40, 233/28, 2–103/101, 2–211/9
'Questiones quodlibitales' 252/23, 2–151/13–17

Aristotle
'Nicomachean Ethics' 107/9, 337/14–18, 2–51/8–9, 2–173/12, 2–197/56, 2–221/41
'Metaphysics' 144/28, 171/59–60, 252/15–16
'On Interpretation' 2–217/7
'On Divination and Sleep' 175/22
'On the Heavens' 95/26, 144/28
'On Politics' 2–51/8–9, 2–197/56

Augustine
'Contra mendacium' 2–213/2, 2–215/54. 2–217/1, 2–218/15,
'De civitate Dei' 110/20, 135/15–19, 2–52/39–46, 2–83//87–90, 2–83/95, 2–117/34, 2–126/6–7, 2–127/26–9, 2–211/9, 2–247/13–44, 2–294/59–60, 2–311/133, 2–313/12–17,
'De doctrina christiana' 2–293/29–30
'De Genesi ad litteram' 127/57–62, 263/19, 270/48, 2–125/52
'De libero arbitrio' 2–36/15–16
'De sermone Domini' 199/12, 2–290/11
'Enarrationes in Psalmos' 106/50, 194/37, 328/23, 335/5, 2–3/30, 2–290/23–5
'Questiones evangelicae' 2–221/52
'Epistolae' 315/16–17, 2–162/77, 2–211/17–21

'Sermones' 134/4, 234/5, 238/15, 299/26, 2–6/65–6, 2–25/42, 2–28/47–8;52–7, 2–31/5–16, 2–67/10, 2–71/5–14, 2–244/96–120, 2–266/8, 2–287/25–6
Untraced: 218/29, 2–2/30, 2–145/23, 2–251/17

Ps. Augustine (Honorius Augustodunensis)
'Dialogus questionum lxv Orosii' 2–112/20

Autisioderensis see William of Auxerre

Balbus, *Catholicon*
2–260/44

Bartholomaeus (*On the* 1*Properties of Things,* trs. John Trevisa)
Bk. 4 var./64, 2–306/1
Bk. 12 308/3, 309/14
Bk. 16 358/52–7
Bk. 18 2–5/28–36, 2–29/64, 2–98/75, 2–123/58

Bede
'Hexaemeron' 2–81/45
'Super acta apostolorum' 93/6
'Super parabolis Salomonis' 2–63/32

Ps.-Bede (Honorius Augustodunensis)
'De gemma anime' 87/5
'De officio divino' 2–230/88, 2–230/2–231/27

Bernard, St.
'Epistolae' 346/22, 2–161/49–50
'Sermones super Cantica' 207/57, 301/3
Untraced: 2–249/38–41

Ps.-Barnard
'Meditationes' 2–103/110–11

Boniface, St. (not 'Pope' as wrongly-stated in text of *D&P*)
'Epistolae' 2–63/51–64/63

'Cato'
2–220/26–7

Chrysostom, St.
'Enarratio in Epistolam ad Hebraeos' 2–291/46
'Sermones' 135/10, 2–242/49(?), 2–244/92–6(?)

Ps.-Chrysostom
'Opus imperfectum' 2–211/24, 2–242/49(?), 2–244/92–6(?), 2–248–9/15–16
Cicero
'De officiis' 2–269/37, 2–269/39–40

Comestor, Peter ('Master of Stories')
'Historia Scholastica' 225/50, 262/79, 2–81/45, 2–106/73, 2–125/66
Untraced: 2–261/75–262/76

Docking, Thomas de
'Super Deuteronomium' 266/32, 2–162/75, 2–162/95, 2–164/137, 2–220/13

Durandus, William de Mende
'Speculum iudicale' 219/56, 237/9, 2–184/5, 2–184/27

Francis, St.
Thomas Celano's 'Second Life of St. Francis' 319/71

Gratian (Francisco Graziano)
Canon law 2–169/39–43

Gregory
'Dialogorum libri' 317/23, 2–189/80–190/97, 2–190/31–7
'Moralia in Job' 177/65, 2–4/12–5/19, 2–86/47, 2–111/46–51, 2–212/44, 2–215/58
'Libri homiliarum' 64/10–12, 132/4, 188/16, 210/33, 331/40–1, 2–19/3–6, 2–190/31–7, 2–240/78, 2–251/5
'Registri epistolarum' 283/25
'Vita' 319/37–8
From 'Speculum Christiani' or untraced: 2–227/27, 2–265/69

Gregory X
Canon law 2–206/71

Grosseteste
'Dictum 13' 2–18/67

Guido di Baysio
'Rosarium' 2–168/16, 2–169/49–50

Hales, Alexander de
'Summa' 106/38

Haymo of Faversham
'Super Hebraeos' 2–59/54

Honorius Augustodunensis see Ps.-Bede

Hostiensis (Henrico de Segusio)
'Summa aurea' 246/39, 256/21, 353/57, 354/91, 2–43/79–80, 2–44/9, 2–166/44, 2–168/24, 2–169/36–7, 2–156/89–90, 2–234–4/64–5

Josephus
'Jewish Antiquities' 225/51

Isidore of Seville
'De summo bono' ('Liber sententiarum') 2–127/26
'Synonima' 225/53
Canon law 235/6

Jerome
'Epistolae' 205/13, 2–27/23, 2–102/93, 2–161/44, 2–164/140
'Commentarium ad Ephesios' 166/13–14, 2–264/54–5
'Commentarium in Mattheum' 348/22
'Commentarium in Michaeam' 2–19/27

John of Freiburg
'Summa confessorum' 219/55, 246/26, 246/36, 246/42–4, 252/23–4, 288/35, 290/32–3, 316/40, 341/18–19, 342/69–70, 2–43/75, 2–46/66, 2–54/50, 2–56/69–70, 2–75/10–11, 2–75/19–20, 2–109/7–8, 2–111/58–9, 2–116/128, 2–151/18, 2–152/39, 2–153/62, 2–176/86, 2–184/27–8, 2–193/8–20, 2–198/6–7, 2–199/58–200/62, 2–202/56, 2–203/87, 2–205/60–206/73, 2–205.62–206/73, 2–235/35–6

Leo I
Sermon 117/91

Nicolaus de Lyra
'Postilla super totam bibliam' 2–94/99, 2–322/1

Origen
'Super Numeros, Hom. 23' 274/1

Peter Lombard ('Master of Sentence')
'Sententiae' 2–127/29, 2–214/51–2

Petrus Tarentinus (Pope Innocent V)
'Super iv Sententiarum' 2–183/85–6

Ptolomy
'Almagest' 125/6–7

Reymond of Peñaforte
'Summa de Poenitentia' 247/2, 249/70,
    267/41, 287/2, 343/8, 245/8–9, 249/
    70, 2–41/38–9;40, 2–130/16–17, 2–
    147/5–6, 2–149/75, 2–166/28–9, 2–
    172/24, 2–176/4, 2–177/55, 2–179/35,
    2–80/91–2, 2–186/23, 2–195/4;8, 2–
    202/55, 2–233/31, 2–290/30

Richard of Middleton
'Commentum super iv libros
    Sententiarum' 104/9–10, 2–221/43–4

Seneca
'De beneficiis' 339/28–9
'Epistolae morales' 2–262/94
Saying attributed to Seneca 2–9/49

Solinus
'Collectanea rerum memorabilium' 2–
    123/58, -209/69–70

William of Auxerre
'Summa aurea' 102/35

William see Durandus

INDEX OF CANON LAW CITATIONS

See Explanatory Notes for references to the Friedberg edition of the *Corpus iuris canonici*.

Abiit, C.11.q.3.c.83 2–236/4
Accepimus, X.5.34.16 246/36–7
Ad apostolicum, X.5.3.42 2–181/36–182/
44
Ad audienciam, X.5.12.12 2–41/17–18
Agnouimus, C.26.q.6.c.13 2–25/26
Apostolicus, C.16.q.1.c.67 2–290/27–8
Apostolicus, et Sacrorum C.12.q.2.c.13 &
15 352/35
Audiuimus, X.5.3.4 2–181/32–5, 2–184/
9–19
Aurum, C.12.q.2.c.70 352/35
Canonum, C.14.q.4.c.3 2–202/48–52
Cauendum, C.10.q.3.c.7 2–19/15–23
Clerici, X.3.1.15 167/25–7
Clericus, D.81.c.20 2–108/26
Clericus, C.12.q.1.c.5 2–164/150–9
Clericus qui adulat, D.46.c.3 2–3/36–7
Conquestus, X.5.19.8 2–198/10–11
Consanguineos, C.35.q.6.c.1 2–236/46–
237/48
Conspiracionum & Coniuraciorum,
C.11.q.1.c.21–2 256/15–16
Constituimus, C.3.q.5.c.9 2–74/91–2
Consulisti, X.3.41.3 352/41
Consuluit, X.5.19.10 2–199/33–9
Cum dilectus, X.1.4.8 2–172/31
Cum homines, X.3.30.71 2–167/61–2
Cum non ab homine, X.2.1.10 2–204/18–
26
Cum omnibus, D.81.c.27 2–108/25–9
Cum per bellicam, C.34.q.1 & 2.c.1 2–
74/101–2
Cum tu, X.2.20.16 2–237/16–18
Cum tu, X.5.19.5 2–205/43–6
De celebracione missarum, X.3.41.2 2–
186/23–187/29
Decernimus, D.28.c.2 2–107/23
Decimas, C.16.q.7.c.7 2–165/15
Decime, C.16.q.1.c.66 317/6, 2–16/22, 2–
166/18–28
De clerico venatore, X.5.24.1 & 2 186/1–
12
Decreuimus, C.10.q.1.c.10 2–168/15–16
De episcopis, C.23.q.8.c.1 2–38/20

De peregrinationis, X.3.34.1 249/70
De purificacione post partum, X.3.47.1 2–
116/6 (see Volens)
De regula iuris vi, Sext.5.12.5 216/77–9
De sortilegiis, X.5.21.2 159/61
Deteriores, C.6.q.1.c.15 2–132/27
Dilectissimis, C.12.q.1.c.2 320/29, 2–136/
48, 2–137/60–1, 2–158/78
Dilectus filius, X.5.3.30 2–177/36
Discipulos, De cons.D.5.c.26 287/24
Discrecionem, X.4.13.6 2–75/113
Duces inquit, C.1.q.1.c.23 2–181/21–5
Duo mala, D.13.c.1 2–137/56
Ecclesiasticarum, D.11.c.5 114/8
Ephesiis, D.43.c.4 2–24/3
Episcopi, C.26.q.5.c.12 158/27–39
Episcopus, C.26.q.5.c.12 186/24
Episcopus, C.35.q.6.c.2 245/41–2
Episcopus, D.35.c.1 167/25–7
Et hec diximus, C.16.q.7.c.9 220/64
Etsi Cristus, X.2.24.26 230/21–2
Ex merito, C.6.q.1.c.13 2–132/37–8
Ex parte, X.2.20.7 2–256/22
Extirpande, X.3.5.30 2–171/98
Filiis, C.16.q.7.c.31 352/25, 353/53
Forus, X.5.40.10 2–50/40
Fraternitatem, X.3.28.3 217/88
Gaudemus, X.4.19.8 2–75/118
Hii quoscumque, C.1.q.1.c.44 2–19/27–
20/29
Homines et Is autem, C.22.q.2.cc.3–4 155/
50
Homicidiorum, C.33.q.3.c.24 (De
pen.D.1.c.24) 2–2/35–6
Ideo permittente, C.25.q.1.c.16 prope
finem 2–117/30–1
Ieiunia, De cons.D.3.c.16 275/19
Ieiunia et Sabato, De
cons.D.3.cc.13;16 173/41, 275/19
Ieiunium, D.76.c.1 296/20–1
Ieiunium, De cons.D.3.c.14 296/20–1
Igitur, C.26.q.3 & 4.c.1 135/18, 136/12–
13, 139/85
Igitur cum, C.23.q.8.c.7 2–43/5
Ille, C.22.q.5.c.5 2–26/5

Impudicas, C.27.q.1.c.11 2–110/16–17
In aliquibus, X.3.30.32 2–172/24–5
In criminali, v. Servi, C.4.q.2 & 3.c.3 2–
    222/4–5
In dolo iurat, C.22.q.2.c.1 237/50
Inhibendum, X.3.2.1 2–108/32–7
In lectum, C.34.q.1 & 2;c.6 2–74/108
In malis promissis, C.22.q.4 &.5.c.5 225/
    53
In nomine, X.2.20.2 2–237/28–9
In nostra, X.2.20.32 2–237/39–41
In omni, X.2.20.4 2–237/28–9
In tantum, X.5.3.36 2–181/30–2. 2–184/
    9–19
Inter cetera, C.22.q.4.c.22 238/14
Interrogo vos, C.1.q.1.c.94 2–23/54
Intimauit, X.2.20.18 2–237/30–3
Ipsi apostoli, C.2.q.7.c.38 2–236/1–3
Irreligiosa, De cons.D.2.c.2 293/21–2
Ita ne, C.32.q.4.c.3 2–74/100
Iudicet, C.3.q.7.c.4 2–74/92–5
Iustum, C.23.q.2.c.1 2–51/49–50
Jacobus, X.5.3.44 2–184/9–19
Legimus, D.37.c.9 139/85–6
Licet, X.2.9.3 288/28
Licet, X.2.19.9 2–237/19–20
Meretrices, C.32.q.4.c.11 2–131/31
Miramur, C.24.q.1.c.37 2–236/57–60
Monasterium, C.16.q.7.c.33 352/45
Mouet te, C.22.q.1.c.16 244/14
Nemo, X.5.3.14 2–183/79–81
Nichil enim prodest, De cons.D.5.c.23 2–
    132/34
Nichil iniquius, C.32.q.6.c.1 2–74/97
Nauiganti, X.5.19.19 2–199/51–8
Nobis fuit, X.3.38.25 352/34, 353/52; 58
Noli, C.23.q.1.c.3 2–55/15–21
Noluit, C.33.q.5.c.16 346/20
Non cogantur, D.41.c.3 2–293/47–8
Non liceat, C.26.q.5.c.3 120/32 (text
    should read 'liceat'), 159/49–59
Non mediocriter, De cons.D.5.c.24 207/
    67
Non obserueitis, C.26.q.7.c.16 157/1
Non omnis, C.5.q.5.c.2 2–291/56–7
Non putes, C.23.q.5.c.36 328/23–31
Non sane, C.14.q.4.q.5.c.15 2–157/39–40, 2–
    232/8
Non satis, D.86.c.14 2–291/52, 2–292/
    25–8
Non semper, C.11.q.3.c.92 339/19
Non solum, C.11.q.3.c.85 2–132/37–8
Nullus, D.32.c.5 2–107/16

Nullus vmquam, C.4.q.4.c.1 2–235/40
Numquam, De cons.D.5.c.33 2–202/48–
    52
Nunc autem diuina, D.21.c.7 217/91
Nupciarum, C.27.q.1.c.41 2–110/16–17
Nuper, X.2.20.51 2–237/39
Occidit, C.23.q.8.c.14 2–38/11
Omnes dies dominicos, X.2.9.1 275/15,
    287/3, 291/29
Omnium sacerdotum, D.32.c.1 2–111/59–
    64
Pasce, D.86.c.21 2–14/5–6, 2–291/52
Pastoralis, X.3.30.28 2–166/37–8, 2–167/
    61–2
Penale, C.14.q.5.c.13 2–131/31
Perlatum ad non, De cons.D.3.c.27 82–3/
    44–5
Per tuas, X.2.19.10 2–237/20–2
Personas, X.2.20.20 2–237/33–7
Peruenit, De cons.D.3.c.12 284/31
Pervenit et Constitutus, X.3.22.2 2–199/
    45–51
Peticio, X.5.12.24 2–41/20–3
Petrus, C.23.q.8.c.16 2–49/80–1
Pie mentis, C.16.q.7.c.26 351/6, 352/38
Plerique, C.2.q.7.c.27 245/41–2
Post miserabilem, X.5.19.2 2–205/56–8
Postquam, C.13.q.2.c.13 2–193/3–8
Postulasti, X.5.12.21 2–44/13
Predicandum, C.22.q.1.c.17 255/2–3
Presbiterium, X.5.12.7 2–41/16, 2–40/
    15–41/16
Preter hoc, C.32.c.6 2–107/16
Preterea, X.3.38.4 352/48
Preterea, X.2.22.7 2–237/25–6
Priusquam, D.28.c.4 2–235/38
Proposuisti, D.82.c.2 2–111/1–4
Quacumque, C.22.q.5.c.9 235/6
Quam pio, C.1.q.2.c.2 2–180/1–8
Quamuis, C.11.q.3.c.75 2–50/36–7
Quatuor, C.11.q.3.c.78 2–248/1–2
Quatuor, C.12.q.2.c.27 2–168/13
Querelam, X.5.4.4 2–179/54–5
Quesitum, X.3.2.10 2–108/46
Questa, C.13.q.2.c.12 219/61–2, 2–193/
    3–8
Qui abstulerit, C.12.q.2.c.1 2–24/14
Quia, X.1.221.6 2–116/130–1
Quia frustra, X.5.19.14 2–204/14–17
Quia in omnibus, X.5.19.3 2–203/1–204/
    10
Quia iuxta, C.16.q.1.c.59 2–166/18–28
Qui crimen, C.6.q.1.c.6 2–74/91–2

Qui Cristi, C.12.q.2.c.1 2–24/14
Quicumque clericus, C.23.q.8.c.4 2–40/1–8
Quicumque, Sext.5.11.11 256/22
Quicumque, C.14.q.7.c.4 2–166/37–8
Quicumque, C.16.q.7.c.30 352/33
Quidam, X.3.41.2 2–186/32–3-187/29
Qui de mensa, D.37.c.11 135/32–3, 139/85–6
Quid in omnibus, C.32.q.7.c.16 2–110/22
Qui diuinaciones, C.26.q.5.c.12 159/49–59
Quiescamus, D.42.c.2 2–291/38
Quisquis, C.17.q.4.c.21 2–165/13
Quod non est licitum, X.5.41.4 250/92, 287/22
Quoniam, X.12.9.21 287/4–7
Quoniam, C.16.q.1.c.68 2–165/169–70
Quoniam enormis, X.5.4.3 2–185/48–52
Quoniam multos, C.11.q.3.c.103 2–291/52
Quoniam quicquid, C.16.q.1.c.68 317/6, 2–16/22
Quorundum, D.34.c.1 186/9
Quum decorum, X.3.1.12 293/21–2
Quum in cunctis, X.1.6.7 354/81
Quum tu, X.2.22.16 2–237/16–18
Reperiuntur, C.1.q.1.c.7 2–178/21
Res ecclesie, C.12.q.1.c.26 2–165/162
Reuertimini, C.16.q.1.c.65 2–166/18–28
Sane, C.15.q.3.c.5 2–236/51–2
Sciendum, C.26.q.4.c.2 152/3
Sciendum, C.27.q.1.c.37 2–110/16–17
Sic non sunt, C.32.q.4.c.10 2–150/94–5
Sicut De cons,.D.1.c.11 287/24
Sicut, D.47.c.8 2–165/166
Sicut, X.2.24.13 237/9
Sicut pro certo, X.5.3.39 2–184/9–19
Sicut tuis literis, X.5.3.33 2–175/73–4
Si ergo, X.4.19.8 2–75/118–19
Si gens Anglorum, D.56.c.10 2–63/51–64/63
Significasti, X.1.6.4 229/10
Significasti, X.5.12.18 2–41/19
Significasti, X.5.16.5 219/50–4
Si homicidium, C.23.q.5.c.41 2–37/40–1
Si motum De cons,.D.1.c.19 219/50–4
Si non licet, C.23.q.5.c.9 2–49/2;7, 2–51/16
Si peccauerit, C.2.q.1.c.19 245/41–2

Si presbiter, C.26.q.6.c.12 2–25/26
Si qui, X.2.20.8 2–237/43–6
Si qui a symoniacus, C.1.q.1.c.108 2–180/85–92
Si quid, D.86.c.33 2–50/36–7
Si quid, C.15.q.7.c.2 2–50/36–7
Si quis, C.26.q.5.c.9 159/49–59
Si quis, C.5.q.6.c.7 2–236/4–6
Si quis, C.22.q.5.c.4 2–236/7–237/16
Si quis amodo, D.81.c.16 2–109/51–2, 2–169/39–43
Si quis etiam extra, De cons.D.1,c,35 196/26–7
Si quis insaniens, C.15.q.1.c.12 2–40/11
Si quis irascitur, C.13.q.1.c.13 2–293/48–53
Si quis non iratus, C.15.q.1.c.13 2–40/15
Si quis ordinauerit, X.5.3.45 2–181/13–21
Si quis per capillum, C.22.q.1.c.10 239/13
Si quis presbiter, D.30.c.17 296/17
Si quis propter necessitatem, X.5.18.3 287/25
Si quis se, C.22.q.5.c.4 2–236/7–237/16
Si qui sunt, D.81.c.15 2–109/52–60, 2–169/49–50
Si quis uxorem, C.32.q.1–2.c.6 2–75/112
Si tantum, C.6.q.2.c.2 245/41–2
Si tu, C.27.q.2.c.24 2–74/99
Sufficiat, De pen.D.1.c.64 123/53–6
Sufficit, De cons.D.1.c.53 2–179/60
Sunt qui, C.17.q.4.c.3 2–110/20–1
Tam literis, X.2.20.33 2–237/41–3
Testes, C.4.q.2&3.c.2 2–235/42–6, 2–236/48–55
Tua nobis, X.3.30.26 2–169/30, 2–170/70–2
Tua nos, X.2.24.11 237/9
Tua nos, X.5.12.19 2–44/13
Tua nos, X.5.19.9 2–204/10–14
Unum, D.25.c.31 2–293/47–8
Usuarum, Sext.5.5.1 2–205/60–206/73
Venerabiles, De cons.D.3.c.28 90/20, 108/36
Veniens, X.5.3.19 2–184/9–19
Veritatis, X.2.24.14 245/8
Vestra, X.3.2.7 2–108/32–7, 2–108/46
Vident, D.86.c.10 186/1–12
Volens, X.3.47.1 2–116/6

BIBLIOGRAPHY

MANUSCRIPTS

Aberystwyth
National Library of Wales
   Peniarth 541C, MS fragment of *Dives and Pauper* (W)

Birmingham
Oscott College Library,
   Pastedown, fragment of *Dives and Pauper* (O)

Chicago, Ill.
Newberry Library,
   MS 167, fragment of *Dives and Pauper* (N)

Glasgow
University Library
   Hunterian 270, *Dives and Pauper* (G)

Lichfield
Lichfield Cathedral Chapter Library
   Lichfield 35 (olim 5), *Dives and Pauper* (L)

London
British Library
   Additional 10053, fos. 94^v-98^r, *Dives and Pauper* (fragment) (A)
   Harley 149, *Dives and Pauper* (H)
   Royal 17 C xx, *Dives and Pauper* (T)
   Royal 17 C xxi, *Dives and Pauper* (R)

New Haven, Ct.
Beinecke Library, Yale University
   MS 228, *Dives and Pauper* (Y)

Oxford
Balliol College
   MS 28, Thomas Docking (Super Deuteeronomium)
   MS 61, Peter Tarentaise (In lib. ii-iv Sententiarum}
   MS 85, William of Auxerre (*Summa aurea*)
   MS 183, Haymo (Super epistulas)
Bodleian Library
   Ashmole 750 (5), fos. 42^r-98^r, *Dives and Pauper* (fragment) (M)
   Bodley 3, 'Pore Caitif'
   Bodley 299, John of Freiburg, *Summa confessorum*
   Bodley 798, Grosseteste *Dicta*

Bodley 830, Grosseteste *Dicta*
Bodley 938, 'Pore Caitif'
Douce 295, *Dives and Pauper* (D)
Eng.th.d.36, *Dives and Pauper* (B)
Eng.th.e.1, *Dives and Pauper* (fragments) (E)
Laud misc. 374, Grosseteste *Dicta*
Lyell 29, 'Pore Caitif'

Salisbury
Salisbury Cathedral Library
  MS 174 (olim 103), *Jacob's Well*

Wiltshire, Longleat House
Library of the Marquess of Bath
  MS Longleat 4, Sermons by the author of *Dives and Pauper*

PRIMARY PRINTED SOURCES

Adam de Usk, *Chronicon Adae de Usk, A.D. 1377–1404*, ed. and tr. Edward M. Thompson (London, 1876)
——, *The Chronicle of Adam of Usk, 1377–1421*, ed. and tr. C. Given-Wilson, OMT (Oxford, 1997)
Aelred of Rievaulx, *Aelred of Rievaulx's 'De Institutione inclusarum'*, ed. John Ayto and Alexandra Barratt, EETS 287 (1940)
——, *Walter Daniel, The Life of Ailred of Rievaulx*, ed. F. M. Powicke (Oxford, 1950; repr. 1978)
Albertus Magnus, *Opera omnia*, 38 vols., ed. Augustus Borgnet (Paris, 1890–9)
Alexander of Hales, *Summa theologica*, Quaracchi (Florence, 1924–48)
An Alphabet of Tales, ed. Mary Macleod Banks, EETS os 126, 127 (1904–5)
Ambrose: Ambrose de Milan, *Traité sur l'Evangile de S. Luc*, 2 vols., ed. Gabriel Tissot (Paris, 1971–6)
——, *Expositio Evangelii Secundum Lucam*, PL 15:1607–1944
——, *Sancti Ambrosii Opera: De spiritu Sancto . . . De Incarnationis dominicae sacramento*, ed. Otto Faller, CSEL 79, Part 8 (Vienna, 1964)
——, *Saint Ambrose: Hexaemeron, Paradise, and Cain and Abel*, tr. John J. Savage (Washington, D.C., 1961; repr. 1985)
Analecta see Drèves
Ancrene Wisse, ed. J. R. R. Tolkien, EETS 249 (1972)
——, *The English Text of the Ancrene Riwle, edited from Magdalene College, Cambridge, Pepys 2498* ed. A. Zettersten, EETS 274 (1976)
——, *The English Text of the Ancrene Riwle Cotton Titus D. xviii and Bodleian MSS. Eng.th.e.70*, ed. Frances M. Mack, EETS 252 (1963)
The Anonimalle Chronicle 1333 to 1381, ed. V. H. Galbraith (Manchester, 1970)

Anselm: 'Cur Deus Homo', ed. F. S. Schmitt, in *Opera Omnia*, 6 vols., 3:38–133 (Seckan, 1938; repr. Edinburgh, 1946–61)

——, *St Anselm: Basic Writings*, tr. S. N. Deane (LaSalle, Ill., 1903; repr. 1968)

An Apology for Lollard Doctrines, ed. J. H. Todd, Camden Society, Series I, 20 (London, 1842; repr. New York, 1968)

The Apostolic Fathers, 2 vols., ed. and tr. Kirsopp Lake, LCL 24, 25 (Cambridge, Mass., 1977)

Aquinas, Thomas, *Catena Aurea in Quatuor Evangelia*, 2 vols., ed. P. A. Guarienti (Rome, 1953)

——, *Commentary on St Paul's First Letter*, tr. F. R. Larcher and M. Duffy, Aquinas Scripture Series 3 (Albany, N.Y., 1969)

——, *Quodlibetal Questions 1 and 2*, tr. Sandra Edwards, Medieval Sources in Translation 27, PIMS (Toronto, 1983)

——, *Sancti Thomas Aquinatis: Quaestiones Disputatae, cum Quolibetis, Opera Omnia, Tom. 9* (Parma, 1859; repr. New York, 1949)

——, *Summa theologiae*, 60 vols., Blackfriars edition (London/New York, 1963-)

——, *Summa Theologica*, 5 vols.+ Index, OP edn. (Rome, 1894)

——, *Summa Theologica*, 5 vols., tr. Dominican Fathers, Christian Classics (Westminster, Maryland, 1981)

Aristotle: *The Complete Works of Aristotle*, 2 vols., ed. and tr. J. Barnes (Oxford, 1984)

——, *De Caelo: On the Heavens*, tr. W. K. C. Guthrie, LCL 338 (Cambridge, Mass., 1939; repr. 1986)

——, *Parva Naturalia*, ed. W. D. Ross (Oxford, 1955)

Audelay: *The Poems of John Audelay*, ed. Ella K. Whiting, EETS, 184 (1931; repr. 1971)

Augustine, *Opera omnia*, PL 33–8; 40–43

——, *Sancti Aurelii Augustini: Sermones de Vetere Testamento*, ed. C. Lambot, CCL, XLI, pars xi, 1 (Turnhout, 1961)

——, *Sancti Aurelii Augustini: Enarrationes in Psalmos*, 3 vols., ed. D. E. Dekkers and J. Fraipont, *CCL* xxxviii, xxxix, xl (Turnhout, 1956–90)

——, *Sancti Aurelii Augustini: In Iohannis euangelium tractatus*, ed. D. R. R. Willems, *CCL* xxxvi (Turnhout, 1990)

——, *St. Augustine, The Literal Meaning of Genesis*, 2 vols., tr. J. H. Taylor, Ancient Christian Writers Series, 41, 42 (New York, 1982)

——, *Sancti Aurelii Augustini: De sermone Domini in Monte, libros duos*, ed. Almut Mutzenbecher, *CCL* xxxv, pars vii, 2 (Turnhout, 1967)

——, *The Works of Saint Augustine: Sermons*, 11 vols., tr. Edmund Hill, ed. J. E. Rotelle (New York, 1990–7)

Ayenbite see *Dan Michael of Kent*

Baker, Geoffrey le: *Galfridi le Baker de Swinbroke chronicon angliae*, ed. J. A. Giles, Caxton Society, VII (1847; repr. New York, 1967)

Balbus see *Catholicon*

Bale, John, *Scriptorum Illustrium majoris Britannicae, quam nunc Angliam et Scotam vacant Catalogus*, 2 vols. (Basel, 1557–9)

Barlaam and Iosaphat, ed. J. C. Hirsh, EETS, 290 (1986)

Bartholomaeus see Trevisa

Bede, *Opera omnia*, PL 90–5

——, *Bedae venerabilis opera, pars II, opera exegetica*, ed. J. E. Hudson, *CCL* cxix B (Turnhout, 1983)

——, *Bede: on the Tabernacle*, ed. and tr. A. G. Holden (Liverpool, 1994)

Bernard of Clairvaux, *Opera omnia*, PL 182–5

——, *Opera*, 8 vols., ed. J. Leclerq, C. H. Talbot and H. M. Rochais (Rome, 1957–77)

[Bible] *The Holy Bible, Douay Rheims version*, 1582–1609, rev. by Bp Richard Challoner 1749–52 (Baltimore, Md., 1899; repr. 1971)

——, *The Holy Bible, Containing the Old and New Testaments with the Apocryphal Books in the Earliest English Version, Made from the Latin Vulgate by John Wycliffe and his Followers*, 4 vols., ed. J. Forshall and F. Madden (Oxford, 1850; repr. New York, 1982)

——, *The New Oxford Annotated Bible, Revised Standard Version*, ed. Herbert G. May and Bruce M. Metzger (Oxford, 1973)

——, *Novum Testamentum Domini Nostri Iesu Christi Latine*, 3 vols., ed. J. Wordsworth and H. J. White (Oxford, 1898–1954)

——, *Septuaginta*, ed. A. Rahlfs (Stuttgart, 1935; repr. 1979)

——, *Biblia Latina cum glossa ordinaria: anastatical reproduction of the first printed edition, Adolph Rusch, Strassburg, 1480/1*, 4 vols., ed. M. T. Gibson and M. Froelich (Louvain, 1992)

——, *Biblia Sacra iuxta vulgatam versionem*, 2 vols., ed. Robert Weber *et al.* (Stuttgart, 1969–83)

——, *The Apocryphal New Testament, being the Apocryphal Gospels, Epistles and Apocalypses*, ed. M. R. James (Oxford, 1924; repr. and corr. 1955)

——, *The Apocrypha and Pseudepigrapha of the Old Testament in English*, 2 vols., ed. R. H. Charles (Oxford, 1913; repr. 1977)

——, *The Old Testament Pseudepigrapha*, 2 vols., ed. James H. Charlesworth (New York, 1985)

Boethius, *The Theological Tractates and Consolation of Philosophy*, ed. and tr. H. F. Stewart, E. K. Rand and S. J. Tester, LCL 74 (Cambridge, Mass., 1918; repr. 1973)

Bokenham, Osbert, *Legendys of Hooly Wummen*, ed. M. S. Serjeantson, EETS 206 (1971)

Bonaventura, *Opera Omnia*, 10 vols., ed. Collegium Sanctae Bonaventurae (Rome, 1882–1902)

Boniface: *The Letters of Saint Boniface*, tr. Ephraim Emerton (New York, 1940)

Boniface VIII: *Les registres de Boniface VIII*, ed. G. Digard *et al.*, Bibliothèque des écoles françaises d'Athènes et de Rome, Ser. 2, iv, iii, No. 5582:888–90 (Rome,1921)

The Book of the Knight of La Tour-Landry, ed. Thomas Wright, EETS os 33 (1906; repr. 1969)

A Book of London English, 1384–1425, ed. R. W. Chambers and M. Daunt (Oxford, 1931; repr. Oxford, 1967)

The Book of Vices and Virtues, ed. W. Nelson Francis, EETS 217 (1942)

Bracton, Henry de, *De Legibus et consuetudinibus Angliae, 1220–1240* ed. and tr. S. E. Thornton (Cambridge, Mass., 1968)

Brantyngham, Thomas, *The Register of Thomas de Brantyngham, Bishop of Exeter, Part I*, ed. F. C. Hingeston-Randolph (London, 1901)

Bridget: *The Liber Celestis of St Bridget of Sweden*, Vol. I, ed. Roger Ellis, EETS 291 (1987)

The Sermons of Thomas Brinton, Bishop of Rochester, 1373–1389, 2 vols., ed. M. A. Devlin, Camden Society, 3rd ser., 85, 86 (London, 1954)

Brooke, Rosalind see Francis

Brown, Carleton, ed., *Religious Lyrics of the Fourteenth Century* (Oxford, 1924; rev. edn. 1957)

——, ed. *English Lyrics of the XIIIth Century*, (Oxford, 1932; repr. 1957)

——, ed. *Religious Lyrics of the Fifteenth Century* (Oxford, 1939; repr. 1962)

Brown, E. see *Fasciculus rerum*

The Brut Parts I and II, ed. Friedrich W. D. Brie, EETS os 131, 136 (1906–1908)

Burchard of Worms *Decretum*, PL 140:537–1058

Bury, Richard de, *Philobiblon*, ed. E. C. Thomas (Oxford, 1960)

du Cange, C. D., *Glossarium mediae et infimae latinitatis*, 7 vols. (Paris, 1840–1850)

Cantor see Peter Cantor

Carpenter, Alexander, *The 'Destructorium viciorum' of Alexander Carpenter* [1428], ed. G. R. Owst (London, 1952)

Catholicon: Joannes Balbus, *Catholicon* (Mainz, 1460; facs. edn. Farnsborough, Hants., 1971)

Catholicon Anglicum, an English-Latin Wordbook (1483), ed. S. J. H. Herrtage, EETS os 75 (1881; repr. 1975)

Cato: *Disticha Catonis*, ed. Marcus Boas (Amsterdam, 1952)

The Chastising of God's Children, ed. J. Bazire and E. Colledge (Oxford, 1957)

Chaucer, Geoffrey, *The Riverside Chaucer*, ed. Larry D. Benson (3rd. edn., Boston, Mass., 1987)

The Chester Mystery Cycle, 2 vols., ed. R. M. Lumiansky and David Mills, EETS ss 3 and 9 (1974–86)

Chevalier, Ulysse, *Repertorium Hymnologicum*, 6 vols. (Louvain, 1892–1920)

Chichele, Henry: *The Register of Henry Chichele*, 4 Vols., ed. E. F. Jacob (Oxford, 1943–7)

de Chobham, Thomas, *Summa de Arte Praedicandi*, ed. F. Morenzoni, CCCM, lxxxii (Turnhout, 1988)

——, *Thomas de Chobham, Summa confessorum*, Analecta mediaevalia Namurcensia 25, ed. F. Broomfield (Louvain; Paris, 1968)

——, *Thomas de Chobham, sermones*, ed. F. Morenzoni, CCCM, lxxxii A (Turnhout, 1993)

Chrysostom, John: Ioannes Chrysostomus, *Opera omnia*, PG 57, 58, 63 (for homilies on Matthew and Hebrews)

——, *The Homilies of St John Chrysostom*, 2 vols., tr. G. T. Stupart (Oxford, 1848–52)

——, *Homilies on the Gospel of Saint Matthew*, ed. Philip Schaff, NAPF 10 (repr. Grand Rapids, Mich., 1978).

Ps.-Chrysostom, *Opus Imperfectum in Matthaeum*, PG 56:611–946

——, *Opus Imperfectum in Matthaeum*, Vol. I, ed. J. van Banning, CCL lxxxvii B, (Turnhout, 1988)

Clement of Alexandria, 'The Rich Man's Salvation', in *Clement of Alexandria*, ed. and tr. G. W. Butterworth, LCL 92 (Boston, Mass., 1919; repr. 1982), 265–367

Comestor, Peter, *Historia Scholastica*, PL 198:1054–1722 (repr. Turnhout, 1966)

Concilia Magnae Britanniae et Hiberniae, 4 vols., ed. D. Wilkins (London, 1737)

Conciliorum Oecumenicorum Decreta, ed. J. Albarigo *et al.* (Bologna, 1972)

Corpus iuris canonici, 2 vols., ed. Æmilius Friedberg (Leipzig, 1879; repr. 1959)

Corpus iuris civilis, 3 vols., ed. P. Krueger, T. Mommsen, R. Schoell, G. Kroll (Berlin, 1862, [1872]-1895)

Councils and Ecclesiastical Documents, 3 vols., ed. W. Haddon and W. Stubbs (London, 1871)

Councils and Synods, with other documents relating to the English Church, II, AD 1205–1313, 2 vols., ed. F. M. Powicke and C. R. Cheney (Oxford, 1964)

Courtesy Book see *Fifteenth Century*

Cursor Mundi, ed. R. Morris, EETS os 57, 59, 62, 66, 68, 69, 99, 101, 1877; repr. 1962–4)

Dan Michel's Ayenbite of Inwyt, 2 vols., ed. Pamela Gradon, EETS 23; 278 (1965; 1979)

De Lyra see Lyra, Nicolaus de

De Vitry see Vitry, Jacques de

Dickinson, F. H., ed., *Missale ad usum Insignis et Praeclare Ecclesiae Sarum*, (Burntisland, 1861–3)

Dictionary of Medieval Latin from British Sources, Fascicules I-V, ed. R. E. Latham *et al.* (Oxford, 1975-)

Dives and Pauper (text), 2 vols., ed. P. H. Barnum, EETS 275, 280 (1976–80)

Drèves, G. M. and C. Blume, *Analecta hymnica medii aevi*, 55 vols. (Leipzig, 1886–1922)

Durandus, William de Mende, *Rationale Divinorum Officiorum*, 3 vols., ed. A. Davril and T. M. Thibodeau, *CCCM* cxl, cxlA, cxlB (Turnhout, 1995–2000)

Early English Homilies, ed. Rubie D.-N. Warner, EETS os 152 (1917; repr. 1971)

Edmund of Abingdon, *Speculum Religiosorum* and *Speculum Ecclesiae*, ed. Helen P. Forshaw, Auctores Britannici Medii Aevi 3, The British Academy (Oxford, 1973)

Elucidarium see Honorius

English Lyrics see C. Brown

English Works see Wyclif

English Wycliffite Sermons see Hudson, Anne

Eulogium Historiarum, 3 vols., ed. Frank S. Haydon, RS 3 (London, 1858–63)

Fasciculi zizaniorum Magistri Johannis Wyclif, cum tritico, ed. W. W. Shirley, RS 5 (London, 1858)

Fasciculus morum, a Fourteenth-Century Preacher's Handbook, ed. and tr. Siegfried Wenzel (Penn State, Pa., 1989)

Fasciculus rerum, 2 vols., ed. Edward Brown (London, 1690; repr. Tucson, Ariz., 1967)

Festial see Mirk

A Fifteenth-Century Courtesy Book and Two Fifteenth-Century Franciscan Rules, ed. R. W. Chambers and W. W. Seton, EETS os 148 (1914; repr. 1962)

Fifteenth Century Verse and Prose, ed. A. W. Pollard (London, 1902)

Fifty Earliest English Wills, ed. Frederick J. Furnivall, EETS os 78 (1882; repr. 1964)

Francis: Rosalind B. Brooke, ed. and tr., *The Writings of Leo, Rufino and Angelo, Companions of St Francis*, Oxford Medieval Texts (Oxford, 1970; repr. 1990)

——, *St Francis of Assisi, Writings and Early Biographies*, ed. Marion A. Habig *et al.* (3rd edn., Chicago, 1973)

Frere, W. H., *The Use of Sarum*, 2 vols. (Cambridge, 1898–1901)

Friedberg see *Corpus iuris canonici*

Sir Gawain and the Green Knight, ed. J. R. R. Tolkien and E. V. Gordon, rev. N. Davis (Oxford, 1967)

Gesta Romanorum, ed. S. J. H. Herrtage, EETS es 33 (1879; repr. 1962)

Gerald of Wales, Gemma Ecclesiastica, in Opera Geraldi Cambrensis, ed. J. S. Brewer et al., RS 21, Vols. 2 and 5 (London, 1861–91)

Getz, F. M., ed. Healing and Society in Medieval England, a Middle English Translation of the Pharmaceutical Writings of Gilbertus Anglicus (Madison, Wisconsin, 1991)

Glanvill: The Treatise on the Laws and Customs of the Realm of England Commonly Called Glanvill, ed. and tr. G. D. G. Hall, Oxford Medieval Texts (Oxford, 1993)

A Glastonbury Miscellany of the Fifteenth Century, a Descriptive Index of Trinity College Cambridge MS. O.9.38, Oxford English Monographs, ed. A. G. Rigg (Oxford, 1968)

Golden Legend: The Golden Legend of Jacobus de Voragine, 2 vols., ed. and tr. William G. Ryan (Princeton, N. J., 1993)

——: Supplementary Lives in Some Manuscripts of the Gilte Legende, ed. Richard Hamer and Vida Russell, EETS 315 (2000)

——: Jacobi a Voragine Legenda aurea, (Strassbourg, 1487), 3rd edn. Th. Graesse (Breslau, 1890)

The Gospel of Nicodemus see Nicodemus

Gower, John, The English Works of John Gower, 2 vols., ed. G. C. Macaulay, EETS os 81, 82 (1900–1; repr. 1969)

——, The Complete Works of John Gower, the Latin Works, ed. G. C. Macaulay (Oxford, 1902)

——, The Major Latin Works of John Gower, tr. E. W. Stockton (Seattle, Washington, 1962)

——, Mirour de l'Omme, tr. W. B. Wilson, rev. by N. W. Van Baak (E. Lansing, Mich, 1992)

Graesse see Legenda aurea

Gratian, the Treatise on Laws, Decretum DD. 1–20, tr. Augustine Thompson, OP, and James Gordley, Studies in Medieval and Early Modern Canon Law (Washington, D.C., 1993)

The Greek New Testament, ed. K. Aland, M. Black, C. M. Martini, B. M. Metzger, A. Wikren (3rd edn., Stuttgart, 1975)

Gregory, Opera S. Gregorii Magni, PL 75–7

——, S. Gregorii Magni, Moralia in Job, libri i–xxxv, 3 vols., ed. M. Adriaen, CCL cxliii, cxliiiA, cxliiiB (Turnhout, 1979–85)

Grosseteste, Robert, De decem mandatis, ed. R. C. Dales and E. B. King, The British Academy (Oxford, 1987)

——, Hexaemeron, ed. Richard C. Dales and S. Green, The British Academy (Oxford, 1982)

——, *Roberti Grosseteste Episcopi Quondam Lincolniensis Epistolae*, ed. Henry R. Luard, RS (London, 1861)

——, *Die Philosophischen Werke des Robert Grosseteste*, ed. Ludwig Baur (Münster, 1912; repr. Austin, Texas, 1993)

——, *The Writings of Robert Grosseteste*, S. Harrison Thomson (Cambridge, 1940)

Guy de Chauliac: *The Cyrurgie of Guy de Chauliac*, Vol. I, text, ed. Margaret S. Ogden, EETS 265 (1971)

Habig see Francis

Hales, Alexander de, *Summa Theologica*, 4 vols., ed. P. B. Klumper *et al.*, Quaracchi (Florence, 1924–1948)

Hali Meiðhad, ed. B. Millett, EETS 284 (1992)

Handbooks of Penance see McNeill

Handlyng Synne see Robert of Brunne

Haren, Michael J. see *Memoriale*

Herbert *Catalogue* see H. L. D. Ward.

Herebert, William, *The Works of William Herebert, OFM*, ed. Stephen R. Reimer, PIMS (Toronto, 1987)

Higdon, Ranulph, *Polychronicon*, 9 vols., ed. C. Babington and J. R. Lumby, RS (London, 1865–86)

Hilton, Walter, *The Scale of Perfection*, ed. E. Underhill (London, 1923)

——, *Walter Hilton's 'Mixed Life'*, ed. from Lambeth Palace MS 472, ed. S. J. Ogilvie-Thomson, SSEL (Stuttgart, 1986)

Hoccleve, Thomas, *Hoccleve's Works, the Minor Poems*, ed. F. J. Furnivall and I. Gollancz, rev. by J. Mitchell and A. I. Doyle, EETS es 61,73 (1892; repr. 1970)

——, *Regement of Princes*, ed. F. J. Furnivall, EETS es 72 (1897; repr. 1997)

——, *Selections from Hoccleve*, ed. M. C. Seymour (Oxford, 1981)

——, *Thomas Hoccleve's Complaint and Dialogue*, ed. J. A. Burrow, EETS 313 (1999)

Holcot, Robert, *Seeing the Future Clearly: Questions of Future Contingents*, ed. Paul A. Streveler and Katherine H. Tachau, Studies and Texts 119, PIMS (Toronto, 1995)

——, *Exploring the Boundaries of Reason*, ed. H. G. Gelber, Studies and Texts 62, PIMS (Toronto, 1983)

Horace, *Satires, Epistles and Ars Poetica*, ed. H. R. Fairclough, LCL 194 (1926; repr. 1978)

Honorius of Autun (Augustodunensis), *Elucidarium*, PL 172:1109–1176

Horstman, Carl, ed., *Yorkshire Writers, Richard Rolle of Hampole and his Followers*, 2 vols. (London, 1895)

Hudson, Anne, ed., *Selections from English Wycliffite Writings* (Cambridge, 1978)

———, and Pamela Gradon, eds., *English Wycliffite Sermons*, 5 vols., (Oxford, 1983–1990)

———, ed., *Two Wycliffite Texts*, EETS 301 (Oxford, 1993)

———, ed., *The Works of a Lollard Preacher*: The Sermon *Omnis plantacio*; the Tract *Fundamentum aliud nemo potest ponere* and the Tract *De oblacione iugis sacrificii*, EETS 317 (2001)

Hugh of St Victor, *De sacramentis*, PL 176

Hugh of Saint Victor on the Sacraments of the Christian Faith [*De scramentis*], tr. R. J. Deferrari (Cambridge, Mass., 1951)

Hunt, Simon, 'An Edition of Tracts in Favour of Scriptural Translation and of Some Texts connected with Lollard Vernacular Biblical Scholarship', 2 vols., D. Phil. thesis (Oxford, 1994)

Innocent III, *De Miseria Condicionis Humane*, ed. Robert E. Lewis, The Chaucer Library (Athens, Ga., 1978)

Instructions for Parish Priests see Mirk, John

Isidore of Seville, *Isidori Hispalensis episcopi etymologiarum sive originum*, 2 vols., ed. W. M. Lindsay (Oxford, 1911; repr. 1975)

Jack Upland, Friar Daw's Reply and Upland's Rejoinder, ed. P. L. Heyworth (Oxford, 1968)

Jacob's Well, Part I, ed. A. Brandeis, EETS, os 115 (1900)

Jacobus de Voragine see Voragine

Jerome, *Opera omnia*, PL 22–30

———, *S. Hieronymi presbyteri opera, pars I, opera exegetica*, ed. P. Antin, CCL lxxii (Turnhout, 1959)

———, *Select Letters of St Jerome*, ed. and tr. F. A. Wright, LCL 262 (Cambridge, Mass., 1963)

John of Damascus, *De fide orthodoxa*, ed. E. M. Buytaert, The Franciscan Institute (St Bonaventure, New York, 1955)

John of Salisbury, *Frivolities of Courtiers and Footprints of Philosophers*, ed. and tr. Joseph B. Pike (Minneapolis, Minn., 1938)

———, *Joannis Saresberiensis, Policraticus*, I–IV, ed. K. S. B. Keats-Rohan, CCCM cxviii (Turnhout, 1993)

John of Wales, *Communiloquium* (originally printed by Jordanus de Quedlinburg, Strasburg, 1489; facs. S. R. Publishers, Yorkshire,1964)

Josephus, *The Latin Josephus I, Introduction and Text, The Antiquities: Bks. I–V*, ed. Franz Blatt (Copenhagen, 1958)

———, *Jewish Antiquities*, 9 vols., tr. H. St.J. Thackeray, R. Marcus, A. Wikgren *et al.*, LCL, vols. 1–7; 242, 281, 365 (1930–1991)

Justinian, *Institutes of Justinian*, ed. Thomas C. Sandars (7th edn., London, 1941)

The Life of St. Katherine, ed. Eugen Einenkel, EETS os 80 (1884)

The Book of Margery Kempe. Vol. I, Text, ed. Sanford B. Meech and H. E. Allen, EETS 212 (1940)

Knaresborough, Robert, *The Metrical Life of St. Robert of Knaresborough*, ed. J. Bazire, EETS 228 (Oxford, 1953; repr. 1968)

Knighton, Henry, *Chronicon*, 2 vols., ed. J. R. Lumby, RS 92 (London, 1889–95)

Knighton's Chronicle 1337–1296, ed. & tr. G. H. Martin, Oxford Medieval Texts (Oxford, 1995)

Langland, William, *The Vision of William Concerning Piers the Plowman, in Three Parallel Texts*, 2 vols., ed. W. W. Skeat (Oxford, 1886)

——, *Piers Plowman (the A version)*, 2 vols., ed. George Kane (London, 1960)

——, *Piers Plowman (the B version)*, ed. George Kane and E. T. Donaldson (London, 1975)

——, *Piers Plowman by William Langland, an edition of the C-Text*, ed. Derek Pearsall, York Medieval Texts, 2nd Series (Berkeley, CA, 1979)

The Lanterne of Liȝt, ed. L. M. Swinburn, EETS os 151 (1917; repr. N.Y. 1971)

A Selection of Latin Stories from manuscripts of the thirteenth and fourteenth centuries, ed. Thomas Wright, Percy Society (London, 1842)

The Lay Folks Catechism, ed. T. F. Simmons and H. E. Nolloth, EETS os 118 (1901; repr. 1997)

The Lay Folks Mass Book, ed. Thomas F. Simmons, EETS os 71 (1879; repr. 1968)

Legenda aurea see *Golden Legend*

Legg, J. Wickham, ed., *The Sarum Missal, edited from the Early Manuscripts* (Oxford, 1969)

Lollard Sermons, ed. Gloria Cigman, EETS 294 (1989)

Lombard, Peter, *Sententiae in IV Libris Distinctae*, 2 vols., ed. Collegii S. Bonaventura, Grottaferrata (Rome, 1971)

Love, Nicholas, *The Mirror of the Blessed Life of Jesus Christ*, ed. Michael G. Sargent (New York, 1993)

Lydgate, John, *The Pilgrimage of the Life of Man, Englisht by John Lydgate A.D. 1426, from the French of Guillaume de Deguileville A.D. 1330, 1355*, ed. F. J. Furnivall and K. B. Locock, EETS es 77, 83, 92 (1899–1904)

Lyndwood, William, *Provinciale, seu constitutiones Angliae, [1470–80] (Oxford, 1679)*

Lyra, Nicolaus de, *Postilla super totam bibliam*, 4 vols. (Strassburg, 1492; facs. repr. Frankfurt/Main, 1972)

The Macro Plays, ed. Mark Eccles, EETS 262 (1969)

Macrobius: Commentary on the Dream of Scipio, tr. and notes by William Stahl (New York, 1952; repr. 1966)

Maidstone, Richard, *Protectorium paupertatis*, ed. Arnold Williams, *Carmelus* 5 (1958), 132–80

Mandeville's Travels, ed. M. C. Seymour (Oxford, 1967)

Mansi: *Sanctorum Conciliorum amplissima collectio*, 31 vols., ed. J. D. Mansi (Florence-Venice, 1759–88)

Map, Walter, *De nugis curialum*, ed. M. R. James; revd. edn. R. A. B. Mynors and C. N. L. Brooke, Oxford Medieval Texts (Oxford, 1983)

Matthew, F. D., ed., 'The Trial of Richard Wyche' *EHR* 5 (1890), 530–44

McNeill, John T. and H. M. Gamer, ed. and tr., *Medieval Handbooks of Penance*, Records of Civilization, Sources and Studies XXIX (New York, 1938; repr. 1965)

Meditations on the Life of Christ, ed. and tr. Isa Ragusa and R. B. Green (Princeton, 1961)

Memoriale: 'A Study of the *Memoriale Presbiterorum* a Fourteenth-Century Confessional Manual for Parish Priests', ed. Michael Haren, D.Phil thesis (Oxford, 1975)

Middle English Sermons, ed. W. O. Ross, EETS 209 (1960)

Mirk, John, *Mirk's Festial: a Collection of Homilies by Johannes Mirkus*, Vol. I, ed. T. Erbe, EETS es 96 (1905)

——, *Instructions for Parish Priests*, ed. Edward Peacock, EETS os 31 (1902)

The Mirour of Man's Saluacioun, A Middle English Translation of 'Speculum humanae salvationis', ed. A. Henry (Aldershot, 1986)

Mommsen, Theodore, *C.Iulii Solini, Collectanea rerum memorabilium* (2nd edn. Berlin, 1895)

Monasticon Anglicanum, 3 vols., ed. R. Dodsworth and G. Dugdale (London, 1655–1673)

Mone, J. F., ed., *Lateinische Hymnen des Mittelalters*, 3 vols. (Freiburg, 1853–5)

Monmouth, Thomas of, *The Life and Miracles of St William of Norwich by Thomas of Monmouth*, ed. Augustus Jessop and M. R. James (Cambridge, 1896)

Monumenta Franciscana, I. Thomas de Eccleston de adventu fratrum minorum in Angliam, II. Adae de Marisco Epistolae, III. Registrum fratrum minorum Londoniae, ed. J. S. Brewer, RS (London, 1858)

Mum and the Sothsegger, ed. M. Day and R. Steele, EETS 199 (1936)

The Myroure of Oure Ladye, ed. J. H. Blunt, EETS es 19 (1873)

The N-Town Play, 2 vols., ed. Stephen Spector, EETS ss 11,12 (1991)

Neckham, Alexander, *De Natura Rerum*, ed. T. Wright, RS (London, 1863)

Nicholas of Lynn, *The Kalendarium*, ed. Sigmund Eisner, The Chaucer Library (Athens, Ga., 1980)

Nicodemus: The Middle English Harrowing of Hell and Gospel of Nicodemus, ed. William H. Hulme, EETS es 100 (1907; repr. 1978)

——: *The Gospel of Nicodemus: Gesta Salvatoris*, ed. H. C. Kim, Toronto Medieval Texts (Toronto, 1973)

Nicolaus see Lyra

Norton, Thomas, *Thomas Norton's Ordinal of Alchemy*, ed. John Reidy, EETS 272 (1975)

Norwich heresy trials see Tanner, Norman

Odo of Cheriton, *The Fables of Odo of Cheriton*, tr. J. C. Jacobs (Syracuse, New York, 1985)

An Old English Miscellany containing a Bestiary, Kentish Sermons, Proverbs of Alfred, Religious Poems of the thirteenth century, ed. Richard Morris, EETS os 49 (1872; repr. 1979)

The Orchard of Syon, I, ed. P. Hodgson and G. M. Liegey, EETS, 250 (1966)

Oresme, Nicholas of, *Nicole Oresme and the Marvels of Nature: a Study of his 'De Causis Mirabilium' with critical edition*, Bert Hansen, PIMS (Toronto, 1985)

Origen: Contra Celsum, ed. and tr. Henry Chadwick (Cambridge, 1953; repr. 1965)

——, *First Principles*, tr. G. W. Butterworth (Gloucester, Mass., 1973)

——, *Opera*, PG 12

Saint Patrick's Purgatory, ed. Robert Easting, EETS 298 (1991)

The Pauline Epistles, ed. M. J. Powell, EETS es 116 (1916; repr. 2002)

Pecham, John, *Fratris Johannis Pecham, tractatus tres de Paupertate*, ed. C. L. Kingsford, A. G. Little and F. Tocco (Aberdeen, 1910; repr. Farnsboro Hants., 1966)

Pecock, Reginald, *Pecock's Donet*, ed. E. V. Hitchcock, EETS os 156 (1921)

——, *Pecock's The Folewer to the Donet*, ed. E. V. Hitchcock, EETS 164 (1924)

——, *The Reule of Crysten Religioun*, ed. W. C. Greet, EETS 171 (1927)

——, *The Repressor of Over-much Blaming of the Clergy*, 2 vols., ed. C. Babington, RS (London, 1860)

Penance see McNeill

Peter of Blois, 'Contra perfidiam judaeorum', *PL* 207:825–870

Peter Cantor, *Verbum abbreviatum*, PL 205:21–370

Peter Idley's Instructions, ed. C. D'Evelyn (London, 1935)

Peter of Riga, *Aurora, Petri Rigae Biblia Versificata, a Verse Commentary on the Bible*, 2 vols, ed. P. E. Beichner (Notre Dame, Ind., 1965)

Pierce the Ploughman's Creed, ed. W. W. Skeat, EETS os 30 (1867; repr. 1969)

The Pilgrimage of the Life of Man, translated by John Lydgate, ed. F. J. Furnivall and K. B. Locock, EETS 77, 83, 92 (1899–1904; repr. 1975)

Pisan, Christine of, *The Epistle of Othea from the French text of Christine de Pisan by Stephen Scrope*, ed. Curt F. Bühler, EETS 264 (1970)

——, *The Book of Fayttes of Armes and of Chyualrye*, tr. William Caxton, ed. A. T. P. Byles, EETS 189 (1932; repr. 1988)

Political Poems and Songs relating to English History, 2 vols., ed. Thomas Wright, Rerum Britannicarum Medii Ævi Scriptores (London, 1861)

Political, Religious and Love Poems, ed. Frederick J. Furnivall, EETS os 15 (1866; repr. 1965)

Pollard, A. W., ed., *Fifteenth Century Prose and Verse* (London, 1903)

——, ed., *Records of the English Bible: The Documents Relating to the Translation and Publication of the Bible in English, 1525–1611* (London, 1911)

Powicke & Cheney see *Councils & Synods*

Praepositinus of Cremona, *Praepositani Tractatus de Officiis*, ed. J. A. Corbett (Notre Dame, 1969)

Pricke of Conscience, ed. Richard Morris (Berlin, 1863)

Promptorium Parvulorum, ed. A. L. Mayhew, EETS es 102 (1908; repr. 1973)

Properties see Trevisa

Raymond of Peñaforte, *Summa de poenitentia et matrimonio, cum glossis Ioannis de Friburgo* (Rome, 1603; facs. Farnsborough, Hants., 1967)

Religious Pieces in Prose and Verse, edited from Robert Thornton's MS, ed. George G. Perry, EETS os 26 (1905; repr. 1969)

Reliquae antiquae, scraps of Ancient Manuscripts Illustrating chiefly Early English Literature and the English Language, ed. Thomas Wright and J. O. Halliwell (London, 1841)

Richard II: *Historia Vita Ricardi Secundi*, ed. G. B. Stow, Jr., Foundation Series 21 (Philadelphia, PA, 1977)

Richard of Middleton, *Super iv libros Sententiarum Petri Lombardi, quaestiones*, 4 vols., (Brixiae, 1591; *Manuscripta*, film, List No. 27, no. 24, St Louis, Mo.)

Robbins, Rossell H., ed., *Historical Poems of the XIVth and XVth Centuries* (New York, 1959)

——, *Secular Lyrics of the XIVth & XVth Centuries* (New York, 1952; repr. 1961)

Robert of Brunne, *Handlyng Synne*, ed. F. J. Furnivall, EETS os 119, 123 (1901–3)

——, *Robert Mannyng of Brunne, Handlyng Synne*, ed. Idelle Sullens, MRTS 14 (Binghamton, N.Y., 1983)

Robert of Flamborough, *Liber poenitentialis*, ed. J. J. F. Firth (Toronto, 1971)

Rolle, Richard, *The Fire of Love*, tr. by Richard Misyn, ed. Ralph Harvey, EETS os 106 (1896; repr. 1979)

——, *Richard Rolle: Prose and Verse*, ed. S. J. Ogilvie-Thomson, EETS, 293 (1988)

Rosarium: The Middle English Translation of the 'Rosarium Theologie', ed. Christina von Nolcken, Middle English Texts 10 (Heidelberg, 1979)

Ross see *Middle English Sermons*

The Sarum Missal see Legg

Three Prose Versions of the Secreta Secretorum, ed. R. Steele and T. Henderson, EETS es 74 (1898)

Seneca, *Moral Essays*, 3 vols., ed. John W. Basore, LCL 214 254. 310 (1935; repr. 1989)

——, *Epistulae morales*, 3 vols., ed. R. M. Gummere, LCL 75–7 (1925; 1989)

Solinus see Mommsen

The South English Legendary, 2 vols., ed. Charlotte D'Evelyn and Anna J. Mill, EETS 235, 236 (1956)

Speculum Christiani, ed. G. Holmstedt, EETS 182 (1933)

Speculum Laicorum, ed. J. P. Welter (Paris, 1914)

Speculum religiorum see Edmund of Abingdon

Speculum Sacerdotale, ed. Edward H. Weatherly, EETS 200 (1931; repr. 1971)

The Stacions of Rome and the Pilgrims Sea-Voyage, ed. Frederick J. Furnivall, EETS os 25 (1867)

Stafford: *The Register of Edmund Stafford (A.D. 1305–1419) an Index and Abstract of its Contents*, ed. F. C. Hingeston-Randolph (London, 1886)

A Stanzaic Life of Christ, compiled from Higdon's Polychronicon and the Legenda Aurea, ed. Frances A. Foster, EETS 166 (1926; repr. 1971)

Tanner, Norman P., ed., *Heresy Trials in the Diocese of Norwich, 1428–31*, Camden, 4th Ser., 20 (London, 1977)

Tertullian: De anima, ed. J. H. Waszink (Amsterdam, 1947)

The Towneley Plays, 2 vols., ed. Martin Stevens and A. C. Cawley, EETS ss 13, 14 (1994)

Trevisa, John, *Dialogus inter Militem et Clericum, Richard FitzRalph's Sermon: 'Defensio Curatorum' and Methodius: þe Begynnyng of þe World and þe Ende of Worldes*, ed. A. J. Perry, EETS 167 (1925)

——, *On the Properties of Things: John Trevisa's translation of Bartholomaeus Anglicus 'De Proprietibus Rerum' A Critical Text*, 3 Vols., ed. M. C. Seymour *et al.* (Oxford, 1975–88)

——, *The Governance of Kings and Princes: John Trevisa's Middle English Translation of the De Regimine Principium of Aegidius Romanus*, ed. David C. Fowler, Charles F. Briggs and Paul G. Remley (New York and London, 1997)

Usk see Adam of Usk

Vernon manuscript: *The Minor Poems of the Vernon MS*. Part I, ed. Carl Horstmann, EETS os 98 (1892; repr.1975)

The Book of Vices and Virtues, ed. W. Nelson Francis, EETS, 217 (1942; repr. 1968)

Vitae patrum, PL 73, 74

Vitry, Jacques de, *The Exempla or Illustrative Stories from the Sermones vulgares of Jacques de Vitry*, ed. Thomas Crane, The Folklorre Society (London, 1890)

Von Nolcken see *Rosarium*

Voragine, Jacobus a, *Legenda Aurea*, ed. Th. Graesse (repr. from 1845 edn., Breslau, 1890)

Richard of Wallingford, 2 vols. ed. J. A. North (Oxford, 1976)

Walsingham, Thomas, *Ypodigma Neustriae a Thoma Walsingham*, ed. Henry T. Riley, RS (London, 1876)

Walther, Hans, *Proverbia, sententiaeque latinitatis medii aeve*, 9 vols. (Göttingen, 1963–9)

Ward, H. L. D. and J. A. Herbert, *Catalogue of Romances in the Department of Manuscripts in the British Museum*, 3 vols. (London, 1883–1910)

The Westminster Chronicle 1381–1394, ed. L. C. Hector and B. F. Harvey (Oxford, 1982)

Westminster Missal: Missale . . . Ecclesie Westmonasteriensis, ed. J. Wickham Legg, The Henry Bradshaw Society (London, 1891; repr. 1999)

Whiting, B. J. and H. W., *Proverbs, Sentences, and Proverbial Phrases from English Writings Mainly before 1500* (Cambridge, Mass., 1968)

Wilkins, D. see *Concilia*

William of Auxerre, *Guilelmus Altissiodorensis Summa Aurea in Quatro Libris Sententiarum* (facs. Frankfurt/Main, 1964)

William de Conches, *De philosophia mundi, libri quatuor*, PL 172:39–102

William of Norwich see Thomas of Monmouth

William Worcestre, Itineraries, ed. John H. Harvey (Oxford, 1969)

Willmott, Adrian, 'An Edition of Selected Sermons from MS. Longleat 4', (Ph.D thesis, Bristol, 1994)

Wirtjes, Hanneke, *The Middle English Physiologus*, EETS 299 (1991)

Wordsworth, J. see *Novum Testamenum*

Wright, Thomas, *Political Poems and Songs Relating to English History, Composed during the Period from the Accession of Edw. III to that of Ric. III*, 2 vols. (London, 1861)

Wyclif, John, *Tractatus de Mandatis Divinis*, ed. Johann Loserth and F. D. Matthew, WS (London, 1922)

——, *Tractatus de civili dominio*, 4 vols., Vol. I ed. Reginald L. Poole, WS (London, 1885); Vol. II ed. Iohann Loserth (London, 1900); Vol. III ed. Iohann Loserth (London, 1903); Vol. IV ed. Iohann Loserth (London, 1904)

——, *Tractatus de potestate papae*, ed. J. Loserth, WS (London, 1907)

——, *Sermones*, 4 vols., ed. J. Loserth, WS (London, 1887–90)

——, *Polemical Works*, 2 vols., ed. R. Buddensieg, WS (London, 1882–3)

——, *Trialogus cum supplemento Trialogi*, ed. G. Lechler (Oxford, 1869)

——, *Tractatus de civili dominio*, 4 vols., vol. 1 ed. R. L. Poole, vols. 3–4 ed. J. Loserth (London, 1885–1904)

——, *Opus Evangelicum siue De antichristo*, 4 vols. in 2, ed. Johann Loserth (London, 1895–6)

——, *De veritate sacrae scripturae*, 3 vols., ed. Rudolph Buddensieg (London, 1907)

The English Works of Wyclif, hitherto unprinted, ed. F. D. Matthew, EETS os 74 (1880; rev. 1902)
Select English Works of John Wyclif, 3 vols., ed. Thomas Arnold (Oxford, 1869–71)
Yorkshire Writers see Horstman, Carl

SECONDARY SOURCES FOR WHICH FULL REFERENCE IS NOT GIVEN IN EXPLANATORY NOTES

Alford, John, 'Literature and Law in Medieval England', *PMLA*, 92, no. 5 (1977), 941–51
——, *Piers Plowman: a Glossary of Legal Diction* (Cambridge, 1988)
——, *Piers Plowman, a Guide to the Quotations*, MRTS 77 (Binghamton, New York, 1992)
Allmand, Christopher, *Henry V* (Berkeley, CA, 1994)
The Anchor Bible Dictionary, 6 vols., ed. David N. Freedman, *et al.* (New York, 1992)
Aquinas, Thomas: *Thomas Aquinas 1274–1974, Commemorative Studies*, 2 vols., ed. A. A. Maurer, *et al.*, PIMS (Toronto, 1974)
Aston, Margaret, *Thomas Arundel: a Study of Church Life in the Reign of Richard II* (Oxford, 1967)
——, 'Lollards and Sedition' (No. 17, April 1960), repr. in R. H. Hilton, ed. *Peasants, Knights and Heretics*, Past and Present Publications 3 (Cambridge, 1976), 273–318
——, *Lollards and Reformers: Images and Literacy in Late Medieval Religion* (London, 1984)
——, 'Gold and Images', SCH 24, ed. W. J. Shiels and D. Wood (Oxford, 1987), 189–207
——, *England's Iconoclasts*, Vol. I: *Laws Against Images* (Oxford, 1988)
——, ed. and Colin Richmond, ed., *Lollardy and the Gentry in the Later Middle Ages* (New York, 1997)
Atkinson, C. W., *Mystic and Pilgrim: the Book and the World of Margery Kempe* (Ithaca, New York, 1983)
d'Avray, D. L., *The Preaching of the Friars* (Oxford, 1985)
——, 'Philosophy in Preaching: the Case of a Franciscan' in *Literature and Religion in the Later Middle Ages, Philological Studies in Honor of Siegfried Wenzel*, ed. R. G. Newhauser and J. A. Alford, MRTS 118 (Binghamton, New York, 1995), 263—73
Baldwin, James F., *The King's Council in England during the Middle Ages* (Gloucester, Mass., 1965)
Baldwin, John W., *Masters, Princes & Merchants*, 2 vols. (Princeton, 1970)
Bammel, Ernst, 'Romans 13' in *Jesus and the Politics of his Day*, ed. E. Bammel and C. F. D. Moule (Cambridge, 1984; repr. 1992), pp. 365–83

Bartlett, Robert, *Gerald of Wales 1146–1223* (Oxford, 1982)

——, *Trial by Fire and Water* (Oxford, 1986)

Beckwith, J., *Ivory Carvings in Early Medieval England* (London, 1972)

Beeson, C. F. C., *English Church Clocks 1200–1850*, Antiquarian Horological Society, Monograph No. 5 (London and Chichester, 1971)

——, *Clockmaking in Oxfordshire, 1400–1850*, Banbury Historical Society (Banbury, 1971)

Bellamy, J. G., *The Law of Treason in England in the Later Middle Ages* (Cambridge, 1970)

——, *Crime and Public Order in England in the Late Middle Ages* (London, 1973)

Bennett, H. S., *The Pastons and their England* (Cambridge, 1968)

Berger, Samuel, *Histoire de la Vulgate pendant les premiers siècles du moyen âge* (Paris, 1893)

Bestul, Thomas H., 'Chaucer's Parson's Tale and the Late-Medieval Tradition of Religious Meditation', *Speculum* 64:3 (1989), 600–619

Blamires, Alcuin, *Woman Defamed and Woman Defended* (Oxford, 1992)

——, *The Case for Women in Medieval Culture* (Oxford, 1997)

Bloomfield, Morton W., *The Seven Deadly Sins, an Introduction to the History of a Religious Concept with Special Reference to Medieval English Literature* (Michigan State University Press, 1952; repr. 1967)

Boniface, St. see Emerton

Boyle, Leonard E. OP, 'The *Summa Confessorum* of John of Freiburg and the Popularization of the Moral Teaching of St Thomas and of John of Freiberg' in *Thomas Aquinas, 1274–1974, Commemorative Studies*, 2 vols., ed. A. A. Maurer, PIMS (Toronto, 1974), 2:245–68

Brady, Sr. M. Teresa, 'The *Pore Caitif*', *Traditio* 10 (1954), 529–48

——, 'Rolle's form of living and 'The *Pore Caitif*' *Traditio* 36 (1980), 426–35

——, 'Lollard Sources of the *Pore Caitif*' *Traditio* 44 (1988), 389–418

——, 'Lollard Interpolations and Omissions in MSS of the '*Pore Caitif*', in *De Cella in Seculum*, ed. Michael G. Sargent (Cambridge, 1989), pp. 183–203

Brooke, C. N. L., D. Luscombe *et al.*, eds., *Church Government* (Cambridge, 1976; repr. 1980)

Broughton, Bradford B., *Dictionary of Medieval Knighthood and Chivalry, Concepts and Terms* (New York, 1986)

Brown, Andrew D., *Popular Piety in Late Medieval England* (Cambridge, 1995)

Brown, A. L., 'The Commons and the Council in the Reign of Henry IV', *EHR* 310 (Jan. 1964), 1–30

Brown, Carleton. 'The Prioress's Tale' in *Sources and Analogues of Chaucer's*

Canterbury Tales, ed. W. F. Bryan and G. Dempster (New York, 1941; repr. 1948), pp. 447–85.

——, and Robbins, Rossell Hope, *The Index of Middle English Verse*, The Index Society (New York, 1943)

Brown, C. S., and R. H. West, 'As by the Whelp Chastised is the Leon' *MLN* 55 (1940), 209–10

Brown, Peter, *Religion and Society in the Age of Augustine* (London, 1972)

Brundage, James A., *Medieval Canon Law and the Crusader* (Madison, Wisc., 1969)

——, *Law, Sex, and Christian Society in Medieval Europe* (Chicago, 1987)

——, *Medieval Canon Law* (London and New York, 1995)

Bryan, W. F. and G. Dempster, ed., *Sources and Analogues of Chaucer's Canterbury Tales* (New York, 1941; repr. 1948)

Bühler, C. F., 'A Lollard Tract on Translating the Bible into English' *MÆ* 7 (1938), 167–83

——, 'Prayers and Charms in Certain Middle English Scrolls', *Speculum* 39 (1964), 270–8

Burr, David, *Eucharistic Presence and Conversion in Late Thirteenth Century Franciscan Thought* (Philadelphia, Pa., 1984; repr. 1986)

——, *Olivi and Franciscan Poverty: the Origins of the 'Usus Pauper' Controversy* (Philadelphia, Pa., 1989)

Burrow, J. A., *Essays on Medieval Literature* (Oxford, 1984; repr. 1985)

——, *The Ages of Man* (Oxford, 1988)

——, ed., *Middle English Literature: British Academy Gollancz Lectures*, The British Academy (London, 1989)

Bynum, Caroline W., *Jesus as Mother: Studies in the Spirituality of the High Middle Ages*, Publications of the Center for Medieval and Renaissance Studies, UCLA (Berkeley, 1982)

Callus, D. A. OP, ed. *Robert Grosseteste: Scholar and Bishop: Essays in Commemoration* (Oxford, 1955)

The Cambridge History of the Bible, Vol. II: *The West from the Fathers to the Reformation*, ed. G. W. H. Lampe *et al.* (Cambridge, 1969)

The Cambridge History of Later Medieval Philosophy, ed. Norman Kretzmann, Anthony Kenny and Jan Pinborg (Cambridge, 1982)

The Canterbury Hymnal, ed. Gernot R. Wieland, Toronto Medieval Latin Texts, PIMS (Toronto, 1982)

Cantica see Dove

Catto, Jeremy I., 'New Light on Thomas Docking, OFM', *Medieval and Renaissance Studies* 6 (1968), 135–49

——, and T. A. R. Evans, eds., *The History of the University of Oxford*, 2 vols., Vol. II *Late Medieval Oxford* (Oxford, 1984–92)

Cayré, F., *Manual of Patrology and History of Theology*, 2 vols., tr. H. Howitt (Paris, Tournai and Rome, 1935)

Chambers, E. K., *The Medieval Stage*, 2 vols. (Oxford, 1903; repr. 1954)

Chambers, R., ed., *The Book of Days: a Miscellany of Popular Antiquities*, 2 vols. (London, 1883)

Charlesworth, James H., ed., *Jesus and the Dead Sea Scrolls* (New York, 1992)

Cheney, C. R., *From Becket to Langton* (Manchester, 1956; repr. 1965)

——, *The English Church and its Laws, 12th-14th Centuries*, Variorum reprints (London, 1982)

Chodorow, Stanley, *Christian Political Theory and Church Politics in the Mid-twelfth Century* (Berkeley, CA, 1972)

Clay, R. M., *The Medieval Hospitals of England* (London, 1909; repr. London 1966)

——, *The Hermits and Anchorites of England* (London, 1914)

Cohen, Jeremy, *The Friars and the Jews: the Evolution of Medieval Anti-Judaism* (Ithaca, New York, 1982)

——, *Living Letters of the Law* (Berkeley, CA, 1999)

Coleman, Janet, 'Medieval Readers and Writers', in *English Literature in History 1350–1400*, ed. R. Williams (London, 1981)

——, 'The Two Jurisdictions: Theological and Legal Justifications of Church Property in the Thirteenth Century' SCH 25, ed. W. J. Sheils and D. Wood (1987) 75–110

[Collectanea]: *A Collection of Curious Discourses written by eminent antiquaries upon several heads in our English Antiquities*, 2 vols., ed. Thomas Hearne (London, 1775)

Constable, Giles, *Monastic Tithes from their Origins to the Twelfth Century*, Cambridge Studies in Medieval Life and Thought, n.s. 10 (Cambridge, 1964)

——, *Three Studies in Medieval Religious and Social Thought* (Cambridge, 1995)

Coopland, G. W., ed. and tr., *Nicholas Oresme and the Astrologers* (Cambridge, Mass., 1952)

Curtius, Ernst R., *European Literature and the Latin Middle Ages*, tr. Willard R. Trask (New York, 1953)

Dahmus, Joseph, *William Courtnay, Archbishop of Canterbury 1381–1396* (University Park and London, 1966)

Daniel, E. Randolph, *The Franciscan Concept of Mission in the High Middle Ages* (Lexington, Ky., 1975)

Davenport, W. A., 'Patterns in Middle English Dialogues', in *Middle English Studies Presented to George Kane*, ed. E. D. Kennedy et al. (Woodbridge, Suffolk, 1986), pp. 127–45

Davis, Norman, D. Gray, P. Ingham, A. Wallace-Hadrill, *A Chaucer Glossary* (Oxford, 1979)

Dawson, James Doyne, 'Fourteenth-century Poverty Controversies' *JEH* 34 (1983), 315–44

Deanesley, Margaret, *The Lollard Bible and Other Medieval Biblical Versions* (Cambridge, 1926; repr. 1966)

——, *The Significance of the Lollard Bible* (London, 1951)

Delaruelle, Etienne, *La Piété populaire au moyen âge* (Turin, 1980)

Delatorre, Bartholomew R., *Thomas Buckingham and the Contingency of Futures* (Notre Dame, Ind., 1987)

De Ricci, S., *Cursus of Medieval and Renaissance Manuscripts in the United States and Canada* (New York, 1935–40)

Dobson, E. J., *Moralities on the Gospels* (Oxford, 1975)

Dobson, R. B., *The Peasants' Revolt of 1381* (London, 1970)

——, and J. Taylor, *Rhymes of Robyn Hood* (London, 1976; revd. edn. 1997)

Doe, Norman, *Fundamental Authority in Late Medieval English Law* (Cambridge, 1990)

Doelger, F. J., *Sol Salutis: Gebet und Gesang im christliche altertum mit besonderer Rücksicht auf der Ostung in Gebet und Liturgie*, Liturgische Forschungen, 4–5 (1920)

Doob, Penelope, *Nebuchadnezzar's Children: Conventions of Madness in Middle English Literature* (New Haven, Ct., 1974)

Doucet, V., *Doctoris Irrefragabilis: Alexandri de Hales Summa Theologica*, Quaracchi (Florence, 1924–1940)

Douie, Decima L., *Archbishop Pecham* (London, 1952)

Dove, Mary, ed. and tr., *Glossa Ordinaria, pars. 22, in Canticum Canticorum* CCCM clxx (Turnhout, 1997)

Doyle, A. I., 'A Survey of the Origins and Circulation of Theological Writings in English in the 14th, 15th and early 16th Centuries with Special Consideration of the Part of the Clergy Therein', 2 vols. (Ph.D thesis, Cambridge, 1953–4)

Duckett, Eleanor S., *Anglo-Saxon Saints and Scholars* (New York, 1947)

Duff, E. Gordon, *Fifteenth-century English Books, a Bibliography of Books and Documents printed in England and of Books in the English Market Printed Abroad*, The Bibliographical Society (Oxford, 1917)

Duffy, Eamon, *The Stripping of the Altars: Traditional Religion in England 1400–1580* (New Haven, Ct., 1992)

Edden, Valerie, 'The Debate between Richard Maidstone and the Lollard Ashwardby, c.1390', *Carmelus* 34 (1987), 113–74

Edwards, Graham R., 'Purgatory: "Birth" or Evolution?' *JEH* 36 (1985), 634–46

Emden, A. B., *A Bibliographical Register of the University of Oxford to A.D. 1500*, 3 vols. (Oxford, 1957; repr. 1989)

Emerton, Ephraim, *The Letters of Saint Boniface*, tr. with Introduction (New York, 1940)

Emmerson, Richard K., *Antichrist in the Middle Ages* (Seattle, WA, 1981)

d'Entrèves, A. P., *Natural Law* (London, 1951; repr. 1972)

Evans, Joan, *English Art 1307–1461* in *The Oxford History of English Art*, Vol. 5 (Oxford, 1949)

Ferguson, George, *Signs and Symbols in Christian Art* (Oxford, 1954; repr. 1966)

Finlay, Alison, 'The Warrior Christ and the Unarmed Hero' in *Medieval English Religious and Ethical Literature: Essays in Honour of G. H. Russell*, ed. G. Kratzmann and J. Simpson (Cambridge, 1986), 19–29

Fletcher, Alan J., 'The Preaching of the Pardoner' SAC 11 (Knoxville, Tenn., 1989), 15–35

——, *Preaching, Politics and Poetry in Late-medieval England*, Medieval Studies (Bodmin, Cornwall, 1998)

Flint, Valerie I. J., 'The Place and Purpose of the Works of Honorius Augustodunensis', *Révue Bénédictine* (1977), 97–127

——, *The Rise of Magic in Early Medieval Europe* (Princeton, 1991)

Flusser, David, 'The Parable of the Unjust Steward', in *Jesus and the Dead Sea Scrolls*, ed. J. H. Charlesworth (New York, 1992), pp. 176–97

Flynn, Maureen, 'The Spectacle of Suffering in Spanish Streets' in *City and Spectacle in Medieval Europe*, ed. B. A. Hannawalt and K. L. Ryerson (Minneapolis, Minn., 1994), pp. 153–68

Forsyth, Neil, *The Old Enemy, Satan and the Combat Myth* (Princeton, 1987)

Fowler, David C., *The Life and Times of John Trevisa, Medieval Scholar* (Seattle, WA, 1995)

Frappier, Jean, 'The Vulgate Cycle', in *Arthurian Literature*, ed. R. S. Loomis (Oxford, 1959), pp. 295–318

Friedman, B., '"He hath a thousand slayn this pestilence": Iconography of the Plague in the Late Middle Ages' in *Social Unrest in the Late Middle Ages*, ed. Francis X. Newman, MRTS 39 (1986), 75–112

Gabel, Leona C., *Benefit of Clergy in the Later Middle Ages*, Smith College Studies in History, 14:4 (Northampton, Mass., 1928–9)

Gaffney, Wilbur, 'The Allegory of the Christ-Knight in *Piers Plowman*', *PMLA* 46 (1931), 155–61

Gallagher, C., 'Canon Law and the Christian Community: the Role of Law in the Church according to the *Summa aurea* of Cardinal Hostiensis', *Analecta Gregoriana* (Rome, 1978)

Gallop, David, *Aristotle on Sleep and Dreams* (Peterborough, Ontario, 1991)

Gerould, G. H., 'The Second Nun's Prologue and Tale' in *Sources and Analogues of Chaucer's Canterbury Tales*, ed. W. F. Bryan and G. Dempster (New York, 1941; repr. 1958), pp. 664–84

Getz, F. M., 'The Faculty of Medicine Before 1500' in *The History of the University of Oxford, Vol. II, Late Medieval Oxford*, ed. J. I. Catto *et al.* (Oxford, 1992), 2:373–405

Gibson, Gail McM., *The Theater of Devotion, East Anglian Drama and Society in the Late Middle Ages* (Chicago, 1989)

Gibson, Margaret T. , 'The Place of the *Glossa ordinaria* in Medieval Exegesis' in *Ad Litteram*, ed. Mark D.. Jordan and Kent Emery Jr. (Notre Dame, 1992), pp. 5–27

Ginsburg, Carlos, *The Night Battles*, tr. J. and A. Tedeschi (New York, 1983)

——, *Ecstasies: Deciphering the Witches' Sabbath*, tr. R. Rosen (New York, 1991)

Giry, A., *Manuel de Diplomatique* (Paris, 1894)

Glorieux, Palémon, *Répertoire des maîtres en théologie de Paris au xiii siècle*, 2 vols. (Paris, 1933)

——, *La faculté des arts et ses maîtres au xiii siècle* (Paris, 1971)

Glunz, H. H., *A History of the Vulgate in England* (Cambridge, 1933)

Goering, Joseph, *William de Montibus (c. 1140–1213), the Schools and the Literature of Pastoral Care*, Studies and Texts, PIMS (Toronto, 1992)

Gradon, Pamela, 'Langland and the Ideology of Dissent' in *Middle English Literature: British Academy Gollancz Lectures*, sel. and introd. by J. A. Burrow, The British Academy (1989), 195–221

Gransden, Antonia, 'Realistic Observation in Twelfth Century England', *Speculum* 47:1 (1972), 29–51

——, 'The Continuations of the *Flores Historiarum* from 1265 to 1327' in *Med. Stud.* 36 (Toronto, 1974), 472–92

——, *Historical Writing in England*, 2 vols. (London/Ithaca, N.Y. 1982)

Grant, Edward, *Planets, Stars, and Orbs: the Medieval Cosmos 1200–1687* (Cambridge, 1996)

Green, R. G., 'John Ball's Letters' in *Chaucer's England* ed. Barbara Hanawalt (Minneapolis, Minn., 1992), pp. 176–200.

Gregorovius, Ferdinand, *Rome and Medieval Culture: selections from Gregorovius' History of the City of Rome in the Middle Ages*, ed. K. F. Morrison, tr. G. W. Hamilton (Chicago, 1971)

Gurevich, Aron, *Medieval Popular Culture*, tr. J. M. Bak and P. A. Hollingsworth (Cambridge, 1988; repr. 1990)

Gy, Pierre-Marie, ed., *Guillaume Durand, Evêque de Mende* (Paris, 1992)

Haines, Roy M., '"Wilde Wittes and wilfulnes": John Swetstock's attack on those "poyswummongeres", the Lollards', SCH 8, ed. G. J. Cuming and D. Baker (Cambridge, 1972), 143–53

Hanawalt, Barbara ed., *Chaucer's England: Literature in Historical Context* (Minneapolis, Minn., 1992)

——, and Katheryn L. Ryerson, *City and Spectacle in Medieval Europe* (Minneapolis, Minn., 1994)

Hanna, Ralph III, 'Sir Thomas Berkeley and his Patronage', *Speculum* 64:4 (1989) 878–916

——, *The Index of Middle English Prose; Handlist XII: Manuscripts in Smaller Bodleian Collections* (Cambridge, 1997)

Haren, Michael, *Sin and Society in Fourteenth-Century England: a Study of the Memoriale Presbiterorum* (Oxford, 2000) [See Haren in *Primary Sources*]

Hargreaves, Henry, 'Popularising Biblical Scholarship: the Role of the Wycliffite *Glossed Gospels*' in *The Bible and Medieval Culture*, Mediaevalia Lovaniensis, Series I / Sudia VII (Louvain, 1979), 171–89

Harrison, F. Ll., 'Music at Oxford before 1500' in Catto, *History* (Oxford, 1992), 2:359–61

Hartung see *Manual*

Harvey, John, *The Perpendicular Style* (London, 1978)

——, *Henry Yevele: 1320–1400* (London, 1944)

Harvey, Margaret, 'Papal Witchcraft: the Charges against Benedict XIII' in *Sanctity and Secularity*, SCH 10, ed. Derek Baker (Oxford, 1973), 109–116

Haskins, Charles H., *Studies in the History of Medieval Science* (Cambridge, Mass., 1927)

Hassall, W. O., *The Holkham Bible Picture Book* (London, 1954)

Heath, Peter, *English Parish Clergy on the Eve of the Reformation* (London and Toronto, 1969)

——, *Church and Realm 1272–1461* (London, 1988)

Heist, William W., *The Fifteen Signs before Doomsday* (E. Lansing, Mich., 1952)

Helmholz, R. H., 'Usury and the Medieval English Church Courts' *Speculum* 61:2 (1986), 364–80

——, *Canon Law and the Law of England* (London, 1987)

Hilton, R. H. ed., *Peasants, Knights and Heretics* (London 1976).

Hirsh, John C., 'Fate, Faith and Paradox in Medieval Unlucky Days as a Context for 'Wytte Wondyr' *MÆ* 66, No. 2 (1997), 288–92

Hocedez, Edgar, *Richard de Middleton* (Louvain, 1925)

Holcot see Streveler

Holkham see Hassall

Hopper, V. H., *Medieval Number Symbolism* (New York, 1938)

Hoppin, Richard H., *Medieval Music* (New York, 1978)

Hudson, Anne, and H. Leith Spencer, 'Old Author, New Work: the Sermons of MS. Longleat 4', *MÆ* 53, No. 2 (1984), 220–38

——, *Lollards and Their Books* (London, 1985)

——, 'A New Look at the Lay Folks' Catechism' *Viator* 16, 243–58

——, *The Premature Reformation: Wycliffite Texts and Lollard History* (Oxford, 1988)

Hughes, Andrew, *Medieval Manuscripts for Mass and Office: a Guide to their Organization and Terminology* (Toronto, 1982)

Hunt, R. W., 'The Library of Robert Grosseteste' in *Robert Grosseteste*, ed. D. A. Callus (Oxford, 1955), pp. 121–45

——, and W. A. Pantin, R. W. Southern, eds., *Studies in Medieval History Presented to F. M. Powicke* (Oxford, 1969)

Hutton, Ronald, *Stations of the Sun, a History of the Ritual Year in Britain* (Oxford, 1996)

The Index of Printed Middle English Prose, ed. R. E. Lewis, N. P. Blake, and A. S. G. Edwards (New York and London, 1985)

Jacob, E. F., *The Fifteenth Century, 1399–1485*, The Oxford History of England 6 (Oxford, 1961)

Joliffe, P. S., *Check-list of ME Prose Writings of Spiritual Guidance*, PIMS (Toronto, 1974)

Jones, Cheslyn *et al.*. eds., *The Study of Liturgy* (Oxford, 1978; rev. edn. New York, 1992)

Jones, W. R., 'Lollards and Images: the Defence of Religious Art in Later Medieval England' *JHI* (Jan.-Mar. 1973), 27–50

——, 'The Heavenly Letter in Medieval England' in *Medievalia et Humanistica* n.s. 6 (1975), 163–78

Jordan, Mark K. and Kent Emery, Jr., eds., *Ad Litteram, Authoritative Texts and their Medieval Readers* (Notre Dame, Ind., 1992)

Julian, John, *Dictionary of Hymnology*, 2 vols. (London, 1892; revd. edn. New York, 1957)

Jüngmann, Josef A., *The Early Liturgy*, tr. F. A. Brunner (Notre Dame, 1959)

Karras, Ruth M., *Common Women* (Oxford, 1996)

Kedar, B. Z., 'Canon Law and Local Practice: the Case of Mendicant Preaching in Late Medieval England' in *Bulletin of Medieval Canon Law* n.s. 2 (1972), 17–32

Keiser, George R., '"Nought how lang man lifs; bot how wele": the Laity and the Ladder of Perfection', in *De Cella in Seculum*, ed. Michael G. Sargent (Cambridge, 1989), 145–59

Kellog, Alfred L., and Louis A. Hasellmayer, 'Chaucer's Satire of the Pardoner', *PMLA* 66 (1951), 251–77

——, *Chaucer, Langland, Arthur: Essays in Middle English Literature* (New Brunswick, N. J., 1972)

Kelly, Henry A., *Love and Marriage in the Age of Chaucer* (Ithaca, New York, 1975)

Ker, N. R., *Fragments of Medieval Manuscripts and Pastedowns in Oxford Bindings*, Oxford Bibliographical Society Publications n.s. 5 (Oxford, 1951–2)

——, *Medieval Manuscripts in British Libraries*, 4 vols. (Oxford, 1969–1992)

Kerby-Fulton, Kathryn, *Reformist Apocalypticism and 'Piers Plowman'* (Cambridge, 1990)

Kieckhefer, Richard, *Magic in the Middle Ages* (Cambridge, 1969; repr. 1992)

King, Archdale A., *Liturgies of the Religious Orders* (London, 1955)

Kingsford, Charles L., *The Grey Friars of London* (Aberdeen, 1915)

——, and A. G. Little, F. Tocco, eds. *Fratris Johannis Pecham, Tractatus Tres de Paupertate* (Aberdeen, 1910; repr. Farnsborough, Hants., 1966)

Kittredge, George L., *Witchcraft in Old and New England* (Cambridge, Mass., 1929)

Knowles, Dom David, *The Religious Orders in England*, 3 vols. (Cambridge, 1955; repr. 1961)

——, *The Monastic Order in England* (Cambridge, 1966)

Kraus, Dorothy and Henry Kraus, *The Hidden World of Misericords* (New York, 1975)

Krautheimer, Richard, *Rome, Profile of a City, 302–1308* (Princeton, 1980)

Kretzmann see *Later Medieval Philosophy*

Krey, Philip D. W. and Lesley Smith, *Nicholas of Lyra: the Senses of Scripture* (Leiden, 2000)

Kruger, Steven F., *Dreaming in the Middle Ages* (Cambridge, 1992)

Kuttner, Stephan, 'Gratian and Plato', in *Church and Government in the Middle Ages: Essays presented to C. R. Cheney*, ed. Christopher Brooke, D. Luscombe, G. Martin and D. Owen (Cambridge, 1976; repr. 1980), pp. 93–118

——, *Medieval Councils, Decretals and Collections of Canon Law: Selected Essays*, Variorum reprints (London, 1980)

——, *The History of Ideas and Doctrines of Canon Law in the Middle Ages*, Variorum reprints (London, 1980)

de Lagarde, Georges, *La naissance de l'esprit laïque*, 5 vols., (Paris and Louvain, 1956–63; repr. 1973)

Lambert, Malcolm, *Medieval Heresy: Popular Movements from the Gregorian Reform to the Reformatiion*, 2nd. edn. (Oxford, 1992)

Lambert, M. D., *Franciscan Poverty* (London, 1961)

Lang, David Marshall, *The Balavariani (Barlaam and Josaphat), a Tale from the Christian East translated from the Old Georgian* (Berkeley, CA,1966)

Langmuir, Gavin I., 'The Jews and the Archives of Angevin England: Reflections on Medieval Anti-Semitism' *Traditio* 19 (1963), 183–244

——, 'Thomas of Monmouth: Detector of Ritual Murder' *Speculum* 59:4 (1984), 820–46

Lea, Henry Charles, *The Duel and the Oath with Additional Documents by Arthur C. Howland*, ed. Edward Peters (Philadelphia, PA, 1886; repr. 1974)

——, *A History of the Inquisition of the Middle Ages*, 3 vols. (New York, 1888)

Leclerq, J., 'Aux origines bibliques du vocabulaire de la pauvreté' in *Etudes sur l'histoire de la pauvreté*, 2 vols., ed. M. Mollat (Paris, 1974), 1:35–43

Leff, Gordon, *Bradwardine and the Pelagians* (Cambridge, 1957)

——, *Heresy in the Later Middle Ages*, 2 vols. (Manchester and New York, 1967)

——, 'The Bible and Rights in the Franciscan Disputes over Poverty' SCH, Subsidia 4, ed. K. Walsh and D. Wood (Oxford, 1985), 225–49

LeGoff, Jacques, *The Birth of Purgatory*, tr. A. Goldhammer (Chicago, 1981)

Leigh, David J., 'The Doomsday Mystery Play: an Eschatalogical Morality' in *Medieval English Drama*, ed. Jerome Taylor and A. H. Nelson (Chicago, 1972), pp. 260–78

Lindberg, David C., ed., *Science in the Middle Ages* (Chicago, 1978)

——, *The Beginnings of Western Science: the European Scientific Tradition . . . 600 B.C. to A.D.1450* (Chicago, 1992)

Lindström, Bengt, 'Four Middle English Passages', *Studia Neophilogica* 46 (1974 [1]), 151–8

——, 'Two Notes on "Dives and Pauper"', *Studia Neophilologica* 46 (1974 [2]), 331–7

——, 'Two Descriptions of the Signs before the Last Judgement', *Studia Neophilologica* 48 (1976), 307–11

Little, A. G., *The Greyfriars in Oxford* (Oxford, 1892)

——, *Studies in English Franciscan History* (Manchester, 1917)

——, *The Franciscan School at Oxford in the Thirteenth Century* (Florence, 1926)

——, *Franciscan Papers, Lists and Documents* (Manchester, 1943)

——, 'Personal Tithes', *EHR* 60 (1945), 57–88

Little, Lester K., *Religious Poverty and the Profit Economy in Medieval Europe* (Ithaca, New York, 1978)

——, *Benedictine Maledictions: Liturgical Cursings in Romanesque France* (Ithaca, New York, 1993)

Logan, F. Donald, *Excommunication and the Secular Arm in Medieval England: a Study in Legal Procedure from the Thirteenth to the Sixteenth Century*, PIMS (Toronto, 1968)

Longère, Jean, *La prédication médiévale*, Etudes Augustinienne (Paris, 1983)

Loomis, R. S., *Arthurian Literature* (Oxford, 1959)

Lubac, Henri de, *Corpus Mysticum: l'eucharistie et l'église au moyen âge* (Paris, 1949)

——, *Exégèse médiévale*, 2 vols. [in four] (Paris, 1959–64)

Luscombe, David, 'The *Lex divinitas* in the Bull *unam sanctam* of Pope Boniface VIII', in *Church Government in the Middle Ages*, ed. Christopher Brooke, D. Luscombe, *et al.* (Cambridge, 1976), pp. 205–21

Mackinnon, H., 'William de Montibus, a medieval teacher', in *Essays in Medieval History presented to Bertie Wilkinson*, ed. T. A. Sandquist and M. R. Powicke (Toronto, 1969), pp. 32–45

McCulloch, Florence, *Medieval Latin and French Bestiaries* (Chapel Hill, N.C., 1960)

McFarlane, K. B., *Lancastrian Kings and Lollard Knights* (Oxford, 1972)

——, *The Nobility of Later Medieval England* (Oxford, 1973)

McGinn, Bernard, *Visions of the End* (New York, 1979)

McGuckin, J. A., 'The Vine and the Elm Tree', SCH 24, ed. W. J. Sheils and D. Wood (Oxford, 1987), 1–14

McHardy, Alison, 'Bishop Buckingham . . .' SCH 9, ed. Derek Baker (Cambridge, 1972), 131–47

——, 'Clerical Taxation in Fifteenth-Century England: the Clergy as Agents of the Crown' in B. Dobson, *The Church, Politics and Patronage in the Fifteenth Century* (Gloucester and New York, 1984), pp. 168–92

——, 'Ecclesiastics and Economics', SCH 24, ed. W. J. Sheils & Diana Wood (Oxford, 1987), 129–38

McIntosh, Angus, M. L. Samuels, and M. Benskin, *A Linguistic Atlas of Late Mediæval English*, 4 vols. (Aberdeen, 1986)

——, and A. M. Laing, 'Middle English *wyndown*, 'Window', a Word-Geographical Note', *Neuphil* 97 (1998), 295–300

McKenna, J. W., 'Popular Canonization as Political Propaganda: the Cult of Archbishop Scrope', *Speculum* 45:4 (1970), 608–23

McKisack, May, *The Fourteenth Century, 1307–1399*, The Oxford History of England 5 (Oxford, 1959)

——, 'London and the Succession to the Crown during the Middle Ages', in *Studies in Medieval History presented to F. M. Powicke*, ed. R. W. Hunt, W. A. Pantin and R. W. Southern (Oxford, 1969), pp. 76–89.

McLaughlin, T. P., 'The Teaching of the Canonists on Usury (XII, XIII and XIV Centuries)', *Medieval Studies* 1 (1939) 81–147

——, 'The Teaching of the Canonists on Usury (XII, XIII and XIV Centuries)' (2) *Medieval Studies* 2 (1940), 1–22

McNeill, John T. and Helena M. Gamer, eds. & tr., *Medieval Handbooks of Penance: a Translation of the Princpal* libri poenitentiales *and Selections from Related Documents* (New York, 1938; repr. 1965)

McNiven, Peter, *Heresy and Politics in the Reign of Henry IV* (Woodbridge; Suffolk, 1987)

Macy, Gary, 'The Dogma of Transubstantiation in the Middle Ages' *JEH* 45, no. 1 (1994), 11–41.

Mâle, Emile, *L'Art réligieuse en France*, 3 vols. (Paris, 1924–1925)

Mann, Jill, *Chaucer and Medieval Estates Satire: the Literature of Social Classes and the Prologue to the Canterbury Tales* (Cambridge, 1973)

Manual: A Manual of the Writings in Middle English, 9 vols., ed. J. B. Severs and A. E. Hartung, *et al.*, Connecticut Academy of Arts and Sciences (New Haven, Ct., 1967–1993)

Marbach, Carolus, *Carmina scripturarum: Antiphonas et Responsoria ex Sacro Scripturae Fonte in Libros Liturgicos Sanctae Ecclesiae Romanae* (Hildesheim, 1963)

Marsilius of Padua, *Defensor Pacis*, ed. and tr. Alan Gewirth (Toronto 1956; repr. 1964)

Masschaele, James, *Peasants, Merchants and Markets: Inland Trade in Medieval England 1150–1350* (New York, 1997)

Matter, E. Ann, *The Voice of my Beloved, the Song of Songs in Western Medieval Christianity* (Philadelphia, PA, 1990)

Maurer, A. A., ed. *Thomas Aquinas 1274–1974, Commemorative Studies*, 2 vols., PIMS (Toronto, 1974)

Mellinkoff, Ruth, *The Horned Moses in Medieval Art and Thought* (Berkeley, CA, 1970)

Miller, Patricia C., *Dreams in Late Antiquity* (Princeton, 1994)

Minnis, A. J., ed., *Late Medieval Religious Texts and their Transmission: Essays in Honour of A. I. Doyle*, York Manuscripts Conference Proceedings, Series 3 (Cambridge, 1994)

Miskimin, Alice, ed., *Susannah: an Alliterative Poem of the Fourteenth Century* (New Haven, Ct., 1969)

Mollat, Michel, ed., *Etudes sur l'histoire de la pauvreté*, 2 vols. (Paris, 1974)

——, *The Poor in the Middle Ages*, tr. Arthur Goldhammer (New Haven, Ct., 1986)

Mooney, L. R., 'The Cock and the Clock', SAC 15 (1993), 101–9

Moore, Ellen W. Moore, *The Fairs of Medieval England*, PIMS (Toronto, 1985)

Moorman, J. R. H., *A History of the Church in England* (London, 1953; 3rd edn. 1975; repr. Wilton, Ct., 1980)

——, *Church Life in England in the XIII Century* (Cambridge, 1955)

Moorman, John, *A History of the Franciscan Order from its Origins to the Year 1517* (Oxford, 1968)

Morey, J. H., 'Peter Comestor, Biblical Paraphrase and the Medieval Popular Bible', *Speculum* 68:1 (1993), 6–35

Morgan, Margery M., 'Pynson's Manuscript of *Dives and Pauper*', *The Library*, 5th Ser., Vol. 8, No. 4 (1953), 217–28

Murray, Valerie, 'An Edition of 'A Tretise of Gostly Batayle' and 'Milicia Christi'' (D.Phil thesis, Oxford, 1970)

Mynors, R. A. B., *A Catalogue of the Manuscripts of Balliol College, Oxford* (Oxford, 1963)

Nelson, Benjamin, *The Idea of Usury, from Tribal Brotherhood to Universal Brotherhood* (2nd edn. Chicago, 1969)

Nightingale, Pamela, *A Medieval Mercantile Community: the Grocers' Company and the Politics and Trade of London 1000–1485* (New Haven, Ct., 1995)

Noonan, J. T., *The Scholastic Analysis of Usury* (Cambridge, Mass., 1957)

——, 'Gratian Slept Here: The Changing Identity of the Father of the Systematic Study of Canon Law' *Traditio* 35 (1979), 145–72

North, J. D., 'Natural Philosophy in Late Medieval Oxford', in *The History of the University of Oxford*, 2 vols., ed. J. I. Catto and T. A. R. Evans (Oxford, 1992), 2:65–102

——, 'Astronomy and Mathematics', in *The History of the University of Oxford*, 2 vols., ed. J. I. Catto and T. A. R. Evans (1992), 2:103–174

Oberman, Heiko, 'Facientibus quod in se est Deus non denegat Gratiam, Robert Holcot and the Beginnings of Luther's Theology', *Harvard Theological Review* 55 (Cambridge, Mass., 1962), 317–42

——, *The Harvest of Medieval Theology* (Durham, North Carolina, 1983)

O'Carroll, Mary E., SND, *A Fourteenth-Century Preacher's Handbook: Studies in MS Laud Misc. 511*, Studies and Texts 128, PIMS (Toronto, 1997)

Oman, Charles, *The Great Revolt of 1381* (Oxford, 1906; repr. New York, 1968)

Opie see *The Oxford Dictionary of Nursery Rhymes*

Opie, Iona and Tatem, Moira, eds., *A Dictionary of Superstitions* (Oxford, 1989)

Orme, Nicholas, *The English Hospital 1070–1570* (New Haven, Ct., 1995)

Owst, G. R., *Preaching in Medieval England* (Cambridge, 1926; repr. New York, 1965)

——, '"Sortilegium" in English Homiletic Literature of the Fourteenth Century' in *Studies Presented to Sir Hilary Jenkinson*, ed. J. C. Davies (London, 1957), pp. 272–303

——, *Literature and Pulpit in Medieval England* (Cambridge, 1933; repr. New York, 1966)

The Oxford Dictionary of English Proverbs, ed. F. P. Wilson (3rd edn. revd., Oxford, 1970)

The Oxford Dictionary of Nursery Rhymes, ed. Iona and Peter Opie (Oxford, 1951; repr. 1962)

The Oxford Dictionary of Popes, ed. J. N. D. Kelly (Oxford, 1986)

The Oxford Dictionary of Saints, ed. David H. Farmer (Oxford, 1978)

Ozment, Steven, *The Age of Reform* (New Haven, Ct., 1980)

Pantin, William A., *The English Church in the Fourteenth Century* (Cambridge, 1955; repr. Notre Dame, 1962)

——, 'Instructions for a Devout and Literate Layman', in *Essays Presented to R. W. Hunt*, ed. J. J. G. Alexander and M. T. Gibson (Oxford, 1976), pp. 398–422

Parkes, M. B., *English Cursive Book Hands 1250–1500* (Oxford, 1969)

——, *Scribes, Scripts and Readers: Studies in the Communication, Presentation and Dissemination of Medieval Texts* (London, 1991)

Patch, Howard R., *The Goddess Fortuna* (Cambridge, Mass., 1927; repr. 1967)

Patterson, Frank A., *The ME Penitential Lyric; a Study and Collection of Early Religious Verse* (New York, 1911; repr. 1966)

BIBLIOGRAPHY

Paues, A. C., *A Fourteenth-Century English Biblical Version* (Cambridge, 1904)

Payer, Pierre J., *Sex and the Penitentials: the Development of a Sexual Code 550–1150* (Toronto, 1984)

Pearsall, Derek, 'Poverty and Poor People in "Piers Plowman"', in *Middle English Studies Presented to George Kane*. ed. E. D. Kennedy, R. Waldron and J. S. Wittig (Woodbridge, Suffolk, 1988), pp. 167–185

——, 'Hoccleve's "Regement of Princes": the Poetics of Royal Self-Representation', *Speculum* 69:2 (1994), 386–410

Pelikan, J., *The Christian Tradition: A History of the Development of Doctrine*, 5 vols.: citations from Vol. 2, *The Spirit of Eastern Christendom, 600–1700* and Vol. 3, *The Growth of Medieval Theology 600–1300* (Chicago, 1971–89)

Peters, Edward, ed., *Heresy and Authority in Medieval Europe* (Philadelphia, PA, 1980)

Pfaff, Richard W., *New Liturgical Feasts in Later Medieval England* (Oxford, 1970)

——, 'The English Devotion of St Gregory's Trental', *Speculum* 49:1 (1974), 75–90

——, *Medieval Latin Liturgy, a Select Bibliography* (Toronto, 1982)

Pfander, Homer G., 'Dives et Pauper', *The Library* 14 (1933), 299–312

——, 'The Mediaeval Friars and some Alphabetical Reference Books for Sermons', *MÆ* 3 (1934), 19–29

——, 'Some Medieval Manuals of Religious Instruction in England and Observations on Chaucer's Parson's Tale' *JEGP* 35 (1936), 243–58

——, *The Popular Sermon of the Medieval Friar in England* (New York, 1937)

Pfeffer, Wendy, *The Change of Philomel: the Nightingale in Medieval Literature*, American University Studies, Series III, vol. 14 (New York, 1985)

Platt, Colin, *The Parish Churches of Medieval England* (London, 1981)

Plomer, Henry R., *Wynkyn de Worde and his Contemporaries from the Death of Caxton to 1535, a Chapter in English Printing* (London, 1925)

Pollard, A. W. and Redgrave, G. R., *A Short-Title Catalogue of Books Printed in England, Scotland, & Ireland, and of English Books Printed Abroad 1475–1640*, 2 vols., The Bibliographical Society (2nd edn. enlarged, London, 1986)

Pollock, Frederick, and Maitland, Fredric W., *The History of English Law before the Time of Edward I*, 2 vols. (Cambridge, 1895; reissued with new introduction and bibliography by S. F. Milsom, 1968)

Portier, Lucienne, *Le Pélican, histoire d'un symbole* (Paris, 1984)

Post, Gaines, 'A Romano-canonical maxim: Quod omnes tangit', *Traditio* 4 (1946), 197–251

Powell, James M., ed., *Innocent III, Vicar of Christ or Lord of the World*, 2nd edn. (Washington, D.C., 1994)

Powell, Sue, 'The Transmission and Circulation of the *Lay Folks' Catechism*, in *Late-Medieval Religious Texts and their Transmisssion, Essays in Honour of A. I. Doyle*, ed. A. J. Minnis, York Manuscripts Conferences: Proceedings Series 3 (Cambridge, 1994), 67–84

Power, Eileen and Postan, M. M., eds., *Studies in English Trade in the Fifteenth Century* (New York, 1966)

Pyper, Rachel, 'An Abridgement of Wyclif's *De mandatis divinis*' *MÆ* 52 (1983), 306–9

Quasten, Johannes, *Patrology*, 4 vols. (Vol. 4 ed. Angelo di Berardino, with Introduction by Johannes Quasten) (Utrecht, 1950, repr. Christian Classics, Westminster, Md., 1983)

Raby, F. J. E., *A History of Christian-Latin Poetry*, 2nd edn. (Oxford, 1953)

Reichl, K. 'No more ne will i wiked be . . .', in *Literature and Religion*, ed. R. G. Newhauser and J. A. Alford (Binghamton, New York, 1995)

Reynolds, Roger, 'Guillaume Durand parmi les théologiens médiévaux de la liturgie', in *Guillaume Durand* ed. P.-M. Gy (Paris, 1992), pp. 155–68

Richardson, H. G., 'Dives and Pauper', *NQ* 11 S.iv (Oct. 21, 1911), 321–3

——, 'Dives and Pauper', *The Library* 15 (1934), 31–7

Richardson, H. G. and G. D. Sayles, *The Governance of Medieval England from the Conquest to Magna Carta* (Edinburgh, 1963)

Rigg, A. G., 'Clocks, Dials and other Terms', in *Middle English Studies Presented to Norman Davis*, ed. D. Gray and E. G. Stanley (Oxford, 1983), pp. 255–274

——, *A History of Anglo-Latin Literature 1066–1422* (Cambridge, 1992)

Robbins, Rossell Hope, and John L. Cutler, *Supplement to the Index of Middle English Verse* (Lexington, Ky., 1965)

Robson, J. A., *Wyclif & the Oxford Schools* (Cambridge, 1966)

Rock, Daniel, *The Church of Our Fathers, as seen in St Osmund's Rite for the Cathedral of Salisbury* (London, 1849; new edn. in 4 vols. by G. W. Hart and W. H. Frere, London, 1905)

Rouse, R. H. and M. A., 'The Franciscans and their Books: Lollard Accusations and the Franciscan Response', SCH 24, ed. A. Hudson and M. Wilks (Oxford, 1987), 369–84

——, *Authentic Witnesses, Approaches to Medieval Texts and Manuscripts*, The Medieval Institute, Vol. XVII (Notre Dame, Ind., 1991)

Rubin, Miri, *Charity and Community in Medieval Cambridge* (Cambridge, 1987)

——, *Corpus Christi: the Eucharist in Late Medieval Culture* (Cambridge, 1991)

——, *Gentile Tales, the Narrative Assault on Late Medieval Jews* (New Haven, Ct., and London, 1999)

Russell, Frederick H., *The Just War in the Middle Ages* Cambridge Studies in
Medieval Life and Thought, 3rd ser., vol. 8 (Cambridge, 1975)

Russell, Jeffrey B., *Witchcraft in the Middle Ages* (Ithaca, New York, 1972)

Russell, Josiah C., 'The Canonization of Opposition to the King in Angevin
England', in *Haskins Anniversary Essays in Medieval History*, ed. C. H.
Taylor and J. L. LaMonte (Boston, Mass., 1929), pp. 179–90

Russell, P. E., *The English Intervention in Spain and Portugal in the Time of
Edward III and Richard II* (Oxford, 1955)

Russell-Smith, Joy M., 'Walter Hilton and a Tract in Defence of the
Veneration of Images', *Dominican Studies* 7 (1954), 180–214

Salzman, L. F., *Building in England down to 1540* (Oxford, 1952)

Sargent, Michael G., ed. *'De Cella in Seculum': Religious and Secular Life and
Devotion in Late Medieval England* (Cambridge, 1989)

Saul, Nigel, E., 'Chaucer and Gentility' in *Chaucer's England, Literature in
Historical Context*, ed. Barbara Hanawalt (Minneapolis, Minn., 1992)

Scase, Wendy, *'Piers Plowman' and the New Anticlericalism*, Cambridge
Studies in Medieval Literature 4 (Cambridge, 1989)

Sewell, W. H., 'The Sexton's Wheel and the Lady Fast', *Norfolk Archaeology*
9 (1884), 201–14

Seymour, William W., *The Cross in Tradition, History and Art* (New York,
1898)

Shailor, Barbara, *Catalogue of Medieval and Renaissance Manuscripts in the
Beinecke Rare Book and Manuscript Library, Yale University*, Vol. I, MSS
1–250, MRTS 34 (Binghamton, N.Y., 1984)

Sharp, D. E., *Franciscan Philosophy at Oxford in the XIIIth Century* (Oxford,
1930)

Smalley, Beryl, *The Study of the Bible in the Middle Ages* (Oxford, 1952; repr.
Notre Dame, 1964)

——, *English Friars and Antiquity in the Early Fourteenth Century* (New
York, 1960)

——, 'Church and State 1300–1377: Theory and Fact', in *Europe in the Late
Middle Ages*, ed. John Hale *et al.* (London, 1965), pp. 15–43

——, *The Becket Conflict and the Schools* (Oxford, 1973)

Snell, F. J., *The Customs of Old England* (London, 1911; repr. 1977)

Somerset, Fiona, *Clerical Discourse and Lay Audience in Late Medieval
England*, Cambridge Studies in Medieval Literature 37 (Cambridge, 1998)

Southern, Richard W., *Robert Grosseteste, the Growth of an English Mind in
Medieval Europe* (Oxford, 1986)

Spargo, John W., 'The Canon Yeoman's Prologue and Tale', in *Sources and
Analogues of Chaucer's Canterbury Tales*, ed. W. F. Bryan and G. Dempster
(New York, 1941; repr. 1958), pp. 685–98

Spencer, H. Leith, *English Preaching in the Late Middle Ages* (Oxford, 1993)

Spicq, P. C., *Esquisse d'une histoire de l'exégèse latine au moyen âge* (Paris, 1944)

Stock, Brian, *The Implications of Literacy: Written Language and Models of Interpretation in the Eleventh and Twelfth Centuries* (Princeton, 1983)

Straw, Carole, *Gregory the Great* (Berkeley, CA, 1988)

Stubbs, William, *The Constitutional History of England*, Vol. III, 5th edn. (Oxford, 1903)

Sumption, Jonathan, *Pilgrimage, an Image of Medieval Religion* (London, 1975)

Swanson, Jenny, *John of Wales a Study of the Works & Ideas of a Thirteenth-Century Friar*, Cambridge Studies in Medieval Life and Thought 10 (Cambridge, 1989)

Swanson, R. N., *Church and Society in the Late Middle Ages* (Oxford, 1989; repr. 1993)

——, 'Literacy, heresy, history and orthodoxy' in *Heresy and Literacy 1100–1530*, ed. P. Biller and A. Hudson (Cambridge, 1994), pp. 279–93

——, 'The "Mendicant Problem" in the Later Middle Ages', SCH, Subsidia 11, Essays in Honour of Gordon Leff, ed. P. Biller and B. Dobson (1999) 217–38

Sweeney, James B., and Stanley Chodorow, eds. *Popes, Teachers and Canon Law in the Middle Ages* (Ithaca/London, 1989)

Szittya, Penn R., *The Antifraternal Tradition in Medieval Literature* (Princeton, 1986).

Taylor, James and Alan H. Nelson, eds., *Medieval English Drama, Essays Critical and Contextual* (Chicago, Ill., 1972)

Thibodeau, T. M., 'Les Sources du "Rationale" de Guillaume Durand', in *Guillaume Durand*, ed. P.-M. Gy (Paris, 1992), pp. 142–53

——, 'The Doctrine of Transubstantiation in Durand's *Rationale*', *Traditio* 51 (1996), 308–17

Thomas, Keith, *Religion and the Decline of Magic* (New York, 1971)

Thompson, A. Hamilton, *The English Clergy and their Organization in the Later Middle Ages*, The Ford Lectures 1933 (Oxford, 1947)

Thompson, Stith, *Motif Index of Folk Literature*, 6 vols. (Bloomington, Indiana and London, 1975)

Thomsom, J. A. F., *The Later Lollards 1414–1520* (Oxford, 1965)

Thomson, S. Harrison, *The Writings of Robert Grosseteste* (Cambridge, 1940)

——, *Latin Book Hands of the Later Middle Ages 1100–1500* (Cambridge, 1969)

Thomson, Williel R., *The Latin Writings of John Wyclif*, PIMS (Toronto, 1983)

Thorndike, Lynn, *History of Magic and Experimental Science*, 8 vols. (New York, 1923–34)

——, *The Sphere of Sacrobosco and its Commentators* (Chicago, 1949)

——, *Latin Treatises on Comets between 1238 and 1368 AD* (Chicago, 1950)

——, 'Unde versus', *Traditio* 11 (1955), 163–93

——, *Michael Scot* (London, 1965)

Thrupp, Sylvia L., *The Merchant Class of Medieval London* (Chicago, 1948)

——, 'The Grocers of London: a Study in the Distribution of Trade', in *English Trade in the Fifteenth Century*, ed. E. Power and M. M. Postan (New York, 1966), pp. 217–92

Tierney, Brian, *The Medieval Poor Law* (Berkeley, CA, 1959)

——, *The Origins of Papal Infalibility 1150–1350* (Leiden, 1972)

——, *Church Law and Constitutional Thought in the Middle Ages*, Variorum reprints (London, 1979)

——, 'Natural Law and Canon Law in Ockham's *Dialogue*' in *Aspects of Late Medieval Government and Society: Essays Presented to J. R. Lander*, ed. J. G. Rowe (Toronto, 1986)

Tout, T. F., *Chapters in the Administrative History of Medieval England*, 6 vols., Historical Series 34, 35, 48, 49, 57, 64 (Manchester, 1820–1933)

Ullman, Walter, *The Growth of Papal Government in the Middle Ages: A Study in the Ideological Relation of Clerical to Lay Power* (London, 1955)

——, *Law and Politics in the Middle Ages: An Introduction to the Sources of Medieval Political Ideas* (Ithaca, N.Y., 1975)

Van Caenegem, R. C., *The Birth of the English Common Law* (Cambridge, 1973; 2nd edn. 1988)

Van de Wiel, Constant, *History of Canon Law*, Louvain Theological and Pastoral Monographs, 5 (Louvain, 1991)

Vogel, Cyrille, *Medieval Liturgy, Introduction to Sources*, revd. and tr. W. G. Storey and N. K. Rasmussen (Washington, D.C., 1986)

Wailes, Stephen L., *Medieval Allegories of Jesus' Parables*, Center for Medieval and Renaissance Studies 23 (Berkeley, CA, 1987)

Waldron, Ronald A., 'Langland's Originality: the Christ-Knight and the Harrowing of Hell', in *Medieval English Religious and Ethical Literature: Essays in Honour of G. H. Russell*, ed. G. Kreutzmann and J. Simpson (Cambridge, 1986), pp. 66–81

——, 'Trevisa's Original Prefaces on Translation: a Critical Edition' in *Medieval English Studies Presented to George Kane*, ed. E. D. Kennedy, R. Waldron and J. S. Wittig (Woodbridge, Suffolk, 1988), pp. 285–9

Walsh, Katherine, *A Fourteenth Century Scholar and Primate, Richard FitzRalph in Oxford, Avignon and Armagh* (Oxford, 1981)

Ware, R. Dean, 'Medieval Chronology: Theory and Practice', in *Medieval Studies, an Introduction*, 2nd edn., ed. James M. Powell (Syracuse, New York, 1992), pp. 252–77

Warner, Sir George and Gilson, J. P., *Catalogue of Western Manuscripts in the Old Royal and King's Collection*, 3 vols. (London, 1921)

Warren, W. L., 'Simon of Sudbury', *JEH* (1959), 139–52

Watson, Nicholas, *Richard Rolle and the Invention of Authority* (Cambridge, 1991)

Wedel, T. O., *The Medieval Attitude Toward Astrology* (New Haven, Ct., 1920)

Welter, J.-th, *L'Exemplum dans la litérature religiouse et didactique du moyen âge* (Geneva, 1927; repr. 1973)

Wenzel, Siegfried, *Verses in Sermons, Fasciculus morum and its Middle English Poems*, The Medieval Academy of America, Publication 87 (Cambridge, Mass., 1978)

——, 'Chaucer's Pardoner and his Relics', SAC 11 (Columbus, Ohio, 1989), 37–41

——, 'The Continuing Life of William Peraldus's *Summa vitiorum*', in *Ad Litteram*, ed. M. D. Jordan and K. Emery, Jr. (Notre Dame, Ind., 1992), pp. 133–63

White, Lynn, *Medieval Religion and Technology* (Berkeley, CA, 1978)

Wilks, Michael, 'Predestination, Property, and Power: Wyclif's Theory of Dominion and Grace', SCH 2, ed. G. J. Cuming (Cambridge, 1965), 225–8

——, 'Early Oxford Wyclif', SCH 5, ed. G. J. Cuming and D. Baker (Cambridge, 1969), 69–98

——, 'Reformatio Regni', SCH 9, ed. Derek Baker (Cambridge, 1972), 109–30

——, 'Royal Patronage', SCH Subsidia 5, ed. A. Hudson and M. Wilks (1987), 135–63

Williams, Arnold, 'Middle English *questmonger*' *Medieval Studies* 10 (1948), 200–4

Wilson, R. M., *The Lost Literature of Medieval England* (London, 1952)

Wilson, E. M. Carus, 'The Overseas Trade of Bristol' in *Studies in English Trade in the Fifteenth Century*, ed. Eileen Power and M. M. Postan (New York, 1966), pp. 183–246

Wood, Chauncey, *Chaucer and the Country of the Stars* (Princeton, 1970)

Wood-Legh, K. L., *Perpetual Chantries in Britain* (Cambridge, 1965)

Woolf, Rosemary, 'The Theme of Christ the Lover-knight in Medieval English Literature' *RES* n.s. 13 (1962), 1–16

——, *The English Religious Lyric in the Middle Ages* (Oxford, 1968)

——, *The English Mystery Plays* (London, 1972)

Workman, H. B., *John Wyclif: a Study of the English Medieval Church*, 2 vols. (Oxford, 1926; repr. Hamden, Ct., 1966)

Wright, John K., *The Geographical Lore of the Time of the Crusades* (New York, 1925)

Wylie, James H., *History of England under Henry the Fourth*, 4 vols., (London, 1884; repr. New York, 1969)

Young, John, and Aitken, P. H., *A Catalogue of the Manuscripts in the Library of the Hunterian Museum in the University of Glasgow* (Glasgow, 1908)
Young, Karl, *The Drama of the Medieval Church*, 2 vols., (Oxford, 1933)
Ziegler, Philip, *The Black Death* (London, 1969)

ERRATA AND CORRIGENDA FOR
D&P I: 1
(not including those printed in vol. I: 2)

vii *for* Frout- *read* Front-
2/21 *for* precepyts *read* preceptys
3/46 *for* diuers *read* dyuers
3/47 *for* , *read* , &
4/78 *for* is is *read* it is
6/var.134 *for* H *read* H
7/var.142 *for* C *read* c
8/var.35: *add square bracket after* sekyrly
19/var.74 *add* amd] can. G
20/var.13 *add square bracket after* þe
44/xii *for* -oun *read* -ioun
52/33 *after* ȝeuere *add* [2 Cor. 9:7]
52/47 *after* nedyσ t *add* [Mt. 6:28–30]
53/10 *after* come *add* [Heb.13:14]
53/39 *after* Pouyl *add* [I Cor. 1:27–8]
54/9 *after* dede *add* [Lc.13:11–17]
54/12 *after* blisse *add* [Lc.16:9]
55/51 *for* 14:23 *read* 14:33
59/19 *for* [9;16] *read* [5:9–16]
59/66 *after* dyshese *add* [Mt.5:14]
63/9 *for* Dominiamini *read* Dominamini
70/2 *for* obiauerunt *read* obuiauerunt
72/2 *for* [25] *read* [35]
72/10 *for* Dominiamini *read* Dominamini
73/27 *for* [38] *read* [35]
77/22 *for* [Lc.6:20] *read* [Mt.5:3]
80/53 *for* [17] *read* [18]
82/21 *for* Exodi xv [1–40] *read* Exodi 24:18
93/8 *after* gallochis *add* [Act.12:8]
99/67 *after* reuerence *add* [Phil. 2:10]
101/53 *add period after* prys
110/14^{va}r. *after* H *add* 15 þe] *om.* Y

112/47 *after* skyis *add* [Eccli.35:21]

115/57 *after* Englysh *add* [Zach.6:12]

119/19 *for* [22] *read* [1]

122/30 *after* Ionas *add* [3:10]

135/12 *after* born *add* [Num. 24:17]

138/73–4 *for* [Act. 5:38–9] *read* [Prov. 21:30]

149/3 *for* may *read* many

150/var.10 *add square barckets after* bokes

153/11 *for* [23–24] *read* [31–32]

154/48 *for* -coun *read* -cioun

155/71 *omit* [2 Par.18:21]

157/34 *for* temptacoun *read* -cioun

157/10 *for* -counys *read* -ciounys

165/88 *for* ȝongrir *read* ȝongere

176/40 *after* wakyn *add* [Eccles.5:2]

184/16 *for* schule *read* schulde

186/18 *for* to *read* to-

190/18 *for* amendyge *read* amendynge

193/21 *for* -coun *read* -cioun

196/27 *after* [etiam] *add* extra

196/38 *for* be *read* ben

199/17 *add* [Eccli.35:21] *after* skyyis

200/6 *for* Mt: *read* Mt.

242/24 *after* betere *add* [Heb.6:16]

252/23 *for* in Questione de quodlibet *read* In questione de quolibet

254/67 *for* [7] *read* [1]

256/22 *for* lii *read* ii (L mkd. for om. in MS)

256/23 *for* Quicunque *read* Quicumque

257/32 *for* [14] *read* [12–15]

258/7 *after* dispysyd *add* [Eccli.27:15]

262/73 *for* knyrede *read* kynrede

263/21 *for* [37] *read* [3]

265/62 *for* [17] *read* 16–17]

272/44 *after* tabernaculys *add* [Lc.16:9]

276/41 *for* 13] *read* 14–15;13]

278/2–3 *for* [7] *read* [8]; *for* [20–6] *read* [25]

286/27 *after* sonne *add* [Mt.13:43]

289/4 and 6 *for* anoþer *read* anoþir

289/9 *for* [14] *read* [15]

289/11 *for* oþer *read* oþir

293/7 *after* sacrifice *add* [I Reg.15:22]
297/45 *stet* baranye *and change note to* barayne *al.*
300/60 *after* þout *add* [1 Cor.2:13]
300/65 *for* worchepith *read* worchepit (h mkd for om. in MS)
302/34 *add* [I Cor. 6:11] *after* Iesus
306/67 *for* gremitus *read* gemitus
307/35 *after* ordenance *add* [II Reg.18]
309/23 *for* lyue. Be *read* lyue, be
310/16 *after* chapitele *add* [I Tim.5:17]
311/31 *omit* [Eccli. 33:19]
311/38 *for* [22] *read* [19–22]
313/11 *for* belue *read* beleue
313/24 *for* belue *read* beleue
324/14 *add* [Reg.I 4] *after* kynrede
325/39 *for* [2] *read* [3]
var./79 *for* [5] *read* [6]
327/4 *for* entry- *read* entyr-
328/45 *for* [4] *read* [2;4]
329/21 *for* ouer- *read* ouir-
333/12 *om.* [Eph.6:5]
334/38 *omit* [I Pet. 2:13]
334/60 *for* [18–25 *read* [13–22]
336/36 *for* [5] *read* [5–7]
341/14 *for* falnesse *read* falsnesse
344/55 *for* pre- *read* per-
346/22 *for* A de *read* Ade
348/20 *after* gospel *add* [Mt.18:10]
352/42 *for* sarum con- *read* sarum, Con-
356/5 *for* vi [1] *read* [5:16]
357/7 *for* worchpeyn *read* worchepyn

ERRATA & CORRIGENDA FOR
D & P I:2

4/40 *omit* [Ez.13:18]
5/16 *after* his hed *add* [Ezec.13:17]
6/65 *after* ende *add* [Mt.25:1–13]
10/18 *after* hem *add* [IV Reg.25:1–7; Ierem.38;39]
11/31 *after* Kyngys *add* [3 Reg.22;6]
16/7 *for* [27] *read* [26–27]
17/43 *omit* [Ez.34:2]
18/57 *for* [3–8] *read* [2–6]
20/39 *for* [1] *read* [1–2]
26/57–8 *omit* [Eccli.5:5–9]
27/33 *after* ourself *add* [Mt.22:36–40]
35/46 *for* [4] *read* [2–5]
50/34 *for* [2] *read* [1–2]
54/43 *for* [33] *read* [28]
62/64 *for* [26–9;22–4] *read* [25;28;22–4]
65/86 *for* kyndam *read* kyngdam
66/9 *for* [24] *read* [21–24]
77/14 *add after* aforn [I Cor.5:11]
78/68–9 *for* [13–21] *read* [20–21]
83/87 *for* pruye *read* pryue
84/112 *for* bacam *read* becam
86/66 *for* [17] *read* [16–17]
91/21 *for* [3–5] *read* [7]
93/91 *for* [13] *read* [11–20]
102/98 *for* deocioun *read* deuocioun
105/25 *for* [17–18] *read* 11–13]
109/51 *after* chirche *add comma*
131/27 *for* f.189 *in margin read* f.189ᵛ
132/28 *for* great *read* gret
132/42 *for* Ecclesiatici *read* Ecclesiastici
153/60 *for* opynl echourys *read* opyn lechourys
154/51 *for* seck *read* seek
156/7 *for* -4] *read* -24]
157/46 *after* dette *add* [Lc.16:1–8]

177/30 *for* [24] *read* [27]
183/91 *for* wihelde *read* withhelde
197/65 *after* nacionys *add* [Deut.23:19–20]
206/67 *for* comentes *read* comontes
222/5 *for* verbo *read* vide
241/7 *for* [cf.I Thess.4:15–16] *read* [Eph.5:14]
242/29 *for* 16] *read* 16–17]
244/92 *for* [18] *read* [21]
247/22 *for* þese *read* þe se
249/28 *for* 42] *read* 42–3]
249/45 *for* netyn *read* metyn
266/8 *for* [12] *read* [13]
271/40 *for* f.249 *in margin read* f.249^r
273/98 *for* Ecclesiastes *read* Ecclesiasticus
287/27 *after* pore *add* ben
292/24 *for* þouert *read* pouert
297/72 *after* wif *add* [Exodi 20:17]
298/20 'of þe . . . coueytise' *is a scribal eyeskip that should have been omitted in text and added to variants*
306/47 *omit* [Gen.4:6]
307/26 *om.* [Eph.6:11]
307/27 *for* [12–17] *read* [11–18]
310/109 *after* warkys *add* [Eph. 6:14–17]
310/110 *for* [Tit.3:8] *read* [II Tim.4:5]
312/169 *for* [2 Tim.3:17] *read* [Eph.6:13]
318/35 *for* partriarchys *read* patriarkys
322/47 *for* worcheþe *read* worchepe
325Plate facing page 325 *for* 210^v *read* 199^r
var./var. *after* calander *read* ii^d 4 lebis